Office 2013
IN DEPTH

Joe Habraken

800 East 96th Street
Indianapolis, Indiana 46240

OFFICE 2013 IN DEPTH

ISBN-13: 978-0-7897-4870-6

ISBN-10: 0-7897-4870-3

Library of Congress Cataloging-in-Publication Data is on file.

Printed in the United States of America

First Printing: March 2013

Trademarks

All terms mentioned in this book that are known to be trademarks or service marks have been appropriately capitalized. Que Publishing cannot attest to the accuracy of this information. Use of a term in this book should not be regarded as affecting the validity of any trademark or service mark.

Warning and Disclaimer

Every effort has been made to make this book as complete and as accurate as possible, but no warranty or fitness is implied. The information provided is on an "as is" basis. The author and the publisher shall have neither liability nor responsibility to any person or entity with respect to any loss or damages arising from the information contained in this book.

Bulk Sales

Que Publishing offers excellent discounts on this book when ordered in quantity for bulk purchases or special sales. For more information, please contact

U.S. Corporate and Government Sales
1-800-382-3419
corpsales@pearsontechgroup.com

For sales outside of the U.S., please contact

International Sales
international@pearsoned.com

Editor-in-Chief
Greg Wiegand

Executive Editor
Loretta Yates

Development Editor
Susan Hobbs

Managing Editor
Sandra Schroeder

Senior Project Editor
Tonya Simpson

Copy Editors
Krista Hansing
Karen Annett

Indexer
Rebecca Salerno

Proofreader
Dan Knott

Technical Editor
Laura Acklen

Editorial Assistant
Cindy Teeters

Book Designer
Anne Jones

Compositor
Jake McFarland

CONTENTS AT A GLANCE

CONTENTS

ABOUT THE AUTHOR

Joe Habraken is a computer technology professional, educator, and best-selling author with more than 25 years of experience in the information technology and digital media production fields. His books include numerous titles on the Microsoft Office application suite, computer networking, and Microsoft's Windows Server network platform. Titles include Que's *Microsoft Office 2010 in Depth* and *Sams Teach Yourself Windows Server 2008 in 24 Hours*. Joe is an associate professor in the department of Arts and Communications at the University of New England in Biddeford, Maine, where he teaches a variety of desktop application, information technology, and digital media courses.

DEDICATION

To my mom, Carolyn, with much love.

ACKNOWLEDGMENTS

It takes a lot of people to create a large and comprehensive book like this; the author (me) is just one of many who spent long hours working hard, staring at a computer screen. It has been a real privilege to collaborate with the team of professionals at Que who have helped make this project (and my other Que titles) a reality and a success. I would like to thank Loretta Yates, our acquisitions editor, who worked very hard to assemble the project team for this book, helped determine the content coverage for the text, and showed the patience of a saint during the actual writing process. I would also like to thank Susan Hobbs, who served as the development editor for this book and who waded through first-draft text and came up with many great ideas for improving its content. Our technical editor, Laura Acklen, did a fantastic job making sure that everything in the book was correct and suggested a number of additions that made the book even more technically sound. I would also like to thank our other team members: managing editor Sandra Schroeder; proofreader Dan Knott; indexer Rebecca Salerno; publishing coordinator Cindy Teeters; interior and cover designer Anne Jones, who made everything look great; and our page layout guru, Jake McFarland. Finally, a huge thanks to our project editor, Tonya Simpson, who ran the last leg of the race and made sure the book made it to press on time—what a fantastic group of publishing professionals!

WE WANT TO HEAR FROM YOU!

As the reader of this book, *you* are our most important critic and commentator. We value your opinion and want to know what we're doing right, what we could do better, what areas you'd like to see us publish in, and any other words of wisdom you're willing to pass our way.

We welcome your comments. You can email or write to let us know what you did or didn't like about this book—as well as what we can do to make our books better.

Please note that we cannot help you with technical problems related to the topic of this book.

When you write, please be sure to include this book's title and author as well as your name and email address. We will carefully review your comments and share them with the author and editors who worked on the book.

Email: feedback@quepublishing.com

Mail: Que Publishing
            ATTN: Reader Feedback
            800 East 96th Street
            Indianapolis, IN 46240 USA

READER SERVICES

Visit our website and register this book at quepublishing.com/register for convenient access to any updates, downloads, or errata that might be available for this book.

INTRODUCTION

Congratulations! You are about to embark on a journey to harness the incredible capabilities of the latest version of Microsoft Office: Office 2013. Microsoft Office has been the gold standard for application suites for many years and provides all the applications you need for a wide variety of tasks. Whether you are writing a novel, balancing your budget, managing your emails and contacts, or creating an important sales presentation, Office 2013 offers all the features and tools you need to get the job done.

If you have never used Microsoft Office, this book gets you started with each of the Office applications and gives you in-depth coverage so that you can tackle any task or feature. If you are a Microsoft Office user but have not upgraded for a few years, you will find that the Office applications have undergone a dramatic transformation: They are more powerful and intuitive, and they embrace cloud file storage wholeheartedly.

As personal computing moved from a somewhat solitary environment to a new world of connectivity and collaboration, Microsoft enriched the Microsoft Office applications to make it easier for you to communicate and collaborate with other users on your business or home network and via the Internet. Office collaboration tools make it easier for you to share files and review documents edited by colleagues.

This latest version of Office also takes into account the fact that we all now work in a much more graphically rich computing environment and typically create files that include images, diagrams, and other graphics. Office 2013 includes many new enhancements, as well as trusted and tested tools that improve your capabilities to enrich your documents, worksheets, and presentations with a variety of digital graphics, including sound and video.

Who Should Buy This Book

This book has been designed to get the Office novice up and running, and to allow the seasoned Office users to flex their application "muscles" and accomplish even more with the likes of Word, Excel, PowerPoint, and Outlook. There are definitely some good reasons why you should consider purchasing this book and making it your Microsoft Office 2013 go-to reference. First, this book is part of Que's *In Depth* series, which is dedicated to providing a series of comprehensive guides for a variety of software applications and operating systems. The highly skilled publishing team at Que Publishing works hard to give you the very best computer reference books.

This particular book is designed for a range of Microsoft Office users, from the novice to the well-seasoned veteran. New users will find it an excellent hands-on tool for learning the basics of the various Office applications. More experienced users will find it a resource that enables them to go well beyond the basic capabilities of powerful application software packages such as Word, Excel, Outlook, PowerPoint, Publisher, and OneNote.

This book's approach is simple: It provides in-depth coverage of Microsoft Office 2013 application features and software tools, and also supplies the context in which to use those particular features or tools as you edit documents, create email messages, or fine-tune complex worksheets. This book serves as a reference for specific application features, but it can also be a resource for learning how to best take advantage of the capabilities of the individual Office applications and to leverage the capabilities of Office as an integrated suite of software tools. As someone whose job it is to teach students the practical application of software in the real world, I have made sure that this book embraces that ideal and enables you to use the various Office applications more completely and effectively, whatever your endeavors.

The book is written in an easy-to-read, conversational style that allows you to concentrate on learning and understanding. Although each of the Office applications provides multiple ways to tackle nearly every task, this book stresses best practices in using applications such as Word, Excel, and PowerPoint to help you achieve better results when using these software tools.

How This Book Is Organized

Microsoft Office 2013 In Depth is organized into seven parts and also includes two appendixes. Each Office application covered in this book is discussed in detail in its own part or section. This makes it possible for you to quickly access information related to a specific Office application: Word, Excel, PowerPoint, Outlook, Publisher, or OneNote. All the most important and useful features and tasks are covered in the application-specific sections of this book. The book also includes an introductory section (Part I) that quickly gets you up to speed with the Office 2013 interface and the new features and tools in this version of the powerful Microsoft Office application suite. Two appendixes are included; one provides insight into using the Office applications in an integrated fashion, and the other is a primer on Office macros.

Part I, "Introduction to the Office 2013 Application Suite," gets you oriented to the Office application interface and geography, stressing Microsoft's Office Fluent user interface approach, and looks at improvements and new features in the Office applications. This section also discusses managing and sharing your Office application files and working with graphics and images in the various Office applications. An introduction to the new Office Web apps is also provided.

Part II, "Word," takes an in-depth look at the Office suite's powerful word processor and desktop publishing application. This section begins with an overview of the Word application environment and how to access essential Word features and tools. Each subsequent chapter in this section builds your Word knowledge base, from commonly used features and commands to advanced subject matter that helps you create more complex and specialized Word documents using styles, tables, and sections. This section also provides complete coverage of advanced features, such as Word's mail merge and forms, and it details approaches for creating larger documents that require a table of contents, footnotes, and cross-references.

Part III, "Excel," quickly orients you to this powerful spreadsheet application so that you can immediately begin to work with worksheets, text labels, values, formulas, and cell ranges. This section then focuses on worksheet management and advanced formatting, and provides an in-depth discussion on using formulas and functions in your Excel worksheets. Charts, pivot tables, and tools for sorting and filtering data are also covered in this section. This part culminates in coverage of Excel's advanced features for validating and analyzing your worksheet data.

Part IV, "PowerPoint," provides a detailed discussion of this powerful presentation tool. Beginning with an overview of the PowerPoint application environment and basic presentation tools and concepts, this section gives you all the information you need to build complex and compelling PowerPoint presentations. Chapters in this section include information on how to build better PowerPoint slides using themes, slide transitions, and special animations. The options and best practices for presenting PowerPoint presentations are also provided, with particular insight into how printed materials such as handouts and notes can make a presentation even more effective.

Part V, "Outlook," covers how to use this powerful information manager in both small office/home office environments and on corporate networks. The chapters in this section give you an overview of the Outlook interface and essential features. The Outlook section then shifts from the general to the specific, by concentrating on each of the diverse capabilities Outlook provides as an email client, contact information manager, calendar manager, and organizer of tasks, notes, and other personal information. Coverage is also given to help you secure the information in Outlook and protect your Outlook Inbox from spam, viruses, and other security threats.

Part VI, "Publisher," discusses the Office suite's dedicated desktop publishing application. Publisher has evolved from a home office–oriented application into an extremely useful and robust design application that enables you to quickly create a variety of visually appealing and professional documents. This section orients you to the basics of creating special documents in Publisher and then builds your knowledge base in the application so that you can create more complex items, including online content.

Part VII, "OneNote," covers the capabilities of this information manager, which enables you to gather, organize, and share information. This section begins with an overview of the OneNote interface and the creation of OneNote notebooks. Chapters in this section walk you through the use of tabs, pages, and tables in your notebooks to store and organize information. This section concludes with a look at how OneNote can be integrated with other Office applications, such as Word and Excel.

The book completes its discussion of the Office applications with Appendixes A and B, which provide information on integrating the Office applications and Office macros, respectively. Each appendix is designed to give you additional information related to the Office applications that can be used to leverage your capabilities when using Office suite members such as Word, Excel, and PowerPoint. In my mind, the appendixes provide information over and above the in-depth coverage on each Office application in the seven sections of the book. You'll want to have a strong working knowledge of the Office applications before you tackle the information in the appendixes, particularly Appendix B, "Office Macros."

Conventions Used in This Book

Special conventions are used throughout this book to help you get the most out of each and every page as you ramp up your knowledge of Microsoft Office 2013.

Key Combinations

Much of what we do in the various Office applications is typically a matter of mouse clicks (if we aren't typing text); however, some commands are key combinations on the keyboard. Key combinations are represented with a plus sign. For example, if the text calls for you to bold text using the Ctrl+B key, the plus (+) symbol denotes that the keys are to be pressed at the same time.

Special Elements

Special elements in this book give you additional information that helps you better understand the text in a particular chapter section or warn you about a potential problem with a particular software feature. These elements help you better navigate the features and tools discussed in this book. They consist of Notes, Tips, Cautions, and Cross-References. The name of each special element provides insight into how you can use the information.

Cross-References

Cross-references point you to other locations in this book or other books in the Que family. They make it easy for you to jump to another part of the book for supplemental information related to the topic in the chapter you are currently reading. Cross references appear as follows:

> ➡ *For information on configuring an Outlook profile and email account the first time you run Outlook, **see** Chapter 22, "Requisite Outlook: Configuration and Essential Features."*

note

The Notes element provides information that expands on information in a chapter. The extra information in Notes isn't essential as you work through a chapter, so you can take advantage of Notes as time allows.

 caution

Cautions warn you about potential pitfalls with an application feature or tool. Heeding the warning provided by a Caution can save you both time and frustration as you navigate a tricky or confusing concept, feature, or tool in an Office application.

 tip

Tips provide best practices and shortcuts as you work with the various Office features and tools. Tips are designed to help you get the most out of a particular software feature and increase your overall efficiency and ability with the application.

GETTING ORIENTED TO THE OFFICE 2013 APPLICATIONS

Microsoft Office 2013 is the latest version of Microsoft's powerful application suite. Office 2013 provides a number of versatile and impressive applications, including Word, Excel, PowerPoint, and Outlook, which enable you to tackle a large variety of business and personal tasks. Whether you are creating reports, crunching budget numbers, organizing a presentation, or managing your email and contacts, Office 2013 gives you all the tools and features you need to get the job done.

This chapter offers an introduction to the Office 2013 application suite, including a look at the different versions of Office 2013 available. The discussion also incorporates licensing information options and highlights some of the new features and tools in Office 2013.

Introducing Office 2013

Upon first inspection, the Office 2013 suite members look similar to their Office 2010 predecessors. The Ribbon is still the go-to apparatus for accessing commands and features in the applications, and the Backstage provides access to tools related to managing, sharing, and printing your files (although there are changes to the Ribbon and the Backstage, so read on).

When you get past the fact that the overall look of the applications hasn't changed dramatically (although the Office application interface is much less "cartoony" and more sleekly designed in Office 2013), you find that Microsoft made improvements and enhancements to each of the applications. For example, Excel provides some great new tools for data analysis. The Quick Analysis gallery enables you to quickly apply formatting, charts, and formulas to the selected data in your worksheet. Figure 1.1 shows the Excel application window and the new Quick Analysis gallery.

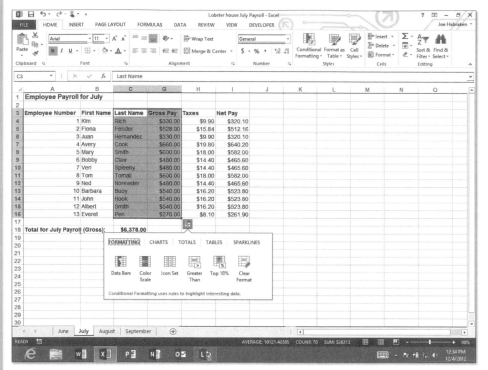

Figure 1.1
Excel 2013
provides the
new Quick
Analysis
gallery.

The Quick Analysis gallery is an obvious change to Excel, as are other changes you experience when using the Office 2013 applications. You also find subtle changes to the applications that don't allow you to accomplish something epic but that do make your life easier. For example, Word and PowerPoint provide the Welcome Back bookmark, which appears when you return to an existing document or presentation, respectively. Figure 1.2 shows the PowerPoint application window. An existing presentation is opened, and you can use the bookmark to jump to the last slide you were working with during your previous PowerPoint session.

One of the biggest changes to the Office 2013 applications isn't apparent when you are working in Word or Excel. Office has embraced the cloud. Office 2013 makes it easy for you to save your files to cloud storage options such as SkyDrive and SharePoint. Saving your files to the cloud simplifies sharing files with other users. Having your files available in the cloud also means that you can easily access your files from different devices running Office 2013. You can save a Word document to your SkyDrive using your computer and then access it later that day on your touchscreen smart device. Microsoft's cloud initiation involving the Office 2013 applications also affects the options for how you purchase and install Microsoft Office 2013 on a computer or other device. Microsoft's Office 365 subscriptions enable you to install the Office suite on multiple devices using Microsoft's new Click and Go technology that installs and updates your Office applications.

Figure 1.2 Use the Welcome Back bookmark to quickly return to the last slide accessed.

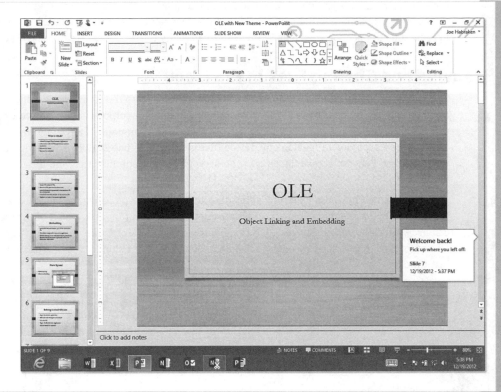

Office 2013 provides an innovative application suite that builds upon the familiar working environment of its predecessor, Office 2010. Not only have the Office 2013 applications been enhanced for use with Windows 8 in the PC environment, but changes to the applications have also been influenced by the fact that Office 2013 is available for devices that use touchscreens as their primary input method.

The following section gives a brief rundown of some other new features of the Office 2013 applications. We then look at the different versions of the Office 2013 suite and options for purchasing and licensing Office.

New Features and Tools in Office 2013

The Office 2013 applications boast many new features and capabilities. Some of these affect all the Office suite members or a subset of the Office member applications. Other changes and improvements are application specific. In this chapter, we explore some of the "global" enhancements that you find in the Office 2013 applications. Individual enhancements to specific applications in the Office suite are also introduced. New features are explored in more detail throughout the book. For example, new Word features are discussed in Part II, "Word."

Let's begin with a discussion of Office and the cloud. We can then look at other enhancements to the Office suite, including the new application Start screen and some of the "high-profile" changes to individual applications, such as Word 2013's capability to edit Adobe Acrobat (PDF) files.

Saving and Sharing Files in the Cloud

The Office 2013 applications encourage you to save your files to the cloud. Depending on the environment where you use Office 2013—home, small business, or corporation—different cloud storage options are available. If you are a home user, you can take advantage of SkyDrive to store your files. You can then access your files on any device that is running Office 2013 or any device that has a web browser. You can access the Office web apps to view or edit files that you have stored on the SkyDrive.

If you are a small business user who subscribes to Office 365, you can save your files to SkyDrive Pro, a SharePoint site that is part of your subscription. As with the free version of SkyDrive, you can access files stored on SkyDrive Pro from multiple devices. Corporate users of Office 2013 can also store files in the cloud by taking advantage of a SharePoint site hosted by their company or institution.

So no matter what kind of user you are, you have a cloud option when you work in Office 2013. Figure 1.3 shows the Save As page in the PowerPoint Backstage. Cloud locations for saving your files are treated the same as "physical" locations, such as your computer.

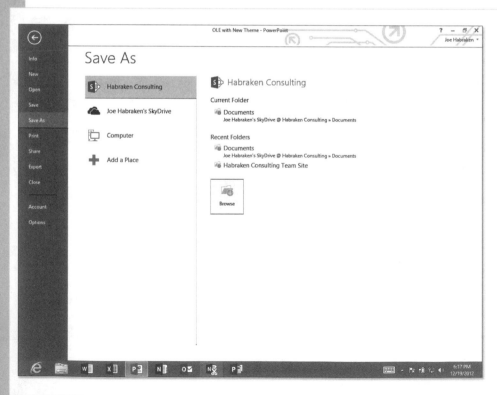

Figure 1.3
You can save files to your SkyDrive or SkyDrive Pro.

When you install Office on your computer, you have the opportunity to sign in using your Office 365 Subscription ID or your Windows Live ID. Signing in sets up your SkyDrive or SkyDrive Pro as one of the places where you can save or open files by accessing the appropriate page in the Backstage.

Saving your files to the cloud on either your SkyDrive or SkyDrive Pro (or your company's SharePoint site) makes it easy to share files with co-workers or colleagues. In fact, to share OneNote notebooks, you must save them to a cloud location.

When you save a file to your SkyDrive (or SkyDrive Pro), you can quickly share the file using the options provided on the Backstage Share page. Figure 1.4 shows the Share page in the Word Backstage.

Figure 1.4
Quickly invite people to share an Office file.

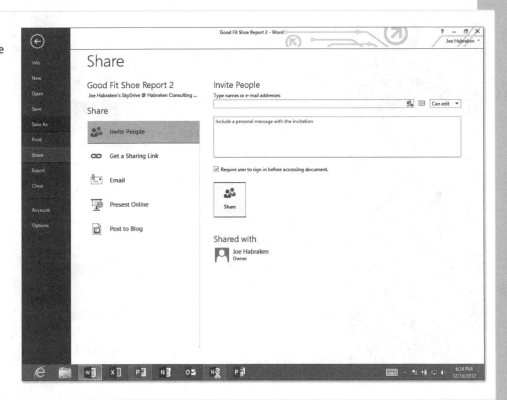

The Office applications provide more than one way to share a file with other users. You can invite people by creating an email message from the Share page, or you can generate a sharing link for your file, which enables you to post the link on a social media site such as Facebook or a corporate website so that a large number of people can access the file. Each Office application also offers a unique way to share a file with others; for example, Word can help you post the current document to a blog.

So saving your files to the cloud provides with easy access to your files from (potentially) multiple devices. Saving to the cloud also makes it easy for you to quickly share a file.

➡️ *For more information on saving files to the cloud,* **see** *Chapter 5, "Using the Office Web Apps."*

New Start Screen

An obvious change to most of the Office 2103 applications (Word, PowerPoint, Excel, and Publisher) is the new Start screen. When you open an application such as Excel, you are taken to the new Start screen. In past versions of Excel (Office 2010 and earlier), a new, blank worksheet opened in the Office application window. The Start screen gives you some choice over what happens when you start an application such as Excel and is similar to the Backstage Open page. The Start screen grants access to templates and themes, including, in the case of Excel, a new Blank workbook. Figure 1.5 shows the Excel Start screen.

Figure 1.5
The Excel
Start screen.

The Start screen also provides a Recent list, which you can use to access recently opened files. If you want to retrieve workbook files not listed on the Start screen, you can quickly switch to the Open page in the Backstage by clicking the Open Other Workbooks link (a similar command is provided on the Word and PowerPoint Start screens). The Open page gives you access to places such as My Computer and your SkyDrive or SkyDrive Pro. You can select any of these file storage options and then use the Browse button to open the Open dialog box. You can use the Open dialog box to browse your files or use the Search box to search for files.

➡ *For more information on saving and opening Office files, **see** Chapter 3, "Managing and Sharing Office Files."*

Editing Adobe Acrobat Files

This enhancement is strictly related to Word. It is a major update for Word but doesn't come with fireworks or blaring trumpets. You can now edit Adobe Acrobat (PDF) files using Word 2013. All you have to do is open the PDF document in Word. The conversion to a "regular" Word document is immediate, with no alarms or an hour-long wait to see whether the file was converted correctly. Because the file is converted to a Word document, your original PDF file is still safe. This feature works well on most Adobe Acrobat files but can have problems reformatting (to a Word document) some complex PDFs.

In terms of editing a PDF in Word, as soon as you open the PDF file (really, you are opening a Word copy of the file), you can begin to edit the content. You can use all the Word features to modify the document. You can then save the edited version in any file format you want, including the Adobe Acrobat file format (PDF). Saving a file as a PDF makes it easy for you to share it with people who do not have access to Microsoft Word. PDF viewers are available on every sort of smart device, so virtually anyone can read the PDF document. When you save a Word document as a PDF (in the Save As dialog box), you can use the Options button to password protect the Adobe Acrobat file you create. Anyone attempting to open the file will need the password.

Other Office 2013 Improvements and Updates

Other new features and enhancements also appear when working with the individual Office applications. Many of these new features are discussed within the application sections of this book. The following list highlights some of my favorite updates to the Office 2013 applications:

- **Theme variations:** Themes have always been a great way to uniformly format the fonts and colors in PowerPoint slides and Word documents. The Office applications now provide theme variants, which make it easy for you to fine-tune the selected theme (for your document, worksheet, or presentation), with different color possibilities.

- **New task panes in PowerPoint and Excel:** When you work with objects such as charts and pictures, task panes provide options for formatting these objects. This is a big improvement over the rather clunky dialog boxes for these objects in previous versions of these Office applications.

- **New chart tools:** When you select a chart in an application such as Excel, three buttons appear on the right of the chart. These buttons—Chart Elements, Layout, and Filter—enable you to quickly change the elements shown on the chart, change the overall layout of the chart, and filter the chart by a particular data series, respectively.

- **Improved conversation view in Outlook:** Outlook provides a new conversation view of your emails so that you can easily work with associated email messages, whether sent or received. You also now have the capability to ignore conversations, which helps cut down on the clutter as you work with your important emails.

- **Live layout and alignment guides:** The Office applications make it extremely easy to place a picture or other graphic in a document. As you drag the picture on the page (or slide), alignment guides help you with its final placement. In Word, you can access text-wrapping layout options for the picture and its surrounding text with one click on the Layout Options button, which appears when the picture is selected.

- **Outlook People Hub view:** This is the new default view for contacts in Outlook. The People hub shows your Outlook contacts (which you likely expect), and it also includes contacts from your social network sites (it works particularly well if you have a LinkedIn account). The new Contact card for contacts (People) aggregates information about a particular person from information gleaned from multiple sources, such as social media websites.

- **Better OneNote integration with the other Office applications:** OneNote is an even more effective organizational tool when it interfaces with the other applications in the Office 2013 suite. You can embed Excel worksheets directly into your notebooks (giving you the power of Excel as you work in OneNote). Integrating Outlook and OneNote also provides new possibilities, including the capability to connect your OneNote notes with Outlook meetings.

- **Better web apps:** The Office web apps have been fine-tuned and work well whether you are using them via your free SkyDrive site or SkyDrive Pro, as part of your Office 365 subscription. The web apps definitely serve you well in a pinch when you don't have access to the installed versions of the Office applications.

This isn't an exhaustive list of changes to the Office applications, but hopefully you get the feeling that Office 2013 is an exciting upgrade of Microsoft's powerful application suite. You can do more in the applications—and do it more effectively.

➡ *For more about the Office web apps, **see** Chapter 5, "Using the Office Web Apps."*

➡ *For more information on views in Outlook, **see** Chapter 22, "Requisite Outlook: Configuration and Essential Features."*

The Office 2013 Suite Applications

The Office 2013 suite applications are bundled in different versions. The Office applications available in your installation depend on the bundle version that you or your company purchased. If your Office installation is part of your Office 365 subscription, the Office applications that are installed depend on the level of your subscription. We sort out the different versions and subscription application mixes in the next section. In this book, we concentrate on the following applications:

- **Web apps:** Although each web app has an Office 2013 suite member counterpart, we cover the web apps in their own chapter (Chapter 5) in Part I, "Introduction to the Office 2013 Application Suite."

- **Word:** The standard for word processing in the Windows environment for many years, Word 2013 has many new features and possibilities. Whether you use Word to create letters, short reports, or lengthy documents that include footnotes, a table of contents, and cross-references, you find in-depth coverage of Word in Part II, "Word."

- **Excel:** This powerful number cruncher provides new features such as the Quick Analysis gallery, new inline chart tools, and Flash Fill. Excel in-depth coverage can be found in Part III, "Excel."

- **PowerPoint:** Your PowerPoint presentations can be even more exciting, with wide-screen slide formats and new theme variations. PowerPoint also enables you to merge multiple shapes. PowerPoint's in-depth coverage is located in Part IV, "PowerPoint."

- **Outlook:** This versatile personal information manager and email client enables you to communicate with co-workers and friends, and manage all your messages, contacts, and appointments. New views for contacts and the capability to connect to popular social media sites make it even easier to manage all sorts of information in Outlook. Part V, "Outlook," covers this app.

- **Publisher:** With Publisher, you can create a range of publication types, from the simple to the complex. Publisher 2013 enables you to drop multiple pictures onto the scratch area and easily prepare publications for commercial printers. Part VI, "Publisher," provides in-depth coverage.

- **OneNote:** OneNote enables you to store information in electronic notebooks, which you can then easily share with other users. OneNote 2013 is more tightly integrated with the other Office applications, making it easy to store a variety of information in your notebooks. Coverage of OneNote is provided in Part VII, "OneNote."

Your Office 2013 installation can also include other applications, such as Microsoft Access, the powerful database application, and Microsoft Lync. Lync is a new communication tool that enables you to hold online meetings, chat with Skype users, and send instant messages. One point to keep in mind as you use the various Office applications is that they are designed as an integrated group of software tools. You can easily share information between applications and use multiple applications to build powerful reports, presentations, and shared content.

The Different Versions of the Office 2013 Suite

Office 2013 comes in different flavors, or versions, that you can purchase. The other route to an Office 2013 installation is an Office 365 subscription. This section looks at the different "install" versions of Office and the Office 365 subscription levels in the context of the office applications that are installed as part of your purchase or subscription. You can review pricing information for these installations and subscription bundles at http://office.microsoft.com. Let's start with the Office bundles for purchase:

- **Microsoft Office Professional Plus 2013 (volume licensing):** This high-end version includes Excel, Outlook, PowerPoint, Word, Access, InfoPath Designer, Lync, Publisher, and OneNote.

- **Microsoft Office Professional 2013:** This version (which is available as a retail product) includes Excel, Outlook, PowerPoint, Word, Access, Publisher, and OneNote.

- **Microsoft Office Home and Business 2013:** This version includes Word, Excel, PowerPoint, OneNote, and Outlook.

- **Microsoft Office Standard 2013:** This version includes Word, Excel, PowerPoint, Publisher, OneNote, and Outlook. It is available through Microsoft's Open Business program and requires a minimum purchase of five licenses.

- **Office Home and Student 2013:** This version (available retail) includes Word, Excel, PowerPoint, and OneNote.

The alternative to purchasing your Office software is to license it as part of an Office 365 subscription. The levels of Office 365 subscriptions are as follows:

- **Business and Enterprise (volume licensing):** This version of the Office 365 subscriptions are priced per user and provide the Office Professional Plus edition of the Office 2013 software. This level of subscription also gives a business other network services, including multiple SharePoint sites and Microsoft Server–hosted services such as Active Directory and Exchange server (the Microsoft communication server). This subscription level is intended for medium-sized and large businesses that do not want to administer their own network infrastructure.

- **Office 365 Small Business Premium:** This subscription provides Word, Excel, PowerPoint, OneNote, Outlook, Publisher, Access, Lync, and InfoPath (the same as the Pro Plus purchase installation bundle). This bundle is user specific and allows a single subscriber to use the Office software on up to five devices.

- **Office 365 Home Premium:** This subscription provides Word, Excel, PowerPoint, OneNote, Outlook, Publisher, and Access (the same as the Pro Plus purchase installation). You can install the Office software on up to five PCs, Macs, or other devices, and this subscription is not user specific.

All the available versions of Office 2013 (both purchase and subscription) provide the core Office applications that include Excel, PowerPoint, and Word. You will want to determine your own needs in relation to the application mix that you purchase or receive as part of a subscription.

 note

Many articles and blogs on the Web debate the pros and cons of an Office 2013 software purchase versus an Office 365 subscription. Your choice should reflect your need and take cost into consideration.

Hardware and Software Requirements for Office 2013

All the bells and whistles of Office 2013 come with hardware requirements. It is always better to have a computer that exceeds the minimum hardware requirements for a software application. The more memory your computer has and the faster its processor is, the more enjoyable your experience will be as you use the Office 2013 member applications. This book concentrates on Office installations on a PC running Windows 8. Office 2013 is available on different operating system platforms across a range of devices. Research the Office 2013 hardware and operating system requirements for your device before you purchase the software or attempt to install it. A good place to start gathering information is www.office.microsoft.com.

The minimum hardware requirements for Office 2013 on a PC, and some realistic recommendations, are as follows:

- **Processor:** 1GHz processor (at least); I recommend at least 2GHz or better to really take advantage of what Office 2013 has to offer—the faster, the better. Any new computer with a dual-core processor (or better) runs the Office applications at peak performance.

- **Memory (RAM):** 1GB for a 32-bit system, and 2GB for a 64-bit system. I recommend a bare minimum of 2GB on a 32-bit system and 4GB for a 64-bit system. Memory is relatively inexpensive. The more RAM you have, the better these applications run, particularly when you want to run multiple applications at the same time.

- **Hard drive space:** The minimum amount required for installing the Office suite is 3GB. If you are running low on the hard drive that also contains your Windows installation, get an external drive such as a USB drive, and clean up your personal files and move them off the main drive. You can then install Office.

- **Graphics card:** You need a DirectX 10–compatible graphics card with a resolution of 1024×576. As with everything else, the more powerful your video card is, the better the graphic-intensive Office features run.

In terms of the Windows operating system and Office 2013 compatibility, you can run the 32-bit version of Office 2013 on a computer that is running Windows 7 or Windows 8. Make sure that your Windows installation is up-to-date on service packs before installing Office. Windows 7 and Windows 8 are both available in 32- and 64-bit versions.

Although it is not a hardware or software requirement for installing Office, get a Windows Live ID if you do not currently have one. A Windows Live ID enables you to use Microsoft's SkyDrive. You can connect your SkyDrive to your Office applications, which gives you with another possibility for saving your files to the cloud. Having access to SkyDrive also gives you access to the Office web apps.

Installing Office 2013

How you purchase your Office 2013 software affects how you install Office 2013. If you purchase your software on DVD (or potentially as a download from Microsoft), you install it by running the Setup file that accompanies the software files. A DVD automatically runs the setup when you load the DVD (typically). After setup begins, you must accept the terms of agreement to proceed; you also have the option to customize the installation (basically, you choose the applications and tools that are installed). When you are past these installation screens, you can sit back and let the installation proceed.

If you subscribe to Office 365, install your Office applications from your Office 365 Admin website. All you do is initiate the installation, and Office 365 downloads the application files to your PC and takes charge of the installation. Figure 1.6 shows an Office installation that was initiated from the Office 365 Office installation page. When you run the executable file, your installation proceeds without any additional interaction required.

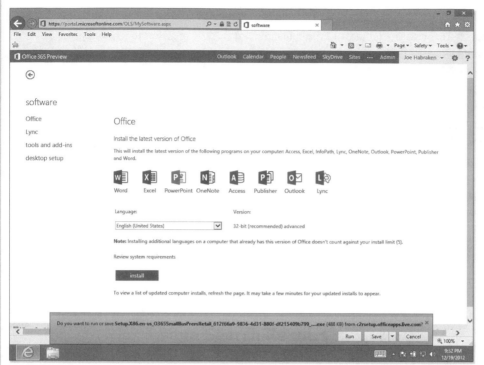

Figure 1.6
The Office installation page on the Office 365 Admin site.

So the Office 2013 installation pretty much takes care of itself. You do have a role in the installation process, though: You must activate the Office suite the first time you launch one of the Office applications. How you activate the installation depends on how you acquired your Office 2103 software.

Launching the Office applications is accomplished in Windows 8 via the Start screen. Tiles are added to the Start screen after you install the Office suite. When you launch an application, the application runs on the desktop. It makes sense to right-click the Office application icon on the desktop's taskbar and pin the application. This provides easy access to that application when you are working on the desktop.

When you launch an Office application immediately after your Office installation, you need to activate the installation. Figure 1.7 shows the Activate Office window.

You have three options for activating your Office installation. Two of the options use Microsoft accounts; the third option uses the product key that came with your Office installation DVD (or other media).

If you subscribed to Office (such as an Office Home and Student subscription) and associated your Windows Live ID with the subscription, select Microsoft Account in the Activate Office window; then enter your Windows Live ID and password to activate Office.

Figure 1.7
The Activate Office window.

Activate Office

To activate this install, sign in with the account associated with your Office product. When you sign in, your Office documents and personal settings are just a click away. You can also save your documents online and get to them from virtually anywhere.

Microsoft account
Sign in with the account you use for SkyDrive, Xbox LIVE, Outlook.com, or other Microsoft services.

Organizational account
Sign in with the account provided by your work or school to use with Office 365 or other Microsoft services.

Enter a product key instead

Learn more | Privacy statement

If you have an Office 365 subscription (or your employer has an Office 365 subscription), select the Organizational account option in the Activate window. Use your Office 365 username and account to activate Office.

If you purchased your Office 2013 application suite and you have a product key, use this to activate Office. Click the Enter a Product Key Instead link at the bottom of the Activate Office window. The Enter Your Product Key window opens. Enter your 25-character product key and then click Continue.

After your Office installation is activated, you can begin to use your installed applications. If you are new to Office, you may want to take a look at Chapter 2, "Navigating and Customizing the Office Interface," and Chapter 3 before tackling the sections of the book that are devoted to specific Office applications, such as Word, Excel, and Outlook.

 note
If you use Office on a corporate network, your network administrator more than likely dictates how you upgrade to or install Office 2013.

 tip
If the DVD does not automatically run, open the File Explorer on the desktop; then you can access the Setup file on the DVD.

 Note
You can quickly switch between the desktop and the Start screen (and vice versa) using the Windows key on the keyboard.

Getting Help in the Office Applications

Help is just a click away when you are working in one of the Office applications. The Help icon resides at the top right of the Office application window. The Help icon is also available in the Backstage (again, at the top right of the window). The Help window for the current application opens when you select the Help icon.

The Help window provides several links to basic information for the current application under a Getting Started heading. Popular searches are also provided in a list and are specific to the application you are working in. If you want to search for specific help, type keywords into the Search box at the top of the Help window and then run the search. Figure 1.8 shows the results of a search in the Excel Help window for the keywords *pie chart*.

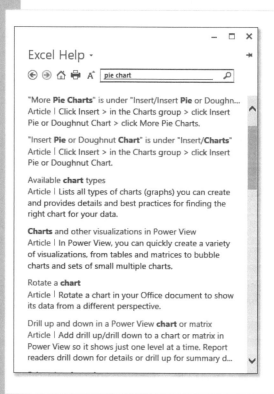

Figure 1.8
The Excel Help window.

Links are provided in your search results that enable you to explore related information. You can return to the Help main page by click the Home icon in the Help navigation bar. You also have the option to print Help information, if needed. When you finish working with the Help window, you can close it.

 tip
You can access Help at any time in the Office applications by pressing the F1 key.

The Backstage can also serve as an informational tool. It doesn't give you help on a particular feature or command or let you search for help by topic. It can, however, give you information on the current document (or file you are working with) and give you information about your Office installation and connected services.

When you enter the Backstage by selecting File on the Ribbon, the Info page is active. This page gives you the properties for the current document. This page also lists the authors who have modified the document. The Info page provides tools that enable you to protect and inspect your file. We discuss how to use these tools in Chapter 3.

Another source of information in the Backstage is the Account page. This page gives you a list of the Office applications installed on your computer and provides a list of all your connected services. Connected services can be your SkyDrive, SkyDrive Pro, the Office store, and other services that you have connected to your Office applications, such as Flickr, YouTube, and LinkedIn. The Connected Services list enables you to manage these connected services, and you can remove a service by clicking the Remove link. Any service that you disconnect can be reconnected at any time.

Another source of information that serves you well as you work with the Office application is Office.com. This website provides tips, ideas, and access to Office templates and clip art. Probably your most valuable resource is your sense of humor. You are going to make mistakes, and sometimes Office can be frustrating. Don't be afraid to laugh once in a while.

NAVIGATING AND CUSTOMIZING THE OFFICE INTERFACE

The Microsoft Office 2013 applications are designed to make it easy for you to concentrate on the file you are creating, whether it is an Excel workbook or a PowerPoint slide presentation, and quickly access the commands and features that you need as you work. The Office 2013 applications provide an interface that is easy to navigate and customize. As with its predecessor, Office 2010, Office 2013 provides the Ribbon as the place to go when you need to access an application command or feature. In this chapter, we take a look at the interface shared by the Office applications (primarily Word, Excel, PowerPoint, and Publisher) and see how best to stay productive as you navigate the various command elements, such as the Ribbon tabs, galleries, dialog boxes, task panes, and even the status bar.

We look at options for customizing the Ribbon and also explore the Backstage. Our discussion includes the Trust Center, which enables you to specify trusted locations for opening files and other security settings.

Getting Familiar with the Office Interface

The Office 2013 applications employ much of the same "application geography" introduced in Office 2007 and then refined in Office 2010. The Ribbon-dominated user interface uses each Ribbon tab for grouping commands into somewhat broad yet related categories. For example, in Word 2013, the Review tab (shown in Figure 2.1) provides groups of commands related to reviewing and finalizing a document.

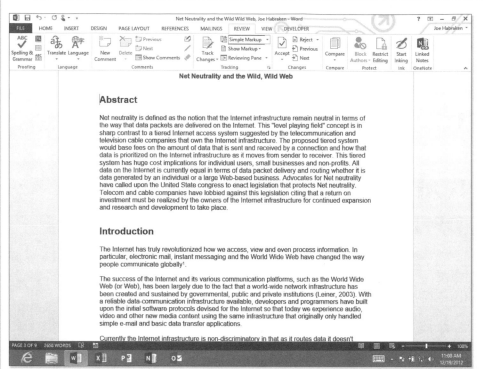

Net Neutrality and the Wild, Wild Web

Abstract

Net neutrality is defined as the notion that the Internet infrastructure remain neutral in terms of the way that data packets are delivered on the Internet. This "level playing field" concept is in sharp contrast to a tiered Internet access system suggested by the telecommunication and television cable companies that own the Internet infrastructure. The proposed tiered system would base fees on the amount of data that is sent and received by a connection and how that data is prioritized on the Internet infrastructure as it moves from sender to receiver. This tiered system has huge cost implications for individual users, small businesses and non-profits. All data on the Internet is currently equal in terms of data packet delivery and routing whether it is data generated by an individual or a large Web-based business. Advocates for Net neutrality have called upon the United State congress to enact legislation that protects Net neutrality. Telecom and cable companies have lobbied against this legislation citing that a return on investment must be realized by the owners of the Internet infrastructure for continued expansion and research and development to take place.

Introduction

The Internet has truly revolutionized how we access, view and even process information. In particular, electronic mail, instant messaging and the World Wide Web have changed the way people communicate globally[1].

The success of the Internet and its various communication platforms, such as the World Wide Web (or Web), has been largely due to the fact that a world-wide network infrastructure has been created and sustained by governmental, public and private institutions (Leiner, 2003). With a reliable data-communication infrastructure available, developers and programmers have built upon the initial software protocols devised for the Internet so that today we experience audio, video and other new media content using the same infrastructure that originally only handled simple e-mail and basic data transfer applications.

Currently the Internet infrastructure is non-discriminatory in that as it routes data it doesn't

Figure 2.1
Ribbon tabs house related command groups.

These groups include the Proofing group, the Language group, the Comments group, the Tracking group, the Changes group, the Compare group, the Protect group, the Ink group (which is designed for use on a touchscreen), and the OneNote group (which enables you to link notes from the current document to a OneNote notebook). All these groups provide commands related to reviewing and fine-tuning the document. For example, you definitely want to take advantage of the Spelling & Grammar command in the Proofing group as you finalize and review your work.

The Microsoft Office user interface also provides consistency across the Office applications. The Home tab in the Word, Excel, PowerPoint, or Publisher application window contains the Clipboard group and other groups related to font formatting, text alignment, and styles. Considering the different purposes of the Office applications, the Ribbon tabs and accompanying command groups obviously vary from application to application in the Office suite. However, the similarities help you quickly adapt your knowledge of one of the applications that you know well (such as Word) to an application that you have not used as much (say, PowerPoint).

 Tip

If you are upgrading to Office 2013 from a pre–Office 2007 version of the Office suite, notice that the menu system has been replaced by the Ribbon. Commands that you would have normally found on the File menu are now available in the Backstage. As you learn where commands are located on the Ribbon, remember that many commands and features are available on shortcut menus. So when you are in doubt about where a command is on the Ribbon, right-click in the work-space and see if the shortcut menu provides the command you need.

Galleries

Certain commands on the Ribbon tabs require that you select from a list of choices. Some of these commands provide a simple list of choices, whereas other commands provide a more visual representation of the choices in a gallery.

A gallery supplies the actual results related to a command. For example, if you want to apply a theme to a PowerPoint presentation, access the Design tab and select from the available theme choices, as shown in Figure 2.2. As you work in the Office applications, you can select theme choices for your documents; each theme also supplies variants, which provide subtle changes to the theme colors, fonts, or effects.

Figure 2.2
Galleries provide result-driven options.

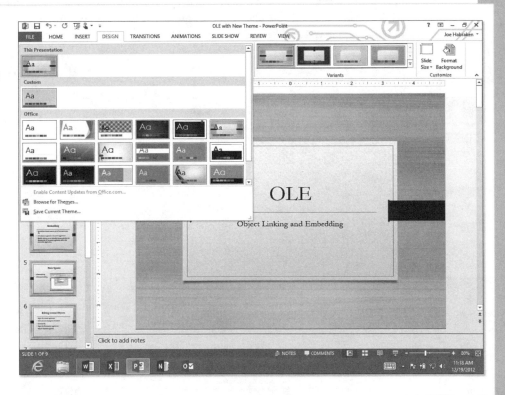

Because many of the galleries are related to the visual appearance or formatting of objects (such as tables or charts) in your documents, slides, and worksheets, a live preview of how that particular option would apply to your application's content is supplied when you place the mouse on that option. Being able to immediately preview and then apply a particular gallery option gives you greater flexibility and efficiency as you work with gallery-driven commands on the various Ribbon tabs.

 note

The ToolTips in Office 2013 have been enhanced and give you more information about a particular command when you place the mouse on it.

tip

The Office applications also provide Paste Preview, which enables you to view options for pasting an object into a file before you commit to the paste. Paste options are available when you select the Paste command in the Clipboard group.

Contextual Tabs

As you work in an Office application, the Ribbon tabs that are available do not remain static and can change depending on the current task you are undertaking. Contextual tabs become available when you are working with a particular object or feature.

For example, if you insert a table into a Word document or PowerPoint slide and then place the insertion point inside that table or select a row or column in the table, two Table Tools tabs appear: Design and Layout. Figure 2.3 shows the Design and Layout tabs of the Table Tools tab, with the Layout tab selected.

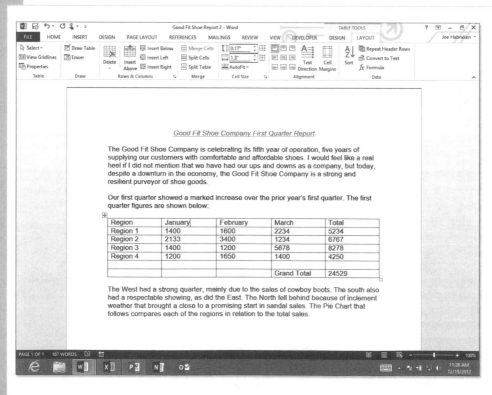

Figure 2.3
Contextual tabs provide tools for the task at hand.

You can use the commands on these contextual tabs related to tables as long as the table object is active. As soon as you click outside the table, the contextual tabs disappear and you return to the Ribbon with only the core tabs available. The core tabs include Home, Insert, and so forth; the specific tabs available depend on the application you are using and the task you are undertaking.

Overview of the Office Application Window

If you are new to the Office Fluent user interface (a more streamlined, less complex application interface that uses the Ribbon to access most commands and tools), it makes sense to take some time to gain familiarity with its various parts. Some of these application window elements have been around as long as Windows applications have. Others are additions to either Office 2007 (which launched the Office Fluent user interface) or Office 2010. Figure 2.4 shows the Excel application window, with callouts for several application window elements.

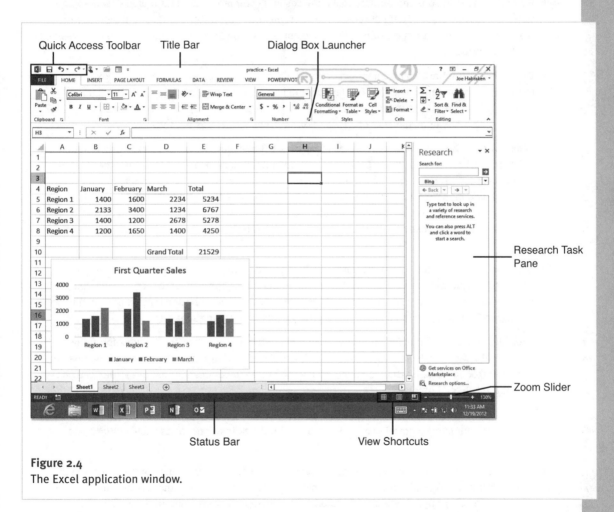

Figure 2.4
The Excel application window.

The following list provides a short overview of several elements common to the Office 2013 application interface:

- **Title bar:** The title bar supplies the application name and the name of your file (after you have saved it). The title bar also includes the Minimize, Maximize/Restore, and Close buttons on the far right.

- **Quick Access Toolbar:** The Quick Access Toolbar is nestled into the left side of the title bar. The Quick Access Toolbar provides the Save, Undo, and Redo buttons, by default. You can customize it to include other commands by using the Customize Quick Access Toolbar button.

- **Ribbon:** The Ribbon is the primary tool for accessing commands and features in Office applications. It contains a set of default tabs for each of the Office applications. Each tab includes command groups, which then contain individual commands. The Microsoft Office Help button resides on the far right.

- **Dialog box launcher:** Some command groups on the Ribbon tabs provide a dialog box launcher to the right of the group's name. The launcher enables you to open a dialog box that contains options related to that particular group. For example, the Font group on Excel's Home tab provides a dialog box launcher that opens the Format Cells dialog box with the Font tab selected.

- **Task panes:** The number of task panes in Office 2013 has increased when compared to Office 2010 and earlier versions of the Office application suite. A task pane is a multipurpose, feature-related window. A good example of a task pane is the Research task pane, which opens via the Research command on the Ribbon's Review tab. Several new task panes found in individual Office applications, such as PowerPoint, enable you to quickly format objects such as text boxes and other shapes. These new task panes replace dialog boxes that were often confusing and difficult to work with.

- **Mini toolbar:** The mini toolbar becomes available when you have selected an object in your application window (such as text in Word). The mini toolbar "ghosts" into view; when you place the mouse pointer on it, you can access its options via the toolbar buttons, many of which relate to various formatting options, such as bold, italics, alignment, and font size.

- **Shortcut menus:** Shortcut menus have been a mainstay of the Office applications for many years. Right-click a selected object to see options related to that object. The shortcut menus are often referred to as contextual menus because they provide commands that are within the context of the selected object.

- **Ruler:** Both vertical and horizontal scrollbars are available in the applications. This enables you to align objects more precisely and to set tabs and indents in applications such as Word and PowerPoint.

- **Status bar:** The status bar provides application information, feature indicators, and view commands. For example, in Word, the left side of the taskbar provides information such as the page number and other application-specific information, including word count and section number. The far right of the status bar provides the View shortcuts and the Zoom slider, by default.

It goes without saying that the individual Office application windows vary depending on the application you are using. Word, Excel, PowerPoint, and Publisher share the most elements of the Office applications (although Publisher does have some specialized interface tools); Outlook and OneNote adhere to the "typical" Ribbon-centric interface as much as possible but also provide unique tools for navigating the application. For example, Outlook provides a Folders pane that enables you to quickly access folders such as your Inbox, Sent Items, or Junk Email. OneNote provides a Notebook pane, which enables you to quickly access your current notebooks. Figure 2.5 shows the OneNote application window.

Figure 2.5
The OneNote application window.

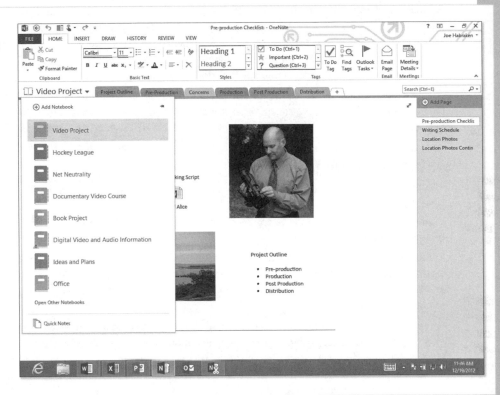

So although the Office applications share many navigation and command elements, the "one size fits all" application geography breaks down when you work with some of the more "specialized" applications, such as Outlook and OneNote. And because each Office application is built around a specific purpose, even Word, Excel, and PowerPoint require unique command elements that enable you to tackle a particular task or work with a specific feature.

 OneNote is discussed in depth in Part VII, beginning with Chapter 30, "Requisite OneNote: Essential Features."

note

Although it's called a dialog box launcher, some of the items that a launcher opens are really task panes instead of dialog boxes. The Styles pane in Word, which is opened with the launcher on the Styles group, is a good example.

➡ *Outlook is discussed in depth in Part V, beginning with Chapter 22, "Requisite Outlook: Configuration and Essential Features."*

Navigating the Office Applications

Because the Office 2013 applications take advantage of the same basic user interface, some universal procedures work for navigating and using the individual applications. However, because each Office application creates different things (say, worksheets versus documents, calendars, or contacts lists), the nuances that make up the more detailed command structures of the individual applications require that you develop some specific knowledge for each application.

As mentioned earlier in this chapter, at the center of the Office user interface is the Ribbon. So the Ribbon is a good place to start an investigation of common features and tools in the Office applications.

Working with the Ribbon

The Ribbon tabs provide a results-driven grouping of application commands that divide closely related commands into groups. Accessing Ribbon commands is just a matter of selecting the appropriate tab and then accessing the command that you want from the group containing the commands related to a particular feature.

For example, in Excel, you might want to insert a Sum function into a selected worksheet cell to total a column of values. You select the Ribbon's Formulas tab, look in the Function Library group, and then select the AutoSum command. The Ribbon's structure makes it easy to quickly drill down to a specific command or feature.

Some of the individual commands in the command groups include a drop-down arrow. Clicking this arrow on some commands gives you a simple list of options related to the command, which might also open dialog boxes associated with that particular feature. For example, clicking the Insert command on the Excel Ribbon's Home tab provides the options Insert Cells, Insert Sheet Rows, Insert Sheet Columns, and Insert Sheet. The Insert Cells option opens the Insert dialog box, where you can specify how the inserted cells should affect existing cells or whether Excel should insert an entire row or column.

Other commands provide access to a gallery of choices related to the command. For example, if you have selected text in a Word document and you want to apply a new style to the selected text, you can do so from the Style gallery, which is available in the Style group on the Ribbon's Home tab.

When you place the mouse pointer on one of the styles provided in the Style gallery, you can preview the style on the selected text (see Figure 2.6). This feature, Live Preview, enables you to test various options as you work in an Office application and apply only the option that works best. This saves you from having to apply a certain option to see how it looks and then using the Undo command to start over when you don't like the results.

The Live Preview feature is most prevalent in Office applications such as Word, Excel, PowerPoint, and Publisher. For example, a number of Word commands bring up Live Preview, including the Line and Paragraph Spacing command in the Paragraph group on the Home tab and the Header, Footer, and Page Number commands on the Ribbon's Insert tab (in the Header and Footer group).

Figure 2.6
Galleries
provide visual
options and
Live Preview.

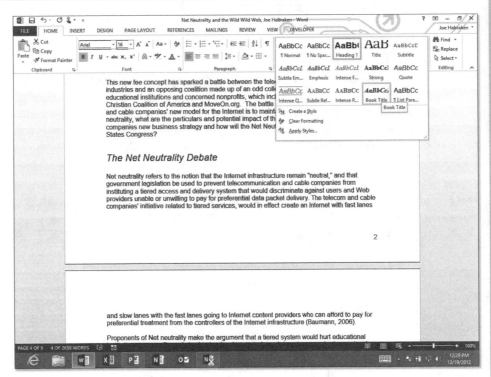

Minimizing the Ribbon

The Ribbon takes up a big chunk of the application window, particularly because it provides visual cues for accessing commands and actually contains some galleries on Ribbon tabs. You can configure how you want the Ribbon to behave in an application window. On the upper right of the Office applications' workspace (the application window) is a Ribbon Display Options button just to the right of the Help icon.

The Ribbon Display Options button gives you three options for dealing with the Ribbon:

- **Auto-hide Ribbon:** This option hides the Ribbon. You can access the Ribbon by clicking at the top of the application window.

- **Show Tabs:** This option shows the Ribbon tabs only. Click a tab to view the associated commands.

- **Show Tabs and Commands:** This option is the default setting and shows the entire Ribbon, including the tabs and the commands available on the currently selected tab.

All the Office applications provide the Ribbon Display Options button except for Publisher. Publisher has a Collapse the Ribbon command (an upward-pointing chevron) just to the right of the Ribbon. Click this button to show the Ribbon tabs only. When you click a tab, the Ribbon commands appear.

Accessing the Ribbon with the Keyboard

You can also access some Ribbon commands using the keyboard. The keystrokes aren't typical keyboard shortcuts, such as Ctrl+B for bold, but they can work for you when you want to keep your hands on the keyboard.

Press (and release) the Alt key, and individual shortcut keys appear for the tabs on the Ribbon. For example, the Home tab is assigned the H shortcut key, the Insert tab is assigned N, and so on. Click one of the Ribbon tabs using the appropriate shortcut key. The tab is selected, and keyboard shortcuts are assigned to the commands on the tab. Figure 2.7 shows the keyboard shortcuts assigned to the Word Ribbon's Home tab.

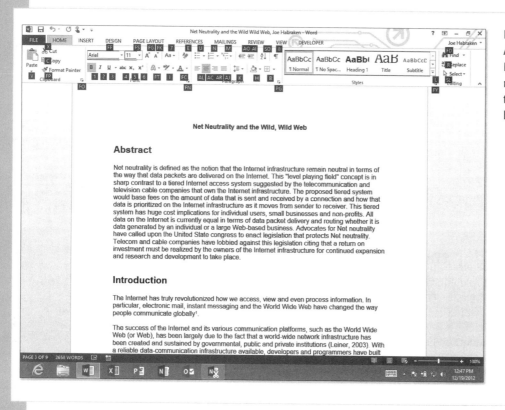

Figure 2.7
Access Ribbon commands from the keyboard.

Individual alphanumeric keystrokes and multiple alphanumeric keystrokes define the commands on the Ribbon tab. To access a particular command, press the key or key combination for that command. For example, you press the N key to access the Numbered List command. Some commands, however, such as the Font Color command, require that you press two keys simultaneously—in this case, F and C.

When you select a keyboard shortcut, the command activates and the keyboard shortcuts on the Ribbon disappear. To exit the current command and go back to the Ribbon with keyboard

 note

When you press Alt to access the Ribbon using keyboard shortcuts, the Quick Access Toolbar buttons are assigned numerical shortcuts.

shortcuts, press Esc. You can toggle off the keyboard shortcuts by pressing Alt or by clicking inside the application workspace.

Working in the Backstage

The Office Backstage has been designed to provide easy access to tasks and settings that are part of the actual work that you do in the application window. So accessing information related to the file you are working with in the application window, accessing print settings, and sharing the file with other users are all relegated to the Backstage.

To access the Backstage, click the File tab on the Ribbon. When you enter the Backstage, the Info page is selected. This page provides information related to the file's properties and also enables you to access document-protection features and inspect a document that you might want to share. Other pages in the Backstage are accessed using the navigation list on the left of the Backstage. If you want to return to the application window, click the Back button at the top of the navigation list. Figure 2.8 shows the Word Backstage with the Info page selected.

Figure 2.8
The Backstage provides access to features such as printing and sharing.

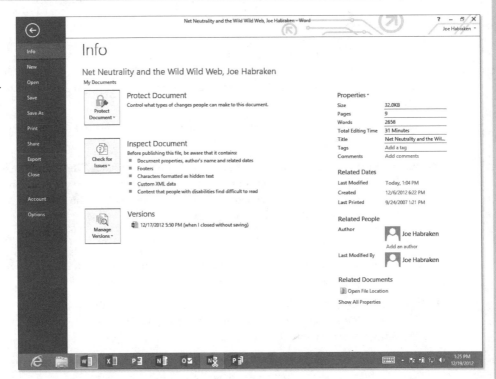

The Backstage pages available in Word, Excel, PowerPoint, and Publisher are the same. This is because these applications all create files as their products. Outlook is different because of the type of "product" that you create in Outlook. You do create entries such as emails and appointments, but they are stored the same way as the individual files you create in an application such as Word. OneNote also has a "modified" Backstage, which is primarily because your OneNote notebooks are saved automatically. So sharing your notebooks is a little different than sharing a file such as an Excel workbook.

As already mentioned, Word, Excel, PowerPoint, and Publisher share the same Backstage pages. To give you an idea of the type of information, commands, or features you can access in the Backstage, let's look at what you would find if you accessed the Backstage in one of these applications (such as Word or PowerPoint). A list of the Backstage pages follows:

- **Info:** Provides access to permission settings (Protect Document) for the file and enables you to check the file for any issues that might cause problems if you share the file with other users. The Info page also provides access to versions of the file that automatically saved during your application session (if you don't save a file when exiting). This page provides access to file properties such as file size and editing time, and lists authors who have worked on the file.

- **New:** Gives you access to templates and themes, which you can use to create a new file. The Search box enables you to search for other templates available on Office.com.

- **Open:** Provides a list of "places" you can use to store and retrieve your files. Your places include My Computer and any cloud storage that you have access to, such as SkyDrive or a SharePoint site. Access to cloud storage requires that you log onto Office using the username and password for these cloud storage possibilities. You can sign into Office when you complete the Office installation. You can also add cloud storage places by using the Login service at the top right of the Backstage.

- **Save:** Saves changes to the current file. The Save command is also available on the Quick Access Toolbar in the application window.

- **Save As:** Shows all the "places" you have available for file storage. The list of places provided includes My Computer and any cloud storage you can access, such as your SkyDrive, SkyDrive Pro, or a SharePoint site. Recently accessed locations are also listed on this page. You can use the Browse button to open the Save As dialog box.

- **Print:** Provides access to print and page setup commands. It also provides a Print Preview pane.

- **Share:** Enables you to share the current file with other users. Options include email sharing invitations and the capability to present the document or presentation online.

- **Export:** Enables you to create a PDF or XPS version of your file that you can then share with other users. The Export page also provides the Change File Type command, which makes it easy to save the file using a different file type.

- **Close:** Closes the current document (workbook or presentation); this also exits the application if this is the only file you currently have open.

- **Account:** Lists user information and shows the Office background and theme that you are using by default. The Account page also shows the connected services you are accessing, such as your SkyDrive or Flickr (for online photo storage). The Account page shows the Microsoft Office product that is activated on your computer and the individual applications that the product contains.

- **Options:** Provides access to the configuration options for the application. We discuss how to change application options later in this chapter.

Using the Backstage requires that you leave behind the application interface. This has been done by design because the Backstage pages are designed so that you can concentrate on particular settings and tasks without worrying about the intricacies of the document itself. When you finish working in the Backstage, you can return to the application window by clicking the Back button.

Customizing an Application Interface

You can customize the Office 2013 application interfaces to suit your own needs. These customization options include customizing the Ribbon, the Quick Access Toolbar, and the status bar.

Before we look at customizing the Ribbon and the Quick Access Toolbar, which really allows you to be selective about the commands and features available, we should briefly discuss the fact that customizing the application interface also relates to whether the application window shows certain elements or tools. For example, we have already discussed ways to show or hide the Ribbon. You also have control over other elements of the application window, such as task panes. Task panes give you the capability to fine-tune a particular feature. For example, when you are formatting elements of a chart in Excel, you can configure each chart element separately in an associated task pane. Figure 2.9 shows the Format Legend task pane, which enables you to configure the various legend options, including position, colors, and effects.

Figure 2.9
The Format Legend task pane in Excel.

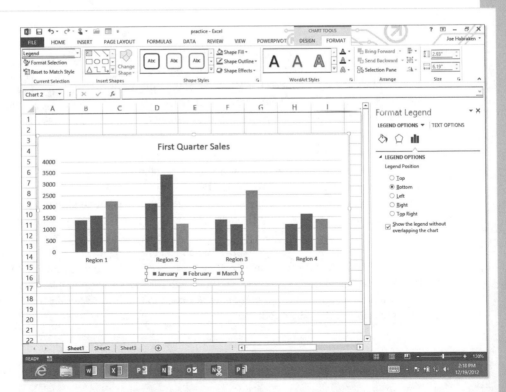

When you open a task pane in an application window, you can choose to leave that task pane floating in the application window or you can close it. For example, the Format Legend task pane (shown in Figure 2.9) enables you to quickly click an element in a legend to access the settings. If you are going to configure multiple elements, it makes sense to leave the task pane in the Excel application window until you have finished with it.

Depending on the application you use, you might also find it advantageous to have the ruler available in the application window, particularly if you are aligning objects on a page or are working in Word or PowerPoint and want to set tab stops or indents using the ruler. To place the vertical and horizontal rulers in the application workspace, click the Ribbon's View tab and then select the Ruler check box. In an application such as Publisher, the ruler is particularly important in aligning objects in your publications, and you can drag guides from the rulers to help you position items on the page.

Customizing the Ribbon

Because the Ribbon is the command center for the Office applications, it certainly makes sense for you to customize it as you see fit. You have control over the tabs available on the Ribbon, as well as the commands available on those tabs. Each Office application has an Options window. One of the options relates to tailoring the Ribbon to your needs. You access the application options, such as Word Options, via the Backstage. Click File to open the Backstage and then select Options. The Options window for that application opens.

Each Options window provides an options list on the left side of the window. To work with the Ribbon, select Customize Ribbon. Figure 2.10 shows the Customize Ribbon settings in the Word Options window.

Let's start our discussion on the right side of the Customize Ribbon window. The list box on the right lists available tabs for the Ribbon. By default, the Customize the Ribbon drop-down box is set to Main Tabs (explained shortly). Some of the tabs are enabled, and the check box for the tab is selected. Other tabs are not enabled or checked, and these tabs are not available on the application's Ribbon.

 note

The status bar can be customized in terms of what appears on the status bar. The next section discusses customizing the status bar.

You can use the Customize the Ribbon drop-down list to view different lists of the tabs available in an application; to see all the tabs available, select All Tabs. As already mentioned, the main tabs are listed by default. The main tabs are the tabs that remain available on the Ribbon no matter what you are working on in the application. The main tabs include the default tabs, such as Home, Insert, and so forth, and other tabs that are not available by default, such as the Developer tab. The tool tabs are a different story; these tabs are the contextual tabs that appear when you are working on a specific application object or element. For example, in Word, Table Tools is a set of contextual tabs (Design and Layout) that appear when you are working on a table. You can enable (show) or disable (hide) either main tabs or tool tabs. Just remember that you don't normally see the tool tabs until they activate when you perform a particular task in the application.

Figure 2.10
The Word Options window, with Customize Ribbon selected.

You can expand a particular tab in the Tabs list to view the groups available on that tab. You can then expand a group on the tab to view the commands available in a group. You can enable a tab in the tabs list, if you want. For example, if you want to create macros in a particular application, you need to have access to the Developer tab. To include the Developer tab on the application's Ribbon, select the Developer tab check box.

Below the Tabs list is a set of buttons that are useful if you want to create new tabs and groups (with the intention that these groups will contain commands). A brief description of each command button follows:

 tip

If you want to rearrange the order of the tabs on the application's Ribbon, you can use the Move Up and Move Down buttons to the right of the Tabs list. Click a tab and then use either button to move the tab.

- **New Tab:** Creates a new tab below the currently selected tab in the Tabs list. When you create a new tab, a new group is automatically created for the new tab.

- **New Group:** Creates a new group below the currently selected group.

- **Rename:** Enables you to rename a tab or group in the Tabs list.

- **Reset:** Enables you to reset the selected Ribbon tab or reset all the customizations that you made to an application's Ribbon. This is useful when you have been overzealous in creating tabs and groups.

- **Import/Export:** Enables you to import a customization file or create a new customization file based on the changes you made to the application's Ribbon. After you have created a customization file for an application's Ribbon, you can import it on other computers running Office 2013. This gives you access to your custom Ribbon at home or the office.

Creating custom tabs with custom groups requires that you use the New Tab, New Group, and Rename commands. After you create your custom tabs and groups, you can add commands to them.

You can add commands to the groups on the existing Ribbon tabs. You can also add commands to a group or groups contained in any new tabs you have created. On the left of the Ribbon settings windows is a list of available commands. By default, popular commands are shown. You can use the Choose commands from the drop-down list at the top left of the window to select the type of commands listed. You can select from command lists such as Commands Not in the Ribbon, All Commands, and commands by tab (such as File Tab and All Tabs). If you want to see all the commands available in an application, select the All Commands option.

Adding a command or commands to a Ribbon tab's group is straightforward. Select the group in the Tabs list. Then select the command that you want to add to the group in the Command list. Click the Add button to add the command to the group. You can repeat this procedure as needed to add commands that you use frequently to existing groups on the main or tools tabs. You can also populate the custom groups that you have created for any custom tabs.

Removing a command from a group requires only that you locate the command (in the group and on the tab) in the Tabs list. Select the command and then click Remove to remove the command.

When you finish modifying the Ribbon, you can close the application's Options window. The changes you made to the Ribbon become available as soon as you return to the application's workspace.

 tip

You can also access the New Tab, New Group, Rename, Move Up, and Move Down commands by right-clicking the Tabs list.

 tip

You can customize (or add) keyboard shortcuts for the various Ribbon commands. Select Customize (below the Command list). Use the Customize Keyboard dialog box to locate a particular command, and then set the new shortcut key for that command.

Customizing the Quick Access Toolbar

The Quick Access Toolbar is located in the upper-left corner of the application window. By design, it gives you a toolbar where you can quickly find commands that you use often. The Quick Access Toolbar provides the Save, Undo, and Redo commands by default.

You can add commands to the Quick Access Toolbar using the list provided on the Customize Quick Access Toolbar menu. Click the Customize Quick Access Toolbar button to the right of the Quick Access Toolbar to access the menu. Figure 2.11 shows the Excel Quick Access Toolbar menu.

Figure 2.11
The Quick
Access
Toolbar
menu.

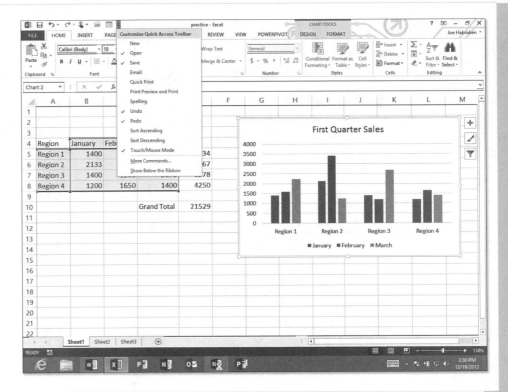

When you want add a command button to the toolbar, select a command on the menu. A check mark appears to the left of the command, and the command button is placed on the Quick Access Toolbar. You can also remove any command button from the toolbar by deselecting it on the menu.

The Customize Quick Access Toolbar menu provides only a short list of commands to add to the toolbar. If you want to add a command not listed, you need to access the Customize the Quick Access Toolbar window. This window gives you a complete listing of all the commands available in the application.

On the Customize Quick Access Toolbar menu, select More Commands. Doing so opens the application's Options window with the Quick Access Toolbar options selected. Figure 2.12 shows the Excel Options window with Quick Access Toolbar selected.

> **tip**
>
> To place the Quick Access Toolbar below the Ribbon in the application window, select Show Below the Ribbon on the Customize Quick Access Toolbar menu.

On the right of the Quick Access Toolbar options is a list of the commands currently on the Quick Access Toolbar. On the left side of the Options window is a list of the popular commands. You can use the Choose Commands from List (on the top left of the window) to view other command sets, such as Commands Not in the Ribbon and All Commands. You can also select a particular Ribbon tab in this list to view the commands on that tab.

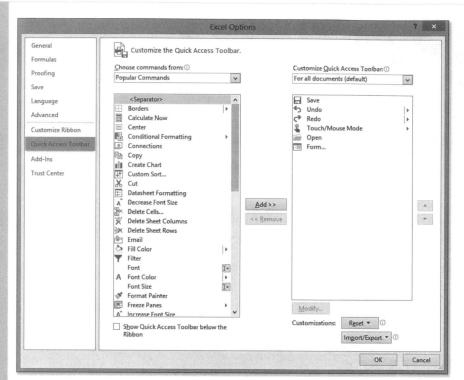

Figure 2.12
Customize the Quick Access Toolbar in the Options window.

To add a command from the Command list, select the command and then click the Add button. The command appears in the Quick Access Toolbar list on the right side of the window. To rearrange the commands in the Quick Access Toolbar list, you can use the Move Up and Move Down buttons as needed. The list order determines the order in which the commands appear on the Quick Access Toolbar. If you decide that you don't want a command on the toolbar, select the command and then click Remove.

You can also create a secondary Quick Access Toolbar for the current file (a Word document, an Excel workbook, and so forth). Note the Customize Quick Access Toolbar drop-down list above the Quick Access Toolbar command list (on the right side of the window). By default, you are customizing the Quick Access Toolbar for all the documents that you create in the application, such as all the workbooks you create in Excel or all the presentations you create in PowerPoint. Any changes that you make to the Quick Access Toolbar will be available whenever you use the application.

 note
You can also add macros that you create to the Quick Access Toolbar and the Ribbon. For a primer on creating Office 2013 macros, see Appendix B, "Office Macros."

If you are creating a template or a document and want to create a Quick Access Toolbar that is available only in that document, you can use the Customize Quick Access Toolbar drop-down list to select the current document. This empties the Command list (on the right side of the Options window); you can select commands in the Command list (on the left side of the window) and then use the Add button to populate the special Quick Access Toolbar for that document. This new Quick Access Toolbar appears to the right of the default Quick Access Toolbar, above the Ribbon, in the application window after you close the Customize the Quick Access Toolbar Options window.

A couple more points about the Quick Access Toolbar options are relevant: If you decide that you don't like the changes you have made to the Quick Access Toolbar, you can click the Reset button at the bottom right of the window. As with custom Ribbons, you can use the Import/Export button to import custom Quick Access Toolbars that you have created on other computers. You can also export your Quick Access Toolbar configuration to an exported Office UI file that can be used on any computer with Office 2013 installed.

 tip

The type of work you do in an application influences the commands that you add to that application's Quick Access Toolbar. However, in terms of good additions to the toolbar in any Office application, I'm partial to the Open, Open Recent File, Paste Special, Save As, and Quick Print commands.

When you finish working in the Options window, click OK. This closes the window and returns you to the application workspace. The changes you have made to the Quick Access Toolbar are immediately available.

Customizing the Status Bar

The Office applications' status bar has historically served as an informational tool at the bottom of the application window. It provides information related to the file that you are working on and lets you know whether certain features (such as overtype) are enabled. The Office 2013 applications' status bar is actually customizable, allowing you to determine what kind of information it provides. We have already discussed the fact that the View shortcuts, Zoom, and Zoom slider tools are on the right side of the status bar and let you control your view of your document in the application window.

You can customize the status bar to show additional information related to your current document (or worksheet or slide). Other informational additions to the status bar, such as Caps Lock, enable you to see from the status bar whether Caps Lock has been enabled.

You can also place options on the status bar that perform an action when you click on them. For example, in Word, you can add Word Count to the status bar and use it to quickly open the Word Count dialog box and view the statistics for the document. A useful status bar option in Excel is the Num Lock option (which not all the applications have) because the numerical keypad on the keyboard is often used to enter values into Excel worksheets.

To customize the status bar, right-click anywhere on it. The Customize Status Bar menu appears. Figure 2.13 shows the Word Customize Status Bar menu.

To add an item to the status bar, click the item. You can also remove items from the status bar by deselecting them (remove the check mark) on the Customize Status Bar menu, as needed.

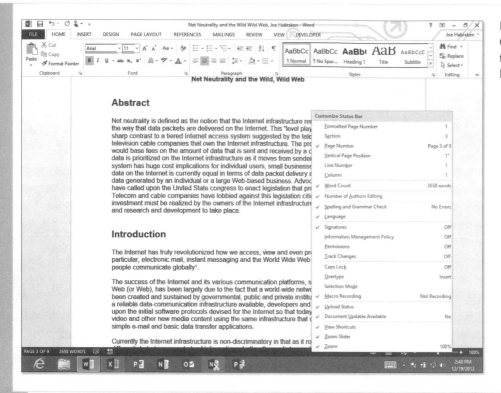

Figure 2.13
Customize
the status
bar.

Configuring Application Options

Microsoft has done a good job of making the tools for configuring the various Office 2013 members extremely consistent across the applications. Excel, Word, PowerPoint, and Publisher use many of the same option categories, such as General, Customize Ribbon, and Add-Ins. Even Outlook and OneNote provide the same overall approach to configuring the application using the Options window.

Obviously, some differences exist in the configuration options provided for the Office applications because each application serves a different function. For example, Excel has a Formulas option category, which makes sense because of Excel's capability to do calculations. In Outlook, configuration options are available for the Calendar, contacts, and mail, which makes sense because of the type of work you do in Outlook.

All the applications in the Office 2013 suite provide an Options link in the Backstage. Select File, Options to open its Options window. Figure 2.14 shows the Excel Options window with the General category selected.

The Options window breaks down the various application configuration possibilities into a series of categories. Each category provides a set of tools for configuring associated features. In Figure 2.14, the General category is selected and provides user interface options such as enabling the

Mini Toolbar and Live Preview. The User Name option, available under Personalize Your Copy of Microsoft Office, is a universal setting, and any change to the username in Excel ports over to other applications such as Word and PowerPoint.

Figure 2.14
Excel General
Options window.

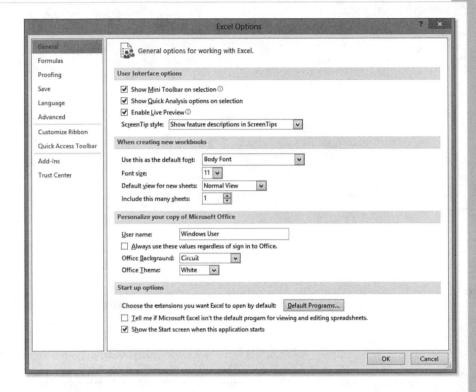

Two other option categories contain settings that can affect multiple Office applications: Proofing and Language. The Proofing options enable you to set the AutoCorrect settings specifically for an application. However, when you select options related to how spelling is corrected in the application or the default dictionary language, other applications also use those settings. Figure 2.15 shows the Excel Proofing options.

Note that many spelling options are controlled using check boxes, and drop-down lists provide options for different language modes and the main dictionary language. The Proofing category provides similar options when accessed in Word or PowerPoint. You need to change Proofing options in only one application, however, for them to be in force in the other applications.

The settings available in the Language options are also Office preferences rather than individual application preferences. Changing settings such as the editing, display, and help languages affects the other Office applications. Think of the Proofing and Language options as universal options that are applied to all the applications.

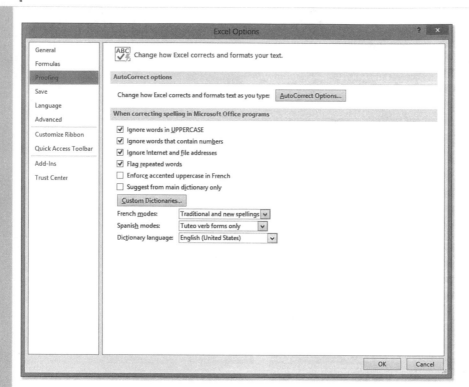

Figure 2.15
Excel Proofing
options.

In terms of options specific to an application (other than the Ribbon and Quick Access Toolbar settings that we have already discussed), most of these are housed in the Advanced category. Advanced options are divided into subcategories such as Editing, Print, Display, and a catch-all General subcategory.

The Advanced options available for each application vary; however, the subcategories (such as Editing and Print) are consistent across the applications, particularly Word, Excel, PowerPoint, and Publisher. Outlook is a good example of the odd man out: It has configuration options that you don't have to deal with in the other applications. These relate to the different types of information that you create and manage in Outlook, such as emails, calendars, and contacts. Outlook's use and configuration is discussed in detail in the Outlook section of this book.

➡️ *Outlook's configuration is discussed in Chapter 22, "Requisite Outlook: Configuration and Essential Features."*

Advanced Option Settings

The Advanced Option settings provide several application-specific settings. Even though these settings are specific to the application you are working in, the Advanced option subcategories that you use in applications such as Word, Excel, and PowerPoint are as follows:

- **Editing Options:** These options relate to editing and selecting items in the application. For example, Word provides an Editing option related to whether selected text is replaced when you type. Excel provides an Editing option that enables or disables Auto-Complete. Look for features in this subcategory that make it easier for you to select and edit information in the applications.

- **Cut, Copy, and Paste:** True to their names, these options relate to settings such as whether the Paste Options button is enabled when you paste an item. They also include settings in Word for setting formatting options related to pasting within the same document, between documents, or between programs.

- **Display:** This set of options provides settings for the number of recent files that are displayed in the Backstage, and contains other settings related to whether formatting marks, such as Tab characters and spaces, are shown on the screen.

- **Print:** These options relate to the quality of certain objects when they are printed. For example, in Excel, you can set a high-quality mode for graphics. In PowerPoint, you can specify that all printing is high quality. Word and PowerPoint also provide options for background printing so that you can continue to use the application as you are printing.

Many of the Advanced options available for Office applications are easy to work with. Most are enabled or disabled via check boxes. You can try out a particular setting by enabling it with a click of the mouse. If it isn't particularly useful, you can return to the Advanced options and easily disable the option with another click.

Add-Ins

One other category of application options to be aware of is the add-ins. Add-ins are additions to an application that increase the application's functionality. Each Office application has add-ins available. Some are added by default when you install the application. Other add-ins are installed when you install Office 2013 but are not added to the application by default. This means that they are inactive add-ins. For example, Excel has add-ins such as the Solver and the Euro Currency Tools. To use either of these add-ins, you must add them to your Excel configuration.

When you select the Add-Ins category in the application Options window, you can view the active and inactive add-ins. To enable an inactive add-in, follow these steps:

1. Select Add-Ins in the Manage drop-down list at the bottom of the Options window (when the Add-Ins category is selected). Then click Go.

2. An Add-Ins dialog box appears that is specific to the application (such as Excel or Word). The dialog box lists the available add-ins.

3. Select an add-in. If you have downloaded an add-in, you can use the Browse button to locate it.

4. After selecting an add-in (or add-ins) to activate, click OK. The Add-Ins dialog box closes.

When you return to the Options window for the application and select Add-Ins, the Active Application Add-Ins list includes the add-ins that you activated. You can now use the add-in as needed in the application.

Adding Apps to the Office Applications

Office 2013 enables you to add apps to your Office applications to extend their functionality. An app is a self-contained mini-application with a particular function. For example, the Merriam-Webster dictionary app helps you look up the definition of a selected word from within an application window such as Word. Figure 2.16 shows the Word window and the Dictionary app (on the right in its own task pane).

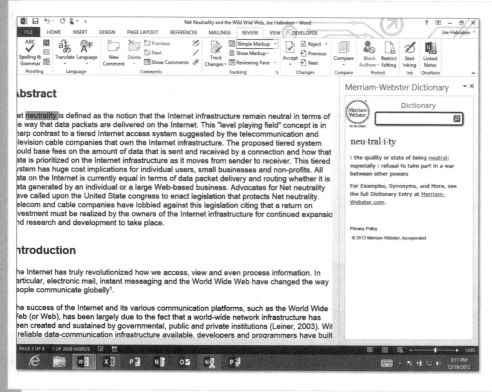

Figure 2.16
The Dictionary app in Word.

You can use the Dictionary app in more than one Office application; you can use it in Word, Excel, or PowerPoint. However, other apps are specific to an application in the Office suite. For example, the Bing Finance app provides real-time stock information and is designed for use within Excel. You can open the Bing Finance app in its task pane (on the Insert tab, select Insert and then Apps for Office to access the installed apps for an application) and then use it to locate information on specific securities. The Bing Finance App is designed to help you quickly build a portfolio table in an Excel worksheet.

You can add other apps to your Office applications as well. Select Apps for Office on an application's Insert tab and then select See All. In the Apps for Office window, click the Find More Apps at the Office Store link. Your browser opens on the Apps page for the application you are using. For example, if you open the Apps web page when you are in Excel, the apps for Excel 2013 appear in the browser window, as shown in Figure 2.17.

Figure 2.17
The Apps for
Excel 2013
web page.

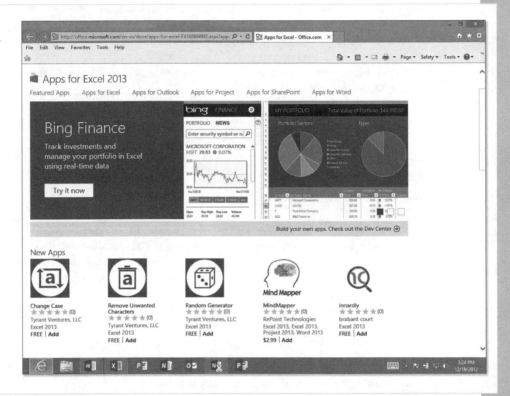

You can browse the apps for the current application or use the links to view apps for other applications in the Office suite. Each app icon provides the cost for the app (many are free) and the company of origin. When you have located an app you want to add to your Office installation, click Add (below the app description). You are taken to a description page that provides more information about the app, including the app's requirements (and terms and conditions). When you are ready to download the app, click Add. You are asked to confirm that you want to add the app. Click Continue.

After the app has downloaded, you can return to the application and give the newly added app a test drive. Navigate to the Ribbon's Insert tab and select Apps for Office. Select See All to open the Apps for Office window. Select your newly downloaded app in the Apps for Office window and then select Insert. The app opens in a task pane or app window. Now you can take advantage of the additional functionality that the app provides your Office application(s).

Using the Trust Center

Keeping your computer secure from attack and protecting personal information on your computer has become a greater challenge as connectivity to the somewhat untrustworthy networking infrastructure of the Internet has become common. We use the Internet in many instances for private communication and to share files (by email and other means) without necessarily considering that we are opening up our files and computer to a public global network. Even extremely secure corporate networks that protect users from the risks of a persistent connection with the Internet can have problems with security and privacy issues.

Microsoft has worked hard to build security and privacy protections into the Office applications themselves, and this is where the Trust Center comes in. Each Office application has its own Trust Center, which provides access to security and privacy settings for the application. You access the Trust Center settings via the Options window of the specific application. To open the Trust Center for an Office application, follow these steps:

1. Select File on the Ribbon to access the Backstage.

2. Select Options to open the Options window.

3. In the Options window, select Trust Center. Because the Trust Center is related to privacy and security settings, the Options window provides a series of links that include access to Microsoft's privacy statement for the current application and Office, and a link for Microsoft Trustworthy Computing. Microsoft recommends not changing the settings in the Trust Center if you want to keep your computer secure. Unless you have a compelling reason to change these settings, it makes sense to go with the defaults. Changing the security settings could open your computer to attack, particularly if you use macros from a source unknown to you.

4. Select Trust Center Settings to open the application's Trust Center. Figure 2.18 shows the Word Trust Center with the Trusted Locations options selected.

The Trust Center for each of the Office applications differs in the options available. For example, Outlook also provides Email Security settings and Automatic Download options (related to pictures in HTML emails). Outlook does not have Trusted Documents or Add-Ins options, as Word does. Word, PowerPoint, and Excel have similar options available in their Trust Centers. Outlook, OneNote, and Publisher provide only a subset of the options in the other applications, but they include some special options related to the function of the application (such as the Trust Center options found in Outlook, as we've already mentioned).

Because Microsoft sees the Trust Center as a way to make your application environment more secure, make changes to these settings only if a change provides greater security or privacy as you work. Although it is easy to select a Trust Center option category and begin to make what seems like good choices, Trust Center options are really "if it isn't broke, don't fix it" settings; don't change them unless you have a compelling reason to do so.

 caution

If you work on a corporate network, or are a small office or home user and don't have an actual need that requires changes to the Trust Center, don't change the settings. A compelling reason might be that you are working with macros or you are considering using add-ins from a source other than Microsoft, and you want the add-ins to be signed by a trusted publisher.

Figure 2.18
The Trust Center.

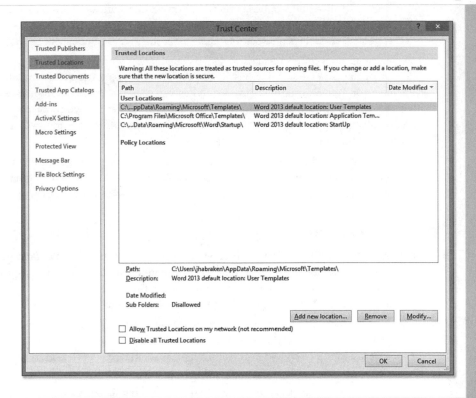

Two options related to the Trust Center that make it easier for you to take advantage of files containing active content, such as macros or ActiveX controls, are the Trusted Publishers and Trusted Documents settings. Both settings are available in the Word, Excel, and PowerPoint Security Centers. This makes sense because Word documents, Excel worksheets, and PowerPoint presentations are most likely to use active content, such as macros. The following information looks more closely at trusted publishers and trusted locations.

Trusted Publishers

If you use macros, add-ins, or ActiveX controls to enhance the capabilities of your Microsoft Office applications and you acquire these application additions from a legitimate developer, you can add the publisher to the Trusted Publishers list. For you to add a publisher to the list, the developer's add-in or ActiveX control must be digitally signed using a digital certificate that the developer or publisher has acquired. The certificate must be from a reputable certificate authority. A number of certificate authorities are available online, such as A-Trust (www.a-trust.at), CertPlus (http://certplus.com), and VeriSign (http://digitalid.verisign.com).

 tip

Remove publishers from the list only when the digital signature has expired or you no longer use content from that publisher.

You don't actually add the publisher to the Trusted Publishers list in the Trust Center. You can use the Trust Center only to view details related to a trusted publisher or to remove a publisher from the list. To remove a publisher, select the publisher in the Trusted Publishers list and then click Remove.

When you attempt to run a macro or ActiveX control that you have acquired, it is disabled by default. A message bar appears below the Ribbon in the application window, letting you know that the macro or ActiveX control is disabled. When you click the Options button in the message bar, the Security Options dialog box for that item opens. In the dialog box, you can see whether the developer/publisher digitally signed the item. You can view details related to the digital signature by clicking the Show Signature Details link.

If you are satisfied that the signed item is using a legitimate digital certificate and you want to add the publisher to the Trusted Publishers list, select the Trust All Documents from This Publisher option in the Security dialog box. Then click OK to add the publisher to the list in that application.

Trusted Locations

In Word, Excel, and PowerPoint, the Trusted Locations list contains the default paths for documents, templates, startup files, and other items, such as add-ins (in Excel). If you are a user on a sophisticated network (other than a home network), some of these locations might be local paths on your computer or might have been edited by your network administrator to use network paths.

The whole purpose of trusted locations is that these folders are used to store files that you trust; you do not want the Trust Center to raise a fuss when you open a file stored in a trusted location. This enables you to place files that contain macros or other content, such as add-ins, in a trusted folder and not have the Trust Center disable any of the content when you open the file.

You can edit the default trusted location path, if you want. Select a user location in the list and then click the Modify button in the Trusted Locations pane. The Microsoft Office Trusted Location dialog box opens. Change the path in the Path box and then click OK to close the dialog box.

In most cases, it is probably advisable not to change any of the default trusted locations, particularly if your Office applications were configured specifically to run on your corporate network. This doesn't mean that you can't create your own trusted locations and use them as depots for files that contain content that must be trusted in order to run correctly (such as macros, ActiveX controls, and so forth).

To create a new trusted location, click the Add New Location button. The Microsoft Office Trusted Location dialog box opens, as shown in Figure 2.19.

Type the path for the new location in the Path text box, or use the Browse button to locate the folder on your computer or your network. If you want to have all the subfolders in the new trusted folder also be trusted, select the Subfolders of This Location Are Also Trusted check box.

You can add an optional description for the new trusted location in the Description box. When you have finished entering the information for the new trusted source, click the OK button.

 note

If you create your own macros or use macros created by co-workers, changes to Trust Center options related to macros might come into play. Appendix B discusses macros in more depth.

Figure 2.19
Create a new trusted location.

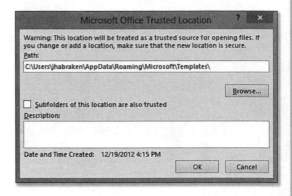

The new trusted location is added to the Trusted Locations list. If you need to remove a location that you no longer use or need, select the location in the list. You can then click the Remove button to remove the trusted location.

MANAGING AND SHARING OFFICE FILES

The Microsoft Office 2013 applications provide you with all the tools you need to create documents, presentations, workbooks, and publications. After you create your various files using the Office applications, it is up to you to manage your files and share them with colleagues and co-workers.

In this chapter, we take a look at the Office file formats used in each of the Office applications. We also look at your options for managing and sharing files.

Understanding Office File Formats

The default file formats for each of the Office applications (all except for OneNote) take advantage of the open XML (eXtensible Markup Language) file standards. The file formats provide benefits in terms of file compaction, improved damage recovery, better detection of files containing macros, and better compatibility with other vendor software.

Although some backward-compatibility issues may be involved when you attempt to share a file using one of these file formats with a user who still works with an earlier version of a particular Office application, most problems have been ironed out. Users still working with earlier versions of the Office applications (including versions of Microsoft Office running in the Mac OS environment) can take advantage of various conversion utilities and software updates that enable them to convert or directly open a file using one of the new file formats. You can also save your files in file formats that offer backward compatibility for co-workers still using older versions of the Office applications. And the Office applications (such as Word and Excel) provide you with compatibility-checking tools that help negate any issues with files shared with users of legacy Office applications.

As already mentioned, Word, Excel, and PowerPoint use the open XML file formats by default when you save a file in these applications. And you have a number of other file format options in these applications, if needed.

Publisher 2013, on the other hand, saves publications by default in the .pub file type, which was first introduced with the Office 2003 version of Publisher. The .pub file type is compatible with both Publisher 2010 and Publisher 2007 (the two previous versions of Publisher). Although Publisher does not enable you to save a publication in the open XML file format, you can save Publisher files in the XPS file type, which is an XML file format for "electronic paper." Publisher also has file types available that you can use to make your publications backward compatible with collaborators who are using previous versions of Microsoft Publisher, such as Publisher 2000 and Publisher 98.

➡ *For more about Publisher file types, **see** "Creating a New Publication," **p. 812.***

Each of the Office applications gives you options in terms of saving a file in different file formats. The following lists provide an overview of some of the file types used in Word, Excel, and PowerPoint, respectively.

Word:

File Extension	Description
docx	XML file type; default file type for Word 2010 and 2013 documents
docm	XML file type; macro-enabled document
dotx	XML file type; Word template
dotm	XML file type; macro-enabled Word template
doc	Binary file type; document compatibility with Word 97–2003
dot	Binary file type; template compatibility with Word 97–2003

Excel:

File Extension	Description
xlsx	XML file type; default file type for Excel 2010 and 2013 workbook
xlsm	XML file type; macro-enabled workbook
xltx	XML file type; Excel template
xltm	XML file type; macro-enabled Excel template
xls	Binary file type; document compatibility with Excel 97–2003
xlt	Binary file type; template compatibility with Excel 97–2003

PowerPoint:

File Extension	Description
pptx	XML file type; default file type for PowerPoint 2010 and 2013 presentation
pptm	XML file type; macro-enabled presentation

File Extension	Description
potx	XML file type; PowerPoint template
potm	XML file type; macro-enabled PowerPoint template
ppsx	XML file type; PowerPoint show
ppsm	XML file type; macro-enabled PowerPoint show
ppt	Binary file type; presentation compatibility with PowerPoint 97–2003
pot	Binary file type; template compatibility with PowerPoint 97–2003

The Office 2013 applications also provide other file formats that make it simple for you to share your documents or workbooks in a format designed for easy viewing. For example, you can use the PDF file format (created by Adobe Systems), which enables users who have the free Adobe Reader software installed on their computer to view your file. Windows 8 also provides a PDF viewer (Windows Reader), to view a PDF document and change from a one-page view to a two-page view. The viewer also enables you to search the PDF document using the Find tool.

The XML electronic paper file format (XPS) also makes it easy for others to view your work. Windows 8 supplies an XPS viewer that enables any Windows 8 user to open and view files in the XPS file type. Figure 3.1 shows the Windows 8 XPS viewer containing a Word document converted to an XPS document (Windows 7 also provides an XPS viewer).

Figure 3.1
A Word XPS document in the Microsoft XPS viewer.

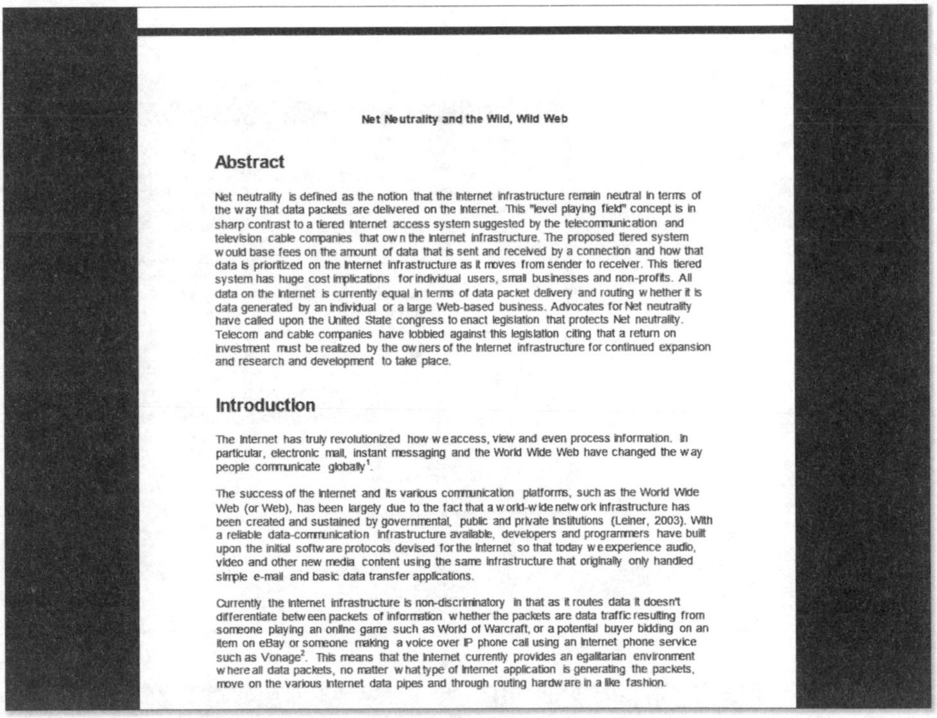

Both the PDF and the XPS file formats are primarily designed to enable you to share a view of a particular file without requiring that the Office applications themselves be installed on the computer of the user who will view the file. Although both the PDF and XPS file types require a particular viewer type to view the file, viewers such as Acrobat Reader and a number of XPS viewers (including Microsoft's XPS viewer) are available for free download on the Web. Most operating systems, including Windows 8, have their own native PDF and XPS viewers.

 tip

This particular chapter doesn't address Outlook because how it stores and works with different items such as emails and contacts is different than in applications in which you create specific files, such as Word or Excel. Part V, "Outlook," covers it in more detail.

Saving Files to Different File Types

When you create a new Word document, Excel workbook, or PowerPoint presentation, you eventually need to save your work to a file. As mentioned earlier, each of these applications uses the open XML file format by default. For example, if you save a new Word document and do not change the Save As Type setting, you get a file with the extension .docx.

When you save a file for the first time, the Save As dialog box opens. At a minimum, you must provide a filename for the new file, and you have the option of specifying the location where the file will be saved. You also have control over the file type used when the file is saved. You can select the file type in the Save As Type drop-down list. Figure 3.2 shows the Word Save As dialog box with the Save As Type drop-down list selected.

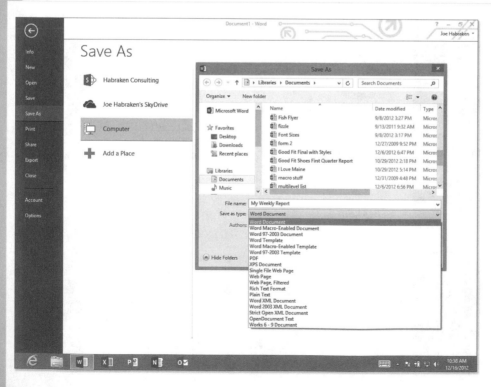

Figure 3.2
Selecting the file type for a Word document.

After selecting the file type, click Save to save the file. When you have saved the file for the first time, the Save button on the application's Quick Access Toolbar saves the changes that you make to the file as you add and edit information to the file.

You can also convert an existing file to another file type by using the Save As dialog box. After you save a file, the only route to the Save As dialog box is via the application's Backstage. Follow these steps to open the Save As dialog box for a previously saved file:

 tip

You can also save Office files such as Word documents, Excel worksheets, and PowerPoint presentations in various web page formats, making it easy to include the content on a website.

1. Select File to access the Backstage.

2. Select Save As. The Backstage Save As page opens.

3. Select a place (location) to save the file on the left side of the Save As page. You can choose from My Computer and cloud places such as your SkyDrive or Sharepoint site.

4. Select Browse to choose your location and open the Save As dialog box.

5. In the Save As dialog box, use the Save As Type drop-down list to specify the file type for the file.

6. You also have the option of changing the name and location for the newly created file.

7. Click Save. The Save As dialog box closes.

The file is saved using the new file format that you selected. The file has a new name and save location, if you chose to change these settings in the Save As dialog box.

Converting Files to Different File Types

So Save As gives you the capability to change a file's current file type to another file type. Another avenue for converting a particular file to a different file type is the Export page in the Backstage. You can access this page by selecting File and then selecting Export.

The Export page provides two possibilities: Create PDF/XPS Document and Change File Type. By default, the Create PDF/XPS Document is selected on the Export page, so to quickly create a PDF or XPS "copy" of the current file, click the Create PDF/XPS button. The Publish As PDF or XPS dialog box opens (it looks much like the Save As dialog box). By default, the file is saved as a PDF, but you can switch to XPS using the Save As type drop-down list. Specify a location and a name for the file, and then select Publish to save the PDF (or XPS) file.

The Export page also provides the Change File Type pane, which is accessed by selecting Change File Type on the left side of the Export page. The Change File Type pane makes changing a file's file type less confusing than just picking a file type from the Save As Type drop-down list in the Save As dialog box. File types are visually represented in the Change File Type pane, and short descriptions of each file type are provided. Figure 3.3 shows the Excel Change File Type pane in the Backstage.

To create a copy of the current file in a new file type, select one of the alternative file types provided in the Change File Type pane. For example, you might want to save an Excel workbook that is currently in the Excel .xlsx file format (the default) to the Excel 97–2003 workbook file type (.xls) so that you can share the file with a colleague who uses an earlier version of Excel.

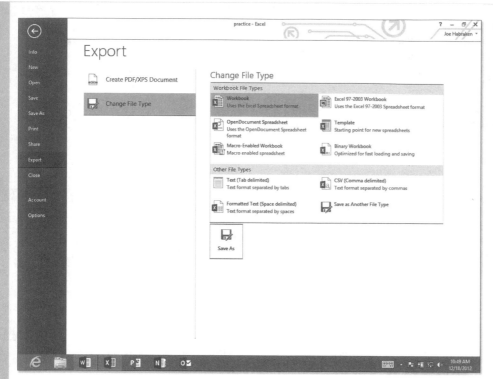

Figure 3.3
The Export
page and the
Excel Change
File Type
pane.

Select the new file type in the Change File Type pane, and the Save As dialog box opens. The file type that you chose in the Change File Type pane is selected in the Save As Type drop-down list. You can change the filename or the file location as needed; then click Save to save a copy of the original file in the file type.

Although going directly to the Save As dialog box via the Backstage Save As command might seem to be a faster option than getting to the Save As dialog box via the Change File Type pane, the latter option does a better job of laying out the possibilities. Until you have a good feel for which file type is which on the Save As Type drop-down list in the Save As dialog box, use the Change File Type pane as an aid to selecting the appropriate file type for the file. Obviously, "appropriate" depends on what you are going to do with the file in its alternative file type.

Configuring Save File Options

When you save a file in one of the Office applications, you have the option to specify the location where the file will be saved. You also have the option of bypassing the Backstage when saving files (and opening files as well). By default, the Office applications are configured to save your files in your Documents folder; however, this doesn't happen automatically because (by default) you are ushered to the Backstage when you want to save a file. Files saved in Office applications are saved to your Documents folder. So if you don't provide an alternative location, the files end up in the default folder.

You can control the save options for an Office application and specify both the default file format for saving files and the default location for files and templates. You can even set an option so that the Backstage won't open every time you save a new file; this option enables you to "jump" right to the Save As dialog box. Other options that you control include the default file location and the default file format used to save files in a particular Office application. The settings for these various options are in the Save pane of an Office application's Options window.

To open the Options window for an Office application, select File to open the Backstage. Then select Options. The Options window for the application opens. Click Save to view the save settings for the application. Figure 3.4 shows the Save pane for PowerPoint. The Save options for PowerPoint, Word, and Excel are similar.

Figure 3.4
The PowerPoint
Save options.

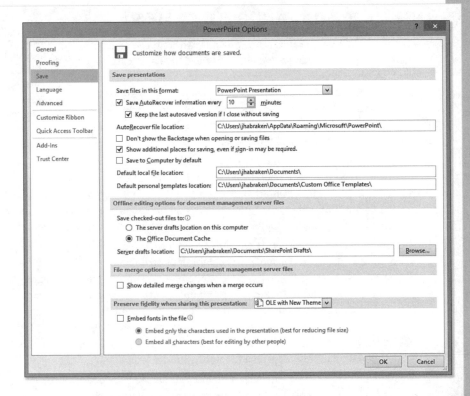

To change the default file format, use the Save Files in This Format drop-down list. Change the file format only if you have a good reason, such as the fact that you always work with people who use a legacy version of an Office application, and you want to match the file type that they use. You can also edit the default file location. The default file location is used only if you also select Don't Show the Backstage When Opening or Saving Files. Selecting this option takes you right to the Save As dialog box when you save a new file for the first time (instead of going to the Save As page in the Backstage).

If you do want to specify the location where your files are stored by default, you can edit the entry in the Default Local File Location box. You are required to type the path, so you may want to use the Windows File Explorer to browse for the path so that you enter it correctly in the Default local file location box.

Other options provided by the Save pane relate to the AutoRecover feature and offline editing options when you work in an environment that uses network servers running SharePoint Server. Leave most of these options at the defaults—particularly those related to offline editing in a server environment.

 Caution

If you work in a networked environment other than a home or small office environment, you might drive your network administrator completely insane if you change the default Save settings for your Office applications. So check with your administrator before you attempt to change these settings.

Creating and Managing Files

The Office 2013 applications provide you with different ways to create new files. When you open one of the Office applications, such as Word, Excel, and PowerPoint, you are taken to the Start screen. The Start screen (which is new in Office 2013) enables you to create a new blank file (such as a new blank document in Word), open files from the Recent list, or take advantage of a huge library of themes and templates.

By design, templates are ready-made blueprints for documents, workbooks, or other Office application files. For example, you might want to create a monthly budget for your household. If you want some help in creating the overall layout that goes into creating this budget in Excel, you can take advantage of a Simple Monthly Budget template that is provided by Office.com and easily opened via the Excel Backstage.

 Note

Everything that you create in the Office applications is based on a template. Each application has a default template. For example, in Word, the default template is the Normal template and is used when you create a new blank document.

Templates often provide layout attributes, text formatting, and even placeholder text. The sophistication of the file created using a particular template depends on the actual template. For example, you might use a Word Memo template that creates a simple memo containing some placeholder text (that you replace) in the To, From, and Re: areas of the memo. Or you might take advantage of the Simple Monthly Budget template mentioned a moment ago. It provides individual tables in a worksheet for items such as projected costs and projected monthly income, and it supplies ready-made charts for your monthly expenses and expenses by category. Figure 3.5 shows a new Excel worksheet opened using the Household Monthly Budget template.

You can also start a new file using a theme. A theme is a collection of colors, fonts, and text effects. Most of the possibilities provided on the Start screen and the Backstage New page are actually themes (unless you do an online search for templates on the Start screen or New page). Themes provide you with an overall document look, as a template does, but using a theme negates having to work within the confines of a template's placeholder text and other document settings. Using themes or templates, however, is a quick way to begin the process of creating an eye-catching document, presentation, or worksheet.

Figure 3.5
Excel's Simple Monthly Budget template.

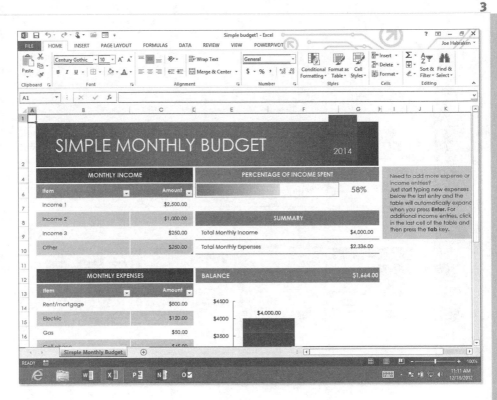

You can take advantage of themes and templates in Excel, Word, PowerPoint, and Publisher. To start a new file based on a template or theme, follow these steps:

1. Select File to open the Backstage.

2. Select New in the Backstage. The New page opens (which is similar to the Start screen). Figure 3.6 shows the Excel New page.

3. Select a template or theme in the New window to preview the template or theme. The Preview window also provides a description of the theme or template.

4. If you want to search for an online template or theme, select one of the suggested searches at the top of the New page or enter keywords in the Search box and run the search.

5. The search results show all the templates available online that match your search criteria. On the right side of the Search results, you find a Category list. The categories listed are keyword subsets of all the templates that were found using your search terms. Each category has a number to the right showing how many of the listed templates fall into the category. You can view a subset of the search results by selecting a category.

6. If you selected a template stored locally on your computer, click Create. If the template is an Office.com template, click Download. In either case, a new file opens in the application window based on the template.

Figure 3.6
Create a new
file based on
a template or
theme.

You determine whether to create your files from new blank documents, workbooks, or presentations, or to take advantage of the various themes and templates available. Working with themes and templates can help you determine how a special document, such as a newsletter, or a special worksheet, such as an invoice, should be laid out. So instead of reinventing the wheel, it makes sense to take advantage of the benefits a template can provide. You can also use themes to great advantage when you are creating a "family" of documents that are related. For example, you might use the same theme for a Word document, an Excel worksheet, and a PowerPoint presentation that are related to a specific project you are developing.

Managing Files

Managing files effectively is a bit of an art form. You need to create some sort of structured environment that keeps your saved files organized but also makes it easy for you to find the files that you work with often. Your particular situation might also require that you store your files in particular network shares (folders) so that others can easily access them. The Microsoft Office 2013 applications have adopted a cloud storage strategy that also makes it possible for you to easily store files on your SkyDrive, SkyDrive Pro (available with an Office 365 subscription), or corporate SharePoint site.

Whether you store your files on your computer's hard drive, on a shared drive on a network server, or in the cloud on your SkyDrive, you still have to adopt a strategy for organizing your files. And whether you are talking about a hard drive or SkyDrive, these storage containers can still be seen as the electronic equivalent of a filing cabinet. Each drawer in the filing cabinet is equivalent to a folder on the drive. The hanging file folders inside filing cabinet drawers are equivalent to the sub-folders inside the main folders.

The naming conventions that you use for the folders and subfolders that you create are really up to you but should reflect some sort of system. For example, you could have a folder named Projects that contains subfolders named for each of the specific projects you are working on. So take some time to figure out your folder taxonomy. If you end up with a folder named Miscellaneous, I recommend that you rethink your naming system.

 note

You might want to use your Documents folder as the parent container for the subfolders you create for your various projects. This enables you to create the necessary folder structure without cluttering the C: drive with a lot of new folders.

This method of organizing files in folders and subfolders works no matter what version of Windows (Windows 8 or Windows 7) you are currently running. However, before you get too far along in your planning, you might want to take a look at a new option—the library—that can help you organize and access files, no matter where you store them on your computer (or your network).

In Windows 8, a library is a container that gathers files from different locations on your computer and your network and displays them as a collection that you can access. By default, Windows 8 provides the Documents, Music, Pictures, and Videos libraries.

So you can go "old school" and create folders and subfolders on your computer's hard drive, or you can take advantage of libraries to give you easy access to the Office files you use. Whether you are creating new folders on your computer or on a network share assigned to you, you can use the File Explorer as your primary tool. The same goes if you want to create new libraries: You use the File Explorer.

The next two sections look more closely at creating folders and libraries on your computer's hard drive. Working in the cloud and organizing cloud storage is similar in most respects to organizing a "physical" drive. You can create folders on both your SkyDrive and SkyDrive Pro (or other SharePoint site). SkyDrive Pro also gives you the capability to create and manage libraries. A SharePoint library is a little different, however, than a library you create on your hard drive using the Windows 8 File Explorer. However, they both serve the same purpose as "virtual" containers that organize your files.

Creating a New Folder

In Windows 8, switch to the desktop and then click the File Explorer icon on the taskbar. File Explorer (shown in Figure 3.7) provides links on the left side of the window, such as various links to the desktop or your current libraries, such as Documents and Music. In its main pane, it provides a listing of the hard drives, DVD drives, CD drives, and so forth on your computer and any network shares (in the Network Location area) configured for your use (including SharePoint sites).

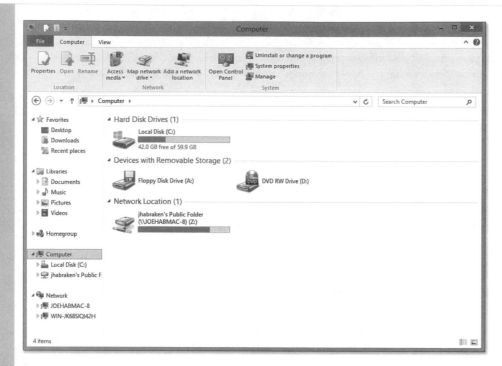

Figure 3.7
Create new
libraries or
folders using
File Explorer.

To view the folders on a particular drive, such as the `C:` drive
(which is typically the default drive on most PCs), double-click
the drive. You can create new folders on any drive or in existing
folders, such as the `Documents` folder. Navigate to the drive or
folder you want to serve as the parent container, and then click
the New Folder button on File Explorer's Ribbon. Type a new
name for the folder, and you are good to go. You can drag existing files and folders into the new folder (using File Explorer) and
specify the new folder when you save an Office file in the Save
As dialog box.

 tip

You can also create new folders in an Office application's
Save As dialog box. Navigate to
where you want to create the
new folder, and then select New
Folder on the toolbar in the Save
As dialog box. Provide a name for
the folder. You can now use the
folder as a location to save the
current file.

Creating a New Library

As already mentioned, a Windows 8 library enables you to view
and access files from different locations on your computer and your network. A library isn't really
a container because a library doesn't store the actual files. A library is a kind of virtual container
that can point to different folder locations and enable you to access related files (such as all the files
related to a particular project).

To create a new library in File Explorer, select Libraries in the links pane (on the left). On the File
Explorer Ribbon, select New Item and then Library. The new library appears in File Explorer. Type a

name for the new library. After you create the new library, you can select folders to be included in it. This inclusion of folders is what provides you access to the various files included in the folders.

Double-click the new library in the File Explorer to open it. Click the Include a Folder button. The Include Folder dialog box opens for the current library. Navigate to a folder that you want to include in the library. Select the folder and then click Include Folder. This closes the Include Folder dialog box. Notice that the subfolders and files included in the folder that you included in the library are now listed in the library.

You can add folders to the library as needed. Use File Explorer to navigate to any folder on your computer or on your network. Right-click the folder and then point at Include in Library. A list of available libraries appears. Select the library.

When you are working in one of the Office applications and want to open a particular file from one of your libraries from the Open dialog box, select the library in the Location list and then locate the file you want to open. You can also save your Office application files to folders in a library when you are in the Save As dialog box.

Viewing File Versions in an Application

When you are working in an Office application such as Word or Excel, the application uses the AutoRecover feature to create different versions of the file you are working on. By default, the Office applications save AutoRecover information for your current file every 10 minutes. If you accidentally close a document or workbook in Word or Excel without saving, the last AutoRecovered version of your file is saved so that you can access it (this is also a default setting in the application's Save options).

When you save a file and close it, all the AutoRecovered versions of the file are deleted. But you can peruse the different versions of your file saved by the AutoRecover feature as you work on the document. This includes any unsaved versions of the document that exist because you did not save changes that you made to the file before you closed it (each unsaved version was automatically saved by Excel even though you didn't save it).

To view any unsaved versions of the current file, such as an Excel workbook, select File to open the Backstage and then click Info. Figure 3.8 shows the Info window for an Excel workbook. The area of interest in this window is the Versions area. Note that, in Figure 3.8, a version of the file exists (from the previous day) because the file was closed without saving changes made to the file.

You can also browse for unsaved versions of a file by clicking the Manage Versions button and then selecting Recover Unsaved Documents. This enables you to browse for any unsaved versions saved on your computer. Any unsaved versions of the current document that have been automatically saved are listed in the Versions area of the window.

You can open a version of the file from the list by selecting it. When you open the automatically saved version of the file (which is labeled "unsaved"), a message bar appears at the top of the document window below the Ribbon. It states that the current document is a Recovered Unsaved File and the file is temporarily stored on the computer. You are provided two options: Compare and Restore. You can select Compare to compare this version of the file with the current version of the file. Any differences between the two files are detailed using the Track Changes feature and are displayed in the document and the Reviewing Pane. You can go through each of the changes marked in the document and accept or reject them as needed.

Figure 3.8
The Excel Info
page.

You also have the option of selecting Restore. This option saves the autorecovered version of the file over the current copy of the file. A message box opens, letting you know that the current version will be overwritten by the restored version. Click OK to overwrite the current version.

Searching for Office Files

If you haven't done a good job of keeping your files organized and can't seem to locate the file you need, you can search for files a couple different ways. First, you can use the Search box provided by File Explorer. Open File Explorer, and then select the location for the search using the icons on the left of the File Explorer window. You can then type the file name or a portion of the file name in the search box; the search begins automatically.

The File Explorer window supplies the results of the search. You can modify the search as needed. You can also open a file listed in the search results. The Close Search button closes the search and returns you to the previous File Explorer window.

 note

The File Explorer provides you with a tab of Search Tools when you run a search. Location commands enable you to specify where the search should take place (current folder versus subfolders). Commands are also available to refine the search, such as Date Modified, Kind, and Size.

Another option for searching your Office files is to do a search in an application's Open dialog box. This is particularly useful if you remember at least part of the filename but don't really remember what folder contains the actual file. To access the Open dialog box, select File to open the Backstage. Then select Open. On the Open page, select a particular location, such as Computer. You can then select the Browse button to access the Open dialog box.

In the Open dialog box, navigate to the drive, folder, or library that you want to search for the file. Type your keywords for the search into the Search box in the upper-right corner of the Open dialog box. Files that match your search criteria have the search keywords highlighted in both the document title and document content, as shown in Figure 3.9.

Figure 3.9
The Word Open dialog box, as it appears after you have searched by keyword.

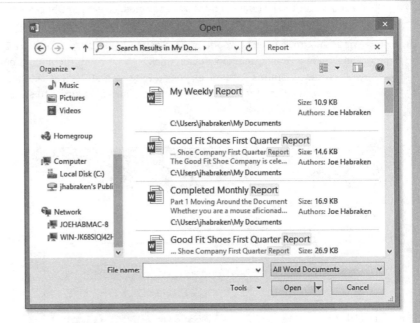

If you want to search a different folder using the search, select that folder in the Organize list and then click the Search box to select your recently used keywords. When you want to open a file that has been identified by the search, double-click the filename to open it in the current application.

 note
If you need a complete reference to Windows 8, check out *Microsoft Windows 8 In Depth,* by Brian Knittel and Paul McFedries.

Sharing Files Using Homegroup

Chapter 5, "Using the Office Web Apps," provides a primer on sharing files in the cloud, specifically SkyDrive and SkyDrive Pro. Cloud strategies for sharing files are available to every kind of Office user. For example, the home user of Office can take advantage of SkyDrive, the small business user with an Office 365 subscription can save files to SkyDrive Pro, and corporate Office users can share files on a local area network or in the cloud on a SharePoint site.

In the small business or home office environment, you can also share resources on your computer using a homegroup. Sharing files and other computer resources such as printers using a homegroup is just one more way to make it easy to collaborate with other users. When you create a homegroup, Windows generates the password used by subsequent users who want to join the homegroup.

The homegroup shares resources on your computer by sharing libraries such as the Documents or Pictures libraries. Libraries enable you to share folders in place. As we discussed earlier in the chapter, a library is really a virtual container that lists the files in a folder that has been added to the library.

To access the homegroup settings (and create a homegroup), right-click the Windows 8 Start screen and then select All apps. On the Apps page, select Control. The Control Panel opens. In the Control Panel, under the Network and Internet settings, select the Choose homegroup and sharing options link.

The Homegroup dialog box opens. To create a homegroup, select the Create a Homegroup button. The Create a Homegroup tool opens. Click Next to begin the homegroup creation process. A list of your current Libraries appears, as does a Printers and Devices category. Choose one of two options for each of the libraries listed: Shared or Not Shared. Figure 3.10 shows the Create Homegroup window and the share list.

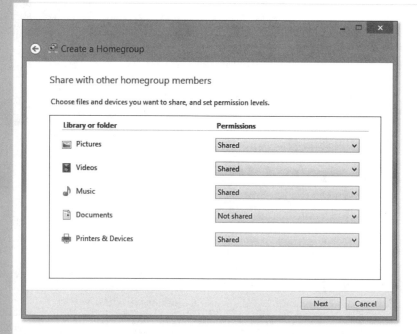

Figure 3.10
Choose the libraries and devices you want to share.

After specifying what you want to share (and not share), click Next. The password for the homegroup is generated. Make sure that you write down the password; you must use it to add other computers to the homegroup.

If you have set up a homegroup, you have probably found that only the default Windows 8 libraries were listed for sharing (or not sharing). You can add your own libraries to the homegroup using the File Explorer. Open the File Explorer on the desktop, and then select the Libraries icon on the left of the File Explorer window. Select a library, and then select Share on the File Explorer Ribbon. You can specify the sharing of the library by selecting Homegroup (view) or Homegroup (view and edit); obviously, the Homegroup (view and edit) setting enables other users to not only view but also edit the contents of the library. You also have the option to share the library with specific people using the Specific People command (the File Sharing command opens, showing the people with whom you are sharing your files).

After you set the access level for the library, it is added to the homegroup. Obviously, you can also remove a library from the homegroup by selecting Stop Sharing on the Share tab when that library is selected in the File Explorer window.

Protecting an Office File

The Office applications enable you to protect a file (such as a document or workbook) that is shared with other users (particularly users on a network). The Protect Document settings help protect the content of the file and can also potentially restrict what can be changed in the document and by whom. To view these options, click the Protect Document button in the Info window as shown in Figure 3.11.

Figure 3.11
Select a document-protection strategy on the Info page.

The following options are available:

- **Mark As Final:** This command marks the file as final and makes the file read-only. All editing commands for the file are disabled; however, any user opening the document can remove the Mark As Final setting in the Backstage. This feature is primarily designed to keep users from inadvertently making changes to a file.

- **Encrypt with Password:** The file is encrypted and protected with a password. When you select this option, you are required to enter a password for the file. Only users with the password can open the file.

- **Restrict Editing:** This command opens the Restrict Formatting and Editing task pane in the document, presentation, or worksheet window. You can restrict formatting to a selection of styles and specify editing restrictions for the document, including making the document read-only.

- **Restrict Access:** This option enables you to take advantage of a Digital Rights Management server. This type of service allows you to assign users different permission levels for the file.

- **Add a Digital Signature:** You can digitally sign a file to prove its authenticity. Signing a file digitally requires that you obtain a digital certificate. A certifying authority can provide digital certificates.

The first three options provided by Protect Document are available to any kind of Office user (home, small business, or big business). The Mark As Final option is useful when you want your collaborators to know that the current version of the document is the final version. This setting also makes the file read-only, but anyone wanting to change the file can remove the Mark As Final attribute and edit away. So this option is not a strong security measure.

Encrypting the document with a password (the second option) definitely limits access to the file because the password is necessary to open it. This means that you also have to keep track of the password because it is the only way to open the encrypted file. This is a strong security measure, but it can backfire if you forget the password for the file.

The Restrict Editing setting enables you to be somewhat selective in what you allow other users to do to the file. You can specify both formatting and editing restrictions using the Restrict Editing task pane. You can also choose parts of a document or worksheet and specify the users who can edit those portions of the file. This feature requires that you have user groups on your network, such as domain user groups on a Windows Server network.

The Restrict Access setting requires that you have access to a Digital Rights Management server (DRM server). So if you work in a corporate environment that provides a DRM server, you can take advantage of this way of securing Office files. Restricting access using a DRM server enables you to specify a particular user (by username or email address) and then assign a level of access to that user.

Digitally signing a file is a way to authenticate that a file is from a trusted source. So adding a digital signature to a file is more about letting users with whom you share the file know that the file is authentic and does not contain any malicious code that might damage their computers or computer files. Adding a digital signature to a file provides protection to your collaborators—the people who review the shared file—more than it protects you from a particular security problem.

To digitally sign an Office file, you need a digital certificate. You can obtain digital certificates from online certifying authorities such CertPlus (http://certplus.com) and VeriSign (http://digitalid.verisign.com). You can also create your own digital certificate using the Digital Certificate for VBA Projects utility that is provided with Office 2013. Appendix B, "Office Macros," provides a complete walkthrough of using this utility in the section "Digitally Signing Macros."

You should digitally sign a file only when you are providing a final draft to your collaborators. Signing the file marks the file as final, which makes it read-only. So when you have a final file and the certificate is on your computer, you are ready to go.

Click Protect Document and then Add a Digital Signature. The Sign dialog box opens, as shown in Figure 3.12.

Figure 3.12
The Sign dialog box.

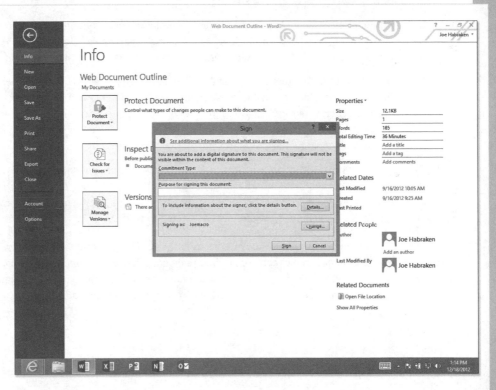

Enter the commitment type and the purpose for signing the file. Your default signing certificate is listed in the dialog box in the Signing As pane. You can click the Change button to locate a different certificate if you have multiple certificates on your computer.

When you are ready to sign the document, click Sign. The Signature Confirmation box opens, letting you know that your signature has been saved with the document. However, if the document is changed, the signature becomes invalid.

Prepare a File for Sharing

The Microsoft Office applications also give you tools for checking a document before you share it. These features are primarily designed for both security and accessibility issues. For example, you can check the document for any personal information that might be contained in it; this is a security check because you don't necessarily want to share personal information in the shared document. Or you might have text in the document that will be difficult for people with disabilities to read; this is an accessibility issue.

The Check for Issues button on the Info window in the Backstage provides three tools that check your file for possible issues related to sharing:

- **Inspect Document:** This tool inspects the document for specific content such as comments, annotations, document properties, and hidden text. The main purpose of the inspector is to help ferret out personal information that you might have inadvertently stored in the document.

- **Check Accessibility:** This tool opens the Accessibility Checker task pane in the document and provides a list of warnings related to accessibility issues in your document. For example, several blank lines between paragraphs might signal to a person using a screen reader that the document has ended. As you select each warning in the task pane, you are presented with information on why you should fix the issue and suggestions on how to fix it.

- **Check Compatibility:** This tool checks the file for items that are not supported by earlier versions of the application that you are using. For example, I might have used the Citation and Bibliography features in Word 2013, but the Compatibility Checker tells me that earlier versions of Word (Word 97–2003) need to convert these items to static text.

As already mentioned, you can run these tools from the Backstage in the Info window. The purpose of these tools is to negate the chance of sharing personal information (inspect document), make sure that the file is accessible to users with disabilities (check accessibility), and ensure that users of earlier Office products can access the file and view its content (check compatibility).

USING AND CREATING GRAPHICS

Each Office application is designed for a particular purpose. Excel is a number cruncher, Word is a powerful word processor, and PowerPoint is a presentation application extraordinaire. Although you use the different Office applications for different purposes, graphics (images, shapes, and clip art) are used for pretty much the same purpose in all the applications. Graphics enable you to enhance information and add interest to the worksheets, documents, and presentations that you create. In Office 2013, the commands and tools used to insert and modify images, shapes, SmartArt graphics, and clip art are pretty consistent across the different applications in the Office suite. So if you know how to use graphics in Word, you can apply that knowledge to another Office application, such as PowerPoint.

This chapter provides an overview of the options for adding graphics to your Office application files. We look at how to insert shapes, SmartArt graphics, images, and clip art. We also look at new features in the Office 2013 applications that make it easier for you to manipulate and insert pictures from online sources such as your SkyDrive and your Flickr.com account.

The Office 2013 Options for Graphics and Pictures

The Office 2013 applications definitely offer you ample ways of enhancing the files you create with graphics. Options for graphics range from basic shapes, to insertion of customizable SmartArt graphics or your own digital images. How you use graphics in your Office application documents (or files, if you prefer) is as important as the type of graphics you use. Graphics are meant to enhance a Word document, Excel worksheet, or PowerPoint slide.

Enhancing your work with graphics can have a different meaning, depending on the type of product you are creating in an Office application. For example, a neighborhood newsletter created in Word might benefit from the use of clip art as design elements or headlines formatted as graphics using WordArt. In another scenario, a PowerPoint slide detailing a particular business process could be greatly enhanced using a SmartArt graphic diagram that provides a visualization of the process described on the slide. Weighing the benefits of adding a graphic to an Office document definitely makes sense; you should avoid graphics that make a document, worksheet, or slide too busy, or that do not enhance the information provided. Make sure that your use of graphic elements increases the impact of information being presented.

Charts, for example (which are discussed in the context of their use in particular Office applications such as Excel and PowerPoint), are extremely useful graphics that provide a visualization of numeric data. Charts can be particularly useful when they accompany worksheet data in Excel or help explain numerical data provided on a PowerPoint slide or in a Word document. Consider the chart as your measuring stick in terms of weighing whether to use a particular graphic type in an Office application. We know how charts enhance the understanding of numerical values in tables, so try to apply the same measuring stick when you plan to use digital images, clip art, and diagrams; make sure that they add to the document and don't just serve as a cute distraction. I realize that pictures of puppies and kitties are popular on the Web (they melt nearly anyone's heart), but using puppy pictures to mask poor sales data on a PowerPoint slide is just plain wrong.

➡ *For information on creating charts in Excel,* ***see*** *Chapter 14, "Enhancing Worksheets with Charts."*

➡ *For information on using charts and other graphics in PowerPoint,* ***see*** *"Adding Charts to Slides," p. 572.*

As already mentioned, the Office applications provide different types of graphical elements that you can use in your Office files. The following list briefly describes the possibilities:

- **Picture:** You can insert your digital pictures into your Office documents. The Office applications support different file formats, including Windows Bitmap (`.bmp`), Graphics Interchange Format (`.gif`), Joint Photographic Experts Group (`.jpg`), Portable Network Graphics (`.png`), and Tagged Image File Format (`.tif`) formats.

- **Clip art:** Each Office application has access to Office.com, which is a huge library of royalty-free clip art images and photos that can provide just about any type of stock image you need.

- **Shapes:** The capability to insert different drawn shapes into an Office application has been around nearly as long as the Office applications. A Shapes gallery provides different shape categories that make it easy to add lines, rectangles, stars, and even callouts to your Office documents. You can also edit and group shapes, for all sorts of possibilities. PowerPoint 2013 provides new Merge Shapes commands that enable you to combine several shapes into a single shape.

- **SmartArt:** This graphic type provides SmartArt diagrams, which include lists, processes, hierarchies, and relationships. Even the most complex SmartArt graphics are designed so that you can easily add text labels and other information to the various parts of the SmartArt.

- **Screenshot:** This tool gives you the capability to take a snapshot of the Windows desktop and/ or any windows open on the desktop. This can be particularly useful if you want to visually document the steps required in a particular feature in one of the Office applications (or any application open on the Windows desktop). You can also use it to capture the screen of messaging platforms such as Skype or the Wall on your Facebook page.

- **WordArt:** WordArt styles are a quick way to add special effects to text in objects such as text boxes. A WordArt quick style includes a number of different text options (formatting possibilities), including Shadow, Reflection, Glow, Soft Edges, and 3-D Format. WordArt is designed for those times when you want text to stand out and add visual interest to your document.

In the past, each of these graphic types has been differentiated by the way you inserted it into a Word document or Excel worksheet. Each was sequestered to its own command on the Ribbon's Insert tab. Office 2013 blurs the lines that differentiate these different types. For example, the Images group (shown on Figure 4.1) includes two commands for inserting pictures: Pictures and Online Pictures. So what is the difference?

Figure 4.1
The Ribbon's Insert tab enables you to insert objects such as pictures, shapes, and SmartArt.

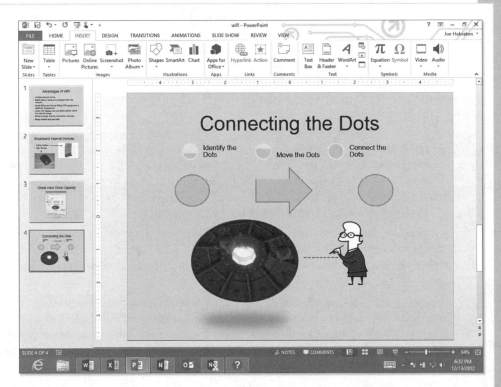

The Pictures command enables you to access the Insert Picture dialog box, which is designed for you to locate pictures on your computer and insert them into your document, worksheet, or presentation slide. However, if you can access your SharePoint site as a mapped drive, you can insert pictures from your SkyDrive Pro (or other SharePoint site), which is "online."

The other command option for inserting pictures, Online Pictures, has replaced the Clip Art command in the previous version of the Office applications. However, when you select it and the Insert Pictures window opens, you can insert clip art, the results of Bing Web searches, files from your Flickr.com account, and picture files saved on your SkyDrive. Figure 4.2 shows the Insert Pictures window.

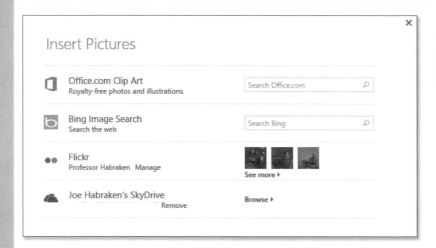

Figure 4.2
You can insert Office.com clip art and your own online pictures using the Online Pictures command.

Microsoft has rethought the commands to insert pictures to make it easy for you to access your cloud-based images (and the Office.com cloud-based images). This is because Microsoft has designed this latest version of the Office applications for cloud computing. You can access your files from anywhere (because they are in the cloud) from any device (using new versions of Office that are forthcoming for tablet computers or the Office web apps).

Another new feature you notice when you insert pictures, SmartArt, or other graphics into a Microsoft Word document (or Publisher publication) is the Layout Options button. The Layout Options button provides quick access to layout settings related to how the text surrounding (or above and below) the graphic wraps.

The Office 2013 applications also embrace some other changes related to graphics, particularly enhancements related to working with pictures and shapes. Let's take a look at working with SmartArt graphics, which are probably the most complex graphic item type that you work with (other than charts). We can then look at some of the other graphic possibilities, including pictures, screenshots, and WordArt.

Working with SmartArt Graphics

SmartArt provides a large gallery of complex graphical elements that you can use to create eye-catching lists and diagrams. You can create lists that use shapes to better define the relationship between text entries in a list, and you can create lists that make it easy to combine text and pictures. Figure 4.3 shows a vertical picture list SmartArt graphic that includes thumbnail photos and text.

Figure 4.3
A SmartArt
vertical
picture list
in Word,
with Layout
Options
shown.

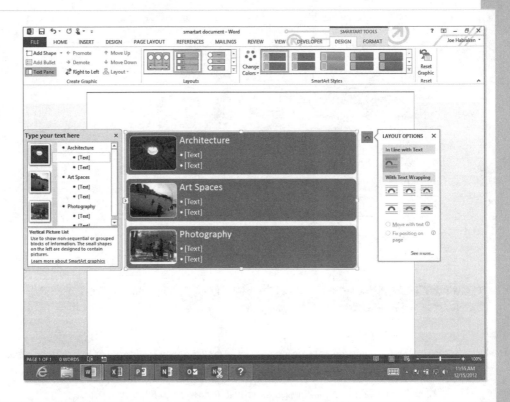

SmartArt lists enable you to go beyond the possibilities normally associated with numbered and bulleted lists. SmartArt lists can be particularly useful in PowerPoint, where you can replace bulleted lists on slides with SmartArt lists. SmartArt lists are better at showing how the different items in a list are related than the typical bulleted list found on a PowerPoint slide.

➥ *For information on converting text to SmartArt in PowerPoint,* **see** *"Converting Text to a SmartArt Graphic," p. 570.*

The SmartArt gallery also provides many different diagram types, including process diagrams, relationship diagrams, and hierarchy diagrams, just to name a few. For example, you can use a hierarchy organization chart in an Excel worksheet to provide information related to how different departments shown in a worksheet relate to each other in terms of corporate structure. Figure 4.4 shows a half-circle organization chart in an Excel worksheet.

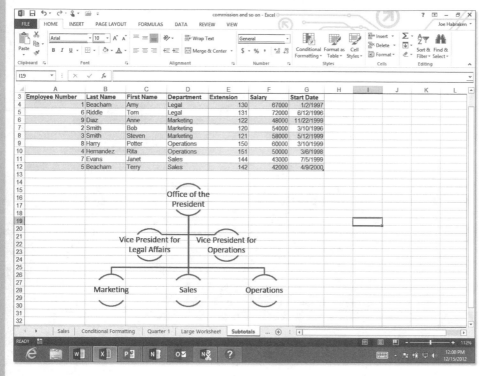

Figure 4.4
Organization charts can be inserted into Excel worksheets or other Office documents.

Each SmartArt diagram category gives you a specific way to represent information visually in your Office documents. The following list briefly describes each SmartArt graphic category:

- **List:** Places text in nonsequential vertical or horizontal lists.

- **Process:** Shows a logical progression or flow, to break down the steps in a process or cycle.

- **Cycle:** Shows the steps in a continuous process.

- **Hierarchy:** Shows the hierarchical relationship between items shown in the diagram. A hierarchy diagram can also show a decision tree.

- **Relationship:** Shows how elements in the diagram are related or connected.

- **Matrix:** Shows how the parts relate to the whole.

- **Pyramid:** Shows both hierarchical relationships and the proportional importance of items in the hierarchy.

- **Picture:** Lists all the SmartArt lists and diagrams that enable you to incorporate images into the SmartArt structure.

- **Office.com:** Provides additional SmartArt graphics provided online via the Office.com website.

SmartArt graphics are easy to create. They are also easy to edit and modify. Let's take a look at inserting SmartArt graphics into the Office applications, and then look at the tools available for modifying and enhancing SmartArt lists and diagrams.

Inserting SmartArt Graphics

SmartArt graphics are inserted using the SmartArt command, which is housed in the Illustration group on the Ribbon's Insert tab. To insert SmartArt into an Office document, follow these steps:

1. On the Insert tab, select SmartArt. The Choose a SmartArt Graphic dialog box opens, as shown in Figure 4.5.

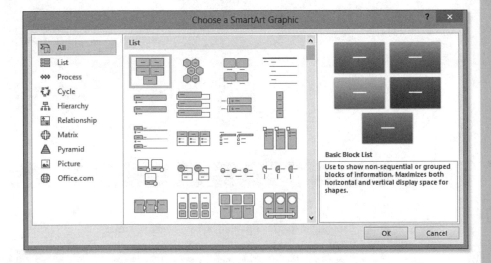

Figure 4.5
The SmartArt Graphic dialog box.

2. Select a SmartArt category to view the individual diagrams provided by a particular category.

3. Select the list or diagram that you want to insert.

4. Click OK. The list or diagram is inserted into your current Office document.

You can now enter the text that you want to place in the diagram. Figure 4.6 shows a Venn diagram SmartArt graphic that has been inserted into a Word document.

You can enter the text for the diagram directly onto the diagram parts by replacing any of the [TEXT] placeholders. You can also enter and edit text entries for the diagram in the Text pane that accompanies each SmartArt graphic (to the left of the SmartArt). You can collapse the Text pane by clicking the pane's Close button. If you want the Text pane to reappear, click the Expand button on the left edge of the SmartArt frame.

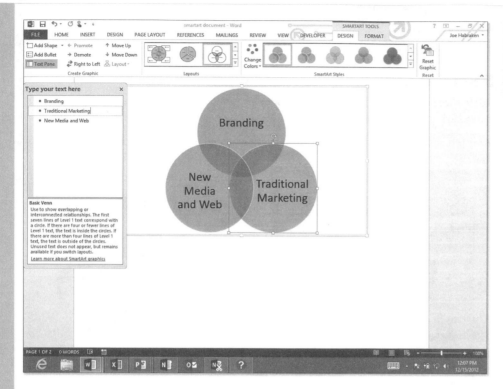

Figure 4.6
Enter the text for the SmartArt list or diagram.

Some SmartArt lists and diagrams enable you to include pictures as part of the list or diagram. After you insert a SmartArt graphic that includes placeholders for pictures, picture placeholders are provided in the different diagram parts and the Text pane for the SmartArt graphic. To replace a picture placeholder, click the placeholder in either the diagram or the Text pane. The Insert Picture dialog box opens. Navigate to the folder that houses the picture graphic, and then select the file. Click Insert to place the picture in the SmartArt graphic.

The picture is sized according to the space allotted for it in the list or diagram. For example, if you insert a picture into a circle that is part of a particular diagram type, the picture is sized to fit in the shape, meaning the circle. This means that you do not have to size or crop images before you insert them into a SmartArt list or diagram. Even the largest digital photo will be sized to fit appropriately into the SmartArt graphic shape.

When you have finished entering the text and pictures (if applicable) for the SmartArt graphic, click outside the graphic's frame. You can now continue to work on the document, worksheet, or

 caution

If you are going to use SmartArt graphics in an Office application, you want to save your file in the current Office 2013 file formats. For example, Word uses the file format .docx, whereas Excel uses .xlsx. Saving a file containing SmartArt graphics in one of the earlier Office formats (such as .doc or .xls) can lead to a loss of functionality and capability when dealing with the SmartArt graphics in the file. So sharing files containing SmartArt graphics with folks using some of the legacy versions of Office (particularly pre-2007) is probably best avoided.

presentation that you are creating. The SmartArt graphic is like any other object, in that you can move or size it as required.

Modifying SmartArt Graphics

When you select a SmartArt graphic in an Office document (it is selected when you first insert it), the SmartArt Tools become available on the Ribbon. The SmartArt Tools consist of a Design tab and a Format tab.

The Design tab is devoted to modifying the SmartArt elements. For example, the Create Graphic group on the Design tab enables you to add shapes and bullets, and promote or demote items in the SmartArt list. Figure 4.7 shows the SmartArt Tools Design tab.

Figure 4.7
The SmartArt Tools Design tab.

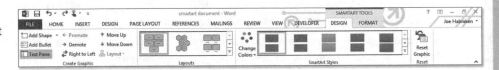

The Design tab also enables you to change the SmartArt layout and to assign different styles to the elements in the SmartArt. For example, from the Layouts gallery, you can choose among different layouts for the particular type of SmartArt list or diagram that you inserted into your Office document. The Change Colors command in the SmartArt Styles group enables you to specify a color combination for the SmartArt graphic based on the current theme, as well as a number of other color categories. After you have specified a color combination for SmartArt, you can use the SmartArt Styles gallery to fine-tune the use of the color scheme selected for the graphic and apply 3D styles to the SmartArt.

Two other command groups serve as the end caps for the Design tab. On the far left is the Create Graphic group, and at the far right is the Reset group. In the Create Graphic group is the Add Shape command, which enables you to add shapes (the same shape used as the primary building block for the SmartArt graphic) to the graphic.

So if you have inserted a SmartArt list that provides three list boxes, you can increase the number of boxes using the Add Shape command. The Create Graphic group has other commands that enable you to promote or demote and move up or move down shapes in the SmartArt graphic. The availability of these commands depends on the type of SmartArt graphic you have inserted into your Office document.

If you make design changes to your graphic using the Change Colors command or the SmartArt Styles gallery, and you just don't like the way things turned out, you can reset the graphic and start over (or leave things well enough alone). Click the Reset Graphic command in the Reset group. The Reset Graphic command does not reset changes that you make using the Layouts gallery or the commands in the Create Graphic group.

The other SmartArt Tools tab is the Format tab, shown in Figure 4.8. The Format tab commands are geared to modify shapes and assign shape styles to the SmartArt graphic. WordArt styles are also provided so that you can manipulate the text elements in the SmartArt graphic.

Figure 4.8
The SmartArt Tools Format tab.

Many of the command possibilities the Format tab provides can apply to the entire SmartArt graphic or the individual shapes (elements) that make up the graphic. This enables you to fine-tune the look of a SmartArt graphic and modify an existing graphic as you require.

For example, you might want to change the shape of a specific element (which is referred to as a shape, so this can be confusing) in the SmartArt graphic. You can select a specific shape and modify it, or you can select a number of shapes (select the first shape or element and then hold down the Ctrl key when selecting the other shapes) and modify them collectively. The Shapes group on the Format tab enables you to change the shape of a selected element or elements using the Change Shape gallery. You can also change the size of a shape or shapes using the Larger and Smaller commands.

In addition, the Format tab enables you to modify the style for a selected shape or shapes and modify shape fill, outline, and effects. The Shape Styles group provides access to the Shapes Styles gallery, which provides different border fill and text styles. Shape Fill, Shape Outline, and Shape Effects enable you to modify these style elements individually.

The WordArt Styles gallery offers WordArt text styles that you can apply to the text in a shape. These styles include color, outline, shadow, and text effects. If you want to fine-tune the WordArt style assigned to a particular shape or a number of selected shapes, you can use the Text Fill, Text Outline, and Text Effects commands as needed. For even greater control over the shape and text options for a SmartArt graphic, select the SmartArt graphic and then navigate to the SmartArt Tools Format tab. Select the dialog box launcher in the WordArt Styles group to open the Format Shape task pane.

The Arrange group commands relate to how a shape is layered with other shapes and how the text in a document such as a Word document deals with the SmartArt graphic. To layer shapes in a graphic, use the Bring Forward and Send Backward command. You can change the alignment and rotation of an entire SmartArt graphic or shape by using the Align Objects and Rotate Objects commands, respectively.

 tip
If you are working with a 3-D SmartArt graphic, you might find it easier to edit the shape settings in 2D. Select the Edit in 2-D command in the Shapes group.

 tip
You can toggle the SmartArt graphic's Text pane on or off using the Text Pane command in the Create Graphic group on the SmartArt Tools Design tab.

 tip
If you are attempting to select a shape in a SmartArt graphic that is behind another shape, the easiest way to select it (instead of using Bring Forward) is to select the shape's text in the Text pane.

Working with Your Digital Pictures

The Microsoft Office applications enable you to insert different digital picture file formats into your Office documents. Because it is true that a picture is worth a thousand words, you can use pictures to enhance your Word documents, PowerPoint slides, Excel worksheets, and even Outlook emails. You can also include images on your OneNote notebook pages. Some of the commonly used digital picture file formats are as follows:

- Windows Bitmap (`.bmp`)
- Graphics Interchange Format (`.gif`)
- Joint Photographic Experts Group (`.jpg`)
- Portable Network Graphics (`.png`)
- Tagged Image File Format (`.tif`)
- Windows Metafile (`.wmf`)

Digital image files are compressed, and the compression scheme a particular file format uses can have an effect on the overall quality of the image. Lossless compression schemes compress the file without discarding any of the file data; the lossy compression scheme actually discards some of the file's data to compress the image file. Image files also differ in the number of colors they can provide, so you will find that each file format definitely has its own plus and minuses.

For example, GIF files provide for a total of only 256 colors, but GIF files are often small (in terms of size) and can be used as pictures on websites. The PNG format provides millions of colors and uses a lossless compression scheme, so you get a fantastic-looking image, but the file size can be quite large. A JPEG image uses a lossy compression scheme; it might not look as good as a PNG file, but it definitely provides with a smaller file size.

Most digital cameras shoot either JPEG or PNG files by default. Most digital cameras also enable you to adjust the number of megapixels used in a shot, which relates to the resolution of the picture and the file size created.

When using digital images in your Office applications, you don't really need to worry about file size, megapixels, or file type. The Office applications can deal with most of the common file types and typically size the image to fit into the shape or frame that holds the image.

Inserting Pictures

The Pictures command is on the Insert tab. To insert a picture, follow these steps:

1. Select the Pictures command. The Insert Picture dialog box opens, as shown in Figure 4.9.
2. Locate and select the picture file that you want to insert.
3. Click the Insert button. The Insert Picture dialog box closes, and the picture is inserted into the document.

Figure 4.9
The Insert Picture dialog box.

After the image has been inserted into the document, you can size the document using the handles provided on the picture frame. You can also modify the image size using the Shape Height and Shape Width spinner boxes, which are provided in the Size group of the Pictures Tool Format tab. The Picture Tools become available on the Ribbon when the picture is selected.

Adjusting Pictures

The Picture Tools Format tab provides commands that modify different aspects of the picture. For example, the Picture Styles gallery enables you to change the border type and the shape, and to apply some 3D effects to the picture. You can access the picture border and the effects applied to the picture, such as settings for the shadow, glow, or 3D rotation, using the Picture Border and Picture Effects commands, respectively.

Many of the commands provided on the Picture Tools Format tab are the same as those found on the SmartArt Tools Format tab. For example, the Position, Wrap Text, and other Arrange group commands are the same for a picture, SmartArt graphic, or shape; however, the Picture Tools Format tab does provide the Adjust group, which contains extremely useful commands specific to digital pictures. The Adjust group commands are as follows:

- **Remove Background:** This command enables you to remove the background from the picture. This is a new tool for the Microsoft Office applications. We look at using this tool later in the chapter.

- **Corrections:** With this command, you can select from a gallery of choices that enables you to sharpen and soften the image or adjust the brightness and contrast. Thumbnails of your image are provided in this gallery, with different correction settings applied to them. All you have to do is select one of the possibilities. To view the brightness and contrast settings for one of the gallery thumbnails, place the mouse on that thumbnail to view a ScreenTip that provides the percent brightness and contrast.

- **Color:** This command provides a gallery of color saturations and tones, as well as recolor settings for your image. Figure 4.10 shows the Color Saturation gallery. Color saturations are denoted by percent saturation, such as 100%, 200%, and so on. The color tones are denoted by degrees Kelvin (lower numbers are "cooler" and tend toward the blues; higher numbers are "warmer" and tend toward yellow). To apply a setting from the gallery, select the thumbnail of your image that provides the color changes you want to make to your picture.

Figure 4.10
The Color gallery for a picture.

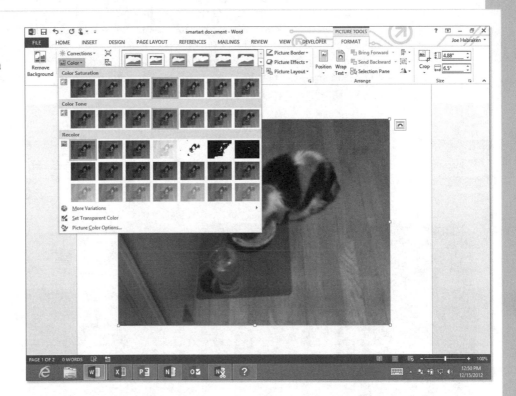

- **Artistic Effects:** This command provides a gallery of photo effects, such as Pencil Sketch, Cement, and Plastic Wrap. You can preview any of the effects on your picture by placing the mouse on a particular effect in the gallery. Some of the possibilities are mind-blowing and really groovy (of course, I grew up in the 1960s).

 tip

To add a caption to a picture (or clip art), right-click the selected picture and then select Insert Caption. You can then set up the caption in the Caption dialog box.

- **Compress Pictures:** This command enables you to compress the image so that its size (in terms of file size, not size in the document) is smaller; therefore, your entire document file size will be smaller. When you select Compress Pictures, the Compress Pictures dialog box opens. It enables you to delete any cropped areas of the picture and to select a target output size, such as 96 ppi, or pixels per inch) for emails and 150 ppi for web pages.

- **Change Picture:** Use this command to open the Insert Pictures dialog box, and select a picture to replace the current image.

- **Reset Picture:** This command throws out all the formatting changes you have made to the picture. You return to Square One.

Although the galleries provided by a number of the Adjust group commands might be sufficient for your needs in changing an image's attributes, you can fine-tune these settings using the Format Picture task pane. You can display the Format Picture task pane by selecting the options link provided at the bottom of the Corrections, Color, and Artistic Effects galleries. For example, if you select Picture Corrections Options at the bottom of the Corrections gallery, the Format Picture task pane opens (see Figure 4.11), with Picture Corrections selected.

Figure 4.11
The Format Picture task pane.

You can use the different settings in the Format Picture task pane to specify the fill, the line color, the line style, and the 3D format and rotation for the image. You can also fine-tune changes that you have made to the picture, such as brightness and contrast corrections, color changes, and artistic effects. For example, you can adjust the Picture Corrections settings (shown in Figure 4.11) using slider bars that soften or sharpen an image or change the brightness and contrast of the image.

Cropping an Image

Another useful command for adjusting an image is the Crop command. Although this command isn't included in the Adjust group, the Crop command is useful when you want to trim unneeded parts of the image. It is located at the other end of the Format tab in the Size group.

The Crop command offers more than one possibility for cropping an image. When you select the Crop command, the following options are provided:

- **Crop:** Select Crop to place the crop frame around the image. You can then adjust the cropping handles as needed. Select the Crop command again to apply your cropping settings.

- **Crop to Shape:** You can apply a shape to the image from the Shape gallery and have the image cropped to that specific shape.

- **Aspect Ratio:** You can have the image cropped using a specific aspect ratio, such as 1:1 (square), 2:3 (portrait), or 3:2 (landscape).

- **Fill:** The image is resized to fill the entire picture area (such as a picture box), and the portions of the image that fall outside the picture area are cropped.

- **Fit:** The image is resized to fit in the picture area, maintaining the original aspect ratio of the image (this is the opposite of cropping).

If you find that you have gone overboard on the cropping, you can remove the cropping by using the Undo command on the Quick Access Toolbar. The Reset Picture command does not undo cropping.

Using the Background Removal Tool

The Background Removal tool can be extremely useful in removing unwanted background information from a picture so that the resulting image completely highlights the subject of the picture. The great part about this tool is that it can differentiate the background from the foreground elements in your photo and automatically selects the background areas to be removed from the photo. How well this works depends on the photo. Some photos contain color combinations or low contrast between the elements in the photo that make it difficult to easily separate the background from the foreground elements; however, after the Background Removal tool takes the first cut at selecting the background of the photo, you can step in and fine-tune the selection so that you end up with some good results.

To use the Remove Background tool, select a photo in your Office application. Then click the Remove Background command. The Background Removal tab appears on the Ribbon, as shown in Figure 4.12.

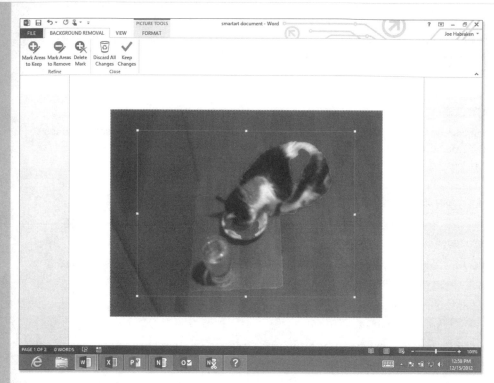

Figure 4.12 The Background Removal tab and a selected picture.

The commands provided on the Background Removal tab are self-explanatory. Two command groups are provided: Refine and Close. The Refine group provides commands that enable you to refine the initial selection of the background. The Close group provides you with two possibilities that enable you to either discard the changes or keep them.

Upon first inspection after selecting the Remove Background command, the background areas marked in the photo for removal are designated by a magenta overlay. A marquee with sizing handles is also floated on your image to specify the area of the image that contains the foreground elements to keep. If the marquee has excluded foreground items that you want to keep, you can change the size of the marquee or move the marquee's position as required.

Adjusting the marquee isn't going to get you much, so for greater refinement, you need to take advantage of the Refine group commands. Let's start with marking areas that you want to keep: Select the Mark Areas to Keep command. The mouse pointer becomes a pencil. Use the pencil to outline each area that you want to keep that has been marked for removal. Click the pencil to place a mark point on an area, and then continue to drag the mouse. Marking points makes it easier to connect the dots and get all of an area that you want to mark to keep. You might find that you enclose only a portion of an area to keep using the mouse when the Background Removal tool suddenly catches on and finishes the selection for you by removing the magenta overlay from that area.

You can also mark areas to remove. Select the Mark Areas to Remove command and use the pencil to mark areas that should be removed. When the area has been marked for removal, the magenta overlay is applied to that area of the image.

When you are ready to complete the process by keeping all the fine-tuning that you did with the Mark Areas to Keep and the Mark Areas to Remove commands, select the Keep Changes command. The background is removed from the image. Now you can take advantage of the picture styles that provide background fill colors or shadow effects.

If you have ever attempted to manipulate digital photos, you are probably aware that many of the possibilities we have discussed here would normally require a sophisticated piece of digital image-editing software. It is pretty amazing that you can quickly correct such image parameters as brightness and contrast, and apply artistic effects to an image from within the various Office applications such as Word and PowerPoint.

Inserting Online Pictures

When working with previous versions of the Office application suite, the only images that were really considered "online" were images stored in Microsoft's online clip art library (Office.com). Office 2013 still provides you access to royalty-free clip art and photos on Office.com, but it expands the definition of what we consider an online image and how we insert these images into the various documents we create with the Office applications.

So the online picture category still provides you with clip art and photos from Office.com. Other sources of online pictures (these are new to Office 12013) include the results of Bing image searches, files saved to your Flickr.com account, and image files stored on your SkyDrive.

When you select the Online Pictures command on the Ribbon's Insert tab (which is in the Illustrations group in Word, Publisher, and Excel and in the Images group in PowerPoint and OneNote). The Insert Pictures window opens, as shown in Figure 4.13.

Figure 4.13
The Insert Pictures window.

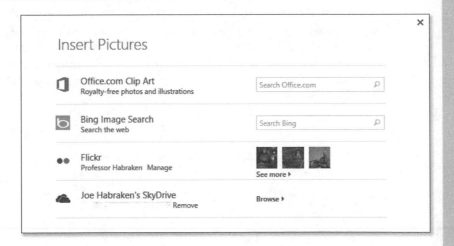

The Insert Pictures window gives you access to all the "online" image resources. Let's look at each of the possibilities, starting with clip art.

Inserting Clip Art

Clip art has been available in the Office applications for a very long time and has served as a way to add design elements and thematic images to Office documents. At one time, clip art was merely a collection of line drawings and cartoons. The clip art library provided by the Office 2013 applications, however, consists of traditional clip art and a large number of high-quality stock photos.

To insert clip art into an Office document from the Insert Pictures window, click in the Search Office.com box and type search criteria in the form of keywords. Then click the Search icon.

A collection of clip art that meets your search criteria is displayed as thumbnails in the results window. To enlarge one of the thumbnails, select the thumbnail and then select the View Larger icon. When you have located the clip art image you want to insert into your document, select the image and then select Insert. The image is downloaded and inserted into your document.

You can manipulate photos that you download from Office.com using the various Adjust group tools, including the Remove Background tool. When you insert clip art files (line art), you cannot use the Remove Background tool or the Artistic Effects gallery, and some of the Format Picture commands found in the Format Pictures task pane are unavailable (they are grayed out).

Inserting Bing Image Search Results

You can also insert images that you find online using a Bing image search. To run a web image search from the Insert Pictures window, click in the Search Bing box and enter your keyword(s) for the search. By default, the Bing image search shows only images found (using your search criteria) that are licensed under Creative Commons. Creative Commons is a nonprofit organization that gives content creators licensing options for sharing their work on the Web. Each image that appears in your search results may have a specific license with specific use restrictions. Figure 4.14 shows the results of a Bing image search with the Creative Commons license message.

When you select an image in the search results, the filename, size (in pixels), and website location appear in the lower left of the Insert Picture window. You can navigate to the source site for more information on the image. When you have located an image that you want to insert (and feel comfortable that you are not violating any use restrictions), select the image and then click the Insert button.

Figure 4.14
The results of a Bing image search.

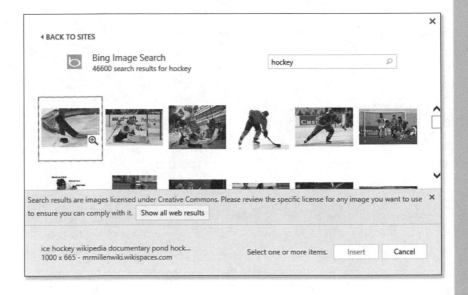

Inserting Flickr.com Images

You can also access images that you have stored using Flickr. You need to sign up for a Flickr account at Flickr.com before you can take advantage of this online image source. When you have a Flickr account, you can associate the account with your Microsoft Live ID (Outlook.com, Hotmail.com, MSN.com—any of these email accounts work).

Open the Insert Pictures window in any of the Office applications via the Ribbon's Insert tab. In the Insert Pictures window, select the Flickr logo box below the Also Insert From heading (at the bottom left of the window). The first time you select the Flickr option, you need to associate your Microsoft account (Outlook.com or Hotmail) with your Flickr logon. To proceed, select Connect and then log onto Flickr using your Yahoo!/Flickr ID (which is the account you created when you signed up for Flickr).

After you have associated your Microsoft account with your Flickr account, you return to the Insert Pictures window; Flickr appears as one of the choices for inserting online pictures. To view the images you have stored on Flickr, click the See More link, which is below thumbnails of images you have stored on Flickr. Your Photostream is loaded into the results window, as shown in Figure 4.15.

If you have many photos in your Photostream, you can use the Search Flickr box to search through your Flickr photos. When you select a photo, the filename and photo size display. To insert a photo, select the photo and then click Insert. The photo is downloaded and inserted.

Photos that you download from your Flickr account are the same as photos that you insert from your computer or other source, such as your SkyDrive (which we discuss shortly). You can manipulate all your digital photos using the Picture Tools and the settings available in the Format Picture task pane.

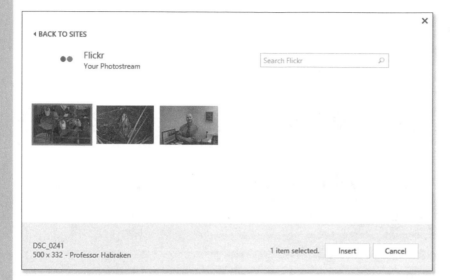

Figure 4.15
You can insert photos from your Flickr.com account.

Inserting Images from your SkyDrive

You can also insert photos you have stored on your SkyDrive from the Insert Picture window. If you have signed into your Office applications using your Windows Live ID (your Outlook.com or Hotmail account), your SkyDrive appears as one of the options in the Insert Picture window.

Click the Browse button to the right of the SkyDrive icon in the Insert Picture window. The Browse window opens, showing all the folders available on your SkyDrive (see Figure 4.16.)

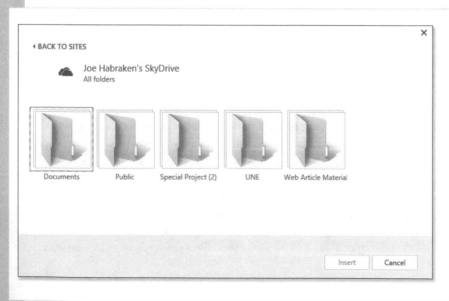

Figure 4.16
You can access photos stored on your SkyDrive.

Select a folder to open it. Photos in the selected folder appear as thumbnails in the image window. If a folder does not contain image files, the message "There are no items in this folder" appears in the image window. You can use the folder links provided at the top of the window to navigate back to your SkyDrive root folder and then select another folder as a source of image files.

When you have located the image you want to insert into the current document, select the image and then select Insert. The image is downloaded and inserted into your document.

 tip
You can upload images to your SkyDrive using your web browser. Log onto your SkyDrive, and then use the Upload link to upload images (or other files) to a specific folder.

Using Shapes and the Office Drawing Tools

The Microsoft Office applications enable you to add a variety of shapes to your Office documents. The Shapes gallery, which you access via the Shapes command on the Insert tab, provides shape categories. You can add lines, rectangles, block arrows, callouts, and other shape types.

One of the available shapes is a text box, which, as its name implies, adds a box containing text to a document. However, other shapes can also contain text; this means that you can use any shape as a design element and get double duty out of it as a text container. This can be useful when you want to add text to a document but also want to add some visual interest—say, in a Word document or a PowerPoint slide. You format the text in a shape using WordArt styles and text fill, outline, and effects tools. This enables you to create shapes with eye-catching text entries that serves an informational purpose in your document.

You can insert multiple shapes into a document, worksheet, or PowerPoint slide. When you insert a shape onto a document page or slide, the shape resides in a layer that is superimposed on the text that already exists on the document page or slide. You can move a shape to any location and also size the image. In Word, you can determine how the image coexists with the surrounding text by clicking the Layout Options button, which appears next to the selected shape. This opens the Layout Options pane, which enables you to quickly determine whether the shape should be in line with the text or whether the text should wrap around the shape in a pattern such as a Square, Tight, Through, Top and Bottom, Behind Text, or In Front of Text.

To insert a shape onto a slide or document, navigate to the Ribbon's Insert tab and then select Shapes. The Shapes gallery appears, as shown in Figure 4.17.

Select a shape in the gallery. The pointer becomes a drawing tool, and you can use it to "draw" the shape on the document page, sheet, or slide. After inserting the shape, you can size the shape using the sizing handles provided when the shape is selected. You can also drag the shape in the document to position it. When the Shape is selected, the Drawing Tools Format tab becomes available on the Ribbon. It supplies commands for formatting the shape and the text that appears in the shape.

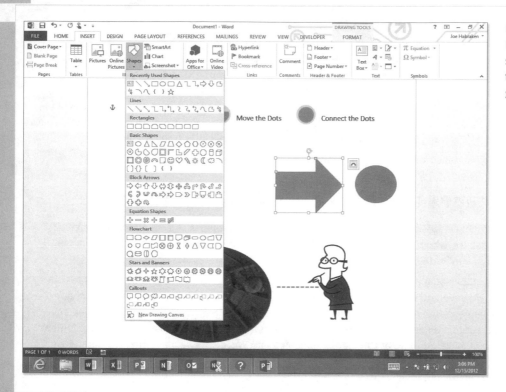

Figure 4.17
Insert a
shape from
the Shapes
gallery.

Adding and Combining Multiple Shapes

Although the SmartArt graphics provide many composite drawings and diagrams that contain different shapes (and can be manipulated individually), you can use the shapes in the Shapes gallery to create pretty much anything you require. In Word and Excel, you can insert multiple shapes and then group them. After the shapes are grouped, you can treat them as a single object on the page.

To create a design element from multiple shapes in Word or Excel, insert the required shapes. Position the shapes as needed and use the Arrange commands to position and layer the shapes.

You can use the Selection pane to change the layer position of the shapes by changing the shape's position in the Selection list. You can also select shapes in the Selection pane (instead of trying to click items on the page) when you want to specify the shapes to be grouped. Figure 4.18 shows multiple shapes selected on a Word document page. Note that the Selection pane provides a list of all the objects on the page (including one clip art picture and one photo).

When you are ready to group the selected shapes (and other objects), select the Group Objects command in the Arrange group. Now when you move or size one shape in the group, all the shapes in the group are moved or sized.

PowerPoint takes the capability to combine multiple shapes even further by offering a Merge Shapes Command. This command is available in the Insert Shapes group on the Drawing Tools Format tab when you have multiple shapes selected on a slide. When you select Merge Shapes, you have five possibilities:

Figure 4.18
Group multiple shapes and objects.

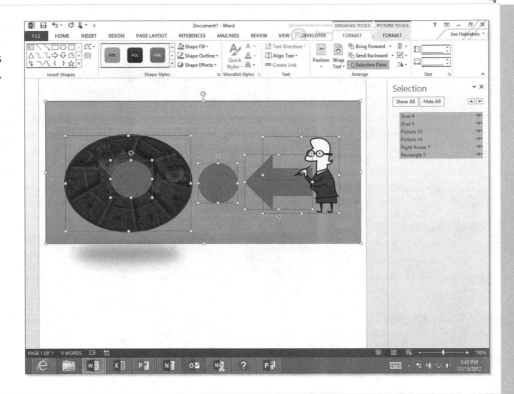

- **Union:** Combines all the shapes into a single shape. You basically end up with a shape that incorporates the outline and internal volume of the original shapes. A one-color shape is created.

- **Combine:** Combines the shapes into a single shape, where any overlapping parts of the original shapes are omitted. A single color shape results, as shown in Figure 4.19.

- **Fragment:** Combines the shapes into a one-color shape that outlines the exterior shape and any parts where the shapes originally overlapped.

- **Intersect:** Creates a combined shape that shows only the parts that originally overlapped.

- **Subtract:** Subtracts the overlapping shapes. For example, if you placed an arrow on top of a circle and selected Subtract, the circle would have an empty space within it in the shape of an arrow.

Using the Merge Shapes commands gives you another way to create custom shapes for your PowerPoint slides. No matter how you create your shapes (Insert Shape, versus Group Shapes, versus Merge Shapes), you can use the various tools in the Shape Styles group to modify fill color, outline, and effects for a selected shape or shapes.

tip
You can add text to any shape. Select the shape and then click the Text Box tool in the Insert Shapes group. The Insertion point is placed in the shape. Type the text.

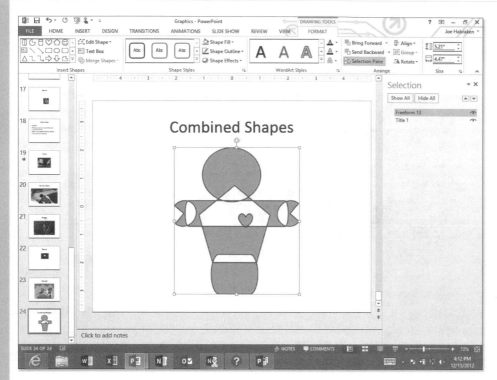

Figure 4.19
Use
PowerPoint's
Merge
Shapes com-
mands to
combine mul-
tiple shapes
in different
ways.

Formatting a Shape with the Drawing Tools

The Drawing Tools Format tab provides all the tools that you need for formatting a shape. The Drawing Tools Format command groups are as follows:

- **Insert Shapes:** This group provides the Shapes gallery and the Edit Shape, Draw a Text Box, and Merge Shapes commands. The Edit Shape command enables you to replace a selected shape or view the edit points on a shape. The edit points enable you to manipulate different parts of a single shape. For instance, on a Smiley Face, the edit points give you control over the placement of the eyes and mouth on the face.

- **Shape Styles:** This group enables you to apply shape styles to your shapes that include fill, outline, and text color formatting. You can fine-tune the style for a shape using the Shape Fill, Shape Outline, and Shape Effects commands. The Shape Effects command enables you to apply different effects to the shape, such as Shadow, Reflection, and Glow. You can also use the 3D Rotation option to add 3D effects to the shape.

- **WordArt Styles:** This group becomes available when you have added text to the shape. You can apply WordArt styles to the text and manipulate the fill, outline, and effects for the text. The Text Effects command provides Shadow, Reflection, and Bevel effects, as well as 3D rotation effects.

- **Text:** This group (available in Word) provides commands for formatting the text in the shape. You can change the text direction and alignment within the shape. When you create multiple text boxes (which again, can be any shape), you can link the shapes containing text using the Create Link command. This causes the text to flow through the linked text containing shapes.

 Tip
You can also right-click on a shape and select Add Text to add text to the shape.

- **Arrange:** This group enables you to position the shape (or multiple shapes on a canvas) with the text layer in a document. In Word the Position command specifies whether the shape is inline with the text. The Wrap Text command then specifies how the text actually wraps around the shape. This group also provides the Bring Forward, Send Backward, and Group commands. PowerPoint also includes this group but does not provide the Position or the Wrap Text commands.

- **Size:** This group contains the Shape Height and Shape Width spinner boxes, for sizing the selected shape.

If you have layered a number of shapes, you might find it difficult to select a specific shape, particularly a shape that is at the back or behind another shape. You can view a list of shapes and the canvas that they are associated with using the Selection pane.

Using the Screenshot Feature

The screenshot feature enables you to capture a screenshot of an open application or a specific area of an application window by using the Screen Clipping tool. This enables you to place screenshots of any application, utility, or web browser window into your Office application documents. For example, you can place a screenshot of an Excel worksheet in a Word document as part of a report, or you can include a screenshot of a website page on a PowerPoint slide. The possible uses of the screenshot feature are really up to you, and this feature can be useful if you are writing a set of procedures on how to use a particular application for a certain purpose.

You can capture screenshots in Word, Excel, PowerPoint, OneNote, and Outlook (when creating new email messages, appointments, tasks, and contacts). The Screenshot command is housed in the Illustrations group on the Ribbon's Insert tab, except for in PowerPoint, where it resides in the Images group on the Insert tab. As already mentioned, you can create a screenshot of an entire application window or specify an area to be captured. To capture an entire window, follow these steps:

1. Open the application window that you want to capture in the screenshot.

2. Switch to the Office application that will serve as the destination for the screenshot. For example, you might insert the screenshot into a Word document or onto a PowerPoint slide.

3. Select the Screenshot command. An Available Windows gallery appears, as shown in Figure 4.20.

4. Select the window that you want to capture. The entire application window is pasted as a screenshot into the current Office application.

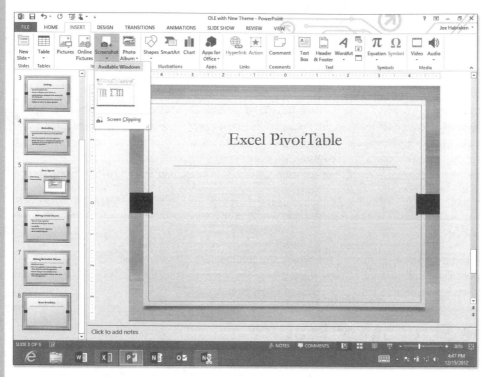

Figure 4.20
Specify a
window for
the screen-
shot.

You can size or move the inserted screenshot; it is no different from any other graphic object. In fact, when the screenshot is selected, the Picture Tools Format tab becomes available on the Ribbon. You can use the commands available to manipulate and format the screenshot as you would a digital image, which we discussed earlier in this chapter. For example, you can crop the screenshot or adjust brightness and contrast settings using the Correction command. You can also add styles to the screenshot using the Picture Styles gallery.

In addition, you can capture screenshots of specific areas of a window. The Screen Clipping tool provided by the Screenshot command makes it easy to use the mouse to specify the area to be captured.

Before you use the Screen Clipping tool, you need to get the open windows cued up so that you have access to the correct application window when you select the Screen Clipping tool. This is particularly important if you have more than two windows open on the Windows desktop; select the application window that contains the area you want to capture using the appropriate icon on the Windows taskbar. This places that window at the top of the windows that are currently open. Switch back to the Office application that will serve as the destination for the screenshot using that application's icon on the taskbar.

Now you can capture the screenshot: Select Screenshot and then Screen Clipping. You are switched to the application window, where you make the screen capture. The mouse pointer becomes a screen-clipping tool. Click and drag the mouse as needed to specify the area of the window that you want to capture. When you release the mouse, you return to the screenshot destination application, and the screen area you selected is pasted into the current Office document as a screenshot.

You can save your screenshots as image files for further use. Right-click a selected screenshot and then select Save As Picture. The Save As Picture dialog box appears. Provide a name for the screenshot, and navigate to the folder that serves as the destination for the file. By default, the screenshot is saved as a PNG file. You can also save the file in other digital image formats, such as GIF and JPEG, and as a bitmap file.

Using WordArt

WordArt enables you to create interesting text effects within your Office application documents. You can use WordArt boxes on PowerPoint slides or as graphic elements in a Word document or an Excel worksheet. You can create a WordArt object from existing text, or you can create a blank WordArt object and then type the required text directly in the WordArt frame.

The WordArt command is on the Ribbon's Insert tab. It is available in Word, PowerPoint, Excel, Publisher, and Outlook when you are creating new Outlook items such as emails, contacts, and appointments.

Inserting a WordArt object into a document is really just a matter of selecting the WordArt command and then selecting one of the WordArt styles from the WordArt gallery. Figure 4.21 shows the WordArt gallery.

Figure 4.21 The WordArt gallery.

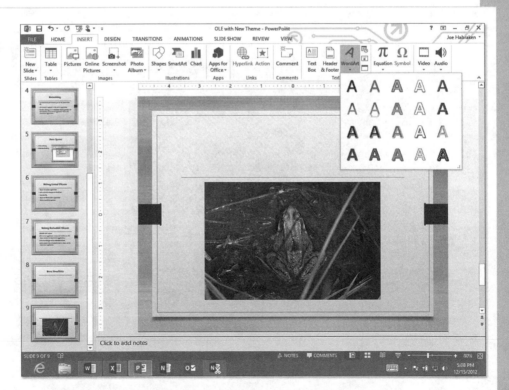

If you formatted selected text as WordArt, your existing text appears in the WordArt frame and is formatted with the selected WordArt style. A new WordArt box contains the placeholder text "Your text here," which you can replace with your own text.

You can move the WordArt in the document as needed and also size the WordArt box. When the WordArt box is selected, the Drawing Tools Format tab appears on the Ribbon. You can change the style of the WordArt box (or frame) by using the shape styles and shape-related commands (such as Shape Fill and Shape Outline) in the Shape Styles group.

The commands that affect the way the WordArt text looks are found in the WordArt Styles group. You can change the WordArt style that you have assigned to the selected WordArt by using the WordArt Styles gallery. The gallery provides styles that incorporate interesting effects, such as bevel and reflection.

The Text Fill and Text Outline commands enable you to control the fill for the WordArt text characters and the outline of the characters, respectively. The really cool part of using WordArt, however, lies in the different text effects that you can apply to the WordArt via the Text Effects command. Figure 4.22 shows the Text Effects gallery, including the Transform gallery.

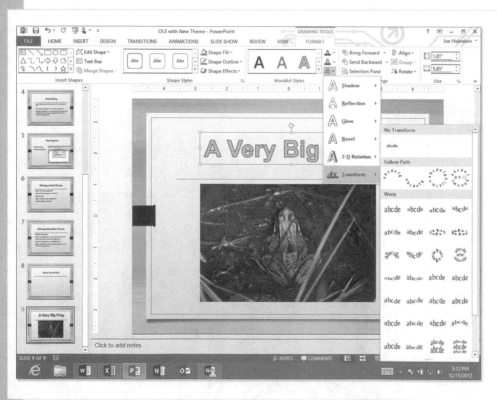

Figure 4.22
The Text Effects gallery.

The Text Effects gallery enables you to apply effects to the WordArt text, including Show, Reflection, Glow, and 3D Rotation. For those of you who lament the loss of the old WordArt utility that operated as a rather clunky add-on to the Office applications before the release of Office 2007, you will find that the Transform gallery gives you all the different text-warping effects that were available in the original WordArt utility. In terms of working with the WordArt object, the other Format tab command groups enable you to manipulate the text direction and alignment, and determine how the object is positioned in relation to existing text in the Office document.

 tip

For more control over the WordArt text effects, right-click the WordArt and select Format Shape to display the Format Shape task pane. It provides shape attributes such as fill and line color, and also enables you to manipulate text effects such as 3D format and rotation.

5

USING THE OFFICE WEB APPS

We have all found ourselves in situations while we're on the road or just away from the office when we would like to be able to look at a Word document recently completed by a colleague or a PowerPoint presentation that you prepared but didn't really have time to fine-tune. Office 2013 has shifted the application suite away from the notion of storing files on your computer. Rather, Office now adopts a new cloud strategy where you are encouraged to save your files to your SkyDrive or a location on a SharePoint server site (for Office 365 subscribers who use SkyDrive Pro). Both of these cloud options then make it easy for you to access your files from any location and device; all you need is a Web browser application. Saving to the cloud also makes it much easier for you to share your files with co-workers or colleagues.

Microsoft provides the Office Web Apps, which allow you to view and modify the files that you store in the cloud. You can also use the Web Apps to create new files and save them to your SkyDrive. As already mentioned, all you need is a device that provides a Web browser. A version of the Office Web Apps is also available to users who have access to a SharePoint site, such as Office 365 Small Business and Enterprise subscribers.

Since being introduced as part of the rollout of Office 2010, the Web Apps have been enhanced and improved, and a new version of the Office Web Apps has been made available as part of the release of Office 2013. Web Apps are available for Word, Excel, PowerPoint, and OneNote.

In this chapter, we look at what the Web Apps can do for you and how you access the Web Apps. We also discuss (more specifically) the Word, Excel, PowerPoint, and OneNote Web Apps.

What the Web Apps Can Do

The Web Apps provide you with the ability to view, edit, and save Office files to an online workspace that can be accessed from any computer or smart device with an Internet connection and a supported Web browser. But the Web Apps are only part of Microsoft's cloud computing initiative. Microsoft continues to provide users with a free SkyDrive account. To take advantage of SkyDrive, you just need to obtain a Windows Live ID (Outlook.com, MSN.com, Hotmail.com—all these account types work as Live IDs). The SkyDrive website (https://skydrive.live.com) provides free storage space for your files and access to the Office Web Apps.

If you are a subscriber to Microsoft Office 365 (Small Business or Enterprise), you are provided access to a SharePoint site. Microsoft calls this SkyDrive Pro. When you sign in to your Office 365 Admin Dashboard, you can access your SkyDrive Pro and the accompanying Office Web Apps. Employees at larger companies that host their own SharePoint sites can also take advantage of the Office Web Apps when accessing files on the SharePoint site.

 note

Office 365 is another important part of Microsoft's cloud computing initiative. When you subscribe to Office 365, the "full-blown" Office applications are installed on your computer or other supported devices via the Web.

The Web Apps provide you with basic capabilities for working with files that you have created using the installed versions of Microsoft applications, such as Word, Excel, PowerPoint, and OneNote. The Web Apps also provide you with the capability to create new files, but the Web Apps are certainly not as full-featured as the installed versions of the Office applications.

Although the Web Apps lack all the capabilities found in the installed versions of the Office applications, there is still a lot that you can do with them. Figure 5.1 shows a PowerPoint presentation that was stored on SkyDrive Pro and opened using the PowerPoint Web App.

Even though you are using the PowerPoint Web App, you can add new slides to the presentation, modify existing slides, and format text on the slides. You can even add a picture or SmartArt to a new slide and then view the presentation as a slide show—all from the Web App.

Note the PowerPoint Web App looks similar to the installed version of PowerPoint. The PowerPoint Web App Ribbon, however, has only a subset of the Ribbon tabs (and commands) provided in the full-featured version of PowerPoint. This is because the Web Apps are designed to be used when you are working on a computer that does not provide the installed Office applications and you just need to do some basic modifications or view a file that you have saved to the cloud.

 note

Whether you use the Web Apps via your free SkyDrive, your Office 365 subscription, or your company's hosted SharePoint site, you are still using the same SharePoint Server technology. The Office Web Apps are pretty much the same in terms of functionality no matter which of these three options you use to access them.

The Web Apps are designed to provide you with a fallback plan when you just don't have access to a device that hosts the installed Office application suite. The fact that they are available from any computer (and many other devices) with a Web browser and an Internet connection means that the Web Apps provide you with a lot of portability and possibilities for accessing your files in the cloud and sharing them with co-workers or colleagues.

Figure 5.1
Files stored on SkyDrive, SkyDrive Pro, or a SharePoint site can be opened in the Web Apps.

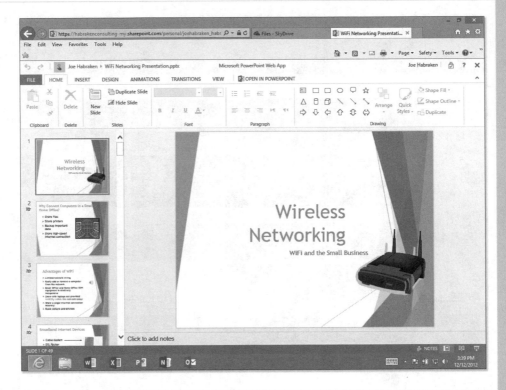

Where the Web Apps Live

As already mentioned, the Office Web Apps operate in your Web browser whether you are using the Web Apps via the Microsoft SkyDrive website, SkyDrive Pro, or a SharePoint Server installation at your company or institution that provides the Web Apps. For the Web Apps to function correctly, you need to be using a supported Web browser. The Office Web Apps rolled out in conjunction with the release of Office 2013 embrace HTML5, which means that the Web Apps do not require browser plug-ins to operate. So the Office Web Apps now work in most Web browsers, including Microsoft Internet Explorer, Google Chrome, Mozilla Firefox, and Apple Safari. To avoid any browser issues, make sure that you are using the most recent version of your chosen Web browser.

Accessing SkyDrive, SkyDrive Pro, or a company-run SharePoint server requires logon credentials: a valid username and password. When you sign in to SkyDrive (https://skydrive.live.com), the SkyDrive main page provides a list of the folders and files you have stored on the site. On the left of the SkyDrive main page, a Navigation pane makes it easy for you to view your recently saved documents (Recent docs) and view files that you have shared (Shared). Figure 5.2 shows the SkyDrive main page.

> **note**
> The latest edition of the Web Apps have also been optimized for "touch" and to run on different form factor devices, such as smartphones, touchscreens, and tablets.

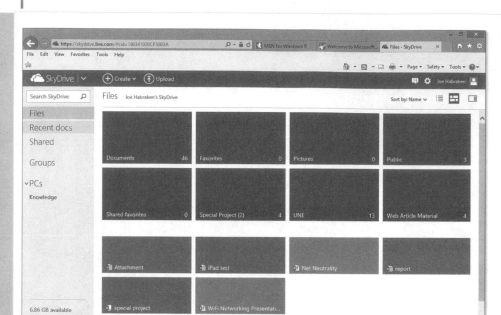

Figure 5.2
The SkyDrive
main page.

To view a file in a Web App viewer, select the file. Figure 5.3 shows a Word document open in the Word Web App viewer.

You are certainly not limited to viewing files when you work in your SkyDrive. You can edit an existing file or you can create new Word, Excel, PowerPoint, and OneNote files by launching the appropriate Web App via the New command. When you choose to edit an Office file stored on your SkyDrive, you can edit the document in Word (if you have Word installed on the device) or you can edit in the Word Web App (these two choices are shown in Figure 5.3).

Accessing files and the Office Web Apps using your Office 365 subscription (logon at https:// login.microsoftonline.com/) or a SharePoint server hosted by your company or institution is a little different than using the free SkyDrive. When you sign in to Office 365, you land on an Admin page. At the top of the Admin page is a list of services. For example, you can check your email and calendar using the Outlook and Calendar apps, respectively. There is also a People app that allows you to access your contacts. These three Office 365 apps are synced with Outlook. So anything you have stored in your installed version of Outlook (emails, appointments, and contacts) is accessible via the Office 365 Admin page. Companies hosting their own SharePoint sites also typically deploy these Web Apps for their users.

Figure 5.3
A Word document open in the Word Web App viewer.

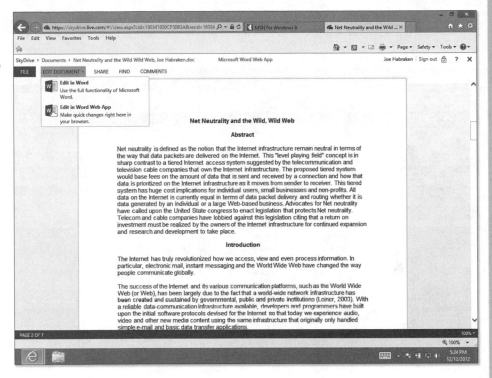

To access your Office 365 SkyDrive Pro, select SkyDrive at the top of the Admin window (the link for SkyDrive Pro is at the top of the page). The SkyDrive Pro window opens, as shown in Figure 5.4. Your documents and any folders that you have created are listed in the Documents window. A default folder named "Shared with Everyone" is also present in your file list. This folder can be used to share files with anyone who has access to your SharePoint network (either other users covered by your Office 365 subscription or with access to a corporate SharePoint site).

 note

Subscribing to Office 365 Small Business and Enterprise services is designed to let small business and entrepreneurs take advantage of Microsoft network services such as Exchange and SharePoint without having to host any servers.

You can view any file listed in a Web App viewer or open the file in the associated Web App to edit the file. When previewing a file, select the Edit Document command on the App Ribbon and then select Edit in Word Web App. As with the free version of SkyDrive, you can also choose to open the file in the installed version of the associated Office application.

SkyDrive, SkyDrive Pro, and corporate SharePoint sites aren't merely a means to an end—the end being access to the Office Web Apps. These cloud networking platforms provide easy-to-access online file storage (from almost any device) and also provide you with the ability to securely share your files with other users. There is no doubt that the Office Web Apps are very intriguing and fun to work with. However, they are best thought of as one aspect of the cloud storage and sharing framework that Microsoft has created. Using the Web Apps in concert with the installed Office 2013 applications should allow you to take full advantage of these productivity tools.

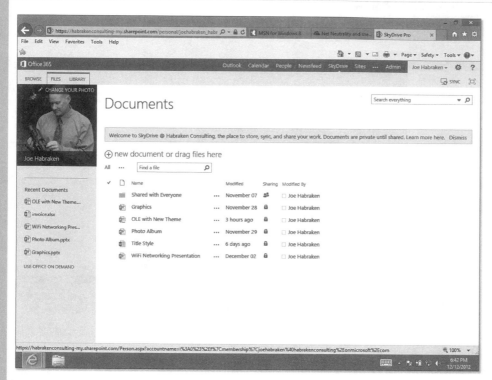

Figure 5.4
The Office 365 SkyDrive Pro Documents page.

Saving Office Application Files to the Cloud

The installed versions of the Office 2013 applications strongly encourage you to save files to the cloud. In fact, saving your Office files to a cloud server such as SkyDrive or SkyDrive Pro is configured at the end of the Office installation process (if you work at a company or institution, your Office installation may be handled by your network administrators). So, at least one cloud location is available by default in all of your Office applications. Saving your Excel, Word, PowerPoint, or OneNote files directly to one of these cloud options allows you to easily access your files from multiple devices and allows you to easily share files with colleagues or co-workers.

So at the end of the Office 2013 installation process, whether you are using an Office installation DVD or installing Office as part of an Office 365 subscription using Microsoft's new Click-to-Run installation technology, you are provided with the option to sign in to Office. The Sign In to Office window allows you to sign in using your personal credentials (a Windows Live account such as Outook.com, MSN.com, or Hotmail.com) or allows you to sign in using your organization or school credentials. The organization or school credentials would cover users in cases where your company or organization is hosting its own SharePoint site. Your network administrator supplies you with the login information. The organization and school option also covers users who have an Office 365 subscription. Subscribers would use the username and password that they established when they signed up for the Office 365 service.

Even though you finalize the Office installation by choosing one of the cloud server possibilities (for example, the free SkyDrive or the Office 365 SkyDrive Pro), you can add additional "places" to your Office configuration. This means that you can configure Office so that you can save to both your free SkyDrive and SkyDrive Pro (from your Office 365 subscription), or you can access your free SkyDrive and your corporate SharePoint site. If you work for a company that provides multiple SharePoint sites, and you have access to these sites, you can add the sites to your Office applications as places (cloud locations to save and retrieve files).

Figure 5.5 shows the Save As page in the Word Backstage. Two cloud locations (or places as Office refers to them) have already been configured for Office (the SharePoint site was added at the end of the Office installation and the SkyDrive was added from the Save As page). You can add additional cloud locations, including SkyDrive and SharePoint sites, by selecting Add a Place. To actually log in to one of the cloud options and add it as a place, select one of the options in the Add a Place list (which appears after you select Add a Place). Figure 5.5 also shows the Sign In to Office window, which allows you to sign in to one of the cloud services and add it as a place in the Backstage.

Figure 5.5
The Word Backstage Save As page and cloud places.

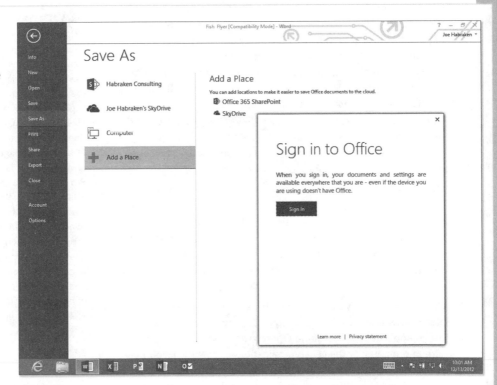

When you add a place to one of the Office applications, you are adding it to all the Office applications. Also accessing these cloud storage sites is going to be the same for most of the Office applications, including Word, Excel, and PowerPoint. Access to these cloud places is also the same when you specify a location for a OneNote notebook in the cloud; however, the process is a little different than Office "standards" like Word and Excel.

Let's take a look at saving files from the Office Backstage to a cloud location such as SkyDrive or SkyDrive Pro. We can then discuss each of the Office Web Apps individually.

Saving a File to SkyDrive or SkyDrive Pro

Saving a file to your SkyDrive or SkyDrive Pro (or any other SharePoint site) is very straightforward. For example, let's say that you want to save a new Excel workbook to your Windows Live SkyDrive. With the workbook open in the Excel application window, select Save on the Excel Quick Access Toolbar. Excel switches to the Save As page in the Backstage. The Save As page provides a list of cloud places (that you have added to the Office configuration); it also provides an icon for your computer (Computer). When you select a particular place such as your SkyDrive (which is signified by a cloud icon) or SkyDrive Pro (which is signified by a SharePoint icon), the folders recently accessed on the site are listed on the right of the Save As window. You can select any of the recent folders to open the Save As dialog box. Or after selecting one of the cloud places, you can browse the site (via the Save As dialog box) by selecting the Browse button. Figure 5.6 shows the Excel Save As page and a selected SharePoint site. The Save As dialog box is also shown.

When you have specified the location in the Save As dialog box for the file, select Save. The Excel workbook (or other Office file—depending on the application you are working in) is saved to the cloud place. You can see that Microsoft has integrated the cloud locations into the Office file storage scheme (for saving and opening files) and the cloud places such as SkyDrive or a SharePoint site are treated the same as a place on your computer (your hard drive) or your corporate network (mapped network drives).

Opening files that you saved to your SkyDrive or other cloud place is no different than opening a file stored locally. In the Office application's Backstage Open page (or the new Start screen provided by the Office applications), recently saved files are listed. If you saved a file to the cloud and it's listed in the Recent list, select the file to open it. If a cloud-based file isn't listed in the Recent list, you can select the appropriate cloud location (in the Open window) and then locate and open the file using the Open dialog box.

 note

Windows 8 can be configured so that you sign in using logon credentials such as your Microsoft Live ID. This configures Windows 8 to include your SkyDrive as a default location (which you can access on the Windows Start page using the SkyDrive tile). Your Office installation can "pick up" on your Windows 8 configuration (and vice versa), so if you are using your Windows Live or Office 365 credentials to log on to Windows, you might find your SkyDrive or SkyDrive Pro has already been configured as a "place" in Office.

 note

Think of the free SkyDrive as "SharePoint Lite." SkyDrive uses SharePoint technology (as does SkyDrive Pro) to provide you with the Web Apps and file-sharing capabilities. However, the file-sharing environment provided by the free SkyDrive is probably not as secure a storage and sharing environment as is a SkyDrive Pro account or a corporate SharePoint site. You can always make your accounts more secure (whether they are free or by subscription) by using more secure passwords that take advantage of capital alphanumeric characters and a clever combination of numbers and letters of the alphabet. Don't make it easy for others to guess your password.

Figure 5.6
The Excel
Save As page
and the Save
As dialog
box.

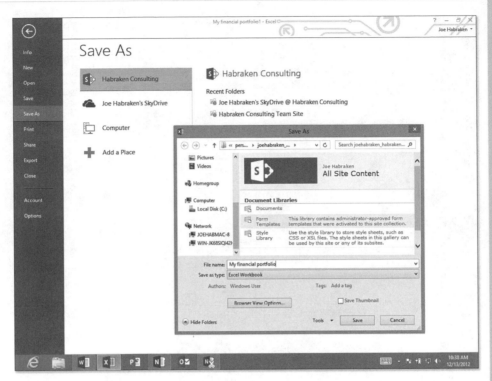

Sharing a File Saved to the Cloud

Office 2013 makes it very easy for you to share a file that you have saved to one of the cloud-based places such as your SkyDrive or SkyDrive Pro. In the case of SkyDrive Pro or corporate SharePoint sites, you can save your files to folders that are already shared with other users. The sharing process is basically the same for the different cloud options. Let's take a look at how you share a Word document that has been stored on SkyDrive. With the document open in Word, select File to access the Word Backstage. In the Backstage, select Share to open the Share page, which is shown in Figure 5.7.

The Word Share page is indicative of what you find in the other Office applications. You are provided with more than one strategy for sharing a file with other users. The sharing strategies make it easy for you to share a file with co-workers or colleagues for the purpose of collaborating. The options are as follows:

- **Invite People:** You can invite other people (users) to access the file on your SkyDrive. This is a great way to share a document that requires collaboration from several co-workers. You can specify whether or not a user has to log in to access the file (in either the SkyDrive scenario or the SharePoint scenario).

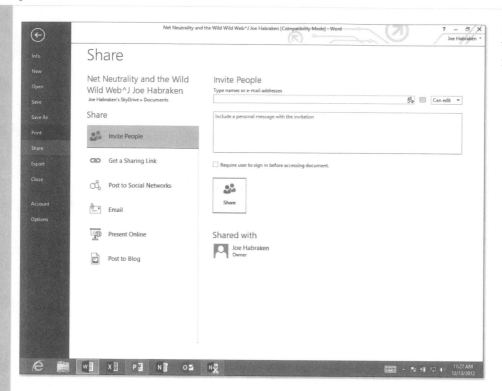

Figure 5.7
The Word
Share page.

- **Get a Sharing Link:** You can use this option to share a file with a large group of people where you would like to post the link to the presentation on the Web or via some medium other than email invitation. Select Create Link to create the link (again this can be used when you have saved the file such as a Word document to your SkyDrive or SharePoint site).

- **Post to Social Networks:** You can post a link to the SkyDrive stored Word document (or other file) via a social media site. You need to associate your Windows Live (such as Outlook.com or Hotmail) account to your Facebook account or other social network site. The possibilities include LinkedIn and Google. This option is useful if you want to share a file with a lot of other people. You can specify whether your social media "friend" (or LinkedIn colleagues) can just view the file or can edit the file.

- **Email:** You can send the file as an email attachment, link, or as a PDF or XPS file. In terms of collaboration, you want all the invitees to work on the same file, so emailing a link is your best bet. This option is no different than the Invite People option if you are sending a link.

I've only highlighted the Word sharing options that allow you to collaborate with others when you share the file. The other options such as Present Online (PowerPoint also provides a similar Present Online option) or Post to Blog are other ways to share the information in the file but it doesn't set up a collaborative environment where users can access the original file and edit it.

Sharing OneNote Notebooks

OneNote notebooks are designed to be stored in the cloud, and they can be useful for managing projects and sharing information when you share a notebook with other users. OneNote notebooks are collections of information tied together for a particular purpose. You can create a notebook related to a party you are planning or create a notebook for an important work project.

It makes sense to save your OneNote notebooks to your SkyDrive, SkyDrive Pro, or other SharePoint site. OneNote apps already exist for smartphones and tablets (including those that run Apple's iOS), which means you can access your notebooks on any device (including any device with a Web browser) to take advantage of the OneNote Web App. So no matter where you are, you can access important notebooks from the cloud.

Sharing OneNote notebooks is similar to sharing files from the other Office applications. Sharing a notebook is accomplished using the Share page in the Backstage. If you have saved a notebook to SkyDrive or a SharePoint site, you can readily share the notebook by inviting people via email or sharing a link (you can also share a notebook via a Lync meeting if you have the Lync communication client installed on your computer).

If you have not saved the notebook to your SkyDrive or SharePoint site (including SkyDrive Pro)—let's say you have saved the notebook to your My Documents folder on your computer—the Share Notebook page only provides you with one option, as shown in Figure 5.8. You have to move the notebook to your SkyDrive or SharePoint site before you can share it.

Figure 5.8
Notebooks have to be saved to your SkyDrive or SharePoint site to be shared.

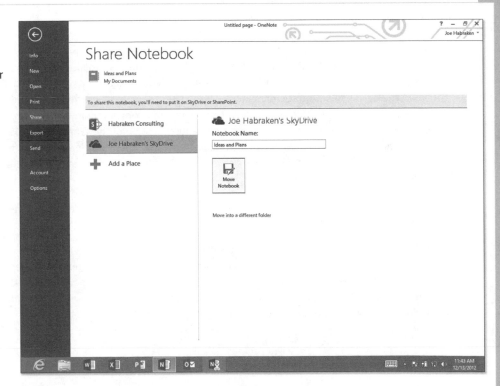

Sharing OneNote notebooks and your other Office files leverages the use of cloud storage by making it easier for you to collaborate with colleagues or co-workers. The Office Web Apps also play an important role in providing you with 24/7 access to the files you store on your SkyDrive or SharePoint site. In the next section, we begin a discussion of each of the individual Web Apps, starting with the Word Web App.

➡ *For much more detail on creating OneNote notebooks and sharing notebooks, **see** "Sharing a Notebook," p. 875.*

Using the Word Web App

The Word Web App provides you with the ability to edit existing documents (stored in the cloud) and create new documents. It supplies a number of commands for working with text, including character- and paragraph-formatting attributes. It also provides you with the ability to insert tables, pictures, and Office.com-sourced pictures into a document. The document views in the Word Web App are limited to the Editing view and the Reading view.

The differences between the Web Apps on SkyDrive and SkyDrive Pro in terms of starting a new file are minimal. There is a slight difference in the location of the New Document command that allows you to start a new file, so to start a new Word document, select New Document and then select Word Document on the Create a New File list. A File Name text box opens and requires you to supply a filename (on SkyDrive and SkyDrive Pro) before the new document opens in the Word Web App. New files created in the Word Web App are saved in the .docx file format. You are not provided the option of saving the document in any other file format; however, if you do need to create a copy of the file in a different file format, such as .doc, which provides backward compatibility with co-workers or friends who are still using an earlier version of the Word application, you can open the file in your installed Word application and save the file in a different format as needed. Files stored on SkyDrive or a SharePoint site in other file formats might not open in the Web Apps, however.

 tip

When you are using SkyDrive to access the Web Apps, the SkyDrive toolbar provides a Create command, which allows you to quickly create a new Office file, including a Word document, Excel workbook, or new OneNote notebook.

➡ *For information on saving Office 2013 application files in different file formats, **see** "Saving Files to Different File Types," p. 56.*

The Word Web App provides you with four Ribbon tabs: File, Home, Insert, and View. The Ribbon also provides a convenient Open in Word command that allows you to open the current document in the installed version of Word if it is present on the device you are using. Perusing the commands available on the Ribbon tabs supplies you with good insight into the overall capabilities that you're afforded by the Word Web App. Let's look at each of the Ribbon tabs and the command groups that they provide.

The File Tab

The File tab (which uses a similar geography to the File tab in the installed Office applications) provides you with access to the Word Web App's Backstage. The Backstage provides you with the ability to open the current document in your installed Word application via the Info tab. It also enables you to save the changes that you have made to the document (Save) and access Save As. The only option provided on the Save As page is to download a copy of the document to your computer.

The Word Web App's Backstage also provides access to a Share page and a Print page. The Sharing options (shown in Figure 5.9) allow you to invite other people to view or edit the document, and you can embed the document in a blog or website to share it.

Figure 5.9
The Word
Web App
Backstage.

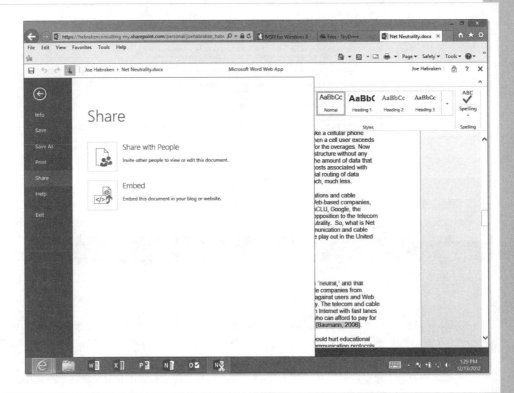

The Print page doesn't allow you to send the document to a printer, but it does allow you to create an Adobe Acrobat file from the file currently open in the Web App. The Web App Backstage also provides access to help for the Web App that you are currently using.

The Word Web App Home Tab

The Home tab in the Word Web App provides a subset of the commands that you would find on the Word 2013 Home tab. The Word Web App Home tab provides you with the ability to change font attributes, set paragraph alignment settings, and assign styles to your document text. Figure 5.10 shows the Word Web App Ribbon's Home tab. The default font and font size for the Word Web App are Calibri, 11 point.

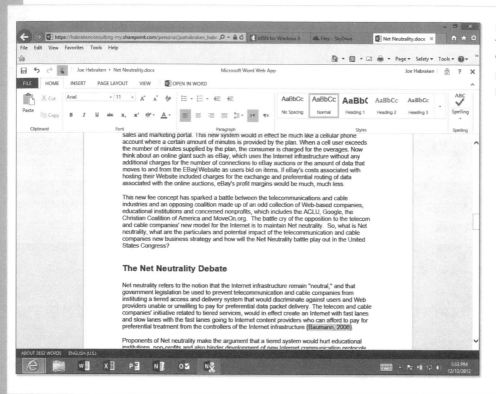

Figure 5.10
The Word Web App Ribbon's Home tab.

Notice that none of the Home tab command groups, such as Font or Paragraph, include dialog box launchers; therefore, the commands available in the groups are limited to those provided on the Ribbon.

The Font group provides you with the ability to change the font, font size, and assign font attributes to your text, such as bold, italic, and underline. By default, the Font group also includes Subscript and Superscript commands.

The Paragraph group provides commands for text alignment and indents and enables you to create bulleted and numbered lists. There are two commands supplied in the Paragraph group that you won't find on the Word 2013 Home tab by default: the Left-to-Right Text Direction and the Right-to-Left Text Direction commands. The Left-to-Right Text Direction command enables you to enter text on the page from left to right, whereas the Right-to-Left Text Direction command enables you to start on the right of the page and enter text that moves from the right to the left.

To assign a style to document text, select one of the styles provided in the Style gallery. The Style gallery also provides access to the Apply Styles dialog box shown in Figure 5.11. Open the Style gallery and then select Apply Styles. Select a style in the Apply Styles dialog box and then click OK. The style is applied to the text.

tip

The Web Apps, such as the Word Web App, also provide a Quick Access Toolbar above the Ribbon. It provides the Save, Undo, Redo, and Touch Mode commands.

The Word Web App also provides access to the Spelling feature via the Home tab and enables you to set the proofing language used by the Spelling feature. The Word Web App flags words that it considers misspelled; you can "fix" a misspelled word by right-clicking on the word and selecting one of the options provided by the shortcut menu that appears.

➡️ *For information on text and paragraph formatting in Word 2013, **see** "Understanding Document Formatting," p. 146.*

Figure 5.11
Apply Styles dialog box.

The Word Web App Insert Tab

The Word Web App Ribbon's Insert tab provides you with a number of possibilities for enhancing your document with a table, picture, or clip art image. The Insert tab also provides you with the ability to quickly insert a link (hyperlink) into your document. You can also insert a table and then add or delete columns and rows as needed. You can also upload pictures from your computer to the document and insert clip art from the Office.com library.

The Table command provides a table grid that enables you to select the number of columns and rows in the new table. After the new table is inserted into the document, the Table Tools Layout tab becomes available on the Ribbon. The Table Tools Layout tab enables you to select the table or the current column, row, or cell. You can then use the commands in the Delete group to delete the table or selected column or row. You can also insert new columns or rows above, below, or to the left or right, respectively, of the currently selected column, row, or cell. Text in the table can be aligned using the commands provided in the Alignment group.

➡ *For information on working with tables in Word 2013,* ***see*** *Chapter 8, "Working with Tables, Columns, and Sections."*

The Insert tab also enables you to add pictures to your document. Select the Picture command to open the Choose File to Upload dialog box. Select the picture file you want to insert and then select Open.

When you insert a picture, the Picture Tools Format tab becomes available on the Ribbon. This tab enables you to specify alternative text for the image (in cases where the document is viewed on the Web and the picture cannot be loaded), and enables you to enlarge, shrink, or scale the image. You will find that large picture files will take a while to load when you insert them into the Web App. If you want to take advantage of a much more complete set of picture commands, you might want to insert pictures into your documents using Word 2013 rather than the Word Web App.

➡ *For information on working with pictures in the Office 2013 applications,* ***see*** *"Working with your Digital Pictures," p. 83.*

The Word Web App View Tab

The Word Web App View tab is definitely bare bones when compared with the possibilities provided by the Word 2013 Ribbon's View tab. The Web App View tab provides two possibilities: Editing view and Reading view.

The Editing view is the view that you are using as you edit the document in the Word Web App. When you select the Reading view, as shown in Figure 5.12, you are taken to the Word Web App view. This is the same view provided when you select and preview a file that is listed in a SkyDrive folder or in your SharePoint site library.

This viewer does enable you to zoom in and out on the document and also to open the Find in Document pane. You can search for text in the document using the search box that this pane provides. You have the option of searching forward or backward in the document.

When you have finished viewing your document, you can then select Edit in Browser to reopen the document in the Word Web App. You also have the option of opening the document in Word 2013 by selecting Open in Word.

Figure 5.12
The Word
Web App
view.

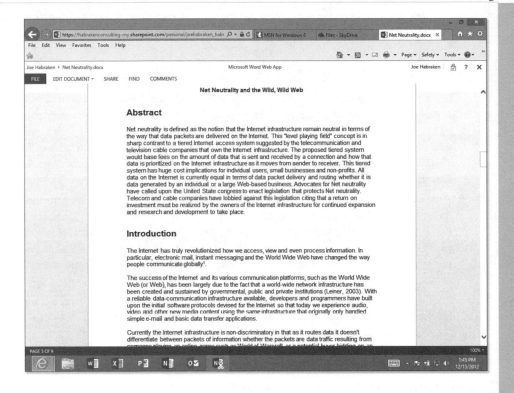

Using the Excel Web App

The Excel Web App rolled out in conjunction with the Office 2013 applications is definitely a stronger app than its predecessor (which was rolled out with Office 2010). The latest version of the Excel Web App allows you to quickly add sheets to the current workbook (the New Sheet command is on the bottom right of the window), and you can quickly insert Excel functions using the AutoSum command in the new Formulas group on the Ribbon's Home tab. The Excel Web App also provides you with the ability to create new Excel workbooks and to edit your existing workbooks that have been saved to your SkyDrive folder or SharePoint.

The Excel Web App provides basic capabilities for formatting text labels (via the Font group) and values using the Number Format gallery. The Excel Web App is probably strongest in working with Excel tables and provides you with the ability to specify a cell range as a table. You can then use the Sort and Filter drop-down lists provided for each field (column) heading to sort and/or filter the table. The Excel Web App also enables you to update connections in a workbook if you are editing a workbook created in Excel 2013 that includes external data sources such as a SQL Server database or other data source accessed through Microsoft Query. Use the Data command in the Data group to refresh all external data sources.

➡ *For information about Excel tables, PivotTables, and data sources, **see** Chapter 15, "Using Excel Tables and PivotTables."*

The Excel Web App File Tab

The Excel Web App provides a Ribbon with three tabs: File, Home, and Insert. The File tab, which is equivalent to the Backstage found in the installed version of Excel, is sparsely populated. You have probably already figured out that the Excel Web App doesn't have a Save button. The files that you create or edit in the Web App are saved automatically to your SkyDrive or SharePoint site. The Web App Backstage does supply a page for each of the following items: Save As, Print, Share, About, and Help.

The Save As page allows you to save a copy of the current workbook in the same online folder as the original. It also provides the ability to download a copy of the current workbook to your computer. The Print page can provide you with a print-friendly view of the current worksheet that you can then print (similar to the PDF option provided by the Word Web App). The Share page allows you to send a share invitation to your collaborators or you can embed a copy of the sheet on a web page or blog.

The About page in the Excel Web App Backstage is purely informational (there is no information related to the Excel worksheet you are working on). This page provides Microsoft's terms of use for the Excel Web App and also provides a primer on how the Web Apps protect your privacy. The Help page provides access to an Excel Web App Help window that allows you to search for help.

Working in the Excel Web App

The Excel Web App provides a pretty strong subset of the Excel 2013 commands so you can build sheets that take advantage of Excel's function library and its ability to manipulate table data as well as visually portray your data in a variety of chart types.

Basic features are covered in the Excel Web App and you can adjust row heights and column widths in a worksheet by dragging the row or column border. The Best-Fit column width function (double-clicking on a column border) is now also available in the Web App, so you can easily size columns to accommodate the longest entry in a particular column. As already mentioned, you can insert new sheets into your workbook and you can delete a sheet in the workbook by right-clicking on the sheet tab and selecting Delete. You can also rename worksheets as needed.

You can view graphics that you have added to a worksheet created in Excel 2013, such as pictures, clip art, and SmartArt, but you do not have the formatting control over them that you do in the installed version of Excel. You can move a graphic such as a picture on a page in the Web App and resize the picture as needed. You can also remove a picture (or other sheet object) by selecting the object and then pressing Delete on the keyboard.

Inserting Functions and Charts in the Excel Web App

Inserting functions into a worksheet when you are working in the Excel Web App can be accomplished using the AutoSum drop-down list provided on the Ribbon's Home tab (in the Formulas group) or the Function command provided on the Insert tab. Selecting More Functions on the AutoSum command (on the Home tab) or selecting the Function command (on the Insert tab) opens the Insert Function dialog box, as shown in Figure 5.13.

Figure 5.13
The Insert Function dialog box.

Select a function category in the Insert Function dialog box and then pick the function you want to insert into the currently selected cell. Select OK and the function is inserted into the sheet; however, you still need to specify the range of cells that are to be used by the function. For example, in Figure 5.14 the MAX function is used to compute the maximum salary in a range of salary data. Simply select the range of cells that you want the function to act upon.

To finish off the function (after selecting the cell range), you have to type a closing parenthesis; then press Enter. The results of the function appear in the sheet. Working with more complex functions in the Excel Web App may be more trouble than they are worth. The installed version of Excel does much more hand-holding when it comes to setting up complex functions.

You can also add your own formulas to a sheet when you are working in the Excel Web App. To add a formula, type the equal sign (=) and then specify the cell addresses and the operators required for the formula. You can use the mouse to specify the cell addresses that appear in the formula as you would in Excel 2013. When the formula is complete, press the Enter key.

In terms of copying a formula or function (or extending a series), you can use the fill handle as you would in the installed version of Excel. You can also take advantage of the Clipboard group on the Home tab to cut or copy a formula or function (or any cell content). The Paste command in the Excel Web App provides a menu that enables you to paste formulas, paste values, or paste formatting. Select Paste Formulas to paste the formula.

You can also insert charts into your sheets when you are using the Excel Web App. Select the cells that will serve as the chart data. On the Insert tab, select one of the chart types. Each chart type provides chart subtypes. Select one of the subtypes and the chart is inserted into the sheet, as shown in Figure 5.15.

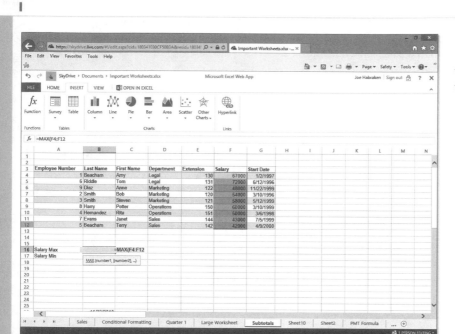

Figure 5.14
Insert a function and then select the range to act upon.

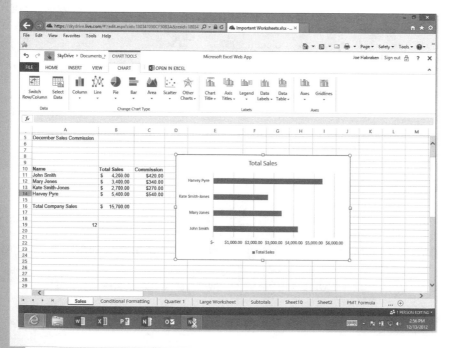

Figure 5.15
Insert a chart into a sheet.

When the chart is selected, the Chart Tools are available on the Ribbon. These Chart Tools are a stripped-down version of the Chart Tools found in the installed version of Excel, but they still provide you with a lot of possibilities. You can manipulate the chart type, and you can modify chart elements, such as the chart title, axes, and gridlines.

 note
The Excel Web App does not include a Save button on the Quick Access Toolbar. Changes you make to an Excel workbook in the Web App are saved automatically.

➡️ *For more information on creating charts in Excel, **see** Chapter 14, "Enhancing Worksheets with Charts."*

➡️ *For more information on Excel formulas and functions, **see** Chapter 13, "Getting the Most from Formulas and Functions."*

Using the PowerPoint Web App

The PowerPoint Web App provides you with a solid collection of commands for creating a new presentation or editing an existing presentation that you have saved to your SkyDrive or SharePoint site library. It is probably the most full-featured of the Office Web Apps. When you create a new presentation, you must provide a filename (as with the other Office Web Apps) and then the PowerPoint Web App opens in your browser window. The first thing that the Web App requires when you create a new presentation is that you select a theme for the presentation. The Select Theme dialog box opens, as shown in Figure 5.16.

Figure 5.16
Select a theme for the new presentation.

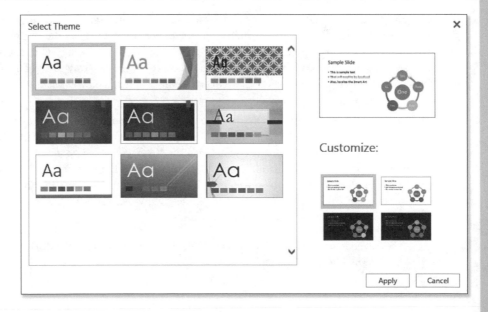

You can scroll through the themes provided in the Select Theme dialog box. After you find the theme you want to use, select the theme, and then click the Apply button. You can change the theme that you initially select using the Themes gallery and the Variants gallery provided on the new Design tab provided by the PowerPoint Web App. The PowerPoint Web App Ribbon provides the File, Home, Insert, Design, Animations, Transitions, and View tabs. The File tab provides you with access to the Backstage and includes pages that allow you to open the presentation in PowerPoint 2013 (Info), print the presentation to a PDF (Print), and share the presentation (Share) with other users.

The Home tab provides you with the Clipboard commands and Slides commands that allow you to insert, duplicate, and hide slides. The Home tab also provides font and paragraph formatting commands and includes a Drawing group that allows you to insert different shapes onto a slide. It also provides you with commands that enable you to format font and paragraph attributes for the text on your slides, including bulleted and numbered lists.

The Insert tab enables you to insert objects, such as pictures, clip art, shapes, SmartArt, and hyperlinks. There is also a Text Box command and a Comment command on the Insert tab, which allow you to insert a new text box or comment, respectively. The PowerPoint Web App also allows you to insert pictures and other graphics onto a blank slide, which you could not do in the previous version of the app.

The Design tab is reserved for the Themes gallery and the Variants gallery, which allows you to change the presentation theme or modify the current theme by selecting a variant, respectively. This tab is really only missing the Slide Size and Format Background commands that you find in the full-blown version of PowerPoint.

Both the Transitions and Animations panes are similar to their namesakes on the installed version of PowerPoint's Ribbon. The installed version of PowerPoint follows the Design tab with the Transitions tab and then the Animations tab, which the Web App reverses (Animations before Transitions). However, both of these tabs provide you with an easy way to add animations and/or transitions to your presentations without ever opening the installed version of PowerPoint.

The Ribbon's View tab provides you with an Editing view and a Reading view (which is the Preview view that is used by SkyDrive or SkyDrive Pro when you preview a presentation file). Other commands available on the View menu include the Slide Show command (which starts the slide show) and the Notes and Show Comments commands. The Notes command opens the Notes pane at the bottom of the slide, so you can add notes to the presentation. If you are sharing the presentation or you have added comments to the presentation, you can open the Comments pane from the Show Comments command. The Notes, Editing View, Reading View, and Slide Show commands are also available on the bottom right of the Web App status bar.

➡ *For more information on working in different PowerPoint views,* **see** *"Working with Slides in Different Views," p. 512.*

Working with Slides

You can add, delete, and duplicate presentation slides. The slide-related commands are on the Ribbon's Home tab. Your new presentation is provided with a title slide by default. You can click on the title slide and enter the title slide text as needed.

To insert a new slide, select the New Slide command. The New Slide dialog box opens, as shown in Figure 5.17.

Figure 5.17
Insert a new slide.

Select a layout for the new slide. If you are going to add an object, such as a picture or SmartArt, select a slide layout that provides a content placeholder. Click Add Slide to insert the new slide.

After you have inserted the new slide, you can enter the text for that slide. You can format the text using the Font and Paragraph group commands provided on the Home tab. You can add other slides as needed. Changes that you make to the presentation are saved automatically.

You can delete elements on a slide; select a text box or content box and then press Delete. You can also rearrange the slides in a presentation in the Web App by dragging the slide thumbnails to a new position in the slide list. To delete a slide, select the slide's thumbnail and then select Delete Slide on the Home tab.

Adding Pictures and SmartArt

To add pictures, SmartArt, or links to a slide using the PowerPoint Web App, all you need to do is navigate to the Insert tab of the Ribbon and then insert the object type. For example, to insert a SmartArt graphic, select the SmartArt command on the Insert tab. The SmartArt gallery opens.

The gallery contains thumbnails of many different types of SmartArt lists and diagrams. Select a SmartArt list or diagram in the gallery to insert it into a content placeholder on the slide.

When a SmartArt graphic is selected on a slide, the SmartArt Tools become available on the Ribbon, as shown in Figure 5.18. You can change the layout of the SmartArt graphic, colors, and also the style for the currently selected SmartArt graphic.

 caution

You can't change a slide's layout (there is no Layout gallery for an existing slide) after the fact in the Web App, so if you insert a slide with the wrong layout, you can wait to change the layout in PowerPoint 2013 or you can delete the slide and insert a new slide with the correct layout.

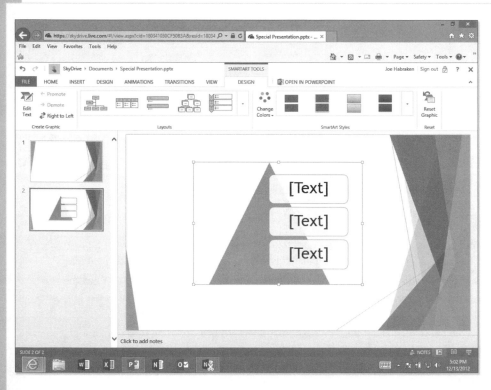

Figure 5.18
A SmartArt graphic and the SmartArt Tools.

To make text entries in a SmartArt graphic, click on one of the text placeholders on the graphic. The text boxes on the SmartArt graphic are temporarily converted to a list; enter your text and then click outside the list and the SmartArt graphic reappears on the slide.

Pictures can also be added to your slides via the Insert tab when you are using the PowerPoint Web App. When an inserted picture is selected, the Picture Tools become available on the Ribbon. Assign a style to the selected picture or you can use the Change Picture command to specify that a different picture file be used in the slide.

> *For information on working with pictures and SmartArt in the Office 2013 applications,* **see** *"Adjusting Pictures,"* **p. 84**.

Using the OneNote Web App

The OneNote Web App enables you to create OneNote notebooks and edit OneNote notebooks that have been saved to your SkyDrive or SkyDrive Pro. A notebook is basically an organizational container like a three-ring binder. A notebook consists of sections that you create to specify the organizational sections of the notebook. Pages can then be inserted into each section. Pages can contain all sorts of information, such as text notes, tables, pictures, and a variety of other items.

The OneNote Web App does a pretty good job in enabling you to create a basic notebook that includes text tags, tables, and pictures. The Backstage in the OneNote Web App provides a Share page, which allows you to invite users to share your notebook. You can also open the notebook in the fully functioning OneNote using the Open in OneNote command on the OneNote Web App's Ribbon.

The OneNote Web App Ribbon's Home tab provides access to Clipboard-related commands and basic text formatting commands, including styles and the Tag command. The Insert tab allows you to insert tables, pictures, and links and also provides the Notebook group, which is where the New Page and New Section commands reside.

The OneNote Web App does not provide the Drawing Tools available in the installed version of OneNote nor does it enable you to check the sync status for a shared notebook. The Web App does provide you enough functionality, however, to get work done on a new or existing notebook. Let's take a look at adding sections and pages to a notebook and then some of the options for inserting objects onto notebook pages.

Adding Sections and Pages

A OneNote notebook is divided into different parts using sections. When you create a new notebook using the OneNote Web App, the notebook is created with one section and one page. You can rename the default untitled section by right-clicking on the section tab and selecting Rename from the shortcut menu. Type the new name in the Section Name dialog box and then click OK.

Each page, including the default page in the default section, contains a header area above a time stamp in which you click to enter a name for the page. The sections that you add to a notebook appear in the Navigation pane on the left of the Web App workspace. Pages contained in a section appear under the section name. The Navigation pane looks a lot like an outline after you have populated it with sections and pages.

To add a new section to the notebook, select the Ribbon's Insert tab and then select New Section. The Section Name dialog box opens. Provide a name for the section and then click OK.

The new section is added to the notebook. When you add a new section, a new untitled page is also added to the section. You can type a name for a new page in its header area.

You can also insert pages as needed into a particular section in the notebook. Select a section in the Navigation pane and then click the New Page icon on the right of the section tab (or select the New Page command in the Notebook group on the Insert tab). You can then type a name for the page in the page's header area. New pages can also be inserted from the Ribbon's Insert tab using the New Page command.

You can rearrange pages in a section by dragging a page to a new position in the Navigation pane. You can also drag a page from one section to another section. Sections in the notebook can also be rearranged by dragging them as needed in the Navigation pane.

➡ *For information on working with sections and pages in OneNote,* **see** *"Working with Sections,"* *p. 879.*

Adding Notes and Note Tags to Pages

The real value of a notebook is the information included on the pages it contains. You can click below the time stamp on a page to add a text note to the page. To add the text note, just start typing at the insertion point. The OneNote Web App enables you to place notes along only the left margin of the page. To add blank lines between the notes on the page, use the Enter key.

Tags or note tags can take the form of preformatted notes, such as to-do lists, contact note boxes, or idea boxes. Some note tags are just icons or text formatting that is applied to the text in a note. Note tags not only make it easy to enter a list or contact information, but also serve as special reminders and enable you to differentiate between the different types of notes that you have added to a page.

To insert a new note tag, select the Tag command on the Ribbon's Home tab. The Tag gallery opens, as shown in Figure 5.19. To view additional tags, select the More Tags option at the bottom of the Tag gallery.

Select a tag from the gallery to insert onto the page. Enter the appropriate text associated with the tag. For example, if you inserted a To Do note tag, type each item in the to-do list as needed. A check box is provided for each item in the list.

You can remove the tag from a note that you have typed. Place the insertion point on the tagged note; then access the Tag gallery and select Remove Tag from the gallery. The note remains on the page; only the tag is removed.

➡ *For information on working with notes and tags in OneNote,* **see** *"Inserting and Formatting Notes," p. 887.*

Figure 5.19
Insert a
note tag on
a notebook
page.

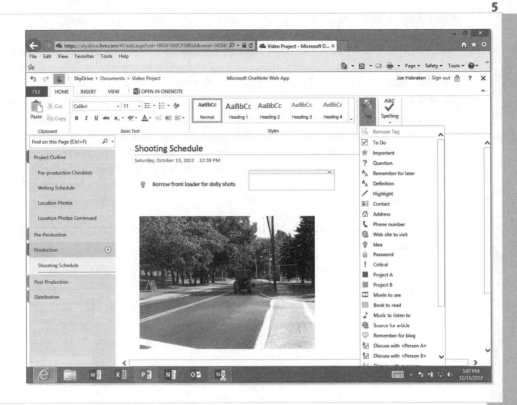

Inserting Tables and Other Objects onto Pages

The OneNote Web App also provides you with the ability to insert tables and other objects, such as pictures and clip art. Tables enable you to organize information in columns and rows. Pictures enable you to provide images that give visual support for notes that you have placed on your notebook pages.

To insert a table, select the Table command on the Insert menu. Use the table grid provided to specify the number of rows and columns for the table. Enter the required text in the table. You can move from cell to cell by pressing the Tab key. You can move backward in the table (from cell to cell) by using Shift+Tab.

You can format the text in the table by using the basic text commands in the Basic Text group and the styles provided in the Style gallery. When the insertion point is in the table, the Table Tools Layout tab is available on the Ribbon. You can use these commands to modify the table, such as deleting columns or rows or inserting columns and rows. You can also use the Align Left, Center, and Align Right commands, which can be used to align the text in a cell or a group of selected cells in the table.

The OneNote Web App includes most, but not all, of the Table Tools Layout commands in the installed version of OneNote. So working with information in tables is one of the Web App's strong suits.

The OneNote Web App's Insert tab also enables you to insert pictures and clip art. When you insert a picture, you select from picture files that are stored on your computer (you can't access your SkyDrive but if you use a SharePoint site, you can access any pictures stored there). When you insert clip art, you are searching Office.com by keyword(s); Office.com houses a huge library of clip art and royalty-free photos. To insert clip art, select the Clip Art command on the Insert menu. The Insert Clip Art dialog box opens. Type a search string for the search and then click the Search icon.

Clip art matching your search string appears in the Insert Clip Art dialog box. Select a clip art image in the dialog box and then click the Insert button. The clip art is inserted onto the notebook page. When the picture is selected, you can take advantage of the Picture Tools Format commands that enable you to enlarge or shrink the image and to specify the image size by using the Scale spinner box. You cannot undo the insertion of clip art onto the page, but you can select the image and then press Delete to remove it.

For information on adding pictures to OneNote pages, **see** *"Adding Objects to Notebook Pages," p. 903.*

REQUISITE WORD: ESSENTIAL FEATURES

Word processing might not seem like the most exciting task. However, Word 2013 can make the document creation process much more productive and creative. In this chapter, we take a look at the Word application window and the basic features and tools this powerful word processor provides.

We cover the options for creating new Word documents and look at ways to navigate the Word application window and your documents. We look at document formatting, including working with fonts and formatting paragraphs. We also work with tabs, margins, and page orientation settings.

Introducing Word 2013

Microsoft Word has been the standard for word processing for nearly two decades. And it is certainly safe to say that it is the most often used member of the Microsoft Office application suite—no matter what our job or endeavor, we all need to create documents. Some of us use Word to create lists, memos, and letters; others create more complex documents, such as reports, newsletters, and forms. Regardless of the type of documents you create, Word 2013 provides all the tools and word-processing features of a full-fledged desktop publishing application. The new Word (2013) also provides some interesting new features that better integrate this powerful application with web content and cloud computing.

The Word 2013 Interface

Word 2013 builds upon the application interface introduced with Office 2007 and then refined in Office 2010. Word 2013 provides many improvements when compared to previous versions of the software application.

The Ribbon is the command center, and it provides you with quick access to logical groupings of commands and features. Each Ribbon tab is divided into groups of related commands and features. With related commands broken into visually separate groups.

Figure 6.1 shows the Ribbon with the Home tab selected. The Home tab is home to command groups that include the Clipboard, Font, and Paragraph groups. Each group contains related commands. For example, the Font group contains font-formatting commands such as Bold, Italic, Font Size, and Font Color.

Figure 6.1
The Word 2013 application window and Ribbon.

The Ribbon also provides a contextual approach to accessing the tools you need as you work on a particular task or with a particular Word feature. For example, you can quickly create a table from the Insert tab of the Ribbon by selecting the Insert tab, selecting Table, and then choosing one of the methods of table creation. When you place the insertion point in the table, a contextual tab, Table Tools, appears on the Ribbon. Selecting either the Design tab or the Layout tab provides tools specific to formatting the table. Figure 6.2 shows the Tables Tools (Layout tab) that becomes available when a table is selected in a document.

The Layout tab enables you to work with rows and columns, merge cells, and change the text alignment in cells. The Design tab enables you to assign styles to the table and set style options.

Figure 6.2
The contextual Table Tools become available on the Ribbon when you work with a table.

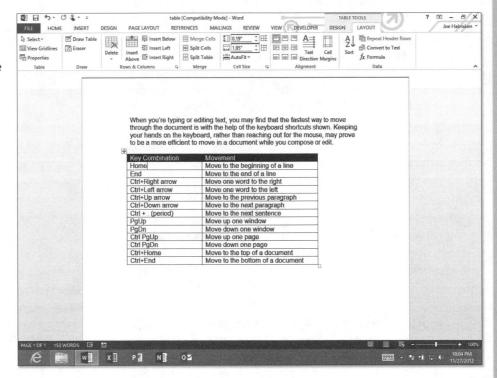

➡️ For information about customizing the Ribbon, **see** "Customizing an Application Interface,"
p. 35.

New Features and Improvements

Word 2013 builds on the tools and features of Microsoft Word 2010 and provides some important enhancements of its own. Some of the more notable improvements to Word 2013 follow:

- **Live layout and alignment guides:** Word 2013 makes it extremely easy to place a picture or other graphic in a document and immediately get a live preview of the picture and its effect on the surrounding text. As you drag the picture on the page, alignment guides help you with its final placement. Text-wrapping layout options for the picture and its surrounding text can be accessed with one click on the Layout Options button, which appears when the picture is selected.

- **Online picture and video insertion:** You can now quickly and easily insert pictures and videos from online sources. The Insert tab of the Word 2013 Ribbon provides an Online Pictures command and an Online Video command. You can insert images by connecting directly to Flickr or by searching other resources using Microsoft's Bing search engine. In addition, you can source video from YouTube or other websites. Both features enable you to search for content without leaving the Word application window.

- **Better table tools:** Word 2013 makes it easy for you to add columns or rows to a table. Place the mouse between two columns (at the top of the table) or between two rows (on the left of the table), and new insert controls appear that enable you to quickly insert a new column or row. The table styles gallery has also been revamped, providing groupings of styles in plain tables, grid tables, and list tables categories.

- **PDF editing in Word:** Word now makes it possible to edit an existing PDF file. Open the Adobe Acrobat file in Word; the text, images, and other material in the PDF are converted to a new Word document. You can then edit the document and save your changes. By default, the new document is saved as a Word document.

 note

As with all software version upgrades, some improvements in Word 2013 are under-the-hood features that most users will not notice.

- **New Start Screen:** When you launch the Word application, you go to the Start screen (instead of opening a new, blank document). The Start screen makes it easy for you to open recent documents or select a document template that you can use to build a new document.

- **Default document saving to SkyDrive:** Word 2013 is embracing cloud computing, which not everyone considers an improvement. By default, your documents are saved to your SkyDrive (or SharePoint, if you have access to a SharePoint server). The idea is to make it easy for you to access your documents from any device: computer, tablet, smart phone, and so on. You should definitely acquire a Microsoft Live ID (go to Outlook.com) by signing up for a Microsoft email account. If you don't want to save your files to SkyDrive, you can change Word's default setting to save your documents to your computer.

 tip

You can pin the Word Start menu icon to the Windows 8 taskbar. With the Word application window open on the desktop, right-click the Word icon on the taskbar and then select Pin This Program to Taskbar. You still need to access the desktop to start Word from the taskbar, but it gives you another possibility for starting applications that you use frequently, such as Word.

Although this is not an exhaustive list of all the new features and improvements in Word 2013, it does give you a heads-up on a number of new possibilities that you can take advantage of as you use Word. Other new Word features are introduced in appropriate context in Chapters 6 through 10.

➡ *For an overview of the new and improved features in Office 2013,* **see** *"New Features and Tools in Office 2013," p. 9.*

Options for Creating a New Word Document

When you start Word, the Start screen opens. This screen lists recently opened documents under a Recent heading. If this is the first time you have started Word, a message stating that you haven't opened any documents recently will reside where the list of recently opened files would normally be. You also have the option to open saved documents not listed under Recent by clicking the Open Other Documents option. The Start screen also provides access to a library of Word document templates. See Figure 6.3, which shows the start screen.

Figure 6.3
The new Start screen makes it easy for you to open an existing document or start a new one.

You have two choices here: Open and edit an existing document (or a copy of a document), or start a new document from scratch. You can quickly start a new, blank document by clicking the Blank document template. This document contains all your default page layout settings, such as margins and page orientation, and uses Word's default font and font attributes. Starting a document from scratch affords you complete control over how the document looks, from the font to the paragraphs to the page. However, you might want to create some sort of specialized document (such as a newsletter), or you might want help with the overall design and look of a document.

 tip
You can quickly open a copy of any document provided in the Recent list. Right-click the document name and select Open a copy from the shortcut menu. You can also pin or remove documents in the Recent list by taking advantage of the options on the shortcut menu.

Creating a particular kind of new document is really just a matter of choosing the appropriate template. The Start screen lists several template options; at the top of the page is a search box for locating templates stored in a large online library of possibilities. We discuss templates in more detail in the next section.

When you start Word, the Start screen options for opening an existing document or starting a new document are self-evident. So, let's say you've completed your initial document task and want to either open an existing document or start a new document. Basically, you want to return to the Backstage and either access saved documents to open an already created document or access templates to create a new document. To return to the Backstage from the Word application window, select File on the Ribbon.

You return to the Open page of the Backstage. This page (shown in Figure 6.4) provides a list of recent documents and provides access to various places you might have stored documents. For example, to open a file on your computer, follow these steps:

1. Select Computer in the Places list. A Browse icon and a list of recently opened folders appear in the right pane of the Open window.

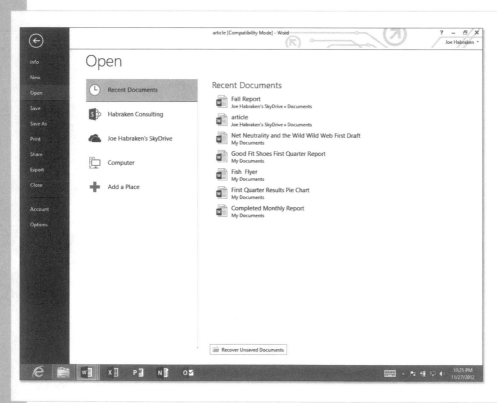

Figure 6.4
Open an existing document from the Recent Documents list.

2. To access one of the recent folders, select the folder or select Browse.

3. The Open dialog box opens (in either the recent folder you selected or your default Windows 8 folder, typically Documents). Navigate as needed to locate the file you want to open.

4. Select the document in the Open dialog box and then select Open; if you want to open a copy of the document, select the drop-down arrow next to Open and then select Open As Copy. The document opens in the Word application window in Read mode.

Read Mode is designed to make it easy for you to read your document no matter what type of device you are using to run Word—a computer, a smartphone, or a tablet. Read Mode formats the document into columns and removes the Ribbon to provide maximum screen space for the document. We discuss Read Mode in more detail in the next chapter.

➡ *For more about using Read Mode and changing the Word document display,* ***see*** *"Changing the Document Display," p. 188.*

Exiting Read Mode is straightforward. Select View (on the "mini-Ribbon" at the top left of the screen) and then select Edit Document from the menu that appears. Now you can edit your document as needed.

Using Templates

As already mentioned in the previous section, one option for creating a new document is to use a template provided on the Start screen or the New page in the Backstage. When you create a new document in Word, you actually always use a template—even blank documents. Blank documents are based on the Normal template, which uses all the default settings such as the default font, margins, tabs, paragraph settings, and the other document layout attributes. If you haven't changed any of the default Word settings (something we talk about later in this chapter), the Normal template presents you with all the default settings that Word provides at installation.

For example, the default margins for the Normal template are 1 inch for left, right, top, and bottom (of the page). The default page orientation is portrait (meaning the page is taller than it is wide, based on the default page size in the United States of 8.5 by 11 inches). The default font is Calibri, with a default font size of 11 points (there are 72 points to an inch). The default line spacing (which is a paragraph setting) is set to Multiple, which is actually 1.08 spaces between each line. This is different than in earlier versions of Word, which use 1 as the default line spacing. Obviously, if you want to create a special document such as a resume, flyer, or restaurant menu, you will want to edit these and other default settings to achieve the appropriate overall design and look for your special document.

By design, templates contain formatting and layout attributes particular to a certain document type. So if you need to create a brochure, you simply select one of the brochure templates provided. The template takes care of the font, paragraph, and page-formatting attributes; all you have to do is provide the content for the document, such as text and pictures. Then you can quickly print your required number of brochures. Figure 6.5 shows one of the Word brochure templates.

Templates also often contain sample text or text placeholders. You replace the sample text with your text or click one of the text placeholders and insert the required text. Some templates also contain borders, shading, and even graphics (some of the graphics might take the form of watermarks on the page). The whole point behind templates is to enable you to quickly and efficiently create a specialized document that typically requires special formatting and layout attributes.

At this point in our discussion, you might not have a complete feel for all the different font, paragraph, and page layout formatting attributes that a Word template can control (although you will after you have perused the Word section of this book). Even without a thorough understanding of all the options, though, you can still take advantage of the templates to create special documents.

(I drive a hybrid automobile but can't really explain the science of how the engine works.) Using a template does not lock you into the formatting attributes provided by the template, however, and you can fine-tune your new template-based document as readily as you can tweak a simple document that you created from scratch (which, as you now know, is based on the Normal template).

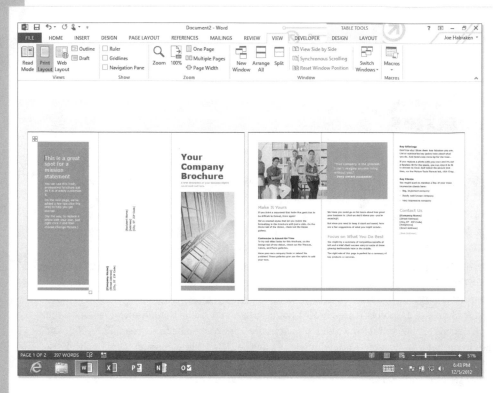

Figure 6.5
Templates, such as this brochure template, enable you to quickly create specialized documents.

If you decide to use a template, you have three options:

- You already have some templates installed on your computer from installing Microsoft Word.

- Office.com provides a huge number of templates that you can preview and then quickly download into your template library.

- You can create your own templates (as you would any Word document) and base new documents on that template.

When you start Word, the Start screen gives you access to the Word templates. If you are already working in Word, the steps for creating a new document using a template are as follows:

1. Open the Backstage (select File on the Ribbon).

2. Select New in the Backstage. At this point, you can select one of the listed templates and then click Create to open the new document based on the template. Steps 3–5 walk you through a template search.

3. To search for an online template, either select one of the suggested searches (Letters, Resume, and so on) or type keywords into the Search Online Templates box and then click the search icon (or press Enter). A List of templates appears; on the right of the New window is a Filter by list that enables you to filter the found templates by category. Figure 6.6 shows the New window and the results of a template search.

4. You can filter the template list provided by selecting a category in the Filter By list. Select the template that best suits your needs.

5. To open a new document based on the template, select Create.

> **note**
>
> Templates take advantage of styles. Styles are a collection of font, paragraph, and other formatting attributes saved under a style name. Styles enable you to apply a number of formatting attributes to text just by assigning the style to the text (such as a heading or a paragraph). Chapter 7, "Enhancing Word Documents," discusses styles in depth.

Figure 6.6
You can access a huge library of Word templates online and then filter the list by category.

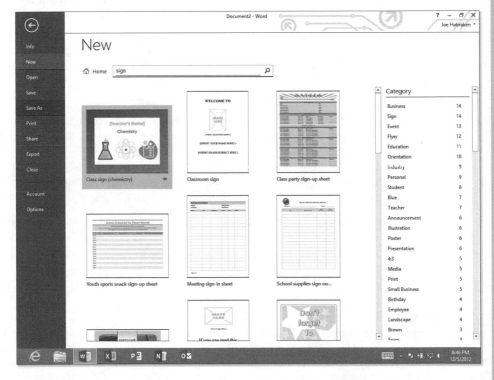

When your new document is open in the Word window, you can edit it as needed. Remember, your changes to the document are reflected in the document only; you are not editing the template itself. When you save the document, the Save As dialog box opens and you can specify a name and location for the document.

Creating a Template

As your knowledge of Word begins to parallel your creativity and need (in creating specialized documents), you will find it extremely advantageous to create your own document templates. Although an incredible number of templates are available on Office.com, you might still want to create templates specific to the type of Word documents you need to create.

tip

After you have selected a template in the New window (or the Start screen), Back and Forward arrows appear on the left and right of the template sample, respectively. You can use arrows to cycle through the list of templates provided by your search. If you want to close the current template and return to the New window, click the Close button in the template box.

Before you can create a personal template, you have to let Word know where you want to save this and all the other templates that you create for your use. This means you have to specify a default location for your personal templates in the Word Options. Select File to get to the Backstage and then select Options. In the Word Options window, select Save.

The Save page is where you specify the folder for your templates. All you have to do is type a path in the Default Personal Templates Location box. Example syntax is C:\Users\Joe\Documents\Templates, using the drive letter, folder, and subfolder. I created a Templates folder in the Documents folder (C:\Users\Joe\Documents) before entering the path in the Word Save options. After specifying the path, select OK to return to the Word application window.

When you return to the Backstage and select New, the New window includes a new template heading to the right of Featured. A Personal heading is now available; when you click this heading, you have access to all your personal templates that are saved in the folder you specified in the Word Save options.

➡ For more about configuring Office application options, **see** "Configuring Application Options," p. 42.

After you have addressed the default personal templates location, you can create a template. First, open a new, blank document (or an existing document). Then configure the various document settings, such as font attributes, paragraph attributes, and page layout settings. You can also create styles in the document that are then available in the template based on the document.

note

As already mentioned, templates can contain pictures, watermarks, and other graphics. They can also contain building blocks (one of the Quick Parts options covered in Chapter 7), which are blocks of text that are saved as part of the template and can be quickly added to a document. In addition, templates can contain macros, which are small, user-coded programs that enable you to automate tasks in Microsoft Office (Appendix B, "Office Macros," discusses macros). Anything that you add to a document saved as a template is available when you base a new document on that saved template.

When the document is finished, you can save it as a template. Follow these steps:

1. Select File and then select Save As in the Backstage. The Save As page appears.

2. Select a location for the file from the Places list. Possibilities include your SkyDrive, your computer, and any other places you have added. (To add a place, simply select Add a Place.)

3. Select a folder from the right pane of the Save As window or double-click one of the locations in the Places list. The Save As dialog box opens.

   In the Save As dialog box, navigate to the folder that you specified in the default personal templates location settings in the Word options.

4. Type a name for your template, and change the Save As Type box to Word Template (see Figure 6.7).

Figure 6.7
Save any document as a template.

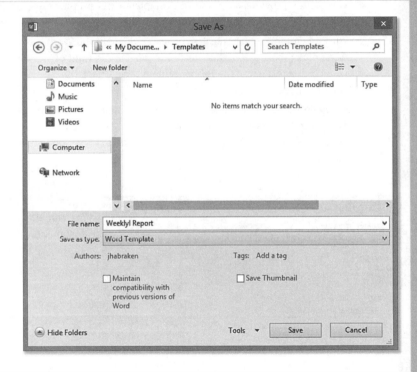

5. Click the Save button to save your new template.

Now when you want to base a new document on the saved template, you can access it (and your other personal templates) by selecting Personal in the Backstage New window (File, New) or the Word Start screen (when you start Word). All you have to do is select the template you want to use, and a new document based on the template opens in the Word window.

Templates can provide both uniformity and efficiency when creating new documents. If you repeatedly create documents that are similar (such as a weekly report), it makes sense to use templates to create those documents.

Attaching a Template

Because templates can include building blocks, styles, and macros, you might find it advantageous to change the template currently assigned to the document you are working on. Attaching a template replaces the template currently assigned to the document.

To attach a template to a document, you need access to the Developer tab on the Ribbon. It is not included by default. The Developer tab provides access to the Templates and Add-ins dialog box, which is where you actually attach the template.

Select File on the Ribbon and then select Options. In the Word Options dialog box, select Customize Ribbon. On the right of the dialog box is a list of the Ribbon's main tabs. Check the Developer check box and then click OK.

The Developer tab now appears on the Ribbon. Select Developer and then, on the Developer tab, click Document Template in the Templates group. The Templates and Add-ins dialog box opens, as shown in Figure 6.8.

 tip

If you are having trouble finding the Templates folder (Users/your username/AppData/Roaming/Microsoft/Templates) that holds your downloaded templates and the Word Normal template, it might be because the Templates folder and its parent folders are typically hidden in Windows 8 by default. Open the Windows 8 Control Panel and then select System and Security. Select Appearance and Personalization, then Folder Options. On the View tab of the Folder Options dialog box, select the Show Hidden Files, Folders, and Drives option and then click OK. Now you can locate this folder when navigating the folders on your computer.

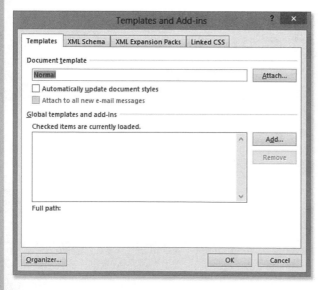

Figure 6.8
You can attach a different template to your document.

In the Templates and Add-in dialog box, click the Attach button. The Attach Template dialog box opens. The templates listed are either the templates you downloaded or templates that were installed with Word (Users/your username/AppData/Roaming/Microsoft/Templates). You can also navigate to another folder to select a template, such as the folder you are using to store the templates you created. After you locate the template you want to attach, select it and then click Open.

The template that you selected appears in the Document Template box on the Templates and Add-ins dialog box. Click OK to close the Templates and Add-ins dialog box. The document now has access to any styles or other items, such as building blocks saved with the template.

Navigating a Word Document

As you create a new document or work with an existing document, you need to move around the document (say, from paragraph to paragraph or page to page). With the understanding that you use different techniques, such as taps, slides, and other manipulations of the touchscreen on a tablet (or other touchscreen device), let's take a look at the basics of moving around a Word document on a PC using the mouse and keyboard. The keyboard provides some nice shortcut key combinations. For example, to quickly go to the bottom of a document, press Ctrl+End. You can return to the top of the document just as easily by pressing Ctrl+Home. Let's look at what the mouse can do in terms of moving around a document and then see what the keyboard can do.

Moving Around a Document with the Mouse

The mouse provides the easiest way to move the insertion point to a new position on the current page: Place the I-beam in the text and then click to fix the insertion point at that position. Obviously, you can also scroll through the document pages using the scroll button on the mouse. The vertical scrollbar provides different ways to move through the document, as listed in Table 6.1.

 caution

When navigating a document with the keyboard versus the mouse, remember that when you use the keyboard shortcut keys or the arrow keys, you move the insertion point to a new position. You can then immediately start typing or editing. When you use the mouse to move around a document (including when you use the mouse and the vertical scrollbar), you change your viewpoint of the document. After you locate the place you intend to go to using the mouse, you need to click the I-beam in the text to place the insertion point.

 tip

If you don't see the vertical and horizontal scrollbars, you might have to activate them via the Word Options. Select File to enter the Backstage and then choose Options. In the Word Options window, select Advanced. Scroll down through the options until you find the Display settings. Select Show Horizontal Scrollbar and Show Vertical Scrollbar, and then click OK.

Table 6.1　Using the Mouse and Vertical Scrollbar

Mouse Movement	Your View of the Document Will ...
Click up scroll arrow	Move up a line
Click down scroll arrow	Move down a line
Click Next Page	Move to next page
Click Previous Page	Move to previous page
Click below scroll box	Move to next screen
Click above scroll box	Move to previous screen
Drag scroll box	Move to a specific page

The vertical scrollbar also provides some options when you right-click it. The shortcut menu that appears enables you to quickly go to the top or bottom of the document or to scroll to the position where you executed your right-click (Scroll Here).

The horizontal scrollbar offers the capability to scroll to the left and right of a document page. The horizontal scrollbar does not appear if the document window is wide enough to display the entire page from left to right. The horizontal scrollbar is useful when you zoom in on a document and need to pan left and right to view all the text and other items (such as graphics) in the document.

 note

More complex documents that contain multiple sections can (and often do) have different page layout settings in each of the sections. For more about sections, see Chapter 8, "Working with Tables, Columns, and Sections."

Moving Around a Document with the Keyboard

Word also embraces a number of keyboard shortcuts that enable you to move around your document. For example, everyone is familiar with using the arrow keys on the keyboard to move around in your document. The up arrow takes you up a line, and the down arrow takes you down a line. By themselves, the arrow keys are not that efficient in moving around your document. Table 6.2 shows some more elegant keyboard shortcuts for moving around a document.

Table 6.2 Using the Keyboard to Move Through a Document

Key Combination	The Insertion Point Will ...
Home	Move to the beginning of a line
End	Move to the end of a line
Ctrl+right arrow	Move one word to the right
Ctrl+left arrow	Move one word to the left
Ctrl+up arrow	Move to the previous paragraph
Ctrl+down arrow	Move to the next paragraph
PgUp	Move up one window
PgDn	Move down one window
Ctrl+PgUp	Move up one page
Ctrl+PgDn	Move down one page
Ctrl+Home	Move to the top of a document
Ctrl+End	Move to the bottom of a document

To a certain extent, your use of the mouse or keyboard for moving around your document relies on personal preference. However, it makes sense to consider keeping your hands on the keyboard as you are initially typing your document instead of constantly reaching for the mouse. Using the keyboard shortcuts can save you some time.

tip

Another useful keyboard shortcut for navigating a document is Ctrl+G. This keystroke combination opens the Find and Replace dialog box with the Go To tab selected. Select an item in the Go To What list and then enter a number in the box to the right. For example, with Page selected, you can enter a page number and then select the Go To button to move to that page. Go To can also quickly move to bookmarks you have placed in a document, as well as to specific document items such as footnotes, tables, and headings.

Selecting Text

When you use the mouse to select text, you actually have a number of options depending on whether the mouse pointer is in the document text itself or along the left margin of the document, which is referred to as the selection bar. The selection bar is the whitespace on the left edge of your document window, just in front of your text paragraphs. When you place the mouse in the selection bar, the mouse pointer becomes an arrow (in contrast to placing the mouse in the document, where the pointer appears as an I-beam). Table 6.3 provides the possibilities for selecting text using the mouse.

Table 6.3 Selecting Text with the Mouse

Text Selection	Mouse Action
Selects the word	Double-click a word
Selects the text block	Click and drag or Click at the beginning of the text, and then hold the Shift key and click at the end of the text block
Selects the line	Click in the selection bar next to the line
Selects multiple lines	Click in the selection bar and drag down through multiple lines
Selects the sentence	Hold Ctrl and click a sentence
Selects the paragraph	Double-click in the selection bar next to the paragraph or Triple-click in the paragraph
Selects the entire document	Hold down Ctrl and click in the selection bar

You can also select text using the keyboard. Hold the Shift key and use the arrow keys to select text as needed. If you work "old school," you can also use the Word Extend feature to select text using the keyboard. Position the insertion point before the word or sentence you want to select. Press the F8 function key to turn on Extend. Press the spacebar to select a word; each time you press the spacebar, you select the next word. To select an entire sentence, turn on the Extend feature and then press the period (.) key. You can select entire paragraphs this way by pressing the Enter key. To turn off the Extend feature, press the Esc key.

Understanding Document Formatting

The overall look of your document depends on different types of attributes and layout settings, which many Word users lump together under the general term of *formatting*. However, text or character formatting relates to how the characters look (settings such as bold, 14 point, and red), whereas paragraph formatting is concerned with line spacing, indents, borders, alignment, and so on. Other document layout settings, such as margins, columns, and page orientation, fall under the Page Layout settings. So when you create documents in Word, you must understand that although they are distinctly different in how they are applied to the document and how they change the document, the character formatting, paragraph formatting, and document layout settings all work together to give the document its overall look.

In terms of simple documents (such as a two-page letter), most people would agree that, when changing a page layout setting such as the margins, they would expect the margins on all the pages to change to the new settings. Page layout settings are pretty much all encompassing when you change them in a document. Character and paragraph formatting, on the other hand, are specific in their application. Read on to learn more about those settings.

Character Formatting Versus Paragraph Formatting

You have probably selected text and then clicked the Bold command on the Home tab of the Ribbon. The selected text becomes bold; it's a simple text-formatting operation. Character formatting relies on you to select the text you want to format and then select a character attribute, such as bold or red, to format the selected text.

Paragraph formatting, such as with line spacing, indents, borders, and other paragraph-formatting attributes, is a little different. For paragraph formatting to completely make sense, you need to understand what Word considers a paragraph.

When you click the Show/Hide command on the Ribbon's Home tab, Word shows you the paragraph marks and the spaces between words. In the discussion here, the paragraph marks are extremely important. Every time you press the Enter key, which creates a blank line, you create a paragraph to Word.

So when you click in a block of text preceded and followed by the paragraph mark symbol, you are in a paragraph—or what Word considers a separate paragraph. With the insertion point in that paragraph, you simply click the Center command on the Ribbon's Home tab to center that text (all the text in the paragraph). You are not required to actually select the text (as you do when you want to change a character formatting attribute such as bold or italic). When you want to apply paragraph formatting to multiple paragraphs, you must select the paragraphs.

 tip

By default, the Show/Hide command shows paragraph marks and spaces between words. You can view other hidden formatting marks on the screen by opening the Word Options window (click the File tab and then Options). Select Display on the left side of the window, and then select the Show All Formatting Marks check box.

Manual Formatting Versus Styles and Themes

You can quickly and easily apply character formatting attributes to text in the document. Making a heading bold and then 14 point, for example, is easy. The same goes for paragraph formatting; after you click in a paragraph, you can change the line spacing, for example, using the Line Spacing command on the Home tab.

The problem with this manual formatting approach to changing the way text and paragraphs look is that building a consistent look throughout a document that consists of several pages can be a real chore.

If you desire a uniform look for a document, taking advantage of styles and themes makes sense. A style can be a collection of character and paragraph formatting attributes saved under a style name. You can repeatedly apply this style to text in the document, providing consistent formatting. A theme, on the other hand, is an integrated set of formatting attributes that provides font, color, and effects settings.

In terms of a consistent look for a document, styles and themes give you a more controlled approach than manual formatting does. Taking advantage of styles and themes makes sense, particularly when you are working on special document types that require a greater amount of overall formatting.

➡ *Read more about styles in the "Understanding Styles" section,* **p. 199.**

➡ *To learn more about themes,* **see** *"Formatting with Themes,"* **p. 172.**

Working with Fonts and Text Formatting

The basic look of the text in a Word document is controlled by the font you are using. Each font set has a particular typeface, meaning the physical characteristic of the characters. Each font also has a particular look that makes it unique. An example of a font set is Calibri, which is the default Word font. A variety of other fonts exist, with names such as Arial, Courier, Times New Roman, Cooper Black, and Bookman Old Style. The fonts you have access to when working in Word depend on the fonts installed on your computer. Most of the fonts you work with are software fonts, or "soft fonts," and are Microsoft Open Type fonts (formally called True Type fonts) provided by your Windows operating system.

Most of the fonts that you use are proportional fonts, meaning that the characters can have varying widths (as opposed to nonproportional fonts, which use a single standard width for all characters, such as in monofont type). For example, in proportional fonts, the letter *W* is wider than the letter *I*. Proportional fonts have a typeset look and not only are easier to read, but also work well in columns and tables. Figure 6.9 shows some of the proportional fonts available in Word.

Proportional fonts are measured in points, which refer to the character height. Each point is 1/72 of an inch. For example, a 12-point font is 1/6 of an inch tall; a 36-point font is 1/2 inch tall.

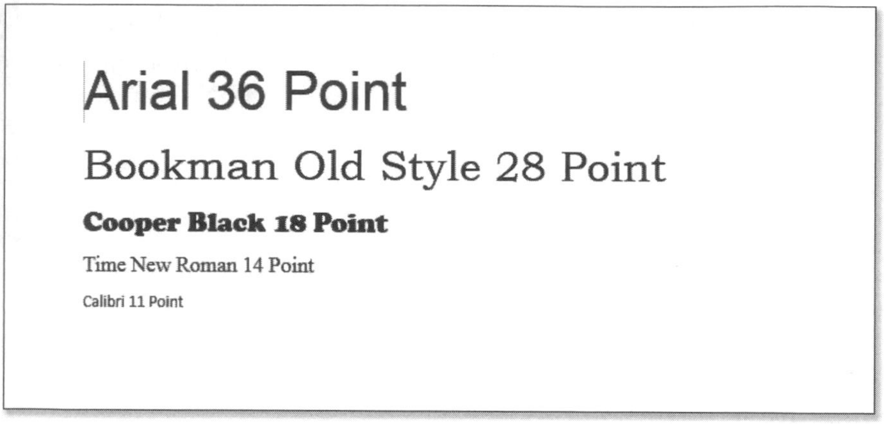

Arial 36 Point

Bookman Old Style 28 Point

Cooper Black 18 Point

Time New Roman 14 Point

Calibri 11 Point

Figure 6.9
Proportional fonts in different point sizes.

You can change the font settings (also known as font characteristics or attributes) before you begin typing in a document, or you can change the various text attributes after the fact and format existing text. If you want to change the font name or font size in a new document before you begin typing, use the Font and Font Size drop-down boxes on the Home tab. Or if you are going to type a heading that you want in bold, press Ctrl+B to turn on the bold and then press Ctrl+B a second time to toggle off the bold. Let's look at using the various text-formatting commands that Word provides.

Formatting Text

The easiest way to change a number of the commonly used font attributes (whether you are typing new text or working with selected text) is to take advantage of the formatting commands in the Font group of the Ribbon's Home tab. This group includes the Font, Font Size, Bold, Italic, Strikethrough, Subscript, Superscript, Text Highlight Color, and Font Color commands, which are straightforward in their use. With drop-down lists such as Font, Font Size, Underline, and Font Color, you can preview the formatting before you apply it to your selected text (this is called Live Preview). Just point at one of the choices, such as a particular size on the Font Size list, to preview the size change directly on the selected text.

Some of the Font group commands warrant additional discussion. The following list provides a brief description of these commands:

- **Text Effects and Typography:** This command provides text effects such as Glow, Shadow, Reflection, and Outline. It also grants access to styles, ligatures, and stylistic sets.

- **Increase Font Size:** This command increases the font by one increment (to the next preset). If the font is currently 18 point and the next increment on the Font Size list is 20 point, the command increases the font size from 18 point to 20 point.

- **Decrease Font Size:** This command decreases the font one increment (down one preset). It is the opposite of the Increase Font Size command.

- **Change Case:** This command provides a drop-down list that enables you to change the selected text to sentence case, lower case, or upper case. It also enables you to capitalize each word in the selection or toggle the case of the text.

- **Clear Formatting:** This command clears all the formatting on the selected text. This includes font-formatting attributes and paragraph-formatting attributes. This command also removes a style from the selected text.

Obviously, these commands are easy to use when you are formatting text that already exists and has been selected. Using these commands as you type might slow you down quite a bit. Table 6.4 provides some of the most often used font-formatting shortcut key combinations.

Table 6.4 Font Formatting Keyboard Shortcuts

Attribute	Shortcut Keys
Bold	Ctrl+B
Italic	Ctrl+I
Underline	Ctrl+U
Double underline	Ctrl+Shift+D
Small caps	Ctrl+Shift+K
Subscript	Ctrl+equals sign (=)
Superscript	Ctrl+Shift+plus sign (+)
Increase size	Ctrl+Shift+>
Decrease size	Ctrl+Shift+<
Toggle case	Shift+F3
Clear formatting	Ctrl+spacebar

Although these keyboard shortcuts are not all-inclusive in terms of font-formatting options, they enable you to quickly toggle a font format attribute on and off. For example, you can press Ctrl+I, type your italicized text, and then press Ctrl+I again to toggle italics off.

 tip

You can copy and then paste font- and paragraph-formatting attributes from one paragraph in a document to another (or to more than one paragraph). Select the text that has the formatting attributes you want to copy. Then click the Format Painter on the Clipboard group of the Ribbon's Home tab. You can click a paragraph to paste the formatting or use the Format Painter mouse pointer to select text, which then has the formatting copied to it. To apply the copied formatting multiple times, double-click the Format Painter initially and use it as needed. When finished, click the Format Painter again to turn off the tool.

The Mini Toolbar

When you select text in a document, a transparent floating toolbar appears near the selected text. This is the Mini Toolbar. It provides quick access to a number of the font-formatting commands (and some paragraph-formatting commands such as Bullets and Number). Figure 6.10 shows the Mini Toolbar with the Font Color palette selected.

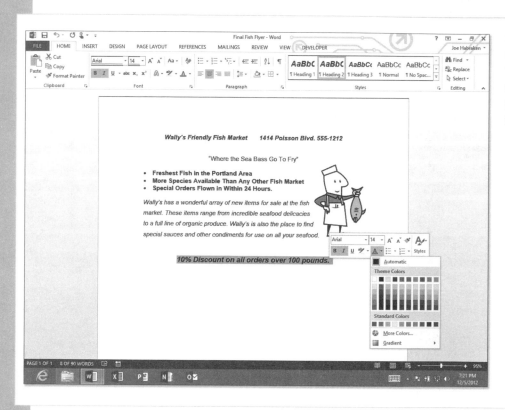

Figure 6.10 Use the Mini Toolbar to quickly format selected text.

To use the Mini Toolbar, move the mouse onto it immediately after it appears near your selected text. Select commands from the Mini Toolbar as you do any of the commands that you work with on the Ribbon's Home tab.

The Font Dialog Box

Although the Font Group on the Ribbon's Home tab and the Mini Toolbar provide you with most of the font-formatting attributes you need, the one place that provides access to all the font attributes and a number of other advanced character settings is the Font dialog box. To open the Font Dialog box, click the dialog box launcher (on the right side of the Font group on the Home tab).

The Font dialog box has two tabs: Font and Advanced. The Font tab provides access to the font, font style (bold, italic, and so forth), and font effects. You can also access text effects from the Font tab. When you select a font attribute, it is applied to selected text in the document.

The Advanced tab of the Font dialog box enables you to control features related to text spacing and Open Type features. First the Character Spacing settings:

- **Scale:** This setting enables you to stretch or condense the text (horizontally). For example, a scale setting of 200% stretches the font characters, making them larger. A scale setting of less than 100% compresses the characters.

- **Spacing:** This setting controls the distance between the characters. Expanded increases the space between the characters; Condensed compresses the spacing.

- **Position:** This setting enables you to raise or lower the selected characters from the text's baseline position.

- **Kerning:** This setting enables you to compress the distance between characters (meaning the space between the characters). You specify a baseline font size, and all fonts of that size (and above) are then kerned.

The OpenType features on the Advanced tab relate to the capabilities of OpenType fonts, which Microsoft and Adobe jointly developed and introduced in Office 2010. Without going into a lengthy discussion of font outline data and font layout tables, suffice it to say that OpenType fonts provide you with more robust font families and special font features such as ligatures and stylistic sets.

A ligature is a combination of two adjacent characters by a common element. For example the letters *f* and *i* can be combined as a ligature using the cross piece in the *f*. Stylistic sets are alternative sets of glyphs (the visual representations of the individual characters) for the font. Selecting a different stylistic set lets you take advantage of a different set of glyphs; for example, a stylistic set might contain all caps and other style differences. If you are interested in typography, you might find ligatures and stylistic sets useful.

Working with Paragraph Formatting

Paragraph formatting encompasses a number of formatting attributes, including alignment (think of centering and aligning text left), line spacing (single spaced versus double spaced), tabs, and indents. However, other settings related to how paragraphs are broken between lines and pages (such as widow/orphan control) play a part in this discussion of paragraph formatting.

As discussed earlier in this chapter, Word sees a paragraph as any text block (or blank line or lines) that is preceded and followed by a paragraph mark (that is, you pressed Enter before the paragraph and after the paragraph). Each paragraph can be assigned different paragraph attribute settings, such as Center or Indent. Each paragraph can also have different tab settings.

You can access all the paragraph settings in the Paragraph dialog box, which you open via the dialog box launcher on the right side of the Paragraph group (on the Home tab of the Ribbon). Settings such as alignment and indentation are available on the Indents and Spacing tab, as shown in Figure

6.11. Widow/Orphan control and other break and formatting options are available on the Line and Page Breaks tab.

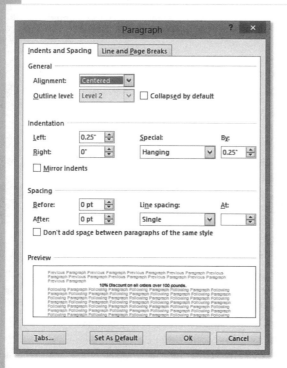

Figure 6.11
You can access all paragraph-formatting options in the Paragraph dialog box.

To apply paragraph formatting to a single paragraph, you simply make sure that the insertion point is in the paragraph. If you want to format multiple paragraphs, you must select those paragraphs. Let's look at the various formatting attributes related to paragraphs, how you can view the formatting present in a document, and how you can copy formatting attributes from paragraph to paragraph.

 tip

You can change font settings in the Font dialog box and make them the default settings for Word (meaning that you change the Normal template). After you select the various font attributes you want to use by default, click the Set As Default button.

Setting Paragraph Alignment

A basic formatting attribute of every paragraph, whether it is a 20-line paragraph or a single-line heading, relates to how that paragraph is aligned on the page in relation to the left and right margins. By default, all text uses the Align Text Left setting, which is characterized by text that is straight or unvarying on the left margin but has a ragged right-edged margin.

Paragraph alignment that varies from the norm of left alignment can set elements of a document apart from other document elements, such as a centered heading. You can also use alignment to provide a document page with a look of uniformity, such as a letter or resume that uses justification on all paragraphs. The following list briefly explains each paragraph alignment possibility.

- **Align Text Left:** This is the default placement for normal text, aligned on the left.

- **Align Text Right:** Text is aligned at the right margin, and text lines show a ragged left edge.

- **Center:** Text is centered between the left and right margins of the page (with both margins having irregular edges).

- **Justify:** Text is spaced across each line so that both the left and right margins are straight and uniform (often used in printed publications such as daily newspapers).

The fastest way to change the alignment of a single paragraph (or many selected paragraphs) is to use the alignment commands provided by the Paragraph group of the Ribbon's Home tab. For example, to center a heading, click the heading and then click Center in the Paragraph group. You can also control alignment using the Alignment drop-down box on the Indents and Spacing tab of the Paragraph dialog box.

Changing Line Spacing

Line spacing is the vertical space between lines of text in the paragraph. The default line spacing is Multiple 1.08 (the actual spacing depends on the height of the font you are using). You can control line spacing options using the Line and Paragraph Spacing command, which is in the Paragraph group on the Ribbon's Home tab. Click Line and Paragraph Spacing and then select one of the line spacing options, such as 1.0, 2.0, 3.0, and so forth.

If you want to set custom line spacing settings, you can do so in the Paragraph dialog box in the Spacing section of the Indents and Spacing tab. The Before and After spinner boxes enable you to set spacing before and after a particular paragraph or paragraphs. This is particularly useful for headings or other special text items. Be advised that the After setting of a paragraph is added to the paragraph that follows, so if you have set a Before setting for the next paragraph, the space between the paragraphs will be the same as the After setting for the current paragraph and any Before setting from the next paragraph.

You can also control the line spacing for paragraphs using the Line spacing drop-down list. It provides the following options:

- **Single:** Spacing accommodates the largest font size found on the lines and adds a small amount of whitespace (depending on the font used) between lines.

- **1.5:** The line spacing is 1 1/2 times greater than single spacing.

 tip

You can also set the alignment for a new line of text using Word's Click and Type feature. Place the insertion point at the beginning of a blank line, and then move the I-beam from left to right on the page, the I-beam becomes an indent pointer, then a center point, and then a justify right pointer. Double-click the mouse to place the insertion point horizontally on the line, based on the current mouse alignment pointer.

 tip

You can set the spacing before and after a paragraph using the spinner boxes on the Spacing portion of the Paragraph group found on the Ribbon's Page Layout tab.

- **Double:** Spacing is twice the size of single-line spacing.

- **At Least:** This is the default setting. Line spacing adjusts to accommodate the largest font on the line and special items such as graphics.

- **Exactly:** All lines are equally spaced, and special font sizes or items such as graphics are not accommodated. If these items are larger than the setting used here, they appear cut off in the text. You can still accommodate these items by using the Multiple box, described next, to shift all the text lines to a higher spacing percentage that accommodates special items.

- **Multiple:** You specify the line spacing by a particular percentage. This feature is used in conjunction with the Exactly option to set a line-spacing percentage that accommodates special font sizes or graphics in the document. For example, if you want to decrease the line spacing by 20 percent, you enter the number 0.8. To increase the line spacing by 50 percent, you enter 1.5.

 tip

If you are using two different fonts in a document, you might find that setting line spacing to Exactly (and a specific point size) in the Paragraph dialog box gives you a more uniform look in the document.

Some of the setting options that you select from the Line Spacing list are influenced by the point size you enter in the At box (this applies only when you have selected At Least, Exactly, or Multiple). Use the click arrows to increase or decrease the point size of the line spacing. The Preview pane gives you an overview of how the line spacing that you set will actually look on the paragraph or paragraphs affected by the line settings.

Setting Line and Page Breaks

The Paragraph dialog box also gives you control over how line and page breaks affect a paragraph or paragraphs. Figure 6.12 shows the Line and Page Breaks tab of the Paragraph dialog box.

By default, Widow/Orphan control is set (note the selected check box for Widow/Orphan control in Figure 6.12). A widow is the last line of a paragraph that appears by itself at the top of a page. An orphan is the first line of a paragraph left by itself at the bottom of the page. Widow/Orphan control keeps the last line or first line of a paragraph from printing on the next or previous page, respectively. The Keep Line Together option keeps the entire paragraph together on a page, and the Page Break Before option forces Word to start the paragraph on a new page if it can't keep it all on the previous page.

The Line and Page Breaks options also provide formatting exception settings that you can apply to your paragraphs. Word can assign line numbers to all the lines in a document (the line numbers setting is in the Page Setup group of the Ribbon's Page Layout tab). If you are using line numbering, you can use the Suppress Line Numbers formatting exception if you want to suppress line numbers for specific paragraphs in a document.

Word does not automatically hyphenate words in paragraphs; it wraps them to the next line. If you have turned on hyphenation (the Hyphenation command is on the Page Setup group on the Ribbon's Page Layout tab), you can use the Don't Hyphenate check box on the Line and Page Breaks tab in the Paragraph Dialog box (click the launcher on the Paragraph group) to turn off the hyphenation on a paragraph or paragraphs.

Figure 6.12
The Line and Page Breaks tab.

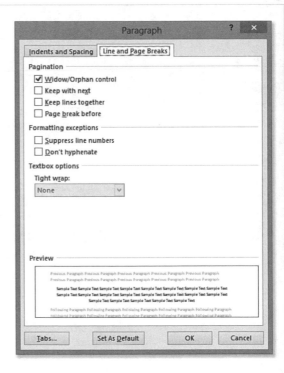

Setting Indents

You can use indents to offset paragraphs (including individual lines such as headings) from both the left and right margins. By default, indents are set every half-inch. The Increase Indent command is in the Paragraph group of the Ribbon's Home tab. Each time you click Increase Indent, you indent the paragraph another half-inch. To decrease the indent, use the Decrease Indent command.

You can also use the ruler to set the indent for a paragraph. The ruler has both a left indent and a right indent marker. It also has a first line indent marker and a hanging indent marker. These two markers are stacked on the top of the left indent marker, but you can move them independently. Figure 6.13 shows the different ruler indent markers.

You can drag the left indent marker or the right indent marker as needed to indent the left or right of a paragraph, respectively. You can also create hanging indents by using the indent markers. Hanging indents are created by separating the first line indent marker from the left indent marker on the ruler.

 tip

To view the ruler (for both the horizontal and vertical rulers), click the Ruler check box in the Show group of the Ribbon's View tab.

 tip

You can also set the left and right indents for a paragraph using the Indent settings on the Paragraph group of the Ribbon's Page Layout tab.

Left Indent Marker   First Line Indent Marker   Right Indent Marker

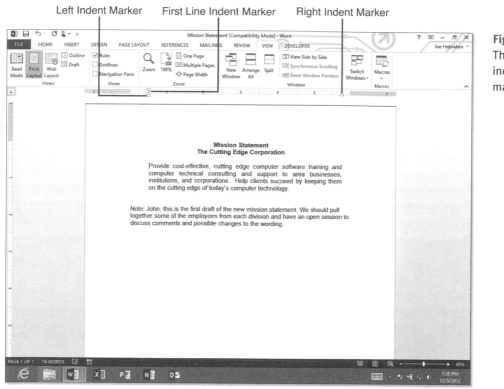

Figure 6.13
The ruler's indent markers.

To create a hanging indent, drag the left indent marker (using the square bottom of the marker) to the position where you want to indent the second and subsequent lines of the paragraph. Then drag the first line indent marker (drag it by the top of the marker) back to the position where you want the first line to begin. Hanging indents are useful when you want to subordinate the remainder of a paragraph under the first line of the paragraph, such as with job descriptions in resumes.

Working with Tabs

You can use tabs to align text in your documents. Most Word users typically think of the tab as a way to offset the first sentence of a paragraph (one tab stop from the left margin) from the rest of a paragraph. Word actually provides different types of tabs that you can use as a way to align items in much the same way (at least visually) that you align items in a table.

By default, Word provides a tab stop every half-inch. Every time you press the Tab key on the keyboard, you offset the text line from the left margin one tab stop. You can set your own tab stops using the Tabs dialog box or the ruler. You open the Tabs dialog box from the Paragraph dialog box (select the dialog box launcher in the Paragraph group). Figure 6.14 shows the Tabs dialog box.

Figure 6.14
The Tabs dialog box.

You can change the default tab stops from .5 inch to any increment using the Default Tab Stops spinner box. To create a new tab, enter a tab stop position (in inches) and then select the alignment for the new tab (Left, Center, Right, and so on). You can also select one of the Leader options for your tab, such as Dot Leader (2). When you have finished setting the tab's options, click Set to create the tab. You can then create the process as needed.

Word provides different tab types; the following list briefly describes each:

- **Left tab:** Aligns the beginning of the text line at the tab stop

- **Center tab:** Enters the text line at the tab stop

- **Right tab:** Right-aligns the text line at the tab stop

- **Decimal tab:** Lines up numerical entries at their decimal point

- **Bar tab:** Inserts a vertical bar at the tab stop (it doesn't actually align text)

Because it provides a more visual medium for setting tabs, the ruler is your best bet for quickly setting tabs and using the different types of tabs Word offers. To set a tab on the ruler, click the Tab button on the far left of the ruler to select the tab type (Left, Center, Right, and so on). Each time you click the Tab button, you cycle to the next tab type. If you go past the type of tab you want to set, keep clicking until the tab type appears on the Tab button.

When you have the appropriate tab type selected on the Tab button, place the mouse pointer on the ruler where you want the tab and then click to place it. If you need to adjust the position of a tab, drag it to a new position on the ruler. Figure 6.15 shows the different tab stop types and how they actually align text at the tab stop.

When you want to remove a tab from the ruler, drag it off the ruler. You can also clear a tab or all your tab settings in the Tabs dialog box.

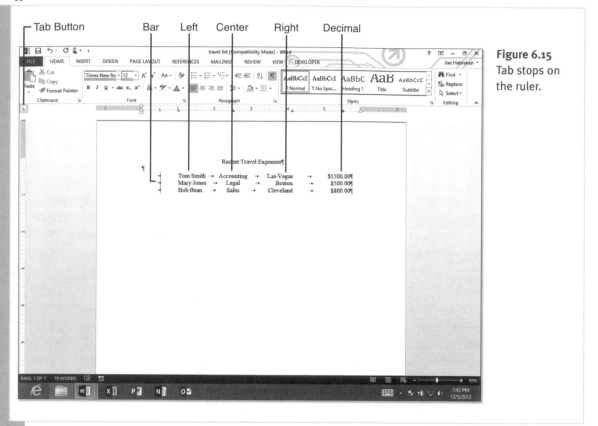

Figure 6.15
Tab stops on
the ruler.

Revealing Format Settings

The Reveal Formatting task pane is a useful feature when you're working with manually assigned font- and paragraph-formatting attributes. This feature enables you to quickly review the font and paragraph formatting that you have assigned to your text.

To open the Reveal Formatting task pane, press Shift+F1. To view the font and paragraph formatting in a particular paragraph, click that paragraph (or select text as needed).

For more detail on the source of the formatting that has been assigned to test, click the Distinguish Style Source check box in the Options area of the Reveal Formatting task pane (see Figure 6.16).

The Reveal Formatting task pane also has a Show All Formatting Marks check box. You can select it to view paragraph marks, spaces, and tabs in the document.

Figure 6.16
The Reveal
Formatting
task pane.

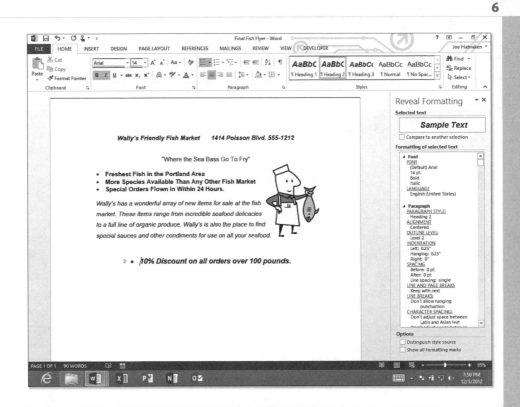

Page Layout: Margins and Page Options

The standard page layout options primarily relate to the document margins, page orientation, and paper size. Other page setup options, such as the paper source settings, are more closely associated with printing documents; we look at printing in the last section in this chapter. Layout settings are related to sections and headers and footers. We discuss headers and footers in Chapter 7 and then look at sections in Chapter 8.

Margins control the amount of whitespace of the page. Four margins exist: top, bottom, left, and right. By default, each of these margins is set to 1 inch. You can change any of the margin settings for your document as needed; you can also change the margins for just a portion of a document. Select the text in the document and then change the margins. The changes affect only the selected text.

 tip

You can have Word mark formatting inconsistencies the same way it marks spelling errors and grammar problems. On the File tab, open Options and then click Advanced. Under Editing Options, select the Keep Track of Formatting check box and the Mark Formatting Inconsistencies box. Now Word marks formatting inconsistencies with a wavy blue line.

Changing Margins

To change the margins for the document or selected text, use the Margins command in the Page Setup group of the Ribbon's Page Layout tab. You can select from one of the margin presets provided, or you can select Custom Margins. This opens the Page Setup dialog box, shown in Figure 6.17.

Figure 6.17
The Page Setup dialog box.

The Page Setup dialog box enables you to set each of the margins. Use the appropriate spinner box, or type a new margin setting.

When you are creating a special document, such as a document with mirror margins or a book-fold document, you can change the Multiple Pages setting in the Pages area of the Page Setup dialog box so that your margins accommodate that type of document. For example, if you select Mirror Margins (the margins on the facing pages will be mirrored) in the Multiple pages drop-down list, you have Top, Bottom, Inside, and Outside margins. You also set a gutter, which provides extra space between the inside margin and the edge of the page. This helps accommodate binding or punch holes if you plan to bind your document in a three-ring notebook.

When you want to change only the document margins forward in the document from where you parked the insertion point, you can select From This Point Forward in the Apply To drop-down box

 note

A document divided into sections can potentially have different margin settings for each section. Sections are discussed in Chapter 8.

 caution

Be advised that your default printer defines the minimum (and maximum) margins for a page. If you set margins less than the minimum, a dialog box appears when you close the Page Setup dialog box, letting you know that your margins are outside the printable area of the page. Click Fix to return to the dialog box and fix the margins.

(this creates a new section in the document). When you have completed your changes to the margin settings, click OK to return to the document.

Changing Page Orientation and Paper Size

The default page orientation in Word is portrait. The default page size (in the U.S.) is Letter (8.5 by 11 inches). You can change both the page orientation and the page size as needed.

To change the page orientation, click Orientation in the Page Setup group of the Page Layout tab. Then select Portrait or Landscape, as needed. You can also change the page orientation on the Margins tab of the Page Setup dialog box.

The Size command in the Page Setup group of the Page Layout tab provides a list of paper sizes, such as Letter, Legal, and Executive. You can select from the list or click More Paper Sizes to open the Paper tab of the Page Setup dialog box and select from a list of preset paper sizes. More important, this option enables you to set the paper size to Custom Size and then set your width and height for the paper.

 tip

You can view your document margins in the Print Layout and Full Screen Reading views. You can also see the margins in Print Preview. To add Print Preview to the Quick Access Toolbar, select the drop-down menu on the right of the Quick Access Toolbar and select Print Preview.

Inserting Page Breaks

As you type your document, Word automatically starts a new page when you fill the current page with text or other document items (such as tables, clip art, and so on). You can insert a page break in your document as needed. You insert page breaks using the Page Break command on the Insert tab of the Ribbon (in the Pages group). You can also insert page breaks from the Break list in the Page Setup group on the Page Layout tab.

 tip

The quickest way to insert a new page break is from the keyboard: Press Ctrl+Enter.

When you want to be able to visually differentiate between the page breaks Word placed in the document and the page breaks you inserted, select the Show/Hide command (on the Home tab) and then go to Draft view using the view icons along the bottom right of the status bar.

Page breaks that you insert show a dotted line and the words Page Break. You can select your inserted page break and then delete them, if needed.

 tip

Type a range of page numbers (for example 1–4,6) below the Print All Pages box. This changes the setting to Print Custom Range and prints only the pages you specify.

Printing Documents

Printing in Word 2013 is accomplished using the various tools provided in the Backstage Print window. This window enables you to select a printer, set printer properties, and control print settings such as page orientation, page size, and margins. The Print window also provides a print preview of a selected page in the document, and you can use the Zoom slider to zoom out and view multiple pages. Figure 6.18 shows the Backstage Print window.

PART II

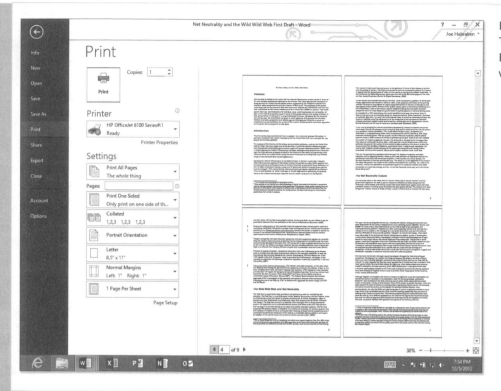

Figure 6.18
The Print Backstage view.

To send the document to the printer, you click the Print button. If you need to change the number of copies, you can use the Copies spinner box. Before printing, you might want to examine some of the possibilities that the new Print Backstage view provides. A number of print-related settings are listed under the Settings area. These options are as follows:

- **Selecting what to print:** By default, Print All Pages is selected and the entire document prints. You can select other options from the list, such as Print Selection, Print Current Page, or Custom Print (which requires that you provide a range of page numbers). You can also choose to have certain lists related to the document's properties printed, such as styles, autotext entries, and a list of customized shortcut keys.

- **Printing One or Two Sided:** This option enables you to set up the print job to print one-sided or print on both sides (if your printer can handle duplex printing). You can also choose to manually print on both sides, which enables you to flip the paper over and reload it in the printer.

- **Collated or Uncollated:** You can choose to have your printout collated or uncollated using this setting.

- **Orientation:** You can choose the printout orientation: portrait or landscape.

- **Paper Size:** You can change the paper size before printing. Remember that this repaginates the document.

- **Margins:** You can change the margins before printing.

- **Pages per Sheet:** You can select how many pages are printed per page. You can also have the document pages scale to the paper size.

In previewing the document, you can use the Zoom slider on the lower-right portion of the screen. A Zoom to Page button zooms you back to a single-page view if you have been previewing multiple pages.

ENHANCING WORD DOCUMENTS

Word provides a number of features that enable you to enhance your documents. This chapter looks at different possibilities for making your documents look more interesting and more professional. It begins with a look at bulleted and numbered lists and then examines formatting options such as themes and styles.

This chapter also explores the use of headers and footers in documents and discusses page-numbering options. We also delve into enhancing your Word documents with pictures, clip art, and charts. Included is a look at different ways to view a document and how to use building blocks and document review tools, including the Spelling feature and the Thesaurus.

Creating Better Documents

When you have a good feel for the typical features used to create, save, and print documents, it is time for you to explore features that enable you to enhance your documents. A broader command of Word's features will not only make you more productive, it also will enable you to create more interesting-looking documents that take advantage of bulleted and numbered lists, borders, shading, and themes. Features and tools such as quick parts and styles also enable you to create documents more efficiently and produce more uniform documents.

Additionally, some tools enable you to root out errors in a document; others make it possible to enhance the actual content of the document. These tools include the review tools, such as Spelling and Grammar, which help you detect errors, and the Research pane and Thesaurus, which enable you to improve the content of the document.

Creating Bulleted and Numbered Lists

Numbered and bulleted lists emphasize information on the page and also provide a visual mechanism for arranging similar items. Bulleted lists work best when you want to separate and highlight items from the other text on a page; however, a bulleted list doesn't necessarily have a particular order or hierarchy. Numbered lists work well when you are detailing a procedure in which the order of the steps is important in accomplishing a particular task.

You can quickly assign both bullets and numbers to existing lists, or you can toggle on bullets or numbering and create your list as you type. You have complete control over the bullet type (using special characters or other graphics) used in a bulleted list and the alignment of the text lines in the list. You can also format numbered lists by specifying the numbering format, including where the numbering starts and the numbered items' text alignment.

The commands for bullets, numbering, and multilevel lists are located in the Paragraph group of the Ribbon's Home tab. Each command also gives you a drop-down list that enables you to fine-tune the formatting related to the particular list type (bullets versus numbers) that you select.

Bulleted Lists

Whether you are formatting an existing list that you have selected or are planning to type the bulleted list on the fly, all you have to do is select Bullets in the Paragraph group on the Ribbon's Home tab.

If you want to select the bullet character used in the list, click the arrow next to the Bullet command to choose one of the bullet characters provided by either the Recently Used Bullets list or the Bullet library. When you are changing the bullet for a selected, existing bulleted list, place the mouse on any of the bullets to preview that bullet on the list. Figure 7.1 shows the Bullet library; the selected bullet is previewed in the document.

 tip

You can also turn on bulleting using the Mini Toolbar, which appears when you select text (such as several lines of text in a list). Click the Bullets icon on the Mini Toolbar. This formats the existing list as a bulleted list and turns on the bullets so that each item you add to the list is also bulleted.

When you want to use a bullet type not provided in the library, select the Bullets command arrow and then click Define New Bullet. The Define New Bullet dialog box opens and enables you to select a new bullet character from available symbols. You can also ramp up the look of your bullets by using bullet pictures (including many available on Office.com) or importing your own pictures to use as bullets. Figure 7.2 shows the Define New Bullet dialog box.

To select a new bullet character from the various symbols installed on your computer as part of your available fonts, click the Symbol button in the Define New Bullet dialog box. The Symbol dialog box provides a Font drop-down box that enables you to select the font or character set from which to select the new bullet character. After you select the new bullet, click OK to return to the Define New Bullet dialog box.

The Define New Bullet dialog box also enables you to select the alignment for the bullet (Left, Centered, Right) and makes it possible to select the font family used to render the bullet (by default, the bullet uses your default font).

Figure 7.1
Change the bullet for the selected list.

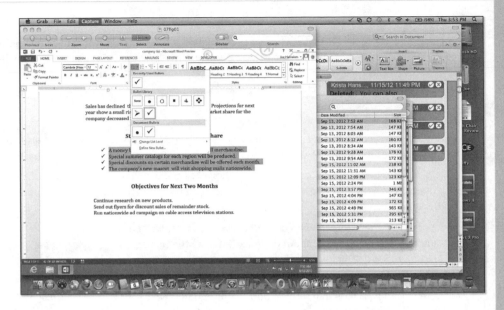

Figure 7.2
Define your own bullets for your lists.

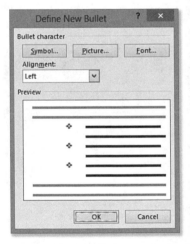

Although we don't typically think of bulleted lists as having different levels, you can change the list level for a bulleted item (or items) in a list. To change the list level, click the Bullets command arrow, point at the Change List Level command, and then select a list level from the list level presets provided (nine list levels are provided).

tip

Some of the more interesting bullet characters are in the Wingdings and Webdings font groups. You can access these and other installed font groups from the Symbol dialog box; just select the Symbol button in the Define New Bullet dialog box.

Numbered Lists

You can create numbered lists in your document as you type, or you can format an existing list as numbered after the fact. You can also take advantage of a variety of number formats.

To start numbering or to format a selected list, click the Numbering command (in the Paragraph group on the Ribbon's Home tab). Doing so brings up a list using the default numbering format (1,2,3) and starting at the number 1.

You can use the Numbering command arrow to access different number formats in the Numbering library (such as the Roman numeral format). This gallery of number format choices also enables you to change the list level for one or more items.

 tip

You can quickly change a numbered list to a multilevel list by changing the list level for items in the numbered list.

If the number formats in the Numbering Library don't meet your needs, you can define your own number format. Use Define New Number Format (in the Numbering command arrow gallery) to open the Define New Number Format dialog box (see Figure 7.3).

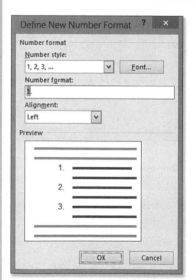

Figure 7.3
Define your own number formats.

In the Define New Number Format dialog box, you can set the number style, the number format, and the alignment of the number (Left, Centered, Right). You can also select the font used for the numbers.

If you want to change the starting number of the list, you can open the Set Numbering Value dialog box (click Set Numbering Value on the Numbering menu). This dialog box also gives you the option to start a new list (the default) or continue the numbering from a previous list. You can also continue from a previous list but set an advance value, which enables you to skip numbers.

Multilevel Lists

You can create outlines or lists that require different levels using the Multilevel List command in the Paragraph group on the Ribbon's Home tab. As with other lists, you can format selected existing text or start a new list. First, select the Multilevel List command and select one of the multilevel list formats from the List Library. You also can define new multilevel lists via the Define New Multilevel List command at the bottom of the library.

When you have the multilevel list format set, you can build your list or edit an existing list. In the case of a new list, use the Tab key to demote an item to the next lower level. For example, if you have already typed a primary-level heading, press Tab and then type the secondary level items that go under that heading.

When you need to move the insertion point up a level in the multilevel list, press Shift+Tab. For example, you might have a secondary-level item that you want to promote to a primary level. You also can change the level of a list item using the Change List Level command. Select the line in the multilevel list you want to promote or demote. Select the Multilevel List command, and then select the Change List Level command (below the List Library). Choose a new level from the levels provided.

 note

Multilevel lists are fine for simple outlines. However, when you need to use outlining as a more advanced organizational tool in complex documents, use the Outline view. It provides tools for designating headings, promoting and demoting paragraphs, and expanding and collapsing levels.

➡️ *For more information about the Outline view, **see** "Changing the Document Display," **p. 188**.*

To select the format for the multilevel list, click the Multilevel List command arrow and select a format from the List library. If you need a custom list format, select the Define New Multilevel List command. This opens the Define New Multilevel List dialog box, shown in Figure 7.4.

You can modify each level, including the number formatting, number style, and position for the level. If you click the More button, you can also select other options, such as specify the start number for the level, select the level to be shown in the gallery, and denote whether the number should be followed with a specific character, such as a tab, a space, or nothing (yes, nothing is a choice).

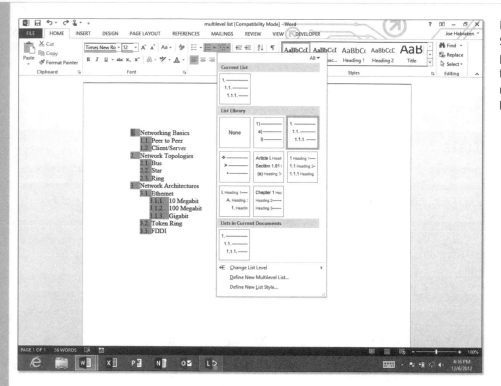

Figure 7.4
Set the
parameters
for a new
multilevel
list.

Working with Borders and Shading

Font-formatting attributes, such as bold, italics, underline, and increased font size, can emphasize specific text in a document. When you want to draw attention to a certain paragraph or heading but want something a little more flashy than a font attribute change or simple paragraph-formatting attributes such as centering or indents, you can take advantage of borders and shading. Borders and shading provide a simple way to add color and graphical elements to a special document such as a report, flyer, or newsletter.

 tip

When you edit a multilevel list, you can use the Decrease Indent and Promote Indent commands in the Paragraph group to demote and promote items, respectively.

You can place a border around any text paragraph or a number of selected paragraphs. To place a border around a single paragraph, make sure that the insertion point is in that paragraph. If you want to put a border around several paragraphs, select them.

To select one of the border options for the paragraph (or paragraphs), select the Borders command in the Paragraph group of the Ribbon's Home tab. The border gallery provides many border options, including Bottom Border, Left Border, and Outside Borders (designed for use on tables). Select an option to have the borders applied to your text.

After you have selected your border, you can place shading behind the text (you can "shade" text that doesn't have a border as well). You apply the shading using the Shading command in the Paragraph group. When you click the Shading command arrow, a palette of theme colors appears (you can also choose from a list of standard colors). To select additional colors, click the More Colors option. This opens the Colors dialog box, where you can select standard colors or mix your own custom colors (on the Standard and Custom tabs, respectively).

> **tip**
>
> The Borders and Shading drop-down list also enables you to insert a horizontal line at the insertion point or draw a table.

> ➡ *To learn more about themes and how they affect formatting options,* **see** *"Formatting with Themes," p. 172.*

If you want greater control over the borders (and shading) you assign to document paragraphs—including settings such as the border's line style, line width, and line color—you can open the Borders and Shading dialog box, shown in Figure 7.5. Select Borders and Shading on the Borders drop-down gallery (click the arrow next to Borders in the Paragraph group to open the gallery).

Figure 7.5
The Borders and Shading dialog box.

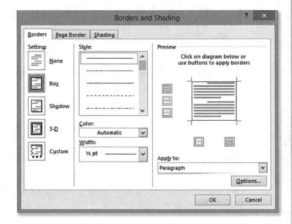

> **note**
>
> On the Custom tab of the Colors dialog box, you can specify a color by its RGB code. This is particularly useful if you want to make sure that you are consistently using the same color for different document elements (such as paragraph shading and font color). For example, to make sure that I am using steel blue as my shading color, I enter the Red Blue Green code of 70– 130– 180. A number of websites provide the RGB color codes—just do a Bing or Google search.

The Borders tab of the dialog box gives you control over the style and color of the line and provides settings that enable you to include a shadow or 3D effect on the border. The Page Border dialog box enables you to place a border around the entire page (or pages), which is discussed in a moment. The Shading tab lets you select a fill color and an optional pattern style for the paragraph shading.

You can also place a border on the pages of your document, using the Page Border tab of the Borders and Shading dialog box. It provides you with options similar to those provided for paragraph borders, such as shadow and 3D effects and the capability to control the line style, color, and width. Page borders can also include repeating art elements (such as palm trees or gingerbread men). You select these border elements by using the Art drop-down list. Word provides a number of color and grayscale elements that you can use for your page borders.

 tip

You can open the Page Border tab of the Borders and Shading dialog box directly using the Page Borders command. This command resides in the Page Background group of the Ribbon's Design tab.

Word also enables you to assign a page background color to a page (or pages). Select the Page Color command arrow on the Page Background group of the Ribbon's Design tab. This opens the color palette, where you can choose from theme colors or standard colors, or open the Color dialog box to choose from the colors or mix your own. You can configure fill effects such as gradients, textures, patterns, and pictures for your page background by selecting Fill Effects from the Page Color palette. This opens the Fill Effects dialog box.

Formatting with Themes

Giving a document a uniform look when you are working with different colors (including font, border, and shading colors), fonts, and text effects can be somewhat difficult. And in some situations, you want the color and font schemes in a Word document to match an accompanying Excel worksheet or PowerPoint presentation. Keeping a document's appearance consistent, particularly when you have used some special formatting attributes, is best done using themes. A theme is a collection of colors, fonts, paragraph settings, and text effects. The Themes gallery provides many different themes, and you can modify existing themes to create your own themes.

Themes are consistent across the Microsoft Office applications such as Word, Excel, and PowerPoint. This means that you can create a family of Word documents, Excel worksheets, and PowerPoint presentations that are consistent in their overall look.

Each Word template (such as the Normal template) has a specific default theme. You can change that default theme to any of the built-in themes, and you can also browse for themes you have created (they are typically saved to the Documents Themes folder: Microsoft/Templates/Document Themes folder on your computer).

 note

The Themes command group in Word 2010 was on the Page Layout tab. Word 2013 has a new Design tab with a Document Formatting group that provides theme-related commands such as Colors, Fonts, and Effects.

➡ *See Chapter 6, "Requisite Word: Essential Features," for more about templates.*

To take advantage of themes, you need to be working with a document that you have saved in the Word 2007–2013 XML-based file format (just save your document using the Word Documents file type in the Save As dialog box). You cannot apply themes to documents that you saved in the Word 97–2003 file format (to provide backward compatibility with users of previous versions of Word).

Word 2013 offers improved capabilities for creating professional-looking documents that also are well designed and visually interesting. One of these improvements relates to themes. Themes now include multiple style sets that change the formatting of built-in styles (and some formatting attributes of styles you have created) you have applied to your document. Although we don't discuss styles until the end of this chapter, suffice it to say that each theme available in Word gives you more choice in how your text looks, which is an improvement over previous versions. These new theme possibilities are housed on the Design tab on the Ribbon; the theme commands are in the Document Formatting group. The only other command group in the Design tab is the Page Background group, so most of the tab is reserved for the Document Formatting gallery and the theme commands such as Themes, Colors, and Fonts.

As already mentioned, themes include color, font, paragraph, and text effects formatting attributes. You don't really see the complete effect of a theme on your document if you don't use the built-in styles provided in the Styles gallery, which is accessed via the Home tab. A style is a collection of saved formatting attributes. Themes are collections of formatting attributes that affect styles. Each theme has a collection of style sets that change how your applied styles look. The current style set dictates the font and paragraph formatting of the text in the document.

It's really an upside-down pyramid with themes at the top, followed by the style sets (found in the Style Set gallery on the Design tab), followed by individual styles (from the Styles gallery on the Home tab). So assume that you have jumped ahead in this chapter and browsed the section on styles, and you want to change the theme of the document (remember that this changes the overall look of the document). To change the current theme, select Themes on the Design tab. The Theme gallery opens (see Figure 7.6).

Place the mouse pointer on a theme to preview how that theme affects the text in your document. When you select a theme, the theme is then applied to your document.

To refine the effect of the theme on the document, you can change the current style set. Click More at the bottom right of the Style Set gallery to view all the available style sets related to the currently selected theme. Place the mouse on a style set to see how it changes the text formatting in your document. Select a style set to apply it to your document.

As already mentioned, the Document Formatting group (on the Design tab) also includes additional commands that enable you to make even finer refinements to how the currently selected theme and style set affect your document: Colors, Fonts, Paragraph, Effects, and Set As Default. The drop-down lists, such as Colors and Fonts, enable you to fine-tune the settings for the current theme and the currently applied style set (from the Style Set gallery). For example, if you select Colors, you see a gallery of color combinations. Place the mouse on one color set to see it previewed in the document. Select the color scheme when you find the one that works best for the current document.

You also have control over paragraph spacing via the Paragraph Spacing command. The Paragraph Spacing gallery shows you the current style set selected in the Style Set gallery and provides access to built-in spacing such as Compact, Open, and Double. You can also preview each spacing scheme by placing the mouse on it. If you want to change the font setting for the currently selected style set and theme, select Fonts and then make a selection in the Fonts gallery, as shown in Figure 7.7.

Style Set Gallery

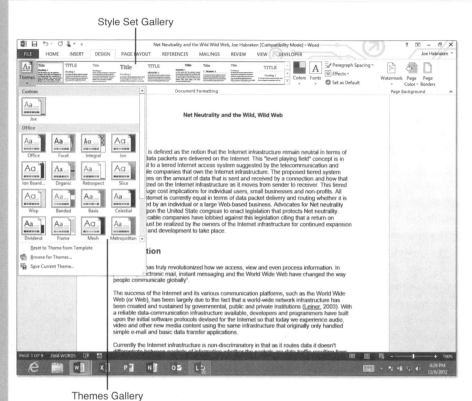

Themes Gallery

Figure 7.6
The Themes gal-
lery.

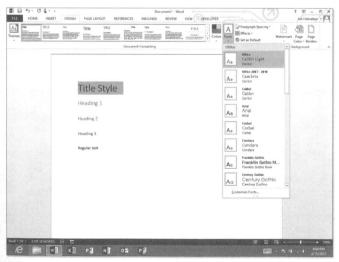

Figure 7.7
The Fonts gallery.

You have the option of creating your own style sets and your own themes. To create a new style set, you first modify the built-in styles that you applied to the parts of your document (such as headings, titles, and so on). See the "Understanding Styles" section of this chapter for all the information on creating and modifying styles (even the built-in styles provided in the Styles gallery on the Home tab).

 For more about working with styles, such as those found in the Styles gallery, **see** *"Understanding Styles," p. 199.*

After you modify and save the styles, go to the Design tab of the Ribbon. Your changes appear as a style set in the Style Set gallery. To save this new style set as a permanent style set in the current theme, click the More button in the Style Set gallery. Select the Save As New Style Set command at the bottom of the gallery. The Save As a New Style Set dialog box opens. Be sure to save the style set in the Users\UserName\AppData\Roaming\Microsoft\ Quickstyles folder (the default folder for style sets). Type in a name for the style set and click Save. The new style set appears in the Gallery. This style set is now available in the Style Set Gallery when you are working on a new document or an existing document.

You can also create your own custom themes; you simply modify the existing document theme (any theme you selected in the Theme gallery). To modify the current scheme, use the Colors, Fonts, Paragraph Spacing, and Effects drop-down lists to modify the current theme-formatting attributes. After you modify the theme, select the Themes command and then select Save Current Theme. The Save Current Theme dialog box opens. Supply a name for the new theme and then select the Save button. Now when you open the Themes gallery via the Themes command, your newly created theme (and any other theme you create) appears in the gallery under the Custom heading. All the built-in themes appear under the Office heading.

Changing the style set or theme when working on a document changes the formatting attributes of the built-in Word styles (that you might have modified), as well as the styles you created. If you don't want to keep a custom style set or a custom theme, you can delete it. In the Style Set gallery, right-click the style set that you created and then select Delete from the shortcut menu. Select Yes to delete the style set. Deleting a theme that you created is just as straightforward; right-click the custom theme in the Themes gallery and then select Delete. Select Yes to confirm the deletion. The theme file you created is deleted, and the theme is removed from the Custom theme list in the gallery.

 tip

If your new style set doesn't differ dramatically from the built-in styles sets, and you are having trouble locating it in the Style Sets gallery, select the More button. The style sets that you created are listed under the Custom heading in the Style Sets gallery.

 tip

You can also create your own custom color sets and font sets. The Colors gallery (select Colors) provides a Customize Colors command, which opens the Create New Theme Colors. The Fonts gallery (select Fonts) provides the Customize Fonts command, which opens the Create New Theme Fonts dialog box. Edit the settings in these dialog boxes to create custom color and font settings for a theme.

PART

II

Creating Headers and Footers

In business documents such as reports, manuals, and even some correspondences, text or even images (such as a company logo) are repeated at the top and/or bottom of each document page. And I'm probably safe in assuming that pretty much everyone has at some point had to create a multipage document that required page numbering on each page.

Headers and footers give you a way to include repeating information on each page of a document, such as a document title, the current date, or the page number. Headers and footers can also contain pictures, design elements, or even clip art. You can format text in a header or footer using the same formatting tools that you use for your text in the document itself.

 note

Documents published either in print or online (such as journal articles, published essays, manuscripts, and so on) typically need to conform to a particular style manual (an example of an often-used style manual is the *Chicago Manual of Style*). The manual provides guidelines on how to structure headers and footers and what information to place in those areas of the document.

The header resides at the top of a page, and the footer resides at the bottom of a page. The header and footer areas are within the top and bottom margins of the document. Because the header and footer cannot grow beyond the limits of the margins (they can't be on unprintable portions of the page), larger headers and footers (meaning a header or footer with many text lines or a large image such as a logo) steal line space from the regular text portion of the page.

How you use headers and footers can depend greatly on the overall structure of your document. For example, say that you have a report document with a title page. All the pages that follow the title page consist of the report details. It is common practice to not include headers and footers, page numbers, the report title, or a draft number on the title page of a report (or any document). So you need different headers/footers settings on the first page because you don't want to include the headers and footers that appear on the rest of the document pages. Word enables you to have different headers/footers on the first page of the document.

Another document structure issue that affects headers and footers arises when you want to bind a document with facing pages (where you have printed on both sides of the pages). Bound documents often use different headers and footers on the odd and even pages of the document (take a look at this book as an example). Word has you covered when creating different odd and even page headers and footers.

Consider one more point related to headers and footers: When working with more complex documents, it is not uncommon to have different document parts that vary greatly in terms of layout, content, and purpose. For example, you could be working on a document that has a table of contents, the main body of the document, and then a bibliography or index. Having different headers and footers for these very different parts of the document would make sense.

Documents can be divided into sections. Sections (which the next chapter discusses) enable you to set different page layout settings, including headers and footers, for each of the sections. So because each section of the document can have its own set of headers and footers, you can give the table of contents its own headers/footers, the body of the document its own headers/footers, and so on.

➡ *For more about sections,* ***see*** *"Understanding Sections," **p. 225**.*

Inserting Headers and Footers

Word 2013 expands and improves upon the Header and Footer tools that the previous version of Word (2010) offered. To insert a header, footer, or page number in your document, you use the Header and Footer commands on the Ribbon's Insert tab (the Header & Footer group). After a header or footer has been placed in the document or in a section of a document, the Header & Footer Tools are activated on the Ribbon. The Design tab provides all sorts of possibilities for modifying, navigating, and fine-tuning the header or footer. We talk about these tools shortly. First, take a look at how you insert a header or footer in a document.

To place a header in the header area, select the Insert tab of the Ribbon and then select the Header command. The Header gallery (shown in Figure 7.8) provides several different header styles, including a blank header. Header styles make it easy for you to insert your text into the header area. For example, the Annual Header style provides placeholder text for the document title and the year. It also provides a horizontal line and the font and paragraph formatting for the header text. In addition, the Header gallery provides the Edit Header and Remove Header commands.

Figure 7.8
The Header gallery.

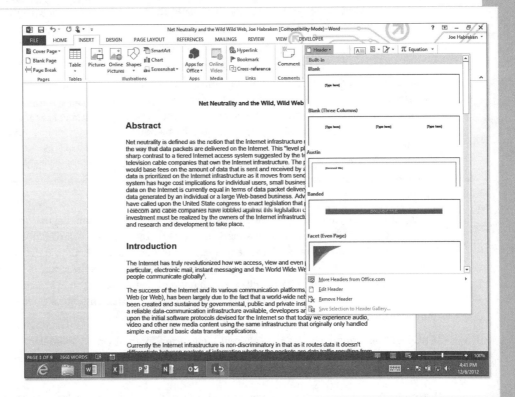

After you select one of the header options in the gallery, the Header area appears at the top of the current page. Replace the placeholder text with your own text. If you select the blank header, type and format your text as needed in the Header area.

Placing a footer in the Footer area involves pretty much the same process as placing a header in the Header area. Select a footer style from the Footer gallery (open it by selecting the Footer command) and, when the insertion point appears in the Footer area, type and format your footer text as needed.

The Header and Footer Tools

When the insertion point is in the Header or the Footer area, the Ribbon takes on the form of the contextual Header & Footer Tools Design tab. This special Header and Footer toolkit contains the following command groups:

- **Header & Footer:** This group provides the Header, Footer, and Page Number commands. These are the same commands found in the Header & Footer group on the Ribbon's Insert tab. We discussed the Header and Footer commands (which place a header or footer) earlier in this chapter. We look at the Page Number command later in this section.

- **Insert:** This group enables you to insert items into the header and footer, including date and time information, quick parts, pictures (including online pictures), and clip art. The Document Info command enables you to quickly add document-creation information to the header or footer, such as the document's author (most likely, your name), the filename, and/or the file path. Inserting informational fields into a document's header or footer can help you keep track of the origin of a document and even sort out various drafts of the same document.

 tip

If you want to go "old school" with headers and footers, you can place the insertion point in the header or footer without using either the Header or Footer command (in the Header & Footer group). Make sure that you are in Print Layout view, and then double-click in the Header or Footer area (top or bottom margin of the page). You can then type the text for the header and footer and format the text as needed. Be advised that even the default header and footer settings include formatting: a center tab at 3.25 inches and a right tab at 6.5 inches.

- **Navigation:** This group of commands enables you to jump between the header and footer in your document and navigate to a particular header or footer, if you have a complex document with multiple headers or footers. An important command in this group is Link to Previous; it controls whether the current header or footer is linked to the previous header or footer in the document (when you have multiple sections in the document and, therefore, multiple headers and footers). If you have independent sections of a document, such as a document with a table of contents or bibliography, you probably do not want to link headers and footers.

- **Options:** This group provides the Different First Page, Different Odd & Even Pages, and Show Document Text check boxes. To have different headers and footers on the first page of the document (different from the rest of the document), select the Different First Page check box.

- **Position:** This group enables you to set the distance for the header in relation to the top of the page and the footer from the bottom of the page (remember that this setting cannot place the header or footer into the unprintable portion of the margin, as dictated by your printer settings). This group also provides the Insert Alignment tab, which enables you to insert an alignment tab at the left, center, or right of the header or footer, and select a leader such as dot leader for the tab setting.

■ **Close:** This group contains the Close Header and Footer command. It closes the Header or Footer area and returns the insertion point to your document text.

When you are working with headers and footers, note that the use of these commands depends on the complexity of your document (such as the Different First Page and Different Odd & Even Pages commands), and the number of headers and footers in the document (such as a document with sections where you need to move from header to header or footer to footer using the Previous and Next commands).

In terms of what you place in your header and footer, the Insert group makes it easy for you to include information such as the current date or a picture such as a logo. This group also makes it easy to quickly create informational headers and footers.

For example, if you need to insert your name (author), your company name, or other document property information (such as the filename or path of the document), you can take advantage of the fields provided by the Document Info command. The Document Property command on the Document Info menu offers many possibilities, including company, company name, keywords, and category. Other potential sources of information that you can insert into a header or footer are items that you have stored as an AutoText entry; you can select the Quick Parts command and then select from your various AutoText entries.

The Quick Parts command also opens the Building Blocks Organizer, which provides access to all default building blocks (including added AutoText entries and added Quick Parts). The Building Blocks Organizer contains some building blocks specifically designed for headers, footers, and page numbering.

Both the Quick Parts command and the Document Info command provide access to the Field dialog box, which enables you to insert additional fields into your header or footer. We look more closely at fields (in relation to Word forms) in Chapter 9, "Managing Mailings and Forms." For now, I want to stress that you can use some fields to great effect in headers and footers. Figure 7.9 shows the Field dialog box.

 tip

Inserting document property information into a header or footer isn't all that useful if you haven't entered any information into the document's properties. You can access the document properties via Backstage View. Select File and then select Info. On the Backstage Info page, select the Properties heading (on the right side of the page), and then select Show Document Panel. You are returned to the Word application window and the Document Panel opens at the top of your document. You can add information as needed in the provided fields. Click the Close button on the far right of the panel when you finish your additions.

As already mentioned, the Document Info menu provides access to useful fields such as Author, File Name, and File Path. You might want to insert other fields into a document, such as insert the PrintDate and SaveDate fields into a header or footer, to show you the last time (date) a file was printed or saved, respectively. The only place where you see a complete list of the fields available in Word is the Field dialog box.

The Field dialog box enables you to list fields by categories via the Categories drop-down list. Three categories that are particularly useful in terms of document information are the Date and Time, Document Information, and User Information categories.

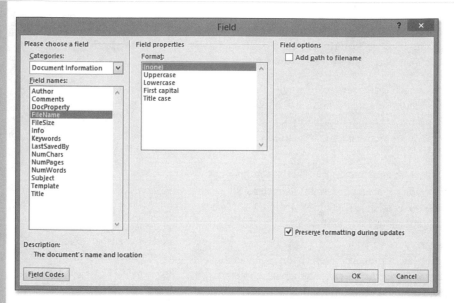

Figure 7.9
The Field dialog box.

When you select a field in the Field dialog box, you also must select from options provided in the Field properties list. For example, if you select PrintDate and the field you want to insert into the header or footer, you also have to select a date format for the date. Or say that you select the Title field from the Document Information category. This field inserts information that you provided in the document properties. So you are inserting field information that is simple text, and the Field dialog box wants you to specify whether it should appear in the header or footer in a particular text format, such as upper case or lower case. Using fields in your header or footer to "tag" a document with important information such as the author, filename, and path is a good practice. Other users editing a document will always know the author of the document if you have used the Author field. If you use the File Name and File Path fields, you can even find a document on your computer (or network) from a hard copy because the header or footer gives the file's name and location on your computer.

Working with Page Numbering

You can quickly place page numbers in the header or footer of the document using the Page Number command (on the Ribbon's Insert tab). A menu gives you various options for the location of the page, such as Top of Page, Bottom of Page, and Page Margins (yes, you can place the page number in the margin or at the current position of the insertion point).

When you select one of the placement options for the page number, such as Top of Page or Bottom of Page, a gallery of different page-numbering formats appears. You can also access more page number formats from Office.com by selecting More Page Numbers from Office.com.

You can modify the number format for your header and footer page numbers. Select the Page Number command (either on the Insert tab or on the Headers & Footers Tools tab if you are already in the header or the footer), and then select Format Page Numbers. The Page Number Format dialog box, shown in Figure 7.10, opens.

tip
When you have text or field information in a header or footer, the Page Number command (from the Ribbon's Insert tab or the Design tab of the Header & Footer Tools) deletes this text. For example, if you have your name and the file path in the footer, then when you select Page Numbering and Bottom of Page, all the footer information is deleted when the page code is inserted. The remedy for this is to place the insertion point where you want the page number to appear (in relation to the other text or fields in the header or footer) and then use the Current Position command to place the page number. You can also use the Page field from the Field dialog box. Insert the field where you want the page number to appear, and format the field as needed.

Figure 7.10
The Page Number Format dialog box.

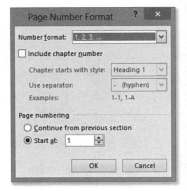

Use the settings in the dialog box to change the number format using the Number Format drop-down list. If you have chapters in your document, you can also have chapter numbers included along with the page number (you specify the style used for your chapter titles, to let Word know where the chapters start). You can also choose to continue the page numbering from the previous section, or you can use the Start At box to specify a number for the start of the page numbering.

Inserting Pictures, Clip Art, and Charts

You can enhance your Word documents using pictures, clip art, and other graphics. Word 2013 gives you options for inserting your own digital photos and also makes it easy to insert pictures from online sources, including a large clip art and royalty-free photo library from Office.com. In addition, you can insert other graphics, such as shapes, SmartArt, charts, and equations, into your documents. As with the other Office 2013 applications, Word 2013 offers some dramatic improvement for working with photos and other graphics. The new Live Layout shows you the position of your graphic in real time as you move or resize it. Alignment guides help you position an item, such as a photo, on the page. Options for formatting how text near the image is aligned are accessed with a single click on the Wrap Text button, which provides picture layout options; the Wrap Text button is available when a picture or other graphic is selected.

➡ *For a detailed overview of working with pictures and other graphics in Microsoft Office 2013,* **see** *Chapter 4, "Using and Creating Graphics."*

Inserting a particular graphic or image is really just a matter of parking the insertion point in the document where you want to insert the item and then specifying the type of graphic—picture, clip art, SmartArt, and so on—that you want to insert. As already mentioned, you can use a variety of image sources, including digital photographs, scanned images, and content from online sources.

Word also gives you a robust set of image-adjustment and formatting tools. You can quickly adjust the brightness or contrast settings for a photo and change the color saturation or tone. The Picture Tools also provide picture styles and arrangement and sizing tools.

Inserting Pictures

The Picture command in the Illustrations group, which resides on the Ribbon's Insert tab, enables you to insert picture files. You can take advantage of many picture file formats in your Word documents. These are some of the image file formats Word supports:

- Portable Network Graphics (.png)
- CompuServe GIF (.gif)
- Encapsulated PostScript (.eps)
- Various paint programs (.pcx)
- Tagged Image File format (.tif)
- Windows bitmap (.bmp and .dib)
- JPEG file interchange format (.jpg)
- Microsoft meta files (.emf and .wmf)

To insert a picture from your computer (or network) into the current document, place the insertion point where you want to insert the picture and then select Pictures on the Insert tab. The Insert Picture dialog box opens. It opens by default to the Picture folder (library). Navigate to the folder that holds your picture file and then select the file. Click Insert to insert the image into the Word document (or double-click on the image to select and insert it).

When a picture is selected on a page (such as the picture you just inserted), the Picture Tools appear on the Ribbon. Figure 7.11 shows an inserted picture file (a .jpg file) and the Picture Tools that are provided on the Ribbon.

➡ *For more about manipulating pictures and other graphics in the Office applications,* **see** *Chapter 4, "Using and Creating Graphics."*

The Picture Tools enable you to adjust the picture (such as its brightness and contrast), select a picture style, arrange multiple pictures on the page, and crop and size the selected picture. The Picture Tools groups are as follows:

Figure 7.11
The Picture
Tools enable
you to adjust
pictures.

- **Adjust:** This group provides tools for altering and fine-tuning the picture settings. You can correct the contrast, make color corrections, add artistic effects, and even remove portions of the photo's background. You can preview the adjustment before applying it to the picture and also compress a picture in a document (it is saved in the document as a .jpg file) so that the overall Word file size is more accommodating if you share the file online or via email.

- **Picture Styles:** This group offers frame formats such as Metal Frame, Center Shadow Rectangle, and Relaxed Perspective White. Place the mouse on a style to preview the style on the picture. This group also enables you to select the color of the picture border and add effects to the picture.

- **Arrange:** You can layer multiple images with this group (using commands such as Bring Forward and Send Backward). You also can group graphics, align images (left, center, right, top, middle, bottom), and rotate and flip pictures. The Position and Wrap Text commands reside in this group as well.

- **Size:** This group provides Height and Width spinner boxes for sizing a picture. You can also use the Crop command to crop the image as needed.

When you have finished working with the Picture Tools, click outside the picture or graphic. This returns the Ribbon to its "normal" set of tabs and command group.

Notice also that when a picture is selected on a page, the Layout Options icon appears next to the upper-right corner of the image. It provides quick access to the layout options (in relation to the surrounding text) for the picture or other graphic. By default, the picture's layout is in line with the text; you can access other possibilities by selecting one of the options provided.

Adding Clip Art

Office.com (the online resource for Microsoft Office) provides a seemingly endless supply of clip art images (and royalty-free photos) that you can use to enhance your documents. How you use clip art to enhance your documents is up to you, but remember that professional documents aren't meant to be cute, and you don't want to overshadow the purpose or impact of the document with unneeded images.

To insert clip art at the insertion point, select the Online Pictures command in the Illustration group (on the Ribbon's Insert tab). The Insert Pictures web browser opens.

The Insert Pictures web browser provides you with more image resources than just the Office clip art. You can also do a Bing image search to locate pictures online and access pictures on your SkyDrive.

Inserting clip art requires that you first do a keyword search for the category of clip art that you want to insert. For example, if you want to insert clip art related to cheese, you type the word "cheese" and then press Enter or select the search icon. Images that meet your keyword search criteria are previewed as thumbnails in the Insert Picture browser. Figure 7.12 shows the clip art and photo thumbnails that resulted from a search for the keyword "cheese."

You can scroll through the thumbnails in the browser. When you locate the clip art image you want to insert into the document, select the thumbnail and then click Insert. If you don't like the thumbnails provided by the search, select the Back to Sites link at the top left of the browser and modify your search for better results.

tip

You can remove all the picture-formatting changes you have made to a picture using the various tools provided by the Picture Tools (except for Change Picture and Compress Picture). Click the Reset Picture command (in the Adjust group).

note

The Insert Pictures web browser makes it easy to insert images you have saved to your Flickr account, so you can quickly access your online photos and videos. Chapter 4 provides an overview of how to create, manage, and use images and other graphics in the files you create using the Microsoft Office applications.

note

You can also insert charts and worksheets created in Microsoft Excel into your Word documents. See Appendix A, "Office Application Integration," for more about sharing information between Office applications such as Word and Excel.

Figure 7.12
The Insert Picture web browser and clip art search results.

Inserting a Chart

You can insert many other graphics into your Word documents, including shapes, SmartArt (both discussed in Chapter 4), and charts. Chart types include column, line, pie, bar, doughnut, and radar charts. To insert a chart at the insertion point, select Chart (in the Illustrations group on the Insert tab). The Insert Chart dialog box opens (see Figure 7.13).

Select a chart type in the All Chart list. You can then select one of the specific chart types for that category of chart (such as Line or Pie). Click OK to insert that chart into the Word document. An Excel worksheet also opens that provides the datasheet for your chart (see Figure 7.14). You can change the category and series names (the column and row headings in the Excel sheet) and the data on the worksheet until they contain the information required for your chart.

➡ *For best practices related to using and selecting charts and entering chart data,* **see** *Chapter 14, "Enhancing Worksheets with Charts."*

When you finish making your changes to the Excel table, you can close the Excel window (you don't need to save the table data). Whenever the chart is selected in your document, the Ribbon provides the Chart Tools, which bring up a Design and Format tab. The Design tab provides access to the data sheet you created for the chart. Use the Edit Data command (in the Data group on the Design tab) to open the data sheet. The Design tab also enables you to change the chart type, add chart elements, and select one of the built-in chart styles.

The Format tab of the Chart Tools enables you to change shape styles and select WordArt styles for the text labels in the chart. You can use the Height and Width spinner boxes to set the size for the chart.

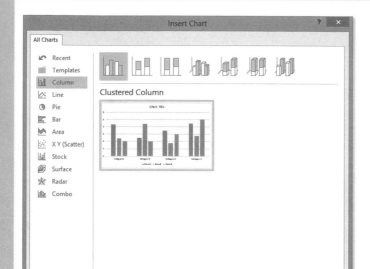

Figure 7.13
The Insert Chart dialog box.

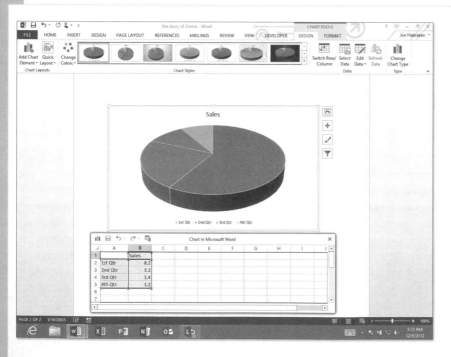

Figure 7.14
Edit the table data to
create your chart.

Creating simple charts within Word is a fairly straightforward process. When you are working with more complex sets of data, you might want to use Excel to create the chart. You can then copy and paste the chart into Word (see Appendix A for more about integrating Word and Excel).

Integrating Text and Images

One of the most important aspects of using pictures, clip art, or charts in Word is integrating the image with the text in the document. This primarily relates to sizing the picture or clip art file and determining how you want the text to wrap in relation to the image.

You can click any image and use the sizing handles that appear on the image to change its size. To maintain the height/width ratio of the image (so that you don't stretch or distort the image), use the sizing handles on the corners of the image and drag diagonally. If you would rather change the size of the image more precisely, you can use the Height and Width spinner boxes on the Size group (you can find this group on the Picture Tools and the Chart Tools).

For more precise control of the height and width of an image, you can use the spinner boxes in the Size group. This group also provides cropping capabilities. For even more control over an image, and to lock the aspect ratio (the height/width) of an image, you can take advantage of the Layout dialog box, particularly its Size tab. To open the Layout dialog box from the Picture Tools (with the Format tab selected), click the dialog box launcher on the Size group. Figure 7.15 shows the Layout dialog box.

Figure 7.15
The Size tab of the Layout dialog box.

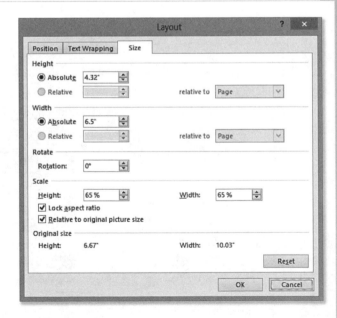

You can use the settings on the Size tab to adjust the height and width and to rotate the image. When you select Lock Aspect Ratio (which is typically set by default), any change to the height or width results in a change to the other measurement; for example, if you change the height, the width changes based on the aspect ratio.

Another aspect of integrating the image with the text relates to the text wrapping you set. By default, the wrapping style is set to In Line with Text. This means that the image is placed between the margins, and text appears over and below the image. You can use the Wrap Text command in the Arrange group of the Picture Tools tab and the Chart Tools tab to change how the text wraps in relation to the image. You can use the Square setting to have the text frame run along the top, bottom, left, and right of the image. You can also use Behind Text or In Front of Text to set the text to appear in front of the image or behind the image, respectively. These settings are available on the Text Wrapping tab of the Layout dialog box or by selecting the Layout Options button, which appears next to the top right corner of any selected image.

Changing the Document Display

Word gives you several viewing possibilities as you work on your documents in the application window. All the viewing options are available on the Ribbon's View tab. The Document Views group provides commands for the different document views, such as Read Mode, Print Layout, and Draft. The Zoom group enables you to access the Zoom dialog box and quickly zoom to 100%. The Window group enables you to arrange the open document windows and view two documents side by side. Figure 7.16 shows the Ribbon's View tab and a document in the Print Layout view with Multiple Pages selected in the Zoom group.

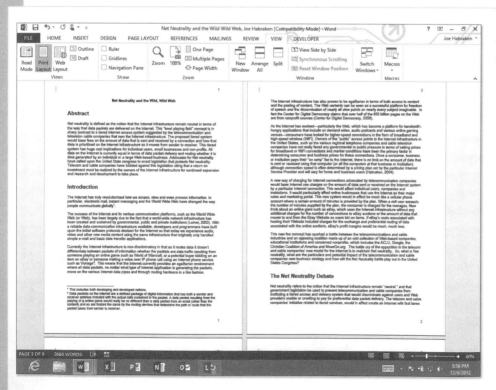

Figure 7.16
The Ribbon's View tab.

Using the different document views to your advantage can help you visualize and create great-looking Word documents. The following list provides an overview of the different document views in the Document Views group of the View tab.

- **Read Mode:** This view is new to Word 2013 and is designed to make reading a document easy whether you are running Word on your personal computer or on a smaller-footprint device such as a tablet or smartphone. Read Mode provides a "magazine" format for the document, dividing the text into easy-to-read columns of information. Navigational arrows move through each screen of the document (both forward and background). The Ribbon is not available in Read Mode, but a menu containing three commands—File, Tools, View—is available in the upper left of the Read Mode window. The File command takes you to the Backstage. The Tools command provides access to tools such as the Find command and the Search with Bing command. The View command provides a list of commands such as Edit Document, Navigation pane, and Show Comments. It also offers the Column Width, Page Color, and Layout commands, which enable you to fine-tune the Read Mode environment and make it easier to view and read your document.

- **Print Layout:** Here you can view your document exactly as it appears on the printed page. Here you can view headers and footers, margins, and other page layout settings. You also can fine-tune graphic placement because pictures and clip art appear as they print in this view.

- **Web Layout:** This view is designed for creating HTML documents for the Web. It does not show margins or other layout attributes; instead, it provides a workspace much like what appears in a browser window when you view a web page.

- **Outline:** This view (select Outline in the Views group) is designed so that you can see the document in an outline format. Headings appear as level 1 of the outline; text that follows each heading displays as secondary-level body text. You can use Outline view to rearrange text in a document by moving a heading and its associated body text. Outline view is also designed for working with master documents, which are discussed in Chapter 10, "Creating Special Documents."

- **Draft:** This view (select Draft in the Views group) displays character and paragraph formatting that you place in the document; however, it does not display the document headers and footers or show graphics in the document as they print. It is an excellent view for finding page breaks that you have placed in the document and for finding section breaks that you have assigned to a document.

Each view provides a different way of looking at your document. Most users create the initial draft of a document in Print Layout or Draft view. For organizing the document text, you might then switch to the Outline view, particularly if you are working with a larger document that contains headings and different document sections. Read Mode enables you to easily read through the document and concentrate on the content rather than the layout.

Using the Navigation Pane

Although it is not designated as a full-fledged view (as are Print Layout and Draft), the Navigation pane enables you to navigate through a document using search results, document headings, or page thumbnails. You enable the Navigation pane by selecting the Navigation Pane check box in the Show group. To navigate using the Search document box in the Navigation pane, type a keyword or phrase in the box and then press Enter or click the Search icon. Select Results to view the occurrences of the keyword or phrase in the document. You can quickly jump to each result of the search by selecting the occurrences listed.

To take advantage of the Headings feature in the Navigation pane, you need to use the built-in Heading styles that Word provides to format the headings in the document (such as Heading 1, Heading 2, and so on). When the Headings feature is selected in the Navigation pane, you can quickly jump to a particular heading in the document by selecting that heading. Figure 7.17 shows the Navigation pane with the Headings feature selected. If you didn't use the Word built-in styles (in the Styles gallery on the Home tab), you can still use the Search box or navigate through the document page by page by selecting Pages in the Navigation pane. To open the Navigation pane, select the Navigation Pane check box in the Show group (of the Ribbon's View tab).

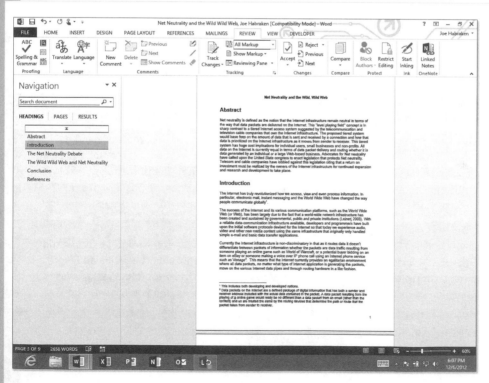

Figure 7.17
The Navigation pane.

When the Navigation pane is active in the Word application window, the Collapse/Expand toggle button appears when you place the mouse just to the left of one of your document headings (headings formatted using the built-in heading styles). Click the toggle to collapse all the text that is subordinate to the heading. In effect, this hides the text that follows that heading in the document (each heading in the document controls the subordinate text that follows it). Now if you move the heading in the document (that is, when you drag it to a new location), the subordinate text goes with it. Expand the heading (with the toggle button) to view the text. This feature is similar to what happens when you expand or collapse text when you are working in Outline view (discussed in the next section). When you have finished working with the Navigation pane, click the Close button to remove it from the application window.

 tip

Another useful view-related tool is the View Side By Side command in the Window group. It enables you to view two different documents side by side. By default, the two documents have their scrolling synchronized. You can click the Synchronous Scrolling command to scroll independently through each document. You can then drag and drop text between the documents and compare the documents as needed.

Using the Outline View

Outline view is probably one of the most misunderstood of the view-related features. Outline view is much more than just a tool for created simple outlines; it is a different way of organizing a complex document. Outline view enables you to quickly move a heading and its associated text to a new location and also allows you to promote or demote an item to a different level in the outline hierarchy. This makes it easy to manage the headings and subheadings in the document.

You can start a new document in Outline view, which helps you build the basic organization of the document. For example, you can brainstorm the main headings and subheadings that appear in the document. You can then build the document as you would an outline by typing the text that goes under each heading (or subheading). You can use Outline view to rearrange the information in the document as needed.

To start a new document in Outline View (or work with an existing document), select the View tab and then select Outline in the Views group. An Outlining tab appears on the Ribbon and gives you the Outline Tools group. When you type the first item in your document, it is assigned Level 1 in the outline hierarchy. You can use the Level drop-down list or the Promote or Demote buttons to change the level of an item in the outline. Be advised that a Level 1 item is assigned the Heading 1 style. Level 2 is assigned the Heading 2 style. Nine heading levels are available in Outline view, and a Body Text level is assigned to text that is not a heading (the actual content of the document). Figure 7.18 shows a document created in Outline view. The document currently contains three levels: Level 1 Headings, Level 2 headings, and body text.

When you are working with the document in Outline view, you can quickly select a heading and its associated subheadings and body text by selecting the Outline level button to the left of the heading. You then drag the heading and all the associated text to a new location in the document. If you want to concentrate on just the Level 1 headings, you can click the Show Level drop-down list and select Level 1. This makes rearranging the document by heading easy because you are not distracted by subheadings or body text. The Move Up, Move Down, Expand, and Collapse buttons (just below the Level drop-down list) move selected outline items up or down in the outline and expand or collapse headings and associated text, respectively.

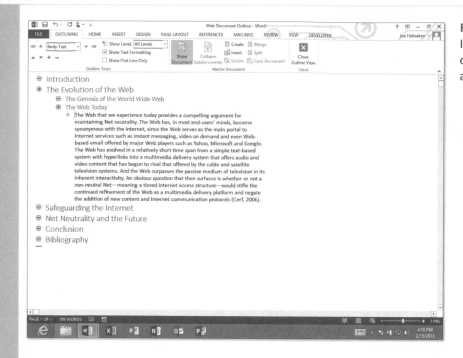

By design, Outline view helps you concentrate on the document's organizational structure. It enables you to concentrate on specific levels of the document and makes it easy to move entire parts of the document based on headings. When you have finished working in the Outline View, select the Close Outline View command. This takes you to the Print Layout view, where you can finalize your document by enhancing it with pictures, charts, or other graphics.

Splitting the Document Window

Another useful view-related tool is the capability to split the current document into two panes. This enables you to scroll to a different part of the same document in the different panes. You can then use two panes to drag and drop information from one part of a document into another. Remember that changes you make in either of the split panes affect the document.

To split the document screen into two panes, select the Split command (in the Zoom group of the View tab). Use the mouse to position the split in the document, and then click the mouse to place the split.

Each of the separate panes can be treated as a separate document. You can use Zoom to change the zoom level of each pane independently, and you can use all the other Word tools as needed in each of the panes. When you have finished working in the split document window, select Remove Split in the Window group to remove the splitter bar from the document.

 note

The AutoCorrect feature corrects some spelling errors automatically. The next section of this chapter discusses this feature.

Using the Review Tools

Even the best-looking document can suffer if it is not error free; it's hard for someone to take your information seriously if you have spelling errors, grammar issues, or errant typos. Word provides proofing tools such as the Spelling and Grammar features, which are designed to ferret out errors in your text. Word proofs your document as you type and automatically flags spelling and grammar errors as you enter text into your document. This enables you to quickly and immediately correct errors as you build your document.

Spelling errors are flagged with a red wavy underscore, and grammar errors are flagged with a green wavy underscore. Right-click spelling errors to access a shortcut menu that provides suggested spellings. You can also right-click grammar errors to view possible corrections. You can use this method to correct errors on the fly, or you might find it more efficient to correct them collectively by running the checks after you have entered all your text.

You can change the default settings associated with the automatic spelling- and grammar-checking features (meaning, turn them off). Click File to go to Backstage view, and then select Options. In the Word Options dialog box, select Proofing. Clear the check boxes on Check Spelling As You Type and Check Grammar with Spelling to turn off these features. Then click OK to return to the document window.

Running Spelling and Grammar

Waiting to correct spelling and grammar errors in a document until you have finished composing enables you to concentrate on getting your thoughts down without interruption. You can then check the entire document. The Ribbon's Review tab provides access to the Spelling and Grammar command and other proofing tools, such as the Thesaurus, the Define command, and the Word Count command.

Word 2013 has improved the spelling- and grammar-checking tools. When you start the Spelling and Grammar "checker," your errors are listed in the new Spelling task pane, which appears on the right side of the Word document window. This task pane enables you to ignore or change spelling and grammar errors, and you can also add items to the dictionary. In addition, the Spelling task pane provides a basic definition of suggested words (to replace your misspelled words). With the audio icon, you can check the pronunciation of the selected word in the suggestion list. To check the spelling and grammar in the document, click the Spelling & Grammar command. The Spelling task pane opens (see Figure 7.19).

Words that are flagged as misspelled appear in the Spelling task pane. To change the misspelling to one of the suggested words, click that suggestion and then click Change. If you know you have misspelled the word consistently throughout the document, you can click Change All.

In terms of grammar errors, the suspected error appears in the task pane, but the task pane heading switches from Spelling to Grammar (letting you know that you are now dealing with a grammar issue). The task pane provides suggested corrections and pronunciation. After you correct or ignore an error, the Spelling and Grammar feature continues to check your document. When it cannot find any additional errors, it opens a message box that the spelling and grammar check has been completed. Select OK to close the message box.

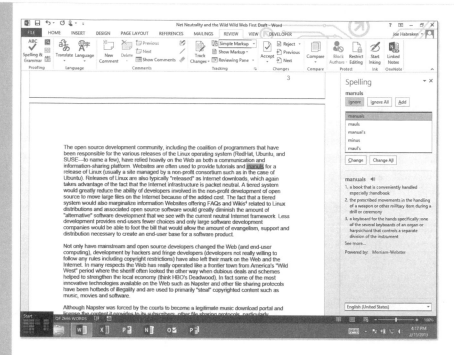

Figure 7.19
Checking the document's spelling and grammar.

Using the Thesaurus

The Thesaurus gives you a tool to find synonyms for the words in your document. Synonyms are words that mean the same thing. Because the Thesaurus can generate a list of synonyms for nearly any word in your document, you can avoid the repetitive use of a particular descriptive adjective (such as *excellent*) and add some depth to the vocabulary in your document.

Click a word in your document and then click the Thesaurus command in the Proofing group. The Thesaurus task pane opens on the right side of the Word window. To replace the word with a synonym, place the mouse on the synonym in the synonym list and then click the drop-down arrow that appears to the right of the synonym. Click Insert from the menu that appears.

If you prefer to forgo using the Thesaurus task pane for synonyms, you can view a short list of synonyms for a selected word by right-clicking the word. Point at the Synonyms command on the shortcut menu, and a list of synonyms for the word appears. Click one of the words provided to replace the word in the document.

 tip

If you want to see a list of synonyms for one of the words that appears in the Thesaurus task pane, click that word.

Using the Define Command

Word 2013 provides a new command in the Proofing group: Define. The Define command gives a definition for the word that currently contains the insertion point or has been selected. You simply click a word in a document and then select Define. The first time you use the Define feature, you need to install a dictionary from the Office store. The dictionaries available are listed in the

Dictionaries task pane that appears when you select Define. The task pane shows the price and rating for each dictionary. Select Download to download and install one of the dictionaries.

After the dictionary has been installed, the name of the dictionary (such as Merriam-Webster Dictionary or Bing Dictionary) appears at the top of the task pane. Click Define a second time so that the dictionary defines the word in the document. The definition of the word appears in the task pane, as shown in Figure 7.20.

Figure 7.20
The
Dictionary
task pane.

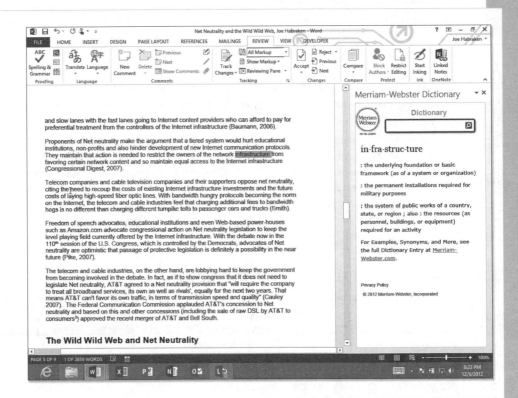

You can also type a word into the Dictionary box in the task pane and then press Enter or click the Lookup button to retrieve a definition of the word. In addition, you can quickly jump to the website for your currently installed online dictionary if you want to see more information (such as the full dictionary entry) regarding your word. When you have finished working with the Dictionary task pane, click the Close button.

 note

The Review tab of the Ribbon also offers a Language tab that provides a Translate command. You can use it to translate selected text (or the whole document) into another language.

Working with Quick Parts

As we create documents, we are always looking for shortcuts and timesavers that help us work more efficiently. The Quick Parts feature gives you access to premade document-building blocks, your own AutoText entries, document properties, and Word fields. Inserting document parts, information, or words and phrases that you use often not only saves you time, but also keeps information consistent in your document or documents.

So what is a building block, compared to an AutoText entry? Building blocks are any words, text lines, paragraphs, or even entire pages that you save as a building block. By definition, building blocks are meant to help you quickly enter often-used text into your documents. Word provides a number of building blocks, such as different headers and footers, page-numbering formats, and even text boxes and watermarks. You can add building blocks as needed and then access your building blocks in the Building Blocks Organizer. Building blocks are organized in galleries. These galleries include possibilities such as cover pages, headers, and tables, among others.

AutoText entries are a type of building block; however, you can insert AutoText entries into a document more quickly than a building block, and the entries are saved in a specific AutoText gallery. Think of the difference between AutoText entries and building blocks as being practical rather than technical. I recommend that you reserve AutoText for words and phrases such as company names, letter closings, and the like—short text entries that you use often. Save the building blocks for more complex items that you insert occasionally—items such as long paragraphs, a particular page type (such as a cover page), or a special table.

Creating and Inserting an AutoText Entry

To create an AutoText entry, select the text you want to save as the AutoText entry. Select the Ribbon's Insert tab and then select Explore Quick Parts. On the Quick Parts menu, point at AutoText and then select Save Selection to AutoText Gallery. The Create New Building Block dialog box opens (see Figure 7.21).

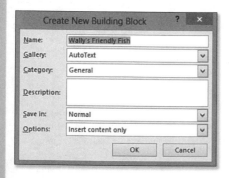

Figure 7.21
The Create New Building Block dialog box.

In the dialog box, provide a name for the new AutoText entry (a name based on the text content is provided by default). You can also choose options related to the entry, such as whether to insert the content only or to insert the content in a separate paragraph or on a separate page. Click OK to create the entry.

To insert an AutoText entry in your document, place the insertion point where you want to place the entry. Select the Explorer Quick Parts command and then point at AutoText. Select the entry you want to place in the document from the choices provided in the AutoText gallery.

 tip

You can provide an optional description for the new entry in the Create New Building Block dialog box. This can be useful if you end up with several AutoText or building block entries that have similar names.

Creating and Inserting Building Blocks

Creating a building block is similar to creating an AutoText entry.
Select the text, table, header, footer, or other object that you want to serve as the building block. Select the Ribbon's Insert tab and then select Quick Parts. On the Quick Parts menu, select Save Selection to Quick Part Gallery. The Create New Building Block dialog box opens (refer to Figure 7.21).

Provide a name for the new building block. You can also select the gallery and category for the building block. More importantly, you can control the options related to how the building block will be inserted into the document via the Options drop-down list.

If the building block contains only text that you want to insert into other paragraphs (much like an AutoText entry), use the Insert Content Only option. The building block is then formatted the same as the surrounding text.

If you are creating a building block with specific formatting or a special building block such as a table, use the Insert Content in Its Own Paragraph option. This maintains the formatting of the block. If you are creating a building block that consists of a page such as a cover page (or a number of pages, such as front matter for a book), select the Insert Content in Its Own Page option. This places the building block into the document as a new page or pages. When you have finished selecting the various options, click OK to create the building block.

When you want to insert a building block that you created into a document, you insert it from the Quick Parts menu (if you used the General category when you built the building block). Select Quick Parts and then select the building block from the menu.

When you want to use building blocks that Word provides or you want to peruse the various building blocks available (including AutoText and building blocks you created), you can open the Building Blocks Organizer from the Quick Parts menu. Figure 7.22 shows the Building Blocks Organizer.

You can insert building blocks from the organizer (select the building block and then click Insert). You can also manage your building blocks by editing their properties and even deleting unwanted building blocks. To change the text or other objects in a building block, you can insert the building block into a document and modify it as needed. You can then save it to the Building Block gallery using the same name and properties. You are asked whether you want to redefine the building block; click Yes, and the building block is modified.

Obviously, building blocks can save you a lot of time and add consistency (in terms of content) to your Word documents. If you create several building blocks, remember to use the appropriate gallery and category for each building block, to help you keep the library of text blocks organized.

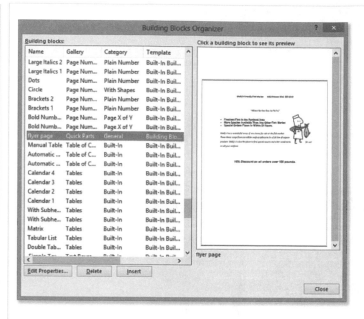

Figure 7.22
The Building Blocks Organizer.

Configuring AutoCorrect

AutoCorrect has remained fairly consistent in terms of its configuration and function, and in Word 2013 it still automatically corrects commonly misspelled words, including words that you add to it. It also corrects issues such as initial caps, automatically capitalizes the first letter of the first word in a sentence, and automatically capitalizes the names of days of the week.

You can access the AutoCorrect dialog box (see Figure 7.23) from the Word Backstage. Select File and then Options. In the Word Options window, select Proofing and then click the AutoCorrect Options button.

You can add entries to the Replace text as you type list. In the Replace box, enter a word as you misspell it. In the With box, enter the correct spelling of the word. Click Add to add the entry to the AutoCorrect list.

You can also access settings related to AutoFormat, such as replacing straight quotes with smart quotes on the AutoFormat tab of the AutoCorrect dialog box. Other options, such as automatic bulleted lists and the formatting of a list item the same as the previous item, are accessed on the AutoFormat as You Type tab.

Figure 7.23
The AutoCorrect dialog box.

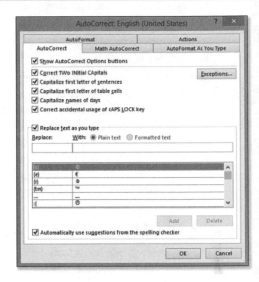

Understanding Styles

When you create Word documents that contain a great deal of formatting attributes for the various headings, special paragraphs, and the like, it makes sense to take advantage of styles. A style is a grouping of formatting attributes identified by a style name. Styles can contain text-formatting attributes such as bold and 14 point, and can also contain paragraph-formatting attributes such as indents and other alignment settings (such as Center or Justify).

The great thing about using styles to format your text is that, when you modify the style itself, the modifications apply to all the text that has been assigned that style. For example, if you have used a style for all the headings in your document and decide that you want the headings to be in bold (along with the other formatting contained in the heading style), you simply modify the style to include the bold attribute.

Word provides Quick Styles that are predesigned styles. Quick Styles, or just built-in styles, if you prefer, come in families or sets of styles to provide consistency in look and formatting when you use them to format the various items in a document, such as headings, titles, and quotes. These style families are called style sets. You can change the style set currently used in the document on the Design tab. The Design tab also provides access to the Themes command, which enables you to change the document's current theme. For more about themes and style sets, see "Formatting with Themes," earlier in this chapter.

Although you might think of styles as formatting that is reserved for the formatting of headings, titles, and other special text that you want to stand out in your document, styles are used to format lists and tables. For example, a multilevel list, such as an outline, contains different levels; each sublevel is indented below its parent level, and a numbering system denotes parent levels and sublevels. For example, the Primary level might be designated with the number 1, whereas the first sublevel is 1.1, the second 1.2, and so on. You can create a numbered list and modify the formatting and level designations. This new list format can then be saved as a new list style.

Styles help with table formatting, too. The Table Tools Layout tab has a gallery of table styles, or you can create your own.

Clearly, styles can help you consistently format the text and other objects in your documents, and you have freedom to create, modify, and delete your own styles, if you want. Tools help you manage your styles; you can quickly inspect a style in a document with the Style Inspector, and you can import and export styles from document to document (or to and from a Word template). Next, you look at how to take advantage of the Quick Styles provided by Word and then how best to create your own styles.

Using the Styles Gallery

You can apply Quick Styles to selected text or a paragraph (remember that Word considers even a single-line heading to be a paragraph). The Quick Styles reside in a style gallery in the Styles group of the Ribbon's Home tab.

After you specify the text that you want to format with the Quick Style, place the mouse pointer on any of the available styles to preview the style's formatting (on your text). To view additional Quick Styles in the current set, use the arrows to the right of the Quick Style gallery. You can also click the More button (just below the arrows) to expand the gallery so that you can see more of the Quick Styles in one view.

If you want to use a different set of styles in the current document, navigate to the Ribbon's Design tab. Select the More button on the Style Set gallery (in the Document Formatting group) to see all the style sets available, including the style set used in the current document and the various built-in styles sets (see Figure 7.24).

If you place the mouse pointer on any of the style sets listed, you get a preview of how the built-in styles that you have already used in your document will look when you apply the new style set. You can also reset your document to the style set used by the current template (which, in many cases, is the Normal template); this also resets all the Quick Styles to their defaults if you have modified any of them.

 tip

To create a list style based on a modified multilevel list, place the insertion point in the list and then click the Multilevel List icon in the Paragraph group on the Ribbon's Home tab. Select Define New List Style in the gallery. The Define New List Style dialog box enables you to specify the settings for the new style and apply the style to the current document and/or all the documents based on the current template.

 caution

The Quick Styles that you have assigned to your document's text are affected (in terms of their formatting attributes, such as the fonts and font colors used) when you change the theme or style set for your document. If you plan to use themes, style sets, and Quick Styles, assign the theme to the document and/ or style set before you begin to create it; then select the appropriate Quick Styles for each text item as needed (such as headings, titles, and body text).

 tip

If you have modified the built-in styles in your document and want to save these changes in a new style set, select Save As a New Style Set in the Style Set Gallery. Provide a name for the new style set in the Save As a New Style Set dialog box. The new style set appears in the Custom list when you expand the Style Set Gallery with the More button.

Figure 7.24
Select a new
style set.

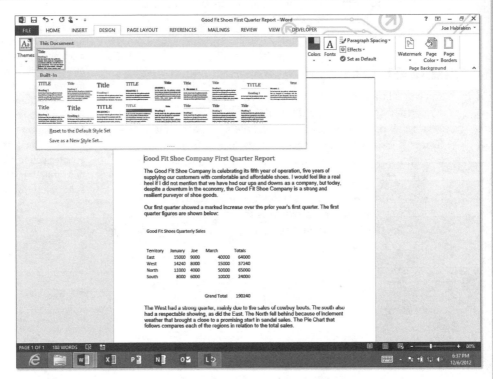

Creating Styles

You can create your own styles quickly and easily by example. Apply font- and paragraph-formatting attributes to selected text. The text can be a single-line heading or an entire paragraph of text. Any of the font-formatting attributes, such as bold, italics, font color, font size, and even font type, are fair game for your style, as are paragraph-formatting attributes related to alignment, line spacing, indents, borders, and shading.

When you have the text formatted, click the More button in the Styles group (on the Home tab), and then select Create a Style. The Create New Style from Formatting dialog box opens, as shown in Figure 7.25.

Figure 7.25
Create a new style from formatting.

Provide a name for the new style in the Name box and then click OK. The new style appears in the Quick Style gallery. You can apply it to your document text as needed.

Editing Styles

You can edit any style in the document, including the built-in style provided by the current template and any styles that you have created. A quick way to view all the styles available in the current document, and to access a particular style for editing, is to open the Styles window (click the Styles window launcher on the edge of the Styles group).

The Style window lists all the styles in the document (see Figure 7.26). If you want to see a preview of the style's formatting attributes, click the Show Preview check box at the bottom of the Styles window.

 tip

If you decide that you want to modify the new style before actually saving it to the Quick Style gallery, click Modify in the Create New Style from Formatting dialog box, and a larger Create New Style from Formatting dialog box appears. The larger dialog box enables you to change the various formatting attributes of the style before you save the style.

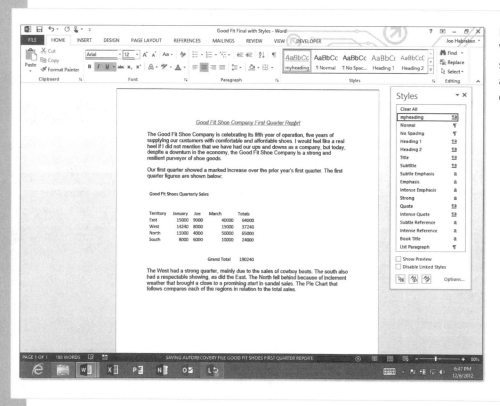

Figure 7.26
View all the styles available in the document.

You can modify a style from the Style window in two ways. You can modify it by example or edit the style's formatting attributes manually.

To modify the style by example, reformat text that has been assigned the style so that it is formatted with the attributes you want in the modified version of the style. Click the drop-down arrow next to the style that you want to modify (in the Style window) and select Update (*style name*) to Match Selection. The style is updated, as is all the text that has been assigned that style.

You can also modify a style using the Modify Style dialog box: Click the drop-down arrow next to the style and select Modify. The Modify Style dialog box provides Formatting toolbars that you can use to change font-formatting attributes and paragraph attributes.

You can also access specific dialog boxes from the Modify Style dialog box to achieve even greater control over the formatting attributes contained in the style. Select the Format button at the bottom-left of the dialog box and select Font, Paragraph, Tabs, Borders, or any of the other dialog boxes listed; that particular dialog box opens (such as the Font dialog box or the Paragraph dialog box).

After you have made changes to formatting attributes in one of the dialog boxes, closing the dialog box (clicking OK) returns you to the Modify Style dialog box. When you close the Modify Style dialog box, you return to your document and the Styles window.

Managing Styles

The Styles window not only gives a comprehensive list of the styles in a document, but it also enables you to quickly modify and even delete styles from the document. The Styles window also provides access to the Manage Styles dialog box, which gives you even greater capability to manage the styles in your document. It even enables you to import and export styles into and from your current document.

In the Styles window, select the Manage Styles button (first button on the right). This opens the Manage Styles dialog box (see Figure 7.27).

This dialog box enables you to modify any of the styles in your document (or template, if you are working on a template), including deleting them, and also to create new styles (directly from the dialog box). The Manage Styles dialog box also enables you to determine which styles appear in the Quick Style gallery and Styles window, as well as specify the order in which the styles appear. In addition, it provides options related to setting some of the font- and paragraph-formatting attributes for the document.

The Manage Styles dialog box provides four tabs:

- **Edit:** This tab enables you to modify and delete styles and to change how the list of styles is sorted on the tab. For example, you can change the sort order to Alphabetical using the Sort Order drop-down list. The default sort order, As Recommended, is based on a numerical system (a style assigned a 1 appears at the top of the list), which you can set on the Recommend tab.

 tip

To quickly view the formatting attributes of a style in your document, select text that has the style applied and then click the Style Inspector button in the Styles window. The Style Inspector provides paragraph- and text-level formatting for the style. The Style Inspector can also clear formatting attributes used in the style.

 tip

If you want to delete a style, click the drop-down arrow next to the style in the Style window and select Delete (*style name*) on the menu. Click Yes to confirm the deletion.

 tip

You can also create a new style from the Styles window by clicking the New Style button at the bottom of the window.

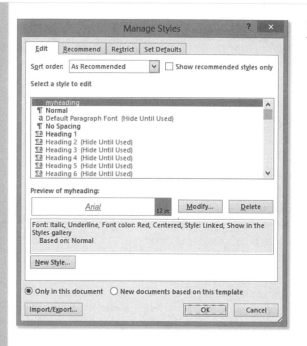

Figure 7.27
The Manage Styles dialog box.

- **Recommend:** The Recommend list is determined on this tab by assigning a particular order number to a style (1 is the highest). The order determined by the Recommend list is basically the priority used to list the styles in the Quick Style gallery and the Styles windows. Use the Move Up, Move Down, and Assign Value buttons to assign the priority number to a style in the list. You can also choose to have certain styles hidden until you use them (via the Hide Until Used button), and you can hide styles. Any styles assigned the Hide Until Used or Hide status can be shown by selecting the style or styles and clicking Show.

- **Restrict:** You can limit access to formatting in the document. This is particularly useful if you are designing a template in which you want users of the template to have restricted access to the formatting tools on the Ribbon and want only certain styles to be used for formatting (in lieu of direct formatting). Select a style or styles in the Styles list to permit or restrict the style. If you want to limit formatting to the permitted styles, be sure to select the Limit Formatting to Permitted Styles check box. This feature grays out formatting commands on the Ribbon's Home tab, making them unavailable.

- **Set Defaults:** This tab enables you to specify some of the default formatting attributes for the current document or documents based on the template that you are creating and configuring. These attributes include Font and Font Size, Paragraph Position, and Paragraph Spacing.

Another tool that you can access via the Manage Styles dialog box is the Organizer. It enables you to copy styles from other documents and templates into your current document (and export them to other documents and templates). After all, sometimes you want to have access to styles that you have created in other documents or that are contained in other Word templates (existing templates and templates that you have created).

➡ **See** *Chapter 6 for more on templates.*

To open the Organizer, click the Import/Export button at the bottom of the Manage Styles dialog box (the button is available on all tabs of the Manage Styles dialog box). The Organizer (shown in Figure 7.28) provides two separate panes that list the styles in the current document (on the left of the dialog box) and the styles in the current document template, which is the Normal template in Figure 7.28.

Figure 7.28
The Organizer dialog box.

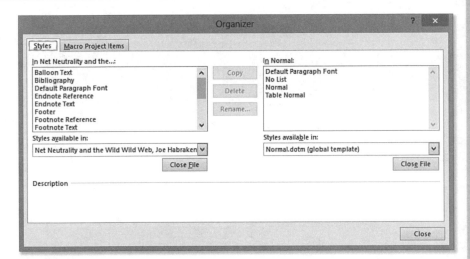

The trick here is to leave the current document and its styles in the Organizer (in the left pane) and to use the right side of the Organizer window to open the document that you want to use when you import (or export) styles. To close the current template file on the right side of the dialog box, click the Close File button.

Now you need to open the document or template that will serve as the source for the styles you want to import or that will serve as the destination for the files that you want to export from the current document. Click Open File on the right side of the Organizer dialog box. The Open dialog box appears. Use it to locate and open the document or template from which you want to copy the styles (or export styles to). Double-click the file in the Open dialog box to open the file.

 tip

If you want to import a style into a document (from a document or template), but that style has the same name as a style that already exists in the document that will receive the imported style, you need to use the Rename command to rename the style before you can import it.

Now all you have to do is import or export the styles. Select a style or styles (use the Shift key to select multiple styles) in the document opened on the right side of the Organizer, and then click Copy to import the styles into your current document. If you want to export styles from the current document, select them on the left and then copy them to the file on the right. The dialog box also enables you to select styles in either style list and delete them.

WORKING WITH TABLES, COLUMNS, AND SECTIONS

Many of the documents that you create probably require you to arrange information on the page in ways other than the typical paragraphs that you find in a simple business letter. For example, you might need to show sales data that is best displayed in a table format, or you might need to create a newsletter that requires your text and images to appear in columns.

Word makes adding tables to your documents relatively simply. It also enables you to create columns on a document page or pages. You might run into a situation when you need to display a large table (in terms of columns) on a page in Landscape view, but you need to have the other pages in the document remain in Portrait orientation. Or you might want a document to have regular single-column text in paragraphs, but then switch at a certain point in the document to a two-column layout.

Sections can handle these types of layout issues. Each section can have its own page layout settings, such as number of columns, margins, and even headers and footers. This chapter first discusses tables, and then moves to columns and, finally, Word sections.

Options for Adding a Table

When you think about the spatial arrangement of text on a Word document page, the positioning of the information is dictated primarily by the document margins and then any paragraph alignment or line-spacing settings that you choose (such as centered or double-spaced text). Tables, however, are containers that provide a way for you to arrange information on a page in a gridlike format. Tables consist of columns and rows, and each intersection of a column and row is referred to as a cell. You enter your data (text or other objects) into the table cells.

Although you can arrange text on a page in a tabular (or tablelike) format using tabs, tables are much more flexible, particularly when the amount of text to be entered into each column is not uniform. The cell's height grows as needed to accommodate your entered text, and you can easily widen the columns when required. Tables can also contain pictures and other graphics, to provide you with layout possibilities that would be nearly impossible to achieve using tab stops.

Word provides multiple options for creating a table in your document. Figure 8.1 shows the possibilities when you select the Table command on the Ribbon's Insert tab. The table-creation possibilities are as follows:

- **Table Grid:** You can insert a table by dragging the mouse on the table grid to select the number of columns and rows that make up the table. You access the table grid by selecting the Table command in the Table group. When you insert a table using the table grid, you are initially limited to a maximum table size of 10 columns by 10 rows, although you can easily insert additional columns and rows afterward.

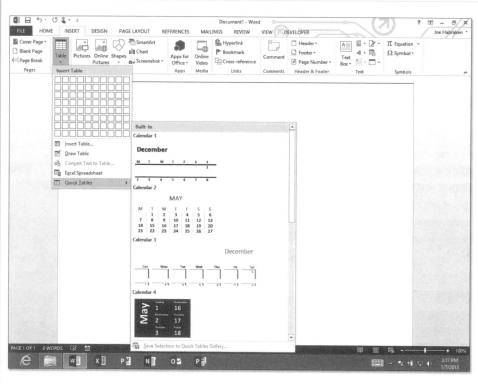

Figure 8.1
Create a new table using one of the options provided by the Table command.

- **Insert Table:** This old-school table option uses the Insert Table dialog box and enables you to specify the number of columns and rows. To open the Insert Table dialog box, select Table on the Insert tab and then select Insert Table.

- **Draw Table:** You can draw your table in the document using a "pencil" mouse pointer. You can add columns and rows using the drawing tool as needed (you can distribute the rows and columns evenly afterward via commands on the Table Tools Layout tab). To draw a table, select Table and then select Draw Table.

- **Convert Text to Table:** You can convert existing text to a table. This is useful when you have used tabs to place text in a tabular arrangement.

- **Excel Spreadsheet:** This option places a new Excel sheet into your document at the insertion point. Whenever the spreadsheet is selected, Excel tabs and commands are available on the Word Ribbon.

- **Quick Tables:** You can select a premade table from the Quick Tables gallery. You access the gallery via the Table command on the Ribbon's Insert tab (select Table and then point at Quick Tables). Quick Tables provide different table layouts and formatting (see Figure 8.1). They also provide sample text, which you can replace with your own text.

 For more about integrating Word and Excel, ***see*** *Appendix A, "Office Application Integration."*

All these options place a table (or an Excel spreadsheet) into the document at the insertion point. However, keep in mind that the differences among these different table-creation methods provide you with a great deal of flexibility in creating a table. For example, if you want to quickly create a table such as a tabular list and are happy with the layout and formatting provided by the Tabular List quick table, it likely will want to use it and then replace the sample text with your own text.

If you are creating a table where you want to more precisely control the number of columns and rows, you can use the Insert Table option. This option also enables you to work through the process of setting the design and layout options for the table and format the cell contents (text). Let's walk through each of the options for creating a table from scratch and then look at fine-tuning tables, including using the Design and Layout Table Tools provided by Word 2013.

Inserting a Table

When you insert a table, you can specify the initial number of rows and columns in the table. You also can specify the position on the page where you want to place the table; you simply park the insertion point where you want to place the table. The insertion point marks the top-left starting point of the table.

> **🔍 note**
>
> You might think it best to use Excel for information that needs to be in a table format and then copy and paste the Excel sheet data into Word. When the data is already in Excel, this makes sense; however, the Word table feature is extremely robust and flexible and provides you with a number of options in terms of table format and layout. Word also enables you to insert formulas into the table so that you can do calculations (as in Excel). So if the data isn't already in Excel and doesn't need to be in Excel, just enter it into a Word table.

Obviously, if you use the Insert Table grid on the Table command's menu, you merely drag the mouse to specify the number of columns and rows. With initial settings, the Insert Table dialog box provides you with more options, so let's assume that you want to go that route to insert the new table. Follow these steps:

1. Place the insertion point in the document where you want to insert the table.

2. Select the Table command on the Ribbon's Insert tab and then select Insert Table. The Insert Table dialog box appears, as shown in Figure 8.2.

Figure 8.2
Insert a table using the Insert Table dialog box.

3. Use the Number of Columns and Number of Rows spinner boxes to specify the number of columns and rows for the table (or type a number in either box).

4. The AutoFit options enable you to specify how the columns in the table behave in relation to the amount of text placed in each column. The options are as follows:

   ■ **Fixed Column Width:** This setting enables you to set a fixed width (an actual number in inches) for all the columns in the table. When you use this option, you must manually resize columns in the table (using the sizing tool) to change any of the column widths.

   ■ **AutoFit to Contents:** Column widths adjust to the amount of text in the column. A column grows in width (at the expense of the other columns in the table) as you enter text.

   ■ **AutoFit to Window:** This option keeps the table aligned between the left and right margins. It is primarily designed for web pages so that the table adjusts its size based on the web browser window size.

5. (Optional) If you want the settings you selected to become the default for new tables, select the Remember Dimensions for New Tables check box.

6. When you have finished setting the options for the new table, click OK.

 tip

To access the AutoFit settings for the table (after you have created the table), use the AutoFit command in the Cell Size group on the Table Tools Layout tab.

The table is inserted into the document. The Ribbon also switches to the Table Tools, discussed later in this chapter.

Drawing a Table

An alternative to inserting a table into your document is to draw the table. When you draw the table, you can make the table any height and width instead of having Word determine the height and width based on the number of columns and rows. You create the outside table borders without any rows or columns; you then must manually insert the rows and columns using the Table Drawing tool.

Although you can build a highly customized table using this method, it is not as fast as inserting a table with a prescribed number of rows and columns (as when you insert a table). Follow these steps:

1. Select Table on the Insert tab and then select Draw Table. The mouse pointer becomes a "pencil" drawing tool.

2. Click and drag to create the table's outside borders (its "box" shape). Release the mouse when you have the outside perimeter of the table completed.

3. To add rows and columns to the table, use the pencil to draw (click and drag) the row and column lines.

4. When you have finished drawing the column and row borders (they do not have to be spaced evenly at this point), select Draw Table on the Design tab of the Table Tools. This turns off the pencil drawing tool.

5. To evenly distribute the drawn rows and/or columns in the table, select the Layout tab (of the Table Tools Ribbon) and then select Distribute Rows and/or Distribute Columns, as needed.

If you click outside the table (in the document's text) when using the table drawing tool, the Draw Table feature is toggled off. All you have to do is click inside the table and then click the Draw Table command on the Table Tools Design tab to reactivate the pencil drawing tool. You can then add tables or rows as needed. You can also use the Eraser tool to erase rows or columns that you have placed in the table. Select Eraser on the Design tab and then click and drag the Eraser to select a row or column border. When you release the mouse, the column or row border is erased. You can also use the Eraser to fine-tune borders and erase parts of a column or row to join cells.

Converting Text to a Table

You can convert existing text to a table. This is particularly convenient when you have used tabs to align text in a tabular format but find that you are better served by converting the text into a table. This is also useful if you have a text file that is delimited with spaces or commas and you want to get the data into a table.

To convert delimited text (some sort of delimiter must exist between each text entry), select the text. On the Ribbon's Insert tab, select Table and then select Convert Text to Table. The Convert Text to Table dialog box opens (see Figure 8.3).

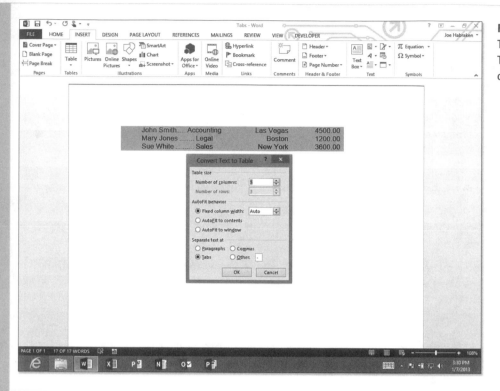

Figure 8.3
The Convert
Text to Table
dialog box.

Select the delimiter that separates the text in the list in the Separate Text At area of the dialog box. You can select from Paragraphs, Commas, Tabs, or designate a delimiter using the Other option. Based on the delimiter, Word specifies a table size showing the number of columns and rows. You can also set the AutoFit behavior in the Convert Text to Table dialog box, if warranted.

When you click OK, the text converts to a table. If the table hasn't perfectly arranged the data, you can insert columns and rows (if needed) and then drag and drop cell entries until you have the data appropriately placed in the table.

 Tip

You can change the line style, line weight, and pen color when you are using the Draw Table feature. Change any of the color or line settings in the Borders group on the Design tab of the Table Tools.

Entering Text and Navigating a Table

When you have the table in your document, you need to add data. In most cases, this is text, although you can also insert pictures and other graphics into a cell. Entering text into the table is straightforward. Click in the first cell of the table and enter the appropriate text. To move to the next cell, press the Tab key. You can continue to move through the cells in the tables by pressing Tab and entering your text. If you want to back up a cell, press Shift+Tab. This moves you to the cell to the left of the current cell. If you move to a cell that contains text, that text is selected. If you type new text, it overwrites the original contents of the cell.

Of course, you can use the mouse to click in any cell of the table at any time. However, if you are entering information into the table, using some of the other keyboard combinations to navigate a table is quicker:

- **Alt+Home:** Takes you to the first cell in the current row

- **Alt+Page Up:** Takes you to the top cell in the current column

- **Alt+End:** Takes you to the last cell in the current row

- **Alt+Page Down:** Takes you to the last cell in the current column

Deleting text from the table is really no different than deleting any other text in a document. Select text in the table and press Delete to remove it. If you want to delete all the text in an entire row, place the mouse pointer at the left edge of the particular row. Click to select the entire row. When you press Delete, all the text in the selected row is deleted. You can also use a column pointer (a solid black arrow; place the mouse at the top of any column) to select an entire column and delete text in that column using the Delete key.

Selecting and Positioning a Table

To select a table, place the mouse just above the top-left corner of the table. The Table handle appears. Click the handle, and the entire table is selected. You can also reposition a table using the Table handle. Use the handle as needed to drag the table to a new position in the document.

Because the text surrounding the table (the text in your para-graphs) basically sees the table as a graphical element, you can configure how the surrounding text wraps around the table (as you can a picture or clip art). Drag the table to position it within a paragraph of text. Right-click the table and select Table Properties from the shortcut menu. The Table tab of the Table Properties dialog box is selected, as shown in Figure 8.4.

In the Alignment area of the Table tab, select Left, Center, or Right to position the table in relation to the text in the paragraph. If you do not want the text to wrap around the table, select None in the Text Wrapping area. To return to the document, click OK.

 tip

The contents of the cells in your table are not limited to text. You can place clip art, pictures, and other graphics in a cell. You can also nest a table in a table. For example, you can include a table of data (in a cell) beside a chart of that data (which is also in a cell). Tables provide a great way to arrange objects on a document page.

 tip

You can select a cell, a column, a row, or the entire table using the Select command on the Table Tools Layout tab.

Formatting Tables

In terms of formatting tables, you work with two broad categories of tools: layout and design. The Layout commands appear on the Table Tools Layout tab. These tools include commands that enable you to insert columns and rows, merge and split cells, and change the text alignment in a cell or cells. Figure 8.5 shows the Layout tab.

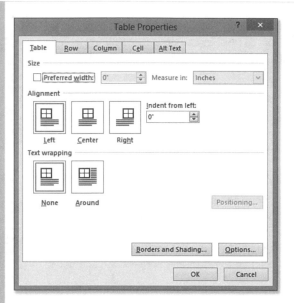

Figure 8.4
The Table Properties dialog box.

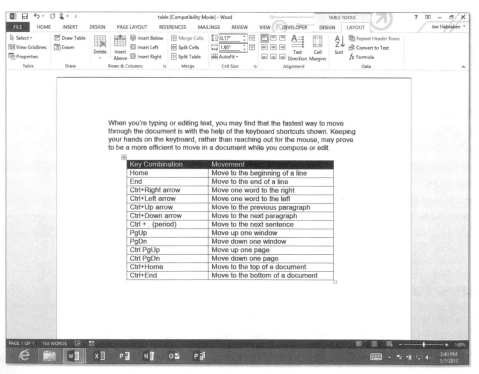

Figure 8.5
The Table Tools Layout tab.

In the design tools are commands related to the use of table styles (many table styles are built into Word) and shading and borders settings. The Draw Borders group is also part of the Design tab of the Table Tools and is shown in Figure 8.6.

Figure 8.6
The Table
Tools Design
tab.

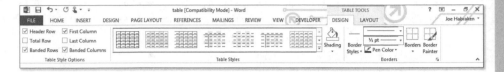

When seeking a unified theme for the Layout commands versus the Design commands, think of the Layout commands as tools that enable you to manipulate the rows, columns, and cells of the table and the text alignment in the cells. The Design commands control more of the overall look of the table by providing access to the table styles, table style options, and commands related to the format of the table's borders.

Adjusting Columns and Rows

The columns and rows provide the table's basic structure, or "bones." You have complete control over the number of rows and columns in your table. You also control column widths and row heights. Word 2013 provides you with new insert controls for quickly inserting columns or rows into a table. To insert a new column, place the mouse on the border between two columns at the top of the table. An insert control appears as a vertical element highlighting the column border. Click the plus symbol on top of the column insert control, and a new column is inserted (between the columns). You can also use the row insert control to add a new row between two existing rows. Place the mouse on the left side of the table between two rows until the insert control appears. Click the plus symbol to insert the row.

The Table Tools Layout tab gives you commands for inserting columns and rows into a table. The possibilities are as follows:

- To insert a column, place the insertion point in the column next to where you want to insert the new column. On the Layout tab of the Table Tools, use the Insert Left or Insert Right command to insert a new column to the left or right of the current column, respectively.

- To insert a row, place the insertion point in a row; then use the Insert Above or Insert Below command to insert a new row above or below the current row.

- If you need to add more than one column or row, select the number of columns or rows you want to add to the table; then use the commands in the Rows & Columns group to insert columns or rows as needed (to the right or left of the selected columns, or above or below the selected rows).

For adjusting column widths and row heights, you can use the sizing tool to visually change the width of a column or the height of a row. To change the column width, place the mouse between two columns until the resizing pointer appears. Drag the mouse to increase or decrease the column width.

To set a more precise width for a column (or selected columns), you can use the Width Spinner box in the Cell Size group of the Layout tab. Use the arrows to increase or decrease the width, or type a measurement (in inches) in the box to specify the width.

You can increase the row height by using the resizing pointer to drag down (on the bottom) the border of a row. To change the height for selected rows, use the Height command spinner box in the Cell Size group.

 tip

If you are working on a table that does not have borders, click the View Gridlines command on the Table Tools Layout tab. Seeing the nonprinting gridlines makes working with the table easier.

You can also set column widths and row heights in the Table Properties dialog box. Click in the column or row that you want to adjust. Select the Properties command in the Table group of the Layout tab. If you are adjusting the width of a column (or columns), select the Column tab of the Table Properties dialog box (see Figure 8.7).

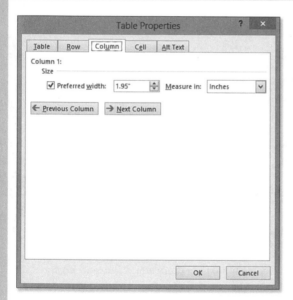

Figure 8.7
The Column tab of the Table Properties dialog box.

Use the Preferred Width spinner box to set the width for the column (the default measurement is inches). You can use Previous Column or Next Column to set the preferred width for columns adjacent to the current column.

For row height, use the Row tab. The Specify Height spinner box enables you to set the row height, and the Row Height spinner box lets you specify that the height of the row is at least or exactly the height you have entered. An option is also available that enables you to specify whether the row should be allowed to break across pages.

Columns and rows can be selected and dragged to new positions in a table. You might also find it necessary to delete columns or rows in the table. Deleting columns or rows is straightforward. Select a column (or columns) or a row (or rows). Select the Delete command on the Layout tab. Use the Delete Columns or Delete Rows command as needed. If you want to delete the entire table, select Delete Table.

> **tip**
>
> The Repeat As Header Row at the Top of Each Page check box on the Row tab enables you to specify that the current row is the header (top row of the table) and should be repeated when the table is broken over multiple pages.

Formatting Cells

Word provides formatting attributes to relate directly to the cells in a table. These formatting features include the capability to merge and split cells. You also have control over how text is aligned in the cell and the cell margins.

Merging cells gives you control over the internal space of the table. To merge cells, select the cells and then click the Merge Cells command in the Merge group of the Table Tools Layout tab. You can also split a cell; use the Split Cells command to split the current cell into two cells.

Another split-related command is available in the Merge group. If you want to split a table into two tables at a particular row, place the insertion point in that row and then click Split Table.

Several other cell-specific commands are in the Alignment group on the Layout tab. These commands control the following cell settings:

- **Alignment Commands:** On the left of the Alignment group are nine commands that control where the text is aligned in a cell (or selected cells): Align Top Left, Align Top Center, Align Top Right, Align Center Left, Align Center, Align Center Right, Align Bottom Left, Align Bottom Center, and Align Bottom Right.

- **Text Direction:** This command enables you to cycle through two text-direction possibilities: On the first click of the command, the text is rotated 90° and placed in the upper right of the cell; the next click rotates the text 180° (from the previous setting) and places it in the bottom left of the cell. The third time you click the Text Direction button, the text returns to its normal text orientation and default alignment.

- **Cell Margins:** This command enables you to set the default cell margins for the table. This is particularly useful if you want to give crowded cells more breathing room and add some whitespace to the interior of the table. When you select the Cell Margins command, the Table Options dialog box opens (see Figure 8.8). You can specify the top, bottom, left, and right cell margins and also set the default cell spacing.

> **tip**
>
> You can adjust the width of an individual cell. Select the cell and then drag the cell border as needed to change the width. Note that this takes the cell out of alignment (in terms of its borders) with the rest of the cells in that column.

One point to remember when working with the individual cell settings, such as the Alignment commands and the Cell Margins command, is that you need to make these types of adjustments *after* you apply a style to the table. Table styles override any specific cell-formatting attributes that you configure except for the Text Rotation setting, which is not affected by assigning a style to a table.

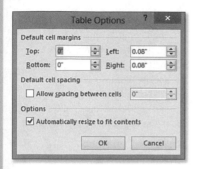

Figure 8.8
Table Options dialog box.

Using Table Styles

Table styles give you a unified design for your tables that includes a number of table-formatting attributes, including fonts, borders, and shading. By default, all new tables created use the Table Grid style, which provides black borders for the table cells. This basic table style uses the default font from the current template (in most cases, Calibri and the Normal template) and applies no shading to the cells. Formatting a table with a table style doesn't mean that you relinquish all control of the table's look. Obviously, you can edit the style. Check boxes provided in the Table Style Options group on the Table Tools Design tab also determine how the table styles will affect certain parts of the table. These options are as follows:

- **Header Row:** The header row is the first row of the table and typically contains the column headings for the table. Because the header row differs from the rows that contain regular data, the table style formats it differently. This option is selected by default.

- **First Column:** The first column often contains the row headings for the table. If you select the First Column option, the table style formats the first column differently than the other columns in the table. This option is selected by default.

- **Total Row:** Totals are typically included in the last row of the table. This option requires the table style to format the last row differently.

- **Last Column:** This option indicates that you want the table style to format the last column differently than the other columns in the table.

- **Banded Rows:** When you select this option, the style formats the odd and even rows in the table differently. This option is selected by default.

- **Banded Columns:** This option allows the table style to format the odd and even columns in the table differently.

When you decide on the options for the table styles by selecting or deselecting options in the Table Style Options group, you can preview how the various styles provided in the Table Styles gallery look when applied to the table (just point at a style to

 tip

You can access the Borders and Shading dialog box for more control over the border and shading options for your table; simply select Borders and Shading on the Borders drop-down list.

preview it). Figure 8.9 shows the Table Styles gallery (click the More button to view the gallery) and the Table Style Options group (on the left).

Figure 8.9
The Table Styles gallery.

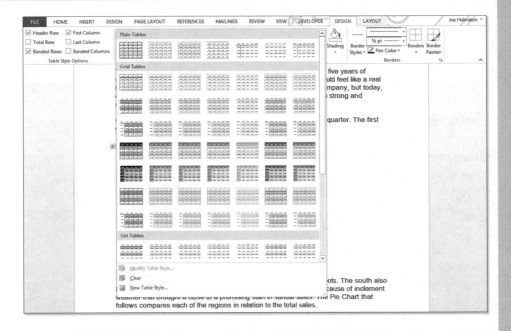

After you apply a particular style to the table, you can change any of the table style options as needed (deselect the check boxes or select different check boxes) and modify other table-formatting attributes supplied by the style, such as the shading or border formats. For example, you can select the Shading command to select a shading color from the color palette. You can select colors from the current document theme or from a list of standard colors. You can also select your own colors by clicking More Colors.

In addition, you have access to a new tool (new to Word 2013) in the Borders group: the Border Painter. Select a border style in the Border Styles list, and the mouse pointer becomes a pen; this is the Border Painter. Use the Border Painter to "paint" the new border style on the borders in the table (click and drag along a border to paint the border with the new format). When you have finished working with the Border Painter, select the Border Painter button in the Borders group to deactivate this feature.

If you modify the table formatting provided by the currently selected table style, you have the option to save the modified style as a new style. You can then use this new style to format any future tables that you create. You can specify whether the new style is available only in the current document or in all new documents based on the current template. Follow these steps to save the modified table style as a new style:

1. On the Design tab of the Table Tools, select the More button on the Table Styles gallery. The Tables Style gallery expands.

2. Select the New Table Style command at the bottom of the gallery. The Create New Style from Formatting dialog box appears (see Figure 8.10).

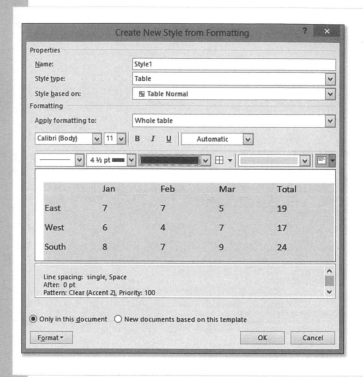

Figure 8.10
The Create New Style from Formatting dialog box.

3. Provide a name for your new style. Use the Apply Formatting To list to specify whether the style is applied to the whole table, the header row, the total row, and so on.

4. Select either the Only in This Document option or the New Documents Based on This Template option.

5. Select OK to save the new style.

The new style is listed in the table style gallery under the Custom heading. You can modify any existing table style as needed. If you format a table from scratch (including borders, shading, and font), you can save the table's formatting as a new style.

You can also easily delete a table style that you have created but no longer need. Right-click the style in the gallery, and select Delete Table Style from the shortcut menu.

 tip

You have complete control over all the format settings in a style when you are in the Create New Style from Formatting dialog box. Select the Format button at the bottom of the dialog box to access Table Properties, Borders and Shading, Banding, and other formatting attributes that you want to modify.

Sorting Table Data

Word enables you to sort data within the table. You can select a group of cells and then sort the data in those cells, or you can sort all the data in the table based on the contents of a particular column in the table. To sort an entire table, your table layout must be consistent; if you have split or merged cells within the table, you must select specific groups of cells for the sort to work correctly.

To sort data in the table, select the cells to be included in the sort, or click anywhere in the table when you are sorting a uniform table with no split or merged cells and no special rows (such as a total row). On the Layout tab of the Table Tools, select the Sort command (in the Data group). The Sort dialog box opens (see Figure 8.11).

Figure 8.11
The Sort dialog box.

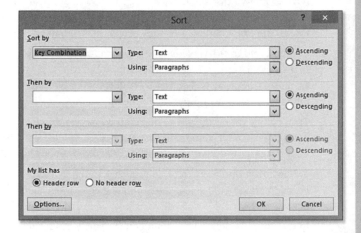

The Sort dialog box enables you to set the sort based on a specific parameter, such as a particular column or row heading. You also can specify the type of data (Text, Number, or Data). If you are sorting an entire table with uniform cells and the table has a header row (meaning column headings in the top row), take advantage of the Header Row option. If you are working with a table or a selected area of a table with column and row headings, the Sort dialog box anticipates the Sort By parameter from the sort and can usually specify the type of data you are sorting (text versus numbers).

The Sort dialog box enables you to sort by three different sort criteria (for example, you can sort by last name and then first name in a table of clients or employees). After you set the various sort parameters, click OK to perform the sort and return to the table.

Using Formulas in Tables

Word enables you to do different types of calculations in your tables. It certainly does not provide the large number of functions you find in Excel, but it provides functions calculations that include average, sum, maximum, and minimum.

Word (like Excel) also has the capability to take an educated guess on the type of calculation you want to make in a table. For example, if you insert a formula at the bottom of a column of numbers, Word assumes that you want to act upon the data above the current cell and suggests the formula =SUM(ABOVE). This is because Sum is also the default formula.

In some cases, Word might not be able to help you by recognizing the group of cells you want to include in the calculation, so you have to know how to specify a group (called a range) of cells to be acted upon by a particular formula. Here is the geography of a table: The first column is A, the second is B, and so on.

The first row in the table is 1, the second row is 2, and so on. The first cell in a table, which is in column A and row 1, is cell A1. Each cell's address is dictated by its location in the table: the column letter followed by the row number.

 note

When you need to do a lot of calculations, you might want to copy and paste the table into Excel. Excel provides greater flexibility and ease of use in working with calculations.

To specify a group of cells to be acted on by a formula, you must specify the first cell in the group and the last cell in the group. For example, if you were adding cells B2, B3, B4, and B5, you designate the cell group with B2:B5. This tells Word where the cells to act on begin and end.

To insert a formula into a table cell, click in the cell where you place the formula. To open the Formula dialog box, select the Formula command in the Data group. Figure 8.12 shows the Formula box.

In the Formula dialog box, you need to specify the formula in the Formula box. As already mentioned, if you are inserting a formula at the bottom of a column of numbers or at the end of a row of numbers, Word provides a formula in the Formula box.

You can specify a formula for the Formula box by selecting a function from the Paste function list. After you paste in the function, you must specify the cells that the formula will act on. To do so, type the cell range (which is the starting cell address and ending cell address) between the parentheses provided in the formula.

You can also use the Number Format drop-down box to specify how the calculation result in the cell should be formatted (such as currency or a percentage). When you finish setting the formula options, click OK to insert the formula.

 tip

You can specify the cell range for a formula in a Word table using a bookmark. Select a group of cells in the table, select Bookmark on the Ribbon's Insert tab, and provide a name for the bookmark. You can now use the bookmark when you create your formula in the Formula dialog box.

Figure 8.12
The Formula
dialog box.

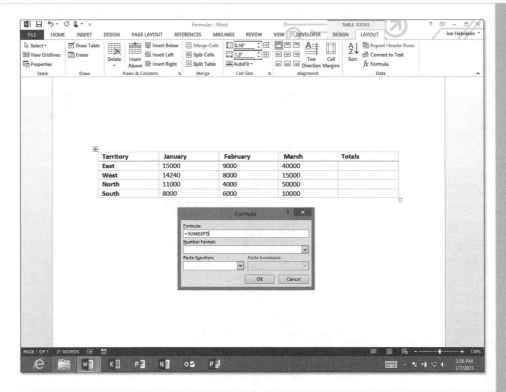

Adding Columns to a Document

The columns that you work with in Word are called newspaper or "snaking" columns. This means that if you have two columns on a page and you fill the first column with text, the additional text snakes over into the second column and continues to be inserted there. Word columns are perfect for newsletters and brochures.

You can format a blank document for columns, or you can select text and then apply column settings to the selected text. You can also have Word begin the column settings at the insertion point and place all the text from that point forward in the number of columns that you have selected. When you apply column settings to any selected text, Word automatically places the text (now in the number of columns you selected) into its own document section. We discuss sections in the next section of this chapter. For now, it is probably clear that the purpose of a section is to separate the new page layout settings from the rest of the document.

To insert columns into a document at the insertion point, select the Columns command on the Ribbon's Page Layout tab. You can select One, Two, or Three from the Columns list that appears. Selecting Two (or more) places columns of equal width on the page. You can also select Left or Right. The Left option places a narrow column on the left and a wider column on the right (a 1.83-inches wide column on the left and a wider right column of 4.17 inches). The Right selection does just the opposite. All the preset selections separate the columns created by a half inch. with a spacing of a half inch.

If you want more control over the column settings, select More Columns. This opens the Columns dialog box (see Figure 8.13).

You can select the presets from the Columns dialog box or specify your own number of columns using the Number of Columns spinner box. After you specify the number of columns, you can specify the width and spacing (between the columns) using the Width and Spacing boxes.

caution

Word columns are not appropriate for arranging text in a tabular format (meaning side-by-side text). Use a table or tabs if you need to arrange text on the page in side-by-side columns.

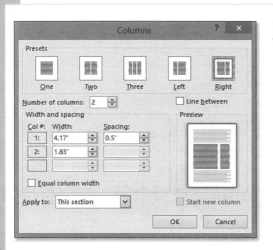

Figure 8.13
The Columns dialog box.

You can also specify whether you want the column settings to apply to the whole document or from this point forward in the document (from the insertion point). If you select This Point Forward in the Apply To drop-down list, a new section is created in the document. When you finish entering your settings for the columns, click OK.

You can edit the columns settings that you have applied to your document (or a section of the document). Make sure that you place the insertion point within a document section formatted for columns. Then click the Columns command in the Page Setup group and select More Columns. This opens the Columns dialog box, and you can edit the current settings as needed.

Because you are working with continuous, newspaper-type column settings, sometimes it is advantageous to force a column break in a column. This enables you to balance the text between columns or end the text in a column at a particular point and force the rest of the text into the next column. To place a column break at the insertion point, select the Breaks command on the Ribbon's Page Layout tab. Select Column on the Breaks list.

tip

If you want to place a line between the columns in your document, select the Line Between check box in the Columns dialog box.

Understanding Sections

Most of the documents that we create (the smaller, less complex documents) typically consist of one section. The page layout attributes such as margins, page orientation, number of columns, and even headers and footers are the same for the entire document. More complex documents can be more challenging in terms of page layout settings; think of a report that has a cover page, a table of contents, the body text of the report, and then a bibliography.

Each of these different parts or sections in this complex document might require different page layout attributes than the other document sections. In Word, a section is designed to meet the different page layouts in a single, complex document. Each section in a document is defined by a section break, and each section can have its own page layout settings, as well as its own headers and footers.

Adding and Removing Section Breaks

When you insert new section breaks into a document, switch to Draft view (Draft on the View tab). This enables you to view the section break and the type of section break that you insert. When you have confirmed that you have the section break in the right place, you can always switch to another view, such as Print Layout, and continue to work on your document. Whenever you need to deal with section breaks, however, particularly when you want to locate and delete section breaks, Draft view is the best view to use.

Place the insertion point in the document where you want the new section to start. On the Ribbon's Page Layout tab, select Breaks (in the Page Setup group). Figure 8.14 shows the various Breaks options, including the section break types (in the lower half of the gallery).

> **tip**
>
> You can copy the formatting from one section to another in a document by copying the section break. In Draft view, select and copy the section break. Then paste it into another part of the document. This creates a copy of the section, including all the page layout settings from the copied section.

Four types of section breaks are listed:

- **Next Page:** A page break is placed in the document, and the new section begins on this new page.

- **Continuous:** The new section starts at the insertion point and continues for the rest of the document (or until it comes to the next section break).

- **Even Page:** The new section starts on the next even-numbered page.

- **Odd Page:** The new section starts on the next odd-numbered page.

Obviously, the type of section break you select depends on the type of document you are creating. If your document has a table of contents followed by the body, using a Next Page section (starting the body of the document on a new page) makes sense. Even page and odd page sections are often used when you create a document with facing pages. Different headers and footers are then created for the even pages and the odd pages.

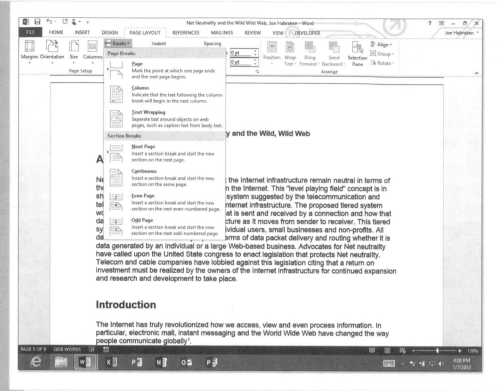

Figure 8.14
The Breaks
gallery.

> *For more about headers and footers, **see** "Creating Headers and Footers," p. 176.*

After you select one of the section break types in the Breaks gallery, the section break is inserted into the document. As already mentioned, you can view the section break in Draft view. This view doesn't give you any insight into the different page layout settings configured before and after the section break, but it is the only way for you to see where the section break has been inserted into the document (in Print Layout view, section breaks look the same as page breaks). To delete a section break in Draft view, select the section break and then press Delete. This removes the section from the document. It also removes all the page layout formatting that was applied to the section. In effect, removing the section resets the text that was in that section. The text does not adhere to the layout attributes that were configured for the section directly above the text that were contained in the deleted section.

Formatting Page Attributes in a Section

After you establish a new section in the document, you can specify the various page layout settings for that section. When you want to format a particular section, make sure you have the insertion point in that section.

Some of the common page layout settings and other document attributes that differ from section to section in the document require use of the Page Setup commands on the Page Layout tab. These commands enable you to change margins, page orientation, and number of columns for each section. Other settings that you might want to configure differently for document sections relate to headers, footers, and page numbering. These commands are located in the Header & Footer group on the Insert tab.

Remember that, to view the actual location of a section break, you use the Draft view. To view the effect of the page layout settings for a section, you use Print Layout view or the Print Preview pane in the Print window (in the Backstage).

9

MANAGING MAILINGS AND FORMS

Creating form letters, mailing labels, and envelopes can be daunting tasks. However, Word takes a straightforward approach to creating all the printed materials necessary for a mass mailing to a group of customers, colleagues, or friends. Word also makes it easy to gather information electronically by creating forms that can be circulated on your network or via email. You can create questionnaires or other materials that make it effortless for the recipient of the form to provide you with the information you need.

In this chapter, we look at how to create mail-related documents such as envelopes and labels. We also perform a mail merge in which you merge names and addresses with a form letter or email message. We wrap up the chapter with a look at how to create forms using form controls.

Options for Mail-Related Documents

Most tasks undertaken in Word relate to communicating with others—creating documents such as letters, emails, and forms. Word gives you all the tools required for letters, envelopes, and mailing labels: You can quickly create any snail mail–related document that you require.

Word also enables you to quickly merge a data source, such as a list of names and addresses, into a document such as a form letter. Merges can also be accomplished using data from Microsoft Outlook that is then merged into an email. Word definitely has you covered in terms of mass mailings.

For mail-related documents, Microsoft Word provides several letter templates. You can use these templates to create a letter to send to an individual or a form letter that can play a part in a merge that produces a number of letters based on a list of names and addresses.

Along the same lines, Word enables you to quickly create a single envelope for a letter or to merge addresses into an envelope form that creates envelopes for your entire mailing list. The same goes for labels; you can create labels that repeat a single address (such as your return address), or you can create labels for each person on your mailing list.

In addition, Word has the capability to build forms. Using form controls on your forms makes it easy for respondents (such as network users or email recipients) to quickly fill the form with responses. These controls can specify lists of responses so that your data collection using the form is more consistent across your respondent pool.

Creating an Envelope

When you create a letter in Word, it typically contains the name and address of the individual whom you want to receive your letter. Having the name and address available in the letter makes it easy for you to then create an envelope for that letter.

Creating the letter and then using the address information in the letter in the envelope makes sense. You can also add the envelope to the letter in a separate section that enables you to print both the envelope and letter at your convenience (or save for later reference). In creating the letter, you can use your own format or one of Word's letter templates.

To create the envelope, select the Envelopes command on the Ribbon's Mailings tab (in the Create group). The Envelopes and Labels dialog box opens, as shown in Figure 9.1. Note that the Envelopes tab of the dialog box is selected.

 tip
You can quickly insert the current date into the letter using the Date and Time command in the Text group of the Insert tab.

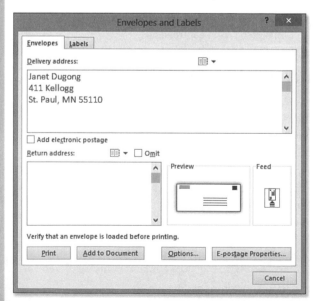

Figure 9.1
The Envelopes and Labels dialog box.

If a delivery address was present in your letter, it should appear in the Delivery address box (in the dialog box). You can type in the address, if needed, or you can use the Address Book icon to add the address from Outlook. You can also type your address in the Return Address box, or you can use the Address Book icon to add your address to the box using your Outlook profile.

The Envelopes and Labels dialog box enables you to add electronic postage to the envelope. To specify the options for your envelope, such as the size and the fonts used, select the Options button in the Envelopes and Labels dialog box. This opens the Envelope Options dialog box (see Figure 9.2).

Figure 9.2
The Envelopes Options dialog box.

You can specify the envelope size and the fonts to use for both the delivery address and the return address. You can also specify the distance from the left and top of the envelope for the addresses. Click OK to return to the Envelopes and Labels dialog box.

You can now print the envelope, if you want. Click the Print button in the Envelopes and Labels dialog box. If you want to add the envelope to the current document (your letter), click the Add to Document button. When you select this option, you are creating a new section in the document (remember that different sections can have different page layout settings). Having the envelope as part of the current document means that you can print the envelope and the letter during the same print job.

Creating a Label or Labels

In Word, you can create a single label for an address or other information. You can also choose to create or print a sheet of labels that all use the same, single address (or other information). This is particularly useful if you want to print a sheet of labels with your return address. If you send mail to a particular addressee frequently, it also doesn't hurt to have ready-made labels on hand for that purpose.

To create the labels (or a single label), click the Labels command on the Ribbon's Mailings tab (print a single label by selecting Single label). The Envelopes and Labels dialog box opens with the Label tab selected. You can enter the address for the label (or sheet of labels) in the Address box or use the Address Book icon (it is just to the left of the Use Return Address check box) to add an address from Outlook.

The default setting for printing labels is to print a full page of the same label. You can print the labels via the Print button or save them as a new document (use the New Document button) and then print them as needed.

After you have specified the address for the full page of labels or a single label, you will want to specify the type of label you will actually use in your printer. Select the Options button (or click the default label shown in the Label box); the Label Options dialog box opens (see Figure 9.3).

The Label Options dialog box enables you to specify the label vendor and the product number of the labels you are using. Select the vendor in the Label Vendors list, and then scroll through the Product Number list and identify your label.

You can access the details for a particular label by selecting the Details button. You can adjust the margins, pitch, height, and width for your label. This should not be necessary if you are using a standard label.

caution

You might think that creating labels in Word is a pretty simple process. However, labels have always been somewhat problematic in Word. I recommend that you purchase labels made by a company on the vendor list and also use labels that appear in the Product Number list. It will make your life a lot easier.

tip

If you have a letter open in Word that contains your return address, you can click the Use Return Address check box to have your address placed in the label's Address box.

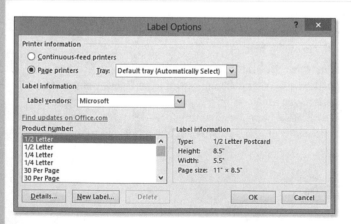

Figure 9.3
The Label Options dialog box.

When you select your label vendor and type (of label), you can choose to immediately print the labels (via the Print button). You also have the option to create a new document (use the New Document button) for the labels. This enables you to save the labels for future printing.

Understanding Word's Options for Mass Mailings

 tip

If you choose the Single label option on the Labels tab of the Envelopes and Labels dialog box, you can specify the row and column of the label that you use on the label sheet when you print. This is handy if you will be using one label at a time and want to use all the labels on the sheet.

We normally equate mass or group mailings with form letters that are then sent by snail mail. In fact, Word's mail merge feature enables you to create a variety of documents, including the typical form letter. Other possibilities include envelopes, labels, and directories. You can also merge information into an email and send it to addressees in a database file or your Outlook Contact list.

To perform a mail merge, you need two things: a mass-produced merge document (one that is created for each recipient, such as a form letter) and the data that goes into the document. The document that is merged with the data can take any form; it is most often a letter or an envelope, but you can merge data into any type of Word document.

As already mentioned, you also need data for a mail merge. This can be a list of names and addresses or a list of email addresses. The data, such as the names and addresses, is stored in a file called a data source. So the big question is, how does the data in the data source know where to end up in a document such as the form letter?

The information in the data source is inserted into the form letter, envelope, or mailing label using placeholder codes called merge fields. Each merge field in the merge document relates to a piece of information in the data source document, such as first name, last name, or street address, and the merge field gets its name from that particular field in the data source.

Performing a Mail Merge

The commands you use to perform a mail merge are found in the Start Mail Merge group (on the Ribbon's Mailings tab). As already mentioned, the merge process requires that you have a document such as a form letter and that you also have a data source. The process of performing the mail merge consists of four distinct parts: creating or opening the merge document; creating or specifying the data source; inserting the merge fields into the main document; and running the merge, which creates the form letters, envelopes, and so on.

Each of these four actions can—and probably does—require that you perform a subset of tasks. For example, to create merged letters during the merge process, you must supply the initial form letter. You can accomplish this by creating the letter during the merge process or by opening an existing letter.

When you need to specify your list of recipients (the data source), you might create the recipients list on the fly, or you might already have the list available (and it might even be in another application, such as Microsoft Outlook). Even if you have the list of recipients available, you might want to edit the list or specify that the merge use a subset of the available recipients. Obviously, what happens during each major phase of the merge is dictated by your particular needs related to the merge document, the recipient list, and the merge fields you are going to use.

To perform the mail merge, you use the Mail Merge Wizard, which walks you through the entire process. To invoke the Mail Merge Wizard, select the Start Mail Merge command and then select Step by Step Mail Merge Wizard. The Mail Merge task pane opens, as shown in Figure 9.4.

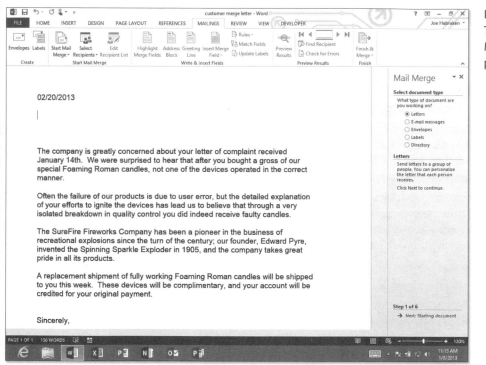

Figure 9.4
The Mail Merge task pane.

The wizard breaks the mail merge process into six distinct steps:

1. **Select Document Type:** This step provides option buttons that enable you to specify the type of merge document you want to create: Letters, Email Messages, Envelopes, Labels, or Directory. A directory does not create a separate document for each of the recipients; an example is a list of names and addresses created from your data source.

2. **Select Starting Document:** Here you specify how you set up the merge document. You can select from the following options: Use the Current Document, Start from Template, or Start from Existing Document.

3. **Select Recipients:** This step not only provides the list of recipients for the merge, but also determines the merge field codes (based on the data source's fields) that are available to insert into the merge document. You can use an existing list, select from Outlook contacts, or type a new list.

4. **Write Your Letter:** In this step, you type your merge document, such as a letter or email, or set up your envelope or labels (if you haven't already done it). This is also the step where you insert merge fields into the document. Merge files included in the task pane are the Address Block, Greeting Line, and Electronic Postage.

> *We look more closely at merge fields in this chapter in the section "Using Merge Fields."*

5. **Preview Your Letters:** This step previews your letters (or other merged documents, such as envelopes or labels). Use the Next and Previous buttons as required to preview the results of the merge.

6. **Complete the Merge:** Finally, you either send the results of the merge to a printer or edit each of the individual documents that resulted from the merge (such as your letter, envelopes, and so on).

caution

Although the Mail Merge Wizard makes sure that you complete all the steps necessary to perform the merge, you might find more flexibility in completing the merge process if you forgo the wizard and use the various commands on the Mailings tab. Let's take a closer look at each major part of the mail merge process and add some depth to your knowledge of the various commands on the Ribbon's Mailings tab.

Using the Mail Merge Commands

If you find the Mail Merge Wizard a hindrance rather than a help, you can forgo using the Mail Merge Wizard and run through the merge process "manually" by using the commands in the Start Mail Merge group. You go through the same overall process to create merged form letters, envelopes, or labels. You simply select your commands from left to right on the Mailings tab as you move through the mail merge process.

To begin the process, select the Start Mail Merge command in the Start Mail Merge group (see Figure 9.5). As you do when you use the wizard, you select the type of document you want to create using the merge: Letters, Email Messages, Envelopes, Labels, or Directory. The Start Mail Merge command provides an additional option: Normal Word Document.

tip

A form letter always contains the current date (typically at the top of the letter). To insert the date into your form letter so that it automatically updates, open the Date and Time dialog box using the Date & Time command on the Insert tab. Select a date format in the dialog box and then select the Update Automatically check box.

For best practices, create your letter or email before you even think about the merge process. In the final analysis, the content of the letter or email is of primary importance (although you do want the merge to work correctly). Make sure that you spend the appropriate amount of thought and time on the correspondence itself.

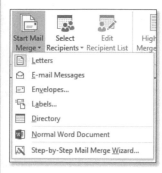

Figure 9.5
Select the type of merge you want to perform.

The two most problematic parts of performing the merge relate to creating and manipulating the recipient list and then inserting (appropriately) the merge fields into your document. Let's look at some issues related to recipient lists and then work with merge fields.

Understanding Recipient Lists

The data source or recipient list (if you prefer) consists of the information that you merge into your form letter, email, envelope, or other document type (for example, you can merge into a memo or a phone list). As already mentioned, data sources used in mail merges are typically names and addresses, but they can also include other information, such as email addresses and telephone numbers. Data sources can include any information that is important and necessary for the merge.

I want to introduce a couple terms that can help you work with data sources: records and fields. A record is the information related to a particular person (or place or thing). So each person in your recipient list has his or her own record.

More important (at least, for understanding the merge process), each piece of information in a record, such as the first name or street address, is called a field. The fields in the data source relate directly to the merge field codes available to insert into your form letter or envelope. Each field code, then, directly relates to information (a field) in each record in your recipient list.

When specifying a recipient list for a particular merge, you have options. You can access these options via the Select Recipients command in the Start Mail Merge group (see Figure 9.6).

 note

If you are using the Mail Merge Wizard, the recipient list is created or specified in step 3 of the wizard's merge process provided in the Mail Merge task pane.

Figure 9.6
Select or create a recipients list.

The options related to the recipient list are as follows:

- **Type a New List:** Use this option to create a new data source using the recipient list tools in Word. We explore this option in more detail in a moment.

- **Use Existing List:** This option enables you to open an existing list created in Word or data sources created in Microsoft Access. The Select Data Source dialog box also provides options for connecting to shared data sources (on your corporate network) via a Microsoft Office Data Connection or a Microsoft SQL database server.

- **Choose from Outlook Contacts:** With this option, you select the names and addresses for the merge from your Outlook contacts. When you select the option on the Select Recipients menu, the Choose Profile dialog box opens so that you can choose the Outlook profile that provides the contacts for the merge. After you select the profile, the Select Contacts dialog box opens to enable you to select an Outlook contact folder to import.

> *Outlook permits multiple Outlook profiles on the same computer. For more about Outlook profiles, **see** "Understanding Outlook Profiles," p. 642.*

Obviously, using existing lists or data sources that are shared on a network makes it easier for you to quickly access the records that you need to include in a merge. However, sometimes you must create the recipient list using the tools Word provides. Thankfully, these tools help you easily create, edit, and manipulate the records in the data source.

> **🔍 note**
>
> You can create mail merge data sources in Word, Excel, and Access (Microsoft's relational database product). You can also import data from a variety of database sources into Excel and Access. For more about Excel and external databases, see Chapter 15, "Using Excel Tables and PivotTables."

Creating a Recipient List

Creating a data source during the Mail Merge process is a straightforward task. Word provides you with a form that you use to enter people's names, addresses, and other information. When you select Type New List on the Select Recipients command menu or in the Mail Merge task pane, the New Address List dialog box opens, as shown in Figure 9.7.

Word provides a default set of fields for the recipient list. The field list includes files such as Title, First Name, Last Name, and so on. If you want to use the default fields (which also serve as the column headings in the New Address List dialog box), you can enter the name, address, and other information that you want to place in the record for the first recipient. To move forward through the field columns, use the Tab key. To back up in a field or fields in a record, use the Shift+Tab keys. You then create subsequent entries by selecting the New Entry button in the Address List dialog box. Each time you click New Entry, a new row is added to the address list.

If you want to modify the field list, it is important that you do so before you begin to enter field information into the address list. Select Customize Columns in the New Address List dialog box, and the Customize Address List opens, as shown in Figure 9.8.

Figure 9.7
Create your records in the New Address List dialog box.

Figure 9.8
The Customize Address List dialog box.

You can add, delete, or rename field names in the list. You can also use the Move Up and Move Down buttons to change the relative position of the field columns. If you want to add a field, click the Add button. The Add Field dialog box opens. Enter the name for your new field and click OK. You can use the Delete and Rename buttons as needed to modify the field list for your own particular needs. When you finish modifying the default field names, click OK to return to the New Address List dialog box.

Whether or not you modify the list's fields, enter your records as needed in the New Address List dialog box. If you want to delete a particular record, select that record and then click Delete Entry. When you finish entering your records, click the Close button on the New Address List dialog box.

The Save Address List dialog box opens (see Figure 9.9). By default, your data sources are saved in the My Data Sources folder, which is a subfolder of your My Documents folder.

Figure 9.9
The Save Address List dialog box.

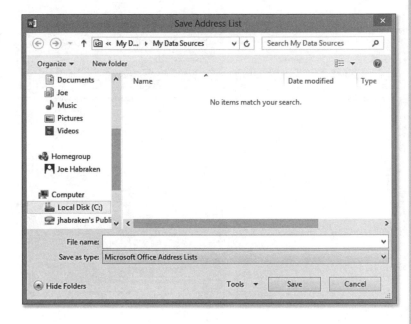

Provide a name for the data source and specify a new location for the file (if required). The file type for the new file is Microsoft Office Address Lists, which is saved with the .mdb extension (the same as Microsoft Access databases). To save the new data source, click the Save button.

Editing and Manipulating a Recipient List

After you create or select a recipient list for the merge, the Edit Recipient List command in the Start Mail Merge group is activated. When you select it, the Mail Merge Recipients dialog box opens, as shown in Figure 9.10.

This dialog box enables you to refine the recipient list using tools such as Sort, Filter, and Find Duplicates. You can also access individual records in the data source and edit them when needed.

You can sort the records in the recipients list by up to three sort criteria. Select Sort to open the Filter and Sort dialog box. You can use the Sort By drop-down list to specify the first field to sort by and then use the optional two Then By drop-down lists to specify a second and third field for the sort, if necessary. In addition, you can specify whether the sort should be ascending or descending using the supplied option buttons. When you are ready to perform the sort, click OK. The records in the Mail Merge Recipients dialog box sort according to your sort parameters.

 note

The Mail Merge Recipients dialog box also enables you to validate addresses in the address list. To do this, you need validation add-on software. Visit www.microsoft.com for more information about address validation options for Office.

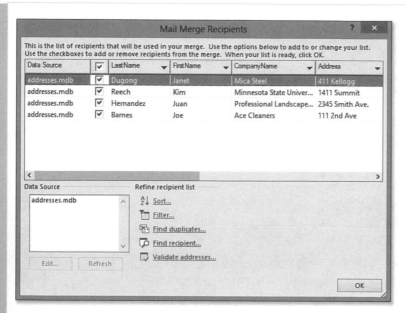

If you want to preclude specific records from being included in the merge, deselect the check box for that record or records. This is a quick fix for removing a recipient from the merge but keeping the record intact in the recipient's list.

You can also filter the records in the data source. This enables you to select a subset of recipients to include in the merge based on specific criteria related to a field or fields. You can filter by up to six fields.

To open the Filter and Sort dialog box with the Filter Records tab selected, select Filter (in the Mail Merge Recipients dialog box). You then specify the field or fields by which you want to filter the data source by using the Field drop-down lists, as shown in Figure 9.11.

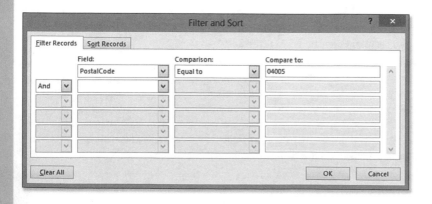

After you select a field, you can specify the type of comparison you want to make to that field's content. You can specify a number of comparisons, including Equal To, Not Equal To, Less Than, Is Blank, and Contains. After you select the Comparison Type (such as Equal To), you type the text to be used by the comparison in the Compare To box for that particular field. For example, you might want to send letters to people on your list who have a particular ZIP code, so you would select the Postal Code field, set the Comparison Type as Equal To, and then type the ZIP code in the Compare To box. You could also create a filter to filter the list for a specific state or use the Not Equal To comparison parameter to filter out people in the list who reside in a specific state (filtering gives you many possibilities for specifying or precluding records in the address list that meet a particular condition or conditions).

note

You can set up conditional statements for your filters combining field criteria using AND, or you can set up a conditional OR statement in which the field criteria can be equal to a particular field or another selected field. Bottom line: You can create some elegant filters using the tools on the Filter Records tab.

After you set your filter parameters, click OK. The records listed in the mail Merge Recipients dialog box are a subset of the original list, based on the criteria you set for your filter.

The Mail Merge Recipients dialog box also gives you access to the Edit Data Source dialog box (which is similar to the New Address List dialog box discussed earlier). In the Edit Data Source box, select the current data source and then click the Edit button. Use the Edit Data Source dialog box to edit records as needed. You can also add records in the Edit Data Source dialog box using the New Entry button.

Using Merge Fields

When the data source is ready for the merge, the next step in the merge process revolves around inserting the appropriate merge fields into the form letter or other merge document. The Field codes are inserted via the Write & Insert group on the Ribbon's Mailings tab.

If you are creating form letters, envelopes, or mailing labels, one of the most often used set of field codes is the Address Block. The Address Block combines the name, company name, and address information, including the state and ZIP Code.

To insert the Address Block in your document (typically three lines below the date in a letter), position the insertion point appropriately and then click the Address Block command. The Insert Address Block dialog box opens, as shown in Figure 9.12.

tip

If your filter doesn't give you the expected results, click Filter to open the Filter and Sort dialog box and then edit the filter settings. If you want to completely clear the filter and return to your original list, click the Clear All command and then click OK.

The Insert Address Block dialog box provides you with different formats for inserting the recipient's name and address information. Choose one of the formats listed. You can also specify whether the Company Name field is included in the address block and whether to include country/region in the address.

When you finish configuring the address block, click OK to insert it into the merge document. The merge code <<AddressBlock>> is placed at the insertion point.

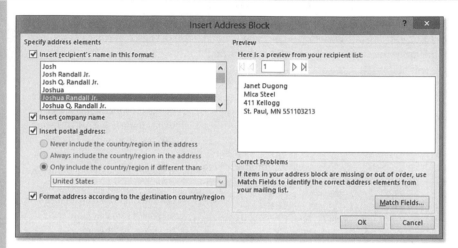

Figure 9.12
The Insert Address Block dialog box.

Another useful merge command is the Greeting Line command. It inserts a salutation such as Dear or To and enables you to specify how the name field data is included with the greeting. In addition, you can control the punctuation used after the greeting (comma, colon, or none). As with the Address Block, the Greeting Line has its own dialog box.

Be advised that the Address Block and Greeting Line are configured to use the default field names that Word supplies you when you create a recipients list (in Word). If your data source originated in another application, such as Microsoft Outlook, Microsoft Access, or an external SQL database, you must match the field names that you used to the typical Word merge fields that specify information such as the recipient's name or address. Click the Match Fields button in the Address Block or Greeting Line dialog box. This opens the Match Fields dialog box (see Figure 9.13). You can also open the Match Fields dialog box using the Match Fields command in the Write & Insert Fields group.

The Word mail merge fields are listed on the left side of the Match Fields dialog box. You use the drop-down boxes to specify the matching field from your data source. Each drop-down list shows all the field names for your recipients list that need to be reconciled with the field names that Word uses. For example, if you used the field name Address for the street and street number in your data source, you match it to the Address 1 Word field. After you match all the fields, you close the Match Fields dialog box by clicking OK.

 tip

You can use the Preview pane in the Insert Address Block dialog box to preview all records in your recipient list. This enables you to catch any records that have blank address fields or other typos.

You can also insert individual field codes into a merge document, if required. Place the insertion point in the merge document where you want to insert the field code. Select the Insert Merge Field command on the Mailings tab, and select a merge field from the list provided. Remember that merge field codes can relate to any data. For example, you can set up a data source that includes information such as the names of your clients' spouses or their favorite sports, and then insert that information into an appropriately crafted merge letter. This enables you to personalize each of the form letters or other merge documents that you create.

Figure 9.13
The Match Fields dialog box.

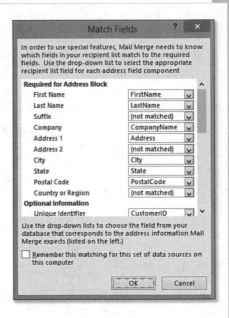

Using Merge Rules

One other merge tool that can help you personalize your merge documents and control the content of the documents created during the merge is the Rules command, found in the Write & Insert Fields group. With this command, you can take advantage of several rules that control the content of merged documents during the actual merge process.

When you click the Rules command, the list of rules appears. The following rules, which are special fields, are provided on the list:

- **Ask:** This field prompts you so that you can enter text during the merge. When you create an Ask field, you create a bookmark that can include a default response; the field appears as an empty bookmark in the merge document.

- **Fill-in:** This field prompts you to enter text that is placed in your document (replacing the field code) after you have completed the merge. The Fill-in field can contain default text, if you want. Figure 9.14 shows the Insert Word Field: Fill-in box. You provide prompt text for the field (that is, the field prompts you for the text to be entered), and you have the option to provide default fill-in text.

 tip

You can also reconcile your field names to the Word field names via the Match Fields command in the Write & Insert Fields group. This command opens the Match Fields dialog box. If you consistently used data sources that utilize the same field names, select the Remember This Matching for This Set of Data Sources on This Computer check box so that you won't have to match the fields each time you do a merge.

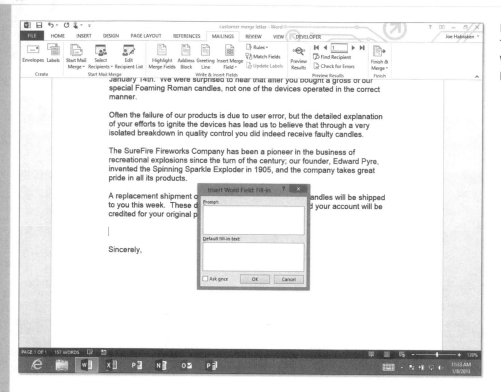

Figure 9.14
The Insert
Word Field:
Fill-in box.

- **If...Then...Else:** This field enables you to enter two different text blocks into the merged documents, depending on whether a condition is met. For example, if you have an actual storefront in a particular state for your business, this field can insert a location (and address) for the store when the recipient's state matches the If statement.

- **Merge Record #:** You use this field to provide a true count of the number of records in the data file even when you use fields such as Skip Record If to merge certain recipients into the same letter or other merged document.

- **Merge Sequence #:** This field counts the actual number of merged documents that result from your merge.

- **Next Record:** This field has Word insert the next data record into the current merged document without starting a new page. This field is used by default when you create mailing labels during a merge.

- **Next Record If:** This field enables you to set a conditional statement; if the statement is met, the next record is merged into the current document without beginning a new document. This can be useful when more than one recipient in your list works at the same company. You can send a single letter to all the recipients that meet the If condition of working at that particular company.

- **Set Bookmark:** This field can control the text referred to by a bookmark, such as the bookmark created by the Ask field. You can also use the Set Bookmark field with a conditional statement such as the If...Then...Else field.

- **Skip Record If:** You use this field to set a conditional statement so that recipients that meet the condition are not included in the merge.

Some of these special fields are useful to you, and some you might not need. Experimenting with these fields, particularly Fill-in and If...Then...Else, definitely makes sense because they can give you added capability to personalize the letters that result from your merge.

 tip

You can highlight the fields that you placed in the merge document when you are previewing the results of the merge. Select the Highlight Merge Fields command in the Write & Insert Fields group. Click the command again to turn off the highlighting.

Previewing Merge Results

When you have your merge document, recipient list, and merge field codes squared away, you can preview the merge results. Select the Preview Results command in the Preview Results group.

You can then use the Next Record and Previous Record buttons to preview each of the resulting merged documents. You can also use the Find Recipient command to open the Find Entry dialog box. You can then search for information in all the merge fields or a specific field. To toggle off the Preview Results feature, click Preview Results.

Another tool that you can use to check the merge results (which can simulate the merge or complete the merge and report errors) is the Auto Check for Errors command. When you select Auto Check for Errors, the Checking and Reporting Errors dialog box opens, as shown in Figure 9.15.

The dialog box provides three options:

- **Simulate the Merge and Report Errors in a New Document:** This option performs the merge and displays a message box detailing whether errors occurred during the merge. When you click OK, you return to your merge document.

- **Complete the Merge, Pausing to Report Each Error As It Occurs:** This option pauses the merge each time an error is detected and then creates a merged document.

- **Complete the Merge Without Pausing. Report Errors in a New Document:** This option completes the merge and details any errors in the newly created merged document.

Each of these options provides feedback regarding whether an issue arose with the merge. They are also useful in saving paper because the merge doesn't go directly to the printer.

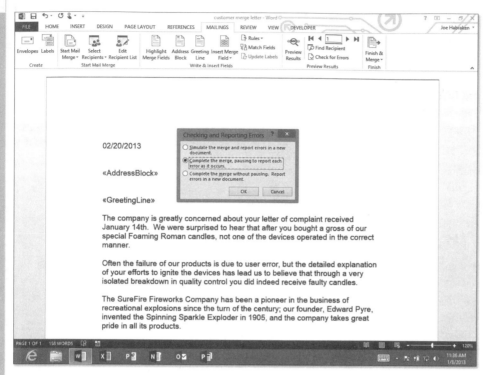

Figure 9.15
The Checking and Reporting Errors dialog box.

Completing the Merge

If you chose either of the Complete the Merge options in the Checking and Reporting Errors dialog box (the second and third options), you have essentially completed the merge. You can save the resulting merged document and then print the document as needed (or, if the merge process has errors, you can correct the errors and run the merge again).

You're not required to check the merge for errors, so you can complete the merge using the Finish & Merge command in the Finish group (it is the only command in this group). Select Finish & Merge and then select one of the following from the list provided:

■ **Edit Individual Documents:** This creates a new merged document. Probably the best choice, it gives you an opportunity to look through the results of the merge before printing.

■ **Print Documents:** This sends the merge results to your printer.

■ **Send Email Messages:** If you performed an email merge, this option sends the resulting emails through your Outlook email client.

After you make your selection, you are finished. You have completed the merge process.

Creating Merged Envelopes and Labels

The procedure for creating envelopes and mailing labels is much the same as the process for creating form letters. You can use the Mail Merge Wizard, or you can cycle through the commands on the Mailings tab of the Ribbon as you complete each step (Start Mail Merge, Select Recipients, and so on.).

For merged envelopes, a crucial step is selecting the appropriate envelope type. When you select Envelopes in either the Start Mail Merge list or the wizard's task pane, the Envelope Options dialog box opens. This dialog box enables you to select the envelope size and select the fonts for the delivery and return addresses. Figure 9.16 shows the Envelope Options dialog box.

Figure 9.16
The Envelope Options dialog box.

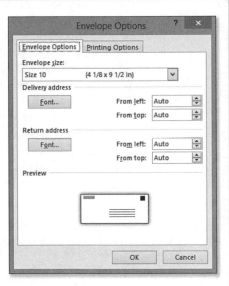

The dialog box also provides a Printing Options tab where you can specify the feed method and the orientation of the envelope in the printer. You can also select the printer tray that contains the envelopes.

After you select the envelope type, click OK to close the Envelope Options dialog box; the envelope then appears in the Word workspace. You can select or create your recipient list and insert the merge fields onto the envelope.

When you select labels for your merge document, the Label Options dialog box enables you to select the label vendor and product number and to specify the tray for the labels. Labels are a bit tricky when inserting your merge fields (after you create or select your data source). Insert the merge field or fields (in most cases, you will probably use the Address Block only) onto the first label.

Now here is the important step in getting the labels to work: Click the Update Labels command in the Write & Insert Fields group. This places the entered field code, such as the Address Block, on all the labels. Note that each label (other than the first label) is automatically assigned the Next Record field, which keeps the labels on the same page when you complete the merge.

Understanding Word Fields

The mail merge process provides a good look at some of the possibilities that can be accomplished using fields. Merge fields pull data from a recipient list and place the data in the merged documents. You can use other fields, such as the Skip Record If field, to preclude certain recipients in your list from being included in the merge (based on a condition).

Word provides a variety of other field types that you can use to enhance your documents and to build online forms. For example, when you insert the current date into a document using the Date and Time dialog box, you have the option of selecting the Update Automatically check box. This option means that Word inserts a date field into your document, and the field is updated (to the current date) each time you open the document. Page numbering in your document is also controlled by a field when you insert the page number using the Page Number command on the Ribbon's Insert tab. So you are using fields even in simple documents, although you might not be aware of it.

You can insert field codes into a document via the Field dialog box. To open this dialog box, access the Ribbon's Insert tab. Then select the Explore Quick Parts command (in the Text group) and select Field on the list provided. Figure 9.17 shows the Field dialog box.

Tip

You can format field codes as if they are text. For example, select a field code such as the Address Block and then make it bold. The resulting merged information appears in bold in the merged documents.

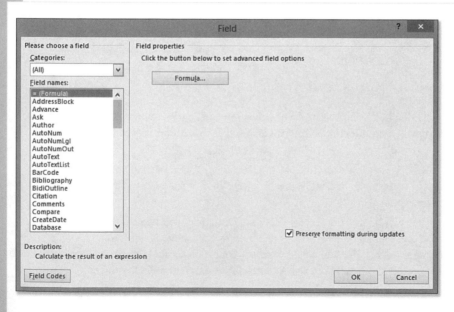

Figure 9.17
The Field dialog box.

Many fields are available in the Field Names list, particularly when you have the Categories selection set to All. You might want to concentrate on certain categories of fields that enable you to easily input information related to dates, document information, and user information. Many of these informational fields are best placed in the header or footer of a document and are particularly useful when users on a network share a document. The fields can serve a housekeeping function by specifying where the document is stored (the path) and which user saved the document in its current form.

For example, when you select the Document Information category, the available fields in the Field Names box include Author, FileName, LastSavedBy, NumPages, and other fields. These fields enable you to stamp a document with information that was stamped on the document at its creation (such as the author and the filename), as well as information that can change during the document's life (such as who last saved the document and the number of pages currently in the document).

 tip

If you are placing fields in a header or footer related to a document's properties, remember that the Document Info command on the Header & Footer Tools Design tab provides easy access to fields such as Author, Status, and Keywords.

You can view the field code for a selected field in the Field dialog box. Select a field and then click the Field Codes button. The field's code displays on the right of the dialog box. Click Hide Codes to return to the default field view.

To insert a field into a document, select the field in the Field Names list (in the Field dialog box) and then click OK. The field is inserted into the document at the insertion point.

When you insert the field, the results of the field (such as the date, page number, or filename) appear in the document. To view the field codes (which help you manage the fields), you can press Alt+F9. To toggle back to the field results, press Alt+F9 again.

 note

You can use ActiveX controls to create a form that is then saved as an HTML document. It can be used on a website as an online form.

You can also change Word's options so that field codes are shown in a document: Select File to open the Backstage view and then select Options. In the Word Options window, select Advanced. In the Show Document Content area, select the Show Field Codes Instead of Their Values check box. You can also specify how fields should be shaded in the document using the Field Shading drop-down box (which is just below the Show Field Codes Instead of Their Values check box in the Options list).

You can delete field codes as you would any Word text. You can also copy, cut, and paste fields as needed.

Building a Form with Form Controls

You can build online forms using form fields, also referred to as form controls. The control is a placeholder for the text that is input by the user of the form. Form controls can consist of text fields, check boxes, or drop-down lists. Your form controls can also include help text, which is useful in getting the appropriate type of response for a particular field on the form.

The various form fields or controls are accessed via the Developer tab of the Ribbon. This tab is not included on the Ribbon by default, so you need to enable it. Select File to go to Word's Backstage. Then click Options.

In the Word Options window, select Customize Ribbon in the Customize Ribbon list (on the right of the window). Select Developer in the Main Tab list. Then click OK. This puts the Developer tab on the Ribbon.

To create a form that any number of users can use (which is particularly useful in a setting where you work on a network), you need to create a template. Open a new blank document and then save the document in the Save As dialog box; be sure to change the Save As Type setting to Word Template.

When the new template is ready to go, you can insert the various form fields that you want to use on the form. Follow these steps:

1. Select the Ribbon's Developer tab. In the Controls group, select Design Mode.

2. The Controls group provides all the control fields you need. Click a control to insert it. The controls are as follows:

   - **Rich Text:** Provides a text block control, and is typically used for text entry that you do not want changed or accessed.

   - **Plain Text:** Provides a text block control.

   - **Picture Content:** Enables the user to select an image to insert into the form.

   - **Building Block Gallery:** Enables the user to select text blocks from a building block gallery.

   - **Check Box:** Provides a check box for user response.

   - **Combo Box:** Enables the user to select a response from a drop-down list or type in a text response.

   - **Drop-Down List:** Provides a list of responses for the user.

   - **Date Picker:** Enables the user to select a date from an interactive calendar.

   - **Repeating Section:** New control type, designed to repeat multiple instances of content (including control content and field information). To take advantage of this control (which is an advanced feature), you must build an XML script that provides the repeating information to the Repeating Section control.

   - **Legacy Tools:** Supplies a list of legacy Word form controls and ActiveX controls, such as the Option button and the Toggle button.

3. Insert all your form fields, as needed, to complete the form.

 note

By default, field codes (that is, their result) are shaded with a gray background when you select the field text.

 note

When designing your form layout, you might want to scratch it out on a piece of paper before creating it in Word. Remember that using various drop-down lists and check boxes on the form require the form to have an easy-to-use layout. You might want to use a table to position the various form fields on the page.

4. Save the document as a new template (change the Save As Type setting to Word Template in the Save As dialog box).

After you insert all the form controls on the template page (or pages), you must go back and set the properties for each of the controls (although you can set the properties for each field as you insert them). For example, if you inserted a Drop-Down List field, you must provide the list of responses that the field provides when selected by the user. Select the field control and then click the Properties command in the Controls group. The Content Control Properties dialog box opens, as shown in Figure 9.18.

Figure 9.18
The Content Control Properties dialog box.

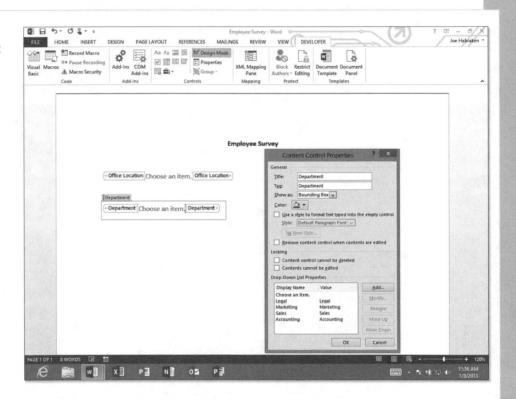

In the Content Control Properties dialog box, you can add an optional title and tag name for the control. You can lock the control using the Content Control Cannot Be Deleted and Contents Cannot Be Edited check boxes. To remove the default value (Choose an Item), select it in the Drop-Down List Properties. Then use the Add button to add the responses you want to include in the drop-down list.

You can change the order of the responses using the Move Up and Move Down buttons. After you edit the control's properties to suit your needs, click OK.

When you have the controls inserted and configured, restrict the editing on the template so that users cannot change it (other than allowing user response) when it is in use. Select the Restrict

Editing command in the Protect group. The Restrict Formatting and Editing task pane opens. In the Editing Restrictions area of the task pane, select the Allow Only This Type of Editing in the Document check box. Then select Filling in Forms from the drop-down list and click Yes, Start Enforcing Protection to protect the template. You must enter a password (twice) in the Start Enforcing Protection dialog box. Save the template, and it is ready for use.

10

CREATING SPECIAL DOCUMENTS

Word provides several features and tools that are designed for creating complex and specialized documents. For example, if you create a large document that requires a table of contents, Word has you covered. Word also enables you to easily divide a large document into different sections; each section can then have its own formatting, including page-layout attributes such as margins and page orientation.

In this chapter, we explore how to create documents that consist of more than just a couple pages. We look at creating a table of contents, adding sections to a document, and working with a table of figures. We also discuss how to create cross-references, indexes, citations, bibliographies, footnotes, and endnotes, and how to track the changes made by multiple authors.

Options for Large Documents

Larger, more formal documents typically have special parts, such as a table of contents, table of figures, index, and/or bibliography. These documents might also require specialized notations, such as cross-references and footnotes or endnotes.

To make it easier to work with more complex documents, you can use bookmarks to quickly navigate to a specific spot (or spots) in the document. You can also add nonprinting comments to the document to help you remember the status of a particular page or the need to revise particular content in the document.

> ➡ *When you work with larger documents, you typically use sections to break the document into different parts so that each section can have its own headers, footers, and page-numbering scheme. Sections are discussed in Chapter 8, "Working with Tables, Columns, and Sections."*

If you are working with a large document, you can keep the different parts of the document in separate files and then use the master document commands on the Outlining tab (available when you switch to the Outline view) to link other documents (such as the chapters of a document) to the current document.

When you are collaborating with other users, you can take advantage of the Track Changes feature. Each user's changes are tracked in the document, and you can accept or reject these changes as needed. You can also compare different versions of the same document. We begin our discussion of Word features for larger documents with an exploration of how to create a table of contents.

Creating a Table of Contents

If you want to make it easy for the reader of a large document to find specific parts or chapters of the document, you really need to include a table of contents. Creating a table of contents in Word relies on the use of specific styles to show the organizational structure of your document. As long as you do this, creating a table of contents is straightforward.

For example, you can use Word's built-in heading styles (Heading 1, Heading 2, Heading 3, and so forth; see Figure 10.1) to format the different levels of headings in the document, or you can create your own styles to do so. Using these headings requires you to use some methodology to break down the contents of your document, such as using section levels or chapter levels. The important point is to use them consistently to format the various headings that you use in the document.

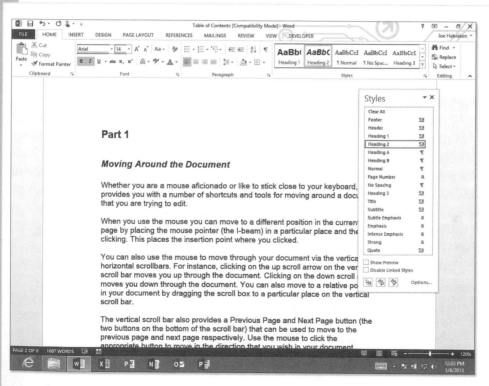

Figure 10.1
Assign styles to your document headings.

A good example is a document that is divided into parts and then further subdivided into chapters (each part contains several chapters). If you use Word's heading styles to format the different division levels in the document, you might use Heading 1 for the parts (Part I, Part II, and so on) and Heading 2 for the chapter titles. By assigning these built-in styles (or your own) to the different headings, you can generate a table of contents that shows two levels: parts and chapters. This process works because Word can pinpoint a particular heading level by the style you've assigned to it.

When you create a table of contents, the page numbers generated depend on the location of the headings formatted with the styles you have specified for the different levels of the table of contents. If you edit the document and move any of the headings, you need to update the table of contents so that it reflects the new page references (meaning page numbers). You can quickly regenerate an existing table of contents by selecting the Update Table button at the top of your generated table of contents or by using the Update Table command in the Table of Contents group. We discuss options for updating a table of contents later in this chapter in the section "Adding Entries and Updating the TOC."

➡️ *For more about styles,* **see** *"Understanding Styles," p. 199.*

So the first step in the process of creating a table of contents is to use styles (either built-in or your own) to mark and format the various heading levels in the document. You can quickly format the different headings in the document (if you haven't already) using the Heading styles on the Ribbon's Home tab in the Styles gallery. You can also mark the headings for the different TOC levels using the Add Text command in the Table of Contents group. Place the insertion point on a heading in the document and then select the Add Text command. Select Level 1, Level 2, or Level 3 to mark the level of the heading. The heading is also formatted using a built-in heading style. Level 1 is equivalent to Heading 1, Level 2 is equivalent to Heading 2—you get the picture. After you have assigned the headings the appropriate style, you can generate the table of contents.

Creating a Table of Contents with Built-in Styles

If you use Word's built-in styles (Heading 1, Heading 2, and so on), you can quickly insert a table of contents into the document. However, before you do so, I recommend that you create a blank page at the beginning of your document for your table of contents. An even better idea is to create a new section (a section break with a new page). That way, you can assign different headers and footers to the table of contents section of the document and use other headers and footers for the remainder of the document.

To insert the table of contents, follow these steps:

1. Park the insertion point where you want to insert the table of contents.

2. Select the Ribbon's References tab.

3. In the Table of Contents group, select the Table of Contents command.

4. From the Table of Contents gallery, choose one of the two built-in TOC styles provided to format the different levels of the TOC, as shown in Figure 10.2.

Tip

You can assign the built-in Word styles to your headings using the quick styles in the Styles group or by opening the Styles window and assigning the quick styles from the window.

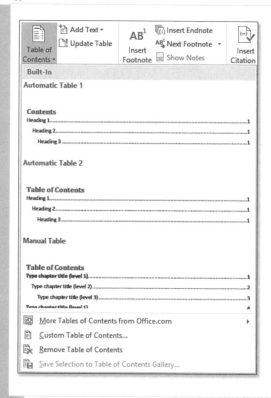

Figure 10.2
Select a TOC style from the gallery.

The table of contents is inserted into the document at the insertion point. The various levels of the table of contents are formatted by the TOC style that you selected in the Table of Contents gallery. When you select the table of contents (click within the table of contents area), a table toolbar appears at the top of the table. On the left of the toolbar is a button that provides access to the built-in table of contents styles and also a command that enables you to remove the table of contents. On the right is a button that enables you to update the table (Update Table) if you have edited the document or added other items to the table of contents using styles.

Creating a Table of Contents with Your Own Styles

The alternative to creating a table of contents based on Word's built-in quick styles (the heading styles) is to create your own styles and use them to format your headings and specify the different heading levels for the table of contents. As with generating a table of contents with built-in styles, the first step in the process is to assign the appropriate level style to each heading in the document.

The trick with using your own styles is that you need to let Word know that these styles replace the heading quick styles that it normally uses to generate the table of contents. You do this in the Table of Contents dialog box.

Park your insertion point where you want to insert the table of contents and then select the Table of Contents command. In the Command gallery, select Custom Table of Contents. This opens the Table of Contents dialog box with the Table of Contents tab selected, as shown in Figure 10.3.

Figure 10.3
The Table of Contents dialog box.

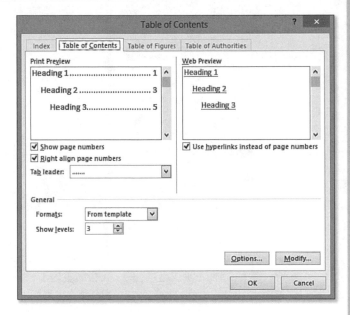

The Table of Contents tab gives you a preview of the table of contents hierarchy for Word's built-in heading styles (by default). It also gives you access to several options, such as whether to use page numbers in the table of contents and the style of tab leader to use. In addition, you can set the number of levels for the table of contents using the Show Levels spinner box.

To force Word to recognize your styles as the TOC levels, you must open the Table of Contents Options dialog box; click the Options button. Figure 10.4 shows the Table of Contents Options dialog box.

By default, Heading 1 is marked as TOC level 1, Heading 2 is marked as TOC level 2, and so on. Individually select the numbers in the TOC level boxes for the default headings and delete them. This removes the check mark for each of the built-in headings. To specify one of your styles as a TOC hierarchical level, type the level number (1, 2, 3, and so on) into the appropriate style's TOC level box. After you have assigned the various TOC levels to your styles, click OK to return to the Table of Contents dialog box. Click OK, and the table of contents (based on your styles) is inserted into the document.

 tip

The entries in your table of contents are links to the headings in the document that you used to generate the TOC. You can use these TOC entries to quickly move to that part of the document. Press the Ctrl key and then click the mouse on an entry to move to that page in the document.

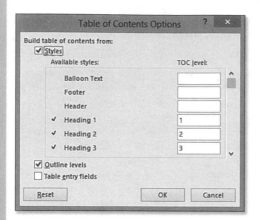

Figure 10.4
The Table of Contents Options dialog box.

Adding Entries and Updating the TOC

You can add entries to the table of contents even after you have inserted the TOC into the document. This is useful if you missed a heading when assigning styles to the TOC levels and, as a result, the heading was not included in the table of contents.

Select the heading and then click the Add Text command in the Table of Contents group. On the Add Text list, select the TOC level to assign to the selected heading (Level 1, Level 2, and so on). Note that the default is Do Not Show in Table of Contents.

Now that you have marked a new entry for the table of contents using the Add Text command, you need to update the TOC. Select the Update Table command in the Table of Contents group (or the Update Table button that appears at the top of your selected TOC). The Update Table of Contents dialog box opens, as shown in Figure 10.5.

Select the Update Entire Table option button. Then click OK to close the dialog box. The table of contents updates, and any headings that you added to the TOC using the Add Text command, are included in the TOC.

If you need to delete a table of contents, you can select the table of contents and then press Delete. You can also delete the TOC from the Table of Contents (command) gallery. Select Remove Table of Contents.

Figure 10.5
The Update
Table of
Contents dia-
log box.

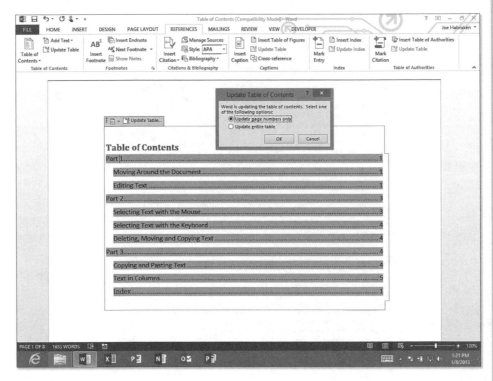

Building a TOC with Field Codes

Another option for building a table of contents in a document uses the TC field code. This method identifies the heading and the TOC level for the heading using the TC, which is placed to the right of the selected text. Because the code is nonprinting, its appearance in the document just serves as a marker. To view the TC field codes as you insert it in the document, click the Show/Hide command on the Ribbon's Home tab.

You can insert the TC field via the Field dialog box (as you can other field codes), but you must know some field switches and edit the field so that it provides the TOC-level information for the entry. Marking items for the table of contents with the TC field is much easier using the Mark Table of Contents Entry dialog box because it enables you to also select the level for the TOC entry.

> ![caution] **caution**
> If the heading you are adding to the TOC using the Add Text command is assigned a different style than the other headings at that level, it is not reformatted with that level's assigned style. Assign the style to the heading and then update the table instead of using the Add Text command.

 Fields are also discussed in Chapter 9, "Managing Mailings and Forms."

Select the text that you want to mark for the table of contents. Press Shift+Alt+O. The Mark Table of Contents Entry dialog box opens, as shown in Figure 10.6.

Figure 10.6
The Mark Table of Contents Entry dialog box.

The text you select appears in the Entry box. The Table identifier is set to C by default and can remain as is. Use the Level spinner box to specify the level for the entry. Then click OK. Repeat the process as needed to mark all the headings with the TC field and the appropriate TOC level. Click Close to close the Mark Table of Contents Entry dialog box.

To generate the table of contents, select the Table of Contents command on the References tab and select Custom Table of Contents. Doing so opens the Table of Contents dialog box.

On the Table of Contents tab, click the Options button. In the Table of Contents Options dialog box, clear the Outline Level check box and select the Table Entry Fields check box (because your TOC is based on field codes instead of styles). Click OK and then OK again to close the two dialog boxes. The TOC is inserted into the document.

Obviously, using styles to designate the TOC level for headings in your document is much more straightforward than using the TC field; however, you might want to generate two different TOCs in the same document. The Word table of contents feature enables you to create only one TOC per document, but you can generate a second TOC in the document if you know how to mark TOC entries with the TC field (and a couple other things that I discuss later).

The procedure for creating two TOCs in the same document is straightforward. Create the first TOC in the document using styles, and then insert the TOC using the Table of Contents command (as you would for a single table of contents). One TOC down, one to go.

Inserting the second TOC is a little trickier. Mark all the entries for the second TOC using the TC field (via the Mark Table of Contents Entry dialog box). Then place the insertion point where you want to insert the second TOC into the document.

Now you need to insert a TOC field code at the insertion point, which generates the second table of contents (using the entries marked with the TC code). Select the Explore Quick Parts command (on the Ribbon's Insert tab) and then select Field. The Field dialog box opens.

In the Categories box, select Index and Tables. Then in the Field Names box, select the TOC field. You must edit the TOC field code with a switch, so select the Field Codes button at the bottom of the dialog box. Then click Options.

In the Switches list, select the \f switch and click Add to Field. Click in the Field codes box and type C. (Remember that C was the table identifier designated in the Mark Table of Contents Entry dialog box.) Figure 10.7 shows the Field Options dialog box with the edited field code.

Figure 10.7
The Field Options dialog box.

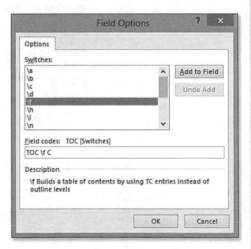

Click OK to return to the Field dialog box. Click OK to close the Field dialog box. When you return to the document, the second table of contents appears at the insertion point.

Working with Captions and Tables of Figures

Business-related reports and articles for scholarly publications often contain tables, images, and other figures that provide supporting material for the text contained in the document. For example, a chart detailing quarterly sales data typically accompanies narrative text related to how the sales for the quarter went. You can add captions to your document figures and generate a table of figures, giving the reader of the document a reference for finding particular figures in the document.

Inserting a Caption

To add a caption to an image or table, select the Insert Caption command on the References tab, or you can right-click the item (such as a photo) and select Insert Caption from the shortcut menu that appears. The Caption dialog box opens, as shown in Figure 10.8.

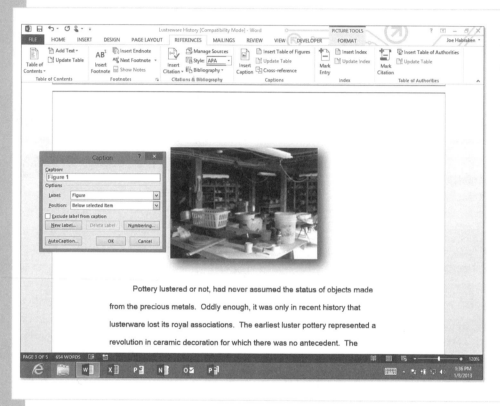

Figure 10.8
The Caption dialog box.

The figure numbers are assigned automatically to each subsequent figure. You can include additional text for the caption by typing it in the Caption text box. In the Options area of the dialog box, you can specify the label type for the figure: Figure, Table, or Equation. You can also use the Position drop-down list to specify the position for the caption and modify the caption numbering for your figures, if needed. Select the Numbering button in the Caption dialog box to access the Caption Numbering dialog box. This enables you to change the format for the numbering, and you can include the chapter number with the figure number by selecting the Include Chapter Number check box. You must specify the style that you used for the heading that starts each chapter.

After you have configured the caption settings for the figure, click OK. This inserts the caption in the document.

 tip

If you want to place several figure objects, such as Excel charts, into a document, you can use the AutoCaption command to automatically add a caption when you insert a particular figure type. The figure types include Excel charts, PowerPoint slides, and Word tables.

Inserting a Table of Figures

Inserting a table of figures is straightforward. The Table of Figures feature uses the figure style that you assigned to the figures via the captions that you inserted.

Park the insertion point where you want to insert the table of figures in the document. On the Ribbon's References tab, select Insert Table of Figures. This opens the Table of Figures dialog box, as shown in Figure 10.9.

Figure 10.9
The Table of Figures dialog box.

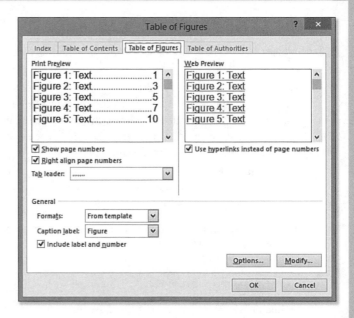

You control whether page numbers are included in the table and the type of dot leader that separates the figure caption from the page number. The most important setting in the Table of Figures dialog box is the Caption Label setting. Its options are None, Equation, Figure, and Table. If you are building a table of figures for items that you assigned the Figure caption label, make sure that it is selected in the Caption Label drop-down list.

When you are ready to generate the table of figures, click OK. The table of figures is inserted into the document. If you add figures (with captions) to the document, you can easily update the table of the figures.

Select the table of figures, and then select the Update Table command in the Captions group. You also can right-click on the table and then select Update Field on the shortcut menu. Both of these possibilities open the Update Table of Figures dialog box. Select the Update Entire Table option button and then click OK. The table updates to include additional figures you have added to the document.

Using Cross-References

Complex documents often require you to provide readers with the capability to quickly reference other information in the document that is pertinent to text they are currently reading. This is where cross-references come in handy. Cross-references are notations in the document that tell the reader where to find additional information on particular subject matter. Cross-references are essentially navigation mileposts within the document that make it easy for the reader to follow the information trail related to a particular topic that is referenced more than once in a document.

Word's cross-referencing capability is extremely flexible, and you can create cross-references associated with a heading, figure, table, or bookmark (so any text bookmarked can serve as a cross-reference). The cross-reference can give you page number information or can reference a particular table or figure number.

The great thing about cross-references is that they react to changes in the document. For example, if you move a figure noted by a cross-reference to another location in the document and renumber it, the cross-reference updates to provide the correct figure number. If text is rearranged in the document and headings associated with cross-references move, the cross-references update to provide the correct page numbers for the cited headings.

Creating a cross-reference is really a two-step process. First, you supply the anchor for the cross-reference. As already mentioned, this can be a table, an equation, or a figure that has been assigned a caption. Other possibilities are as follows:

- **Numbered Item:** Text in the document that has been numbered using the Numbering command

- **Heading:** Text headings that have been assigned one of Word's built-in heading styles

- **Bookmark:** Any text that has been assigned a bookmark (we discuss bookmarks later in this chapter)

- **Footnote:** Any footnote that you have placed in the document

- **Endnote:** Any endnote that you have placed in the document

 caution

If you want to create cross-references for tables, figures, or equations, you must use the Caption tool to assign captions to your tables, equations, or figures. The caption provides the cross-reference with the information that it needs to locate the figure or table and specify the figure or table number.

To create a cross-reference, place the insertion point in the document where you want to insert the cross-reference. Type the introductory text for the cross-reference, such as "For more information, see page."

Select the Ribbon's References tab and then click the Cross-Reference command in the Captions group. This opens the Cross-reference dialog box.

Select the Reference type for the cross-reference (such as Heading, Bookmark, Figure, and so on). The items available in the list box reflect the reference type that you selected. For example, if you select Heading as the reference type, all the headings (that have been assigned Heading quick styles) in your document appear in the For Which Headings box, as shown in Figure 10.10.

Figure 10.10
The Cross-reference dialog box.

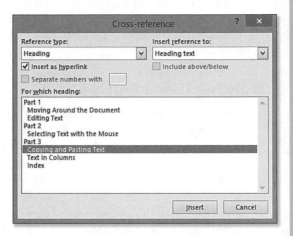

After you select the reference type and the item in the document that you want connected to the cross-reference (such as a heading or bookmark), you need to determine what the cross-reference itself should consist of. For example, you can use a heading as the reference anchor and then select Page Number in the Insert Reference To drop-down list. This inserts the page number for the referenced heading into the document as your cross-reference.

Each reference type has choices for what you insert into the document as the cross-reference. A figure reference type can provide the entire caption, the label and number, or the page number for a figure. A bookmark used as a cross-reference can include the bookmark text, the page number of the bookmark, or even the paragraph number. After you select your options for the cross-reference in the Cross-Reference dialog box, click Insert. You add additional cross-references as needed using the Cross-Reference dialog box. When you are finished, click the Close button on the Cross-Reference dialog box.

To follow a cross reference (go to the referenced text or heading) that you inserted as a hyperlink (the default), place the mouse pointer on the cross-reference text. A message box appears that says Ctrl + Click to Follow Link. Hold down the Ctrl key and click on the cross-reference; you will "jump" to the location of the cross-reference in your document.

 tip

To view the field codes placed in a document when you insert cross-references, press Alt+F9. Press Alt+F9 again to hide the cross-reference fields.

Generating an Index

Another useful addition to a long document is the index. An index provides a list of important terms and other keywords from the document and gives a reference to the page number (or numbers) where the term appears. An index in a document is generated in a similar manner to creating a table of contents or a table of figures. To specify entries for the index, you mark the appropriate text items in the document.

The commands that you need to create your index are available in the Index group on the Ribbon's References tab. The first step in creating the index is to mark the index entries throughout the document.

Marking Index Entries

Select a text entry for the index, and then select Mark Entry to open the Mark Index Entry dialog box. The selected text appears in the main entry box of the Mark Index Entry dialog box, as shown in Figure 10.11. You don't have to use the default text in the main entry box; you can type over the text to revise the main entry.

If you want to create a subentry to accompany the main entry in the Index, type the text in the subentry. For example, if your index entry is footnotes, but the index actually points to a passage that discusses converting footnotes to endnotes, you can add the subentry of "converting to endnotes." The index entry in the index then contains "footnotes" followed by an indented "converting to endnotes" on the next line (which would also include the page number of the entry).

 note

Indexes are meant to contain key terms and major concepts in the document so that the reader of the document can quickly locate that information in the document; don't commit overkill when marking text entries for the index, and don't completely skimp on entries for the index. It is a *Goldilocks and the Three Bears* dilemma: The index needs to be "just right."

Figure 10.11
The Mark Index Entry dialog box.

By default, the index entry includes the page number (the page where your index entry actually resides in the document). You can also specify a page range for the index entry by selecting the Page Range option button and supplying the name of a bookmark you created that includes the page range you want to assign to the index entry.

Bookmarks are discussed later in this chapter, in the "Building a Better 'Big' Document" section.

The Mark Index Entry dialog box also provides an option for creating a cross-reference for the index entry. For example, the main entry might be "data source," and you want to include a cross-reference in the index entry that states, "See mail merge." To use the cross-reference option, select the Cross-reference option button and enter the required text. This type of entry does not include a page number reference, but is designed to have the reader look elsewhere in the index to locate the document information.

The Mark Index Entry also supplies two check boxes (Bold, Italic) that enable you to select formatting for the page numbers included with the index entries. After you specify the parameters for your index entry, select Mark. Because the dialog box stays open as you mark the various index entries for the document, you can mark additional entries and then click Close when you finish marking all the index entries in the document.

Inserting the Index

After marking the index entries, you can insert the index. Park the insertion point in the document where you want to insert the index. You might want to start a new page or even a new section in the document for the index.

To insert the index, click the Insert Index command in the Index group. The Index dialog box opens, as shown in Figure 10.12.

Figure 10.12
The Index dialog box.

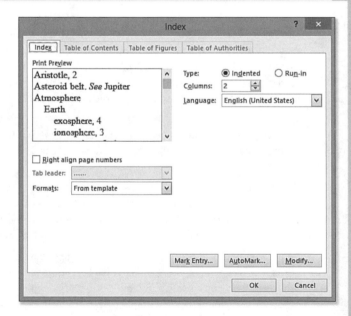

By default, the index is set up indented in two columns. You can change the number of columns and other settings as needed. When you are ready to insert the index, select OK. The index is inserted into the document.

If you modify your document (move pages, delete pages, or insert additional pages) and you mark additional entries for the index, you need to update the index in your document. Select the Update Index command in the Index group to update the index.

 tip

If you want to go beyond the main entry and subentry levels and add a tertiary-level entry to the index, type a colon (:) after the subentry text and then enter text for the tertiary-level index information.

 note

Different style manuals exist for publications. Word provides citation and bibliography formatting for 10 different sets of style guidelines including the Modern Language Association (MLA), the American Psychological Association (APA), and the *Chicago Manual of Style*.

Working with Citations and Bibliographies

If you are working on a journal article, a paper for conference proceedings, or some other document that requires a listing of your sources at the end of the document, you can take advantage of Word's citation and bibliography features. Citations are short references to articles, papers, books, or other material that you consulted that appear directly in the text of your document. For example, if you need to cite an article you read that was written by Jane Smith in 2012, the citation in the document would appear directly after any reference that you have made to Smith's article. A format that the citation might appear in would appear as: (Smith, 2012).

The full reference for the article, including the author's name, the article title, the publication date, and the publication in which the article appeared, are provided in the bibliography itself. So a bibliography is really a comprehensive list of all the source materials you have referenced in your citations.

When you insert a citation into the document (that is, when you create the citation), you provide all the information related to the article or book, such as the title, author, date published, and so forth. When you generate the bibliography, the bibliography entries created for each of the publications cited are based on the information that you provided for each of your citations.

Before you begin to insert the citations into the document, make sure that you understand the style guidelines you use for your publications. Style guides supply the rules for citing the borrowing of other works in your own documents. For example, many educational institutions use the MLA style guidelines in the humanity disciplines and the APA style guidelines for the social sciences. Other groups, such as book publishers, use the *Chicago Manual of Style* as a resource for their writers.

So the first step in the citation-to-bibliography process is to choose the style guidelines to use for your citations and bibliography. All the commands that you need for creating citations and the bibliography are on the Ribbon's References tab in the Citations & Bibliography group.

To specify the style guidelines that you want, select the Style drop-down box (the default is APA) and select one of the listed styles. Now you can begin to create the citations for the document.

Creating Citations

Citations include all the information related to the publication that you are citing in your document. Park the insertion point at the end of a sentence where you want to insert the citation, and then follow these steps:

1. Select the Insert Citation command in the Citations & Bibliography group.

2. On the Insert Citation gallery, select Add New Source. The Create Source dialog box opens (see Figure 10.13).

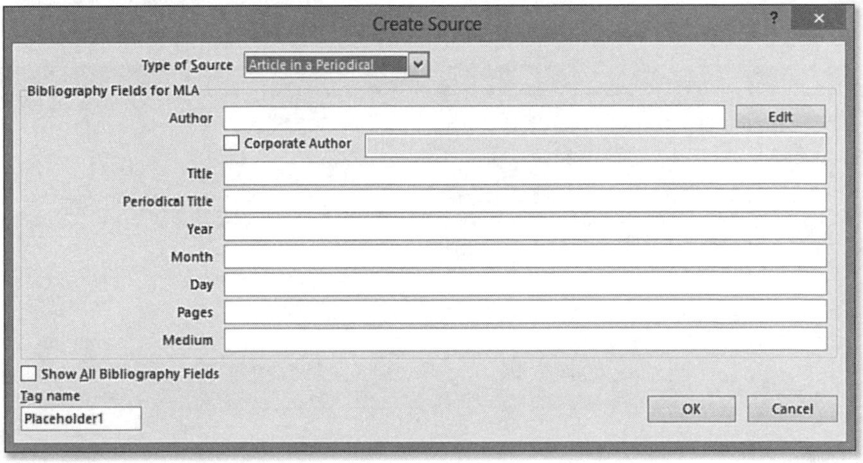

Figure 10.13
Enter the information for the publication in the Create Source dialog box.

3. Use the Type of Source drop-down list to select the type of publication you are citing (Book, Journal Article, Report, and so on). The type of publication you select determines the number of fields of information you must fill in for a complete citation.

4. Enter the appropriate information into each of the text boxes in the Create Source dialog box. A tag name is created for the citation, based on the author's name and the year of publication.

5. When you finish entering the data for the source, click OK.

The citation is placed at the insertion point in parentheses. The appearance of the citation depends on the style you are using. For example, the APA style includes the author's last name, followed by the year of publication. The MLA style uses only the author's last name for the citation.

Repeat the insert-citation process as needed to create all the citations for the document. When a citation has been created, it appears on the Insert Citation menu and can be quickly inserted into the document by selecting the Insert Citation command and then selecting the citation. Remember that the citation is inserted into the document at the insertion point. If you need to edit a citation, click the citation in the document (if there are multiple occurrences of the citation in the document, any instance will do). A drop-down arrow appears to the right of the citation. Select the drop-down arrow and then select Edit Source. The Edit Source dialog box opens; it is identical to the Create Source dialog box. Edit the citation as needed and then click OK to return to the document. Any changes you have made to the source are updated in the citations you already inserted into the document.

Managing Citations

You can manage the citation sources that you create using the Source Manager. The Source Manager provides a master list of citations compiled by Word (as an XML document) as you create the citations in your various documents. To open the Source Manager, select Manage Sources in the Citations & Bibliography group. Figure 10.14 shows the Source Manager.

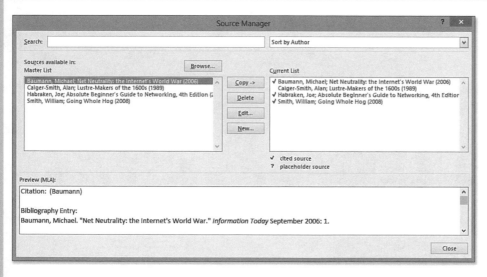

Figure 10.14
The Source Manager dialog box.

The Source Manager provides two different lists. In the left pane is the master list, which is a compilation of all citations that you created. In the right pane are the citations in the current document. You can select a citation in either the master list or the current list and copy it to the other list. For example, if the master list contains a citation that you want to include in the current list, select the citation and then click Copy.

If you have a large number of sources in your lists, you can quickly filter both the lists (the Master List and Current List) simultaneously using the Search box. Type a keyword or keywords into the Search box, and the lists filter using your terms. Delete the search terms in the Search box to refresh the lists. You can also use the Sort box on the top-right of the Source Manager dialog box. A drop-down list enables you to sort your sources by such things as author, title, and year.

The Source Manager also gives you tools to delete, edit, or create a new source. To delete a source, select the source (in the Master List or the Current List) and then select the Delete button. If you need to edit an existing source, select the source in the Source Manager and then click the Edit button. This opens the Edit Source dialog box.

The New button in the Source Manager opens the Create Source dialog box. If you want, you can open the Source Manager and create all the citation sources for your document before you enter any of the citations into your document. When the sources are ready to go, you can quickly add citations from the Insert Citation command, which provides a list of all the sources you have created for the document.

Inserting the Bibliography

After you insert your citations into your document, you can use the citation sources (that you already created) to insert a bibliography into the document. As with a table of contents or table of figures, you insert the new bibliography on a new blank page or (even better) in a new document section—particularly if you want to have different headers or footers for the portion of the document that contains the bibliography.

Creating the bibliography is straightforward: Place the insertion point where you want to insert the bibliography. Select the Bibliography command in the Citations & Bibliography group. The Bibliography gallery opens (see Figure 10.15).

 tip

You can save an inserted bibliography that you modified or one that you created from scratch to the Bibliography gallery, which is one of the Building Block galleries. Use the Save Selection to Bibliography Gallery command in the Bibliography command's gallery.

Figure 10.15
Select a style for the bibliography from the gallery.

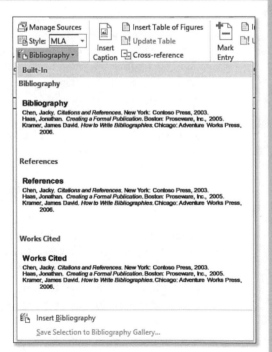

The gallery provides you with built-in bibliography styles. Select one of the styles: Bibliography, References, or Works Cited. The bibliography is inserted into your document using the selected style. If you don't want to use of the built-in styles, you can insert a more generic bibliography (without a title) by selecting Insert Bibliography (in the Bibliography gallery). If you don't like the look of the bibliography style that you have inserted, select the Undo command on the Quick Access Toolbar. If you want to delete the bibliography, select it and then click the Delete key.

 tip

You can save an inserted bibliography (that you modified) or one that you created from scratch to the Bibliography gallery, which is one of the Building Blocks galleries. Use the Save Selection to Bibliography Gallery command in the Bibliography command's gallery.

Inserting Footnotes and Endnotes

Footnotes and endnotes serve as explanatory additions to the text in your document. Similar to citations, both footnotes and endnotes can be used to reference published information that you consulted as you created your own work. Obviously, footnotes appear at the bottom of the page (in the footer area) and are included at the bottom of the same page where you inserted the footnote or footnotes. Endnotes appear at the end of the document.

As you insert footnotes or endnotes into a document, they are numbered sequentially. If you delete a footnote or endnote, the remaining footnotes or endnotes renumber automatically. In addition, if you add footnotes or endnotes to the document, the existing footnotes or endnotes renumber as needed.

 tip

To view the text for the footnote or endnote nearest to the insertion point, select the Show Notes command in the Footnotes group. It takes you either to the footer area to see the next footnote or to the last page of the document to view the current endnote.

Whether you use footnotes or endnotes depends on the type of document you are creating and also (somewhat) on the style manual you are using as the guide for your document formatting and structure. The great thing about footnotes and endnotes is that footnotes can be converted to endnotes, and endnotes can be converted to footnotes. If you start out using footnotes and determine that you should have been using endnotes, you can quickly remedy the problem.

The commands that you use to insert a footnote or an endnote are in the Footnotes group on the Ribbon's References tab. To insert a footnote or endnote, place the insertion point where you want to place the footnote or endnote reference number in the document. To insert a footnote or an endnote, click the Insert Footnote or Insert Endnote command, respectively. Doing so places the note number in the text and also moves the insertion point to the appropriate place in the document for you to enter the note text.

When you insert a new footnote, your insertion point moves to the footer area of the current page. Type the text for the footnote. When you insert a new endnote, the insertion point moves to the last page of the current document. Enter the text for the endnote.

You can navigate from footnote to footnote (or endnote to endnote) using the Next Footnote command in the Footnotes group; its menu provides Next Footnote, Previous Footnote, Next Endnote, and Previous Endnote.

If you need to modify the number format or other settings related to your footnotes or endnotes, you can do this in the Footnote and Endnote dialog box (see Figure 10.16). To open the dialog box, click the Footnote and Endnote dialog box launcher on the Footnotes group.

Figure 10.16
The Footnote and Endnote dialog box and the Ribbon's References tab.

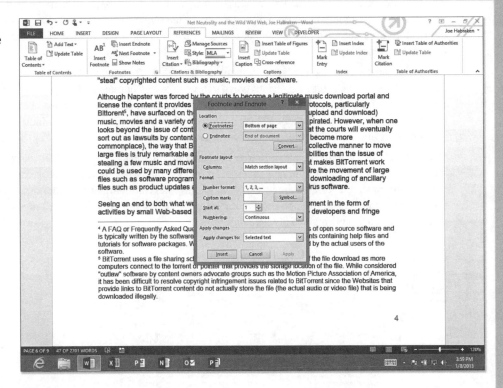

The Footnote and Endnote dialog box also enables you to convert your footnotes to endnotes, and vice versa. Select the Convert button in the Footnote and Endnote dialog box. The Convert Notes dialog box opens and provides three options:

- **Convert All Footnotes to Endnotes:** Your footnotes become endnotes.

- **Convert All Endnotes to Footnotes:** Your endnotes become footnotes.

- **Swap Footnotes and Endnotes:** Any footnotes are converted to endnotes, and any endnotes are converted to footnotes.

Select the appropriate option button and click OK. This returns you to the Footnote and Endnote dialog box, which you can then close.

Tracking Document Changes

If you work in an environment where you collaborate with coworkers on Word documents such as reports, employee handbooks, and other materials, you can track the changes made by the various collaborators in the document. This enables you to keep track of changes made by each individual; in fact, each individual's changes are tagged with a username. After the various participants have made all their changes to the document, you can review it and determine the changes that you will accept and reject.

Word 2013 provides some new enhancements to the Track Changes feature. These changes help clear up the screen clutter that results when you use Track Changes and make it easier for collaborators working on the document to communicate in real time. The most obvious change to the Track Changes feature is the new Simple Markup view. Simple Markup is now the default view for the changes that are marked in a document when Track Changes is enabled.

Figure 10.17 shows a document in Simple Markup view. A vertical line in the left margin denotes an edit in the document. Comments inserted in the document are represented by comment balloons in the right margin. Select a comment balloon to view the comment. Simple Markup removes all the balloons, insertions, and deletions that cluttered the document page when Track Changes was turned on in previous versions of Microsoft Word.

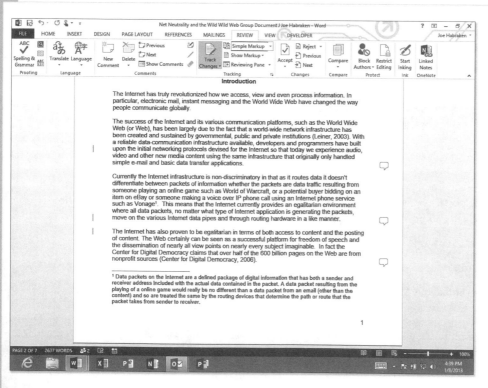

Figure 10.17
Simple Markup view.

You can switch from Simple Markup view to All Markup view (the view that was the standard for Track Changes in previous versions of Word) with one click of the mouse. Click a vertical edit mark in the left margin, and the edit (and other edits on the page) appears as an inline edit, such as the edits shown in Figure 10.18. The text associated with the edit is also selected. Any nearby comments also appear.

Figure 10.18
Click a vertical edit mark to switch to All Markup view.

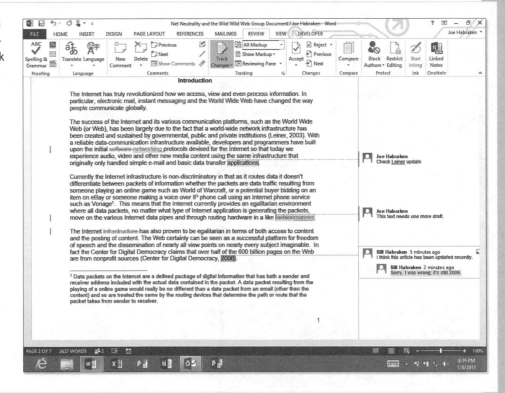

Another improvement related to the collaborative editing of a document concerns comments that are inserted into a document. Comments now enable users to exchange comments in real time. This "chat" allows users editing the same document to have a dialogue related to any changes made to the document. Figure 10.18 shows two comments; the top comment contains entries from two users who are simultaneously editing the document.

Be advised that you don't have to work in Simple Markup view when you use Track Changes. If you were happy with the way previous versions of Word displayed edit and comment information in an edited document, you can switch to All Markup view by clicking the Display for Review drop-down list (in the Tracking group) and selecting All Markup.

All the commands related to the Track Changes feature are located in the Tracking group on the Ribbon's Review tab. Before you begin tracking changes in the document, you might want to peruse and even change the various settings related to the tracking options. You can select or deselect markup options in the Show Markup drop-down list. You can control what is shown (such as comments or formatting) and whether balloons are used to show revisions or comments.

All these options are also provided in the Track Changes Options dialog box. Click the dialog box launcher on the bottom-right corner of the tracking group to open the Track Changes dialog box. You can specify what is shown in the document and how balloons are used. If you want control over more options related to the appearance and color of deletions or insertions, select the Advanced Options dialog box to open the Advanced Track Changes Options, which is shown in Figure 10.19.

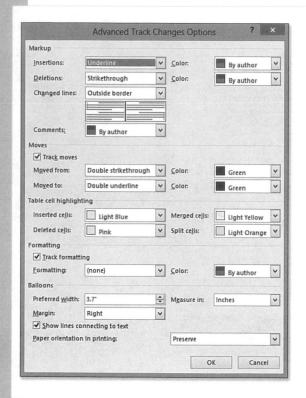

Figure 10.19
The Advanced Track Changes Options dialog box.

In the Advanced Track Changes Options dialog box, you can configure different options related to how editing changes such as deletions and insertions are formatted and colored in the document. The Advanced Track Changes Options dialog box is divided into category areas including Markup, Moves, Formatting, and Balloons.

Each grouping, such as Markup, uses formatting attributes and color to specify a particular type of change. For example, the Markup group includes insertions, deletions, and changed lines. By default, insertions are formatted using an underline, whereas deletions are formatted with a strikethrough.

You can determine whether changes that do not remove or insert text, such as moves and formatting, are tracked (using the appropriate check box). This dialog box also provides settings related to balloon size and margin.

You can change color settings for the various markup items, such as insertions or deletions. However, because the point of this feature is to differentiate the changes made to the document by different individuals working on the document, I do not recommend changing any of the color settings for items that have the By Author selection by default. This includes items such as insertions, deletions, and formatting.

Options for Viewing Changes

When you are ready to begin tracking the changes in a document, select the Track Changes command in the Tracking group and then select Track Changes. As you edit, changes are marked in the document; when you share the document, any changes by your collaborators are also marked in the document.

caution

Unless you have some compelling reason to make a change, in most cases, you can use the default formatting and colors provided by the Advanced Track Changes Options dialog box.

As already discussed, the new default view for Track Changes is Simple Markup. To toggle between Simple Markup and All Markup, just click one of the vertical edit marks in the left margin of the document. The Display for Review drop-down list in the Tracking group also provides other possibilities for changing the view when Track Changes is enabled. One possibility, No Markup, removes all editing marks from the document and shows you the document with all the editing changes that have been made; changes are displayed as regular text, as if you had accepted each change.

Another possibility provided by the Display for Review drop-down list is Original view. When you select Original, the original version of the document (the document before editing) is displayed. If you attempt to edit the document while in Original view, the display immediately changes to Original: Show Markup view. This view shows you all the edits and comments in the document (the same view provided by All Markup if no changes have been accepted or rejected since editing began).

The Show Markup menu (select Show Markup in the Tracking group) gives you quick access to a list of items that control what is shown in the document when All Markup is the selected view, such as comments, insertions, and deletions or formatting. You can use the Specific People selection on the menu to show or hide the changes made by certain reviewers (that's what Word calls your collaborators) in the document; point at Specific People to see a list of all the reviewers of the document. If you want to hide changes made by other authors, deselect the Other Authors command on the Show Markup menu.

Reviewing Changes

When you have all the reviewers' changes marked in the document, you can review the document and determine which changes you want to accept and which you want to reject. The commands related to reviewing the document, such as the Accept and Reject commands, are in the Changes group on the Ribbon's Review tab.

To aid you in reviewing the various edits made throughout the document, you can open the Reviewing pane in a vertical or horizontal orientation. Select the Reviewing Pane command in the Tracking group, and then select Reviewing Pane Vertical or Reviewing Pane Horizontal. Figure 10.20 shows the vertical reviewing pane.

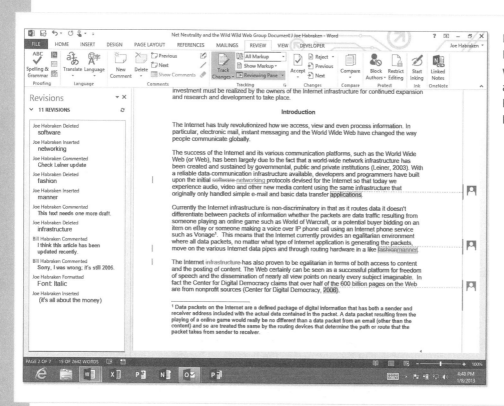

Figure 10.20
Document with changes and the Reviewing Pane.

To begin the process of reviewing the document changes, go to the top of the document (Ctrl+Home) and then click the Next command in the Changes group. You are taken to the first change in the document. At this point, you can take advantage of the Accept or Reject command and the choices on their menus.

The Accept command and the Reject command enable you to accept or reject a change and then move to the next change—just accept or reject the change, or accept or reject all changes.

After you have accepted (or rejected) changes in the document, you can save the final version of the document. It makes sense to use Save As and save the document under a new filename detailing that the document review has taken place.

Comparing Documents

You might want to reconcile the text in two different drafts of a document or combine revisions from multiple authors (in different documents) into a single document. This is particularly useful if you did not circulate a single copy of a document with the Track Changes feature enabled among the various authors involved in the project. The Compare command has its own Compare group on the Ribbon's Review tab.

To compare two versions of a document, select the Compare command and then select Compare on the Compare menu. Doing so opens the Compare Documents dialog box. To view all the settings available in this dialog box, click More (see Figure 10.21).

Open the original document on the left side of the dialog box and open the revised version of the document on the right side of the dialog box. The Label Changes With boxes enable you to specify the author name used to label the changes found between the documents when the comparison is made.

note

Ink is an option on the Show Markup menu. It refers to pen markup made to a document on a tablet PC.

note

You can control the type of changes and the level of access that reviewers have to a document. Use the Restrict Formatting and Editing pane (select Restrict Editing in the Protect group) to limit formatting and editing restrictions.

Figure 10.21
The Compare Documents dialog box.

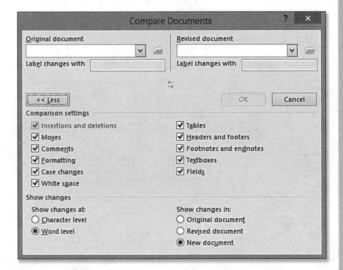

You can select the various comparison settings in the Comparison Settings pane (select More). This enables you to select specific actions for comparison, such as moves, comments, formatting, and so forth.

You also have control over how Word displays the differences in the two documents. You can choose to show the changes in the original document, the revised document, or a new document (with the latter being both the best option and the default).

After you specify the documents for comparison and set the various parameters in the Compare Documents dialog box, click the OK button. A document opens (a new document, if you went with the default setting) in Word that has automatically marked changes to the original document based on the revised version you specified. The Vertical Reviewing pane also opens, detailing the changes that have been marked in the document. You can now review the changes in the document as if you had the Track Changes feature enabled during the entire editing process. Figure 10.22 shows the results of a comparison between two different versions of the same document. The Compared Document pane provides the results of the comparison between the original document and the revised document. The original and revised documents are also shown in their own panes in the Word application window. As you scroll through the compared document, you move through the original and revised documents at the same time. The summary of revisions made appears in the Reviewing pane on the left of the Word window. You can choose to accept or reject changes as you would any other document that has been edited by multiple authors using Track Changes.

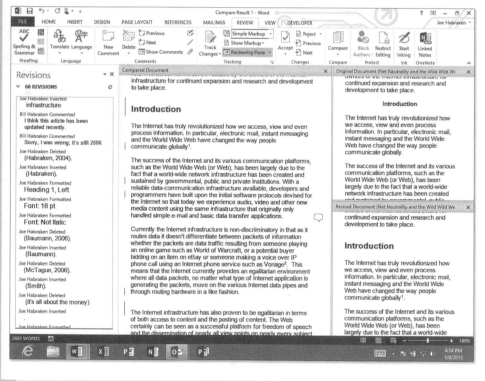

Figure 10.22
Review the changes resulting from the comparison of two versions of the same document.

The Compare command in the Compare group also provides the Combine command. This command opens the Combine Documents dialog box, which is structured the same as the Compare Documents dialog box. Use the Combine command and the Combine Documents dialog box when you want to quickly reconcile the changes that have been marked in two different versions of the same document. A new document is created, and you still have the opportunity to accept or reject changes made to the document (which are shown as inline edits in the new document created). The major difference between Compare and Combine is appearance. Compare creates a new document and also shows the original and revised versions of the document. Combine provides a new document only. Both scenarios, however, enable you to fine-tune any edits made to the original document.

Building a Better "Big" Document

So far in this chapter, we have looked at how to insert special document parts, such as tables of contents, indexes, and bibliographies, into larger, more complex documents. We have also discussed tools for documents with multiple authors, including the Track Changes feature and the Compare command. Working on a large, complex document can be a daunting task; tools and features in Word make it easier to navigate, comment on, and build a bigger document both when you are the sole author and when you are collaborating with multiple authors.

Creating Bookmarks

Bookmarks mark the location of specific text blocks or other items in a document. You can use bookmarks to generate cross-references in a document and to create the page run for an index entry that encompasses multiple pages. In their simplest function, bookmarks are a good way to navigate a large document because they point to a specific place in the document; you can easily "jump" to any bookmark in the document.

The Bookmark command is in the Links group on the Ribbon's Insert tab. To create a bookmark, simply select text in the document or park the insertion point at a particular place in the document, and then click Bookmark. The Bookmark dialog box opens, as shown in Figure 10.23.

Type a name for the new bookmark (no spaces are allowed). Then click the Add button to add the new bookmark to the list.

The Bookmark dialog box enables you to specify how the bookmark list is ordered; it can be sorted by name or location. You can delete bookmarks in the Bookmark dialog box (select a bookmark and click Delete), and you can use the Go To button to go to a selected bookmark.

After you have inserted a number of bookmarks into a document, you can move to a specific bookmark by using the Go To tab of the Find and Replace dialog box. To open the find dialog box with the Go To tab selected, select Find on the Ribbon's Home tab and then select Go To. You can open the Find dialog box with the Go To tab selected by pressing Ctrl+G on the keyboard.

 note

Documents that you share with other users on your SkyDrive (or SharePoint site) allow them to edit the document in Word or use the Word Web app. You can view a list of users currently editing a document by selecting the author's icon on the Word status bar. If you have track changes turned off, Word highlights (in green) edits made by other authors.

 tip

Much of the information that we work with on a daily basis is web content. Referencing a web page in a Word document is a common occurrence. To insert a hyperlink into a Word document, open your web browser and navigate to the page addressed in the hyperlink. Select Hyperlink on the Insert menu. The address for the page is in the Address box of the Insert Hyperlink dialog box. Provide the text you want to display in the document (for the hyperlink), and then click OK to insert the hyperlink.

Figure 10.23
The Bookmark dialog box.

On the Go To tab, select Bookmark in the Go To What list. Then select a specific bookmark from the Enter Bookmark Name drop-down list. Select the Go To button to move to the selected bookmark. Close the Find and Replace dialog box when you have finished using your bookmarks to navigate the document.

Inserting Comments

Earlier in this chapter, we discussed the fact that the Word Comment feature enables you to use an inserted document comment as a platform for communication among multiple authors editing the same document. Comments are not reserved for multiauthor documents, and you can insert non-printing comments into your document that you use as reminders. For example, you might insert a comment such as "Finish this chapter" to remind you to complete a particular portion of the document. Comments left for other users editing a document are an extremely useful way to discuss changes made to the document in real time.

The Comments group is on the Ribbon's Review tab. To insert a new comment, park the insertion point and then select the New Comment command (the New Comment command is also on the Insert tab in the Comments group). A new comment balloon opens. Enter the text for the comment. The new comment is marked with your username and initials and a time stamp.

In Print Layout view, comments appear as comment balloons. In Draft view, a comment appears as pink highlighting on the document text where the comment was inserted. You can view a comment by placing the mouse pointer on that particular comment. A preview box opens, showing the author of the comment, the date and time the comment was inserted, and the comment text. You can view all the comments in the document as a list in the Reviewing pane; select Reviewing Pane in the Tracking group. You can also move from comment to comment using the Go To tab of the Find and Replace dialog box (Find and then Go To). Select Comment in the Go To What list and then use the Enter reviewer's name drop-down list to go to a comment made by a specific reviewer (click Previous or Next to move to a comment).

The Comments group also provides two commands for moving to comments in the document: Previous and Next. The Delete command enables you to delete a selected comment, all comments shown, or all the comments in a document, as needed.

---

 note

Using comments is a great way to communicate with other authors working on the same document. With Word now available as a web app and on multiple devices (PCs and tablets), collaboration with coworkers has become even more important as users take advantage of Word's capabilities on multiple computing devices.

---

 tip

You can delete comments from the Reviewing pane. Right-click a comment to open the shortcut menu, and then select Delete Comment.

Creating a Master Document

An extremely useful feature when you are collaborating with multiple authors who are responsible for specific parts of a larger document (such as chapters) is the Master Document feature. The Master Document feature enables you to insert links to other documents. These links can be chapters or other document parts being written by other users. In essence, the Master Document feature has one great and noble purpose: It enables you to create a master document outline of the entire document, even while the various parts of the document are still being created. When the various authors complete the linked subdocuments that make up the master document, your master document is also complete. It can then be printed and distributed, or it can be saved as a PDF file and made available to anyone who needs a copy.

---

 tip

Use a new blank document for the master document so that you have complete flexibility in inserting and rearranging the subdocuments that link to the master.

The Master Document feature provides an outline view of the entire document that allows you to expand and collapse the subdocuments using the Outlining tools. You can insert new subdocuments as links to other document files, or you can create a new subdocument for the master document from scratch directly in the outline.

You can create global items, such as page numbering, for the master document and then apply them to the various linked subdocuments that make up the master document (keep in mind that all these subdocuments are separate files linked by the master document). When you generate the table of contents for a master document, the "master" table of contents includes all the "TOC" headings in the various linked subdocuments. And when you are working with a master document in Word in

Print Layout or Draft view, it ends up looking like any other Word document, although it is a series of links to the various subdocuments.

Working in Outline View

As already mentioned, the master document is an outline of linked subdocuments. You work with a master document in Outline view. This enables you to view the linked subdocuments and use the various Outline tools for arranging and manipulating the subdocument links in the master document outline. Figure 10.24 shows a master document that contains three linked subdocuments. The Show First Line Only check box is selected in the Outline Tools group so that all three subdocuments are on the screen. Normally, expanded subdocuments show all the pages in the subdocument.

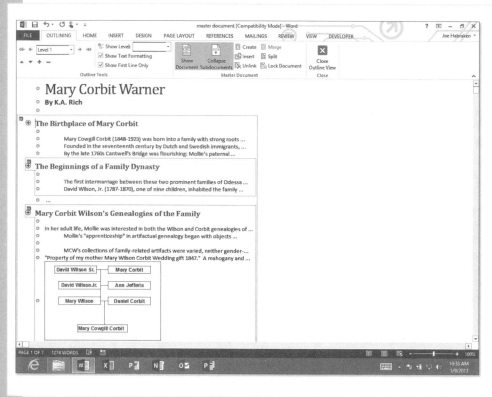

Figure 10.24
A master document with linked subdocuments.

To begin the process of creating a master document, open an existing document or a new document. If you are using an existing document as a master document, it can contain text entries and other objects. Be advised that any content in the master document (prior to creating the subdocument outline) is part of the "assembled" content that is realized when you link the subdocuments into the master document outline. So, the master document can be a "chapter" that is part of the larger master document you are creating; the master doesn't necessarily have to be a new blank document.

When you have the document open (new or existing) that serves as the master document, switch to Outline view; then select Outline on the Ribbon's View tab. Outline view (which appears on the Ribbon as an Outlining tab) provides commands (in the Outline Tools group) that enable you to promote and demote items in the outline to different levels. You can also select levels by using the Level drop-down list. Tools such as Move Up, Move Down, Expand, and Collapse enable you to move through the outline and expand or collapse outline parts, respectively.

After you are in Outline view, you also need to be aware of the commands in the Master Document group on the Outlining tab. When working in Outline view on your master document, make sure to select the Show Document command in the Master Document group. This "activates" the other Master Document tools. Now you are ready to create or insert the subdocuments that make up the master document.

Creating Subdocuments from Scratch

Creating new subdocuments from scratch is just a matter of using the Create command in the Master document group. This adds each new subdocument that you create to the master document outline. Each time you add a new subdocument to the master document outline, a new blank Word document (the subdocument) is also created in the folder where you have stored the master document. For example, if I have a master document saved to My Documents (on my computer's hard drive) and I create a new subdocument in the outline titled "Chapter 1," a new blank Word document is created in My Documents named Chapter 1 (when I save the changes that I have made to the master document).

If you are working in the cloud (SkyDrive or SkyDrive Pro) or on a network where you can easily share files with other users, the subdocuments that are automatically created as you build the master document outline can be shared with other users. These other users can then add the content to the subdocument, which is then available when you open the Master document.

To create a new subdocument (from scratch) in the master document, place the insertion point in the outline where you want to insert the blank subdocument. Make sure that the outline level at the insertion point is set to one of the heading levels (1–9); it cannot be set to body text. To set the heading level, select the Outline Level drop-down list (in the Outline Tools group) and specify the

note

Outline view uses the built-in Word heading styles to denote the different levels in the outline. For example, Level 1 in the level list is really the Heading 1 style. Regular text in the outline uses the Body Text designation, which is the Normal style.

level (the levels 1–9 in the Outline Level list correspond to Word's built-in heading styles 1-9). Make sure the Show Document command is activated in the Master Document command group; then select the Create command. A new subdocument (it's a rectangle with an Expand button) appears in the master document outline, as shown in Figure 10.25. You can repeat the process as needed to add other subdocuments to the master document outline. Make sure that you type a heading for the new subdocument (which also serves as the filename for the new subdocument that is saved when you save the modified master document).

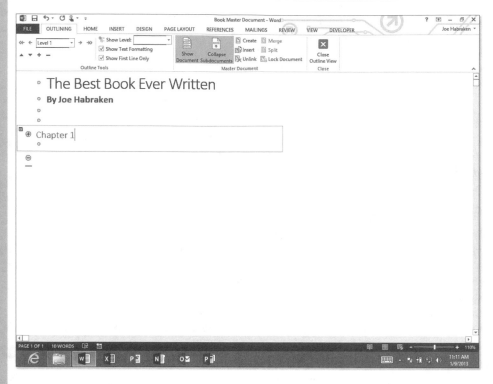

Figure 10.25
A new sub-
document
added to the
master docu-
ment outline.

If you want, you can enter the contents for a particular subdocument directly into the master document outline. This includes text, pictures, and any other content that you would insert into a "regular" Word document. As already mentioned, when you save the master document, all the subdocuments that you created in the outline are saved as separate files using the subdocument heading as the filename. The fact that each subdocument exists as a separate Word document file makes it easy for you to assign parts of a master document to coworkers or colleagues, and also makes it easy for you to concentrate on a particular part of the master document. For example, you can work on Chapter 1 by opening the Chapter 1 document and adding content as needed. The next time you open the master document, the content you added to the Chapter 1 document file appears in the master document outline.

Inserting Existing Document Files into a Master Document Outline

You have an alternative to creating empty subdocuments in the master document outline. You (and your collaborators) can create the various Word documents that will be the subdocuments in the master document before you create the master document outline. This enables each collaborator to concentrate on the chapter or part of the master document they need to create. When all the subdocuments are saved as Word document files, you can easily build the master document outline that links all that content together.

To insert an existing Word document file into a master document outline as a subdocument, switch to Outline view and make sure that you have selected the Show Document command in the Master Document group. Place the insertion point in the outline where you want to insert the subdocument. You don't have to change the outline level for the line (to a heading level) as you are required to do when you create a new subdocument in the outline from scratch (as discussed in the previous section). However, you might want the same heading level for each subdocument that you insert, so that the document titles are at a consistent level in the outline (particularly if you want to drag an entire subdocument section to a new position in the master document outline).

To insert the subdocument link into the master document outline, select the Insert command on the Master Document group. The Insert Subdocument dialog box opens, as shown in Figure 10.26. You can repeat the process to insert other subdocuments as needed.

Figure 10.26
Select the subdocument to be inserted into the master document outline.

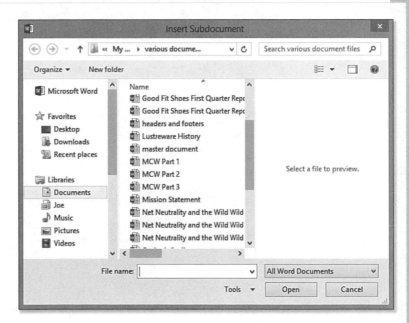

Because the subdocuments that make up the master document are separate files, they can be edited and re-edited (separately) as needed. When you open the master document file, all revised subdocument content is shown in the master document outline.

Manipulating the Master Document

You can fine-tune your master document using the other tools provided in the Master Document group on the Outlining tab. For example, if you want to unlink a subdocument from the original file (that is, you don't want to make changes to the subdocument itself), select a particular subdocument in the outline and then select Unlink. The subdocument content is copied into the master document. Any changes made to the "unlinked" subdocument file (from that point on) will not be included in the master document (because the subdocument file is no longer linked, or talking to, the master document).

You can use the Merge and Split commands to either merge two subdocuments in the outline or split a subdocument at a particular place into two subdocuments. If you want to protect the actual files that make up the subdocuments, you can use the Lock Document command. This enables you to make changes to the master document (such as styles, headers, footers—you name it) and not have them propagate back to the original subdocuments.

When you are finished working with the Outlining tools and the various tasks related to constructing the master document, click Close Outline View. In the other Word views, such as Print Layout or Draft, the master document appears like any other document that you work with, even though it consists of linked content held in multiple Word document files.

11

REQUISITE EXCEL: ESSENTIAL FEATURES

Whether you create simple worksheets to track your small business income or you do a complex statistical analysis of migrating bird populations, Microsoft Excel gives you all the tools and features you need to assemble your data, calculate results, and then analyze those results. Excel continues to be the gold standard for spreadsheet software. Excel 2013 builds on the features and tools provided by earlier versions of this powerful spreadsheet application and offers a number of improvements and new features.

In this chapter, we take a look at new features in Excel 2013. We also look at the process of building Excel worksheets, including entering data. In addition, we examine how to best navigate the Excel workspace and work with and manage Excel worksheets.

Introducing Excel 2013

Excel 2013 provides all the number-crunching power of its predecessors and offers many new features and enhancements. When you open the Excel 2013 application window, the New Start screen greets you. In earlier versions of Excel, you were pretty much on your own when it came to building a new workbook. Upon startup, Excel opened a blank worksheet, and everything else was up to you. Excel's new Start screen, shown in Figure 11.1, grants quick access to a new, blank workbook. However, Excel now also provides quick access to workbook templates. You can choose from templates available on the Start screen, such as My Financial Portfolio, Quarterly Sales Report, or Expense Report. You can also use the Search box at the top of the Start screen and search through the huge Excel template library available on Office.com.

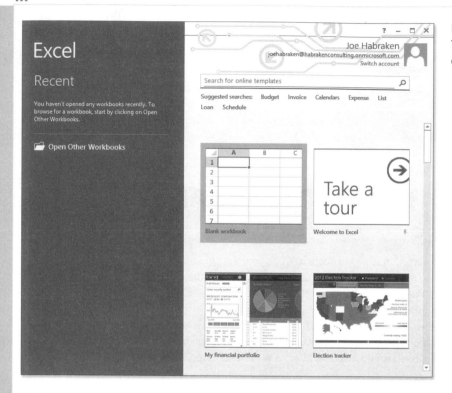

Figure 11.1
The new Start screen offers you templates.

The Start screen also lists recently opened workbooks (under the Recent heading on the left of the Start screen). If you want to open a workbook that is not listed, you can access your computer, SkyDrive, SharePoint site, or network drives by selecting the Open Other Workbooks link.

The Start screen is just one of many enhancements that you encounter as you work in Excel 2013. Some of the changes to Excel 2013 are quite noticeable, such as the Start screen and the new Quick Analysis feature (which we discuss shortly). Some new updates are more under-the-hood enhancements that you won't really notice. These changes make Excel run better or do a particular task faster.

Excel 2013 and the entire Office 2013 application suite make it easier for you to share your work with other users. The default location for saving new Excel workbooks is either your SkyDrive or a SharePoint site (SkyDrive Pro), depending on whether you log onto Office using your Windows Live ID or your Office 365 Subscription ID. In both cases, Excel is ready to save your files to the cloud.

When you open multiple workbooks in Excel, each workbook is in its own window. This makes it easier to switch between the two workbook windows and also copy or move data from one sheet to another.

Some of the other more obvious user-friendly updates to Excel include the Quick Analysis tool, the Recommended Chart command, and the new Flash Fill feature. Let's take a quick look at each of these new features. Chapter 12, "Worksheet Formatting and Management"; Chapter 13, "Getting the Most from Formulas and Functions"; Chapter 14, "Enhancing Worksheets with Charts"; Chapter 15, "Using Excel Tables and PivotTables"; and Chapter 16, "Validating and Analyzing Worksheet Data" cover other new Excel features within the appropriate subject matter context.

Quick Analysis

The new Quick Analysis tool enables you to quickly access different analysis tools and features and then quickly apply them to the selected data in your worksheet. Figure 11.2 shows a select data range in a worksheet and the Quick Analysis gallery. You open the gallery by clicking the Quick Analysis button, which appears at the bottom right of a selected cell range.

Figure 11.2
You can quickly apply Quick Analysis options to your data.

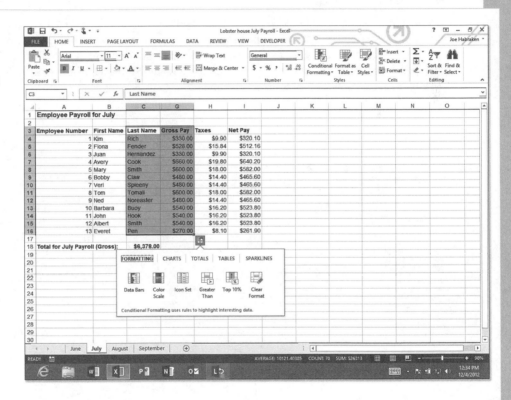

The Quick Analysis gallery gives you formatting options, including data bars and conditional formatting possibilities (Greater Than and Top 10%). The gallery also makes it easy for you to represent the date visually in a chart or sparklines. You can quickly add functions such as Average, Count, or % of Total from the Totals sections provided in the Quick Analysis gallery. Furthermore, you can quickly format your selected cell range as a table and use various Data tools to filter and summarize the data (on the Ruler's Data tab). The Quick Analysis gallery also automatically creates pivot tables associated with your data that you can view and manipulate.

 For more information about using charts and sparklines, ***see*** *Chapter 14, "Enhancing Worksheets with Charts."*

For more information about tables and pivot tables, ***see*** *Chapter 15, "Using Excel Tables and PivotTables."*

note

The Quick Analysis gallery grants quick access to many data-manipulation and analysis tools that are spread across the various Excel Ruler tabs. This is a particularly great feature if you have a touchscreen device.

Recommended Chart

Visually representing the information in an Excel worksheet as a chart makes it easier for you (and anyone else who sees the worksheet) to understand what the data is actually "saying." And although selecting a chart type has always been pretty straightforward in Excel, Excel 2013 provides recommended charts based on the selected cell range. Figure 11.3 shows the Insert Chart dialog box and recommended charts for a data range.

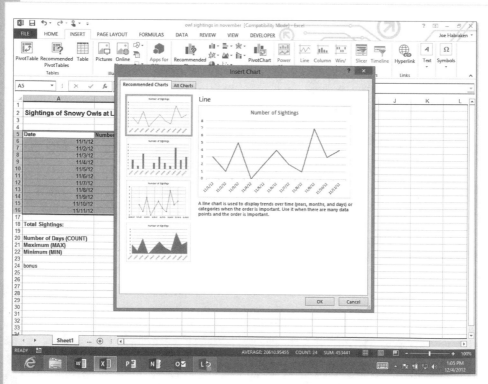

Figure 11.3
Excel provides recommended charts for your data.

You can access the recommended charts for your selected cell range by clicking Charts in the Quick Analysis gallery and then clicking the More Charts icon. A Recommended Charts command is also available in the Charts group on the Excel Ribbon's Insert tab.

Flash Fill

When you take data from other sources (other people can be other sources), particularly the Web, and "shoehorn" it into Excel (let's say you copy some data from a web table and then paste it into a worksheet), you can end up with columns of information that need to be further divided into additional columns. For example, you might have a names column that contains both the first and last names of a list of people. You want to break out the first names and last names into separate columns. The Flash Fill feature is designed to recognize data entry patterns in your worksheet and fill in the rest of the data for you. Figure 11.4 shows how the Flash Fill feature has inserted the first names into the First Name column based on the entry of only the first two names (Kim and Fiona).

Figure 11.4
The Flash Fill feature can automatically enter data into your worksheet.

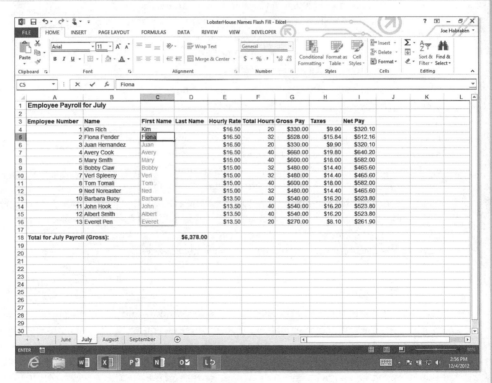

The Flash Fill feature isn't limited to recognizing patterns in text entries that use a space as the divider (such as in the case of a name). You can also use it in other instances. For example, if you had a long list of social security numbers in a column, you could create a column of "last fours" that shows only the last four digits of the social security number. Just start the new column and type the first couple last fours, and Flash Fill takes care of the rest. Flash Fill needs to merely discern a pattern in existing data to automatically fill entries for you. If you aren't consistent in the way you enter information into a worksheet, the Flash Fill feature probably won't be able to determine the data you are trying to "fill" in a particular column or row.

Navigating the Excel Workspace

When you open Excel, you land on the new Start screen. You can quickly begin a new presentation from any of the templates provided on the Start screen, including the Blank workbook template. You can also search for other templates online at Office.com by taking advantage of the Search box at the top of the Start screen.

If you have created a new workbook and saved it or you have worked with existing workbooks, these are listed under Recent on the left side of the Start screen. You can use the Open Other Workbooks link to open any of your other workbooks and access your computer, local area network, and other locations, including your SkyDrive (if you have signed into Office).

When you start a new workbook or open an existing workbook, you find yourself in the Excel application window. As with the other Office applications, the tools and features that you use to build and then enhance your Excel workbook are found on the Ribbon and its various tabs. Excel 2013 (and the other Office applications) have been built with touchscreen computing in mind, so you can find some interesting ways to access features and tools without necessarily having to access the Ribbon (the commands, tools, and functions that the Quick Analysis gallery provides are an example of this). Some changes also have been made to the Excel Ribbon, as we discuss in the next section.

The Excel Ribbon

The Ribbon sits at the top of the Excel application window and provides access to the commands and tools you use as you work on your Excel worksheet. Excel 2013 provides a cleaner, more "metro" Ribbon (Windows 8 is Microsoft's standard for the metro interface) and has added commands to specific Ribbon tabs. Another Office 2013 addition to the Ribbon is the Ribbon Display Options button just to the right of the Help icon at the right top of the Excel window. The Ribbon Display Options enable you to autohide the Ribbon, show just the Ribbon tabs (their names), or show the tabs and commands all the time. A short description of the Excel Ribbon tabs follows.

tip

If you haven't signed into Office using your Windows Live ID (Outlook.com or Hotmail account) or your Office 365 ID (or both), you can do so at the top right of the Start screen. Signing into Excel (and Office) makes your SkyDrive and/or SkyDrive Pro (Office 365 subscription) available as a place to save Excel files or retrieve existing files.

note

Excel 2013 provides one sheet in a new workbook (instead of the three it provided in the past). A New Sheet button to the right of the Sheet1 tab makes inserting a new sheet into the current workbook easy and quick.

note

If you are using Excel for the first time, you should know that a worksheet is divided into columns and rows. There are 16,000 columns (designated by letters) and 1,048,576 rows (designated by numbers). The intersection of a column and a row is a cell (designated by its column letter and row number). Cells are designed to hold information.

- **Home:** This tab (which is the same as the Excel 2010 Home tab, except for a minor facelift) provides the Clipboard group and groups that are associated with formatting and editing the worksheet data. The tab provides font, paragraph, and number formatting, and provides access to formatting features such as conditional formatting, table formatting, and a gallery of cell styles. The Editing group provides quick access to functions such as AutoSum and provides the Fill, Sort & Filter, and Find & Select commands.

- **Insert:** This tab enables you to insert objects into an Excel worksheet, including pivot tables, pictures, shapes, and charts. New commands available on this tab include the Recommended PivotTables command, Apps for Office (enables you to add applications that enhance an application such as Excel), and Recommended Charts (if you have Office 2013 Professional installed, the Insert tab includes the Power View command). The Insert tab also provides access to features such as sparklines, slicers, and the new Timeline command. The Insert tab provides access to the sheet header and footer as well. Figure 11.5 shows the Ribbon's Insert tab.

Figure 11.5
The Ribbon's Insert tab.

- **Page Layout:** This tab, which has not changed in Excel 2013, enables you to select a theme for your sheet and to manipulate the margins, orientation, and paper size for the sheet. The Page Setup group also enables you to place page breaks in a worksheet and select a background image for the sheet. Other commands available on this tab enable you to scale the worksheet for printing and select sheet options such as gridlines and headings. The Arrange group helps you manipulate and group multiple objects on a worksheet.

- **Formulas:** This tab provides easy access to the function library by function type. The long horizontal set of function categories in Excel 2010 has been arranged vertically in a more compact function library. This tab also provides the Defined Names tab, which enables you to define names for cells and cell ranges in the worksheet. Commands are provided for auditing formulas, including Trace precedents and Evaluation Formula. The Watch Window command helps you monitor specific cells (their results) as you add or manipulate the data in the worksheet.

- **Data:** This tab makes it easy for you to import external data from other applications or the web into Excel. Other commands available on this tab enable you to sort and filter data and specify data validation settings. The What-If Analysis command enables you to access tools for data analysis, such as the Scenario Manager and Goal Seek.

- **Review:** This tab provides proofing tools such as the Spelling feature and enables you to manage comments added to cells in your worksheet. Commands are also available that enable you to protect a worksheet or the entire workbook. Commands related to sharing a workbook are also provided.

■ **View:** This tab provides access to the various workbook views and also enables you to zoom in and out on the current worksheet. Other commands, such as Freeze Panes and View Side by Side, give you options for viewing a worksheet or multiple workbooks.

In addition, you should be familiar with some other areas of the Excel workspace. The Name box, on the far left, shows the address of the currently selected cell in the worksheet. The Name box also shows the name of a range when a named range is selected (we talk about naming ranges in Chapter 12). To the right of the Name box is the formula bar, which does a couple different things. As you enter information into a cell, it appears in the formula bar. The formula bar shows information that has been entered into the currently selected cell. You can also click in the formula bar to place the insertion point and edit the cell entry. When you work with formulas or functions, the result of the formula or function is shown in the cell that contains it. To view the formula or function, select the cell; the formula bar shows you the formula or function as it was entered.

At the bottom of the Excel application window, to the left of the vertical scrollbar, is the Sheet1 tab. Just to the right of the tab is the New sheet command. Use it to add sheets to the current workbook. Individual sheets are selected by their tab. You can rename a sheet by double-clicking the tab and typing a new name.

At the very bottom of the Excel application window (just below the horizontal scrollbar) is the Excel status bar. On the far right of the status bar are the View shortcuts and the Zoom slider. You can customize the status bar by right-clicking it and then selecting the various options from the shortcut menu that appears.

Moving Around a Worksheet

Moving around a worksheet is basically a matter of moving the mouse (or your finger, in the case of a touchscreen device) and "pointing out" the cell that you want to move to or select. If you are using a device with a keyboard, you can speed up your data entry by using keyboard shortcuts to move around the worksheet. Obviously, the arrow keys move you one cell in the direction specified by the key, but other options exist as well. Table 11.1 provides some of the keyboard shortcuts available in Excel.

Table 11.1   Using the Keyboard to Move in a Worksheet

Key Combination	Result
Tab	Moves one cell to the right
Shift+Tab	Moves one cell to the left
Ctrl+Right arrow	Moves right to the last occupied cell in the current row (before a blank cell)

Key Combination	Result
Ctrl+Left arrow	Moves left to the first occupied cell in the current row (before a blank cell)
Ctrl+Up arrow	Moves to the topmost occupied cell in a column (before a blank cell)
Ctrl+Down arrow	Moves to the last occupied cell in a column (before a blank cell)
Ctrl+End	Moves to the first empty cell below the bottom-most right occupied cell in sheet
Ctrl+Home	Moves to cell A1 in the worksheet
Enter	Enters data into the cell and moves down one cell

The mouse also gives you other possibilities for interacting with the worksheet cells. You can double-click in a cell to insert the insertion point and edit the data directly in the cell. You can also click directly in the formula bar and edit the current cell entry there. You can use the mouse to zoom in or out on the current worksheet: Hold down the Ctrl key and then use the mouse wheel to zoom in or out as needed.

Creating Workbooks and Worksheets

We already discussed the new Excel Start screen, which is designed to let you either start a new workbook or quickly open an existing workbook. In terms of creating a new workbook, you can use the blank workbook template and build a new workbook from scratch. The alternative to building a workbook from scratch is building a workbook based on one of the many workbook templates that are provided by Excel and the template library at Office.com.

If you are already working on a workbook in Excel and you would like to open a new workbook, you can quickly access the New page in the Excel Backstage. Select File and then New. The New page is similar to the Excel Start screen; however, it does not provide a list of recently opened workbooks. The New Page, shown in Figure 11.6, is all about creating a new workbook.

To create a new blank workbook, you simply have to select the Blank workbook template; wait a moment, and you see a lot of blank columns and rows. The alternative to using the blank workbook is to take advantage of an Excel template. We discuss the Office.com templates in the next section.

Figure 11.6
The New
page in the
Backstage.

Using Office.com Templates

Office.com provides you with different types of Excel templates; you can download budgets, calendars, invoices, plans, and schedules. To view the templates available in one of the template groups, select a group such as Invoices. The number of templates available in a particular group depends on the group you have selected. Each group provides several possibilities. In some cases, you might find more templates of a particular type than you need.

You can preview the templates by selecting a template in the list; the preview appears in the Preview pane of the Available Templates window. When you are ready to create a new workbook based on a particular template, make sure that the template is selected, and then click either Create (for templates stored on your computer) or Download to download a template from Office.com. Figure 11.7 shows a new workbook based on an invoice template downloaded from Office.com.

The template that you select will provide the formatting, the placeholder text, and the specific formulas and functions that will be present in your new workbook (based on the template). A template such as the invoice template shown in Figure 11.7 creates a new workbook with one worksheet sheet, named Sales Invoice.

Other templates, such as several of the report templates, create multiple worksheets in the workbook. For example, the Home Remodel Budget template creates three worksheets: Dashboard, Cost Input, and Setup. The Dashboard provides a summary of estimated and renovation costs and provides a chart of costs versus budget. The Cost Input sheet provides cost input by date and is configured as a table, which can be filtered by column headings such as Area, Room, and Item. The Setup worksheet provides the individual tables that populate the drop-down lists for the Cost Input worksheet. All three of the worksheets are tied together by information that is linked between the sheets.

Figure 11.7
A new work-book based on an invoice template.

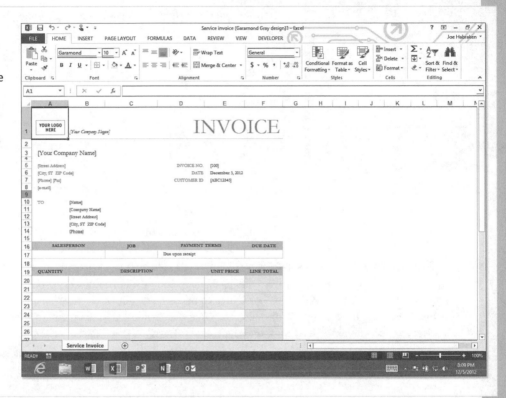

Some of the templates not only create multiple worksheets, but also include ready-made charts on some worksheets in the new workbook. The great part about templates is that even if you don't find a template that completely fits your needs, you can modify the worksheets a template provides. You can also add worksheets to any workbook, as discussed in the next section.

Inserting and Rearranging Worksheets

You can insert new worksheets into any workbook. If you add more worksheets than you need, you can easily delete them. You can also name, rename, copy, and move worksheets. You determine the order of worksheets (or sheets, as they are also referred to) in a workbook.

You can insert a new worksheet into a workbook in a couple ways. You can quickly insert a new sheet using the New Sheet button, which is located just to the right of the sheet tabs (at the bottom of the Excel window). You can also insert a new sheet using the Insert command in the Cells group on the Ribbon's Home tab. To name a new sheet, double-click the sheet tab and type the new name.

You can also reorder the sheets in a workbook. Grab the sheet tab and then drag the worksheet to a new location in the sheet hierarchy. Rearranging the worksheets in a workbook is also accomplished in the Move or Copy dialog box, shown in Figure 11.8.

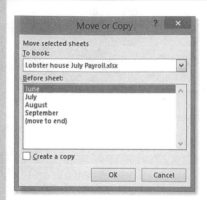

Figure 11.8
Rearrange worksheets using the Move or Copy dialog box.

To open the Move or Copy dialog box, right-click a sheet tab and then select Move or Copy. You can move the selected sheet before any of the listed sheets in the workbook. You can also use the Move or Copy dialog box to create a copy of a worksheet by selecting the Create a Copy check box.

The Move or Copy dialog box enables you to move or copy the currently selected sheet or sheets to another workbook. The other workbook needs to be currently active in Excel, so you need to open it before accessing the Move or Copy dialog box. Use the To Book drop-down list to specify the workbook that accepts the move or copy, and then click OK.

To rename a sheet, right-click the worksheet tab and then select Rename from the shortcut menu. The current name is selected (such as Sheet 1, Sheet 2, and so on). Type the new name for the sheet.

To delete a worksheet from the shortcut menu, right-click any worksheet tab and then select Delete. If the worksheet contains data, you get a warning box alerting you to the fact that data might exist on the sheet you are deleting; click the Delete button in the warning box to continue. Be careful when deleting worksheets in a workbook: The Undo command on the Quick Access Toolbar can't undo a sheet deletion.

 tip

Double-click a worksheet tab to select the current name if you want to rename the sheet.

Managing Excel Workbooks

The first time you save a new workbook, Excel takes you to the Save As page in the Backstage. The Save As page shows the various places where you can save the new Excel workbook. Figure 11.9 shows the Save As page.

Figure 11.9
Specify the location for your new Excel workbook on the Backstage Save As page.

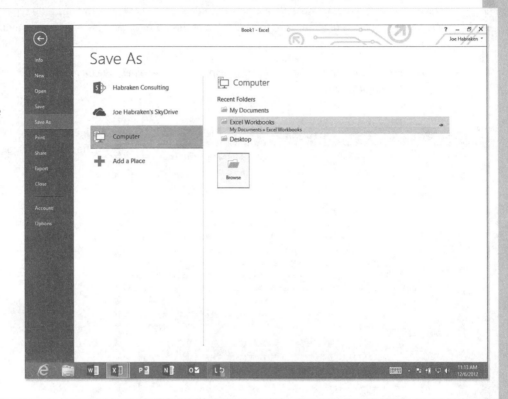

Locations (or places) provided on the Save As page include My Computer and optional places such as your SkyDrive or your Office 365 SharePoint (if you have signed into Office using your SkyDrive and/or Office 365 username and password). If your SkyDrive or your SharePoint site is not shown, you can quickly add it to the page using the Add a Place command.

When you select one of the places listed (such as Computer, as shown in Figure 11.9), recent folders opened from that location (or place) are available on the right side of the Save As page. A Browse button enables you to browse for other locations on the selected place.

Your job on the Save As Page is to locate a place for the new Excel workbook. When you select a recent folder or the Browse button, the Save As dialog box opens, as shown in Figure 11.10. After you have navigated to the folder location for the new workbook, provide a filename for the file and then click Save.

When you save an Excel workbook, it is saved in the .xlsx (XML file type) default file format. You can save your workbook in other file formats, including Excel 97-2003 Workbook, Single File Web Page, or Excel Template. The Save As Type drop-down list shows the different file types. If you have already saved a file and want to save it in another format, use the Save As command in the Backstage.

 *For more about Excel and other Office application file types, **see** Chapter 3, "Managing and Sharing Office Files."*

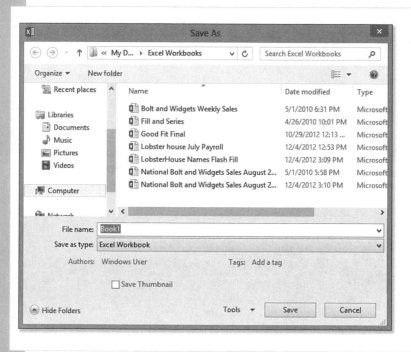

Figure 11.10
The Save As dialog box.

---

tip

If you don't like "landing" in the Backstage when you save a workbook for the first time (or when using the Open command that you can add to the Quick Access toolbar), you need to change the Excel Save options. In the Backstage, click Options in the Excel Options window, and then click Save. In the Save Workbooks settings, select the Don't Show the Backstage when Opening or Saving Files check box.

Another Backstage page that provides you with workbook management tools is the Backstage Info page. This page provides access to the workbook protection settings (Protect Workbook) and privacy and compatibility settings (Check for Issues); all these settings can be an issue if you are going to share (publish) this workbook with other users. The Info page provides access to the different versions of your workbook that the Autosave feature has created. Figure 11.11 shows the Backstage Info view.

Figure 11.11
Backstage
Info view.

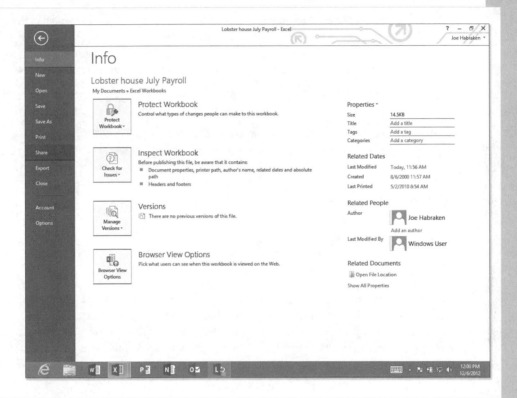

Excel 2013 (and all the Office 2013 applications) was designed to promote collaboration. Two important aspects of sharing a workbook with other users relate to controlling what kind of changes people can make to your workbook and determining whether the workbook itself is compatible with other versions of Excel that your collaborators might be using. Let's look at workbook protection more closely and then cover inspecting a workbook that you want to share.

Protecting Workbooks and Worksheets

You can configure the workbook to limit changes made by other users you share the file with. You can make the workbook read-only (meaning no changes allowed), or you can restrict permissions by individual users. The Protect Workbook command in the Info window provides these possibilities:

- **Mark As Final:** This command marks the file as final and makes it read-only. All editing commands for the file are disabled. This feature is primarily designed to keep users from inadvertently making changes to a file, because a user can change Mark As Final in the Backstage.

- **Encrypt with a Password:** The file is encrypted and protected with a password. When you select this option, you are required to enter a password for the workbook. Only users with the password can open the workbook.

- **Protect Current Sheet:** This option opens the Protect Sheet dialog box, which enables you to password-protect the sheet or specify individual sheet-related capabilities. such as Format Cells, Insert Hyperlinks, and Delete Columns. You also can configure interaction with locked cells in this dialog box. We discuss locked cells and sheet protection in more detail shortly.

- **Protect Workbook Structure:** You can use this option to keep users from changing the number of sheets in the workbook. This means that worksheets cannot be deleted or added.

- **Restrict Access:** This option enables you to connect to a digital rights management server, which gives you the capability to assign users different permission levels based on user authentication. To take advantage of this feature, you need to work in an environment that provides a digital rights management server to authenticate users. At the time of writing, Microsoft no longer appeared to be offering the free Information Rights Management Service made available to users of Office 2010.

- **Add a Digital Signature:** You can digitally sign a file to prove its authenticity. Signing a file digitally requires that you obtain a digital certificate from a certifying authority (you can locate a digital certificate authority on the Web).

You can see that the Info window provides some protection schemes that are all-or-nothing propositions, such as Mark As Final and Encrypt with a Password. Instead of protecting an entire workbook, you can choose to protect only certain cells on a sheet (before you share it with other users). For example, you might want to lock cells that contain formulas and functions so that the person doing the data entry does not accidentally overwrite or delete the worksheet formulas or functions. Let's look at how you lock cells in a sheet.

Locking Cells

Locking cells in a sheet is a two-step process. You must first select and lock the cells. Then you must turn on protection on the entire worksheet for the lock to go into effect.

Select the cells in the worksheet that you want to lock. These can be cells containing formulas, functions, or column and row labels (or names, Social Security numbers, or anything you want to protect). If you need to select noncontiguous cells, hold down the Ctrl key and then click a cell to include it in the selected range of cells.

On the Home tab, select the Format command in the Cells group. Then select Format Cells. This opens the Format Cells dialog box with the Protection tab selected. The Locked check box should be selected by default, as shown in Figure 11.12.

Figure 11.12
The Protection tab of the Format Cells
dialog box.

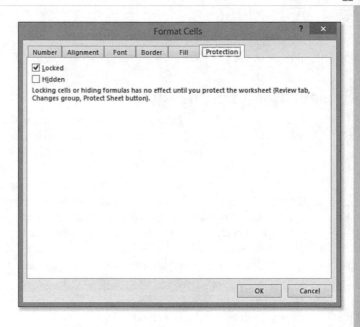

To close the Format Cells dialog box, click OK. Now you need to protect the sheet. Select the
Ribbon's Review tab and then select the Protect Sheet command in the Changes group. The Protect
Sheet dialog box opens, as shown in Figure 11.13.

Figure 11.13
The Protect Sheet dialog box.

You can enter a password to protect the sheet, if you want. You can also select other options related
to what users can do to the worksheet, such as formatting cells, columns, or rows and inserting
hyperlinks. To protect the locked cells on the sheet and allow data entry in other cells, you need not
change any of the settings in the Protect Sheet dialog box. Even the password is optional. Click OK
to close the dialog box.

When you (yes, you) or another user attempts to enter data into the locked cells on the worksheet, a message box opens to let you know that the cell is protected and is read-only. No data entry is allowed in the cell.

 tip
To unprotect a protected worksheet, select the Unprotect Sheet command on the Review tab.

Specifying Edit Ranges

You can protect cells in a sheet in another way. With the cell lock approach, you specify the cells that should be unavailable. You can also do the opposite by specifying the range of cells that other users can edit. This method seems easier to configure than the method discussed for locking cells, but be advised that specifying edit ranges is primarily designed for use in network environments. In fact, it is really designed for situations in which you use Excel on a Microsoft Windows Server network. Because users are listed in a global catalog provided by the Active Directory (which is a catalog of all the objects on the network, including users, computers, and networks), setting permissions for specific users or groups related to ranges that you password-protect is easy. This method certainly is not restricted to corporate networks because you can specify users who have been set up on your local computer using the Add or Remove User Accounts link in the Control Panel.

To specify the ranges that users can edit, you specify the ranges in the Allow Users to Edit Ranges dialog box. Each range can be protected by a different password so that you can provide access to some cells to certain users and other cells to other users. This provides a little more fine-tuning in terms of cell access than the method that we looked at involving locking cells and then protecting the sheet. In the Changes group on the Ribbon's Review tab, select the Allow Users to Edit Ranges command. This opens the Allow Users to Edit Ranges dialog box, shown in Figure 11.14.

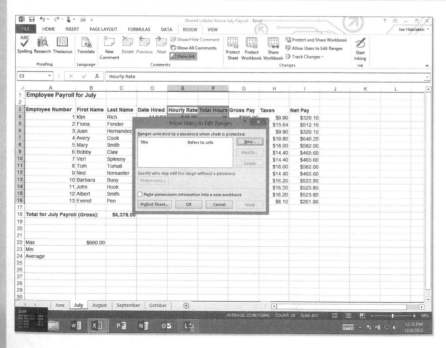

Figure 11.14
The Allow Users to Edit Ranges dialog box.

To specify an editable range, click the New button. This opens the New Range dialog box. Provide a title for the range. Click in the Refers to Cells box, and you can then select the range of cells in the worksheet. You can select contiguous cells or noncontiguous cells, as needed.

After specifying the range in the New Range dialog box, provide a password in the Range Password text box. You can also specify permissions related to the password-protected range. Select the Permissions in the New Range dialog box, and the Permissions dialog box for the range opens.

You can use the Add button to open the Select Users or Groups dialog box. You can then add users or groups to the list provided in the Users or Groups dialog box. User accounts or groups added to the list can be local accounts (accounts that you have added to your Windows 8 users) or can be user accounts and groups that are housed on your network server, such as a domain controller in a Microsoft Windows Server network.

 tip

Whenever you are working with passwords, you need to make sure you record the passwords and keep them in a safe place. Forgotten passwords don't do anyone any good.

After specifying users and groups, click OK to return to the Permissions dialog box for the range. You can select a group or username in the Permissions dialog box and then specify whether you allow or deny access to the range without a password. The default setting is Allow, so you should change this—the whole point of this process is to password-protect a specific range.

When you have specified the individual permissions for each user or group, click OK to return to the New Range dialog box. You can click OK to close the dialog box. A Confirm Password dialog box opens, requiring that you re-enter the password you set for the range. Enter the password and then click OK to return to the Allow Users to Edit Ranges dialog box. The new range appears in the range list. You can repeat the process to add other ranges to the Allow Users to Edit Ranges dialog box. When you finish adding the ranges, click OK to close the dialog box.

For editing ranges to work, you still need to lock all the cells in the worksheet and then protect the sheet. Use the Sheet Selector button (the box just to the left of column A and above row 1) to select the entire worksheet. Then select the Format command on the Home tab and select Lock Cell on the menu provided. All the cells on the sheet are now locked.

Navigate to the Review tab of the Ribbon and select Protect Sheet. When the Protect Sheet dialog box opens, the Protect Worksheet and Contents of Locked Cells check box is selected, which should stay selected. However, you can also specify a password that can be used to unprotect the sheet (which can be useful if you want to allow a coworker complete access to the cells in a protected sheet). Other settings in this dialog box enable you to set exceptions to your sheet protection, such as allowing users to select locked cells, insert columns, or delete rows. You can select any of these exceptions via the appropriate check box. When you have finished fine tuning your settings, click OK to protect the sheet.

So let's say that you share the workbook with another user or users. When they attempt to access locked cells on the sheet, they are greeted by a message box letting them know that the cell is locked and is read-only. When the user attempts to enter data in a cell that is in one of the edit ranges that you specified, the Unlock Range dialog box opens. The user needs to provide the password that unlocks the range. Formatting a sheet with edit ranges provides other users with access to cells in the sheet so that they can enter data. Cells that contain formulas or functions are protected from accidental deletion or editing. Even the cells in the edit ranges are secure and require a user to enter the password to access the edit range cells.

Preparing a Workbook for Sharing

The Check for Issues button in the Backstage Info window provides commands that enable you to check a workbook for hidden or personal information and for any accessibility or compatibility issues with your workbook. When you select the Inspect Document command, the Document Inspector opens, as shown in Figure 11.15.

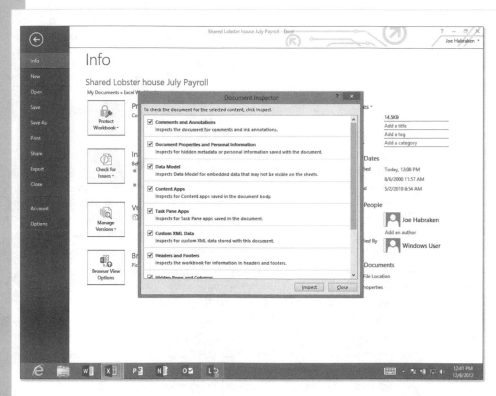

Figure 11.15
The Document Inspector.

The primary job of the Document Inspector is to scour your workbook for any personal or sensitive information that you might not have realized the workbook contains. This includes information that you might have placed in comments or the headers and footers of the worksheets. The Inspector also checks for hidden items such as rows, columns, and sheets. When you select Inspect in the Document Inspector dialog box, an inspection runs on the workbook.

When the inspection has completed, a list of results appears in the Document Inspector. For example, personal information might have been included in the workbook properties, and this is flagged as a possible problem. As already mentioned, headers and footers might include information that you do not want to share with others, so if the workbook contains any headers or footers, they are flagged as a potential problem.

The Document Inspector does provide remedies for these issues, but they are pretty much the equivalent of blowing up your entire backyard to get rid of a few hungry moles. For example, if headers and footers are present, the Document Inspector's solution is Remove All, meaning that all the information in the header or footer area is removed. The same goes for information in the document properties.

Instead of going with the nuclear option that the Document Inspector provides, you might want to use the information in the Document Inspector as a checklist of things you need to look at before sharing the document.

Managing Versions

The options provided by the Versions area of the Info window relate to autosaved copies of your workbook and any draft versions that have been created for the workbook in cases when you did not save changes to the workbook and then closed it. This includes situations in which you lost power to your computer.

You can open any of the autosave versions of your workbook by clicking the link provided. The auto-save versions are time-stamped, so you know when that particular version was created. Be advised that when you save and exit the current workbook, the various autosave versions of the workbook are deleted. You need to use these versions during your current editing session.

In the case of working with any saved draft versions, click the Manage Version button and then click Recover Draft Versions. This opens the Open dialog box, and any draft versions of the current workbook (or other workbooks) are listed. All draft copies of workbooks have "UnSaved" included in the filename. Select a draft version, and then click Open to open the draft in Excel. You can then use the Save As command to change the filename if you want to keep the draft.

 tip

If you don't need any of the draft versions saved by Excel, select Manage Versions and then Delete All Unsaved Workbooks to remove them from your computer.

Entering Data in a Worksheet

Entering data in a worksheet is just a matter of clicking a particular cell and then typing the information. When you work in Excel, you enter different types of information, such as text, numbers, dates, times, formulas, and functions. In terms of the raw data that you enter (precluding the insertion of formulas or functions), you are really working with two different types of information: labels and values.

A label is typically descriptive information, such as the name of a person, place, or thing, or a time designation such as the day of the week or month of the year. A label has no numerical significance in Excel; labels provide context for the values in the worksheet. Now, don't get me wrong—dates can have numerical significance and can be used in formulas and functions. For example, you can subtract today's date from the date of an upcoming holiday, such as Labor Day or Thanksgiving, and compute how many days remain until that particular holiday. Social Security numbers, on the other hand, are numbers, but they are descriptors and do not have numerical significance; we don't add or subtract Social Security numbers.

A value is data that does have numerical significance. Values can be numbers, dates, and even times. Values can be acted upon by formulas and functions. A value could be the monthly payment you have made on an automobile or the water levels you have measured over the course of the year on a nearby lake. Values are the fuel that drive Excel's number-crunching engine.

Entering Labels

As already mentioned, text entries in the worksheet serve a descriptive purpose; they are labels. Text can be used as row and column headings and can describe particular cells. In fact, as soon as you press one of the letters of the alphabet, Excel aligns the text entry on the left side of the cell. Excel knows the basic difference between labels and values.

When you type a label into a particular cell, you need to seal the deal by pressing Enter, navigating to another cell (arrow keys or Tab), or selecting Enter (the checkmark) in the Formula bar. Any of these actions enters the information into the cell.

In some situations, you want to enter numbers but have them "seen" by Excel as text entries. You can select the cells that contain the numerical labels and format the cells as text before entering the actual numbers. Follow these steps:

 tip

If you find that a text entry is cut off when you enter data in the next cell to the right, all you have to do is widen the column by dragging the column border to accommodate the entry in the cell.

1. Select the cells that contain the numbers that serve as labels.

2. On the Home tab, select the General command in the Number group.

3. In the Number format gallery that appears, scroll to the bottom and select Text.

4. Enter the numbers (including leading zeros) in the formatted cells.

The numbers entered into these text-formatted cells are left-aligned in the cells (the same as any text entry). The next chapter has more about formatting cells.

➥ *For more about formatting cells,* **see** *Chapter 12.*

Entering Values

Values provide the raw data to be used in a calculation performed by a formula or function. You can enter values using the 0–9 keys on the keyboard or the numeric keypad. You are not required to enter commas, dollar signs, or percentage signs in the cell when you enter a value. Formatting the value can come afterward, using the number formats Excel provides. You are required to place the decimal point in the correct place, however.

Excel right-aligns values in the worksheet cells. Make sure that you check any values that you enter into your cells. Typing mistakes make up most of the errors typically found in a worksheet. Although a misspelled label might be embarrassing, an erroneous formula or function result due to incorrect data entry can be damaging to your credibility and business.

Dates and times that you enter into an Excel workbook can have numerical significance. Excel sees a date as a number that reflects the number of days that have elapsed since January 1, 1900. Even though you won't see this number (Excel displays your entry as a normal date), the number is used whenever you use the date in a calculation. Times are also considered values. Time is computed as a percentage of 24 hours. To you, 10:45 a.m. might be time for a coffee break, but to Excel, it is the decimal value of .4479.

You can enter a date into a cell using more than one date shorthand or format. For example, you can use the MM/DD/YY or MM-DD-YY format. You can also enter a date in the format MONTH DAY, YEAR, such as August 9, 2011. If you need to specify a year earlier than 2000, include the entire year information, such as 1954.

tip
To insert the current date into a cell, press Ctrl+; (semicolon).

Dates entered have the default date format applied to them. You can change the formatting for dates via the Number tab of the Format Cells dialog box, which can be opened using the dialog box launcher on the Font group on the Ribbon's Home tab. Chapter 12 discusses formatting cell entries.

The format for entering time is HH:MM. You can specify a.m. or p.m. with a or p (following the time), respectively. You can also enter time using the 24-hour international time format.

tip
If you enter a value, particularly a date, and the entry is shown as #####, you need to widen the column to accommodate the value.

Using AutoComplete

AutoComplete can take some of the drudgery out of entering the same label multiple times in a worksheet column. Excel keeps a list of all the labels that you enter in a worksheet column. For example, suppose you have a worksheet tracking sales in Europe, and you are entering country names, such as Germany, Italy, and so on, multiple times into a particular column in the worksheet. After you enter Germany the first time, it becomes part of the AutoComplete list for that column. The next time you enter the letter G into a cell in that column, Excel completes the entry as Germany.

tip
To quickly access the AutoComplete list in the current cell, press Alt+down arrow.

AutoComplete works with text entries and entries that contain a combination of text and numbers. Depending on the similarities of labels in a particular column, you might have to type several characters before Excel provides you with the correct match. When the AutoComplete entry appears in the cell, press Enter.

You can also choose to select an AutoComplete entry from a drop-down list. All the entries available for a particular column appear in the list. Right-click a cell and then select Pick from Drop-down List on the shortcut menu that appears. A drop-down list of AutoComplete entries appears, as shown in Figure 11.16.

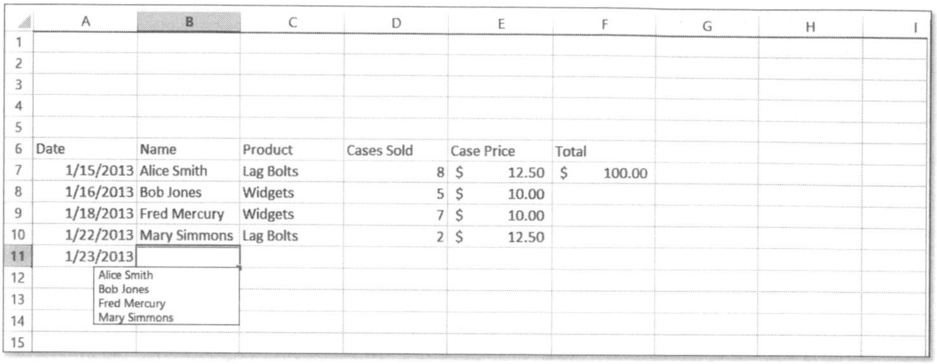

	A	B	C	D	E	F	G	H	I
1									
2									
3									
4									
5									
6	Date	Name	Product	Cases Sold	Case Price	Total			
7	1/15/2013	Alice Smith	Lag Bolts	8	$ 12.50	$ 100.00			
8	1/16/2013	Bob Jones	Widgets	5	$ 10.00				
9	1/18/2013	Fred Mercury	Widgets	7	$ 10.00				
10	1/22/2013	Mary Simmons	Lag Bolts	2	$ 12.50				
11	1/23/2013								
12									
13									
14									
15									

Figure 11.16 AutoComplete drop-down list.

Select an entry from the list. The entry is entered in the cell. Using the list enables you to see the available entries, which can be particularly useful in large worksheets that contain many different labels in a particular column.

Filling and Entering Series

The capability to automatically fill cells with information is a useful and time-saving trick that can help you avoid data entry drudgery and also decrease the possibility of data entry errors in your worksheets. A couple different techniques help in filling cells with information.

We discussed the new Flash Fill feature earlier in the chapter. Flash Fill is used primarily to separate into multiple columns text information that has been lumped together in a column. For example, if you have to fix a poorly designed worksheet where first and last names have been combined in a single column; the Flash Fill feature helps you "type" the first names into a new column as soon as it recognizes the "entry" pattern for the information. Flash Fill is kind of a hybrid tool, a cross between Autocomplete and Fill.

You probably won't use Flash Fill often (unless you have a coworker that keeps designing "bad" worksheets). One tool that you will use quite often to extend or copy a label or value series is the Fill handle.

Another option for filling data series is the Fill command in the Editing group of the Home tab, which can be used to enter value series where you can specify the type of series (such as linear or growth) and provide the step value for the series. The step value serves as either the amount that the value in each subsequent cell is increased (in a linear series) or the multiple used to increase each subsequent entry in the series (in a growth series). Data series can also be created where the step value provides the increment for specifying each subsequent date in the series.

Using the Fill Handle

The Fill handle can help you quickly create series for days of the week and months of the year. It can also provide a series for labels that contain a number. For example, if I divided my sales territory into regions specified as Region 1, Region 2, and so on, all I would have to do is enter the Region 1 label in a cell and then use the Fill handle to drag the rest of the series into other adjacent cells, as needed. The Fill handle can create a series in a column or a row.

The Fill handle is the small black box in the lower-right corner of a selected cell's border. The mouse pointer becomes a small + symbol when you are on the Fill handle. To use the Fill handle, drag it in the direction you want the fill to take place. For instance, if you are filling cells in a column, you can drag down or up (probably down); if you are filling cells in a row, you can drag to the right or left.

To create a fill series, such as the days of the week or months of the year, follow these steps:

1. Enter the first item in the series, such as Monday or January.

2. Grab the Fill handle and drag in the appropriate direction to extend the series. ScreenTips appear as you drag across the cells, showing a preview of each item that will be placed in each subsequent cell.

3. Release the mouse to enter the series items.

When you release the mouse, the series items appear in the cells. The AutoFill Options button appears, as shown in Figure 11.17.

Figure 11.17
A filled month series and the AutoFill Options.

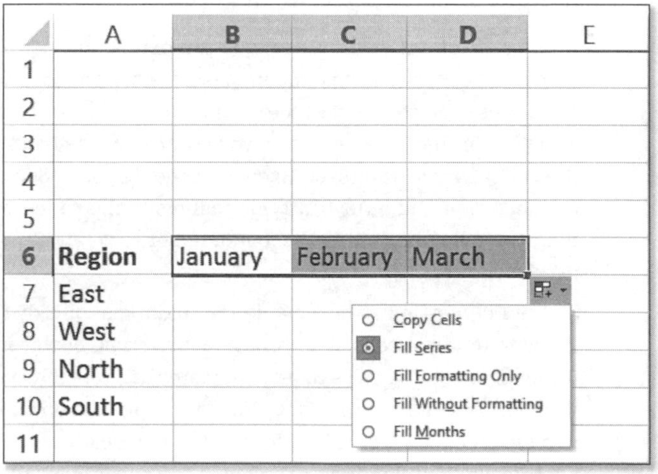

The AutoFill Options menu (accessed when you select the AutoFill Options button) provides a series of options related to dragging the Fill handle. Although we are using the Fill handle to extend a series, you can see from Figure 11.17 that other options are possible. These options vary depending on whether you are using the Fill handle to copy an item (such as a formula, a function, or even a heading) or creating a series, as discussed here. The possibilities the AutoFill Options menu provide can include the following:

- **Copy Cells:** The Fill handle might have created a series when you wanted to copy the entry in a cell to other cells using the Fill handle. Select this option to copy rather than fill.

- **Fill Series:** If the Fill handle has copied the entry in the cell, you can select this option to get an extended series.

- **Fill Formatting Only:** This option fills the cells that you move across using the Fill handle with the formatting provided by the selected cell. The contents of the cell are not copied (or extended) into the subsequent cells in the fill range.

- **Fill Without Formatting:** This option creates a series but does not include any formatting that has been applied to the cell that you "extended" using the Fill handle.

You can also use the Fill handle to extend numerical series, date series, and even text series (where a number is included with a text entry, such as Region 1). When you use the Fill handle to extend a date series, the AutoFill Options menu provides other options, such as Fill Days, Fill Weekdays, Fill Months, and Fill Years. So no matter what type of date series you are trying to create from a source date, the Fill handle can create the series for you.

The Fill handle can also be used to copy a cell's content, including formulas for functions, to a range of cells. Remember that if you don't get the result you seek, you might have to consult the AutoFill Options menu and then select the option that provides the needed fill or copy.

 tip

When you copy formulas and functions to multiple cells in a column or row, you typically employ the Fill handle rather than copy and paste.

In the case of numerical series, you can extend any series as long as Excel knows what the step is between the numbers in the series. The step is the incremental difference between the numbers in the series, so when you enter 2 in a cell and then 4 in the cell below it, you tip off Excel that the step is 2. Select both of the cells containing the first two numbers in the series, and then drag the Fill handle on the second number to create the series as needed.

So the Fill handle can create a series, and it can quickly copy items to multiple cells. It does have a limitation, however, in terms of copying a cell's content in more than one direction (such as down and then to the right). You can copy only down or up in a single column, or to the right or left in a single row. If you

 note

If you are attempting to fill cells with a series that is already contained in the worksheet, you can select Flash Fill in the AutoFill Options to enter the existing data.

need to copy into multiple columns or rows, you have to extend the series in one direction and then extend the series a second time in the second direction. This makes more sense when you attempt to copy formulas or functions to cells in a range that encompasses multiple columns or rows.

➡ *For more about copying formulas and functions,* **see** *"Copying and Moving Formulas and Functions," p. 387.*

Creating Custom Fill Lists

You can also create custom fill lists and then apply them using the Fill handle. For example, you might have a group of employee names or location names that you always enter in the same order in different worksheets. When you create the custom fill list, all you have to do is enter the first item in the list in a cell and then use the Fill handle to extend the rest of the custom fill list into the required cells.

A custom list can consist of text entries or text mixed with numbers. So custom lists are reserved for a series of labels. You can create a custom fill list from a range of cells that already exist in a worksheet, or you can create a custom list by typing in the entries for the list manually. Custom fill lists are created in the Custom Lists dialog box, shown in Figure 11.18.

 note

The Fill command also provides a menu of commands for filling down, right, up, or left. You can use these commands to copy information from a cell to a group of selected cells.

Figure 11.18
The Custom Lists dialog box.

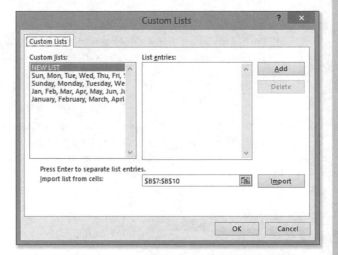

To access the Custom Lists dialog box, select File on the Ribbon to enter Backstage view and then select Options to open the Excel Options window. Select Advanced, and then scroll down in the Advanced options; the Edit Custom Lists button is near the bottom of the General category.

If you want to import a selected range of cells into a custom list, you can specify the range by selecting the Shrink button to the left of the Import button. This gives you access to the worksheet. Select the range, and then click the Expand button to re-enter the Custom Lists dialog box. You can then click the Import button. The new list is placed in the Custom Lists pane, and the entries in the list are shown in the List Entries pane.

If you want to create the custom list from scratch, select New List in the Custom Lists pane and then click Add. You can then type the entries in the List Entries pane. Press Enter after each entry. When you are ready to add the list, click the Add button in the Custom Lists dialog box.

You can now use the custom list or lists that you created in your worksheets. Type the first entry in a custom list in a cell, and then use the Fill handle to extend the range. The new range consists of the entries you placed in the custom list.

 tip

To delete a custom list that you have created, select the list and then click the Delete button in the Custom Lists dialog box.

Creating Custom Series

Another option for creating a series (a series of values, including dates) in a worksheet is to take advantage of the Series dialog box. The Series dialog box gives you complete control over the series you want to create, including the step value (the increment between each subsequent cell and the cell before it) and the stop value. You can also create different types of series:

- **Linear:** This series type uses the starting value provided in the worksheet and then uses the step value to create a linear progression.

- **Growth:** This series type uses the starting value provided in the worksheet and then multiplies each value in the series by the step value to enter each subsequent value in the range. So this type of series is really a geometric progression.

- **Date:** This series type enables you to specify a date unit, such as Day, Weekday, Month, or Year. The step value is then added to each subsequent date in the series.

- **AutoFill:** This type of series mimics the use of the Fill handle. You do not enter a step value for this type of series.

Enter the start value for the series you want to create in a cell in the worksheet. You can then select the cell and the range of cells that will be filled by the information you enter into the Series dialog box. To open the Series dialog box, select the Fill command on the Home tab and then select Series. Figure 11.19 shows the Series dialog box.

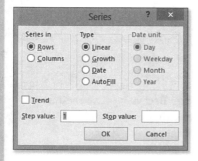

Figure 11.19
The Series dialog box.

Select the appropriate option to specify whether the series appears in rows or columns. Select the type of series you want to create, such as linear, growth, or date. Enter the step value for the series in the Step Value box. If you did not select the cells that you want to fill using the series, you can enter a step value for the series. This specifies the end of the series and also dictates the number of cells the series fills. When you are ready to create the series, select OK.

Copying, Moving, and Deleting Cell Contents

We have already discussed how to use the Fill handle to copy data (both labels and values) from one cell to a range of cells (or from a range to a range). You can also use the Copy command in the Clipboard group to copy a cell's content to another cell. Cell ranges can be copied and then pasted, and a single cell's content can be pasted to a range of cells. In addition, you can move cell data using cut and paste, or drag and drop cells or cell ranges in new locations on a sheet.

Copy-and-paste and cut-and-paste are pretty familiar to even the most novice Office user, so no quantum physics are involved in selecting a cell and then using Copy or Cut to place it on the Clipboard. The different possibilities the Paste command provides get a little confusing, but they give you a lot of possibilities for what is pasted from a selected cell or cell range to another cell or cell range. In terms of the possibilities of the Paste command, some of the options are related to information that you copy from another worksheet in your workbook or another workbook (you can open multiple workbooks and copy or cut and then paste cell information, as needed). Sometimes you want only the cell contents, not the formatting found on the cells (such as borders or colors) or formatting used on the cell contents (such as the number format).

 tip

You can use Ctrl+C to copy, Ctrl+X to cut, and Ctrl+V to paste. When you use Ctrl+V, the Paste icon appears below the pasted items, enabling you to adjust the type of paste you make.

Select a cell or range of cells to be copied. Then select Copy or Cut as needed from the Clipboard group on the Ribbon's Home tab. When you select the Paste command, a gallery of different paste options appears, as shown in Figure 11.20.

Figure 11.20
The Paste gallery.

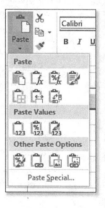

The Paste gallery divides the different paste options into categories. Each of the options found in the categories provides a ScreenTip when you place the mouse on a specific option icon. The options available depend on what you have copied to the Clipboard; the option you select, obviously, depends on the results you require. The Paste gallery categories follow:

- **Paste:** This category provides, from left to right, the following options: Paste, Formulas, Formulas and Number Formatting, and Keep Source Formatting. The Paste option pastes the contents, but they are formatted according to the formatting that has been applied to the new location. If you want to keep the original formatting, use the Keep Source Formatting option. If you are pasting formulas or functions, take advantage of the Formulas option; if you want to keep the original formatting that was applied to the cells containing the formulas, use the Formulas and Number Formatting option.

- **Paste Values:** If you want to paste the values calculated by a formula or function, instead of pasting the formula or function itself, you can use the options provided in this category. Options are provided to paste the value only (Value), the value and its number formatting (Values and Number Formatting), and the value and the cell formatting (Values and Source Formatting).

- **Other Paste Options:** You can paste the formatting of the select cell (or cell range) using the Formatting option. If you want to link the copied data to the destination cell or cells, use the Paste Link option. Linked data updates automatically when you change the values (such as the results of a formula or function) in the source cell or cells.

When you select one of the options and paste the cell or range into a worksheet, the Paste Options button appears just below the pasted content. You can access the same options that were available in the Paste gallery from this button. The cell or range that you originally copied still has a marquee (that sparkly rectangle thing) denoting that the cell or cells have been copied to the Clipboard. Press Esc to get rid of the marquee.

You can access the Office Clipboard to view cells or cell ranges that have been copied or cut to it. This enables you to reuse items on the Clipboard. For example, you can paste any of the items on the Clipboard, so if you have cut and then pasted a range, you can paste that same range again from the Clipboard to the current worksheet or another worksheet in the workbook.

To view the contents of the Clipboard, select the Clipboard launcher at the bottom right of the Clipboard group on the Ribbon's Home tab. The Clipboard appears as a pane on the left side of the Excel workspace, as shown in Figure 11.21.

The Office Clipboard can hold up to 24 items, which makes it easy to paste data from worksheet to worksheet or even to another Excel workbook. When you place the mouse on an item stored in the Clipboard, a drop-down menu arrow appears. You can use the menu to paste the item. You can also remove it from the Clipboard by selecting Delete on the drop-down menu. You can paste all the items on the Clipboard using the Paste All command. If you want to remove all the current items on the Clipboard, click the Clear All button.

Figure 11.21
The Office Clipboard pane.

Using the Paste Special Dialog Box

The Paste gallery provides a number of possibilities in terms of what is pasted after you copy or cut a cell's or range's data. The Paste Special dialog box provides even more possibilities. Many of the options provided in the Paste Special dialog box relate to pasting cells (that have been copied or cut) from one worksheet to another worksheet, or cells from one workbook to another. Because worksheets can be formatted differently, the options in the Paste Special dialog box are designed to enable you to fine-tune what is pasted and how it affects the worksheet where the cells are pasted. To open the Paste Special dialog box (after you copy or cut a cell range), select Paste and then Paste Special. Figure 11.22 shows the Paste Special dialog box.

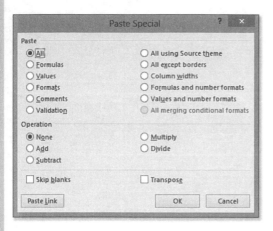

Figure 11.22
The Paste Special dialog box.

Most of the options provided in the Paste area of the Paste Special dialog box have names that give you a good idea of what the option does. Some of the options paste the contents of the cell or range in the worksheet. For example, Values converts formula and function results to the actual value calculated when the cells are pasted. The Formats option pastes the cell formatting. The Formulas option pastes the formulas or functions in the range but does not include any of the formatting provided by the source range. Some of the other options paste only formatting or other attributes. For example, the Formats option pastes only the cell formatting found in the range and any formatting that has been applied to the text or values found in the cells. Another example is the Column Width option, which pastes only the column width from the source range.

Using the Paste Special Operation Options

The Paste Special dialog box goes beyond the various options you might need for pasting cells and cell ranges into a worksheet. The Operation options enable you to perform an operation on a selected range of cells based on a value supplied in the copied cell. You don't actually paste a cell or range of cells for the operation to take place; the Paste Special dialog box uses the originally copied value to adjust the values in a second range of cells. You can add, subtract, multiply, or divide the values in the range.

 tip

The Skip Blanks check box in the Paste Special dialog box enables you to skip blank cells when pasting ranges in your worksheet.

For example, you might have a list of products in a worksheet that is accompanied by a range of prices for the products. If your supplier raises your cost for each item by 2%, you can multiply the values in the range of prices by 1.02 to raise your prices by 2%. So for lack of a better name, we can call the cell containing the 1.02 the adjustment value. The cells that are adjusted using the adjustment value can be referred to as the adjusted range.

To use the Operation option, enter a value in a cell that serves as the adjustment value. Then copy the cell to the Clipboard using the Copy command (Ctrl+C). The marquee appears around the cell. Now select the range of cells that you want to adjust. The marquee remains around the copied adjustment value even though the range of cells to be adjusted is currently selected. Select Paste and then Paste Special to open the Paste Special dialog box. In the Operation options area of the Paste Special dialog box, select the operation that you want to take place, such as add, subtract, multiply, or divide. Then click OK. The selected range (the adjusted range) adjusts according to the operation you chose and the adjustment value you originally copied to the Clipboard.

Transposing a Cell Range

The Paste Special dialog box can also be used to transpose a range of cells that are currently in a row to a column, or vice versa. This is particularly useful if you want to change the column headings that you have placed in the top row of your worksheet into row headings. To transpose a range of cells, you typically use the Cut command (because you are moving the cells) and then the Paste Special dialog box, which provides the Transpose option.

Select the range of cells that you want to transpose, and then select Cut on the Home tab. The marquee marks the range of cells that have been cut. Click in a cell that is the first cell in the range where you transpose the cut range. Make sure that there are empty cells below (if you are transposing a row to column) or to the right (if you are transposing a column to a row) of the cell that you selected after cutting the range to be transposed. Then open the Paste Special dialog box by selecting Paste, Paste Special.

In the Paste Special dialog box, select the Transpose check box and then click OK. The range of cut cells is transposed to the new location.

Moving Cells and Ranges

For moving cell content from one place to another in a worksheet, you can use Cut and Paste if you choose; however, dragging and dropping is much easier. You can drag cell content to a new location, and you can drag the contents of a range of cells to a new location. If you drag and drop a range onto a cell or cells that already contain data, the data is replaced by the data in the range that you are moving.

Select a cell or cell range to be moved, and drag the border of the selected cell or cells to the new location. To insert the range between existing cells in a worksheet, hold down the Shift key as you drag. You can also move the data to another worksheet in the current workbook. To move the data to a different worksheet, press the Alt key and drag the selection to the worksheet's tab. You're switched to that sheet, where you can drop your selection at the appropriate location in the worksheet.

 tip

If you want to copy a range using drag-and-drop, hold down the Ctrl key as you drag a copy of the range to a new location.

Clearing and Deleting Cells

A cell and its content are two different entities when you start looking at the possibilities for removing content from a worksheet. You can quickly remove a cell's content or the content of a number of cells in a selected range by pressing the Delete key on the keyboard. You can use the Clear command to clear the contents of a cell, but it also gives you some options for clearing formatting that was applied to a cell or range of cells or comments that have been added to a cell. The Clear command is in the Editing group on the Home tab (its icon is an eraser). The Clear gallery provides the following options:

- **Clear All:** This option clears formatting, content, and comments.

- **Clear Formats:** This option clears the formatting that has been applied to the cell, including font, alignment, and number formatting. This option also clears any conditional formatting or cell styles that have been applied to the cell or cells.

- **Clear Contents:** This option clears the contents of cell or range of cells (much like the Delete key).

- **Clear Comments:** A comment can be added to a cell to give you additional information about the cell's content. You can remove the comment from a cell or remove the comments on cells that are in a selected range by using this option on the Clear menu.

- **Clear Hyperlinks:** This option removes a hyperlink from the selected cell or range of cells.

- **Remove Hyperlinks:** This option deletes a hyperlink from a cell or cells and removes the formatting.

Clearing cells is foolproof: You select the cell or a range of cells and then use the Delete key or one of the options on the Clear command's menu. If you want to remove cells from the worksheet, you need to determine how you want the cells around the deleted cells to be repositioned. Remove cells only if you want the other cells in the worksheet to shift to new positions. Otherwise, just delete the data in the cells or type new data into the cells.

To remove cells from a worksheet, select the cell or cell range and then select the Delete command in the Cells group of the Ribbon's Home tab. The Delete command provides a gallery that enables you to delete cells, rows, columns, or an entire worksheet. To open the Delete dialog box, select Delete Cells. Figure 11.23 shows the Delete dialog box.

Figure 11.23
The Delete dialog box.

The Delete dialog box enables you to select whether the remaining cells shift left or up to fill the space left by the deleted cells. You can also choose to delete the entire row or column by selecting the appropriate option. When you are ready to delete the cells, click the OK button. The cells are removed from the worksheet, and the remaining cells move to fill the gap left by the deleted cells.

➡ *For information on inserting cells into a worksheet,* ***see*** *"Inserting Cells," **p. 354**.*

Editing Cell Content

Accurately entering information into the cells of your Excel worksheet is extremely important, particularly in the case of values. A worksheet boasting the most complex functions Excel can offer still calculates incorrect results if you have made an error when entering the data onto the worksheet.

While entering text or values in a cell, you do have the capability to edit your work if you make a mistake. As you are entering data, you can quickly back up and delete a typo by using the Backspace key. If you've already entered the data and moved on to another cell before noticing that it is incorrect, you have a couple options.

If the data entered is really a mess, click the cell and retype the entire entry. When you press Enter or move to another cell, your new entry replaces the original data in the cell.

If the data contains only a one- or two-character mistake, you might want to edit the entry. Double-click the cell with the error; the insertion point appears on the far right of the cell. You can use the mouse or the keyboard to move the insertion point and correct the errors in the entry. Several keystrokes that are useful when editing data directly in the cell follow:

- **Right or left arrow keys:** Moves one character to the right or left
- **Home:** Moves to the beginning of the entry
- **End:** Moves to the end of the entry
- **Delete:** Deletes the character to the right of the insertion point

After editing the data in the cell, press Enter or click the Enter button on the formula bar to enter the changes to the data. You can also edit your cell data in the formula bar. Select a cell to edit and then use the mouse to place the insertion point in the formula bar. The various movement keystrokes listed earlier also work in the formula bar. When you have finished editing the cell, click the Enter button in the formula bar or move to another cell.

 tip

You can also check for typos using the Spelling feature. Select the Spelling command on the Review tab or press F7.

Viewing Worksheets

Excel provides different workbook views and makes it easy for you to zoom in and out on the current worksheet. Changing the view has no effect on how your worksheet looks when printed (unless you have hidden rows or columns, which are discussed in Chapter 12). The Ribbon's View tab, shown in Figure 11.24, provides the Workbook Views, Show, and Zoom groups, which enable you to manipulate the basic view of the current worksheet and the Excel window.

The View tab provides other commands for manipulating the worksheet and viewing multiple workbooks. Chapter 12 discusses the various commands found in the Window group.

Figure 11.24
The Ribbon's
View tab.

The Workbook Views group gives you different views of the current worksheet. The Normal view, which is the default view, provides the basic landscape that we use to enter values, labels, formulas, and functions in the worksheet. Because we spend most of our time working in the Normal view, we aren't always cognizant of where the page breaks are located in the worksheet and how the worksheet translates to the printed page.

To get a better idea of the overall layout of the worksheet and to view any page breaks in the worksheet, select the Page Layout command. The amount of information that you can place on one Excel page is based on the default paper size and page orientation that is configured for Excel. In most cases, in the United States, the paper size is letter (8.5 × 11 inches) and the orientation is portrait. So page breaks are automatically placed in the worksheet when you exceed the usable space on any page. Figure 11.25 shows a worksheet that has a page break between the last two columns of the sheet.

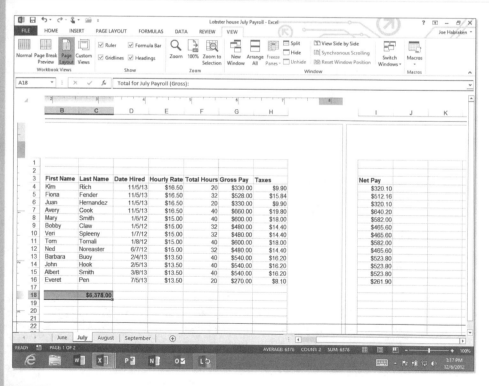

Figure 11.25
Page Layout
view.

After you have an indication of the overall layout of the sheet, particularly in the case of the page breaks, you can attempt to remedy any issues before you print the worksheet. For example, the worksheet shown in Figure 11.25 would print on two pages, essentially orphaning the last column of the worksheet. You have options related to this problem. If the cell range that is pushed onto the second page (or any number of pages) is fairly small (such as a column or two or a row or two), you can have Excel scale the worksheet to fit on one page when you print the worksheet (discussed in the next section). However, doing so reduces the font size on the printout, and you don't want to end up with a printed page that requires a magnifying glass to read.

After you use Page Layout view to take a look at your worksheet, dashed lines appear on the worksheet in Normal view. These are the page breaks present in the worksheet.

Another option is to adjust the page orientation or the paper size, perhaps even the margins. For example, a worksheet with a lot of columns might print on one page if you switch the orientation from portrait to landscape using the Orientation command on the Page Setup tab (discussed in the next section of this chapter).

The Workbook Views group also provides a possibility for adjusting a page break or breaks: You can use the Page Break Preview command. When you select Page Break Preview, Excel zooms out on the worksheet and shows the page breaks as dashed lines. The Welcome to Page Break Preview dialog box also appears, letting you know that you can drag page breaks to a new position in the worksheet as needed. Click any of the page breaks and drag to a new location.

tip

You can also use the View short-cut icons on the status bar to switch between Normal view, Page Layout view, and Page Break Preview.

You can also get a larger view of the current worksheet by using Full Screen view. This command blows up your current view (such as Normal or Page Layout) on the screen by removing the title bar, Ribbon, and status bar from the Excel window. You can still access the worksheet tabs at the bottom of the worksheet. To exit Full Screen view, press the Esc key.

When you are working in Normal view, Page Layout view, and Page Break Preview, you can use the Zoom slider on the status bar to change the zoom level. You can also take advantage of the commands in the Zoom group on the View tab. To open the Zoom dialog box, select the Zoom command. The Zoom dialog box enables you to set a specific magnification from a range of options, includ-

tip

You can also use the mouse wheel to zoom in and out on your worksheet. Simply hold down the Ctrl key as you use the mouse wheel. Rolling the mouse wheel away from you zooms in, and rolling the mouse wheel toward you zooms out.

ing 200%, 75%, and 25%. You can choose to fit the current selection (a selected range) on the screen using the Fit Selection option. If you want to set a custom zoom level, use the Custom box in the Zoom dialog box.

You can quickly zoom to 100% using the 100% command. If you want to focus on a particular range of cells, you can zoom to a certain selection. Select the range and then select the Zoom to Selection command. You can then use the Zoom slider as needed to zoom in or out on the current selection.

To finish the first three groups on the View tab, we should probably take a quick look at the Show group. This group enables you to remove items from the Excel workspace, such as the formula bar, the row and column headings, and the gridlines from the worksheet. This group provides four check boxes that toggle the feature on or off; these commands are Ruler, Gridlines, Formula Bar, and Headings. The Ruler command is inactive in Normal view and is available only in Page Layout view. This makes sense because Page Layout view shows you how your worksheet will appear on the printed page. You can use the ruler to align objects such as charts and images on a worksheet.

Printing Worksheets

Printing worksheets is a two-step process. As you enter information on a worksheet, you don't need to worry about the overall layout of the sheet until you need a hard copy. The Page Layout tab of the Ribbon provides all the commands you need to adjust the overall layout of the sheet, including page orientation, margins, and page sizes. You can also scale the sheet and insert page breaks into the worksheet as needed.

After you have adjusted the various page layout settings using the Page Layout tab, you can open the Backstage Print page, which enables you to specify the printer for the printout and also configure other print settings, such as what is to be printed, how many copies should be printed, and how the printouts should be collated. Let's look at the Page Layout command and then the Print page options.

Using the Page Layout Commands

The Ribbon's Page Layout tab provides several groups of commands that relate to getting the worksheet ready to print. The Page Setup, Scale to Fit, and Sheet Options groups enable you to control the size and orientation of the worksheet pages, scale the worksheet data to fit on a page, and include gridlines or heading in the printout, respectively. The Page Layout tab, shown in Figure 11.26, also includes the Themes group and the Arrange group; Chapter 12 discusses Themes.

Figure 11.26
The Page Layout tab of the Ribbon.

The Page Setup group on the Page Layout tab provides commands that are important in terms of configuring the page settings for the worksheet. Commands are provided for everything from setting the margins to specifying print titles that consist of row or column headings that are repeated on each page of the printout. The commands provided in the Page Setup group are as follows:

- **Margins:** The Margin command provides three different margin settings in a gallery: Normal (top and bottom .75 inch, left and right .7 inch), Wide (top, bottom, left, and right 1 inch), and Narrow (top and bottom .75 inch, left and right .25 inch). You can also access the Margins tab of the Page Setup dialog by selecting Custom Margins.

- **Orientation:** This command enables you to switch from portrait to landscape, or vice versa.

- **Size:** This command provides a gallery of page sizes, such as Letter, Legal, Executive, and A3 through A5. Select More Paper Sizes to open the page tab of the Page Setup dialog box. You can use the Paper Size drop-down list to select other page sizes available on the default printer.

- **Print Area:** This command enables you to set a print area based on a selected range in the worksheet. You can also use this command to clear a print area that you have previously set.

- **Breaks:** This command provides a menu of commands that enable you to insert a page break, remove a page break, or reset all the page breaks in the worksheet.

- **Background:** This command enables you to select an image that is used as a background for the worksheet.

- **Print Titles:** This command opens the Sheet tab of the Page Setup dialog box. Print titles are column or row headings that you want repeated on each page of the printout. This is an extremely useful feature when working with large worksheets that span multiple pages.

The Scale to Fit group on the Page Layout tab enables you to scale the worksheet by width, height, or scale. By default, the scale is set to 100%, and you can decrease or increase the scale as needed to either shrink or expand the size of the worksheet. The Width command shrinks the width of the worksheet on a page or pages. The default width is set to Automatic, so the width of the actual sheet determines the number of pages to be used. If you want to shrink a worksheet that has a minimal number of columns that are outside the first page, you can select 1 on the Width menu to shrink the worksheet to fit on one page (by width). You can specify from one to nine pages on the Width menu.

The Height command also provides a menu of page number selections from 1 to 9. It is best used when you have a worksheet with many rows and want to make a few errant rows fit onto a page.

Both the Width and the Height menus provide a More Pages selection that opens the Page tab of the Page Setup dialog box, as shown in Figure 11.27. You can use the Fit To option and the accompanying spinner boxes for width and height to scale the worksheet to a specific number of pages wide and a specific number of pages tall.

The page tab of the Page Setup dialog box also provides an Adjust To option that enables you to scale the worksheet as a percentage of its normal size. This is the same setting as the Scale setting found in the Scale to Fit group on the Page Layout tab.

The Sheet Options group on the Page Layout tab provides check boxes related to gridlines and headings. If you want the gridlines on the worksheet to print, select the Print check box under Gridlines. You can also have the column and row headings print by selecting the Print check box under Headings.

 tip

You can remove a page break in the Page Break Preview by dragging the page break off the worksheet.

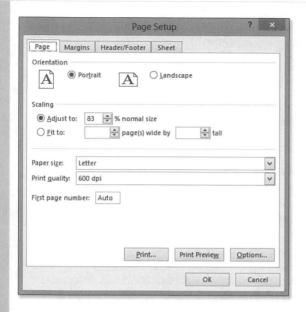

Figure 11.27
The Page tab of the Page Setup dialog box.

Setting a Print Area

You do not always have to print an entire worksheet; instead, you can easily tell Excel what part of the worksheet you want to print by selecting the print area yourself. If the area you select is too large to fit on one page, no problem—Excel breaks it into multiple pages. Print areas are useful when you want to print only a portion of a worksheet.

To set a print area, select the range in the sheet that serves as the print area. Select the Print Area command and then select Set Print Area. The print area is denoted by a dashed-line frame. When you open the Print page in the Backstage, only the print area is previewed. You can also clear a print area, if needed. Select the Print Area command and then select Clear Print Area.

Inserting Page Breaks

Excel determines the page breaks in the worksheet to be printed based on the paper size, the margins, and the print area (if one has been selected). Excel does not do any thinking when it places page breaks in your worksheet. It places them where they are needed, even if it breaks up the continuity of the data that you have entered in the sheet's columns and rows. To make the pages more presentable and understandable, and to break information in logical places, you can insert your own page breaks into the worksheet. You can insert page breaks into the worksheet in Normal view, Page Layout view, or Page Break Preview.

To insert a page break to the left of a column, select the column in the worksheet (click the column's heading). Select the Breaks command and then select Insert Page Break. You can also insert a page break, specifying a row as the break position. The page break is inserted above the selected row.

You can also specify that a page break be inserted above and to the left of a cell in the worksheet, meaning that you get two page breaks: one along the row and one along the column. This can be useful when you are working with a large worksheet that might contain various sections, such as four quarters of data positioned on the worksheet into obvious quadrants. All you have to do is select the cell that is below and to the right of where you want the page breaks to be inserted, select Breaks, and then select Insert Page Break.

After inserting page breaks, take the time to peruse your worksheet in Page Layout view or Page Break Preview (particularly if you want to adjust the location of page breaks). You can also use the Backstage Print page to preview the printout of the worksheet. If you want to start over and remove the page breaks that you have inserted in the worksheet, select the Breaks command and then select Reset All Page Breaks.

Setting Print Titles

If you will have a multiple-page worksheet and you have either many rows or many columns, it makes sense to set print titles for the worksheet. Print titles enable you to specify a rows or rows where you have entered column names or headings and repeat these on each sheet of the printout. You can also specify a column or columns that contain row headings and have these repeat on each page of the printout.

To access the Sheet tab of the Page Setup dialog box, select the Print Titles command. In the Print Titles area of the Sheet tab is a Rows to Repeat at Top box and a Columns to Repeat at Left box. To specify rows to repeat, click the Shrink button on the right of the Rows to Repeat at Top box. The dialog box rolls up, or shrinks. Select the row or rows to be repeated using the mouse. Click the Expand button on the dialog box to return to the Sheet tab. If you need to also include columns as print titles, click the Shrink button to the right of the Columns to Repeat at Left box and repeat the process by selecting the columns that you want to print. When you have completed the process, click OK to close the Page Setup dialog box.

 tip

You can access the Page Setup dialog box by selecting the dialog box launcher on the Page Setup, Scale to Fit, or Sheet Options groups.

Working on the Print Page

When you have the Page Layout settings the way you want them, you can access the Backstage Print page to finalize settings for your sheet printout (you can actually print multiple sheets in a workbook). To access the Backstage, select File on the Ribbon. In the Backstage, select Print. Figure 11.28 shows the Excel Print page.

The Print page gives you a preview of your printout. You can use the page indicators on the left of the preview to move through the pages of the printout. You can also use the Zoom to Page command to zoom in and out on the current page.

The Print page enables you to set the number of copies you want to print and also to choose the printer for the printout. In addition, you can adjust printer properties for the selected printer.

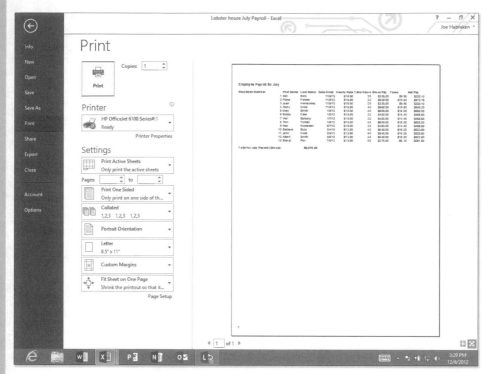

Figure 11.28
The Backstage Print page.

The Settings area of the preview window enables you to control options related to the printout, including what is actually printed and how the printout and settings relate to page size, margins, and scaling. The options provided on the Print page follow:

- **Print Active Sheets:** By default, this menu is set to Print Active Sheets; it determines what you print. You can also choose to print the entire workbook (all the sheets in the workbook) or only a selection in the current worksheet. To print only certain pages, enter the page numbers of the pages you want to print in the Pages boxes.

- **Print One Sided:** Again, this is the default setting for this menu. You can also choose to print on both sides of the paper. Two settings for two-sided printing are supplied; one is for flipping pages on the long edge, and the other is for flipping pages on the short edge.

- **Orientation:** This menu enables you to switch between portrait and landscape orientation.

- **Page Size:** The Page Size menu is set to the page size you specified on the Page Layout tab of the ruler. You can change the page size via this menu. Letter is the default.

- **Margins:** This drop-down menu enables you to change the margin settings that you might have set via the Margins command on the Page Layout tab. You can choose from margins provided in the gallery or select Custom Margins to access the Margins tab of the Page Setup dialog box, as shown in Figure 11.29. You can use the spinner boxes as needed to set the margins for the worksheet. You can also specify a header or footer area using the appropriate spinner box.

Figure 11.29
The Margins tab of the Page Setup dialog box.

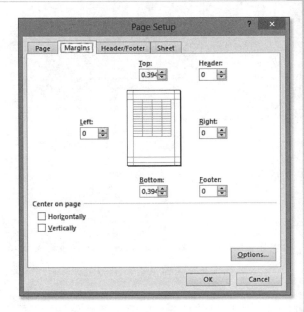

- **Custom Scaling:** You can scale the worksheet using the options provided on this menu. You can choose to have the entire sheet print on one page (this is useful when the sheet has a page break between most of the columns and one or two "straggler" columns) or choose to fit either all the columns or all the rows on one page.

There is also a Page Setup link at the bottom of the various print options. This link opens the Page Setup dialog box. Before we end our discussion of worksheet printing (which is just a matter of clicking the Print button on the Print page), we need to look at how to specify headers and footers for your worksheet printouts.

Inserting Headers and Footers

To open the Page Setup dialog box, click Page Setup. To access the header/footer information for the worksheet, select the Header/Footer tab.

The Header/Footer tab provides a preview of the current header and footer (which means there is probably not a header or footer). The tab also provides check boxes that enable you to determine whether there are different headers and footers for odd and even pages and whether the first page is different (in terms of headers and footers) from the rest of the printout.

To specify a header for the worksheet, click the Custom Header button. This opens the Header dialog box, shown in Figure 11.30. You can specify a header for the left, center, and right sections of the worksheet.

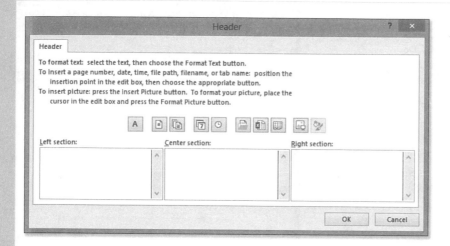

Figure 11.30
The Header dialog box.

For example, you might want to place your name in the left section of the header, the title of the worksheet in the center, and perhaps a draft number or the date in the right section. Enter the text for a header section. You can then select the text and use the Format Text button to open the Font dialog box and format the selected text.

A number of buttons are provided that insert information into the header, such as the page number, date, file path, and sheet name. You can even insert and format a picture such as a logo into the header. When you have the information for the various sections of the header, click OK to return to the Header/Footer tab. A preview of the header is provided.

If you want to include a footer, click the Custom Footer button. The Footer dialog box opens. The Footer dialog box is basically a replica of the Header dialog box and gives you the same three section panes and tools. Enter the footer information as needed in the three footer sections, and then click OK to return to the Header/Footer tab of the Page Setup dialog box. When you have finished specifying the options for the header and/or footer, click OK to return to the Print page.

The header and/or footer information appears in the preview provided by the Print page. When you are ready to print your worksheet, click the Print button.

WORKSHEET FORMATTING AND MANAGEMENT

Entering data into a sheet, such as labels (text), values, formulas, and functions, is only one aspect of creating a sheet. Formatting entries in cells so that certain information is highlighted or certain cells are emphasized can also be important. Creating a sheet that has visual appeal as well as a sensible layout can help to make all those columns and rows of information easier to understand.

In this chapter, we look at formatting cell entries. We look at how to format text labels, including how to wrap text in a cell or joined cells and also how to work with the formatting of values, such as numbers and dates. Coverage is provided on manipulating cells and cell entries as well as columns, rows, and entire sheets. We also discuss how to add graphics to Excel sheets for more visual appeal.

Formatting Text Entries

Formatting text entries, or labels (as we like to call them in Excel worksheets), can be as simple as assigning different font settings or alignment attributes to a cell or a range of cells. Formatting text in Excel isn't really that much different from formatting text in Word or PowerPoint. You can easily add bold or italic to the contents of a cell or cells using commands on the Ribbon. You can also change the font and font size used by a range.

Excel also provides some cell formatting features that are a little more "flashy" than your basic font formatting attributes, such as bold, italic and underline. For example, the Orientation command enables you to rotate text in a cell or cell range. This can be particularly useful in cases when you want to create eye-catching row or column headings but want to do it without greatly increasing the row or column size.

The Ribbon's Home tab provides all the commands for the basic formatting attributes. The Font group provides you with the ability to change the font and font size and to select font attributes, such as bold, italic, underline, and font color. The Font group also includes the Border and Fill Color commands, which we discuss later in the chapter.

The Alignment group contains the vertical alignment commands—Top Align, Middle Align, and Bottom Align—that enable you to control the vertical alignment of text in a cell. The horizontal alignment tools are also present in this group—Align Text Left, Center, and Align Text Right—as are the Decrease Indent and Increase Indent commands.

To format labels in a cell or cell range, select the cells that are to be formatted. Then select the attributes that you want to apply to the text labels by using the commands in the Font and Alignment group.

 note

The Ribbon's Home tab is consistent in Excel, Word, and PowerPoint. The Home tab always provides the Clipboard group and also includes the Font and other command groups, such as Alignment or Paragraph, that are related to formatting or aligning the text in cells.

Accessing the Format Cells Dialog Box

Font and alignment attributes can also be controlled via the Format Cells dialog box. Because all the information that we put into a worksheet is placed in cells, it makes sense that all the various formatting attributes we assign to sheet labels would be considered cell formatting.

To format the text in a cell or cell range, select the range and then open the Format Cells dialog box. You can open the Format Cells dialog box by selecting the dialog box launcher in the Font, Alignment, or Number groups. The group dialog box launcher that you use to open the dialog box dictates the tab selected. For example, if you launch the Format Cells dialog box from the Font group, the Font tab is selected when the dialog box opens.

You can also open the dialog box from the Format command in the Cells group; select Format, then Format Cells. Figure 12.1 shows the Font tab of the Format Cells dialog box.

The Font tab of the Format Cells dialog box provides you with access to the same font attributes provided by the commands in the Font group. The Font tab, however, provides you with some additional font attributes, such as the accounting underline styles (single and double accounting) and provides you with effects, such as strikethrough and superscript and subscript.

Although font formatting is meant to make your sheet look "better," too much font formatting can be distracting. You might want to limit yourself to only a font type or two and only use

 tip

You can also use keyboard shortcuts to format cells such as Ctrl+B for bold, Ctrl+I for italic, Ctrl+U for single underline, and Ctrl+5 for strikethrough.

 caution

The discussion in this section focuses on the formatting of text entries. You can also apply any of the font formatting and alignment settings to values (numbers) in your sheets to make them stand out or otherwise be differentiated from the surrounding data. A very useful tool for formatting values is the conditional formatting tool; it allows you to format values (including the results of formulas) based on whether or not a value meets a particular condition. We discuss conditional formatting in this chapter.

bold, italic, and other formatting attributes, such as a font color when you are sure that they truly enhance the sheet.

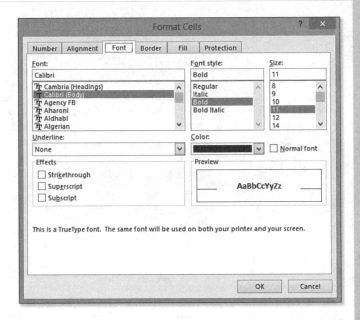

Figure 12.1
The Font tab of the Format Cells dialog box.

Changing Text Orientation

You can change the orientation of text in a range of cells by using the Orientation command in the alignment group. This is useful in cases where your labels must conform to very narrow columns or in cases where you want to align labels on the diagonal so that they are readily noticeable or you just want to add a little bit of design drama to the top of the sheet.

Select the cell range that you want to format with the Orientation command. Then select Orientation in the Alignment group. The orientation possibilities are as follows:

- **Angle Counterclockwise:** Tilts the text upward on the diagonal in a counterclockwise direction, as shown in Figure 12.2.

- **Angle Clockwise:** Tilts the text onto the diagonal clockwise.

- **Vertical Text:** Aligns the text vertically in the cells expanding the row height as needed to accommodate the longest entry in the row.

- **Rotate Text Up:** Rotates the text up vertically.

- **Rotate Text Down:** Rotates the text down vertically.

- **Format Cell Alignment:** Opens the Format Cells dialog box with the Alignment tab selected.

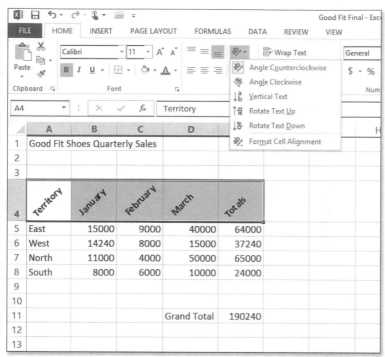

Figure 12.2
Rotate text labels using the Orientation command.

The options provided by the Orientation command are limited to five different orientations for the text. If you want to create a custom rotation, you can do so on the Alignment tab of the Format Cells dialog box. Drag the Orientation Degree dial to specify the orientation for the text visually. Or you can specify the orientation by specifying the actual degrees of the angle to be used using the Degrees spinner box. Positive angle values give you a text up rotation, and negative angle values give you a text down rotation. When you finish setting the orientation on the Alignment tab, click OK to close the Format Cells dialog box.

Formatting Values

The number formats provided by Excel for the numerical values in your sheets are extremely useful for differentiating the different types of values present. You want to make it easy for anyone viewing the sheet to be able to quickly distinguish between the different types of data in a sheet, such as currency, percentages, or dates. Obviously, you can format values as you format text in a sheet with settings, such as bold and italic or a font color; however, assigning actual numeric formatting to a value (such as currency or percentages) gives that value or range of values immediate meaning.

Although you can enter numbers with formatting as you type, such as $20.50 or 2,300 (Excel automatically recognizes this number formatting), it is much easier to enter the values and then format them after the fact. Excel provides you with more than one way to format the values in your sheet.

The most obvious path for formatting numeric values in a sheet is to take advantage of the commands in the Number group on the Ribbon's Home tab. This group provides commands related to specific number formats, such as the percent style, and provides you with the ability to increase or decrease the decimal places in cell values. It also provides a gallery with access to several number formats. The Number group commands are as follows:

- **Number Format:** Provides 11 different numeric formats, such as Number, Currency, Fraction, Scientific, and Text, on the drop-down gallery, which is set to General by default. It also provides access to the Number tab of the Format Cells dialog box via the More Number Formats command.

- **Accounting Number Format:** Provides different accounting or currency formats. The default is U.S. dollars. This command also includes other international accounting formats, such as British pounds, the Chinese yuan (People's Republic of China), and the euro.

- **Percent Style:** Displays the number as a percentage.

- **Comma Style:** Displays the number with commas as the thousands separator.

- **Increase Decimal:** Increases the number of decimal places.

- **Decrease Decimal:** Decreases the number of decimal places and rounds the number as needed.

The Number Format command's gallery provides the greatest number of options in terms of formatting values in a sheet. There are additional numeric formats available in Excel in the Format Cells dialog box. You can use the More Number Formats command at the bottom of the Number Format gallery or the dialog box launcher at the bottom of the Number group to open the Format Cells dialog box. The Number tab is selected in the dialog box. This tab provides a Category list of different number formats, as shown in Figure 12.3.

Figure 12.3
The Number tab of the Format Cells dialog box.

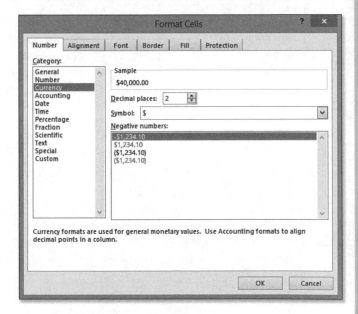

Using the Format Cells Dialog Box

The Number tab of the Format Cells dialog box provides several categories of number formats. Table 12.1 provides a list of these different number formats provided on the Number tab of the Format Cells dialog box and a short description of each.

Table 12.1 Excel Number Formats

Number Format	Examples	Description
General	10.6	No specific number format.
Number	3,400.50	The default number format providing two decimal places and commas as separators. Negative numbers are shown in red.
Currency	$3,400.50	The default Currency format including the default symbol ($ for U.S.). Negative values are shown in red.
Accounting	$3,400.50	Aligns currency symbols and decimal points for values vertically (in a column).
Date	11/7/2010	The default Date format is the month, day, and year separated by a slash.
Time	10:30:45 PM	The default time format is the hour, minutes, and seconds separated by a colon; AM or PM is also designated.
Percentage	99.50%	The default percentage format has two decimal places.
Fraction	1/2	The default fraction format provides for up to one digit on either side of the solidus, or fraction slash as the slash dividing the two numbers is also referred to.
Scientific	3.40E+03	The default scientific format has two decimal places and can be used to display extremely large numbers.
Text	123456	Use the text format to format numbers as text.
Special	44240	This format is designed to display ZIP Codes, phone numbers, and Social Security numbers correctly so that you don't have to enter any special characters, such as hyphens or parentheses.
Custom	00.0%	Use this format to create custom number formats. You can edit any of the existing codes as you create your own custom formats.

Several of the number formats enable you to control the number of decimal places used by the format and also how negative numbers to which a particular format are assigned appear in the sheet. Some formats also enable you to include or preclude the thousand separator—the comma. A sample of how the selected number format looks in your sheet is provided on the right of the Number tab.

After selecting a format (or designing your own format using the Custom category), click OK. The format is assigned to the selected cell range in the sheet.

Creating Custom Number Formats

Although there are probably more than enough built-in number formats for most Excel users, you might find yourself in a situation where you really need to create a custom format. To create a custom format, select the Custom Category on the Number tab, as shown in Figure 12.4.

Figure 12.4
Creating a custom number format.

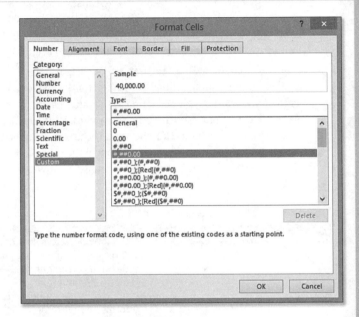

If you want to base your number format on an existing format, select that format; then click Custom to view the codes for that format. You can then edit the existing number format and create your custom form in the Type box. As you specify the custom format, a sample is provided above the Type box. Probably the best way to learn to create your own formats is to look at the format codes that have been created for the different numerical formats provided by Excel.

The rules for creating custom formats are straightforward. Each custom format can consist of up to four sections. The sections are divided by semicolons. Each section has a specific purpose in terms of the state of the value to be formatted. The first section serves as the format for the number if it is positive, the second section provides the formatting if the number is negative, the third section provides the formatting for zero values, and the fourth section provides the formatting for text. So, a custom format would follow the pattern of POSITIVE; NEGATIVE; ZERO; TEXT. A sample numeric format code with all four sections might look something like this:

#,##0.00;[Red] -#,##0.00;0.00;[Blue]"Replace with Value"

The number sign (#) serves as a digit placeholder and the zeros in the code pad the format with zeros when necessary to fill the format. The commas serve as thousand separators. The color codes, [Red] and [Blue], dictate the colors for those sections of the custom format. Note that the second section, which is used for negative numbers, also includes a hyphen (-) that serves as a minus sign.

Your custom format does not necessarily need to include all four sections. For example, you could create a custom format that includes only two sections such as #,##0.00;[Red] -#,##0.00;0.00, which specifies how to format the values when they are either positive (the first section) or negative (the second section).

After you have determined the number of sections you are going to create in the custom format, you can enter the codes that supply the formatting guidelines for each section. The codes that you use in the custom formats are straightforward. We have already looked at how you use the number sign (#) and zeros in a custom format. Table 12.2 provides a list of some of the other codes you can use in your custom formats and examples of how the codes would be used.

 note

The text formatting section of a custom number format might seem counterintuitive because we are talking about formatting numbers. You can use this section of the format code to let users who enter data in the sheet know that they can't put text entries in cells formatted with the format. For example, you could set up the text section of the format as; [Blue]"Replace with Value" so that any text entered is replaced with the text Replace with Value in blue.

Table 12.2 Excel Custom Format Codes

Code	Example	Usage
#	#,###	Digit placeholder; this particular example provides for no decimal places but does insert a comma at the thousands mark. The number of # placed in the code for your format does not limit the number of characters that you can type in a cell formatted with the code.
0	#,##0.00	Digit placeholder; use to pad format.
?	#0.0?	Digit placeholder; does not display the insignificant zeros but can be used to add spaces on either side of the decimal point to align numbers in a column by the decimal point.
.	#,##0.00	Specifies the decimal place in the code.
%	0.000%	Percentage; formats the number as a percentage (meaning Excel multiplies the number by 100). This example includes three decimal places.
_	#,##0.00_	Space; creates a space in the format that is one character width.
" "	#,##0.00 "Profit"	Quotation marks; use to include text in codes (with or without numbers). In this case, a positive number format includes the text "Profit."
$	$###.##	Currency; designates that the numerical format following the $ code should be formatted as U.S. currency. Other codes that display without quotation marks include the /, &, -, and =.

Code	Example	Usage
m, d, y	m/dd/yy	Date; displays the current month (1–12) without leading zeros. The day would be displayed as two digits with leading zeros, as would the year.
h, m	hh:mm	Time; displays the hour and minutes as a double-digit number.

Table 12.2 provides only a subset of the different codes that you can use to create custom formats. As already mentioned earlier in this section, you can modify any of the format codes provided in the Format Cells dialog box to meet your needs. Just select a code such as a currency code and then click Custom to view the code and modify it as needed. Using the provided format codes as the starting point for your own custom number formats provides you with the basic design for custom formats for currency, dates, fractions, or scientific notation.

Adding Comments to Cells

Providing an explanation for the contents of a particular cell can be useful both to you and to others accessing your Excel workbooks. A comment enables you to include a brief text notation that describes what the content of a cell means or how you came up with a particular value. It can also be useful for annotating complicated formulas or functions that are placed in a cell.

To add a comment to a cell, click on the cell to select it. You can then navigate to the Review tab of the Ribbon and select the New Comment command. A new Comment box opens, as shown in Figure 12.5.

Figure 12.5
A new Comment box.

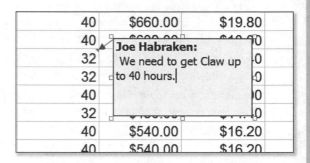

Type the comment text. When you have finished typing the comment, click elsewhere in the worksheet. The cell has a small red triangle in the upper-right corner of its border denoting that a comment has been added to the cell. To view a cell's comment, place the mouse on the cell. The Comment box opens. If you want to edit the comment, you can select the cell containing the comment and then click the Edit Comment command in the Comments group. You can add or delete text as needed.

Formatting Comment Text

You can also modify the font attributes for the text in the Comment box using some of the Font commands on the Home tab. Select the text when editing (or creating) a comment; you can then change settings such as the Font (type), Font Size, and formatting such as bold, italic, and underline. You can also use the vertical and horizontal alignment commands in the Alignment group such as Top Align and Middle Align or Center and Align Text Right. Some of the settings in the Font and Alignment groups are not available for formatting comment text (and are "grayed out").

If you want to radically change the formatting of the comment text, you need to open the comment for editing; right-click the cell that contains the comment, and then select Edit Comment on the shortcut menu. Now you can open the Format Comment dialog box and format the text in the comment. Right-click the comment (which is open for editing) and select Format Comment on the shortcut menu. The Format Comment dialog box opens; you can select the font, font style, and size for the comment and you can also change the color of the font. In addition, effects such as strikethrough, superscript, and subscript can be applied to the text if needed. When you click OK, the Format Comment dialog box closes and you return to the comment.

note

You can also add a comment to a cell by right-clicking on the cell and then selecting Insert Comment.

Deleting and Viewing Comments

The Comment group also provides you with the ability to delete comments—select the cell and then click the Delete command. If you want to cycle through the comments in a sheet, you can use the Previous and the Next commands. To open a comment and leave it open in the sheet (even if you click elsewhere in the sheet), select a cell containing a comment and then click the Show/Hide Comment command. You can leave the comment open in the sheet as needed and then select the cell and click Show/Hide Comment to hide the comment again.

If you want to open all the comments in a sheet, use the Show All Comments command. Click the Show All Comments command a second time to close the comments.

A couple of other things related to comments: You can size the Comment box when a comment is open, and you can drag the comment to a new position on the screen. This doesn't detach the comment from the cell, but it does enable you to get the comment off of other important data as you are perusing a particular area of the sheet. You can tell which cell is associated with the comment because an arrow (think of it as a leash for the Comment box) is attached to both the cell and comment with the arrow pointing at the cell. The comment stays at the new position you have placed it in until you drag it back to the edge of the cell.

Using Themes

Themes provide a way for you to apply cell formatting and create a uniform-looking sheet. A theme is a collection of colors, fonts, and text effects. Themes are consistent across the Office applications, such as Excel, Word, and PowerPoint. This enables you to create a group of related Office application files (document, workbook, and presentation) that have the same overall look.

The Themes gallery is accessed using the Themes command, which is available in the Themes group on the Ribbon's Page Layout tab. The Themes group also houses the Colors, Fonts, and Effects commands. Figure 12.6 shows the Themes gallery.

Figure 12.6
The Excel Themes gallery.

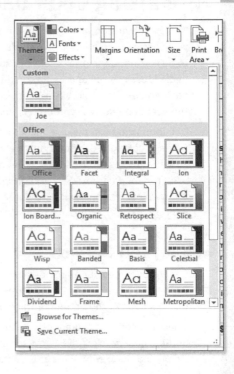

To preview a theme, place the mouse on that theme. When you have found the theme that you want to use for the sheet, select the theme.

As already mentioned, a theme controls the colors, fonts, and effects (formatting settings) when you apply a theme to a sheet. You can change each of these theme attributes using the Colors, Fonts, and Effects commands. If you adjust any of these theme attributes and want to save the result as a new theme, access the Themes gallery and then save the theme using the Save Current Theme command. You can then browse for saved themes using the Browse for Themes command.

You can also create custom theme colors and theme fonts. To create custom theme colors, select Customize Colors in the Colors gallery. This opens the Create New Theme Colors dialog box, which enables you to set the theme background color, accent colors, and hyperlink colors. In the case of theme fonts, select Customize Fonts in the Fonts gallery and the Create New Theme Fonts dialog box opens, enabling you to specify the heading and the body font for your custom theme. The theme feature is pretty consistent across the Office applications (particularly Excel, Word, and PowerPoint). If you are interested in reading more about working with themes, see Chapter 18, "Advanced Presentation Formatting, Themes, and Masters," in the PowerPoint section of this book.

➡ *For more information on working with themes,* ***see*** *"Working with Themes," **p. 539.***

Formatting Cells Using Borders and Color

The overall design of a worksheet is often dictated by the results that the sheet is to produce. Data is sometimes arranged in columns and rows so that formulas or functions can be strategically placed to do calculation on the data. This doesn't always result in a sheet that provides visual cues that make it easy to see and understand the purpose of the sheet. This is where cell borders and cell background or fill colors can be useful. You can use borders and colors to highlight certain areas of the sheet and draw attention to a specific cell or range of cells.

Cell formatting can make a sheet look more visually appealing, but it can also emphasize cells or cell ranges, making it easier for anyone perusing the sheet to have a more immediate understanding of how the results shown in the sheet relate to the data that is used in the calculations. Borders can be used to group certain cells or highlight individual cells, and you can use cell fill color to emphasize or group cells using color. The Borders command and the Fill Color command are both housed in the Font group on the Ribbon's Home tab.

Adding Cell Borders

The Borders command provides a gallery of different border types, such as Bottom Border, Top Border, All Borders, and so on. Figure 12.7 shows the Borders gallery, which includes the Draw Borders tools at the bottom of the gallery.

Select the cell or cell range to which you want to apply the border and then select a border from the Borders gallery (click the arrow to the right of the Borders command). The Borders gallery provides single and double-line border formats as well as thick border formats.

You can also choose to draw the border for a cell range. The Draw Borders area provides a drawing tool—Draw Border—and it also provides the Line Color and the Line Style menus that enable you to select the color for the border line and the line style, such as a single line, dashed line, double line, or thick line.

To draw the border using the default line settings, select the Draw Border command and then use the pen mouse pointer to select the cells that you want to format. You can select the attributes for the line using the Line Color and Line Style menus. When you have finished working with the border drawing tool, press the Esc key or click the Draw Border Line command to turn off the feature (this is the Borders command in the Font group).

For maximum control over the borders you want to place on a selected range of cells, you can use the Border tab of the Format Cells dialog box. To access the dialog box, select More Borders in the Borders gallery. Figure 12.8 shows the Border tab of the Format Cells dialog box.

 note

The Draw Border Grid option in the Borders gallery enables you to draw both internal and external borders on a cell range.

Figure 12.7
The Borders gallery.

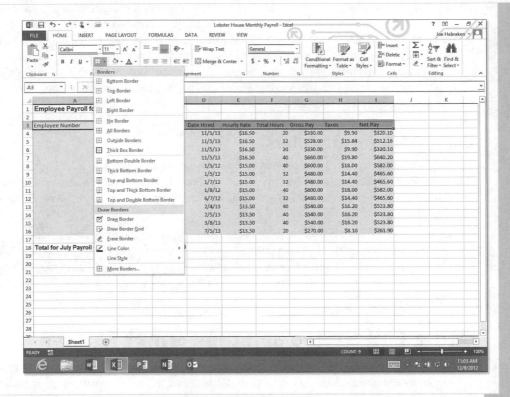

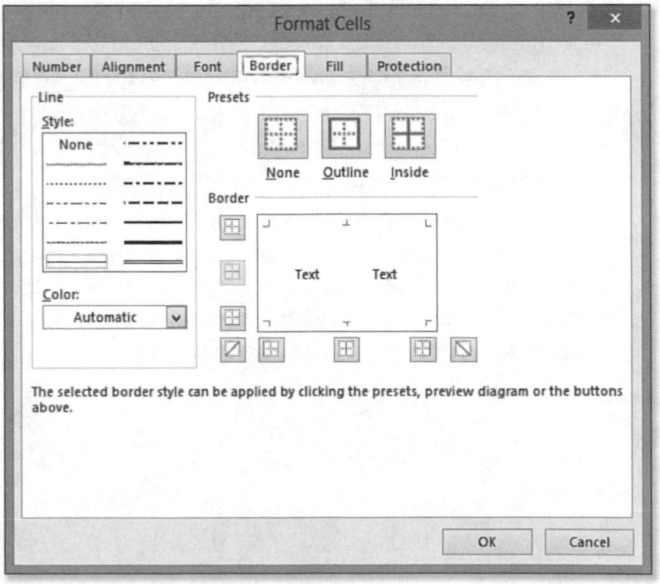

Figure 12.8
The Border tab of the Format Cells dialog box.

The Border tab provides you with border presets as well as all the tools that you need to create your own custom borders. You can use the Style box to select the line for the style and use the Color drop-down palette to specify the color for the line. You can use the various Border buttons provided adjacent to the border preview diagram to specify the borders that you want to apply to the cells. You can also click inside the preview diagram to place the borders. When you have completed specifying the options for your custom borders, click OK. The borders are applied to the selected cell range in the sheet.

Using Background Colors

Backgrounds or cell fill colors provide you with an excellent way to add color to your sheets. The fill colors available are based on the current theme that you have selected for your sheet. You can quickly add a background color to a selected cell or cell range using the Fill Color command in the Font group.

Select the range of cells to which you want to add a fill color. Then select the drop-down arrow for the Fill Color command. The Color palette provided gives you access to the current theme colors and provides standard colors that you can apply to your cell range. If you want to select a custom color, you can click More Colors; this opens the Colors dialog box where you can specify a custom color for the range.

Using Cell Styles and the Format Painter

An easy way to apply cell formatting to a range of cells that includes font, border, and fill settings is to take advantage of the cell styles provided by Excel. These cell styles are more than just ways of adding color and formatting to a sheet, however. Excel provides specific cell styles for helping you denote cells that need to be checked or results that should be considered bad or good. Other cell styles are provided specifically for headings and results, and there are also cell styles provided for number formatting. The Cell Styles command is in the Styles group on the Home tab. When you select the Cell Styles command, the Cell Styles gallery opens, as shown in Figure 12.9.

There are a number of useful cell styles in the Cell Styles gallery. There are Good, Bad, and Neutral categories of styles and also Data and Model styles. A number of themed cell styles are also provided based on the current sheet's current theme.

The Cell Styles gallery is designed as a set of samples. As already mentioned, cell formatting can be used to differentiate cells that contain particular content; so, the cell styles provided are really to get you thinking about the possibilities for showing information more clearly in a sheet by using cell styles. You can use the cell styles provided, but this feature becomes even more useful (and particular to your purposes) if you create your own cell styles.

Figure 12.9
The Cell Styles gallery.

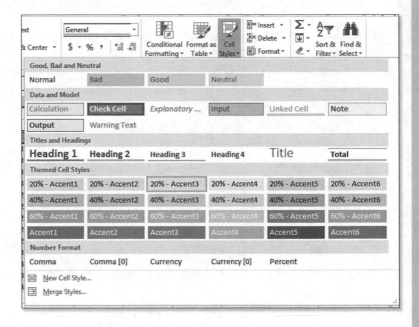

Creating a Cell Style

You can create a cell style by example. Format a cell or range of cells with font and cell attributes (such as font settings and border and fill settings); you can also specify number formatting for the style by formatting the contents of the cell (or the cell range) with the different number formats provided in the Number group or the Number Format gallery.

When you are ready to create the cell style, select the Cell Styles command and then select New Cell Style in the Cell Styles gallery. The Style dialog box opens, as shown in Figure 12.10.

Figure 12.10
The Style dialog box.

By default, the style includes the Number, Alignment, Font, Border, Fill, and any Protection settings assigned to the cell. If you provided all these attributes by example, you can leave all the check boxes enabled. If there is a particular attribute that you do not want to include in the cell style, clear the appropriate check box.

If you want to fine-tune any of the attributes that you have set for the cell style (your examples), click the Format button. This opens the Format Cells dialog box. Although we have discussed most of the tabs provided by this dialog box, the following list provides a quick review:

- **Number:** This tab is where you set the number format for the values that use the style. The formats include Number, Currency, Date, Time, and Percentage.

- **Alignment:** This tab enables you to specify the Horizontal and Vertical alignment of the cell content. You can also rotate text using the Orientation dial.

- **Font:** This tab provides all the font attributes, such as the Font, Font Style, Size, Underline, and Color.

- **Border:** Use this tab to specify a border for the cell style, including the Line Style and Color.

- **Fill:** Select from a number of background colors and fill effects provided. You can also specify custom colors.

- **Protection:** You can lock cells that contain formulas or functions or data that you do not want others to be able to edit. Locking cells does not protect areas of the sheet until you choose to protect the sheet.

➡ *For more information on locking cells and protecting sheets*, **see** *"Protecting Workbooks and Worksheets," p. 303.*

When you have finished working with the various cell attributes for the style in the Format Cells dialog box, click OK to return to the Styles dialog box. Make sure that you provide a name for the style in the Style Name text box. When you click OK, the new cell style is created and is placed in the Custom category area in the Cell Styles gallery. You can now access your new cell style as needed by selecting the Cell Styles command and then selecting your style from the gallery.

Using the Format Painter

You can also copy the cell formatting from a cell to a cell or to a range of cells using the Format Painter. This is useful in cases where you just want to have consistent formatting in a sheet but don't want to have to deal with cell styles.

Select a cell that has the formatting that you want to copy. Click the Format Painter command in the Clipboard group. You can then click on a single cell to paste the format or you can click and drag to format an entire range of cells. If you want to copy the formatting to multiple noncontiguous ranges or from a sheet to two or more other sheets, double-click the Format Painter. You can paste the format as many times as needed. When you have finished working with the Format Painter, click the Format Painter command to toggle it off.

Using Conditional Formatting

So far we approach cell formatting from a static viewpoint; any formatting applied to cells was our job, even in cases where we wanted to highlight certain cells because of their contents using cell formatting. Conditional formatting provides a more dynamic (and often useful) way to use formatting to "point out" cells in a sheet that meet certain conditions. For example, if you want to format all the monthly sales totals in a sheet that fall below a certain conditional amount, you can use conditional formatting to do just that. The cells that meet the condition you set could be formatted with any of the cell-formatting attributes we have discussed. In the example we are discussing, a condition could state that all monthly sales figures that fall below 2,500 are then formatted in red with a blue border. Both the condition that you set and the formatting that is applied are completely up to you. Just make sure that you select cell-formatting attributes for the conditional formatting that stand out from the other formatted cells on the sheet. You are also not limited by the number of conditions that you can apply to a cell. The conditional formatting can be based on an unlimited set of conditions. Obviously, conditional formatting is an excellent tool to apply to cells that contain the results of formulas or functions.

When you select the Conditional Formatting command in the Styles group, the Conditional Formatting gallery opens. It provides you with several different options related to applying conditional formatting to the selected range of cells in the sheet. Figure 12.11 shows the Conditional Formatting gallery with the Highlight Cells Rules command selected.

Figure 12.11
The Conditional Formatting gallery.

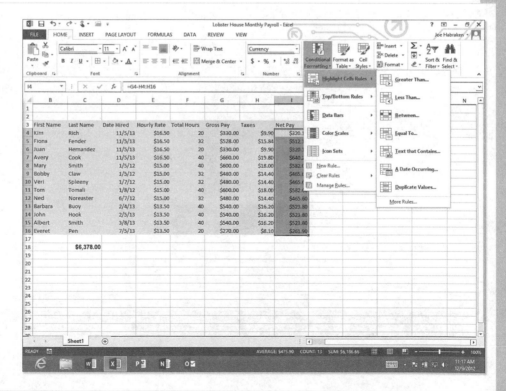

You will find that the conditional formatting feature provides you with more than just the ability to apply a condition or conditions to a cell range. Let's look at each of the options provided in the Conditional Formatting gallery and the possibilities that they present.

Using Highlight Cell Rules

When you select Highlight Cells Rules, you are provided with a list of conditions or rules such as Greater Than, Less Than, Between, and Duplicate Values. For example, if you select the Greater Than rule, the Greater Than dialog box opens.

To take advantage of this "prepackaged rule," specify a value on the left side of the dialog box that serves as the condition. You can type a value in the box or you can click the Collapse button and specify a value by selecting a cell in the sheet. When you return to the Greater Than dialog box (after specifying a cell in the sheet), you can fine-tune the formatting that is used by selecting the formatting drop-down arrow. A series of formatting attributes is supplied by default for the rule. You can specify a custom format for the rule by selecting Custom Format. This opens the Format Cells dialog box, which provides you with control over all the cell-formatting attributes applied by the rule. Figure 12.12 shows the Greater Than dialog box containing a condition and format. The Net Pay column is formatted by this conditional formatting.

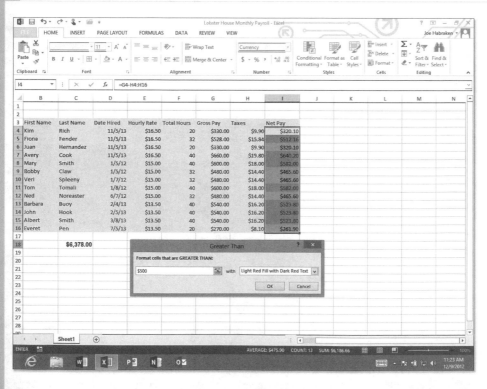

Figure 12.12 The Greater Than dialog box and affected cell range.

When you are ready to apply the rule to the selected range, click OK. The conditional formatting is applied to the cells that meet the conditions of the rule. You can apply additional rules to the range of cells as needed. Remember, you are not limited to the number of conditions that you apply to a cell or a range of cells. However, make sure that you keep track of the formatting that each rule applies to the range so that if a particular cell or cells meets more than one condition that is applied, you can tell by the formatting that the cell meets multiple conditions.

 tip

To clear the conditional formatting rules from a range, select Conditional Formatting, Clear Rules and then Clear Rules from Selected Cells. You can also clear all the rules on a sheet by selecting Clear Rules from Entire Sheet.

Using Top/Bottom Rules

The Top/Bottom rules enable you to quickly apply conditional formatting to cells in a range that fall into the top or bottom 10 items and the top or bottom 10% of the values in the range. You are not locked into the top or bottom ten values in your range when you use the top or bottom 10 items rules. The dialog box for each of these rules provides spinner boxes that enable you to specify the number of items that are used by the rule. For example, if you want to see the bottom 5 items in the selected range, you can change the 10 in the Bottom 10 Items dialog box to 5 by using the spinner box (or by selecting the 10 and typing 5).

There are also two rules available in the top/bottom rules based on the average of the values in your selected range: Above Average and Below Average. You don't need to worry about calculating the highest 10 values or computing the average. The rule takes care of this and based on that computation, it applies the conditional formatting.

To apply one of the top/bottom rules, select Top/Bottom Rules in the Conditional Formatting gallery and then select one of the rules provided. When you select a rule such as Above Average, a dialog box specific to that rule appears. Select the formatting for the condition and then click OK.

Using Data Bars

If you like to visually compare data in a range of cells without resorting to a chart or sparklines, you can take advantage of the data bars provided in the Conditional Formatting gallery. The data bars are actually bar graphs that are placed in the cells of the selected range. This enables you to quickly see how the various values in the range compare with each other. Figure 12.13 shows a range of values that is formatted using data bars.

When you select Data Bars in the Conditional Formatting gallery, you can choose from bars that use a gradient fill or a solid fill. The data bars might skew the concept of how you think about conditional formatting, but they do provide you with another option for quickly comparing sheet values.

 note

Sparklines are mini-charts placed inline with a row or column of values (so they look similar to the data bars feature). Sparklines are another easy way to add visual information to a worksheet without creating a full-blown chart. Sparklines are discussed in Chapter 14, "Enhancing Worksheets with Charts."

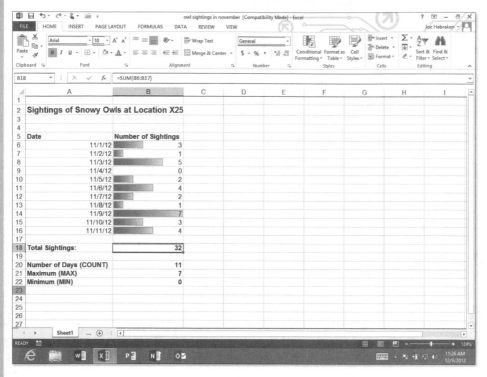

Figure 12.13
Data bars enable you to visually compare values in a range.

Using Color Scales

Another possibility provided by the Conditional Formatting gallery is the color scale. Each color scale consists of a set of colors. There are three-color scales and there are two-color scales.

When you apply a three-color scale to a range of cells—such as the Green-Yellow-Red Color Scale—you separate the values into three subsets based on the values in the cell. The top third is formatted with the first color (green), the middle third with the second color (yellow), and the bottom third with the third color (red). As already mentioned, there are also two-color scales, which divide the values in a top and bottom half using the two colors provided.

As with data bars, the color scales are used for relative comparison of the values in the cell range. They enable you to see by color the cells that fall in the same tier with the range. There are six preset three-color scales and six preset two-color scales available. Each scale uses a different set of colors.

Using Icon Sets

The Conditional Formatting gallery also provides you with icon sets that can be used to format the values in a selected range. The icon sets are somewhat similar to the color scales in that the icons are in groups that enable you to differentiate where the values in the range fall in relation to each other.

When you select Icon Sets in the Conditional Formatting gallery, you are provided different categories of icon sets, such as Directional, Indicators, and Ratings. The number of icons in the set you select specifies how the values in the range are grouped. An icon set containing five icons formats the values in the range based on five groupings of the values (highest to lowest). A three-icon set groups the values in three different groupings (thirds).

Creating Conditional Formatting Rules

You are certainly not limited to the rules provided by the various rule categories listed in the Conditional Formatting gallery. You can create your own highlight cells rules, top/bottom rules, or other rule types as needed.

New rules are created in the New Formatting Rule dialog box. You can open this dialog box by selecting New Rule in the Conditional Formatting gallery, or you can select More Rules when you have accessed a rule category, such as Highlight Cells Rules or Color Scales. Figure 12.14 shows the New Formatting Rule dialog box.

Figure 12.14
The New Formatting Rule dialog box.

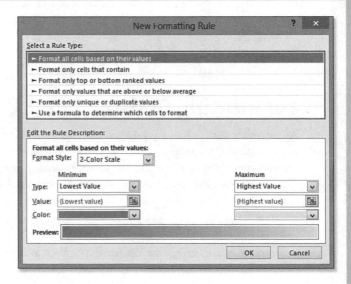

Creating a new rule is a two-part process. First, you select the rule type in the Select a Rule Type list. For example, if you want to create a rule that formats cells in the sheet that contains values that fall between two values, you choose Format Only Cells That Contain in the Select a Rule Type list.

You then select a condition for the new rule. For example, you might set the condition as Between. The rule also needs to know what two values specify the range that cell values would have to fall between to satisfy the rule. You can do this two ways: You can type the two values (the low and high value for the range) in the dialog box. The other possibility is to specify two cell addresses that contain the values that specify the range of values to be used by the rule.

As already mentioned, you can also create other rule types, such as top or bottom rules or above or below average rules. To create a top or bottom rule, select Format Only Top or Bottom Ranked Values in the Select a Rule Type list. You can then specify whether you want to format the top or bottom of the values and specify the number of values you want the rule to format. The default number is 10, but you can specify any number you want. In the case of the above- or below-average rules, all you have to specify is whether the rule formats values above or below the average.

 tip

You can manage the rules that you create in the Conditional Formatting Rules Manager dialog box; select Manage Rules in the Conditional Formatting gallery. You can edit existing rules, delete rules, and create new rules from this dialog box.

The second part of the process of creating a new rule is specifying the formatting that applies to cells in the range that meets the condition of the rule. The New Formatting Rule dialog box provides a preview of the formatting for the new rule. However, it starts out as No Format Set, meaning you have to specify the formatting before the rule is ready to go.

Click the Format button in the New Formatting Rule dialog box. This opens the Format Cells dialog box. Use the tabs on the dialog box to specify the formatting for the new rule. You can work with any of the cell-formatting attributes, including font, border, and fill. When you click OK in the Format Cells dialog box, you return to the New Formatting Rule dialog box. Click OK and your rule is applied to the selected range.

Manipulating Cells and Cell Content

As you enter data in Excel, you might find that you need to add additional cells to the worksheet to accommodate the information that you need to include in the sheet. You might also find that there are occasions when you want to add long text entries or explanatory text, and want the information to span several cells and to wrap in the cells as text would in a paragraph. The solutions to these various minor issues are easy to come by in Excel.

You can easily insert cells and join cells, if necessary, and then wrap text in a cell or joined cells as needed. In cases where you have entered repeating labels or values into your sheet and find that you need to either change the text entries or change the values, Excel also has you covered with the Replace feature, which shares the Find and Replace dialog box with the Find feature.

Inserting Cells

You can insert single or multiple cells into a sheet. Inserting cells causes the data in the adjacent cells to shift down a row or over a column (to the right) to create a space for the new cells.

The number of cells inserted depends on the number of cells that you select prior to inserting the new cells. To insert cells into a sheet, follow these steps:

1. Select the cell range where you want the new cells to be inserted. Excel inserts the same number of cells as you select.

2. Select the Insert command on the Home tab and then select Insert Cells. The Insert dialog box opens, as shown in Figure 12.15.

Figure 12.15
The Insert dialog box.

3. The Insert dialog box provides you with options for how the current cells are affected by the insertion of the new cell. Select Shift Cells Right or Shift Cells Down. If you want to insert an entire row or column, select the appropriate option.

4. Click OK. Excel inserts the cells and shifts the adjacent cells according to the option you specified in the Insert dialog box.

Inserting cells is useful if you have inadvertently mismatched data in your cells as you have entered it. For example, you might have entered an employee's name and then entered a portion of another employee's data. If you insert the required number of cells, you can fix the input problem by quickly adding the new data and editing the mismatched data without deleting a lot of information or messing around inserting new rows or other information. You can even drag the incorrect data to its appropriate location by dragging the information to the new cells.

Merging Cells and Wrapping Text

You can merge cells on a worksheet. This can be particularly useful when you want to add a large heading to a sheet or need to add a paragraph or two of explanatory text and want it to appear directly on the sheet. You can merge cells that are contiguous in a particular row (from left to right) or you can merge cells that are contiguous in a column (from top to bottom). You can also merge cells that are contiguous and span more than one row or column.

Excel provides you with options for merging cells. Select the cells you want to merge and then select the Merge & Center command in the Alignment group. The Merge & Center command provides four different options:

- **Merge & Center:** This option merges the cells and takes the content (such as a large heading) and centers it across the newly merged cells.

- **Merge Across:** Use this option to merge all the cells in a selected row or rows.

- **Merge Cells:** Use this option to merge contiguous selected cells in a single column or row or in multiple columns or rows. This option does not center the content across the merged cells.

- **Unmerge Cells:** This option enables you to unmerge cells that you have merged. All you have to do is select the merged cells and then use this option to put the cells back in their unmerged condition.

Selecting one of the merge options provided by the Merge & Center menu merges the cells. When you have the cells merged, you can take advantage of the various alignment commands in the Alignment group to align the text in the merged cells as needed.

If you are working with a large block of text, you can wrap the text within the merged cells. As you type text, even in merged cells, the text consists of a single line of text that bleeds over into the cells to the right of merged cells. As soon as you enter other data in the cells to the right of the merged cells, your large text entry is truncated (as is any entry that is too large for a cell). To wrap the text within the merged cells, select the merged cell and then select the Wrap Text command in the Alignment group. The text wraps in the merged cell, filling the cell much like a text box. The width of the cell that was created by merging the multiple cells dictates the number of times your text needs to wrap.

 tip

You can find merged cells using the Find feature. Use the Format option provided by Find to search for merged cells.

Finding and Replacing Cell Items

Sheets can become quite large (there are a lot of columns and rows that can be filled), so there might be occasions where you want to find specific cell content and the easiest way to find it quickly is using the Find and Replace feature. The Find and Replace feature is also useful in situations where you have entered a particular label or value into the sheet and find that you have consistently entered it incorrectly. A great way to change multiple occurrences of a label or value is using Excel's Replace feature; you can locate data in the sheet and replace it with new data as needed.

The Find and Replace feature can do more than just find text strings or values in cells and replace them with other information; it can also be used to search for cell formatting and optionally replace that formatting with formatting that you specify. To open the Find and Replace dialog box with the Find or the Replace tab active, select the Find & Select command in the Editing group and then select Find or Replace, respectively. Figure 12.16 shows the Replace tab of the Find and Replace dialog box with the options expanded.

Figure 12.16
The Find and Replace dialog box.

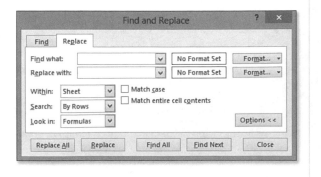

The Find and Replace tabs function similarly. The only real difference is that the Replace tab also provides a Replace With box, enabling you to specify the content or formatting that will be used to replace the item or formatting that is to be found in the worksheet. If you want to match the case of your entry in the Find What box, select the Match Case check box. If you want to locate cells that contain exactly what you have entered into the Find What text box, select the Match Entire Cell Contents check box.

You can use wildcards in the Find What box to aid in your searches. You can use the question mark (?) as a wildcard for a single character. The asterisk (*) can serve as a wildcard for any number of characters. Enter text in the Find What box (on either the Find or Replace tab) and then use the Format button to specify any formatting that you might want to include in the search; the Format button (to the right of the Find What box) opens the Find Format dialog box and provides you with access to all the cell-formatting possibilities.

If you want to provide the formatting by example (the format to be found), click the Format button's drop-down arrow, and then select Choose Format from Cell. The mouse pointer becomes an Eyedropper tool. Click it in a cell that contains the formatting that you want to find. You will be returned to the Find and Replace dialog box. After you specify formatting using either the Find Format dialog box or the Eyedropper tool, the format is previewed in the box to the right of the Find What box.

Because we are talking about finding formatting and then replacing it, you also need to specify the format to be used as the replacement. This is accomplished by providing a format to the right of the Replace With box. Select Format to open the Replace Format dialog box. You can specify the formatting using the tabs in this dialog box. You also can specify the "replacement" format using the Eyedropper tool. Select the Format drop-down arrow, and then select Choose Format from Cell. Click a cell that contains the format you want to use.

 tip

You don't have to include a search string if you are searching for formatting only. Just specify the formatting and then run the search. You can also specify formatting only as the replace options for a find and replace.

So, let's look at what happens after you set up a search using the Find tab. When you are ready to conduct your search, you can use the Find Next button to find the next occurrence of the search string (or formatting). Click the Find Next button as needed to cycle through the found cells that match your search criteria. If you want to find all the cells that contain your search string, click the Find All button. A list of all the cells found by the search will be listed in the bottom of the Find and Replace dialog box. The sheet, cell address, and value found are supplied in the list. To navigate to a particular cell (that was found), click the cell reference in the list.

When you are working on the Replace tab, you can replace each subsequent occurrence of the found string or formatting using the Replace button. If you have set up your find and replace carefully and are sure that items will be replaced correctly, click Replace All and take care of all the replacements in one fell swoop.

The Go To feature is also accessed via the Find & Select menu, and specific items that you can go to are specified on the Find & Select menu, such as Formulas, Comments, and Conditional Formatting.

This provides a quick way to select occurrences of specific items or formatting in the sheet. For example, if you select Formulas, the formulas in the sheet are selected.

Working with Columns and Rows

Manipulating columns and rows in your sheets is straightforward. You can easily change the column width for a column or columns and adjust row heights. You can also insert or delete columns and rows as needed. Inserting or deleting columns or rows doesn't change the number of columns or rows in the sheet; the number of columns or rows in a sheet is fixed. In the case of inserting columns or rows, however, it does enable you to open up some whitespace in a sheet when you need to add data. When you delete columns or rows, you remove them from their current position; they aren't removed from the sheet.

You can also hide columns and rows in the sheet. This is particularly useful in cases when you have data in the sheet that you do not want prying eyes to see or information that you do not want to include in a printout. For example, you may want to print an employee list but do not want to include the columns that list employee salaries.

Changing Column Width and Row Height

You have probably noticed that the default column width is not all that wide; it is 8.43 characters to be exact, and it doesn't readily accommodate long text entries or values that have been formatted as currency or other numeric formats. You might have found entries in certain cells change to ########. This lets you know that you need to adjust the column width so that it can accommodate the entry and its formatting.

To adjust a column's width, position the mouse pointer on the column's right border. The mouse becomes a sizing tool. Drag the column border to the desired width. You can also change a column's width using AutoFit, which adjusts the column widths to accommodate the widest entry within the column; to use AutoFit, double-click the sizing tool on the column border. The column immediately adjusts to its widest entry.

 tip

You can also access the Insert and the Delete commands from the shortcut menu. Right-click on selected columns or rows and then select Insert or Delete as needed.

If you want to adjust several columns at once, select the columns. Place the mouse on any of the column borders and drag to increase or decrease the width. Each selected column is adjusted to the width you select. You can also double-click to use AutoFit to adjust the width of the selected columns.

If you want to specify a more precise column width for a column or a number of selected columns, select the Format command (in the Cells group on the Home tab), and then select Column Width. The Column Width dialog box opens. Specify the width in the Column Width text box, and then click OK.

 tip

The Format command also provides an AutoFit Row Height and an AutoFit Column Width option.

You can also adjust row heights, if you want, using the mouse; just drag the bottom border of a row to adjust the height.

However, your row heights automatically adjust to any font size changes that you make to data held in a particular row. Row heights also adjust if you wrap text entries within them. You may need to adjust column widths in your sheets far more often than row heights.

You can adjust row heights using the Row Height dialog box. Select the Format command and then Row Height. Adjust the row height in the Row Height text box by typing a new value (the default is 15) and then click OK.

Inserting Columns and Rows

You can insert a single column or row or multiple columns or rows as needed. To insert a single column, click in the column that is to the right of where you want the new column to be inserted. Click the Insert command in the Cells group and then select Insert Sheet Columns. The new column is inserted to the left of the currently selected cell (and its column).

For inserting a single row, click in a cell in the row that you want to insert the new row below. Click the Insert command and select Insert Sheet Rows. The new row is inserted below the current row.

To insert multiple columns or rows, select the number of columns or rows you want to insert. In the case of columns, drag over the column headings; for rows, drag over the row numbers. Then use the Insert Sheet Columns or Insert Sheet Rows to insert the columns or rows specified. New columns are placed to the left of the selected columns and the selected columns are pushed to the right. The new rows are placed below the currently selected rows.

Deleting Columns and Rows

You can also delete a column or row from the sheet. In either case, select either the column or row you want to remove by clicking on the appropriate column or row heading (drag to select multiple columns or rows).

Select the Delete command in the Cells group and then select Delete Sheet Columns or Delete Sheet Rows as needed. The columns or rows are removed from the sheet. Remember that any data that is included in the columns or rows is also deleted. It makes sense to make sure that you have laid out your sheet in a way that is appropriate to your needs from the get-go. This saves you a lot of time dragging information around on the sheet and possibly negates the need for a lot of inserting new columns or rows or deleting columns and rows in the sheet.

Hiding Columns and Rows

As already mentioned, there may be occasions when you want to hide certain columns or rows in a sheet both on the screen and when you print the sheet. Hiding columns or rows is straightforward and the process is easy to reverse.

In the case of columns, select the columns you want to hide. Select the Format command and then point at the Hide & Unhide option. Select Hide Columns and the columns are hidden.

The same process can be used for rows. Select the rows and then select Format, Hide & Unhide and then Hide Rows. The rows are hidden.

Reversing the process is just a matter of accessing the Hide & Unhide options provided by the Format command. Select Unhide Columns to get your columns back and Unhide Rows to see those hidden rows.

Working with Worksheets

We had the opportunity to look at the various views that can be used when you are examining a sheet in Chapter 11, "Requisite Excel: Essential Features." There are also some other tricks related to viewing sheets that can help you when you are working with large sheets that contain many columns or rows or in cases when you want to see two disparate parts of the same large sheet at the same time. As with columns and rows, you can also hide sheets if needed.

➡️ *For more information about viewing Excel worksheets, **see** "Viewing Worksheets,"*
   p. 323.

Freezing Rows and Columns

Adding data or just viewing the data can be problematic in a large worksheet that contains many columns, rows, or both. Because the column labels or row labels are not visible when you scroll down or to the right, respectively, determining what you should type in a certain cell can be a mystery. For example, you might be entering employee information and the employee names are in the first and second columns of the sheet. If you scroll to the right any distance (when you have a number of columns of data to work with), the names provided are no longer visible in the Excel workspace. This makes it difficult to add new data or even determine what the data in a particular cell represents.

You can freeze your column and row labels so that they remain on the screen no matter how far you scroll to the right or scroll down in the sheet. The Freeze Panes command is in the Zoom group on the Ribbon's View tab. The Freeze Panes command enables you to freeze panes (both column and row labels), freeze the top row (the column labels), or freeze the first column (the row labels).

The Freeze Top Row and the Freeze First Column options on the Freeze Panes gallery are self-explanatory and require nothing from you other than just choosing one of these options after selecting the Freeze Panes drop-down arrow.

If you want to use the Freeze Panes option, you need to specify the rows and columns you want to freeze. This is accomplished by selecting the cell that is below the row you want to freeze and to the right of the column you want to freeze.

Figure 12.17 shows a sheet where the Freeze Panes command has been used to freeze columns A through C and rows 1 through 5 (1–4 are unimportant; we are mainly concerned with freezing row 5, which contains the headings for the columns) and to freeze column A. Notice that cell D6 was selected before the panes were frozen. This is because cell D6 is one cell below the last row to be frozen and one cell to the right of the last column to be frozen.

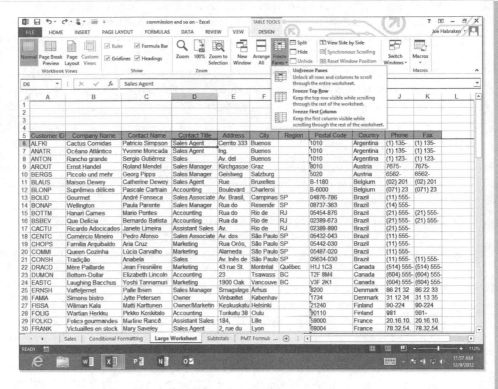

Figure 12.17 Freeze panes to keep column or row labels on the screen when you scroll.

When you have identified the cell you want to use to specify the rows and or columns to freeze, select the cell. A vertical "freeze" borderline is placed between the frozen columns and the other "active" columns. A horizontal borderline is placed between the frozen rows and the active rows.

Then all you have to do is select Freeze Panes to freeze the specified row and column in place. You can now scroll either down or to the right in the sheet and the row and column labels should stay on the screen as you scroll. When you finish working with the frozen panes, you can easily remove them. Select the Freeze Panes drop-down arrow and then select Unfreeze Panes.

Splitting Worksheets

Another useful trick for dealing with large sheets is the Split command. You can split the current worksheet window into multiple panes. Doing so enables you to view different parts of the same large worksheet in different panes simultaneously. This is useful for looking at data or the results of calculations that are typically quite distant in the geography of a large sheet.

To split the current sheet into multiple panes, select the cell where you want the split to occur. When you specify a cell, the split appears below the selected cell or to the right of the selected cell. After specifying the cell, select the Split command on the View tab. You can use the mouse to drag the split to a new location as needed.

You can also manually place splits in a sheet. A horizontal split box sits just above the vertical scrollbar. Drag the horizontal split box onto the sheet to create a horizontal split. There is also a vertical split box just to the left of the horizontal scrollbar. Drag the vertical split box onto the sheet to create a vertical split.

After you have your splits on the Excel screen, you can scroll within each of the independent panes to locate certain parts of your sheet. When you have finished working with the split panes, select the Split command to remove all the splits from the sheet window.

Hiding Worksheets

We have already discussed hiding worksheet columns and rows, but you can also hide an entire sheet in your Excel workbook. This enables you to hide sensitive information as you work on the other sheets in the workbook.

The sheet you want to hide should be the active sheet. If it isn't, click the sheet's tab to make it the active sheet. Select the Format command on the Home tab; then point at the Hide & Unhide option. Select Hide Sheet to hide the current sheet. Other sheets in the workbook will still be available. You can hide other sheets in the workbook by repeating the process.

When you need to work on a sheet that you have hidden, you are only a few mouse clicks away from unhiding it (yes, *unhiding* sounds wrong; I guess Microsoft didn't want to make *found* the opposite of *hidden*). Select Format and then point at the Hide & Unhide option. Select Unhide Sheet. The Unhide dialog box opens. The Unhide dialog box lists the sheets that you have hidden in the current workbook. Select the sheet you want to unhide and then click OK.

 tip

You can hide an entire open workbook via the Ribbon's View tab. Use the Hide command to hide a workbook window and then use Unhide to unhide it.

Naming Ranges

When you work with values in an Excel worksheet, they typically make up a range of cells that contain like values. For example, all the cells containing employee salaries are typically located in the same column and so constitute a contiguous range of cells. You can then use this range for a number of calculations, such as total company salary, or compute the average or the mean for the salary range.

You can select a range of values and give the range a range name. For example, the salary range discussed in the previous paragraph could be given the name "salary." The range name could then be used directly in formulas or functions as a substitute for the range, which is specified by the beginning and ending cell addresses in the range. Range names can be quite useful, and remembering a range name is a lot easier than remembering the cell range in terms of the cell addresses.

You can use range names in calculations (in both your own formulas and Excel functions) to create charts and to move to a particular place in a sheet using the Go To feature (press Ctrl+G to open the Go To dialog box).

Creating a range name for a selected range of cells is easy. There are some rules related to naming ranges, however. You are limited to 255 characters for a range name. You cannot use spaces. You also cannot use most of the symbols on the keyboard. The underscore and the period are allowed.

You can use alphanumeric characters (A to Z and 0 to 9), so range names can consist of a combination of numbers and letters. You can also use the underscore in the place of a space where you want to create range names that describe the cell range, such as gross_income or taxable_income (these two types of income are the same if you don't have any tax_shelters).

There is more than one way to create range names. You can select a range of values and then define the name, or you can have Excel generate range names for the selected values using the column or row headings as the range names. To specify a range name for a selected range, select the range and then click the Define Name command in the Defined Names group of the Ribbon's Formulas tab. The New Name dialog box opens, as shown in Figure 12.18.

Figure 12.18
Create a range name for a selected range of cells.

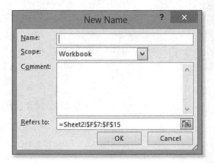

Provide a name for the range in the Name text box. By default, the scope of the range name is at the workbook level, meaning you can specify this range anywhere in the workbook using the range name. You can change the scope to a specific sheet in the workbook. Select the Scope drop-down list, and select a sheet from the provided list.

You can also enter optional comments related to the range and its name in the Comment text box. Before you create the new name, take a moment to check the range specified in the Refers To text box. You can adjust the range if it is incorrect by selecting the Collapse button. You can then reselect the range in the sheet and then click the Expand button to return to the New Name dialog box. Click OK to create the range name.

Creating Range Names from Selections

You can also create range names based on the column labels or row labels that you have created in the worksheet. For example, if you have several columns of numbers, such as sales figures for different regions by month (January, February, March), you can quickly create a range name for each of the columns using the column labels. To create range names from row or column labels, select the ranges (either in columns or rows) and make sure that you include the row or column containing the descriptive labels for the range. Then click the Create from Selection command in the Define Names groups. The Create Names from Selection dialog box opens, as shown in Figure 12.19.

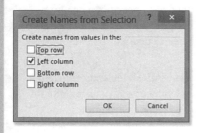

Figure 12.19
The Create Names from Selection dialog box.

Select the location of the labels that you want to use as the range names using the check boxes provided: Top Row, Left Column, Bottom Row, or Right Column. If the labels are in the top row of the selected range and the values are arranged in columns, select Top Row. If the labels are in the first column (the left column) and the values are arranged in rows, select Left Column. When you are ready to generate the range names, click OK.

Managing Range Names

You can view and manage your range names in the Name Manager. The Name Manager enables you to create new range names, edit existing range names, and delete range names that you no longer want.

To open the Name Manager, select the Name Manager command in the Defined Names group. Figure 12.20 shows the Name Manager.

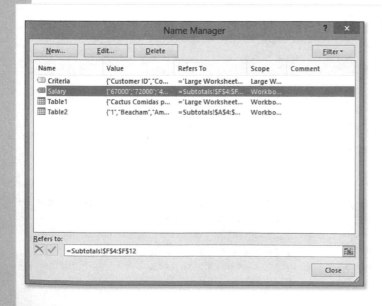

Figure 12.20
The Name Manager.

All the range names in the current workbook are listed in the Name Manager. You can filter the list using the Filter drop-down button on the right side of the dialog box. You can filter by scope (sheet or workbook) and filter for names that contain errors.

If you find that you need to edit a particular range name, select the name in the list and then click the Edit button. This opens the Edit Name dialog box, which enables you to modify the name, comments, or the range for that particular name.

To create a new range name, select the New dialog box. This opens the New Name dialog box. Specify a name, a cell range, and optional comments for the new range name. When you click OK to create the new name, you return to the Name Manager.

You can also delete range names from the Name Manager. Select a name in the list and then click the Delete button. You are asked if you are sure you want to delete the name. Click OK. The name is removed from the list.

Remember that the main reason you create range names is to use them as a way to specify a range of values in a formula that you design or an Excel function that you use. Range names can be quickly inserted into a formula or function via the Use in Formula command, which provides a list of your range names.

> *For more information about using range names in formulas and functions,* **see** *"Using Range Names in Formulas and Functions," p 383.*

Adding Images and Graphics to Worksheets

You can add pictures, clip art, shapes, and SmartArt graphics to your Excel worksheets just as easily as you can add these items to Word documents or PowerPoint presentation slides. For example, you can quickly insert a company logo graphic or insert a picture of the salamander species that is the subject of a population study you have detailed in your Excel sheet.

The Insert tab provides the Illustrations group, which enables you to insert digital pictures (Pictures), clip art (Online Pictures), shapes (Shapes), and SmartArt graphics (Insert a SmartArt Graphic). Pictures can be useful if the image directly relates to the subject matter of the sheet. Clip art is less useful, and overly cute clip art can diminish the impact of the facts and figures that you have included in the sheet. Office.com provides you with more than just clip art, however, and also houses a large number of royalty-free photos in the online clip art and photo library (accessed using the Online Pictures command).

SmartArt graphics provide you with the possibility of creating illustrative graphics that can help make sense out of the information in the sheet. For example, if you create a sales report that details the quarterly sales of your sales force by region, you can include an organizational chart showing the report structure for the regions. You can do this by creating an organizational chart using one of the SmartArt graphics provided in the Hierarchy category.

> *For an overview of using images and graphics in the Office applications,* **see** *Chapter 4, "Using and Creating Graphics."*

Obviously, the graphic type that you use most often in Excel is going to be a chart based on the data in a sheet. Other graphical possibilities that help provide meaning to data visually are sparklines and conditional formatting graphical options, such as data bars, color scales, and icon sets.

➡ *For information on adding charts to your Excel worksheets,* **see** *Chapter 14, "Enhancing Worksheets with Charts."*

Excel differs from Word or PowerPoint in that Excel worksheets must be designed and formatted so that they can provide a meaningful snapshot of often complex numerical information. Use graphical elements such as pictures and graphics sparingly and only when they are an aid to understanding the data provided in the sheet.

13

GETTING THE MOST FROM FORMULAS AND FUNCTIONS

Excel's real power lies in its ability to do calculations. We enter values into Excel to have those values acted upon by formulas or functions; Excel is all about answers and the answers are provided by the results of the various formulas and functions in a sheet. Whether you are a biologist using statistical functions to enumerate a population study of snowy egrets in the Hudson River valley or a financial maven tracking your investments, Excel provides you with all the tools that you need to do the math.

In this chapter, we look at the basics of building simple formulas and taking advantage of Excel's huge library of built-in formulas—functions—to do calculations. We explore a number of different function categories, including statistical, logical, date, and financial functions. We also discuss best practices for entering, copying, moving, and proofing your formulas and functions.

Performing Calculations in Excel Worksheets

Excel provides you with two different possibilities for doing calculations in your worksheets: formulas and functions. Formulas are do-it-yourself math. You specify the cells to be referenced in the calculation and you also provide the operators, which determine what kinds of calculations actually take place. Formulas are best reserved for simple calculations, such as subtraction, multiplication, and division. Figure 13.1 shows a subtraction formula that subtracts the payment to the instructor (G10) from the Tuition Total for that class (D10).

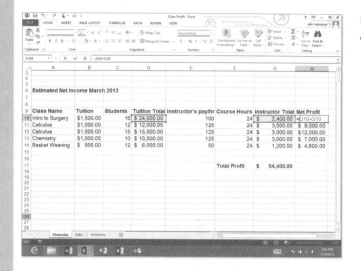

Figure 13.1
A subtraction formula.

Note that the formula (=D10-G10) is shown in H10 and in the formula bar. When you place the insertion point in the formula bar, the cells involved in the formula are selected using a different color for each cell address included in the formula.

Functions, on the other hand, are built-in formulas provided by Excel. The Excel Function Library is huge; it provides more than 300 functions, grouped into categories that include date and time functions, engineering functions, financial functions, math and trigonometry functions, statistical functions, and even text functions. Figure 13.2 shows the PMT function, which is an Excel function used to determine the periodic payment on a loan that has a fixed interest rate.

> **note**
>
> You can show the formulas and/ or functions in a sheet by selecting the Show Formulas command. The command is found in the Formula Auditing group on the Ribbon's Formulas tab.

Note that the function is designated by the function name (PMT). The cells that are to be acted on by the function are B6 (the interest rate), C6 (the term: 60 months), and D6 (the actual cost of the car or the principal). Note that the only operator you see in the function is the /. This is because the annual interest rate needs to be divided by 12 so that you are calculating the monthly payment.

Creating your own formulas is best reserved for situations where Excel doesn't provide you with a function that will do the same job. As already mentioned, most of the formulas that you need to create take care of simple math problems that are used to subtract or divide values (or results from other formulas or functions). Developing an awareness of what the Excel functions can do in terms of complex calculations is time better spent than attempting to create your own arcane and elaborate formulas.

Figure 13.2
The PMT
function.

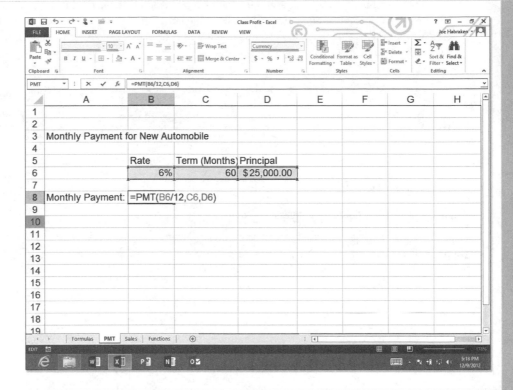

Relative Versus Absolute Referencing

Understanding how Excel references cells in your worksheets when you specify them in a formula or function is fundamental to the overall understanding of how best to use formulas and functions in your sheets. If you are ever going to copy a formula or function in a sheet (and you will need to), you need to understand how both relative referencing and absolute referencing work in Excel.

When you create a formula or function and designate cell references, Excel uses a form of referencing called relative referencing. When you copy a formula or a function from one cell to another cell, the cell references in the formula or function are rewritten to adjust to its new location. For example, Figure 13.3 shows a simple worksheet that uses the SUM function to add the January through March sales totals for each of the regions designated in column A. The SUM function was entered once in cell E4 and then copied (using the fill handle) to cells E5, E6, and E7.

 note
When you select a cell containing a formula or function and place the insertion point in the formula bar, the range finder highlights the cells referenced in the formula or function.

Note that as the function was copied down into the other total cells, the function adjusted to its new location and specifies the correct range of cells to be acted on by the function. This is because of relative referencing. Although you specified a range of cells to be summed in cell E4, what Excel saw was that it was to take the three cells to the left of the cell containing the function (E4) and add them together. So, when you copy the function down to cells E5 through E7, Excel just takes the three cells to the left of the function and adds them together. This is what relative referencing is all about and why it is so easy to copy a formula and function in a worksheet and get the correct answer or answers.

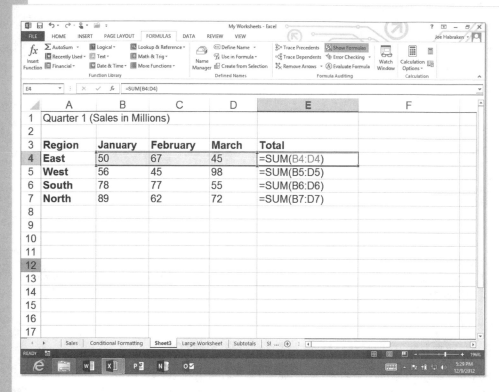

Figure 13.3
Relative referencing enables you to quickly copy a function to multiple cells.

In some situations, you need to override Excel's relative referencing so that a formula or function does not change all the cell references when you copy it to a new location. This is where absolute referencing comes in. Suppose that you have a worksheet that computes the commission made on sales by each of your salespeople. The commission rate is specified in one cell. Figure 13.4 shows the simple multiplication formula that was created to multiply the total sales (in column B) by the commission percentage, which is located in cell B17. The formula was entered in cell C11 and then copied to cells C12 through C14.

Note that the commission percentage (B17) is specified in the formula as B17. This is because you want the commission formula (you created) to always (absolutely) reference cell B17 even when you copy the formula to other cells. Note that cell B11 (which is the total sales for John Smith) is included in the formula in C11 as a relative reference (no dollar signs are used on B11 to "lock" the column or row designation).

Figure 13.4
Absolute
referencing is
used to override relative
referencing.

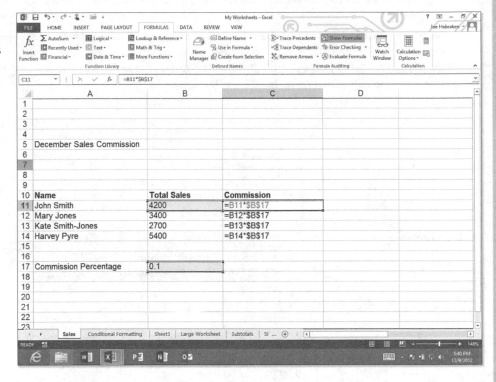

As the formula was copied down, B11 is adjusted to the new location and is automatically changed in each subsequent cell, first to B12, then B13, and then B14. If cell B17 was not designated in the formula as an absolute reference, as soon as the formula was copied from C11 to C12, the formula would no longer work. That is because the formula would attempt to adjust the relative reference for B17 to B18. B18 is empty (it contains no value) so that would result in no calculated value in C12 (you multiply something by 0 and you get 0).

To specify a cell reference as absolute, add a $ (dollar sign) before the column letter and before the row number that make up the cell address (such as our example of an absolute reference: B17). The easiest way to add the dollar signs to an absolute reference is to press F4 after you have specified the cell address in a formula or function.

In our example, we looked at a single cell as an absolute reference. You can also have the situation where you only designate the column or row in a cell address as absolute rather than making both the column and row designation absolute. Remember that cell references are two parts: column designation and row designation. So, you can make a reference in a formula or function where

 note

In Figure 13.4, I used my own formula =B11*B17; I could have also used the Excel function: =PRODUCT(B11,B17).

 note

Using range names in formulas and functions can negate the need to use absolute references. We discuss using range names in formulas and functions later in this chapter.

only the column is absolute and the row reference is still relative. This is referred to as a mixed reference.

Let's look at an example, using the PMT function as the function we want to copy in a worksheet. Figure 13.5 shows the PMT function as it was originally written in cell C7. A row of car amounts (principals) are listed in row 5 and different interest rates are listed in column B. Only one term (the number of monthly payments) is listed in cell C14.

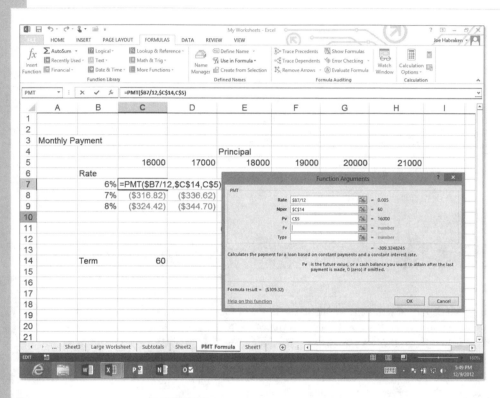

Figure 13.5
Mixed references can be used in cell addresses.

When the function is copied across the columns, you always want the function to look for the rates in column B. So, column B is designated as absolute in the function ($B). You also want the function to continue to look in row 5 for a principal when it is copied down, so row 5 is designated as absolute in the function ($5). Finally, the term in C14 must always (absolutely) be referred to by the function, no matter where you copy it. So, it is designated as an absolute as C14. So, we have mixed references and one absolute reference in the same function.

Using absolute references and mixed references can be a little tricky. If you enter a formula or a function with incorrect absolute or mixed referencing, Excel typically lets you know. For example, if you neglect to make column B absolute in the example in Figure 13.5, as soon as you copy the function to the next column, you get the message #NUM in the cells. This is because there is a number error in the function. All you have to do is fix the function and then recopy it to the other cells in the sheet to fix the problem. Excel also offers a number of other tools for correcting formulas and functions, including the ability to trace precedents and dependents and do error checking on formulas and functions. We look at some of these tools later in this chapter.

Creating and Editing Formulas

Creating formulas in Excel is straightforward. You can include cell addresses, values, and even functions in your formulas. The values in the formula (specified by cell addresses) are then acted on by an operator or operators that you specify in the formula. When you begin a new formula in a cell, you start the formula's notation with the = sign. This lets Excel know that you are entering a formula. You can then specify the cell addresses for the formula and the required operators. For example, you might enter the formula:

=B6-C6

You are specifying that Excel should take the value in C6 and subtract it from the value in B6. The result is placed in the cell where you entered the formula. Table 13.1 shows some of the common arithmetic operators used in Excel formulas.

Table 13.1 Arithmetic Operators

Operator	Performs	Examples
+	Addition	=A1+B1
–	Subtraction	=A1-B1
*	Multiplication	=A1*C12
/	Division	=A1/B3
^	Exponentiation	=A1^2

Excel also provides other operators that are referred to as comparison operators. These operators can compare two cells and return one of two logical values: TRUE or FALSE. Table 13.2 provides a list of comparison operators.

Table 13.2 Comparison Operators

Operator	Comparison	Examples
=	Equal	=A1=B1
>	Greater than	=A1>B1
<	Less than	=A1<C12
>=	Greater than or equal to	=A1>=B3
<=	Less than or equal to	=A1<=2

Obviously, after you know what operator or operators you are going to use, the rest of the formula typically consists of the cell addresses that are to be acted on by the formula. The values in those cell addresses that you reference are referred to as operands. Operands in a formula can consist of a cell range, single cell addresses, constants (values, dates, or text you enter as part of the formula), or range names.

Understanding Operator Precedence

An important aspect of creating formulas is understanding operator precedence. In simplest terms, operator precedence means that certain operations in a formula take precedence over (or take place before) other operations in a formula. For example, in the formula =B2+B3*C2, the multiplication of B3*C2 takes precedence, so B3 is multiplied by C2 and then B2 is added to that result. The order of operator precedence is as follows:

1. Parentheses ()

2. Exponent ^

3. Multiplication *, Division /

4. Addition +, Subtraction −

5. Equal to =, Less than <, Greater than >

In the case of the formula =B2+B3*C2, if you want the formula to add B2+B3 before multiplying the result by C2, you would have to write the formula as: =(B2+B3)*C2. Operations enclosed in parentheses take precedence over operations that are not in parentheses.

Entering Formulas

You can enter formulas in one of two ways: by typing the entire formula, including the cell addresses, or by typing the formula operators and selecting the cell references. Because many of the errors found in Excel typically relate to incorrectly entered information, it makes sense to point to the cells or cell ranges that are included in a formula. This makes it less likely for an incorrect cell address or range to be placed in the formula. Follow these steps to enter a formula:

1. Select the cell that will hold the formula. Type = to begin the formula.

2. Click on the first cell that will be referenced in the formula. The cell address is entered in the formula in the formula bar.

3. Enter the appropriate arithmetic operator after the value to indicate the operation you want to perform.

4. Click on the next cell that will be referenced in the formula.

5. Repeat steps 3 and 4 if necessary. You can also enter constants into the formula as needed.

6. When the formula is complete, click the Enter button on the formula bar or press Enter. The formula is entered in the current cell.

After the formula has been entered in the cell, the result of the formula appears in the cell. When you select the cell, you can view the formula in the formula bar. If you click in the formula bar, the range finder highlights the cells that you specified in the formula.

 tip

If you are entering a formula and want to get rid of it and start again, press Esc.

Editing Formulas

Editing formulas in Excel is straightforward. You can edit a formula in the formula bar or directly in the cell. To edit the formula in the formula bar, select the cell containing the formula; then place the insertion point into the formula (in the formula bar) and edit as needed. As soon as you place the insertion point in the formula bar, the range finder highlights the cells referenced in the formula.

You can use the arrow keys to move within the formula bar. To go to the beginning of the formula in the formula bar, press the Home key; the End key takes you to the end of the formula. You can also do in-cell editing: Double-click on a cell to place the insertion point into the contents of the cell such as a formula.

When you need to edit a cell reference (or references) in a formula, it is probably easiest to do this in the formula bar. Select the cell address in the formula that you want to change. You can type the changes required; however, it is more foolproof to click on the cell and that cell's address is inserted into the formula, replacing the selected cell reference. When you have finished editing the formula, click the Enter button in the formula bar or press the Enter key.

➡ *For more information about editing a cell's content,* **see** *"Entering Data in a Worksheet," p. 309.*

Working with Excel Functions

Formulas provide you with a way to do simple arithmetic and some logical expressions, but most of the heavy lifting you do in terms of calculations in Excel is accomplished using functions. Functions can do everything from adding a range of numbers, to counting the number of entries in a range, to providing you with the return on an investment when you have a constant interest rate and consistent monthly deposits. And you can bank on the fact that my previous statement doesn't even scratch the surface of possibilities in terms of the different kinds of functions that Excel provides.

Functions consist of two parts: the function name and the cell addresses that are to be acted on. These cell ranges or individual cell addresses are also referred to as the function's arguments because they are used by the function to arrive at an answer. One of the most common functions used is the SUM function, which is also referred to as the AutoSum function because Excel has provided an AutoSum command in just about every version of Excel that I can remember. It is designed to quickly add a range of numbers. So, the SUM function might look like this in a worksheet: =SUM(B4:D4), where the argument is the range of cells B4 to D4, which will be added by the SUM function. The SUM function can also add cells that are not in a contiguous range using the syntax =SUM(B3, C6, D12); individual cell addresses serve as the arguments in the function and are separated by commas. The number of arguments (or cell addresses) that can be placed in the SUM function is endless, meaning that many functions do not control the number of legal arguments specified in the function.

Some functions do not have any arguments. For example, the =NOW() function, which is a date function, returns the current date and time formatted as a date and time. It does not require an argument in the parentheses to work.

The number of arguments allowed in Excel functions can vary, and some functions allow optional arguments. For example, the FV function, which calculates the future value of an investment that has a constant interest rate and the same payment amount over the investment period, allows for an optional present value of the investment if you have rolled money over into a new money market account, certificate of deposit, or other investment instrument. Figure 13.6 shows a simple future value worksheet that includes an optional present value (the initial investment on the worksheet).

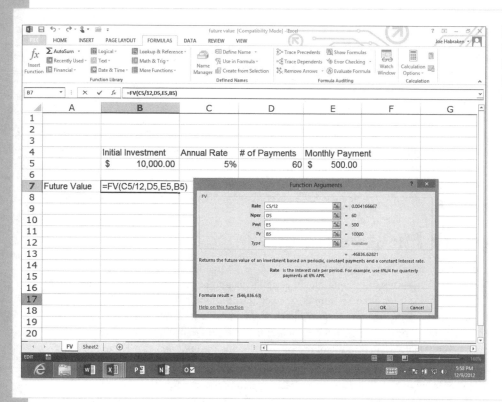

Figure 13.6
Supplying a Future Value function with arguments.

Figure 13.6 shows the Function Arguments dialog box, which is used to build a function. The Future Value function (FV) requires that a Rate (the interest rate divided by the number of payments in a year), the Nper (the total number of payment periods in the investment), and the Pmt (the actual payment) be supplied for the function to work. It also allows for an optional PV (or Present Value) to be included.

Entering a Function in a Cell

Excel provides different methods for inserting a function into your worksheet. You can type in a function (as you can a formula) by typing an equal sign (=) followed by the name of the function. The cell references for the function are then provided within the parentheses that follow the function name.

Typing functions can be just as fraught with potential errors as typing in formulas. Excel provides you with two methods for inserting functions: the Insert Function dialog box and the category commands provided in the Function Library. Both of these avenues get you to the same place: the Function Arguments dialog box. The Function Arguments dialog box enables you to specify the arguments to be used by the function. This can require that you specify a range of cells or individual cell addresses. Because the Function Arguments dialog box breaks the required arguments for the function, you can use the mouse to easily specify the arguments directly on the worksheet. This can greatly cut down on the possibility of specifying the wrong range or cell address in the function.

Although using the Function Arguments dialog box is relatively straightforward, some of the more commonly used functions such as SUM, AVERAGE, and other statistical functions such as MAX (maximum) and MIN (minimum) can be inserted in a more direct way via the AutoSum command. Let's look at AutoSum and then we can return to our discussion of inserting functions using the Function Arguments dialog box.

Using AutoSum

As already mentioned, the SUM function is probably the most used function in Excel; we are always adding things together, such as the total number of employees, the total number of widgets in our inventory, or the total amount of money in our bank account.

You can insert the SUM function into a worksheet using the AutoSum command on the Ribbon's Home tab or the AutoSum command in the Function Library of the Ribbon's Formulas tab. Select the cell where you want to place the SUM function. Typically, you choose a cell that is at the bottom of a column of values or at the end of a row of data. This makes it easy for AutoSum to figure out the range of cells that it should include in the SUM function.

When you select the AutoSum command, AutoSum inserts =SUM and selects the range of cells to be included in the function. The range is also specified in the function. Figure 13.7 shows the SUM function inserted by the AutoSum command and the range of cells that is included in the function.

Note that the range of cells is specified as B6:B17. The beginning and end of the range are separated by a colon (:). AutoSum does not always select the correct range of cells. When you insert the SUM function using AutoSum in a cell that is at the bottom of a column and at the end of a row, AutoSum selects the cells in the column. Blank cells within a range stop AutoSum from selecting the entire cell range you might want to specify in the function. You can change the range selected as needed. Use the mouse to extend or reduce the selection marquee or select an entirely new range of cells. After you have the correct range specified, click the Enter button in the formula bar or press the Enter key. The SUM function is placed in the cell and returns a result.

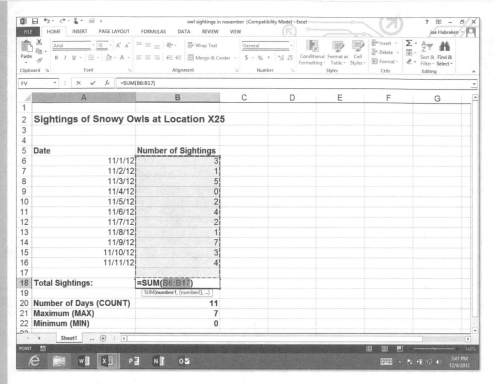

Figure 13.7
AutoSum attempts to select the range of cells to be added.

You can also insert other statistical functions from the AutoSum drop-down menu. These functions include Average (AVERAGE), Count Numbers (COUNT), Maximum (MAX), and Minimum (MIN). To enter one of these functions, such as AVERAGE, select the cell that contains the function and then select the drop-down menu for the AutoSum command on the Home tab or the Formulas tab. The function is entered in the cell. The function attempts to select a range; however, how successful this is depends on where you are placing the function and how the values that you want to be acted on are arranged in the worksheet. Use the mouse if you need to specify the range for the function and then press Enter. The result of the function appears in the cell.

 tip

The Count Numbers or COUNT function does not count blank cells or cells containing text. If you want to count values, use COUNT. If you want to count the cells in the range no matter what is in the cells (excluding blank cells), use the COUNTA function.

Using the Status Bar Statistical Functions

Because we are talking about some of the statistical functions, such as Average (AVERAGE), Count Numbers (COUNT), Maximum (MAX), and Minimum (MIN), and how to insert them, I want to take a short side trip and discuss the statistical counters or Autocalculate fields that are provided by the Excel status bar. When you select a range of cells, the status bar can automatically calculate such things as the average, count, minimum, maximum, and sum for the range. The result is shown in the status bar (not in the sheet).

To activate these statistical counters, such as Average, Count, or Sum, right-click on the status bar to open the Customize Status Bar menu. Select a statistical function such as AVERAGE,COUNT, or MIN (you can enable as many of these statistical counters as you want).

Now when you select a range of cells in the sheet, the results of the enabled statistical functions appear on the status bar. These status bar statistical functions provide you with a quick statistical summary of any selected cell range.

Using the Insert Function Dialog Box

The Insert Function dialog box can be accessed via the AutoSum drop-down menu; select the AutoSum drop-down arrow on the Home tab of the Ribbon and then select More Functions. You can also access the Insert Function dialog box from the Insert Function command on the Ribbon's Formulas tab. In either case, the Insert Function dialog box opens, as shown in Figure 13.8.

Figure 13.8
The Insert Function dialog box.

The Insert Function dialog box is designed to help you find a function in cases where you have a good idea of what you want to do in terms of a calculation in the worksheet but aren't sure which function to use or can't remember the name of a function that you use occasionally. To search for a particular function, type a brief description of what you want to do in the Search for a Function box and then click Go. For example, you could type "investment value," and Excel would list financial functions (among other functions) that help you calculate the present or future value of an investment.

 tip

If you need more help with a particular function, select the function in the list and then click Help on This Function to open the Excel Help window.

If you want to see functions that you have recently used, you can use the Or Select a Category drop-down list to view the most recently used functions. You can also peruse the functions by category, such as Financial, Date & Time, Statistical, Logical, and so on, by selecting a particular category of functions via the Category drop-down box.

When you select a function in the Select a Function list box, the syntax for the function appears below the function list. A definition of the function is also provided.

After you have located the function that you want to place in the worksheet, make sure that the function is selected and then click OK. The Function Arguments dialog box opens. Provide the various arguments for the function as required by the function and then click OK. This places the function in the worksheet and returns your result.

Using the Function Library

Another alternative for inserting a function into a sheet is to use the function category commands that are provided in the Function Library group on the Ribbon's Formulas tab. The Function Library group also provides access to the Recently Used command, which lists recently used functions as well as the Insert Function command and the AutoSum command, which has a drop-down list that includes other statistical functions, such as AVERAGE and MIN.

Each of the Function Library categories provides access to an entire category of functions. For example, selecting the Financial command lists Financial functions in alphabetical order. Figure 13.9 shows the Ribbon's Formulas tab.

Figure 13.9
The Ribbon's Formulas tab.

The Formulas tab provides more than just access to the Function Library. It also provides commands that are related to range names, auditing formulas and functions, and determining when and how results should be calculated in the worksheet. The command groups on the Formulas tab are as follows:

- **Function Library:** This group provides function category commands that enable you to specify a function to be inserted into a worksheet. Commands include Insert Function, AutoSum, and Recently Used. Category commands, such as Financial, Logical, Text, and so on, enable you to access specific lists of commands by category. The More Functions command provides access to additional function categories, such as Statistical, Engineering, and Cube.

- **Defined Names:** This group provides the commands for creating, accessing, and managing range names. Using range names in formulas and functions is discussed in the next section in this chapter.

For more information about creating range names, **see** "Naming Ranges," **p. 362**.

- **Formula Auditing:** This group provides tools that enable you to check formulas and functions for errors. It also enables you to show the formula and functions in a worksheet (rather than their results) and activate the Watch Window, which is used to monitor the values in certain cells as changes are made to the values in the worksheet. Proofing your formulas and functions is discussed later in this chapter.

- **Calculation:** This group enables you to immediately calculate the results in a sheet (Excel automatically calculates results by default) and also change calculation options such as switching from automatic calculations to manual.

To take advantage of the Function Library, select a function category to view the functions in that category. Place the mouse on a function (in a category list). A ScreenTip appears that provides you with a brief description of the function. For example, Figure 13.10 shows the Logical gallery (opened by selecting Logical in the Function Library) with the ScreenTip for the IF function.

Figure 13.10 The Logical gallery and the ScreenTip for the IF function.

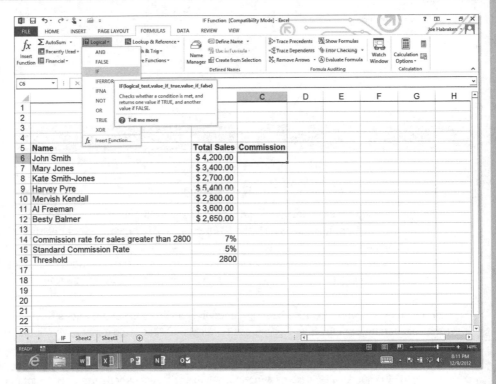

After you locate the function that you want to insert into the worksheet, select the function in the gallery. The Function Arguments dialog box opens, as shown in Figure 13.11.

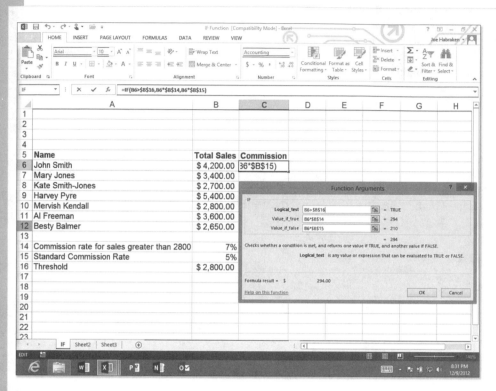

Figure 13.11
The Function Arguments dialog box for the IF function and the accompanying sheet.

The Function Arguments dialog box lists both the required (and in some cases optional) arguments for a function. In Figure 13.11, the IF function is shown, which requires that a logical test be provided along with a value if true and a value if false. The logical test can include cell addresses, operators, and a constant, if needed. The value if true can be a calculation, a cell address, or a text string. When you include text strings in functions, you need to place quotation marks around the text.

In the sheet shown in Figure 13.10, the function is inserted in cell C6 and is then copied down so that the commission for each salesperson is calculated. The logical test requires that the total sales for a salesperson be greater than cell B16 (which holds the value of 2,800.00). If the logical test is true (if total sales exceeds B17) then the commission rate is calculated by multiplying the total sales by cell B14 (7%). A salesperson selling more than the threshold amount gets a higher commission because the commission is figured at the higher rate (7%). If the value is false, the total sales is multiplied by the standard commission rate in cell B15 (5%).

After you have provided the various arguments required by the function, you can click OK. This closes the Function Arguments dialog box; the function is placed in the worksheet and provides you with a result.

Using Range Names in Formulas and Functions

Range names can be used in both your formulas and functions to reference cell ranges. Because range names are often descriptive in terms of the cell or cell range defined by the name, range names provide you with a more meaningful way (in terms of your own thought process) to specify the arguments in a formula or function.

Using range names for cells that provide constants or other arguments for a formula or function can also negate the need to use absolute referencing in the formula or function. The range name is, in effect, an absolute reference of a specific cell or cell range by virtue of the range name itself. This can be particularly useful in cases when you are building formulas or functions that pull data from multiple sheets in the same workbook. The range names help you differentiate arguments and can also cut down on the possibility of incorrectly specified cell addresses or ranges in a formula or function.

All the range names that you create can be accessed via the Use in Formula drop-down list. The Use in Formula command is housed in the Defined Names group on the Ribbon's Formulas tab. The Use in Formula drop-down list is available when you are typing a formula or function into a cell from the keyboard or inserting a function using the Function Arguments dialog box.

➥ *For details on ways to create range names,* ***see*** *"Naming Ranges," **p. 362**.*

Inserting a Range Name into a Formula

You can insert range names into your formulas as you create them in a cell. Begin the formula by typing the equal sign (=); specify any cell addresses to be included in the formula by clicking on that cell or selecting the cell range. Add operators as needed to the formula. When you want to specify an argument by range name, select the Use in Formula command and select the range name from the list provided. Figure 13.12 shows a formula being created in cell C11. The Commission Percentage range name, which is the range name for cell F18 (the commission percentage value), is pasted into the formula.

When you have pasted the range name into the formula, you can complete the formula as needed. If you need to paste additional range names into the formula, repeat the process using the Use in Formula command. Press Enter when you have finished creating the formula.

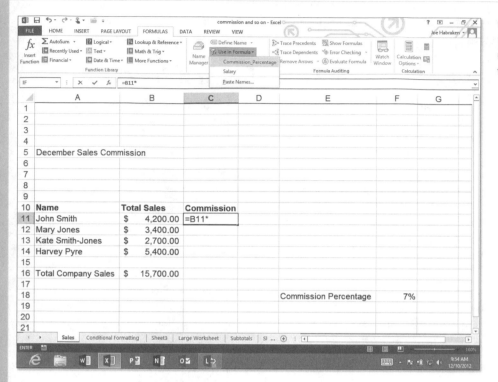

Figure 13.12
Insert range
names into a
formula.

Inserting a Range Name into a Function

You can also insert range names into the functions that you use in your worksheets. Select the function you want to use from the Function Library category commands or the Insert Function dialog box. Specify the range names to be used by the function in the appropriate argument box in the Function Arguments dialog box. For example, let's say you are using the PMT function to figure out monthly payments at different interest rates and principals. You want to insert the term (Nper) into the Function Arguments dialog box but don't want to have to use absolute referencing and so you specify the cell using an already defined range name.

Figure 13.13 shows the Function Arguments dialog box for the PMT function and the Use in Formula range name list. The Nper box in the Function Arguments dialog box is the "target" for the pasted range name.

When you are inserting range names into the Function Arguments dialog box (or directly into a formula or function in a cell), you can insert the range name from the Use in Formula range name list or the Paste Name dialog box. The Paste Name dialog box also allows you to view range names available in the current workbook. To open the Paste Name dialog box, select the Use in Formula command and then select Paste Name.

Figure 13.13 Insert range names into the Function Arguments dialog box.

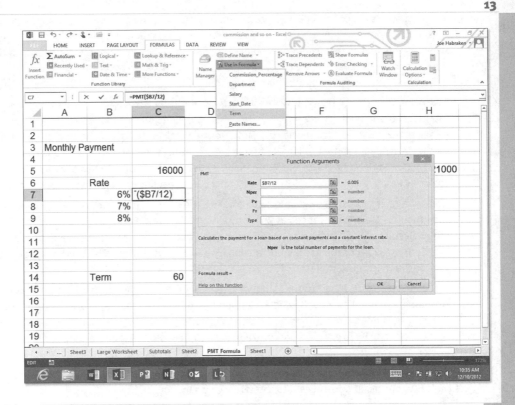

The Paste Name dialog box is useful in cases where you have created a large number of range names for the sheets in your workbook. A long list of range names in the Use in Formula range name list can make it hard to find the range name you want. The Paste Name dialog box, on the other hand, allows you to scroll up and down through the Paste Name list. Selecting a range name in the Paste Name dialog box also does not immediately insert the range into the function (as does the Use in Formula range name list). The Paste Name dialog box requires you to click OK after specifying the range name to be pasted.

Referencing Cells or Ranges on Other Worksheets

When you work in situations where data that spans more than one sheet in an Excel workbook must be summarized, you need to include cell references in a formula or function that consist of cell addresses or ranges that are not on the current worksheet (the worksheet that contains the formula or function). For example, you might have created a different worksheet for each quarter of the year that details your sales figures or expenditures, and you want to have a worksheet in the workbook that provides summary information for all four quarters.

The syntax for a cell reference on a worksheet that is in the same workbook as the sheet you are working on is `'sheet name'!cell address`. The single quotation marks are required for the sheet name reference only if the sheet's name contains spaces.

The best way to specify a cell address on another sheet in the same workbook, or a range of cells in the same workbook, is to select the cell or range of cells as you create a formula or function that includes this information as an argument. By pointing out the arguments contained on the other worksheet or worksheets, you don't have to worry about the syntax related to how you refer to a cell on another sheet; Excel takes care of that for you.

For example, let's say that you want to add your quarterly sales totals, each of which is on a separate quarterly worksheet in an Excel workbook. All you have to do is select the AutoSum command to insert the SUM function in the cell. Now, you can show Excel the cells that are to be added. Click on the worksheet tab that holds the first quarterly total. Then click on the cell containing that total. The first cell reference is added to the function. Before navigating to the next worksheet, type a comma (,) after the first cell address entry to separate each of the cell references in the function.

Go to the next worksheet and select the total for the next quarter; then type a comma. As you build the function, the cell references appear on the formula bar. Repeat the process as needed, separating each cell reference with a comma. After specifying the last cell reference to be included in the function, press Enter (do not include a comma after the last entry). The SUM function returns the sum of the four quarter totals.

You can also insert cell addresses that specify cells on other worksheets into the Function Arguments dialog box, which is used to build functions. Select the appropriate argument box in the Function Arguments dialog box and then navigate to the worksheet that contains the cell or cell range. Select the cell or range and it is added to the Function Arguments dialog box.

Figure 13.14 shows a function and a formula that reference cell addresses on other worksheets in the workbook. Specifying these addresses using the point-and-click method is much easier than trying to type the cell references into the formula or function.

You can also reference cell addresses that are in other workbooks (meaning a separate Excel file). The syntax for cell addresses referenced in other Excel workbook formulas or functions is as follows:

```
'[workbook name]sheet name'!cell address
```

This is the syntax used when the other workbook is open. The syntax for a closed workbook is a little more involved:

```
'drive letter:\folder\[workbook name]sheet name'!cell address
```

The easiest way to reference cells or ranges in other workbooks is to open all the workbooks involved. You can then switch between the workbooks to specify the cell addresses used in a formula or function in much the same way that you can move from worksheet to worksheet in a single workbook and then select the cells to be used as operands or arguments.

 tip

To view two open workbooks side by side, select the View Side By Side command on the Ribbon's View tab.

 tip

Another way to reference cell ranges on other sheets in a workbook (sheets other than the one where you are inserting a formula or function) is to use range names to specify the ranges. A range name can basically be a description of location in terms of the sheet that it is on. This may make it easier for you to visualize a formula or function that calculates a result using cell ranges from several sheets in a workbook.

Figure 13.14
Functions
and formulas
can contain
references
to cell
addresses
outside the
current work-
sheet.

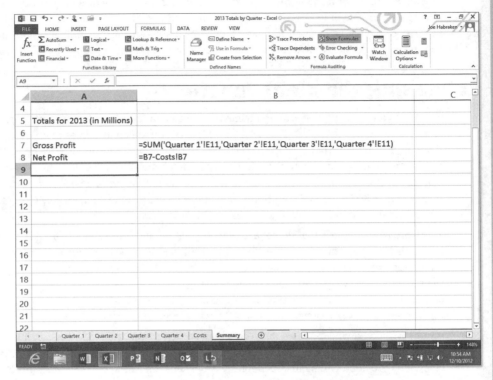

Copying and Moving Formulas and Functions

Copying and moving formulas and functions is straightforward as long as you remember the fact
that Excel uses relative referencing by default. This makes it easy to copy a formula or function that
acts on rows or columns that are similar to the row or column where you first inserted the formula
or function. For example, if you have several rows of values that contain the same number of cells,
you can use the SUM function to total the first row and then drag the SUM function down using the
fill handle to copy it so that it totals each subsequent row in the worksheet. The cell references in
the function change relative to its position because of relative referencing and so you get the correct
total for each row.

You can copy formulas or functions using the fill handle (when appropriate) and you can also use the
Copy and Paste commands. Remember that copying a formula or function can be tricky if you have
not specified any absolute references that basically lock the address of certain values in the formula
or function. If you get an error value such as #NUM, Excel's relative referencing is wreaking havoc
with your copied formula or function.

For more about relative and absolute referencing, **see** *"Relative Versus Absolute Referencing,"*
p. 369.

Moving a formula or function can be accomplished by dragging the formula or function (the cell containing the formula or function) to a new location on the worksheet. You can also use Cut and Paste as needed. Even if you move a formula or function, it still returns the original results, meaning it continues to reference the cell addresses originally specified when you built the formula or function.

Choosing the Right Function

Excel functions provide you with ready-made formulas for just about any type of calculation you want to undertake. Statistical, Financial, and Math & Trig are all examples of function categories that supply functions that do calculations. Statistical functions, such as COUNT and AVERAGE, are designed for doing statistical analysis. Financial functions, such as PMT and FV, compute the monthly payment on a car or house or the return on an investment, respectively. Math & Trig functions, such as SINE and COS, return the sine or cosine of an angle, respectively (sorry for dredging up any potential trigonometry nightmares).

There are also functions that do not actually do what we typically think of as calculations, meaning math. There are the lookup functions HLOOKUP and VLOOKUP, which are designed to look up information in a table and then return that value to a cell. The logical function IF provides you with the ability to set up a conditional statement and then have the IF function perform one action if the condition is true and another action if the condition is false. And I haven't even mentioned the text functions, which are designed to manipulate text strings in your worksheets.

It goes without saying (but obviously, I am going to say it) that there are a lot of different possibilities in Excel functions. Just take a tour of the possibilities by perusing through the different function categories provided in the Function Library. An exhaustive listing of Excel functions and their uses are beyond the scope of this book. However, the information that follows is designed to provide you with some help in understanding some of the most-often-used functions in your worksheets.

Financial Functions

The financial functions provide you with the ability to do all sorts of different financial calculations; there are depreciation functions, financial functions (related to securities), and investment and annuities functions. Many of these functions are related to finance and accounting principles that require a solid knowledge base to use them correctly. However, there are other financial functions that just about anyone can take advantage of. For example, you can easily calculate monthly payments on loans, compute the present value of an investment, and determine the future value of an investment.

When you are working with financial functions, there is some basic terminology that you need to have under your belt, particularly if you want to take advantage of some of the financial functions that enable you to compute the return on an investment or the periodic payment on a loan. For example, to compute the current value of an investment, you need to know the Rate, Nper, and the Pmt.

The Rate (which is what Excel asks for in the Function Arguments dialog box when you are setting up a financial function such as PV or Present Value) or interest rate is straightforward. We have all at the very least had an interest-bearing checking account that is tied to a particular interest rate. The rate supplied to you for both investments and loans is typically the APR or the annual percentage rate. This means that when you provide the rate for a financial function such as PV, you need to divide the annual interest rate by the number of payments you make each year to provide the function with the interest rate per period.

Another piece of information that you need to supply to a financial function such as PV is the total number of payment periods in the investment or Nper; the Nper is based on the number of payments you make annually. So, if you make monthly payments on the investment for five years, the Nper is 60 (5*12).

The PV function also needs to know how much the payment was each period. For PV to work, the payment must be the same for each period during the life of the investment. Figure 13.15 shows a simple worksheet that uses PV to compute the value of a five-year investment.

Figure 13.15
PV uses the Rate, Nper, and PMT to calculate the value of an investment.

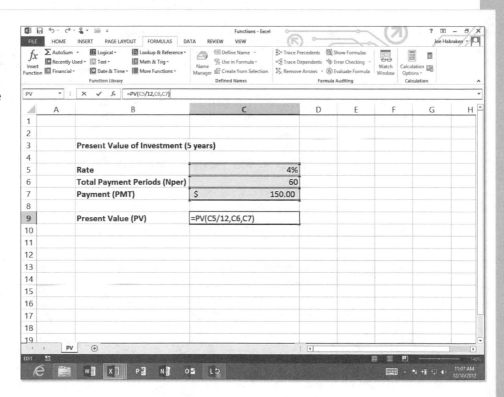

If you understand one financial function such as PV, you can probably work your way through similar functions such as FV (Future Value), NPER (number of payment periods for a loan), and PMT (loan payment), because they use similar arguments such as the Nper and Rate when you build the function. For example, the syntax for the PMT function is

```
=PMT(Rate, NPER, PV)
```

When using the PMT function and other financial functions that include the Rate (interest rate), remember that it needs to be divided by the number of payments that you make in a year. For monthly payments, you would divide the rate by 12; for quarterly payments, you would divide by 4.

Logical Functions

Logical functions enable you to evaluate conditional statements. The IF function is probably the most used of the logical functions and provides you with the ability to include other formulas or functions as part of the true or false answer that is derived from your conditional statement. The syntax for the IF function is as follows:

```
=IF(logical_test, value_if_true,value_if_false)
```

The logical test can use operators such as less than ($<$), greater than ($>$), and equal to ($=$). The *value_if_true* or the *value_if_false* can consist of values, formulas, functions, or text strings. If you use text strings as the true or false values, the text must be enclosed within quotation marks such as "text".

In terms of providing an example to illustrate the use of the IF function, let's say that you have total sales figures for your sales personnel and you want to calculate the commission for each salesperson. You have two commission rates: a low commission rate and a high commission rate. Any salesperson selling more than $28,000.00 of merchandise receives the high commission rate. Those who fall below $28,000.00 receive the low commission rate. A breakdown of the IF function just described would be as follows:

```
Logical_test: total sales > $28,000.00
Value_if_true: total sales*High Commission Rate
Value_if_false: total sales*Low Commission Rate
```

Figure 13.16 shows a sample worksheet that uses the IF function. The cells containing the low commission rate, high commission rate, and the threshold (B15, B16, and B17) have all been named using the row labels to the left. So, the range names have been used in the Function Arguments dialog box (which negates the need to use any absolute references, if you want to copy the function to other cells).

When you have finished entering the arguments for the IF function in the Function Arguments dialog box, click OK. You can then drag the fill handle down and copy the function to the other commission cells that are associated with each employee.

Figure 13.16
The IF func-
tion.

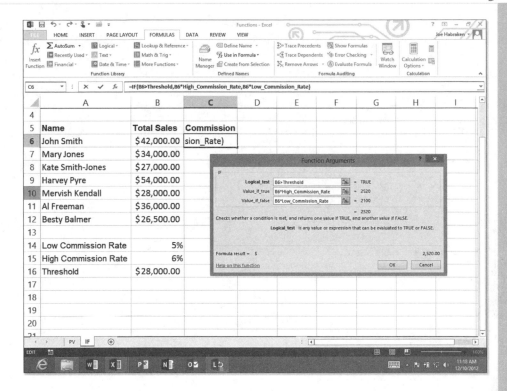

Statistical Functions

The statistical functions provide you with often-used functions, such as SUM, AVERAGE, COUNT, MAX, and MIN. There are more complex statistical functions, such as CORREL (correlate changes in compared variables), CHISQ.TEST (test how actual data compares to a random distribution), and FREQUENCY (used to analyze a series of values and group them in frequency ranges). So, whether you use basic statistical functions or perform fairly heavy-duty statistical analysis, the Excel Statistical functions provide you with all the analysis functions you need. Figure 13.17 shows the COUNT, MAX, and MIN for a range of values.

Note that when you use the Show Formulas command on the Formulas tab to see the formulas rather than the results, the dates are changed to numerical values. The syntax is pretty consistent for the relatively simple statistical functions, such as AVERAGE and MAX, and some of the more esoteric statistical analysis functions, such as MEDIAN (computes the median for a range of cells) and STDEV.P (calculates the standard deviation of a range of values). The syntax for the AVERAGE function follows:

```
=AVERAGE(cell range)
```

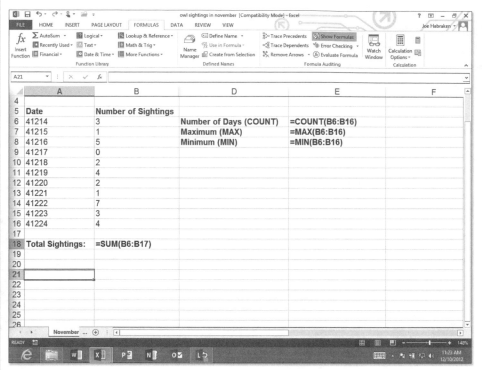

Figure 13.17
Many of the
Statistical
functions cal-
culate a result
on a range of
cells.

The AVERAGE, COUNT (Count Numbers), MAX, and MIN functions can be quickly inserted into a function using the menu
provided by the AutoSum command on the Formulas tab and the
AutoSum command on the Home tab. For example, to insert the
AVERAGE function, select AutoSUM and then AVERAGE. Use
the mouse to specify the range for the function to act on and then
press Enter or click the Enter button on the formula bar.

 tip
You can access all the Statistical
functions by selecting the More
Functions command and then
pointing at Statistical.

Lookup & Reference Functions

The Lookup & Reference functions provide a number of different functions, such as HYPERLINK
(enables you to specify a link to a local or remote file), TRANSPOSE (converts a vertical range to a
horizontal range or vice versa), and the Lookup functions VLOOKUP and HLOOKUP. VLOOKUP and
HLOOKUP can be quite useful and they work in much the same fashion. They can look up values
from a table and place the value in the cell that holds the LOOKUP functions. Let's take a closer look
at VLOOKUP.

VLOOKUP does a vertical lookup and returns a value from an array (which is just another word for a
multi-column lookup table) based on the search criterion. For example, you can create a four-column
array that contains employees' last names in the first column, the first name in the second column,

the department in the third column, and the phone extension of each employee in the fourth column. It is this fourth column that serves as the information that VLOOKUP inserts into the worksheet.

Place the VLOOKUP function in the Extension column of the sheet (directly to the right of the employee name column); the function then automatically looks up the phone extension based on the information in the employee name column. Figure 13.18 shows the VLOOKUP function that has looked up the phone extensions for each employee as the names were entered in the first column.

Figure 13.18
VLOOKUP can look up information in an array and insert it into a cell.

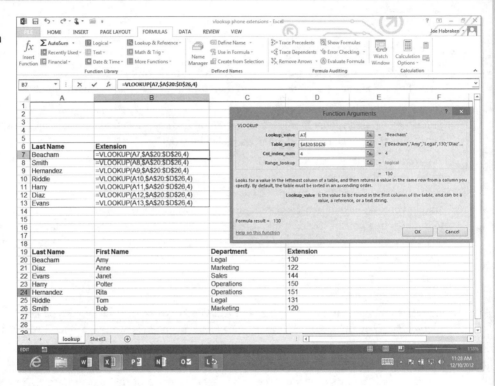

The syntax for VLOOKUP is as follows:

```
=VLOOKUP(Lookup_value,Table_array,Col_index_num
```

The Lookup_value is the cell that contains the information that the function uses to look up the information in the table array. So, the Table_array is the range or range name that specifies the table that contains the information. The Col_index_num tells VLOOKUP which of the columns in the table array should be placed in the cell that contains the VLOOKUP function. In Figure 13.18, the information is in column 4 of the table array.

When you create the VLOOKUP function, it makes sense to name the table array. If you don't name it, make sure that you specify the table array range as an absolute reference. That way, the

VLOOKUP function is always looking in the correct place (the table array) when you copy the function to other cells. The VLOOKUP function can be accessed via the Lookup & Reference command on the Ribbon's Formulas tab. If your information is in rows rather than columns, you can use HLOOKUP, which is set up in a very similar manner to VLOOKUP.

The LOOKUP functions can do more than just return the extension numbers for employees. It can also be used for such things as price lists. You can create a worksheet using either VLOOKUP or HLOOKUP and when you enter the name of a product, the price is returned by the LOOKUP function.

Date & Time Functions

Excel views dates and times as values. Dates are based on the starting point of January 1, 1900. So, if you enter this date in a worksheet and then format the date as a general number, the value shown is 1.

Time is also perceived by Excel as a value. Times are seen as a fractional part of a day. For example, 12:00 p.m. is equivalent to 0.5; whereas 9:00 a.m. would be 0.375.

You don't typically have to convert dates or times to their actual value equivalents. The fact that dates and times are seen as numerical values means that you can include dates and times in your formulas and functions. In terms of date and time functions, Excel provides you with functions that enable you to quickly place the date and/or time into your worksheet or to calculate values related to date or time entries. For example, the NETWORKDAYS function can return the number of workdays between two dates as long as you also supply the number of holidays that fall between the two dates. The NETWORKDAYS function uses the syntax:

```
=NETWORKDAYS(Start_date, End_date, Holidays)
```

The start and end dates are the beginning and end date for the time span. The holidays are also specific dates of when the holidays actually fall. The holidays (if there are multiple) can be entered as a range into the function. The NETWORKDAYS function is an excellent way to determine how many working days there are during a particular project cycle.

The date and time functions are accessed via the gallery provided by the Date & Time command on the Formulas tab. Two simple-to-use functions that place the current date into a worksheet are NOW and TODAY. NOW enters the current date and the time. The TODAY function enters the current date only.

These two functions are dynamic and so they change to the current date and/or time when you open the workbook. If you want a static date on a worksheet that serves as a time stamp of when you started the worksheet, enter the date and/or time manually.

Text Functions

You might find it odd that Excel also provides a number of functions designed to work with cells containing text entries or labels. As we discussed at the outset of the Excel section of this book, Excel knows when you have entered text in cells and it knows when you enter numbers—values—into cells. It automatically left-aligns text and right-aligns values because it knows which is which.

The text functions provided by Excel enable you to split text entries in cells, combine text entries, manipulate the case of text, and convert numbers to text.

If you want to join text entries in two or more columns into a single column, you can take advantage of the CONCATENATE function. You can join the text from 255 different text strings into a single text string (in a single cell) using this function. The syntax for the CONCATENATE function is as follows:

= CONCATENATE (text1, text2, ...text255).

To insert cell addresses in the text boxes provided in the CONCATENATE function's Function Arguments dialog box; click in an argument box (such as Text1) and then click on the cell you want to reference. Repeat this process, placing the text string cell addresses in subsequent argument boxes. As already mentioned, you can specify 255 cell addresses.

You can also type text in the argument boxes in the CONCATENATE function's Function Arguments dialog box. This enables you to add a text string to the text concatenated by the function that does not exist in a cell in the worksheet. This text must be placed between quotation marks. For example, if you are combining information and you need to include a space between text strings (such as the combination of first and last names shown in Figure 13.19), you can insert a space (it must be surrounded by quotation marks) in a text box that is between the text entries that are combined (such as first and last names).

> **tip**
>
> The new Flash Fill feature makes it easy for you to separate text strings that have been inadvertently combined in a column of information. See Chapter 11, "Requisite Excel: Essential Features," for an introduction to the Flash Fill feature.

Figure 13.19
Use the CONCATENATE function to combine text strings.

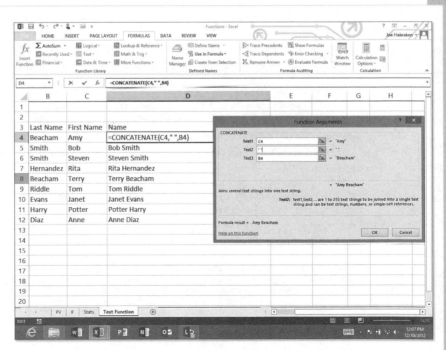

Other useful text functions relate to problems you might have with information that you import into Excel, such as imported text that contains extra spaces or unprintable characters. The TRIM function can be used to remove extra spaces. If you want to remove any unprintable characters from imported text, use the CLEAN function. The TRIM and CLEAN functions make a copy of the text contained in the cell or cell ranges specified in the function (TRIM or CLEAN). So, you end up with multiple copies of the text string in your worksheet (the before and after). You can't delete the original text with too many spaces (or in the case of the CLEAN function, the unprintable characters) because the function no longer has the original text to reference and provide you with the result.

You can convert the result of either the TRIM or CLEAN function to a value using Copy and Paste and then discard the original text that was imported. This leaves you with the trimmed or cleaned result.

Select the cell containing the TRIM or CLEAN function and then click Copy in the Clipboard group. Then select Paste. In the Paste gallery, select the Values option. Now when you select the cell or cells that originally contained the TRIM or CLEAN function, you find that the function has been converted to a text string. You can go ahead and delete the original, imported text.

 tip
Another easy way to join or concatenate text from multiple cells is to set up your own formula using the following syntax: cell address&" "&cell address. The ampersand (&) serves as the operator in the formula.

Other Function Categories

Excel also contains other function categories than those that we have discussed thus far. As already mentioned, there are more than 300 functions available in Excel. Many of the function categories relate to specific disciplines such as accounting, finance, statistical analysis, and engineering. When you select the More Functions command, several function categories are listed, such as Statistical, Engineering, and so on. We have already discussed the statistical functions. The list that follows provides a description of the other function categories found in the More Functions gallery:

- **Math & Trig:** This group provides a combination of useful mathematical and trigonometric functions. Functions such as COS (cosine), SIN (sine), and TAN (tangent) are used in computations related to a right-angled triangle. Another useful math function is ROUND, which enables you to specify the number of decimal places that a range of cell values should be rounded to. There are also the EVEN and ODD functions, which can be used to round values to even or odd numbers, respectively.

- **Engineering:** Excel provides a number of functions that are useful for various engineering-related applications. For example, there is CONVERT, which converts measurements from one system to another (such as miles to kilometers). Another conversion function provided in this category is the BIN2HEX function, which can be used to convert binary numbers to hexadecimal.

- **Cube:** The cube functions are used to interact with external data that is derived from an analysis services cube. The data is served up from a Microsoft SQL Server that provides the analysis services.

- **Information:** These functions enable you to derive information concerning a cell, such as the content or formatting of a cell. For example, the ISERR function returns the statement TRUE if an error exists in a cell (meaning an incorrectly designed formula or function) or FALSE if there is no error in a cell. ISBLANK is similar in that it returns either TRUE or FALSE based on whether or not a cell is blank.

- **Compatibility:** This category consists of functions that were native to earlier versions of Excel (many were native to Excel 2007) but have been replaced by new functions in Excel 2013. You would use the compatibility functions only in cases where you share your workbooks with co-workers or colleagues who still use earlier versions of Excel, such as Excel 2007. You can determine the Excel version of a Compatibility function by reading the function description in the Insert Function dialog box.

Remember, you are not required to use every type of function provided by Excel. Make sure that you test functions that are new to you. Use sample data that enables you to easily determine whether you are getting the appropriate result when you plug the data into the function.

Proofing Your Formulas and Functions

Just because a formula or function returns a value, it doesn't necessarily mean that it's correct. Making sure that your formulas and functions are providing the correct results in your worksheets is incredibly fundamental; yet many Excel users assume that if Excel came up with that answer, it has to be right. Fortunately, Excel provides tools that can help you proof your formulas and functions.

There can be different causes for formulas or functions to return an incorrect value. For example, you might have made a syntax error in actually creating the formula or function. You might not have included the appropriate operators for a formula or you did not provide a function's arguments in the correct order. This is why it makes sense to build functions using the Functions Argument dialog box rather than trying to type a function into a cell.

Errors can also result from incorrect cell references. You have the syntax for the formula or the function correct, but you did not reference the correct cells or range of cells.

Although Excel provides error messages in cases where a formula or function cannot calculate a return because of an obvious reason, the error messages will not save you when a formula or function contains an error that still allows it to return an answer—albeit an incorrect answer.

Excel provides a number of different error messages that can help you proof a problem formula or function. Other tools, such as the ability to view formulas in the worksheet and the fact you can also trace the cells related to a particular problem formula or function, can also help you fix issues related to calculations.

Common Error Messages

Excel seems to have an endless supply of error messages, and it does have your back when a formula or function contains an egregious error. Excel flags the problem formula or function with a specific error message. Some of the most common error messages are provided in Table 13.3.

Table 13.3 Common Error Messages

Error Message	Description
#REF	A cell referenced in the formula or function cannot be found. This can be the result of an incorrect range name or specifying a range that no longer exists.
#NAME?	Excel does not recognize text included in a formula or function such as a range name. This can be a syntax error (an incorrectly spelled function name) or a problem with a range name specified in the function.
#DIV/0!	The formula or functioning is attempting to divide by 0. This is typically due to an incorrectly referenced cell in the formula or function (a cell that does not contain a value).
#VALUE	An incorrect argument is present in the formula or function. This can be caused by referring to both text and value entries in the same formula or function. You can't add words to numbers.

These errors can often be easily corrected by carefully examining your formula or function. In the case of the #NAME? function, check to see whether you have misspelled the function name or have missing parentheses in a function. The #DIV/0! error can occur if you have copied a formula or function and have not taken into account cell referencing in the formula or function. You might have to use an absolute reference so that the cell you are dividing by is always referenced in the formula or function.

When an error message appears in a cell, a smart tag is provided for the error. When you select the smart tag, the menu provided identifies the error type and also provides you with access to help on the error. Other options provided enable you to view the calculation steps for the formula or function and an option to edit the function in the formula bar.

An error message that you want to definitely pay attention to is the Circular Reference Warning. When you attempt to create a formula or function that includes the formula or function within the range of cells that the formula or function acts on, you have a circular reference.

If you suspect that circular references are contained in workbooks that have been created by co-workers or colleagues, you can check them using the Circular References command in the Error Checking gallery. Any circular references in the worksheet are listed. The Circular References check is just one of the possibilities provided by the Formula Auditing command group found on the Ribbon's Formulas tab. Let's look at some of the other tools.

 tip

You can configure the Error Checking settings such as background error checking and the error-checking rules that are enabled in the Excel Options window. Select File and then click Options in the Backstage. Select Formulas to view the error-checking settings.

Using the Auditing Tools

One of the easiest auditing tools to use is the Show Formulas command. It shows you all the formulas and functions in a worksheet rather than their results. This enables you to peruse your formulas and functions for any possible issues that need to be addressed but were not of a nature that resulted in an error message being placed in the cell where the formula or function resides.

Two extremely useful formula auditing commands are Trace Precedents and Trace Dependents. To display the cells that are referenced by a particular formula or function—the precedents—select a formula or function in the worksheet and then select the Trace Precedents command. Blue arrows are drawn from the precedents for the currently selected function or formula, as shown in Figure 13.20.

Figure 13.20
Trace precedents for a formula or function.

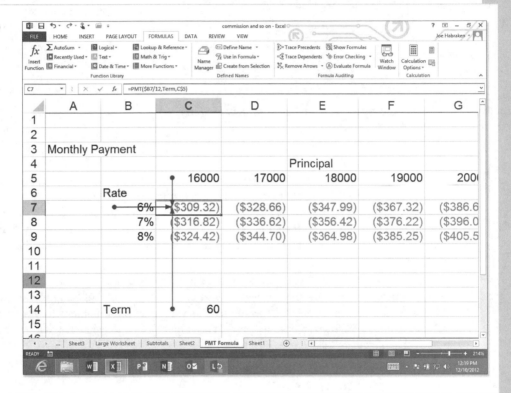

You can repeat the command as needed to view the precedents for other formulas or functions on the sheet simultaneously. When you want to remove the arrows from the worksheet, select the Remove Arrows command or one of its subcommands: Remove Precedent Arrows or Remove Dependent Arrows.

You can also trace the dependents for a particular value or range of cells. Select the cell or range of cells and then select the Trace Dependents command. Trace arrows are drawn from the cell or cell range to any formulas or functions that depend on that value or values.

When an error message is shown in a cell, you can use the Trace Error command to show the cells or cell range involved in the bad formula or function. Select the cell containing the error message and select the Error Checking drop-down arrow; select Trace Error and the precedents for the cell are shown.

Another useful auditing command is the Error Checking command. It can be used when a cell contains an error message. The command opens the Error Checking dialog box, as shown in Figure 13.21.

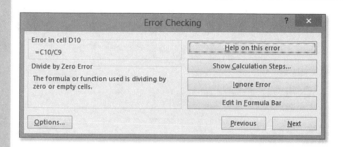

Figure 13.21
The Error Checking dialog box.

The Error Checking dialog box enables you to access help in the Excel Help window related to the type of error present in the cell. It also enables you to show the calculation steps and evaluate the formula. When you select Show Calculation Steps, the Evaluate Formula dialog box opens. Select Evaluate to begin evaluating the formula or function. You can also step in and out on the different portions of the formula or function until you find the portion of the formula or function that is causing the error.

The Error Checking dialog box can also act as a sort of spell checker for errors. After you have dealt with one error in a worksheet, you can click Next in the Error Checking dialog box and proceed to the next error found in the sheet. After you have repaired that error (perhaps by viewing the calculation steps), you can then proceed to the next error and so on until you have dealt with any and all cells in the worksheet that contain errors.

Using the Watch Window

Although it is not an auditing tool per se, the Watch Window can be a useful tool in monitoring certain cells in a worksheet in terms of how the entering of worksheet data or the editing of worksheet data affects those cells. The Watch Window can be particularly useful in cases where you have formulas or functions that are dependent on cell addresses or ranges that span multiple worksheets in a workbook. For example, you might have a summary worksheet that summarizes data from other worksheets in the workbook that provide detailed information for each quarter of your fiscal year.

 tip
You might want to name cells that you plan to watch in the Watch Window. A descriptive range name makes it easier to differentiate among multiple cell references that you place in the Watch Window.

To open the Watch Window, select the Watch Window command in the Formula Auditing group. Figure 13.22 shows the Watch Window. The Watch Window floats on top of your worksheets and remains in view even when you switch worksheets in a workbook. In fact, the Watch Window is also visible even when you switch to a different Excel workbook. So, the Watch Window is also useful in cases where you have cells in other workbooks that provide precedents to the cell that you have included in the Watch Window.

Figure 13.22
Keep an eye on specific workbook cells in the Watch Window.

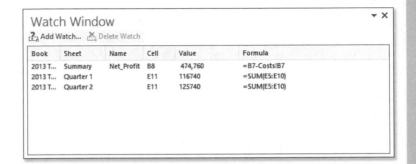

To add a cell to the Watch Window, navigate to the sheet that contains the cell or a cell range and then select Add Watch in the Watch Window. The Add Watch dialog box opens. Select the cell or cell range, and the reference is added to the Add Watch dialog box. When you click Add and return to the Watch Window, the cell reference is listed. It supplies the book, sheet, name, cell, and the current value of the cell as well as any formula or functions that reside in the cell. You can add additional cells to the Watch Window as needed.

Any changes that you make to cells that are precedents for the cell or cells you are watching in the Watch Window are reflected in the Watch Window. For example, if you entered data on a worksheet for first quarter sales and you are watching the yearly total SUM function on a summary sheet, the cell's value in the Watch Window reflects any data additions or changes.

To remove references from the Watch Window, select a listed reference and then click the Delete Watch command. When you are finished using the Watch Window, click its Close button. Even if you close the Watch Window, it retains the list of cell addresses that you have added to it.

14

ENHANCING WORKSHEETS WITH CHARTS

There is little doubt that Excel's incredible capabilities provide you with the tools to create complex and meaningful worksheets that serve all sorts of purposes from basic accounting to statistical analysis to complete mathematical mania. Excel has evolved far beyond the early spreadsheet programs that were first available for the personal computer. However, Excel still uses the very same classic spreadsheet geography of columns and rows of numbers used by these earlier programs. All those cells containing values, labels, formulas, and functions can be quite difficult for many people to readily understand. That is where charts come in. Charts provide you with the ability to take a visual snapshot of worksheet data and represent it as a graphic. Charts can greatly enhance the understanding of worksheet data and how the data is related.

In this chapter, we look at how to create charts in Excel. We also discuss what type of charts to use in particular situations and how you can modify and manipulate charts and chart elements. We look at sparklines and also take advantage of the new Recommended Charts command, which helps you select an appropriate chart type to accompany your sheet data.

Understanding Excel Charts

Excel charts provide a pictorial representation of worksheet data. Charts not only provide a way for people to better grasp trends or relationships in the worksheet data, but they can also add visual impact to your Excel worksheets. Charts are objects (just like an image or a SmartArt graphic) that can be included anywhere on a worksheet. Charts can also be created so that they reside on their own worksheet in a workbook. This is particularly useful for charts that contain a lot of detail and don't fit particularly well on a large worksheet that contains the data used to create the chart.

Chart Terminology

Working with charts is pretty straightforward. It does not hurt, however, to have a handle on some of the terminology you will run across when creating charts; a list of basic chart terms follows:

- **Chart area:** The area inside the object frame that contains the chart, the axes, the data point labels, the legend, the chart title, and other chart elements.

- **Plot area:** The area of the chart between the chart axes. This is where the data points are plotted.

- **Data series:** Related data points are referred to as a data series. A data series typically corresponds to a particular row or column of values in your worksheet (depending on how you have arranged your data in the worksheet). Each data series in a chart has its own pattern or color. Single-line charts or pie charts are examples of charts that have only one data series. In bar charts, particularly in cases where you are comparing entities over time—such as the performance of sales regions over time—multiple data series are present on the chart (one series for each region).

- **Categories:** Categories reflect the number of elements in a series. For example, on a chart that charts regional sales totals, the x-axis consists of the names of the regions, which are the categories for the chart.

- **Axis:** A two-dimensional chart, such as a line chart, has an x-axis (horizontal) and a y-axis (vertical). The x-axis contains the data series and categories in the chart. If you have more than one category, the x-axis often contains labels that define what each category represents. The y-axis reflects the values of the bars, lines, or plot points. In a three-dimensional chart, the z-axis represents the vertical plane, and the x-axis (distance) and y-axis (width) represent the two sides on the floor of the chart.

- **Legend:** The legend provides the key for how color coding or patterns have been used to differentiate the different elements in a data series on the chart. For example, a pie chart uses a different color to show the various categories that appear as parts of the pie.

- **Data labels:** Labels that appear on the chart denoting the value of the data points used to create the chart.

- **Gridlines:** Gridlines help visualize the value of a particular data point on the chart. Gridlines are typically used along the y-axis (where the value data points originate), but you can also include gridlines for the x-axis, which can be useful in situations where you have created a combination chart.

- **Background:** The background consists of the space behind and below the chart area. For example, the chart wall is the area directly behind the plot area and any gridlines shown on the chart. The chart floor of the chart is the bottommost part of the chart area.

Figure 14.1 shows a line chart embedded in a worksheet. This line chart contains one data series: the measured lake level for each month of the year. The x-axis consists of the labels associated with the data points: in this case, the months of the year, January through December. The y-axis consists of the scale for the values represented by the chart, in this case, a scale in feet. The x-axis lists the categories for the chart—each month is a specific category.

Figure 14.1
A line chart.

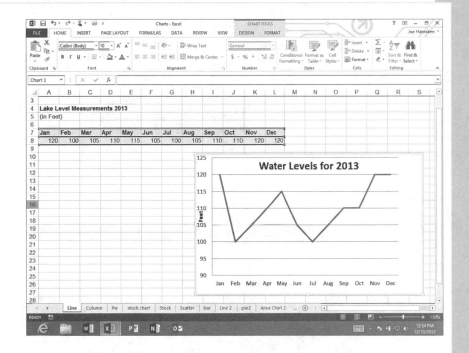

Notice that when a chart is selected in a worksheet (as it is in Figure 14.1), the contextual Chart Tools appear on the Ribbon and consist of Design and Format tabs. We explore the specific commands and tools provided by the Chart Tools as the chapter progresses.

Charts can also be created that have multiple data series. Figure 14.2 shows a bar chart that has four data series—one data series for each of the sales region's monthly totals. The chart in Figure 14.2 also includes a legend that shows the color coding for the different data series (each region's sales) displayed on the chart.

You can also build combination charts in Excel so that you can visualize the data series in a worksheet in a unique way that enables you to emphasize or differentiate different sets of data points. Figure 14.3 shows a combination chart that includes both a line chart and a column chart.

The columns in the chart show the sales for four regions—East, West, South, and North—over a three-month period (January through March). Total sales are also included in the chart and have been formatted as a line chart that shows the growth of overall sales during the three-month period. Combination charts provide you with the ability to have your chart emphasize more than one set of data points by combining two different chart types.

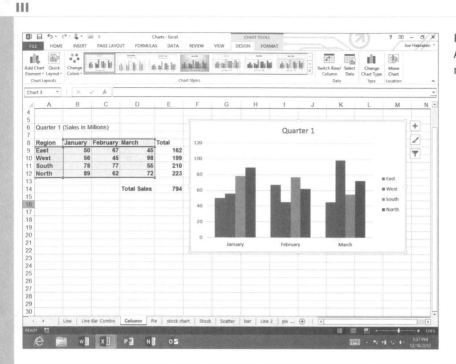

Figure 14.2
A column chart with multiple data series.

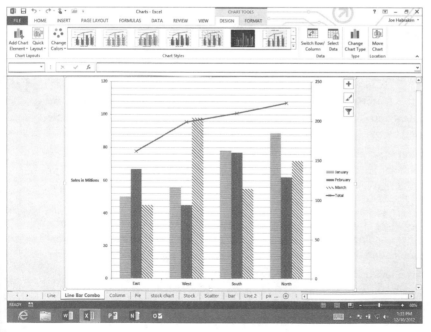

Figure 14.3
A combination chart graphs data series separately using different chart types.

Using Different Chart Types

Excel provides you with a number of different chart types. It is important that you develop an understanding of the purpose of each chart type and then use the appropriate chart type when charting your data. Using a chart type that isn't designed for your purpose doesn't really enhance anyone's understanding of the worksheet data and might misrepresent what is going on with the data.

For example, a line chart would do an excellent job of showing the change over time of the sales figures for a particular product or company. However, place that same data in a bar chart and the changes are less marked. Finally, throw that same data into a pie chart, which is completely wrong for showing change over time, and all of a sudden the sales figures (even poor sales figures) look relatively the same. This is not to say that people deliberately choose the wrong chart type to hide the true nature of worksheet data and any associated trends; however, Excel offers so many different chart types that it is easy to inadvertently select the wrong type of chart for a particular situation. Let's look at the different chart types that Excel provides.

Column Chart/Bar Chart

The column/bar chart is probably one of the most commonly used business chart types. These types of charts work very well in showing how different data series or groups of data points compare. Figure 14.4 shows a bar chart that displays the total sales for each salesperson listed in the worksheet.

Figure 14.4
A bar chart comparing total sales.

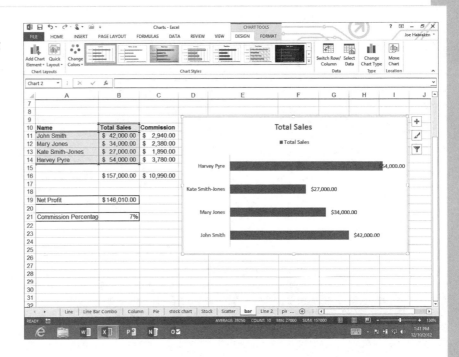

Column and bar charts make it relatively easy to quickly discern the highs and lows in terms of the data points charted. Column or bar charts are often used to show the relative success of salespeople or franchise locations, or can even be used to compare the number of home runs hit during a season by a group of baseball players. If you have totals you want to compare, column and bar charts are the route to go. Obviously, the tallest column in a column chart shows the highest data point; in a bar chart, it is the longest horizontal bar.

Line Chart

Line charts are perfect for showing change over time. Line charts are straightforward two-axis charts, with numerical values plotted on the y-axis in relation to labels provided on the x-axis that describe what is actually being measured. Line charts are often used to depict business growth or business decline.

For example, you might plot the monthly profits of your small company over the past 12 months. The y-axis consists of the net profits for each month and the x-axis consists of the months of the year, January through December. Line charts work very well when you want to discern the highs and lows in productivity or value. Line charts are not particularly good if you want to compare the relative success of one data series against another data series. Figure 14.5 shows a line chart that provides a separate line for each region's sales data points from January, February, and March.

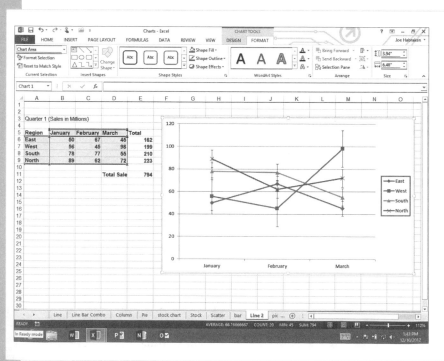

Figure 14.5
A line chart depicting different sets of data points.

Although the line chart makes it easy to track the changes over time for each of the regions in terms of their sales figures for the January through March time frame, the lines do not provide a good way to compare the overall performance of each region. This is accomplished better by using a column/ bar chart.

Pie Chart

Pie charts enable you to show how the various parts relate to the whole. For example, you might be trying to keep track of your monthly expenses. A pie chart would enable you to visually represent the relative size of each of your monthly expenses as compared with your total expenses.

Pie charts are great for showing how costs, sales, or other data series for a group of categories relate to each other. Figure 14.6 shows a pie chart that has a single data series: the individual values for different monthly expense categories.

Figure 14.6
Pie charts show how the parts relate to the whole.

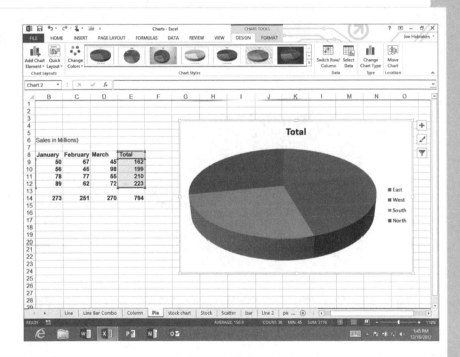

Pie charts can support only one data series and differ from other chart types such as bar charts and line charts, which can show multiple data series on the same chart. If you need to show multiple data series in a pie chart–like format, you can use a doughnut chart.

In the case of the pie chart shown in Figure 14.6, it is clear that the South (the light green pie piece) realized the most sales when compared to the other "sales" regions (West has the second high- est sales total, followed by North and East). Pie charts showing percentages make it even easier to determine the percentage of a particular item plotted on the chart in reference to the whole (meaning 100%).

Area Chart

Area charts enable you to show trends using cumulative totals over time. These types of charts emphasize the general direction of the data series up or down and show the magnitude of change. Area charts are somewhat similar to line charts; however, area charts show not only trends over time, but can also show how data series shown in the chart relate to the whole and each other. This enables you to view trends related to each data series and to compare data series. Figure 14.7 shows an area chart that tracks sales from different regions over 12 months of the year (January through December).

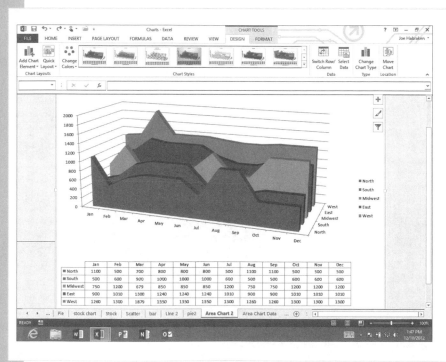

Figure 14.7
Area charts show trends and enable comparison of data points.

The chart uses the 3-D area chart type, which uses three axes—x, y, and z—to provide the vertical, horizontal, and depth aspects for the chart. The 3-D area chart shows the trends for the sales in each region and provides for a comparison of the regions. The 3-D layout, however, can be problematic if you have a set of data points that are much smaller or larger than the other data sets depicted in the chart. Go with a line chart that depicts each data series using a separate line rather than trying to use the area chart.

X Y (Scatter) Chart

Scatter charts enable you to determine whether the data points in a series fall on the chart in a pattern called a cluster. Scatter charts are used to see whether there is a correlation between values. One set of values is plotted on the x-axis and the other set of values is plotted along the y-axis. Figure 14.8 shows a scatter chart.

Figure 14.8
Scatter charts enable you to see the relationship between associated data series.

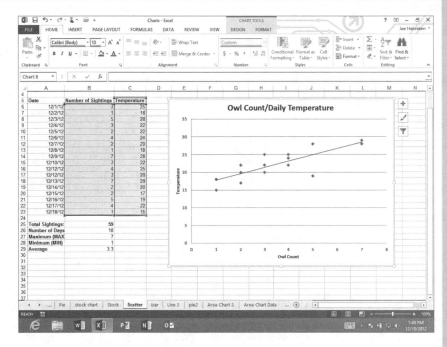

The scatter chart in Figure 14.8 plots owl count against the temperature taken each day the count was conducted. Let's say you want to see whether there is a correlation between owl activity and temperature. You could plot the daily count versus the daily temperature.

Because scatter charts are meant to determine the correlation between two different sets of values, you typically need a large number of data points to get a discernable pattern on the chart. Remember that both the x-axis and y-axis on a scatter chart consist of values. If you have a situation where only one set of data is values, you should use a line chart.

Stock Chart

Stock charts (also known as box plots, box and whiskers plots, or candlestick plots) are particularly useful when you are tracking a particular stock that is in your stock portfolio or that you are considering making part of your portfolio. Stock charts can be created using three different data series, four different data series, or five different data series—all of which are related to the price of the stock. For example, the three data series stock chart uses the daily high, low, and close value of the stock. The four data series stock chart uses the open, high, low, and close price for the stock.

Figure 14.9 shows a stock chart tracking Microsoft stock during January of 2013. Stock charts not only show you the range of a stock's price on a particular day, but the chart can also show trends over the time frame that you have charted.

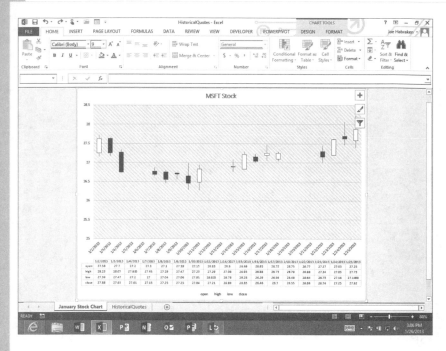

Figure 14.9
Stock charts provide trends while tracking multiple fluctuating data points.

 note

Scatter charts use Cartesian coordinates (two different sets of values) to create the points that appear in the chart plane. René Descartes came up with the Cartesian coordinate system in the seventeenth century. Remember this the next time you get a Descartes question during trivia night.

 note

Finding stock information—such as the daily open, high, low, and close value of a particular stock on the Web—is pretty easy. You can use the Microsoft MoneyCentral website, Yahoo! Finance, or Google Finance.

The stock chart can be used for data types other than stock prices. You can use it in any situation where you have a particular data point that fluctuates during a specific time frame. For example, you might want to chart data related to the daily change in water temperature of a vernal pool that you are using for a salamander population study.

Other Chart Types

We have already looked at the stock chart provided in the Other Charts command's drop-down gallery. There are four other chart types provided in this gallery. The list that follows provides a brief description of each chart type:

- **Surface chart:** This type of chart is designed to group related values by color or pattern. A 3-D surface chart looks a lot like a relief or topographic map and can be used to determine how one variable can be affected by two other variables. Surface charts are created using an x-axis data series, a y-axis data series, and a z-axis data series. There must also be a z-axis value for each x-axis and y-axis pair. So, basically, the surface chart shows how the z-axis data is affected by two variables: the x-axis data and the y-axis data.

- **Doughnut chart:** This chart type is designed to show how the parts compare with the whole, much like a pie chart. A doughnut chart, however, can include more than one data series, which a pie chart cannot. You can use a doughnut to compare the sales of different regions over a specific time frame or show your monthly expenses for more than one month for comparison.

- **Bubble chart:** This chart type is similar to a scatter chart. However, a scatter chart can use only two sets of variables (one for the x-axis and one for y-axis); a bubble chart can work with three sets of values. The third value set determines the size of the bubbles. So, the bubble chart shows related x and y data in clusters and shows the relative value of each z-axis data point as a gradation of bubble sizes.

- **Radar chart:** This chart type can plot multiple data sets. The values from each category are plotted along a separate axis line that radiates out from the chart's center point. The scale for each data set to be included on the chart must be the same. Radar charts can be used to show business performance measurements or compare safety features on different automobiles. These charts work best with a limited number of categories so that each data set is discernable on the chart.

Although each chart type has a specific purpose and requires that the appropriate data be supplied in your Excel worksheet, creating charts in Excel is straightforward (in fact, Excel can help you choose the correct chart type). After you have created a particular chart type, the commands and tools available for changing the design and formatting of the chart and chart elements are a consistent proposition, no matter what chart type you have created. Let's look at how to create a chart and then look at the options Excel provides for modifying the chart and chart elements.

Creating Charts

Charts reflect the data in a worksheet and so you need to make sure that the values and labels in the worksheet provide the information in a way that allows for charting. You should arrange the worksheet data in a consistent manner, either horizontally in rows or vertically in columns. Also avoid empty cells, rows, or columns within the areas of the worksheet that serve as the data series for your chart or charts.

Although a chart is based on the values in your worksheet, your sheet labels provide the categories and information used as axes titles and legend information. It makes sense to make row and column headings (your labels) very descriptive yet short enough to fit well on the chart as a chart element.

When building a worksheet that includes a chart, place the data on the sheet so that the sheet can also easily accommodate an inserted chart below or to the right of the data range. This enables you to easily view or print the worksheet data and the accompanying chart. Charts with a large amount of detail and those derived from large worksheets would probably best be created on their own worksheet.

Excel provides you with different ways to insert a chart into a worksheet as an object. You can also choose to move a chart from the sheet containing the data to its own sheet. Excel 2013 makes it even easier than previous versions of Excel (Excel 2010 and earlier) to take your worksheet data and represent it as a visually interesting and meaningful chart. Let's take a look at how you insert a chart into a sheet and then look at two new features for creating a chart: recommended charts and the Quick Analysis gallery.

Inserting a Chart from the Ribbon

Inserting a new chart into the current sheet is a two-step process: Specify the data you want to chart and then select the chart type to insert. So select the range to be charted. If you are not selecting a contiguous range for the chart, select the first range of cells to be included in the chart and then hold down the Ctrl key to select other cells or ranges for the chart.

To choose the chart type, switch to the Ribbon's Insert tab. The Charts group provides commands for specific chart types, including Insert Column Chart, Insert Line Chart, and Insert Pie or Doughnut Chart. Select the drop-down arrow to the right of any of these chart commands to select a chart subtype. For example, when you select the Insert Pie or Doughnut Chart command, you can select from three different subtypes: 2-D Pie, 3-D Pie, and Doughnut. After you make a selection, the chart is inserted into the current sheet.

If you like to be able to peruse all the chart types (in a list) before inserting a chart, you can open the Insert Chart dialog box from any of the chart type commands. In the case of the Insert Pie or Doughnut Chart gallery, select More Pie Charts. The Insert Chart dialog box (shown in Figure 14.10) provides a list of all the chart types and also provides a gallery of subtypes for the current chart type (in 14.10, it's a pie chart and its subtypes). After selecting a chart type and/or subtype in the Insert Chart dialog box, click OK to insert the chart.

 tip

ScreenTips can be accessed for any of the chart types that are provided by the chart type command's gallery. These ScreenTips provide a brief explanation of the chart type.

Figure 14.10
The Insert Chart dialog box lists all the available chart types.

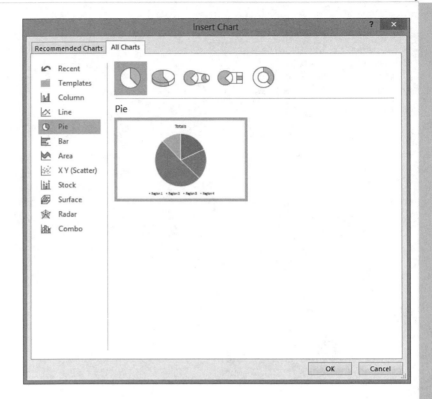

Selecting a Recommended Chart

A new option for inserting a chart into a sheet is the Recommended Charts feature. This feature helps you determine the best chart type for your data, and it can be particularly useful in situations where you aren't quite sure what type of chart would best represent the data in the sheet.

To view recommended charts for your data, select the cell range for the chart and then navigate to the Insert tab. Select the Recommended Charts command in the Charts group. The Insert Chart dialog box opens with the Recommended Charts tab selected, as shown in Figure 14.11.

The recommended charts for your data are listed on the left of the Recommended Charts tab. To view a preview of a particular chart type, select the chart thumbnail. The chart preview also provides a definition of each recommended chart type under the chart preview (on the right of the Recommended Charts tab). To insert one of the recommended charts, select the chart thumbnail and then click OK.

Figure 14.11
Excel provides you with a list of recommended charts for your sheet data.

Inserting Charts with the Quick Analysis Gallery

Another option for inserting a chart into your worksheet is the Quick Analysis gallery. The Quick Analysis gallery is a new addition to Excel 2013. This feature provides quick access to conditional formatting settings, charts, statistical functions, table settings, and even sparklines. Think of the Quick Analysis gallery as a way to quickly access different analysis features from one location (the Quick Analysis gallery), negating the need to switch to the Ribbon's Home tab or Insert tab or Formulas tab—you get the picture; the Quick Analysis gallery is quick.

To insert a chart using the Quick Analysis gallery, select the cell range for the chart. The Quick Analysis button appears at the very bottom right of the selected range. Click the button, and the gallery opens; select Charts to view the Quick Analysis charting options. Figure 14.12 shows selected data and the Charts options provided in the Quick Analysis Gallery.

The Quick Analysis Gallery provides recommended charts for your selected data range. You can select one of the options provided to insert that chart type. If you want to access the Recommended Charts tab of the Insert Chart dialog box, select the More Charts option. The Recommended Charts tab provides the same chart type options that are available in the Quick Analysis Gallery. However, the Recommended Charts tab does allow you to preview each of the recommended chart types before inserting one of them into the sheet. Whether you select one of the recommended charts from the Quick Analysis Gallery or the Recommended Charts tab of the Insert Chart dialog box, your chart still ends up as an object on the current worksheet.

Figure 14.12
The Quick Analysis
Gallery provides recommended chart types.

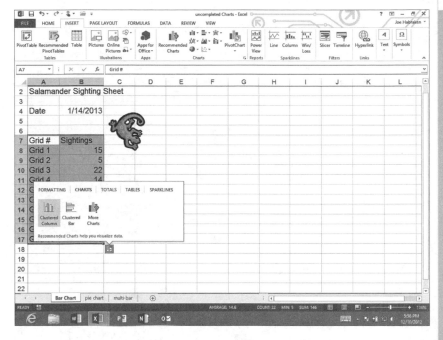

Tools for Quickly Customizing a Chart

The chart is selected when you insert a new chart into the current sheet. Three new tools that allow you to quickly customize the chart are available next to the chart's right border: Chart Elements, Chart Styles, and Chart Filters. Here is what they do:

- **Chart Elements:** Click the Chart Elements button to open the Chart Elements list. This list (which appears on the left side of the chart) allows you to select or deselect the chart elements to be shown in the current chart. The chart elements listed depend on the type of chart (and chart subtype) you selected when you inserted the chart.

- **Chart Styles:** Click the Chart Styles button to open a Chart Styles gallery for the current chart type. The Chart Styles gallery provides you with a number of different chart styles, as shown in Figure 14.13. Select a particular style to see how it affects the chart. You can also select from a number of color schemes by selecting Color in the Chart Styles gallery.

- **Chart Filters:** Click the Chart Filters button if you want to filter the chart in place. The Filters gallery provides you with a list of the data series and categories in the current chart. You can select a particular series or category to view the portion of the chart that relates to that data. You can also deselect series or categories to see how this changes the chart when that series or category is removed. When you have finished filtering the data, you can reselect all the series and categories and then click Apply to put the chart back into its original condition.

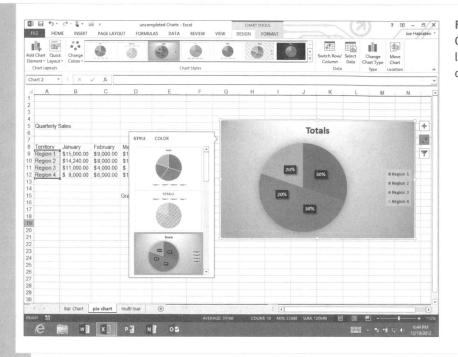

Figure 14.13
Quickly select from a
list of chart styles and
colors.

When you have finished working with one of the quick format tools, you can switch to one of the other tools (for example, from the Chart Styles gallery to the Chart Filters feature) by selecting a different tool button. If you want to shut down the gallery for one of the tools, reselect the tool button. If you have finished manipulating the chart using these tools and want to return to the sheet, click outside the chart to deselect it.

Moving, Copying, or Deleting a Chart

When a chart is selected in a sheet, the Chart Tools are available on the Ribbon. If you want to move the chart to its own chart sheet (rather than as an object in the current worksheet), select the Move Chart command on the Chart Tools Design tab (the last command on the right). When you select the Move Chart command, the Move Chart dialog box opens.

You can move the chart to a new sheet by clicking the New Sheet option button in the Move Chart dialog box. You can also specify the name for the new sheet by typing the name in the text box to the right of the New Sheet option button. The Move Chart dialog box also provides an Object In option button. You can use this option to move the selected chart to any of the other sheets in your current Excel workbook.

Select the Object In drop-down list and then select the worksheet that will be home to the chart object. When you are ready to move the chart (to a new sheet or a different worksheet), click OK.

Chart objects (on a sheet) can be treated like any other object you place on an Excel worksheet, such as a picture, clip art, or SmartArt graphic. You can use copy and paste to make copies of the chart and cut and paste to move the chart. You can also remove unwanted charts. To remove an embedded chart in a worksheet, select the chart and then press the Delete key. If you want to delete a chart that is on its own sheet (a chart sheet), right-click on the worksheet's name tab and then select Delete. The sheet is removed from the workbook.

> **caution**
>
> When you delete a chart object on a worksheet, you can use Undo to get it back. When you delete a chart sheet in a workbook, Undo does not bring back the deleted sheet.

Modifying a Chart

After you have the chart embedded on the current worksheet (along with the worksheet data the chart uses) or moved to a new sheet, you can modify the chart's design, layout, and format. We've already talked about the new Charts Tools provided by Excel 2013 (the Chart Elements, Chart Styles, and Chart Filters buttons) that appear to the right of the chart when the chart is selected. When a chart is selected, the Chart Tools become available on the Ribbon.

The Chart Tools have been streamlined in Excel 2013 and are now divided between two Chart Tools tabs: Design and Format (as opposed to three tabs in Excel 2010). The Design tab provides commands that enable you to manipulate the various chart elements (such as the chart title, data labels, and trendlines) and change the chart layout or colors. The Chart Styles gallery on the Design tab allows you to select from a number of chart styles for the current chart type. Other commands provided on this tab include the Switch Row/Column and Change Chart Type commands. The Design tab also provides the Move Chart command, which allows you to move an embedded chart to its own sheet or any other sheet in the workbook.

The Format tab provides the command groups that you would find for modifying other graphic object types, such as text boxes or pictures. These groups include the Insert Shapes, Shape Styles, and the WordArt Styles groups. The Arrange group provides commands for arranging objects on the sheet (remember that a chart is just another object type). The Current Selection group on the far left of the Format tab provides you with the ability to select a particular chart area and then apply the various formatting commands available to that area (such as the whole chart or the Chart Title or a particular data series).

> ➡ *For an overview on working with and formatting objects such as images and SmartArt graphics in the Office applications,* ***see*** *Chapter 4, "Using and Creating Graphics."*

In terms of modifying a chart (rather than just another object on a sheet) you will probably spend more time fine-tuning the chart elements and chart display using the commands on the Chart Tools Design tab. Let's take a look at how some of these commands are actually applied to a chart.

Changing Chart Type or Chart Data

As already discussed, the Chart Tools Design tab enables you to modify the chart type, manipulate the data used by the chart, and select a layout or style for the chart. If you find that you have created a chart that doesn't provide a proper picture of the data that you selected to include in the chart, you might want to rethink the chart type that you have selected. You might also need to change how the chart is looking at your data (in rows instead of columns), or you might even need to change the data selection that the chart is using.

Changing the chart type doesn't mean that you necessarily have to switch to a completely different chart type such as a line to bar—it also is a way to fine-tune the chart type you have currently selected by going with a different chart subtype. For example, you might be using the 3-D pie chart type but want to switch to the exploded pie in 3-D to better differentiate the parts of the pie.

To change the chart type, select the Change Chart Type command in the Type group. The Change Chart Type dialog box opens. This dialog box is the same as the Insert Chart dialog box. Select a chart type and/or subtype as needed to change the chart type of the currently selected chart. To apply the change in type or subtype, click OK.

Another command that can be useful in cases where a chart doesn't look quite right is the Switch Row/Column command. This command can be used in cases where the chart has based the x-axis or y-axis on column data rather than row data and you want to swap the data on the x-axis with the y-axis or vice versa.

This command can also be used to manipulate a single axis, such as the x-axis, when you have labels at the top of your data columns and labels for each data row. A bar chart by default charts the column labels along the x-axis. However, if you want the x-axis to show you data related to the row columns, such as the names of your salespeople or regions or the fruits and vegetables that you ate last week, you can use the Switch Rows/Columns command to switch the label data shown on the x-axis and the legend.

In cases where you have selected an incomplete or incorrect data range for a chart, you can modify the data selection used by the chart using the Select Data command. Click the Select Data command and the Select Data Source dialog box opens, as shown in Figure 14.14.

 tip

Right-click on a chart and then select Change Chart Type to open the Change Chart Type dialog box.

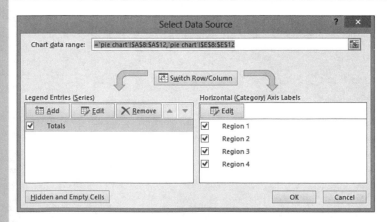

Figure 14.14
The Select Data Source dialog box.

To change the data range for the chart, select the current data range in the Chart Data Range text box and then use the Shrink button to access the worksheet data. Select the range to be used by the chart and return to the dialog box.

You can also use the Switch Row/Column button in the Select Data Source dialog box to swap the series or axis data. Using the Switch Row/Column command in the Select Data Source dialog box might make more sense to you because you see how the series and axis labels are swapped rather than how the chart itself is changed. You can add entries, such as legend entries, to the Select Data Source dialog box. You can also edit and remove labels as needed.

The Select Data Source dialog box also makes it easy to deal with hidden or empty cells that fall within the data range being used by the chart. Click the Hidden and Empty Cells button to open the Hidden and Empty Cells Settings dialog box. By default, empty cells are shown as gaps in the chart. You can also choose to have empty cells shown as zero or you can have the chart connect data points with a line so that gaps are effectively ignored. As for hidden rows or columns that fall into the chart data source range, you can choose to ignore the hidden data, or you can click the Show Data in Hidden Rows and Columns option button to include this data in the chart. When you finish working in the Hidden and Empty Cell Settings dialog box, click OK to return to the Select Data Source dialog box. To close the Select Data Source dialog box and return to the chart, click OK.

Selecting Chart Layouts and Styles

Each chart type has a number of different chart layouts available. A chart layout provides specific chart elements, such as title, legend, and data labels. You can use a chart layout (also referred to as a quick layout) to quickly add needed chart elements to a chart and then you can further modify the layout as needed.

The various layouts for the currently selected chart can be accessed for a specific chart type by using the Quick Layout button, which is located on the Design tab's Chart Layouts group. Figure 14.15 shows the Quick Layout gallery for a pie chart.

You have to select a layout based on the thumbnail provided. Place the mouse on a layout thumbnail and it is previewed on the chart. The layouts differ in the chart elements that they provide, such as the legend and axis titles, and in the position of these elements on the chart. Some layouts also provide data labels and data tables; data tables are particularly useful when you place a chart on its own sheet. Because the data for the chart is in the data table, you don't have to switch back and forth between the chart sheet and the sheet where the data is held.

You can also control chart elements using the Add Chart Element command. This command provides a list of elements supported by the current chart type. You can add or remove elements and specify where a chart element should appear on the chart.

You can also modify the chart using one of the chart styles provided in the Chart Styles gallery. Figure 14.16 shows the Chart Styles gallery and the chart styles available for a bar chart. These styles affect the data series and the background of the chart (such as the back wall, floor, and so on). Color schemes for a particular style can be controlled using the Change Colors command (also in the Chart Styles group).

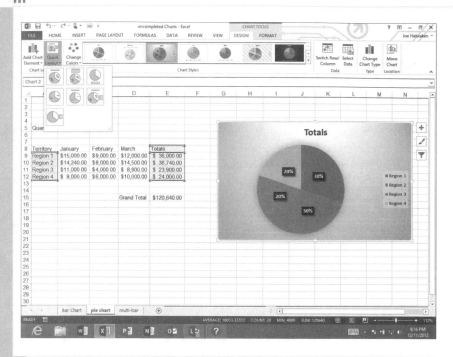

Figure 14.15
The Quick Layout gallery.

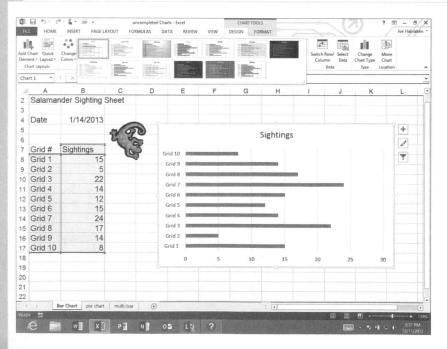

Figure 14.16
The Chart Styles gallery.

When working with the Change Colors gallery, you can select one of the multicolor color schemes for your chart or you can select from a large number of monochromatic color schemes. Monochromatic color schemes, particularly the grayscale schemes, can be used to make the chart information more readable on a printout. The grayscale color schemes, obviously, serve you well if you are going to print a chart on a grayscale printer such as a laser printer.

 tip

Remember that you can select any chart element, including data points, data series, and the chart title or legend, using the selection drop-down list in the Current Selection group on the Chart Tools Format tab.

Working with Chart Elements

Although we think of a chart as a single object, it is actually made up of a number of different elements that can be manipulated individually. Elements on a chart that contain text such as the chart title and axes titles can be moved, sized, and formatted in place. We discussed the Quick Layout gallery in the previous section and how it provides different chart layouts. Each layout can include a different mix of chart elements in terms of the chart elements that are included and how they are arranged in the chart frame.

You can select a chart element (including the chart area) using the Current Selection group's drop-down list. The Current Selection group is on the far left of the Chart Tools Format tab. The Current Selection group also provides the Format Selection command. This command opens the Format task pane for the currently selected chart element. For example, if you select the Legend in the Current Selection drop-down list, the Format Legend task pane opens when you select the Format Selection command.

The various Format task panes for your chart elements are new to Excel 2013. Excel 2013 does away with the Chart Tools Layout tab that was found in Excel 2010. Chart Elements can now be manipulated using the Add Chart Element command on the Chart Tools Design tab. Adding and removing chart elements from a chart can also be accomplished using the Chart Elements button (the Plus symbol button) immediately to the right of a selected chart. Figure 14.17 shows the Add Chart Element gallery and the Chart Elements quick access pane.

Both the Add Chart Element gallery and the Chart Elements quick access pane enable you to add (or remove) the elements on the currently selected chart, including data labels, error bars, gridlines, or a legend. The Add Chart Element gallery lists the different chart elements (such as Axes or Legend), and when you select an *active* chart element in the Add Chart Element gallery, you are provided with a submenu of choices. (I use the term *active* because some elements are grayed out or inactive depending on the chart type you are working with.) So, let's say that you want to add data labels to a bar chart, such as the chart shown in Figure 14.17. Select Data Labels in the Add Chart Element gallery; the choices provided on the Data Label submenu are related to the placement of the data labels in reference to the bars on the chart and include Center, Inside End, Inside Base, and Outside End.

The Chart Elements quick access pane is much simpler than the Add Chart Element gallery in that it only enables you to add or remove an element by toggling a particular chart element on or off using the appropriate check box. For example, if you want to add data labels to the current chart, select the Data Labels check box in the Chart Elements quick access pane to place the data labels in the outside end position.

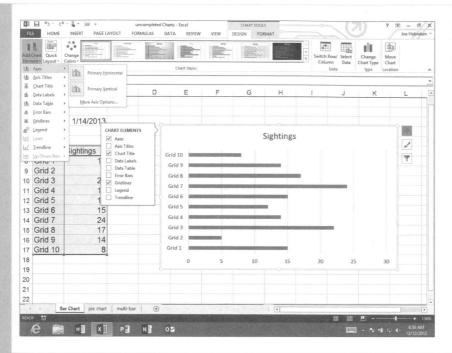

Figure 14.17
The Add Chart Element gallery and the Chart Elements pane.

If you need more control over a particular chart element, you can open the element's formatting pane. Figure 14.18 shows the Format Data Labels task pane. You can open a format task pane for a particular chart element using the Add Chart Element command; select Add Chart Element, then point at the chart element you want to format. On the submenu for the chart element, select the More (name of element) Options command. You can also double-click on a chart element in the chart frame to open the associated format task pane.

The options provided by various chart element format task panes are relatively consistent. There are options specific to the element. You can control settings such as the Fill and Line, Effects, and Size & Properties. Other options for elements relate to what an element contains and its position within the chart frame. For example, data labels have both check boxes for what each label should contain, such as the Series Name, Value, and/or Legend key. Other options relate to the position of the label, such as Center, Inside End, or Outside End.

Although chart elements are a special kind of object and live inside the chart's plot area (or frame), both the Fill & Line and Effects formatting options for chart elements are similar to those that you find when formatting a shape, a SmartArt graphic, or other graphic element.

Chart elements such as data labels and titles also have text options associated with them. These options include text fill and text outline settings. You can also switch between the various chart elements from within the current element's task pane. Select the Options drop-down list for the current element and select another element to format. For example, you can quickly switch between the Format Axis settings to the settings for the chart title. The discussion that follows provides information on manipulating specific chart elements starting with titles and data labels.

Figure 14.18
The Format Data
Labels task pane.

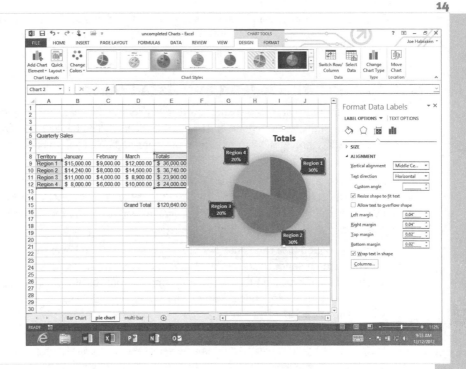

 tip

You can format text elements in a chart, such as a label or text in the legend, as you would any text in any of the Office applications. Select the text and use the formatting options provided by the mini toolbar or the text formatting commands on the Ribbon's Home tab.

➡ *For an overview on working with and formatting objects such as images and SmartArt graphics in the Office applications,* ***see*** *"The Office 2013 Options for Graphics and Pictures," **p. 73**.*

Modifying Titles and Data Labels

Chart titles provide descriptive text for the chart and other elements, such as the axes. Editing the chart title text or other text-based elements such as the axis titles can be done by inserting the insertion point in the text box that serves as a particular chart element such as the title. You can then edit the text as needed.

Data labels are different from the other text boxes on the chart in that the values shown for the data labels are derived from the worksheet data that you used to create the chart. So, you cannot edit a data label in situ. The value changes only if you edit the worksheet data related to the chart.

To change the position of a chart title or axis title, you can drag the selected title object to a new position on the chart. You can take advantage of the commands in the Add Chart Element gallery to specify a position for an element such as the chart title or axis title. You can also position data labels using the Data Labels commands in the Add Chart Element gallery and access the Format Data Labels task pane.

Working with the Legend and Data Points

The legend for the chart is the color or pattern key for the data series represented on the chart. You can move and size the legend on the chart as needed. The Legend command in the Add Chart Elements gallery provides different legend positions and gives you the option of turning off the legend.

You can access additional formatting options for the legend by opening the Format Legend task pane. You can open the task pane for the Add Chart Element gallery by double-clicking on the legend's frame. The Format Legend task pane enables you to control the fill, border color, and effects for the legend as well as the position of the legend.

The Format Legend task pane does not provide you with control over the color scheme used to differentiate the data series on the chart. Colors are automatically assigned to the different data series based on the chart type (and theme you are using for your Excel worksheet). You can change the color scheme for the chart, which changes the legend, using the Change Colors command on the Chart Tools Design tab.

If you want complete control over the legend, you can replace the default colors for the data series on the chart. The fastest way to do this is to select the data point such as a column in a column chart or a pie slice in a pie chart. A shortcut formatting toolbar appears; select a new fill color using the Fill color palette, as shown in Figure 14.19. You can also use this shortcut toolbar to change the outline color for the data series.

If you want even more control over the fill color or the border on the data series, you can double-click on a data point such as a column or pie slice to open the Format Data Series task pane (see Figure 14.19). If you are working with multiple data series that are associated (such as sales figures for a particular salesperson over the course of several months), the double-click I suggest does not open the Format Data Series task pane for all the associated data series—just the one you double-click on). So select one of the data points, which should select all of the other associated data points. You can then right-click on one of the data points and select Format Data Series to open the Format Data Series task pane.

Opening the Format Data Series task pane allows you to select gradient or pattern fills and also manipulate the border for the data point or series. Any format changes you make to a data point or data series are reflected in the chart's legend.

 tip

The formatting attributes for a chart element that relate to how the data is portrayed in the chart are found in the Format task pane for a particular element by clicking the Options button that looks like an Excel column chart.

 tip

If you are going to use different patterns, textures, or gradients to differentiate data points on a chart, make sure that each data point can be readily identified — meaning don't select patterns for the different data points that are hard to tell apart.

Figure 14.19
The Format Data Series task pane.

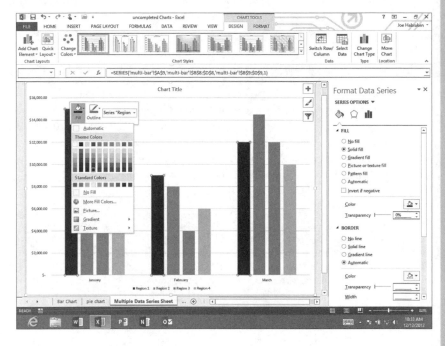

Manipulating Axes and Gridlines

If you are working with a chart type that shows the vertical and horizontal axes in the chart area, such as a line chart or a bar chart, you can manipulate the scale on the value axis. Double-click on the axis frame (you might have to select it before you can double-click on it, just so you can see it) to open the Format task pane for the axis. Axis options allow you to set the bounds for the axis and also the minimum and maximum for the access. You can also specify the major and minor units for the axis.

In the case of a value axis (such as the primary vertical or y-axis on many line and column charts), you can choose to display the axis using numbers represented in the thousands, millions, or billions. You can also choose to show the axis with a log 10–based scale. This is also known as a logarithmic scale because it uses a specific quantity to create the scale on the axis. In the case of the log 10–based scale, the scale would consist of 1 then 10 then 100 then 1,000 and so on. This type of scale is extremely useful in cases where you have data that encompasses a very large range of values.

Gridlines make it easier for you to determine the values associated with a particular data point on a chart, particularly in cases where you have not included data labels. Depending on the chart layout that you select for your chart via the Chart Layouts gallery, your chart might already contain the major gridlines, which are placed perpendicular to the value axis on your chart.

Because this is the y-axis in many chart types, the primary horizontal gridlines provide you with horizontal lines on the chart that serve as reference points for the value units placed on the y-axis itself. The easiest way to access the gridline settings for a selected chart is to select the Add Chart

Element command and then point at Gridlines in the Add Chart Element gallery. Gridline options allow you to specify horizontal or vertical primary major and minor gridlines. You can access the Format Gridlines task pane to format the fill and shadow settings for the specified gridlines.

Adding Trendlines, Drop Lines, and Bars to a Chart

You can add additional elements to your charts, such as trendlines, drop lines, and error bars. A trendline provides the overall slope or trend of the data points and is based on the relationship between each set of x and y values shown on a chart. Figure 14.20 shows a linear trendline that has been added to a stock chart (which is also known as a candlestick or box plot). The trendline is based on the close value for the stock shown. The trendline provides an overall analysis of how the stock has done over the time frame shown on the chart.

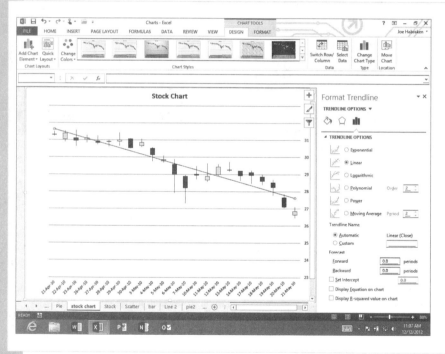

Figure 14.20
Trendline added to stock chart.

You can add trendlines to a number of Excel 2-D chart types, including line, column, bar, area, stock, scatter, and bubble charts (you can't add a trendline to a 3-D chart). Excel provides a number of different trendline types via the Trendline command in the Add Chart Element gallery (select Add Chart Element and then point at Trendline). The trendline types include Linear, Exponential, Linear Forecast, and Moving Average. Additional types of trendlines can be accessed in the Format Trendline task pane (shown in Figure 14.20). The type of trendline that you use depends on the type of data that you are working with and the type of analysis you want to make with the trendline. The trendline possibilities are as follows:

- **Exponential:** This type of trendline provides a best-fit curve that is best used in cases where the data points rise or fall in constantly increasing rates and then level off. For example, an exponential trendline could be used to analyze production data for a factory that has rapid growth in its production rate until it reaches maximum capacity and levels off.

- **Linear:** This type of trendline creates a best-fit straight line based on the data points in the series that you have specified for the trendline. This type of trendline is best used in cases where you want to see whether your data points are trending up or down; this trendline can be useful for a quick look at trends in sales figures.

- **Logarithmic:** This trendline type provides a best-fit curved line that projects future data trends when the data used to create the chart changes dramatically (either up or down) but then levels out again. Logarithmic trendlines are best for showing long-range trends where the percent change is reflected in the trendline rather than the absolute change (in values).

- **Polynomial:** This trendline type is basically a way to do linear regression on data that fluctuates greatly and where there is not necessarily a true linear relationship between the x and y variables.

- **Power:** This trendline is a curved line that can be used to show the relationship between two sets of values (x and y) when there is an increase or decrease at a specific rate.

- **Moving Average:** This trendline averages the data points found in two periods and draws a trendline based on the averages. You can specify the period for a moving average trendline by formatting the trendline in the Format Trendline task pane.

The settings for any of the available trendline types can be fine-tuned in the Format Trendline task pane. You can open the Format Trendline task pane by double-clicking on a trendline in the chart or by selecting Trendline then More Trendline Options in the Add Chart Element gallery.

You can also change other formatting options related to a trendline in the Format Trendline task pane. You can change both the line formatting and the effects settings (shadow, glow, etc.).

 note

When you are using trend-lines on your charts, you are performing linear regression, which analyzes the relationship between data points on the x and y axes of your chart. The validity of a trendline is measured by determining the square of the correlation coefficient R, which is a fractional number between 0 and 1. The closer R2 is to 1, the greater the correlation between the x and y variables—meaning as x changes, y also changes in a somewhat consistent manner.

Using Drop Lines and High-Low Lines

Drop lines are lines that extend from the data points on the chart down to the horizontal or x-axis. The drop lines are used to make the chart easier to read and the drop lines enable you to more easily determine the x-axis attributes of the data points used to create the chart. You can use drop lines on line and area charts. To add drop lines to a chart, select Lines and then Drop Lines in the Add Chart Element gallery.

You can also add high-low lines to your 2D charts. The high-low line extends from the highest to the lowest value in each chart category. For example, you might create a line chart that compares your actual monthly expenses (one data series for the chart) with a budget (another data series on the chart) that you create. The high-low lines connect the high value in each category (say you have categories such as food, utilities, entertainment, rent, and so on) with the minimum value in each category.

You can format your drop-lines or high-low lines by double-clicking on a drop-line or high-low line on the chart. This opens the Format Drop Lines or the Format High-Low Lines task pane, respectively. These task panes provide you with control over line and effect formatting.

Adding Error Bars and Up/Down Bars to a Chart

You can also add error bars and up/down bars to your charts. Error bars are used to reflect uncertainty or variability in the data that has been charted and can help show the potential amount of error relative to the data points in a chart data series. Error bars can be used in 2-D area, bar, column, line, scatter, and bubble charts.

The error bars are created on the chart based on an error amount. You can quickly create error bars that use the standard error, percentage, or standard deviation as the error amount. Select Add Chart Element, point at Error Bars, and then select one of the error bar types. Figure 14.21 shows standard error bars on a scatter chart. The figure also shows the Format Error Bars task pane.

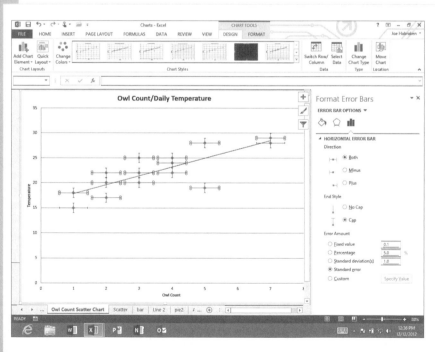

Figure 14.21
A scatter chart with error bars and the Format Error Bars task pane.

If you want to specify an error amount or change other settings related to the error bars on your chart, double-click on an error bar to open the Format Error Bars task pane. The task pane allows you to specify the direction of the error bar and also to select the end style for the error bar. More importantly, you can set the error amount from the standard error to one of the following:

- **Fixed Value:** You can specify a fixed amount as the error value.

- **Percentage:** A percentage can be specified as the error value.

- **Standard Deviation:** Excel computes the standard deviation for the chart data and uses it as the error amount for the error bars.

- **Standard Error:** Excel uses the standard error equation to compute the standard error for the chart data.

- **Custom:** You can specify the positive error value and the negative error value for the error bars. When you select Custom in the Format Error Bars dialog box, you must then specify the error values by clicking Specify Value. The error values (positive and negative) can be based on data ranges in the worksheet or you can specify them as a series of values separated by commas.

 tip

After you refine a chart's layout, color, and style, you can save that chart as a template. This allows you to quickly insert a new chart based on the settings in your chart template. To create a chart template, right-click on a selected chart and select Save as Template on the shortcut menu. Chart templates are saved to the user name\AppData\Roaming\Microsoft\Templates\Chart folder. You can access your saved chart templates in the Insert Chart dialog box on the All Charts tab. Select the Templates icon in the chart type list to list your chart templates.

Up/down bars are used to show the difference between the first and the last data series on the chart. For example, if you are comparing two data series, you get an up bar when the data point in the first series is less than the second series. You get a down bar when a data point for the first series is greater than the second series. You can take advantage of up/down bars in 2-D line charts that use multiple data series.

To assign up/down bars to your chart, select Add Chart Element, point at Up/Down Bars, and then select Up/Down Bars. You can format the fill and the effect settings for up/down bars in the Format Up (or Down) Bars task pane. Double-click any up or down bar in the chart to open the task pane.

Creating a Combination Chart

Before we end our discussion of Excel charts, we should look at how you create a combination chart. A combination chart combines two or more chart types in a single chart. Excel provides premade combination charts such as pie of pie and bar of pie charts. A pie of pie chart is shown in Figure 14.22.

A pie of pie chart (or a bar of pie chart) enables you to separate out certain data points into the secondary chart, meaning the second pie. This can be extremely useful when you have a situation where a few large data points dominate the pie chart and you would like to make smaller slices of the pie more visible by moving data points that represent smaller values to the secondary pie.

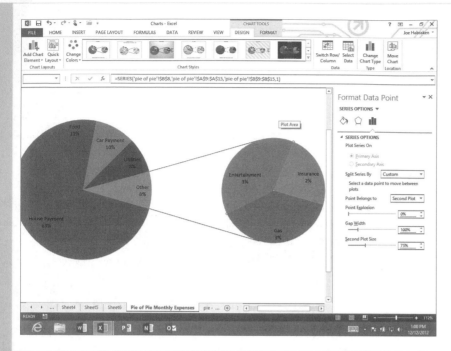

Figure 14.22
Pie of Pie chart.

Working with a Pie of Pie Chart

Because pie charts enable you to specify only a single data series, how the different data points end up in the primary and the secondary plot or pie depends on how you have the data series arranged in a column or row in your worksheet. By default, Excel uses the last third of the data points listed in the chart data range to create the secondary chart. Remember that this is the default setting for a pie of pie chart, and you do have options regarding how the data series is split between the two charts in the combination chart. If you want to go with the default, you can arrange your data in the worksheet so that it is sorted from high to low based on the values you chart (use the Sort & Filter command on the Home tab to quickly sort ascending or descending as needed). This means that the lower values, which typically make up the smallest slices on the pie, are placed at the bottom of your values and so appear in the secondary pie when you are creating a pie of pie chart.

You can fine-tune the pie of pie chart by specifying whether or not a data point (pie piece) is shown on the primary pie or the secondary pie. You can also change other settings such as the gap between the two plots and the second plot size in the Format Data Point task pane. Double-click on a pie piece (data point) in either the first plot (large pie) or the second plot (small pie) to open the Format Data Point task pane (see Figure 14.22).

You can determine how to split the series by position value or percentage value using the Split Series drop-down list. You can also specify where a data point (pie piece) belongs using the Point Belongs To drop-down list. As with other chart elements, the Format Data Point task pane also allows you to control the fill and effects settings for the data point.

Creating a Custom Combination Chart

You are certainly not limited to the combination chart types that Excel provides such as the pie of pie; charts are created by virtue of the fact that you supply a data series of values for the chart. If you have more than one data series in a chart, you can apply different chart types to the different data series, creating a combination chart that combines two or more of the different chart types supplied by Excel. This means that you can combine a line chart and a bar chart in the same combination chart or even have a combination chart that combines multiple chart types such as a line, bar, and pie. The possibilities are dictated by your data and your need for showing the relationships between the various data series visually.

For example, you can easily create a column and line chart combination. Let's say that you have sales figures for each of your sales regions (East, West, South, and North) for the months January, February, and March. It certainly is not difficult to calculate the quarter total for each region using the SUM function and to include this information in the worksheet.

You could then create a chart that places the sales figures for each region using the region names as the category names along the x-axis. The months (January through March) would serve as the data series for the chart (along with the values associated with the sales for each month by region), and so the legend would supply the color coding for each of the data point values by month.

The totals data series (the total sales for each region) would also be included on the chart. This data series could then be formatted as a line chart, providing you with a column chart that provides a comparison of the monthly sales of each region and a line chart that provides a look at the trend of your total sales for the quarter.

To create a combination chart, select all the data that you want to include in the chart, including the data series that serves as the secondary plot. Select the Insert tab and then use the chart type commands to insert the chart that serves as the primary plot or chart.

Now you need to select the series that you want to convert to a secondary chart. Use the drop-down list in the Current Selection group (on the Chart Tools Format tab) to select the data series that provides the values for the secondary plot. To change the series data to another chart type, right-click on the selected data series and select Change Series Chart Type. This opens the Change Chart Type dialog box, as shown in Figure 14.23.

Select the Chart Type drop-down list for the selected series. For example, Figure 14.23 shows a clustered column chart; I've changed the Totals series to a Line. This created a custom line and column combination. After you have made your changes in the Change Chart Type dialog box, click OK. Your original chart is now a combination chart.

You can create a number of different combination charts, including column/line, column/area, and even pie/area. Remember that each data series can be formatted separately, meaning that the attributes of each of the charts—the primary and secondary plots—can be modified as needed. This includes applying data labels to the different series and using things such as drop lines and other descriptive chart elements, such as axis titles and gridlines, to make the chart readily meaningful.

 note

The Format Data Series task pane can also be used to set a number of options related to the data in a chart. In the case of pie charts, you can set the pie explosion percentage and the size of a secondary plot.

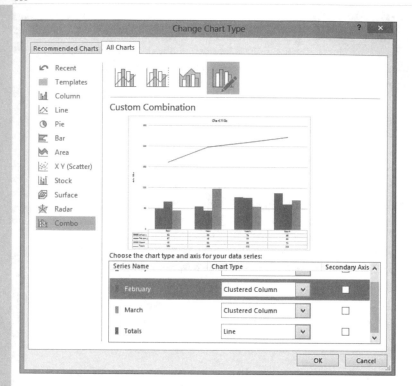

Figure 14.23
Change the chart type for a data series to create a custom combination chart.

Using Sparklines

Sparklines are small charts that are embedded in sheet cells; sparklines can be inserted in rows or columns. You can position sparklines so that they appear at the bottom of a column of values or at the end of a row of values (including formula or function results). This enables you to place the sparklines directly inline with the data that they visually represent. Sparklines are not meant to replace full-blown charts in Excel, but can be used to accompany data series in the worksheet.

A sparkline can take the form of a line, column, or win/loss chart. Sparklines can be inserted in a single cell or multiple cells (for multiple rows or columns of data). You can also insert a sparkline for a row or column of values and then drag the sparkline's fill handle to copy the sparkline to other rows or columns as you would an Excel formula or function. When you change the data in a row or column that has an associated sparkline, the sparkline chart is immediately updated.

Creating Sparklines

As already mentioned, three different types of sparklines can be inserted in a worksheet: line, column, and win/loss. A line sparkline can be used to show a trend in the data. A column sparkline enables you to visually compare different data points. Win/loss sparklines can be used to show the win/loss trend over time for such things as investments or even the performance of a sports team.

You can insert a sparkline in a cell or a range of cells. The different types of sparklines are available in the Sparklines group on the Ribbon's Insert tab. To insert a sparkline, follow these steps:

1. Select the cell or cell range where you want to insert the sparkline.

2. Select the sparkline type that you want to insert from the Sparklines group. The Create Sparklines dialog box opens, as shown in Figure 14.24.

Figure 14.24
The Create Sparklines dialog box.

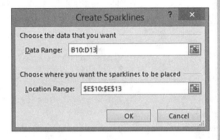

3. The Create Sparklines dialog box requires that you specify a data range and a location range. To specify the data range, click the Shrink button and then select the cells that contain the values that are used to create the sparklines. Do not include cells containing labels as you would for an Excel chart.

4. If you selected the cell range where the sparklines were to be inserted, a location range is already shown in the Location Range text box. If you need to specify the range or edit the current range, click the Shrink button and select the location range.

5. After the data range and the location range have been selected for the sparklines, click OK. The sparklines appear in the location range cells. Figure 14.25 shows a range of cells containing sparklines that use values arranged in rows.

When you select a sparkline in a range, the other sparklines in that range (meaning the cells in the range) are also selected. As with a number of other features in Excel, a specific set of contextual sparkline tools is provided when a cell containing a sparkline is selected. Let's look at the Sparkline Tools Design tab's commands.

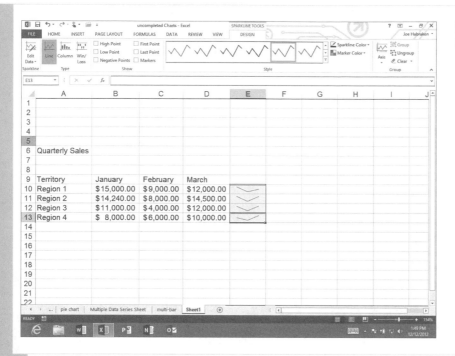

Figure 14.25
Sparklines in a sheet.

Modifying Sparklines

The Sparkline Tools Design tab provides a number of different options for modifying and enhancing the sparklines that you inserted into a worksheet. You can change the type of sparkline you have inserted after the fact, and you can change the style assigned to the sparklines. The command groups provided by the Sparkline Tools Design tab are as follows:

- **Sparkline:** This group contains the Edit Data command. This command enables you to edit the group and data location for all the sparklines in a specific group. The Edit Single Sparkline's Data command enables you to edit a specific cell containing a sparkline without editing the values used by the other sparklines in the group. A Hidden and Empty Cells command enables you to specify whether hidden and empty cells should be treated as gaps or zeros and whether the data should be shown that is included in any hidden rows or columns included in the data range for the sparkline.

- **Type:** You can change the type of sparkline you have inserted using the Line, Column, or Win/Loss commands provided by this group.

- **Show:** You can highlight certain data points in the sparklines, including the high point, low point, and negative points. You can also specify that markers are shown on the sparklines, which shows the number of data points used to create the sparkline.

- **Style:** The Style gallery provides you with a number of different sparkline styles for each sparkline type: Line, Column, or Win/Loss. Sparkline Color and Marker Color commands are also provided that enable you to select your own colors for the sparklines and the markers that you are including on the sparklines (selected via the Show group), respectively.

■ **Group:** This group provides commands that can be used to group or ungroup sparklines. A Clear command is provided that enables you to clear the selected sparklines or selected sparkline groups. An Axis command enables you to modify the horizontal and vertical axis options. You can change the horizontal axis type, and specify minimum and maximum values for the vertical axis.

Sparklines provide you with another possibility for providing a visual representation of the data in a worksheet. And although sparklines do not provide the detail you find in an Excel chart, they can be useful in doing quick comparisons of a range of data values or to show a trend in the values.

USING EXCEL TABLES AND PIVOTTABLES

Although we primarily think of Excel as a number cruncher, it also provides a number of capabilities for working with collections of information—databases. Excel enables you to view and manipulate data records and field information in a database table. You can sort records in your table, filter the records, and import or connect to external data sources.

In this chapter, we look at Excel's database capabilities, including a number of different table manipulation tools and data tools. We also look at grouping and ungrouping ranges in a table and creating subtotals in a table. We wrap up this chapter with a discussion of PivotTables, which provide you with a dynamic way to view and analyze worksheet data.

Excel and Databases

A database is a collection of organized information. The basic container used to hold data in a database is the table, and complex databases can consist of many tables. Excel provides you with the ability to interact with and manipulate tables by using a number of different tools. You can create your own tables in Excel or import or connect to data provided by other databases external to Excel. The fact that database information is held in discrete tables means that you can interact with database information that lives in a number of different database platforms, including Microsoft Access, the Web, and server-based database systems such as those provided by Microsoft SQL Server. Excel tables can also be shared via a SharePoint Services server (such as a server running SharePoint 2013).

A table looks much like any other Excel worksheet, with the data arranged in columns and rows. However, it is important that a database table be structured correctly for you to take advantage of the commands and tools provided on the Ribbon's Data tab; a table must have the data arranged in records and fields.

Each column in the table is a field. Each field consists of a discrete piece of information such as an employee's phone number or department. The very first row in the table consists of field names or headings, which defines what is contained in each field. The field headings play an important role when you are filtering data in the table.

Each row in the table is a record. A record is all the information related to a particular person, place, or thing. The record comprises the field entries made for that particular record. For example, if you have a table of employees, each record in the table is the record for a different employee.

You might be wondering why you would want to tackle database tables in Excel when there is more powerful relational database software such as Microsoft Access. The best answer is that when looking at individual tables, Excel provides a number of tools that enable you to view the data in different ways using sort and filter commands. Excel's ability to do calculations also enables you to use formulas, functions, and other Excel features to quickly go beyond the data analysis that you could do easily in a particular database software application. So, don't think of Excel as the database creation application as much as the analysis engine that can be used after the database has been created. Your Excel (database) tables really look no different from other worksheets you create in Excel. The information still appears in columns and rows.

note

Tables that you create in Excel are referred to as flat-file databases because you cannot set up relationships between associated tables in Excel such as an employee table with an employee sales table. Relational databases created in Microsoft Access use related tables to create the structure and data relationships for the database. Tables in a relational database will each contain a primary key, which is a field (such as an employee number or invoice number) that discretely identifies each record in the table.

Defining a Table Range

To define a table in Excel, you use the Format as Table command on the Ribbon's Home tab. Before you can define the table, you need to create the table or import it from a source external to Excel. We look at working with external data later in the chapter, so let's concentrate on issues related to creating your own table directly in Excel.

Before you begin banging away on the keyboard, you might want to take a moment and do a little planning related to your table. It makes sense to determine the fields that you want to include in the table and that make up each record. You also need to determine the purpose of the table; is it truly a data repository or is it a way to list some data and then manipulate it? If you are building the table for analysis purposes, you don't necessarily have to include all the information that you have collected for the database as you would if you are building a table that serves primarily as an information resource.

tip

You might want to include a key field in your table. This provides a field column that contains a unique identifier for each record in the table, such as employee number or invoice number. You can then use the key field to quickly sort your records back into the original order. You can use the fill handle to quickly create a series and assign unique numbers in the key field column as needed.

For example, if you are working with employee salary data or sales information for your sales force and want to be able to filter and sort the data to get a better picture of performance, do you need to include extraneous information in the table such as the employee's phone number or the names of a particular salesperson's children? So, the first thing you need to decide is what fields to include in the table. After the fields are entered in the top row of the table, you can then enter each of the records that make up the table.

 note

When you scroll down through a large table in Excel, the field headings now remain on the screen as you move down through the records in the table.

After you have the table in an Excel worksheet, defining the actual table range is very straightforward. Follow these steps:

1. Select the cell range for the table, including the field names in the top row of the table.

2. Select the Ribbon's Insert tab and then click the Table command in the Tables group. The Create Table dialog box opens, as shown in Figure 15.1.

Figure 15.1
The Create Table dialog box.

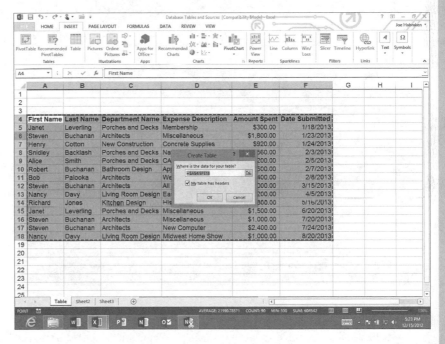

3. Make sure that the range specified in the Create Table dialog box encompasses your entire table range. You can modify the range by clicking the Shrink button and then selecting a new range for the table.

4. Click OK. The range is now defined as a table.

As soon as you close the Create Table dialog box, the table is formatted with the default table style and drop-down lists appear on each field heading in the table. These are the AutoFilters for each field in the table. The AutoFilters enable you to sort and filter the records in the table by each field.

Creating a Table Using Styles

You can also create your database table by selecting a table style in the Table Styles gallery, which is accessed via the Format as Table command on the Ribbon's Home tab. This enables you to specify your table range and pick a table style—all pretty much at the same time.

Select the cell range for the table. Then select the Format as Table command in the Styles group on the Ribbon's Home tab. The Table Styles gallery appears, as shown in Figure 15.2.

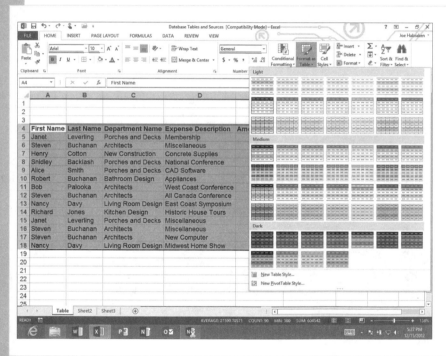

Figure 15.2
The Table Styles gallery.

Select one of the table styles in the gallery. When you select the style, the Table Styles gallery closes and the Format as Table dialog box opens. Make sure that the data range for the table is correct and then click OK. The table is created and assigned the table style you selected.

Database tables do not necessarily need to be discrete tables on their own worksheets. You can also create tables by selecting a subset range of the original worksheet. Think of the table feature as a way to access data analysis tools on the Data tab of the Ribbon. This enables you to use the table and accompanying tools as a way to work with existing data in large worksheets that contain information arranged in the appropriate table format of field columns and record rows.

You can also define multiple tables within a single worksheet, which enables you to group data in such a way that you can do some meaningful manipulations of the information by using the commands on the Data tab.

Using the Table Tools

After the table range has been specified, you can take advantage of the Table Tools to change the table style and other options related to the table style. You can also refresh data that comes from an external source, export the table to a SharePoint list, or convert the table back to a normal worksheet range. Figure 15.3 shows the Table Tools Design tab. It is another example of Excel's (and the Office applications') contextual tool sets.

**Figure 15.3
The Table
Tools Design
tab.**

Basic commands related to the table style and table options are available to you whether the data is external or internal to Excel. The commands available in the External Table Data group are limited to the Export command if you are working with a table created in Excel. The Table Tools Design tab command groups are as follows:

- **Properties:** This group provides the table name (which you can edit as needed) and also a Resize Table command. You can resize the table to include more or fewer rows and columns if required, meaning you are changing the table range.

- **Tools:** This group provides you with the ability to create a PivotTable from the current table (we discuss PivotTables later in the chapter). A Remove Duplicates command is also provided that enables you to specify a column that contains duplicate entries and delete them. This group also provides the Convert to Range command, which converts the table data range back to a regular worksheet data range.

- **External Table Data:** This group provides the Export command, which can be used to export your Excel table to a SharePoint list. Other commands in the group relate to external table data and enable you to refresh the data, view the data properties, and unlink from the external data source.

- **Table Style Options:** This group provides a series of check boxes that enable you to fine-tune the table. For example, you can include or preclude a header row or a total row. The Banded Rows formatting can also be turned on or off. You can also choose to format the first column or last column in the table and add banded columns to the table.

- **Table Styles:** This group provides access to the Table Styles gallery. Place the mouse on a style in the gallery to preview that particular style on your table. The More button enables you to view the entire gallery. Click a style to assign it to the current table.

Although the Table Tools Design tab becomes active when you select a cell range that falls in the table range, the commands that are the real meat and potatoes of table manipulation are provided by the AutoFilters placed on each of the table field headings and the commands provided on the Ribbon's Data tab. Two of the most fundamental manipulations of table records are sorting and filtering.

Sorting Table Data

Sorting by the fields in a table enables you to quickly place the records in the table based on your sort criteria. You can sort data by using the sort commands on a field's AutoFilter menu or by selecting one of the Sort commands in the Sort & Filter group on the Ribbon's Data tab. To quickly sort the table by a particular field, select that field's AutoFilter arrow, as shown in Figure 15.4.

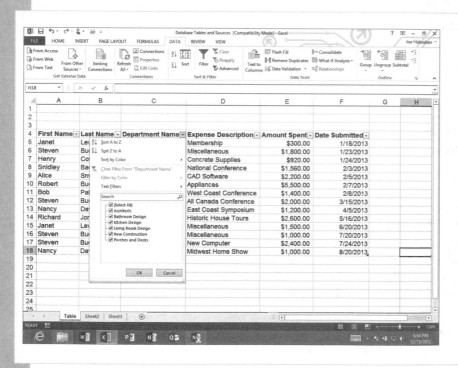

Figure 15.4
The AutoFilter menu for a table field.

You can then select Sort A to Z (ascending) or Sort Z to A (descending) as needed on the AutoFilter menu. The records in the table are sorted by the field you selected in the direction you selected (ascending or descending). You can use the Sort commands in the Sort & Filter group. Click in the field column that you want to use as the sort field. Then select either the Sort A to Z or Sort Z to A command. The table records are sorted by the field you specified.

You can also sort by multiple fields in the table. For example, assume that you have a table where the last name field column is followed by the first name field column. You can select any two cells in these two field columns and then select either the Sort A to Z or Sort Z to A command in the Sort & Filter group to sort the table by the last name field followed by the first name field.

This enables you to sort out all the Smiths and Jones that appear in your table. In terms of a more generic application of this multiple field sorting, Excel sorts by the first selected field column (starting on the left) and then moves to the right, sorting by each subsequent field column that has been selected.

How Excel Sorts Data

When Excel sorts the records in a table, it follows rules for how the data is actually sorted. Numbers appear first in a sort list and in the case of an ascending sort (A to Z) are sorted from the smallest (negative numbers qualify as small numbers) to the largest. Numbers (or values) include dates, which Excel perceives as values. Keep in mind that Excel looks at the content of the cell, not the formatting of the content. So, even a date that appears as December 1, 2015, is still a number to Excel.

In the case of text entries, the field column data are sorted by punctuation and special characters such as #, &, *, and so on (in the order you find them on the keyboard) followed by the letters of the alphabet (A through Z). Text with numbers would follow regular text entries when doing a sort. If you have a field column that contains numbers, text, and text with numbers, the ascending sort would use this sort order: numbers, followed by text, and then numbers with text.

Using the Sort Dialog Box

In cases where you cannot conveniently sort by multiple fields because of the location of the fields in the table and you would like more control over the number of levels in the sort, you can use the Sort dialog box. The Sort dialog box enables you to specify 64 levels for your sort.

To open the Sort dialog box, select Sort in the Sort & Filter group. Figure 15.5 shows the Sort dialog box.

Figure 15.5
The Sort dialog box.

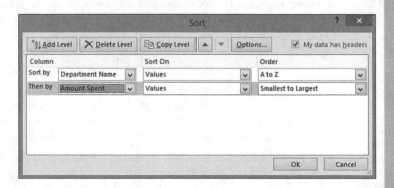

The first sort level is available when you open the Sort dialog box; specify the first field name in the first level's Sort By drop-down list, which lists all the fields in the table. By default, sort levels sort on the values that are in the field column you have specified in the primary sort level (or key, as sort levels are also known). You can choose to sort by values, cell color, font color, or cell icon. The cell and font color can be specified by cell attributes that you have manually assigned to cells. These attributes can also be the result of conditional formatting. This includes the possibilities of the field column's cells containing cell icons that have been inserted into cells that have met certain criteria related to conditional formatting that you have assigned to the table cells.

> ➡ *For information on using conditional formatting including icon sets,* **see**" *Using Conditional Formatting," p. 349.*

After you have specified what column should be sorted and what the sort should be performed on (values, cell colors, and so on), you can specify the order of the sort level. For cells containing text, this is A to Z or Z to A, and for numerical values, it is smallest to largest or largest to smallest. Dates are oldest to newest or newest to oldest.

You can also create custom sort lists to determine the sort order. Select Custom List in the Order drop-down box and then create the custom list in the Custom Lists dialog box. Custom lists were discussed in Chapter 11, "Requisite Excel: Essential Features," in reference to creating custom series, but the lists can also be used to determine the sort order of information in a field column.

After you have specified the parameters for the first sort level, click the Add Level button to add an additional level to the Sort dialog box. Configure the level by going through the same steps you used to configure the first level. You can also delete levels if needed and you can copy levels to hasten the configuration process for field columns that are similar in contents and how you want them to be sorted.

tip

If you don't see the AutoFilter arrows on the table field headings, make sure that you select a cell within the table range and then select the Filter command on the Ribbon's Data tab.

You also have the option of changing sort options related to the case of text entries and the orientation of the sort. By default, the case of the text is ignored during sorting and Excel assumes that you have placed your fields in columns and your records in rows. When you click the Options button in the Sort dialog box, the Sort Options dialog box opens. The Sort Options dialog box is extremely simple. It provides a Case Sensitive check box, which you can select to specify that case be considered during the sort. Uppercase text is sorted before lowercase text when this check box is enabled.

A sort typically takes place from top to bottom, meaning the rows are rearranged. This is why Sort top to bottom is the default option selected in the Sort Options dialog box. If you have a situation where you want to sort the columns instead of the rows, you can switch the sort to Sort Left to Right (this would be useful in cases where you want to sort a worksheet arranged in columns rather than rows, such as a database table is). Click OK to close the Sort Options dialog box.

After you have specified your sort levels and the information for each level, you can run the sort. Click OK and the sort takes place in the table.

Filtering Table Data

Although sorting helps you arrange the records in the table in a particular order, filtering enables you to view subsets of the table records based on specific criteria. One option for filtering the data in the table is to use the AutoFilter lists on each of the table field headings. AutoFilter enables you to quickly filter the table in place.

When you select the AutoFilter arrow for a particular field, the AutoFilter menu provides a list of all the entries for that particular field. By default, all the values are selected, meaning there is no filtering currently applied to the table based on that field. Figure 15.6 shows the AutoFilter list for a table field (a date field, which provides months of the year in the filter list).

Figure 15.6
The AutoFilter drop-down menu.

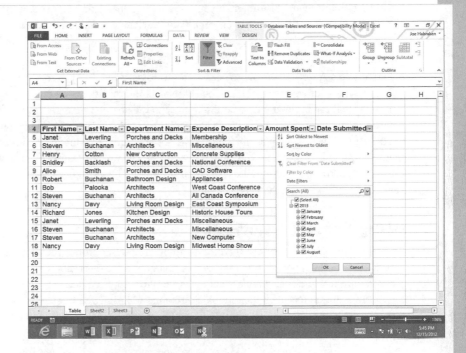

The most straightforward method of filtering the table by a specific field is to deselect the Select All check box in the field list and then select the field value that you want to use to filter the table. You can select more than one value in the field data list. Remember that the purpose of the filter is to show a subset of the table records, so you can specify multiple criteria for a single field. When you are ready to run the filter based on actual field values, click OK. The table records will be filtered based on your selection or selections in the AutoFilter list.

AutoFilter enables you to filter by more than one field, so you can create filters based on criteria for more than one field in the table. Simply use the AutoFilter drop-down list to specify the filter criteria for each field. The field or fields that you have used to filter the table will have a small filter icon (it looks like a funnel) on the AutoFilter drop-down arrow. This serves as a reminder as to which fields in the table have been used to filter the data.

You can clear a filter that is specific to a field. Select the AutoFilter drop-down arrow and then select the Clear Filter from "Field Name" on the AutoFilter menu. Any other filters applied to the table remain in force. If you want to clear all the filters that you have applied to the table, select the Clear command in the Sort & Filter group.

Using the AutoFilter Search Box

Each of the AutoFilter drop-down menus for your field columns contains a Search box (just above the field value list). The Search box can be used to quickly search for data that appears in that field. This can be particularly useful when you are working with a database table that has a large number of records. The list of field values for each field, obviously, is as numerous as the number of records in the table, so having a Search box that can be used to find a specific field value quickly can speed up the filtering of the table.

Select a field's AutoFilter arrow to access the AutoFilter menu. Click in the Search box. As you begin to type your search entry, matches appear in the results list as you enter each character for a number (value) or a text entry. Continue to type the search parameter string until you have the desired results listed. For example, to view all the people with the last name of *Smith*, you might need to type *smi* to view just the Smiths and not any Smythes. The data found by the search in that field column are listed below the Search box and the check box for matches to your search string are selected. To run the AutoFilter based on the search results, click OK. If you need to fine-tune the search string, do so and then run the filter.

Creating Custom AutoFilters

So far we have looked at filtering tables as an all-or-nothing proposition. Either the records completely met the field parameters that were set via the AutoFilter menu on a field or fields or the records didn't. You can also create custom AutoFilters that provide you with the ability to create more robust filters based on conditional statements. These conditional statements enable you to filter the table records for a range of field values or text entries rather than an exact match to a particular criterion.

The AutoFilter menu provides number, date, and text filters that are designed to help you create more complex filters for each of these specific data types. For example, when working with a field column that contains numbers (values), you can specify filter criteria based on conditional statements such as equals, does not equal, is greater than, between, and so on. For text entries in a field column, you can also create conditional statements such as equals, begins with, ends with, and contains. In the case of dates, you can use conditional statements such as equals, before, and after, and you can also choose from a wide variety of data filters such as tomorrow, yesterday, next week, next quarter, and year to date. Figure 15.7 shows the different data filters provided for a field column that contains dates.

As already mentioned, each data type filter, such as those for numbers or for text, enables you to quickly create a custom AutoFilter based on a conditional statement that you select from a list. For example, if you want to see employee expense records that fall into a certain data range, you could select the Between filter on the Date Filters list. This opens the Custom AutoFilter dialog box, as shown in Figure 15.8.

Figure 15.7
Custom AutoFilters such as Date Filters enable you to quickly filter by a data type.

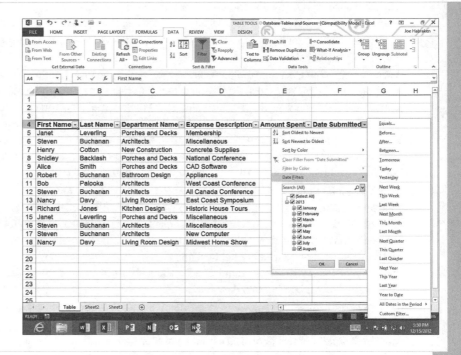

Figure 15.8
Creating a date range AutoFilter in the Custom AutoFilter dialog box.

By selecting the Between filter (for a date filter), the Custom AutoFilter dialog box has automatically entered two criteria for the filter: is after or equal to and is before or equal to. All you have to do is specify the two dates that provide the beginning and end of the data range that you want the filter to use. The Custom AutoFilter dialog box even provides Calendar icons so you can insert the dates directly from a particular calendar month (as shown in Figure 15.8).

Creating a Custom AutoFilter for a number field, such as a salary field, is every bit as straightforward as working with date fields. Selecting a Between filter for a number field allows you to select Is Greater Than or Equal To in the Custom AutoFilter dialog box as the start point for a numerical range and Is Less Than or Equal To as the end point.

When you use the Custom AutoFilter dialog box, you can modify the filter criteria by using the criteria drop-down lists. You specify the values, dates, or text entries for the AutoFilter by using the field content drop-down lists, which are to the right of the criteria lists. You can specify the specific value or text entry that should be used by the AutoFilter for each criteria by selecting a field column entry in the drop-down list. You can also type in filter parameters and use the question mark (?) to represent single characters and the asterisk (*) to represent a series of characters. These two wildcards are most useful in situations where you are working with a field that contains text entries.

When you are ready to run the AutoFilter, click OK. The table is filtered based on the criteria set for the field's custom AutoFilter. You can apply custom AutoFilters to multiple field columns to filter by more than one field in the table. For example, you could do a custom AutoFilter that will filter a Department Name field by specific departments using the And operator. You could then run a Between AutoFilter on a Salary field column to see who (which employees) in the specified departments (specified by the department filter) made a salary that fell in the range specified by the custom AutoFilter applied to the Salary field.

If you want to create a custom AutoFilter that isn't listed in the set of filters provided for a particular field, you can open the Custom AutoFilter dialog box and set up your filter from scratch. Select Custom Filter at the bottom of any of the different data type (numbers, text, or dates) filter lists. The Custom AutoFilter dialog box opens and you can set the filter operators and criteria as you require.

You can clear custom AutoFilters in the same way that the quick AutoFilters are cleared: by using the field's AutoFilter menu. If you want to clear all the custom AutoFilters that you have applied to a table, click the Clear command on the Sort & Filter group.

 tip

You can quickly filter a number field using the Top 10 number filter. The Top 10 AutoFilter enables you to quickly show the top or bottom items in a field column (10 is the default number but you can change it) based on the values in the field or a percent. For example, you could find the top 10 sales representatives based on the percent of sales.

Filtering Tables with Slicers

Another option for filtering table data is the slicer. The ability to use slicers to filter Excel table data is a new feature in Excel 2013. A slicer is similar to a filter in that it filters a table in place and shows only the data that meets the slicer's criteria.

To create a slicer for a table, select any cell in a defined table area. Click on the Table Tools Design tab to access the Insert Slicer command, which is in the Tools group. When you select Insert Slicer, the Insert Slicers dialog box opens, as shown in Figure 15.9.

The Insert Slicers dialog box lists the fields (column headings) available in the table. You can select one field in the Insert Slicers dialog box to create a slicer that filters by that one field or you can specify more than one field and build a separate slicer for each field selected. Each slicer you create can only be related to one field in the table.

Figure 15.9
Specify the fields to be used by the slicer to filter the table.

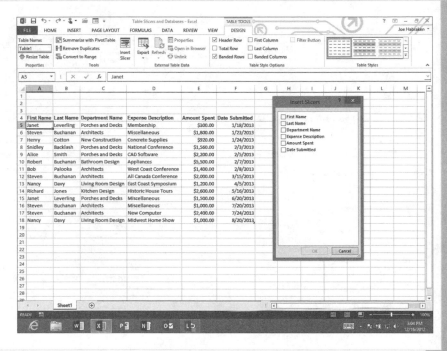

After selecting the fields in the Insert Slicers dialog box, click OK. A slicer is created for each selected field. The slicer for a particular field lists all the data entries that appeared in that particular field column. Click one of the specific field entries to filter the table by that entry.

Figure 15.10 shows a slicer that was created to filter a table by the Department Name field. The figure also shows the results of selecting Porches and Decks in the Department slicer.

Slicers are an easily accessible sheet object and can be moved and arranged on the worksheet as any other object (such as a chart). When a slicer is selected, the Slicer Tools Options appear on the Ribbon (see Figure 15.10).

You can change the style for the slicer by selecting one of the styles in the Slicer Styles gallery. You can also change the slicer settings by selecting the Slicer Settings command in the Slicer group. This opens the Slicer Settings dialog box.

By default, a slicer filters the data and also sorts the data in ascending order (A to Z). You can change the sorting direction to descending by clicking the Descending option button in the Slicer Settings dialog box. By default, a slicer also visually indicates items that contain no data; you can change this setting by selecting the Hide Items with No Data check box. When you have finished modifying the settings in the Slicer Settings dialog box, click OK to return to the current sheet.

 note

Slicers were introduced in Excel 2010 as a way to filter PivotTables. Slicers can now also be used to filter your Excel 2013 data tables.

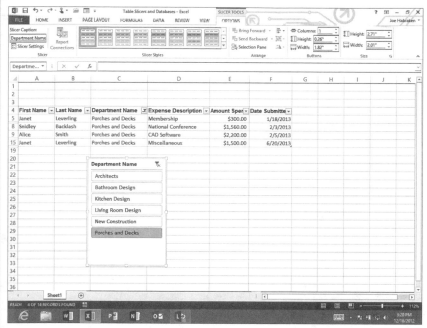

Figure 15.10
A slicer filtered table.

Creating Advanced Filters

You might find that even the custom AutoFilters are limiting in terms of the number of fields that you can use to filter the table and are rather cumbersome in terms of having to work in a different Custom AutoFilter dialog box for each field that you want to filter. Custom AutoFilters are best used for comparisons, and any filter that goes beyond a couple of comparison criteria is going to require that you set up your table for advanced filtering.

Advanced filters enable you to filter a database by as many fields as you want. Advanced filters use a criteria range to set the filter criteria (which we get to in a moment). Advanced filters can filter the table in place or they can copy the results of the advanced filter—the filtered records—to a specified range on the current worksheet.

Before you can create an advanced filter, you need to create a criteria range for the table. The criteria range consists of an exact duplicate of the field headings found in the table. The criteria range also consists of at least one empty row below the copied field headings. If you are going to use multiple criteria for a particular field, you need multiple blank rows below field headings you designate as the criteria range. It is in the cells directly below each of the field heading copies that you place the filter parameters for the advanced filter.

So, first copy the row that contains the field headings for the table. You can then paste these headings somewhere onto the worksheet so that there is at least one empty row below the copied field names. It makes sense, however, to have multiple empty rows available for multiple criteria for a single field.

You can place the copied field headings above or below the database table; it's up to you. Just make sure that there is clear separation between the table and the criteria range that you specify when you run the advanced filter. Figure 15.11 shows a database table (A4:F18) and an accompanying criteria range (A20:F21).

Figure 15.11
A table, criteria range, and Advanced Filter dialog box.

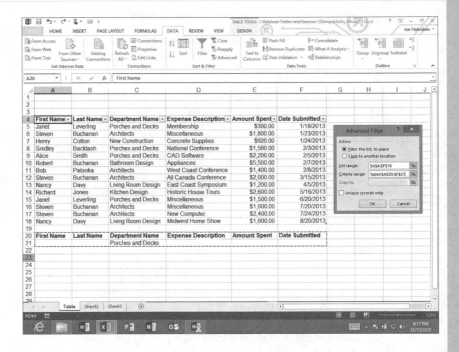

In this case, the criteria range consists of the cells containing the copied field headings and the row below the copied field headings. A criterion, "Porches and Decks," has been typed below the Department Name field heading in the criteria range. The Advanced Filter dialog box is configured to filter the table in place. Both the List range (the table range) and the Criteria range are specified in the Advanced Filter dialog box.

It is the criteria that you place below the field names included in the criteria range that enables you to filter the table records. For example, in Figure 15.11, when OK is clicked in the Advanced Filter dialog box, the table is filtered to show only the records that have Porches and Decks specified in the Department Name field column. This example shows only a single criterion, but you can specify multiple criteria and use different operators, such as greater than (>) or less than (<), as part of the criteria.

In cases where you have criteria for more than one field column in the same criteria range row, you are creating an And statement. The advanced filter bases its results on the first criteria *And* the second criteria (and additional criteria if included). In cases where you are specifying multiple criteria for a single field column, you are creating an Or statement.

Although advanced filters might look like more trouble than they are worth, they are the only way to filter a table using a number and variety of criteria. Advanced filters can be used to copy records from a large table to a table that includes only a subset of records based on the filter. This makes it easier to work with subsets of the records provided by the table.

After you have copied the field headings for the advanced filter to an area that can serve as a criteria range, you are ready to create the advanced filter. Follow these steps:

1. Enter criteria for the filter under the criteria range field headings. You can enter filter criteria for more than one field (type the criteria below the field name) or you can enter multiple criteria for a single field: Type the multiple criteria in the required number of cells below the field name.

2. Click in the database table that you are filtering. Because you have defined this range as a table, it is automatically specified as the List range for the advanced filter.

3. Select the Advanced command in the Sort & Filter group. The Advanced Filter dialog box opens.

4. Set the action for the filter. You can filter the list in place or copy the results of the filter to another location on the worksheet. If you are going to copy the results to another location, make sure that you give yourself plenty of open space (meaning empty cells) for the copied results.

5. The List range is the range for the table. If you performed step 2, the range shown in the List range box should reflect the range for the table. If not, click in the worksheet and select the range for the table.

6. Click in the Criteria range box. Select the field headings and the number of rows below the field heading you have copied to provide the criteria range. If you are specifying criteria only in the row below the copied field headings, you only need to specify the field heading row and the row below it. If you are specifying multiple criteria for a single field (or fields), make sure that each row that contains a criterion statement is included in the criteria range.

7. (Optional) If you select the Copy to Another Location option button as the action for the filter, you need to specify where the filter should place its results. All you really need to do is click in the blank cell that serves as the upper-left limit for the filter results. The results then spill over into other cells as needed.

8. When you are ready to run the filter, click OK.

The results of the advanced filter appear in the table if you filtered the table in place. If you chose to have the filter results copied to another area of the worksheet, the results appear there. If you filtered the table in place, you can clear the advanced filter by selecting the Clear command in the Sort & Filter group.

Each time you change the criteria in the criteria range, you need to rerun the filter. Select Advanced in the Sort & Filter group and make sure the List range and Criteria range are correct for the filter you want to run. Then click OK to run the filter.

 tip

You can use the question mark (?) and the asterisk (*) as wildcards when building filters for text fields. In cases where you want a filter criterion to find a specific occurrence of a specific text string when it is not part of a larger text string, use the format ="=text string".

 tip

If you want the results of the advanced filter to show only unique records, select the Unique Records Only check box in the Advanced Filter dialog box.

Using the Data Form

When Excel 2007 adopted the new Ribbon-based user interface, the data form lost its place as one of the readily accessible data tools on the Data menu. The form is not available via a command on the Ribbon's Data tab. This also holds true in Excel 2013 and so if you want to take advantage of the data form to enter or find records in your database table, you need to add the Form command to the Excel Quick Access Toolbar. The form can be quite useful when you are working with extremely large tables. Figure 15.12 shows the form containing a table record.

Figure 15.12

The data form can be used to view and edit individual records.

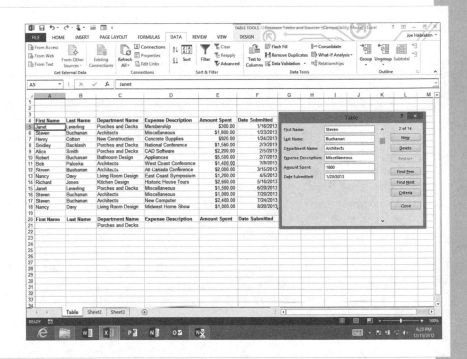

The form provides you with the ability to view, edit, and add records to the table individually. It also enables you to quickly search the database table to find records.

You can quickly add the Form command to the Excel Quick Access Toolbar from the Excel Options window. Follow these steps:

1. Select the Customize Quick Access Toolbar menu and then select More Commands. The Excel Options window opens with the Quick Access Toolbar settings selected.

2. In the Customize Quick Access Toolbar pane of the Options window, select the Choose Commands from List, and then select All Commands.

3. Scroll down through the commands listed in the Command pane and select Form.

4. Click the Add button to add the Form command to the Quick Access Toolbar. Then click OK to return to the Excel window.

Now you can open the form as needed when you are working with a table. Click in a record (a row in a table) and then click the Form command on the Quick Access Toolbar. The record opens in the Form window. You can edit a record or delete a record from the Form window. You can also enter new records to the table by selecting New. The new record is inserted at the bottom of the table.

If you want to find a particular record or records, click the Criteria button. Enter criteria in a field or fields and then click the Find Next button. The first record that meets your criteria is shown in the Form window. You can click the Find Next button to move to the next record that matches your criteria. When you have finished working with the form, select Close.

Creating Outlines and Subtotals

The Ribbon's Data tab also provides an Outline group that provides the Group, Ungroup, and Subtotal commands. The Group command enables you to create outline groups in a worksheet. The groups can then be individually expanded or collapsed, so you can hide information at a particular outline level and view only a summary of the data (such as sales totals by regions or salary data by department) rather than each individual row of data.

The purpose of an outline is to take advantage of a hierarchy that is already present in the worksheet. If you think about a text outline, it is made up of different levels of information such as primary levels, secondary levels, and so on. In Excel, the hierarchy is based on logical groupings of information. Typically the key to grouping several rows of information is that they are tied together by a summary row. This row can be above or below the detail rows, but it has to be in the same place for you to create an outline. For example, you might have a sales sheet that shows the monthly sales figures for each of your regions for an entire year. At the end of each quarter, a summary row provides a total for each region's sales for that quarter. Figure 15.13 shows a worksheet that has been formatted as an outline using the Group command.

Note that each group in the outline has a button that can be used to collapse grouped rows. You can collapse a particular quarter group and view the summary row for only that particular group. You can click the control for a collapsed group and expand the group to show all the data in a particular group. Level numbers are also provided at the top of the worksheet area just above the row numbers and to the left of the column letters. You can use these buttons to collapse the outline to level 1 or to expand the outline to level 2 as needed.

To create an outline, you have two choices: You can create the outline manually or you can allow Excel to create an auto outline. If you are working with a range of cells that has been formatted as a table, you can't use the auto outline possibility. So, you might want to use the Convert to Range command on the Table Tools Design tab to convert the table back to a regular worksheet. It definitely makes sense to try the auto outline scenario first because Excel is good at recognizing the groupings in a worksheet.

Select the worksheet and then click the Group command, and then select Auto Outline. If auto outline doesn't group the data in the worksheet as you anticipated, you can go the manual outline route. If you need to clear the outline grouping provided by auto outline, select the Ungroup command and then select Clear Outline.

Figure 15.13
You can group related data into outlines.

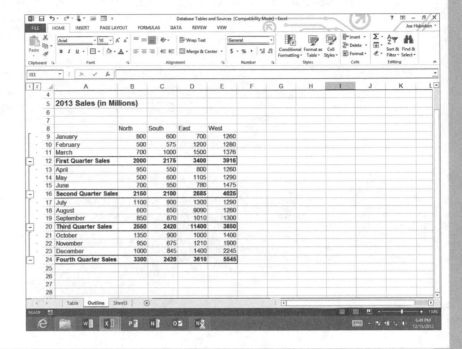

To manually create the outline, select the worksheet data and then click the Group command. Select Group and the Group dialog box opens. This dialog box provides you with two options: Rows and Columns. Click the appropriate option button for grouping the data and then click OK. The worksheet is converted to an outline. If you don't get a proper outline, you can clear the current outline and then rearrange the data as needed so that it can be placed in an outline. Remember it is all about establishing a hierarchy in the worksheet that is consistent throughout the worksheet.

> **tip**
>
> You can also collapse or expand the detail in your outline groups by using the Show Detail and Hide Detail commands in the Outline group, respectively.

Another possibility provided by the Outline group is the Subtotal command. The Subtotal command is easier to work with than the Group command because it automatically inserts subtotal rows for you in the worksheet and can also provide summary data. The trick with subtotals is that you need to have a data column that provides a way to group associated rows of data.

For example, an employee list that includes a Department column could be sorted by department, grouping all the employees in the worksheet in their respective departments. You can then have the Subtotal command act on other column data; for example, if a Salary column is also included in the worksheet, the Subtotal could group the employees by department and then provide a salary subtotal for each department. So, to use the Subtotal command to both group data rows and provide subtotals based on those groupings, you need one column of information that can provide the grouping and another column of information that provides the values that are used to compute the subtotals for each group.

To apply the Subtotal command to a worksheet, sort the rows by the column data that provides the logical grouping of the row data. Then click the Subtotal command. The Subtotal dialog box opens, as shown in Figure 15.14.

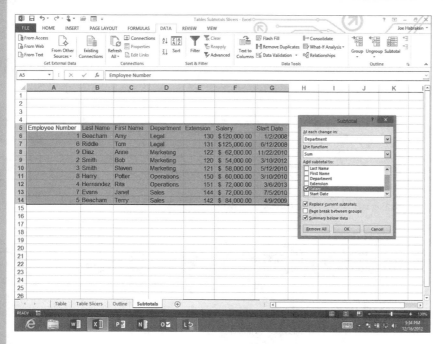

Figure 15.14
A data table and the Subtotal dialog box.

Use the At Each Change In drop-down list to specify the column title (or field name) that serves as the grouping mechanism for the rows in the column (this would be the column that you used to sort the worksheet). In the Use Function drop-down list, select the function that you want to use for the subtotal rows in the worksheet. The default is SUM, but you can also use other statistical functions such as COUNT, AVERAGE, and MAX.

 note
You can't use the Subtotal command on a worksheet range that has been formatted as a table.

In the Add Subtotal To box, select the check box for the column that contains the values you want to use in the subtotal calculation. This is a column that contains numerical values.

Other check boxes provided in the Subtotal dialog box enable you to replace any current subtotals in the worksheet, or place page breaks between the groups, which can be useful on large worksheets that are then printed. A check box is also provided that includes a summary, including a grand total below the worksheet data. When you are ready to add the subtotals and groupings to the worksheet, click OK. Figure 15.15 shows a worksheet that has been grouped by department.

Figure 15.15
A worksheet configured with subtotals.

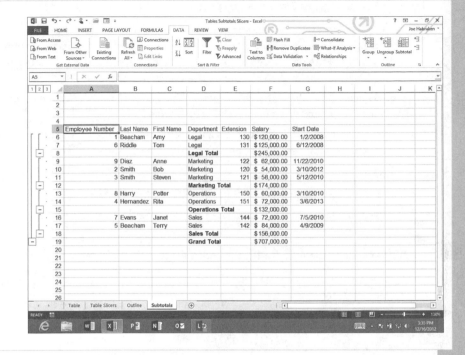

The Subtotal command placed a subtotal for each department in the Salary column. A grand total has also been placed at the bottom of the worksheet range. Controls are also provided that enable you to expand and collapse the different levels created in the worksheet by the Subtotal command, creating an outline in the worksheet.

Working with External Data

Excel provides you with a number of options for getting external data into a worksheet. After you import data from another source or connect to a data source such as a database server, you can then use Excel's wide variety of capabilities to work with the data. The fact that Excel is an extremely powerful number cruncher means that you can probably perform calculations and data analysis that would be extremely time consuming or very labor intensive in another software application, such as Microsoft Access.

Excel makes it easy to import data from other applications or database servers. The Get External Data group commands on the Data tab enable you to import data from Access, web tables (on websites), text files, and other database sources, such as a Microsoft SQL Server. Let's look at the possibilities.

Importing Data from Access

Access is a powerful desktop relational database application and it can also be used as the front-end client for databases hosted by a database server such as a server running Microsoft SQL Server. Access 2013 is the most recent version of the Access software, and whether Access is installed depends on the Office 2013 version that you purchase.

Access uses the table as the data container for its database records. Most Access databases (of any complexity) contain a number of related data tables.

Even though each database contains multiple tables, it is not that difficult to specify a specific table in the Access database and import it into Excel. Follow these steps:

1. Select the cell in the current worksheet (an empty worksheet would be a good idea), which serves as the upper-left corner of the imported table data.

2. Select the From Access command in the Get External Data group. The Select Data Source dialog box opens.

3. Navigate to the folder or the network drive that contains the Access database and then select it.

4. Select Open in the Select Data Source dialog box. The Select Table dialog box opens, as shown in Figure 15.16.

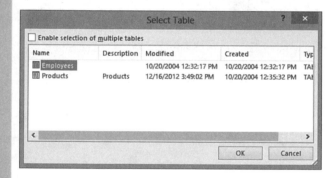

Figure 15.16
The Select Table dialog box.

5. The Select Table dialog box lists the tables and the queries (queries look like tables and consist of columns and rows of data) in the database; select a specific table and then click OK. The Import Data dialog box opens.

6. The Import Data dialog box enables you to specify whether the data should be imported as a table, PivotTable report, or a PivotChart and PivotTable report. We talk about PivotTables later in the chapter, but because we are discussing importing tables in this section, we import the Access data as a table. Click an option button in the dialog box (such as Table). You can also choose to have the data imported into the current worksheet (at a particular place) or you can specify that the imported data be placed on a new worksheet.

7. Click OK and the table is imported.

The table is imported as an Excel table, so it is formatted as a table. You can use any of the Table Tools Design commands to change the look of the table. The Field heading drop-down lists also are available on the imported table (as it would be for an Excel table), enabling you to sort and filter the table. The table you have imported is linked to the Excel worksheet, so changes made to the Access database are reflected in the worksheet when you update the link between the external data and Excel. To refresh a link to an Access database or other external databases, select the Refresh All command on the Data tab. You can use the Refresh All command to refresh all the links to external data or refresh the data on the current worksheet by selecting Refresh.

Importing a Web Table

You can also import data from any table that appears on a web page. The Web Query tool that is used to select a web table to be linked to an Excel worksheet is actually quite good at identifying table data on websites. You can import data from a table on the Web that is static, meaning the data in the table is not updated. You can also import data from a table that is dynamic, meaning the data is updated in the table over time. For example, you might want to include stock data that is published in a table on the Web and that is periodically updated. Because Excel imports the external data as a link, the linked data can be refreshed in the Excel worksheet.

When you create a link to a web table, you must specify the site that contains the table. So, before opening the New Web Query window, you might want to use your web browser to navigate to the website. You can then select the website's URL and copy it so that you can paste it into the New Web Query's Address window.

To open the New Web Query window, select the From Web command in the Get External Data group. Figure 15.17 shows the New Web Query window.

You can type or paste a URL into the Address box and then click Go to navigate to a specific website using the New Web Query window. It is basically a web browser with the ability to specify tables on a web page. All tables (the ones that can be identified as such) on the web page are denoted by a yellow box containing an arrow. When you place the mouse on a specific table arrow, a blue border appears, denoting the boundaries of that specific table.

To import a particular table, select the arrow icon for that table. A check mark appears in the box (that contained the arrow) and the table is highlighted. Click the Import button in the bottom-right corner of the New Web Query window to import the current table.

The New Web Query window closes and the Import Data dialog box opens. You can specify that the imported data is placed in the current sheet (or other sheet in the workbook) or into a new sheet. After specifying your preference, click OK to import the table. It might take a moment for the data to appear in the worksheet. Web table data imported into Excel is not automatically formatted as a table. You can select the imported data range and format it as a table if you choose. Even if you do not format the imported web table as a table, you can use many of the commands on the Data tab to manipulate the data, and you can add formulas and functions to the data for calculations or create a chart based on the data.

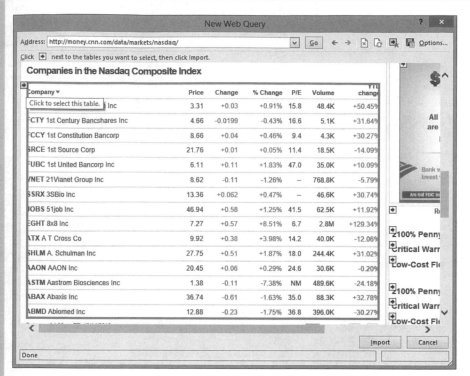

Importing Text Files

There are a lot of different database management software applications available; some are stand-alone and some use a server. For example, Outlook can be used as a standalone contact management application or it can be integrated into a Microsoft Exchange Server environment.

When users of one product attempt to share information with users of another product, they typically must resort to exporting data as delimited text files. These text files can then be imported into a product such as Excel. However, you need to tell Excel what type of delimited text file it is dealing with—there are tab-delimited text files, comma-delimited text files, and other text files that use other characters to delimit its fields and records.

To import a text file into Excel, select the From Text command in the Get External Data group. The Import Text File dialog box opens. Locate and select the text file you want to import and then click Import. The Text Import Wizard opens.

On the first wizard screen, you need to specify whether the text file is delimited or fixed width. A fixed-width text file has the fields aligned in columns, with space between each field. Select Delimited or Fixed Width and then click Next. The Step 2 window of the Text Import Wizard appears, as shown in Figure 15.18.

Figure 15.18
The Text Import Wizard.

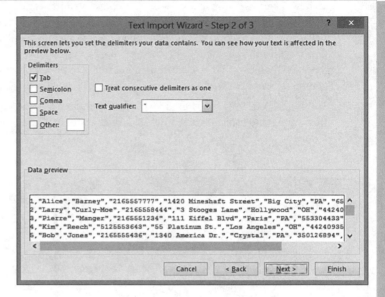

Specify the delimiter used for the text file, such as tab, semicolon, comma, and so on. Then click Next to continue. The next wizard screen enables you to specify the data format in each column shown in the bottom pane of the wizard screen. Select a column and then specify the data type for that column: General, Text, Date, or Do Not Import Column (Skip). Repeat the process until you have formatted all the columns you will import.

When you are ready to import the text file, select Finish. The Import Data dialog box opens. Specify whether you want to import the data in the current worksheet or a new worksheet, and then click OK. The text file is imported. You can format the imported data as a table or otherwise manipulate it using the various Excel commands and functions.

 note

Many nonprofit corporations and government entities that provide data from various studies or government reports on their websites typically provide the data as a text-delimited file. This makes it usable because you can import the information into Excel.

Connecting to Other Data Sources

You can connect Excel to a number of other data sources, including hosted data services such as Windows Azure Marketplace, which is a data services subscription service hosted by Microsoft. The different data sources to which you can connect are listed on the From Other Sources gallery, which is accessed by selecting the From Other Sources command in the Get External Data group. Many of the external data sources available on the Web are powered by Microsoft SQL Server (Azure Marketplace is an example).

SQL Server is a powerful network database platform. If you do a lot of work with information in a corporate or other large institution environment, chances are that you work with data that is stored on a SQL server or one of Microsoft's database platform competitors. Both Excel and Microsoft Access can be used to connect to a SQL server and work with the data on the server. Microsoft Access is often used in a SQL Server environment as the client for database end users. So, Excel doesn't have the capabilities that Access does in terms of working with SQL databases. However, that doesn't mean that table information can't be pulled off of the SQL database and then analyzed and manipulated in Excel.

To connect to a SQL Server database, select the From Other Sources command in the Get External Data group and then select From SQL Server. The Data Connection Wizard opens, as shown in Figure 15.19.

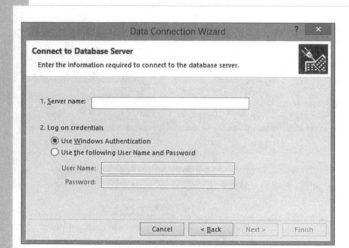

Figure 15.19
The Data Connection Wizard.

To log on to the server and import a data table, you need to know the server name and your logon credentials. In the case of SQL Server, you can log on in some situations using Windows authentication or you can log on using a username and password recognized by SQL Server. Enter the server name and then your logon information. Then click Next to continue.

The next screen provided by the Data Connection Wizard requests that you select a table or tables in the database. Figure 15.20 shows the Select Tables screen of the Data Connection Wizard.

Select a table or tables using the check boxes provided, and then click Next. The Import Data dialog box opens; you can import the data as a table, PivotTable report, or a PivotChart and PivotTable report. You can also specify that the imported data be placed starting at a particular cell in the current worksheet or a new worksheet. Click OK when you are ready to import the SQL data.

The Data Connection Wizard can also be used to connect to a number of different database server types and is not limited to a SQL Server connection. You can start the Data Connection Wizard from the From Other Sources command's gallery. Remember that the whole point of connecting to external data is so that you can use Excel's capabilities to analyze the data in a worksheet format. So, import tables that contain information that you can work with in Excel. Sales data, inventory data—any table with values—can then be manipulated, charted, and analyzed to your heart's content.

Figure 15.20
Select a table or tables.

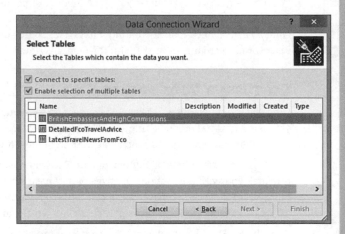

 note

Windows Azure Marketplace is a subscription data resource website hosted by Microsoft. You can access a number of free data sources on the Azure site and import them into Excel for subsequent analysis (in tables or PivotTables). All you need to sign up for an Azure Marketplace account is a Windows Live account (such as Outlook.com, MSN.com, or Hotmail.com). Check out Azure Marketplace at http://datamarket.azure.com/.

Using Microsoft Query

Although the Data Connection Wizard provides you with the ability to connect to a number of different database server platforms, there may be some occasions when you want to connect to a database source and run a query to select the data that you import into Excel. A query is really a question that you pose to a database. Queries enable you to extract data from more than one related table by specifying the field information that is to be included in the query. For example, you could design the query to extract data related to specific products that you sell from a products table and also extract data from a suppliers table that provides information about the suppliers that provide you with your products. For queries to work, there needs be a relationship between the tables that you use in the query. So, you should have some familiarity with the database itself and how the database is structured before you attempt to create queries in Excel to access information in the database.

Microsoft Query enables you to connect to common data sources such as Access and Excel files and also dBASE files (dBASE was one of the first PC-based relational databases). You can also create queries to access data in a SQL Server database. After you create a query, you can then use the query in the future; the query can be used in other Excel worksheets and the query can be modified if needed. The data sources that you identify during the process of creating the query are also available in the future. This makes it easy to reconnect to a particular database or database server from Excel.

When you create a new query, you must identify or create a data source for the query first. You can then create the query using the Query Wizard. Let's look at creating a new data source and then walk through creating a query with the Query Wizard.

 note

You can also import XML files into Excel; the From Other Sources gallery provides the From XML Data Import command.

Creating a Data Source

Creating a data source establishes a connection to the database you use when you create your query. To open the Choose Data Source dialog box, select the From Other Sources command and then select From Microsoft Query.

The Choose Data Source dialog box opens. The Databases tab of the Choose Data Source dialog box provides you with four options in terms of database sources: New Data Source, dBase Files, Excel Files, or MS Access Database. Excel can retrieve data from a number of database types, including dBase, Microsoft FoxPro, Microsoft SQL Server, Oracle, and Paradox.

The Choose Data Source dialog box is designed to allow you to create a query for a new data source, such as a dBase or FoxPro or one of the other database platforms previously mentioned. So, to begin

the process of creating the new query, select <New Data Source> and then click OK. The Create New Data Source dialog box opens. The Create New Data Source dialog box walks you through the steps in creating the new data source.

The first step you must perform in the Create New Data Source dialog box is to enter a descriptive name for the data source. Create a name for the source that makes it apparent what database platform you are accessing and the database you will use in the query. After you have named the data source, select a driver for the type of database you want to access. You can choose a driver for a large number of different database types, including those we have already mentioned in this section, such as dBASE, Access, FoxPro, SQL, and Oracle.

 note

ODBC stands for Open Database Connectivity and is a standard (supported by Microsoft) for accessing different database file types and platforms. It is ODBC that allows Microsoft Query to connect to different types of databases. Figure 15.21 shows the Create New Data Source dialog box and the list of database types.

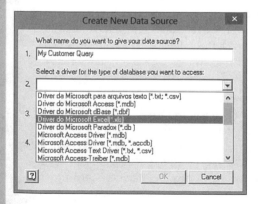

Figure 15.21
Select the driver type for the data source.

After you have selected the driver for the data source, click the Connect button. What happens next depends on the driver you selected for the database. If you select a driver for a database file type, such as Access, dBASE, or Paradox, you need to specify the location of the file on your computer or network.

If you select a database type that is a hosted database service using server technology such as SQL or Oracle, you have to log on to the server. For example, if you select SQL Server as the driver type, when you click the Connect button in the Create New Data Source dialog box, the SQL Server Login dialog box opens. Provide your logon credentials in the SQL Server Login dialog box and then click OK to connect to the server. A SQL server can be the home for more than one database, so you may have to click the Options button to specify the database for your connection.

Creating the Query

After you have connected to your database, which can be your own Access database or a remote database on a SQL server, the Query Wizard opens, as shown in Figure 15.22.

Figure 15.22
The Query Wizard.

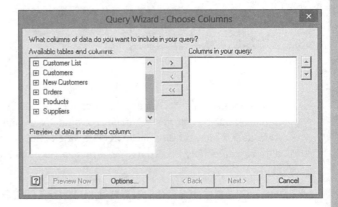

On the left of the Query Wizard dialog box is a list of the tables in the database. Expand a table and then choose specific fields that you want to serve as the columns in your query; select a field and then click the Add button to add it to the columns in your query list. You can use fields from multiple tables if required; it is important, however, that a relationship exist between the tables in the database.

If you attempt to create a query using fields from multiple tables that are not related, the Query Wizard requires that you create the joins between the tables. This would require that a key field in a table also exist as the foreign key in a second table for you to be able to create the relationship. This discussion is a little beyond the scope of this book, so I would say that if you are going to work with database tables in Excel, you should spend some time working with the databases in their native application (such as Access) to make sure you understand how relational databases work.

After you have specified the columns for your query, click Next. On the next screen, you can specify that the data be filtered by a particular field or fields, which establishes the row in the table that is created by the query. Set the filters for the query (if required) and then click Next. On the next screen, you can specify that the data be sorted by a field or fields. After specifying the sort fields and sort order, click Next.

The final Query Wizard screen enables you to save your query, so that it is available in the future in the Choose Data Source dialog box on the Query tab. Select Save Query and then use the Save As dialog box to name and save the query. You then return to the Query Wizard's Finish screen; click Finish. The Import Data dialog box opens, as shown in Figure 15.23.

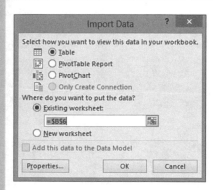

Figure 15.23
The Import Data dialog box.

You can import the data as a table or as a PivotTable Report (or as a PivotChart). The data can be imported into the current worksheet or a new worksheet. Specify the various options in the Import Data dialog box and then click OK. The data is imported into an Excel table. You can manipulate the data as you do any Excel data, including sorting and filtering.

Viewing and Refreshing Connections

If you are working with external data in Excel tables, you might want to view the connections for your Excel workbook. You can also refresh connections to take advantage of the fact that when the data source is updated, this information is also available in Excel after the link to the source has been refreshed.

To view the connections for the current Excel workbook, select the Connections command in the Connections group on the Ribbon's Data tab. The Workbook Connections dialog box opens, as shown in Figure 15.24.

You can refresh or remove a connection listed in the Workbook Connections dialog box. You can also set properties related to a particular connection such as the refresh properties for the source; click the Properties button to open the connection's Properties dialog box. The Usage tab enables you to specify refresh-related settings and also some formatting and drill-through (the number of records to retrieve) settings for OLAP (Online Analytical Processing) databases.

Although refresh options can be set for a data source using the connection's properties dialog box, you can also manually refresh the connections in the workbook or the current worksheet. Select the

Refresh All command to refresh all the connections in the workbook or only connections on the current worksheet.

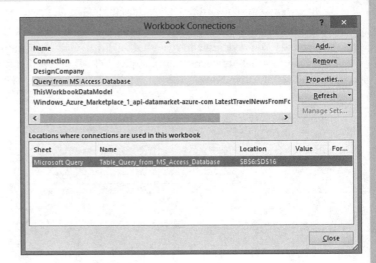

Figure 15.24
Workbook Connections dialog box.

Additional options related to the data source in the current worksheet can also be controlled via the External Data Properties dialog box, which is opened using the Properties command in the Connections group. You can control data formatting and layout features, such as preserving cell formatting and layouts. You can also specify what happens in the case of changes in data that affect the number of rows in the table (which typically relate to the adding or deleting of records in the data source).

Working with PivotTables

PivotTables enable you to analyze and summarize table data. You can use an Excel PivotTable to create a report for a table that you created in a worksheet and you can also create a PivotTable from data that you import into an Excel worksheet, such as an Access database table or a table from another data source. A PivotTable can even be used to analyze data that you imported into Excel using Microsoft Query.

An Excel PivotTable is called a PivotTable because it enables you to arrange table data in a cross-tabulated report. You can pivot or rearrange the information in the PivotTable to analyze the data it contains. You not only determine which table fields are used as row and column headings in the PivotTable, but you also specify fields that contain the values you want to analyze and summarize using the PivotTable. PivotTables can also specify fields that serve as filters for the data that is summarized in the PivotTable.

To take advantage of what a PivotTable can do with table data, you need a source table that has certain attributes. The table that you specify as the data source for the PivotTable needs to contain at least one field in the table (meaning a column of data in the table) that contains repeating data. For example, you might have a table that shows the weekly sales for your sales force. A column in the table lists the product names that have been sold. Because your salespeople sell the same products, there are repeated product names in the Product column.

Another requirement for a PivotTable is that the source table contains at least one field that consists of values. You need numerical data if the PivotTable is going to provide you with summary information, such as subtotals and totals. Figure 15.25 shows a simple table that benefits from being analyzed using a PivotTable.

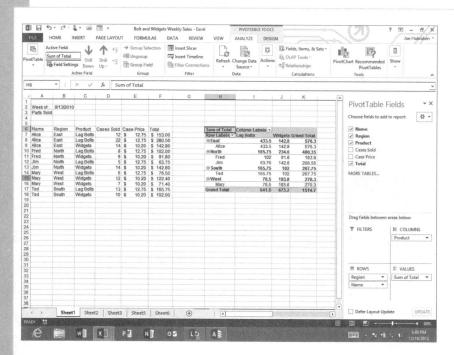

Figure 15.25
PivotTables enable you to analyze table data.

Figure 15.25 shows the source table on the left of the worksheet and the PivotTable is directly to the right of the source table. The PivotTable Field List (the task pane on the right side of the Excel window) provides the Field Section (a list of the fields in the source table) and the Areas Section, which provides the different areas of the PivotTable.

The row labels for the PivotTable, which are contained in the Row Labels section of the PivotTable task pane, are the Region entries followed by the Name column. The regions can then be expanded or collapsed to show or hide the name of the sales representatives in the region, respectively.

The column labels, which have been added to the Column Labels area, consist of the products listed in the source table's Product field. The Total field has been added to the Values area section. The fields placed in the Values area are automatically acted on by the PivotTable, and by default sums are provided for the values. The subtotals provided by the PivotTable enable you to see how each salesperson did on each product item, and the PivotTable can also be collapsed by region to view the region subtotals only.

You can quickly rearrange the field information that you have placed into the various areas of the PivotTable task pane to quickly pivot the data shown in the PivotTable. You can also remove fields or add fields—whatever it takes to enable you to see the data in the PivotTable as you require.

Excel provides you with two options for creating a new PivotTable. You can create a PivotTable from scratch (which we discuss in detail in a moment) or you can insert a recommended PivotTable. Recommended PivotTables are a new feature in Excel 2013. Using the recommended PivotTables is a good way to get familiar with how PivotTables are structured and how they can be used to create different "views" of the same data. Let's take a look at how to insert a recommended PivotTable and then look at inserting your own PivotTable.

> **note**
>
> Specifying row labels, column labels, and values is straightforward. Specifying a report filter can be a little confusing. Think of the report filter as a field or fields that you want to use to see a subset of the data. For example, if you have sales representatives names set as your row labels, you could then use a grouping field such as region to quickly filter the data by including the region field in the Report Filter area. Slicers also enable you to filter data, so you might find slicers even more useful than filters.

Using the Recommended PivotTables Command

The Recommended PivotTables command is in the Insert tab's Tables group. Although you can specify the data source for a recommended PivotTable, the Recommended PivotTables command works best (and fast) when you are on a sheet that contains a table and you have already selected the table range that you want to use as the data source for the PivotTable. Then all you have to do is select Recommended PivotTables. This opens the Recommended PivotTables dialog box, as shown in Figure 15.26.

The Recommended PivotTables dialog box provides a list of recommended PivotTables on the left. Select one of the thumbnails to preview it. When you have found the recommended PivotTable that you want to insert, click OK. The PivotTable is inserted into a new sheet. The PivotTable Fields task pane also opens to the right of the new PivotTable. You can manipulate an inserted recommended PivotTable as you would a PivotTable you create from scratch, which is our next subject.

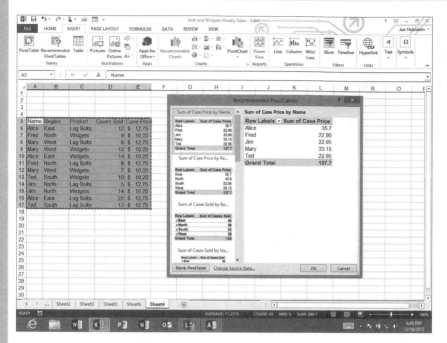

Figure 15.26
Quickly insert a
PivotTable based on a
selected table using
the Recommended
PivotTables command.

Creating a PivotTable

You can also create a new PivotTable using the Create PivotTable dialog box, which is opened using the PivotTable command on the Ribbon's Insert tab. You can insert a PivotTable on the current worksheet or on a new worksheet.

The PivotTable can use a table on a worksheet in the current Excel workbook as the data source or you can connect to an external data source. The real nuts-and-bolts portion of the PivotTable creation process relates to the field placement in the PivotTable. You need to determine the fields that serve as rows headings, column headings, and values to be acted on by the PivotTable. The great thing about the PivotTable is that you can quickly rearrange the field placement and look at the data in a number of different ways.

It makes sense to get your table in shape before you create the PivotTable, although you can edit a table and update the associated PivotTable or PivotTables (yes, you can have multiple PivotTables for a single data source). If you are going to use an external data source, use the Get External Data commands on the Data tab to connect to the data source. This enables you to spend some time looking over the data before you create the PivotTable.

You can create a PivotTable from any data source connection, even data connections in other workbooks. However, I think it is easier to create the PivotTable based on a table (external data or something you have input in Excel) that you can see on a worksheet in the current workbook. To insert a PivotTable, follow these steps:

1. On the Ribbon's Insert tab, select PivotTable and then click PivotTable on the gallery provided. The Create PivotTable dialog box opens, as shown in Figure 15.27.

Figure 15.27
Specify the table range and the PivotTable location in the Create PivotTable dialog box.

2. To create the PivotTable from a table or range on the current worksheet or in the current workbook, click on the Table/Range box and then select the range. If you are going to use an external data source, click the Use an External Data Source option button and then click the Choose Connection button. In the Existing Connections dialog box, select a data source and then click Open.

3. After you have specified the range for the PivotTable or specified a connection, select either the New Worksheet or Existing Worksheet option button to specify where the PivotTable is created. In the case of the Existing Worksheet option, also specify a location for the PivotTable. All you need to do is select the cell that serves as the upper-left corner for the PivotTable.

4. Click OK and the new PivotTable's blank frame is inserted into the current worksheet or a new worksheet. The PivotTable Fields task pane also opens on the right of the Excel window, as shown in Figure 15.28.

5. The PivotTable Fields task pane is used to specify the data source table fields that are used in the PivotTable. Select the fields that you want to add to the PivotTable report. You can drag the field names to the different report areas or you can click in an area and then select the check box next to a field. As you specify the fields for the PivotTable, the PivotTable begins to appear on the sheet.

Remember that a PivotTable is meant to provide you with a dynamic report. If the field arrangement that you have specified for the PivotTable isn't working, or you want to rearrange the fields, you can do so in the PivotTable Fields task pane. When you have finished working with the fields, you can close the PivotTable Fields task pane.

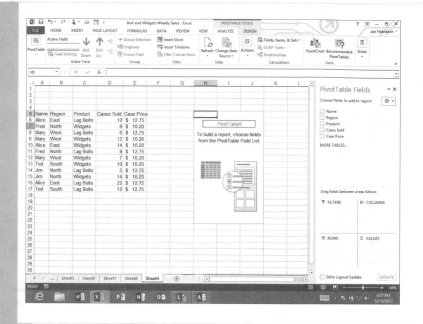

Figure 15.28
PivotTable Fields task pane.

The PivotTable contains Expand and Shrink buttons as well as drop-down lists for the column and row labels. You can use the field drop-down lists to sort or filter the data in the PivotTable. Figure 15.29 shows the list provided for the row labels.

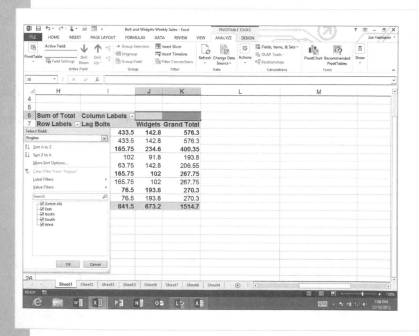

Figure 15.29
A field's drop-down list.

The list enables you to change the sort order of the selected field and to also select the field value (or values) that you want to use to filter the PivotTable. You can use the Select field drop-down box to toggle between the fields that serve as row or column labels as needed.

Working with the PivotTable Tools

When you select a cell in the PivotTable, the PivotTable Tools become available on the Ribbon. There is an Options tab and a Design tab. The Options tab enables you to specify PivotTable and field settings, and to specify how values are summarized and are shown. The Design tab is dedicated to the layout of the PivotTable and enables you to apply styles to your PivotTable.

The PivotTable Tools Analyze Tab

The Analyze tab enables you to manipulate the fields in the table and also filter the data in the PivotTable; for example, you can insert a slicer for the PivotTable. You can use the Expand Entire Field or Collapse Entire Field commands in the Active Field group to expand or collapse the currently selected field or fields as needed.

The Group commands allow you to group a selection of fields and then ungroup them if needed. The Filter group contains the Insert Slicer and Insert Timeline command. We look at inserting slicers in a moment. The Insert Timeline command is interesting in that it allows you to filter the data in a PivotTable so that only the data that falls within the date range you have specified on the Timeline slicers shows in the PivotTable. Figure 15.30 shows a PivotTable and a Timeline slicer for that PivotTable. Selecting a date range on the Timeline slicer hides the data that does not fall within that time range.

Figure 15.30
A Timeline slicer allows you to filter PivotTable data.

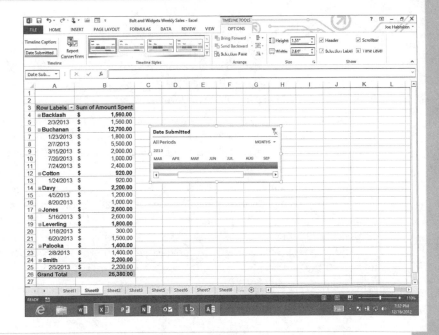

The Analyze tab also provides the Data group that supplies you with commands that enable you to refresh the data source for the PivotTable or to change the data source. The Actions group provides commands that allow you to clear or move the PivotTable and to select elements of the table such as values and labels.

If you need to access the PivotTable Fields task pane (or Field List as it is also known), select the Show command in the Show group and select Field List. The Show command also provides access to the Buttons command and the Field Headers command. The Buttons command allows you to toggle the Expand and Collapse buttons in a PivotTable on or off. The field Headers button toggles the field headers on or off.

The PivotTable Tools Design Tab

The PivotTable Tools Design tab enables you to manipulate the layout of your calculated fields and to also assign styles to the PivotTable. The Layout group provides the Subtotals, Grand Totals, Report Layout, and Blank Rows commands.

The Subtotals command enables you to hide the subtotals or to specify that the subtotals appear at the bottom (the default) or top of a group in the PivotTable. The Grand Totals command enables you to turn the grand totals off or on for rows and columns or specify that grand totals are shown only for the rows or columns only in the PivotTable. The Report Layout command enables you to choose from a number of different formats for the PivotTable, such as Compact, Outline, and Tabular. The Blank Rows command is used to insert or remove blank lines after each item in the PivotTable.

The PivotTable Styles gallery provides a number of different styles that can be applied to the PivotTable. If you apply a particular style, you can then use the PivotTable Style Options check boxes to hide or show elements such as row headers, column headers, or banded rows and columns.

Using Slicers

We already addressed slicers earlier in this chapter when we applied slicers to a table. You can also use slicers to filter the data in a PivotTable. A slicer is an easily accessible workspace object that resides on the sheet with the PivotTable. You can select and deselect items on the slider to quickly filter the PivotTable using different data parameters.

You can create multiple slicers for a PivotTable. For example, you could create a slicer that filters row data and a slicer that filters column data. To create a new slicer, select the Insert Slicer command on the PivotTable Tools Analyze tab. The Insert Slicers dialog box opens and shows all the fields available to your PivotTable.

A slicer can filter the data in the PivotTable by only a single field. However, you can create multiple slicers by selecting more than one field in the Insert Slicers dialog box. After selecting a field (for a single slicer) or multiple fields (for multiple slicers), click OK. The new slicer (or slicers) appears on the current worksheet. The slicer lists the field values in the field that you selected in the Insert Slicers dialog box. Select a particular field value to filter the PivotTable by that value. To remove the filter, click the remove filter icon in the upper-right corner of the slicer's frame.

When you have a slicer selected, the Slicer Tools Options tab becomes available on the Ribbon. You can use the styles available and the size settings to format the slicer. If you have multiple

PivotTables on a worksheet, you can associate the slicer with those PivotTables. This enables you to filter more than one PivotTable using a single slicer. Select the PivotTable Connections command and the PivotTables Connections dialog box opens. Select the PivotTables listed in the dialog box that you want to associate with the slicer. Then click OK to close the dialog box.

Slicers can be moved on the worksheet as needed, and you can also delete a slicer that you no longer need. Make sure that the slicer is selected and then press Delete on the keyboard.

 note

Slicers can also be used to filter data in a PivotChart. A PivotChart is a visualization of PivotTable data and can be quickly created via the PivotChart command on the PivotTable Tools Analyze tab.

VALIDATING AND ANALYZING WORKSHEET DATA

Excel provides you with very powerful capabilities for analyzing worksheet data. Even the most elegant data analysis, however, won't mean much if you have incorrect data in a worksheet.

In this chapter, we look at Excel's data validation features. You can create data validation rules that greatly cut down the possibility of data being entered into a worksheet incorrectly. We also discuss Excel's tools for analyzing worksheet data. We look at the data table feature and the Scenario Manager, which both provide you with the ability to do a what-if analysis of your worksheet data. Coverage is also provided of Goal Seek and Solver, both of which enable you to derive values based on a predefined goal.

Taking Advantage of Data Validation

Even a worksheet containing the best-built formulas and the most advanced Excel functions can still end up providing you with invalid results for the various sheet calculations. This is because people can make mistakes when entering the data into the worksheet. No matter how well designed the worksheet is, incorrect values in cells still render invalid results when they are acted upon by formulas and functions.

A strategy for greatly reducing the possibility of an invalid entry in a cell or cell range or a field column in an Excel table is to use data validation rules. Data validation simply means that the data entered into a cell range that has a validation rule applied to it must meet the criteria specified by the validation rule. For example, the validation criteria for a data validation rule might specify that only a date can be entered into the cell range to which you have applied the rule. You can then specify a valid range of dates that can be entered. For example, you might be creating a quarterly expense report for your sales force, and the only valid dates that can be entered into the range controlled by the validation rule are specified by a date range that you designate when you create the data validation rule.

You can also create validation rules that control the number of characters that can be entered into the cells in a particular range. For example, you might create a validation rule for a cell range where a U.S. state must be entered and you want the state to always be entered using the two-character state abbreviation; the validation rule can limit the text length in the cell range to two text characters (such as IN or ME).

A validation rule can do more than limit entries to a specific length, however. You also can create a validation rule that allows only entries from a list of values that has been entered in a range elsewhere on the sheet. For example, if you have sales regions such as north, south, east and west, you can specify in the validation rule that only these entries are valid in the Region column. The rule wouldn't negate someone entering the wrong region in a cell, but it greatly limits (by virtue of the validation list) what can be entered into the cells "controlled" by the validation rule.

Data validation rules can help you when you are inputting data into a worksheet that you use only occasionally or a large worksheet where it might be difficult to concentrate on what needs to be input into a particular range of cells. The validation rule can provide an input message that clearly tells you what a valid entry would be for each cell in the range. In cases when incorrect data is entered into a cell in a range that is governed by a validation rule, the validation rule can also provide an incorrect data message that alerts you to the incorrect entry and provides help on the data that can be entered into the cell.

Data validation can also be extremely useful in situations where you design a worksheet that is used by co-workers, colleagues, or subordinates. Creating data validation rules can help make sure that whoever ends up entering information into the worksheet does it correctly.

 note

You can create validation rules for any worksheet. This includes ranges in a worksheet that you have formatted as tables. When creating rules in tables, you need to select only a field column heading to apply the rule to all the cells in that particular column.

Specifying Validation Criteria

Creating a validation rule is straightforward. You specify the criteria for the rule and then you have the option of also providing an input message and an error alert for the rule. The Data Validation command is in the Data Tools group on the Ribbon's Data tab.

To create a new data validation rule, select the cell range to which you will apply the rule. On the Ribbon's Data tab, select the Data Validation command and then select Data Validation. The Data Validation dialog box opens.

The criterion for the validation rule is specified on the Settings tab. The Allow drop-down list provides the following options:

- **Any Value:** The default setting has no restrictions. So, why is it even available? You can create a validation rule that doesn't restrict data input but provides an input message as a way to coach users to place certain data in a range of cells. Using this criterion does not restrict users from entering whatever they want in the cell, however.

- **Whole Number:** Select this setting to restrict the data entry to numerical values with no decimals.

- **Decimal:** This setting restricts data entry to numerical values but allows decimals.

- **List:** This setting restricts the data entry to the entries that you specified in a list that you created elsewhere on the worksheet or workbook. Only the items in your list are considered valid entries in the cell range.

- **Date:** This setting allows only calendar dates to be entered into the cell range validated by the rule.

- **Time:** This setting restricts the data entry to time values.

- **Text Length:** This setting enables you to restrict the entry of text in the cell range by a specific number of characters.

- **Custom:** This setting enables you to use a formula (or function) as the criterion for data validation. For example, you might have a total budget for a project of $5,000.00. You can specify that the sum of the range of individual expenses entered in the cell range do not exceed 5,000; this would look something like =SUM(range of cells)<=5000. The cell range in the parentheses must be specified as absolute references for this scenario to work. You can also use other functions, such as the IF function, to validate whether an entry is true or false based on the condition set up in the IF function. Create the formula or function in a cell in the worksheet and then specify the cell's address when you specify the custom criterion.

Select the Allow criterion that you want to use for the validation rule. If you select Whole Number, Decimal, Date, or Time, you have the option of setting up a conditional statement for the rule. You can select from a number of different inequality statements, including Between, Not Between, Equal To, Less Than, and the like using the Data drop-down list.

For example, if you select Between, you then need to provide the starting and ending value for the allowed range of data entries. Figure 16.1 shows the Data Validation dialog box with the Settings tab selected.

Figure 16.1
The Settings tab of the Data Validation dialog box.

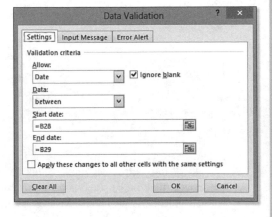

In Figure 16.1, the Allow setting is configured as Date. The Data option has been set to Between, which requires that a start date and end date be specified for the allowed data range.

When you use inequality statements such as between or greater than, you can specify the date, time, or numerical value by typing the value in the text boxes provided at the bottom of the Data Validation dialog box. For example, you could type the start date and end date for the allowed range.

You do have another alternative for providing the start and stop values of an allowed range when you use between or another inequality expression such as greater than; you can specify the start and stop values for the allowed range by specifying cell addresses in the worksheet that provide the values. For example, you might put the start date and end date in cells in the worksheet and then specify these values by entering the appropriate cell address in the Start Date and End Date text boxes.

 tip

You can use the =TRIM function to keep users from inadvertently adding leading or trailing spaces to text entries in a cell. This is useful when employee numbers (which are not values) or other identifying information needs to be entered in a cell range. The Custom criterion formula would be =cell range =TRIM (cell range). Both references to the cell range must be made absolute references for this to work.

Configuring Input Messages and Error Alerts

After you have configured the validation criteria for the data validation rule, you can configure an optional input message and error alert for the rule. The input message is specified on the Input Message tab of the Data Validation dialog box.

The input message is made up of a title and an input message. Figure 16.2 shows the Input Message tab of the Data Validation dialog box.

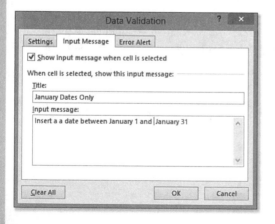

Figure 16.2
Enter an input message for the validation rule.

The input message is designed so that it appears when you or another user click on a cell that has been assigned the data validation rule. The more specific you are when entering the input message, the easier it is for users to comply with the validation rule as they enter data.

You can also configure an error alert for the validation rule. The purpose of the error alert is to give the user some sort of direction in terms of correcting the entry of invalid data. Figure 16.3 shows the Error Alert tab of the Data Validation dialog box.

Figure 16.3
Create an error alert for the validation rule.

Error alerts can be configured so that they provide different levels of protection in terms of whether invalid data is even allowed to be entered into the cell. Three different error alert styles are provided as follows:

- **Stop:** This error message style provides an error message box that enables you to retry or to cancel the entry. Data that violates the rule cannot be entered into the cell range assigned this rule.

- **Warning:** This error message style provides a warning box. The user has the option to continue by selecting Yes. This means that incorrect data can be entered in the cell range. The user is also provided the option of selecting No or Cancel in the warning box, which removes the entry from the cell.

- **Information:** This error message style provides an informational box. Incorrect data can be entered in the cell and all you have to do is click OK in the message box. You can retry the entry by clicking Cancel.

It makes sense to use the Stop error message style when it is imperative that data entered in a cell range be completely valid as dictated by the validation rule. You can make use of the Warning and Information styles when you want to suggest how data be entered in a cell range, but it isn't crucial that data be entered in a form other than that dictated by the validation rule.

When you have completed configuring the validation rule, click OK to close the Data Validation dialog box. You can now enter data into the range governed by the validation rule.

If you decide that you want to remove a validation rule from a cell range, select the range and then select the Data Validation command to open the Data Validation dialog box. You can clear the rule by clicking Clear All on any of the dialog box tabs.

Circling Invalid Data

If you create validation rules that use the Warning and Information error message styles, users can potentially insert invalid data into the range where you have applied the validation rule. Users can also use the Clipboard to paste information into a cell, bypassing a validation rule.

You can circle the invalid data that appears in a cell range where a validation rule has been applied. Figure 16.4 shows invalid data that has been circled in a worksheet.

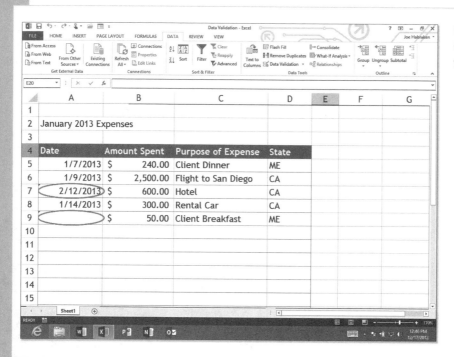

Figure 16.4
Circle invalid data in a worksheet.

To circle invalid data, select the Data Validation command and then select Circle Invalid Data. Any cells that contain invalid data and are governed by a validation rule are circled. You can correct the cell entries as needed. To remove the validation circles from the worksheet, select the Data Validation command and then select Clear Validation Circles.

You can also do error checking related to your validation rules via the Error Checking command in the Formula Auditing command group on the Formulas tab. The Error Checking dialog box flags validation errors as you use it to move through a worksheet. More about the auditing tools is discussed in Chapter 13, "Getting the Most from Formulas and Functions."

➡ *For information on error checking, **see** "Using the Auditing Tools," **p. 398**.*

Performing a What-If Analysis

Excel provides you with the ability to perform a what-if analysis on worksheet data. An analysis of the data in a worksheet can really be approached in two different ways: manipulating values to affect outcomes or specifying an outcome such as a required net profit, and allowing Excel to determine the values required to give you the desired outcome.

As already mentioned, the first possibility for conducting a what-if analysis consists of varying key values in a worksheet, which enables you to see how these changes to the key values affect the result of a particular formula or function. For example, you might want to analyze how different variable costs, such as marketing and supplies, affect your net profits.

There are two different ways to perform a what-if analysis where you specify changes to key values to affect the results of formulas or functions (meaning the outcomes). A data table enables you to vary one or two input values. The changes in input are then reflected in the results of formulas or functions also included in the table.

The other possibility for performing a what-if analysis where key values are varied to provide different calculated outcomes is the scenario. Scenarios enable you to create different versions of the same worksheet where certain values in the worksheet are changed. Each scenario then provides a different outcome. For example, you might be selling your house and the only variables that are fluid are the sales price that you get and the real-estate broker's fee. You can create different scenarios that show different sales prices and broker's fees to see the different possible profits you might make on the sale of your home.

The other approach to analyzing data is to specify an outcome and then work backward (sort of a reverse what-if analysis) to see what key values must be in the worksheet to get the desired outcome. For example, you might want to save 200 dollars a month in an IRA. You can do a worksheet that shows your monthly income and fixed monthly expenses (such as your mortgage). You can also include expenses that are not fixed, such as entertainment and travel, and allow Excel to determine how much you can spend on these variable costs and still sock away the desired amount of money in your retirement fund each month.

There are two different tools that enable you to start with an outcome value (the result of a formula or function) and then work backward to determine what key values must be to get the desired results. Goal Seek enables you to determine the value that you need in an input cell to get a desired result. The other tool is the Solver add-in, which can be used to help you find an optimum value in relation to limitations that are provided by the values in other cells in the worksheet, such as the fixed and variable expenses that we discussed in relation to specifying a monthly contribution to your IRA account.

The Goal Seek tool is limited to determining one key value. Solver can help you determine the value for more than one variable based on a desired result.

Let's look at working with data tables and the Scenario Manager to determine how changes in values affect outcomes. We can then look at how you can work backward from a particular outcome and determine the values necessary to reach your specified goal.

Creating a Data Table

Creating a data table is a straightforward way to vary one or two values involved in a worksheet calculation (or calculations) and then view the results based on the changes that were made to the value (or values). Data tables are a quick way to see how a single varied input cell affects calculations performed by formulas or functions. If you are going to tackle multiple variables for a what-if analysis, it probably makes more sense to use the Scenario Manager, which we discuss in the next section. So, the discussion that follows looks at how to create a one-value data table.

The data table is really an addition to your worksheet. The first thing that you need to do is create the worksheet that contains the values, formulas, and functions that provide you with results.

For example, let's say that you want to see how different automobile values (ranging from $14,000 to $25,000) affect your monthly payment when you have a four-year loan (48 months) with a fixed interest rate of 6%. You can use the PMT function to quickly calculate the monthly payment at $14,000 by using the Functions Arguments dialog box to specify the cell location for the Rate (divided by 12 for monthly payments), Nper (the term in months), and Pv (the present value or cost of the car).

When you have your simple worksheet complete and it is returning results from the formulas or functions you placed in the worksheet, you can build the data table as an accessory to the worksheet. Placement of the data table isn't really crucial, but the layout of the data table certainly is. Figure 16.5 shows a simple car loan worksheet that uses the PMT function in cell D9.

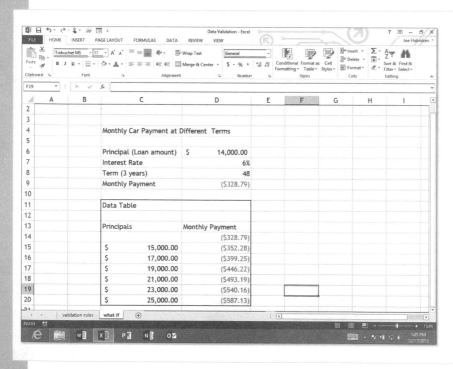

Figure 16.5
Create a data table for your what-if analysis.

The leftmost column of the data table is where you can place range of values that serve as the values that replace the original input cell in your worksheet. In our example, the input cell is the principal for the loan, which is in cell D6 of the worksheet. The values in the data table that you use to replace the input value are in the range C15:C20.

Leave a blank cell between the first value in the leftmost column of the data table and the heading for that column. In Figure 16.5, the blank cell is C14.

The top row of the data table is where you reference any formulas or functions in your worksheet that you want to calculate different results based on the range of possibilities provided in the first column of the data table. In our example, the worksheet contains only one function in cell D9. You reference this function in the top row of the data table (Row 14) by typing an equal sign in cell D14 and then clicking on cell D9. This places =D9 in cell D14 and is basically a pointer to cell D9, which contains the PMT function.

After you have the data table set up, you can have Excel work its magic and calculate the different monthly payments for each of the principal values that you have input in the data table. Select the empty cell above your range of different principals (input values) and make sure that the selection range includes all the cells to the right of the input values, including the cell that references the function (or functions) back in the worksheet. In the example shown in Figure 16.6, the data table range would be C14:D20. After you have selected the cells in the data table, select the What-If Analysis command on the Data tab and then select Data Table. The Data Table dialog box opens, as shown in Figure 16.6.

 note

Think of the data as a cross-tabulated report. The range of different values is placed in the first column of the table and, in the case of a two-variable input table, also in the first row of the table. The results in the table then relate to the formulas or functions that act on the variable data ranges.

Figure 16.6
The data table and the Data Table dialog box.

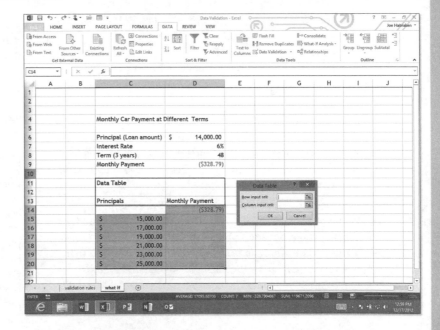

In the Data Table dialog box, you specify the row input cell and/or the column input cell. When you are using only one variable for the data table, as we have in the example provided here, only the Column Input cell needs to be specified. This would be cell D6 where the principal for the loan was specified in the worksheet.

After specifying the input cell addresses, click OK. The values appear in the data table. After you get a feel for the general layout of a data table, you can use it with worksheets that contain more than one formula or function. The great thing about a data table is it provides you with a whole range of possible values based on the varied input values.

Creating Scenarios

The Scenario Manager enables you to create different scenarios or models of what the results might be in a worksheet when different values are placed in key cells in the worksheet. For example, you might be selling your house and want to calculate different scenarios related to the profit that you will make. Two key values related to calculating your net profit that might be variable are the real estate broker's commission and the actual sales price of the home.

You can put your data (and appropriate formulas and/or functions) in a worksheet that provides baseline calculations. For example, in the case of the home sale, you would create a worksheet that calculates your net profit on the sale based on your costs related to the sale and a specific sales price for the house. The worksheet can be structured to provide the most realistic calculation of the net profit for the sale.

You can then create different scenarios that enable you to see how changes in the sales price and brokerage fees (let's say you are talking to different agents who charge different percentages) affect the amount of money you walk away with at closing. For example, you could create a scenario that provides the best-case scenario where you are paying the lowest brokerage fee but selling your house for the highest possible price. You might also create a worst-case scenario that shows your net profit when you sell your house for a lower sales price and pay a higher brokerage fee.

Each scenario created provides you with a different potential outcome. When you create scenarios, you can vary a number of data values in a worksheet to view different potential outcomes for the formulas and functions that are affected by the changing cells you specify for the worksheet's scenarios.

To create scenarios for a worksheet, build a worksheet as you would any other worksheet. Enter your data, formulas, and functions. When you are ready to begin the scenario creation process, select the What-If Analysis command on the Data tab and then select Scenario Manager—the Scenario Manager dialog box opens. Click the Add button to create a new scenario. The Add Scenario dialog box opens, as shown in Figure 16.7.

 note

You can specify up to 32 changing cells for a scenario, meaning you can vary the values in 32 different cells in a worksheet for your what-if analysis.

 tip

If you are working with a large number of changing cells for your scenario, you might want to name those cells and then specify the Changing Cells addresses using the cell names rather than the cell addresses. This helps you keep the different values you're working with straight as you specify the different values for each scenario.

Figure 16.7
The Add Scenario dialog box.

Enter a name for the scenario in the Scenario Name text box. Use a descriptive name for the scenario because you might create multiple scenarios for the worksheet. For example, you might name the scenario "best case" if you will provide values for the changing cells that are optimum values. You might also name the scenario "most likely" or "reality" if you will provide values for the changing cells that are extremely realistic.

The most important aspect of creating the new scenario is to specify the cells in the worksheet that serve as the changing cells for the scenario. The changing cells are the cells in the worksheet that can be varied. In our home sale example, the sales price of the house and the broker's fee were both considered values that could be changed and so the cells in the worksheet that contain these values would be listed in the Changing Cells text box.

Select the changing cells as needed. To select a contiguous range, drag with the mouse. You can select noncontiguous cells by selecting the first cell and then holding down the Ctrl key as you select other cells. Cell addresses inserted into the Changing Cells text box are specified as absolute references.

When you have provided the name and changing cells (there is also an optional Comment text box), click OK. The Scenario Values dialog box opens, as shown in Figure 16.8.

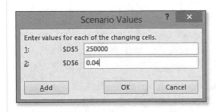

Figure 16.8
The Scenario Values dialog box.

Enter a value for each of the changing cells that you specified in the Add Scenario dialog box in the Scenario Values dialog box. When you have completed entering the values, click OK.

The Add Scenario dialog box opens; create your next scenario for the worksheet. This cycle continues (Add Scenario dialog box to Scenario Values dialog box) as you create each additional scenario. When you finish creating all of the scenarios for the worksheet, click Cancel to close the Add Scenario dialog box.

Viewing Scenarios and Creating Reports

You can view the scenarios that you create for your worksheet by using the Scenario Manager. The Scenario Manager not only enables you to quickly plug the changing cells values into your worksheet based on each scenario that you created, but you can also add additional scenarios or edit or delete existing scenarios.

To open the Scenario Manager, select the What-If Analysis command and then select Scenario Manager. The Scenario Manager lists all the scenarios that you have created for the worksheet, as shown in Figure 16.9.

Figure 16.9
The Scenario Manager dialog box.

To view the results of a particular scenario in your worksheet, select the scenario in the Scenarios list and then click the Show button. The results of formulas and functions in the worksheet are recalculated based on the values for changing cells specified in the scenario. You can select any of the scenarios and quickly view the outcomes provided by that specific scenario.

The Scenario Manager dialog box not only provides you with the ability to view the results provided by each scenario and manage your scenarios (such as edit or delete scenarios), but it also provides you with the ability to create reports or summaries of the scenarios that you have created for a worksheet.

The summary of the worksheet scenarios that you have built can take the form of a scenario summary that lists each scenario and the changing values provided by the scenario. Summary information includes the results of formulas or functions in the worksheet that were affected by the changing cells specified for the scenarios. Figure 16.10 shows a scenario summary for a worksheet that had three different scenarios.

Figure 16.10
A scenario summary for a worksheet with multiple scenarios.

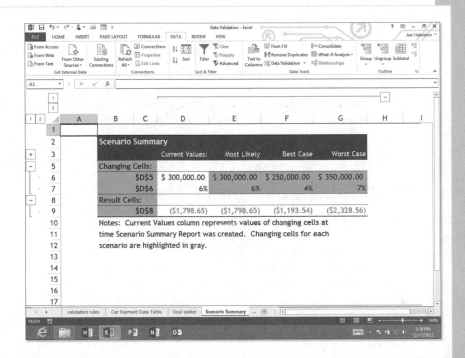

The summary lists the changing cells and specifies how result cells were affected by the changing cells in each scenario. The result cells are the cell addresses for the cells that contain the formulas or functions affected by the changing cells.

Your scenario summary can also take the form of a PivotTable report. The PivotTable report enables you to sort and filter the data provided in the report as you would data in any Excel PivotTable. The PivotTable report can be useful when you have a large number of different changing cells in your worksheet scenarios and the changing cells affect a number of different cells containing the results of formulas or functions.

➡ *For information on using PivotTables, **see** Chapter 15, "Using Excel Tables and PivotTables."*

To create a new scenario summary from the Scenario Manager dialog box, click the Summary button. The Scenario Summary dialog box opens, as shown in Figure 16.11.

Figure 16.11
The Scenario Summary dialog box.

Select the report type: Scenario Summary or Scenario PivotTable Report. In the Result Cells text box, specify the cells that contain results (formulas and functions) that are affected by changing cells in your scenarios. When you click OK, the report is created on a new worksheet.

 note

If multiple copies of a particular worksheet exist (in different workbooks) and different users have created scenarios for that worksheet, you can merge the scenarios into a single worksheet using the Merge command in the Scenario Manager dialog box.

Using Goal Seek and Solver

As mentioned earlier in this chapter, Excel also provides two other analysis tools: Goal Seek and Solver. Goal Seek is designed to work backward from a desired outcome. Goal Seek determines that value that is required for a particular input cell to get a specific result in a dependent formula or function. Goal Seek is designed to help you determine the value of only one input cell involved in the calculation, so although it can be extremely useful, it is also fairly limited.

Solver, which is an Excel add-in, provides you with the ability to find the required value for a number of input cells involved in a predetermined calculation result. So, Solver can be used in situations where you want to determine the value for more than one input cell involved in the calculation result provided by a dependent formula or function.

Working with Goal Seek

To use Goal Seek, create your worksheet, including the formula or function that is dependent on the input value that Goal Seek determines for you. For example, let's say that you put together a worksheet that uses the FV (Future Value) financial function to determine how much you need to put into an investment account each month over a 10-year period to end up with 20,000 dollars in the account when you are getting a 3% annual interest rate.

The FV function uses the format =FV(Rate, NPER, PMT) where the Rate is the interest rate, the NPER is the total number of payments, and PMT is the payment made each period. You want Goal Seek to determine the PMT because you already know the interest rate (3%) and the number of payments, which is 120 (12 monthly payments × 10 years).

➡ *For more information on using financial functions,* **see** *"Financial Functions," **p. 388**.*

After you have your worksheet set up, all you need to do is give Goal Seek three pieces of information: the cell address, the desired goal amount for the dependent, and the changing cell address for which Goal Seek determines the value. Select the What-If Analysis command and then select Goal Seek. The Goal Seek dialog box opens, as shown in Figure 16.12.

Figure 16.12
The Goal Seek dialog box.

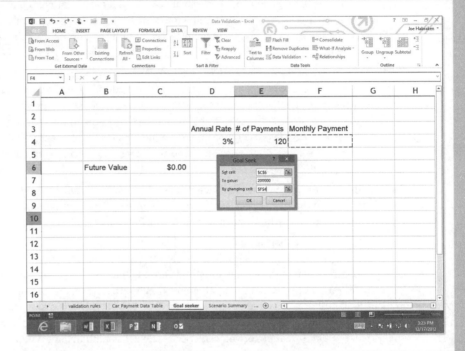

Specify the Set Cell address, which is the cell containing the formula or function. Enter the desired goal for the value in the To Value text box. Specify the address of the cell for which Goal Seek determines a value in the By Changing Cell text box. Click OK, and Goal Seek determines the changing cell value and shows your goal value in the cell containing the formula or function.

The target value and found value (in the changing cell) are inserted into the worksheet. The Goal Seek Status dialog box opens, letting you know that Goal Seek found a solution. Click OK to close the Goal Seek Status dialog box.

In some cases, Goal Seek might not be able to find a value that provides you with the goal that you have specified. You can use the Goal Seek Status dialog box to step through the calculations to see where the problem might be or why Goal Seek was not able to arrive at a solution. If you are using Goal Seek in relatively simple worksheets that do not use a long change of calculations to arrive at a particular specified goal, Goal Seek is able to provide a solution in most cases.

Working with Solver

If you need to determine the values for multiple adjustable or changing cells based on a desired out-come, you can take advantage of Solver. Solver not only provides for multiple changing cells, but it also enables you to set constraints on the value that a changing cell can have to satisfy the desired outcome. This means that you could specify a value that a particular changing cell must be above or below when Solver determines the value for that cell based on the outcome value. Solver is (as is Goal Seek) an optimization tool and enables you to find the best solution in a worksheet that has obvious constraints on certain values. This can be useful when you want to optimize sales or pro-duction or find the best mix of variable values related to a particular outcome.

Before you take advantage of Solver, which is an Excel add-in, you need to enable it. Open the Excel Options window in the Backstage by selecting Options. In the Excel Options window, select Add-Ins. At the bottom of the Add-ins settings, select Excel Add-ins in the Manage drop-down list and then click Go. The Add-Ins dialog box opens, listing a selection of available add-ins, which includes Solver. Select the Solver Add-in check box and then click OK. Solver is added to an Analysis group available on the Ribbon's Data tab.

As with the other analysis tools we have discussed, such as scenarios and Goal Seek, you build your worksheet including the formulas and functions required. You can then put values in the cells that serve as changing cells when you configure Solver.

As already mentioned, Solver enables you to place constraints on the values allowed in a changing cell. For example, you might be looking at how you want to allocate your small business's monthly budget dollars based on the total budget and certain limitations you have set for budget line items, such as marketing or travel. Let's say that you would rather see more money go toward marketing in a particular month, so you are setting a ceiling on travel (which is also a changing cell). You can place the constraint amounts directly on the worksheet (in an area near the monthly budget work-sheet that you have created), or you can specify the constraint amount when you specify the con-straint in the Add Constraint dialog box (which is accessed via Solver).

Placing the constraint amounts on the worksheet itself means that you can always go back and change those amounts and then rerun Solver to see how changed constraints have affected the changing cell values that were used by Solver to adhere to your specified outcome. Solver can save its findings as scenarios, which you can then access as needed using the Scenario Manager.

To configure Solver, click the Solver command in the Analysis group. The Solver Parameters dialog box opens, as shown in Figure 16.13.

Click in the Set Objective text box and then click on the cell that provides the outcome for Solver to use to calculate the values of changing cells. If you want to maximize the set objective (such as maximize your profits), click the Max option button in the To area of the dialog box. You can also click the Min option button to minimize the value. If you want the set objective to be a specific amount, click the Value Of option button and specify the value for Solver to use as a goal.

In the By Changing Variable Cells text box, specify the cells that Solver can change as it attempts to reach your set objective. You can select a range of cells or select multiple noncontiguous cells by holding down the Ctrl key as you select each cell.

Figure 16.13
The Solver Parameters dialog box.

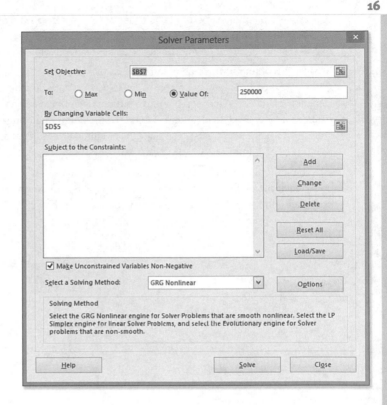

After you have the variable cells specified, you can set any constraints that should be applied to changing cells as Solver works to set values for your specified goal. To add a constraint, click the Add button. The Add Constraint dialog box opens. Specify the changing cell's address in the Cell Reference text box; you can then specify that the cell reference be less than or equal to, equal to, or adhere to another constraint parameter provided by the drop-down list.

In the Constraint text box, specify the value that should be used to constrain the changing cell. You can type the value in the Constraint text box or specify a cell address in the worksheet that contains the constraint value. For example, Figure 16.14 shows a constraint that specifies that the value in the changing cell F5 must be less than or equal to a constraint value specified in cell C14.

Figure 16.14
Create a Solver constraint in the Add Constraint dialog box.

You can add as many constraints as needed. All the constraints are listed in the Subject to the Constraints list in the Solver Parameters dialog box. Your constraints can be changed and deleted as needed using the Change and Delete buttons, respectively.

If you are working with some functions that use payments (which are considered negative numbers) or you want Solver to be able to make certain variables negative numbers, deselect the Make Unconstrained Variables Non-Negative option. Solver also provides you with different solving algorithms, such as the GRG Nonlinear, LOM Simplex, and Evolutionary Engines. For most financial and statistical functions, you can use the GRG Nonlinear default setting.

When you are ready to run Solver, click the Solver button. The Solver Results dialog box opens and lets you know whether Solver was able to find a solution. If you want to save a solution as a scenario, click the Save Scenario button. To keep the Solver solution and exit the Solver Results dialog box, click the Keep Solver Solution option button and then click OK.

REQUISITE POWERPOINT: ESSENTIAL FEATURES

Microsoft PowerPoint is the standard "visual aid" software application for providing informative presentations. Whether you are giving a presentation at an important business meeting or showing pictures of your latest journey to a group of travel enthusiasts, PowerPoint provides an easy-to-use yet powerful presentation platform. PowerPoint not only is a powerful tool for presenting "live," but it also is useful at demonstration tables and kiosks for playing self-running presentations.

In this chapter, we look at the essential tools and features of this powerful presentation application. As you get familiar with the PowerPoint interface and workspace, we also look at the basics of constructing a PowerPoint presentation, including the options for creating a new presentation. In addition, we spend time looking at how to best create and manipulate your presentation slides.

New Features in PowerPoint 2013

Microsoft PowerPoint 2013 builds on the changes and functional improvements that were part of the PowerPoint 2010 release. PowerPoint 2013 also provides some improvements that are certainly worth noting.

A new PowerPoint 2013 feature greets you as soon as you start the application. Instead of opening a new, blank presentation (as PowerPoint 2010 did), PowerPoint provides a new Start screen. This Start screen or Launch page gives you different possibilities for starting a new presentation or opening an existing presentation. Figure 17.1 shows the new Start screen.

You can start a new presentation by selecting one of the templates (including the Blank Presentation template) or themes provided on the

Start screen, or you can use the Search box at the top of the page to search for online templates and themes (we discuss the differences between templates and themes later in this chapter). Suggested searches are also provided on the Start screen, enabling you to quickly look for presentation templates or themes that fall into a particular category such as Business, Education, or Nature. The Start screen also provides the Open Other Presentations command, which enables you to open a recent presentation or browse your SkyDrive, computer, or other location for existing presentations.

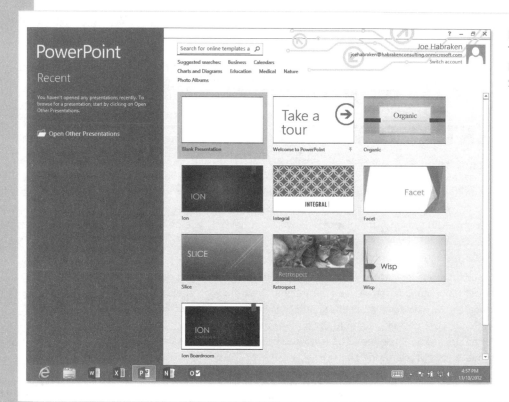

Figure 17.1
The new PowerPoint Start screen.

The Start screen is just one of the new or improved features in PowerPoint 2013. Other new PowerPoint feature additions or improvements include these:

■ **Widescreen capable:** PowerPoint 2013 is ready for widescreen presentations. Because most monitors are now widescreen (as is the aspect ratio for HD LCD video projectors), PowerPoint provides a Widescreen (16:9) slide size by default. If you are working on a standard monitor or plan to show your presentation on an older video projector, you can change the slide size back to the Standard (4:3) setting.

■ **Theme variants:** Themes have always been a great way to uniformly format the fonts and colors in the slides of a PowerPoint presentation. PowerPoint now provides theme variants, which make it easy for you to fine-tune the selected theme with different color possibilities. Themes and their variants work in both the Widescreen (16:9) and Standard (4:3) slide sizes.

- **Merge shapes:** PowerPoint has always made it easy to add simple shapes and SmartArt graphics to slides. You can now easily merge shapes from the Shapes gallery and create more complex objects. PowerPoint also provides inline guides that make it easy to position objects before you merge them.

- **Video and audio enhancements:** PowerPoint supports more video formats, including `.mov` and `.mp4`. A new audio feature enables you to select an audio file (such as a song) and have that audio play for the duration of the PowerPoint presentation. This is perfect for photomontage presentations, particularly self-running presentations that require no narration.

This is just a subset of the improvements in PowerPoint 2013. Other new features that we explore in the PowerPoint section of this book run the gamut of possibilities and include diverse tools such as the new eyedropper tool for color matching and the updated presenter view. Let's start our discussion of PowerPoint with a look at the different ways you can create a new presentation.

Options for Creating a New Presentation

PowerPoint provides different options for creating a new presentation. As already mentioned in this chapter, PowerPoint 2013 now opens a Start screen (look back at Figure 17.1) when you start the application. This screen provides different possibilities for starting a new presentation or opening an existing presentation. In previous versions of PowerPoint, a new blank presentation automatically opened in the PowerPoint workspace when you started the application.

The Start screen is similar to the New page in the PowerPoint Backstage (which is shown in Figure 17.2). The only difference between these two screens is that the Start screen provides a list of recent presentations and a link for opening other presentations (Open Other Presentations). The Start screen also does not provide access to the other Backstage pages (such as Open, Print, Share, and Export). You have to start a new presentation or open an existing presentation to get past the Start screen and on to the PowerPoint workspace.

The New page, which gives you the same possibilities for starting a new presentation as the Start screen, is accessed via Backstage by selecting File on the Ribbon and then New. So now that we've sorted out the Start screen and the New page, we can discuss the various options for creating a new presentation.

You can create a new presentation based on a template. A template is a presentation blueprint that provides a presentation theme, individual slides with specific slide layouts, and, in a number of cases, placeholder text and other design objects already on the individual slides. Templates provide the greatest amount of handholding in terms of placing content on the presentation slides and determining the type of information that should be available on each individual slide.

You can also create a new presentation based on a theme. A theme provides the font family, color scheme, and (typically) design elements for the slides in the presentation. PowerPoint 2013 now offers variations for many of the themes provided, expanding the color schemes available.

You can also create new presentations based on an existing presentation. This option opens a copy of an existing presentation, including the theme, slide layout, and slide content from the presentation. You can then edit the presentation copy as needed to create a new presentation.

Figure 17.2
The New page in the PowerPoint Backstage.

Obviously, creating a new blank presentation is always an option. Both the Start screen and the New page provide access to the Blank Presentation template. Creating a presentation from scratch using the Blank Presentation template gives you the most control over both the design elements of the presentation and the layout of individual slides (all items we discuss in the PowerPoint section of this book).

Let's take a more detailed look at the options for creating a new presentation. We start the discussion with a look at templates.

Using Templates

PowerPoint 2013 draws a fine line between what constitutes a template and what constitutes a theme. A template typically provides an overall "look" for a presentation (including screen colors and fonts, meaning a theme) and includes placeholder text on several sample slides. A template typically includes design elements on slides, which can be edited as needed. For example, a sample company logo on the master slide of the template can be replaced with your own logo. So templates were (and still are) a prepackaged presentation that you edit and add to, making it your own.

A theme has always been seen as a combination of font and color attributes that can be assigned to a presentation to provide uniform colors and fonts on each slide in the presentation. Both the Start screen and the Backstage's New page provide access to many possibilities for creating a new presentation. Most of the choices provided, such as Ion, Facet, Slice, and Dividend, are themes rather than full-blown templates. Some of these themes do provide page number or header and footer placement, which is typically something you see in the realm of the template. However, based on the fact that variants are provided for each of these new presentation possibilities, we are definitely looking at themes. So we need to find some templates if we are going to create a new presentation based on a template.

You can search for online templates (on Microsoft.com) using the Search box on either the Start screen or the New page. You can even create your own templates and then use them as starting material to create new presentations (we talk about creating a template in a moment). Click in the Search box and then type your search criteria. You can also select any of the suggested searches listed below the Search box. Figure 17.3 shows the results of an online search (using the search term "business plan").

The search results show all the templates available online that matched your search criteria. Some templates provide all the slides that you need for your presentation; all you have to do is customize them for your purpose. Other templates provide a few sample slides and the overall look for a presentation.

> **note**
>
> If you do a PowerPoint template search on your computer using the File Manager (search for `*.potx`), you will find that a few PowerPoint templates are installed on your computer in the `Program Files\ Microsoft Office 15\ Root\Templates\1033` folder (they are put there during the Office installation process). These installed templates (which don't show up on the Start screen or the New page) include QuizShow, Pitchbook, and Training.

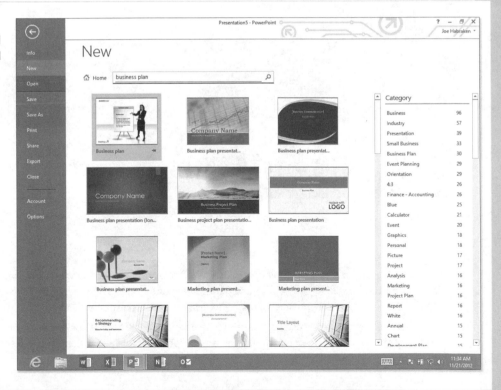

Figure 17.3
Do a keyword search to find PowerPoint templates online.

On the right side of the Search results is a Category list. The categories listed are keyword subsets of all the templates found using your search terms. Each category has a number to the right showing how many of the listed templates fall into the category.

You can view a subset of the search results by selecting a category. For example, if you know that you are going to be presenting on an older video projector, you can select the 4:3 category so that the search results list only templates that use the 4:3 standard slide size. You can also filter the search results by additional categories. For example, after selecting 4:3 in the Category list, you might select Chart and then Picture. You see a filtered list of the search results where the slides sized to 4:3; the

template includes at least one chart sample and at least one picture sample. If you want to remove a category filter or filters you have placed on the search results, click the Close button to the right of the selected filters (the "enabled" category filters appear at the top of the Category list and are highlighted in pink).

When you locate a presentation template in the search results that you want to check out, click the template's sample picture to see a preview of the presentation, as shown in Figure 17.4. To view more images of the template, use the navigation buttons at the bottom of the preview window.

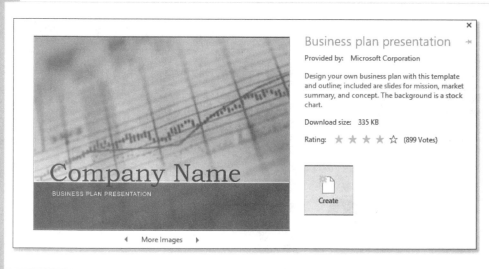

Figure 17.4
You can preview any of the presentation templates.

If you don't want to use the template, click the Close button to return to the search results. When you do find the template you want to use and have opened its preview window, click the Create button. This opens a new presentation in PowerPoint based on the template.

Figure 17.5 shows a new presentation based on a template. Note that the overall look (the theme) for the template sets up the presentation as a number of sample slides containing placeholder text and sample objects. You can edit the slides and their content to modify and complete your presentation. You can also insert additional slides and add objects to those slides, if needed.

Figure 17.5
Modify the slides provided by the template.

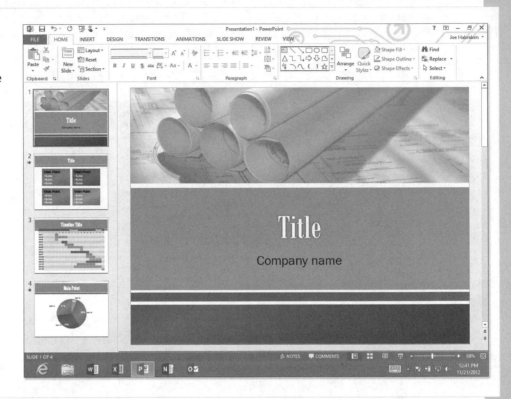

tip

If you find a presentation template during a search that you like but aren't going to use immediately, you can pin it to the Template/Theme list that is provided on the Start screen and the Backstage's New page. This makes it easy for you to use the template later without searching for it again.

Using a Theme to Create a New Presentation

If you want to specify the overall look of a new presentation but don't want to have to edit a lot of slide content, such as placeholder text and other objects that a presentation template provides, you can specify a theme for the new presentation. A theme is a collection of colors, fonts, and text effects. Most of the possibilities provided on the Start screen and the New page are actually themes (unless you do an online search for templates, as discussed in the previous section).

To preview a theme, select the theme's sample picture. A sample image is provided for the theme's title slide (see Figure 17.6). You can use the navigation buttons to view more slide samples for the theme. The theme preview window lists color variants for the theme on the right. To preview one of the variants, select it. You can then use the navigation buttons to preview the slide samples for the theme to see how they look when a particular theme variant is selected. If you don't want to use a theme or one of its variants, click the Close button. When you are ready to use a selected theme, select Create. A new title slide opens in the PowerPoint workspace using the theme you selected.

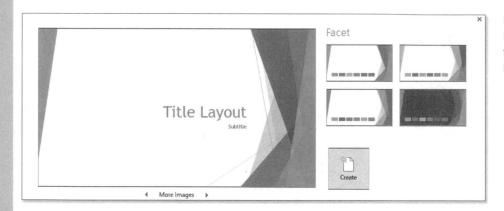

Figure 17.6
Preview a theme and its variants.

 tip

If you want to find online themes (rather than templates and themes), using the Search tool, include the word "theme" in your search criteria. You can also point your web browser to www.office.com. This page provides a Templates link, which gets you to the Microsoft templates page. You can select PowerPoint on this page and browse the theme and template library.

➡ For a discussion on changing themes in a presentation, **see** "Working with Themes," **p. 539**.

Creating a Presentation from an Existing Presentation

You can create a presentation based on any existing presentation. This enables you to make a copy of the existing presentation and then edit it as needed to create a whole new presentation.

If you have just started PowerPoint and are on the Start screen, you can quickly open a copy of any of the presentations listed under Recent. Right-click a listed presentation and then select Open a Copy. A copy of the presentation opens in the PowerPoint workspace. Make sure you save this "new" presentation, which hasn't been named.

If the presentation isn't in your Recent list, you can still open a copy. Select Open Other Presentations; this maneuver takes you to the Backstage's Open page. Select a location, such as your computer or your SkyDrive, and then navigate to the folder that holds the presentation you want to copy. This opens the Open dialog box, as shown in Figure 17.7. Locate the presentation file and then select it. Click the Open button's drop-down arrow and then click Open As Copy. A copy of the presentation opens in the PowerPoint window. Note, however, that this copy is a little different from the copy we made by right-clicking a presentation in the Recent list. This copy (opened using the Open dialog box) has the name "Copy (1)filename" (where filename is the original name of the file). So if you want to give the presentation a new name (to get rid of "Copy" in the name), you must use the Save As command, select File, and then select Save As. In the Save As dialog box, provide a new name for the "copied" presentation and a new location, if necessary.

Figure 17.7
Use the Open dialog box to open a copy of a presentation.

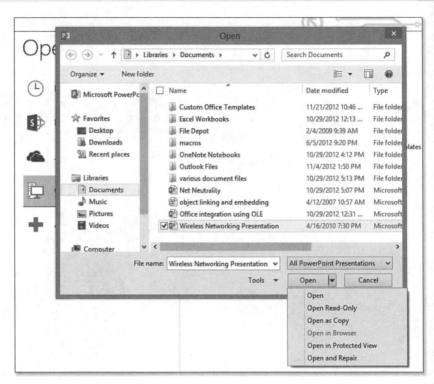

If you are already working on a presentation, you can go to Backstage (File) at any time and also open a copy of any presentation that is listed in the Recent Presentations on the Open page. If you have to locate the file via the Open dialog box, you need to use the Open As Copy command, as already discussed.

Inserting Slides from the Reuse Slides Task Pane

We have already looked at how to open a copy of an existing presentation. PowerPoint also makes it easy for you to insert slides from an existing presentation into your current presentation (which can be a new presentation). The Reuse Slides task pane enables you to use any or all slides in an existing presentation. The Reuse Slide task pane is opened using the Reuse Slides command, at the bottom of the New Slide gallery. To insert existing slides into your current presentation, follow these steps:

1. On the Ribbon's Home tab, select the New Slide command and then select Reuse Slides. The Reuse Slides task pane opens on the right side of the PowerPoint application window.

2. In the Reuse Slides task pane, click the Open a PowerPoint File link (or select Browse and then Browse File). The Browse window opens.

3. Locate the PowerPoint presentation that supplies the slides for the current presentation. Then click Open. The slides in the presentation are listed in the Reuse Slides task pane, as shown in Figure 17.8.

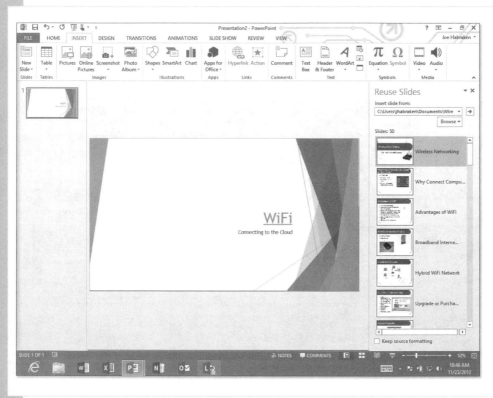

Figure 17.8
Use the Reuse Slides task pane to insert slides from an existing presentation.

4. To add a slide from the Reuse Slides task pane to the current presentation, select a slide. By default, it is formatted using the theme that has been set for the current presentation. Add other slides as needed to build the new presentation.

5. When you have finished working with the Reuse Slides task pane, select its Close button.

The Reuse Slides task pane closes. You can now insert new slides or modify the slides that you "copied" using the Reuse Slides task pane.

---

 tip

If you want to keep the original formatting for a slide (or slides) that you insert using the Reuse Slides task pane, check the Keep Source Formatting check box at the bottom of the task pane.

---

 tip

If you work on a network that provides a SharePoint server, you can save presentations to a slide library. This library can then be available to you and other users on the SharePoint network. Go to the Share page in the Backstage (click File, then Share), and use the Publish Slides command to build a slide library.

Creating a Template

You can create your own templates from your PowerPoint presentations. These templates can include custom logos, special design elements, and even custom color combinations and fonts (themes). You can share templates with coworkers, which can be useful if you want to create consistent-looking presentations for your small business or club. Templates can be fairly bare boned (with little or no slide content), or they can include any number of slides containing text, pictures, and other objects.

You can save any presentation as a template. To create your own template from the current presentation, follow these steps:

1. Select File to open the PowerPoint Backstage, and then select Save As.

2. On the Save As page, select Computer and then select Browse. The Save As dialog box opens.

3. In the Save As Type drop-down box, select PowerPoint Template. When you select the template file type, the folder location defaults to your Custom Office Templates folder (Username\ Documents\Custom Office Templates).

4. Specify a name for the template.

5. Click Save.

The new template is saved to your Custom Office Templates folder. Before you can access your custom template (or templates) from the Start screen or the Backstage's New page, you need to set the default personal templates location in the PowerPoint Options window. Because your new template was saved to the custom template folder (in your Documents folder), you use the location syntax C:\Users\Username\Documents\Custom Office Templates, where Username is the logon name you use for Windows 8.

To open the PowerPoint Options window, select File and then Options. In the PowerPoint Options window, select Save. In the Default personal templates location box, enter `C:\Users\User Name\Documents\Custom Office Templates`, as shown in Figure 17.9. Then click OK to close the PowerPoint Options window.

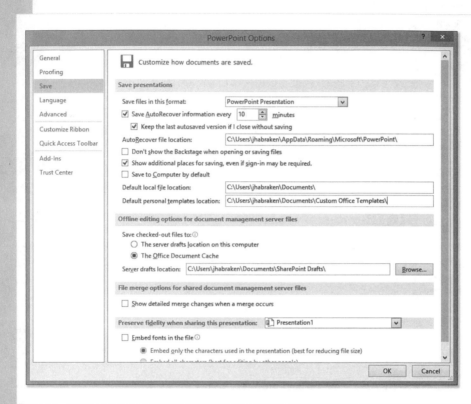

Figure 17.9
Specify the default location for your custom PowerPoint templates.

Now you can access your own template or templates from the Start screen or the New page. A Personal category now appears on the Start screen or the New page (just to the right of the Featured heading). To view your custom templates, select Personal. Thumbnails of your templates are previewed. Select the custom template you want to use for a new presentation. You can use the navigation buttons to see a few more images of the template (as you could with any template available on the Start screen or New page). Select Create to open a new presentation based on the template.

Inserting New Slides

When you create a new presentation using a template (even the Blank presentation template) or a theme, you are almost always provided a title slide. The title slide contains two text boxes: one for the title and one for a subtitle. All the text on your slides resides in text boxes or table boxes (all objects appear on a slide in their own frames, for easy manipulation). To enter text on a slide, such as the title text box, click in the text box and type your text.

After you fill the text box or boxes on a slide, you are probably ready to insert another slide into the presentation. Select the layout for the new slide. The new Slide command is in the Slide group, which resides on the Ribbon's Home tab. Other slide-related commands, such as the Layout, Reset, and Section commands, are also in the Slides group.

When you select the New Slide command, a gallery of slide layouts is provided for common slide types, such as Title Slide, Title and Content, and Blank. Figure 17.10 shows the Slide gallery. The slides available in the gallery are based on the currently selected presentation theme (which is listed at the top of the gallery).

Figure 17.10
Insert a new slide into the presentation.

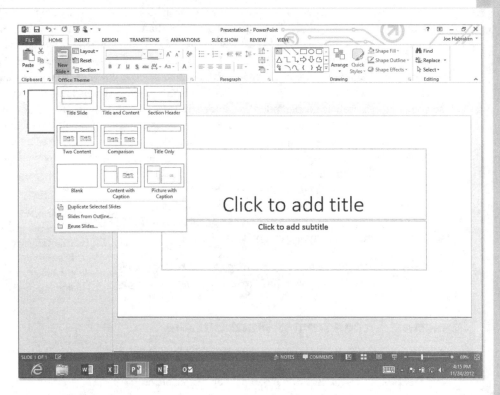

To insert a particular slide layout type, select it in the gallery. The new slide opens in the Slide pane and is added to the list of thumbnails. You can click in the provided text boxes, such as the slide title, and add text as needed. Most of the slide layouts include a content area that can contain text or other objects, such as a table, picture, or clip art.

Entering Text

Each new slide has at least a title text box (unless you insert a blank slide) and a content area box. If you want the content area of a new slide to contain text (instead of other content, such as a table or a picture), select the Click to Add Text placeholder and type the text for the slide. The default formatting for content text is a bulleted list.

PowerPoint provides an alternative to entering text on each slide in the Slide pane. You can switch to Outline view and enter slide text in an outline format. You can also add new slides when you are working in Outline view. To switch to Outline view, click the Ribbon's View tab and then select Outline View (in the Presentation Views group).

Each slide in the presentation is represented in the outline as a primary heading. The text used is the title text for the slide. To add text to a slide (such as a bulleted list below a slide heading), click below the heading (in the outline) and then enter the text. Each time you press Enter, you add another item to the bulleted list. You can switch from the secondary level of the outline (the bulleted or numbered list level) by pressing Shift+Tab. This places you at the primary level in the outline, and each new heading that you type creates a new slide. You can switch back to the secondary outline level to add text items to a slide by pressing Tab. Multiple levels are available in each slide, so you can press Tab as needed and then enter text at that level of the outline. The whole point of Outline view is to make it easier for you to concentrate on the text and the sequencing of your text as you build a presentation with a clear beginning, middle, and end (Aristotle came up with this concept, not me). You can easily rearrange the text on your slides using Outline view. For example,

you can drag an entire bulleted list from one slide to another in Outline view. You can also move items around in Outline view as needed to organize the presentation. When you want to return to Normal view, select Normal on the View tab or click the Normal icon on the right side of the PowerPoint status bar.

 For more information on formatting and working with slide text, **see** "Working with Text Boxes and Formatting," **p. 523**.

 tip

With the new Presentation dialog box, you can use templates that you previously downloaded from Office.com. You can even access the templates when you are not online.

Inserting Slides from a Word Outline

Another option for creating slides in a presentation is to create slides based on an outline created in Microsoft Word. This option quickly creates new slides that contain slide titles and accompanying slide text based on the text in the outline. You can insert as many slides as the outline provides.

To insert a Word outline into PowerPoint as presentation slides, select the New Slide command on the Home tab and then select Slides from Outline. The Insert Outline dialog box opens.

Select the Word outline document and then click Insert. The new slides (based on the outline) are inserted into the current presentation. You can edit the new slides as you would any other slide, including adding objects to the slides as needed.

 note

Creating an outline of your presentation in Word enables you to concentrate on the text in the presentation and makes it easy to arrange your thoughts. You can add pictures and other objects after you insert the outline into PowerPoint.

Inserting Other Object Content

If you want an object other than text in a slide's content pane, you can use the icons provided in the content pane of a newly inserted slide to select the type of object to insert. We discuss working with tables, graphics, and media such as sound and movies in subsequent chapters, but let's walk through the basics of inserting an object.

On a new slide, select an object icon, such as Picture. The Insert Picture dialog box opens, as shown in Figure 17.11. The Windows 8 default library for pictures is Pictures; this is the folder that opens when you select the Picture object icon. So we assume that you have some pictures from your digital camera or other source stored in the Picture library.

Figure 17.11
The Insert Picture dialog box.

All you have to do to insert one of your pictures is select the picture in the Insert Picture dialog box and then click Insert. The picture is placed on the slide. The process for inserting other object types is fairly similar to that of inserting a picture and is fairly simply: You specify the object type to be inserted, PowerPoint gives you a dialog box for choosing the specific item, and you insert it onto the slide.

Modifying a Slide's Layout

You might find that you need to modify the initial slide layout you selected for a slide. For example, you might want to make a slide that has a title text box and a single content pane into a slide with two content panes. You can then have one pane with bulleted text and another pane with an object such as a picture. You can change the layout for any slide in the presentation. Even if you have already entered text or other objects on the slide, you can modify the layout.

Select the thumbnail for the slide you want to modify (or select multiple slide thumbnails in the navigation pane, if you want to modify several slides). Select the Layout command in the slides group. The Layout gallery opens. The Layout gallery is similar to the New Slide gallery. Select a new layout from the gallery. The new layout then is applied to the currently selected slide or slides.

Working with Slides in Different Views

PowerPoint can display your presentation in different views. These views are available in the Presentation Views group on the Ribbon's View tab, and each view is designed for a particular purpose. For example, Normal view is designed for building your presentation and provides you with the Slide pane, which enables you to insert text and other objects onto the selected slide. Each slide is also represented by a thumbnail, which makes it easy to select a specific slide in the presentation (or several slides at once). By contrast, Notes Page view concentrates on the speaker's notes that you are creating for your presentation and de-emphasizes the actual slides.

Slide Sorter view is useful in arranging and rearranging your presentation slides. This view provides thumbnails of all the slides in the presentation and is designed for arranging your presentation slides into the proper order. Slide Sorter view also enables you to create sections so that you group together "parts" of the presentation. The different views provided on the Ribbon's View tab (in the Presentations Views group) follow:

- **Normal:** This is the default view, which includes the Slide pane, the Notes pane, and a navigation pane that includes thumbnails of all the slides in the presentation.

- **Outline view:** This view enables you to view the slides in an outline format that concentrates on the text on each slide. You can add new slides directly to the outline and add slide text at different levels in the outline. Tab and Shift+Tab are used to move up or down a level in the outline, respectively.

- **Slide Sorter view:** This view shows all the slides as thumbnails so that you can easily rearrange them by dragging slides to new positions in the presentation. Figure 17.12 shows Slide Sorter view.

- **Reading view:** This view plays the presentation as a slide show. However, it shows the slide show so that it fits within the current PowerPoint window, even when the window is not maximized. This enables you to view the presentation and work with another application on the Windows desktop. You can go back to the previous view (from Reading view) by pressing the Escape key.

- **Notes Page:** This view enables you to see the current slide and its accompanying notes page. This view is designed for you to enter and review the speaker notes that you are creating to go with each slide in the presentation. Figure 17.13 shows Notes Page view.

Figure 17.12
Slide Sorter view.

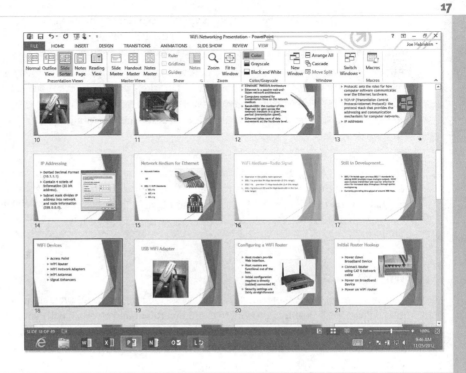

Figure 17.13
Notes Page view.

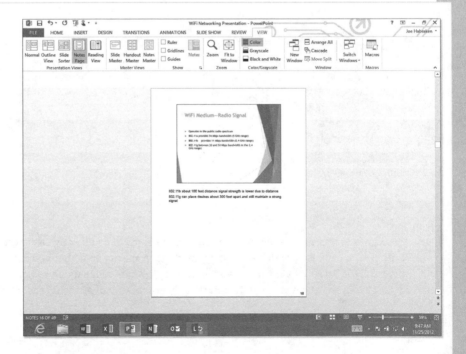

You can switch between these different views using the commands in the Presentation Views group. Some of these views also have icons in the PowerPoint status bar. Icons are provided on the right side of the taskbar for the Normal, Slide Sorter, and Reading views.

Another possible view of a presentation is as a slide show. This view isn't available on the View tab; it is an option in the PowerPoint status bar (the icon just before the zoom slider). We talk more about the different possibilities and views when you run your slide show in Chapter 21, "Delivering a Presentation and Creating Support Materials."

You have options in switching views in the PowerPoint work-space. You can take advantage of the view shortcuts on the PowerPoint status bar. Icons are provided on the right side of the taskbar for the Normal, Slide Sorter, Reading, and Slide Show views. The Slide Show icon plays the slide show beginning with the current slide.

caution
You can't edit the slide content when you are in Slide Sorter or Notes Page views; however, you can double-click a slide in either view to return to Normal view.

Zooming In and Out

As you work on the content of individual slides, you might want to zoom in or out on a slide. You also might find it useful to be able to zoom in and out as you work with your slides in Slide Sorter view. You can use the Zoom slider to zoom in and out on presentation slides or slide content when you are in Normal, Slide Sorter, or Notes Page views.

You can also change the zoom level using the commands in the Zoom group on the View tab of the Ribbon. When you select Zoom, the Zoom dialog box opens, as shown in Figure 17.14.

Figure 17.14
The Zoom dialog box.

You can select any of the available presets in the Zoom dialog box by clicking the appropriate option button. You can also use the percent spinner box to specify an actual percentage. The Zoom group provides the Fit to Window command as well. Select this command in either Normal view or Slide Sorter view; the zoom percentage adjusts so that the slide or slides fill the window.

Rulers, Gridlines, and Guides

PowerPoint provides tools that help you better arrange objects on your slides. Most of these tools have been available in PowerPoint for several versions, but one new possibility is worth noting: smart guides. Smart guides are guides that appear automatically when you move an object on a slide (a text box, picture, chart, or any object). The smart guides tell you when objects on the slide are even or when they are spaced evenly. The best way to experience the smart guides is to place some objects on a slide and then drag them around to see what happens. The View tab also provides additional commands that help you work with object placement. The Show group provides the Ruler, Gridlines, and Guides commands.

To view the horizontal and vertical rulers, select the Ruler check box. When the rulers (horizontal and vertical) are placed in the workspace, the horizontal and vertical positions of the mouse pointer are shown as tick marks on the horizontal and vertical rulers as you move the mouse on the slide.

If you want more help in aligning objects on the slide, you can turn on the gridlines; select the Gridlines check box. The gridlines are nonprinting horizontal and vertical lines. For even more precision, you can use the guides. When you select the Guides check box, a horizontal and vertical guideline appear on the slide. You can move either of these guidelines as needed on the slide's surface. You can then use either guide to help you more accurately align objects on the slide. Clearing any of these command check boxes removes those particular items from the workspace.

If you want to specify settings related to the gridlines and the guides—including the smart guides— you can open the Grid and Guides dialog box. Select the dialog box launcher at the bottom of the Show group. Figure 17.15 shows the Grid and Guides dialog box.

Figure 17.15
The Grid and Guides
dialog box.

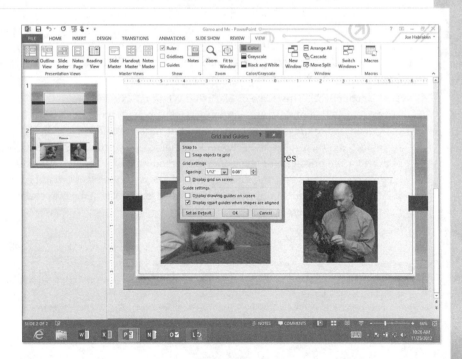

By default, the Snap Objects to Grid option is disabled. When you enable the Snap To feature, objects are "snapped' to the nearest intersection of the grid as you drag the object. If you are using Snap To, you might also want to select the Display Grid on Screen check box so that you can see the grid as you align objects. You can also change the default spacing for the grid using the Spacing box, as well as enable the Display Drawing Guides on Screen option, which places a vertical and horizontal guide that intersect at the middle of the slide. The check box for the Display Smart Guides When Shapes Are Aligned feature is also in the Grid and Guides dialog box. It is enabled by default, and I can see no real reason why you would want to disable it. When you have finished working in the Grid and Guides dialog box, select OK.

Color/Grayscale Commands

By default, your presentation slides are shown in color. The Color command is selected (by default) in the Color Grayscale group. You can view your presentation in grayscale or black and white and then customize how the various colors are translated to grayscale or black and white. This translation can be done on an object-by-object basis, so you have complete control over how a particular object, such as a clip art image or table, looks in grayscale or black and white. The purpose of these commands is to control how a printout of your presentation looks when you print in black and white, such as when you use a laser printer. This is useful when you want to provide your audience with grayscale or black-and-white handouts.

To view the slides in grayscale or black and white, select either the Grayscale command or the Black and White command. You switch to Grayscale or Black and White view, and the Ribbon shows the Grayscale or Black and White tab. This tab provides a series of commands that enable you to change the grayscale or black-and-white characteristics of a selected object on the slide. Figure 17.16 shows the grayscale view of a slide and the Grayscale tab on the Ribbon.

 note

If you still create black-and-white overhead projector transparencies from your presentation slides, the grayscale and black-and-white possibilities are useful.

The commands the Grayscale or Black and White tabs provide are extremely straightforward. For example, if you want an object to be rendered to grayscale or black-and-white automatically (based on its actual color), select the object and then select the Automatic command. The other commands provide more definitive options for the grayscale or black-and-white rendering of an object. For example, when you select an object and then select the Black command, the object is black when printed on a black-and-white printer. You can select multiple objects and then assign the same grayscale or black-and-white attribute to several objects at once.

Figure 17.16
The Grayscale tab and associated commands.

When you finish working with the Grayscale or Black and White commands, select the Back to Color View command. This returns you to the Ribbon's Home tab rather than the View tab.

Opening a New Presentation Window

You can open a second window that shows the current presentation; this enables you to view a presentation in two different views at the same time. For example, one window could use Normal view, and the other window could use Slide Sorter view. This enables you to manipulate the same presentation in different ways. For example, you could cut and paste or copy and paste an object from slides in one of the windows to the other window. Changes that you make to the presentation in either window are reflected in both windows.

To open a second presentation window, select the New Window command. A second window containing the current presentation opens on the Windows desktop. To arrange the two open presentation windows side by side, select the Arrange All command. Figure 17.17 shows two windows containing the same presentation. Normal view is used on the left window, and Slide Sorter view is used in the right window.

 tip

If you don't want an object to be included in a black-and-white printout of the slide, select the object and then select the Don't Show command.

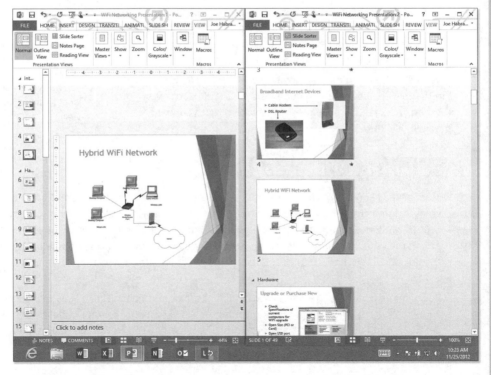

Figure 17.17
You can open multiple windows containing the same presentation.

You can close either window at any time. When you close one of the windows, maximize the remaining window so that PowerPoint takes full advantage of the space available on the Windows desktop.

Rearranging and Deleting Slides

When you have a few slides in a presentation, you might want to rearrange them. You can reorder slides in Normal view and Outline view by dragging slide thumbnails or outline headings to new locations in the presentation, respectively. I prefer Slide Sorter view; depending on the size of the presentation, you might be able to view many, if not all, the slides in the presentation when you are in Slide Sorter view; this makes rearranging the slide order easy.

To switch to Slide Sorter view, select Slide Sorter on the View shortcuts, or select Slide Sorter on the View tab. Drag the slide to its new location; a vertical line shows the position of the slide as you drag it in the presentation. If you need to drag the slide to a location that is not in Slide Sorter view, drag the slide downward to scroll through the slides in the presentation.

You can also copy a slide in Slide Sorter view as easily as you can move a slide. Simply hold down the Ctrl key while you drag the slide. When you release the mouse, PowerPoint inserts a copy of the selected slide into the presentation.

As already mentioned, the slide thumbnails found in Normal view can also be dragged to new locations as needed. Drag up or down in the navigation pane to scroll up or down in the slides list. Release the mouse when you reach the position in the presentation where you want to place the slide.

You can delete a slide easily by selecting a slide (or slides) in either of the Slides/Outline pane tabs or in Slide Sorter view. When you have the slide or slides selected that you want to delete, click the Delete key.

 note

The Slides tab in Normal view probably works best for moving slides when you have only a few slides in a presentation. When you have many slides, you might want to switch to Slide Sorter view.

Modifying Bulleted Lists

Most of the slide layouts in the New Slide gallery provide a title text box and other object place-holders. For example, there are layouts for a title and content, a title and two contents, a title and a caption, and so on. Because the bulleted list is such an important mainstay of a PowerPoint presentation, the object boxes enable you to immediately begin entering text in a bulleted list. This makes the object content box a text box. Each time you press Enter, you can create a new bulleted item in the list.

Because presentations are really a collection of topics and points that you want to bring to your audience's attention, most of your presentation slides probably contain bulleted lists. Again, by default, typing in any content box or text box provided by the New Slide gallery produces a bulleted list.

You can control the bullet formatting of your bulleted lists using the Bullets gallery. The gallery enables you to change the bullets used in the list. If you want even more control over the bullets for the list, you can access the Bullets and Numbering dialog box.

You can change the bullet options before you begin typing your bulleted list, or you can modify an existing bulleted list. To modify a bulleted list already on a slide, select the bulleted text. Select the Bullets command arrow to access the Bullets gallery. You can preview any of the bullet formats provided in the gallery by placing the mouse on that bullet type.

When you are ready to assign a new bullet format to the slide, select one of the bullet styles provided in the gallery. To specify a custom bullet shape for a bulleted list, you need to access the Bullets and Numbering dialog box. Select the Bullets command arrow and then select Bullets and Numbering in the Bullets gallery. The Bullets and Numbering dialog box opens with the Bulleted tab selected, as shown in Figure 17.18.

Figure 17.18
The Bullets and Numbering dialog box.

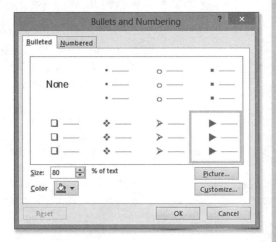

You can select any of the bullet shapes provided on the Bulleted tab. You can also customize the bullets by using a picture as a bullet or by selecting a new symbol to be used as a bullet. If you want to specify a picture as the bullet shape, select the Picture button in the Bullets and Numbering dialog box. The Insert Pictures dialog box opens. You can use any pictures on your computer, Office.com pictures, or pictures stored online, including on Flickr and your SkyDrive. If you use a picture on your computer, use the Browse button to locate the picture and then insert it.

To search for a picture (or clip art) on Office.com, use the Search Office.com search box. You can also search the web for pictures using the Bing search box. In either case, the Insert Picture dialog box lists pictures that match your search. Select an image and then click Insert. The picture is assigned to your bulleted list as the bullet.

You can also specify a new bullet type using any of the many symbols that are installed with the fonts on your computer. In the Bullets and Numbering dialog box, click the Customize button. The Symbol dialog box opens, as shown in Figure 17.19.

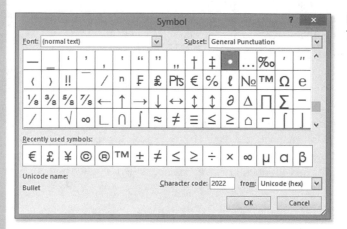

Figure 17.19
The Symbol dialog box.

You can use the Font drop-down list to select different font symbol sets. Some of the most interesting symbols are found in the Wingdings and Webdings font sets, but all the font families you have available provide symbols.

To select a particular symbol, select the symbol in the list provided. Then click OK to return to the Bullets and Numbering dialog box. The new bullet symbol is added to the list of bullets provided on the Bulleted tab. You can change the size or color of the new bullet symbol (which is selected) by using the Size spinner box or the Color drop-down list, respectively.

When you have finished making modifications to the new bullet symbol, select OK to return to the current slide. The new bullet is applied to your selected bulleted list.

 note

If you insert a text box from the Ribbon's Insert tab and want to type a bulleted list, you need to turn on bulleting by selecting the Bullets command on the Home tab.

 tip

You can insert your own pictures as bullets. You don't have to do anything special to the picture. Select the Picture button in the Bullets and Numbering dialog box, and click the Browse button to locate your picture. You also can "create" bullets from the Office.com clip art and photos you have stored on your Flickr site and SkyDrive.

Using Numbered Lists

Because your presentation might also provide step-by-step procedures or a sequence of topics, you can use numbered lists on some of your presentation slides. Numbered lists operate pretty much the same as bulleted lists in terms of creating a new list or modifying an existing list. If you have inserted a new slide with a default bulleted list, you can switch from bullets to numbering by selecting the Numbering command in the Paragraph group. You can also select an existing list and change it to numbering by selecting the Numbering command.

If you want to select a different numbering style (the default is the Arabic system—1,2, 3, and so on), select the Numbering command arrow; the Numbering gallery opens. Select a number style from the gallery.

You can modify the size and color settings for a numbered list and specify the number to start the list in the Bullets and Numbering dialog box. Being able to change the start number for a numbered list is useful if you have two associated slides and you want the list on the second slide to pick up where the numbering on the previous slide's list left off.

To open the Bullets and Numbering dialog box, select the Numbering command arrow and then select Bullets and Numbering in the Numbering gallery. The Numbered tab is selected when the Bullets and Numbering dialog box opens. You can choose from any of the numbering styles provided on the tab; however, they are the same styles as provided in the Numbering style gallery.

If you want to change the starting number for the numbered list, use the Start At spinner box to specify the "start at number." You can also change the size or color of the numbering by using the Size spinner box or the Color drop-down list, respectively. When you have finished modifying the numbering settings, click OK. You return to your slide, and the new settings are applied to the numbered list.

Viewing a Presentation During Editing

As you begin to build your slide presentation, check to see how your slides look when displayed in a slide show. The Slide Show tab of the Ribbon provides commands that enable you to view your presentation as a slide show; these commands are in the Start Slide Show group. The From Beginning command and From the Current Slide command can be used to start the slide show from the first slide or the currently selected slide, respectively. Figure 17.20 shows the Ribbon's Slide Show tab. The Start Slide Show commands are on the far left of the tab.

Figure 17.20
The Slide
Show tab of
the Ribbon.

What happens when you select either the From Beginning command or the Current Slide command depends on whether you have multiple monitors on your computer. If you have multiple monitors on your computer, PowerPoint shows your presentation in Presenter view. Presenter view is enabled by default and gives you a view of the current slide, the next slide, and any notes associated with the current slide on your primary monitor. The other monitor shows the current slide only in typical Slide Show view. Other presenter tools available in Presenter view include pen and pointer tools and a Zoom feature. Presenter view is designed to help you present. It gives you notes on the screen (instead of requiring a printout of your notes), and it shows you the next slide (before your audience sees it). This view also provides a timer that enables you to see the elapsed time the current slide has been on the screen (the timer is also associated with slide timings, which we discuss in Chapter 21).

If you don't have multiple monitors on your computer, selecting the From Beginning command or the Current Slide command shows the first slide or current slide (depending on the command you selected) of your presentation in a full-screen slide-show view. You can advance to the next slide by clicking the mouse. You can also press the Page Down key, the right arrow key, or the down arrow key to navigate to the next slide in the slide show.

If you want to back up a slide, press the Page Up key (you can use the up arrow or left arrow keys as well). You can also back up a slide by right-clicking the mouse and selecting Previous from the shortcut menu that appears.

When you finish viewing the slide show, you can end the slide show and return to the PowerPoint workspace; press the Esc key, or right-click the mouse and select End Show to return to the slide that was last viewed in the slide show.

This short discussion of previewing a slide show as you begin to piece together your presentation is provided to get you in the habit of previewing your slides in slide-show format. We look at issues and PowerPoint features related to planning and preparing a professional presentation in Chapter 21.

 *For a more complete look at the Slide Show commands and how to finalize a presentation, **see** "Running Through a Completed Presentation," p. 612.*

 tip

Even if you don't have multiple monitors, you can open your presentation in Presenter view. Press Alt+F5 (you don't have to be on the View tab), and the presentation opens.

tip

You can also start the slide show from the current slide by clicking the Slide Show button in the View shortcuts on the PowerPoint status bar.

ADVANCED PRESENTATION FORMATTING, THEMES, AND MASTERS

Creating PowerPoint presentations that are both informative and visually appealing means you must walk a fine line between the actual purpose of your presentation and its overall design. To get your message across, you must create slides that are both easy to read and easy to understand. PowerPoint slides are meant to hit the high points related to your subject matter and provide a guide to both you and the audience as you walk them through the information.

Even the most informative and easy-to-understand presentation, however, can be plagued by visually unappealing slides or slides that are not uniform in fonts, colors, and design elements. In this chapter, we look at options for formatting slide text and arranging text in both text boxes and tables. We also discuss the possibilities for manipulating slide color and other attributes using themes and background styles.

We also look at the possibilities for inserting repeating information or elements in slides using headers and footers. Our look at overall design considerations and repeating objects also includes a discussion of slide masters. In terms of organizing the overall presentation into subgroups of information, we look at the sections feature.

Working with Text Boxes and Formatting

Most of the text found on your presentation slides is typically held in a frame called a text box (although tables can also hold text as can other objects). When you insert a new slide into a presentation, you are provided several layout options for that slide. The new slide can use such layouts as Title and Content or Two Content. To add text to a text content box, place the insertion point in a title box or content box (both are default text content boxes) with placeholder text, and then enter the text. The default for content boxes is a bulleted list.

To edit existing text in a text box, select the current text or place the insertion point and then edit the text. The only time that you will need to create a new text box is when you want to place text on the slide in a position other than what is provided by the default text box or text boxes on the slide (which are provided by the slide layout you select).

Inserting a Text Box

Text boxes are "drawn" onto a slide using the Text Box command in the Text group of the Ribbon's Insert tab. Not only do you have control over the format of the text within the box, including the text direction and special text effects, but you also have options for formatting the text box itself, including outside borders and fill color.

To create a new text box on a slide, follow these steps:

1. Select the Text Box command on the Insert menu.

2. Place the mouse pointer on the page, and drag diagonally to create the text box.

3. Release the mouse button, and the insertion point appears in the text box.

Figure 18.1 shows a new text box on a presentation slide (to the right of two pictures). To enter text in a text box, type the text as required.

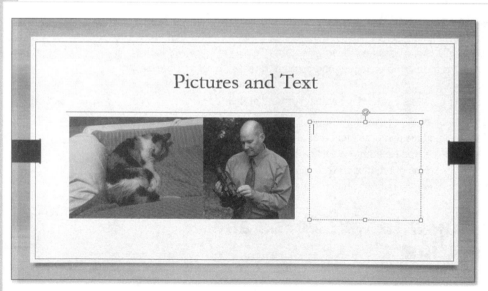

Figure 18.1
A new text box.

You can type the text and then format the text after the fact or you can immediately take advantage of the various font and paragraph-formatting tools provided on the Home tab to apply basic formatting attributes before you type. These attributes include options such as bold, italic, and bulleted or numbered lists.

In the next section, you see that the possibilities for formatting the text in the text box are not limited to the various font and paragraph commands on the Home tab. Other tools that provide you with the ability to add text effects and WordArt styles to your text are provided by the Drawing Tools.

 note

You can add text to nearly any inserted shape. Select the shape and then select the Text Box command on the Drawing Tools Format tab.

note

The text you enter into a text box you have created uses the default font and font size for body text, which is Calibri, 18 point.

Basic Text Formatting

The typical formatting commands for both the font and paragraph attributes of the text in a text box are provided in the Font and Paragraph groups on the Home tab. The Font group provides control over the font type, size, color, and other attributes such as bold, italics, and underline. The Paragraph group enables you to change the horizontal alignment of the text, create bulleted and numbered lists, change the line spacing, and indent text. Figure 18.2 shows the Home tab, including the Font and Paragraph groups.

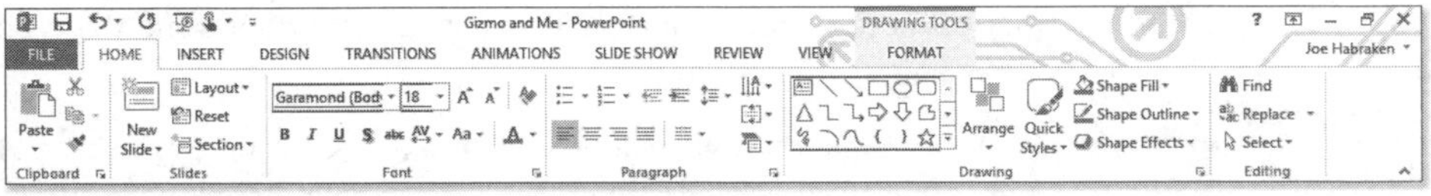

Figure 18.2
The Ribbon's Home tab.

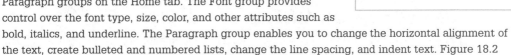

Changing Font Attributes

To change the font attributes of selected text, select the text attribute by clicking the appropriate command (or commands) in the Font group. If you find that you want to remove the text formatting that you have applied to text in a text box, select the Clear All Formatting command to remove all the formatting from the selected text.

 note

You can select text in a text box and change font and paragraph attributes, or select the text box itself and then change attributes for all the text in the text box.

You can also access additional font attributes such as strikethrough, superscript, and small caps by using the Font dialog box. To open the Font dialog box, select the dialog box launcher on the Font group. Figure 18.3 shows the Font dialog box.

The Font dialog box offers you control over the same font attributes available in the Font group on the Home tab. However, other font-formatting possibilities, such as strikethrough, superscript, subscript, and small caps, are also available as check boxes in this dialog box.

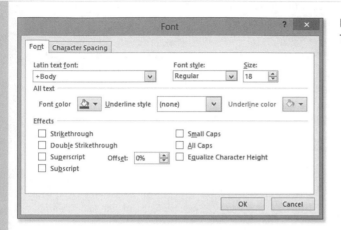

Figure 18.3
The Font dialog box.

Changing Paragraph Attributes

Paragraph attributes include settings such as paragraph alignment (left, center, right, and justify), indents, columns, bulleted and numbered lists, and line spacing. You can assign any of these paragraph settings to selected text (including an entire selected text box). You can also select a specific command, such as numbered list, and then type new text as needed.

The Paragraph group also offers three additional commands that go beyond the typical paragraph formatting. These commands are as follows:

- **Text Direction:** This command provides a gallery of text orientations, including Horizontal, Rotate All Text 90°, and Stacked. Hover the mouse over a text direction setting in the gallery to preview the setting on the currently selected text box.

- **Align Text:** This command provides a gallery of settings that change how the text is aligned within the text box. Settings provided for Align Text are Top, Middle, and Bottom. You can access more alignment settings by selecting More Options; this opens the Format Shape task pane, which provides a larger list of alignment possibilities in the Vertical alignment drop-down list.

 tip

You can copy and paste text formats using the Format Painter on the Home tab.

- **Convert to SmartArt:** This command provides a gallery of SmartArt shapes. You can convert the text box to any of the shapes provided. Place a mouse on a SmartArt shape in the gallery to preview the shape on the currently selected text box.

> *We discuss SmartArt in more detail in Chapter 19, "Better Slides with Clip Art, Pictures, and SmartArt."*

You can also access the more basic paragraph settings for selected text or a text box via the Paragraph dialog box. Select the dialog box launcher in the Paragraph group. The Paragraph dialog box provides more precise setting possibilities for indents and line spacing, including spinner boxes for Before and After, which enable you to set the amount of whitespace before and after a text line, respectively. The Paragraph dialog box also provides access to the Tabs dialog box, which you can use to set tab stops for a selected text box.

➡️ *Setting tabs in PowerPoint, both in the Tabs dialog box and directly on the ruler, is similar to creating tab settings in Word. **See** "Working with Tabs," **p. 156**.*

Formatting a Text Box with the Drawing Tools

Possibilities for formatting a text box and its contents way beyond the more basic settings found on the Home tab are provided by the Ribbon's Drawing Tools. When you select a text box on a slide, the contextual Drawing Tools Format tab appears on the Ribbon. Select Format and the various Drawing Tools command groups are made available. These commands are used to format a PowerPoint object that you add to a slide, which includes AutoShapes and text boxes. The Drawing Tools Format tab and its various command groups are shown in Figure 18.4.

Figure 18.4
The Drawing Tools Format tab.

The commands directly associated with the changes that you can make to the text box and the text within the text box are primarily housed in the Shape Styles and WordArt Styles command groups. The Shape Styles commands are used to apply formatting to the text box. The WordArt Styles group enables you to apply special text effects and control the text fill and outline.

Selecting Quick Styles and Shape Attributes

Shape styles or quick styles, as they are also referred to, are sets of formatting attributes that affect the text box border, font color (and bullet color if applicable), and text box background (fill) color. The shape styles are housed in the Shape Styles gallery. You can use the scroll arrows to scroll through the styles provided, or you can click the More button to view the entire gallery, as shown in Figure 18.5.

The fills (text box background) and styles provided are based on the current theme. You can view additional theme fills by selecting Other Theme Fills at the bottom of the gallery. These fills do not provide changes in the font color. You can change the font color by using the Font Color command on the Home tab.

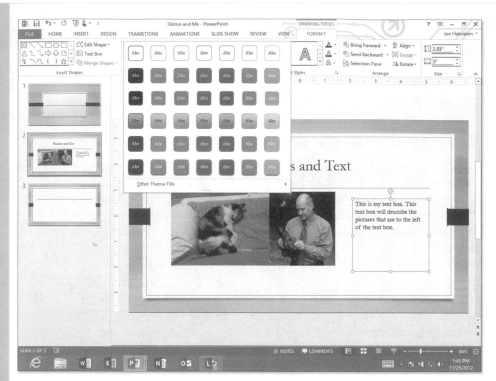

Figure 18.5
The Shape Styles gallery.

Shape Fill, Outline, and Effects

The alternative to selecting one of the quick styles is to change the shape fill, outline, and effects manually. The Shape Fill, Shape Outline, and Shape Effects commands are also available in the Shape Styles group (make sure the Format tab is selected on the Ribbon under Drawing Tools).

To change the text box (or other shape) fill, select the Shape Fill command and select a color from the theme colors provided. You can also choose from standard colors or select More Fill Colors to choose a color from the Colors dialog box. Standard colors can be selected on the Standard tab of the Colors dialog box. If you want to select a custom color or specify a color by its RGB (Red, Green, and Blue) number, you can use the Custom tab of the Colors dialog box.

PowerPoint 2013 provides the new Eyedropper tool, which can be used to copy a color from an object on a slide and then applied as the color for the shape fill or the shape outline. For example, you might have a picture on a slide and want to "steal" a color from the picture and apply it to the fill for your text box or other shape. To use the Eyedropper tool, select Shape Fill (or Shape Outline) and then select Eyedropper. Move the Eyedropper (the mouse pointer) to the object that contains the color you want to use. When you click on the color, the text box is formatted with the color. The Eyedropper tool also works when you apply a text fill or text outline color to the text in a text box (which we discuss in the next section).

The Shape Fill command provides more options for a text box background than just colors. You can select Picture to specify a picture as the background; all you have to do is specify the picture file in the Insert Picture dialog box. When the picture appears in the text box, you can use the Picture Tools to customize the image so that it works well as a background for the accompanying text in the text box.

 Editing pictures in the Office applications, including PowerPoint, is discussed in Chapter 4, "Using and Creating Graphics."

The Shape Fill command does not limit you to color and pictures as a text box background. You are also provided with gradients and textures. When you select the Gradient command, a gallery of gradients appears. Point at a gradient to preview it on the text box.

Textures are also an option as the fill for the text box. Select Texture on the Shape Fill menu and a gallery of textures appears. Preview a texture or textures by moving the mouse over the possibilities in the gallery.

After you have selected a fill for the text box, you can use the Shape Outline command to specify the color for the text box border. You can select from theme or standard colors or use the Color dialog box to specify a custom color. The Shape Outline command also enables you to specify the weight for the text box border and the dash style for the line. The default is a solid line.

To put the finishing touches on the text box, you can add an effect using the Shape Effects command. This command provides a number of different effects that are grouped in galleries under a particular effect category. These categories include Preset, Shadow, Reflection, Glow, and 3-D Rotation. Select any of the specific shape effects in the category galleries to preview the effect on the text box.

> **tip**
>
> You can also assign quick styles to text boxes and other shapes from the Quick Styles command on the Home tab.

Fine-Tuning Shape Formatting

Although the Shape Styles group commands take care of most of the possibilities in formatting the appearance of a text box (or any other shape you insert onto a slide), you can fine-tune these settings using the Format Shape task pane. This is a new feature in PowerPoint 2013 and replaces the Format Shape dialog box. Not only does the new Format Shape task pane provide more possibilities for formatting a shape (such as a text box), but it also allows you to immediately see the results of changes that you make because you don't have a pesky dialog box perched on the screen.

To open the Format Shape task pane, select the dialog box launcher on the bottom right of the Shape Styles group. Figure 18.6 shows the Format Shape task pane with the Fill options expanded in the task pane.

The Format Shape task pane provides options for both the shape and the text in the shape. Let's look at the shape options first. We then look at the text options in the next section.

The Fill and Line options are available in the task pane when the Fill & Line icon is selected below the Shape Options heading. To access the various Fill or Line settings, click Fill or Line to expand that node in the task pane. The Fill settings (when expanded) provide a variety of possibilities, including Solid Fill, Gradient Fill, Pattern Fill, and Slide Background Fill (the text box picks up the fill color from the slide). When you select a Fill option, you can select from Preset Gradients or set the Type, Direction, and Angle of the gradient manually. Color, Position, Transparency, and Brightness settings are also available as Fill options.

Figure 18.6
The Format Shape task pane.

The Line settings enable you to specify the line type (Solid or Gradient) and the line color. Other settings include line Transparency, Width, Compound Type, Dash Type, Cap Type, and Join Type.

When you select the Effects icon at the top of the Format Shape task pane, you are provided with access to all the different shape effect possibilities. Most of these effects, such as Shadow, Reflection, and Glow, provide access to several presets but also provide you with the ability to set custom sizes, colors, and transparency level. The full list of Effects settings is as follows:

- **Shadow:** This shape effect can be used to specify a shadow type for the text box using a gallery of presets. Additional settings, including Transparency, Size, Blur, Angle, and Distance, enable you to fine-tune the overall look and size of the shadow.

- **Reflection:** Another of the shape effects; select a preset from the provided gallery. You can then fine-tune the reflection using the Transparency, Size, Distance, and Blur settings.

- **Glow:** This effect adds a glow to the edges of the shape. You can select from a number of presets and then fine-tune the Color, Size, and Transparency of the glow.

- **Soft Edges:** This effect can be specified by selecting from several presets (that are based on point size, 1 through 50). You can also fine-tune the size of the soft edges, if needed. You can then control the Color, Size, and Transparency of the glow and the size of the soft edges.

- **3-D Format:** You can specify a 3-D bevel effect for the text box (or other shape) based on the Bevel, Depth, Contour, and Surface settings for the object. Galleries are provided by both Top bevel and Bottom bevel, and you have control over the Depth and Contour by selecting a color and adjusting the setting using the accompanying spinner box. Figure 18.7 shows the various settings provided by the Format Shape task pane for 3D custom formatting of a text box.

Figure 18.7
The 3-D Format settings in the Format Shape task pane.

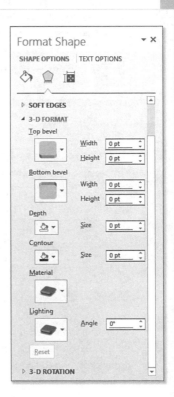

- **3-D Rotation:** This shape effect allows you to rotate a 3-D version of the text box or shape by selecting from a gallery of presets. You can then customize the rotation axes by specifying the X, Y, and Z settings using the provided spinner boxes or a direction button such as Left, Right, Up, or Down. You can also choose to keep the text flat in the 3-D object.

Fortunately, both the 3-D Format and the 3-D Rotation settings also provide you with a Reset option. Manipulating the 3-D options for a particular shape can be trial and error at best. You might need to take advantage of the Reset button that both of these rather complex formatting options provide for your convenience. After you have specified the settings in the Format Shape dialog box, select Close to return to the PowerPoint workspace.

Using WordArt Styles and Text Settings

The Drawing Tools Format tab also provides you with special settings for the text that is contained in a text box or other shape. You can assign WordArt styles to the text, which are text effects that definitely surpass the regular text-formatting possibilities provided on the Ribbon's Home tab.

The WordArt styles provide a gallery of different effect styles that can be directly assigned to the text. You can also set your own text fill, outline, and effects if you want. The Format Shape task pane also provides even more granular settings for text settings, including the fill, outline, and effect for the text as well as the text alignment and direction.

To take advantage of the WordArt Styles gallery, scroll through the possibilities provided in the gallery. If you want to see the entire gallery, click the More button. The WordArt Styles gallery is shown in Figure 18.8.

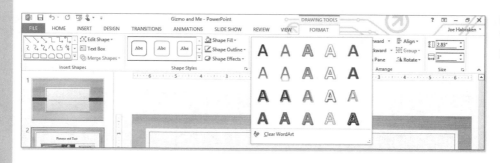

Figure 18.8
The WordArt Styles gallery.

Place the mouse on a style to preview the style on the text in the text box. Select a style to assign it to the text in the text box (or other shape). You can clear a previously assigned WordArt style from the text by using the Clear WordArt option in the WordArt Styles gallery.

Text Fill, Outline, and Effects

If you don't want to use a WordArt style provided in the gallery, you can customize the text by assigning your own fill, outline, and effects settings to the text. The Text Fill command enables you to apply a text color, picture, gradient, or texture to the text in the text box. You can select a color from the colors provided or you can select More Fill Colors to access the Color dialog box. You can also use the Eyedropper tool to copy a color from any object in the Slide pane.

You can also use a picture as the fill for text in a text box; select Picture and then specify and insert the picture file from the Insert Picture dialog box. You might wonder why you would want to use a picture to provide the fill for text given that you won't actually see the entire picture, but think of this possibility in terms of the colors provided by the picture rather than the picture itself. Assigning the background colors to the text using the Text Fill command would enable you to match the text nicely with the accompanying picture on the same slide. Both would use the same color palette, making you look like a design guru. The text fill can also consist of a gradient or texture. Either of these possibilities can be selected from the Text Fill command.

In terms of the text outline, you can use the Text Outline command to select from a variety of colors, or you can use a color you select from the Color dialog box (use the More Outline Colors setting). The Text Outline command also enables you to set the weight and dash style used by the text outline color you select.

The Text Effects command enables you to select from a number of different effects galleries, including Shadow, Reflection, Glow, and Transform. Select a category such as Transform and then preview the possibilities provided in a specific gallery by mousing over a choice or choices. Figure 18.9 shows the Transform gallery provided by the Text Effects command.

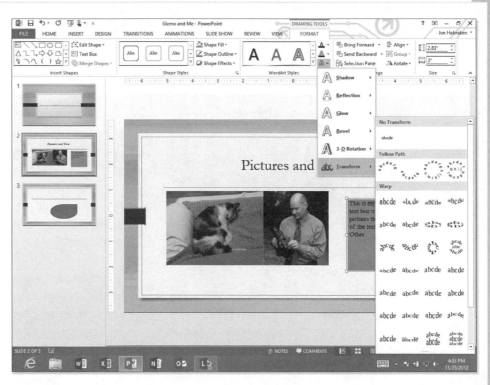

Figure 18.9
Use the Text Effects command to assign special effects to your text.

Although the various text effects are certainly more exciting than what we typically think of as text formatting, I suggest that you use these possibilities judiciously. Cramming a slide with text that has had different effects applied to it might be hard to read or just might be jarring in terms of design sensibility. Use the effects to best effect, which means use them sparingly and appropriately. The effects should add to the slide's appeal, not take away from its ability to communicate.

Setting Text Effects in the Format Shape Task Pane

You can configure and fine-tune text effect settings in the Format Shape task pane (just as you can fine-tune shape settings). To open the Format Shape task pane with the Text Options selected, select the dialog box launcher on the WordArt Styles group.

Figure 18.10 shows the Format Shape task pane with the Text Effects icon selected and the Shadow and Reflection settings expanded. As with the Shape Options we discussed in the previous section, expand one of the setting groups, such as Shadow, Reflection, or Glow, and then change the settings as needed. The Text Effect settings (Shadow through 3-D Rotation) work exactly the same as the effect settings we discussed for formatting shapes (see the list in the previous section).

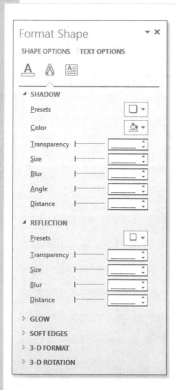

Figure 18.10
The Text Effects in the Format Shape task pane.

The Format Shape task pane also provides you with access to other text settings (not just the text effects). To access the Text Fill or Text Outline settings, select the Text Fill & Outline icon at the top of the Format Shape task pane. You can then expand the Text Fill or Text Outline settings in the task pane.

The Text Fill settings can consist of No Fill, Solid Fill, Gradient, Picture, Texture, or Pattern. When working with the Solid Fill option, you can select a Color and Transparency level for the text. The Gradient option provides you with the ability to set the Color, Direction, Type, and Angle of the gradient. You can then use the Gradient Stops slider to set the stops for the gradient. The Picture or Texture Fill option enables you to select from provided textures or use a picture or clip art as the fill for the text. The last of the fill options, the Pattern Fill, enables you to select a Pattern and Foreground and Background Color.

The Text Outline (meaning the text border) can be a Solid Line or a Gradient Line (or No Line). When you select the Gradient Line option, you can set the Preset Colors, Type (Linear, Radial, Rectangular, or Path), the Gradient Stops for the gradient, and the Brightness and Transparency of the gradient.

You can also access the Text Box settings in the Format task pane. These settings allow you to control the vertical alignment and direction of the text. You can also specify margins for the text box (or other shape containing text) and determine if the text should wrap in the shape (or not). After you have modified the settings in the Format Shape task pane, you can close it by clicking the Close button.

 tip

You can move the Format Shape task pane anywhere in the PowerPoint application window by dragging its top (the top of the task pane). To place the task pane back in its original position, drag it against the right side of the PowerPoint window until it "snaps" back into place.

Arranging Text in Tables

Another option (other than a text box) for placing text on a slide is the table. A table can be very useful when you want to display numerical information in an easy-to-read format or want to arrange information in columns or rows. The intersection of a table column and row is referred to as a cell.

The easiest way to create a table on a slide is to create a new slide that uses the Title and Content layout (or use any slide with a content option); insert the new slide using the New Slide command on the Home tab. In the content area of the slide, select the Insert Table icon. The Insert Table dialog box opens, as shown in Figure 18.11.

Figure 18.11
The Insert Table dialog box.

Specify the number of columns and the number of rows for the new table using the spinner boxes provided. When you are ready to place the table on the slide, click OK. The table is placed on the slide.

Inserting a Table on an Existing Slide

You can also insert a table onto an existing slide. This enables you to include a table on a slide in cases where you don't want to change the slide's layout (particularly in cases where the slide already contains content) or just want to place the table on the slide as an object.

Switch to the Ribbon's Insert tab and then select the Table command; you can select the columns and rows for the table by using the table grid provided by the Table command. When you release the mouse, the table is placed on the slide. You can drag the table to the appropriate position on the slide as needed. You can also use any of the sizing handles to size the table so that it is appropriate for your purposes.

Formatting a Table

After you have the table on the slide, you can enter text into the cells provided by the table. The easiest way to move forward (left to right) from cell to cell in the table is to use the Tab key. Shift+Tab moves you backward (right to left) from cell to cell. As you type text in a cell and exceed the width of the column, the text is wrapped and the cell height increases to accommodate your entered text. You can widen a column by dragging the border on the column.

PowerPoint also provides specific tools for working with both the layout and design of a table. When you select a table (as an object) or place the insertion point in a cell, the Table Tools appear on the Ribbon.

The Layout commands appear on the Table Tools Layout tab. These tools range from commands that enable you to insert columns and rows, merge and split cells, and change the text alignment in a cell or cells. The Design commands, which appear on the Table Tools Design tab, control the overall look of the table by providing table styles and commands that enable you to configure the shading, border, and effects for the table.

 note

You can draw a new table on a slide. Select the Table command on the Insert tab and then select Draw Table. You can then use the mouse to draw the outside borders of the table and the interior row and column borders. If the columns and rows are uneven, use the Distribute Columns or Distribute Rows commands on the Table Tools Layout tab as needed.

Table Layout Commands

The Layout tab houses several command groups that enable you to manipulate your rows, columns, and cells and also work with the text alignment within the cell. Figure 18.12 shows the Table Tools Layout commands.

Figure 18.12
The Table Tools Layout commands.

The Layout command groups are as follows:

- **Table:** This group provides the Select, View Gridlines, and Delete commands. The Select command provides you with the ability to select the table, the current column, or the current row. The Delete command enables you to delete selected columns, selected rows, or the entire table.

- **Rows & Columns:** These commands enable you to insert rows and columns into the table. You can insert rows above or below a selected row or rows. You can also insert columns to the left or right of the selected column or columns. If you select multiple rows or columns, that is the number of new rows or columns that will be inserted into the table.

- **Merge:** You can select cells and then merge these cells into a single, larger cell using the Merge Cells command. Use the Split Cells command if you want to split a cell (a regular cell or a merged cell) into two or more cells. You specify the number of columns and rows created when a cell is split by using the Split Cells dialog box, as shown in Figure 18.13.

Figure 18.13
The Split Cells dialog box.

- **Cell Size:** You can change the width or height of the current row or column (or selected rows or columns) by using the Width and Height spinner boxes, respectively. If you want to evenly distribute the columns or rows in the table, use the Distribute Columns or Distribute Rows commands, respectively. Using both of these commands makes all the cells in the table the same size.

- **Alignment:** This group provides commands such as the Align Left and the Center command that can be used to specify the horizontal alignment of the text within a cell or cells. If you want to specify the vertical alignment of text in a cell or cells, use the Align Top, Align Center, or Align.

- **Bottom commands:** This group also provides commands for specifying the text direction in a cell or cells and internal cell margins for a cell or cells.

- **Table Size:** This group contains the Height and Width spinner boxes, which can be used to adjust the size of the table. If you want the height and width ratio to remain the same when you change the height or width of the table, select the Lock Aspect Ratio check box.

As already mentioned, many of the command options provided on the Layout tab can be used on an individual cell or a group of selected cells. The easiest way to select entire columns or rows is to place the mouse at either the top of a column or on the left of a row until the mouse pointer becomes an arrow. Then use the arrow to drag and select multiple columns or rows as needed.

Table Design Commands

The Table Tools Design tab provides commands that enable you to quickly format the table, including its shading and borders. Commands are also available that enable you to apply quick styles and other WordArt formatting to the text within the table cells.

The first set of commands on the Design tab is housed in the Table Style Options group. Because tables often contain headings in the top row or can contain important information in the first column, the Table Style Options group provides check box commands that enable you to emphasize certain rows and columns in the table. For example, you can emphasize your column headings (which appear in the first row) by selecting the Header Row check box. If you are planning on having totals or other summary information in the last row of the table, you can use the Total Row check box to emphasize the last row of the table. The colors used by the Table Style Options command are based on the table style currently assigned to your table.

You can choose an alternative table style by selecting a style from the Table Styles gallery. You can scroll through the table styles available in the gallery or you can click the More button to view the entire gallery, as shown in Figure 18.14.

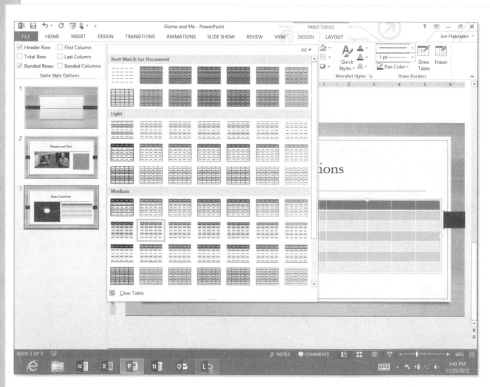

Figure 18.14
The Table Styles gallery.

In cases where you want to specify shading for the table that is not available in one of the table styles provided in the gallery, you can use the Shading command to select a color, picture, gradient, or texture for the fill. You can specify the external and internal borders for the table using the Borders command and its accompanying gallery. You can even specify Diagonal Down and Diagonal Up borders for table cells.

If you would like to add 3D effects to table cells, the Effects command enables you to select bevels, shadows, and reflections for a cell or cells. The effect choices are similar to the effect possibilities that we discussed earlier in the chapter when we looked at the Drawing Tools shape effects provided in the WordArt Styles group. And as with text in a text box, you can choose to format the text in your table with WordArt Styles or specify text fill, lines, and effects using the commands available in the WordArt Styles group.

Working with Themes

PowerPoint pioneered the concept of the theme, which is best described as a unified collection of font, color, and design attributes that can be applied to all the slides in a presentation. This provides an overall look of uniformity for the slides in the presentation, even when the slides use different layouts or contain different types of objects. PowerPoint provides a number of different themes, and you can modify these themes to create your own custom themes. In PowerPoint, a theme controls the slide colors (including the background), the fonts, and the effects. It also controls the layout of the title and content areas on a slide. So, a theme also affects how information is laid out on each slide.

You already know that you can base a new presentation on a template or a theme. Because each template has its own theme, you assign the template's theme to your new presentation (and get some sample slides and object placeholders in the bargain). When you base your new presentation on a theme, you get a title slide and all the theme's attributes, such as the slide background, fonts, and other design elements. So, whether you use a template or a theme to initiate a new presentation (on the Start screen or the New page), it is the theme that dictates the colors, fonts, effects, and the background style for your presentation slides. When selecting a template or theme for a new presentation, try to keep the purpose of your presentation in mind. If you are giving a presentation on major cost-cutting measures that must be enacted at your company, you want to use slide colors, fonts, and design elements that match the tone of the presentation. You probably don't want to use a theme such as the Black Tie theme because it uses a lot of black and muted grays, which makes it seem like you are presenting at a funeral (and people are going to be depressed enough when you talk about budget cuts). On the other hand, you probably wouldn't want to use the Opulent theme, which uses a lot of violet and gradient effects and might be a bit too cheery and contrast with the seriousness of the information being presented.

Remember that the presentation theme you select also controls the position and orientation of title and content boxes on the slides, controlling the layout for each slide. If a particular theme doesn't provide slide layouts that you find appropriate for the type of content you are presenting, you can go with another theme or adjust how the theme affects the different layout masters for the presentation. We discuss the slide master and the layout masters later in this chapter.

➡ *Presentation templates are discussed in Chapter 17, "Requisite PowerPoint: Essential Features."*

Applying Themes

When you create a new presentation using a template, a theme, or an existing presentation (if that presentation had a theme applied to it), you are assigning a theme to your slides. Selecting a theme that you can live with at the outset of the presentation creation process negates you from having to do a lot of work rearranging objects on your slides because you have changed to a radically differ-ent theme (radically different from your "starting" theme). Different themes have different layout restrictions, and you don't want to go back and rearrange text and other content boxes when they are adjusted by the layouts provided by a new theme. I'm not saying that you should never change a presentation's theme; I just want you to be mindful that there might be consequences.

A theme can be applied to your current presentation by selecting a theme in the Themes gallery. The Themes gallery (shown in Figure 18.15) is on the Ribbon's Design tab. To preview a theme on the current presentation, place the mouse on a particular theme. When you have found the theme that you want to use for the presentation, select the theme. It is applied to all the slides in the presentation.

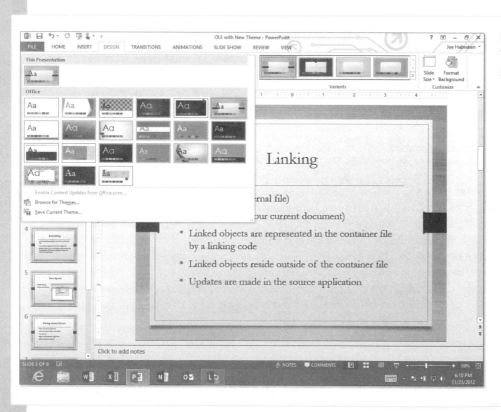

Figure 18.15
The Themes gallery.

Working with themes is not an all-or-nothing proposition. If you don't like the color scheme or design elements of an existing theme, you do have options for modifying a theme. A quick fix in cases where you don't like the color scheme or background of a theme is to apply a variant of that theme. We discuss theme variants in the next section. You also have the option of modifying the colors, fonts, effects, and background settings for a theme (and any of its variants). Changes that you make to a theme or one of its variants can be saved as a custom theme. So, read on as we discuss variants, colors, fonts, effects, and background styles.

Applying Theme Variants

PowerPoint 2013 also provides a new twist on themes called variants. In previous versions of PowerPoint, if you wanted to see what your slides would look like if you varied some of the theme's elements, such as the colors or effects, you had to tweak the colors or effects settings manually (which you can still do if you want). In PowerPoint 2013, a Variants gallery, as shown in Figure 18.16, provides variations of the current theme (the variations in most cases are different color schemes and backgrounds). To see how the variation looks on the current slide, place the mouse on the variant.

Figure 18.16
The Variants gallery and Colors gallery.

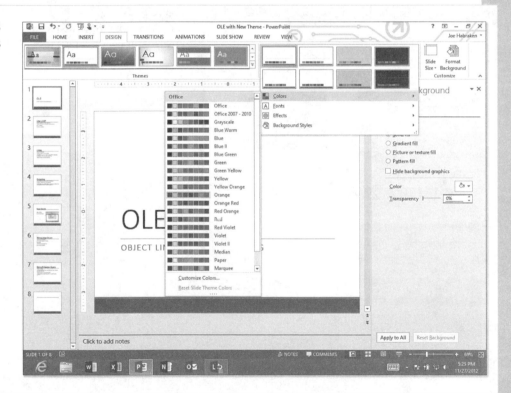

You can expand the Variants gallery by clicking the More button on the right side of the gallery. When you locate the variant you want to use, select that variant. As mentioned in the previous section, you can select a theme variant and then modify the colors, fonts, and effects as needed.

Theme Colors

Each theme and theme variant has a color scheme. As already mentioned, you can adjust the colors for the current theme by selecting a variant. You can also adjust the color set using the Colors command, which is located in the Variants gallery. Click the More button in the Variants gallery to access the Colors gallery, as shown in Figure 18.16. This gallery provides a number of built-in color schemes. You can preview the colors on the current slide by placing the mouse on one of the theme color sets.

If you want to create your own theme colors, you can do so in the Create New Theme Colors dialog box (as shown in Figure 18.17). To open this dialog box, select Customize Colors in the Colors gallery. Use the various color drop-down palettes to select the specific colors for the theme color set. When selecting a color, you can use theme colors or standard colors. To access more colors (more than the theme and standard colors), select More Colors, and the Color dialog box opens.

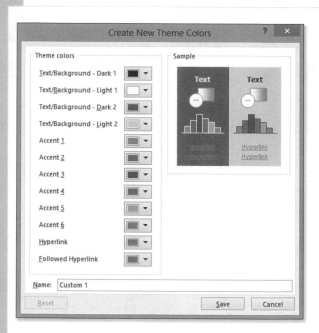

Figure 18.17
Use the Create New Theme Colors dialog box to create your own color sets.

When you have selected the colors for the new theme colors, provide a name in the Name text box. When you click Save, the color theme is added to the Colors gallery under the Custom heading.

Theme Fonts

You can also adjust the fonts used by the current theme (or theme variant). Expand the Variants gallery and then select the Fonts command. A gallery of different font sets opens. Each font set provides the appropriate font sizes for the different title and text boxes that appear on your different slide layouts.

If you want to create your own theme fonts, you can select Customize Fonts in the Fonts gallery and the Create New Theme Fonts dialog box opens. Use the Heading font and Body font drop-down lists to specify the heading and body fonts, respectively. A sample of your font selection is provided in the dialog box.

Enter a name for the new theme fonts and then select Save. The new theme fonts appear on the Fonts gallery under the Custom heading.

> **tip**
>
> If you want to delete custom theme colors or custom theme fonts that you have created, right-click on them in their respective gallery (Colors or Fonts gallery) and then select Delete from the shortcut menu.

Theme Effects

Theme effects can also be modified for the current theme or variant by selecting a built-in effects set from the Effects gallery. Expand the Variants gallery and then select the Effects command; the Effects gallery appears, as shown in Figure 18.18.

Figure 18.18
The Effects gallery.

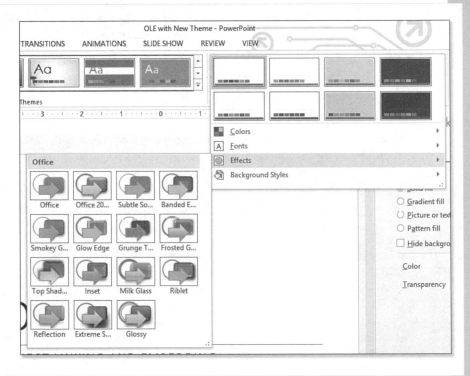

You won't see dramatic changes to your slides when you change the theme effects. Think of the effects as theme design refinements. You also can't create your own effects sets, but you can save effects changes that you have made to the current theme by creating a custom theme (which we talk about in a moment).

Theme Backgrounds

PowerPoint 2013 also makes it easy for you to fine-tune the background style for the selected theme or theme variant. In earlier versions of PowerPoint, background formatting and presentation design elements were typically dealt with on the presentation's slide master (which we talk about in a few pages); however, this also meant that all the slides in the presentation had the same background. PowerPoint 2013 provides options for changing the background on all the slides in the presentation or specific slides in the presentation.

You can apply a new background style to the current theme or variant via the Background Styles gallery. Expand the Variants gallery and then select Background Styles. Select a background style from the gallery. The background style is applied to the slides in the presentation.

You can also format the background manually using the Format Background task pane. You can open the Format Background task pane by selecting Format Background in the Background Styles gallery or by selecting the Format Background command in the Customize group on the Ribbon's Design tab.

Figure 18.19 shows the Format Background task pane with the Gradient fill option selected. You can select from a number of fill options. These options are as follows:

- **Solid Fill:** This option allows you to specify a Fill Color and Transparency.

- **Gradient Fill:** You can select from a number of Preset Gradients and also create a custom gradient where you control gradient attributes, such as the Type, Direction, Color, and Position of the gradient.

- **Picture or Texture Fill:** This option allows you to specify a picture or texture as the background fill. You can insert your own picture or a picture from Office.com for the background, and you can tile the picture as texture if you want. You can also set the offset and scale axes for the gradient and specify the alignment.

- **Pattern Fill:** You can specify a pattern as the background fill for your slides. You also control the foreground and background color from the pattern.

You can apply your background settings to the current slide (which is done automatically as soon as you change any of the background settings), or you can apply the new background to all your slides by clicking the Apply to All button. If you want to "throw out" the background changes you have made (so that they aren't applied to either the current slide or any of the slides in the presentation), click the Reset Background button. When you have finished working with the Format Background task pane, you can select Close to close it.

 tip

If you want to hide background graphics provided by a theme on a particular slide, select the Hide background graphics checkbox in the Format Background task pane when that slide is selected in the Slide list.

Figure 18.19
The Format
Background
task pane.

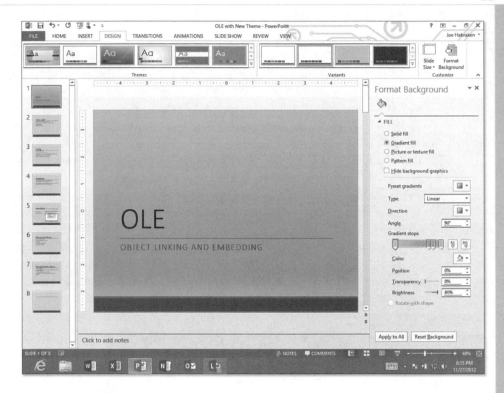

Creating a Custom Theme

We have already looked at options for saving custom color sets and font sets. You can also save all the modifications that you make to a theme as a custom theme. This includes changes you have made to colors, fonts, and background styles. You can then access your custom themes for future use.

To create a custom theme, make modifications to the current theme or a variant (change theme elements such as colors, fonts, and background settings). Select Save Current Theme in the Themes gallery. The Save Current Theme dialog box opens. By default, your custom themes are saved to `Users\User Name\AppData\Roaming\Microsoft\Templates\Document Themes`. Make sure that you save your theme to this folder so that you can easily access it (and other custom themes that you create) from the Themes gallery.

Enter a name for the custom theme and then select Save. Now when you access the Themes gallery, your new custom theme appears under the Custom heading. You can also open saved themes using the Browse for Themes command in the Themes gallery. This is useful if you didn't save a theme to the default folder, and the theme is not listed in the Themes gallery.

Using Headers and Footers

Although each slide contains information that is different from every other slide in the presentation, it is not uncommon to add repeating information to the slides in a presentation. For example, you might want to include the date and a slide number at the bottom of every slide. And in cases where you are providing your PowerPoint slides to others, you might want to place your name on each slide so that it is apparent that you were the creator of the presentation.

You can add footer information to the slides in your presentation as needed. The footer information can appear on specific slides, or it can appear on all the slides in the presentation. If you choose to include the information on all the slides, there is a setting that you can enable to keep the footer information off of the title slide (which is pretty common practice).

You can place footers on your slides, and you also have the option of creating headers and footers that are designed to appear on your note pages and handouts. All the settings related to headers and footers are located in the Header and Footer dialog box. A tab is provided for slides, and a tab is provided for notes and handouts.

To open the Header and Footer dialog box, navigate to the Ribbon's Insert tab. Then select Header & Footer in the Text group. Figure 18.20 shows the Header and Footer dialog box with the Slide tab selected.

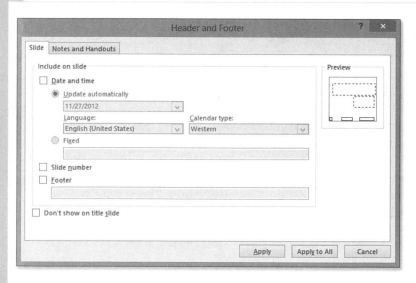

Figure 18.20
The Header and Footer dialog box.

On the Slide tab, you can specify that the date and time are included in the footer and whether or not the date should be updated automatically. A check box is also provided for the slide number, which places a slide number in the footer. If you also want to include additional footer information, such as your name, select the Footer check box and then enter the text into the Footer text box provided.

If you want to apply the footer settings to the current slide only (or a group of selected slides in the Slide Sorter or on the Slide tab), click the Apply button. If you want to apply the footer settings to all the slides in the presentation, click the Apply to All button. If you apply the footer settings to all slides, you might want to take advantage of the Don't Show on Title Slide check box because footer information is typically not included on the presentation's title slide.

➡ *Headers and footers can also be set for your presentation notes and handouts. For information on working with the notes and handout masters,* **see** *"Working with the Notes and Handouts Masters," p. 626.*

Understanding Masters

When you assign a theme to a presentation or add footers to the presentation slides, you are manipulating the master slide for the presentation. The master slide isn't actually a slide, but is the design blueprint for all the slides, including the background fill, colors, fonts, and effects provided by the current theme. The master slide also provides the positioning and the size of the content placeholders—the title text box and the bulleted list text box—which are present on most slides.

Whatever you do to the master slide is inherited by all the slides in the presentation (that use the master slide for their formatting). For example, if you place a graphic of your company logo on the slide master, the logo appears on all the slides in the presentation. Or if you change the background style for the master slide, the background style changes on all the presentation slides.

This ability to modify the master slide goes beyond broad changes, such as applying a background style or placing an image on the master slide. If you change the bullet character or change the indents for the different levels of the default bulleted list in the bulleted list placeholder on the master slide, these changes propagate to all slides in the presentation, including slides that you add to the presentation.

To view the slide master for your presentation, select the Ribbon's View tab. Select the Slide Master command in the Master Views command group. The slide master and its accompanying layout masters appear in the PowerPoint application window. Select the slide master (the first and largest thumbnail) in the master list, and the slide master appears in the Slide pane, as shown in Figure 18.21.

In the Slide pane, all the layout masters for the presentation (based on the template and theme) are listed as thumbnails to the left of the slide master, appearing below the thumbnail for the slide master (it is the larger thumbnail at the top of the thumbnail list). Note that a dotted line connects each of the layout masters with the slide master. The layout masters provide the different slide layouts you access when you use the Insert Slide command or the Layout command on the Ribbon's Home tab. Each and every slide you insert into your presentation is associated with one of the layout masters. If you place the mouse on a layout master, the name of the layout master appears and a list of the slides that have been assigned that layout master is also provided.

Any changes that you make on the master slide are inherited by the various slide layout masters; the dotted connection line that runs from the master slide to the layout masters illustrates the fact that thematic changes (colors, fonts, and so on) propagate to the layout masters. The opposite is not true, however. If you make changes directly on a layout master, these changes do not propagate back to the slide master.

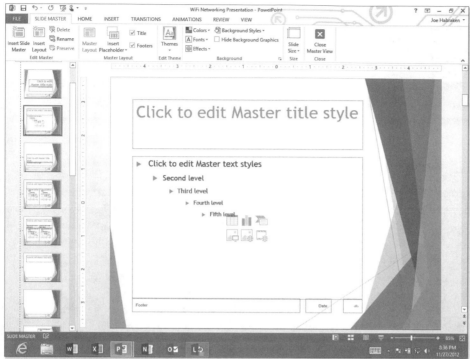

Figure 18.21
The slide master.

So, in cases where you want a unified, consistent look for a presentation, you should edit the master slide. You might be tempted to edit individual layout masters to suit a particular purpose, but it is probably a better idea to create a new layout master that is specific to your purpose. This gets you your special layout without changing any of the default layouts provided. The next section discusses altering and creating master slides and is followed by a section that discusses working with layout masters.

Altering and Creating Master Slides

When you are in the Master view, the Slide Master tab appears on the Ribbon. The Slide Master tab provides different command groups related to modifying and/or creating master slides and layout masters. These command groups are as follows:

- **Edit Master:** This group enables you to insert a new slide master or layout master. Commands are also provided for deleting and renaming masters.

- **Master Layout:** This group enables you to specify the master slide layout's default placeholders (title, text, date, and so on) via the Master Layout command. By default, all placeholders are present on a master slide. The Insert Placeholder command is used to insert placeholders on layout masters, and check boxes are also provided in this group for including a title and footers on layout masters.

- **Edit Theme:** This group provides access to the Themes gallery.

- **Background:** This group provides access to the Colors, Fonts, and Effects commands, which can be used to modify the theme on a master slide. If you want to change the background style on a master slide or layout master, you can use the Background Style command. A check box is also provided to hide background graphics that you might have inserted onto the slide master.

- **Size:** You can change the default slide size from Standard (4:3) to Widescreen (16:9) or vice versa (depending on the original size setting). This command also allows you to access the Slide Size dialog box, which can be used to create a custom slide size and control the orientation of slides, notes, and handouts.

You can change the slide master as you require. This includes rearranging and sizing the content placeholders on the master slide. You also have control over any of the theme-related settings (colors, fonts, and effects) and background styles for the slide master using the Edit Theme and/or Background group commands.

When altering the slide master, you should be aware of a couple of things. If you radically change the location of the title or content placeholders provided on the master slide, or move the footer content boxes to another location on the slide, this can negatively affect the layout masters. For example, if you move the default title placeholder down on the master slide, it might overlay other content placeholders that are on individual layout masters. This means slides that you base on particular placeholders might look really messed up because of changes that were made to the slide master.

In situations where you feel that you need a slide master with a dramatically different look, it makes better sense to create a new slide master. You can then apply the new slide master to only the slides that require this dramatically different look.

To create a new slide master, select the Insert Slide Master command in the Edit Master group. The new slide master is inserted into the Slide Master pane. A default set of layout masters is also created and associated with the new slide master. You can modify the new slide master as needed. Creating a second slide master is the easiest way to employ two different themes in the same presentation. The first slide master can be formatted with one theme, and the second slide master can be formatted with a second theme.

When you use two or more slide masters, the number of layouts available for a new slide multiplies (in the case of two slide masters, the number of layouts available doubles). Figure 18.22 shows the New Slide gallery, which is opened via the New Slide command on the Home tab (when you are working in Normal view). Note that two different sets of slide layouts are provided; the set at the top (the default slide master) has been assigned a theme, and the second set (a new slide master) has not been assigned a theme. Note also that the "added" master slide provides slide layouts that are categorized under the Custom Design heading in the New Slide gallery.

 tip

When you are in Master view, you can delete a slide master by selecting it and then selecting the Delete command in the Edit Master group.

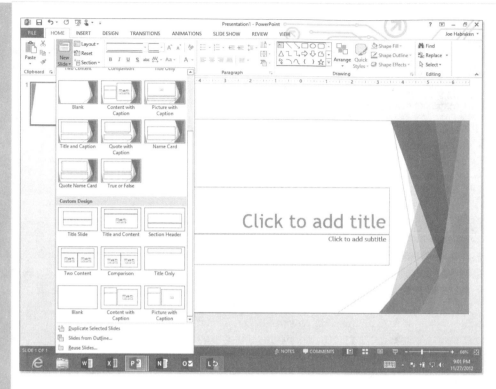

Figure 18.22
Multiple
slide masters
increase the
slide layouts
available.

The changes that you make to your second slide master are not limited to theme formatting. As with any other slide master, you can add graphics and rearrange the content placeholders on the slide master as needed.

When you are in Master view, you can check which slides have been assigned a particular slide master or a particular layout master. Place the mouse on the slide master or the layout master and a message box appears, detailing which slides are associated with the master.

If you create additional slide masters and then find that you don't use them, you can delete them from the Slide Master pane. By default, new slide masters are preserved in the Slide Master pane, whether or not you use them. This isn't a bad thing; it just keeps your added slide masters as part of the presentation regardless of whether you use them. If you are uneasy about having slide masters that you do not use still hanging around, deselect the Preserve command after you create a new slide master. If you don't use the slide master, it is not preserved.

Creating Layout Masters

You also have the ability to create new layout masters. You can create a new layout master for the default slide master or you can create a new layout master for a slide master that you have added to the presentation.

Creating your own layout masters enables you to specify layouts for special slides. This negates the need for radically changing the layout of individual slides in the presentation. You can probably create a new layout faster than you can edit an existing slide in the presentation.

When you create a new layout master, it is associated with the master slide. If you have more than one master slide, make sure that you click on the thumbnail for an existing layout master that is associated with the slide master you want to associate with your layout master (check the dashed lines and the connections between the slide master or slide masters and their associated layout masters).

To insert the new layout master, select the Insert Layout command in the Edit Master group. The new layout master appears in the Slide pane and is added as a thumbnail to the list of masters on the left of the screen. By default, a title placeholder and footers are added to the layout master. You can remove the title or the footers by deselecting the Title or Footers check boxes in the Master Layout group.

To add placeholders to the new layout master, select the Insert Placeholder command in the Master Layout group. Figure 18.23 shows the different placeholder types provided by the Insert Placeholder command.

Figure 18.23
Insert a placeholder on the new layout master.

You can add a number of different placeholder types to the layout master, including text, picture, and chart. Then when you use the layout master to create a new slide, the content specified on the layout master is provided in the new slide.

For example, to place a content box on the layout master, select Content in the Insert Placeholder gallery. You then use the mouse to draw the content placeholder box. You can size the placeholder and arrange the placeholder on the layout master as needed. Arranging and sizing placeholders is no different from working with content boxes on a regular slide—it is all mouse work.

 tip

You can change the background style for a layout master. This change does not affect the other layout masters associated with the slide master.

As already mentioned at the beginning of our discussion related to the slide master and layout masters, I think it is better to create custom slide masters and layout masters rather than radically changing the default slide master and its associated layout masters. In most cases, radically different slide looks and layouts are used minimally in a presentation. So, create your own masters for these exceptions, and rely on the default masters for the more typical slides in your presentation.

 tip

When you have finished working in the master view, select the Close Master View command to return to your presentation.

Using Slide Sections

A great way to organize a presentation with a large number of slides is to break the presentation into parts using sections. Slide sections do not affect the layout or look of slides, but they do provide you with an organizational tool for grouping associated slides in a presentation into a specific section. Having the slides in a presentation grouped by sections makes it easy for you to arrange large parts of your presentation without dragging individual slides around. This is particularly useful when you are fine-tuning the sequence of slides in your presentation. Sections can be collapsed, which enables you to focus on the section itself. This makes it even easier to move a section within the presentation.

The best view to work in when you are creating and rearranging sections is the Slide Sorter. You can switch to the Slide Sorter by using the Slide Sorter button on the PowerPoint status bar or by switching to the View tab on the Ribbon and then selecting Slide Sorter.

The Section command is on the Ribbon's Home tab in the Slides group. The easiest way to create a new section is to select the first slide that appears in the section. Then select Section and then Add Section. A new section is placed between the selected slide and the slides that precede the selected slide in the presentation. You can then navigate to the next slide that starts a new section in the presentation and create a new section at that point. Repeat the process until you have grouped all the slides in the presentation into specific sections.

When you insert the section into the presentation, the section is listed as "Untitled Section." If you select the section, you can then rename it by clicking the Section command and then selecting Rename Section. The Rename Section dialog box opens. Type a name for the section and select Rename.

You can rename any section that you create, and rename the Default Section if it is created automatically. If you are working on a Ribbon tab other than the Home tab, right-click on a section and then select Rename Section to access the Rename Section dialog box. This forgoes the necessity of switching back to the Home tab.

When you have the presentation divided into sections, you can easily rearrange the presentation. Each section has a collapse/expand button on the left side of the section bar. You can collapse a section or sections as needed. If you want to collapse all the sections in the presentation, right-click on any section and then select Collapse All from the shortcut menu provided. Figure 18.24 shows a presentation with four sections; three of the sections have been collapsed and one section shows thumbnails of the slides in that section.

> **note**
>
> If you create a new section in the presentation in a place other than the very beginning of the presentation, the slides that precede the new section are automatically placed in a section titled Default Section.

Figure 18.24
Collapsed sections in the Slide Sorter.

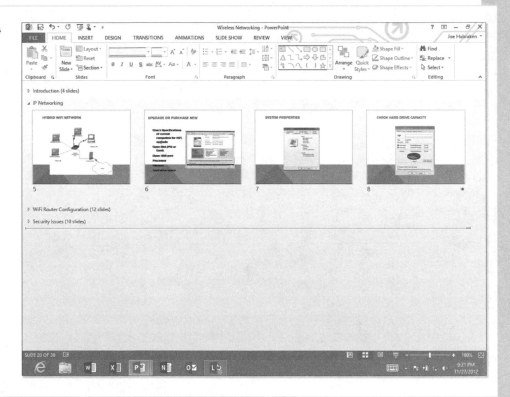

You can drag a section to a new position in the presentation to rearrange the presentation as needed. The number of slides in a collapsed presentation will be noted to the right of the section title.

You can also copy all the slides in a section and paste the entire section into another presentation. Select a section and then select Copy on the Home tab. You can then open an existing presentation or start a new presentation and paste the slides into the presentation. You can also cut and paste slide sections from one presentation to another.

Sections provide markers in your presentation that make it easy to jump to a particular part of the presentation when you are running a slide show.

For more information about showing presentations as a slide show, **see** "Running Through a Completed Presentation," **p. 612**.

BETTER SLIDES WITH CLIP ART, PICTURES, AND SMARTART

PowerPoint presentations are meant to tell a story. Whether you are providing coworkers an update on the company's quarterly sales or sharing your latest vacation photos and experiences with your travel club, a presentation needs to be succinct and complete (with a beginning, middle, and end). Much of the information can be shared as text, but images and other graphics can greatly enhance the audience's understanding of the presented information. Clip Art, pictures, and SmartArt can also make slides more visually interesting and appealing.

In this chapter, we look at adding graphics such as Clip Art, pictures, and SmartArt to your PowerPoint slides. We explore how graphics can serve as informational objects, such as pictures and charts, and how objects such as Clip Art and SmartArt can be used as design elements on your slides. We also discuss working with object layers and how to group related objects. Our discussion includes adding hyperlinks to slides and using hyperlinks to access external information on the Web and point to information in a presentation.

Using Graphics to Enhance Slides

The graphics you place on your PowerPoint slides can be informational in nature or just serve as design elements (or both). In terms of information, a chart or picture can often be more effective than text in getting across an idea or concept. For example, a chart of recent sales figures gives the audience a better feel for recent sales trends than a table of numbers. Graphics can also add visual interest to your slides. Office.com provides enough Clip Art images and pictures to add items to your slides that match the theme of a slide (or the entire presentation). For example, if you are giving a presentation at a town meeting related to the need for a new playground, you can do a search for *playground* in the Insert Picture dialog box. You can then select from a number of playground-related images for your slide or slides.

PowerPoint enables you to insert different visual objects onto a slide. Several of the possibilities are as follows:

- **Picture:** You can insert your digital pictures directly into your presentation slides. PowerPoint supports a number of digital picture file formats. PowerPoint also provides tools that enable you to modify inserted pictures. You can crop, correct, and add effects to your images.

- **Online Pictures:** This possibility isn't a single item, but rather a grouping of different online picture sources. You can access both Clip Art and royalty-free photos on Office.com. PowerPoint 2013 offers you other "cloud" scenarios for inserting online pictures, including the ability to search the Web using Bing and access your images stored on your SkyDrive (or a SharePoint site). You can also insert pictures that you store on Flickr.com into your slides.

- **Screenshot:** You can capture a screenshot of any open window using the Screenshot command. You can then add these screenshots directly to a slide. This is extremely useful when you want to include a screenshot of another application window (such as Excel) on a presentation slide.

- **Shapes:** You can insert many different shapes into your slides (or into the master slide) to add visual appeal to a slide. PowerPoint provides a Shapes gallery that has an enormous number of shapes, including lines, rectangles, block arrows, flow charts, banners, and callouts.

- **SmartArt:** SmartArt gives you access to all sorts of diagrams that enable you to create block diagrams, flow charts, organizational charts, and even pyramid diagrams. If you've ever had to place an inverted pyramid on a slide and tried to draw it in another software package or construct it from shapes, you understand how useful SmartArt can be.

- **Charts:** You can add column, line, pie, bar, and other chart types to your PowerPoint slides. The chart data is entered into an Excel worksheet, making it easy to provide the information that makes the chart a reality. You can edit the chart data at any time.

> *You can also link Excel worksheet data and Excel charts to PowerPoint slides.* ***See*** *Appendix A, "Office Application Integration," for more information.*

PowerPoint provides other objects that can also be considered graphics or design elements. For example, you can insert WordArt text boxes. These special text boxes add interesting text elements to a slide. You can also add equations to your slides. PowerPoint provides a gallery of equations, including the area of a circle, the binomial theorem (one of my favorites), and the Pythagorean theorem (okay, this is my favorite). You can also insert new equations that you create.

> *Video and sound can also enhance your slides. For more about adding video and sounds to your PowerPoint presentations,* ***see*** *"Adding Sound to a Slide,"* ***p. 600.***

There is more than one way to insert a graphic such as a picture or Clip Art to your slides. When you insert a new slide into a presentation, most slides have content areas that provide icons for inserting a chart, SmartArt, a picture, or Clip Art. When you select one of these content options, the graphic is inserted onto the slide, replacing the content frame.

You can also insert items such as pictures and shapes as objects within their own frame. The Ribbon's Insert tab, shown in Figure 19.1, provides the commands for inserting the various graphic object types into your slides.

Figure 19.1
The Ribbon's Insert tab.

After you insert a visual on a slide, contextual tools that relate to the particular graphic type appear on the Ribbon. For example, when you insert a picture, the Picture Tools Format tab appears on the Ribbon. When you insert a SmartArt graphic, the SmartArt tools become available on the Ribbon. PowerPoint 2013 makes it easier to insert and then manipulate graphics on your slides than in previous versions of PowerPoint.

➡ *For an overview of working with graphics in Office 2013,* **see** *Chapter 4, "Using and Creating Graphics."*

Inserting a Picture

You can quickly insert a picture file that you have stored on your computer using the Pictures command in the Images group. PowerPoint supports several popular picture file formats, including Windows Bitmap (.bmp), Graphics Interchange Format (.gif), Joint Photographics Expert Group (.jpg), Portable Network Graphics (.png), and TIFF, Tagged Image File Format (.tiff).

To open the Insert Picture dialog box, select the Pictures command on the Insert tab. If you are working with a new slide that contains content placeholders, you can also open the Insert Picture dialog box by selecting the Pictures icon in the content placeholder. Figure 19.2 shows the Insert Picture dialog box.

The default location for the Insert Picture dialog box is the Pictures library. If you need to navigate to another location on your computer or computer network, do so. When you have located the picture you want to insert, select the picture and then click Insert. The picture is inserted onto the current slide.

When the picture is selected on the slide, the Picture Tools Format tab appears on the Ribbon. Figure 19.3 shows the Picture Tools Format tab.

Figure 19.2
The Insert Picture dialog box.

Figure 19.3
The Picture
Tools Format
tab.

The picture tools enable you to adjust the picture (such as brightness and contrast), select a picture style, arrange multiple pictures on the page, and crop and size the selected picture. The Picture Tools groups are as follows:

- **Remove Background:** This command enables you to remove the background from the picture. When you select the Remove Background command, the Background Removal tab appears on the Ribbon. You can mark areas to keep in the picture or mark areas to remove from the picture. Figure 19.4 shows a picture with the background to be removed and the Ribbon's Background Removal commands used to fine-tune the removal of the picture's background.

- **Adjust:** This group provides commands that enable you to adjust the sharpness, brightness, and contrast, and to make color corrections to the picture, including its saturation and tone. You can also add artistic effects to the picture and reset the picture settings, if needed.

- **Picture Styles:** Picture styles provide you with different frame formats, which include frame shapes and frame border styles. You can preview a style on the selected picture by placing the mouse on any of the styles in the gallery.

Figure 19.4
Remove the background from a picture.

- **Arrange:** This group enables you to layer multiple images (using commands such as Bring Forward and Send Backward). It also enables you to group graphics and align images (left, center, right, top-middle, bottom), and provides you with the ability to rotate and flip pictures.

- **Size:** This group provides Height and Width spinner boxes for sizing a picture. You can also use the Crop command to crop the image as needed.

When you finish manipulating the picture, click outside the picture frame to deselect it. The picture tools are also removed from the Ribbon.

> *For detailed information on working with pictures in the Office applications, **see** Chapter 4, "Using and Creating Graphics."*

Adding Online Images to Slides

Office.com provides an extremely large library of Clip Art and stock photo possibilities. Clip Art can be a little too cutesy at times, but it can also add visual interest to slides if used judiciously and can (at the right time) even add a little humor to your presentation. The Office.com image library consists of photos in the JPEG format (`.jpg`), illustrations and cartoons in the Windows Media File format (`.wmf`), and animated GIFs in the GIF format (`.gif`).

When you open the Insert Picture window, the Office.com image library is not the only possible source of online images. You can also use Bing to do an image search (by keyword) on the Web. Other possibilities include images stored on your SkyDrive and images you have stored on your flickr.com account site.

To open the Insert Pictures window, select the Online Pictures command in the Images group. You can also open the Insert Pictures window by clicking the Online Pictures icon in a new slide's content area. Figure 19.5 shows the Insert Pictures window.

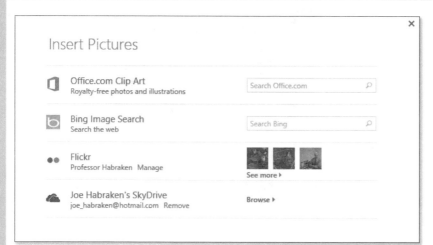

Figure 19.5
The Insert Pictures window.

To insert a photo or illustration from the Office.com Clip Art library, type a search string into the Search Office.com box and then press Enter. The search results appear in the Insert Picture window. You can use the vertical scrollbar to scroll through search results. If you want to zoom in on a particular image, place the mouse on the image and then click the View Larger icon that appears (click the Close button on the enlarged image to close it). If you didn't get the results that you anticipated, you can modify your search criteria in the Search box and search again. After you have located the image you want to insert into the slide, select the image and then click Insert.

Another of the online options for inserting pictures is the Bing image search. All you have to do to locate web-based images is place the insertion point in the Search Bing box, type your search string, and then press Enter (or click the Search icon). The results of your search appear in the Insert Pictures window. You can zoom in on any of the images and refine your search, if necessary.

By default, the Bing image search shows only images found (using your search criteria) that are licensed under Creative Commons. Creative Commons is a nonprofit organization that gives content creators licensing options for sharing their work on the Web. Each image that appears in your search results may have a specific license with specific use restrictions. When you select an image in the search results, the filename, size (in pixels), and website location appear in the lower left of the Insert Picture window. You can navigate to the source site for more information on the image. When you locate an image that you want to insert (and are confident that you are not violating any use restrictions), select the image and then click the Insert button.

If you store your own photos online, you can also access them using the Insert Picture window. If you sign into your Office applications using your Windows Live ID (with your Outlook.com or Hotmail account), your SkyDrive appears as one of the options in the Insert Picture window. Use the Browse button to locate an image. Select the image you want to insert, and then click the Insert button. The Image is placed on the slide.

You can also insert photos that you have stored on your photostream at Flickr.com. In the Insert Pictures window, select the Flickr logo box below the Also Insert From heading (at the bottom-left of the window). Associate your Microsoft account (Outlook.com or Hotmail) with your Flickr logon the first time you select the Flickr option. To proceed, select Connect and then log onto Flickr using your Yahoo! ID (which you created when you signed up for Flickr—if you haven't signed up for Flickr, you can create a Yahoo! ID at this point in the process and then log in).

After you associate your Microsoft account with your Flickr account, you return to the Insert Pictures window, and Flickr appears as one of the choices for inserting online pictures. When you select Browse (to the right of the Flickr logo), your Flickr Photostream opens, as shown in Figure 19.6. You can enlarge individual photos for a better view. To insert a photo into the current slide, select the thumbnail of the photo and then click Insert.

 tip

The Clip Art and photos that Office.com provides are royalty free. This means that you don't have to worry about copyright issues if you use an image in a presentation. Images you find using the Bing image search may have licensing restrictions (in terms of use), so track down the licensing terms for an image if you are going to use it for any "professional purpose." You can read more about Creative Commons and content licensing at http://creativecommons.org/licenses/.

Figure 19.6
Access your Flickr Photostream photos.

‹ BACK TO SITES

●● Flickr
Your Photostream

Search Flickr

DSC_0269
500 x 332 - Professor Habraken

1 item selected.   Insert   Cancel

After you have inserted an image into the slide—whether it is an image from your computer or Clip Art from Office.com—the Picture Tools Format tab appears on the Ribbon. You can adjust the various settings from the image as needed; however, if you are working with Clip Art files that have the `.wmf` or `.gif` file extensions, the Remove Background tool is not available (as it is for other picture file types).

 tip

If you want Clip Art or a picture to repeat on every slide (say, for a logo), place the image on the presentation's master slide.

Creating a Photo Album

If you have a bunch of digital photos that you want to get onto PowerPoint slides with a minimal amount of hassle, you can create a PowerPoint photo album. The Photo Album tool is perfect for quickly placing your digital vacation photos on a series of slides. The Photo Album command is on the Insert tab in the Images group.

When you use the Photo Album command, a new presentation is created, including a title slide for the presentation. Different picture layouts enable you to specify the number of pictures placed on each slide on the album. You also have control over the frame shape for each picture inserted into the photo album, and you can assign a theme to the photo album. All these settings are housed in the Photo Album dialog box, so you can specify the pictures for the album and then quickly create the entire album without manipulating individual slides or pictures.

You can use the Photo Album command even if you are currently in the middle of another presentation. Because a new presentation is created for the photo album, the slides in the current presentation are not disturbed.

To create a new photo album, select Photo Album on the Insert tab and then select New Photo Album. The Photo Album dialog box opens. The first step in the process of creating the photo album is to specify the pictures to include in the album. Select the File/Disk command, and the Insert New Pictures dialog box opens. This dialog box opens to the Pictures library by default. Locate the pictures that you want to use for the photo album. It makes sense to select as many of the pictures as you can at this point. Select the first picture and then select subsequent picture files by holding down the Ctrl key. To select a series of pictures, select the first picture series, and then select the last picture in the series with Shift+Click. This selects all the pictures in the series. After you have selected the pictures, click the Insert button in the dialog box.

You return to the Photo Album dialog box, shown in Figure 19.7. You can now manipulate the picture order in the album, choose picture options, and specify the layout for the album.

If you need to change the order of the pictures in the album, select a picture and then use the Move Up or Move Down buttons to change the position of the picture in the album list. If you decide that you don't want a particular picture in the album, select the filename and then click the Remove button.

 tip

If you need to add pictures to the photo album that are in a different location than the pictures already inserted, select File/Disk and use the Insert New Pictures dialog box to locate and add the pictures to the Photo Album dialog box.

Figure 19.7
The Photo Album dialog box.

Adjusting Picture Settings

The Photo Album dialog box also provides a series of buttons that enable you to adjust settings for each individual picture. You can use the Rotate Left or Rotate Right buttons to rotate the currently selected picture 90 degrees to either left or right, respectively. You can also adjust the contrast or brightness of the selected picture up or down using the appropriate buttons. You can adjust other picture options as well, such as selecting to have all the pictures changed to black-and-white.

If you want to include a text box on each slide that is created in the photo album, select New Text Box. The text box is added to the Pictures in Album list. The text box appears on each slide; after the photo album is created, you can add text to the text box to describe the picture on the slide or provide ancillary information related to each picture.

Setting Album Layout Settings

By default, each picture listed in the Photo Album dialog box is placed on a separate slide and is fitted to the slide, so you don't have to worry about the potentially different sizes of the pictures that you want to add to the photo album. The Fit to Slide option does not enable you to select the frame shape for the inserted pictures.

The Picture Layout drop-down list (in the Photo Album dialog box) does give you other options for how the pictures appear on the slides. The one picture, two pictures, or four pictures options place the specified number of pictures on each slide. These settings also enable you to specify the frame shape for the picture by selecting a shape from the Frame Shape drop-down list. A number of frame shapes are available, including Rounded Rectangle, Simple Frame, White, Center Shadow Rectangle, and Soft Edge Rectangle.

If you want to include a title text box on each slide, you can select the layout of one picture with a title picture. Options for two and four pictures with a title are also included in the Picture Layout drop-down list. Selecting any of the options that include a title also enables you to specify the frame shape for the pictures. Both the number of slides you specify in the layout and the frame shape you select are previewed in the Album Layout area of the Photo Album dialog box.

You also have the option of specifying a theme for the new photo album presentation. Click the Browse button next to the Theme box. This opens the Choose Theme dialog box. The Choose Theme dialog box opens to the default Office themes folder, and the themes are listed by name. You can't view a preview of the theme, but if you have a good feel for the overall look and layout of a particular theme or themes, you can select a theme and then click Open to apply it to the new photo album. This returns you to the Photo Album dialog box. When you have all your settings squared away for the new photo album, select Create. The photo album opens in the PowerPoint workspace with the title slide selected. Figure 19.8 shows a photo album in Normal view.

 caution

If you aren't too familiar with the frame shapes and presentation themes available in PowerPoint, you might want to wait and adjust these settings on the photo album after creating the album. You can then take advantage of the Themes gallery and the Pictures Style gallery, which both provide visual examples of the themes and styles available.

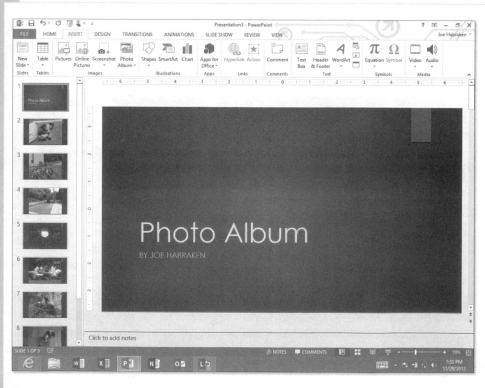

Figure 19.8
A photo album in Normal view.

Because the photo album is no different from any other PowerPoint presentation, you can modify presentation settings such as the theme for the presentation. You can also edit each slide in the presentation, which is required if you specified that a text box or title box be included on each slide when you configured the settings for the photo album in the Photo Album dialog box.

If you want to add photos to the photo album or change any of the settings related to the photo album, you can do so in the Edit Photo Album dialog box. Select the Photo Album command and then select Edit Photo Album. The Edit Photo Album dialog box provides all the settings that were available in the Photo Album dialog box. You can insert additional pictures, modify picture settings, or change the picture layout and frame shape as needed.

When you have finished making changes to the album settings, click the Update button to return to the photo album. Remember that the photo album is a new presentation, so click the Save button on the Quick Access Toolbar and specify a name and location for the photo album in the Save As dialog box.

Working with Shapes

You can add shapes to your slides as design elements and also use them as interesting text boxes (many of the shapes can contain text). When you work with shapes, remember that less is always better, so don't crowd your slides with a lot of rectangles and circles. Proper slide design relates to balance, and emphasis is not on the quantity of shapes and other graphic elements crammed on each slide.

To insert a shape, select the Shapes command on the Ribbon's Insert tab. The Shapes gallery appears, as shown in Figure 19.9.

Figure 19.9
The Shapes gallery.

The shapes provided in the gallery are divided into categories, including lines, rectangles, block arrows, and callouts, just to name a few. When you have located the shape that you want to use, click it. A drawing tool replaces the mouse pointer. Drag on the slide to draw the shape. You can size and position the shape on the page as needed.

When the shape is selected, the drawing tools are available on the Ribbon. Shape styles are provided in the Shapes Style gallery, and you can change the shape fill, outline, and effects as needed using the appropriate command in the Shape Style group.

If you want to place text in a shape, select the Text Box command in the Insert Shapes group and then click in the shape to place the insertion point. You can type your text as needed. You can then use the WordArt Style gallery to format the text. You configure individual WordArt text settings using the Text Fill, Text Outline, and Text Effects commands.

➡ *For more details on working with shapes and the drawing tools,* ***see*** *"Using Shapes and the Office Drawing Tools," p. 93.*

Using SmartArt Graphics

SmartArt graphics provide different diagram types that you can use to visually illustrate information on a slide; SmartArt isn't just a series of design elements or shapes, however. You can use SmartArt to show relationships between text entries, producing slides that make important concepts easy for your audience to understand. And bottom line: SmartArt graphics look professional and are impressive additions to your slides in both visual and informational terms.

PowerPoint provides different types or categories of SmartArt, with each type having a particular purpose. For example, the Cycle category creates diagrams that represent sequential cycles or a process that takes place in a circular flow. Figure 19.10 shows a cyclical diagram on a slide in Slide Show view. The SmartArt diagram not only gives the audience a picture of an overall process, but it gives you the outline for your talking points related to that particular slide.

As already mentioned, SmartArt graphics come in many categories. Because SmartArt is designed to enable you to communicate visually, each SmartArt type or category offers SmartArt slanted toward a particular purpose. The following list describes the SmartArt categories:

- **List:** The SmartArt lists enable you to go beyond the typical PowerPoint bulleted list and better show the relationship of items in a list. You can arrange text in both vertical and horizontal lists that include shapes to emphasize the text. The List SmartArt graphics can also provide insight into the relative importance of the list items or the sequence in which the listed items occur.

- **Process:** This group of SmartArt graphics shows a progression of items. It can provide the sequential steps in a task or process and can give a visual representation of linear workflow or display how parts of an information sequence relate to the whole.

- **Cycle:** This category provides graphics related to the process cycle and the circular flow of events or steps. Some diagrams emphasize the steps in the process cycle; others enable you to better describe the overall process and the relationship of the various segments.

Figure 19.10
A cyclical
SmartArt
graphic.

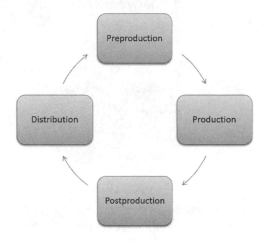

- **Hierarchy:** These SmartArt graphics provide you with diagrams such as the classic organizational chart in a branching tree format, and enable you to emphasize the hierarchical relationship of items in a diagram. There is even a Picture Organization Chart SmartArt graphic that makes it easy to construct an organizational chart with photos of the individuals listed in the chart. Other diagrams in this category help you show how items in the diagram build upon each other.

- **Relationship:** This category provides relationship diagrams that enable you to show the hierarchy of related items and illustrate how concepts or ideas relate to a central theme. This group also includes the basic Venn and radial Venn diagrams. Venn diagrams show the possible or logical relationship between different items. Figure 19.11 shows an example of a basic Venn diagram.

- **Matrix:** The matrix SmartArt graphics are designed to show the relationship of different items or quadrants to the whole. These graphics enable you to create affinity diagrams, which are designed to organize information based on natural relationships. A cycle matrix is included that shows how items are related to a central cyclical process. A good example of this is the basic communication process, which requires listening, interpreting, and responding.

- **Pyramid:** This group provides both a basic pyramid and an inverted pyramid. Pyramids show both hierarchical relationships and the proportional importance of items in the hierarchy. Maslow's hierarchy of needs uses a classic pyramid diagram that shows the basic human needs, from physiological needs such as food and water to the more creative aspects of self-actualization. Figure 19.12 shows a basic pyramid diagram.

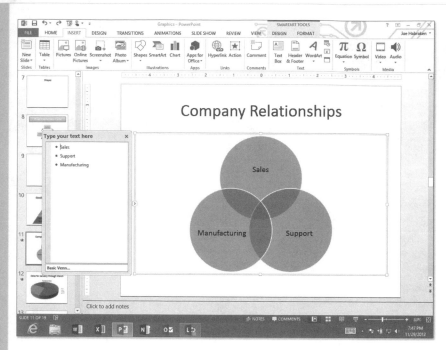

Figure 19.11
A SmartArt Venn diagram.

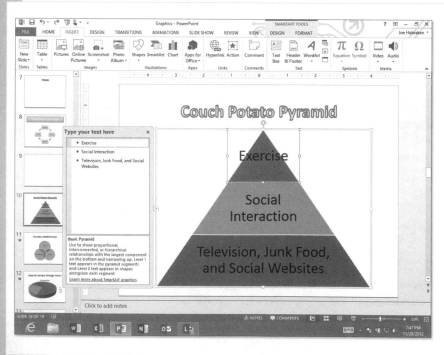

Figure 19.12
A pyramid SmartArt graphic.

- **Picture:** This group pulls together all the SmartArt graphics from the other categories that help you incorporate pictures into the diagram. These possibilities include the continuous picture list, the captioned pictures diagram (which provides multiple levels of pictures), and the hexagon cluster (which provides a grouping of clustered images with minimal accompanying text).

- **Office.com:** This group provides additional SmartArt graphics provided online via the Office.com website.

You can add a SmartArt graphic to a slide and then enter the accompanying text and pictures, or you can format existing text on a slide, such as a bulleted list, with any of the SmartArt graphics in the SmartArt Graphic gallery. When you insert a SmartArt graphic on a slide or convert existing text to a SmartArt graphic, you are provided with the SmartArt tools, which include both a Design tab and a Format tab. So even after you insert a SmartArt graphic onto a slide, you can enhance the graphic's layout, style, and overall formatting (including the text that the SmartArt graphic contains).

Inserting a SmartArt Graphic

You can insert a new SmartArt graphic on a slide via the Insert SmartArt Graphic icon in a slide content box, or you can select the SmartArt command on the Ribbon's Insert tab. In both cases, the Choose a SmartArt Graphic dialog box opens, as shown in Figure 19.13.

The graphic categories are located on the left side of the dialog box. All is selected by default. Select the category of SmartArt graphic you want to create. The graphics in the category are listed.

 note

You can add animation schemes to your SmartArt graphics to create slides with even more visual impact. See Chapter 20, "Enhancing Slides with Animation, Transitions, and Multimedia."

Figure 19.13
The Choose a SmartArt Graphic dialog box.

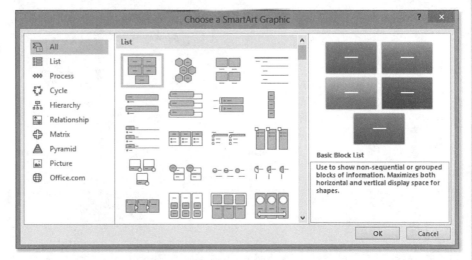

To preview an individual SmartArt graphic, select the graphic; a preview and description of the graphic appears on the right slide of the dialog box.

When you have located the diagram that you want to use, make sure that the graphic is selected and then click OK. The SmartArt graphic is placed in the current slide.

You can enter the text for the diagram directly on the diagram parts itself (such as the item boxes in a cyclical diagram). Just select any of the [TEXT] placeholders in the diagram and type the required text. You can also add the text for the diagram using the Text pane that accompanies the SmartArt graphic (to the left of the slide). Replace the [TEXT] placeholders in the list with your text. You can collapse the Text pane by clicking the pane's Close button, and you can then expand it when needed by using the Expand button on the left side of the graphic. Remember that diagrams visually communicate an idea, process, or relationship, so the diagram should not require much text; in fact, your text entries should be considered the labels for the diagram parts—that's it.

Converting Text to a SmartArt Graphic

You can also convert existing text in a text box to a SmartArt graphic. This enables you to quickly convert a bulleted list on a slide (or other text) into an appropriate diagram. To convert text to a SmartArt graphic, follow these steps:

1. Select the text box that contains the text you want to convert. This can be any text box on a slide, including bulleted lists.

2. On the Home tab, select the Convert to SmartArt command in the Paragraph group. The SmartArt gallery opens, providing a subset of the available SmartArt graphics (see Figure 19.14).

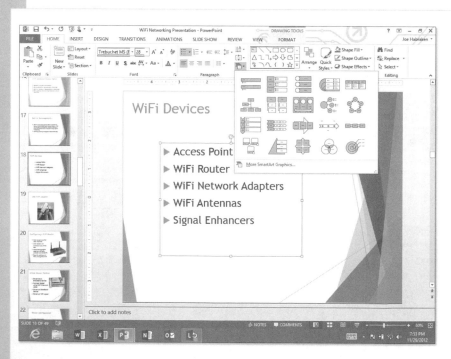

Figure 19.14
The SmartArt Graphic gallery.

3. Select a graphic from the gallery, or access more graphics by selecting More SmartArt Graphics and selecting a graphic. This opens the Choose a SmartArt Graphic dialog box.

4. If you select a diagram in the gallery, the text in the text box is immediately converted. To do the conversion from the Choose a SmartArt Graphic dialog box, select a graph and then click OK.

The existing text is placed in the text placeholders on the SmartArt diagram. The diagram replaces the original text box. You can edit the text as needed on the diagram or use the SmartArt's accompanying text pane.

Using the SmartArt Tools

Whether you create a SmartArt graphic from scratch or convert existing text to a SmartArt graphic, when the diagram is on the slide and selected, the SmartArt tools appear on the Ribbon. Two different tabs of SmartArt tools appear: Design and Format.

The Design tab provides commands that enable you to manipulate the number and position of individual graphics in the diagram and to change the layout and style of the SmartArt graphic. Figure 19.15 shows a Vertical Box List SmartArt graphic and the Design tab commands.

Figure 19.15
The SmartArt Tools Design tab.

The commands groups on the Design tab are as follows:

- **Create Graphic:** This group enables you to add elements (shapes) to the diagram and change the positioning of the shape. For example, if you have a box list graphic, you can add another shape (a box) before or after the currently selected shape by using the Add Shape command. You can also reorder the shapes in the list using the Reorder Up and Reorder Down commands, and change the positioning of the diagram from Right to Left (or vice versa) using the Right to Left command. The commands available in this group depend on the type of SmartArt graphic you inserted into the slide.

- **Layouts:** The layouts available in the Layouts gallery are specific for the type of SmartArt graphic that you placed in the slide. For example, if you inserted a basic cycle diagram into the slide, you can change the layout from the Basic Cycle to the Block Cycle or Radio Cycle by selecting a new layout in the Layouts gallery. More layouts are provided in the Choose a SmartArt Graphic dialog box, which is also accessible from the Layouts gallery.

- **SmartArt Styles:** This command group provides the Change Colors command, which specifies a new color scheme for the SmartArt graphic. The schemes available are specific to the type of diagram that you placed in the slide. You can also change the style for the diagram by selecting one of the styles from the SmartArt Styles gallery. These styles are specific to the type of diagram that you inserted and include 3D possibilities.

- **Reset:** If you don't like the changes that you have made to the SmartArt graphic, you can select the Reset Graphic command. The Convert command enables you to convert the SmartArt graphic to text or convert the diagram to a group of shapes.

When you have finished working with the Design tab commands, deselect the SmartArt graphic's frame to remove the SmartArt Tools from the Ribbon.

The SmartArt Tools Format Tab

The SmartArt Tools Ribbon tab also has a Format tab. This tab provides commands related to the formatting of the SmartArt graphic frame (not the individual items) and the text within the various shapes that populate the diagram.

You can use Shape Fill, Shape Outline, and Shape Effects to format the SmartArt graphic's outside frame. This enables you to select a fill color for the SmartArt background (this does not fill the individual shapes in the diagram) and format the SmartArt graphic with different effects such as the Shadow, Reflection, and 3D Rotation settings.

The WordArt Styles gallery and the Text Fill, Text Outline, and Text Effects commands in the WordArt Styles group can be used to change the formatting of the text that has been entered on the various shapes in the diagram. When you use these commands to format the text, it is a one-size-fits-all scenario. All the text on the various shapes that make up the diagram are formatted in the same manner.

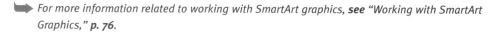 *For more information related to working with SmartArt graphics, **see** "Working with SmartArt Graphics," p. 76.*

Adding Charts to Slides

Charts can be inserted into slides to visually represent important data. Because many people do not immediately relate to tables full of numbers, an accompanying chart gives your audience a better understanding of everything from sales trends to population figures, to quarterly earnings. Charts digest all those numbers, providing with a much more meaningful pictorial view of the information.

When you insert a chart, you use an Excel worksheet to enter the data for that chart. You also use the Excel chart feature, so many of the considerations that go into creating a chart in Excel are applicable when you insert a chart into a PowerPoint slide.

You also have tools for working with charts on your PowerPoint slides. The Chart Tools contextual Ribbon addition provides three tabs of commands: Design, Layout, and Format.

 *Charts are covered in detail in the Excel section of this book. **See** Chapter 14, "Enhancing Worksheets with Charts."*

Inserting a Chart onto a Slide

You can insert a chart using the Chart command on the Ribbon's Insert tab, or you can select the Insert Chart icon in a content box. Both scenarios open the Insert Chart dialog box, shown in Figure 19.16.

Figure 19.16
The Insert Chart dialog box.

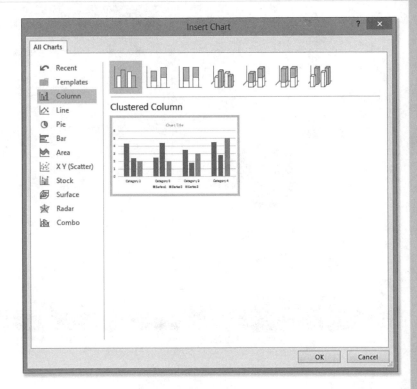

The chart types are listed on the left side of the Insert Chart dialog box. Select a particular chart type, such as Column or Pie. Note that each chart type also provides different formats. For example, the column chart type can be inserted into different formats, including a clustered column, stacked column, and clustered cylinder. The pie chart formats include a 3D pie and an exploded pie. Select the format type for the selected chart type (chart types are along the top of the dialog box), and then click OK.

The chart is inserted into the slide, and a worksheet window opens, containing generic labels and data points for the chart. At this point, the chart doesn't reflect your data or text labels. You need to modify the labels (text entries) and the numerical data on the worksheet. When you do so, the chart immediately reflects the new data. Click in the appropriate cells on the worksheet, and enter your text labels and data as needed. If you need to add more data points than those provided, you can drag the data range border (the lower-right corner) to extend the data range and enter more labels and numerical information. Figure 19.17 shows a pie chart on a PowerPoint slide and the data range for the chart in an accompanying Excel worksheet.

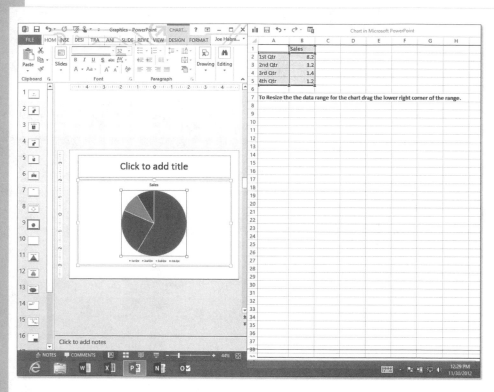

Figure 19.17
An inserted chart and the associated Excel worksheet.

You can also access all of Excel's commands and features as you enter data or otherwise modify the sheet related to your chart. Click the Edit Data in Microsoft Excel icon at the top of the worksheet.

When you finish editing the data on the Excel worksheet, you can close the worksheet. You don't need to save the worksheet; the data that you entered in the sheet remains linked to the chart on the PowerPoint slide. If you do need to reopen the worksheet, you can do so by selecting the Edit Data command on the Chart Tools Design tab (when the chart is selected on the slide).

 caution

You must enter your data and text labels within the data range provided on the worksheet for the chart to reflect the modifications that you make in the chart.

Modifying and Formatting a Chart

When the chart is selected on a slide, the Chart Tools are available on the Ribbon. You can use the various tools to modify the chart layout and style; edit the chart title, legend, and data labels; and format the chart's frame and text using the shape styles and WordArt styles. Although the chart is based on data that was entered in a separate worksheet (separate, in that it was really created in Excel), the chart itself behaves like any other object that you place on a slide, such as SmartArt or a picture. You can size and move the chart on the slide as needed.

To make any substantive changes to the chart, you can rely on the Chart Tools. The various commands provided by this contextual Ribbon addition are divided between two tabs: Design and Format.

The Design tab provides commands related to the chart's type and layout, and gives you the ability to edit the data used to create the chart. The Change Chart Type command enables you to change the current chart to another type. If you then need to edit the data for the chart, select the Edit Data command. This tab also provides a Quick Layouts gallery, which enables you to adjust the overall layout of the chart. Each chart type has specific layouts available. The Add Chart Element command also makes it easy to fine-tune your chart's layout by adding various chart elements. You can change the style of the chart by taking advantage of the Chart Styles gallery. Figure 19.18 shows the Design tab on the Ribbon.

Figure 19.18
Modify the chart's design using the Design tab commands.

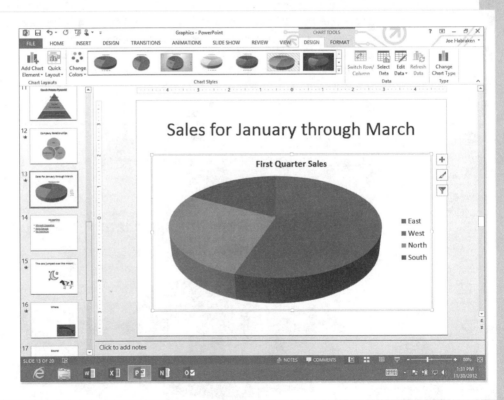

The Format tab grants access to Shape styles to modify the frame of the chart; you can also change the fill, outline, and effects for the chart frame. When you select text objects on the chart, such as the title or legend, you can take advantage of the WordArt Styles gallery and the other text settings on this tab. This tab also enables you to add shapes to the chart and arrange objects in the frame.

PowerPoint 2013 provides new inline command buttons that enable you to manipulate chart elements, change the chart style. and filter the data sets on your chart. When the chart frame is selected, these command buttons appear on the right side of the slide. When you select one of these commands, a pane opens on the left of the slide, giving you various choices (related to the command you selected). Figure 19.19 shows the Style/Color pane, which is opened by selecting the Style/Color command (it looks like a paint brush). More information on these three commands follows:

- **Chart Elements:** This command pane provides a list of the chart elements available for the chart, including the chart title, data labels, and legend. You can select and deselect these elements as needed.

- **Style/Color:** When Style is selected, this command pane houses several chart styles for the current chart type. When you select Color, you see different color schemes that you can apply to the chart.

- **Filter:** You can quickly filter the chart by values or names using this command. When Values is selected in the command pane, you can select or deselect series and/or categories (depending on the complexity of the chart) to view the chart with only a subset of the data represented. Mouse over the categories list (categories are the y-axis values for the chart) to see only the values represented on the chart. When you select Names in the Filter pane, you can control whether the chart shows series and categories names. After making a change on either the Values or Names tab of the pane, click the Apply button.

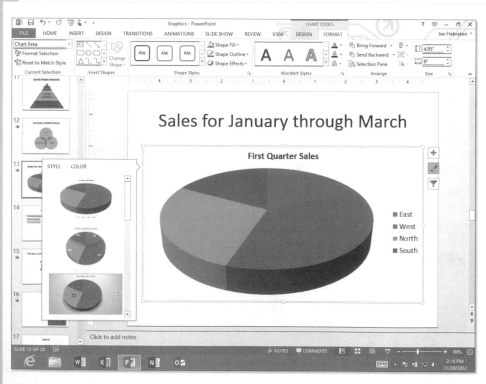

Figure 19.19
New inline chart commands enable you to quickly manipulate a chart.

Although I have stressed the construction and formatting of a chart, you also need to use charts appropriately. In other words, the chart type that you select should match the purpose of using the chart in the first place: to show data pictorially. This means choosing the right chart type for the situation. If you are showing the relationship of parts to a whole, such as how your individual monthly expenses relate to your total monthly expenses, use a pie chart. If you want to show change over time, such as changes in your retirement account, use a line chart (if you do chart your retirement account, avert your eyes to avoid complete shock, please). Make sure that you understand how the chart type you pick translates the numerical data into a visual representation. Selecting the wrong chart type for the situation and the data provides useless information to your audience.

➡ *For more about choosing the right chart type,* ***see*** *Chapter 14.*

Working with Slide Objects

An object can be anything you place on the slide. In this chapter, we looked at a number of object types, including pictures, Clip Art, shapes, and Smart Art. Text boxes qualify as objects as well. Resizing and rotating objects is straightforward. To resize an object, drag the sizing handles on the object's frame as needed. If you want to maintain the height/width ratio of an object, drag the lower-right sizing handle diagonally to size the object.

You can also easily rotate a selected object, such as a shape. When you select the object, the rotation handle (the green dot) appears at the top of the object. Place the mouse on the handle; when the Rotation icon appears, drag the rotation handle to rotate the object.

PowerPoint makes it simple to position multiple objects and even deal with layered objects on a slide. If you need to be accurate in placing items on a slide, you might want to take advantage of the ruler, gridlines, or guides. You can turn on any of these items by using the commands in the Show group on the Ruler's View tab. By default, objects are snapped to the grid. If you are placing objects close together, you can also have objects snap to other objects. You can specify the grid and guide settings by selecting the dialog box launcher on the Show group. This opens the Grid and Guides dialog box, which provides the snap, grid, and guide settings for the presentation.

Grouping Objects

Grouping objects enables you to fine-tune the positioning of any number of objects on a slide. You might have already placed the objects exactly the way you want them in terms of their positioning to each other. You then might need to adjust the overall positioning of all the objects in relation to the top or bottom of the slide or the slide title.

You can group the objects on the slide and then move them as a group. Select all the objects on the slide by using the mouse to drag a selection box around the objects. You can also click to select an object and then hold down the Ctrl key to select subsequent objects as needed.

When the objects are selected, click the Format tab of the drawing tools. Use the Group command in the Arrange group to group the objects. A frame appears around the grouped objects. You can now position or rotate the grouped objects as if they were a single object. If you need to ungroup the objects, select the group's frame; select Group and then select Ungroup. The objects become individual items with their own frames.

Layering Objects

In some cases, you might end up with fairly complex slides that contain many objects. You might have even deliberately layered objects on a slide. For instance, you might be using a combination of shapes, text boxes, and pictures to build a custom logo or other layered item. Or you might overlap adjacent objects using layering to provide additional visual interest.

You can use the Bring Forward command to bring an object forward in the stack (one object) or to bring it to the front of the stack (so that it is on top). The Send Backward command enables you to send a selected object backward (one layer) or to send it to the bottom of the object pile using the Send to Back option. When you have the objects layered correctly, select the entire stack (drag the mouse around the object stack). You can then group the layered objects using the Group command. This enables you to move the stack without messing up the layers.

> **note**
>
> When you align two or more objects on a slide (vertically or horizontally), smart guides appear automatically. This enables you to align objects in relation to each other without using the gridlines or guides.

Adding Hyperlinks to Slides

You can add hyperlinks to your PowerPoint slides. Hyperlinks enable you to jump to external information such as web pages or even files on your computer. For example, you could use a hyperlink to open an Excel worksheet that is associated with a chart that you have copied and pasted into a slide. Hyperlinks can also jump to a bookmark, which can point to a slide in the current presentation. This is useful when you anticipate that a slide shown later in the presentation will elicit requests from the audience to see the earlier slide. You can be ready for the question by placing a hyperlink to the slide on the current slide.

Hyperlinks are added to a text box on a slide using the Insert Hyperlink dialog box, shown in Figure 19.20. You open the Hyperlinks dialog box using the Hyperlink command on the Insert tab.

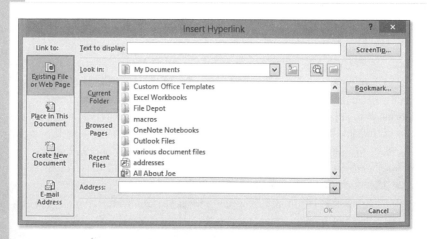

Figure 19.20
Insert a hyperlink into the current slide.

By default, the Existing File or Web Page setting is selected in the Link To box. This setting enables you to create a hyperlink to a file on your computer or a web page. By default, the contents of the My Documents folder are displayed in the Insert Hyperlink dialog box. If the hyperlink is to an existing file, you can select any document in the folder or navigate to another folder to specify an existing file. You can also select Recent Files to view a list of files you have recently opened. This provides another option for specifying an existing file as the destination for the hyperlink.

If you want to create a hyperlink to a web page, you can type the URL for the site in the Address box. If you select Browsed Pages, you are provided with a list of recently browsed web pages. You can select from this list to specify the web address for the hyperlink.

As another alternative, open Internet Explorer or your default web browser and navigate to the website. When you return to PowerPoint, the address of the website that you navigated to in your web browser appears in the Address box.

When you want to specify a slide as the destination for the hyperlink, select Place in This Document in the Link To box. A list of slides in the presentation appears in the Insert Hyperlink dialog box. Select the appropriate slide in the list.

Before you click OK, which closes the Insert Hyperlink dialog box and creates your hyperlink on the slide, you need to take care of one more task. Enter the text that you want to display on the slide when the hyperlink is inserted. The text can be any text you choose; it won't affect the hyperlink's ability to navigate to the destination. For example, the hyperlink text displayed on the slide does not have to be the URL for the website the hyperlink takes you to. When you have finished configuring the hyperlink, click OK to return to the slide.

The hyperlink isn't active on the slide when you are in Normal view. You need to run the slide in a slide show to test your hyperlink. Click the Slide Show shortcut on the right side of the PowerPoint status bar. The slide show begins from the current slide, which is the slide that contains the hyperlink to be tested. If the hyperlink is to a website, your web browser opens and navigates to the site. If you selected a file as the destination, the application in which the file was created opens and loads the file. And if you specified a slide in the presentation as the hyperlink destination, you are taken to that slide in the slide show. You can press Esc to return to the PowerPoint workspace.

 note

You can also create a ScreenTip for the hyperlink. Select ScreenTip in the Insert Hyperlink dialog box, and then specify the ScreenTip text in the Set Hyperlink Screen Tip dialog box.

20

ENHANCING SLIDES WITH ANIMATION, TRANSITIONS, AND MULTIMEDIA

As Microsoft PowerPoint has become more sophisticated over the years in terms of the enhancements that you can apply to your presentation slides, people have come to expect flashier and more graphically rich presentations. Whether you regularly give PowerPoint presentations as part of your profession or just use PowerPoint for your travel club or to show family pictures, your audience expects a visually compelling slide show. You can't just click through a static series of slides without any special effects or multimedia.

In this chapter, we look at animation effects, including how you can apply them to slide objects and customize these animations. We also discuss the use of slide transitions and the addition of sound and video to a presentation.

Animations Versus Transitions

Before we dive into working with animation effects and slide transitions, we need to discuss how they differ and how each of them affects a slide and its contents. Animations are special effects that are added to an object or objects on the slide. Animations can be applied to text boxes, pictures, clip art, SmartArt graphics—any object type.

Animations are designed to emphasize objects on a slide and can also control the entrance or exit of objects as the slide is viewed during the slide show. Animations affect objects such as clip art and SmartArt a little differently than text boxes. For example, if you assign an animation to a clip art object such as the Fly In animation, the clip art will fly onto the slide when you click the mouse or after a delay timer expires (we talk more about setting timers for animations later in this chapter, in the section "Setting Timings for Animations").

In the case of text boxes that include bulleted lists or text in paragraphs, each paragraph is animated by the animation effect. So if you have a text box that includes four items in a bulleted list (each item in the list is considered a separate paragraph), then by default, you have to click the mouse four times to get the entire bulleted list to appear on the slide. Each bulleted item flies in separately upon each subsequent click of the mouse.

You are not limited to one animation per slide: You can apply an animation effect to each object on a slide, if you choose. You can also apply multiple animations to a particular object. For example, you could apply an entrance effect for a bulleted list and then assign a secondary animation to the bulleted list that emphasizes each item in the list.

When you assign animation effects to objects, a number is placed to the left of the object to show that an effect has been applied. The number also tells you the sequence in which the effects are applied to the objects when you run the slide show. Figure 20.1 shows a slide with multiple objects. An animation effect has been applied to the title text box and is the first effect in the animation sequence (thus, it is assigned the number 1). An animation effect has also been assigned to the clip art on the right side of the slide (2).

> ### 🔍 note
> You have complete control over how and when objects assigned animation effects appear on or exit from the screen. We discuss this in detail in the sections of this chapter that cover animation effects.

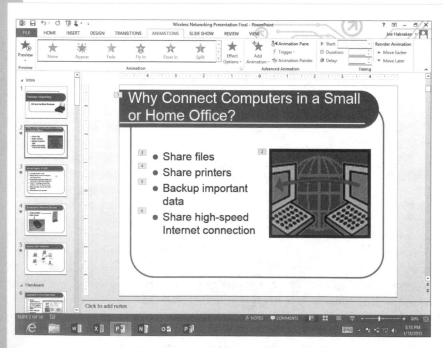

Figure 20.1
A slide that includes multiple animation effects.

The slide also includes a bulleted list consisting of four bulleted items. An animation effect has been applied to the text box that contains the bulleted list. Notice that the individual bulleted items have been numbered in sequence from 3 through 6.

When this slide is viewed during a slide show, only the title of the slide appears when you switch to the slide. On the first click of the mouse, the title text appears; with the next click, the clip art appears. On subsequent clicks of the mouse, the bulleted list items appear in sequence. So animation effects are designed to add effects to the objects on the slide.

Transitions, which are also referred to as transition effects, can also give you a way to add special effects to a presentation. Transitions are assigned to slides. A transition goes into effect during the slide's entrance in the slide show. So transitions are more of an all-or-nothing proposition. You can't have the transition affect apply to only certain objects on the slide; it is applied to the entire slide.

PowerPoint provides several different transition effects. Some of the transition effects are based on film and video transitions, which are used to switch between scenes in a film or television program; these effects include the fade, wipe, and dissolve. Other transitions, such as shred, vortex, and ripple, provide visually exciting transitions that wow your audience.

When using animation effects and transitions in your slide presentations, keep certain points in mind. The list that follows provides some tips for using special effects appropriately and judiciously.

- **Less is better.** Remember that your presentation is meant to convey information, not hypnotize the audience (or make their eyes hurt). You don't have to animate every object on every slide or necessarily assign transitions to every slide. Use these features sparingly to get the most bang out of them when you do use them.

- **Give the audience a rest.** There is no crime in showing slides that have no animations or transitions. After animating several slides in a row or having slide transitions for several slides in a row, put in a slide or two with no effects. This is particularly useful when you are showing a slide that contains important information. You stress the information by not dressing it up with an animation or transition.

- **Use effects to best effect.** Both the animations and transitions provide effects that can be of thematic value to your presentation. For example, if you are discussing issues related to the proper disposal of hard-copy proprietary information, what better slide transition to use than the shred transition? Or if you are emphasizing the spiraling value of a company's stock using a chart, why not animate that chart with the spin animation?

Be sure to think about how you use special effects such as animations and transitions when you are developing the overall design plan for your presentation. How you present the information can be as important as the information itself. You can take advantage of special effects to add interest to your presentation, but don't let them take over your presentation or obscure the information you want to provide your audience.

Assigning Animation to a Slide Object

The Animations tab of the Ribbon provides all the commands related to the application and modification of animation effects. Animating an object or objects on a slide is an easy three-step process.

Select an object on the slide, select an animation from the Animation gallery, and then use the Effect Options gallery to fine-tune the selected animation. Figure 20.2 shows the Animation gallery.

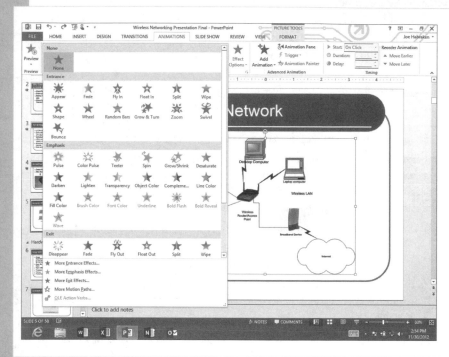

Figure 20.2
The Animation gallery.

The Animation gallery groups the animation effects into four categories: Entrance, Emphasis, Exit, and Motion Paths. The first three categories—Entrance, Emphasis, and Exit—are self-explanatory. Let's look at these standard animation effects; we pick up motion paths in their own section later in the chapter.

The Entrance category provides animations that dictate how the object enters the slide when the animation plays. The Emphasis group provides animations that enable you to emphasize objects such as the items in a bulleted list. For example, as you talk about a particular item in the list, you can click the mouse so that the bulleted item is emphasized with a pulse or spin. The Exit category provides animations that remove items from the slide. For example, if you assign an exit animation such as the Fade effect, the items in the bulleted list fade (sequentially) each time you click the mouse.

To assign an animation effect to an object or objects on a slide, follow these steps:

1. Select the object or objects on the slide. You can select multiple objects by clicking the first object and then holding down the Ctrl key as you click subsequent objects.

2. Select the Animations tab on the Ribbon.

3. Place the mouse on an animation in the Animation gallery to preview an animation on the slide object. If you want to access the entire gallery, click the More button.

4. Select the animation you want to use to close the gallery and assign the animation to the slide object.

You can repeat this process as needed to apply other animation effects to other objects on the slide. When you want to preview the animation effects assigned to the objects on a slide, click the Preview button on the Animations tab. This gives you a preview of the animation effect or effects in Normal view.

Accessing Additional Animation Effects

The Animations gallery provides only a subset of the animation effects available. You can access additional animation effects via a set of dialog boxes that open via the Animations gallery. Each animation effect type—entrance, emphasis, and exit—has a separate dialog box. For example, the Change Entrance Effect dialog box, shown in Figure 20.3, offers many different entrance effects.

Figure 20.3
The Change Entrance Effect dialog box.

The entrance effects in the Entrance Effect dialog box are grouped into categories titled Basic, Subtle, Moderate, and Exciting.

The categories are based on the "specialness" of the effects they include. The Exciting category provides more elaborate animation effects than the Basic category. For example, the basic entrance effect called Fade fades the object or object elements, such as a bulleted list, onto the slide. In contrast, the Pinwheel entrance effect in the Exciting category spins the object elements onto the slide, providing a much more exciting and elaborate entrance. It's kind of like the difference between a magician walking onto the stage from behind the curtain or appearing on the stage in a flash of light or smoke.

To access the dialog box for a specific effect type, click the More button on the Animation gallery. You can then use the More Entrance Effects, More Emphasis Effects, and the More Exit Effects commands at the bottom of the gallery to open the Change Entrance Effects dialog box, the Change Emphasis Effects dialog box, or the Change Exit Effects dialog box, respectively.

By default, each dialog box provides a preview of the effect you select, and the effect is previewed on the selected object or objects. You might want to drag the dialog box off the Slide pane so that you can see the preview of the effect on the slide. The selected effect is not assigned to the object until you click the OK button in the dialog box and return to the PowerPoint workspace.

If you want to preview the animation after you have closed the dialog box, select the Preview command on the Animations tab. You can also open the slide show at the current slide by clicking the Slide Show button on the status bar. This enables you to view the animation as it appears during the slide show. When you want to stop the slide show and return to Normal view, press the Esc key on the keyboard.

Using Motion Paths

Another animation effect type enables you to put your slide objects in pretty much any pattern you want. Motion paths are effects that enable you to move an object on a slide in a prescribed path. Motion paths can emphasize objects in much the same way you use emphasis animation effects such as the Spin or Underline effects. Motion paths can move an object in a circular, octagonal, or trapezoidal path. A vertical figure eight motion path even moves an object in a figure-eight pattern.

However, motion paths do not necessarily have to move objects only in place on the slide. You can also use a custom motion path to relocate an object on a slide. For example, you might want to have a chart and a text box switch positions on the slide, to get your audience to concentrate more closely on the chart itself. Or you might want to use a motion path to have an object interact with another object. Figure 20.4 shows a clip art image of a cow that has been assigned a custom motion path that makes the cow jump over the clip art moon.

Figure 20.4 shows the path for the clip art image with a dotted line that appears on the slide. A green triangle shows the beginning of the motion path, and a red arrow designates the endpoint for the motion path.

When you are working with the standard motion paths (the motion paths other than the custom path), such as lines, arcs, or shapes, PowerPoint 2013 has a new twist. When you select and change the position or the size of the motion path, a ghosted image of the object appears at the new exit point for the path. This is useful in seeing where the object (such as a picture or clip art) ends up on the slide when the motion path actually runs in your slideshow; you can preview the motion path at any time by selecting the motion path and then selecting the Preview command in the Preview group (just to the left of the Animation group).

Figure 20.4
A custom motion path assigned to a clip art object.

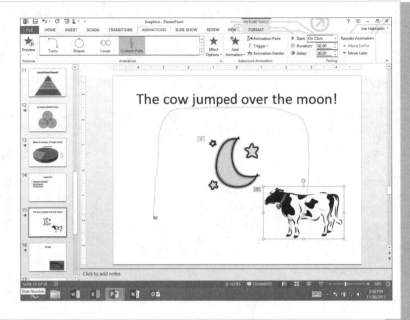

Applying a Motion Path

To apply a motion path to a selected object or objects, scroll through the Animations gallery until you can access the Motion Paths category area provided in the gallery. You can also open the entire gallery by clicking the More button (you still might have to scroll down to see the available motion paths).

On first inspection, the available motion paths in the Animation gallery might appear to be rather meager. However, the motion paths are a little different from the other animation effects available in the gallery. Although you can change some options related to the entrance, emphasis, and exit animation effects, such as the direction and whether a compound object (such as a SmartArt Venn diagram) is animated as a whole or as parts, motion paths give you more customization possibilities. For example, you can control the length of the path, the position of the path, and other path attributes, such as the shape of the path and the path direction. So think of the motion paths available in the Animations gallery as just types of motion paths that you can then customize; this gives you more options than you might at first expect.

To assign a motion path to an object on a slide, select the object. Then select a motion path in the Animation gallery, such as Lines, Arcs, or Loops. If you want to access additional motion path animations, select the More Motion Paths command at the bottom of the gallery. The Change Motion Path dialog box opens, as shown in Figure 20.5.

The Motion Path dialog box is divided into different categories of paths. These categories are as follows:

- **Basic:** This category provides different path shapes, including circle, hexagon, and square paths, as well as several star paths.

- **Lines and Curves:** This category provides different arc, line, and curve paths, and includes special paths such as funnel, heartbeat, and spring shapes.

- **Special:** This category provides unique paths such as bean, loop de loop, peanut, and neutron shapes. It also includes different figure-eight paths.

Figure 20.5
The Change Motion Path dialog box.

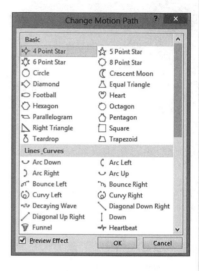

When you select a motion path in the Change Motion Path dialog box, it is previewed on the selected object. To assign the motion path to the object, click OK to close the Change Motion Path dialog box.

Editing a Motion Path

After the path has been assigned to the object, the path itself is represented by a dotted line (when the Animations tab is selected on the Ribbon). The beginning of the path is designated by a green triangle, and the end of the path is designated by a red triangle. The path also has its own sizing handles.

Using the mouse, you can change some of the motion path's attributes, such as its size and its location in relation to the object. The path's start point begins at the center of the object assigned the

motion path, and the object moves through the path to the end point, which also occurs when the center of the object reaches the red triangle (in the case of loops and circular paths, the start point and endpoint are the same). You can change the position of the start point and endpoint, and change the relative positioning of the path itself in relation to the object.

Additional motion path settings are accessed via the Effect Options command. The options available in the Effect Options gallery, which are shown in Figure 20.6 for a horizontal

 note

Fine-tuning a motion path can be a little tricky. After each change made to the motion path, use the Preview command. If you don't like a particular change, take advantage of Undo.

figure-eight effect, depend on the motion path that you select. Some motion paths have alternative motion paths, such as the horizontal and vertical figure eights. You can switch between these two orientations via the Effect Options gallery.

Figure 20.6
Change the motion path options.

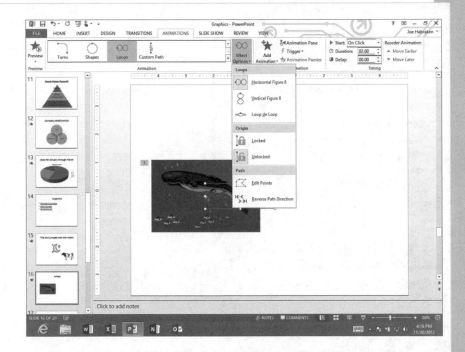

The options typically available on the Effect Options gallery enable you to reverse the path direction and edit individual points in the path. When you select the Edit Points command, a series of point handles becomes visible on the motion path. You can drag any of these handles to change the path. For example, on a figure-eight motion path, you can stretch the size of either oval in the figure eight or change the ovals into any shape you desire.

In the Effect Options gallery, two commands are grouped in an Origin category: Locked and Unlocked. These options do not dictate whether you can make changes to the motion path animation (such as locking the settings for a motion path); they relate to what happens when you move the motion path or the object that has been assigned the motion path.

By default, the motion path is unlocked. This means that when you move the object on the slide, the motion path moves with it. If you select Locked, the path does not move when you move the object. So, in a sense, these two options are a little counterintuitive. You would probably think that the Locked setting would keep the object and the motion path locked, but the reality is just the opposite.

The locked and unlocked options do not differ when you move the motion path itself. In both cases, moving the motion path does not also move the object that the path has been assigned to.

Although the Effect Options gallery is rather limited in terms of the different possibilities for modifying a motion path, you can access additional options in a dialog box that is specific to the motion path you have selected. All you have to do is select the dialog box launcher under the Effect Options command. Figure 20.7 shows the Horizontal Figure 8 dialog box.

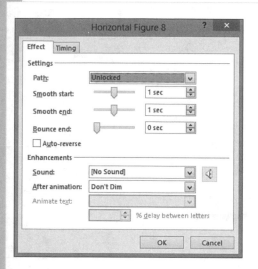

Figure 20.7
A motion path's dialog box.

The dialog box gives you an Effect tab and a Timing tab. The Effect tab enables you to set the path for the animation to Locked or Unlocked (the default). You can also use the available sliders to change the start, end, and bounce intervals for the animation. For example, to lengthen the duration of the start, move the Smooth Start slider bar to the right. This takes duration time away from the Smooth End setting (and the Bounce End setting, if there is a bounce at the end of the animation). By default, animations are provided for a duration of 2 seconds. You can modify the duration on the Timing tab using the Duration drop-down list.

The Effect tab also enables you to include enhancements to the animation, such as sounds, and specify what happens after the animation ends, including settings such as Hide After Animation or Hide on Next Mouse Click (we talk more about animation and sound later in this chapter). Colors are provided in the After Animation drop-down list to enable you to change the fill color for the object upon the completion of the animation. If you choose the same fill color as that used by the slide, the object disappears after the animation plays.

I've already mentioned that the motion path animation's duration can be set on the Timing tab of the dialog box. This tab also enables you to set the Start parameter for the animation by selecting On Click, With Previous, or After Previous. You can also set a delay for the animation or choose to have the animation repeat.

In addition, The Timing tab enables you to specify the trigger for the animation. A trigger can be any object on the slide. For example, you can specify the title text box as a trigger for an animation. When you click the title on the slide, the animation plays. Triggers can also be related to playing other animations or events on the slide. For example, if you have a video or sound file on the slide, the animation can be triggered to play upon playing that other object (the video).

When you have finished editing the settings for the motion path, click OK. This enables your new settings on the motion path animation and returns you to the Normal view.

Creating a Custom Motion Path

You can also create a custom motion path. This is easier than it sounds and really is just a matter of recording the path of the object as you drag it with the mouse. Because most of the motion paths PowerPoint provides are designed to move an object in place, creating a custom motion path for an object enables you to dictate the final position of the object on the slide after the motion effect animation plays.

To create a custom path, follow these steps:

1. Select the object to which you want to assign the custom path.

2. Navigate to the Animations tab and open the Animations gallery.

3. In the Motion Paths category of the gallery, select Custom Path.

4. Place the mouse pointer on the center of the object to which you want to assign the custom path.

5. Hold down the left mouse button; the mouse pointer becomes a drawing tool. Draw the custom path on the slide.

6. When you reach the endpoint for the custom motion path, double-click the mouse.

A preview of the custom path plays. The path itself is represented on the slide as a dotted line.

As with any motion path, you can change the settings for the path using the mouse (and the sizing handles) or the options in the Effect Options gallery. You can also access a Custom Path dialog box by selecting the dialog box launcher under the Effect Options command. This enables you to change the effect settings (including the addition of a sound), timing, and triggers for the custom path, as discussed in the previous section. You can preview any of the changes that you make to the custom path by selecting the Preview command.

Advanced Animation Techniques

PowerPoint gives you additional tools and options for fine-tuning animation effects. We have already looked at effect options related to motion paths; however, you can modify even simple entrance effects, particularly when you assign an animation to a bulleted list, a SmartArt graphic, or a chart that contains multiple items in a sequence.

PowerPoint also enables you to add more than one animation effect to an object. Although restraint is in order here—you don't want to pile animation effects onto your objects—you can add an entrance effect to an object such as a bulleted list and then also assign an emphasis effect, which enables you to revisit each bullet point on the slide to emphasize and review important information before changing to the next slide.

PowerPoint also provides the Animation Painter, which is in the same vein as the Format Painter (used to copy text formatting). The Animation Painter enables you to copy the animation effects assigned to an object (including any effect options that you have fine-tuned) to another object.

The Advanced Animation group provides access to the Add Animation, Animation Pane, Trigger, and Animation Painter commands. We discuss all these commands in later sections, including how to set triggers for an animation, which is considered one of the options when you set the Timing options for an effect in that effect's dialog box. You can open the dialog box associated with a selected animation using the dialog box launcher below the Effect Options command in the Animation group.

The Trigger command enables you to specify how a particular animation is triggered or started. You can specify the trigger to be the click of a particular object on the slide. For example, you can specify the title text box as a trigger for an animation. When you click the title on the slide, the animation plays. You can specify any object on the slide as the trigger for an animation. The animation does not have to be applied to the trigger object, so you can click a clip art image or picture on a slide, and this action can trigger an animation on another. The trigger can also be set so that an animation begins after reaching a particular bookmark in a sound or video object on the slide.

Changing Effect Options

To modify the effect options for an animation assigned to an object, select the object and then navigate to the Ribbon's Animations tab, if necessary. The Effect Options command provides a gallery of options that relate to the type of animation effect, meaning whether you have assigned an entrance, emphasis, or exit animation. The options available in the Effect Options gallery are also specific to the type of object assigned the animation. For example, text boxes have options beyond a clip art image or a SmartArt graphic that has been assigned an animation effect. Objects that consist of multiple paragraphs, such as a text box or a SmartArt graphic that includes many shapes in the graphic, have options for animating all the object parts one by one or all at once.

To change the options for an animation effect, select the object assigned the animation. Then select the Effect Option command to access the options available for that effect and object type. Figure 20.8 shows the Effect Options gallery for a bulleted list assigned an entrance animation.

Both entrance and exit animations provide effect options that enable you to specify the direction of the object's entrance or exit, such as to the bottom, left, top, and so on. Emphasis animations have effect options that relate to the color or the level of the animation effect. For example, if you use the Fill Color animation, the effect options provided include a color palette that enables you to select the fill color for the animation. In the case of the Transparency animation, you select the level of transparency assigned to the objects in the Effect Options gallery.

As already mentioned, the type of object also has a bearing on the effect options available for a particular animation. When you access the effect options for an object that has multiple parts, such as a bulleted list, you provide sequence options that enable you to determine whether the object should be animated all at once or whether the individual parts should be animated separately.

If you want to fine-tune the options for an animation, you can open the animation effects dialog box. Select the dialog box launcher below the Effect Options command. The dialog box for a particular animation type provides options related to the effect itself and supplies enhancement possibilities, such as whether to play a sound with the animation effect. The dialog box for an animation also provides a Timing tab where you can set options related to the start, delay, and duration of the animation. We discuss animation sound and timing options later in the chapter.

Figure 20.8
The Effect Options gallery.

Because the dialog box is specific to a particular type of animation, the settings available vary in the dialog box, as do the options that are available for that animation type in the Effect Options gallery. For example, the dialog box for an entrance or an exit animation has options for setting the direction of the effect and provides slider bars that enable you to specify the duration of the "smooth start" or "smooth end" for the animation. In contrast, the dialog box for an emphasis animation includes options only for the inclusion of a sound and timing settings related to the animation effect.

Adding Additional Animations

The Advanced Animation command group on the Animations tab provides you with the Add Animation command. This command opens the Add Animation gallery, which is really a duplicate of the Animation gallery provided in the Animation group. You can add any of the available animation effects to the current object. The added effect is numbered sequentially in relation to the other animations that have been already added to the slide.

The added animation occurs after the primary animation that you add to the object. So if you plan to use both an entrance and an exit animation on a particular object, make sure that the entrance animation occurs in the animation sequence before the exit animation. It makes sense to assign the entrance animation to the object via the Animation gallery and assign the exit animation, which is really the secondary animation for the object, using the Add Animation command.

 note
The default animation setting for text boxes is to animate the object by paragraph. This is what enables you to bring in each item in a bulleted list separately when you use an entrance animation.

As already mentioned, the Add Animation gallery is much the same as the Animation gallery. At the bottom of the Add Animation gallery is a series of commands, such as More Entrance Effects and More Emphasis Effects. Use any of these commands to open the corresponding dialog box for that type of animation. You can then select from the larger library of animation effects (by type) provided in the specific dialog boxes.

Using the Animation Painter

The Animation Painter enables you to copy the animations that have been applied to an object and "paint" these animation settings onto another object or objects. This enables you to fine-tune animations on a particular object and then apply the animation or animations to other objects on the same slide or other slides in the presentation. This can be particularly useful if you want to have an overall scheme related to the animations that you use and you want particular animations to be repeated on like objects that appear throughout the presentation.

To use the Animation Painter, select an object that has been assigned the animation or animations you want to copy. Then select the Animation Painter in the Advanced Animation command group. The mouse pointer includes a paintbrush, letting you know that the Animation Painter is active. Navigate to the slide that contains the object that you want to assign the animations that have been copied from the previous object. Then click the object to assign the animations to the object. A preview of the pasted animations plays as soon as you click the Animation Painter on the object.

One click on the Animation Painter command enables you to apply the copied animations to one object. As soon as you click that object, the Animation Painter applies the animations and then becomes inactive. You can use the Animation Painter to apply copied animations to multiple objects in the presentation by double-clicking the Animation Painter command. When you have finished assigning the animation or animations to objects in your presentation, select the Animation Painter command again to deactivate the tool.

Including Sound Effects with Animations

You can enhance your animations by adding sound effects to them. When the animation plays, the accompanying sound also plays. PowerPoint supports many popular sound file formats, including the following:

- **Wave:** The Waveform Audio file format (`.wav`) stores sound as a waveform file. These files are relatively small when compared to some of the other sound file formats.

- **MIDI:** The MIDI, or Musical Instrument Digital Interface file format (`.mid`), contains a series of control information that can be played back on a MIDI-enabled device such as a computer.

- **MP3:** The Moving Picture Experts Group audio file format (MPEG 3 or `.mp3`) is a popular compressed file format.

- **WMA:** The Windows Media Audio file format (`.wma`) is a compressed music file format developed by Microsoft.

- **AIFF:** The Audio Interchange File Format (`.aiff`) is an uncompressed waveform sound file type originally used by Apple computers.

■ **M4A, MP4:** PowerPoint 2013 now supports these advanced audio and video coding file formats. M4A and MP4 are known collectively as MPEG-4 Part 14. M4A is an audio codec and MP4 is an audio and video codec.

To specify a sound for an animation, select the object assigned to the animation and then click the dialog box launcher under the Effect Options command. This opens a dialog box for the animation effect assigned to the object. Figure 20.9 shows the dialog box for a Fly In animation applied to a bulleted list.

Figure 20.9
The Sound drop-down list in the Fly In dialog box.

The Effect tab of the dialog box controls settings related to the direction and start and end of the animation. More important to our discussion of sound, the Enhancements area of the Effect tab enables you to specify a sound file to be played with the animation.

The default sound setting for all animations that you have assigned to slide objects is No Sound. When you select the Sound drop-down list, you are presented with a list of sound files that can be applied to the animation. These sounds include applause, camera, chime, and window. Select a sound provided in the list (these sounds consist of .wav files). Click the Sound icon to set the volume level for the sound.

If you want to use a sound file other than the ones PowerPoint provides, you can access these sounds via the Other Sound option in the Sound drop-down list. Selecting the Other Sound option opens the Add Audio dialog box. You can take advantage of any sound files that you have created or downloaded to your computer. However, to use the sound file, it must be in one of the supported file formats discussed earlier in this section.

When you have added the sound to the animation, you can click OK to close the animation's dialog box. Click the preview button on the Animations tab to preview the animation with the assigned sound.

 tip

If you have assigned multiple animations to an object, the easiest way to open the options for a specific effect is to use the Effect Options command that is available for each animation listed in the animation pane.

Setting Timings for Animations

You can set the timing for an animation using the commands available in the Timing group on the Animations tab. The Start command enables you to set how the animation is started. The default setting is On Click, but you can specify that the animation start with the previous animation (With Previous) or after the previous animation has ended (After Previous).

The Duration command provides a spinner box that enables you to set the actual duration of the animation. You can speed up or slow down animations as you require. If you want to have the animation play automatically after a specified delay, use the Delay spinner box to specify the actual time for the delay.

Although it is not included in the Timing group, the Trigger command in the Advanced Animation group also has some bearing on the mechanism for starting an animation; the Trigger command enables you to specify how a particular animation is triggered or started. You can specify the trigger on the click of a particular object on the slide. For example, you can specify the title text box as a trigger for an animation. When you click the title on the slide, the animation plays. You can specify any object on the slide as the trigger for an animation. The animation does not have to be applied to the trigger object, so you can click a clip art image or picture on a slide and use that to trigger an animation on another object (such as a bulleted list).

In addition, you can set the timing settings for an animation in the animation's dialog box on the Timing tab. Figure 20.10 shows the Timing tab of the Fly In animation's dialog box.

Figure 20.10
The Timing tab of the Fly In dialog box.

On the Timing tab, you can set the start, delay, and duration settings for the animation. The dialog box also enables you to configure the animation to repeat using the Repeat drop-down list. If you want the animation to rewind when it finishes playing (which is useful if you have used an animation such as a motion path that moves an object on the slide), you can check the Rewind When Done Playing check box. You can also set the trigger options for the animation via the Triggers drop-down command provided on the Timing tab. You can specify any object on the slide as the trigger for the animation.

When you finish setting the timing-related settings for the animation in the dialog box, click OK to return to the PowerPoint workspace. Take advantage of the Preview command to preview the settings you have configured for the animation.

Managing Slide Animations

An extremely useful tool for managing, reordering, and fine-tuning the animations that you have assigned to the slide objects on a particular slide is the Animation pane. The Animation pane lists all the animations that have been assigned to objects on the current slide. To open the Animation pane, select the Animation Pane command in the Advanced Animation group. Figure 20.11 shows a presentation in Normal view with the Slide pane present on the right side of the PowerPoint workspace.

Figure 20.11
Slide with assigned animations and the Animation pane.

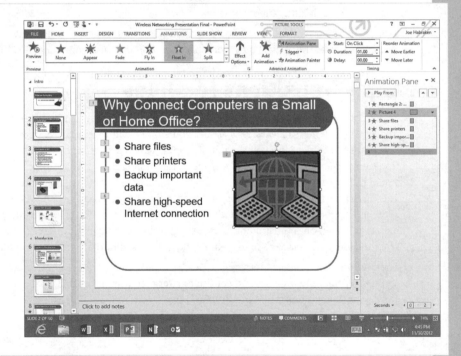

You can use the Slide pane to accomplish a variety of animation-management tasks, including reordering, deleting, and modifying animations. To reorder the animations in the Animation pane, you have a couple options. You can select an animation and then move it up or down in the Animation pane using the Move Earlier or Move Later arrows at the bottom of the Animation pane. You can also drag an animation to a new position in the Animation pane to reorder the sequence of the animations. In addition, you can set the action for when an animation should begin, and you can access effect options and timing settings by clicking the drop-down arrow next to a selected animation.

The bottom of the Animation pane provides delay and duration information for the animation (delay is on the left, and duration on the right—both in seconds). You can use the Seconds drop-down button to zoom in or out on the advanced timeline information to the right of each of the animations. This gives you the relative timing of the animation as it compares to the other animations placed on the slide.

If you want to delete an animation from the slide, select the animation in the Animation pane and then either press the Delete key on the keyboard or select Remove from the drop-down list to the right of the animation. This drop-down list also enables you to set the start for the animation and access the timing settings for the animation.

The Slide pane is particularly useful in sorting out multiple animations that you added to an object. For example, you might have assigned both an entrance and an exit animation to an object. Both these animations are listed separately in the Animation pane. This makes it easy to access the dialog box for an animation by selecting the drop-down list next to the animation and then selecting Effect Options.

tip

You can also reorder animations on a slide without using the animation pane. Use the Reorder Animation commands on the Animations tab.

When you finish working with the Animation pane, you can close it using its Close button. This frees up more of the PowerPoint workspace for working with your slides in Normal view.

Adding Transitions to Slides

Transitions give you another effect type to add visual interest and perhaps even a little excitement to your PowerPoint presentations. When you show a slide show of a presentation that does not contain any slide transitions, you are doing what is called a straight cut in film terminology. The change from the current slide to the next slide is abrupt and can be jarring to the audience. There is no visual buffer between the content of the two adjacent slides. A transition is a special effect that provides a visual shift between slides rather than an abrupt cut or switch. The transition between the slides is triggered when you navigate from the current slide to the next slide (either by a click of the mouse or based on a timing) and that next slide has been configured with the transition. So if you want a transition between slide A and slide B, you assign the transition to slide B.

The Ribbon's Transitions tab provides the command groups that enable you to select a transition, configure transition options, and configure sound and timing settings for a transition. Figure 20.12 shows the Transitions tab of the Ribbon.

Figure 20.12
The Ribbon's Transitions tab.

The Transitions tab also provides a Preview command, making it easy for you to preview a transition assigned to a slide. The Preview command is greatly improved in PowerPoint 2013, in that it shows the transition as the changeover is made between the two slides.

PowerPoint provides several transitions, including the wipe, split, dissolve, checkerboard, and blinds transitions. The Transitions gallery groups the transitions into three categories: subtle, exciting, and dynamic content.

Before we review how to assign a transition to a slide or slides, let me say a couple words about transitions in general. Remember that these are special effects, like the animation effects. Use them to add visual interest to the presentation, not make the audience feel like they are sitting in front of a strobe light at a 1970s disco. Also take into account the additive effect of animations and transitions. If you use a slide transition to get to a slide, is it really necessary to also load up the slide with animations? For example, if you use the Glitter transition, followed by objects on the slide configured with the Grow and Turn animation effect, you might have too much going on in terms of visual interest. That is not to say that transitions and animations can't be used together; you can do so, but you don't want to randomly mix different types of effects. Plan the look that you want for the slide, taking into consideration your purpose and the presentation's topic, and then plan your use of transitions and animations appropriately.

You can assign transitions to your slides when you are working in Normal view or the Slide Sorter. If you want to apply the same transition to several slides, you can easily do this in Slide Sorter view by selecting multiple slides. And although the preview is obviously smaller in Slide Sorter view, you can get previews of all the selected slides and the assigned transition by selecting the Preview command.

To assign a transition to a slide, select the slide. You can then scroll through the Transition gallery (which is in the Transition to This Slide group) to select a transition. Or you can click the More button to view the entire gallery. When you place the mouse on a specific transition, it is previewed on the selected slide or slides. To assign a transition, select the transition in the gallery.

Modifying Transitions

After you have assigned a particular transition in the gallery to a slide, you can modify the transition. The Effect Options command provides a gallery of options related to the transition you selected. Figure 20.13 shows the Effect Options gallery for the Wipe transition.

Figure 20.13
The Effect Options gallery for a Wipe transition.

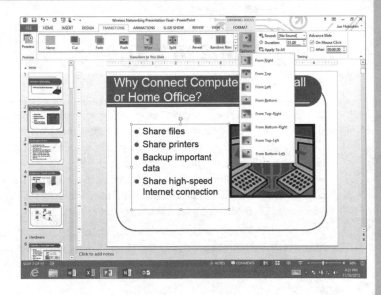

The options provided in the gallery are specific to the transition. For example, the Wipe transition can be modified in terms of its direction, such as from right, from top, and from bottom, as shown in Figure 20.13. Other transitions have other options, which, again, depend on the transition itself. For example, the Split transition enables you to configure the split to go either in or out; you can also choose whether the split is vertical or horizontal. The Checkerboard transition can be configured to occur from the left or from the top. Some transitions, such as the Honeycomb transition, have no options.

Not only do you have control over transition options (if available), but you can also control the duration of the transition and determine whether a sound plays when the transition plays. To set the duration of the transition, use the Duration spinner box in the Timing group of the Transitions tab.

If you want to have a sound play with the transition, select the Sound drop-down list in the Timing group. It provides a number of sound files, including Applause, Chime, and Voltage. If you want to use a sound that you have recorded or downloaded to your computer, you can select the Other Sound command in the Sound drop-down list. This opens the Add Audio dialog box. Navigate to the folder that holds the sound file, and then select the appropriate file; click OK to assign the sound file to the transition.

You can also specify how the slide is advanced. By default, slides are advanced by a click of the mouse. You can specify a time in the After spinner box. The slide then automatically advances based on that setting. You can clear the On Mouse Click check box in the Timing group if you plan to use the timing to advance the slide, or you can leave the option selected. Doing so enables you to advance the slide before the timing you have set. It's always good to have options.

 For more details on working with slide timings and recorded slide shows, **see** *"Creating a Self-Running Presentation,"* **p. 618.**

 tip

If you want to apply a selected transition to all the slides in the presentation, select the Apply to All command on the Transitions tab.

Adding Sound to a Slide

Sounds can add emphasis to information on slides or can serve as actual content to your presentation (such as a sound clip from a famous speech). The sound can consist of a sound effect or narration. You can insert a sound clip as an object onto a slide. The sound plays when you click the image that represents the sound object during a slide show. PowerPoint enables you to insert sound files that have been sourced in different ways. For example, you might already have sound files that you have created or downloaded to your computer. You can insert these sound files into a slide. You can also record sound, such as narration, directly to a slide by using the Record Sound utility. Office. com provides a library of prerecorded sound effects as well. When you get your sound on a slide, PowerPoint provides tools for modifying and enhancing the audio.

First, you have to get some audio onto a slide before you can take advantage of Audio Tools. The Insert tab of the Ribbon includes the Media group, which provides commands for inserting video and audio onto your presentation slides. When you select the Audio command, you have three options:

- **Online Audio:** This command opens the Insert Audio window. A search box enables you to search Office.com for royalty-free sound clips.

- **Audio on My PC:** This command opens the Insert Audio dialog box, which enables you to insert prerecorded sound files (see the supported sound file types listed earlier in this chapter) stored on your computer.

- **Record Audio:** This command opens the Record Sound utility. This feature enables you to record narration and other sounds using the microphone on your PC.

All three of these options produce the same result; an image is placed on the slide to represent the associated sound file. You can then edit options related to the sound file using the contextual audio tools, which appear when the image representing the sound file is selected on the slide.

Editing Sound Options

After you add an audio file to a slide, you have a great deal of control over both the graphic that represents the sound file and the audio file embedded in the slide. When you insert the audio into the slide, it is represented by a sound image and has a control bar that enables you to play the sound, rewind the sound, and adjust the sound volume. Figure 20.14 shows a sound file that has been inserted into a slide and also shows the Playback tab of the Audio Tools.

Figure 20.14
A sound file on a
PowerPoint slide.

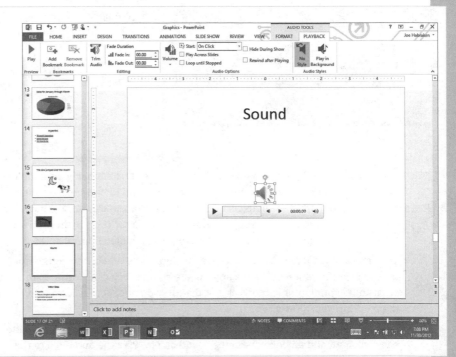

You can replace the standard sound icon picture that is inserted into the slide. The Audio Tools Format tab provides many of the same commands used to adjust the settings of a picture, including a Picture Styles gallery and tools for cropping and sizing the image. So when you change the sound file's picture, you can edit the new picture's settings if you want. For example, you may want to change the picture style and adjust picture attributes such as brightness, contrast, and color.

To change the default sound icon picture, select the Audio Tools Format tab and then select the Change Picture command in the Adjust group. The Insert Pictures window opens, and you can insert a replacement picture from your computer, Office.com, Bing search results, or your Flickr account.

> ➡ *For detailed information on working with pictures in the Office applications,* ***see*** *"Working with Your Digital Pictures,"* ***p. 83.***

The Audio Tools Playback tab enables you to trim your audio clip, apply fades to the audio, and adjust how the audio clip is started during the slide show. The Playback tab also provides a Play command, enabling you to preview any changes that you make to the audio clip.

If you want to trim the audio, you can select the Trim Audio command, which opens the Trim Audio dialog box shown in Figure 20.15. The timeline provided in the Trim Audio command has both a start marker (green) and an end marker (red).

Figure 20.15
The Trim Audio dialog box.

You can trim the clip from the beginning using the start marker. This enables you to cue up the audio to start at a particular point. If you want the clip to end before it plays in its entirety, you can move the end marker to establish a new end time for the marker. Spinner boxes are also provided for the start and end times, and you can use them to set the starting and ending points of the clip. When you have finished working in the Trim Audio dialog box, click OK.

You can also add a fade to either the beginning or the end of the audio clip. Specify the Fade In or the Fade Out duration using the appropriate spinner box. The fades enable you to put some dead air at the beginning or end of a clip so that they do not seem to start or end abruptly when you play them during your presentation.

If you want a slide animation to play when a sound object file reaches a certain point during playback, you can add a bookmark to the sound object. Play the audio file to the point where you want to place the bookmark. Then on the Audio Tools Playback tab, select the Add Bookmark command.

This places the bookmark in the sound file. If you need to remove a bookmark in a sound file, select the bookmark on the sound object's playback bar and then select the Remove Bookmark command.

Adding Video to a Slide

You can also add video to your PowerPoint slides. You can insert online videos, such as a YouTube video, or you can insert video that you have created. PowerPoint 2013 has increased the number of options for inserting online video. The possibilities now include video files stored on your SkyDrive (which are not really online videos—they are just stored online instead of your computer), videos from YouTube, and any online video that has a video embed code. You paste the embed code onto the slide, and the code serves as the conduit to the video content on the Web.

Working with video content in PowerPoint was a rather dicey experience in previous versions of PowerPoint (including PowerPoint 2010). PowerPoint 2013 supports additional video file formats, including `.mp4` (MPEG 4) and `.swf` (Adobe Flash), and also makes it easy to insert online video directly onto a slide. Inserted video can greatly enhance your presentations by providing actual examples of concepts you are presenting, and these videos can also be used as icebreakers to warm up the crowd early in your presentation. Let's take a look at inserting online video and then examine the process for inserting your own video files.

Inserting Online Video

The potential number of online videos you can use in your PowerPoint presentations is huge, and growing every day. I'm not saying that every video you find on the Web can work on your PowerPoint slides, but you can use video clips from popular video websites, including YouTube, Veoh, and Yahoo!. If you decide to use embedded web video clips in your presentation, be advised that you need to be sure you have an Internet connection on your computer when you play your presentation as a slide show. Also be aware of the fact that websites can be down, and video websites sometimes remove videos. So although this is a great way to include video in your presentation, there is a chance that it might not work. Certainly don't make it the center of your presentation.

Also make sure you have the most recent version of Adobe Flash, Windows Media Player, and Microsoft Silverlight installed on your computer. You can get the Flash player at www.adobe.com, and get Silverlight and the Windows Media Player from www.microsoft.com.

To insert an online video clip into the current slide, you need to open the Insert Video window. You can open it by selecting Video and then Online Video on the Ribbon's Insert tab. You can also open the Insert Video window by selecting the Insert Video icon in a content area. Figure 20.16 shows the Insert Video window.

You can locate video clips on the Web using the Bing Video Search feature; just enter your search criteria in the Bing search box. You can also search YouTube to locate a particular video by keyword search. The Insert Video window makes it easy for you to insert your own video file stored on your SkyDrive or insert a video embed code on a slide (we talk about embed codes in a moment).

When you run a search using Bing or the YouTube search box, the results of your search are listed as thumbnails in the results window. You can play videos listed in your search results by selecting the thumbnail for the video and then selecting the View Larger icon. The play icon appears in the middle of the video (after the video is loaded). All you have to do is click Play to preview the video.

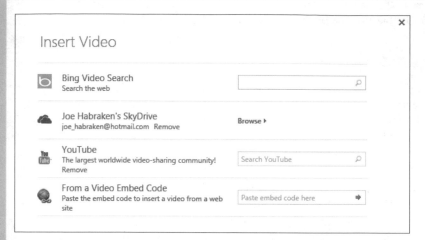

Figure 20.16
The Insert Video window.

When you locate the video that you want to insert into the current slide, select the video and then select Insert. The video is inserted into the slide. You can size the video and move it on the slide as you require. When the video frame is selected, the Video Tools appear on the Ribbon. The Format commands (shown in Figure 20.17) are similar to the Format commands provided for pictures or shapes; they enable you to change the style of the video frame, including the shape and border. Useful commands are provided on the Format tab, in the Adjust group. You can correct the brightness and contrast of the video using the Corrections command. You can also colorize the video using the Color command. The Crop command is another useful command at the other end of the Ribbon. You can crop the video frame if you want to concentrate the viewer's attention on a particular part of the video frame when the video plays.

 note

If you insert a video from your SkyDrive, the video file is downloaded to your computer. This is different from the way other online videos are "coded" onto a slide. The video is still on the Web. So SkyDrive-sourced videos are really no different from videos stored on your computer that you then insert onto a slide (which we talk about in the next section).

You can also use a video embed code to insert a video clip onto a slide. The embed code is really just an HTML/XML pointer to the video clip on the Web. When you "activate" the embed code, the video plays on the slide. If you want to use a video embed code to insert video content onto a slide, you first need to locate the video on a website such as YouTube using your web browser. You then copy the video's embed code to the Clipboard. Different video sites provide different ways to access the video embed code for a video. In the case of YouTube videos, the embed code is accessed by clicking the Share button and then the Embed button (just below the clip's video window). Also make sure that you select the Use Old Embed Code check box below the video. You can use the Copy command on your web browser's edit menu, or use Ctrl+C to copy the selected embed code using the keyboard.

After you copy the embed code for the video, you can open the Insert Video window and then paste the code in the From a Video Embed Code box by pressing Ctrl+V on the keyboard. You then click the Insert button (in the embed code box) to insert the video code into the slide.

Figure 20.17
Online video clip
inserted into a slide.

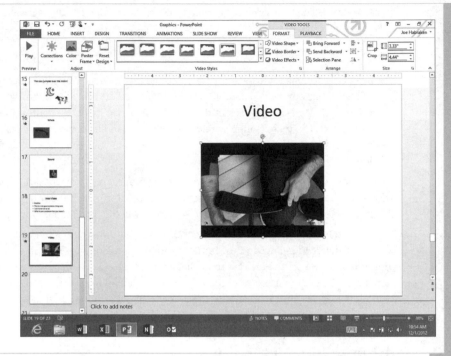

When you select the video embed code box (which looks just like an inserted video box), all the commands available on the Video Tools Format tab are available to modify the video frame (as they are for an inserted web video). When you switch to the Video Tools Playback tab, most of the group commands are grayed out, as they are for inserted online video clips. The Playback commands are accessible only when you insert your own video files into a slide, which we talk about in the next section.

Inserting a Video File

When inserting video files that are stored on your computer (or on your SkyDrive), your video file must be in a file format that PowerPoint supports. The following file types are supported:

- **Windows Video File:** The Audio Video Interleave file type (.avi) is a commonly used video format and has been the standard for Microsoft Windows for years. It uses the Microsoft Resource Interchange file format to store compressed audio and video information.

- **Movie File:** The Moving Picture Experts Group file format (.mpg or .mpeg) has been around for years and was one of the first standards for video and audio compression.

- **Windows Media Video:** The .wmv file format provides highly compressed video and audio in a file that requires minimal space when stored on a computer.

- **Windows Media File:** Yet another Microsoft media file type, the .asf file format is used to stream video and audio over a network.

- **MP4 Video:** This collection of Apple and QuickTime video file types includes `.mp4`, `.m4v`, and `.mov`.

- **Adobe Flash Media:** Flash videos (`.swf`) are also supported.

You have two options for inserting your video file into a slide. You can select the Insert Video icon in a slide content box, or you can go to the Ribbon's Insert tab, select the Video command, and then select Video on My PC. If you select the Insert Video icon in a slide content box, the Insert Video window opens. The Insert Video window enables you to insert video files from your computer, SkyDrive, or directly from YouTube. To insert video from your computer, click the Browse button to the right of the From a file option. This opens the Insert Video dialog box.

If you aren't working on a slide that contains a content box (as discussed in the previous paragraph), you can still insert video files from your computer; select the Video command on the Insert tab (in the Media group), and then select Video on My PC. The Insert Video dialog box opens.

So, both the Insert Video icon in a content box and the Video command on the Ruler's Insert tab get you to the Insert Video dialog box. In the Insert Video dialog box, navigate to the folder that holds your video file. Select the file and then click Insert. The video is inserted into the slide. An accompanying control bar enables you to play the video, rewind or fast-forward the video, and change the sound level for the clip. You can size the video frame, if required, and move the video on the slide as you would with any other slide object.

Modifying Your Video Clips

When an inserted video file is selected on the slide, the Video Tools become available on the Ribbon. As already mentioned, the Video Tools consist of two tabs: Format and Playback. The Format tab has many similarities to the Format tab of the Picture Tools and can be used to modify the frame, correct brightness/contrast issues, or change the color of the video. The tools that enable you to manipulate the video, such as trim the video or add a fade, are on the Playback tab, shown in Figure 20.18.

 tip

If you are working with a very large video file, you can link it to the PowerPoint slide instead of embedding it. Select the Insert drop-down arrow in the Insert Video dialog box, and then select Link to File.

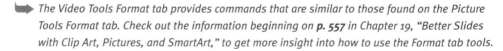 *The Video Tools Format tab provides commands that are similar to those found on the Picture Tools Format tab. Check out the information beginning on **p. 557** in Chapter 19, "Better Slides with Clip Art, Pictures, and SmartArt," to get more insight into how to use the Format tab tools.*

You can use the Trim Video command to trim the beginning or end of the video. This enables you to specify a new start or stop point in the video so that you show only the portion of the video clip that is important to your presentation.

The Playback tab also provides the Bookmarks group. You can use the Add Bookmark command to insert bookmarks into the video object. Bookmarks in a video file can trigger animation effects that you have configured on other objects on the slide. For more about triggering animations, see "Advanced Animation Techniques," earlier in this chapter.

Figure 20.18
An inserted video file
and the Playback Video
Tools.

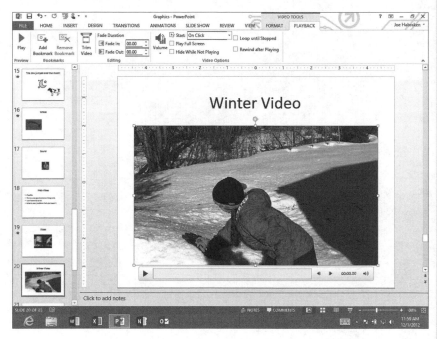

You can also set fades at both the beginning and end of the clip using the Fade In and Fade Out commands, respectively. You can specify that the video be played in full screen mode, when you play the presentation as a slide show. Select the Play Full Screen check box in the Video Options group.

You can test any of the playback changes that you make to the video. Use the Play button as needed. If you want to get a better idea of how the changes you made will appear in the slide show, select the Slide Show icon on the PowerPoint status bar to start a slide show from the current slide.

DELIVERING A PRESENTATION AND CREATING SUPPORT MATERIALS

After you have created and fine-tuned your presentation, you are ready to show it to your audience. Traditionally, the slide show is a speaker's aid and provides the audience with important points and visuals related to the presentation. However, PowerPoint gives you other possibilities for sharing a presentation with an audience. You can create a self-running presentation, which allows individuals or small groups to view the presentation at a conference booth or in a kiosk setting. In addition, PowerPoint enables you to show a presentation on the Web, making it easy for anyone who has the URL for the presentation to view it.

A presentation often involves more than just the slide show itself. Audience members may expect you to provide handouts or other supporting material related to the presentation. PowerPoint makes it easy to print handouts and speaker notes for your presentation.

In this chapter, we look at the different ways of showing your presentation to others. We discuss finalizing your presentations, creating self-running presentations, and broadcasting presentations on the Web. We also look at how to create ancillary materials such as handouts.

Planning Your Presentation

Before we look at some of the aspects involved in getting a PowerPoint presentation finalized and ready to deliver as a slide show, I want to say a few words about planning your presentation. This isn't related to planning the presentation outline and the content, but it is about the preplanning involved in the delivery of the presentation.

Even if you create the most incredible PowerPoint presentation ever seen, you still need to do some planning related to the implementation of your presentation. PowerPoint gives you a technological edge when you are speaking to your audience; however, it won't save you if you haven't done your homework related to your audience, the purpose of the event, and the questions your audience might pose. So, it really makes sense to know the following as you finalize your presentation:

- **Audience:** You need to have a good idea of who will be in the audience when you give your presentation. This affects not only the level of the information you are providing, but also, to some degree, the tone of the presentation, including your use of slide styles, animations, transitions, and multimedia. For example, if you are presenting a sophisticated engineering project to a neighborhood association, keep the technical aspects of the presentation simple. Likewise, consider your audience's visual literacy. A presentation using a lot of bells and whistles, such as animations and multimedia, is easier to digest for a crowd that is technically attuned to graphics and special effects.

- **Purpose:** You must have a good feel for why you are giving the presentation. If you are trying to drum up investors for a construction project, the slide show must help sell the need for the project and make it clear to the audience that you have the expertise to execute the project. Remember that most people can remember only a few major points from even a short presentation, so hit the most important information more than once, and provide a solid conclusion that pulls together the major concepts for the audience.

- **Place:** You really need solid information about the venue where you plan to give your presentation. If you have included a lot of web hyperlinks and perhaps web videos in your presentation, but the site has no Internet connection, you will have to do a lot of dancing to make up for all that missing information. You need to be ready for anything. Always bring your own laptop. You might also want to have hard copies of the presentation ready, in case no video projector is available or the projector light bulb blows just before you take the stage. Oh, and don't count on any kind of audio system that you can use for sound during your presentation.

So you must tailor your presentation for the audience and the venue. Your presentation also needs to have an extremely clear purpose (clear to the audience, not just you). Remember that you can hope to make only a few main points; any more than that, and the audience will be bordering on information overload. Reaffirm your main points in the conclusion of the presentation.

As both a speaker and an attendee at a multitude of educational and technical conferences, I have seen a nearly endless list of things that can go wrong with a presentation—be ready for any eventuality. Spend some time both planning the delivery of your presentation and anticipating some of the potential problems you might face. Doing so will make the presentation go so much more smoothly.

Checking the Presentation for Spelling and Grammar Errors

Making sure that your presentation slides are free of spelling and grammatical errors is important in protecting the veracity of the information in the presentation. If you have obvious spelling errors, for example, the audience will have a hard time taking you seriously. You are probably familiar with the

Spelling and Grammar features in Microsoft Word and the fact that they flag spelling and grammar errors automatically: red wavy lines for spelling errors, green wavy lines for grammar errors.

PowerPoint 2013 now provides the same spelling- and grammar-checking capabilities as Word and the other Office applications. Grammar checking in PowerPoint is not enabled by default, but you can do so in the PowerPoint Options window. Select File and then, in the Backstage, select Options. The PowerPoint Options window opens. Select Proofing to access the spelling and grammar settings, as shown in Figure 21.1.

Figure 21.1
The PowerPoint proofing options.

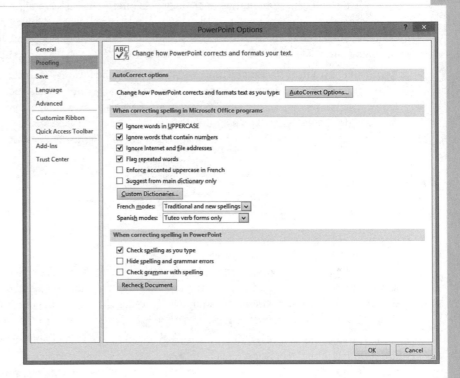

The Check Grammar with Spelling check box is at the bottom of the Proofing options; select it to enable grammar checking. Most of the other Proofing settings are enabled by default. Click OK to save changes and return to the PowerPoint application window.

Do not be complacent about spelling errors and grammar problems because you think PowerPoint is catching them all (it flags misspellings by default and grammar errors after you enable the feature). Run the spelling tool after you complete your presentation; also, do not forget to visually inspect your slides. Proofread your slides and check for contextual errors, such as using the word *there* when you should have used the word *their*. Because PowerPoint text usually consists of short, bulleted fragments, it is easy to make a spelling error that the Spelling feature doesn't flag.

➡ *For more general information about the Spelling feature in Office applications,* **see** *"Running Spelling and Grammar," p. 193.*

note

Use the thesaurus to find synonyms for specific words on your slides. You can also translate slide text using the Translate command in the Language group.

Running Through a Completed Presentation

Before you show your presentation to an audience, run through it several times, checking that the slides are in the right order and that the object animations and slide transitions work correctly (particularly where you have assigned triggers or timings to animations or transitions). Running through the presentation also enables you to practice your prepared speech as you show your slides.

The Slide Show tab of the Ribbon provides all the commands you need to run through your presentation. A Present Online command even allows you to show your presentation via the Web. The Slide Show tab provides commands to create custom slide shows, hide slides in a presentation, and record slide show timings for a self-running show. We discuss these possibilities later in this chapter in the section, "Creating a Self-Running Presentation." Figure 21.2 shows the Slide Show tab.

Figure 21.2
The Ribbon's Slide Show tab.

The Start Slide Show group on the Slide Show tab provides two commands for starting the slide show. The From Beginning command and the From Current Slide command operate exactly as advertised. You can use either command to fire up your slide show, depending on whether you want to start from the beginning or with the slide you are currently editing.

After you start the slide show (from the commands on the Slide Show tab or the Slide Show button provided in the View shortcuts on the status bar), you typically click the mouse as needed to advance through the slides. If you have set timings for slides via slide transitions, you can sit back and practice your narration as the slides change automatically (we talk more about setting slide timings later in the chapter).

In terms of navigating the slide show itself, PowerPoint gives you some easy-to-access tools when you are in Slide Show view. Move the mouse over the bottom-left area of the current slide to access a collection of six tools. From left to right, these tools are as follows:

- **Previous:** The Previous arrow quickly returns to the previous slide.

- **Next:** The Next arrow advances to the next slide in the presentation.

- **Pointer Gallery:** Select the Pen icon to change the mouse pointer into a laser pointer, pen, highlighter, or eraser (if you have already drawn on a slide). You can also select the color used for the pointer.

- **See All Slides View:** A new possibility in the PowerPoint 2013 Slide Show window is the See All Slides View button (to the right of the Pointer Gallery button). Click this button to get a thumbnail view of all the slides in the presentation. You can't move the slide thumbnails around in this view (as you can when you are working in Slide Sorter view), but you can quickly jump to any slide in the presentation by selecting the slide.

- **Zoom:** The Zoom tool enables you to specify an area of the slide and then zoom in on it with an additional click of the mouse.

- **Menu:** This tool enables you to jump back to the last viewed slide, switch to the presenter view (which we discuss in the next section), and set arrow options or end the slide show.

You can also access these different command options from a shortcut menu that is provided when you right-click a slide. You can stop the slide show at any time by pressing the Esc key or selecting End Show on either the shortcut menu or the Slide Show menu. If you run through all the slides in a presentation in Slide Show view, a black screen appears when you proceed beyond the last slide. Click the mouse to exit the screen and return to the PowerPoint application window.

Using the Presenter View

You present your slide show using the "regular" Slide Show view that we discussed in the previous section, or you can show your slide show in Presenter view. Presenter view is designed with you (the presenter) in mind. It is geared toward providing the speaker with the information that the speaker needs while running the slide show. Figure 21.3 shows Presenter view. Previous versions of PowerPoint required that you have your computer connected to at least two monitors for Presenter view to even be an option. PowerPoint 2013 enables you to run Presenter view on a single computer screen, which is a great way to practice your presentation before you hook up your notebook or touchscreen device to an external monitor such as a video projector.

If you have two monitors connected to your computer, check the Use Presenter View check box on the Slide Show tab of the Ribbon. Now when you start the slide show, it opens with Presenter view on your primary monitor and Slide Show view on the secondary monitor. If you find that this isn't happening automatically, select the Monitor drop-down list on the Slide Show tab (in the Monitors group) and select Primary Monitor.

If you have only one monitor on your computer, you can still use Presenter view to practice your presentation. Start the slide show, right-click the first screen in the slide show, and select Show Presenter View from the shortcut menu.

Presenter view divides your computer screen into different panes. On the left of the screen, you see the current slide and can access the Slide Show tools (such as the Pointer gallery or the Zoom feature) and a set of navigation buttons. Above the current slide is a timer that shows you the amount of elapsed time since the current slide has been on the screen.

A Ribbon sits at the top of the left side of the Presenter view screen. This Ribbon provides three commands: Show Taskbar, Display Settings, and End Slide Show. The Show Taskbar command shows the Windows at the bottom of the screen and enables you to quickly switch to another application that is open on the desktop.

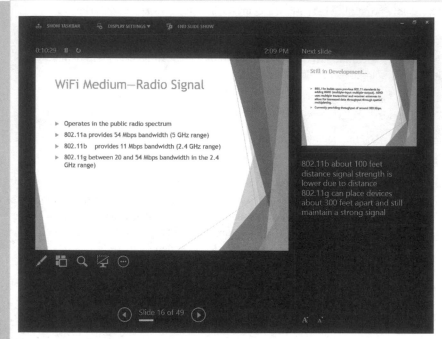

Figure 21.3
Presenter view.

The Display Settings command provides a drop-down list that can be useful when you are working with multiple monitors. The first command, Swap Presenter View and Slide Show, enables you to swap what is being shown on two monitors connected to your computer. I have seen PowerPoint presentations in which the speaker had Presenter view on the audience's "big screen" and was trying desperately to swap it with the slide show that was on the presenter's laptop. The other command, Duplicate Slide Show, places the "basic" slide show on both screens.

The End Slide Show command is self-explanatory. When you want to end the slide show, select End Slide Show.

On the right side of Presenter view, the next slide is shown as a thumbnail. If you have notes associated with the current slide, they appear below the thumbnail of the next slide. This pane of the right side of the Presenter view screen also provides a Make the Text Larger icon and a Make the Text Smaller icon that enable you to zoom in or zoom out on your notes.

Using Hidden Slides

At the outset of this chapter, we discussed the fact that you need to anticipate potential problems when you actually deliver your presentation. Presenter view, discussed in the previous section, can help you keep track of your slides (you always know what slide is up next), and you can also view your notes.

You also need to anticipate, as much as possible, what type of additional information your audience might request during your presentation. For example, if you show a chart on a slide, someone in the audience might ask you about the raw data on which the chart is based. Even though you didn't originally plan to show the data during the presentation, wouldn't it be great if you already had the data arranged in an easy-to-read table on an available slide? This is where hidden slides come in. These are slides that you prepare in anticipation of audience questions or follow-up that you might want to make on your topic if you have extra time at the end of your presentation. The slides are saved in the presentation but are hidden, however, and aren't shown when you run the presentation as a slide show.

The Hide Slide command is housed on the Ribbon's Slide Show tab in the Set Up group. You can hide a slide or slides when you are working in Normal view or in the Slide Sorter. To hide multiple slides, select the slide or slides and then select the Hide Slide command.

A hidden slide is marked with a diagonal slash through the slide's number (which you can see in both Normal view and the Slide Sorter). Hidden slides are also "ghosted" in Slide Sorter view. Remember that a hidden slide still remains in the presentation; however, it is not shown during the slide show. Figure 21.4 shows a presentation in Slide Sorter view. Slides 16, 17, 19, and 20 are marked as hidden.

 tip

To unhide a slide or slides, select the slide or slides and then click the Hide Slide command a second time.

 tip

You can right-click a slide thumbnail in Normal view or in Slide Sorter view and select Hide Slide from the shortcut menu.

Figure 21.4
Slides in the presentation can be hidden.

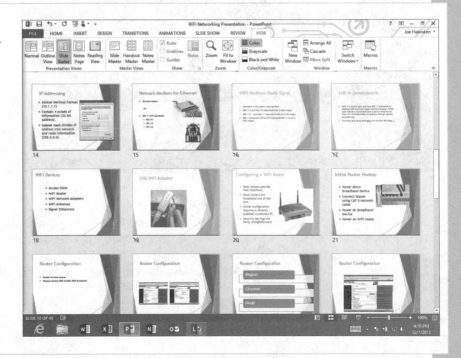

Hidden slides can be anywhere in the presentation; you don't necessarily have to group them. However, you might want to keep them in sequence with slides that cover similar information. If you have a lot of slides in your presentation, you can also divide the presentation into sections and create a specific section to house the hidden slides. That way, the hidden slides aren't mixed in with the rest of the slides.

To access a hidden slide during a slide show (in either Slide Show view or Presenter view), click the See All Slides icon. Thumbnails of all your slides (including the hidden slides) appear on the screen. Hidden slides are ghosted, as shown in Figure 21.5. To open a hidden slide, select the slide. You return to either Slide Show view or Presenter view with the hidden slide displayed.

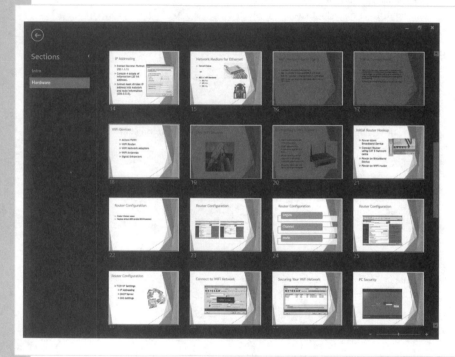

Figure 21.5
Select a hidden slide from the See All Slides pane during a slide show.

If you decide to use hidden slides in your presentations, determine some sort of structure for their placement. If you have a few hidden slides, you might want to keep the hidden slide near the other slides in the presentation that it pertains or refers to. If you have an extremely large number of slides, it might make sense to cluster all the hidden slides in a section or place them at the end of your presentation for easy access (if and when you need them).

Creating a Custom Slide Show

The Slide Show tab has an option for creating a custom slide show. The Custom Slide Show command enables you to take a subset of your current presentation and designate it as a custom show. This means that you can create shorter presentations from the contents of a lengthy presentation.

For example, you might have given a two-hour presentation at a conference and now want to break the presentation into two one-hour custom shows that you can give as lunchtime seminars. You can create any number of custom shows from a single PowerPoint presentation.

To create a custom slide show, select Custom Slide Show on the Slide Show tab and then select Custom Shows. The Custom Shows dialog box opens. From here, you can create new custom shows and modify existing custom shows. After you create a custom show, it appears in the Custom Shows list. To create a new custom show, click the New button. The Define Custom Show dialog box appears.

All the slides in the presentation are listed in the Slides in Presentation list. To add a slide to the custom show, select the slide and then click the Add button. You can select multiple slides (select the check box for each slide) and then click Add to add multiple slides to the custom show. Slides added to the custom show are listed in the Slides in Custom Show list, as shown in Figure 21.6.

Figure 21.6
Create a custom show in the Define Custom Show dialog box.

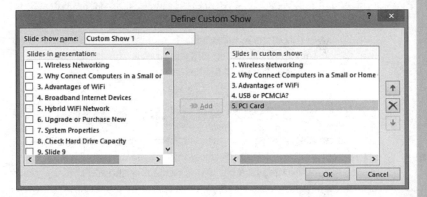

When you have specified the slides for the custom show, click in the Slide Show Name text box and type a name for the custom show. To create the custom show and return to the Custom Shows dialog box, click OK. The new custom show is listed in the Custom Shows dialog box, as shown in Figure 21.7.

Figure 21.7
Custom shows are accessed using the Custom Shows dialog box.

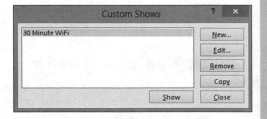

You can edit a custom show by selecting the show in the Custom Shows dialog box and then clicking Edit. This opens the Define Custom Show dialog box. You can use the Add and/or Remove buttons to add slides to the custom show or remove slides from the show. You can also use the Up or Down arrows to reorder the slides in the Slides in Custom Show list.

The Custom Shows dialog box also enables you to remove a custom show or copy a custom show. Making a copy of a custom show lets you add or remove slides from the copy and specify a new name for the copy. This provides a quick way to repurpose an existing custom show.

When you are finished working in the Custom Shows dialog box, click Close to return to the PowerPoint workspace.

The custom show or shows that you create for a presentation are listed on the menu that is provided when you select the Custom Slide Show command. To show a custom show as a slide show, click the custom show's name on the menu. The custom show begins to play. The custom show performs in Slide Show view the same as any other PowerPoint presentation; any settings that you assigned to the slides in the original presentation that are part of the custom show, including animations and transitions, are in force during the showing of the custom show.

 tip

You can run a custom show as a slide show from the Custom Shows dialog box. Select the show in the Custom Shows list and then select Show.

Creating a Self-Running Presentation

A self-running presentation means different things to different people. For example, you might want to create a self-running slide show that advances each slide after a specified period. However, you plan to provide the narration that accompanies the slides in person. You are configuring the slides with timings because you want to concentrate on your speech instead of changing the slides. This scenario requires that you spend time practicing the presentation so that the slides don't get ahead of you or you don't get ahead of your slides as you deliver the narrative.

Another type of self-running presentation is one that runs at a trade show booth or in a kiosk. A live speaker does not accompany this type of self-running show, so you record the narration that goes with the slides as part of the presentation. Two "viewing" options exist for this unaccompanied self-running show: You can allow a user (such as an interested customer) to browse the presentation interactively (which we discuss in the next section), or you can have presentation run itself by looping continuously. The Set Up group on the Ribbon's Slide Show tab provides the commands that help you add timing to a presentation and also record a slide show. When you record a slide show, the timings are set and narration can also be recorded.

Setting Up a Slide Show

You can specify settings for a slide show, including the show type, the slides shown during the slide show, the selection of a custom show, and other options related to the slide show, such as how the slides are advanced and whether you want to use the Presenter view (for a presentation given by a speaker). You open the Set Up Show dialog box by selecting the Set Up Slide Show command in the Set Up group. Figure 21.8 shows the Set Up Show dialog box.

Figure 21.8
The Set Up Show dialog box.

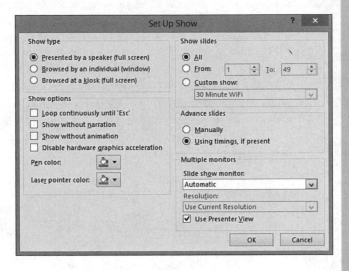

Specify the show type by selecting one of the option buttons provided. The default show type is presented by a speaker (full screen). If you are setting up a self-running show, you can specify either Browsed by an Individual (window) or Browsed at a Kiosk (full screen) options.

Show options also enable you to loop the show continuously, turn off the animation, or turn off any animation in the presentation. When you select Browsed at a Kiosk (Full Screen) as your show type, the Loop Continuously Until Esc option is automatically selected. Options are also provided for the pen and laser pointer color (hold down the Ctrl key and press the left mouse button during the slide show to access the laser pointer). The Pen Color option is available only when you are setting up a show that is to be presented by a speaker. Other settings in the Set Up Show dialog box enable you to specify the slides to be shown, or you can choose from a list of custom shows. You can also specify how the slides should be advanced in the presentation. Using Timings, If Present, is the default setting. This option makes the best sense for self-running presentations, unless you want to include action buttons on slides that enable users to interact with the presentation.

 tip

If you are configuring a slide show that you plan to present, make sure that the Use Presenter View option is selected. This enables you to see your notes and the next slide in the presentation, and also helps you stay on top of your presentation and reduces presentation anxiety.

With the Set Up Show dialog box, you also can specify the monitor to use when you have multiple monitors available (including video projectors). When you finish setting the options for the slide show, click OK to return to the PowerPoint workspace.

Rehearsing Timings

If you want to set the timings for a self-running presentation that do not include narration, you can use the Rehearse Timings command on the Slide Show tab. This scenario works when you want to set the timings for a self-running show that will run in a kiosk or in a case, and you want the slides to advance automatically when you are presenting and narrating the slide show. Remember that setting up the timings does not only involve solely moving from slide to slide; it also includes timing the animations that you set for the various objects on the slides. For example, if you configure entrance animations for objects, particularly bulleted lists, you need to step through the animation to set the appropriate timing for the animation.

When you are ready to rehearse the timings for the slide show, select the Rehearse Timings command. The slide show begins. A Recording toolbar is present in the upper-left of the show window, as shown in Figure 21.9.

 tip

If you want to stop recording, click the Close button on the Recording toolbar. You have the option to save the timings that have been made thus far.

Figure 21.9
The Slide Show window with Recording toolbar.

The toolbar includes a timing counter that times the slide show. The Recording toolbar also provides a Next button, which works the same as a mouse click in terms of advancing to the next slide or stepping through an animation sequence. A Pause button enables you to pause the timer as needed. If you want to reset the timer for a particular slide and start the timing for that slide over, you can click the Repeat button on the Recording toolbar.

After you select the Rehearse Timings command, the clock is ticking, so be ready. Work through the slides as you give your narration if you are setting up timings for a slide show that you will present. When you complete the slide show, a message box opens and provides the total time for the slide show. If you want to keep the slide timings for the show, click Yes; click No if you want to dump the timings and try again.

Recording a Slide Show

You can also record a slide show that has the timings for the slides and animations and includes recorded narration and laser pointer actions. The Record Slide Show command enables you to record the slide show from the beginning or from the current slide.

The recording process is similar to the process for rehearsing timings, as discussed in the previous section. The big difference is that you are able to record audio (meaning your narration) and record your mouse laser pointer actions as if you were giving the slide show. The recorded show can then be played back as a self-running show. You can use the Set Up Show dialog box to configure the slide show to loop continuously.

To start the slide show recording, select the Record Slide Show command and then select Start Recording from Beginning or Start Recording from Current Slide. In both cases, the Record Slide Show dialog box opens, as shown in Figure 21.10. In this dialog box, you can select options related to what is recorded. By default, slide and animation timings are recorded, as are narration and your use of the laser pointer. You can deselect options such as Narrations and Laser Pointer, as needed. If you don't record the narration, you are basically doing the same thing as with the Rehearse Timings command: You are recording the timing for the slide changes and the animation effects on the slides.

Figure 21.10
The Record Slide Show dialog box.

When you are ready to begin, click the Start Recording button in the Record Slide Show dialog box. The slide show starts, and the Recording toolbar is present in the upper-left corner of the slide show window. As already mentioned, you can use it to pause the recording or to restart the recording for the current slide, as needed.

When you have finished recording the timings, the presentation opens in Slide Sorter view (the timings are saved automatically, unlike the Rehearse Timings command). The timing for each slide appears to the left and below each slide in the presentation.

You can clear the timing and/or narration for the currently selected slide or all the slides in the presentation. Select the Record Slide Show command and then point at Clear. Choose the appropriate option from the menu provided (such as Clear Timing on Current Slide). If you clear timings and/or narrations on a particular slide, you can then go back to that slide and redo the recording. With the slide selected in the Slide Sorter, select Record Slide Show and then select Start Recording from Current Slide. Click the Start Recording button in the Record Slide Show dialog box.

Record your timing and narration for the slide (including the timing for any animations on the slide). When you finish with that slide, immediately click the Close button on the Recording toolbar to return to the Slide Sorter; the new timing is shown for the slide.

To play your automated slide show, click the From Beginning button on the Slide Show tab. The slide show plays using the timings that you set and includes recorded narration (if you recorded the narration).

Creating an Interactive Presentation

If you are considering creating a slide show for a trade show booth or some other venue where the audience for the show consists of only one or two people at a time, you might want to give your audience the capability to control the show instead of creating a self-running show. Obviously, turning over control to your audience is fraught with danger, but you might find that more people are likely to tune in if they can interact with it instead of just passively standing by and watching it.

You can use action buttons to place different controls on the slides, meaning that you place the action button on a slide, and a particular action takes place when it is clicked. Action buttons can perform all sorts of different actions. PowerPoint provides premade controls, including buttons that enable you to go back or forward and buttons that play a movie or a sound. You can also configure a custom action button to meet your particular needs, such as moving to a particular slide in the slide show, running an application, or running a macro that you have recorded.

➡ *For more information about enabling and recording macros,* **see** *Appendix B, "Office Macros."*

The use of action buttons on slides is certainly not limited to slide shows in which you want to give the audience interactive capabilities. You can use action buttons on slide shows that you present. They can make it convenient for you to go back to a particular slide or open another application as you show your slides.

The action buttons are found in the Shapes library provided by the Shapes gallery on the Ribbon's Insert tab. Most of the Shapes gallery is devoted to different shapes that can be added to a slide as graphical elements. Action buttons look like a shape but are also designed to make a particular action happen. To insert an action button, follow these steps:

1. In Normal view, navigate to the slide that holds the action button.

2. Select the Ribbon's Insert tab.

3. Select the Shapes command in the Illustrations group. The Shapes gallery opens, as shown in Figure 21.11.

4. Select an action button from the Action Buttons section of the Shapes gallery (at the bottom of the gallery). The mouse pointer becomes a drawing tool.

5. Drag the drawing tool on the slide to create the action button shape. The Action Settings dialog box appears.

6. You can set up the action settings for the action button so that a mouse click or a mouseover activates them. A single action button can do one action on a mouse click and then do a second action on a mouseover. Select the dialog box tab you want to configure based on how you want the action to be activated (the settings on the Mouse Click and Mouse Over tabs of the dialog box are the same).

Figure 21.11
The Shapes gallery, including the action buttons.

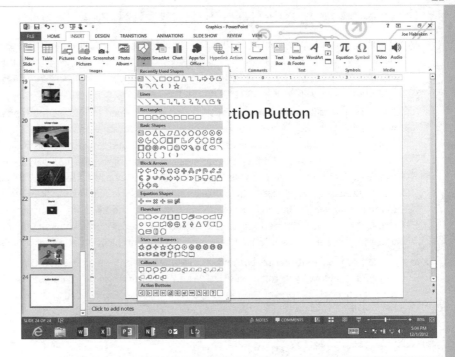

7. Specify the action for the action button by using the option buttons on the dialog box tab that you selected.

8. When you finish setting the options for the action button, select OK to return to the slide in Normal view.

To test your action button, click the Slide Show shortcut on the status bar to start the slide show from the current slide. Click the action button to see whether you get the expected results. You can add multiple action buttons to a particular slide, if needed. If you want to set up the same action buttons on all your slides, such as Backward and Forward Action buttons for navigation of the slide show, place the action buttons on the slide master for the presentation.

 *The slide master is discussed in Chapter 18, "Advanced Presentation Formatting, Themes, and Masters." **See** "Understanding Masters," **p. 547**, for more information.*

note

Action buttons are just like any other shape or object that you place on a slide. You can move them, size them, or delete them.

Presenting a Slide Show Online

Another option for presenting your slide show is to present it online. PowerPoint makes it extremely easy for you to stream a slide show to online participants, and PowerPoint provides two ways to present online. You can present the slide show in a Lync meeting, or you can "broadcast" the presentation using the free Office presentation service.

Lync is Microsoft's communication client and can be used for videoconferencing, text messaging, and online meetings. The Lync client, which is fully integrated with the Office 2013 application suite, requires that you have access to a Lync server and an account on the server. In the past, having access to any sort of online communication platform required employment at a large company that had servers for that purpose. However, if you purchased Office 2013 as part of an Office 365 Small Business, Pro Plus, or Enterprise subscription, you can take advantage of Lync using your Microsoft subscription user account (Microsoft hosts the Lync server as part of your subscription). Other Office users covered under your Office 365 license can also use Lync and its services, meaning you can present a PowerPoint presentation to your employees or coworkers using Lync.

The other possibility for presenting online takes advantage of the free Office presentation service. This option allows you to "broadcast" your presentation to the Web, and participants in the broadcast can access the presentation using a web browser. No special software is needed. You (the broadcaster) need to have a Windows Live ID (meaning an Outlook.com or Hotmail account).

Presenting Online with Lync

An extremely detailed discussion of Lync is beyond the scope of this book. Suffice it to say that Lync can be used to host online meetings with coworkers or colleagues. If you have the appropriate level of Office 365 subscription, Lync is installed along with the other Office applications. The Lync window is extremely simple to use, and you log onto Lync using your Office 365 username and password. You can start a meeting in Lync and then present the presentation, or start a new Lync meeting from PowerPoint.

To get the presentation up and running online, open the presentation in PowerPoint. The Present Online command is on the Ribbon's Slide Show tab. Select the Present Online command and then select Microsoft Lync. The Present This Slide Show in a Lync Meeting dialog box opens. To start a new Lync meeting and present the slide show online, select OK. A message box opens and asks you to join the meeting audio. Select OK. A new conference call starts and a presentation window opens, as shown in Figure 21.12.

You can click the People icon at the bottom of the presentation window and open the Participants pane. This provides access to the Invite More People button, which you can use to access your Lync contacts and invite participants. When you have all your participants, you can present the slide show.

You can access slide thumbnails and your speaker notes using the commands on the lower-right slide of the presentation window. When you have finished broadcasting the presentation, click the Stop Presenting button. You can then close the presentation stage by clicking the Close button.

Figure 21.12
The online presentation in a Lync meeting window.

Presenting Online with the Office Presentation Service

The other option for presenting online is to take advantage of the Office presentation service. Open the presentation you want to broadcast. On the Slide Show tab, select Office Presentation Service. The Present Online dialog box opens. This dialog box explains the Office Presentation Service and also offers some cautions related to file size issue or unsupported content. When you are ready to connect to the Office Presentation Service, click Connect. You are connected to the broadcast service, and the slide show is prepared for broadcast. The Present Online dialog box displays a link to your online presentation, as shown in Figure 21.13.

You need to share that link with your audience. You can copy the link and then paste it into a page that you place on a website, or you can use the Send in Email or Send in IM commands to send the link information in an email or an instant message using Outlook or Lync, respectively.

You probably don't want to present the slide show online forever. Make it clear in the invitation message when you will begin presenting and when you will stop presenting. You can also create an automated slide show and let it run a number of times before ending the presentation. This should allow most of your invitees to view the content.

After you have sent the web link to your attendees, you can start the slide show. Select the Start Presentation button in the Present Online dialog box. The presentation opens in Slide Show view. You can show your presentation, and your online audience can follow along. The slide show can be a manual slide show (in which you advance the slides), or you can set up an automated slide show that loops.

Figure 21.13
A web link is created for the online presentation.

When your presentation finishes and you exit the slide show, you are still in online presentation mode. The Ribbon displays the Present Online tab, which enables you to restart the online presentation, share meeting notes (using OneNote), and send additional invitations. When you have finished running the online presentation, select the End Online Presentation command. A warning box opens to tell you that anyone currently viewing the presentation will be disconnected. Select End Online Presentation (in the warning box). The Ribbon returns to the Slide Show tab, and your online presentation terminates.

Working with the Notes and Handouts Masters

Although most of PowerPoint's capabilities are slanted toward creating slide shows, you can create ancillary printed materials from your presentation slides. I'm talking about notes and handouts. Notes are the script that you create to go with the slide show. Your notes may provide only a few facts or other key points that are not included as actual slide content, or you might create detailed notes for every slide. Your choice depends on the type of presentation you are creating. For example, you might be creating training materials that include a PowerPoint presentation, and you want to include a detailed script for use by the trainers who give the presentation to your employees or clients. Or you might be assembling a presentation about a topic that you can pontificate on for hours, so you may not even need any notes.

Handouts are an ancillary product derived from your presentation slides that you can give to the audience. Handouts can make it easier for your audience to follow the presentation and perhaps use the handout as a convenient place to take notes of their own. You can even print handouts that provide every slide in the presentation. You can determine the number of slides that are included on each of the pages of the handout, and you can specify a range of one to nine slides per page.

PowerPoint provides masters for both the notes and the handouts. Each master determines the header and footer information to be included in the resulting printout and can be configured to use a particular theme or background style. Page setup attributes for both the notes and the handouts are also controlled by their respective master. You can access the master for either your handouts or your notes on the Ribbon's View tab. The Handout Master and the Notes Master commands are in the Master Views group.

Setting Handout Master Options

To access the handout master, select the Handout Master command on the View tab. The Handout Master tab appears on the Ribbon, and the handout master opens in the application window, as shown in Figure 21.14.

Figure 21.14
A presentation's Handout Master and the Ribbon's Handout Master tab.

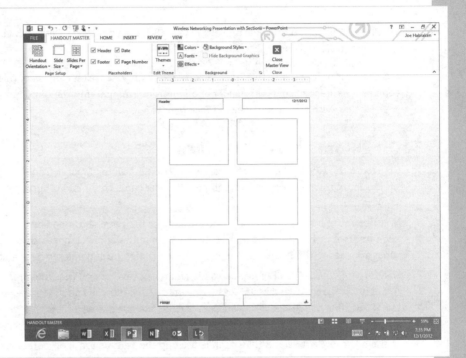

You can configure page settings, determine the placeholders on the handout master, and set a theme or background for the handouts. The Handout Master tab provides the following groups:

- **Page Setup:** This group provides commands that enable you to set up the page size using the Page Setup dialog box. It also provides commands for changing the handout orientation from portrait to landscape. You can change the slide orientation on the page and select the number of slides to show on each page. You can select from one to nine slides per page or provide an outline view of the slides on the page.

> **note**
>
> Determining whether you should distribute your presentation handouts before or after the presentation is always hard. Sometimes handouts can be a distraction and the audience is more absorbed in reading the handouts than watching your presentation. Decide what works best for you.

- **Placeholders:** This group is a set of check boxes that enable you to determine whether a header or footer appears on the page. Options are also provided for including the date and numbering pages.

- **Edit Theme:** The choices in the Theme gallery are grayed out. Because the design of the slides printed in the handout depends on the theme you set for the presentation, you won't have access to these commands when working on the handout master.

- **Background:** You can fine-tune the colors, fonts, and effects for the currently assigned presentation theme, and you can specify a background for the handout pages by using the Background Styles gallery.

- **Close:** This group provides one command: Close Master View. Click this view when you want to return to Normal view.

For the header and footer text, placeholder text is provided. You can select this text and then replace it as needed to insert header and footer information into the handout master. When you finish working with the master, select Close Master View.

Setting Notes Master Options

To access the Notes Master from the View tab, select Notes Master. The Notes Master tab appears on the Ribbon. The Notes Master tab provides the same command groups provided by the Handout Master tab.

You can use the Page Setup commands to change the page setup and also to change the page and slide orientation. The Placeholders group has a number of check boxes that enable you to determine what appears in the header and footer areas on the page, such as the date and page number.

In addition, you can manipulate the slide and notes text box on the Notes Master. For example, if you want the slide to take up less space on the master, you can select the slide box and size or move the slide as needed. You can then expand the notes area.

By default, the master text box is configured to include a five-level outline. You can select the text in the master text box and then change it using the various font and paragraph commands available on the Home tab. You can also select the Format tab of the drawing tools (which appears when you select the text box) and change any desired settings. When you finish setting the options for the notes master, click Close Master View on the Notes Master tab.

Printing Presentations, Notes, and Handouts

You can print the slides in your presentation as needed. You can also print your speaker notes and print handouts for your audience. Printing these various items is accomplished from the PowerPoint Backstage. To access the Backstage, select File on the Ribbon. To access the Print window, select Print. The Print window opens, as shown in Figure 21.15.

You can specify the number of copies you want to print and specify both the printer and its properties for the print job. The Settings area of the window lists the various options related to printing your presentation slides.

Figure 21.15
The Backstage Print window.

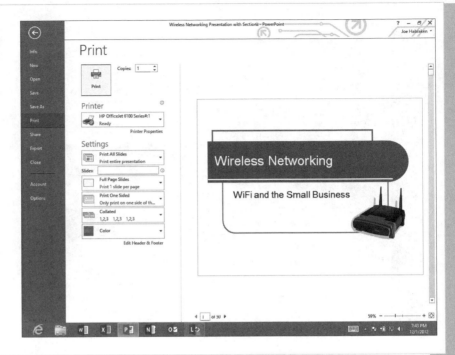

 note

If you are creating printed notes for yourself, you might not want to bother with the Notes Master. Notes are just notes, after all. If you are distributing the notes to other speakers, you might want to take the time to make the notes look a little more formal by fine-tuning the Notes Master's settings.

By default, all sides will print. You can change this setting to print the current slide, or you can specify a custom range in the Slides box. For example, you can specify a range such as 1–23 or specify slides that are not in a range by using commas (for example, 2, 5, 8, and so forth).

By default, each slide prints on a separate sheet. Because printing one slide per page is the last thing I want to do, it makes sense to change the Full Page Slides setting. To change this setting, click the arrow to the right of the Print All Slides setting. The Print Layout gallery appears, as shown in Figure 21.16.

You can choose among different layouts for the printout. If you want to print your notes, select the Notes Pages layout. An Outline layout also is provided for printing the presentation as an outline.

When printing handouts, you can choose among different layouts that enable you to specify the number of slides that print on each page. You can also select special options related to the printout, such as Frame Slides (a frame prints around each slide), Scale to Fit Paper, and High Quality (which provides a printout of the highest quality your printer can produce).

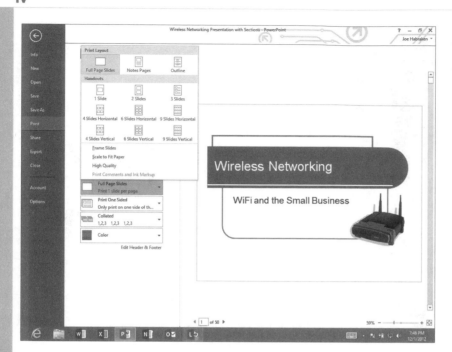

Figure 21.16
The Print Layout gallery.

After you determine the layout for the printout, you can specify whether the printout should print on one or both sides of the paper (if you have a printer that provides this option).

If you print multiple copies of the printout, you can also specify whether the print job should be collated. An orientation drop-down menu enables you to specify the orientation for the printout as well. Portrait is the default, but you can switch to landscape.

You might want to take advantage of one more option, depending on the printer you are using and whether you are going to make grayscale copies of your printout. The Color menu enables you to specify Color, Grayscale, or Pure Black and White for your printout. The Color setting is straightforward; there are some differences between the Grayscale and Pure Black and White settings, however.

No difference exists between the Grayscale and Pure Black and White settings when you print text, fill, lines, clip art, and slide backgrounds. The only differences between these two settings relates to shadows and charts. The Grayscale setting uses grayscale to print these items, whereas the Black and White setting uses black for the shadows and white for charts. In most cases, particularly when you have a laser printer that provides excellent print density, you want to go with a grayscale printout. You can always print a slide page as a test using the Grayscale setting and then apply the Pure Black and White setting to determine the best setting for your particular printer.

When you finish setting the options for your printout, click the Print button in the Print window. Your printout then is sent to your printer.

Exporting a Presentation

Thus far in this chapter, we've looked at strategies for delivering a slide show or online presentation and printing the content in your PowerPoint presentation. PowerPoint also offers different possibilities for exporting a presentation file. For example, you can create an Adobe Acrobat (PDF) version of the slide presentation, which makes it easy to email or post your presentation on a website. Other Export options include creating a video of the presentation and packaging the presentation for a CD.

The PowerPoint Export tools are accessed in the Backstage; select File and then Export. Figure 21.17 shows the Export page in the Backstage.

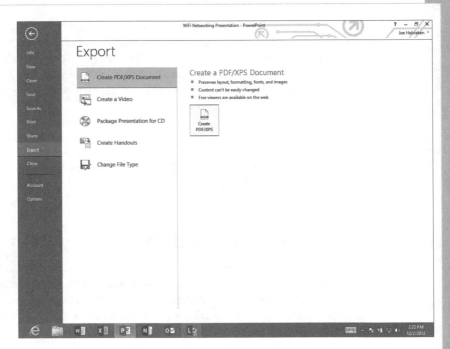

Figure 21.17
The Export Page in the PowerPoint Backstage.

- **Create PDF/XPS:** This command creates a PDF or XPS document of your slide presentation. Both file formats preserve the slide layout and formatting (including fonts and images).

- **Create a Video:** This saves your presentation as an MP4 digital video. All timings, narration, and even recorded mouse gestures (such as laser pointer or pen use) are preserved in the video version of the presentation. The video also incorporates your animations, transitions, and any inserted media, such as sound or movie files. You can save the video at different resolutions, which means you can dictate the file size of the video (the lower the resolution, the lower the file size).

- **Package Presentation for CD:** If you want to give someone a complete and working copy of your presentation, or if you want to transport your presentation to another computer, you might want to package the presentation for CD. This process makes sure that any linked or embedded items are packaged with the presentation content (linked or embedded items can include videos, sounds, charts from Excel—anything that is external to the actual PowerPoint presentation file).

■ **Create Handouts:** We discussed formatting and printing handouts in the previous section. However, you can create handouts that place your slides and notes in a Word document. You can then format the handouts using Word's powerful layout and formatting features. The Word handouts are configured so that if you make any changes to the slides in the presentation, the handouts are updated to reflect those changes. You can fine-tune the colors, fonts, and effects for the currently assigned presentation theme, and you can specify a background for the handout pages by using the Background Styles gallery.

■ **Change File Type:** The Change File Type option enables you to select from a number of different file formats. For example, you can save your presentation in the PowerPoint 97-2003 file format if you need to collaborate with a user of this earlier version of PowerPoint. You can also save your presentation as a PowerPoint picture presentation, with each slide in the presentation represented as a picture. An option is also provided on the Change File Type pane for saving the current presentation as a PowerPoint template.

The Export page provides a range of possibilities for transforming your presentation into a file type that you can easily share with your audience. PowerPoint also provides the Share page in the Backstage, which offers additional options for sharing presentations with collaborators and taking advantage of the cloud in publishing and presenting presentation content. We talk about sharing in the next section.

Sharing Your Presentation

You can collaborate with colleagues and co-workers as you build your PowerPoint presentations. Multiple users can edit a PowerPoint presentation in a networking environment that supports the sharing process. You can share presentations on your SkyDrive or on a SharePoint server (available if you subscribe to Office 365 or work at a company that hosts a SharePoint site). You can also share a presentation via email as attachments.

The Share page in the PowerPoint Backstage provides different strategies for sharing your presentation files with other users. We already mentioned sharing in terms of collaboration. The Share page enables you to post your presentation to social networks, present online, and even send a link to the presentation in an Instant Message. Figure 21.18 shows the Share page.

As already mentioned, the Share page provides a diverse list of options for sharing your presentation:

■ **Invite People:** When you save your presentation file to your SkyDrive or a location on a SharePoint site, you can invite other people (users) to access the file. This is a great way to share a presentation that requires collaboration from several co-workers. You can specify whether a user must log in to access the presentation file (in either the SkyDrive scenario or the SharePoint scenario).

Figure 21.18
The Backstage Share
page.

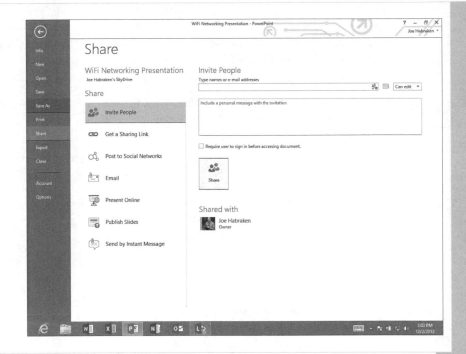

- **Get a Sharing Link:** You can use this option to share a presentation with a large group of people when you want to post the link to the presentation on the Web or via some medium other than email invitation. Select Create Link to create the link (again, this works when you have to save the presentation to your SkyDrive or SharePoint site).

- **Post to Social Networks:** You can post the presentation to a social network such as Facebook. Associate your Windows Live (such as Outlook.com or Hotmail) account to your Facebook account or other social network, including LinkedIn and Google.

- **Email:** You can send the presentation file as an email attachment, a link, or a PDF or XPS file. Remember that if you send the presentation as an attachment, other users can make changes to the presentation. If you send it as a PDF or XPS file, you protect the original content of the presentation.

- **Present Online:** You can give the presentation in a Microsoft Lync meeting or broadcast the presentation on the Web using the Office presentation service. Both options are discussed earlier in this chapter, in the section "Presenting a Slide Show Online."

- **Publish Slides:** You can save the presentation to a slide library on a SharePoint site. Other users can then access the slides in the library, and you can track and review changes made to the presentation slides. You can enable email notification so that you receive an email when changes are made to the presentation.

■ **Send by Instant Message:** This option enables you to send a link to your presentation using Instant Messaging in the Microsoft Lync communication client. You need Lync installed on your computer, and you also need a user account and access to a Lync server. If you are a Small Business or Enterprise Office 365 subscriber, Lync and Lync server are two benefits of your subscription.

As you can see, the possibilities on the Share page range from the practical (Invite People) to options that border on the absurd (Post to Social Networks). Use these options to your benefit and not your dismay.

REQUISITE OUTLOOK: CONFIGURATION AND ESSENTIAL FEATURES

Outlook has long been the communication hub for the Office application suite. Outlook 2013 is no different; it gives you the capability to communicate with others and also to stay organized and productive. Outlook is the tool of choice for sending and receiving emails, scheduling appointments and meetings, and recording tasks and journal entries.

Outlook 2013 adopts the cleaner and sleeker metro look that was pioneered in the Windows 8 environment. Outlook also continues to keep pace with the times and integrates Outlook's powerful personal information-management tools with the social media data that you access on social network websites such as Facebook or LinkedIn. In this chapter, we begin our discussion of Outlook 2013 with a brief look at some of its newest features and enhancements.

Much of the chapter is dedicated to configuring Outlook and taking advantage of its basic features. The discussion includes an overview of the Outlook application environment and includes information on how to organize Outlook items using categories and import/export data.

Introducing Outlook 2013

Microsoft Outlook 2013 builds upon the features found in previous versions of this powerful personal information manager and includes a number of new features. Outlook continues to be a multifaceted communication application, enabling you to work with and manage many different types of information. Although many of us think of Outlook as our email client, it really is so much more; Outlook enables you to create and manage a number of different items, such as emails, appointments, meetings, tasks, and contacts.

Outlook 2013 has new enhancements that make it an even better personal information manager. Some of these new possibilities follow:

- **People Hub View:** This is the new default view for contacts. The People hub shows your Outlook contacts, as expected, and also now includes contacts from your social network sites. The new Contact card for contacts (People) aggregates information about a particular person from information gleaned from multiple sources, such as social media websites.

- **Access Outlook.com calendar, contacts, and tasks:** Previous versions of Outlook made it easy for you to add your Hotmail email address to your Outlook configuration. But now Hotmail is Outlook.com, and you can configure Outlook 2013 so that you can access your Outlook.com email as well as your calendar, contacts, and tasks. These new possibilities result from the addition of the new Exchange ActiveSync feature to Outlook and other members of the Office 2013 application suite, such as OneNote.

- **New Weather bar in the calendar:** The Outlook Calendar provides a new Weather bar that enables you to view real-time weather forecasts. By default, you see a three-day overview of the weather, and hovering over a particular day gives more forecast details. You can add multiple locations to the Weather bar so that you can check the weather at a particular location before using the calendar to schedule that long weekend golf getaway (er, I mean, important sales meeting).

> **tip**
>
> Outlook 2013 is designed to be touch-friendly, for users who take advantage of the application on touch devices such as tablets and other smart devices. Windows 8 is also touchscreen ready and is featured (as is Windows 8 RT version) on Microsoft's new table device, the Surface. Office 2013 is also available for the Surface tablet.

We discuss other Outlook enhancements and changes as we encounter them in the Outlook section of this book. Some new features are more transparent than others and help Outlook function more than they give you a new tool or function. These under-the-hood improvements include Outlook's capability to turn off any add-ins that adversely affect the performance or reliability of Outlook. Outlook 2013 also starts and exits faster than its predecessor, Outlook 2010.

Outlook and Email Accounts

Outlook supports different types of email accounts; you can use Outlook as your email client for an Internet email account from your Internet service provider, a web-based email account such as Microsoft's Outlook.com (formerly Hotmail), or a Microsoft Exchange mail account hosted by an Exchange server on your corporate network. In fact, you can configure Outlook to manage multiple (and different types of) email accounts at the same time.

When you start Outlook for the first time, you are presented with the option to set up your email account. However, as already mentioned, you are not limited to a single email address when you use Outlook. You can easily add email addresses even after you have configured the initial email account when you first ran Outlook.

As already mentioned in this section, you can add different types of email accounts to Outlook. Email accounts are considered a service in Outlook; when you add an email account, you are adding a service. Figure 22.1 shows the Choose Service window that appears when you add a new email account to Outlook. Notice the three possibilities: Microsoft Exchange Server or compatible service, Exchange ActiveSync, and POP3 or IMAP. Obviously, these three possibilities are different, but what do they really mean? The following information looks at each of these email types and how you configure them. We begin with a look at Exchange Server email accounts.

 tip
When you add a new email account to Outlook, Outlook can attempt to configure the email account settings (such as the incoming and outgoing mail servers) purely based on the email account that you provide. Sometimes this works, and sometimes it doesn't.

Figure 22.1
The Add Account window asks you to choose a particular type of new email account.

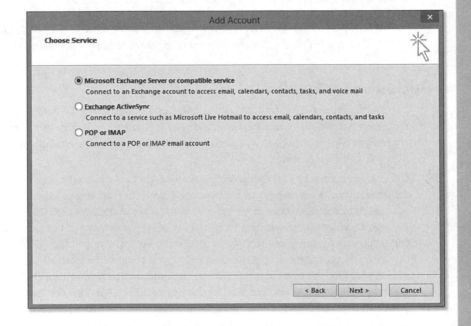

Exchange Server

No one would deny that Outlook was originally conceived as the client software for Exchange Server accounts. And Outlook really shines when you are connected to Exchange Server (which is the server software that hosts the email accounts, shared calendars, and other Outlook features in a networked environment); you can easily share calendars, tasks, meetings, and all sorts of information with other Exchange users.

If you are using Outlook on a corporate network that deploys an Exchange server, the network administrator typically sets up your account on your computer (this also establishes your profile for you). The name of the Exchange Server and your network username are required to complete the configuration. An Exchange Server network provides several email features that are not available when you use Outlook for Internet email (such as a POP3 account from your ISP). These features include the capability to redirect email replies, set message expirations, and even grant privileges to other users, who can then monitor your email, calendar, contacts, and tasks (just to name a few possibilities).

Historically, Outlook's capabilities in an Exchange Server environment were available only to users who worked at companies or institutions that used Exchange as their communication hub on the network. However, now anyone who subscribes to Microsoft Office 365 can use Outlook in an Exchange environment. Office 365 provides hosted email (using Exchange) for each of the different subscription tiers provided by the service. So if you acquired Office 2013 as part of an Office 365 subscription, you have an Exchange Online email account (at least one, depending on the service level of your subscription). Chapter 1, "Getting Oriented to the Office 2013 Applications," discusses the details of purchasing Office 2013 and the Office 365 subscription.

➡ *The different options for buying and licensing the Microsoft Office 2013 application suite are discussed in Chapter 1, "Getting Oriented to the Office 2013 Applications."*

Outlook.com Email

The second type of email that you can add to Outlook is listed in the Add Account window as Exchange ActiveSync; what it should really say is "Outlook.com (formerly Hotmail)." The Exchange ActiveSync feature gives you access to your Outlook.com email, your Outlook.com online contacts (People), and your calendar.

Outlook can configure your Outlook.com email account automatically; you simply need to provide the email account username and the password. So setting up access to your Outlook.com email account from within Outlook is no big deal if you want to do it yourself. In fact, Outlook 2013 makes it easier to add your Outlook.com email than in previous versions of Outlook. Back in the days when Outlook.com was still Hotmail, Outlook 2010 required that you add the Microsoft Outlook Hotmail Connector to your Outlook configuration before you could add a Hotmail account. You can now access your Outlook.com contacts and calendar information from within Outlook, which might make it worthwhile to add Outlook.com as an Outlook email service. This can be particularly useful when you want to reserve your default Outlook email account, such as an Exchange account, for business use only. If you do have to send out a personal email, you can quickly do it using your Outlook.com email account without minimizing Outlook or opening a web browser window to access the Outlook.com web page.

Internet Email

Nearly all of us use an Internet service provider (ISP) for our home or small business Internet connections. The ISP also typically gives you email accounts, such as yourname@providername.com. Most providers supply you with multiple accounts, and you can configure the email account names (the domain name, such as brighthouse.com or Comcast.net will be determined by your provider). Other options for Internet email are popular services such as Google Mail (Gmail) and Yahoo! Mail. Internet email accounts can use one of two different types of email retrieval systems. These email types are based on the protocol used by the email server: POP3 (Post Office Protocol version 3) and IMAP (Internet Message Access Protocol). Outlook supports both of these mail-retrieval protocols.

POP3 has been the standard protocol for Internet email for years, and ISPs typically use POP3 on their mail servers. A POP3 email server really functions as a mail drop, meaning that your email is forwarded to the POP3 server and sits there until you connect with your email client (Outlook) and download the mail to your computer. The great thing about POP3 accounts (at least, for ISPs) is that you download your email from their server. This means that you get it off their server, and they don't have to store it for you.

> **note**
>
> You might wonder why I'm not including web-based HTTP (Hypertext Transport Protocol) email accounts such as Microsoft's Hotmail as a type of Internet email account. Outlook 2010 uses an add-on service called the Microsoft Outlook Hotmail Connector for your Hotmail accounts. We discuss the Connector later in this section.

If you are using a POP3 account, the Post Office Protocol handles only the receive part of the send-and-receive process for your email. Your ISP also provides an SMTP (Simple Mail Transport Protocol) server. This server handles the email that you send from Outlook, over the Internet, to a final destination. That destination is typically the POP3 server that serves as the mail drop for the person to whom you are sending the Internet email.

IMAP is a protocol that allows an email client to download email from an IMAP mail server. IMAP differs from POP3, in that connecting to the server with your email client (Outlook) does not remove your email from the mail server. Instead, you receive a list of saved and new messages, which you can then open and read. However, you can delete messages from the IMAP server.

IMAP is particularly useful when you access one email account on more than one computer or other device (such as a mobile phone or other smart device). Because the email is not downloaded to the email client as POP3 email is, you can access it on the IMAP sever as needed from different devices. Examples of IMAP-based email systems are Google Mail and Yahoo! Mail. We typically interact with these email accounts using a web browser; however, Outlook's capabilities as an email manager might make it worthwhile to add your Gmail account (or other IMAP account) to Outlook's configuration. Obviously, having an email client such as Outlook that can access and manage Internet email accounts using either POP3 or IMAP provides you with a single resource for managing multiple and different types of email accounts.

> Configuring the different types of email accounts is discussed in Chapter 23, "Managing Email in Outlook."

Configuring Outlook at First Start

When you run Outlook for the first time, you have the opportunity to configure your email account. When configuring your email account, Outlook also creates a profile that contains your email account information, the location of your data files, and the location where your emails reside. We discuss Outlook profiles in the next section, but it should be made clear at this point that the profile created is closely associated with the first email account that you create in Outlook. So if you use Outlook primarily as an Exchange Server client, configure your Exchange email account as the initial account in Outlook. If you use Outlook as an Internet email client only, configure Outlook at first start for Internet email.

To get this show on the road, start Microsoft Outlook. The Outlook Startup window opens. The screen welcomes you and explains that it can help you add your email account to Outlook. Click Next to begin the process.

The next screen, Auto Account Setup, can be used to attempt to automatically configure your email account by providing a minimal amount of information. Figure 22.2 shows the Auto Account Setup screen.

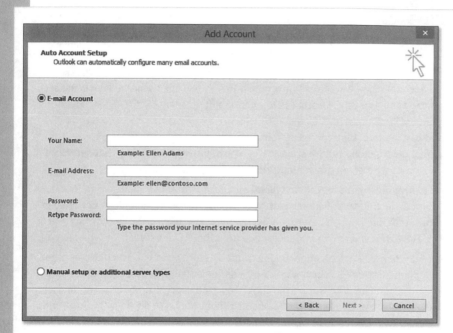

Figure 22.2
Outlook can attempt to automatically set up your email account.

On the Auto Account Setup screen, you enter your email account information, including your name, email address, and password (twice). Outlook refers to this method of configuring your email account as "auto" because it relies on Outlook's capability to search the network, including the Internet, for your account information. This allows Outlook to configure the email server settings for your account based on your email address. When you have entered the required information, click the Next button to continue.

 note
You can create more than one profile for Outlook. This makes it easy to create one profile for an Exchange Server account and one for Internet email. The next section discusses profiles in more detail.

Outlook establishes a network connection and searches for the email account's server settings. If you are on a network that has its own Microsoft Exchange Server or you are using an Exchange online account that is part of a Microsoft Office 365 subscription, the Auto Account Setup is typically successful. In corporate or institutional Exchange Server environments, the network administrator typically sets up your Outlook client, profile, and email accounts for you, so you probably won't have to walk through these steps in Outlook's configuration at first start. If you are using an Office 365 subscription, all you have to do is provide the email account and password and then click Next. It takes a couple minutes, but the email account should be set up for you.

In situations involving Internet email accounts that you get from your Internet provider (ISP), this online search for your server settings might not work. Outlook is attempting to make an encrypted connection to your mail server to verify your email account. Your ISP's mail server might not be capable of dealing with the encrypted connection or verifying your server settings based on your email account. Other reasons for failure are firewall settings or other connectivity issues.

So if Auto Account Setup fails, the next screen lets you know that an encrypted connection to your mail server wasn't available. Select Next if you want to give auto setup another shot using an unencrypted connection. If the unencrypted attempt also fails, you need to manually configure the account settings. Click the Back button to go back to the Auto Account Setup screen. Click the Manual Setup or Additional Server Types option button in the bottom left of the Auto Account Setup screen (the screen notes that the online search failed), and then click Next.

The next screen, the Choose Service screen, asks you to select one of the following: Microsoft Exchange Server or compatible service, Exchange ActiveSync (adds your Hotmail or Outlook.com email to Outlook), or POP or IMAP (both server types that are used for Internet email accounts). As mentioned earlier, Outlook does a good job of setting up email accounts that are "served up" from Microsoft Exchange Server. Problems with auto setup usually are related to trying to autoconfigure a POP or IMAP Internet email account. So let's assume that you are going to select the POP or IMAP option and then click Next.

Figure 22.3 shows the next screen, POP and IMAP Account Settings. It requires that you supply user, server, and logon information to configure the account.

Figure 22.3
You can manually config-ure your Internet email account.

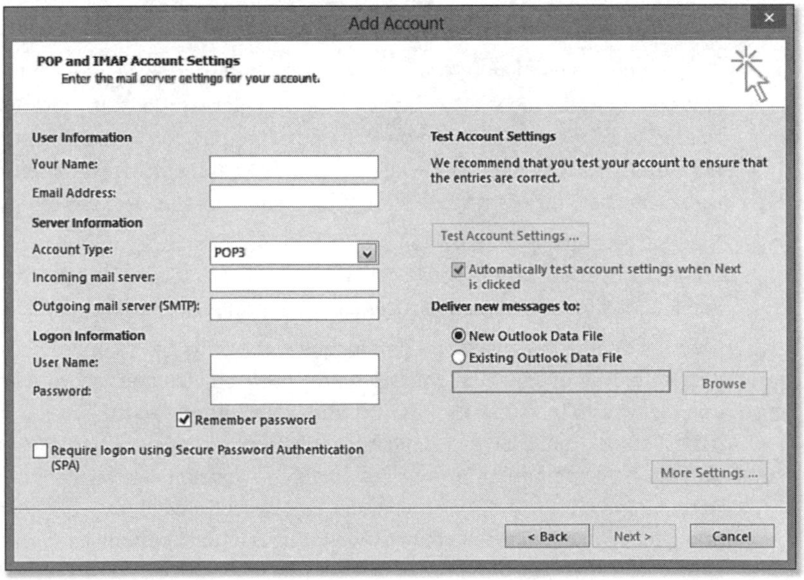

Enter your name, email address, username, and password, and then select either POP3 or IMAP as the account type. You also must provide the name of your ISP's POP3 or IMAP server (incoming server) and SMTP server (outgoing server) in the appropriate box.

If your ISP uses Secure Password Authentication, which provides a second layer of authentication for its mail servers, click Require Logon Using Secure Password Authentication (SPA). If SPA is used, you receive a second username and password (other than your email username) to log on to the servers. Most ISPs do not use SPA.

You can test your new account settings to make sure they work. A dialog box opens with your username and password; click OK. After testing the account settings, click Close to close the Test Account Settings dialog box.

After the account has been set up and tested, you can advance to the last screen in the setup process. Click Finish to end the process. Outlook starts and opens to your email inbox.

After configuring the first email account, you can begin to use Outlook. You can add email accounts as needed or change the configuration information for existing accounts. The next chapter discusses more information related to working with email accounts.

> *For more about working with Outlook email accounts, including Hotmail accounts, **see** "Managing Email Accounts," p. 696.*

 caution

Attempting to configure Internet email accounts using Auto Account Setup might be a non-starter for you. You might find it easier to just manually configure an Internet email account. All you need to know to manually configure the account is your email address and password and the server names (such as the POP3 and SMTP server names), which your Internet service provider can provide.

Understanding Outlook Profiles

Outlook creates an Outlook profile upon initial startup when you configure an email account in Outlook. That profile is loaded every time you start Outlook. It provides information to Outlook related to your email account (or accounts) configuration. You can use different types of email accounts in Outlook and have only one Outlook profile. However, multiple profiles can help sequester settings for different types of email accounts in their own related profiles.

Email accounts are contained in profiles. An email profile comprises email accounts, data files, and information about where your email is stored. Outlook automatically creates a new profile when you run Outlook for the first time. After that, the profile is loaded every time you start Outlook.

Most users need only a single profile, even when you have configured Outlook for multiple email accounts. However, you might find it advantageous to create more than one profile for yourself. This enables you to have one profile related to your Internet email account, meaning your personal email, and another profile for your Exchange email account. This is useful when you want to use Outlook on your home computer for Internet email, but you can also connect to your Exchange server and network via a secure connection (such as a virtual private network connection over the Internet) and check your Exchange email as well. The different profiles keep the two types of email accounts separate and sequestered.

Creating a New Profile

As already mentioned in this chapter, as soon as you configure an email account in Outlook, you also create a profile. If you need to create a new profile or manage existing profiles, you use the Mail Setup dialog box, which you access via the Windows Control Panel.

In Windows 8, right-click on the Start screen and select All Apps. You can then select the Control Panel icon. In the Control Panel, select User Accounts and Family Safety. In the Accounts and Family Safety pane, select Mail. The Mail Setup dialog box opens, as shown in Figure 22.4.

The Mail Setup dialog box enables you to manipulate Outlook settings without being in Outlook. You can create email accounts, change data file settings, and also create and manage profiles. Because you can't create a profile from within Outlook, you do it outside Outlook.

 tip

If multiple people use the same computer to access their email accounts in Outlook (and they do not log on as separate users in Windows), you likely want each person's email account kept in a separate specific profile. This is a case in which multiple profiles are necessary to provide privacy and security.

Figure 22.4
The Mail Setup dialog box.

To create a new profile, follow these steps:

1. In the Mail Setup dialog box, click Show Profiles. The Mail dialog box opens, with the General tab selected (it is the only tab).

2. Select Add. The New Profile dialog box opens.

3. Type a name for the new profile; then click OK.

As soon as you click OK, the Add New Account window opens. This is the same tool that opens at Outlook's first start, as discussed in the previous section. To summarize that discussion: You can enter your name, email address, and password, and then Outlook attempts to connect with your mail server and automatically configure your account. Alternatively, you can manually configure the server settings for the account.

When you click Finish on the last screen of the Add New Account process (after configuring the email account), you return to the Mail dialog box. The dialog box lists your new profile.

Managing Profiles

The Mail dialog box not only lists the profiles set up on your computer, but it also gives you the capability to manage them. You can remove a profile if you no longer need it; select the profile and then click Remove.

You can also edit the properties of a profile. In editing the properties of a profile, you have two possibilities: the email accounts associated with the profile and the data files used to store documents. Select a profile in the Mail dialog box, and then select Properties. This opens the Mail Setup dialog box for the selected profile, as shown in Figure 22.5. (This is not the same as the Mail Setup dialog box shown in Figure 22.4.)

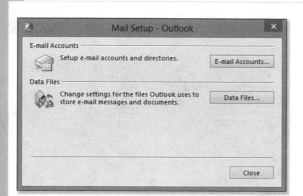

Figure 22.5
The Mail Setup—Outlook dialog box.

If you want to change the email account settings in the profile, click the Email Accounts button. This opens the Account Settings dialog box. This dialog box, which you can also access directly from Outlook via the Backstage Info window (select Account Settings), provides access to many Outlook settings. For example, you can edit data file settings on the Data Files tab. You can also edit other settings, including the RSS feeds, calendars, and address books. Figure 22.6 shows the Account Settings dialog box with the Email tab selected.

In changing the email settings for the current profile, you can add an email account, repair an existing email account, or remove an account. You also can change the folder the account uses when new messages arrive.

The Data Files tab of the Account Settings dialog box enables you to view the location of the Outlook data files associated with the current profile. We discuss managing Outlook data files in the next section, "Understanding Outlook Data Files." When you click Close in the Account Settings dialog box, you return to the Mail Setup dialog box. Click the Close button again, and you return to the Mail dialog box and your list of profiles.

Figure 22.6
You can change email and data file settings in the Account Settings dialog box.

Because you can manage both the email accounts and data files from inside Outlook, we work with these different settings in the appropriate context in other chapters found in the Outlook section of this book. However, it is important to understand that you can access profile-related setting issues via the Mail dialog box, which you reach using the Windows Control Panel. In some situations, you have to change settings related to a profile from the Mail dialog box. For example, adding or deleting an Exchange Server account from within Outlook while Outlook is running can be a problem. (This relates to the fact that Outlook is currently using your default profile and data file to operate.) So you might find that adding or deleting email accounts by accessing the Account Settings dialog box via the Control Panel is less problematic than attempting to do it from "inside" Outlook.

➡ *For information about adding and editing email accounts in Outlook,* **see** *Chapter 23, "Managing Email in Outlook."*

Loading Profiles

One other issue to discuss about using multiple Outlook profiles relates to which profile should be loaded when you start Outlook. The Mail dialog box (select Mail when you are in the User Accounts and Family Safety Control Panel window to open it) provides option buttons related to loading profiles in the lower portion of the Mail dialog box. Look for the When Starting Microsoft Outlook, Use This Profile statement in the lower part of the Mail dialog box. You have two different options, which are as follows:

- **Prompt for a profile to be used:** If you select this option button, a Choose Profile dialog box opens when you start Outlook, enabling you to select the profile that will be loaded from a drop-down list. This is useful if you have multiple profiles for different types of email accounts—say, Internet email versus Exchange Server email. This setting is a necessity when you have multiple users accessing their Outlook email accounts on the same computer. The user can select his or her specific profile.

- **Always use this profile:** Select this option if you want to specify a default profile to be loaded when Outlook starts. Use the drop-down list to select the profile name.

Whether you need to deal with multiple profiles and profile settings depends on your particular work environment. If you are a home or small business user, you might need to create and manage Outlook profiles. In corporate network environments, particularly those that use an Exchange Server for email accounts, a network administrator takes care of email account configurations and profile settings. So even though you might feel empowered after reading this material on profiles, I recommend that you leave the profile and email settings completely alone unless you determine that you really need to create and control multiple profiles.

Understanding Outlook Data Files

When you work in Outlook, you manage and manipulate different types of items, such as email, appointments, contacts, and tasks. These different items have their own homes in Outlook. For example, new email messages are in the Inbox, whereas the To Do list displays tasks. You might find it odd to learn that these different Outlook items are stored in a single Outlook data file. So, all your Outlook items are contained in this data file, which is referred to as a personal storage folder, or .pst file. This file is essential to Outlook's operation and your access to your emails, appointments, tasks, and meetings.

The personal storage folder is actually created when you create your Outlook profile and configure Outlook with a POP3 or IMAP email account. The pst file is actually stored on your computer. Outlook stores its data differently when it serves as an Exchange Server client or for web-based email such as Outlook.com. That data file is actually kept on the Exchange mail server and made available to you when you log on to the mail server.

So we assume, at least in the next paragraph or so, that you configured the first email account on Outlook as a POP3 or IMAP account. As already mentioned, when you configure the first email account for Outlook, it creates the default profile and your Outlook personal storage file, or pst data file. By default, the profile's name is Outlook. The data file's name is *your email account*.pst, meaning that the .pst file is named after the first email account you configured in Outlook. The .pst file is often referred to as the personal folders file.

When you consider how important the personal folders file is to Outlook and to you (in terms of all those emails that you have in Outlook), you understand that, in most cases, you should not play around with this file. That's not to say that you shouldn't back up the personal folders file, which we discuss in a moment. But you should have a compelling reason for other manipulations of the personal folders file, such as changing the file's location or renaming the file—both of which you can do.

Configuring Outlook as an email client for Microsoft Exchange Server does not create a personal folders file. In the Exchange Server environment, your email and other items are stored on the server running Exchange Server. Outlook does create a local data file, however, so you can use your Exchange account offline. This data file has the extension `.ost`; it contains a copy of the items stored on the Exchange server. This file is referred to as the offline Outlook data file. Microsoft's Outlook.com email service (formerly Hotmail) also uses a data file with the `.ost` extension. This is because a copy of your email folders (such as emails, contacts, and the calendar) is also stored on Microsoft's server. The offline Outlook data file just provides you with a copy of your personal files.

To view the default personal folders file (`.pst`) or the offline Outlook data file (`.ost`), or both, select the Outlook Ribbon's File tab to access the Outlook Backstage. Select Info and then select the Account Settings button. Select Account Settings on the menu to open the Account Settings dialog box.

The Account Settings dialog box opens to the Email tab by default. Select an email account from the Settings list, and the Outlook data file for that account (either a `.pst` or an `.ost` file) appears in the lower pane of the dialog box. You can select the Data Files tab to view the Outlook data files associated with the current Outlook profile. Figure 22.7 shows the Accounts Settings dialog box with the Data Files tab selected. Two email accounts are associated with the profile; one is an Internet email account (with a `.pst` file), and the other is an Exchange account (with an `.ost` file).

Figure 22.7
You can view the data files associated with the current profile.

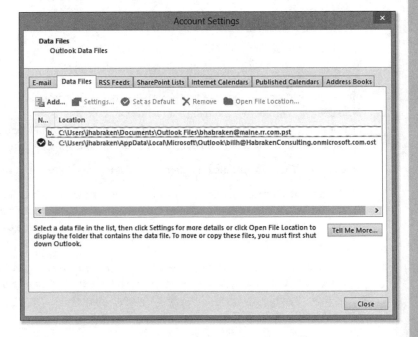

The type of data files shown in the Account Settings dialog box depend on the type of email accounts you have configured. Any POP3 account has an associated personal folders file, and an Exchange account has an offline Outlook data file.

The Account Settings dialog box enables you to change the default data file for the Outlook profile. You can also open the file location for a selected data file. In addition, you can use the Remove command to remove an unneeded data file.

You can view the settings for a personal folders file or an offline Outlook data file. Select the data file in the list, and then select Settings on the Account Settings toolbar. This opens the Outlook Data File dialog box.

For personal folders files, the Outlook Data File dialog box provides the alias or name of the data file, as well as the filename and path for the data file. You have two options related to a personal folders file. You can use the Change Password button to assign a password to the Outlook data file; if you want to reduce the size of your Outlook data file (they can become quite large when you have a lot of Outlook items), you can take advantage of the Compact Now button.

This is useful if multiple users share the same computer. You can also use the Compact Now button to compact the data file. This reduces the size of the file.

If you open the settings for an offline Outlook data file (`.ost`) associated with your Exchange Server account, the Microsoft Exchange dialog box opens. This dialog box provides four different tabs of settings. Remember that your network administrator probably configured your Exchange server account for you; I do not recommend changing any of the settings provided by the Microsoft Exchange dialog box. Consider the explanation of the dialog box tabs that follows purely informational:

 note

Depending on how Outlook was initially configured (and by whom), your profile might not be named Outlook. The name of your personal folders file might also vary. Remember, it has the extension `.pst` or `.ost` (depending on the type of email you use), no matter what the name is.

 note

When you add an Outlook.com email account to Outlook, an offline Outlook data file is also created on your computer.

- **General:** This tab specifies the name of the Exchange Server and the account mailbox name.

- **Advanced:** This tab enables you to add mailboxes that should be open when Outlook connects to the Exchange Server. You also have the option of using the cached exchange mode (which places the `.ost` file on your computer) so that you can work offline. The default setting enables the cached Exchange mode.

- **Security:** This tab provides options related to encryption and user identification. By default, Outlook and Microsoft Exchange trade encrypted data. You can also choose to have user identification required at logon. The type of authentication used is another selection you can make on this tab.

- **Connection:** This tab enables you to select the connection type that you use to reconnect to Exchange when you have been working offline. You can connect to Exchange via your local area network or phone line, or via HTTP by using Outlook Anywhere.

When you close either the Outlook Data File dialog box or the Microsoft Exchange dialog box, you return to the Account Settings dialog box. Click Close to close this dialog box and return to the Outlook application window.

Creating Personal Folders Files

Outlook gives you the capability to create new personal folders files. This can be useful if you want to create a personal folders file for a particular project and then place items from your current Outlook Inbox or other email folders into the new personal folders file. This is useful because it removes the emails from your default personal folders file and cleans up your Outlook folders. It also creates an archive of the project. Obviously, if you have used earlier versions of Outlook, you are already aware of Outlook's capability to archive older emails. So if you are good about archiving Outlook items, you might not feel a huge need to be moving things into secondary .pst files that you create. Think of the use of secondary .pst files as a potential convenience, not something that you have to do.

> ➡ *Outlook enables you to archive old email messages and items. Outlook saves these items in another personal folders file. **See** Chapter 27, "Securing and Maintaining Outlook," for more information.*

You can create a new Outlook personal folders file from the Account Settings dialog box (with the Data Files tab selected) or the Outlook application window. From the Outlook window, follow these steps:

1. Select the Ribbon's Home tab.

2. Select the New Items command in the New group.

3. Point at More Items and select Outlook Data File. The Create or Open Outlook Data File dialog box opens.

4. The Data File dialog box shows the default Outlook data file and any other created data files. Type a name for a new data file in the File Name box and then click OK.

The new data file appears in the Outlook Navigation pane below your email account's Inbox and other mail folders. You can create folders in the new data file and then copy or move email messages to the data file. So you can use the secondary data file to back up specific items or to group items related to a specific project that you no longer need to keep in your current Inbox or other folders.

Repairing Outlook Data Files

Personal folders files can become damaged or corrupt. A sure sign that your default personal folders file is corrupt is that Outlook cannot open it when you start Outlook.

You can use the inbox repair tool (scanpst.exe) to try to correct problems with a personal folders file. You must exit Outlook to run the tool. The tool is typically placed in the \Program Files\

`Microsoft Office\Office15` folder, which is the same folder that holds the installed files for the Microsoft Office 2013 applications.

Exit Outlook and then open the Windows File Explorer. (Open it via the Taskbar icon on the Windows 8 Desktop, or select File Explorer on the Start page after right-clicking and selecting All Apps.) To locate the `scanpst.exe` program file, click in the Search box to open the Search Tools in File Explorer. Make sure you select Computer and then All subfolders before you enter the search term "scanpst." The results of the search should list the scanpst program. Double-click scanpst in the search results, and the Microsoft Outlook Inbox Repair Tool dialog box opens, as shown in Figure 22.8.

Figure 22.8
Use the Inbox Repair tool on damaged personal folders files.

Enter the name of the file you want to scan, or use the Browse button to locate the file. The default folder for your personal folders file is `Documents\Outlook Files`. After entering the filename, click the Start button. The Inbox Repair tool checks the file, and a message box opens, letting you know the level of the problems identified during the scan.

You can have the Inbox Repair tool make a backup copy of the file before repairing it. This is the default setting and a good idea, particularly if the repair process further damages an already corrupted file. The Inbox Repair tool places the backup copy in your Outlook Files folder with the extension `.bak`.

Click the Repair button, and the Inbox Repair tool attempts to repair the file. When the process is complete, the Repair Complete message appears; click OK to close it. You can now open Outlook with the repaired `.pst` file.

If the Inbox Repair tool recovered folders and items, a Lost and Found folder in your folder list (in the Navigation pane) displays. At this point, you should probably create a new Outlook personal files folder (using the method we discussed in the previous section). Drag the items in the Lost and Found folder to the new `.pst` file. You can also drag additional items to the new personal folders file and then make the new `.pst` file the default personal folders file for Outlook by using the Accounts Settings dialog box (accessed via the Backstage). Restart Outlook, and it loads the new `.pst` file. Delete the old personal folders file using the Account Settings dialog box.

Offline Outlook data files (.ost files) can also become damaged. However, these are easier to re-create because the Exchange Server contains the working copies of all your email and other items. Open the Mail Setup dialog box from the Control Panel (select Mail in the User Accounts and Family Safety group). Select Show Profiles, select the Exchange Server profile in the profile list, and then select Properties. This opens the Account Settings dialog box with the Email tab selected. Select the Exchange Server email account in the list of email accounts, and then select Change. The Change Account dialog box opens. Clear the Use Cached Exchange Mode check box, immediately below the Microsoft Exchange server name box.

Now open the Microsoft Exchange dialog box; select More Settings in the Change Account dialog box (in the lower right). In the Microsoft Exchange dialog box, select the Advanced tab. On the Advanced tab, select the Outlook Data File Settings button to open the Outlook Data File Settings. Select Disable Offline Use and then click OK. Click Yes to verify the change. You have turned off the offline use feature, which synchronizes your Exchange Server folders with the .ost file. Now all you have to do is turn this feature back on to create a new .ost file (replacing the damaged file).

You should still be in the Microsoft Exchange dialog box, on the Advanced tab. Select the Use Cached Exchange Mode check box. Then click OK. This closes the Microsoft Exchange dialog box and returns you to the Change Account dialog box. You can click the Next button and then Finish to close this dialog box. Now all you have to do is close the Account Settings, Mail Setup, and Mail dialog boxes. You can return to Outlook, and your Exchange folders should replicate with the .ost file.

Importing and Exporting Data

You can import and export information to and from Outlook. The types of information that can be imported include RSS feeds, mail account settings, Internet email, addresses, calendars (.ics and .vcs), and Outlook personal folders files (.pst). For example, you might be migrating from another personal information manager or email client to Outlook and want to import your address book or contacts list; Outlook can import this type of information in a number of different file formats, including comma-separated values (.csv) and vCards (.vcf).

You might also need to export data from Outlook to another application. You can export Outlook data to Excel and Access, and in several different file types, including as comma-separated values, tab-separated files, and Outlook data files (.pst).

The Backstage Open window handles both the import and export of data. This is where you can access the Open Calendar command to open a calendar file, as well as where you access the Import and Export Wizard, which takes care of both the import and export of a number of different data types.

 tip

You can quickly import your entire contact list or specific groups of contacts from Google Mail to Outlook. Select Contacts in the Gmail window and then click the More button. On the More menu, click Export. You need to export the contacts to a CSV file (the actual export file type in Gmail is Outlook CSV) for import into Outlook or another application. When you have the CSV file, you can import it into Outlook using the Import and Export Wizard.

Importing Data

To import data into Outlook, open the Backstage by selecting File on the Ribbon. Then select Open & Export. The Open window provides you with several commands. The Open Calendar command enables you to open a calendar file in Outlook such as an exported iCalendar or Gmail calendar. To use the command, select Open Calendar. The Open Calendar dialog box opens. Navigate to the path that contains the calendar file and then click OK. The calendar is added to your My Calendars list under Other Calendars.

The Open Outlook Data File command enables you to open any Outlook .pst file. The folders and other data provided by an Outlook data file are added to your Outlook configuration when you open the data file.

The Import/Export command opens the Import and Export Wizard, which we look at in a moment. The Open command set is rounded out by the Other User's Folder command. This enables you to open an Outlook folder such as a Contacts folder when another user has shared it. This feature is limited to when you are working with Exchange email.

If you want to import contacts or emails, use the Import/Export command, which opens the Import and Export Wizard. Follow these steps:

1. Select Import/Export. The Import and Export Wizard opens (see Figure 22.9).

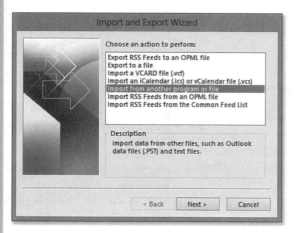

Figure 22.9
The Import and Export Wizard.

2. Select the type of data you want to import (such as a VCARD file or iCalendar file), or select Import from Another Program or File for a data type not shown (for example, a comma-separated file exported from another program such as Excel). Then click Next.

3. On the next wizard screen, select the file type to import from the list. Click Next.

4. On the next wizard screen, use the Browse button to select the file to import. You can also select options related to the import, such as Replace Duplicates with Items Imported, Allow Duplicates to Be Created, and Do Not Import Duplicate Items. Click Next.

5. On the next screen, select the destination folder, such as `Calendar` or `Contacts`. Then click Next.

6. The next screen lists the file to be imported and the folder that Outlook imports it into. At this point, you can choose to map custom fields. This enables you to match the field names used in the import file with the field names used in Outlook, such as the field names used in the `Contacts` folder. Select Map Custom Fields.

7. (Optional) Drag the field names from the source file on the left of the Map Custom Fields box to the Outlook field names on the right (see Figure 22.10). When you have finished mapping the fields, click OK.

Figure 22.10
Map the fields from the import file to the Outlook fields.

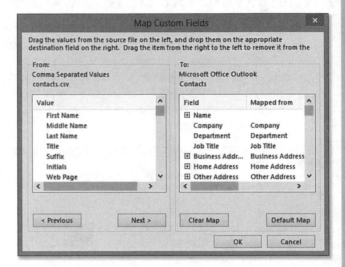

8. Click Finish.

Outlook places the imported data in the Outlook folder that you selected during the import procedure. For example, if you imported contacts, select `Contacts` in the Navigation pane to display the imported contacts.

Exporting Data

You can also use the Import and Export Wizard to export Outlook data into a variety of file formats. Open the Import and Export Wizard from the Backstage Open window (select Import/Export). On the first wizard screen, select Export to a File and then click Next.

On the next wizard screen, you can select the file format for the export. File types include tab- and comma-separated values. You can also import to Access and Excel file formats or export the data as an Outlook data file. When you have selected the export file type, all you have to do is select the

Outlook folder that contains the data that you want to export. Specify an export filename and a location, and you can then export the data.

---

 note

The steps involved in exporting data from Outlook are pretty much the same as the steps for importing data. You specify the file type, the Outlook folder involved, and the location of the file to be created. I guess that isn't exactly the same, but you get the picture.

Navigating the Outlook Workspace

Outlook is all about accessing and managing different types of items, so the Outlook application window makes it easy for you to access and manage your emails, calendar, contacts, and tasks. Outlook 2013 adopts many of the user interface improvements provided in Outlook 2010 and also takes advantage of the simpler and more functional application layout that is indicative of the Metro look provided by Windows 8. Figure 22.11 shows the default Outlook application window, with Mail currently selected in the navigation bar.

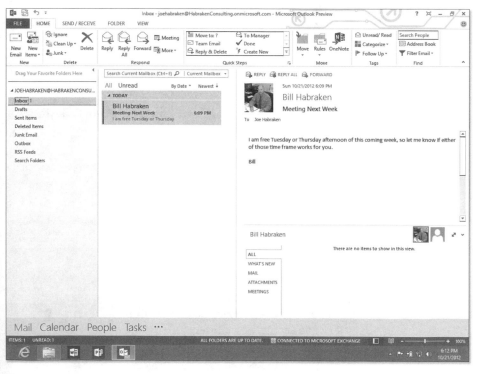

Figure 22.11
Outlook gives you easy access to your email and other items.

The various parts of the Outlook application window are as follows:

- **Folder pane:** The Folder pane enables you to navigate individual folders related to the currently selected Outlook item as Mail (email), Calendar, or People (contacts). The Folder pane also provides a customizable area (at the top); you can drag your favorite folders to this area so that you have access to them no matter what Outlook items you currently have selected. You can also minimize (hide) the Folder pane, if necessary; select the Minimize Folder Pane arrow at the top of the pane.

- **Navigation bar:** The Navigation bar is a horizontal element near the bottom of the Outlook application window, and it serves as the main navigational tool for Outlook. A link to each of the Outlook items—Mail, Calendar, People, and Tasks—is easily accessible.

- **Reading pane:** The Reading pane enables you to view (and read) the currently selected email or task.

- **Details pane:** The Details pane provides a list of available items in a folder, such as your emails or tasks.

- **To Do bar:** The To Do bar provides a calendar and a list of appointments for the currently selected date (which, by default, is the current date). The To Do bar also provides a list of tasks for the day and enables you to quickly add new tasks. The To Do bar is off by default.

 tip

You can grab the top of the Navigation pane's button area and drag it upward to view more Outlook item buttons, such as the Notes and the Folder list.

- **People pane:** The People pane gives you additional information about the currently selected email sender. The People pane uses Outlook's capability to connect with online social networks, such as LinkedIn and Facebook, allowing you to communicate directly (through Outlook) with your Facebook friends and LinkedIn connections.

- **Status bar:** The Status bar provides the View shortcuts and Zoom slider. You can add other information, such as quota information, to the Status bar, and you can also remove features as needed via the Customize Status Bar menu (right-click on the Status bar).

You can manipulate the layout of the various Outlook panes, such as the Folder pane and the To Do bar, on the Ribbon's View tab. The Folder pane, Reading pane, and To Do bar have drop-down menus that enable you to view the panes in different views. You can also use the commands provided to turn off a particular pane and hide it from view.

Accessing Outlook Items Using the Navigation Bar

The Navigation bar provides quick access to the different Outlook items. When you select a particular item, such as Mail, the Folder pane provides a list of folders associated with that item. In the case of Mail, you can access the Inbox, Drafts, and Junk Email, along with other associated mail folders.

The Navigation bar shows links to the Mail, Calendar, People, and Tasks items. At the bottom right of the Navigation bar, there is also an ellipsis (signifying More), which provides access to Other

Outlook items and navigation options. For example, to open your notes, select the ellipsis (or More) and then select the Notes icon.

This menu also provides access to the Folders command. When you are in Mail view and select Folders (via the Navigation Bar ellipsis), all the Outlook folders become available in the Folder pane. The folders listed include `Calendar`, `Contacts`, `Journal`, and `RSS Feeds`. Select any folder to access that particular item. Having the folders listed in the Folder pane makes it easy for you to quickly switch from your Inbox to your contacts, then to your calendar, and finally back to your Inbox. To do this quick switching, you must select the folders in the Folder pane. If you select one of the navigation links, such as Calendar or People, the Folder pane goes back to the default list of folders (for example, your Inbox and Sent Items when Mail is selected).

You can access Outlook information by hovering the mouse over an Outlook item in the Navigation bar. For instance, if you place the mouse on Calendar, you are provided a thumbnail calendar of the current month with a list of any appointments that you have scheduled for the day. Hover over People, and you get access to a Search People box and a list of any contacts that you have added to your Favorites list. Place the mouse on Tasks, and you can see a list of current Tasks. As we work with Outlook in the Outlook section of this book, you learn that Outlook 2013 provides a number of enhancements that enable you to do your work quickly and efficiently, whether you are working with a keyboard and a mouse or on a device with a touch screen.

Customizing Navigation Options

You can use the Navigation Options dialog box to change the order in which Outlook items are displayed in the Navigation bar, as well as how many items are shown; by default, four items are visible—Mail, Calendar, People, and Tasks—but you can increase (or decrease) this setting as needed. Select More (the ellipsis) in the Navigation bar and then select Options. This opens the Navigation Options dialog box. Figure 22.12 shows the Navigation Options dialog box.

tip

You can also open the Navigation Options dialog box via the Ribbon's View tab. Select the Folder Pane command in the Layout group, and then select Options.

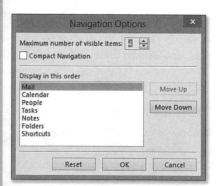

Figure 22.12
You can modify the Navigation bar.

You can use the Move Up and Move Down buttons in the Navigation Options dialog box to change the order of the commands shown in the Navigation bar. You can also change the number of visible items using the spinner box at the top of the dialog box (the default is 4). If you select the Compact Navigation setting in the Navigation Options dialog box, the Navigation bar is "compacted" so that it fits neatly at the bottom of the Folder pane. Icons replace each of the text links that represented the various Outlook items, such as Mail, Calendar, and People.

You can return to the default settings for the Navigation bar at any time. Open the Navigation Options dialog box and select Reset. When you want to return to the default settings for the Navigation bar, you can select Reset.

Working with Views in Outlook

As you work with the different items in Outlook, the Outlook panes provide you with a default view for each item type. For example, Outlook uses the Compact view as the default for mail. Other views for mail can be accessed using the Change View gallery on the Ribbon's View tab. You can also view your mail using the Single or Preview views. In Compact view, each email's subject line and first line of the message show in the email list. (By default, only the first line of the message shows, but you can increase the message preview to up to three lines.)

Messages are listed individually by date, but you can change this by clicking the drop-down arrow (next to By Date) and selecting any of the view options, such as From, Categories, and Importance (we talk more about working with email in the next chapter). And if you yearn for the default Conversation view provided by Outlook 2010 (which arranged emails by conversation), you can select the Show As Conversations check box in the Messages group on the Ribbon's View tab.

Each of the Outlook items has different views available. For example, the default view for your contacts is People. This view lists your contacts in the Details pane (including pictures, if available) and provides detailed information on the selected contact in the Reading pane. Other views are available for your contacts, including Business Cards and Card.

As already mentioned, the Change View command on the Ribbon's View tab provides you with the different views available for the currently selected Outlook item. Figure 22.13 shows People view for the Contacts folder and also shows the other view options for contacts in the Change View gallery (Business Card, Card, Phone, and List).

Not only do you have access to different views of each of the Outlook items (such as mail or tasks), but you also can manipulate the settings for the current view. For example, you might want to change the settings for the Single view provided for emails. Select View Settings in the Current View group. The Advanced View Settings dialog box opens for the current view (such as the Single view for emails). You can change settings related to the view, such as the sort order for the view (using the Sort button). You can also use the Filter button to modify the current view so that it filters the item list using keywords, categories, or other parameters, such as

 tip

If you change the current view using the Advanced View Settings, you can save the "changed" view as a new view. Change the settings as needed and then select Change View on the Ribbon. Select Save Current View As a New View. The Copy View dialog box opens; provide a name for the new view. You can then specify whether the view should be available to all mail and post folders or the current folder. When you have finished with the process, click OK to close the Copy View dialog box.

whether the item is unread or has an attachment (in the case of emails). Other settings that you can change for the current view are the font and the size of the items in the view.

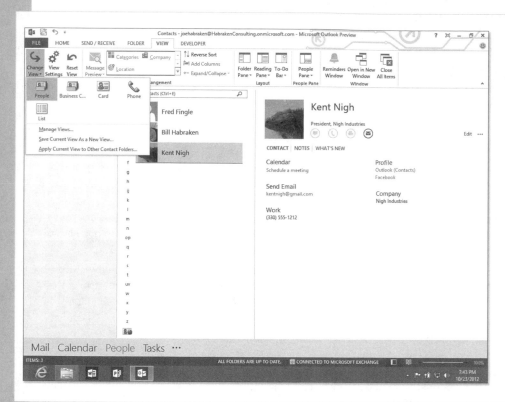

Figure 22.13
Change the view for the current folder.

You can also create custom views for the information in your Outlook folders. Select Change View on the View tab, and then select Manage Views to open the Manage All Views dialog box. The dialog box shows the preconfigured views for the current folder (such as Mail or Contacts). You can use commands in this dialog box to copy, modify, and rename views. You can also use the Reset button to change a view back to its default settings, which is useful when you have modified a view and want to put it back to the way it was by default.

To create a new view, select the New button to open the Create New View dialog box. In this dialog box, you supply the name for the new view, the type of view, and the folders on which Outlook can use the view. You have several options for the type of view you select for the new view:

- **Table:** Presents items in a grid of *n* rows and columns. Use this view type to view mail messages, tasks, and details about any item.

- **Timeline:** Displays items as icons arranged in chronological order from left to right on a time scale. Use this to examine journal entries and other items in this type of view.

- **Card:** Presents items such as cards in a card file. Use this to view contacts.

- **Business Card:** Presents items in a business card format that provides details for the contact, such as name, email, address, and so on.

- **People:** Presents items by photo plus name. Details for each entry are included in the Reading page. This view is used to view contacts.

- **Day/Week/Month:** Displays items in a calendar view in blocks of time. Use this type for meetings and scheduled tasks.

- **Icon:** Provides graphical icons to represent tasks, notes, calendars, and so on.

Obviously, most of the view types relate to a particular Outlook folder. For example, Business Card relates to contacts, whereas the Day/Week/Month type is suited for calendars. You can specify additional options related to the view, such as whether the view is used on the current folder and visible to everyone or is visible only to you. Another option allows Outlook to use the view on all mail and post folders.

After you select the type of view (such as Table or Timeline) and folder options for the new view, click OK. The Advanced View Settings dialog box opens. Figure 22.14 shows the Advanced View Settings dialog box. You can use it to specify how information is grouped (by such things as creation date or categories), sorted, or filtered. You also can specify the fields that should be included in a new view (such as a table). Each field would represent a column and each field column would provide specific information. The field column possibilities include Importance, Reminder, Icon, Flag Status, and Attachment (and there are many others).

Figure 22.14
Advanced View Settings dialog box.

After you configure the new view and click OK, you return to the Manage All Views dialog box. If you need to change a view that you have created, select the view and then select Modify. You can then modify the view as needed. When you close the Manage All Views dialog box, Outlook adds your new view to the Change View menu. You can select it when needed, as you do with the default views provided.

Categorizing Outlook Items

You can assign categories to Outlook items to aid you in locating and organizing information in Outlook. When items have been assigned categories, Outlook can then organize the items in a particular view by a particular category. You can also use Search to locate items assigned to a category, and you can create Search folders that find items based on category.

By default, each Outlook category is color-coded. The categories have names such as Blue Category, Green Category, and so on. To open the Color Categories dialog box shown in Figure 22.15, select Categorize on the Ribbon's Home tab and then select All Categories.

 tip

If you decide that you don't want a view you created, you can delete it in the Manage All Views dialog box.

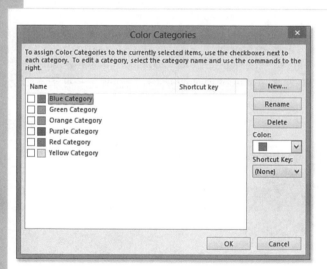

Figure 22.15
The Color Categories dialog box.

You can rename the various color categories to assemble your own list of categories that you can then assign to your Outlook items. If you exhaust the default categories, you can create new categories in the Color Categories dialog box. You can open this dialog box no matter what type of item you are working with. For example, when you are working with an appointment, the Categorize command is on the Appointment tab of the Ribbon. When you are working with an open email, you can access the Categorize command on the Message tab. The first time you assign one of the color categories to an Outlook item, the Rename Category dialog box opens. You can quickly rename the category by typing a new name in the Name box.

When you have renamed categories, you can assign them to your Outlook items as needed. Then when you select the Ribbon's View tab in one of the Outlook folders, you can use the Categories command to arrange the items in the current folder by category. You can filter items in a particular view by using the Search box. Click in the Search box and then select the Categorized command provided in the Refine group (a set of contextual tools provided when you are using the Search box). Select a category, and the list of items is filtered by that category.

Searching for Outlook Items

Outlook provides you with some different possibilities for finding items in your various Outlook folders. The simplest way to search for items in the current folder is to click in the Search box. When you place the insertion point in the Search box, the search tools appear on the Ribbon with the Search tab selected. Figure 22.16 shows the Search Tools on the Ribbon.

Figure 22.16
The search tools.

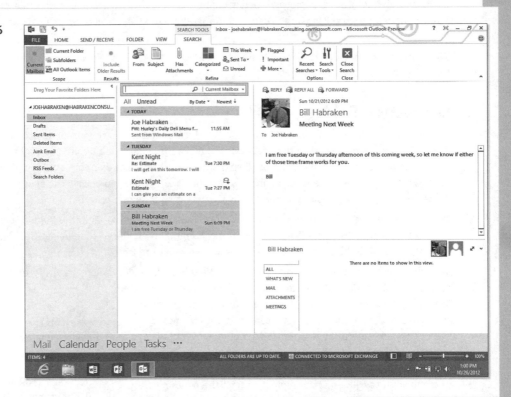

The Search Tools provide a number of options. You can specify the scope for the search, such as the current folder, all subfolders, or all Outlook items. You can also use commands in the Refine group to search for items that have attachments, a particular subject, or the flag or importance level assigned to the item.

After you specify the various options for the search, type your search terms into the Search box; Outlook provides the results of the search. You can modify the search on the fly and enable or disable search parameters on the Ribbon as needed. When you finish the search, click the Close Search command to return to the current folder view.

Using Advanced Find

If you prefer, you can use the Advanced Find dialog box to conduct your search. Click in the Search box; the Search Tools appear on the Ribbon. Select the Search Tools command and then select Advanced Find. This opens the Advanced Find dialog box.

The Advanced Find dialog box enables you to specify the type of item you want to find and the location you want to search. You can also specify parameters such as who a message is from or its recipients. Advanced Find enables you to specify keywords for different fields, such as the subject field. Additional search parameters on the More Choices tab enable you to specify categories to be used in the search and other parameters, such as items that are unread or have a particular importance. The Advanced tab enables you to specify parameters by field, such as address fields and date/time field.

When you have specified the parameters for the search, select Find Now. Outlook lists the items found by the search.

Using Search Folders

Search Folders are containers that you can use to locate mail items in your email accounts. The Search Folders don't really contain mail items, but they provide you a listing of email items that meet your search criteria, meaning the Search Folders criteria. For example, you could search for all unread emails or all emails from a particular person. Then when you access the search folder in the Folders pane, you have access to the emails that meet your search criteria.

To create a new search folder for an account, right click Search Folders in the Folders pane (it's probably directly under RSS Feeds, if you haven't added any folders); then select New Search Folder. The New Search Folder dialog box opens, as shown in Figure 22.17.

You can select a search folder provided by the New Search Folder dialog box. Different categories, such as Reading Mail, Mail from People, and Lists and Organizing Mail, provide specific types of searches that you can assign to the folder. For example, to create a search folder for unread mail, select Unread Mail in the Reading Mail category. If you select a search folder such as Mail from Specific People, you must use the Customize Search Folder option to specify the person or persons you are talking about (you can select the contact or contacts from your Contacts folder by using the Choose button).

After you have selected the type of search folder and supplied the additional information needed, click OK. The new search folder appears in your email folder list. Select the search folder to view the mail items that meet the folder's search criteria.

 tip

You can create custom search folders by selecting Create a Custom Search Folder in the New Search Folder dialog box (it's at the bottom of the criteria under Custom; click Choose after selecting it). This opens the Custom Search Folder dialog box, which you can use to specify custom criteria for the search folder.

Figure 22.17
The New Search Folder dialog box.

Printing Outlook Items

You can print Outlook items in the Outlook Backstage. Select File on the Ribbon. (You can access the Backstage from any item Ribbon, such as the Message Ribbon or Event Ribbon.) Accessing the Backstage from any item type enables you to quickly print the item you are working with (be it a message, contact, task, or event). Outlook also provides options for printing the entire contents of a folder, such as the People (contacts) folder. Because the Print window combines print settings, such as the selection of the print style and print preview, you can fine-tune your print job before printing.

Open a specific Outlook item, or open an Outlook folder, such as your mail or tasks. To access the Backstage, select File on the Ribbon. Select Print to open the Print window. Figure 22.18 shows the Print window.

You can select the printer for the print job by using the Printer drop-down menu. The Print What area of the window provides a list of the different styles available for the current item type that you want to print. The styles vary, depending on the type of item you are printing; for example, an email uses the Memo Style by default, and all the emails in a folder print using the Table Style. For contacts, individual contacts print by using the Memo Style, but entire contacts list print using the Card Style, Small Booklet Style, or Phone Directory Style. Because you are provided a preview of your printout after you select a style, you can try different styles until you find the one most appropriate for the printout you want to create.

If you want to control the number of copies, how the copies are collated, or other print parameters, such as the page range, select the Print Options button on the Print window. This opens the Print dialog box.

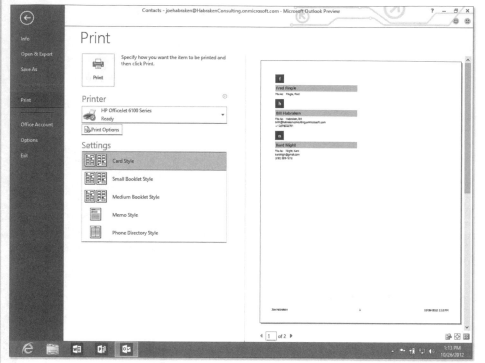

Figure 22.18
The Print window.

You access print settings via the Print dialog box, where you can choose print options such as the fonts used in the printout and the paper type. You can even specify a header or footer to print on each page of the printout. Click the Page Setup button to set the format, paper, and Header/Footer settings in the Page Setup dialog box.

When you change options in the Print dialog box, it makes sense to click the Preview button to return to the Print window. This provides a print preview using the settings you configured in the Print dialog box. You can use the various preview buttons, such as Actual Size, One Page, and Multiple Pages, to preview your printout. When you are ready to send the print job to the printer, click the Print button on the window.

MANAGING EMAIL IN OUTLOOK

Although Outlook is a multitasker's dream for its different functions, one of its primary purposes is that of email client. Considering that most of us (no matter what our vocation) send and receive large volumes of email, Outlook takes the "mess" out of messages (as opposed to putting the "fun" in dysfunctional) and enables you to communicate with others in an organized and effective manner.

Outlook's mail client supports a number of email account types, including Internet mail (email provided by your ISP), Microsoft Exchange Server mail, Microsoft Outlook.com, and Gmail. In this chapter, we look at Outlook's email management tools and features, starting with basic concepts related to creating and sending and receiving emails. We also look at Outlook's capabilities for managing and organizing emails and setting email account configurations and other email settings.

Working in the Mail Folder

After you have configured the initial email account on Outlook's first start (as discussed in Chapter 22, "Requisite Outlook: Configuration and Essential Features"), you are ready to begin creating, sending, and receiving emails. Remember that you are not limited to a single email account in Outlook: You can configure multiple email accounts (and different types of email accounts), as discussed later in this chapter in the section "Adding an Email Account."

➡ *For information about configuring an Outlook profile and email account the first time you run Outlook,* **see** *Chapter 22, "Requisite Outlook: Configuration and Essential Features."*

The Outlook Mail folder provides access to the specific email folders that hold different types of messages, such as received and sent messages. Select Mail in the Navigation bar to view the default email folders, as shown in Figure 23.1.

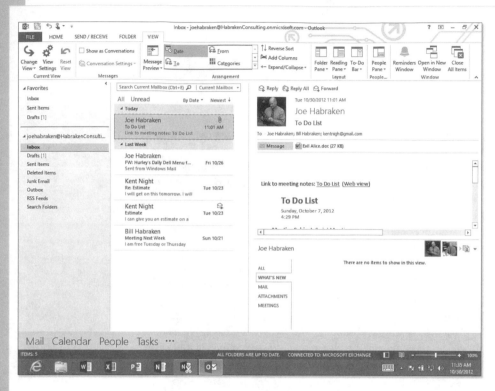

Figure 23.1
The Outlook Mail folder.

When you select the Inbox folder, the Details pane lists the emails in the Inbox. The Reading pane shows currently selected email. Just below the Reading pane is the People pane, which provides information compiled about the contact from social media websites such as Facebook and LinkedIn.

Favorites appears at the top of the Folder pane (on the left of the Outlook window), which provides shortcuts to the Inbox, Sent Items, and the Deleted Items folders, by default. You can add folders to the Favorites list as required. Drag any folder from an email account folder (showing in the Folder pane) to the list. This duplicates the folder and includes it in the Favorites list. You can right-click on a folder in the Favorites list and select Remove from Favorites on the shortcut menu to remove the folder from the list.

You also have the option of closing the Favorites list if you find it distracting or want more room in the Navigation pane for multiple email accounts and their associated folders. On the Ribbon's View tab, select Folder Pane and then clear the check box for Favorites.

 tip
You can add any folder to the Favorites list: Select the folder and then open the Folder tab commands on the Ribbon. Select the Show in Favorites command, and the folder is added to list.

Each Outlook email account has its own set of associated mail folders, such as the Inbox, Drafts, and Sent Items folders. You can collapse an email account in the Navigation pane to hide the folders associated with the account; click the Collapse button for the account. A second click expands the account, showing the associated folders. The default folders for your primary or default email account are as follows:

- **Inbox:** Outlook places received mail in the Inbox by default. When you select the Inbox, the Details pane lists emails by date order.

- **Drafts:** The Drafts folder can potentially contain any email that you compose and then close without sending. When you close an unsent email message, Outlook prompts you to save the email as a draft.

- **Sent Items:** Emails that you send from the email account are stored in this folder. Sent emails display in date order.

- **Deleted Items:** Outlook places deleted emails in this folder. You have the option of letting Outlook empty the Deleted Items folder when you exit the application.

- **Junk Email:** This folder sequesters emails flagged as junk email by Outlook.

- **Outbox:** When you send a message, Outlook places it in the Outbox folder until sending the email by connecting to the outgoing email server.

- **RSS Feeds:** This folder is not mail related, but it gives you a way to access Really Simple Syndication (RSS) newsfeeds in Outlook. You can read content from an RSS feed in the Outlook window in much the same way that you read an email. We discuss RSS feeds at the end of this chapter.

- **Search folders:** A search folder isn't an actual folder. Instead, it consists of search conditions that you can set so that emails meeting your conditions display in the search folder.

As already mentioned, Outlook arranges email in your Inbox folder by date. In the previous version of Outlook (2010), the messages were also arranged in conversations by default. Viewing your email messages in conversations means that even messages contained in other folders, such as the Sent Items folder, appear in the Inbox in Conversations view. This makes it easy for you to view associated messages that relate to a particular mail message subject. If you want to give Conversations view a try, select the View tab on the Ribbon and then enable the Show As Conversations command in the Messages group. A Microsoft Outlook message box opens, asking whether you want to arrange messages in conversations in all your mailboxes or just the current folder. Select the option that works for you. You can toggle off Conversations view by deselecting the Show As Conversations command.

Creating an Email Message

You can send an email message to anyone for whom you have an email address, whether that address is in your list of contacts or scribbled on a scrap of paper. You can even email groups of people listed in your various distribution lists.

You can attach Outlook items and other files to your emails. Because Word is the default email editor for Outlook, you can use all of Word's capabilities to create emails that include formatted text, charts, and SmartArt. You can use the Review tab's tools to check the spelling and grammar in the message or to open the Research pane to find information important to your message.

When you are in the Mail folder, you can quickly open a new email message; select the New Email command on the Ribbon's Home tab. If you happen to be in one of the other Outlook folders, select the New Items command and then select Email Message. Whichever route you take (there are more possibilities than the two mentioned, which we discuss in a moment), a new message window opens, as shown in Figure 23.2.

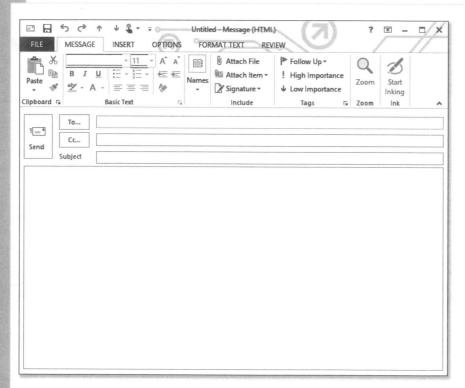

Figure 23.2
A new message window.

If you have not changed the message type for Outlook, the new message appears in HTML format; Outlook sends the message from your default email account. You can change both of these settings via commands provided by the message Ribbon. The list that follows provides a brief description of the command sets found on each of the message Ribbon's tabs:

- **File:** Provides access to the Backstage. You can set permissions for the mail message and properties such as the importance, sensitivity, and delivery options.

- **Message:** Provides access to the Clipboard commands, basic text formatting, and the Outlook Address Book (Names). Other commands available include Attach File, Attach Item, Signature, and message tags such as Follow Up and High Importance.

- **Insert:** Provides commands for different types of attachments (including files and Outlook items such as Business Cards and Calendars). Other items, such as tables, pictures, shapes, and hyperlinks, can also be inserted from this tab.

- **Options:** Enables you to assign a theme to the message. Other options available include additional fields for the message (BCC), voting buttons, delivery and received receipts, and options related to saving and delivering the message.

- **Format Text:** Enables you to change the format of the message (from HTML to plain text, for example). The various text-formatting options provided, such as font, paragraph, and style settings, are also available on this tab.

- **Review:** Provides proofing aids such as the Spelling & Grammar tool and the Thesaurus, and includes language options such as Translate.

 tip

You can create a new message as plain text, Rich Text, or HTML. Select New Items, point at Email Message Using, and then select either Plain Text, Rich Text, or HTML for the message format.

No matter what enhancements or options you select for your message, you need to supply the body of the message, a subject for the message, and the email address of the recipient (or addresses of the recipients). Obviously, you can type an email address in the To box to specify the recipient. You can also enter multiple email addresses by separating the addresses with a semicolon. A better way to address mail messages, however, is to use the Outlook Address Book.

Using the Outlook Address Book

Outlook has the capability to access different stores or lists of information that can provide you with people's email addresses and other contact information, such as phone numbers and addresses. The Address Book is a catchall repository for address lists and can be used to access your Outlook Contacts list, contacts associated with a particular email account (such as your Microsoft Hotmail account), and other directory lists, such as mobile lists and lists provided by other email and communication servers. For example, in a corporate network, a Microsoft Exchange Server provides a global address list shared by all users on the Exchange network.

The different stores or collections of email addresses you have access to depend on the type of email account you use (Exchange Server email versus Internet email). This also depends on whether you have connected Outlook to any social media sites, such as LinkedIn. If you are using Outlook for home or small business email via an Internet email account from your Internet service provider, you won't have access to the Global Address List that an Exchange Server environment provides to a corporate user (although small business and home users can subscribe to Office 365 and get Exchange email accounts).

The Address Book provides access to different collections of contact information (meaning email addresses), including the names that you place in the Outlook People (Contacts) folder. When you are composing a new message in the message window, you can open the Address Book by selecting To in the message window or selecting Names on the Ribbon's Message tab. Figure 23.3 shows the Address Book dialog box.

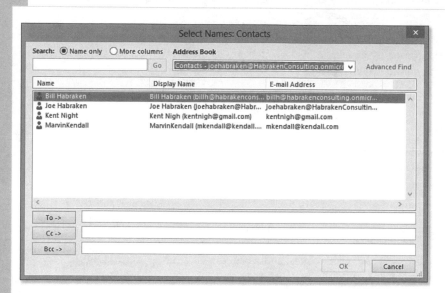

Figure 23.3
The Address Book dialog box.

The Address Book drop-down list in the Address Book dialog box enables you to select the list you want to access to address the email, such as your contacts, an Exchange global address list, or a list from a social media site such as LinkedIn. You can also search a selected address list using the Search box. By default, the Search feature is set to search the selected address list by name only. Enter a name and then click Go. Outlook highlights the first record in the current address list that matches the search term (such as the first or last name of a contact). By default, the Search tool is set to Name only; however, you can search other fields in the selected list's records by selecting More Columns and then running your search.

You can also do a more advanced search (it doesn't work on the Outlook contacts list) of certain address lists (such as your Exchange global address list or offline global address list) by selecting the Advanced Find link. This enables you to look in the fields contained in the records in the address list. You then can search for people in the list from a particular city or with a particular company name, for example. When you select Advanced Find, the Find dialog box opens as shown in Figure 23.4.

The Find dialog box enables you to devise a more complex search than the Search box permits. You can specify information in different fields and then click OK to search the address list. After you have located the email address you want to use to send the message, select the address and then click the To button in the lower part of the Address Book dialog box. Repeat as necessary to add email addresses. You can also add contacts to the Cc box or the Bcc box, as needed. After specifying the destination addresses for the message, click OK to close the Address Book dialog box.

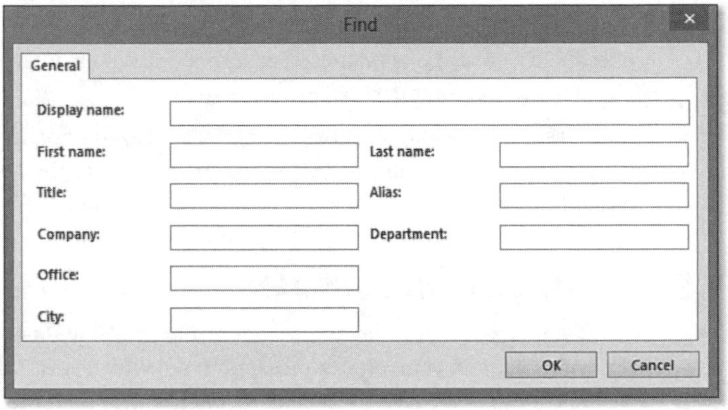

Figure 23.4
The Find dialog box.

Find	
General	
Display name:	
First name:	Last name:
Title:	Alias:
Company:	Department:
Office:	
City:	
	OK Cancel

If you are using Microsoft Exchange Server as your email server, Outlook immediately checks the validity of the email addresses that you have entered in the To, Cc, and Bcc boxes. If you have entered an invalid address because of a typo or have entered an email address that is no longer on the Exchange Server, Outlook lets you know. It places a message below the Ribbon in the message window stating that the email message cannot be delivered to the email address you have supplied because it is no longer valid.

Even if you do not use Exchange Server as your email server, you can check the email addresses that you have added to the address boxes in the message, such as To and Cc, to see whether you entered them correctly. Select Check Names on the Ribbon's Message tab. This process checks Internet email addresses for proper email format (*name@something.com*) and checks the email address against those you have listed in your Contacts folder. If an incorrect or incomplete email address is entered in a To, Cc, or Bcc box, the Check Names dialog box opens. It attempts to provide a suggestion for the correct email address. The Check Names dialog box also gives you access to the Address Book so that you can check the email address manually and provide the correct address.

When you have the message addressed correctly, you can move on to the subject of the email and the actual body of the message. If you want to put the message aside and are not ready to complete and send the message, you can save it as a draft.

Click the Close button in the Message window. A message box opens and asks whether you want to save changes to the email; click Yes. Outlook places the message in the Drafts folder. To access the message later, open the Drafts folder and double-click the message to open it in its window. You can then complete the message and send it.

 note

After you address the mail message, the People pane appears at the bottom of the message window, listing the recipients. If the recipient is one of your contacts, you can use the information provided in the People pane to view different interactions you have had with the contact, such as mail, meetings, and so on.

Setting Message Options

Outlook provides options that enable you to configure the email format, importance, sensitivity, and security settings for a message. You can also specify voting and tracking options for the message and specify delivery options, such as the email address to use when recipients send replies to the message. Other options relate to the format for the email and policies for the message with regard to archiving and retention.

In accessing these various message options, they are not on a single Ribbon tab but are somewhat dispersed among the tabs. A Properties dialog box for the message provides the greatest aggregate of the different settings. We look at this dialog box in a moment.

Specifying Email Format

When you create a new email message using the New Email Message command, Outlook creates a new message in your default message type, which is HTML if you haven't changed the Outlook settings. You might have some mail recipients who prefer to receive email messages in a particular format, such as plain text, because of the email client that they are using. You can select the email format when you use the New Items command to create a new email. After clicking the New Items command (on the Outlook Home tab), select the Email Message Using submenu and then select one of the email formats listed: Plain Text, Rich Text, or HTML.

You can also change the email type of an existing new message. Select the Format Text tab on the message's Ribbon. The email format commands are located in the Format group. Outlook highlights the current format for the message in the group. To change the format of the message, select one of the other formats provided. If you select Plain Text as the message type, most of the Font and Paragraph commands on the Format Text tab are not available, nor are the Basic Text group commands on the Message tab.

Setting Message Flags, Importance, and Sensitivity

Outlook provides you with a number of ways to "label" messages related to follow-up (by you or the recipient), message importance, and message sensitivity. These message tools, including follow-up flags and message importance, are accessed via the Ribbon's Message tab when you are working in a message window (for a new message or a message you are forwarding) or on the Compose Tools Message tab (on the Outlook Ribbon) when you are working on a message within the Reading pane (such as a message you are forwarding or answering). In both cases, commands related to flags, importance, and sensitivity can be accessed via the Tags group or the Message Options/Properties dialog box, which is accessed via the dialog box launcher provided by the Tabs group.

Let's take a look at using follow-up flags. We then discuss the other tag-related features: importance and sensitivity.

Message Flags

You can add follow-up flags to a message as a reminder to you or the message recipient. You can also assign an importance level to the message so that the recipient knows whether the message is of high or low importance.

The message flag assigned to a message appears at the top of the message window. Messages that you have flagged and then sent are listed in your Sent Items folder and are marked by a flag. If the recipient also uses Outlook, any messages sent with flags are "flagged" in the recipient's Inbox folder.

To assign a follow-up flag to the current message (a message you are creating), select Follow Up on the Ribbon's Message tab and then select one of the flags from the flag list, such as Today, Tomorrow, This Week, and so on. Outlook places the flag information at the top of the message window below the Ribbon.

If you want to set a custom flag for you or the recipient (or recipients) of the message, select the Follow Up command and then select Custom. The Custom dialog box opens. You can use the dialog box to set a flag for yourself (in the Flag for Me section) and/or a flag for the recipients. Figure 23.5 shows the Custom dialog box with both the Flag for Me and Flag for Recipients check boxes selected.

Figure 23.5
The Custom dialog box enables you to select flags for the message.

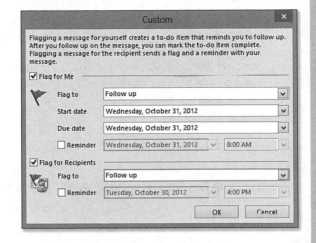

Use the Flag To drop-down list to select the flag type, such as Call, Do Not Forward, Follow Up, For Your Information, and so forth. You can also specify a start date and a due date for the flag. If you want to set a reminder for the flag, select the Reminder check box and specify a date and time for the reminder.

To set a flag for the recipient or recipients, select the Flag for Recipients check box. Then use the Flag To drop-down list to specify the flag type. You can also set reminders for recipient flags: Select the Reminder check box, and specify the date and time for the reminder.

Importance Level

There are three importance levels for Outlook messages: low, normal, and high. By default, Outlook assigns all messages the normal importance level. You can change the importance level to high or low importance, as needed. The High Importance and Low Importance commands are in the Message tab's Tags group.

Assigning an importance level to a message is a one-click endeavor. Select either High Importance or Low Importance on the Ribbon. If you assigned high importance, you can toggle off the setting by clicking it a second time. This resets the importance level to normal (you can also toggle off the low importance setting in the same manner).

Sensitivity Level

You can set the sensitivity level for a message that you are sending or forwarding. You can access the sensitivity settings and a number of other settings related to a message via the Properties dialog box. In the message window, select the dialog box launcher on the lower left of the Tags group to open the Message Options/Properties dialog box (for the current message).

By default, the Sensitivity level for a message is set to Normal. To change the sensitivity setting, select the Sensitivity drop-down list (in the Properties dialog box) and then pick one of the options provided: Personal, Private, or Confidential. You can close the Message Options/Properties dialog box by selecting the Close button. Marking the message with a sensitivity level, such as Confidential, is only to suggest how the recipient should handle the contents of the message. The sensitivity setting does not preclude the recipient from forwarding the message, for instance.

 tip

If you are using Outlook in an Exchange Server environment, you can specify permissions for a message that enable you to set an expiration date for the message and control whether a recipient can forward a message. The Permission settings (if available) are accessed using the Permission command on the message window's Ribbon (in the Options group).

Configuring Voting Buttons, Receipts, and Delivery Options

When you are working in a message window, the Options tab of the Ribbon provides several useful commands in the Tracking and More Options groups. The Tracking options enable you to insert voting buttons on an email that allow the recipients to respond with a click of the mouse. Voting buttons can include items such as Approve and Reject or Yes and No options. The Tracking options also include commands that enable you to receive notification that the recipient of the message has received the message or opened and read it, respectively.

Let's look at voting buttons and then discuss receipt requests and options related to message delivery.

Using Voting Buttons

Voting buttons enable you to make it easy for a recipient or recipients to respond to your email content, such as a question that requires a yes or no answer or a suggestion for either approval or rejection. To add voting buttons to a message, select the Use Voting Buttons command in the Tracking group, as shown in Figure 23.6.

Select any of the following: Approve, Reject; Yes, No; and Yes, No, Maybe. If you want to create a custom set of voting buttons, select Custom. This opens the Message Options/Properties dialog box for the message. You can type possible responses for the voting buttons in the Use Voting Buttons text box. Separate the selections using a semicolon.

Figure 23.6
The Use
Voting
Buttons com-
mand menu.

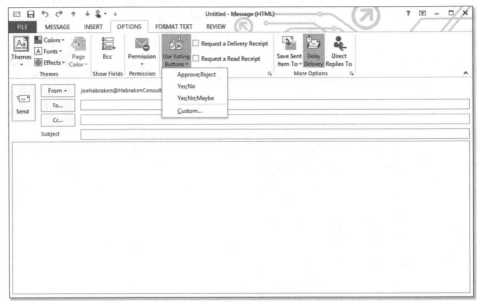

When the recipient votes using the vote buttons on the received message, a message box opens and asks whether Outlook should send the vote response immediately or whether to allow the recipient to edit the message before sending. If the recipient closes the email without sending his or her vote, you won't get that vote even if the recipient used the voting buttons.

Requesting Receipts

You can request receipts for your mail messages using the receipt commands in the Tracking group. Outlook provides two possibilities via check boxes. Select Request a Delivery Receipt to receive an email notification that the intended recipient has received the message. Select Request a Read Receipt to receive email confirmation that the recipient has opened the message.

Even if you select either of these options, the recipient can choose not to send the receipt. The dia-log box that opens when the recipient opens the message provides the opportunity for the recipient to say no to the request for a receipt.

Setting Delivery Options

You can set certain delivery options, such as where a sent message is saved (the folder used when it is saved upon sending—by default, this is the Sent Items folder), when the message is actually sent (delay delivery), and the email address replies are directed to. These options can be useful when you want certain emails placed directly into a folder related to a particular project rather than thrown in with all the other sent emails in the Sent Items folder. They are also handy when you are sending an email and you want all the replies to that email to go to a third party. An example is having all the replies to an invitation for a special event go to the person who is in charge of tracking who will attend the event; it's not uncommon for a department head or other supervisor to send an email invitation and then have a subordinate track the responses. These various delivery options are in the More Options group on the Ribbon's Options tab.

To specify a folder as the location for a saved sent item, select the Save Sent Item To command. By default, the message is saved to the default folder, which is the Sent Items folder. Select Other Folder. The Select Folder dialog box opens, as shown in Figure 23.7.

 note

If you don't want to save a copy of a sent message (for some reason), select Do Not Save on the Save Sent Item To menu (accessed via the Save Sent Item to command in the More Options group).

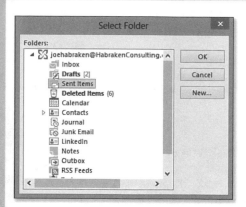

Figure 23.7
The Select Folder dialog box.

Select a folder in the list. If you want to create a new folder, click the New button. The Create New Folder dialog box opens. Type the name of the new folder, and select where you want to place the new folder in the folder list; then click OK. After you have specified the folder (or created a new folder), select OK to close the Select Folder dialog box.

If you want to specify a delivery date for the message, select the Delay Delivery command. The Properties dialog box for the message opens. By default, Outlook selects the Do Not Deliver Before check box in the Delivery Options area of the Properties dialog box. Specify a date and time for the delivery. Then click Close to close the dialog box.

The Message Options/Properties Dialog Box

Most of the message settings that we discussed in the previous sections—everything from flags to delivery options such as delay delivery—are available in the Message Options/Properties dialog box for a new, forwarded, or reply message. If you are going to set a number of message options, it makes sense to select your settings in the Message Options/Properties dialog box.

You can launch the dialog box from the dialog box launcher provided by the Tags group (on the Message tab), the Tracking group, or the More Options group (both Tracking and More Options are on the Options tab). Figure 23.8 shows the Properties dialog box for a message.

Figure 23.8
The Message Options/Properties dialog box provides access to all the options for a message.

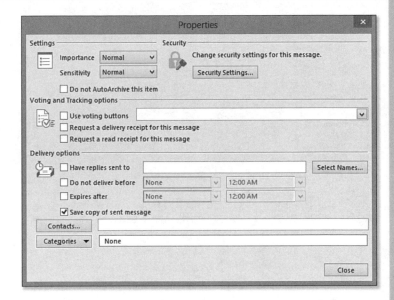

In the Settings area of the Message Options/Properties dialog box, you can set the importance and sensitivity of the message (which we already discussed). You can also configure other message properties that we have discussed, including the Voting and Tracking options and the delivery options.

> *Security settings can also be set in the Properties dialog box; **see** Chapter 27, "Securing and Maintaining Outlook."*

In addition, the Message Options dialog box enables you to link a contact or contacts to a message and assign categories to a message. Linking a contact to a message enables you to view the message on that contact's Activities page when you are viewing that particular contact's record in the Contacts folder.

When you associate contacts and categories to messages, you are just applying organizational tags to the emails. You can then view all the email sent to a particular contact in the Contacts folder or sort sent email by a particular category. The recipient of email that you have tagged in this manner does not know that you have assigned the contact or the category to the message.

To assign a contact to a message, click the Contacts button in the Message Options dialog box. The Select Contacts dialog box opens, as shown in Figure 23.9. This dialog box shows all the people in your Outlook Contacts folder. Double-click a contact to add that person to the Contacts box on the message's Options dialog box. Repeat as necessary.

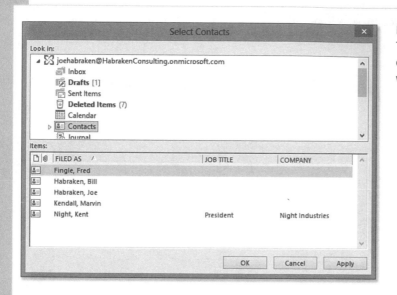

Figure 23.9
The Select Contacts dialog box enables you to associate contacts with a particular message.

You can also add categories to a message from the Message Options/Properties dialog box. Click the Categories drop-down list to assign a category to a message. You can select All Categories on the Categories drop-down list to open the Color Categories dialog box. You can assign a category (or categories) to the message by selecting a category or categories in the Color Categories dialog box. You can also create new categories or rename existing categories, if needed. Click OK to close the Color Categories dialog box and return to the Options dialog box for the message. When you have finished setting options related to the message, select Close to exit the Options dialog box.

 *More about categorizing Outlook items is available in Chapter 22, "Requisite Outlook: Configuration and Essential Features."*

 tip
If you only occasionally set properties related to your email messages and you are not consistently using the same settings, you can use the various commands on the Ribbon or the Options dialog box. If you find that you always use the same options for your mail (other than the defaults), change the Mail Options in the Outlook Options window. Mail options are discussed later in this chapter, in the section "Setting Outlook Mail Options."

Attaching Files and Items to a Message

You can attach files and Outlook items to your email messages. You can send Word documents, Excel workbooks, a family photo, or any other file you want, including a collection of files in various archive formats, such as ZIP (which you can create using the Windows 8 File Explorer). You can also send Outlook items, such as business cards of your contacts. Commands for attaching files and Outlook items are available on the Message tab and the Insert tab of the message window's Ribbon. If you are replying to a message or forwarding a message from within the Reading pane, the Compose Tools Message tab provides the Include group, which houses both the Attach File and Attach Item commands.

When you attach a file to a message, it appears as an icon in an attachment box that resides in the message window right below the Subject box. If you want to view an attachment in the parent application (such as an Excel workbook in Excel), double-click the attachment in the message; the attached file opens in the appropriate application.

You can attach multiple files to an email, as needed. To attach a file to a message, select the Attach File command on the Ribbon's Message tab in the message window. The Insert File dialog box opens, as shown in Figure 23.10. By default, your Documents library folder opens.

Figure 23.10
The Insert File dialog box.

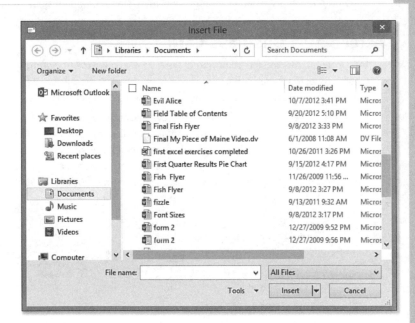

Select the file (or files) that you want to attach to the message, and then click Insert. The Attached box lists the attached file or files. If you attach a file and then decide that you don't want it attached to the message, select the attachment in the Attached box and delete it by pressing the Delete key.

If you are working in Windows Explorer and you want to send a file listed, right-click on the file and select Send To, then Mail Recipient from the shortcut menu. This opens a new message in Outlook with the file attached.

caution

The number and overall size of attachments can be problematic, particularly when you have an Internet email account that limits the size of attachments. The size allowed can vary from provider to provider, so read the provider's FAQ or call your provider to determine attachment limits before you try to send all your family reunion photos attached to a single email message.

In addition to attaching files from other programs, you can attach an Outlook item to a message. An Outlook item can be any item saved in one of your personal folders, including an appointment, a contact, a note, and so on. Outlook makes it easy for you to attach business cards of your Outlook contacts and calendars. The recipient can view calendar items even if he or she does not use Outlook.

To attach an item, select the Attach Item command on the Message tab. This command provides a menu of three possibilities: Business Card, Calendar, and Outlook Item.

Attaching a Business Card

To attach a business card of one of your contacts, select Attach Item, Business Card. The submenu lists any contact cards that you recently attached to messages. To view a list of all your contacts, select Other Business Cards to open the Insert Business Card dialog box.

Use the Look In drop-down list to select the Contacts list that you want to view in the dialog box. The list can include contacts on social media sites such as Facebook or LinkedIn (if you have connected Outlook to them). To preview a contact as a business card, select the contact. When you are ready to attach the business card, select OK. Outlook attaches the card to the message, and the card is inserted into the body of the message, as shown in Figure 23.11.

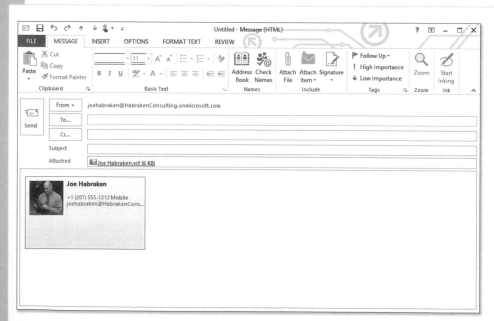

Figure 23.11
Attach a business card to a message.

If you don't want to include the business card in the body of the message, select the business card and then press Delete. The card itself remains as an attachment in the Attached box. You can also delete it from the Attached box if you decide not to send the business card: Select the card in the Attached box, and press Delete.

Attaching a Calendar

You can attach a calendar as an item to your mail message. The recipient need not use Outlook to view the calendar information. The attached calendar can consist of the current date (Today) or a range of dates. You also have control over the level of detail provided in the calendar.

To send a calendar via the message, select Attach Item and then Calendar. The Send a Calendar via Email dialog box opens, as shown in Figure 23.12.

Figure 23.12
Attach a calendar to the message.

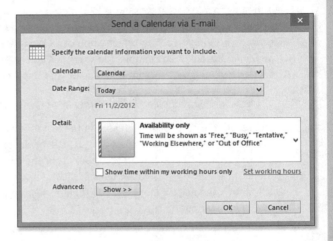

Use the Calendar drop-down list to select the calendar that supplies the information for the attachment (if you have multiple calendars in your Calendar folder). Select the Date Range drop-down list to select the range of dates for the calendar. You can select set ranges, such as Tomorrow and Next 7 Days, or you can click the Specify Dates button and provide the start and end dates for the range.

The Detail settings for the calendar relate to the amount of detail you want to provide the recipient. By default, the detail level is set to Availability only, which shows time as free, busy, tentative, and so on. If you want to include the availability and the subjects of your calendar items (within the date range), select the Limited Details setting. For full disclosure, you can select the Full Details setting.

If you select either the Limited Details or the Full Details setting, Outlook gives you additional options in the Advanced area of the dialog box. You can choose to include the details of items marked private, and in the case of the Full Details setting, you can also include items attached to calendar items within the date range you have selected.

You can also specify the format of the attached calendar. Select the Show button to view the advanced settings. Select Email Layout to choose the layout for the calendar; you can select from Daily Schedule (the default) or List of Events. When you have completed your selection related to the attached calendar, click OK to close the dialog box. Outlook inserts the calendar in the Attached box and the details of the calendar into the body of the message. Users of Outlook can open the attached Calendar (`.ics`) file in Outlook. If you are going to send the calendar to someone who does not use Outlook, you might want to delete the calendar file in the Attached box and leave the calendar embedded in the body of the message. The calendar provides links from a calendar to a list of specific appointments it includes.

Using Themes and Email Stationery

If you use the HTML or Rich Text message format for your email messages, you can take advantage of themes to make your messages look more interesting and appealing. A theme provides formatting attributes for the colors, fonts, and effects used in the message. Because you are using Word as your message editor, you are, in effect, applying a Word theme to the body text of the message. Themes are useful because they enable you to have a consistent look across a family of associated items, such as mail messages, Word documents, and Excel worksheets.

 *For information on using themes in Word,* **see** *Chapter 7, "Enhancing Word Documents."*

Email stationery has been available in the last few versions of Outlook. Stationery gives you an overall look for the message's text and includes backgrounds for the body of the message. You can use stationery when you compose HTML emails. Let's look at assigning a theme to a message and then discuss creating a message using stationery.

To select a theme for the message, follow these steps:

1. Type the body of your message, or make sure that the insertion point is in the body of the message.

2. Select the Options tab of the Ribbon.

3. Select the Themes command. You can preview any of the themes in the gallery by placing the mouse on a particular theme.

4. When you have decided on a theme, click the theme to assign it to the message.

 tip

You can select the Show Time Within My Working Hours Only check box and then set your working hours in the Send a Calendar via Email dialog box. This precludes any appointments or items that fall outside your regular working day from being included with the calendar that is attached to the email message.

You can fine-tune the themes by using the Colors, Fonts, and Effects commands to adjust the settings of the current theme. If you want to add a background color to the body of the message, use the Page Color command to select from the various theme colors. You can preview the colors by placing the mouse on a color in the palette.

If you want to use Outlook stationery for a new message, you must select the stationery as you create the message. On the Home tab of any of the Outlook folders, select the New Items command, point at Email Message Using, and then select More Stationery. The Theme or Stationery dialog box opens, as shown in Figure 23.13.

Figure 23.13
Select stationery for the new message.

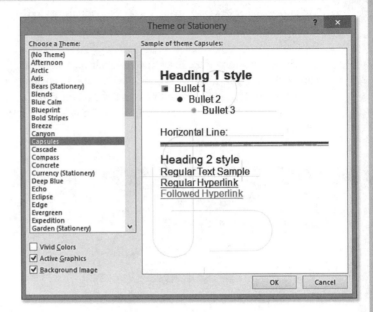

This dialog box provides a list of available themes and installed stationery. The stationery is marked with the parenthetical tag (Stationery). Select the stationery (such as Bears, Currency, or Garden), and a preview of the stationery displays in the dialog box. When you have found the stationery that you want to use, select OK to apply it to the new message and return to the message window.

Adding a Signature

You can further personalize your emails by adding a signature to the message. A signature can be as simple as just your name. A signature can also include your phone number, extension, and other information. Some people even add a favorite quote to their signature. If you use HTML as your message format, you can insert a signature file that contains graphics such as your picture. If you want, you can insert your electronic business card as the signature information (you should always include yourself in your Contacts list). Plain-text signatures (for use with plain-text messages) consist of text characters only.

You can create more than one signature for your mail messages. This enables you to have a different signature for your business emails and your personal emails. You can also create signatures for your plain-text messages and HTML messages.

To create a signature, select the Signature command on the message Ribbon's Message tab and then select Signatures. The Signatures and Stationery dialog box opens. The Email Signature tab of the dialog box contains a list of your signatures in the Select Signature to Edit box. If you haven't created any signatures, there obviously won't be any signatures in the list.

To create a new signature, click the New button. The New Signature dialog box opens. Type a name for the new signature, and click OK. The signature appears in the signature list. Now you can edit the signature using the various tools shown in the Edit Signature pane (see Figure 23.14).

 note

Signatures for your emails are not the same as digital signatures. Digital signatures ensure that a mail message comes from a trusted source. Chapter 27 discusses digital signatures.

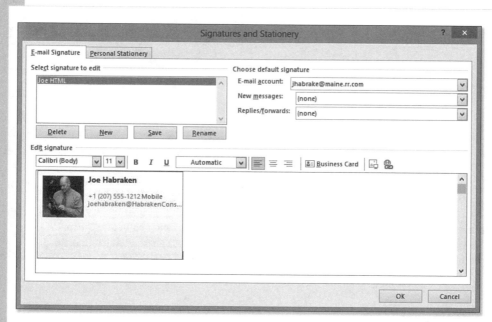

Figure 23.14
Create signatures in the Signatures and Stationery dialog box.

Type the text for the signature, and use the various drop-down formatting lists to format the text. You can also insert a business card or pictures and links in the signature. When you are finished creating the signature, you can repeat the process to create other signatures, as needed. When you click OK, the Signatures and Stationery dialog box closes. You can now use the Signature command to select from the list of the signatures that you have created and add them to the email.

Sending Mail

When you have completed your email message, you can send it. Click Send, and Outlook places the message in your Outbox folder. If you have a persistent connection to your outgoing mail server, Outlook sends the message immediately and places a copy of the message in your Sent Items folder (or the folder that you specified using the Save Sent Item to command on the Options tab).

If you are working offline, Outlook places the message in your Outbox folder. The message remains in the Outbox until you connect to your network (or the Internet, if you are using Internet email) and uses the Send and Receive command. If you configured the message with delivery options that specified a delivery date, the message stays in the Outbox until the delivery date arrives.

Recalling a Message

If you work on a network that uses Microsoft Exchange Server as your email messaging server, you can recall sent messages. You must recall the message before the recipient opens, deletes, or moves it to another folder. This feature is useful if you inadvertently sent an incomplete message or forgot to include an important attachment with the message. The recall feature actually gives you two possibilities: You can recall the message and delete unread copies of the message, or you can recall the message and replace it with a new message, such as a message that includes the attachment you wanted to send.

To recall a message, follow these steps:

1. With the Mail folder selected, select the Sent Items folder.

2. Double-click the message that you want to recall, to open it.

3. On the Ribbon's Message tab, select Actions and then Recall This Message. The Recall This Message dialog box opens, as shown in Figure 23.15.

Figure 23.15
Recall a message.

4. Two options are available related to recalling the message: Delete Unread Copies of This Message (the default) and Delete Unread Copies and Replace with a New Message. Select the option you want to use.

5. If you use the default option to recall the message, select OK. The Recall Message dialog box closes. If you select the Replace with a New Message option, a new message opens. Create the message that replaces the recalled message, and then click Send.

 tip

You can also send an email by pressing Ctrl+Enter. The first time you press this key combination, Outlook asks you to verify it as a shortcut for sending email. Click Yes.

You eventually receive a notification in your Inbox folder (as new mail) notifying you of whether the recall was successful. Remember that this feature is for Exchange Server mail accounts; you cannot recall messages sent via Internet email accounts.

Although you can't recall Internet email messages, you can use this feature to notify the recipients of a particular email message that you want them to ignore. Use the message recall feature as detailed in the steps in this section. When you "recall" the message, Outlook sends a new message to the original recipients stating that you would like to recall the previous message. This doesn't remove the original message from the recipients' inboxes, but it at least gives them a follow-up message that the original message is essentially invalid.

 note

By default, Outlook provides information on whether the recall succeeds for each message recipient.

Working with Received Email

New email is downloaded when you open Outlook and it connects to your mail server (you must be connected to the Internet or your corporate network for this to happen). When Outlook opens, it selects your email inbox (by default) and lists your emails in the Details pane, including any new email messages that have been downloaded from your mail server. The most recent message (the newest) in the Inbox appears at the top of the list and is also previewed in the Reading pane. This is because Outlook groups your email in your inbox by date, by default.

Reading mail is really just a matter of selecting the message that you want to read; the message appears in the Reading pane. You can also open a message in a separate window: Double-click the message in the Details pane.

After you read a particular message, you typically answer it, forward it, or delete it. Outlook tracks each of these actions. For example, when you reply to a message, the original message in the Inbox folder is marked with a Replied symbol. Outlook saves the reply message in the Sent Items folder.

Deleting an email message is straightforward. Select the message (or messages) and then press the Delete key. When you delete a message, Outlook moves it to the Deleted Items folder. When you empty the Deleted Items folder, that message (and anything else in the Deleted Items folder) is gone.

Organizing Messages in the Inbox

You can modify the default view for the Inbox using the options at the top of the Details pane. By default, All is selected, and all your messages are shown in the Details pane. You can quickly filter the list to show only messages that you have not read; select Unread.

If you want to change how the emails are listed in the Details pane (remember, it's by date, by default), you can select the drop-down arrow next to By Date and select other options for organizing the messages in the Inbox, such as From, Categories, Subject, and even Importance (now you can see the value of using message tags and assigning messages categories). If you want to change the order of the messages, you can use the command just to the right of the command list (the list that enables you to view by Date, From, and so on). Click the order arrow (it's called Newest when you sort the email by date) to change the order of the messages. For example, if you select Newest when your email is sorted by date, it changes to Oldest, and now the oldest email is at the top of the email list in the Details pane.

You can also change the current view of the Inbox using the Arrangement commands found on the Outlook Ribbon's View tab. For example, you can select To or From to change how the messages are sorted. The Reverse Sort button changes the order of the messages (which is based on the Arrangement command you have selected, such as Date, To, and From Categories).

Other commands that you can take advantage of on the View tab are in the Layout group. These commands—Folder Pane, Reading Pane, and To-Do bar—enable you to determine whether these panes are shown in the Outlook application window. For example, by default, the Folder Pane and the Reading Pane are shown. If you also want to view your to-do list (tasks) when working with your Inbox messages, you can select the To-Do Bar command and then select Tasks. If you want to hide the To-Do Bar (or the Folder or Reading panes), select the command and then select Off.

Showing Messages As Conversations

Another useful way to view your emails in the Inbox is to arrange the messages by conversation. But what does it mean to arrange messages in conversations? A conversation is emails that are associated to a particular mail message subject. For example, if you received an email in your Inbox and then replied to it, both the original email and the reply would be shown in your Inbox as a conversation group. The conversations are listed by date and in convenient date groupings, such as Today, Last Week, Two Weeks Ago, and Older, enabling you to quickly locate messages that relate to a particular time period. You can collapse and expand a time period group, such as Last Week, to make it easier to concentrate on other date groupings of email conversations listed in the Inbox folder.

To arrange your messages in conversations, select the Ribbon's View tab and then select the Show As Conversations command (in the Messages group). A message box opens and asks you whether you want to apply the conversation view to all mailboxes or just this folder. Click the response that works best for you (I usually just select This Folder so that the Inbox is in conversation view; I don't like my Sent Items or Deleted Items as conversations because it's too confusing). Figure 23.16 shows the Inbox arranged in conversations, with a conversation titled Estimate expanded so that the different emails in the conversation are shown.

You can expand conversations as needed to view all the messages in a particular conversation. Because the conversations are listed by date, you can also change the order of the messages from newest to oldest by selecting the toggle at the top right of the Details pane.

If you are using Conversations view, when you respond to a message, the reply appears in the Inbox folder as part of the conversation. The same is true for forwarded email, which is marked with a Forwarded symbol in the Inbox folder (remember, all these sent emails end up in your Sent Items folder).

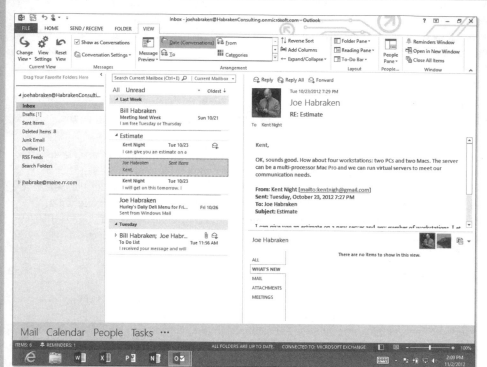

Figure 23.16
Messages in the Inbox can be arranged in conversations.

Filtering Email

The Arrangement commands change how Outlook arranges the messages in a folder such as the Inbox, but you might also want to view a subset of the messages in the Inbox folder, based on certain criteria, such as only messages flagged as high importance or only emails that have attachments. You can filter email using the Filter Email command on the Outlook Ribbon's Home tab. The command uses the Outlook Search feature to filter the messages in the Inbox folder.

Select Filter Email and then select one of the available filters, such as Unread, Has Attachments, or Flagged. The list filters based on your selection, and the Search Tools tab appears on the Ribbon. This tab enables you to set the scope for the filter, such as the current folder or all subfolders, and refine the search. Search refinements enable you to add criteria to the search. For example, if you filtered your Inbox folder by Has Attachments, you could select the Categorized command to add a category to your search filter. You could add another refinement, such as importance, by selecting the Important command.

Several filter-refinement commands (which add criteria to the search filter) are available in the Refine group of the Search Tools tab, including Categorized, Sent To, and Flagged. You can access additional refinement criteria by selecting the More command, which provides the Common Properties list. This list enables you to refine the search by all sorts of criteria, including Bcc, Cc, Due Date, From, and Received.

When you have finished your work with the Search Tools and want to remove the filter you have placed on the current folder, select the Close Search command. Outlook returns you to the folder, such as the Inbox, and removes the filter, showing the entire contents of the folder.

Managing Email

Managing email is really just a matter of determining what to do with your received email messages, although you can manage the Sent Items folder and messages that you save in other folders for later consideration. Whether you read your messages in the Reading Pane or prefer to open them in a separate window, all the commands that you need to manage individual messages are easily accessible via the Ribbon. If you are working in the Inbox folder, the Mail Ribbon provides most of the message-management commands on the Home tab. If you are working with a received message that you have opened in its own window, the message-management commands are on the Ribbon's Message tab (which is the only tab available, other than the File tab that takes you to the Backstage). More commands related to dealing with a message are on the Message tab of the message window's Ribbon. So you might want to open a message if you want to quickly perform an action related to that message. Figure 23.17 shows the message window's Ribbon with the Message tab selected.

Figure 23.17
The Ribbon's Message tab.

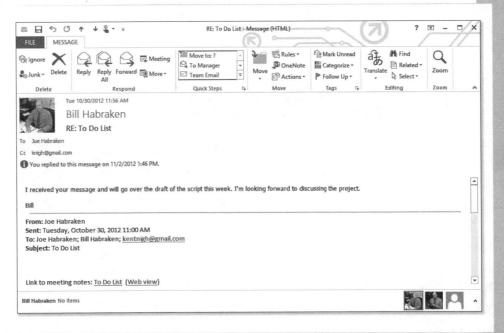

Outlook dedicates most of the command groups on the Message tab to managing received messages. For example, the Delete group provides options for dealing with messages that you no longer want, and the Respond group provides different commands for replying to or forwarding a message.

The Quick Steps group provides access to Quick Steps, which are commands that combine multiple actions in one click. Let's take a more detailed look at how to use Quick Steps.

Using Quick Steps

As already mentioned, Quick Steps are commands that combine multiple actions in one click; For example, the Move To Quick Step (one of the default Quick Steps) enables you to mark an email as read and move it into a particular folder. The Reply & Delete Quick Step opens a reply message for a selected message and, after you have completed and sent your reply, deletes the original message. To view all of the default Quick Steps in the Quick Steps gallery (on the Message tab), select the More button.

Some of the default Quick Steps, such as the Move To and Done commands, require a brief setup the first time you select them. For example, if you are working in a message window and then select the Move To Quick Step, the First Time Setup dialog box opens, as shown in Figure 23.18.

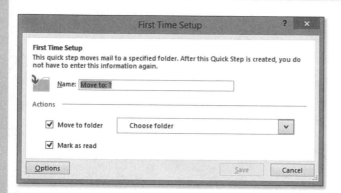

Figure 23.18
The First Time Setup dialog box for the Move To Quick Step.

By default, this Quick Step moves items to the specified folder and marks them as read. Use the Choose Folder drop-down to specify the folder that the Quick Step should use. The name of the Quick Step changes to the name of the folder that you select. However, you can change the name as needed in the Name box. When you have finished setting up the Quick Step, click Save.

You aren't limited to the default Quick Steps provided in the Quick Steps group. You can create additional Quick Steps by selecting the dialog box launcher in the Quick Steps group. This opens the Manage Quick Steps dialog box, shown in Figure 23.19. You can use the dialog box to edit, duplicate, and delete existing Quick Steps. You can also change the order in which the Quick Steps appear in the Quick Steps group. Use the Move Up and Move Down buttons in the Manage Quick Steps dialog box, as needed.

Figure 23.19
The Manage Quick Steps dialog box.

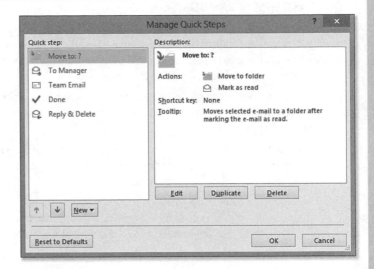

You can also create your own custom Quick Steps. To create a new Quick Step, follow these steps:

1. In the Manage Quick Steps dialog box, click the New button and then select the type of Quick Step you want to create, such as Move to Folder, Categorize and Move, Flag and Move, and so on. When you select the Quick Step type, the First Time Setup dialog box appears.

2. Click the Options button in the First Time Setup dialog box to expand the dialog box. This enables you to see the current actions for the Quick Step and to add actions, if needed.

3. Specify options related to the actions. For example, if the action is Move to Folder, select the folder the mail should move to.

4. If you want to add an action to the Quick Step, click the Add Action button; then select the action you want to take place (such as Categorize Message or Flag Message) from the Choose an Action drop-down list for the new action.

5. (Optional) Select a shortcut key for the Quick Step from the Shortcut Key drop-down list.

6. (Optional) Type text in the ToolTip text box (which appears when you hover the mouse over the Quick Step).

7. Type a name for the Quick Step in the Name box.

8. Click the Save button.

Outlook adds the Quick Step to the Quick Step group. You can also edit, duplicate, and delete Quick Steps in the Manage Quick Steps dialog box, as needed.

 tip

The Quick Steps group is also available on the Home tab of the Outlook Ribbon. Quick Steps aren't reserved for working with mail messages; you can create Quick Steps that also enable you to manage other Outlook items, such as tasks or contacts.

Answering a Message

Answering or replying to a message can take the form of a simple reply to the sender of the message or can encompass a reply that goes to everyone who received the original message and the sender of that message. The Respond group on the Ribbon's message tab provides several commands related to responding to a message.

To simply reply to the sender of the message, select the Reply command. A new message window opens, containing the original message text. Type your response to the message and then select Send.

If you want to reply to the sender and all the recipients of the original message, select Reply All. This opens a new message window addressed to the sender and all recipients, including those listed in the Cc or Bcc address boxes.

The next time you open a message to which you've replied, a reminder at the top of the message window tells you the date and time you sent your reply. Don't forget that the Replied To arrow next to a message in the Inbox window also shows that you have responded to the message.

Forwarding a Message

You can forward received mail as needed to coworkers or other concerned parties. When you forward a message, you can add text to the email and include new attachments to the message, if you so choose. Forwarded mail includes any attachments that were part of the originally received message.

Open the message that you want to forward, or select the message in the Inbox folder. Select the Forward command in the Respond group. A new message window opens. Provide the addresses of the individuals that you want to receive the forwarded message. Select Send to send the forwarded message. Outlook places a copy of the forwarded message in your Sent Items folder and tags the original message as forwarded.

Saving an Attachment

When you receive messages with attachments, you might want to save those attachments to folders on your computer for later examination or reference, or even for editing. You can pick out messages with attachments in your inbox because a paper clip icon beside the message subject represents a message attachment.

Select (in the Inbox) or open the message that contains the attachment that you want to save. The attachment appears as an icon above the message area. To save the attachment, select the attachment icon. Outlook previews the attached item either in the Reading Pane (if you have not opened the message) or in the

 note

Attachments are not included with your response to the message, so if you add recipient addresses to an email reply, they will not receive any attachments related to the original message.

 tip

You can right-click a message and then select Reply or Reply All from the shortcut menu that appears.

 caution

Attachments can pose a security hazard. Do not open attachments from unknown email senders. Even email from known parties merits at least some scrutiny. Save attachments to your computer, and then scan them with antivirus software before opening.

message window, as shown in Figure 23.20 (which shows the attachment in the message window). The Attachment Tools also become available on the Ribbon (as shown).

Figure 23.20
Preview the
attachment.

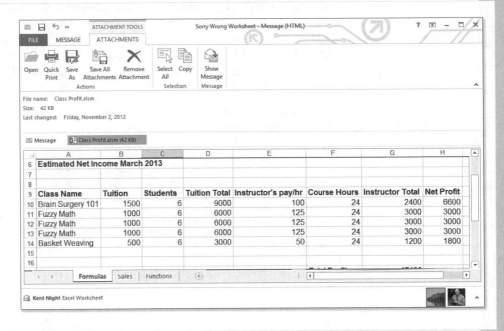

The Actions group on the Attachment Tools tab enables you to open, print, save, or remove the attachment. To save the attachment to your computer, select the Save As command. The Save Attachment dialog box opens. Navigate to the folder where you want to save the attachment. You can also change the filename of the saved version of the attachment, if needed. Select Save to save the attachment.

You can toggle between the message and the attachment preview using the Message and attachment icons provided above the message text. If you do not want to preview the attachment before saving it, right-click the Attachment icon and select Save As from the shortcut menu. You can then save the file via the Save Attachment dialog box, as previously discussed.

If a message contains multiple attachments and you want to save them without previewing or opening them, select Save Attachments in the Actions group. The Save All Attachments dialog box opens. You can specify which attachments to save in the dialog box.

When you are ready to save the attachments, click OK. The Save Attachments dialog box opens. Specify the folder where Outlook should save the attachments, and then select OK. The attachments are saved.

➡️ *For more about attachments and Outlook security settings,* **see** *Chapter 27, "Securing and Maintaining Outlook."*

Deleting Messages

You have options when you delete messages. (This is true for messages in your Inbox folder and other mail folders.) As already mentioned, the commands related to deleting mail messages are in the Delete group (this group is available on the Home tab of the Outlook Ribbon and the Message group of a message window's Ribbon). The most straightforward way to deal with a selected message or group of selected messages that you no longer want is to select the Delete command. The message or messages are moved to your Deleted Items folder. Outlook provides three other possibilities in the Delete group:

- **Ignore:** This command moves the currently selected message and any future messages in the conversation (based on the subject) to the Deleted Items folder.

- **Clean Up:** This command provides a list of three related commands: Clean Up Conversation, Clean Up Folder, and Clean Up Folder & Subfolders. If you select Clean Up Conversation, Outlook moves redundant messages in the conversation to the Deleted Items folder. Remember that the Conversation view can include messages that are present in other Mail folders, not just the Inbox folder. The Clean Up Folder and Clean Up Folder & Subfolders commands remove redundant messages in the current folder or the current folder and its subfolders, respectively.

- **Junk:** This command provides an options list that enables you to block the sender or to never block the sender or the sender's domain (such as @*whatever.com*). This command also enables you to access the Junk Email Options dialog box for your email account.

> For more about dealing with junk email, and using message rules **see** Chapter 27, "Securing and Maintaining Outlook."

The various commands provided in the Delete group make removing items from the Inbox folder or another mail folder a more constructive process in terms of keeping the Inbox free of unwanted, redundant, and spam email. Email messages can also be managed using rules, which are discussed later in the book.

When your emails are in the Deleted Items folder, they are destined for oblivion (although you can move a message in the folder to another folder if you decide you want to keep it). To permanently delete a message in the Deleted Items folder, select the message (you can select multiple messages) and then click the Delete command. A message appears asking whether you want to delete the selected item or items permanently. Click Yes to permanently delete the message or messages.

If you typically are confident about the status of messages that you delete (you know that you won't want to undelete them), you can empty all the messages in the Deleted Items folder instead of emptying it message by message. Right-click the Deleted Items folder and select Empty Folder. Click Yes to verify the permanent deletion of the items in the Deleted Items folder.

You can also configure Outlook so that your Deleted Items folder empties when you exit Outlook. Select File to open the Backstage, and then select Options. In the Outlook Options window, select Advanced and navigate to the Outlook Start and Exit settings. Select the Empty Deleted Items Folders When Exiting Outlook check box. Now Outlook empties your Deleted Items folder (or folders, if you have multiple email accounts) when you exit.

Printing Mail

You can print your email messages in multiple ways. To send a message to the printer without previewing it, right-click the message and select Quick Print from the shortcut menu. This sends the message directly to your default printer.

If you want to specify the printer, the print options, or the print style for the printout, select File and then Print. The Print window opens and provides a preview of the message. You can change the settings related to the print job, such as the printer and the print style, as required.

Moving Email

You can also organize your mail messages by moving the messages from your Inbox folder to other folders. You can use the Move command on the Home tab of the Ribbon to move and copy messages from one folder to another. This provides you with alternative places to store items and can make finding them in the future easier than having all your messages languish in the Inbox folder in one huge mess.

To move a message, select the message in the Details pane. Then select the Move command on the Ribbon's Home tab. If you want to move the selected messages to another folder, select Other Folder. The Move Items dialog box opens, as shown in Figure 23.21.

Specify the folder that you want to move the items to. If you need to create a new folder, select the New button. The Create New Folder dialog box opens. Type a name for the new folder, and then select the location in the folder list where you want to place the new folder. Click OK to close the Create New Folder dialog box; you return to the Move Items dialog box. Click OK to move the items and to close the Move Items dialog box.

 tip

You can create your own filters directly in the Search box. Just type your keywords for the filter, and the messages that meet your criteria are listed in the Details pane.

 tip

If you have a lot of messages in the Inbox, you might want to filter the messages using particular criteria and then move those messages *en masse* to another folder, such as a folder where you keep all your excess emails.

Figure 23.21
Move messages to another folder.

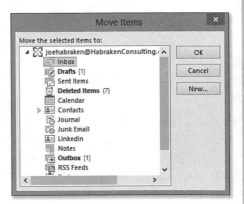

If you don't like working with the Move Items dialog box, you can also create folders directly in the Navigation pane's folder list and then drag items from the current folder, such as the Inbox, to another folder. Right-click a particular email account and select New Folder from the shortcut menu. Provide a name for the folder, and it's ready to go. You can then select items in the current mail folder in the Details pane and drag them to the new folder.

Managing Email Accounts

As we discussed in Chapter 22, Outlook makes it easy for you to configure your default email account the first time you run Outlook. You can also add or delete email accounts as needed (you aren't stuck with a single email address or the email address you first configured on Outlook). You can also change the configuration settings for any existing email accounts. Outlook supports four types of email accounts:

- **Microsoft Exchange Server (or compatible service):** This type of account makes Outlook an Exchange Server client; mailboxes and other resources, such as shared public folders, are managed on the Exchange Server on your network. Your network system administrator likely will configure this or provide you with the settings for an Exchange account.

 note

An excellent way to keep your mail messages organized is to use rules that automatically determine what happens to an email message or messages that meet particular conditions. These rules move or delete messages, depending on the rule actions. See Chapter 27 for more about rules.

- **POP3 Account:** POP3 (Post Office Protocol 3) is a protocol that most ISPs use, which allows a POP3 email server to function as a mail drop. This means that your incoming email arrives at the POP3 server and sits there until you connect with your email client (Outlook) and download the mail to your computer. The home email accounts provided by your Internet service provider are almost always POP3 accounts.

- **IMAP Account:** IMAP (Internet Message Access Protocol) is a protocol that allows Outlook to download email from an IMAP mail server. IMAP differs from POP3, in that your email is not removed from the mail server when you connect to the server with Outlook. Instead, Outlook provides you with a list of saved and new messages, which you can then open and read. IMAP is particularly useful when more than one device, such as your computer and a smartphone or other mobile device, can access a single email account. An example of an IMAP-type account is a Yahoo! Webmail account.

- **Outlook.com or Exchange ActiveSync–compatible service:** This is a new possibility provided by Microsoft (replacing the Hotmail Connector) that enables you to configure an Outlook.com (Hotmail) account for use in Outlook. Exchange ActiveSync was originally developed so that Microsoft Exchange email users could access their email on smart devices such as smart phones. The bottom line with this new service is that it gives you access to your Outlook.com (Hotmail) account, including your contacts and calendars. It also gives you the option of connecting Outlook to other web-based email services such as Gmail.

To access your Outlook account settings, select File and then Info. In the Backstage Account Information window, select Account Settings. If you are using Outlook for Internet email only (POP3), only Account Settings and the Social Network Accounts are available on the Account Settings menu. If you use Outlook as an Exchange Server client, you also have access to Delegate Access, Download Address Book (the Global Exchange Address Book for your Exchange Server network), and Manage Mobile Notifications. Select Account Settings on the menu. The Account Settings dialog box opens. The Email tab of the Account Settings dialog box lists your currently installed email accounts, as shown in Figure 23.22.

 note

Both POP3 and IMAP accounts have to be configured with the outgoing mail server information, which is the SMTP server. SMTP is the Simple Mail Transport Protocol and is used to get your mail from your computer to your provider's SMTP mail server and then on to the Internet for delivery.

Figure 23.22
The Account Settings dialog box with the Email tab selected.

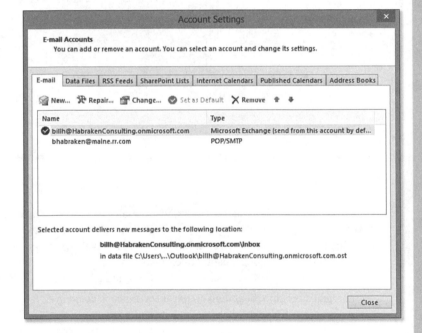

Editing Email Account Settings

To view the current settings for an email account, double-click the account (in the Account Settings dialog box). The Change Account dialog box opens, as shown in Figure 23.23 (which you can also open by selecting the account and then clicking the Change icon on the toolbar). You can view the user information, server information, and logon information for the account. You can edit account settings, if necessary, and then use the Test Account Settings button to see whether the new account settings work correctly. Change account settings only if your ISP sent you a notice to change settings or if the account was not working correctly. When you open the Account Settings dialog box for an Exchange Server account, the information provided is much more limited than that shown for a POP3 account (such as the account shown in Figure 23.23) You really can't edit anything related to the account in the Account Settings dialog box.

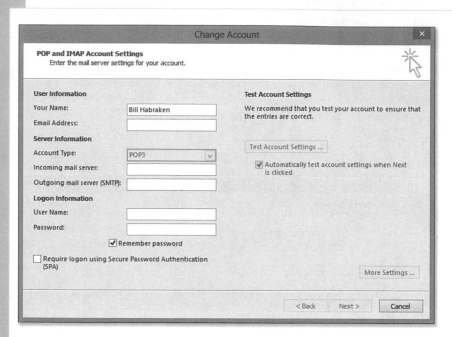

Figure 23.23
The Change Account dialog box for a POP3 mail account.

If an account is not working correctly, you can also use the Repair command to open the Auto Account Setup tool in the Repair Account dialog box. The Auto Account Setup is the same tool you use when you add a new account to Outlook, and it walks you through all the steps of setting up the account; this might be useful in correcting any problems with the account, particularly if you have entered information incorrectly that is required for Outlook to set up the mail account.

If an email account that you no longer have or use is listed in the Account Settings dialog box (for instance, you have changed ISPs), you can delete an account from the list. Select the account and then click the Remove button. Outlook asks you to verify the removal. If you truly want to remove the account, select Yes.

You have control over the email account considered the default account for Outlook. Typically, you send new mail messages from the default account. Select an account in the account list, and then click the Set As Default button. Outlook designates the default account with the default icon (a circle with a checkmark). This change does not take place until you close the Account Settings dialog box and restart Outlook.

 tip

Both POP3 and IMAP accounts have to be configured with the outgoing mail server information, which is the SMTP server. SMTP, the Simple Mail Transport Protocol, is used to get your mail from your computer to your provider's SMTP mail server and then on to the Internet for delivery.

Adding an Email Account

You can add email accounts to the Outlook configuration as needed. All you have to do is select New on the Email tab of the Account Settings dialog box. This opens the Add Account dialog box. You can also open this dialog box from the Outlook Backstage Info window using the Add Account button. The Add Account dialog box provides the Auto Account Setup tool, which can automatically configure most new email accounts.

If you have an Exchange Server account at your company or institution, your network administrator typically sets it up for you unless he or she likes living dangerously. I have never worked in a business environment where Exchange users set up their own accounts, other than perhaps downloading a configuration file that set up the account automatically.

If your Exchange account is part of your Office 365 subscription, you determine the email address during the initial signup process for Office 365. A password for your account is also set up. You can then use this email address/password combination to configure the email account in Outlook using the Auto Account Setup window. All you have to do is supply your name, the email address, and your password (you enter your password twice for confirmation); then you simply select Next. An encrypted connection is made with the Exchange mail server (for Office 365 accounts), and the account is automatically configured in Outlook. At the completion of the configuration process, select Finish. When you add an Exchange account to Outlook, you typically have to restart Outlook for the changes to take effect.

If you are configuring an Internet email account that your Internet service provider (ISP) supplied you, you can also attempt to have Outlook automatically set up the account using the Auto Account tool. However, most ISPs don't provide for an encrypted connection; this means that Outlook tries to locate the mail servers for the account and fails. However, the Auto Account Setup tool gives you the option of running auto setup again without using an encrypted connection. Most email accounts are automatically set up when you run the unencrypted search for the email servers. Select Finish at the end of the process.

If auto setup doesn't work for you, you can manually configure your account. In the case of Internet email from an ISP, the ISP supplies you with the POP3, MAPI (Messaging Application Programming Interface), and SMTP (Simple Mail Transfer Protocol) server names. With these types of email accounts, your ISP also typically provides you with a master logon name and password; you can then specify the username and password for email accounts associated with your ISP account. You typically do this on the ISP's website.

To correctly configure the email account settings, you need to know the incoming mail server name (POP3 or IMAP), the outgoing mail SMTP server name, your account name, and your password.

 tip

If you are having a problem adding an Exchange Server email account to Outlook (particularly if you configured an Internet email account as your first Outlook email account), you might have to close Outlook and open the Account Settings dialog box using the Mail command in the Windows 8 Control Panel. Open the Control Panel, select User Accounts and Family Safety, and then select the Mail icon. In the Mail Setup–Outlook dialog box, click the Email Accounts button. This opens the Account Settings dialog box, and you can select New to add the Exchange mail account.

So how does the manual configuration of an email account play out in the Add Account dialog box? Select the Manually Setup or Additional Server Types option button at the bottom of the Add

Account dialog box. Then click Next. The next screen asks you to select the type of service you want to add. The choices are as follows:

- Microsoft Exchange Server or compatible service

- Outlook.com or Exchange ActiveSync–compatible service

- POP or IMAP

As already discussed, Exchange Server accounts are typically set up for you (by your network administrator) or are easily configured by you using auto setup. We discuss the configuration of an Outlook.com (Hotmail) account in the next section. In most cases, the only account type that might require manual setup is a POP or IMAP account (meaning Internet email). So assume that you are dealing with an uncooperative POP or IMAP account, and have the email name, password, and server names ready to manually enter. Click Next. The POP and IMAP Account Settings screen appears, as shown in Figure 23.24.

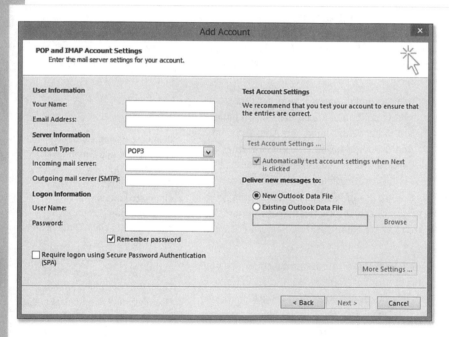

Figure 23.24
The POP and IMAP Settings screen.

Enter your name, the server information, and the logon information for the account. Click the Test Account Settings button to make sure that the settings work as you have entered them. If you entered all the information correctly, the account should work. Select Next and then Finish. When you return to the Account Settings dialog box, it will list the new email account.

caution

Outlook email accounts and Outlook profiles are closely wound entities. I recommend that you look over Chapter 22 and read the sections "Configuring Outlook at First Start" and "Understanding Outlook Profiles" before you add email accounts to Outlook's configuration.

Adding an Outlook.com Mail Account

You can also add a Microsoft Outlook.com (formerly Hotmail) account to your Outlook configuration. In Outlook 2010, you had to use the Outlook Connector to add a Hotmail account to your Outlook configuration (and you even had to download the connector). Luckily, those days are over, and your Outlook.com (yes, that is what they are calling Hotmail now) mail account uses Microsoft's Exchange ActiveSync technology to "talk" with Outlook. This means that you not only have access to your emails, but you also can access your Outlook.com calendars, contacts, and tasks.

You can quickly add your Outlook.com account to Outlook using the Auto Account Setup tool. Enter your name, email address, and password (twice) on the Auto Account Setup screen, and then click Next in the Add Account dialog box.

Outlook adds mail folders (Inbox, Drafts, Sent Items, Deleted Items, Junk Email, Outbox, and Search Folders) for the Outlook.com (or Hotmail) account to the Folder Pane. The Calendar for the Outlook.com account is added to your My Calendars list, the Contacts (People) list from the account is added to your People lists, and any tasks that you created using the Outlook.com account are available in the My Tasks list when you select Tasks on the Navigation bar.

 note

Outlook 2013 better integrates Outlook.com email accounts with the other accounts that you typically use in Outlook, such as Exchange Server and POP or IMAP accounts. It also makes it a lot easier to add an Outlook.com email account to your Outlook configuration.

Setting Outlook Mail Options

We have already discussed options that can be set for individual Outlook mail messages, such as tracking options and delivery options. You also have the option of configuring different email settings using a more "global approach" by accessing the Outlook Options window. You access these various settings and options via the Backstage. Select File and then Options; the Outlook Options window opens. Select Mail to access the mail-related options, as shown in Figure 23.25.

The Mail options window provides a number of categories of options:

- **Compose Messages:** These settings include the default message format (HTML, Rich Text, or plain text) and whether Outlook spell-checks messages before sending them. Other options involve the creation and modification of signatures and address whether Outlook uses personal stationery when creating new messages.

- **Outlook Panes:** This group provides access to the Reading Pane dialog box. You can select options such as when items are marked as read and whether to enable single key reading using the spacebar.

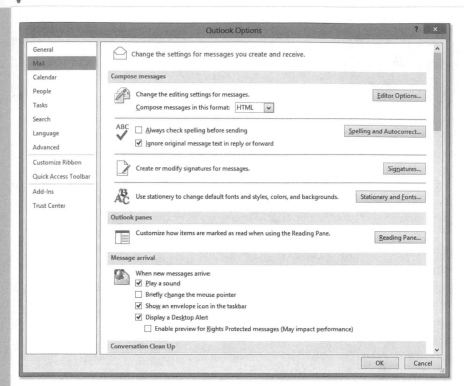

Figure 23.25
Outlook mail
Options.

■ **Message Arrival:** These options relate to what happens when a new message arrives in the Inbox folder. Options include playing a sound, changing the mouse pointer, and displaying an envelope icon in the taskbar. You can also enable an automatic preview for messages that have been assigned rights protection.

■ **Conversation Cleanup:** These options relate to how Outlook cleans up the Inbox folder when you select the Clean Up command. You can specify the folder that cleaned-up items move to, and you can specify that Outlook not move messages that meet certain criteria, such as unread, categorized, or flagged messages.

■ **Replies and Forwards:** These options include one for automatically closing the original message window when you reply to or forward the message. You can also specify whether the original message text is included in your replies or forwarded messages.

■ **Save Messages:** These options relate to saving drafts and whether Outlook saves forwarded messages in the Sent Items folder. You can set when a draft of a message should be saved, based on the minutes it has been opened and not yet sent. You can also determine whether forwarded messages should be saved if copies of sent messages are being placed in the Sent Items folder.

■ **Send Messages:** These options enable you to specify the default importance and sensitivity levels and to specify an expiration date for messages. Other settings include automatic name checking (of email addresses) and whether Outlook should delete meeting requests and notifications from your mailbox as you respond.

- **MailTips:** These options enable you to specify when MailTips display. You make settings in the MailTips options dialog box and can assign them to specific email accounts. MailTips options include options for special message circumstances, such as when the recipient address is not valid, when the message is too large to send, and when the recipient is external to your network (in the case of an Exchange Server environment). You might want to leave all these settings alone because these tips can help you avoid issues with messages, particularly those related to mail addressing.

- **Tracking:** These options enable you to require delivery and read receipts for all your messages, and always to send a read receipt when you receive a message with Read Receipt Required specified.

- **Message Format:** These options primarily relate to HTML emails. You can send HTML messages using cascading style sheets and reduce message size by removing formatting that is not essential to display the message properly.

- **Other:** These options include shading message headers when you are reading messages and specify whether Outlook shows the Paste Options button when you paste content into a message.

Two additional options are related to the Inbox and Deleted Items folders. When you select Advanced in the Outlook options window, look at the Outlook start and exit options. By default, Outlook starts with the Inbox folder selected. You can change this to one of the other Outlook folders, if you want, such as the Calendar or Contacts folders. However, because email seems important to everyone, why not leave it set to the Inbox folder? A check box related to the Deleted Items folder is also available in this set of options. If you want to empty your Deleted Items folder, select Empty Deleted Items Folders When Exiting Outlook. Then click OK to close the Outlook Options window.

USING THE CALENDAR FOR APPOINTMENTS AND TASKS

Staying organized can often seem like a futile endeavor. However, Outlook provides a pretty painless way for you to keep track of your busy life. Outlook's Calendar provides an effective yet easy-to-use environment for managing your schedule. In fact, Outlook can help you juggle multiple calendars so that you can easily track both your work and personal appointments and events. You can keep track of one-time appointments and events and also easily schedule recurring appointments and tasks.

The fact that Outlook can manage multiple calendars means that you can use it to manage your professional and personal calendar or manage calendars related to different projects. For example, you can have a calendar associated with each email account that you manage using Outlook; this includes Outlook.com (Hotmail) accounts. You can also create calendars that enable you to manage different types of events. For example, you can have a calendar for work-related events and a calendar for personal appointments and events. In this chapter, we look at navigating the calendar and working with multiple calendars, including shared calendars. We also look at working with appointments and tasks, and setting Calendar and tasks options.

Navigating the Calendar

To access the Outlook Calendar folder, select Calendar in the Navigation bar. By default, the Calendar is in Month view. The File pane shows the current and next month and also provides a list of all your calendars in the My Calendars list. The Details pane shows the current month, and the current day is highlighted. Figure 24.1 shows the default view for the Calendar.

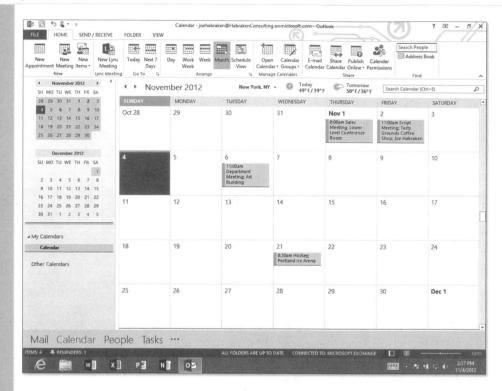

Figure 24.1
The Outlook
Calendar in
the Month
view.

Any appointments or other events that you have entered are now visible on the calendar. (Some events might have been assigned to you by other users, particularly if you share your calendar with other users.) Each event on the calendar provides you with the start time, the name of the event, and the location. If you place the mouse on a particular appointment or other event, a ScreenTip appears and provides the details for the appointment, including the start and end times, the location, the name of the meeting organizer (if it is someone other than you), and whether a reminder has been set for the event.

As already mentioned, a small version of the current month and the next month appears on the Folder Pane. This is referred to as the Date Navigator. The current date is highlighted on the Date Navigator. Any dates that have scheduled appointments or events are shown in bold.

If you select a date on the Date Navigator, the Calendar switches to Day view, which shows the currently selected day in detail. It lists the appointments and events that you have scheduled for the day. You can scroll through the hours of the day to view scheduled appointments, as needed. Figure 24.2 shows the Calendar's Day view.

When you view a date in Day view that does not contain any appointments, two navigation tools appear on the page for that day: Previous Appointment (on the left) and Next Appointment (on the right). You can click Previous Appointment to move backward through the calendar to the closest (to the current day) appointment. If you click Next Appointment, you move forward in the calendar to the next scheduled appointment or event. You can also navigate Day view using the Back and Forward buttons on the left corner of the Calendar.

Figure 24.2
The Outlook
Calendar in
Day view.

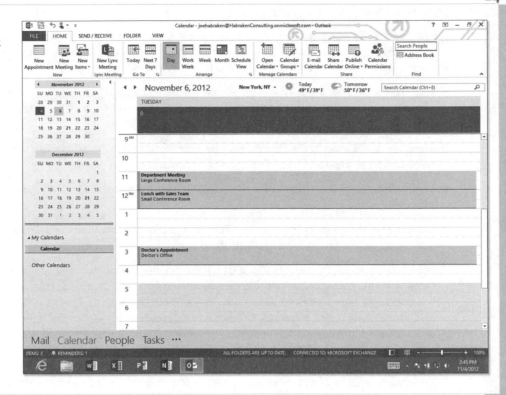

You have also probably noticed that the weather is provided for the current day and the next day (Today and Tomorrow) at the top of the Reading pane when you are working in any of the Calendar views. You can change the location for the streamed two-day weather by selecting the drop-down arrow next to the current city. Select Add Location and provide the city and state information. You can select any of the locations in the list as you require. If you want to remove a location from the list, place the mouse on the location and click the X.

 tip
To view more months in the Date Navigator, drag the border between the navigator and the calendar list downward in the Navigation pane to expand the navigator area. Do the opposite if you want to see fewer months.

 note
If you have multiple email accounts, such as a POP3 account and an Outlook.com account, multiple calendars appear in the My Calendars list and when in Month view (by default).

Changing the Calendar View

You can quickly change your view of the Calendar information by using the commands in the Arrange group. These commands are available on both the Ribbon's Home tab and the View tab when you are working with the Calendar. The Calendar views are as follows:

- **Day:** This shows the current day. You can use the Calendar Navigator to quickly change the current day shown in the Reading Pane. You can use the Back and Forward buttons to move back or forward in the calendar, day by day.

- **Work Week:** This shows the current work week of Monday through Friday. Select any date on the Calendar Navigator to view a different work week.

- **Week:** This shows the current week. Use the Calendar Navigator to specify a different week for this view.

- **Month:** This shows the current month. When you change the month in the Calendar Navigator, that particular month is shown in the Reading Pane.

- **Schedule View:** This view is designed for comparing multiple calendars. If you have multiple email accounts configured in Outlook, these accounts also have associated calendars. For example, you might have a work email account configured in Outlook and a personal account such as an Outlook.com account. Figure 24.3 shows two calendars in Schedule view, which enables you to compare multiple people's calendars in the same window and easily schedule meetings that include these individuals. Schedule view lists the time across the top of the calendar in a horizontal layout. The Calendars included are arranged vertically along the left side of the view. Use the Horizontal scrollbar along the bottom of the Reading Pane to scroll through the time scale.

When navigating within a particular calendar view, you can use the Back and Forward buttons at the top left of the Reading Pane to change to one of the other views, such as Work Week or Month. Select the appropriate command in the Arrange group.

The Calendar folder's Ribbon also provides a Go To group on the Home tab that can be useful for going to a particular day or range of days. To return to the current day (no matter which view you are currently using), select the Today command. If you want to view the next seven days, which uses a format similar to the Work Week and Week views, select the Next 7 Days command in the Go To group.

If you select the Dialog Box Launcher at the bottom right of the Go To group, the Go to Date dialog box opens. This dialog box enables you to specify both a date and a view. You can use the Date drop-down list to open a Calendar Navigator and then specify the date that you want to go to. You can then use the Show In drop-down list to specify the view that you want to use, such as Week Calendar, Month Calendar, and so on.

 tip

You can add other users' shared calendars (this is pretty typical in an Exchange Server environment) to your Outlook Calendar folder. Select the Add a Calendar button in the lower part of the Schedule view. Sharing calendars is discussed in more detail later in this chapter in the section, "Sharing a Calendar."

Figure 24.3
Schedule view makes it easy to compare multiple calendars.

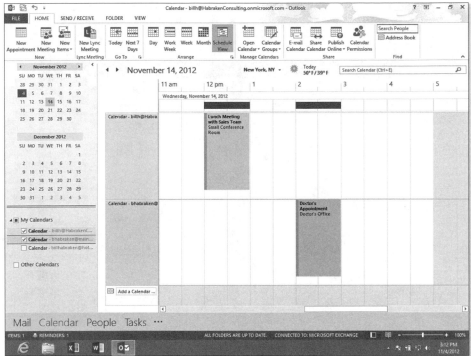

Change the Time Scale and Time Zone

When you are working in a particular view, you might want to change the time scale that is currently being used in that view. By default, the time scale is set to 30 minutes. You can change the time scale using the Time Scale command in the Arrangement group on the View tab (the Time Scale command is not available on the Home tab).

If you decrease the time scale, you have more space for viewing the details related to your various scheduled appointments and events. If you increase the time scale, you have less space to view the details related to your appointments but are able to condense the timeline for that particular view and see a greater range of time.

You can change the time scale in the following views: Day, Work Week, Week, and Schedule View. To change the time scale, select the Time Scale command and then select a different time scale interval, such as 60 minutes, 15 minutes, and so on.

You can also use the Time Scale command to change the current time zone. This is particularly useful when you are on the road and are operating in a different time zone. Changing the time zone ensures that any set appointment or task alarms are operating in the correct time zone. The default time zone set for Outlook is based on the time zone that you selected for your Windows installation. The time zone information is located in the Outlook options for the Calendar, which are typically accessed via the Options command in the Backstage.

PART

V

However, you can quickly access the Calendar options via the Time Scale command. To change the current time zone, select the Time Scale command and then select Change Time Zone. The Outlook Options window opens with the Calendar selected, as shown in Figure 24.4.

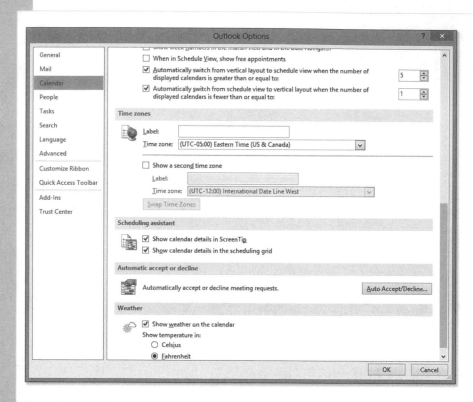

Figure 24.4
The Outlook Options window.

Select the Time Zone drop-down list and select a new time zone for Outlook. Then click OK. This closes the Outlook Options window and returns you to the calendar.

 note

You can add a second time zone to the Outlook calendar. Select the Show a Second Time Zone check box in the Time Zones pane of the Outlook Options window. You can then select the time zone using the Time Zone drop-down list. This can be useful if you work with people who are located in a different time zone.

Scheduling an Appointment

You can quickly create appointments in any Calendar view. You also have different options for creating appoints; two possibilities are using the New Appointment command on the Ribbon's Home tab and double-clicking on a specific day and time in the Reading Pane. Either option opens the Appointment dialog box, shown in Figure 24.5.

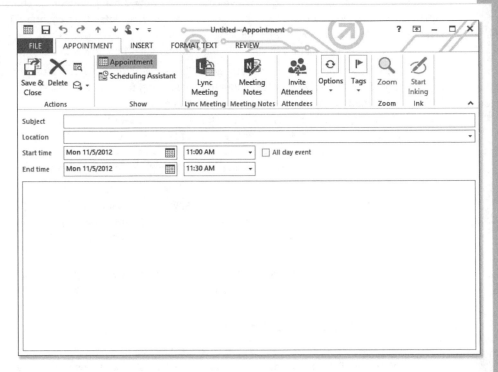

Figure 24.5
The Appointment dialog box.

Enter a subject for the appointment in the Subject box. You can also enter a location. Make sure the appropriate date and start time are entered in the Start Time box. You can use the Start Time drop-down box to access a Calendar Navigator and then specify the date for the appointment. You can also set the time. If you double-click on a particular time in the Calendar in the Reading Pane, the date should be correctly specified when the Appointment dialog box opens.

You might also want to adjust the End Time for the meeting. By default, Outlook schedules each appointment for one half-hour. Use the End Time box's time drop-down list to specify the end time for the appointment.

Each appointment has a body text area that enables you to add notes related to the appointment. You can also insert Business Cards, Outlook items, pictures, or other items related to the appointment using the various commands on the Insert tab. You can also attach files to an appointment, if needed.

If you want to specify a time zone for the start time or end time, which can be extremely useful if you are traveling between time zones, select the Time Zones command in the Options group (if you have reduced the size of the appointment window, you might not see the whole Ribbon; click Options and then Time Zones). This places Time Zone drop-down lists to the right of the Start Time and End Time boxes. You can select a time zone from the appropriate time zone drop-down list as you require.

When you create an appointment, you have control over how the appointment is shown on the calendar. Appointments are shown on the calendar as Busy, by default. To change this setting, select the Show As drop-down list in the Options group to select an option other than Busy for the appointment; other possibilities include Working Elsewhere, Tentative, and Out of Office.

You can also set a reminder for the appointment. Outlook automatically specifies a 15-minute reminder, by default. You can select the Reminder command to select from a list of different time increments (5 minutes, 10 minutes, 1 hour, 1 day, and so on). By default, a reminder sound is played when the Reminder box opens for the appointment. You can select the Sound command at the bottom of the Reminder list to open the Reminder Sound dialog box. Use the Browse button to locate a different sound file if you want to use a sound other than the default. If you do not want a sound to play when the reminder opens, deselect the Play This Sound check box in the Reminder Sound dialog box.

You can also tag an appointment with categories, specify importance levels, or mark the appointment as private using the commands available in the Tags group (on the Appointment tab). When you mark an appointment as private, the details of the appointment are not shown to other users with whom you have shared your calendar.

After you have specified the various parameters and options for your new appointment, select the Save & Close command on the Appointment tab. The appointment is added to the calendar.

Scheduling a Recurring Appointment

If you have a weekly, monthly, or otherwise consistently recurring appointment, you can quickly schedule it on your Outlook Calendar. The appointment must recur at a set time interval, such as weekly or monthly. To create a recurring appointment from the Calendar folder, select the New Items command on the Home tab, point at More Items, and then select Recurring Appointment. The Appointment Recurrence dialog box opens, as shown in Figure 24.6.

In the Appointment Time area, enter the Start and End times for the appointment. Outlook calculates the duration of the appointment for you. In the Recurrence Pattern area, indicate the frequency of the appointment: Daily, Weekly, Monthly, or Yearly. After you select the recurrence pattern, you are provided with options such as day of the week (for a weekly recurring appointment) or day of the month (for a monthly recurring appointment). Specify how often the appointment recurs and the time period (such as day of the week).

In the Range of Recurrence area, enter appropriate time limits using the following guidelines:

- **Start:** Select the date on which the recurring appointments begin.

- **No End Date:** Select this option if the recurring appointments are not on a limited schedule.

- **End After:** Select this option and enter the number of appointments if there is a specific limit to the recurring appointments.

- **End By:** Select this option and enter an ending date to limit the number of recurring appointments.

Figure 24.6
The Appointment Recurrence dialog box.

After you have set all the recurrence options for the appointment, select OK to close the Appointment Recurrence dialog box. This takes you to the Appointment dialog box for the recurring appointment. The start and stop options for the appointment have been replaced by recurrence information, which specifies when the appointment recurs, when it starts (an effective date), and the time for the recurring appointment.

Enter a subject for the appointment; you can also add a location and other information in the appointment body. In addition, you can specify the reminder settings for the appointment and tag the appointment as you would any other appointment. When you are ready to place the recurring appointment on the calendar, select Save & Close.

Scheduling an Event

An event is really just an appointment that lasts an entire day (24 hours or longer). You can use events to block out larger timeframes on your calendar than you would for a normal appointment. As with appointments, you can also schedule recurring events, such as a monthly seminar or some other event that lasts an entire day. To quickly create a new event, select a time slot in the Calendar (to specify the date for the event) and then select New Items and then All Day Event. The Event dialog box opens, as shown in Figure 24.7.

The Event dialog box is almost exactly the same as the Appointment dialog box, but the Start Time and End Time boxes are deactivated because the event lasts all day. You can edit the date for the Start Time and End Time (the same day), if required. Specify a subject for the event and an optional location. As with appointments, you can set reminder options for the event and assign tags to the event, such as categories and importance levels.

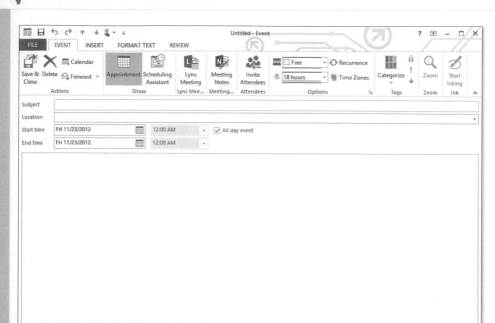

Figure 24.7
The Event
dialog box.

You can also make the event a recurring event. Select the Recurrence command in the Options group, and the Appointment Recurrence dialog box opens. Set the recurrence parameters, and click OK to close the dialog box and return to the event. When you are ready to add the event to the Calendar, select Save & Close.

When viewing your Calendar, you have probably noticed that appointments appear in the Calendar in their specific time slots. Events are listed just below the day designation in Calendar when you are using the Day, Work Week, or Week views. When you use Month view, you can tell events from appointments because events are shown in bold on the calendar day.

 tip

You can make any appointment (new or existing) a recurring appointment. Select the Recurrence command on the Appointment tab to open the Appointment Recurrence dialog box.

 tip

Any appointment can become an event. In the Appointment's dialog box, select the All Day Event check box.

Editing and Managing Appointments

You can edit appointments (or events) in the Calendar, as you require. Double-click on an appointment in the Calendar, and the appointment's dialog box opens. You can change the subject, location, date, and time for the appointment. You can also add information to the appointment body or change other settings related to the appointment using the various commands on the Ribbon. After making changes to an appointment, recurring appointment, or event, select the Save & Close command.

You can also manage appointments directly on the Calendar. To change the appointment subject, select the appointment on the Calendar and then click inside the subject text. You can edit the text as needed.

You can also move an appointment to a different time or day on the calendar; to change either of these appointment parameters, drag the appointment to a new location (in terms of date and time). If you want to change the time for the appointment by dragging, make sure that you are in the Day, Work Week, or Week view. You can also drag appointments to a different date in Month view, but you cannot change the time of the appointment. You can quickly edit the time, however, by double-clicking the appointment and then editing the time in the Appointment dialog box. You can view the time range for an appointment in any of the Calendar views; hover the mouse over the appointment.

When you do select an appointment in the Calendar, the Calendar Tools appear with the Appointment tab. Options such as the reminder settings and tags can be quickly selected for the appointment.

You can also delete unneeded appointments from the Calendar. Select the appointment and then press the Delete key. You can also delete a selected appointment or event from the Calendar using the Delete command in the Action group on the Ribbon. In either case, the appointment is removed from the Calendar.

Searching the Calendar

Outlook provides a robust and flexible Search tool that you can use to search your calendar or any shared calendars. The Search Calendar box is on the top right of your calendar (no matter what view you are using). When you click in the Search box, the Search Tools and Search tab appear on the Ribbon, as shown in Figure 24.8.

Figure 24.8
The Ribbon's
Search Tools.

One way to search the Calendar is to type keywords into the Search box. The appointments and events that match the search terms are displayed in the Reading Pane, sorted by date. Appointments are listed in a tabular format that provides field names such as Subject, Location, Start, and End as the field column headings. You can reorder the list of appointments found by clicking on any of the field headings. To clear the search, click the X to the right of the Search box.

As already mentioned, a number of commands are provided by the Search Tools, which are activated on the Ribbon as soon as you click in the Search box. You can use commands in the Refine group to conduct a new search or refine a search that was based on keywords. For example, you can view appointments that have file attachments by selecting the Has Attachments command. If you have categorized appointments or events, you can use the Categorized command to select a specific category; then only messages that have been assigned that category will appear in the search results.

To access additional properties for your search criteria, you can select the More command. This gives you a list of Common Properties, such as Attachments, Categories, Importance, and Recurring (select Recurring and then Yes in the Recurring box to quickly find recurring appointments). It also enables you to specify more exacting parameters for your search. For example, you can select Body in the Common Properties list, and a Body box appears below the Search box. You can type text in the Body box (yes, that sounds scary), and the search lists appointments that have the search text in their appointment bodies.

You can also use the Common Properties to search for appointments that have a particular start or end time, using the Start and End properties, respectively. For example, if you select Start, the Start box appears below the Search box. Click the Start box to select Start criteria such as Today, Tomorrow, Next Week, and so on. When you have finished working with the Search feature, you can quickly return to the Calendar by selecting the Close Search command.

➡ *For an overview of the Outlook Search feature,* **see** *"Searching for Outlook Items,"* **p. 661.**

Sharing Calendars

Outlook gives you different options for sharing your calendar information with coworkers, colleagues, friends, and family. One of the easiest ways to share Calendar information such as an appointment is to use the Forward command on the Appointment tab to quickly send an open appointment to a coworker or colleague. Other options for sharing your calendar depend on whether you use Outlook as an Exchange Server client. The Exchange environment enables you to share your calendar and also allows others to share their calendars with you. Exchange environments have typically been restricted to bigger companies and institutions; however, Office 365 subscriptions for small business combine the power of Exchange with Outlook at the smallest businesses. Other possibilities for sharing your Outlook calendar include the capability to email calendar information and to publish your calendar online.

Sharing Your Calendar

If you are using Outlook as an Exchange Server client, your calendar is stored on the Exchange server, making it easy to share your calendar with other users on the Exchange network.

To share your calendar, select the Share Calendar command on the Home tab. A Sharing invitation opens, as shown in Figure 24.9. To address the Sharing invitation, select the To button (or select the Address Book command on the Ribbon). The Global Address List opens in the Address Book dialog box. Add a recipient or recipients from the list; select a recipient or recipients, and then click the To button. You can also add recipients from your Contacts list if the recipient is an Exchange Server client.

Figure 24.9
A sharing invitation for your Calendar.

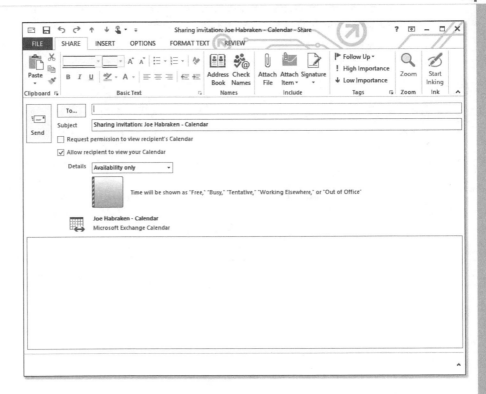

Figure 24.9
A sharing invitation for your Calendar.

The invitation also provides several settings. By default, the Allow Recipient to View Your Calendar check box is selected. If you want to be able to view the calendar of the invitation recipient, select the Request Permission to View Recipient's Calendar check box.

You can control the amount of detail shown when the recipient views your calendar. Select the Details drop-down list; the default setting is Availability Only, but you can also select Limited Details and Full Details. Obviously, Full Details shares all the information on the Calendar, including appointment body notes. After you have addressed the Sharing invitation and set the other options, select Send. The invitation is sent to the recipient or recipients.

 note

Calendars can also be shared by users on a Microsoft SharePoint Server.

 note

If you are using Outlook for Internet-only email (POP or IMAP), the Share Calendar and Calendar Permissions commands in the Share group are grayed out because they are unavailable.

Opening a Shared Calendar

If coworkers or colleagues share a Calendar with you, you receive a Sharing invitation email, as shown in Figure 24.10. To add the Calendar to your Calendar list, select the Open This Calendar command on the Share tab. The Calendar is added to the Shared Calendars group in the Navigation pane. The level of detail that you can view in the Calendar depends on the detail setting that was selected by the user who is sharing the calendar. You can view the shared Calendar as you would your own calendar using the various Arrange and View commands provided on the Ribbon.

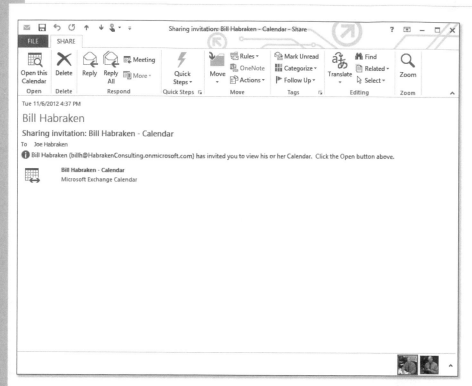

Figure 24.10
A received Sharing invitation.

Viewing Multiple Calendars

Multiple calendars can be opened in the Reading Pane. Select the check box for each calendar that you want to view (in the Folder Pane). Each calendar you have opened resides in its own pane in the Reading Pane. When you are working with multiple and shared calendars, Outlook gives you two useful tools that enable you to compare your appointments and events with another user's Calendar (or users' calendars). These two tools are the overlay feature and Calendar groups (although the Schedule View that we discussed earlier in the chapter is also useful when viewing and comparing multiple calendars).

The overlay feature enables you to superimpose calendars. This can be useful if you want to take a quick look at multiple calendars to check for overlapping or conflicting appointments. To overlay multiple calendars, select the calendar in the Folder Pane. On the Ribbon's View tab, select the Overlay command. The calendar is superimposed, as shown in Figure 24.11.

The calendar in the front of the overlay displays its appointments in bold. You can click the tab for a calendar to bring it to the forefront. If you want to close a calendar, select the Close Calendar button (X) on the calendar.

Figure 24.11
Calendars in
Overlay view.

If you view multiple Exchange (or SharePoint) calendars in Outlook often, you might want to create calendar groups. A calendar group is a listing of multiple calendars. You can quickly open the calendars in a group by selecting that group (instead of the individual calendars).

The easiest way to create a new calendar group is to first open the calendars you want to include in the group in the Reading Pane; then select each calendar in the Folder Pane. On the Home tab, select Calendar Groups and select Save As New Calendar Group. The Create New Calendar Group dialog box opens. Provide a name for the new group, and click OK. In the future, you can quickly open all the calendars in the group by selecting the group in the Folder Pane (the group appears as another category of calendar in the Folder Pane with My Calendars and Shared Calendars).

Emailing a Calendar

Even if you don't have the calendar-sharing capabilities provided by Exchange Server, you can email content from your Calendar to others. The Email Calendar command is in the Share group on the Ribbon's Home tab (when you are in the Calendar folder).

With your Calendar open in the Reading Pane, select the Email Calendar command. The Send a Calendar via Email dialog box opens, as shown in Figure 24.12.

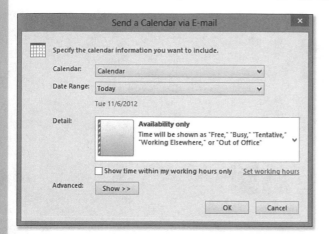

Figure 24.12
The Send a Calendar via Email dialog box.

In the Date Range drop-down list, select the calendar range that you want to include in the email message. You choose details such as Today, Tomorrow, and Whole Calendar. You can also specify a range of dates.

Use the Detail drop-down list to specify the level of detail that you want to provide in the Calendar information: Availability Only, Limited Details, or Full Details. You can also choose to show only time within your working hours by selecting Show Time Within My Working Hours Only. Click the Show button to set advanced parameters related to the Calendar, such as the layout in the email: Daily Schedule or List of Events.

After you have specified the settings for the email calendar, select OK. The Calendar information is embedded in the email message and also attached to the email as an .ics calendar file. Click Send to send the Calendar information to the recipient or recipients.

 note

You can also publish calendars to custom servers (other than Office.com). For example, you can publish calendars to SharePoint servers.

 note

You can set permissions for calendars shared on an Exchange network. Use the Calendar Properties dialog box to set permissions for your shared calendar.

Publishing a Calendar Online

Another way to share a calendar is to publish the calendar online. Whether you can take advantage of this feature depends on the type of computing environment you work in when using Outlook. For example, if you work on a corporate network that provides Exchange email and a SharePoint server or other WebDAV (Web Distributed Authoring and Versioning) server, you will be able to publish a calendar online. If you subscribe to Office 365, you can publish your calendar to Outlook.com, which is the Outlook web client for Outlook users with access to Exchange server email accounts (meaning your calendar is published online). If you are using Outlook for Internet email only, your options are fairly limited; you need to come up with a WebDAV server to which you can upload the calendar (Outlook 2010 took advantage of the Office.com WebDAV server, but this isn't available in Outlook

2013); you can set up an account on a free WebDAV server such as mydisk.com and then publish the calendar to that site (although this might require more work than sharing the calendar through other means, such as email).

Publishing your calendar online is a two-part process. You publish the calendar to a specific server (such as Outlook.com or a WebDAV or SharePoint server provided by your company), and then you invite users to subscribe to the calendar. Let's take a closer look at the process by publishing a calendar to Office 365 (meaning that you are taking advantage of an email address that is provided because you have an Office 365 subscription).

On the Ribbon's Home tab (with the calendar that you want to publish open), select Publish Online, and then select Publish This Calendar. A Calendar Publishing web page opens, as shown in Figure 24.13. Set the level of detail you want to provide to coworkers or colleagues who have access to your published calendar. Select the Publishing details: drop-down list; you can select from the following options:

- **Availability Only:** This option shows availability as Free, Busy, Tentative, or Away with no other details.

Figure 24.13
Publish the Calendar online.

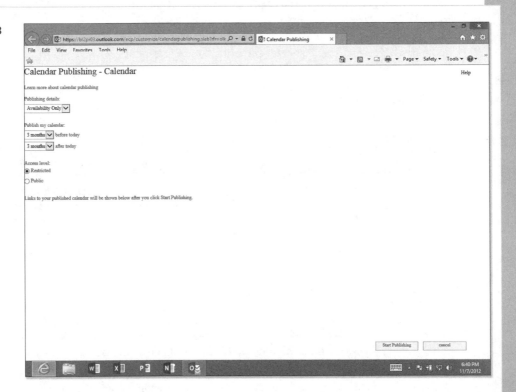

- **Limited Details:** This option shows availability as Free, Busy, Tentative, or Away and includes meeting subject lines.

- **Fill Details:** This option shows all event details.

After selecting the level of publishing details for the calendar, use the Publish My Calendar drop-down lists to set the date range for the calendar. The default settings are 3 months before today and 3 months after today. You can set the date range increments from 1 day to 1 year.

You can also set the access level for the calendar. By default, access is set to Restricted. This means that only invited users can subscribe to the calendar. If you want to allow anyone to subscribe to the calendar, select the Public option button. To publish the calendar, select the Start Publishing button.

After you publish the calendar, two web links are provided on the Calendar Publishing page. One link is for users to subscribe to the calendar, and the other is for a link that allows a user to view the calendar in a web browser.

You can copy the web links provided to the Windows Clipboard by selecting the Copy links to the Clipboard. You can then paste the links into a Word document or an Outlook note—anywhere that is convenient. Then all you have to do is email the link (copy and paste the link into the email) for subscribing to the calendar to your colleagues or coworkers who need access to the calendar. You can also email the link for viewing the calendar in a web browser, as needed. The whole point of publishing the calendar to the Web is to make it easy for people to view your availability (or lack of availability) within the calendar time frame you have published.

When the calendar subscription link is activated (by clicking) by a recipient of your email invitation, the View Downloads window opens. To view the calendar, the recipient simply needs to select Open. A message box then asks how the file opens. The Outlook (desktop) icon is selected, and the calendar is opened in the Outlook Calendar folder.

 note

Web Distributed Authoring and Versioning (WebDAV) is an extension of the HTML tag language used to build web sites. WebDAV's purpose is to provide a collaborative environment for users who want to share files (such as a published Outlook calendar). Some free WebDAV servers are available on the Web: these include mydisk.com. If you have your own server (and the inclination and time), you can also set up your own WebDAV server using different web server software platforms, such as the Apache web server and Microsoft's Internet Information Server (IIS).

Setting Calendar Options

The Calendar options can be accessed via the Outlook Options window. Select File to access the Backstage, and then select Options. The Outlook Options window opens. Select Calendar in the options list to access the Calendar options. Figure 24.14 shows the Outlook Options window with Calendar selected.

The Calendar options enable you to set your work time, reminder defaults, and other options, such as the current time zone. The Calendar options categories are as follows:

- **Work Time:** These options enable you to set the start and end time for your work hours, as well as specify the days in your work week. You can also set the first day of the week and the first week of the year.

Figure 24.14
The Calendar
options.

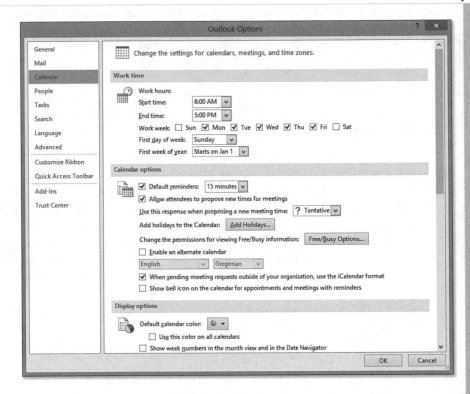

■ **Calendar Options:** These options include the default reminder time and settings related to meetings, such as allowing attendees to propose new times for meetings. You can also add holidays to the calendar, set permissions for the viewing of Free/Busy times, and enable an alternative calendar (useful if you keep separate work and personal calendars).

■ **Display Options:** These options enable you to control the default calendar color and also specify the Date Navigator prompt. Other settings include switching from vertical layout to schedule view based on the number of opened calendars.

■ **Time Zones:** These options enable you to set and label (give it a descriptive name) the current time zone. Options are also available for showing a second time zone.

■ **Scheduling Assistant:** These options enable you to show calendar details in a ScreenTip when using the Scheduling assistant and also specify whether calendar details are shown in the scheduling grid.

■ **Automatic Accept or Decline:** This feature enables you to configure the calendar so that meetings are automatically accepted or declined (declined based on time conflicts), and canceled meetings are automatically removed from the calendar. Meetings are discussed in Chapter 25.

➡ *Meetings are discussed in Chapter 25, "Working with Contacts and Planning Meetings."*

- **Weather:** The Weather bar, which shows at the top of the calendar, by default, can be "turned off" by deselecting the Show weather on the calendar option. You can also choose to show the temperature in either Celsius or Fahrenheit (the default in the United States).

When you have finished setting the various Calendar options, select OK to close the Outlook Options window and return to Outlook.

Working with Tasks

All of us keep a list of tasks. The "to-do" list might be scribbled on scraps of paper or on a paper calendar, but we all have tasks that we have to manage and complete pretty much daily. Outlook makes it easy for you to create and manage tasks. You can include a reminder when you create a task, and you can assign tasks to coworkers and colleagues (and you can be assigned tasks as well).

When you open Outlook, the default view (if you haven't changed it) is the Mail folder; this view includes (again, by default) the Folder list, the Details pane (showing your email in the Inbox), the Reading pane, and the People pane. An easy way to include tasks in this view is to add the To-Do Bar to the Outlook window. There are even options related to what information the To-Do Bar provides.

Select the Ribbon's View tab. The To-Do Bar command is in the Layout group. Select the command, and then select the options that you want to appear in the To-Do Bar: Calendar, People, and/or Tasks. Because we are talking about working with tasks in the To-Do Bar, I recommend that you add at least the Calendar and Tasks to your To-Do Bar.

You can quickly create a task using the To-Do Bar. One option is to click in the Type a New Task box in the bottom pane of the To-Do Bar and then enter a subject for the task. When you press Enter, the task is added to the Task list in the To-Do Bar. Creating a task in this way doesn't open the new Task dialog box, which provides you with access to all the fields for a task (such as Start Date, Due Date, and Status). So another way to create a new task via the To-Do Bar is to double-click in the Task list at the bottom of the To-Do Bar; the new Task dialog box then opens, as shown in Figure 24.15.

Follow these steps to create the new task:

1. Enter the subject of the task into the Subject box.

2. Enter a date on which the task should be complete, or click the Due Date list arrow to open the Date Navigator and then choose a due date.

3. Enter a start date, or use the Date Navigator to select a start date.

4. From the Status drop-down list, choose the current status of the project: Not Started, In Progress, Completed, Waiting on Someone Else, or Deferred.

5. Enter any comments, descriptions, or other information related to the task in the body of the task.

Figure 24.15
The new Task
dialog box.

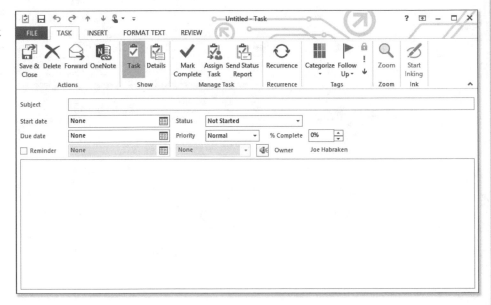

You can use the Task tab of the Ribbon to set other attributes related to the task (in much the same way that you assign options to an appointment). You can use the Categorize command to assign a category or categories to the task. You can also tag the task with a flag using the Follow Up command. If the task is private, high importance, or low importance, use the appropriate command in the Tabs group to set options for the task. When you are ready to place the task on the Task list, click Save & Close. The task is listed in the Task list on the To Do Bar.

Using the Task Folder

You can also create, view, and manage tasks from the Task folder. Select Tasks in the Navigation bar. Your list of tasks (grouped by date ranges such as Today, Next Week, and so on) are listed in the Details Pane in a To-Do list. Select a task to view its details in the Reading Pane. When you use the Task folder, to manage your tasks, you can work with the To-Do list (as shown in Figure 24.16); alternatively, you can select Tasks in the Folder Pane, and your tasks are then listed in a columnar format, with the different fields (such as Subject, Due Date, and Categories) as the column headings.

 tip
If you want to add the Calendar (or Date Navigator, as it also is referred to) to the Tasks folder, select the View menu, click on the To-Do Bar, and select Calendar.

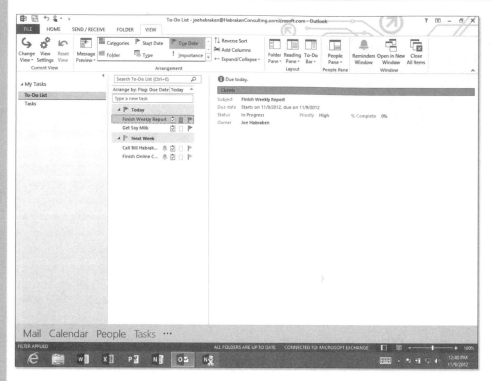

Figure 24.16
The Task folder.

Creating a New Task from the Task Folder

You can also create tasks when you are working in the Task folder. One option is to select the New Task command on the Ribbon's Home tab. This opens the untitled (meaning new) Task dialog box. All you have to do is enter the necessary information for the task and then click the Save & Close command. You can also open the new Task dialog box by double-clicking in the empty part of the To-Do list or below your listed tasks when you have Tasks (instead of the To-Do List) selected in the Folder Pane.

Another possibility for quickly adding a task without entering all the details for that task (we talk about editing a task a little later in the chapter) is to click on the Type a New Task box at the top of the To-Do list and then enter a subject for the task. Press Enter, and the task is added to the Today group tasks.

Creating a Recurring Task

You can create recurring tasks. For example, you might have to provide a weekly report each Friday, so it makes sense to schedule a recurring task that reminds you to get that weekly job done. Recurring tasks can easily be created to recur daily, weekly, monthly, or yearly.

You can create a recurring task from an existing task or by creating a new recurring task. Just open an existing task or create a new task. If you aren't in the Tasks folder (you can create a task or recurring task from any Outlook folder), select the New Items command on the Home tab and then select Task. A new Task dialog box opens. Type a subject for the task; then select the Recurrence command on the task's Ribbon. The Task Recurrence dialog box opens, as shown in Figure 24.17.

Figure 24.17
The Task Recurrence dialog box.

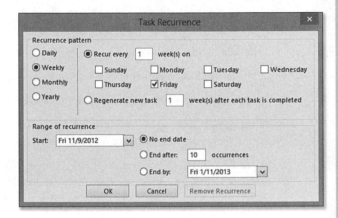

In the Task Recurrence dialog box, set the Recurrence pattern by selecting Daily, Weekly, and so on, and then specify the Recur Every increment (such as 1 week or 2 weeks). Also specify the day that the recurring task recurs using the day check boxes (Sunday through Saturday). You can specify when a new task should be regenerated as the previous recurring task was completed.

In the Range of Recurrence area of the Task Recurrence dialog box, specify the start date for the task. You can then specify the end date for the task using the following options:

- **No End Date:** No end date is specified for the recurring task.

- **End After:** Specify the number of occurrences that should take place before the recurring task is ended.

- **End By:** Specify an end date for the recurring task.

When you have finished setting the options for the recurring task, select OK to return to the Task dialog box. The recurrence information for the task (and the next due date) appears above the subject of the task. You can assign policies (on an Exchange Server network), categories, and other tags, such as follow-up flags, to the recurring task, as needed. When you have finished setting the options for the task, select Save & Close.

Assigning and Accepting Tasks

There is probably no greater joy in the workplace than being able to pass off a task to a coworker or colleague. You can assign tasks to other people, such as coworkers or subordinates. Be advised that your co-workers (and even your subordinates) can also assign you an Outlook task or tasks. Everyone using Outlook has the power to create a task and then assign it to another user. Assigned tasks (meaning tasks you assign to others) appear in your Task list and on the To-Do Bar (if you have it open in other folder views, such as Mail). An assigned task also appears on the To-Do list of the person to whom you assigned the task.

To assign a task to a coworker or colleague, follow these steps:

1. Select the New Task command (from the Tasks folder), or double-click on the To-Do list or the To-Do Bar (or use the New Items command, if you are in a folder other than the Tasks folder). A new Task dialog box opens.

2. Enter the subject and other details for the task.

3. Set options for the task using the appropriate commands on the Ribbon.

4. Select Assign Task. A To: box (just like the To: box that appears on a new email) appears above the Subject box so that you can address the task.

5. Select To or Address Book on the Ribbon to open the Address Book. You can use the Global Address List on an Exchange Server network to add the recipient or recipients of the assigned task, or you can switch to your Contacts list and select the names as needed. Click OK to close the Address Book.

6. When you are ready to assign the task, select Save & Close.

The task can now be managed by the assignee of the task (although you can view it). By default, you receive a status report (via email) when the task is complete. Also by default, an updated copy of this task is kept on your task list so that you can view any changes that have been made to the task, such as whether the task has been started and the percent of the task that has been completed.

Paybacks can be nasty, and in the case of tasks, there is no doubt that those who give shall also receive. When a coworker or manager assigns you a task, the assigned task is sent as a mail message. Double-click the message to open the task. The Respond group on the Ribbon provides the necessary commands for you to respond to the assigned task including Accept and Decline. Select the Accept command to accept the task. If you select Accept, the Accepting Task message box opens. This dialog box enables you to immediately send a response that you are accepting the task. It also gives you the option of editing the Accept response before it is sent. Select OK in the Accepting Task message box and the task will be added to your Task list.

If you want to decline the task, select Decline. The Declining Task dialog box opens. When you decline a task, a message is sent to the originator of the task, and the task is moved to your Deleted Items folder. You also have the option of editing your response (that you are declining the task) before sending it.

 note

You can reply to a task "invitation" before accepting it. Use the Reply command in the Respond group. This enables you to get more information on a task before you decide to "own" it.

Viewing and Managing Tasks

Outlook provides you with different options for viewing your tasks. As mentioned earlier, when you work in the Tasks folder, you can view the tasks in a To-Do list or in a columnar format (by selecting Tasks in the Folder Pane). Outlook provides you with commands that enable you to further manipulate the view of your Tasks folder. The Arrangement group on the View tab provides commands that enable you to arrange the Task list by categories, start date, due date, and importance. The Reverse Sort command can be used to quickly reverse the sort order of the To-Do list.

The Ribbon (when you are in the Tasks folder) provides other commands for managing your tasks. These commands include Delete, Mark Complete, and various commands in the Follow Up, Actions, and Tags groups.

Viewing the Tasks List

When you select Tasks in the Folder Pane, your tasks are listed in a tabular format; this view includes field columns for Subject, Due Date, and Categories. The tasks are listed by due date in ascending order. You can use a column heading to quickly sort the list by subject or category and change whether the tasks are listed in ascending or descending order by that field. In this default Simple List view of the Task list, you are provided basic information for each task, and each task has a check box that makes it easy to select a task or tasks.

You can change the Simple List view of the Tasks list to a different view using the Change View group commands on the Ribbon. Figure 24.18 shows the different views available in the Current View gallery.

Figure 24.18
The Change View gallery.

Each view provides a different tabular view of the tasks, including different fields. The different views available on the Current View gallery are as follows:

- **Detailed:** Displays the subject, status, date modified, and date completed, in the folder and categories.

- **Simple List:** Shows the subject, due date, and categories.

- **To Do List:** Changes to To-Do List view (which can also be accessed via the Navigation pane).

- **Prioritized:** Groups the tasks by priority.

- **Active:** Shows the active tasks, including the status, due date, percent complete, and categories.

- **Completed:** Filters the list to show completed tasks only.

- **Today:** Lists the tasks with "today" as the due date.

- **Next 7 Days:** Lists the tasks with a due date that falls in the next seven days, and includes the status, percent complete, and categories.

- **Overdue:** Filters the task list and lists overdue tasks only.

- **Assigned:** Filters the task list to show tasks that others have assigned to you.

- **Server Tasks:** Lists tasks stored on the Exchange server (which is all tasks that you have created and been assigned from other users on the Exchange server network). This view is not available when you use Outlook as an Internet email client only.

You can add columns to any of the tabular views provided in the Change View gallery, as you require. Select the Ribbon's View tab and then select Add Columns. The Show Columns dialog box opens, as shown in Figure 24.19.

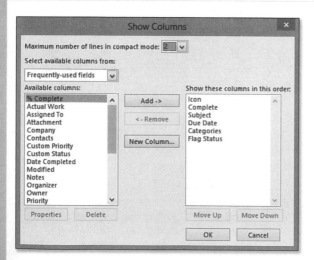

Figure 24.19
The Show Columns dialog box.

Select a column in the Available Columns list, and then click the Add button to add the column to the current view. By default, frequently used fields are shown in the list, but you can use the drop-down list to select other field categories, such as Info/Status fields, Date/Time fields, or All Task Fields.

When you click OK, the Show Columns dialog box closes and you return to the Tasks list. The column or columns that you added using the Show Columns dialog box appear in your current view of the tasks.

If you want to return a particular view to its default, you can reset any view that you have modified using the Show Columns dialog box. On the View tab, select the Reset View command. A message box opens. Select Yes to reset the current view.

 tip

When you view other items, such as emails or contacts, in a tabular view, you can use the Add Columns command to add columns as required.

Editing Tasks

You can edit any task in the Tasks list or the To-Do list. Double-click on the task, and the task's dialog box opens. You can edit any of the fields related to the task, and you can also tag the task with categories, follow-up flags, and level of importance.

When you want to add information to a task, particularly information related to the number of hours required to complete the task or other information, such as mileage or the company you did the work for, select the Details command on the Task tab. Fields are provided for total work, actual work, mileage, and billing information. Enter the information as needed, and be sure to select Save & Close when you finish editing the task's details.

In the case of tasks that you have assigned to others, you can rescind the task. Open the task first; then on the Task tab of the Ribbon, select Cancel Assignment. The name of the assignee or assignees is removed from the task. The task still exists; however, it is now your task and is no longer assigned to a coworker or subordinate. To save changes that you have made to a task in the task's dialog box, select Save & Close.

You can generate a status report for your tasks and then send the report to a coworker or colleague. This is particularly useful when you are working with a task that has been assigned to you, and you want to provide an update to the assigner of the task. In the task's dialog box, select the Send Status Report command (on the Task tab). A new email message appears, including the status of the task in the body of the message. Address the message to the appropriate recipient or recipients, and then click the Send button to send the status report.

 note

By default, assigned tasks generate a status report when they are completed. The report is forwarded to the assignor of the task.

Managing Tasks

Outlook also provides tools for managing your tasks. When you select the check box for a particular task, that task is marked as complete. You can also mark a selected task or tasks using the Mark Complete command on the Home tab. If you want to remove a task or tasks from the list, select the Remove from List command.

You can also mark tasks for follow-up using the various flags provided in the Follow Up group. For example, if you wanted to follow up on a particular task in your task list tomorrow, you could mark it with the Tomorrow follow-up flag.

In some situations, you might want to move tasks from the Tasks folder to an Outlook folder that you have created. For example, you might want to keep tasks that you consider personal (perhaps you have even categorized them as personal) in a "personal" folder. You can create your own folders within any of the default Outlook folders. For example, you can create a new subfolder in your Tasks folder. You can create the folder using the New Folder command on the Folder tab, or you can create the folder during the process of actually moving the tasks (or any Outlook item) to their new home.

To move specific tasks, select those tasks in the task list; then select the Move command on the Ribbon's Home tab. Select Other Folder to open the Move Items dialog box, which lists the default Outlook folders, such as Calendar or Inbox, and any folders that you have created. You can use the New button to create a new folder, if necessary. To move tasks from your Tasks folder to another folder, select the folder in the Move Items dialog box and then click OK. The dialog box closes, and the task or tasks are moved to the folder that you selected.

 tip

You share your tasks with other users (just as you can share your calendar). If you work in a network environment that provides Exchange or SharePoint, you can share tasks using the Share Tasks command on the Ribbon's Folder tab. You can also open tasks that others have shared with you using the Open Shared Tasks command.

Setting Tasks Options

The Tasks options settings can be accessed in the Outlook Options window. Select File to open the Outlook Backstage, and then click Options to open the Outlook Options window.

When you select Tasks in the Outlook Options window, a limited number of options specifically relate to tasks. In fact, there are only two groups of options: Task options and Work Hours. Figure 24.20 shows the Task options.

The Task options include settings related to task reminders, reports, and task flags. You can choose to have reminders set for all tasks with due dates and set a default reminder time. In relation to tasks that you assign to other people or that are assigned to you, you can choose to keep updated copies of tasks that you assign in your Tasks list and also have a status report sent automatically when you complete an assigned task. Both of these settings are enabled by default.

You also have control over the color of overdue and completed tasks. Select the Overdue task color or the Completed task color to change the default color for either of these task types. You can also set a Quick Click flag for flagging tasks with a particular flag type. This feature enables you to add a flag to a task in the Task list with a single click. To specify the flag type for the Quick Click feature, select Quick Click and then use the Set Quick Click dialog box to choose the flag type, such as Today, Tomorrow, or Complete.

The other options group for Tasks is the Work Hours group. There are two possible settings: Task Working Hours Per Day and Task Working Hours Per Week. The default settings for these two options are 8 hours per day and 40 hours per week. You can use the spinner boxes for either of these settings to change the defaults, if required.

Figure 24.20
The option settings
for Outlook tasks.

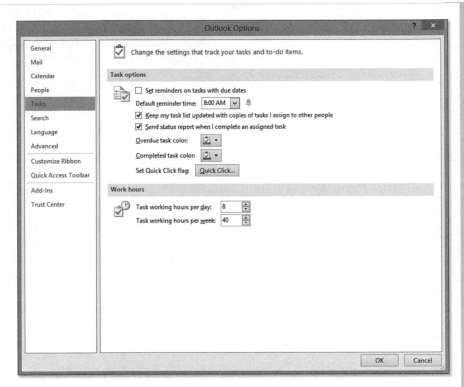

tip
You can copy tasks from your Tasks list to another folder using the Copy to Folder option on the Move command's menu.

WORKING WITH CONTACTS AND PLANNING MEETINGS

Although Outlook is primarily seen as an email application, it is also a powerful contact-management tool that enables you to easily communicate with your coworkers, clients, and friends. Outlook also enables you to access contact information in a variety of lists, including your Contacts list, Exchange global address lists, and social media web sites such as LinkedIn and Facebook. Outlook doesn't just provide access to contact information; it also provides you with tools for better communicating with these contacts. For example, you can quickly send a group email to your customers or schedule a meeting with your coworkers.

In this chapter, we take a look at the possibilities for creating and managing contact data in Outlook and explore how the Contacts folder's data becomes a key part of using Outlook to communicate with others. We look at how you can access contact information on social media websites such as Facebook. Outlook also provides a number of tools related to scheduling meetings with your contacts, and we examine how meetings are scheduled and managed.

Navigating the Contacts List

The Outlook Contacts folder is accessed via the Navigation bar. Select People, and the Contacts folder opens in the Outlook window, as shown in Figure 25.1. Contacts are selected in the Folder Pane. If you are also connected to a social network, the site is listed below the Contacts folder; for example, if you are connected to LinkedIn, LinkedIn appears as a folder choice in the Folder Pane (we talk more about social media websites and Outlook contacts later in the chapter in the section "Accessing Contacts on Social Networks").

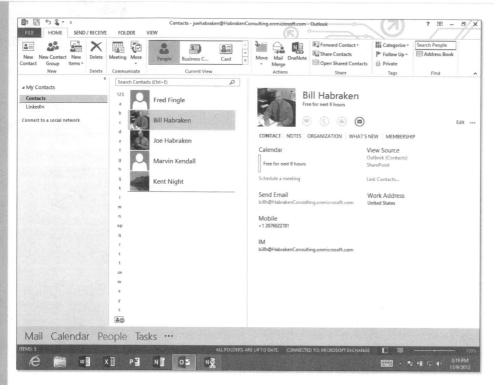

Figure 25.1
The Outlook
Contacts
folder.

The default view for the Contacts folder is People view. The contact list is provided in the Details pane. Information for the currently selected contact is provided in the Reading Pane. You can quickly change the view using the commands in the Current View group on the Ribbon's Home tab. These views are as follows:

- **People:** The default view for the Outlook People folder (Contacts) provides a photo (if available) and the name of the contact. When the contact is selected in the Details pane (Contacts list), additional information (in a tabbed format) is provided for the contact in the Reading/Preview pane, such as the email address, mobile phone number, and instant messaging address. If you are using Outlook in an Exchange Server or SharePoint server environment, you can also see whether the contact is currently available.

- **Business Card:** This view provides the name, phone number, title, company, and address of the contact, and can include a photo of the contact. This is the default Contact view.

- **Card:** This view provides more detail than Business Card view and includes more field information, including assigned categories and notes. This view does not show photos of contacts (when you have inserted a digital photo of the contact in the Contact information).

- **Phone:** This view provides a tabular view of your contacts and includes filed columns for the business phone, business fax, home phone, and mobile phone. It is extremely useful for making phone calls to your contacts.

- **List:** This view provides a tabular format for the contacts and includes a number of field columns for Full Name, Job Title, Company, Department, and Business Phone.

You can further manipulate the view (whatever view you have selected in the Current View gallery) using the commands provided on the Ribbon's View tab (see Figure 25.2). The amount of fine-tuning you can do to the Contacts list depends on the view you have selected. For example, if you have List selected as the current view, you can use the commands in the Arrangement group to sort contacts based on a common element. For example, if you want to group your Contact list by company, select Company.

Figure 25.2
The Contacts folder's View tab, including the Arrangement group.

The Arrangement group commands include grouping commands such as Company, Categories, and Location, and commands also are available for reversing the current sort direction and adding columns to the current view. The Arrangement commands, such as Company and Location, are not available when you are using the People, Business Card, or Card views. When you do group your Contact list by Categories or Company, make sure that Show in Groups is selected in the Arrangement gallery. This lists categories or company names and then lists contacts in the appropriate group.

The Reverse Sort command works no matter what view you are currently using. When you are in a tabular view, such as the List or Phone views, you can also use the field column headings (such as Full Name or Department) to sort the list by that particular field.

If you want to change the view when you have the Ribbon's View tab selected, use the Change View command in the Current View group. If you modify a particular view and want to reset it, select the Reset View command. A message box opens and asks you to verify the reset of the view; select Yes.

Creating a New Contact

You can create a new contact in Outlook either from scratch or based on another item, such as an email. To create a new contact from scratch, you can use the New Contact command on the Home tab of the Contacts folder's Ribbon, or you can create a new contact from any of the Outlook folders using the New Items command (and then selecting Contact).

As already mentioned, you can also add a contact to the Contacts folder based on information found in another Outlook item. For example, you can right-click on an email address in the From, Cc, or Bcc of a received message and then select Add to Outlook Contacts; this opens a new Contact dialog box, and the name and email information is automatically entered for the contact. All you have to do is supply the other information you want to enter.

Contacts don't always have to be entered (by you typing the information) in your Contacts folder; they can be found in global address lists or shared by other users when you use Outlook as an Exchange Server client. We discuss the sharing of contacts with others later in this chapter.

Let's take a look at creating a new contact from scratch. In the Contacts folder, select New Contact on the Home tab. A new Contact dialog box opens, as shown in Figure 25.3.

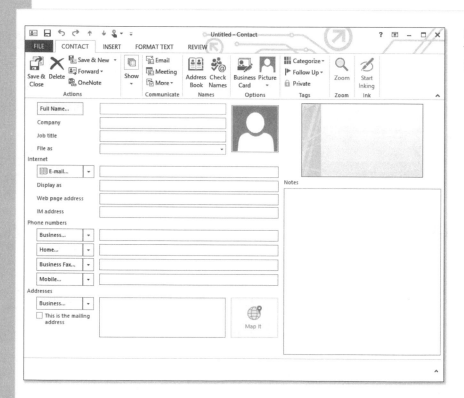

Figure 25.3
The new Contact dialog box.

A wide variety of information can be added for the contact. You don't have to use all the fields provided in the dialog box, but it does make sense to enter the information that is useful to you in terms of communicating with the contact. To make the Contacts folder more than just a glorified email address list, I recommend entering the following field information:

- Name

- Company

- Job title

- Email address

- Web page address

- IM address

- Phone numbers (business, home, business fax, mobile)

- Address (street, city, state, ZIP code, and country)

When you are working in the various fields in the Contact dialog box, you can use the Tab key to quickly navigate from field to field (or Shift+Tab to move backward from field to field). Some fields, such as Full Name and Addresses, provide you with dialog boxes that make it easy for you to enter (and check) all the information possible for that particular field. For example, when you select the Full Name field, the Check Full Name dialog box opens, as shown in Figure 25.4.

Figure 25.4
The Check Full Name dialog box.

This dialog box enables you to enter a contact's title, such as Miss, Ms., Dr., or Mr., and also the first, middle, and last name, including a suffix such as Jr. After you have entered the information in one of the Check dialog boxes, click OK to return to the Contact dialog box.

As you enter the information for the contact, a business card is built for the contact on the right side of the dialog box. Depending on the purpose of your Contact list, you might want to include images of your contacts, which then appear in the Contacts folder when you use People view or Business Card view. This can be particularly useful when you have clients or customers in your Contacts folder you don't see often and need a reminder of their appearance (you can't remember everyone's face).

 caution

If you have saved and closed a contact's record and you are using People view, you might be going crazy trying to get the Contact dialog box open for that contact (or any contact in the list). When you are in People view, the details for the currently selected contact are shown in the Reading Pane. Even when you click Edit in the Reading Pane, you are expected to edit the contact information using the fields in the Reading Pane. To open a Contact's dialog box, change to one of the other views (anything other than People) and then double-click a contact. The contact dialog box opens.

To add a digital photo of the contact to the Contact dialog box, select the Add Contact Picture box (it is a silhouette of a person). The Add Contact Picture dialog box opens. Navigate to the folder that contains the picture, and then select the picture. Click OK to add the picture to the contact's information. You are returned to the Contact dialog box.

Entering Contact Details

The level of detail you enter for a particular Outlook contact is up to you; however, I think that, in most cases, having more information about a contact makes the listing more useful. You can enter all sorts of information related to a contact, such as department, office, title, and manager's name—even a nickname. Personal information about the contact, such as spouse/partner or birthday, can also be included (all these fields are included by default in the Contact dialog box). To enter additional information related to a contact (when you are in the contact's dialog box), make sure the Contact tab is selected on the Ribbon, and then select Details in the Show group. Figure 25.5 shows the details fields.

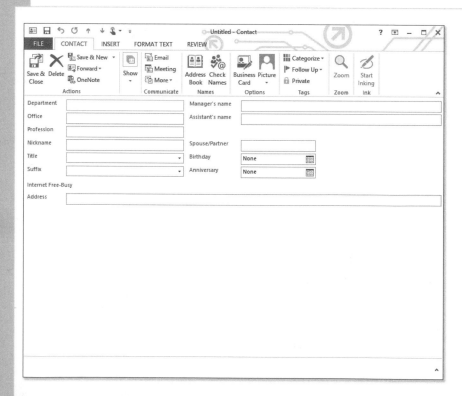

Figure 25.5
The new contact's details fields.

tip

If you make an Outlook window such as the new Contact dialog box smaller, this compresses the Ribbon and changes how some commands are displayed. For example, the Show group provides commands such as Details and All Fields. If you make the contact dialog box smaller, the Show group disappears, and the Ribbon provides a Show command (like a drop-down list) that offers a list of commands such as Details, Certificates, and All Fields.

Adding Fields for a Contact

You also have the option to add fields to the contact's information. This can be useful if you want to include information that isn't included as a default field, such as the contact's children's names or the contact's assistant's phone number. To add fields, follow these steps:

1. Select the All Fields command in the Show group. A blank field pane opens in the Contact dialog box.

2. Use the Select From drop-down list to select a field category, such as Frequently Used fields, Miscellaneous fields, or Personal fields. When you select one of the field groups, a list of specific fields is listed in the field pane. For example, the Personal fields supply fields such as Birthday, Children, Hobbies, and Language.

3. Select a field (on the All Fields screen) and then enter the information for the field in the Value column. You can return to the Select From drop-down list to view other fields and enter information in those fields.

4. When you have finished working with the additional fields, you can return to the general contact information for the contact by selecting General in the Show group.

 tip

You don't necessarily have to worry about the file size of the picture that you use for a client; it is sized appropriately to appear in the Contact dialog box. If you want to change the picture after you have inserted it, use the Picture command in the Options group.

 tip

You can also create user-defined fields. This enables you to include any data you want in the contact information. To create a user-defined field, click the New button at the bottom of the Contact dialog box (when All Fields is selected). Provide a name, type, and format for the new field in the New Column dialog box. Any fields you create are added to a contact's data using the user-defined fields in this item category (via Select from the drop-down list when All Fields is selected in the Show group).

Adding field data only strengthens your informational IQ for the contacts you place in your Contacts folder. Viewing the information you place in these additional fields requires you to use the All Fields command. You can then select the category of fields you used (via the Select From drop-down list) when you entered additional field information for the contacts.

After you enter all the information for a new contact, select Save & Close. This places the contact in the Contacts list and returns you to the Contacts folder.

Editing Contact Information

You can open a contact's record to access field data and add information or edit specific fields. If you are in People view, you can edit the contact's information inline in the Reading/Preview Pane. Select a contact and then click Edit in the Reading Pane. You can then edit the "general" fields for the contact, as shown in Figure 25.6. Click an information category's plus (+) symbol to expand that category, such as in Phone, Work, or Address. Then enter the data in that field. When you have finished editing the contact's information, select Save.

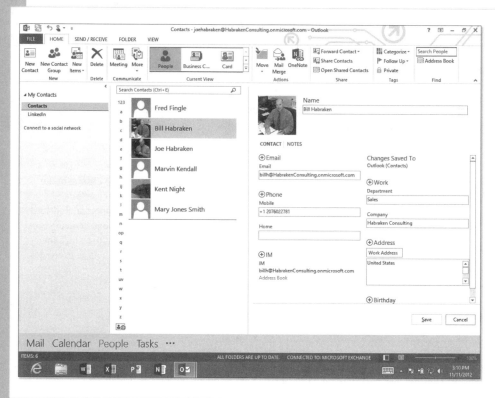

Figure 25.6
Enter contact information inline in People view.

If you find the inline editing too restrictive and you want to update or edit a contact's information in the Contact dialog box, switch to one of the other views, such as Business Card or List (any view other than People works), and then double-click on a contact. The Contact dialog box for that contact opens. Enter new data or edit the existing data for the contact. Remember that you can access additional fields using the commands available in the Show group (such as All Fields).

If you want to enter information about a contact that is more narrative in nature (meaning that it needs more space), you can use the Notes box, which is located on the right of the Contact dialog box. You can enter any type of information in the Notes box, such as notes on a conversation that you had with the contact or the fact that the contact is not very good at golf (no golf invitation for that contact). Editing contact information typically relates to making sure that the contact's information is accurate, but it also pertains to having any and all information that you can accumulate for that contact.

If you prefer to work with your contacts in a view that enables you to edit and enter contact data in a more tablelike environment (columns and rows), you can switch to List view (select List in the Current View gallery). Using the field column names as a reference, click in one of the field positions in a Contact's record (each row of information in the list is the record for a specific contact), and then enter the information for that field. Working in List view also enables you to quickly update information in multiple records without having to open the Contact dialog box for each individual contact.

Editing a Business Card

When you enter the information for a contact, a default business card is created for that contact. You can edit the layout and fine-tune the field information in the business card. Creating a more custom layout for contact business cards can be useful if you have a contact listing for each of your employees and colleagues. When you provide their information to a potential customer or client, you furnish an electronic business card that is extremely informational and also visually appealing. It also makes sense to create your own contact entry and then build your own electronic business card for inclusion with your own emails.

To edit the business card for a contact, double-click the contact in the Contacts list to open the contact's dialog box. Then select the Business Card command in the Options group. The Edit Business Card dialog box opens, as shown in Figure 25.7.

Figure 25.7
The Edit Business Card dialog box.

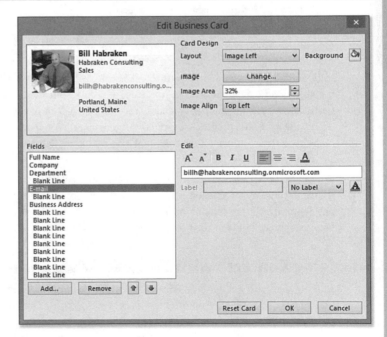

The Edit Business Card dialog box gives you control over the fields shown on the business card, the position of the image, and the fonts used on the business card. Let's start with the fields.

The fields currently used on the business card are listed in the Fields box. You can select a field and then use the Remove button to remove the field from the card. You can also add fields to the business card. Select the Add button. A menu appears and provides categories of fields that you can add to the card. For example, the Organization group provides the Company, Department, and Job Title fields. The Address group lists the Business Address, Home Address, and Other Address fields.

Use the Add Field menu to add fields to the business card as needed. This menu also provides you with a Blank Line option and a Custom Field category. After you have removed or added fields, you can use the Move Field Up or the Move Field Down buttons to rearrange the fields on the business card.

If you have not added an image to the business card or you want to change the image on the business card, select the Change button to open the Add Card Picture dialog box. Locate the image, select it, and click Open.

You also have control over the layout of the business card in terms of where the image is positioned and whether you use a background color. You can use the Layout drop-down list to position the image as follows: Image Left (the default), Image Right, Image Top, Image Bottom, Text Only, or Background Image. If you want to add a background color to the card, select the Background button and choose a color from the Color dialog box.

Depending on the layout setting that you select for the image in the Layout drop-down list, you can select the actual alignment of the image using the Image Align drop-down list. For example, if you choose the Image Bottom Layout setting, you can then align the image on the bottom of the card using the Bottom Right alignment setting.

You can use the various font and alignment settings in the Edit area of the dialog box to change the attributes for the text on the business card. For example, you might want the company name to be in italics, or you might want to use a bold, red font for your name. Having options related to text color and appearance can be particularly useful if you have used a background color or used the image as a background (not unlike a watermark). You can make sure that you use a text color and size that is readable on the background.

When you have finished editing the business card, click OK to return to the contact's dialog box. The new layout for the business card appears in the business card preview to the right of the various contact fields in the contact's dialog box.

 tip

You can also open the Edit Business Card dialog box by double-clicking the business card preview in the contact's dialog box.

 tip

If you don't like the changes you have made to a business card, you can use the Reset Card button in the Edit Business Card dialog box to reset the card to the Outlook defaults.

Tagging Contacts with Flags and Categories

Although you are not actually editing the contact's information, tags such as categories and follow-up flags can enhance (informationally) a contact's record. The various tag commands are provided in the Tags group on the Contact tab of the Ribbon.

To add a category to a contact, select the Categorize command and choose a category from the list provided.

You can also flag contacts for follow-up. For example, you might have had an appointment with a contact recently and want to follow up with that contact sometime this week. You then can flag the contact with the This Week flag. To select a flag for a contact, select the Follow Up command.

Although a follow-up flag serves as a visual reminder that you need to follow up with the contact, you might also want to create a reminder to accompany the flag. That way, Outlook reminds you to follow up with the contact. Select Follow Up and then Add Reminder. The Custom dialog box appears, as shown in Figure 25.8.

Figure 25.8
The Custom dialog box.

Specify the flag type in the Flag To drop-down list. You can also specify a start date and a due date for the follow-up. Use the reminder date and time settings to specify when you want to receive the reminder related to the flag. Select OK to return to the contact's dialog box.

 note

Using follow-up flags is just one way to tag a contact for follow-up. You can also create a task or a specific appointment in the Calendar, which reminds you to follow up with that contact.

Mapping a Contact's Address

Despite the fact that we rely on email, texting, instant messaging, and social media to communicate with customers and colleagues, sometimes you still need to meet face to face. Outlook can help you on your journey by mapping the contact's address.

In the contact's dialog box (to the right of the contact's address), select Map It. Your default web browser opens a map of the address using Bing.com. You can select the Directions link on the left side of the website and then enter your location to get directions to the contact's address. You can then use the Send command to send the directions to an email address or to a mobile device. You can also print the directions from the web browser window. When you close the web window, you return to Outlook.

Searching the Contacts Folder

If you have many contacts in the Contacts folder, you might need a tool to help you locate a particular contact quickly. If you are in the People, Business Card, or Card views, you can jump alphabetically around your Contacts list using the Index on the left side of the Preview pane. This doesn't help you find a specific contact or a group of contacts that work at the same company or reside in the same state, however.

To find contacts that meet certain search criteria, you use the Search Contacts box at the top of the Reading/Preview Pane. Enter a search string in the Search Contacts box; for example, you might type in a portion of a last name to filter the Contacts list. Or you might type in a particular ZIP code or state to filter the list. Using the Search Contacts box as a filter enables you to potentially see a subset of contacts in the Contacts folder based on your search string.

When you place the insertion point in the Search box, the Search Tools become available on the Outlook Ribbon. These Search commands enable you to control the scope of the search (you can search in the current folder and include subfolders), refine the search, and set options related to the search. The Refine group is particularly useful and enables you to refine a search. For example, you can do a search by business name (type the business name in the Search Contacts box) and then use the Has Address command in the Refine group to show only contacts who work at the company (entered in the Search Contacts box) who work at a particular *branch* of the company (based on the business address). Figure 25.9 shows the Search Tool, including the Refine group commands.

Figure 25.9
The Search Tools' Refine group.

The Refine commands provided for searches in the Contacts folder are as follows:

- **Categorized:** This command allows you to search for contacts by category.

- **Has Phone Number:** Enables you to filter the Contacts list by the phone fields: business phone, home phone, or mobile phone. For example, if you select Has Business Phone, only the contacts who have a business phone listed are shown in the Reading Pane.

- **Has Address:** Filters the Contacts list based on whether specific address fields contain information. The possibilities are Has Email Address, Has IM Address, Has Business Address, and Has Home Address.

- **More:** Provides access to additional properties for your search criteria via a list of Common Properties. These properties include Business Phone, Company, Home Address, and Street Address.

You can also access recent searches and other search tools via the Search Tools command groups. To access recent searches that you have used, select the Recent Searches command and select a search from the list provided.

If you want to access advanced search tools, select the Search Tools command. A particularly useful search tool in relation to a large Contacts list is the Indexing Status command. Select this command to have Outlook index your contact entries. This makes your searches faster and more efficient. When you have finished working with the Search feature, you can quickly return to the Contacts by selecting the Close Search command.

➡ *For an overview of the Outlook Search feature*, **see** *"Searching for Outlook Items," p. 661.*

Organizing Contacts with Groups

We have already discussed ways to visually organize your Contacts folder using different views and the Search box. You can also quickly sort contacts in Phone or List view using the field headings to sort the list by name, company, or category, for example.

Another way to organize your contacts is to use contact groups. By default, the Contacts list is one big list with no real subdivisions. You can use contact groups to group contacts by such things as company or location. You can also create a personal group and a business group, to provide some functional division between the types of contacts you store in your Contacts folder.

To create a new contact group, select New Contact Group on the Ribbon's Home tab. The new Contact Group dialog box opens, as shown in Figure 25.10.

Figure 25.10
The Contact Group dialog box.

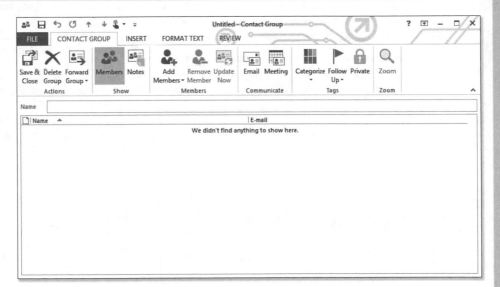

Type a name for the new group in the Name box. You can then add contacts to the group. Select the Add Members command, and then select From Outlook Contacts (you can also add contacts from the Address Book). The Select Members: Contacts dialog box opens, with your Contacts list selected.

Select a contact or contacts in the list, and then click the Members button. When you have finished adding members to the new group, click OK to close the Select Members: Contacts dialog box. You return to the Group dialog box, and the new members are listed. If you want to remove a member or members, select the member (or members) and then click the Remove Member command.

To close the new Contact Group dialog box, select Save & Close. The new contact group appears in your Contacts folder (meaning in the Reading pane) with your contacts. To view the contacts in a contact group, open the contact group. You can open a specific contact in the group by double-clicking on the contact.

Including a contact in a contact group does not remove the contact from your Contact list. It basically creates a shortcut to the contact. So if you remove a contact from a contact group, you are not removing the contact from the Contacts folder. The great thing about contact groups is that you can basically treat them like a contact. If you find that you are sending email messages or assigning tasks to the same group of recipients, create a contact group and then address the email to the contact group. Contact groups can also be used to send multiple meeting invitations. (Scheduling meetings is discussed later in this chapter in the section "Scheduling Meetings.")

Forwarding and Sharing Contacts

You can share your Outlook contacts with coworkers and colleagues. Whether you use Outlook as an Internet email client or use Outlook in an Exchange Server environment, you can quickly forward contact information to anyone with an email address. In Exchange Server environments, you can share your Contacts folder with other network users, and these users can share their Contacts folder with you.

Figure 25.11 shows the Share group on the Contacts folder Ribbon's Home tab. This group provides the Forward Contact, Share Contacts, and Open Shared Contacts commands.

These commands can also be accessed via the Ribbon when you are working in the dialog box for a particular contact. The Share group is located on the Contact tab.

 note

You can assign categories and flags to contacts in contact groups, and you can assign categories and flags to contact groups. Contact groups can also be forwarded to other users.

Figure 25.11
The Contacts folder Ribbon and Share group commands.

Forwarding Contacts

When you forward a contact or contacts to other people, the contact information comes in the form of an email attachment. The contact information can be attached to a message in two different formats:

- **Business Card:** This format is also known as a vCard and uses the VCard file extension .vcf. The vCard is considered the standard for electronic business cards and can be interpreted by most email and contact-management software packages.

- **Outlook Contact:** You can also attach a contact or contacts to a message as an Outlook Contact item. Contacts attached as an Outlook Contact item can be opened by both recipients who use Outlook and recipients who use an email client that supports the Outlook Contact file format.

You can also forward contacts group via a mail message. However, contacts groups can be sent only as Outlook Contact items. You cannot send an Outlook contacts group as a vCard attachment.

To forward a contact or contacts from the Contacts folder, select the contact or contacts in the Contacts list. Select the Forward Contact command in the Share group, and then select one of the commands on the menu provided: As a Business Card or As an Outlook Contact. A new message opens. Figure 25.12 shows a message with a contact's business card being forwarded. The business card is also embedded in the body of the message. When you forward the contact information as an Outlook Contact item, the contact information is not embedded in the body of the message.

Figure 25.12 Mail message with attached contact information.

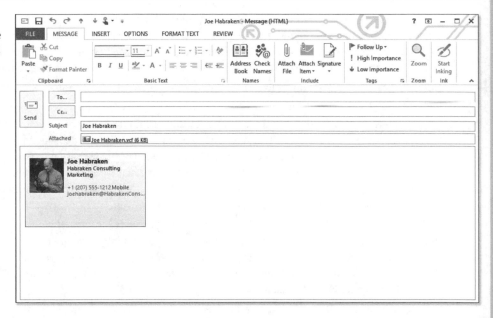

Specify the recipient or recipients for the message as you would any other email message. You can include explanatory text or other text in the body of the message. You can also choose to attach other files to the message, as needed. When you are ready to forward the contact information, select Send.

If you are the recipient of contact information as a business card (vCard) or as an Outlook item, double-click the attachment in the received message. This opens the forwarded contact's dialog box. Select Save & Close, and the contact is added to your Contacts list.

Sharing Contacts

If you are working in an Exchange Server environment or have an Office 365 subscription for your business, you can share all your contacts with other users on your network (or part of your Office 365 subscription). And when I say *all* of your contacts, I mean all of your contacts in the "main" Contacts list. So you might want to consider a couple of possibilities for protecting contact information that you don't really want to share. One possibility is to tag specific contacts as private. Users with whom you share your Contacts list cannot view the details for any contacts you have tagged as private. So select those contacts in the Contacts list and then select the Private command on the Home tab.

note

If Outlook has been configured for text messaging (in an Exchange Server environment or if you subscribe to Office 365 or a third-party text message service), you can also forward contact information in a text message. When you select the Forward Contact command, a Forward As Text Message choice is included on the menu (again, if Outlook is configured for text messaging).

Another possibility is to create a new folder in your Contacts folder and move contacts you don't want to share to this new folder. In the Navigation Pane, right-click on the Contacts icon and then select New Folder. Use the Create New Folder dialog box to specify a name for the new folder and click OK. Drag contacts that you do not want to share from your Contacts list to this new folder.

Now you can share the Contacts list. Select Share Contacts on the Home tab. A Sharing invitation message opens, as shown in Figure 25.13.

Specify the recipients for the sharing invitation by addressing the message as you would any other email message. You can also add text to the body of the message, if needed. A check box in the message specifies that you allow the recipient (or recipients) of the invitation to view your Contacts folder. You can also select the Request Permission to View Recipient's Contacts Folder check box if you want to be able to view the recipient's Contacts folder. Click Send. A message box opens and asks you to verify that the Contacts folder is shared as Reviewer/Read Only (which is a good thing, in most cases). Click Yes, and the invitation is on its way.

When the recipient receives the sharing invitation and opens it, all he or she has to do is select the Open This Contacts Folder command at the top of the email (in the Reading Pane). This places your Contacts list on the recipient's Folder Pane in a Shared Contact group folder. Figure 25.14 shows a shared Contacts list in the Contacts folder.

If you also requested that the recipient share contacts with you, the recipient needs to select the Allow command on the Share message's Ribbon. An Outlook message box opens and asks whether the user wants to share the Contacts folder with you (a read-only version). When that person clicks Yes, a sharing message is sent to you. All you have to do is use the Open This Contacts Folder command when you open the message, and you can view the shared contacts. Now everybody is happy.

Figure 25.13
Share your contacts.

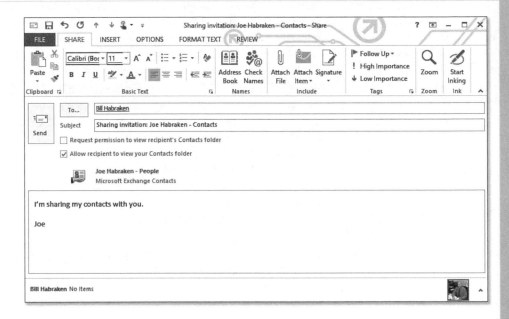

Figure 25.14
Shared contacts can be accessed via the Navigation pane.

 tip

If you have opened a sharing invitation email, make sure the message's Share tab is selected on the Ribbon; then click the Open This Contacts Folder command to switch to Contacts and view the shared Contacts folder.

Accessing Contacts on Social Networks

Outlook 2013 makes it easy for you to expand your contact database by connecting to your social networking accounts. The Outlook Social Connector creates a link between social networking sites such as Facebook and LinkedIn and enables you to view and use the information available on these sites. For example, you can view an Outlook contact's activities on Facebook by connecting to that person's profile. If you have a LinkedIn account, you can access your LinkedIn contacts and send them emails without leaving Outlook.

The idea of connecting Outlook to a social networking site (or sites), even a business-oriented site such as LinkedIn, might make you a little squeamish because of security and privacy issues. Microsoft assures Outlook users that connecting to these sites in Outlook does not put your Outlook contact or account information at risk. The Social Connector pulls information from your social networking sites into Outlook. The only thing that the social network is seeing in terms of Outlook information is email addresses included in the message (so not all your information is necessarily hidden).

To connect to Facebook, you need a Facebook account; to connect to LinkedIn, you need a LinkedIn account. Outlook does not pull information from Facebook related to a contact in your Contacts list unless you are "friends" with that contact on Facebook. In fact, Outlook bases the "friendship" on the email address that you enter for the contact. If it is the same email that is entered in the contact's Facebook profile, Outlook pulls information from Facebook, such as the friend's picture, to populate the image field for the contact. When you receive an email from a Facebook friend or a LinkedIn colleague who is also in your Contacts list, the People pane at the bottom of the email message (in the Reading pane) can give you updates about that person that are pulled from a social network site (such as Facebook).

Be sure to weigh the pros and cons of connecting Outlook with social media sites. Social media is certainly breaking down the wall between our professional and personal lives. If you decide that you want to fire up the Social Connector and connect Outlook to sites such as Facebook, the process is straightforward.

In the Contacts folder, select the Connect to a Social Network link in the Folders list. This opens the Social Network Accounts dialog box shown in Figure 25.15. Select the social networks you want to connect to. You must provide a username and password for each of the social networks you select. Enter the information as needed. When you have finished entering the required information, select Finish. A Congratulations message box opens, letting you know that you are now connected; select Close.

Figure 25.15
You can connect Outlook to popular social networks.

If you connected to LinkedIn, LinkedIn is included in your Folder Pane when you are in the Contacts folder. When you select LinkedIn (under the Contacts link), you can access LinkedIn profiles and use them to send emails and schedule meetings on your Outlook calendar. You can also apply different views to the LinkedIn list (such as Business Card or List), and you can use the Search box to filter the LinkedIn contact list as you would your own Outlook Contacts list.

Communicating with Contacts

Creating and maintaining a contact list in Outlook really has one purpose: We accumulate people's contact information so that we can communicate with them. The Contacts folder's Ribbon (the Home tab) provides the Communicate group commands. These commands provide different options for communicating with your contacts, including emails, meeting requests, and task assignments.

When you are in People view, you are not provided all the commands available in the Ribbons Communicate group (for example, the Call command is not available on the More gallery); switch to one of the other views, such as the Business Card view or List view (any view other than People), to access all the available Communicate commands. We talk in a moment about what I mean by "available" commands.

The full set of Communicate commands follows:

- **Email:** This command enables you to quickly send an email to the selected contact or contacts.
- **Meeting:** This command opens a new meeting request for the selected contact or contacts.
- **Assign Task:** This command opens a new Task message for the selected contact or contacts.
- **Reply with IM:** You can get in touch with the selected contact via instant messaging using Microsoft Lync (part of the Microsoft Office 2013 application suite).
- **Call:** You can have Outlook (with a little help from Windows) dial a phone number for a client if you have a modem or other telephony connection to your computer. This command can be used to dial any of the phone numbers listed for the selected contact.

The Communicate group commands that are available in your installation of Outlook 2013 depend on your Outlook configuration and your computer hardware. For example, if you don't have a dial-up modem or some other type of telephony connection to your computer, you won't be able to dial a contact's phone number and talk to them by phone.

Instant Messaging (IM) is another communication option that might not be available in your Outlook setup. Outlook uses the Microsoft Lync communication software as its IM client. To establish an IM session with a selected contact, you need to have Lync installed (and running). You also need to subscribe to a service that supports IM (as does the contact you want to communicate with). Microsoft Office 365 Small Business and Enterprise subscriptions enable you to communicate via Microsoft Lync using IM and also to videoconference with Skype users (or other Lync users). Many "corporate" Outlook users also have IM and other communication services via Exchange servers and SharePoint servers. Figure 25.16 shows a Lync IM session that was initiated by selecting a contact in the Outlook Contacts folder and then selecting the IM command on the More gallery.

Figure 25.16
Use the Communicate commands such as IM to communicate with your contacts.

At the outset of this discussion related to the Communicate group, I stated that not all the Communicate commands are available on the Ribbon when you are in People view (for example, the Call command is not available). However, when you are in People view and have selected a contact, you can access a number of communication-related commands directly in the Reading Pane (which shows the contacts information). Icons just below the contact's name provide the IM, Call, Videoconference, and Email commands. Again, the communication options that you have available depend on your computer hardware and service connection options (provided by your company or Microsoft subscriptions).

> **note**
>
> If you do have the capability to conduct IM and/or videoconferencing sessions with other users via Lync, Outlook keeps track of your conversations. A Conversation History appears as a subfolder in your Mail folder. Each entry in the Conversation History is a transcript of any IM sessions that you have held with your various contacts.

Contact Actions

The Contacts folder Ribbon also provides you with the Actions group. The commands in this group enable you to interact or "take action" relative to a contact or contacts. The Actions group commands are as follows: Move, Mail Merge, and OneNote.

The Move command is self-explanatory; you can use it to move contacts from the primary Contacts list to other folders within the main Contacts folder. When you select Move, then Other folder, a list of your Contacts folders, is shown. You also have the option of copying selected contacts to a folder.

The Mail Merge command enables you to merge all your contacts or selected contacts into a Word document. Figure 25.17 shows the Mail Merge Contacts dialog box, which opens when the Mail Merge command is selected.

Figure 25.17
Create a mail merge using your contacts.

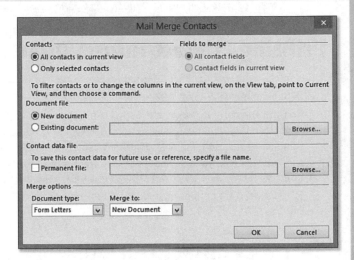

The Mail Merge Contacts dialog box provides options for merging the contact date to a new or existing document. You can also specify that the contact data be saved as a Word data source. You can then use the data source for future merges by selecting the file when using Microsoft Word.

When you select OK, the Outlook data is provided to Word, and a new or existing document (depending on the option you selected in the Mail Merge Contacts dialog box) opens in the Word application window. You can use the Mailings tab to enter the merge fields into the new letter as needed and then complete the merge.

➡ *For a discussion of the Word mail merge feature, **see** Chapter 9, "Managing Mailings and Forms."*

The OneNote command enables you to create notes in a OneNote notebook that are linked to an Outlook contact. Select the contact or contacts in the Contacts folder, and then select the OneNote command. The Select Location in OneNote dialog box opens and provides a list of all your currently open OneNote notebooks. Expand a notebook to select the section where you want to insert the linked note (or notes). When you click OK, OneNote opens to the section you selected and inserts the contact's name, picture (if available), and other information, such as address, email, and phone. Enter notes as needed under the contact information. When you finish entering the note information (which can include file attachments and other items such as tables or file printouts), close the OneNote window and return to Outlook.

When you want to open the OneNote notes linked to a contact, select the contact in the Contacts folder and then select the OneNote command. OneNote opens to the page that contains the linked notes, which you can then modify, if required.

➡️ *For more about using Outlook and OneNote,* ***see*** *"Integrating OneNote and Outlook,"* ***p. 922.***

Printing Contact Information

You can print your contact information in a variety of formats. These formats include an alphabetical card style, a memo style, and a phone directory style.

To print the current Contacts list (this can be the main Contacts list or any lists that you have created in separate folders), select File to access the Outlook Backstage. Then select Print. The Print window opens, with a preview of the default print style. A number of print styles are available in the Settings box. You can choose from different print formats for your contact list, such as Card Style, Small Booklet Style, and Phone Directory Style. You can also specify the printer for the print job and set print options as needed. When you are ready to print the Contacts list, click the Print button.

Setting Contact Options

The setting options for the Contacts folder are found in the Outlook Options window, which is accessed in the Outlook Backstage. Select File on the Ribbon; then in the Backstage, select Options. To view the options for People (contacts), select People in the Options list. You will find that the options for how you work with your contacts are fairly sparse and are pretty straightforward. The options are as follows:

- **Names and Filing:** These options include the full name order for contacts, as well as the default order for filing contacts (by name). The default Full Name order is First (Middle) Last. The Default File As order is Last, First. Use the drop-down lists to change the default settings. The Names and Filing options also include a check box that has Outlook check for duplicates when saving new contacts.

- **Contacts Index:** You can specify that an additional index be shown for the Contacts in a language other than the default language configured for Outlook.

- **Online Status and Photographs:** If you have configured the Social Connector for Outlook or you are using instant messaging (via Lync), you can display the online status of your contacts. This setting is enabled by default. By default, user photographs are also shown when available.

When you have finished working with the People options, select OK. The Outlook Options window closes and returns to the Outlook application window.

Scheduling Meetings

This chapter has already discussed communicating with your Outlook contacts and taking various actions related to a contact or contacts: We've looked at sending messages to contacts and using other methods of communicating with your contacts, such as task assignments and instant messaging. You can also schedule meetings quickly and efficiently using the information in your Contacts folder. Because scheduling meetings also relates to the Outlook Calendar, you can sort out who is available for a particular meeting using the Scheduling Assistant. In environments that enable you to share calendars on the network, such as an Exchange Server or SharePoint environment, you can accurately tell when a contact is available and when a contact is busy.

➡️ *For more about the Outlook Calendar,* **see** *Chapter 24, "Using the Calendar for Appointments and Tasks."*

When you create a new meeting, you provide the time and date of the meeting, identify the subject and location of the meeting, and invite contacts to attend the meeting. You can create a new meeting from any of the Outlook folders using the New Items command. When you create a new meeting from the Contacts folder, you can select the contacts you want to invite to the meeting in the Contacts list before you select the Meeting command.

So, when you are in the Contacts folder (or a folder for LinkedIn or any other folder that contains contacts), select the contacts you want to attend the meeting and then select the Meeting command in the Communicate group. The Meeting dialog box opens, as shown in Figure 25.18.

Figure 25.18
Create a new meeting.

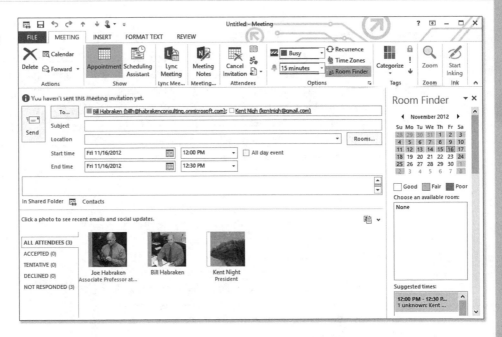

The contacts you preselected in your Contacts list appear in the To box. You can add contacts using the Address Book command in the Attendees group. This means that you can invite attendees to the meeting who are not in your Contacts list but are in other lists in the Address Book, such as the Global Address List that is provided to you when you use Outlook as an Exchange Server client. You might also have lists in your Address Book that you imported from other software applications that can be accessed to build the list of attendees for the meeting. When you use the Address Book dialog box to specify attendees for the meeting, you can specify both required and optional attendees for the meeting.

Enter a subject for the meeting in the Subject box. You can also specify a location for the meeting in the Location box, such as a particular conference room, building location, or site external to your company or institution (say, a local coffee or doughnut shop). You should also specify the start and end time for the meeting (including the date and the time). If you are scheduling an all-day event, select the All Day Event check box.

As with any Outlook item, you can use the Options and Tags group commands to specify options related to the meeting. For example, you can specify when the reminder for the meeting should be provided, details on whether the meeting is recurring (use the Recurrence command), and any possible multiple time zones for the meeting (particularly if it is a videoconference or an online meeting). You can also tag the meeting with categories and importance level flags.

Because the meeting information is sent to the potential attendees as an email message (these are invitations, after all), you provide additional information regarding the meeting in the message body box. You can tell attendees more about what the meeting entails and whether they should bring anything to the meeting.

Selecting the Meeting Location

If you are using Outlook as an Exchange Server client, you can click the Rooms button to the right of the Location box. The Address Book opens, showing the Global Address List for your Exchange Server network (or SharePoint server environment), which might also include a listing of meeting rooms for your corporation or institution. You can select any room listed in the address list and specify it as the location for the meeting by selecting Rooms. Click OK to return to the Meeting dialog box. The meeting room then is listed in the Location box and the To box because the room itself becomes a participant (albeit a location) for the meeting.

An alternative to the Rooms command is the Room Finder pane, which you can open using the Room Finder command in the Options group. The Room Finder command opens a calendar of the current month and also opens a list of available rooms (again, if you are working in a networked environment that provides this information). You can use the date selector (the calendar), the available room list, and the suggested times list (all these tools are in the Room Finder pane) to determine the best room availability based on date and time.

 caution

Many people use Outlook as an Internet email client but do not get to take advantage of all of Outlook's bells and whistles that are provided to users who use Outlook on an Exchange Server network. So don't be disheartened when you can't take advantage of absolutely every Outlook feature. Outlook is a powerful piece of software no matter what type of environment you use it in. You can still schedule meetings, specify the meeting location, and invite attendees.

Using the Scheduling Assistant

While finding a conference room or other venue for a meeting might be an issue, one of the biggest headaches related to scheduling a meeting is finding a date and time that works for all the participants. The Scheduling Assistant can help you ferret out potential conflicts and schedule your meeting when most, if not all, participants are available.

To open the Scheduling Assistant, select the Scheduling Assistant command in the Show group on the Meeting tab. The Scheduling Assistant opens, including the Room Finder Task pane, as shown in Figure 25.19.

Figure 25.19
The Scheduling Assistant and Room Finder.

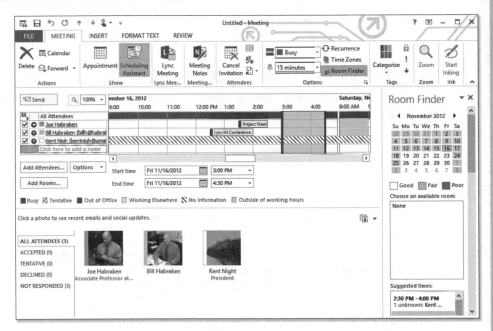

The Scheduling Assistant lists the participants in the All Attendees List. The date (the meeting date) is broken down in a tabular format, with the column headings defined by hours. Each attendee's free/busy time for the date is shown on the timeline.

A blue vertical line shows the start time and end time for the meeting. You can drag the start and end time lines on the time grid to specify a meeting time that does not have any conflicts. You can also cross-reference information provided in the Room Finder Task Pane to make sure there is no room conflict at the newly specified meeting time.

The Scheduling Assistant also enables you to add attendees and rooms so that you can build a meeting directly from the Scheduling Assistant before you add an attendee or other information to the meeting (meaning that you can open a new Meeting dialog box and enter attendees, meeting time, and room from the Scheduling Assistant).

When you have finished fine-tuning the meeting time and other settings in the Scheduling Assistant, select the Appointment command in the Show group to return to the Meeting dialog box. Before you send the meeting invitations, you might want to alter the Response options available on the Response Options command in the Attendees group. By default, a response is requested to the invitation, and attendees are provided the option of proposing a new time for the meeting. If you do not want to allow new time proposals, deselect the Allow New Time Proposals option.

If you send the invitation to possible attendees for which you manually entered the email address or when you are not sure whether an email address is valid, select the Check Names command (in the Attendees group). If there is a problem with an address or name, Outlook provides a message box detailing the problem.

When you are ready to send the meeting, click Send. The meeting invitations are sent to the attendees. The meeting is also added to your Outlook Calendar as an appointment.

Viewing and Editing Meeting Information

You can open a meeting on your Calendar and view or edit the meeting details as needed. Double-click the meeting in the Calendar (which appears as an appointment), and the Meeting dialog box opens.

If you want to quickly track responses for the meeting invitations that were sent, select the Tracking command in the Show group (the Tracking command is available only for sent meetings) and then select View Tracking Status.

A list of the attendees and the status of their responses displays. If an attendee has not responded, the Response is labeled as None. Attendees can also respond to the invitation using Accept, Tentative, or Decline.

You can also edit the meeting parameters. You can change the time and date of the meeting, and you can edit the list of attendees for the meeting. If necessary, you can use the Scheduling Assistant to reschedule the meeting and specify a new location for the meeting. You can even use the Cancel Meeting command to cancel the meeting.

If you make substantive changes to the meeting, you can send these changes to the attendees. When you have finished making your changes, select the Send Update button. Updated invitations are sent to the attendees. If you have changed the date or time for the meeting, the meeting also is moved on your Calendar.

When you do receive meeting response messages from attendees, the message details whether a specific attendee has accepted, tentatively accepted, or declined the invitation. The email also provides tracking information related to the number of accepted, tentative, and declined responses you have received related to the meeting.

Responding to Meeting Requests

When you are a potential attendee for a meeting, you receive a meeting invitation from the meeting organizer. The invitation comes in the form of an email. The invitation provides the details of the meeting and also enables you to accept or decline the meeting invitation. If you accept the meeting invitation, the meeting is automatically added to your Outlook Calendar.

Double-click a meeting invitation in your Inbox to open it. Figure 25.20 shows a meeting invitation message.

Figure 25.20
A meeting invitation message.

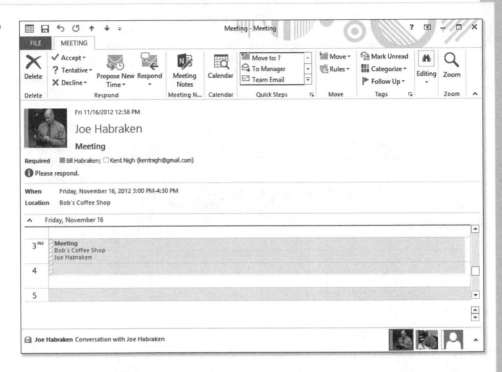

The Respond group provides five alternatives for responding to the meeting: Accept, Tentative (accept tentatively), Decline, Propose New Time, and Respond. The Propose New Time command enables you to either accept tentatively and propose a new time or decline and propose a new time. The Respond command enables you to reply to the sender of the invitation or forward the invitation without accepting or declining the invitation.

 tip

If you select a meeting invitation in your Inbox, you can also respond to the invitation using the response commands at the top of the Reading Pane.

When you select the Accept, Tentative, or Decline commands, you are provided with three options related to your response to the originator of the meeting:

- **Edit the Response Before Sending:** This command enables you to include additional comments with your response message. Selecting this command opens a new message, and you can add text to the body of the message, attach files, or do anything that you can normally do to an email message, such as address or copy the message to other recipients.

- **Send the Response Now:** This command sends a response immediately without additional comments or information.

- **Do Not Send a Response:** This command adds the meeting to your Calendar, in the case of an acceptance or tentative acceptance response from you, but does not provide a response to the meeting planner. If you decline the meeting and use this option, the originator is able to track your response in the meeting's tracking information.

As already mentioned, you can also propose a new time and accept tentatively or decline the message. When you select the Propose New Time command, you have two options: Tentative and Propose New Time, or Decline and Propose New Time. When you select either of these possibilities, the Propose New Time dialog box opens (see Figure 25.21).

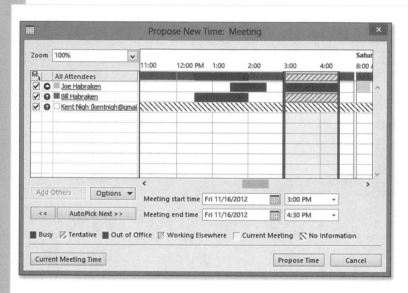

Figure 25.21
You can propose a new time for the meeting.

This dialog box is basically a compact version of the Scheduling Assistant. You can use the Start and End lines (drag them to a new position on the timeline) to propose a new start and end time for the meeting. You can also use the AutoPick Next button to find the next available time slot for all the participants. AutoPick Next enables you to search forward in the timeline. The Back button to the left of the AutoPick Next button enables you to search backward in the timeline.

After you have specified your proposed time for the meeting, select the Propose Time button. A new message opens with both the current and proposed times for the meeting detailed. You can add information to the body of the message as needed. When you are ready to send the message, click Send.

26

USING THE JOURNAL AND NOTES

Outlook not only helps you manage emails, contacts, and tasks, but it can also assist you in developing an "informational trail" related to your interactions with your contacts. Outlook's Journal feature can be used to create a timeline of important interactions with your contacts, including emails, phone calls, and meetings (both "in person" and online). You can also create Journal entries that relate to work that you do in other Office applications, including Excel, PowerPoint, and Word. In this chapter, we look at how you can track information in the Outlook Journal.

Other times, you just want to get some information onto a piece of paper for later reference. It always seems that those sticky notes are buried somewhere under a pile of papers or are being used as a coaster for your coffee cup. Outlook has you covered: You can create electronic notes in Outlook. You can then use the information on those notes as you create other Outlook items, such as emails, or enter information for a new contact.

Using the Outlook Journal

You can use the Outlook Journal to track your work, communications, and meetings. The Journal is really designed to keep track of "billable hours," so you can track various activities such as telephone calls or meetings and then determine the time that you spent on a particular activity or task.

You can also include information in the Journal that is related to your use of other Office applications, including Excel PowerPoint and Word. For example, you might want to keep track of how long it takes you to complete an Excel worksheet that is part of a project you are doing for a client. So the Journal entry enables you to determine the amount of time you put into that part of the project.

The Journal is not included in the Navigation bar, so to view the Journal in the Outlook window (in the Folder list), you need to select the More command (the ellipsis) in the Navigation bar. On the shortcut menu that appears, select Folders. This shows all your folders (including Contacts, Notes, and Calendar) and the Journal.

To access the Journal, select the Journal icon in the Folder list. The Journal window shows a timeline with the current day selected. Because you haven't entered any content into the Journal thus far, the message "We didn't find anything to show here" appears below the timeline. To use the Journal to track your activities, you have to create Journal entries. Let's take a look at how to create Journal entries, including using the timer; then we can take a look at how you view the information that has been entered into the Journal.

> **⚡ caution**
>
> The Journal feature provided by Outlook 2013 is definitely different from the Journal found in Outlook 2010 (and even earlier versions of Outlook). The Outlook 2013 Journal does not allow automatic journaling, which enabled you to record Outlook items automatically when they were related to specific contacts in your Contacts folder. The Journal options have also been removed from the Outlook Options window (as have the Notes options). Still, the Journal continues to provide you with a lot of possibilities for tracking your work (particularly billable hours) and creating entries that pull together information from Outlook items and external files such as Excel workbooks, Word documents, and PowerPoint presentations.

Creating a New Journal Entry

If you are going to use the Journal to keep track of your activities, particularly the time it takes for you to complete an activity, such as writing and sending an email, assigning a task, or even making a phone call, you have to create the Journal entry just before you begin the activity. You can then start the timer in the Journal entry. When you have completed the activity, you can stop the timer.

Journal entries can be associated with contacts, and they can also be categorized. You can also insert Outlook items and attach files to a Journal entry. So a Journal entry basically becomes a log entry that provides you with information about a specific activity and can include references to Outlook contacts and attached files and Outlook items. To create a new Journal entry, follow these steps:

1. Select the Journal icon in the Outlook Folder pane. (If you don't see the Journal icon, select More in the Navigation bar and then select Folders.)

2. In the Ribbon's New group, select Journal Entry. A new Journal entry opens, as shown in Figure 26.1.

3. Enter a subject for the new Journal entry.

4. To specify the entry type for the new Journal entry, use the Entry Type drop-down list. Outlook provides a number of possibilities, including Conversation, Email Message, Letter, Meeting, Meeting Request, Note, Phone Call, and Task. The Phone Call entry type displays in the Entry Type box by default.

Figure 26.1
The Journal Entry dialog box.

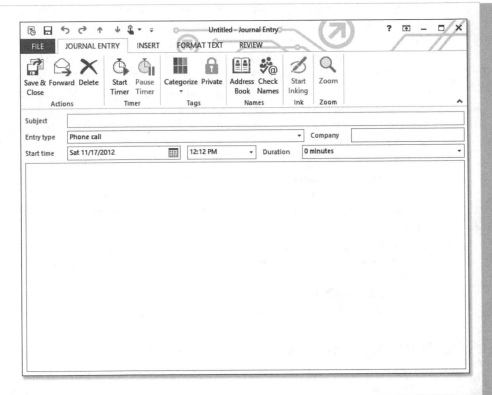

5. Enter other information for the entry as needed (such as the company name related to the entry), including text in the body of the entry.

You can save and close the Journal entry at this point by selecting the Save & Close command in the Actions group. However, if you aren't quite finished with the entry and you want to use the timer or insert Outlook items into the entry, you can save the Journal entry and keep it open in the Outlook window by selecting the Save icon in the Quick Access Toolbar.

 note

As soon as you open a new Journal entry, it is time-stamped with the date and time. You can change the date and the time for a Journal entry, if you want, but that negates the benefit of using the time to track the actual time that a particular task, conversation, or other activity took (although you can estimate the duration and enter that in the Duration box, if you want).

Using the Timer

The Journal entry timer enables you to record an accurate timing of a task, such as a phone call, IM, or even face-to-face meeting, while you are engaged in that activity. You can use the Journal entry timer for new Journal entries, or you can use the timer for an existing Journal entry.

You might think that the Start time entered for an existing Journal entry affects the duration of a "timed entry." Actually, the timer doesn't reference the entered start time; the timer just starts when you select Start Timer and enters the elapsed time (in minutes) until you select Pause Timer. Because you are all about recording an activity in real time, it makes sense to create a new Journal entry just before you begin the task.

If you don't complete a task or other activity that you are "recording" in a Journal entry using the timer, you can pause the timer and Save & Close the entry. You can go back later, open the Journal entry, and restart the timer, adding more time to the duration. So the start time stamp (the date and the time) doesn't necessarily relate to the cumulative duration that you record for an activity that you do over time at a number of sittings (such as writing a long report).

To use the timer to record the timing for an open Journal entry, select Start Timer (in the Timer group). The timer begins running and uses minutes as the base time increment (it doesn't provide the time down to the second). As the minutes pass, the duration provides the running time for the entry.

To stop the timer, select Pause Timer. As already mentioned, when you end the timing, you pause the timer (you do not reset it). You can always return to the Journal entry when needed and time the performance of additional work or tasks related to the entry's purpose. If you work on a project on several different dates, you can always record additional dates when you worked on the activity (because there can only be one start time and date) in the body of the Journal entry.

Adding Tags and Names to a Journal Entry

You can tag a new or existing Journal entry and also associate the entry with a contact or contacts. Adding tags to a Journal entry makes it easier to locate entries that have been tagged with a particular category. Adding Names (contacts) to Journal entries also makes it easy to locate entries associated with a particular contact.

To add a category tag to an open Journal entry (this can be a new or existing entry), select the Categorize command in the Tags group. This provides you with the Category gallery, shown in Figure 26.2. You can add multiple Category tags to a Journal entry. Category tags added to a Journal entry appear above the entry's Subject box. You also can add category tags to a Journal entry by right-clicking on the Journal entry in the Journal folder and selecting Categorize from the shortcut menu that appears.

You can also associate a Journal entry with a contact or contacts. In the Journal Entry dialog box, select the Address Book command in the Names group. The Select Contacts dialog box opens and is divided into two parts. The Look In pane at the top of the Select Contacts dialog box enables you to select the folder that contains the contact or contacts that you want to associate with the Journal entry. You can switch to another folder, including social networking sites such as LinkedIn, if that folder contains the contact or contacts you want to add to the entry.

The bottom half of the Select Contacts dialog box, the Items pane, lists the contacts found in the currently selected folder (in the Look In pane). If you are going to associate only a single contact with the Journal entry, select the contact and then select OK. When you want to add multiple contacts to a Journal entry, select a contact and then select Apply; repeat as necessary. When you want to close the Select Contacts dialog box, select OK. When you have finished associating contacts with a Journal entry, select Save & Close to save and then close the Journal Entry dialog box.

Figure 26.2
Add a
Category tag
to a Journal
entry.

Adding Outlook Items and Inserting Files

You can also add Outlook items to a Journal entry, including emails, appointments, tasks, and Contact cards. Adding Outlook items allows you to include the actual subject of a Journal entry in the entry. For example, if you have created a Journal entry with the Entry type of email message, it makes sense to include the email that you created. You would simply include the email (from your Sent Items folder) in the Journal entry. Adding Outlook items to a Journal entry makes the entry a more complete record of the activity. Not only do you have duration information and also (possibly) tags and contact information that help describe the activity documented in the entry, but you also have the Outlook item that you created related to the Journal entry.

To add an Outlook item to an open Journal entry, select the Outlook Item command in the Include group on the Ribbon's Insert tab. The Insert Item dialog box opens, as shown in Figure 26.3. Use the Look In pane to navigate to the Outlook folder that contains the Outlook item you want to attach to the Journal entry. When a folder is selected, the contents of the folder appear in the Items pane (the bottom pane) of the Insert Item dialog box.

When you insert a selected Outlook item, you have three possibilities for how the item is inserted. The options are Text Only, Attachment, and Shortcut. Inserting an item as text only means that the text from the item is pasted into the body of the Journal entry. For example, if you insert an email address into a Journal entry as text only, all the text from the message, including the From, Sent, To, and Subject fields, is inserted into the entry.

The Attachment option for an inserted Outlook item attaches the item to the Journal entry. The item can then be accessed by double-clicking the attachment icon that is placed in the body of the Journal entry. The Shortcut option also places an icon for the Outlook item in the body of the entry; this icon looks exactly like the icon that the Attachment option creates. When you double-click the

Shortcut link in the entry, the Outlook item opens. When you use the Shortcut option, a warning box opens and asks whether you trust the embedded object that you are opening. Select Yes to open the item.

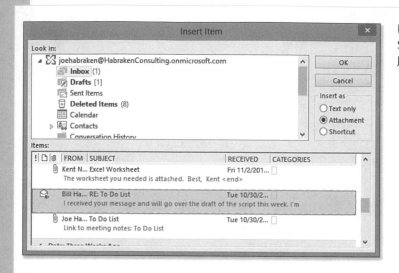

Figure 26.3
Specify an item to add to the Journal entry.

Another possibility for making a Journal entry a more complete record of an activity is to attach a file to an entry. For example, you might have been working on an Excel workbook as part of a project or creating a PowerPoint presentation for a client; in either case, you can attach the actual file you created to the Journal entry.

With a new Journal entry or an existing entry open in the Outlook window, make sure to set the Entry type of the Journal entry to the type of file you attach to the entry. For example, if the entry you are creating is designed to tell you how long (duration) you spent creating a particular Excel worksheet, you want to set the Entry type to Microsoft Excel.

 note
You can attach multiple Outlook items to a Journal entry. You can also attach multiple files to an entry. The more information you include as part of the entry, the more informational the Journal entry becomes when you use it to review the activity.

When you are ready to attach a file to the Journal entry, select the Insert tab and then select Attach File (in the Include group). The Insert File dialog box opens, as shown in Figure 26.4. Locate the file you want to attach to the Journal entry; select the file and then select Insert. An icon for the inserted file appears in the body of the Journal entry.

When you want to view a file that is attached to a Journal entry, double-click the icon for the file. The file's application opens; for example, if the attachment is an Excel workbook, Excel opens and loads that workbook. Attaching files to Journal entries can be useful in recording the amount of time it takes you to create or edit a particular file. Attaching the file (such as an Excel workbook or PowerPoint presentation) enables you to open the file from the Journal entry. You can start the timer in the Journal entry and then open the file from the Journal entry. When you complete your work, you can save the file and then return to the Journal entry to pause the timer.

Figure 26.4
Specify a file to attach to the Journal entry.

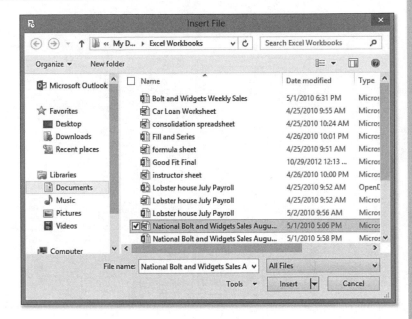

Journal Actions

You can also perform actions on a Journal entry that you have selected in the Journal (you can select multiple entries). The Action group of the Ribbon's Home tab provides two commands: Forward and Move.

If you want to forward an item to a contact, select the item's icon in the Journal (select the icon and title that represent the item on the timeline) and then select the Forward command. A new email message appears, with the Journal item as an attachment (see Figure 26.5).

You can manipulate this email as you do any other email, such as adding a flag or specifying an importance level for the message. Remember that you are attaching a Journal item, which opens in the recipient's Journal. You are not attaching the original item itself, such as an email or a logged application file (for example, a Word document logged in the Journal).

The Move command enables you to move items in the Journal to other folders and locations. Select an item or items in the Journal, and then select Move in the Actions group on the Journal Ribbon. The Move menu provides destination options for the move, such as the Deleted Items folder and the Inbox. To access an Outlook folder not listed on the Move menu, select Other Folder on the menu. This opens the Move Items dialog box, shown in Figure 26.6.

Select a folder from the list provided (the dialog box lists all your Outlook folders). If you want to create a new folder, click the New button to create a new Outlook folder using the Create New Folder dialog box. After you have specified a folder (or a new folder), select OK to close the Move Items dialog box.

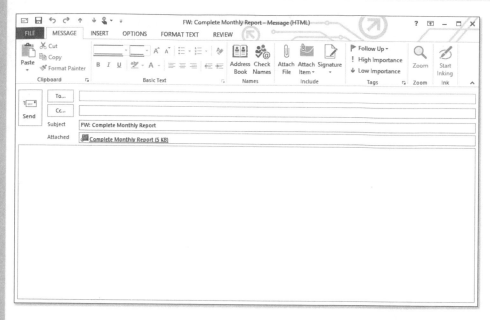

Figure 26.5
You can forward a Journal item as an email attachment.

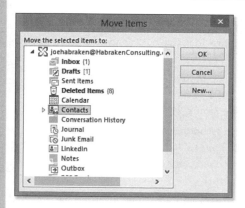

Figure 26.6
Use the Move Items dialog box to specify a destination folder.

If you want to copy the selected Journal item to a folder instead of moving it, select the Copy to Folder command on the Move menu. The Copy Items dialog box opens. Select the destination folder for the copy, or create a new folder as needed.

Viewing the Journal

By default, the Journal provides a Timeline view, with a date range arranged by week along the top of the timeline. The Timeline view also categorizes the Journal entries by entry type (you specified the entry type when creating the Journal entries). For example, any Journal entries that you specified as Email Message types appear under the Entry Type: Email Message heading. You can expand or collapse the entry type categories as necessary. Figure 26.7 shows the Outlook Journal in Timeline view.

Figure 26.7
The Journal timeline with Journal entries.

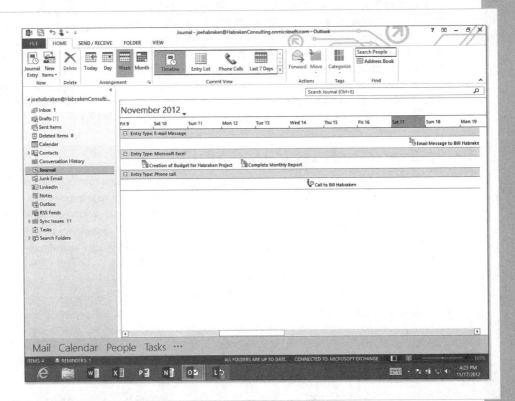

Manipulating the Journal View

You can use the commands in the Arrangement and Current View groups on the Ribbon's Home tab to manipulate your view of the Journal. The Arrangement group enables you to view the timeline by day, week (the default), and month. The Current View group provides different views of the Journal:

- **Timeline:** The default view for the Journal, this view groups entries by entry type and enables you to change the interval for the timeline (day, week, or month).

- **Entry List:** This view displays the entries in a columnar arrangement that includes column headings such as Entry Type, Subject, Start (the date and time you placed the item in the Journal), Duration, and Contact. By default, Outlook lists the items in order by start date, with the newest item listed first.

- **Phone Calls:** This view lists only phone calls in a tabular format, much the same as the Entry List view. So this view is really a filter for phone call entries.

- **Last 7 Days:** This view arranges the item in the same columnar format as the Entry List but shows only items logged in the Journal during the last seven days.

You can manipulate the items in a particular view. For example, in Timeline view, you can collapse or expand the entry type listings; doing so enables you to focus on the entries of a particular type by collapsing all the other entries in the different types. When you are using Entry List view (or the Phone Calls or Last 7 Days views, which also use a columnar format), you can click on a column heading to order the items by the heading. For example, you could list the items by contact (click the Contact column heading) in either an ascending or descending order.

tip

In the Timeline view, the current month is listed at the top of the timeline. Click on the drop-down arrow on the right of the month banner to open a calendar box showing the entire month.

Using Search to Filter Journal Entries

You can use the Instant Search box at the top of the Journal timeline to filter the entries in your Journal. For example, you can have the Search tool list only the Journal entries in a particular category or those that were modified in a certain timeframe. You can also filter the entry list by Journal entries that include attachments or are associated with a particular contact. For example, to view the Journal entries related to a particular contact, click in the Search Journal box and then type the name of the contact. When you press Enter or click the Search icon to run the search, your Journal shows only the entries that reference the contact's name. When you have finished viewing the results of a search, select the Close button (the X in the Search box).

As soon as you place the insertion point in the Search Journal box, the Search Tools appear on the Ribbon. As already mentioned you can use these tools to refine any search. For example, you might want to search by a particular contact's name but also see only the entries related to the contact that have also had a particular category applied to them. To search for a particular category, select the Categorized command in the Refine group and then select the category for the search.

After you have used the various tools provided by the Search tab of the Ribbon, you can return to the Journal Ribbon by selecting Close Search. When you close the search, the "filter" is removed from the Journal entry list, and all the Journal entries are again listed in the Journal timeline.

Working with Notes

Outlook notes are the electronic equivalent of all those scraps of paper in and around your desk that you've used for quickly scrawled notes. Creating notes in Outlook doesn't take any more time than handwriting a note, but Outlook notes are easier to access and use than the paper equivalent. You can use Outlook notes to write down reminders, names, phone numbers, directions, or anything else you need for later reference.

You can quickly create a note while you are working in any of the Outlook folders; select the New Items command, point at More Items, and then select Choose Form. The Choose Form dialog box opens. In the Choose Form dialog box, select Note and then select Open. A new note opens in the Outlook folder in which you are currently working, as shown in Figure 26.8.

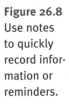

Figure 26.8
Use notes to quickly record information or reminders.

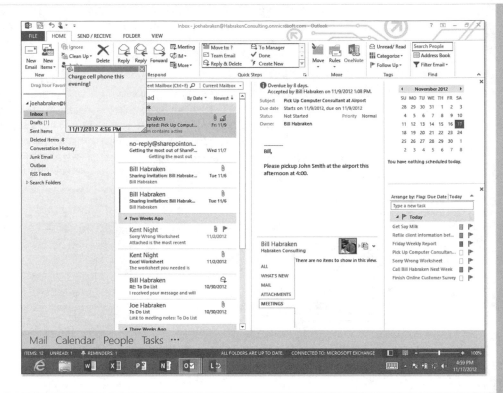

All you have to do is type the information that you want to appear on the note and then close it. You don't have to save the note; Outlook automatically saves it in the Notes folder. You can then use the Navigation bar to quickly switch back to the Mail, Calendar, or Tasks folders without missing a beat.

A note consists of your typed text; you can type as much text as required for the note; however, remember that Microsoft designed notes to be quick reminders. Outlook notes automatically record the time and date when they were created.

The note's window includes a Close button on the right and a menu button on the left. You can use the menu to save the note in a variety of formats, including text. You can also categorize the note or associate the note with a particular contact. If you have a lot of text on a note, you can enlarge the note by using the sizing handle on the bottom right.

As already mentioned, you can create a note from any Outlook folder by using the New Items command. If you are working in an email window or with a particular contact or appointment, you can open a new note by using the shortcut keys Shift+Ctrl+N.

Viewing and Managing Notes

Outlook keeps all your notes in the Notes folder. To open the Notes folder, select the ellipsis (...) to the right of the Tasks link in the Navigation pane. Then select Notes. Another way to open the

Notes folder is to open all your Outlook folders in the Folder pane (this enables you to quickly switch between folders such as your Contacts, Journal, and Notes). Select the ellipsis to the right of Tasks (it really can be considered the Navigation pane's More button), and then select Folders. The Notes folder is listed in your Folders list, which appears in the Folder pane (on the left side of the Outlook window).

The default Notes folder view shows the notes as icons. You can drag the notes within the Notes folder and order them as you like in this view. There are also two alternative views: Notes List and Last 7 Days. Notes List view uses a columnar format that includes a Subject column, a Created column, and a Categories column. Figure 26.9 shows the Notes List view of the Notes folder.

tip
You can drag a note icon from Outlook onto the Windows desktop to place a copy of the note on the desktop. The copy functions as any other note would even if Outlook is not running.

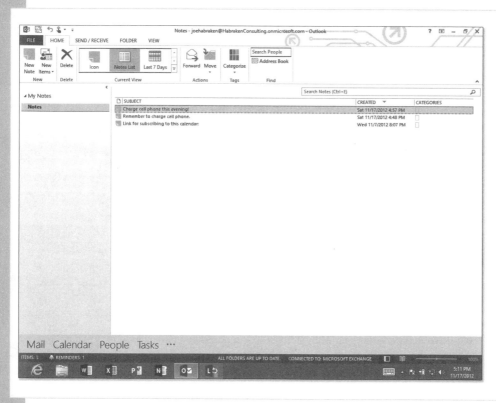

Figure 26.9
Inspect your notes using different views.

In the Notes List view, Outlook sorts the notes by creation date in descending order (newest to oldest). You can click on any column heading, such as Subject or Categories, to sort the notes by that particular column. A second click on a column reverses the order of the sort. Last 7 Days view filters the list of notes and shows only the notes from the last seven days. You can also use the column headings to sort the notes when you are in this view.

➡️ *You can create your own views for the Notes folder (and any other Outlook folder).* **See** *Chapter 22, "Requisite Outlook: Configuration and Essential Features."*

If your Notes folder contains a large number of notes, you can find individual notes using the Search Notes box. Type a search term into the box; only the notes that meet the search criteria appear in the Notes folder.

When you are in the Notes folder, you can quickly create a new note using New Note on the Ribbon's Home tab. The Home tab also provides commands in the Actions group that enable you to forward notes to your contacts or move notes to other folders, such as the Journal and Deleted Items folders. You can also move notes to secondary data files that you have created to back up Outlook items.

To open an existing note, double-click that note in the Notes folder. You can edit the text in the open note as needed. If you want to copy, print, or delete a note, right-click on the note. The shortcut menu that appears provides Copy, Quick Print, and Delete commands (among others).

Creating Appointments and Tasks from Notes

Because notes often contain information that you might want to transfer to another Outlook item, such as an appointment or a task, you might want to create an Outlook item from a note. For example, you might have a note that reminds you to take a report with you when you meet a colleague for lunch; you want to make sure that you create a lunch appointment in your calendar that includes this information.

You can quickly create a new appointment by dragging a note onto the Calendar heading in the Navigation bar. A new appointment dialog box opens, as shown in Figure 26.10.

The subject of the appointment contains the text from the note. You can enter the time, date, and place for the meeting, as needed. You can also modify the subject and body of the appointment, if necessary. When you select Save & Close, Outlook adds the new appointment to your calendar.

You can also quickly create tasks from your notes. Simply drag the note onto the Tasks heading on the Navigation bar. Outlook creates the new task, using the note's text as the task's subject. You can modify the task as needed, including the subject, start date, due date, status, and priority. When you select Save & Close, Outlook saves the changes to the task and returns you to the Notes folder.

 tip

You can also quickly create new tasks from notes by dragging a note onto the Tasks pane in the To-Do Bar. The To-Do Bar isn't included in the Notes folder view by default. Use the View commands on the View tab of the Notes' Ribbon for the To-Do Bar to add it to the Notes window.

PART V

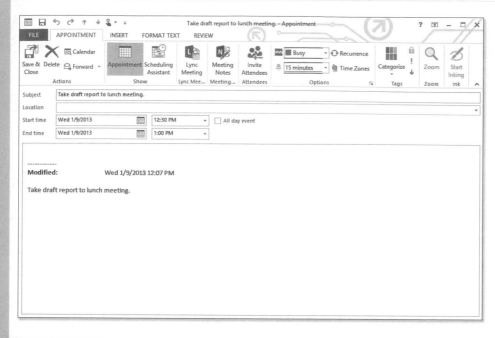

 caution

The Notes options found in the Outlook 2010 Options window have been removed from Outlook 2013. All notes are yellow and have a default size of medium, have a default font of 11-point Calibri, and display the date and time the note was last modified. You cannot change any of these default settings; however, how many of us really modified these settings when we could in Outlook 2010? Notes still provide you with a quick way to get information logged for later use or reference.

SECURING AND MAINTAINING OUTLOOK

Outlook's capabilities for communication are based on the fact that Outlook is connected to a data network. Whereas some Outlook users take advantage of Outlook's features in controlled and secure corporate network environments, many of us use Outlook as a tool for communicating over the Internet. This potentially opens our computers to outside attack by viruses and other malware. Even the most secure network environments fail to completely protect Outlook users from malicious email file attachments or junk email.

In this chapter, we take a look at some of the ways to secure Outlook. This chapter also discusses some of the maintenance tools you can use to keep your Outlook environment more organized, such as email rules and the Outlook archiving feature. We even look at how to configure Outlook to autoreply to messages that you receive when you are out of the office.

 tip

A complete discussion of computer and network security is beyond the scope of this book. For more information on securing Windows 8, check out Que's *Microsoft Windows 8 In Depth,* by Brian Knittel and Paul McFedries.

Security Overview

The fact that Outlook receives data from other people (in some cases, people unknown to you) makes Outlook a potential source of attacks on your computer. These attacks can include the appropriation of information that you store in Outlook, such as your Contacts list. Nothing is more embarrassing (and potentially damaging) than having an infected file attachment "take over" Outlook and send copies of itself to everyone in your address book.

Attacks on your computer are not limited to email attachments and code embedded in HTML messages (which we discuss later in this chapter). Hackers have been known to exploit imperfections in software packages such as Microsoft Outlook and the other Office applications. Operating systems (such as Windows) and applications use TCP/IP ports for communication between your computer and the Internet. Remember that most of us now use persistent Internet connections, such as broadband and DSL, which means our computers are constantly connected to a public network. This gives hackers the ability to potentially invade our computers.

 note

The TCP/IP (Transport Control Protocol/Internet Protocol) protocol stack is the protocol that your computer uses to communicate on IP networks such as the Internet.

Protecting your computer potentially involves a number of different measures. Attacks via TCP/IP port exploits can be countermanded by using a firewall such as the Windows firewall or the firewall capabilities of your WiFi router. A firewall is software or a device that sits between your computer (or computer network) and the Internet. A firewall examines data coming into the computer network or network and can filter out data that does not adhere to the firewall's rules.

Although this chapter primarily looks at what Outlook has to offer in terms of security features, it's not a bad idea to have a good feel for the type of threats you might face. Earlier we briefly discussed IP port exploits and how a firewall can help protect your computer. Let's discuss viruses and other malware a little more closely and also look at some basic things beyond using the Outlook security settings that you can do to protect your computer.

Malware and Antivirus Software

It seems that malware—software designed to do your computer harm, such as viruses—has been around as long as personal computing. All of us who use Windows as our computer operating system know that we must install some sort of antivirus and antimalware software that helps defend our computer and the information stored on our computer from attack.

Malware (or "bad software") comes in a variety of flavors. There are self-replicating viruses, which can easily spread from computer to computer via infected email attachments. Viruses typically require that you activate them, so don't open attachments in emails from senders you don't know. However, even a friend can inadvertently send you an infected file.

 note

Outlook automatically blocks a lot of file extensions that prevent you from receiving malware attachments. For example, program files such as `.exe`, `.com`, and `.app` files are blocked, as are Active Server Pages (`.asp`) and Basic Source Code (`.bas`).

Worms also can infect your computer and do not require you to activate them. They can quickly spread to computers on the same network (yes, even a home or small business network). Trojan horses are malware programs that are disguised as something else. For example, you might receive a file that claims it is a slideshow of firework displays from around the world. If the file is a Trojan horse, there will be fireworks, but just in terms of the havoc that will be wreaked on your PC.

The best way to protect against viruses and other malware is to use an antivirus program. Windows 8 has Windows Defender built into the operating system; it provides you with antivirus protection without adding third-party software. However, if you are particularly fond of a third-party vendor's antivirus software or feel otherwise compelled to purchase additional protection, other antivirus software packages are available for Windows 8, including Kaspersky Antivirus, Panda Antivirus, and Norton Antivirus. (You can check the Web for reviews and other information on these and many more antivirus programs.)

If you use Windows 7, you can install Microsoft's Security Essentials for free. It is available in the Microsoft Safety & Security Center web page, which is accessible from the www.microsoft.com website. And again, if you prefer to use a third-party antivirus program, plenty of options are available.

You might find that some antivirus programs (from third-party vendors) have features that are directly integrated with Outlook, so some antivirus/spam protection programs might add a spam or antispam folder to your Outlook Folders pane (in addition to the Outlook default Junk Email folder).

Some antivirus programs also add new commands to the Outlook Ribbon. For example, you might find commands for the immediate scanning of email items or attachments. It makes sense for you to spend a little time getting to know your antivirus program and how it operates. If the antivirus program also provides integrated functionality with Outlook, it makes sense to take advantage of the spam filters and file attachment scans that it provides. Outlook offers a number of built-in features related to spam control (which we get to later in this chapter in the section, "Coping with Junk Email").

Strong Password Protection

Your email account is password protected. After you configure an email account for use in Outlook, you don't have to re-enter that password to access the account—but that password is still protecting the email account. Windows 8 gives you the option to password-protect your computer by requiring that you enter a logon name and password. This logon name and password can be a Windows Live account name, such as your Outlook.com username and password. So your computer's protection really relies on the strength of the password that you use, as does your Outlook email account.

Not all attacks on your email account and your computer are related to nefarious and complex viruses attempting to infiltrate Outlook and your operating system. Many hackers rely on extremely weak and easily guessed passwords to hijack your email account or gain access to your computer. If you use a weak, easily guessed password (or no password), nearly anyone can log onto your computer and access your data. Or if someone knows your email account name (which is easy to find online) and a little bit about you (also found online), a hacker can probably guess your "easy" password.

The only way to avoid the easy password hack is to protect your computer and your email account or accounts with strong passwords. A strong password (as defined by Microsoft) is a password with at least seven characters. The strong password also uses a combination of numeric and alphanumeric characters and does not include easy-to-guess or personal information. For example, if I use the password "joseph" as my Windows account password, I'm making it easy for someone else to guess my password. Create a more complex, strong password, but make sure that you remember the password. Of course, scribbling passwords on scraps of paper that are easily accessible by anyone walking in the door doesn't set up a very secure environment, either, even if you have created the strongest of passwords.

You probably have noticed that a logon password is not required when you start Outlook (unless you use Outlook in a work environment where the network administrator has configured the software to require a logon at startup). So if your computer is running and you are away from the computer, anyone can start Outlook and poke around in your Mail, Contacts, or Calendar folders.

You have two options for requiring a logon when you start Outlook. If you are using Outlook in an Exchange Server environment (which includes those of you with Office 365 subscriptions), you can configure Outlook so that it always requires user identification upon startup. If you use Outlook for Internet email (such as a POP3 account), you can password-protect your Outlook data file. Both of these Outlook logon-protection schemes are set up in the Outlook Account Settings dialog box, which is accessed in the Outlook Backstage.

To configure Outlook to require user identification (when you are using an Exchange email account), follow these steps:

1. Select File to open the Backstage.

2. With Info selected in the Backstage, select Account Settings and then select Account Settings (again). The Account Settings dialog box opens.

3. Select the Data Files tab in the Account Settings dialog box.

4. Select your Exchange email account data file in the list provided by the Data Files tab.

5. Click Settings. The Microsoft Exchange dialog box opens.

6. Click the Security tab.

7. On the Security tab (see Figure 27.1), select the Always Prompt for Logon Credentials check box; then click OK to close the Microsoft Exchange dialog box.

You can close the Account Settings dialog box to return to the Outlook application window. When you start Outlook in the future, you are required to log in by entering your username and password.

If you are using Outlook for Internet email, you can password-protect Outlook by actually password-protecting your Outlook data file (.pst file). You are then required to provide the data file password when you start Outlook. Don't password-protect the Outlook data file unless you really feel it necessary (for example, when you share a computer with others).

The Outlook data file is accessed via the Account Settings dialog box. Open the Account Settings from the Backstage using the Account Settings button (just as you did in the steps provided a couple paragraphs ago).

On the Data Files tab of the Account Settings dialog box, select the data file for your Internet email account; then select Settings. In the Settings dialog box, select Change Password to open the Change Password dialog box. Enter a new password, and then verify the new password (also make sure you remember this password; if you do write it down, keep it in a safe and secure place). To save the password in your Windows password list, select the Save This Password in Your Password List check box. Then click OK to close the Change Password dialog box. You can also close the Account Settings dialog box.

Figure 27.1
The Security tab of the Microsoft Exchange dialog box.

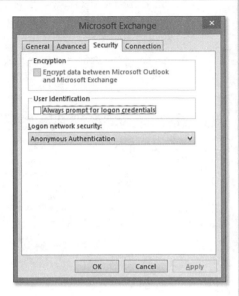

The data file is now password-protected. The next time you start Outlook, you are asked to provide the Outlook data file password. Enter the password, and then click OK to open Outlook.

 caution

If you don't share your computer with other users or don't work in an environment where other users can access your computer (such as your own office), there is no real advantage to requiring a logon when starting Outlook (in an Exchange Server setting) or password-protecting your Outlook data file (when using Internet email). And if you forget the password, it is a real disadvantage. Also, in corporate Exchange Server environments, the network administrator probably does not want you to change any of your Outlook settings.

Configuring Outlook Security Settings

Microsoft Office 2013 has bundled the security settings for each of the member applications in the Trust Center. Each application, such as Outlook, has its own Trust Center where you can view and configure the various security settings.

➡ *For an overview of the Trust Center,* **see** *"Using the Trust Center," p. 48.*

To access the Outlook Trust Center, follow these steps:

1. Select File to open the Outlook Backstage.

2. In the Backstage, select Options. The Outlook Options window opens.

3. Select Trust Center; an Options window opens that provides a series of links to Outlook and

Office privacy statements, as well as to Microsoft Trustworthy Computing. Microsoft also supplies a recommendation that you not change the settings in the Trust Center, if you want to keep your computer secure.

4. To access the Trust Center settings, select the Trust Center Settings button. The Trust Center opens, as shown in Figure 27.2.

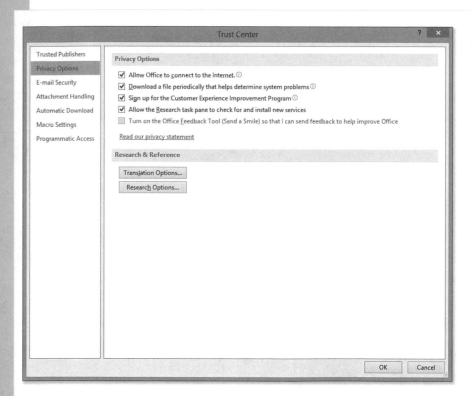

Figure 27.2
The Outlook Trust Center.

The Trust Center provides different categories of privacy and security settings. Figure 27.2 shows the Privacy Options. Categories such as Trusted Publishers and Macro Settings are found in the Trust Center of other Office applications, such as Word and Excel. Trusted Publishers are discussed in Chapter 2, "Navigating and Customizing the Office Interface" and the Macro Settings options are discussed in Appendix B, "Office Macros."

→ *For an overview of the macro-related Trust Center settings, **see** Appendix B, "Office Macros."*

The Trust Center categories that are directly related to the Outlook application environment are as follows:

- **Privacy Options:** The privacy options are all check boxes related to connecting Office applications to the Internet (for software updates), the Microsoft Customer Experience Improvement program, and the installation of new services for the Research task pane. You can determine which privacy options you disable. The options for updating content should remain updated. The Privacy Options window also provides settings for research and reference. You have the option to select language pairs for translation (Translation options), and you can select the reference books and research sites used by the Reference task pane using the Research options.

- **Email Security:** The security options provide encrypted mail settings and the capability to manage digital IDs for sending encrypted and secure mail. You can also choose to read all your standard mail in plain text. We talk about encrypted email options in the next section.

- **Attachment Handling:** These options relate to the inclusion of personal information when sending Office documents as attachments and attachment preview for received emails. These options are discussed in more detail in the "Dealing with Message Attachments" section in this chapter.

- **Automatic Download:** These options relate to the download and display of pictures in email messages. Junk email senders can use pictures in HTML messages to increase the number of junk emails you receive. For more about these settings, see "The Perils of HTML Email," later in this chapter.

- **Programmatic Access:** These settings allow you to enable warnings that alert you when another program accesses the Outlook address book. For example, you might use a smartphone or smart device that syncs your contacts, calendars, or email with the device. This is considered access by another program but is okay. Other access might be the work of a virus or other malware. You can also set a warning for your antivirus program; Outlook can let you know whether it is inactive or outdated.

Many of these Trust Center options can be left with the default options enabled. Change the security settings only if you have a compelling reason to do so. In some networking environments (such as an Exchange Server environment), the network administrator determines the settings for your Outlook mail client.

 caution

If you are going to send encrypted email to another user, that user also needs to have a Digital ID. You and the other party must then exchange emails that are digitally signed. When you add that person to your contacts (or update the contact information), the digital certificate is added to the contact information. The person on the other end must also add you to the Contacts folder in the same manner.

Encrypting Email and Using Digital Signatures

You can choose to raise the bar for email security by encrypting your email. Encrypted email is mail that has been transformed using a mathematical algorithm. The only way to read encrypted mail is to decrypt the mail. Outlook uses digital certificates to verify the sender of encrypted email. If you don't want to encrypt your emails, you can use a digital certificate (also known as a digital ID) to verify the authenticity of the email that you send.

To send encrypted email, you must obtain a digital certificate. If you work at a company that wants you to encrypt your email, it should provide you with a digital certificate. If you run your own small business or work at home and feel the need to encrypt messages, you need to obtain your own digital certificate from a certifying authority. A number of certificate authorities are available online, including A-Trust (www.-a-trust.at), CertPlus (http://certplus.com), and VeriSign (http://digitalid.verisign.com).

The settings related to encrypted email and digital certificates are in the Outlook Trust Center's Email Security options. Figure 27.3 shows the Email Security options.

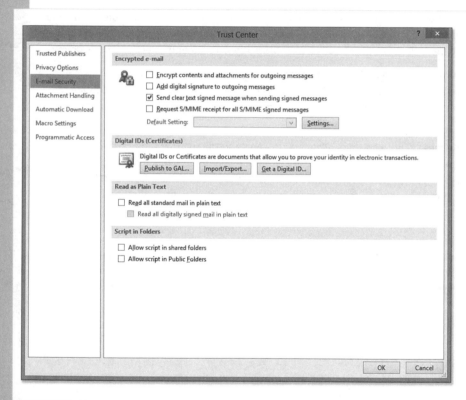

Figure 27.3
Email Security options.

Before you use the Encrypted email settings, you need to either import an existing digital ID or get a digital ID online. If you need a digital ID, click the Get a Digital ID button. This starts your web browser and opens a Microsoft-sponsored web page that provides a list of certificate authorities. Select a certificate authority, and you are walked through the process of obtaining (meaning paying for) a digital certificate.

If you have a digital ID that your company has provided, it might have already been configured on your computer. If a digital certificate has been exported from another computer, you can import the ID into the Trust Center. Click the Import/Export button and then use the Import/Export Digital ID dialog box to specify the filename, password, and digital ID name for the certificate. Then select OK.

If you have purchased your own digital ID, you need to install it on your computer. The certificate installation process is typically provided to you in an email from the certifying authority. Many certifying authorities provide a link that takes you to an installation web page.

Encrypted email uses a private key and a public key. The email is encrypted by the public key associated with your digital ID. The private key, which is then used on the receiving end to decrypt the message, is stored in the recipient's Contacts folder in your contact entry. Anyone intercepting or otherwise pirating the message cannot decrypt the message content or attachments.

Options for Encrypting Email

You have options for encrypting your email. If you want to encrypt all outgoing email and attachments, you can specify that fact in the Encrypted Email section of the Email Security options (open the Trust Center via the Trust Center link in the Outlook Options window). Select the Encrypt Contents and Attachments for Outgoing Messages check box.

You can also choose to encrypt individual emails. This makes more sense than sending all your email encrypted, particularly if you need to share encrypted messages with only one or two recipients. Remember that you and the recipient must share Digital ID information before you can send encrypted emails.

When you have a new message open that you want to encrypt, select the Ribbon's Options tab. In the Permissions group, select the Encrypt command. Prepare your mail message, including attaching files or items as needed. You can then send the message.

If you send an encrypted message to an individual who does not have a digital signature (or if you haven't added the individual to your Contacts folder), Outlook opens an Encryption Problems dialog box and lists recipients of the email. You can click the Send Unencrypted button to send the email as a regular message. Otherwise, click Cancel, and make sure that the recipient is in your Contacts folder. Then attempt to send the message again.

 tip

You can check to see if a digital certificate is installed and available to Outlook. In the Email Security options window, click the Settings button. The Change Security Settings dialog box should list your digital ID in the Signing Certificate and Encryption Certificate boxes.

 note

If you don't have a digital ID, the Options tab does not list the Encrypt and Sign commands.

Digitally Signing Emails

You can also use your digital ID to digitally sign email. This does not encrypt the message content or attachments, but it does verify you as the sender. You can choose to send a digital signature with all your outgoing messages by selecting the Add digital signature to outgoing messages check box in the Encrypted Email section of the Email Security options.

Because you are using a digital signature as a security measure, it makes sense to receive confirmation that your digital signature is validated by the recipients and that messages are received unaltered. This notification can also tell you when a message was opened and by whom. In the Encrypted Email section of the Email Security options, select the Request S/MIME Receipt for All S/MIME Messages check box.

You can also choose to digitally sign specific messages (instead of signing all messages). With a new message open, navigate to the Ribbon's Options tab. Then select the Sign command in the Permission Group. When you send the email, a message box opens and asks you to grant permission to use the key (associated with the digital ID) to sign the message. Click Grant Permission, and then select OK to send the message. When the recipient receives the email, it provides a Signed By statement and includes a digital certificate image in the header of the message. The recipient can click the digital certificate to view details related to the digital ID.

The Perils of HTML Email

Believe it or not, HTML email can pose a threat to your computer. HTML email can include active content such as Active X controls and scripts, and these can potentially be malware. HTML email can also include graphic images. These images can include a web beacon.

A web beacon is basically HTML code that is typically used on websites to count the number of people who access the website; however, web beacons can also be used to send information to a website. So web beacons in HTML emails can verify that your email address is valid (you activate the web beacon when you open or view the email). The verification of your email address is sent to the "owner" of the web beacon and results in you receiving much more junk email.

 note

Outlook can serve as your RSS (Really Simple Syndication) feed reader. Right-click the RSS Feed folder in your Mail folder, and then select Add a New RSS Feed. You can copy and paste the URL for any website that provides an RSS feed into the New RSS dialog box. You can then use Outlook to read the feeds from the RSS source.

To turn off HTML email as the format for received messages, select the Read All Standard Mail in Plain Text check box in the Read As Plain Text section of the Email Security options. Even if you choose to receive plain-text messages, you can quickly switch a message from plain text to HTML when viewing the message. The message Infobar displays "This message was converted to plain text. Select the message and then select Display as HTML."

If you still decide to receive messages as HTML email (I mean, who really wants to receive text-only email messages?), Outlook blocks automatic picture downloads for external sources, by default. And because many web beacons are associated with images, you are protected, to a certain extent. The settings related to picture download and other download-related options, such as RSS item downloads, are in the Automatic Download options of the Outlook Trust Center. Because you can specify safe senders and safe recipients in the Junk Email filter (which we discuss later in this chapter in the section, "Coping with Junk Email"), you can leave the Don't Download Pictures Automatically in HTML Email Message or RSS Items setting enabled. You can then place friends and family members (or other trusted individuals) in the Safe Senders and Safe Recipients lists (as discussed in "Coping with Junk Email").

Dealing with Message Attachments

Outlook blocks many file types as mail attachments. When a blocked file type is included in a message that you receive, Outlook provides a message that a potentially unsafe file type was blocked. Message attachments can certainly contain malware, so blocking file types that are programs or executable files makes sense. Table 27.1 lists some of the blocked file types.

Table 27.1 A Subset of Blocked File Types

File Extension	Description
.app	Executable application file
.asp	Active Server page
.bat	Batch processing file
.chm	HTML help file
.com	Command file
.crt	Certificate file
.hlp	Windows Help file
.js	JavaScript source code
.jse	JScript encoded script file
.msh	Microsoft Shell
.prf	Windows System file
.prg	Program file
.scf	Windows Explorer command
.scr	Windows Screen Saver
.vbp	Visual Basic project file
.vbs	Microsoft Visual Basic for Applications script (or Visual Basic script)

These file types and a number of others are blocked because they are considered potential vehicles for malware. If you glance at the subset of blocked files listed in Table 27.1, you can see why these file types are on the blocked list. Malware masquerading as any of these file types can do a lot of bad things to your computer.

 caution

In an Exchange Server environment, your administrator can tweak the blocked file list. If you are using Outlook for Internet email, you can change settings in the system Registry to unblock specific file types. I don't think this is a good idea unless you are very familiar with editing the Windows Registry. The Microsoft Support website (support.microsoft.com) provides the steps for editing the Registry. Do a search for "Outlook blocked unsafe attachments."

No configuration settings in Outlook can be adjusted to allow blocked file types. If you attempt to send one of these file types as an email attachment, Outlook alerts you that the recipient will not be able to receive the attachment (this is definite if the recipient uses Outlook). If you have to send a blocked file type, there is a way around this.

The first possibility for sending a blocked file type to an Outlook user is to change the file extension on the file. For example, you can change a blocked extension to .txt or .blk (for "blocked"). When you send the attachment to the recipient, make sure you direct him or her in the message to rename the file and change the extension back to the original (such as .chm or .js).

The second possibility for sending blocked file types is probably easier and a little more fool-proof than messing around with the filename the default extension: You can place the file in a zipped folder (archive) and then send the zipped file as the attachment. The recipient can unzip the file and access the original file.

In Windows 8, you can right-click on any file in the File Explorer and access a shortcut menu. Point at Send To, and then select Compressed (zipped) folder. This compresses the file (s) (or a folder) into a ZIP archive. Windows 7 also provides this option for zipping a file or group of selected files.

Before we end our discussion of attachments and Outlook, we need to address two settings in the Attachment Handling options of Outlook's Trust Center. Figure 27.4 shows the Attachment Handling options.

Figure 27.4
Attachment
Handling options.

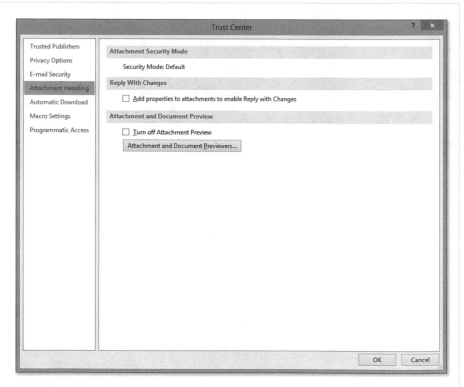

When you select the Add properties to Attachments to Enable Reply with Changes check box, you are allowing Outlook to send personal information that has been placed in a document that you have edited using the Track Changes feature. Information such as your name or email address can easily end up in the properties of an Office file that you have worked with.

If you don't want Outlook to share this personal information in the file's properties, be sure to clear the Add Properties to Attachments to Enable Reply with Changes check box (it is cleared by default). This keeps your personal information out of the attached document; however, this also makes it impossible for you to track changes that others might make to a document that you send them. You must decide whether it's more important to track changes or protect your personal information.

One other setting that can help protect you from security issues with attachments is the Turn Off Attachment Preview check box. If you want to negate a preview of attached files, make sure that the check box has been cleared.

Coping with Junk Email

Junk email is certainly a scourge. It fills up your Inbox with a lot of spam that you just don't want; taking the time to delete this stuff is a pain. And junk email can be more than just a nuisance—it can also potentially serve as part of a phishing scam. In a phishing scam, you receive what appears to be a legitimate email message from a business that you frequent on the web (Amazon, eBay, or any other website where you buy stuff or do financial transactions). These businesses typically keep your personal information, including credit card numbers, on file. The phishing email asks you to update personal information or provides a link that takes you to a fake website where you are asked to supply your password or other personal information. When the phisher has the info, all sorts of bad things can happen.

Outlook's junk email filtering relies on message content, including keywords and phrases, to determine whether a message is junk. Sometimes it places a legitimate message in the Junk Email folder.

The Junk Email filter can also block senders in your blocked sender list. So although Outlook tries its best to ferret out junk email, you can help it by providing information such as safe senders, safe recipients, and blocked senders, to make the Junk Email filter more efficient.

The Junk Email filter can provide different levels of protection from junk email. By default, the filter is set to Low, which moves messages received in the Inbox to the Junk Email folder only if they are obvious junk email messages (at least, obvious to Outlook in terms of content and overall structure). You can change the level of protection using the Junk Email Options dialog box, which we discuss shortly.

Working with the Junk Email Commands

The commands for dealing with individual messages and their junk email status (whether they are or they aren't) are in the Delete group of the Ribbon's Home tab (when the Mail folder is selected in the Folder Pane). Figure 27.5 shows the Junk command and its menu of associated commands.

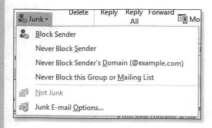

Figure 27.5
The Junk commands.

You can use the commands on the Junk command's menu to specify the "junk" status of a message, no matter what mail folder you are working in (meaning the Inbox or the Junk Email folder). First, let's look at options related to legitimate messages that are marked as junk and placed in the Junk Email folder.

As you receive email, the Junk Email filter moves any email that it considers junk to the Junk Email folder. You can view mail that has been placed in the Junk Email folder by selecting Junk Email in Navigation pane (when the Mail folder is selected).

If you find a message listed in the Junk Email folder that is not junk, you can mark it as "not junk" and have it moved to the Inbox. Select the message in the Junk Email folder, and then select Junk and then Not Junk. The Mark As Not Junk dialog box opens, letting you know that the message was moved back into the Inbox folder. An option box is also included in the dialog box that enables you to always trust email from the sender of the message. This option adds the sender of the message to your Safe Senders list; you have to decide whether you want to leave this check box selected (by default) or choose to deselect it. To close the Mark As Not Junk dialog box, select OK.

You can also add email senders to the Safe Senders list by selecting any message in any folder (including the Junk Email folder) and then selecting the Never Block Sender on the Junk command's menu. A message box opens, letting you know that the sender has been added to your Safe Senders List. Using this Junk option does not move the email from the Junk Email folder.

You can also place a sender's entire domain on the Safe Senders list using the Never Block Sender's Domain command. This command also does not move the email from your Junk Email folder to the Inbox (same as the Never Block Sender command); you need to drag the email (or emails) to the Inbox or use the Not Junk command, as discussed earlier.

When you are working in the Inbox, you can specify a message or messages as junk. Select the message or messages and then select Block Sender. The sender of the message (or messages) is added to the Block Sender List. The message is also moved to the Junk Email folder.

Setting Junk Email Options

You can set the level of protection that the Junk Email filter provides and also work with your safe senders, safe recipients, and blocked senders lists. Select the Junk command, and then select Junk Email Options. The Junk Email Options dialog box opens, as shown in Figure 27.6.

Figure 27.6
The Junk Email Options dialog box.

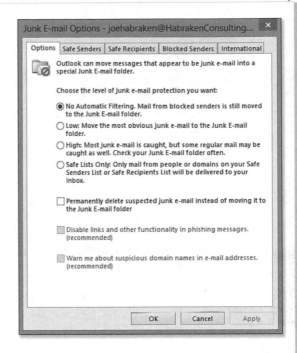

The dialog box provides five tabs:

- **Options:** The Junk Email options are a series of option buttons and check boxes (see Figure 27.6). The Low, High, and Safe Lists Only option buttons determine the level of protection. Low, obviously, is the lowest setting; Safe Lists Only is the highest level. The higher the protection level settings, the greater the number of received messages that will end up in your Junk Email folder. The Options tab also enables you to specify whether junk email should be deleted rather than moved to the Junk Email folder. By default, links are disabled in phishing messages, and you are also warned when a suspicious domain name appears in an email address. By default, your sent emails are postmarked, to help the receiver distinguish them as regular emails.

- **Safe Senders:** This tab provides a list of safe senders that you might have created using the Never Block commands on the Junk menu. You can also add, edit, or remove senders from the Safe Senders list on this tab. You can import a list of safe senders from a delimited text file or export your list to a text file. Two other options provided by this tab are two check boxes: Also Trust Email from My Contacts and Automatically Add People I Email to the Safe Senders List. Both of these check boxes are designed to keep your frequent contacts' and email recipients' messages out of the Junk Email folder.

- **Safe Recipients:** This list might seem a little odd because you are receiving the message that must be either marked as junk or not. If you receive emails that include other recipients (such as a particular contact group that the sender has created), you can specify that any or all of these recipients be added to the Safe Recipients list. This gives Outlook another parameter in determining a received message's junk status. You can add, edit, or remove safe recipients as needed. You can also import a list from a file. This tab works in much the same way as the Safe Senders tab.

- **Blocked Senders:** This is your rogues' gallery of blocked senders. You can add, edit, or remove blocked senders on this tab. You can also import a list of blocked senders or export your list. Remember, any messages from an address or domain name on the Blocked Senders list are treated as junk email.

- **International:** This tab enables you to block top-level domains, meaning that you can block emails from senders who are from specific countries or regions. Countries have their own top-level domain designation, such as .aq (Antarctica), .ba (Brazil), and .nz (New Zealand)—all places I want to go. To block all emails ending in a specific top-level domain, click the Blocked Top-Level Domain List button. Select from the list provided, and then click OK. You can also block emails that are encoded in a particular character set; this means that you can block email sent in specific languages. Click the Blocked Encodings List button, and then specify by language the mail you want to block.

 note

When a message is postmarked, it is tagged with unique information related to that message, such as the list of recipients and the time the message was sent. The postmark is valid only for that message. Postmarking a message means that the message takes a little longer to be processed and to leave your Outlook Outbox. Outlook does not view postmarked emails as junk. Spammers would find it a burden to postmark all their messages; sending tons of spam requires a lot of computing power, and postmarking all spam would take increased computing power. This means that postmarking spam would cost spammers money.

The strength of the Junk Email filter is directly related to the time you take to fine-tune the various options provided in the Junk Email Options dialog box. If you are fairly diligent about specifying safe senders and blocked senders, and if you increase the level of junk email protection on the Options tab, you should see a decrease in junk email. However, remember that spam email is an industry, and those in this industry are constantly looking for ways to get around junk email filters and other types of spam protection. I doubt whether any of us will ever be completely free from spam.

Creating Email Rules

You can automate management of your Mail folder using Outlook rules. A rule can delete, flag, or move messages. For example, a rule can be used to automatically move messages in the Inbox from a particular sender to a particular mail-related folder. This can help you keep organized, particularly if you need to place mail from a particular sender in a folder other than the Inbox. Although rules can't necessarily be considered a security feature, they do give you control over the disposition of the email messages that you receive.

Outlook rules are basically a set of conditions. When the conditions of the rule are met by an email message, the rule acts on the message. Rules can take all sorts of things into account, such as sender, message subject, and message body content. Rules can be simple or complex; it all depends on what you want the rule to do.

Creating a Quick Rule for a Specific Sender

Outlook makes it easy for you to create rules based on the properties of a selected email. For example, you can quickly create a simple rule that moves email from a particular sender from your Inbox to another specified location. Follow these steps:

1. Select a message from a sender in your Inbox.

2. Select the Rules command in the Move group.

3. Select Always Move Messages From *name of sender*. The Rules and Alerts dialog box appears, as shown in Figure 27.7.

Figure 27.7
The Rules and Alerts dialog box.

4. Select a folder in the Rules and Alerts dialog box, or use the New button to create a new folder using the Create New Folder dialog box (and then select the new folder).

5. Click OK.

The new rule is created. The selected message moves to the folder that you specified when you created the rule. Messages in the Inbox that also meet the conditions of the rule (the single condition of a specified sender) move to the folder you chose in the Rules and Alerts dialog box.

Creating Complex Rules

You can also create rules that are more complex. Rules can use multiple criteria and perform multiple actions. Outlook provides a Rules Wizard that makes it fairly straightforward to create rules with multiple criteria and multiple actions.

If you have an email message that meets the criteria (or some of the criteria) that you include in a rule, you can speed up the creation of the rule by selecting that message. To open the Create Rule dialog box, select the Rules command and then select Create Rule. Figure 27.8 shows the Create Rule dialog box.

Figure 27.8
The Create Rule dialog box.

The Create Rule dialog box provides a number of check boxes and other options that enable you to create a rule based on the currently selected message. The criteria for the rule can consist of the sender, the subject text, and the message recipient (or recipients, if the message was sent to more than one recipient). To set the criteria or conditions for the rule, select the appropriate check boxes and provide additional information, as required (such as subject text).

Because rules need to "do something" based on your conditions, you are provided several check boxes in the Do the Following area of the dialog box. You can have the rule provide a new alert window when a message is received that meets the conditions of the rule. You can also choose that a sound be played when the rule's conditions are met. You can use the Browse button to use any .wav sound file on your computer for this purpose.

You also specify that the rule move the item to a particular folder. The Select Folder button specifies a folder as needed.

So the Create Rule dialog box limits you to three different conditions (sender, subject, and receiver) and can open an alert window, play a sound, and/or move the message to a specified folder. This doesn't seem much better than the rule we quickly created in the previous section based on the sender of the email. There has to be a tool that enables you to beef up a rule with more conditions and multiple actions. There is—read on.

The Rule Wizard

Complexity and functionality can be added to a rule using the Rule Wizard. With the Create Rule dialog box open, select the Advanced Options button in the lower-right corner. The Rules Wizard opens, as shown in Figure 27.9.

The first wizard screen asks you to select all the conditions to be used by the new rule. These conditions can be related to sender, subject, message importance, specific words in the body, flags, categories, and messages with an attachment. Many of the conditions that you select in the conditions list require you to provide additional information in the Edit the Rule description box of the Rules Wizard to flesh out that particular condition. So select conditions using the check boxes provided in the Step 1: Select Condition(s) Box.

Figure 27.9
The Rules Wizard: Set conditions.

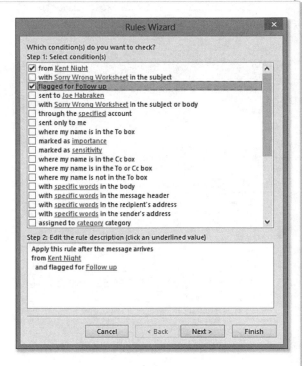

In the Step 2: Edit the Rule description box, select any underlined items associated with the conditions you select in the Step 1 box. Provide the information required by each condition; for example, Specific Words in the Body Condition requires that you click the specific words link and supply a list of words for the rule to use. At this point in the process, you are provided only the conditions for the rules, not what the rule will do. After providing and fine-tuning your conditions, click Next.

 note

Rules can be created for your RSS feeds. See the RSS feed conditions provided by the Rules Wizard on the condition screen.

On the next wizard screen, you specify the actions that you want the rule to perform. Figure 27.10 shows the What Do You Want to Do with the Message screen.

Select an action or actions in the Step 1: Select Action(s) box. If you select an action that contains a link, you need to provide the details for the action in the Step 2: Edit the Rule description box. For example, if you select the Forward It to People or Public Group action in Step 1, you need to specify the people or public group in Step 2 (specify the people using the Address Book).

After you specify the action or actions for the rule and provide the details for the action, click Next. The next wizard screen enables you to configure any exceptions that you want to have for the rule. These exceptions could relate to mail from specific people, messages that are flagged for a particular action, or messages with specific words in the subject or body. Use the check boxes in the Step 1 box to select individual exceptions to the rule. For example, if you create a rule that moves messages to a particular folder (the action) based on the subject line or keywords in the body (the condition), you can set an exception for the rule, such as ignoring the rule if the message is from a particular person.

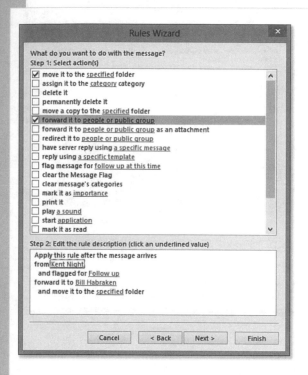

Figure 27.10
The Rules Wizard: Specify the actions for the rule.

You are certainly not required to specify an exception or exceptions for a rule. However, if there are exceptions, use the exceptions check boxes in the Step 1 box to specify them. Then provide the underlined value information for any exception you have selected for the rule in the Step 2 box.

When you are ready to continue the rule creation process, click Next. The Finish Rule Setup screen appears, as shown in Figure 27.11.

Specify a name for the new rule (or you can go with the default, which is based on the first action you selected when you started this process). The Turn On This Rule check box is selected by default, so the rule is enabled. You can choose to run the rule on messages already in the Inbox by selecting the appropriate check box. This screen also enables you to review your rule, including

 note

Although the Rule Wizard provides a separate screen for the rule's conditions, actions, and exceptions, configuring each of these items for a rule is similar. You specify a condition, action, or exception on the appropriate wizard screen (Step 1) using a check box. Then you provide the details for the condition, action, or exception in the Step 2 box.

the conditions, actions, and exceptions. When you are sure that everything is configured correctly, click the Finish button. The Rule is created and added to your Rules and Alerts list. If you chose to have the rule act on messages already in the Inbox, the rule does its stuff based on your rule settings.

Figure 27.11
Final Rules Wizard step: Name and review the rule.

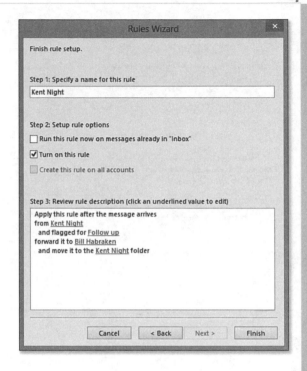

You can run rules that you have created at any time by accessing the Clean Up commands on the Ribbon's Folder tab. Select the Run Rules Now command to run all your rules.

Managing Rules

You can manage your rules using the Rules and Alerts dialog box. This dialog box enables you to edit existing rule settings, delete rules, create new rules, and run rules in the Rule list. It also enables you to determine the specific order that rules run in, which is important if the rule sequence is of consequence to your overall plan related to using rules. To open the Rules and Alerts dialog box, select the Rules command and then select Manage Rules & Alerts. Figure 27.12 shows the Rules and Alerts dialog box.

The rules are listed on the Email Rules tab. You can select a message in the dialog box and then use the Rule description area to edit the values for the rule's conditions, actions, or exceptions. Other commands provided in the Rules and Alerts dialog box are as follows:

- **New Rule:** This command opens the Rules Wizard so that you can create a new rule. When you open the Rules Wizard from the Rules and Alerts dialog box, you have the option of starting the new rule by choosing a rule template from three different categories: Stay Organized, Stay Up-to-Date, or Start from a Blank Rule. After you select a rule template, the process for creating the rule is the same as discussed earlier in this chapter.

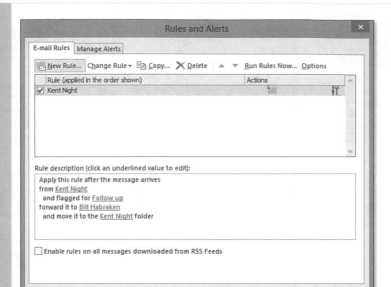

Figure 27.12
The Rules and Alerts dialog box.

- **Change Rule:** This menu enables you to edit a rule's settings, rename a rule, change the alert for the rule, and move or copy the rule to a folder.

- **Copy:** You can copy the rule to another Outlook message folder.

- **Delete:** You can delete the selected Rule.

- **Move Up/Move Down:** Use these buttons to change the order of the rules. Remember that the rules perform their actions in the order they are listed in the Rules list.

- **Run Rules Now:** This command opens the Run Rules Now dialog box. You can select a rule or rules in the dialog box and specify a folder in which the rules run. You can apply the rule (or rules) to all messages, unread messages, or read messages. After making your choices in the Run Rules Now dialog box, select Run Now to run the rules.

- **Options:** This command opens the Options dialog box. You can use the commands in this dialog box to export or import Outlook rules.

If you make changes to your rules, you can immediately apply the changes by selecting Apply. When you are finished working in the Rules and Alerts dialog box and you want to close the dialog box, click OK.

Archiving Outlook Items

Another Outlook management tool is the AutoArchive feature. Older mail messages can be periodically and automatically archived in an archival Outlook data file. This `archive.pst` file is kept in the same location on your computer's hard disk as the Outlook data source file that holds your Outlook profile information. You can archive mail messages and calendar items, such as appointments and tasks.

The point of archiving is to save email messages for later reference, but also to remove some of the older items that are floating around your mail folders. Items autoarchived by Outlook are also compressed, to take up less space.

Archived messages are still accessible. You can access them as needed from the Archive folders that are made available in the Folder Pane when you enable the AutoArchive feature. You have a couple of options for archiving information in an Outlook mail-related folder. You can use the AutoArchive feature, or you can manually archive specific folders.

The great thing about using the AutoArchive feature is that you can specify global archiving settings that affect all your Outlook mail folders. If you don't like a one-size-fits-all approach to folder archiving, you can breathe a sigh of relief: You can also set the AutoArchive settings for individual folders, if required.

Configuring AutoArchive Settings

The AutoArchive feature is configured in the AutoArchive dialog box. You can open this dialog box from the Outlook Advanced options window (select Options in the Backstage and then Advanced) using the AutoArchive Settings button. Figure 27.13 shows the AutoArchive dialog box.

Figure 27.13
The AutoArchive dialog box.

By default, the AutoArchive feature is disabled. To enable the feature, select the Run AutoArchive every 14 Days check box. This means that, every 14th day, the AutoArchive feature automatically archives the contents of the Inbox and other email folders. You can use the day spinner box to specify a different interval for running the AutoArchive feature. You have probably noticed that a lot of settings are crammed into the AutoArchive dialog box:

- **Prompt Before AutoArchive Runs:** If this item is enabled, Outlook displays a dialog box each time it is about to perform the AutoArchive; you can click OK to continue or Cancel to stop the operation.

- **Delete Expired Items (Email Folders Only):** Check this box to have Outlook delete messages from the Inbox after archiving them.

- **Show Archive Folder in Folder List:** This option makes the archive folder available from the Mail Folder list, making it easier to access archived files.

- **Clean Out Items Older Than:** Use this spinner box to specify the increment, and then use the drop-down list to specify Months, Weeks, or Days. The default age for older items is 6 months.

- **Move Old Items To:** This setting provides the path and filename for the archive file. The default name is `archive.pst`, and the location is `My Documents\Outlook Files`. You can use the Browse button to specify another location (or filename), if needed.

- **Permanently Delete Old Items:** Select this option if you want to delete old items rather than archive them.

When you have specified the settings for the AutoArchive feature, you can apply these to the Outlook folders (those that can be archived, such as the Inbox, Tasks, and Calendar folders). Select the Apply These Settings to All Folders Now; then click OK to close the dialog box.

Setting AutoArchive Options for a Folder

If you do not want to apply the AutoArchive options that you set in the AutoArchive dialog box to all Outlook folders (such as the Mail, Tasks, and Calendar folders), you can set AutoArchive options for each folder individually.

Select a Folder in the Folder Pane (you can list all your folders in the Folder Pane by selecting More and then Folders in the Navigation bar), and then select the AutoArchive Settings command on the Ribbon's Folder tab. Figure 27.14 shows the AutoArchive tab of the Inbox Properties dialog box.

To set custom archiving options for the folder, select the Archive This Folder Using These Settings option button. You can then set the increment and time frame (months, weeks, or years) for the age of items to be archived. By default, the Move Old Items to Default Archive Folder option is selected. You can choose to use the Move Old Items To option button to specify another archive file and/ or path, or you can choose the Permanently Delete Old Items option button to delete the old items rather than archive them. Click OK to close the dialog box.

Figure 27.14
The AutoArchive tab of the Inbox Properties dialog box.

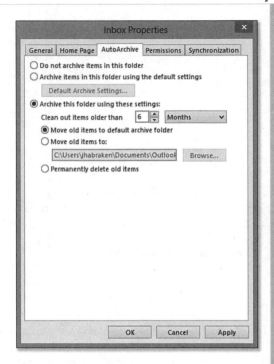

Archiving Manually

If you don't want to use the AutoArchive feature or you feel the need to archive a folder outside the archiving cycle that you have established in the settings for the AutoArchive feature, you can choose to archive folder items manually. This feature enables you to archive one folder at a time (and any subfolders it might hold). The manual archive can be run using the current AutoArchive settings for a folder (such as the age of items that should be archived), or you can select new age parameters while doing the manual archive.

To open the Archive dialog box, select File on the Ribbon and then select Info in the Backstage. On the Info window, select the Cleanup Tools button and then select Archive. The Archive dialog box appears, as shown in Figure 27.15.

Choose one of the following options in the Archive dialog box:

- **Archive All Folders According to Their AutoArchive Settings:** Use this option to manually archive all the Outlook folders using their individual AutoArchive settings. Using this option is no different from running an AutoArchive, except that you are prompting Outlook to archive the folders immediately.

- **Archive This Folder and All Subfolders:** Select this option to archive the selected folder. Using this option requires that you provide an age date for items to be archived. You can also specify the path for the archive to be created.

Figure 27.15
The Archive dialog box.

If you selected to archive the folder selected in the Folder list, provide an item age (Archive Items Older Than) using the drop-down list. You are specifying the age by an actual date. You can also choose to include items that have been flagged as Do Not AutoArchive (in their own Properties dialog boxes). You can also specify an archive file other than the default using the Browse button. When you have finished specifying your settings for the manual archive, select OK.

 note

Another tool that you might find useful is the Mailbox Cleanup tool, which is available in the Backstage Cleanup Tools. Use it to find old and large items and manage the size of your mailbox.

Whether you use autoarchiving or manual archiving is up to you. After you archive items in Outlook, an Archive group appears in the Navigation Pane and provides a list of folders that have been archived. You can access archived items by selecting the appropriate archived folder and selecting the item.

Configuring an Autoreply Message

Outlook users who work in an Exchange Server environment at a corporation or institution, or who subscribe to Office 365 Small Business or Enterprise, can take advantage of the Automatic Replies command in the Outlook Backstage (on the Info window) to configure an automatic out-of-office reply. This reply goes out in response to any received messages. The autoreply message can be useful if you are going to be away for a period of time when you cannot check your Outlook email using another device.

When you select the Automatic Replies command, the Automatic Replies dialog box opens, as shown in Figure 27.16. To configure your automatic reply, select the Send Automatic Replies option button. You can then specify a start and end time for the time span during which the automatic reply should be active.

Figure 27.16
The Automatic Replies dialog box.

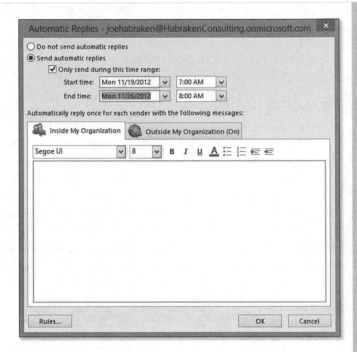

The Automatic Replies dialog box also enables you to configure a separate out-of-office reply for people inside your organization and people outside your organization. Select the Inside My Organization tab to enter an internal message. To create an autoreply message for outside your organization, select the Outside My Organization tab.

By default, the Outside My Organization reply is configured to auto-reply to all message senders outside your organization. You can specify that the autoreply go to only your contacts by selecting the My Contacts Only option button.

When you finish configuring your automatic reply, you can click OK to close the Automatic Replies dialog box.

If you use Outlook for Internet email (such as a POP3 account), you don't have the option to use Automatic Replies dialog box to configure an autoreply message (the Automatic Replies command isn't even on the Info window in the Backstage). You can, however, use an Outlook rule and template to create an automatic reply system for when you are out of the office. This helps keep your Inbox from being crammed to the max upon your return because message

 tip
You can apply rules to an automatic reply that you have configured in the Automatic Replies dialog box. Click the Rules button (at the bottom of the dialog box), and the Automatic Reply rules dialog box opens. Use the Add Rule button to create new rules that apply to incoming messages while you are out of the office. For example, you might want to create a new folder and have a new rule move all emails you received during the automatic reply time span to that folder. When you come back from your vacation, you can go right to that folder and deal with any pressing messages.

senders receive a reply message that you are out of the office. This might make them hold back additional messages until your return (or so we can hope).

The first task that you should do to create your automatic reply is to open a new mail message. Because you want the reply to reach everyone who sends you a message, it makes sense to create the email as a plain-text message. On the Ribbon, select New Items and then point at Email Message Using. Select Plain Text.

Type a subject for the new message, such as "Out of Office," "On Vacation," or any subject that works best for you to let recipients know that you are currently unavailable. Also enter body text for the message, to provide any other information that you feel is required for the automatic reply being created.

After you have entered the subject and the message body text, save the message as an Outlook template. Select File to open the Backstage; then select Save As. In the Save As dialog box, change the Save As Type entry to Outlook Template. Supply a filename and path for the message, and then select Save. You can then close the message without saving it.

Now you can create the rule, which uses the template as the automatic reply message. In the Ribbon's Move group, select Rules and then Create Rule. In the Create Rule dialog box, select Advanced Options. The Rules Wizard opens. In the condition box, select the Sent Only to Me check box; then select Next.

On the Action screen, select the reply using the specific template check box. In the Step 2 box of the Action screen, select the specific template value to open the Select a Reply Template dialog box. In the Look In box, select User Templates in File System. Select the template that you created in the template list (use the Browse button if you saved your template to a folder other than the default path for user templates). Figure 27.17 shows the Select a Reply Template with a user-created template selected.

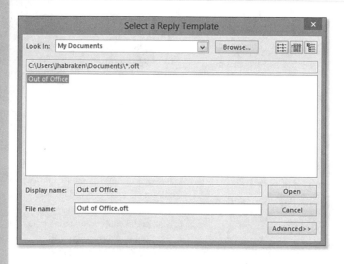

Figure 27.17
The Select a Reply Template dialog box.

After you have selected the template, click Open. The Select a Reply Template dialog box closes, and you return to the Rules Wizard. The path and template name now appear in the Step 2 box with the Reply Using action. Click Next. You can add any exceptions to the autoreply rule on this wizard screen. Then click Next.

You are almost finished; provide a name for the rule. By default, the Turn on This Rule check box is selected. All you have to do is click Finish. Now when you receive a message in your Inbox, your autoreply rule sends a response to the sender using your mail template.

REQUISITE PUBLISHER: ESSENTIAL FEATURES

Most desktop publishing applications are developed for well-schooled designers who create complex publications using fairly complicated software tools. These complex software applications were not designed for the average user and required a steep learning curve to take full advantage of the software's capabilities. Microsoft introduced Publisher in 1991 as an easy-to-use publication design application that enabled even the novice user to create a wide variety of publication types.

Microsoft Publisher has evolved over the years from a somewhat basic application for creating simple publications into a powerful desktop publishing tool. In this chapter, we look at the features you need to know to begin creating your own publications in Microsoft Publisher 2013.

Introducing Publisher 2013

Publisher 2013 takes full advantage of the improvements that were made to the previous version of Publisher (Publisher 2010) and offers some new enhancements of its own. For example, you can now quickly select a photo or other image file to serve as a page background in your publication. The picture can either fill the background or be tiled, depending on your needs. You also find other improvements related to working with pictures in Publisher; even the Backstage has been given a makeover, making it easier for you to access your publications or start a new publication. Some of the enhancements you find in Publisher 2013 are as follows:

- **New Start page:** When you open the Publisher application window, you "land" on a new Start page. This Backstage page provides easy access to your recently opened publications. It also enables you to quickly start a new publication based on a large library of publication templates. You can even search for more publication templates on Office.com using the Start page Search box.

- **Capability to insert online pictures:** Publisher 2013 makes it easy for you to insert pictures from the Web into your publications using the new Online Pictures command on the Ribbon's Insert tab. Online images can be sourced from the Office.com clip art library, Bing image searches, and your SkyDrive. You can also configure Publisher (and the other Office applications) to connect to your Flickr account and access your Flickr photos.

- **Feature to drop multiple pictures on the scratch area:** You can insert multiple pictures from your computer or online sources via the commands in the Insert tab's Illustrations group. When you insert multiple pictures, the pictures are placed in the scratch area of the Publisher application window. You can then drag the pictures onto the publication pages, as needed. Pictures dragged into picture placeholders provided by a publication have pink borders when the picture is appropriately positioned in the placeholder.

- **Capability to prepare publications for printing:** Publisher now makes it easy for you to prepare your publication for printing at a photo center or commercial printer. The publication can be exported in a variety of image file types for photo center printing or can be exported as a PDF for commercial printing.

This is just a subset of some of the new features and improvements that you encounter as you work with Publisher 2013. The Publisher chapters (Chapters 28 and 29) of this book highlight and explain other new features.

 tip

Publisher makes it easy to swap two photos on a publication page: Just drag a picture onto another picture on the page. When the outline of the picture frame turns pink, drop the picture (you are dragging), and the two photos exchange positions—they are swapped—on the page.

Planning Your Publication

Although Publisher makes it easy to create a variety of publication types, you should still spend some time planning a new publication before you actually assemble it in Publisher. If you are poised to create a business card, newsletter, or flyer, you have already established that you have a need for a particular publication type. However, you should also look at the core purpose of the publication and determine how to approach the overall look, feel, and theme of the publication. For example, a newsletter for your book club might have a colorful, friendly look and light, playful content. On the other hand, a publication for business clients would likely have a more "professional" layout, color scheme, and tone.

Another important aspect of planning a new publication is assembling the different objects and text that make up the publication. Because Publisher is a design and layout tool, it makes sense to have a folder on your computer that contains all the pictures, images, and perhaps even pretyped text blocks to use as you create the layout for the publication. Of course, you can create these items (particularly the text) as you assemble the publication, but doing so takes some of your concentration away from creating a professional and eye-catching publication.

PART VI

Here are some other points to keep in mind as you get ready to create a new publication in Publisher:

- **Know your printer:** Printers differ in the amount of whitespace they require on the outside edge of a printed page. Inkjet and laser printers have different requirements as well. If you plan to do bleeds off the page for brochures or flyers, you need to know whether your printer is capable of this task before you set up the publication with that particular design feature. If you need professional-looking results for your finished publication and your printer isn't up to the task, consider using the Export possibilities in the Backstage Export page. You can save the publication pages as a JPEG or TIFF file and then print the pages at a center that provides photo printing. The Export page also gives you the option to save your publication for a commercial printer that has the proper equipment.

- **Consider print publications versus electronic paper publications:** As already mentioned, the printer you use can affect the overall quality of a printed Publisher publication. Publisher provides alternatives to a printed publication. You can save your publication as either a PDF or an XPS document. These file types preserve your fonts, formatting, and images as you laid them out. Publisher also gives you the option to create an HTML version of your publication, which you can publish directly to a web page. Consider using these electronic publication possibilities if you don't need to distribute hard copies of your publications to your target audience.

- **Balance objects on the page:** Effectively using the whitespace on a page is important in creating an eye-catching layout. Consider balancing the layout of a page on the diagonal (the upper-left part of the page should balance with the lower-right part of the page), and align items with respect to the outside borders of the page instead of in the center of the page. A publication with everything centered on the page looks unprofessional and doesn't use the page space effectively. The best way to get a feel for balanced publications is to examine flyers, brochures, or ads that you feel are designed well and then adapt these overall layout concepts to your own Publisher publications.

- **Size items according to their importance:** The relative size of an item on the page reflects the importance of that item. Make sure that the objects on the page that are important to the overall theme or message of the publication are sized to have maximum impact.

These are just a few of the points to keep in mind when designing a new publication. Ultimately, you must remember the importance of emphasizing the purpose of a particular publication while also exercising your artistic sensibilities. Even the most eye-catching publication ultimately will fail if it doesn't get its message across.

Working with Publication Templates

When you begin a new publication in Publisher, you typically start by selecting one of the many publication templates available. Publisher 2013 has a large library of built-in templates and also provides access to a huge number of templates on Office.com. When you start Publisher, you are greeted by the Start landing page (see Figure 28.1). This page gives you access to any recently opened publications (select a publication to open it). It also grants access to the publication templates.

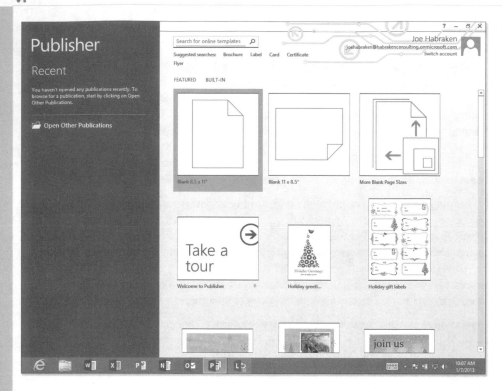

Figure 28.1
The Publisher
Start page.

By default, the Start page lists featured templates, which is a subset of the available templates. To see all the built-in templates provided, select Built-In at the top of the templates list.

The built-in templates are housed in categories such as Advertisements, Brochures, Calendars, and so on. To access the individual templates in a template category, select one of the categories. If you want to search for a particular type of template, use the Search Online Templates box in the upper part of the template window (we talk more about searches in a moment).

When you select a particular template category, such as Business Cards, a list of installed templates appears in the Built-In Templates window. Most templates provide a specific color and font scheme and also contain sample text and images, which you can replace with your own. Some template types (again, business cards are an excellent example) also provide templates that are vendor specific. Many business form vendors make business card sheets, so if you want to build your business cards based on a particular manufacturer's business card sheet size and orientation, you can select from the sheets provided in the manufacturers' folders at the bottom of the template list. For example, the Business Cards category provides manufacturers' folders for Avery, Formtec, Office Depot, and Staples, just to name a few. Most publication types provide you with a large number of predesigned templates but also give you blank sizes so that you can start from scratch when you create a new publication.

If you do want to use a preformatted template, you still have control over options related to the template's color scheme, font scheme, and page size. When you select a particular template, a Customize pane appears on the right side of the Built-In window. It provides a larger preview of the template and its Color scheme, Font scheme, and Page Size drop-down lists. You can use any of these options to modify the default settings for the publication. Figure 28.2 shows the Customize pane and a preview of the selected business card template.

Figure 28.2
You can modify the default settings for the selected template.

Any changes that you make to the template appear in the preview provided. By default, the template preview uses your default business information set, which is information such as your name, title, business name, address, and phone number.

You can create many business information sets that enable you to change the information Publisher places in the publication template. You can use the Business Information drop-down list to select the information set that you want to use for the publication(the default is Custom 1). You certainly want to create at least one information set, particularly if you create publications such as business cards, business forms, invitation cards, or emails.

➡️ *To learn more about creating and editing business information sets, **see** "Creating a Business Information Set," **p. 821**.*

Even if you select one of the blank templates provided in a publication category, you can customize it. You have control over the color scheme, font scheme, and business information set, as you would for any other Publisher template. Because blank templates do not provide placeholder text or default design elements and graphics, you don't see a preview of the publication in the Customize pane. You do, however, get a description of the template and its dimensions, such as the page size and sheet size.

Publisher's Start page is designed to help you quickly start a publication. If you need to access Publisher templates after you begin or finish a publication, you simply go to Publisher's Backstage. In the Publisher application window, select File to return to the Backstage. Select New to open the Backstage New window. The New page looks the same as the Start page; it provides access to templates and also enables you to search online for additional templates.

 tip

If you select a template category or even a specific template and still want to return to the Start page, click the Home button. If you want to go back one level, click the level heading to the right of the Back button (which also takes you back).

Before walking through the process of creating a new publication using a template (both preformatted and blank), an explanation of the difference between a page and a sheet is in order. A page is exactly what you think a page is: it is represented in the Publisher Workspace as a whitespace (in the dimensions that you selected when you selected the template) where you place the objects to appear in the publication. You can navigate from page to page in the publication by using the Page pane.

A publication can have multiple pages. You can modify page dimensions by using the Page Setup commands on the Page Design tab and the Page Setup dialog box.

A sheet is the actual piece of paper that you use when you print the publication. You can specify the sheet size, the orientation, and other settings for the sheet in the Backstage Print window. If you use a template based on a paper size, the paper and the sheet are the same. In some cases, the sheet size can be bigger than the actual publication. For example, when you create a business card, the page is the size of one business card, with the understanding that you print multiple pages on a single (and larger) sheet.

Creating a New Publication

Selecting a route for creating your new publication depends on your experience with Publisher and the particular design requirements of your publication. The various publication templates give you a lot of help as you initially design your publication: They create placeholder objects in your new publication that you can replace with your own pictures or design elements.

Creating a new publication using a blank template requires more initial layout and design work, but depending on your desktop publishing abilities, you might find that creating your own publications from scratch gives you the end product that you desire.

Using a Template

We have already discussed the overall geography of the Start page (and the New page) in Publisher's Backstage. In terms of template selection, you can use one of the built-in templates or search for a template on Office.com. If you use one of the built-in templates, you can choose either a preformatted template or a blank template. In both cases, you can customize the settings for the template, such as the color scheme, font scheme, and business information set. After selecting the template and making the necessary adjustments to color or font settings, select Create to open the publication in the Publisher workspace.

If you decide to search for a template on Office.com, the results of your search appear in a list on the Start or New pages (see Figure 28.3). You also can filter the results by category. Select a category in the Category list to filter the search results. You can filter by multiple categories. To remove a category filter from the Filter by list, point at the selected category and then click the Close button on the right of the category.

Figure 28.3
You can filter your search results by category.

When you find the online template that you want to use, select the template. A template window opens and provides the name (and provider) of the template. Depending on the type of template, navigation arrows enable you to see more images of the template. A Create button is also provided in the template window but you are not offered the customization options that are provided for the built-in templates. Any modifications that you make to the template must be made in the Publisher workspace after you have downloaded the template. Select the Create button. The template downloads, and your new publication opens in the Publisher workspace.

Using Blank Sizes

When creating a publication from scratch based on sheet size and orientation, blank templates are available when you start Publisher (on the Start page) or when you access the Backstage and then select New (the New page). The two most easily accessed blank templates are available in the Featured (template) list and consist of the Blank 8.5x11" and Blank 11x8.5" templates. These provide a blank portrait or blank landscape page, respectively. If you want to access more blank page templates (which relate to a specific publication category), select Built-In and then select the category of publication you want to create. For example, the Brochures category provides blank sizes in both portrait and landscape orientation. To see the blank sizes offered by a particular template category, scroll down in the category's list. Figure 28.4 shows the blank sizes available in the Brochures category.

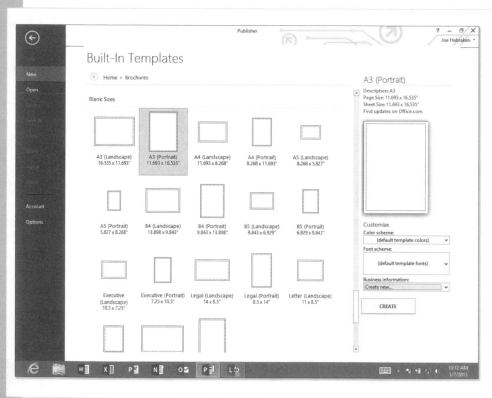

Figure 28.4 Each template category provides blank sizes.

Blank templates are also found in the various manufacturers' folders available in specific template categories, such as business cards or labels. For example, in the labels category, you find blank templates for such specific label manufacturers as Ace Label, Adetec, Avery US Letter, and Office Depot.

When you locate the blank template you want to use, select it. You can then customize the color or font scheme or change the business information to be used for the publication. When you click Create, the new publication (based on the template) opens in the Publisher workspace.

Creating a New Template

If you want to base new publications on a publication you have already created, you can save that publication as a template. Your custom template is then available in the template list provided in the Backstage. Before you can take advantage of your own templates, you need to let Publisher know where you want to save any personal templates that you create.

Go to the Backstage (File) and then click Options. This opens the Publisher Options window. Select Save in the options list on the left of the window. Type the complete path for your personal template folder in the Default Personal Templates location box. You can use any folder on your computer. For example, I create a folder called templates in my Documents folder. I then let Publisher know that the path is C:\Users\my user name\My Document\templates, where C: is my hard drive letter.

If you want to go "old school," you can use the default folder for templates in Publisher, which is Users\your user name\AppData\Roaming\Microsoft\Templates. Where you keep your Publisher templates is up to you; just make sure you type the correct path in the Default Personal Templates location box. After you have specified the folder location, select OK.

Now you can base a new template on any publication you have created (or create a new one). And although this is a little like putting the cart before the horse (because I haven't discussed all the ins and outs of the various Publisher commands and tools), here is how you do it:

> ### ⚠ caution
>
> If you don't specify a default folder for your personal templates in the Publisher Save options, Publisher will not provide a Personal heading on the Start or New pages in the Backstage.

1. Create a new publication or open an existing publication.

2. In the Publisher workspace, modify the current publication as needed. You can insert objects, including pictures and page parts. You can also modify the page setup and color scheme settings on the Page Design tab.

3. When you have modified the publication to meet your needs (meaning that you are ready to save it as a template), select File to access the Backstage.

4. In the Backstage, select Save As and then Select Computer in the Places list.

5. Select Browse on the Save As page. The Save As dialog box opens.

6. Select the Save As Type drop-down list, and select Publisher Template. The Save As dialog box automatically navigates to your default Publisher template folder (as you specified in the Publisher Options).

7. Provide a filename for the template, and then select Save to save the template. The new template saves to your default template folder.

Now when you go to either the Start page or New page in the Backstage (where the templates are accessed) a new heading, Personal, appears between the Features and Built-In headings. Select Personal, and any template that you have saved to your template folder is listed. To start a new document from the template, select the template.

Navigating the Publisher Workspace

When you select a template (preformatted, blank, or your own), a new publication opens in the Publisher workspace. The Ribbon borders the top of the workspace, and the status bar is at the bottom. The View shortcuts (Single Page and Two-Page Spread) and the Zoom slider are on the right side of the status bar, which makes it easy to change the current view of the publication and to zoom in and out of the publication page. Figure 28.5 shows the Publisher workspace.

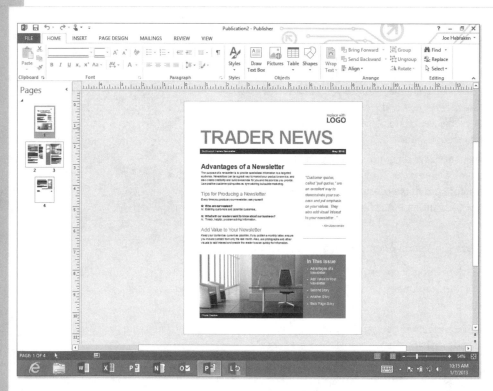

Figure 28.5
The Publisher workspace.

The Pages pane, on the left side of the workspace, helps you navigate the various pages in the publication. A thumbnail is provided for each page in the publication. The gray area surrounding the current publication page is the scratch area. You can drag items from a publication page and place them on the scratch area. Objects in the Scratch area are available even when you switch between pages in the publication or open a different publication. Think of the scratch area as a place to leave logos, headings, or other items that you use as you work on a particular publication. Parking the object on the scratch area is also the easiest way to move an object from one page to another.

Using the Rulers and Guides

Bordering the top and left sides of the scratch area are the horizontal and vertical rulers, respectively. You can use the rulers to place objects on a publication page. When you move the mouse on the page, the vertical and horizontal positions of the mouse pointer are shown as tick marks on the vertical and horizontal rulers. When you drag an object on the publication page, the position (horizontal and vertical) of the mouse pointer also displays on the Publisher task bar. You can thus precisely place objects on a page.

You can also drag horizontal or vertical guides from the rulers onto the publication page. Place the mouse on the horizontal or vertical ruler edge, and drag the ruler guide onto the publication when you see the guide mouse pointer. These light-green ruler guides are nonprinting, and you can use them to align objects on the page more precisely. In fact, when the Align to Guides check box is checked on the Ribbon's Page Design tab, objects dragged onto the publication snap to a grid line, making it easy to align the object (such as an image). Just move an object near a guide, and the guide is highlighted as the object snaps onto it.

If you want to remove a ruler guide, drag it off the publication page. Grabbing a guide is easiest if you select it in one of the page margins. That way, you aren't inadvertently selecting objects that are within the confines of the page itself.

At this point, we should mention that Publisher provides with another category of guide (other than the ruler guide): the layout guide. Layout guides are also used to position objects precisely on a publication page. Different kinds of layout guides exist: margin, column, row, and baseline. These types of guides appear as light blue lines on the publication page (by default); however, you can't drag them off the page as you do a ruler guide. The layout guides are on the master page (or master pages) of the publication and so appear on all the pages in the publication (ruler guides appear only on the page where you place them). The master page, as its name implies, provides the page setup and other publication settings for new pages inserted into the publication. The next chapter talks more about using layout guides and editing master pages.

➡ *You can use layout grids on master pages to help you align objects in a publication. For more about master pages and layout grids,* ***see*** *"Working with Master Pages," **p. 848**.*

 tip

If you don't like using ruler guides, you can move either of the rulers right onto the publication page. Hold down the Shift key and drag a ruler (vertical or horizontal) onto the publication. Repeat the process to place the ruler back in its original position adjacent to the Scratch area.

So if you want to add ruler guides to a particular publication page, you can quickly drag a new ruler guide from either the horizontal or the vertical ruler. Several preset ruler guide configurations are provided in a Guides gallery, making creating ruler guides less of a drag. To open the Guides gallery, select the Ribbon's Page Design tab and then select the Guides command in the Layout group. The Guides gallery opens, as shown in Figure 28.6.

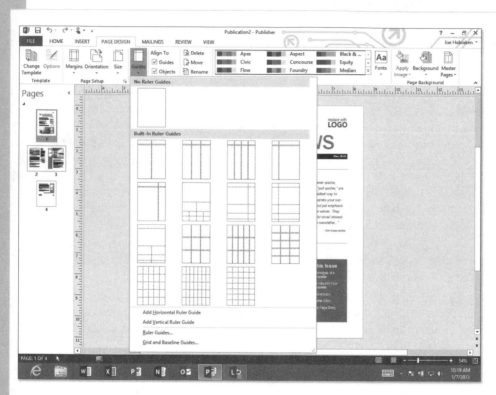

Figure 28.6
The Guides gallery.

You can choose from any of the built-in ruler guides provided in the Guides gallery. If you want to add a single horizontal or vertical ruler guide, use the Add Horizontal Ruler Guide or Add Vertical Ruler Guide commands, respectively.

If you find that the built-in ruler guides don't give you the guide layout you want, you can create your own custom ruler guides. Select Ruler Guides in the Guides gallery to open the Ruler Guides dialog box, as shown in Figure 28.7.

The Ruler Guides dialog box provides both a Horizontal tab and a Vertical tab. To set the guide position on the Horizontal tab, specify a position in the position box (such as 4 for 4 inches) and then click the Set button. Each time you specify a position and click the Set button, Publisher adds a guide to the guide list.

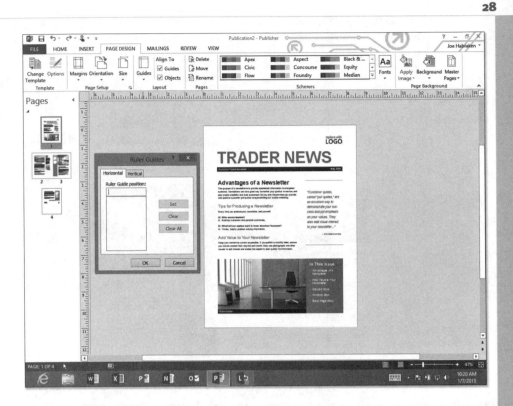

Figure 28.7
The Ruler
Guides dia-
log box.

You can select the Vertical tab of the Ruler Guides dialog box and set vertical guides as needed by providing a position and then clicking the Set button. You can clear individual guide positions on either tab by selecting a position and then clicking the Clear button (Clear All clears all the guides). When you click OK, the Ruler Guides dialog box closes and the guides you specified appear on the publication.

You can quickly clear all the guides (those selected from the gallery or those that you created) on the publication page by using the Guides command. Select Guides and then select No Ruler Guides in the gallery.

Options for Viewing the Publication

As already mentioned, the Pages pane provides a thumbnail of each page in your publication. You can use the Pages pane to quickly move from page to page in your publication. You can also collapse or expand the Pages pane by using the button at the top of the pane. If you want to increase the size of the page thumbnails on the Page pane, you can drag its border (on the left side of the vertical ruler) toward the scratch area as needed.

Because the Publisher workspace contains both your actual publication and other tools, such as the Ribbon, the rulers, the Pages pane, and (potentially) guides, it makes sense that you might want to manipulate the view in the Publisher workspace. The Ribbon's View tab provides command groups for changing the view and the items shown in the workspace, and for manipulating the current zoom level for the publication. Figure 28.8 shows the Ribbon's View tab.

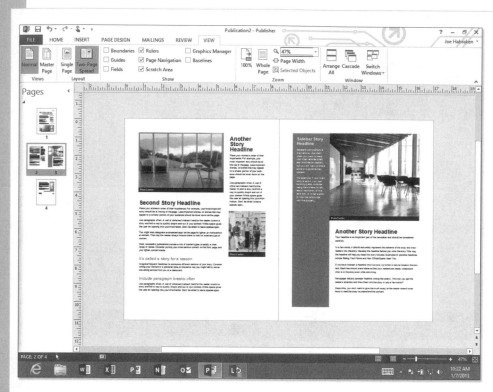

Figure 28.8
The Ribbon's View tab.

The Views group on the View tab enables you to switch between Normal view (the view of your publication pages) and Master Page view (the next chapter covers master pages). The Layout group enables you to view a single page or view two facing pages using the Two-Page Spread Command. The Show group has check boxes that enable you to view different items in the workspace. These commands are as follows:

- **Boundaries:** This command enables you to view the boundaries for the objects on the page, such as images, text boxes, and shapes.

- **Guides:** To view guides on your publication, this command must be enabled (it is enabled by default).

- **Fields:** Select this command to show fields in the publication. The mail merge process uses fields as placeholders for names and addresses in your recipient list.

- **Rulers:** Enabled by default, this command shows or hides the rulers.

- **Page Navigation:** When you select this command, the Page pane displays on the left side of the Publisher workspace. Clear the Page Navigation check box to hide the Page pane.

- **Scratch Area:** Enabled by default, this command shows the Scratch area and any objects you might have dragged to the Scratch area.

- **Graphics Manager:** This command opens the Graphics Manager task pane. The Graphics Manager provides a list of pictures on the publication. You can select from the picture list to select a picture in the publication.

- **Baselines:** This command shows the baseline guides set for the publication. You can use baseline guides to align text to the guides, which controls the spacing between text lines in a story (we discuss text and stories later in this chapter).

The other command groups on the View tab include the Zoom commands and the Window group. The Zoom commands include 100%, Whole Page (the default), and other zoom settings. If you want to change the zoom on a particular item, select the item and then click the Select Objects command.

You use the Window commands to arrange open publication windows. You can tile (Arrange All) or cascade (Cascade) the open publication windows, which is particularly useful if you want to drag an object from one publication to another or do a copy-and-paste between publications.

Creating a Business Information Set

Before you get too far into the publication-creation process, you will want to create one or more business information sets. A business information set is a collection of information about you (and your company). Publisher uses the information in the business information set to automatically fill in information needed by Publisher templates such as business cards, brochures, and envelopes.

The best part of a business information set is that you enter the information once and then can use it again and again as you create your various publications. Publisher even enables you to create multiple business information sets, which is extremely useful if more than one person is using Publisher on the computer or if you create publications for both personal and business uses on the same computer.

Creating a New Business Information Set

You can create a new business information set or edit an existing business information set in the Publisher Backstage (if you have already created one). You have the option to select or create a business information set every time you select one of the built-in templates to create a new publication (in the Start or New Backstage pages). Let's assume that you haven't created the default information set: In the Backstage, select the Info command and then click the Edit Business Information button. The Create New Business Information dialog box opens, as shown in Figure 28.9.

Provide the information required in each field of the Create New Business Information Set dialog box (Individual Name, Tagline or Motto, Address, and so on). You can also specify a logo for your company: Simply select the Change button, use the Insert Picture dialog box to specify the new logo for your company, select a new image file, and then select Insert. Publisher places the new logo in the Logo box. When you have finished editing the information set, specify the name for the set in the Business Information Set Name box (the default is Custom 1); then click Save to save the information. If you are currently working on a publication that uses the default business information set, you are asked to update the publication (with the information you just placed in the information set); select Update Publication.

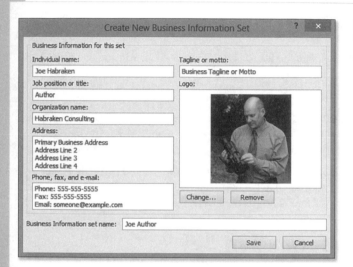

Figure 28.9
The Create New Business Information Set dialog box.

Now you have your initial (and default) business information set. If you need to edit the information, go to the Info page of the Publisher Backstage. To access your default business information, select Edit Business Information. The Business Information dialog box opens. Use the drop-down list to select a business information set, and then select Edit. The Edit Business Information Set dialog box opens—it is basically the same as the Create New Information Set dialog box. After you have edited the business information set, you can click the Save button to save your changes and close the Edit Business Information Set dialog. You then return to the Business Information dialog box. If you want to update the information used in the current publication, click the Update Publication button; otherwise, click Close.

Creating Additional Business Information Sets

If you use Publisher to create publications for both personal and business use, or if multiple people use the same computer (and Publisher), you might want to create multiple business information sets. You can open the Business Information dialog box from the Backstage by clicking the Edit Business Information button in the Info window. You can also open the Business Information dialog box as you work on a publication. Select the Business Information command on the Ribbon's Insert tab (in the Text group), and then select Edit Business Information. Figure 28.10 shows the Business Information dialog box.

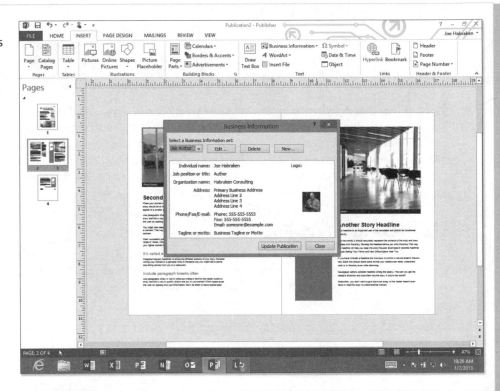

Figure 28.10
The Business
Information
dialog box.

To create a new business set, select New. The Create New Business Information Set dialog box opens (refer to Figure 28.9). Supply the information for the set using the various field boxes. You can also specify a logo for the new information set. Type a new name for the set in the Business Information Set Name box, and then click the Save button to save the new information set.

When you open the Business Information dialog box in the future, you can specify the business information set you want to use. Use the drop-down box to select a specific information set. You can change the information set for the current publication—select the information set from the list, and then select Update Publication.

You can also edit the current business information set, create a new set, or select a different information set for the current publication from the Publisher workspace. Select the Ribbon's Insert tab and, in the Text group, select the Business Information command.

You can use the Business Information Fields list to insert any of the field information in the information set directly into the publication. If you want to edit the business information set or create a new set, select the Edit Business Information command on the Fields list. The Business Information dialog box opens. Use the Edit or New commands in the dialog box, as needed. You can delete an information set by selecting the set in the drop-down list and then clicking the Delete button.

Working with Text

When you work with text in Publisher, a text box called an object frame encloses the actual text. Publisher gives you complete control over the look and formatting of the text in the object frame, including the font style, font size, font attributes (such as bold and italic), and color of your font. You can edit any or all of these font parameters for a particular text box.

Working with text in Publisher is more than just typing inside boxes. You have control not only over the format of the text within the box, including the text direction and special text effects, but also over formatting of the text box itself, including outside borders and fill color. You can create text boxes as spaceholders as you design your publication and then add the text to the box at your convenience. You can even insert text files into your publication that you have typed in other applications.

Editing Text in a Text Box

If you use a template that contains text boxes with placeholder text, you need to edit the text in each of the text boxes. Select the text in a specific text box and then type the text that replaces the placeholder text. Figure 28.11 shows selected placeholder text in a template text box.

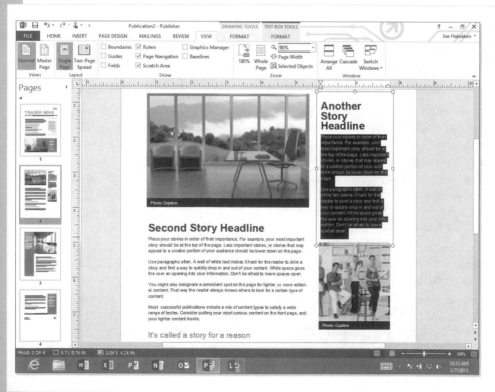

Figure 28.11
Edit the text in a text box.

The new text uses the same font attributes as the placeholder text. If you want to change the font or paragraph attributes for text, select the text that you want to format (in the text box) and then use the Font and Paragraph commands on the Home tab, as needed. You can also create bulleted and numbered lists inside a text box by using the Bullets and Numbering commands in the Paragraph group.

When you use templates to create your publications, you might also find two or more text boxes linked together—that is, clicking the text in one of the text boxes on the publication page selects the text in more than one text box. This means that the text actually flows from one text box to the other (it can flow through several text boxes). The text in a text box or linked text boxes is also referred to as a story. We look at creating linked text boxes shortly.

Creating Your Own Text Boxes

You can insert a new text box on any publication page, as needed. The Draw Text Box command is on the Ribbon's Insert tab. Follow these steps:

1. Select the Draw Text Box command.

2. Place the mouse pointer on the page and drag diagonally to create the text box (in the required dimensions).

3. Release the mouse button. The insertion point appears in the text box.

4. Use the Font commands on the text box tools Format tab to set the font size and attributes for the font, such as font color, or switch to the Home tab to use the font, paragraph, and styles commands that it provides.

5. After specifying your font attributes, type the text that you want to place in the box.

When you have finished entering the text into the text box, click outside the text box to deselect it. You might find that it makes sense to zoom in on the text box when you are entering the text. This is particularly true if you are looking at a large publication page in Whole Page view.

Formatting Text Boxes

As already mentioned in the discussion of text boxes, you have control over the text inside the box, as well as the text box itself. When you click inside a text box to select text, two sets of contextual tools appear on the Ribbon: Drawing Tools and Text Box Tools. You use the drawing tools (available when you select Format under the Drawing Tools tab) to format the text box itself, including the shape style, fill, outline, and special effects.

The text box tools (available when you select Format under the Text Box Tools tab) enable you to change text, font, and alignment settings. This set of tools also provides the commands for linking text boxes and adding effects to your text. Typography settings are available that enable you to use the Drop Cap feature and special typographic features, such as ligatures.

 tip

You can format selected text in a text box using WordArt Styles. Publisher provides different style formats in the WordArt Styles gallery.

Using the Drawing Tools

To format the text box itself, select the text box and then click Format under the Drawing Tools tab to access the various tools for formatting an object (remember that text boxes, pictures, and clip art are all Publisher objects). Figure 28.12 shows a selected text box and the Drawing Tools Format tab on the Ribbon.

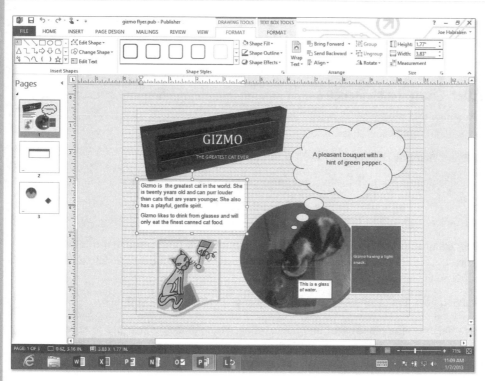

Figure 28.12
Use the Drawing Tools to enhance a text box.

Publisher 2013 has reduced the number of command groups in the Drawing Tools. This makes working with the Drawing Tools less complicated. However, the tools themselves are more sophisticated than those in the previous version of Publisher. The Drawing Tools command groups are as follows:

■ **Insert Shapes:** This group provides a Shapes gallery divided into categories that include Lines, Basic Shapes, and Callouts. The shapes in the gallery can be inserted onto the current page by selecting a shape and then "drawing" it (clicking and dragging) on the page. Inserting a new shape does not affect the currently selected text box or other shapes. You can use the Edit Shape command to edit the currently selected text box (or other object). On a text box, you can edit wrap points, which enables you to change the shape of an object such as a rectangle and determine how the text wraps within the edited object (which is why they are called wrap points). The Insert Shapes group also provides the Change Shape gallery, which enables you to change the current shape of the object (a rectangle, for a text box). If you want to edit the text in a text box or add text to a new shape that you have inserted into the page, use the Edit Text command when the object is selected.

- **Shape Styles:** This group provides a gallery of Shape styles that you can assign to the currently selected text box (or the currently selected shape). Click the More button (underneath the Shape Styles scroll arrows) to see the entire gallery, which provides shape styles with color gradients and other shading possibilities. The Shape Fill command provides access to a Scheme Colors palette that enables you to change the current color scheme. You can also add gradient textures and patterns using this command. The Shape Outline command enables you to specify a new scheme color (which affects the lines, including the outside lines) of the object. You can also use this command to specify tints, line weight, dashes, and patterns for the currently selected shape.

 tip

The Shape Fill command provides a Sample Fill Color tool (which looks like an eyedropper). You can use it to clone a color from any object in your publication and then use that color as the fill for the currently selected object. Select Sample Fill Color and then click an object on the page.

- **Arrange:** This command group enables you to change how the text wraps around other objects on the page (if you have a large text box containing other objects). Wrapping options include Square (the text wraps around the object in a square), Top and Bottom, and Through. The Wrap Text command also provides access to the Edit Wrap Points command and the More Layout Options command, which opens the Format Text Box dialog box. The dialog box gives you control over all aspects of a text box related to colors, lines, size, and layout. The other commands in the Arrange group relate to arranging a text box on the page in layers with other objects. You can change the layer position of an object using the Bring Forward or Send Backward commands. The Align command enables you to change the alignment of an object in relation to the page margins (such as Align Left or Align Top). You can also choose to distribute multiple, selected objects using the Distribute Horizontally or Distribute Vertically commands. The Group or Ungroup commands enables you to either group or ungroup several selected objects. Grouping objects helps maintain their position in relation to each other. A Rotate command is also provided in this group and can be used to either rotate or flip a selected object, such as a text box or picture.

- **Size:** This command group provides measurement spinner boxes that adjust the height and width of the text box. You can also access the Format Text Box dialog box by selecting the dialog box launcher at the bottom of this command group.

All the commands that we discussed that relate to a text box apply to another Publisher object: the shape. Aligning and layering multiple objects on a page can be complicated, so we revisit the Arrange command group in the next chapter when we look at working with multiple objects on a page.

Aligning and layering multiple objects can be tricky. **See** *"Manipulating Publication Objects," p. 854.*

Using the Text Box Tools

As already discussed, you can use any of the font and paragraph attributes to format the text in a text box using the commands on the Home tab. If you want to use special formatting attributes, use the text box tools. The Text Box Tools go beyond the settings for basic font attributes and enable you to do more complex manipulations, such as specifying the text's direction and how it fits in the box (including special alignment commands). You can also add effects and special typography settings to the text, including WordArt Styles. Figure 28.13 shows the Text Box Tools tab.

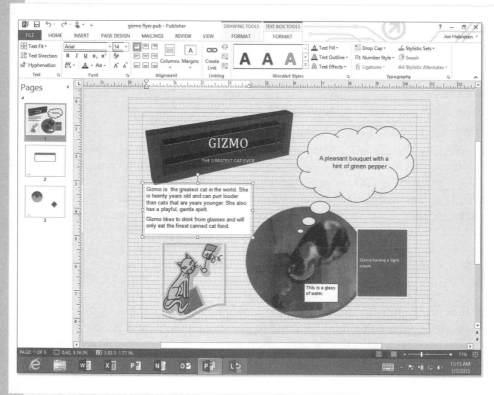

Figure 28.13
Format the text in the text box using the Text Box Tools.

The command groups provided on the Text Box Tools tab are as follows:

- **Text:** These commands fit text in the box, change the text directions, and set the hyphenation for the text. The Text Fit command enables you to use best fit to change the size of the text so that it fits in the box. You can also choose to grow the text box or shrink text upon overflow. The Text Direction command enables you to rotate the text from horizontal to vertical. The Hyphenation command opens the Hyphenation dialog box and enables you to change the hyphenation zone or manually hyphenate the text.

- **Font:** This command group provides font attribute settings (such as size, bold, italics, and font color) and enables you to adjust the character spacing (normal, tight, loose, and so on). A Clear Formatting command enables you to clear all formatting on the selected text.

- **Alignment:** These commands enable you to align the text in reference to the borders of the text box. For example, the Align Top Left command moves the text to the top-left corner of the text box. Nine alignment options exist. The Columns command enables you to create columns in the text box. You can select from one to three columns on the Columns menu, or you can select More Columns to open the Columns dialog box. The Margins command enables you to set the margins for the text (the margins in the box) using presets such as Narrow, Moderate, and Wide. You can select the Custom Margins command to open the Format Text Box dialog box and set custom margins for the text box.

- **Linking:** The Create Link command links two or more selected text boxes. We look at linking text boxes in the next section.

- **WordArt Styles:** This group provides a WordArt Styles gallery with styles that you can assign to selected text. The group also provides commands that enable you to fine-tune the formatting provided by the currently selected WordArt style. You can modify the fill color for the text using the Text Fill command. To manipulate the outline color or the weight of the font border, use the Text Outline command. If you want to change the text effect for the text, you can use the Text Effects command, which enables you to manipulate the shadow, reflection, glow, and bevel of the text characters.

- **Typography:** These commands add items such as a drop cap to text, set the number style, or add special typography formatting, such as ligatures and stylistic sets. Ligatures are text characters tied together using a common design element (common to the text characters). The Drop Cap command provides a gallery of drop caps, as shown in Figure 28.14. You can preview any of the drop cap styles in the gallery or use the Custom Drop Cap command to set your own drop cap in the Drop Cap dialog box. The stylistic sets provide alternative character shapes for the selected text. Not all font families provide this option; some font families also enable you to turn on flourishes using the Swash command.

If you want additional control over settings related to the text box and the text inside the text box, you can go "old school" and open the Format Text dialog box. On the Text Box Tools tab, select the dialog box launcher at the bottom of the Text group. Figure 28.15 shows the Format Text Box dialog box.

The Format Text Box dialog box has five tabs that provide control over such things as text box lines and fill, size, layout, alignment, and margins. The Color and Lines tab enables you to set the fill color and level of transparency, as well as the line color, style, and weight. You can use presets or set your own borders. You can even use the Border Art button to select from a list of available borders with titles such as Apples, Baby Pacifier, and Candy Corn.

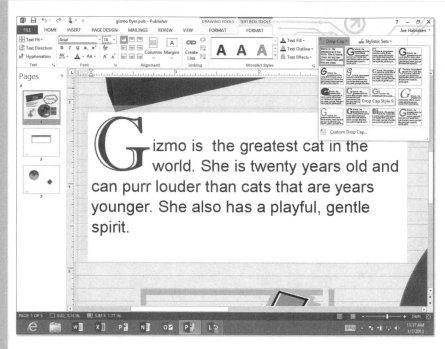

Figure 28.14
Select a drop cap style.

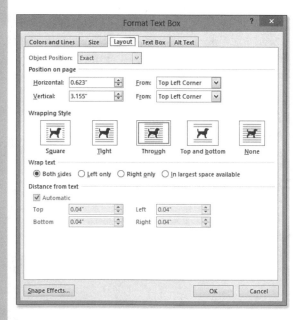

Figure 28.15
Set text box options in the Format Text Box dialog box.

The Size tab provides settings for the size and rotation of the text box. It also provides scale settings for the height and width and enables you to lock the aspect ratio. The Layout tab provides settings for the position of the text box on the page and the wrapping style if an image is included in the text box. The Text Box tab is where you set the margins for the text box and specify the vertical alignment of the text in the box. The Alt Text tab is reserved for alternative text descriptions of the objects on your publication page, which are useful to people with impairments (such as vision) who want to view your publication.

 note

Because you can add text to any shape you insert into a publication, both the Drawing Tools and Text Box Tools discussed in this chapter are applicable to any shapes you place.

Linking Text Boxes

If you want text to flow from one text box to another, you can link the text boxes. Publisher then considers the text that fills the text boxes to be a single story. You might find many linked text boxes in the flyer and brochure templates, among other Publisher preformatted templates. Linking the text boxes makes it easier for you to keep the text formatting consistent in a longer or more complex publication.

To create your own linked text boxes, follow these steps:

1. Use the Draw Text Box command to create a new text box, and enter text into that text box as needed.

2. Create a second text box using the Draw Text Box command.

3. Select the first text box.

4. Select the Text Box Tools tab on the Ribbon.

5. Select the Create Link command in the Linking group. An ellipsis symbol appears on the selected text box.

6. The mouse pointer becomes a pitcher (like a pitcher of water). Navigate to the text box that you want to link to the currently selected text box, and then click the mouse. The text boxes now are linked.

You can tell when two (or more) text boxes are linked because, when you select a linked text box, the Next symbol (a right-pointing arrow) or the Previous symbol (a left-pointing arrow) appears on the edge of the text box frame. You can use these buttons on the text box frame to move to a linked text box from its partner.

After you fill the first text box with text (either by typing the text or by inserting a text file, as discussed in a moment), the text flows into the next text box. Figure 28.16 shows three linked text boxes. Note the Previous and Next symbols on the middle text box (showing that it is linked to both the top and the bottom text boxes).

Note the Previous button and Next button on the text box in the center of the page (between the top and bottom text boxes). One point to keep in mind is that, as you size either of the boxes, the

 note

If you don't like typing text in the text boxes, create your text in Word and then copy and paste the text into your Publisher text boxes. You can link as many text boxes as necessary in a publication.

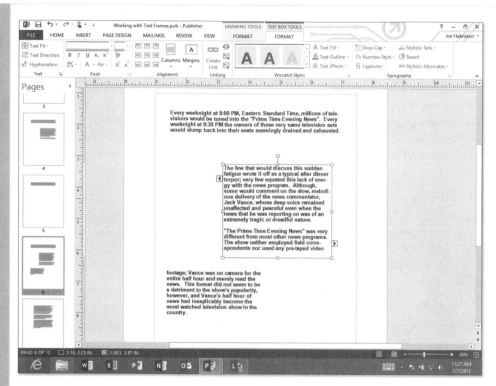

Figure 28.16
Link text
boxes.

amount of text in the boxes shifts from one box to the other, particularly if you make the primary box in the linked pair larger or smaller.

When you enter more text into a text box than it can hold (or copy and paste more than it can hold), an ellipsis (...) button appears on the text box frame. This means that the text box contains more text than it can accommodate. This also means that you have the Do Not Autofit command selected on the Text Fit command menu. You can fix this problem by creating another text box and then clicking the ellipsis button. The mouse pointer shows the Create Link icon (the pitcher); click it on a text box to link the boxes. The overflow text (the text that you can't see) flows into the second text box.

Inserting a Text File

You can insert text files directly onto a publication page. This is extremely useful when someone is creating the publication copy (the text) as you design the publication in Publisher. You can easily insert files created in Word. The Word document can even have images and other objects embedded in the text (such as pictures or even Excel worksheets). If you are using some other word processor, you should save the text document as plain text (.txt) or in Rich Text Format (.rtf).

You can insert a Word document or text file directly onto a publication page, and the Insert feature creates its own text boxes to accommodate the text as needed; however, you have greater control over the process if you create your own text box and then insert the file text directly into it. If you know that the text file requires more than one text box, create the text boxes and then link them. You can then have the story flow from the initial text box into the other text box (or boxes). To insert a text file into your publication, follow these steps:

1. Draw a text box (or linked text boxes) on the publication page.

2. Click inside the text box (or in the first of the linked text boxes).

3. Select the Insert tab on the Ribbon.

4. In the Text group, select the Insert File command. The Insert Text dialog box opens.

5. Locate the file using the Insert Text dialog box, and then select the file you want to insert.

6. Select OK.

Publisher inserts the text into the text box (or linked text boxes). You can modify the formatting for the text as needed by using the font- and paragraph-formatting attributes on the Home tab or the additional text-formatting tools on the Text Box Tools tab.

Inserting Illustrations

Publisher gives you a lot of flexibility in the types of illustrations you can add to your publication pages. You can add a picture file in many image file formats, and you can add a clip art image from the extensive clip art library on Office.com. You can also add a variety of shapes to your publication pages using the Shapes gallery. Publisher 2013 makes it even easier for you to add your own pictures to publications via the Online Pictures command. You can use Bing to do an image search on the Web, or you can insert a picture from your SkyDrive. If you use Flickr to store photos, you can also connect to flickr.com to access images.

Images on a publication page not only add interest to the publication, but can also greatly enhance the probability that your publication will get its intended purpose across to the reader. Although adding graphic elements to a publication is fun, make sure you place and size key graphics, particularly important pictures, for maximum visual impact.

 note

If you misjudge the size of your text box (or linked text boxes) to accommodate all the text in an inserted text file, Publisher creates an additional linked text box to make sure that all the imported text is taken care of. Resize your original text boxes and then delete the added text box.

Options for Inserting Pictures

Publisher supports a wide variety of picture file formats that you can insert into a publication. File formats that do not require you to add a graphics filter are as follows:

- Windows Bitmap (.bmp)

- Graphics Interchange Format (.gif)

- Joint Photographic Expert Group (.jpg)

- Portable Network Graphics (.png)

- TIFF, Tagged Image File Format (.tif)

- Windows Metafile (.wmf)

➥ *More details related to working with pictures and other graphics in the Office 2013 applications are provided in Chapter 4, "Using and Creating Graphics."*

When inserting a picture into your publication, you can insert the picture directly onto the publication page or you can insert a picture placeholder. Inserting a large image onto a page requires that you size and/or crop the image to get it into a manageable size. Of course, the size of the image on the page depends on the size of the image file. I think using the picture placeholder is preferable. The picture placeholder provides an already cropped and sized version of the picture by conforming to the picture placeholder. You have the option to move the Crop markers (if you want to make the placeholder bigger), and you can also move the picture within the picture placeholder to make sure that you determine the center of the photo in relation to the placeholder. By default, the placeholder places the center of the inserted picture in the center of the placeholder box. Whether you insert your pictures directly on the page or into picture placeholders is up to you. Let's look at both options, starting with inserting a picture.

Insert a Picture

Inserting a picture is really just a matter of selecting a picture file and having Publisher plop it onto the current publication page. To insert a picture, follow these steps:

1. Navigate to the page where you want to insert the picture.

2. Select the Insert tab of the Ribbon.

3. Select the Pictures command. The Insert Picture dialog box opens.

4. Navigate to the folder that holds the picture you want to insert; then select the picture file.

5. Click Insert.

Publisher places the picture on the publication page. The picture tools become available on the Ribbon. You can size the picture and position the picture on the page as needed.

Insert a Picture Placeholder

We have already discussed that the alternative to inserting a picture directly onto the page is to insert a picture placeholder. You can insert a picture into the placeholder frame. This enables you to presize the picture based on the picture placeholder size.

On the Insert tab, select the Picture Placeholder command, and then size and position the picture placeholder as needed. When you click the picture icon in the middle of the picture placeholder, the Insert Picture dialog box opens. Locate your picture file, select it, and then click Insert. Figure 28.17 shows an inserted picture on the left and the same picture placed directly into a picture placeholder.

Figure 28.17
Inserted picture versus picture in a placeholder.

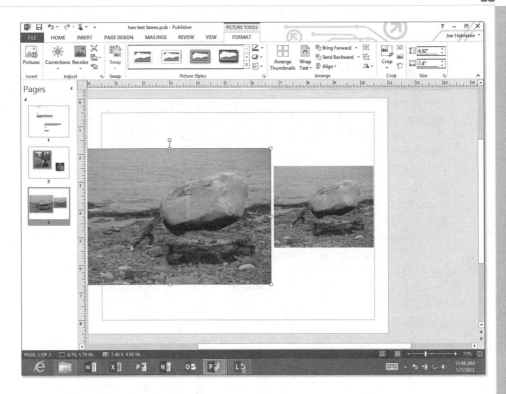

Notice that Publisher sized the picture in the placeholder appropriately for the publication page. The picture on the left is quite large and needs some work in terms of sizing and placement. You don't have to use picture placeholders, but they do allow you to lay out a page before you add photos or other images. They also help by presizing and precropping the picture for you.

After you place a picture on a page, you might find that you want to replace it with another picture. If both of the pictures are already on the page, you can drag one image onto the top of the other to have the two pictures swap positions. This maneuver is a little tricky, so make sure you are dragging the picture by the picture icon that appears in the center of the picture when you select it. Also, don't let go of the picture you are dragging until the pictures actually swap places. In addition, you can select two pictures and then swap them using the Swap command on the Picture Tools tab (which appears when you have selected a picture or pictures). The Swap command also enables you to swap the formatting between two pictures. Swapping formatting means that any adjustments you made to a file using the Adjust group commands are swapped between the photos.

If you want to replace a picture on the page with a picture that is on your computer, on SkyDrive, on Office.com, or somewhere on the Web (you can search with Bing), you simply select the picture and then select the Change Picture command in the Adjust group of the Picture Tools tab. Select Change Picture on the menu to open the Insert Pictures dialog box. Select one of the options for pictures (such as From a File, Office.com Clip Art, or your SkyDrive). Then insert the "replacement" picture. The inserted picture replaces the current picture and conforms to the frame that was inhabited by the "replaced" picture. The picture that was replaced is put in the Scratch area for subsequent use.

Formatting a Picture

After you have inserted a picture onto the publication page, you are provided with the Picture tools, which enable you to enhance and fine-tune the picture (and the frame around it). Select any picture, and then click Format under the Picture Tools tab to make the various picture tools available on the Ribbon. Figure 28.18 shows the picture tools.

You can use the various commands to adjust the picture and its border as needed. On the far left of the Picture Tools is a Picture command that enables you to insert another picture onto the page. The Adjust group of commands, which includes Corrections (brightness and contrast) and Recolor, can enhance the image itself. This group also includes the Compress Pictures (which reduces the picture files sizes to keep the publication file size down), Change Picture, and Reset Picture (resets all your changes) commands.

 note

When you replace a picture with another picture, any changes you made to the frame around the picture, such as a picture style or sizing, are used by the new picture. If you made any adjustments to the original picture, such as corrections or recoloring, these settings are not adopted by the replacement picture.

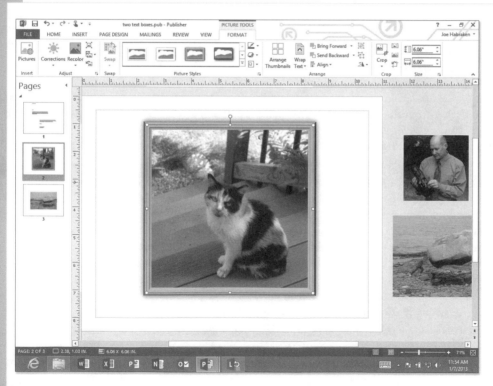

Figure 28.18
The Picture Tools.

The Picture Styles group provides commands that enable you to change the shape and style of the picture frame (the Picture Styles Gallery) and also control the picture border's line color and weight. Additionally, you can add special effects to the photo and its frame using the Picture Effects command. This group also makes it easy to add a caption to a picture using the Add Caption command. The Picture Tools tab includes command groups that were available on the Text Tools tab (which we discussed earlier). The Arrange group provides commands that enable you to layer objects on the page and rotate objects. The Crop and Size groups allow you to crop or size the picture, respectively. For a primer on working with pictures and other graphics, see Chapter 4.

➡ *For an overview of working with graphics in Office 2013,* **see** *Chapter 4, "Using and Creating Graphics."*

Inserting Clip Art

Another way to add pictures to your publication pages is to use clip art. Microsoft's clip art library, Office.com, provides a seemingly endless supply of clip art files and royalty-free photos.

Inserting clip art into your publications can be entertaining, but remember that images you add to your publications are meant to enhance your publications. Don't overdo the cutesy clip art. Always gauge the tolerance of your audience for clip art and use it as much as you want in your personal publications. Use clip art sparingly in any publications that you are creating for use in a professional context.

To insert clip art into the current publication page, select the Ribbon's Insert tab. Then click the Online Pictures command in the Illustrations group. The Insert Pictures window opens. Use the Office.com Clip Art search box to specify search criteria for the type of clip art you want to use. Select the clip art image that you want to insert in the results window, and then select the Insert button. When you select the inserted clip art image on the publication page, the Picture Tools become available on the Ribbon.

Inserting Shapes

You can insert any of the shapes available in the Shapes gallery. These shapes include lines, arrows, and flowchart parts, among other possibilities.

To insert a shape, select the Shapes command (on the Insert tab). Locate the shape in the gallery that you want to use and then select the shape (such as Rectangle, Arrow, or Rounded Rectangular Callout). A drawing tool replaces the mouse pointer. Drag on the page to create the shape. You can size and position the shape on the page as needed.

When you select the shape, the Drawing Tools become available on the Ribbon. These are the same tools that become available when you select a text box on a page. We discussed formatting text boxes earlier in this chapter, and the same commands and tools apply to formatting shapes. If you want to place text in a shape (and, in effect, turn it into a text box), select the shape on the page and then select the Edit Text command in the Insert Shapes group. This places the insertion point in the shape.

Using Building Blocks

Another option for adding graphical elements to a Publisher publication is a building block. The Building Blocks group on the Insert menu provides premade graphics that you can use to enhance your pages. These items range from headings and pull quotes to calendars and advertisements. The commands in the Building Blocks group are as follows:

- **Page Parts:** The page parts are a gallery of items that include ready-made headings, sidebars, and stories. The stories are preformatted text boxes containing placeholder text and an image; you can replace these placeholders with your own text and objects. The page parts are well designed and provide items that you can add to your publications to make them look more professional.

- **Calendars:** This command provides a gallery of calendars that you can insert into your publication. Calendars are available for the current month (This Month) and the next month (Next Month). If you want more control over the month and year for the calendar, select the More Calendars option on the bottom of the Calendars gallery. The Building Block Library window opens. It offers a large number of calendar designs and enables you to set the month and year for the calendar you insert into the publication page.

- **Borders & Accents:** This command provides a gallery of box frames and accents that you can use to enhance your publication. Selecting More Borders takes you to the Building Block Library window, which provides additional borders and accents, as well as frames and lines.

- **Advertisements:** The advertisements range from simple graphic elements, such as attention-getters, to more complex advertisements that are predesigned text boxes containing pictures, text, and other graphic elements. You can modify the text in even the simplest of the attention-getters, if required. You open the Building Block Library window by selecting More Advertisements in the Advertisements gallery. The library provides other items as well, including coupons.

Inserting a building block is just a matter of selecting one of the building block commands, such as Page Parts or Advertisements, and then selecting a particular item provided in that command's gallery.

Printing Publications

When you are working in Publisher, you are, in effect, always seeing each page as it will print. This means that objects, pictures, and text boxes appear on the Publisher pages as they look on printed pages.

The best strategy for previewing your publication is to go from the general to the specific. Zoom in and make sure that individual objects are correctly set up and that text boxes do not contain typos.

When you zoom out on the publication, you can check placement of objects, the overall design of the publication, and the use of color.

 tip

Don't forget to take advantage of the Spelling feature on the Ribbon's Review tab; you can correct any typos or misspellings before you print your publication.

When you are ready to print your publication, select File to open the Backstage. In the Backstage, select Print. The Print page opens, as shown in Figure 28.19.

**Figure 28.19
The Print
page.**

As with any other Office application, you can use the printer settings to specify the printer for the print job and specify properties for your printer. The actual settings for the publication specified in the Settings area depend on the type of publication you are printing. For example, if you are printing a flyer, the setting of one page per sheet makes sense. However, if you want to print multiple business cards to a blank sheet of perforated business cards, select multiple copies per sheet and then specify the number of items that should print on each sheet.

For double-sided printing, you have the option of flipping the page on the long edge or on the short edge. Select the option that makes it easiest for the recipient of your publication to read the front side and then the flip side without having to rotate the page.

In most cases, it is assumed that you will print your publication to a color printer. However, if you plan to print to a black-and-white printer, switch the publication color from composite RGB (red, green, blue) to composite grayscale. This results in a more readable product than just sending the RGB print job to a black-and-white printer.

When you are ready to print your publication, click the Print button. This closes the Print window and sends your publication to the specified printer.

ADVANCED PUBLISHER FEATURES

Microsoft Publisher 2013 provides templates for all the common publication types, such as brochures, flyers, newsletters, and business cards. And you probably figure that using a template is the way to go if you want a professional-looking product. However, always relying on Publisher templates means that your publications are going to look similar to the publications created by other Publisher users. So how do you make your publications stand out and look unique? Publisher offers advanced tools and features that can greatly enhance even the simplest of publications.

In this chapter, we look at some of the more advanced features of Microsoft Publisher. We start with an exploration of features related to the pages in a publication, including master pages. Master pages make it easy to include design elements and ensure consistent layout options across the pages of a publication. We also look at using tables in a publication and manipulating multiple objects on a page. We close the chapter with a look at merging information into a publication and fine-tuning your publications.

Adding Pages to a Publication

At some point, you will need to add blank pages to your publication. Whether you create your publication from scratch (using a blank template) or use one of Publisher's preformatted templates (such as a newsletter or menu), the process for adding pages is straightforward and risk free. The Page command is on the Ribbon's Insert tab in the Pages group. The Pages group contains only two commands: Page and Catalog Pages. We discuss the Catalog Pages command later in this chapter.

When you select the Page command, you have three possibilities: Insert Blank Page, Insert Duplicate Page, and Insert Page. The Insert Blank Page command inserts a blank page after the currently selected page. The page is the same size and has the same orientation and margins as the page that was selected in the Pages pane (before you inserted the new page). So other than the fact that the page is blank, it is the same as the original page in terms of the page setup.

The page has the same page settings because Publisher bases these on the master page for the publication, which dictates the page setup for all the pages in the publication (unless you have more than one master). We talk more about master pages later in this chapter. For now, you just need to know that the master page contains the page-layout information for the pages in the publication and can contain other elements that you want to appear on every page, such as a logo or information in headers and footers. Each publication has a single master page, by default (although you can create additional master pages for a more complex publication).

If you are using a template that provides objects that you don't think you can duplicate, you can choose the Insert Duplicate Page option on the Page command to create a duplicate of the currently selected page. You can then remove the objects that you don't need or rearrange the objects to create your new page.

When you want to add multiple pages before or after the current page, and you want to have control over the objects (duplicates and otherwise) that appear on the new pages, use the Insert Page command on the Page gallery. This opens the Insert Page dialog box, shown in Figure 29.1.

tip

To delete a page from a publication, right-click the page in the Pages pane and select Delete from the shortcut menu.

Figure 29.1
The Insert Page dialog box.

Specify the number of new pages needed, and state whether you want the new pages to be added before or after the currently selected page. For objects, you have three options for the new page or pages: You can insert blank pages (with no objects), create one text box on each new page, or duplicate all the objects on a specified page in the publication. After setting the options in the Insert Page dialog box, click OK. Publisher adds the pages (based on the options you chose) to the publication.

Be advised that, when you are working on a publication that has facing pages, such as a publication based on one of the newsletter templates, the options available in the Insert Page dialog box are different than those shown in Figure 29.1 (which shows the choices available for a document that does not contain facing pages). With the facing pages selected in the Pages pane, the Insert Page dialog box provides the Before Left Page, After Right Page, and Between Pages options, which enable you to specify where a new set of facing pages is inserted into the publication in reference to the currently existing two-page spread.

Configuring Page Settings

The commands related to formatting your publication pages are found on the Ribbon's Page Design tab. The command groups Template, Page Setup, Layout, Pages, Schemes, and Page Background populate this tab. The Page Setup group provides commands that enable you to quickly and easily change page attributes such as margins, page orientation, and size. For example, the Orientation command has two possibilities: Portrait and Landscape. However, if you have a publication in landscape and you want to change the orientation of a single page (the currently selected page) to portrait, all the pages change orientation when you select Portrait on the Orientation gallery.

So using the term "Page Setup" as the name for this command group might be a little misleading because you are changing the settings for the master page on which your document pages are based. Be advised that Publisher applies any changes you make using the Page Setup commands to all the pages in your publication.

The Margins and the Size commands both provide a number of presets. For example, the Margins command provides a gallery of margin possibilities, as shown in Figure 29.2.

 note

You can have more than one master page for a publication, which means that you can mix pages that use different page setup attributes in the same publication. We discuss master pages later in this chapter.

Figure 29.2
Select from a gallery of margin presets.

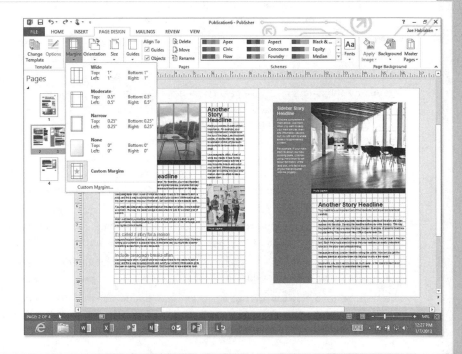

You can select from the margin presets: Wide, Moderate Narrow, and None. You have no preview for the margin changes, so you need to select one of the presets to see how it affects the objects currently on the page. If you want to set custom margins, select the Custom Margins command in the Margins gallery. The Layout Guides dialog box opens (see Figure 29.3).

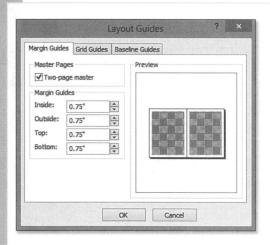

Figure 29.3
Set custom margins in the Layout Guides dialog box.

Use the margin spinner boxes to set the margin guides for the pages in the publication. Remember, you are setting the margins for the master page for the publication. When you have finished configuring the margin guides, click OK. The new margin guides appear on the pages of the publication.

The Size command also provides a list of preset page sizes, such as A5 (Landscape), Letter (Landscape), and Tabloid (Landscape). The available preset page sizes depend on the template you used for your publication.

Again, any selection in the Size gallery changes the size of all the pages in the publication. If you select More Preset Page Sizes, the Preset Page Sizes window opens. This window provides different publication sizes in folders (such as Standard, Booklets, and Postcards). The contents of these page size folders are the blank pages sizes and the manufacturer's blank page sizes that you have access to when you are using the Backstage's Start or New page to create a new publication using a blank template (of a particular page size). To view the page sizes provided by a particular page size group, select that group by clicking the folder. Figure 29.4 shows the page sizes available when you select the Standard group.

When you find the page size you want to use, select the page size and then click OK. You return to the Publisher workspace, and the page size you selected is applied to the pages in the publication.

The Size gallery also provides a Page Setup command, which opens the Page Setup dialog box. This dialog box, shown in Figure 29.5, gives you settings for all the various page options.

The Page Setup dialog box gives you access to the page size and margin guides settings. It also provides you with settings for the number of pages per sheet and the settings for the target paper.

Figure 29.4
Select a page
size from the
Preset Page
Sizes win-
dow.

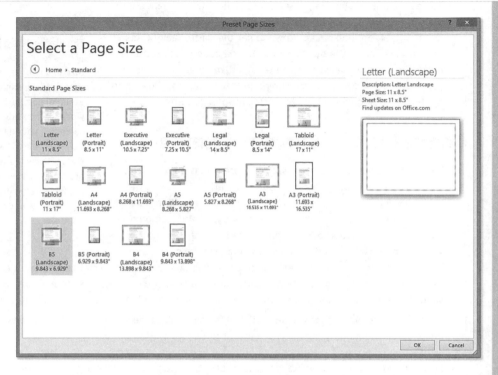

Figure 29.5
Set the page configuration
options in the Page Setup
dialog box.

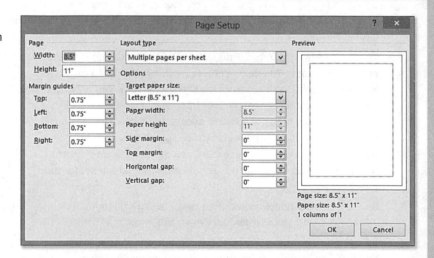

Remember that sheets are what the printer produces; each sheet in the publication can have multiple pages (think of mailing labels or business cards). To set the number of pages per sheet, use the
Layout Type drop-down list.

To set the options for the printer paper that is used, select a target paper size in the drop-down list, or select Custom and then use the page option spinner boxes to set the width, height, margins, and so on for the target paper. As you change the settings in the Page Setup dialog box, the results display in the preview pane. When you finish setting the page setup options, click OK to apply the settings and close the Page Setup dialog box.

Changing the Current Template

Whether you use a blank page size or a preformatted template, you still use a template to build your publication. You have the option to change the template for the current publication. This can be tricky, particularly if you have already established objects such as text boxes and pictures on the pages of the publication. There is no risk, however, because if you choose to apply a new template to the current publication, Publisher can create a new publication based on the change in template; the current publication is unaffected. In fact, you can then decide whether you want to save the new publication and continue to edit it, or discard it and return to your original publication.

 tip

The Size gallery also provides access to the Create New Page Size dialog box. This dialog box is exactly the same as the Page Setup dialog box, except it provides a Name box so that you can name your new page size. Use the Create New Page size dialog box when you want to create a new custom page size. Use the Page Setup dialog box when you want to modify the current page size.

Making a template change (instead of starting over with a new template) is really based on how much work you already put into the current publication. Whether you want to attempt a change in templates depends on the number of changes you made to the current document and the type of template you used when you began the publication-creation process. If you used one of the preformatted templates, such as a brochure or business card template, you are probably better off starting a new publication and copying the objects you created from the original publication to the new publication. The preformatted templates contain a lot of default objects that might not translate well to a different template.

To change the current template, select the Change Template command on the Page Design tab. This opens the Change Template window (which is similar to the Start and New pages that you access via the Backstage). The window defaults to a listing of various flyer templates, but you can select Home at the top of the window to access any of the built-in templates or search for templates on Office.com. If you use one of the built-in templates, you can use the Customize settings to change the color scheme, font scheme, or business information set for the publication.

 caution

Apply the template to your current publication only if you are sure that it will not negatively affect the publication layout. It really makes more sense to create a copy; you can discard it later if you don't like it.

Select your new template and then click OK. The Change Template dialog box appears, as shown in Figure 29.6.

By default, the Change Template dialog box specifies that a new publication is to be created using the new template. This is probably the best way to proceed. When you are ready to create the copy of the current publication based on the new template, click OK. It might take a moment, but the new publication displays in the Publisher workspace.

Figure 29.6
The Change Template dialog box.

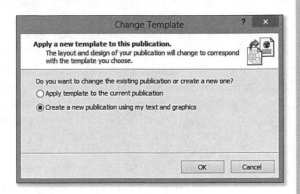

How successful the template change was in the layout and look of the new publication is a matter of how well the new template was able to "digest" the objects that you placed in the original publication. If Publisher was unable to place objects on the pages (mainly due to available space or page formatting), the Extra Content task pane appears as shown in Figure 29.7.

Figure 29.7
The Extra
Content task
pane.

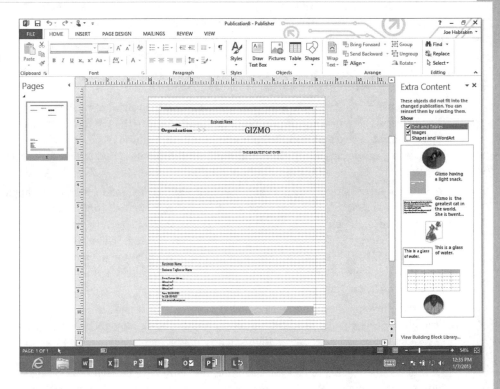

The Extra Content task pane lists all the objects that did not fit into the changed publication. You can choose to view subsets of different object types not placed using the Show check boxes: Text and Tables, Images or Shapes, and WordArt.

To place an object in the new publication from the Extra Content task pane, select the arrow to the right of the object and then click Insert. You can repeat this process as needed to place all the unused objects on the publication page or pages. If you find that most of the objects that you inserted on the original publication pages are showing up in the Extra Content task pane, you might want to abort this entire mission and try again with a different substitute template. If you don't want the new publication based on the new template, close the publication. A message box opens to let you know that you have not used all the items in the Extra Content task pane. Click OK to close the message box. Another message box appears alerting you that you have not saved changes to the publication (meaning the new publication); select Don't Save, and the publication closes.

 tip

You can save items in the Extra Content task pane to the Building Block library. Select the object arrow and then select Save As Building Block.

Working with Master Pages

The term *master page* was already introduced in our discussion of page setup attributes such as margins and page orientation. When you create a new publication, whether based on a blank template or a preformatted template, Publisher creates a master page that supplies basic page-formatting attributes to the pages in the publication. If you are creating a simple publication that consists of pages with the same formatting, this single master page approach (meaning that every page uses the master page settings) can probably work for you.

Master pages can also include information and objects that you want repeated on every page of the publication. For example, if you want to include a logo on the top-right corner of every page, it makes sense to place that logo on the master page. You can also place header and footer items on the master page, which can include page numbering and other information, such as a draft number or date.

You are not responsible for making sure that the master page (and its settings) is applied to the page or pages in your publication. By default, Publisher assigns the default master page to the pages. However, if you have pages in the publication that you do not want affected by changes to the master page, you can select those pages and then choose None on the Master Pages gallery (select Master Pages on the Page Design tab). This breaks the tie between the page and the master page. You can always associate the page with the master page (if required) by selecting the master page in the Master Pages gallery.

Even though you have the option of whether to apply master page settings to the pages in the publication (because you can specify None as the master page setting for a page), you might still need to create multiple master pages. Multiple master pages can be useful when you are working with a more complex publication that requires different page setup values (such as page orientation) for some of the pages. Each master page you create can have its own settings and objects, which repeat on the pages assigned that master page. You can even create a two-page master for publications that contain facing pages (such as a booklet).

note

Although many of the commands on the Ribbon's Page Design tab affect all the publication pages because they change the master page settings, the Background command in the Page Background group changes only the background on the selected page.

Placing Objects on the Master Page

If you want to place a repeating object on your publication pages, such as a logo, you can place the object on the master page. Any page in the publication that has been assigned the master page (which is all the pages, by default) "inherits" the object or objects. Any object (and I do mean *any* object) that you place on a master page is placed on all the pages that are associated with the master.

To edit a master page (in most situations, it is the only master page for the publication), select the Master Pages command on the Page Design tab and then select Edit Master Pages. This switches you to Master Page view. Publisher lists the master page (or pages) for the publication in the Pages pane, and the Master Page tab appears on the Ribbon. The current master page displays in the Publisher workspace. Figure 28.8 shows Master Page view.

Figure 29.8 Master Page view and related Ribbon commands.

Master pages are designated by letters of the alphabet. For example, the default master for a publication is master page A. You can change the name or ID of a master page using the Rename command, but Publisher provides only a one-character ID (so you can't create a descriptive ID for a master page).

In many respects, a master page is no different than a "regular" publication page. You can use the various tools on the Ribbon's Insert tab to add objects to the master page. These objects, such as a text box or a logo, display on each page in the publication (controlled by the master you are working on).

Select the Insert tab and add objects to the master page as needed. If you want to have repeating page parts, borders, accents, or advertisements in the publication, use the Building Blocks group commands (on the Ribbon's Insert tab) to insert items. You can also insert pictures, clip art, and shapes as needed (and as you would on any page in a publication).

The Apply To command on the Master Page tab enables you to apply the master page (and the changes you have made to the master) to all the pages in the publication, the current page, or a specific range of pages. Use the Apply to All Pages option to assign the change to all pages in the publication. Apply to Current Page affects only the page that was selected when you switched to the Master Page view.

To specify a range of pages, select Apply Master Page; the Apply Master page dialog box opens. It has options for all pages, a range of pages, or the current page. To set a range of pages, select the Pages option button and then use the From and To boxes to specify the page range. When you have finished working in the dialog box, click OK.

When you have finished working with the master page (or pages, if there are multiple masters), select the Close Master Page command on the Master Page tab. This returns you to your publication.

 tip

You can also quickly apply a master page (or None) to the pages using the Master Pages command on the Ribbon's Page Design tab. Select a page or pages in the Pages pane, and then click the Master Pages command. You can select a master page or None, as needed.

Inserting Headers and Footers

You can use headers and footers to add repeating information to the pages in your publications. For example, you can insert page numbers, dates, and any other information that you want to repeat. The header or footer for a publication (a publication with only one master) resides in the master page and propagates to the pages assigned that master page (typically, all the pages in a publication with one master page).

You can add headers and footers to a master page in the Master Page view; the related commands are in the Header & Footer group. To show the header on the selected master page, select the Show Head/Footer command. Publisher selects the header area on the master page; it appears as a selected text box. You can type text into the header or use the Insert tab to insert objects such as pictures or other items. To move to the footer area of the master page, select the Show Head/Footer command a second time. Each time you select this command, you toggle between the header and footer (or vice versa).

Three other commands in the Header & Footer group are extremely useful. The Insert Page Number command inserts the page number symbol (#) in a header or footer. This places the appropriate page number on the pages in the publication. You can add text before or after the page number symbol. For example, you can type the word Page before the inserted page number symbol.

The Insert Date command enters the current date, and the Insert Time command enters the current time. You can use these commands to add information in either the header or the footer. When you have finished working in the header or footer of a master page, click in the body of the master page to deselect the header or footer box.

 tip

You can also access the header and footer for a publication using the Header and Footer commands in the Insert tab's Header & Footer group. This group includes a handy Page Number command that provides a gallery of page number positions, including Top Left, Bottom Left, and Center. This gallery also gives you access to the Page Number Format (select Format Page Numbers), which enables you to select the number format and specify the start number for the page numbering in the publication.

Creating Master Pages

You can add master pages to your publication in the Master Page view. You can also rename and/or delete master pages, if needed. One option for adding a new master page is the Add Master Page command. When you select the Add Master Page command, the New Master Page dialog box opens, as shown in Figure 29.9.

note

If you want to create a new master page that is a duplicate of an existing master page, you can use the Duplicate command in the Master Page group. This creates a new master page with a new ID that is a duplicate of the currently selected master. You can then edit the duplicate master as needed and assign it to pages in the publication.

Figure 29.9
The New Master Page dialog box.

By default, Publisher sets the page ID to B (which you might as well leave as is). If you want, you can add a description for the new master page. When you click OK, Publisher adds the new master page to the Pages pane. The new master page is also selected so that it is the active page in the

Publisher workspace. You can modify the master page as already discussed and then use the Apply To command to apply the new master page to specific pages in the publication.

Having more than one master page enables you to create a publication that contains pages with different layouts and default objects, including different headers and/or footers. For example, you can have a master page that does not include a header or footer and a master page that does include a header or footer. Assigning the master page without a header or footer to the first page in the publication enables you to follow the general rule that page numbers and headers/footers are not typically included on the first page of a publication. All the subsequent pages in the publication can be assigned a master page that includes header and footer information, such as page numbering. Remember that you can assign master pages to selected publication pages when you are working on the pages in the workspace. Use the Master Pages command on the Page Design tab to assign a master page to the current publication page by selecting from the master page gallery.

Using Tables in Publications

You can use tables on your publication pages to arrange objects on the page. When you place a table on a page, you are inserting a Publisher object, just like a text box or picture. You can thus size and move the table on the page as needed. You can place text in the table cells, and you can place other objects, such as pictures, in the cells. Although you might think of a table as columns and rows that enable you to enter text information into a cell, you can also consider a table as a potential layout tool for positioning objects on the page. This can be an especially useful strategy when working with pages that have a lot of objects.

You insert a table into a page using the Table command on the Ribbon's Insert tab. You have two options for creating the table. First, you can select the Table command and then use the table grid to specify the number of columns and rows for the table using the mouse. When you release the mouse button, Publisher inserts the table into the publication.

Second, if you want to specify the number of rows and columns for the table without having to drag the mouse onto the table grid, you can select the Insert Table command, below the table grid. Selecting Insert Table opens the Create Table dialog box. It provides a spinner box for both the number of rows and the number of columns. Specify the number of columns and rows as needed and then click OK.

When you insert the new table, the table is the selected object on the page. The table tools appear on the Ribbon. The table tools consist of two different tabs: Design and Layout.

Table Design Commands

The table tools Design commands consist of commands related to the overall look of the table, such as the table's format, the fill color, and border parameters for the table. You can use the Table Formats gallery to select a format for the table from the supplied gallery. Place the mouse on a format in the gallery to preview the format on your table. If you do not want to use a table format, you can use the Fill command to select a fill color for the table. The commands in the Borders group enable you to select a line weight and color and to specify the location of the border in the table.

When you are working with text in the table, you can use the WordArt styles to add interest to all the text in the table or specific cells. The Text Fill, Text Outline, and Text Effects commands in the WordArt Styles group modify the WordArt style you assign to the table text.

The Typography group enables you to add drop caps, select different number styles, and change the stylistic set for the current style being used. The Table Design commands share a great deal of similarity with the Text Box Tools Format group of commands. Both of these command groups include the WordArt Styles and Typography group.

Because you are working with a table that consists of separate cells, you can format the entire table by selecting the table frame. If you want to format specific cells or ranges of cells in the table, select those cells and then use the commands provided in the various Design groups, as needed.

Table Layout Commands

Publisher also provides commands related to the layout of the table, which include commands for inserting rows and columns and aligning text (or other objects) within the table cells. To access the Layout commands for a table, select the table and then click the Layout tab under Table Tools (see Figure 29.10). The table tools Layout command groups are as follows:

- **Table:** This group provides the Select command. You can use the options on the Select command menu to select a cell, column, or row, or the entire table. The View Gridlines command shows the gridlines in a table that does not have formatted borders. The Delete command provides options for deleting columns, rows, or the entire table.

- **Rows & Columns:** This group provides insertion commands for rows and columns. You can insert above or below a row and to the left or right of a column. Select multiple rows or columns to add a like number using these commands.

- **Merge:** The Merge Cells command merges selected cells. If you want to split merged cells, use the Split Cells commands. The Diagonals command enables you to divide a cell or cells on the diagonal either downward (Divide Down) or upward (Divide Up).

- **Alignment:** This group controls how the text is aligned in the current cell or selected cells. The specific commands are Align Top Left, Align Top Center, Align Top Right, Align Center Left, Align Center, Align Center Right, Align Bottom Left, Align Bottom Center, and Align Bottom Right. This group also provides the Text Direction and Cell Margins commands. The Text Direction command toggles the orientation of the text from horizontal to vertical (and vice versa). The Cell Margins command enables you to set the table's default cell margins.

- **Arrange:** These commands enable you to control the text-wrapping properties in the table or selected cells. Other commands in this group relate to changing the layer position of an object in a table cell and grouping or ungrouping objects. A Rotate command enables you to rotate or flip an object.

- **Size:** You can change the height or width of the table using the appropriate spinner box. The Grow to Fit Text check box is enabled by default and allows the table cells to group to accommodate text that you type. The dialog box launcher for this group opens the Format Table dialog box, which gives you control over the color, lines, size, and layout of the table.

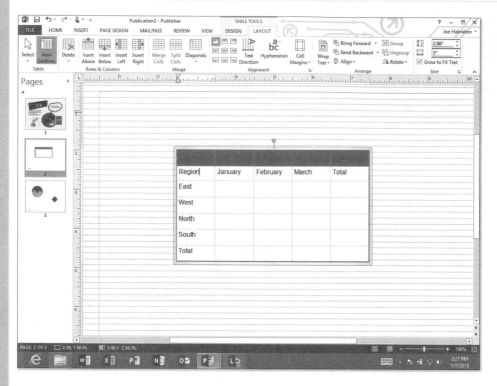

Figure 29.10
The Table
Tools Layout
commands.

Remember that a table is more than just a container for text. It is a structured layout tool that you can use to arrange a variety of object types on a page.

Manipulating Publication Objects

Publisher enables you to manipulate the objects on a page. You can group objects, layer objects on a page, and even swap images between two picture frames and maintain the size settings for each of the picture placeholders involved in the swap.

Grouping Objects

Grouping objects lets you fine-tune the positioning of any number of objects on the page. For example, after you have placed objects on a page, you might want to adjust the overall positioning of all of them in relation to the top or bottom of the page or some other special element on the page (such as a large heading). Moving each object individually can be time-consuming and frustrating, especially if you have the objects currently positioned exactly where you want them to be in relation to each other.

To group objects, use the mouse to click and drag a selection box around the objects. If you don't want to select all the objects on a page, select the first object and then select subsequent objects by holding down the Control key as you click on them. After you select all the objects that you want to include in the group, select the Group command on the Home tab. Figure 29.11 shows a group of several objects on a page.

Figure 29.11
Grouped objects.

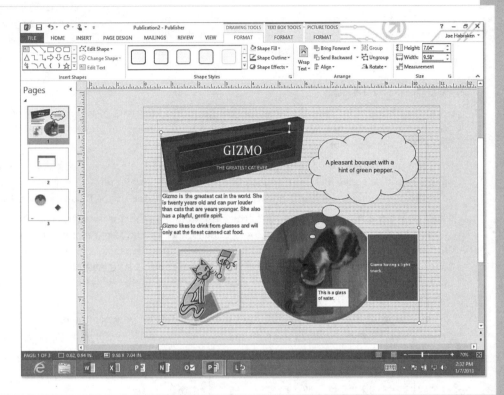

A group has its own frame, and you can use the frame to move the entire group on the page. Place the mouse on the group frame and then drag it to a new position. You can also use the group frame to size the entire group of objects at the same time; click and drag the sizing handles as needed.

You can delete a group and all the objects in the group at once, or copy the objects and then paste them on another page in your publication. When you finish manipulating the grouped objects, click anywhere outside the group to deselect it.

Layering Objects

You can also layer objects in a stack. For example, you might use a combination of shapes, text boxes, and pictures to build a custom logo or other layered item. You can also overlap adjacent objects by layering to provide the page with more visual interest.

Layering objects is just a matter of dragging the objects onto each other and then sorting out the layers using the commands in the Arrange group. You can use the Bring Forward command to bring an object forward in the stack (one object) or to bring it to the front of the stack (on top). The Send Backward command enables you to send a selected object backward (one layer) or to send it to the bottom of the object pile using the Send to Back option.

When you have the objects layered correctly, select the entire stack (drag the mouse around the object stack). You can then group the layered objects using the Group command. This enables you to move the stack without messing up the layers.

 note

Use the Ungroup command to separate the objects in a selected group.

Swapping Images

A nice addition to Publisher's overall capabilities for working with pictures is the Swap command on the picture tools Format tab. It enables you to swap the pictures in two selected picture frames or swap the formatting of two selected picture frames.

Select a picture on a page; then hold down the Ctrl key and select a second picture. The Swap command becomes active on the Ribbon (on the Picture Tools Format tab) as soon as you select the second picture. Select the Swap command. On the menu provided by the Swap command, select Swap.

This swaps the two pictures but keeps the formatting of the picture frame the same. In fact, the pictures adapt to the size of the frame. For example, if you swap a larger picture with a small picture (in terms of the picture frame size), the large picture takes the place of the smaller picture and, in effect, becomes the smaller picture. The real value of being able to swap the pictures without disturbing the placement and formatting of the picture frame is that you don't disrupt the overall balance of your publication page.

When you want to swap the formatting of the picture frames between the two selected pictures, select Swap Formatting Only on the Swap command menu. This swaps the formatting of the frames but does not change the size, content, or placement of either frame.

Merging Data into a Publication

You can perform a variety of data merges into Publisher publications. You can do a mail merge to envelopes, mailing labels, addressable brochures, and other publications. You can also perform email merges to an email publication. A catalog merge enables you to merge text or picture entries into a publication. For example, you might want to generate a product list using a data file that contains the name and perhaps even pictures of your products. Publisher merges each product and any accompanying information related to the product to a new publication page.

When you conduct a merge, whether a mail merge or a catalog merge, you need two items: the publication that you want to merge the information into (such as a postcard that you send to multiple clients) and the information that you merge, such as names and addresses. This information is saved in a data file. Publisher inserts the information in the data file, known as the data source, into the postcard, envelope, or mailing label using placeholder codes called merge fields. Each merge field in the merge publication relates to a piece of information in the data source, such as first name, last name, or street address.

The publication that you use as the destination for the merged information can be any publication that you create in Publisher. For example, you might want to use an envelope template if you want to do a merge of client name and address information to envelopes that you can then print. The merge publication is only the model for the merge, and Publisher creates multiple copies of the merge publication (such as an envelope or a catalog page)—one for each record (or each person, in the case of clients) in the data file.

note

The data file used for a merge in Publisher can be created in Microsoft Excel, in Microsoft Word, or directly in Publisher as you perform the merge.

Performing a Mail Merge

To perform a mail merge, create a new publication. For example, you can create a new postcard using one of the postcard templates. Most of the envelope, postcard, and other mail-related templates have reserved areas on them for the recipient's address. You want to place the merge fields (which are codes that correspond to field information in your data source) in that area of the publication. Delete the text box text reserved for the address information on the publication. The commands that you use to perform the merge are on the Mailings tab.

For the merge, you first must supply an address list, or a data source, for the merge. You can create it or use an existing list. Publisher saves the data source in the Microsoft Access database format with the extension .mdb.

To begin the merge and create a new address list, follow these steps:

1. Select the Mail Merge command and then select Mail Merge. The Select Recipients command in the Start group becomes active.

2. Click the Select Recipients command. You can specify the recipients for the merged publication in either a new list or an existing list.

3. Let's assume that you need to create a new list. Select Type New List. The New Address List opens, as shown in Figure 29.12.

tip

If you are entering individual fields using the Insert Merge Field command, you can put spaces or blank lines between fields, as needed. Line up the fields as you would the address information on an envelope or other publication to be mailed.

tip

When working in the New Address List dialog box, use the Tab key to move forward a field, and use Shift+Tab to move back.

4. Each column in the address list is a different field. Each row is a different record. Type the field entries for the first recipient (that is, first name, last name, and so on).

5. To enter additional records, select the New Entry button, as needed.

6. When you have finished entering the recipients in the address list, click OK. The Save Address List dialog box opens.

7. Specify a name and location for the list, and then click Save. The Mail Merge Recipients dialog box opens. You can clear recipient check boxes so that those people are not included in the merge.

8. Click OK to close the dialog box.

Figure 29.12
The New Address List dialog box.

After you have specified the recipient list for the merge, commands in the Write & Insert Fields group, such as Insert Merge Field, Address Block, and Greeting Line, become active. This is because you have provided the merge fields for the merge by creating the recipient list. You can enter individual field names from the Insert Merge Field command; it provides a list of all the field names in the recipient list.

If you are creating envelopes or mailing labels, the easiest way to get the name and address on the envelope or label publication is to use the Address Block command. Position the insertion point on the publication where you want the recipients' names and addresses to reside—for example, in a text box on an envelope. Then select the Address Block command. The Insert Address Block dialog box opens, as shown in Figure 29.13.

 note

The Mail Merge Wizard walks you through the steps of the merge, but using it is more trouble than just using the commands supplied on the Mailings tab and your own common sense.

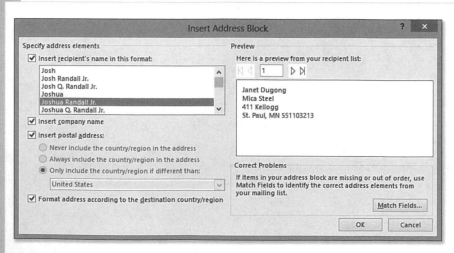

Figure 29.13
The Insert Address Block dialog box.

Select a recipient name format and then deselect items that you do not want to include in the address block, such as Insert Company Name. You can also specify that the country/region not be included in the address. A preview appears on the right side of the dialog box. When you are ready to return to your publication, click OK. The address block field appears on the publication page as <<AddressBlock>>.

When the merge fields are on the publication, you are ready to perform the merge. You can select the Preview Results command and then preview each of the merged publications (such as individual envelopes) if you are unsure of how the results of the merge will look. When you are ready to complete the merge, select the Finish & Merge command.

The Finish & Merge command provides three options: Merge to Printer, Merge to New Publication, and Add to Existing Publication (in the case of an email merge, it supplies Send Email Messages). I recommend merging to a new publication, which enables you to closely examine the results of the merge before you print the merged publication pages. When you complete the merge and create a new publication, a multipage publication opens in Publisher. A copy of the publication is created for each of the recipients. For example, if you used a two-page postcard publication as your starting material, a two-page postcard would be created for each recipient.

Performing a Catalog Merge

Another Publisher tool that enables you to merge date into a publication is the Catalog Merge feature. This merge tool creates product lists in catalogs. The data placed into the catalog comes from a data source of products. You can use an existing list or create the list when you create the catalog pages.

To begin a catalog merge into the current publication, select the Insert tab and then select Catalog Pages. A catalog merge area (in the form of a text box) appears on a new, blank page in the publication. In the Pages pane, the new page appears as a stack of pages because Publisher considers it a catalog. The catalog tools become available on the Ribbon. These commands walk you through the process if you start on the left (with the Start group) and then take advantage of the subsequent commands as they become active on the Ribbon.

You can size or move the catalog merge area as needed on the blank publication page. Remember that it contains the fields that specify what information to merge into the catalog pages using the information in the data source. You cannot insert tables or other objects in the catalog merge area.

You can specify the number of entries that will appear on each catalog page, but not until you get a little further along in the merge process.

The next step in the process is to specify a product list for the merge. This serves as the data source. Select the Add List command. You can type a new list or use an existing list. Again, let's assume that you need a new list. Select Type New List. The New Product List dialog box opens, as shown in Figure 29.14.

 tip

To specify pictures for the product list, you need to type the picture filename into the Picture field, including the file extension for the picture (such as .jpg, .png, and so on). You also need to specify the folder that will hold the picture files, but that happens later in the process.

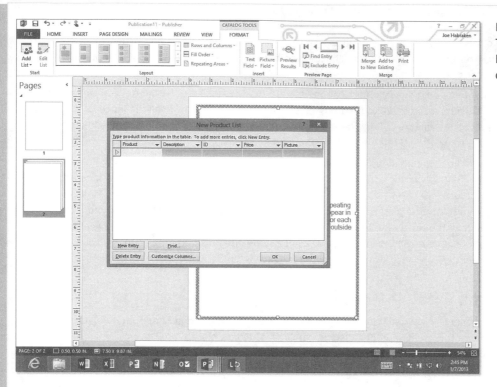

Figure 29.14
The New
Product List
dialog box.

Enter the field information into each of the fields for your first product. Repeat as needed to build your product list. If you want to add fields to the product information, select the Customize Columns button. The Customize Product List dialog box opens. You can add fields, rename fields, or delete fields, as needed. When you click OK, you return to the New Product List dialog box.

When you have completed your data entry, click OK. The Save Address List dialog box opens. Specify a name and location for the list, and click Save. Publisher saves the file, and the Catalog Merge Product List opens. You can deselect records that you do not want to include in the merge by deselecting the check box for that item. Then click OK to close the dialog box.

After you have specified the data source for the catalog merge (or created it), many of the catalog tools become active on the Ribbon. You can use the various layout commands, such as the Layout gallery, to specify how you want the catalog entries to appear on the page, including the number of entries per page. You can also use the Rows and Columns command to manually set the number of columns and rows in the catalog merge area if you do not like any of the presets in the Layout gallery.

When you have a layout selected, you can insert the merge field codes into the catalog merge area. When you select the layout, Publisher inserts placeholder text into the catalog merge area; you can replace this text with merge fields. Select the appropriate placeholder text and then use the Text Field command to enter the field name. Repeat this process as necessary to add all the field codes to the catalog merge area.

If you included a picture field in the product list, a picture placeholder appears in the catalog merge area. Click the picture placeholder; the Insert Picture Field dialog box opens. Select the Picture field and then click the Specify Folders button. You can specify the folder that holds your pictures by using the Add button. This opens the Browse dialog box; use it to specify the folder that contains the pictures (such as the My Pictures folder), and then click OK.

You are almost finished. Now you can use the Preview Results command to preview the results of the merge. When you are satisfied with the results, use the Merge to New or Add to Existing commands to merge the catalog to a new publication or an existing publication document, as needed. I recommend merging to a new publication. When you are sure that the catalog data has merged correctly into the new publication, you can print the results.

Fine-Tuning Your Publications

Before you print a hard copy of the final product, be sure to correct all the errors in the publication and to check the overall design. Publisher offers several tools that enable you to fine-tune your publication.

The Spelling Feature

The Spelling feature checks your documents for misspellings and typos. It is available in the Proofing group of the Ribbon's Review tab. The Proofing group also provides access to the Research task pane and the Thesaurus, which you can use as resources for finalizing text in your publication.

You can set spelling options for Publisher in the Publisher Options window. Select File to open the Backstage, and then select Options. Select Proofing to select (or deselect) settings related to spelling, such as Flag Repeated Words and Ignore Words That Contain Numbers.

Hyphenation

Another element of fine-tuning a publication is determining where words hyphenate in your text boxes. You can have Publisher automatically hyphenate the text in your text frames, which means it determines where to break words with a hyphen and continue the remaining portion of the word on the next line. Because Publisher enables automatic hyphenation by default, it places hyphens only as needed. The great part about the feature is that, if you edit the text, Publisher automatically removes unnecessary hyphens and places new hyphens as needed.

You can also specify the hyphenation zone for new text boxes in the Publisher Options window. Go to Publisher Backstage (File) and then click Options. In the Publisher Options window, select Advanced; the hyphenation-related settings display in the Editing Options area. By default, Publisher automatically hyphenates text. You can set the hyphenation zone as needed.

If you want, you can manually hyphenate text in a text box by selecting the Hyphenation command in the Text group of the Text Box Tools Format tab. When you select Hyphenation, the Hyphenation text box appears. You can clear the Automatically Hyphenate This Story check box and then change the hyphenation zone. To manually hyphenate the story, click Manual.

Design Checker

The Design Checker is another great tool for helping you fine-tune your publications. The Design Checker looks at the design elements and objects in your publication and helps you find empty frames, improperly proportioned pictures, font problems (such as too many fonts), and other design problems. The Design Checker also offers you help when it identifies a potential design problem.

To run the Design Checker on the current publication, select File to access the Backstage. Then select Info. In the Info window, select the Run Design Checker button. The Design Checker reviews your publication. When it is finished, you return to the Publisher workspace. The Design Checker task pane appears on the right side of the workspace, as shown in Figure 29.15.

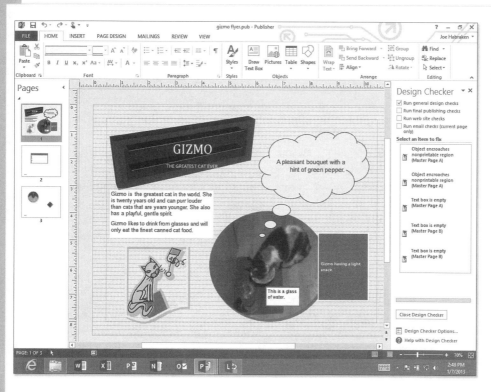

Figure 29.15
The Design Checker task pane.

By default the Design Checker runs a general design check. Any problems it unearths display in the Select an Item to Fix list. The Design Checker flags problems on publication pages as well as master pages associated with the publication. You can quickly go to a flagged item in the publication by selecting the item in the list. As soon as you fix the problem, such as placing text in an empty text box or deleting the empty text box, Publisher removes the item from the Design Checker list.

If you want to run additional tests, which include design checks for commercial printing (Run final publishing checks), web publishing (Run web site checks) and email publishing (Run email checks), select the appropriate check boxes in the Design Checker task pane. When you select one of the additional test possibilities, the Design Checker immediately begins inspecting the publication.

If you want to fine-tune the type of problems that the Design Checker flags, you can open the Design Checker Options dialog box; click the Design Checker Options link in the task pane. The Design Checker Options dialog box has two tabs: General and Checks. The General tab enables you to specify the display options for the list of problems and the page range to examine when you run the Design Checker (you can select all pages or the current page).

The Checks tab lists the items that the Design Checker uses when it checks the publication. It looks for problems such as Picture Is Missing, Object Is Overlapping Text, and Text Is Too Big to Fit in the Frame. You can clear any of the check boxes, if necessary. The Design Checker then no longer flags items that meet that particular condition as items to fix. When you have finished with the Design Checker Options dialog box, click OK. You can close the Design Checker task pane by clicking its Close button.

REQUISITE ONENOTE: ESSENTIAL FEATURES

Organizing information efficiently and continually is truly a battle that never ends; there is always more information. Contact information and important notes can end up on a scrap of paper or a sticky note stuck on your desk. Important information can end up buried in a pile of papers or get lost.

Microsoft OneNote 2013 provides an organized environment for your ideas, notes, and other important information. Adding information to OneNote and then accessing that information when you need it is uncomplicated. Each OneNote notebook can contain a variety of information, including your notes, digital pictures, screen clips from other applications, and even drawings that you create using the tools provided on the OneNote Ribbon's Draw tab. You can even keep track of important files created in the other Office applications that play a part in a project or presentation; all the information can be part of a OneNote notebook.

In this chapter, we look at how to navigate the OneNote application workspace. We also discuss the basics of creating OneNote notebooks and adding sections and pages to them. We examine how to add tables, notes, and tags to a notebook page. We also cover sharing notebooks and syncing notebooks accessed by multiple users.

Introducing OneNote

OneNote provides you with digital notebooks that can keep your projects organized whether you are using OneNote at work or at home. For example, at work, you might be putting together an important presentation to a group of investors; OneNote enables you to organize your thoughts, important project files, and digital content such as pictures, audio, and video. Any information related to your presentation can be contained in or linked to a OneNote notebook that is specific to the presentation.

At home, you might be planning a graduation party or building an addition onto your home. OneNote can keep track of lists of party supplies and guests or information on building subcontractors and scanned images of building plans. Bottom line: Use OneNote any time you need to keep a lot of information organized—and use a OneNote notebook for just about any type of information you need.

OneNote not only helps you stay organized, but it also provides you with an information platform that you can access from a variety of devices. Your OneNote notebooks (and the notes that they contain) are saved in the cloud by default. This means that you can access your notebooks on your PC, tablet, or smartphone. Because a OneNote web app is available on your Microsoft SkyDrive, you can also work with notebooks on computers that do not have OneNote installed.

New Features in OneNote 2013

OneNote 2013 builds on the capabilities provided by OneNote 2010, which supplied a solid footing for this powerful information organizer. OneNote 2013 is even more attuned to sharing your information with others and storing your information where it is the most accessible: your SkyDrive (or your organization's SharePoint site). By default, all your notebooks are stored on your SkyDrive. This means that your notebooks can be synched across multiple devices. Update a notebook on your PC, and then later access that same notebook (with any updates you have made) on your tablet or smartphone. Because your notebooks are saved in the cloud, you can also share the information with other users, including coworkers, collaborators, or family members. Other improvements to OneNote 2013 are as follows:

- **Improved Send to OneNote tool:** OneNote 2013 enables you to quickly clip information from your current window, whether you are working in a web browser, Microsoft Word, or any other application. The tool sends anything you clip to the current OneNote notebook. You can also quickly jot down notes via the Send to OneNote tool by adding a new quick note. The quick note is saved in a special Quick Notes area that is accessible no matter what notebook you are currently accessing.

- **New table features:** OneNote 2013 provides improved support for formatting and enhancing tables. The Table Tools Layout commands give you the capability to manipulate the rows and columns in the table and format the table's borders and cell shading. You can even convert a OneNote table to an Excel spreadsheet.

- **Better integration with the other Office applications:** OneNote is an even more effective organizational tool when it interfaces with the other applications in the Office 2013 suite. You can now embed Excel worksheets directly into your notebooks (giving you the power of Excel as you work in OneNote). Integrating Outlook and OneNote also offers new possibilities, including the capability to connect your OneNote notes with Outlook meetings.

You can find other improvements and changes in OneNote 2013 as well (if you were a OneNote 2010 user). Some of these changes relate to new or improved features. Some of the updates are under-the-hood types of changes that aren't apparent but make OneNote run more smoothly on your computing device.

How OneNote Notebooks Are Organized

OneNote notebooks are a lot like outlines; they provide a hierarchy that enables you to organize information at different levels. As you drill down through each level in a OneNote notebook, you can access information that is more specific. In OneNote, you use different containers to define the hierarchical levels, with the top-level container being the notebook. The following list describes the different types of OneNote "information containers":

- **Notebook:** This is the container file for OneNote. The notebook contains all the sections, pages, and information that you place on the pages.

- **Section Group:** A group enables you to place associated sections together. This is particularly useful when a notebook contains many sections. Section groups are optional.

- **Section:** This is a tabbed divider that enables you to group pages related to a particular topic or project phase. Each section provides delineation in the notebook and serves as the main topical level in the notebook's hierarchy.

- **Page:** You place your notes and other items on the notebook pages. The Page Tabs pane lists pages in a selected section.

- **Subpage:** Subpages enable you to break up information normally placed on a single page. The subpage serves as the lowest level in the notebook's structure. Subpages are listed below the page that they are associated with in the Page Tabs pane.

 note

OneNote can be particularly useful on a tablet or smartphone where you can write directly on OneNote pages and use the Draw tab commands to create your own drawings. You can also convert OneNote "ink" to text and convert handwritten math equations to text.

It really makes sense to think of a OneNote notebook in the same way you would a three-ring binder. The different sections in a OneNote notebook are synonymous with the colored tabs you place in a regular binder. Each binder tab (or section in OneNote) organizes pages of information into logical groupings. You then place individual pieces of information on the pages. When you need a way to manage a notebook that contains a lot of sections, you can add another level of organization to the notebook by creating section groups and placing related sections in a particular group.

This analogy holds true only in terms of the organizational structures in OneNote notebooks and an actual three-ring binder. When you see how easy it is to insert all sorts of digital information into your OneNote notebooks, including audio and video, you probably won't ever consider using a "real" three-ring binder again.

Navigating the OneNote Workspace

When you open OneNote for the first time, a sample notebook called Personal opens. This notebook provides a Quick Notes section with an overview of OneNote and even gives some introductory video material to help you get started. This notebook also includes an Unfiled Notes tab. You can add pages to the Unfiled Notes tab and practice working in the OneNote workspace. You can also add sections and pages (we talk about adding items to a notebook later in this chapter).

If you find the default Personal OneNote notebook a distraction or you have already gleaned all the information you can from this sample notebook, you can close it. Right-click the Show Notebooks list (it is on the far left of the window and shows a notebook icon and the name of the currently open notebook—in this case, Personal). Then select Close This Notebook. That removes the notebook from the OneNote workspace (it doesn't delete the notebook—it just closes it). A Quick Notes tab appears. This isn't a new notebook, but rather a container that holds any notes you send to OneNote using the Send to OneNote command. This command is one of the OneNote Clipping tools, which load automatically when you start OneNote. The OneNote Clipping tool icon appears on the Windows taskbar as a pair of scissors resting on a piece of yellow paper. We talk more about the clipping tool in the next chapter.

Before we begin the process of creating a new notebook, let's look at OneNote's screen geography. The OneNote application workspace is similar to the other Office 2013 applications, and it still uses the Ribbon as its command center. However, the Ribbon is hidden until you select one of the tables, such as Home Insert. As with the other Office applications, a Quick Access Toolbar provides the Undo command. However, the Quick Access Toolbar does not include a Save command. Your notebooks are saved automatically as you work on them. Figure 30.1 shows the OneNote application window containing a sample notebook.

To access the Ribbon commands, click any of the Ribbon tab names, such as Home or Insert. The Ribbon appears, and you can then use any of the commands available on that tab. As soon as you click the current page in the selected section or move to a different page or subpage using the Page Tabs pane (on the right of the application window), the Ribbon is hidden again.

Unfortunately, when the Ribbon is active, the list of sections in the notebook is obscured by the Ribbon. However, the "pinned" Ribbon (as it is referred to) gives you more screen space to work on as you manipulate the information on a particular notebook page, particularly when the Ribbon is hidden. If you find the Ribbon's comings and goings annoying and you want to see the Ribbon commands on the selected tab at all times (and also see the section names in the current notebook), you can unpin the Ribbon. Right-click any of the Ribbon tab names and then select Unpin the Ribbon on the shortcut menu that appears (to clear that selection). The Ribbon appears with the Home tab selected (and your section names visible). Figure 30.1 shows the OneNote workspace with the Ribbon included.

tip

To delete a notebook after closing it, first use Windows Explorer to navigate to your Libraries\Documents\OneNote Notebooks folder. Then select the notebook and press the Delete key to remove it from your computer.

The OneNote Ribbon

The OneNote Ribbon provides seven different tabs; each tab contains different command groups. The OneNote Ribbon tabs are as follows:

Figure 30.1
The OneNote
workspace.

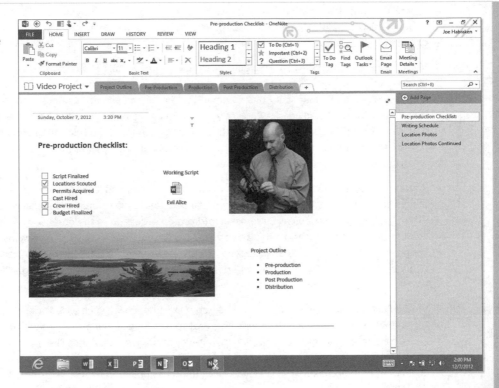

- **File:** This tab provides access to the OneNote Backstage. The Backstage gives information on your notebooks and enables you to access sharing settings for the current workbook. The Backstage also provides access to the Open and Print pages and enables you to access configuration options for OneNote via Options.

- **Home:** This tab provides the Clipboard group and three groups designed for working with the text on your notebook pages. The Basic Text and Styles groups enable you to change text-formatting attributes and assign styles to text, respectively. The Tags group enables you to assign tags to page notes and provides a tool for locating tags in notebooks. The Email group provides one command, the Email Page command, which makes it easy for you to email a copy of the current notebook page.

- **Insert:** This tab enables you to insert different objects into a page, such as tables, pictures, and links. It also enables you to insert printouts of files or scanned items from your scanner. In addition, the Insert tab provides commands for recording audio and video directly onto a page and adding time stamps, equations, and symbols. New additions to the Insert menu include the Spreadsheet command, which enables you to embed an Excel worksheet into a page, and the Page Templates command, which allows you to quickly add special page types, such as to-do lists, meeting notes, and even decorative pages.

- **Draw:** This tab provides tools and shapes for creating your own drawings on your notebook pages. It also supplies commands for highlighting information on a page and arranging multiple objects that you have stacked or overlapped.

- **History:** This tab provides commands that enable you to check revisions and other activity in a shared notebook. You can quickly move to an unread note on a page using the Next Unread command. You can use the Recent Edits command to find changes that have been made in a specific time frame. You can also check which of your coauthors changed information in the notebook using the Find by Author command. With the History group on the History tab, you can view different versions of notebook pages and open the notebook's Recycle Bin, in case you want to see what has been discarded.

- **Review:** This tab provides access to the Spelling, Research, and Thesaurus tools, as well as the Language group, which provides the Translate and Language commands. A Password command in the Section group enables you to password-protect a section in the notebook, which can be useful when you are sharing a notebook with other authors and want some sections of the notebook locked. The Linked Notes command on this tab enables you to take linked notes in a docked window. The linked note that you create links to the information you are looking at, such as a PowerPoint presentation or a particular web page.

- **View:** This tab provides access to the different OneNote views, such as Normal view and Full Page view, and enables you to change page setup parameters, such as the page color. The Rule Lines command enables you to place horizontal or grid lines on a page. The View tab also provides the various zoom commands and enables you to open a new OneNote window or a new docked window for taking notes as you work in other applications.

OneNote differs from the other Office applications, in that it doesn't provide quite the level of redundancy that you find in Word or Excel, which offer a number of ways to access a particular command or feature. In fact, some commands that you can access via other areas of the OneNote workspace or via shortcut menus aren't even available on the Ribbon. For example, you insert a new section using the Create a New Section command, which is just to the right of the last section in the notebook. You add pages by clicking the New Page command in the Page Tabs task pane.

Shortcut menus also provide some commands that you won't find anywhere else. For example, when you right-click a section tab, you find commands specific to sections, such as the Merge into Another Section command and the Password Protect This Section command. Even the Section Color command is available only on the shortcut menu and is not included on the Ribbon.

The Notebook Pane

After you create a new notebook or open an existing notebook, the notebook's name is placed in the Notebook pane. This pane is opened by selecting the Show Notebooks command; this command is accessed via the down-pointing arrow just to the right of the current notebook's name. The Notebook pane lists all your open notebooks. To make one of the notebooks in the list "current" (meaning that it opens in the OneNote workspace), click that notebook.

The Notebooks list can also be pinned to the OneNote workspace. Select the Pin Notebook Pane to Side command (it is a pin icon in the upper right of the Notebook pane). Pinning the Notebook pane to the side makes the pane smaller (so that it doesn't take up as much of the workspace) and provides arrows that can be used to expand or collapse the contents of a notebook or notebooks. When you expand the contents of a notebook, you can see all the sections in the notebook, and you can drag sections or pages from the current notebook into any of the notebooks listed in the Notebook pane. You can also expand multiple notebooks in the Notebook pane and rearrange the sections as needed.

In addition, the Notebook pane provides an Open Other Notebooks command that takes you to the Open page of the OneNote Backstage. This page provides a list of notebooks available on your SkyDrive (if you are currently logged in via Windows 8). It also shows a list of recently accessed notebooks (in the Recent Notebooks list) You can browse other locations for notebooks (including your computer) by selecting the Browse button. This opens the Open Notebook dialog box.

One other command provided on the Notebook pane is the Add Notebook command. When you select this command, you go to the New Notebook page of the BackStage, where you can create a new notebook. The next section looks at the ins and outs of creating a new notebook.

Creating a Notebook

You can create a new notebook for any project, plan, or other endeavor. Creating a new workbook for each of the different projects or major tasks you want to undertake makes sense, whether you are using OneNote at work or at home. For example, having one notebook named Work probably will get you just a big mishmash of information stored together with no obvious relationship, even though you can use sections to divide even a poorly conceived notebook (for more about modifying a notebook, see "Modifying a Notebook," later in this chapter).

Try to plan ahead for what should go in a particular notebook and what should not; think of the notebook as a container for just the information related to one plan or project. There is certainly no penalty for having a lot of specific OneNote notebooks. For example, you might have a notebook related to every report or project assigned to you. Your notebooks should not become like that miscellaneous drawer in your filing cabinet that contains everything from old reports and project files, to loose paperclips and rubber bands, to a dirty coffee mug and spoon.

You create new notebooks in OneNote via the Backstage. Select File to go to the Backstage, and then select New. This takes you to the New Notebook page. You also can navigate to the New Notebook page (in the Backstage) by selecting the drop-down arrow next to the current notebook name and then selecting Add Notebook. The New Notebook page is shown in Figure 30.2.

You have different options for where to store the new notebook. The default place for the new notebook is your SkyDrive (or your organization's SharePoint site). OneNote assumes that you might want to work on the device using multiple devices and/or with other authors. So the cloud storage option (SkyDrive or SharePoint) makes synchronizing across devices and collaborating with other users pretty much a no-brainer. Unless you have a compelling reason to save the notebook to your own computer or a network location, you might as well embrace the cloud. To save the new notebook to your SkyDrive, all you have to do is provide a name for the notebook and then click the Create Notebook button.

➡ *For information on using SkyDrive and the OneNote web app, **see** "Using the OneNote Web App," p. 127.*

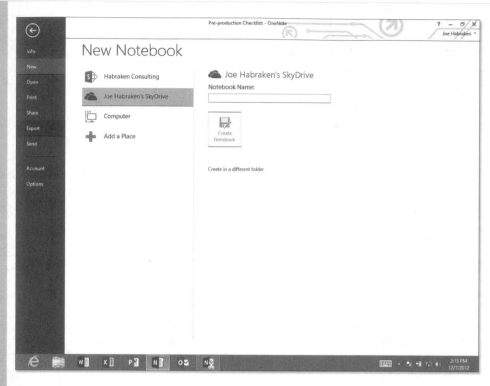

Figure 30.2
The Backstage New Notebook window.

As already mentioned, you can save your notebook to your computer, your local area network, or a SharePoint site. To save the new notebook to your computer, select Computer in the Places list. When you click Create Notebook, the new notebook is typically saved in your Documents folder (or other default folder; the \Users\ *username* \Documents\ path is the default location for new notebooks stored on your computer). You can choose the folder for the new notebook by selecting Create in a Different Folder. This opens the Create New Notebook dialog box, which enables you to navigate to any folder on your computer or network.

 tip

If some pages in a notebook really belong in a new or different notebook, you can easily copy or move notebook pages.

If you want to add a place such as an Office 365 SharePoint site or a SkyDrive site (and you haven't logged into Windows 8 using your Windows Live ID, which is typically also your SkyDrive username and password), click the Add a Place selection. This opens the Add a Place options.

If you select the Office 365 SharePoint option, a Sign In dialog box opens, requesting your user ID and password. After you have provided this information, click Sign In. When the logon is complete, a new Sharepoint site appears in your Places list on the New Notebook page. You can select it and then save your notebook to your organization's Sharepoint site (or Microsoft's Sharepoint site, if you are subscribing to Office 365).

If you select the SkyDrive option, a dialog box opens that asks you to enter your user name and password. This adds the SkyDrive site to your Places list.

After you have specified the place for your new notebook (SkyDrive, Computer, or other place, such as a SharePoint server) and the name for the new notebook, you simply click the Create Notebook button. One more point: You are asked in a OneNote message box whether you want to invite people to share the notebook or whether you are finished for now. We discuss sharing notebooks shortly, so if you have been following along, just select I Am Done for Now. The new notebook opens in the OneNote workspace. You are now ready to build the sections and pages in the notebook.

 tip

You can sign in to any of the Office applications using your Office 365 or Windows Live username. Signing in to one application (such as OneNote) enables your SkyDrive or SharePoint site (SkyDrive Pro) in all the Office applications (including Word, Excel, and PowerPoint). Access to the Accounts dialog box is available in the upper-right corner of all the Backstage pages in all the Office applications except for Outlook. Your Office account settings are accessible in Outlook's Backstage on the Office Account page.

Modifying Notebook Properties

When you create a new workbook, it contains a single section (New Section 1) that contains a single untitled page. Although a lot of whitespace is staring you in the face at the outset, immediately begin building an organizational structure in your notebook is not too difficult using sections. You can then create pages in the sections and insert the notes and other information that make up the content of the notebook. We discuss working with sections and pages later in this chapter.

You also have control over the properties and settings for a notebook that you create. You access these settings via the Notebook Information window in the OneNote Backstage. To access these notebook options, select File on the Ribbon to access the Backstage.

The Notebook Information window provides a list of notebooks that are currently available (select Info if you don't see the Notebook Information page). Each notebook has a Settings button that you use to access the share settings for the notebook and other notebook properties. You can select the Share or Move commands to share the notebook with other users or move the location of the notebook (we talk about sharing a notebook in the next section). You can also sync the notebook by selecting the Sync button; this synchronizes all changes made to the notebook by any users who share the notebook. Any changes you made using additional devices are also synchronized (we discuss synchronization in more detail as well). If you have multiple notebooks open, each notebook is listed on the Notebook Information page (in the Backstage) and has its own Settings button.

To open the Properties dialog box for a notebook, select Properties on the Settings menu (for that notebook). Figure 30.3 shows the Properties dialog box for a notebook.

The Properties dialog box gives you the option to change the display name or the color for the current notebook. You can also change the location of the notebook.

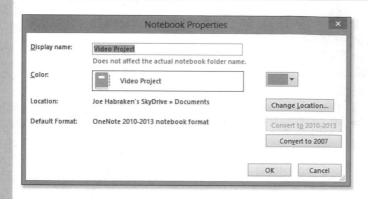

Figure 30.3
The Notebook Properties dialog box.

You can edit the display name as needed. This does not change the notebook folder name created when you originally created the notebook. This is a necessity of shared notebooks because a change in the name of the notebook folder changes the path (location) for the shared notebook.

You can also use the Change Color drop-down box of the notebook icon that represents the notebook in the Navigation pane. Select the Color drop-down box, and select a new color. The Color palette provided contains 16 different notebook color possibilities.

You can also choose a new sync location for a notebook. This is particularly useful for notebooks shared on a local area network. When you select the Change Location button, the Choose a Sync Location for This Remote Notebook dialog box opens. You can use it to browse your network to find a specific share or network folder that serves as the new location.

Because a local cache keeps track of changes that you make to a shared notebook and syncs them with the remote notebook folder (as it does for other users who access to the notebook), you can change the location of a shared notebook. However, it probably makes more sense to establish the permanent path for the notebook when you first create it. This is particularly true for notebooks that you are sharing via Microsoft's SkyDrive service or on a SharePoint site.

The Notebook Properties dialog box also enables you to convert a notebook to the OneNote 2007 file format. This can be useful if you need to share notebooks with users who are still working with OneNote 2007. Be advised, however, that if you convert a notebook to the 2007 format (using the convert to 2007), you negate some of the features in OneNote 2013.

Similarly, the Notebook Properties dialog box enables you to convert a OneNote 2007 notebook to the 2010–2013 format. This type of conversion allows you to take advantage of new features (new in OneNote 2010 and 2013, that is), such as linked notes, math equations, and notebook history. Select the Convert to 2010–2013 button if you are converting a OneNote 2007 notebook.

 tip

If you find that converting a notebook's format has caused problems for other users (or yourself), you can always convert the notebook back to its original format via the Notebook Properties dialog box.

Whether you select the Convert to 2010–2013 button or the Convert to 2007 button in the Notebook Properties dialog box, a Convert dialog box opens and provides a warning related to the type of conversion you are making. To continue, click OK, and OneNote converts the notebook.

Sharing a Notebook

You can share a notebook whether you have saved it to your SkyDrive, your organization's SharePoint site, or your local area network. Even a notebook that you have saved to your computer can be "moved" to your SkyDrive or SharePoint site afterward if you determine that you need to share it. You probably have already noticed that, when you create a new notebook and save it to SkyDrive or your SharePoint site, you are immediately asked whether you want to share the notebook. If you didn't share the notebook initially, you can easily share it afterward. So we are really looking at three different scenarios: sharing notebooks on SkyDrive or SharePoint sites, sharing notebooks saved to your local area network, and sharing notebooks you have saved to your computer's hard drive. To share a notebook, you need to navigate to the OneNote Backstage. When you select File on the Ribbon, you go to the Info page (which lists all your open notebooks). To open the Share page for the current notebook, select Share. As an alternative to selecting Share, you can access the share settings for any of the notebooks listed on the Info page by selecting a particular notebook's Settings button and then clicking Share or Move. Figure 30.4 shows the Share Notebook page for a notebook saved on SkyDrive (the choices available on the Share Notebook page are the same for a notebook saved to a SharePoint site).

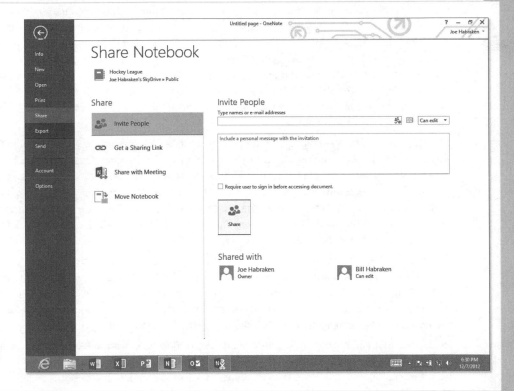

Figure 30.4
The Backstage Share Notebook page.

The easiest way to share a notebook on SkyDrive or a SharePoint site is to invite people. Supply names or email addresses in the Invite People box. You can select recipients from your address book by selecting the Address Book icon. A drop-down list just to the right of the Address Book icon provides two options: Can Edit and Can View. Select the appropriate setting (*edit* can mean *destroy*, so choose wisely). You simply include a message to go with the invitation and then determine whether you want to make users sign in before accessing the notebook. Select Share; the invitations are sent to the recipients, and the notebook is shared.

 tip

You can quickly share a page of notes from a notebook via email. Go to the page you want to send and then select Email Page on the Ribbon's Home tab. An Outlook message window opens. Provide the recipient's address, and send the email. The notes are on their way.

The Share Notebook page also offers two other possibilities for sharing the notebook. The Get a Link option enables you to create a link that can be made available to any number of users (by email or otherwise). You can create a view link or an edit link. Be advised that anyone with a view link or an edit link can view or edit the notebook, respectively.

The third option provided by the Share Notebook page is Share with Meeting. This option requires that you have Microsoft Lync running and connected to your company's Lync server. (Lync is the Microsoft Office communication tool and provides instant messaging and audio- and video-conferencing capabilities.) When you select Share with Meeting on the Share Notebook page, the Share with Meeting button becomes active. Select the Share with Meeting button. A Share Notes with an Online Meeting window opens. If you have a current conversation or meeting underway in Lync, you can select that meeting and then click OK. (You can also start a new Lync meeting from the Share Notes with an Online Meeting window, if needed, and then click OK.) You are returned to the current notebook, and any notes inserted into the notebook are shared with the conversation or meeting participants.

We still need to discuss how to share a notebook that has been saved to your local area network. Anyone who can get to the notebook can access it, meaning that access is controlled by your local area network access rights. If someone has access rights to the folder, that person can get to the notebook. You can alert the users whom you want to access the notebook by selecting the Settings button on the Notebook Information page (in the Backstage). Select Share or Move on the Settings menu; this opens the Share Notebook page for the notebook (you can also select the Invite people to this notebook link to open the Share Notebook page). Figure 30.5 shows the Share Notebook page for a notebook that has been saved to a network share.

To let other users know about the shared notebook, select the Email Others About the Notebook link on the Share Notebook page. This opens Microsoft Outlook, enabling you to email a link that points to the network location where the notebook resides. Send the email to your collaborators; to access the notebook, they simply have to click the link in the email address.

Notebooks that you have saved on your computer need to be moved to SkyDrive or SharePoint if you want to share them with other users. To begin this process, select the Share on Web or Network link below the notebook's name (on the Notebook Information page), or select Settings and then Share or Move. This opens the Share Notebook page, shown in Figure 30.6.

Figure 30.5
The Share Notebook page for a notebook saved to your network.

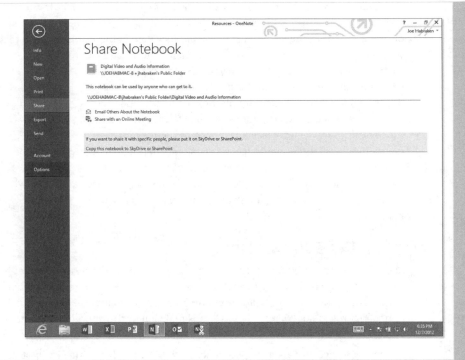

Figure 30.6
The Share Notebook page for a notebook saved on your computer.

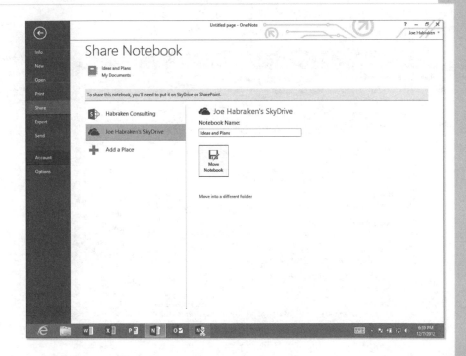

On the Share Notebook page, select your SkyDrive or SharePoint site in the Places list (you can add a place using the Add a Place command). Recent folders you have accessed appear on the right side of the page. For example, if you choose your SkyDrive in the Places list, the recent folders opened on your SkyDrive appear on the right. If you want to access a folder that is not listed, you can navigate your SkyDrive or SharePoint site using the Browse button. Both selecting a folder in the Recent Folders list and selecting the Browse button open the Move Notebook dialog box. Provide a name for the notebook, and then select Move. The notebook is moved to the new location. A message box opens when the move is complete, letting you know that the notebook is now syncing to the new location. You can then share the notebook as needed by inviting people to share the notebook or by sending a link or sharing the notebook in a Lync meeting.

 tip

Remember that the Notebook Information page of the OneNote Backstage is the starting point for the process that enables you to quickly share your SkyDrive, SharePoint, or network notebooks.

Viewing the Sync Status

Shared notebooks are synchronized with a cached copy of the notebook (that is, a local copy is kept cached on your computer). You configure the synchronization of your notebooks so that the sync occurs automatically, or you can configure it so that synchronization is manual. (Manual might be an option when you don't have a persistent connection to the Internet, meaning your SkyDrive or your Sharepoint site.)

To view the sync status for the workbooks you currently have open in OneNote, select File and then Info. On the Notebook Information page, select the View Sync Status button. The Shared Notebook Synchronization dialog box appears as shown in Figure 30.7.

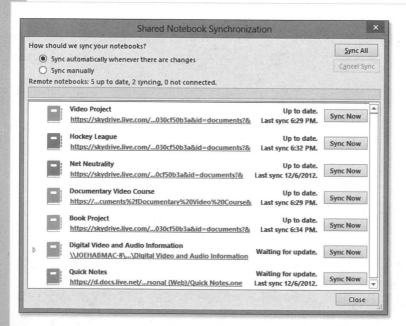

Figure 30.7
The Shared Notebook Synchronization dialog box.

The Shared Notebook Synchronization dialog box shows you the sync progress for your open notebooks, as well as their locations. By default, the sync option is set to Sync Automatically Whenever There Are Changes. If you want to work offline or sync the notebook only at certain times, click the Sync Manually option button. If you select this option, you have to access the Shared Notebook Synchronization dialog box whenever you want to sync a shared notebook or notebooks via the Sync Now command. When you are ready to exit the Shared Notebook Synchronization dialog box, select Close; you are returned to the active notebook in the OneNote workspace.

Working with Sections

Sections give you important organizational containers for your notebooks. Similar to the file folders you use in a file cabinet drawer, sections enable you to group related pages both for easy access and to logically keep similar or associated information together.

When you end up with a lot of sections in a notebook, you can group related sections into a higher-level storage container called a section group. Using section groups as a way to organize related sections means that the section group functions much like a hanging file folder, and the sections become the manila file folders that you use to divide information in each hanging file folder. You certainly are not required to use section groups, but doing so is a good way to organize notebooks that contain a large number of sections. The whole purpose of using OneNote in the first place is to organize a lot of disparate information.

Creating or Deleting a Section

You can quickly add a new section to the current notebook. Select the Create a New Section tab to the right of any existing sections. A new section then is added to the notebook. The new section contains a new, untitled page, as shown in Figure 30.8.

Figure 30.8
A new section containing an untitled page.

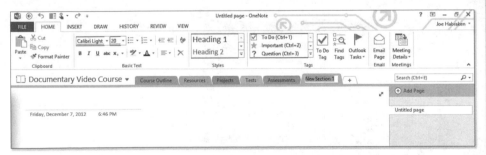

To name the section, double-click the New Section 1 placeholder text on the section's tab. Type the name for the section. You can add sections to the notebook as they are needed.

If you end up with a section that you don't need, you can quickly remove it. Right-click the section's tab and then select Delete. A message box opens asking if you want to move the section to the notebook's Recycle Bin; click Yes to confirm the deletion. Deleted sections and pages are stored in the notebook's Recycle Bin for 60 days and can be restored to a notebook if needed; we discuss the Recycle Bin later in this chapter.

Modifying Sections

You can make certain modification to a section. You can change its name and the color of its tab. You can also move or copy a section within a notebook or to another notebook. You can password-protect a section and merge a section into another section to combine two sections.

To change the name of a section, double-click the current name on a section's tab and then type a new name. To change the color of the section's tab, right-click the section and then point at Section Color on the shortcut menu. A color palette opens; select a new color on the palette.

Copy, Move, or Merge Sections

You can quickly rearrange the sections in a notebook. Drag a section to a new location in the note-book by grabbing its tab with the mouse. You can also drag a section from one notebook to another notebook; simply pin the Notebook pane to the OneNote workspace (open the Notebook pane and then click the pin). Expand notebooks as needed in the pinned Notebook pane. You can then drag a section from one notebook to another (including dragging sec-tions or pages from the current notebook into any notebook listed in the Notebook pane). When you move a section, you cannot reverse the action with the Undo command on the Quick Access Toolbar. You can also move or copy a section within the notebook or between other open notebooks by using the Move or Copy Section dialog box. Right-click a section's tab and then select Move or Copy. The Move or Copy Section dialog box appears, as shown in Figure 30.9.

 tip

You can also rearrange sections in a notebook or move sections between notebooks using the expanded Navigation pane.

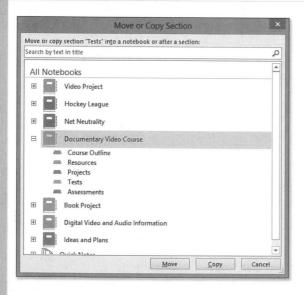

Figure 30.9
The Move or Copy Section dialog box.

You can expand any of the projects listed in the All Notebooks list to view the sections in a particular project. Select the section in a project to which you want to move or copy the current section. The current section is copied or moved to a position after the selected section. After you have provided the positioning for the moved or copied section, select the Move or Copy button at the bottom of the dialog box. The section is moved or copied, depending on your choice in the dialog box.

Password-Protect a Section

If you have a section in a notebook that contains private or proprietary information and you share the notebook online or on your network, you might want to password-protect that section. When you password-protect a section, only users who have the password can access that section.

To password-protect the current section, right-click the section's tab and select Password Protect This Section on the shortcut menu. The Password Protection pane appears on the right side of the OneNote window, as shown in Figure 30.10.

Figure 30.10
The Password Protection pane.

Click the Set Password button, and the Password Protection dialog box opens. Enter the password for the section and then confirm the password. Click OK to set the password for the section.

Password-protect only sections that truly contain highly sensitive information. If you forget the password, OneNote does not have a method of recovering the password, so use the password protection feature only when it is absolutely necessary.

After you have set the password for the section, you can lock the section and any other sections that you have password-protected. Click the Lock All button in the Password Protection pane.

When any user attempts to access the password-protected section, a message appears on the section to let the user know that it is locked. Click the section or press Enter to access the Protected Section dialog box. Provide the password for the section and then click OK.

If you decide that the section doesn't need to be password-protected, right-click the section's tab and select Password Protect This Section on the shortcut menu. You can use the Remove Password button to remove the protection from the section. Enter the password in the Remove Password dialog box, and then click OK.

Merging a Section

You can merge a section in a notebook with another section in that notebook or any other notebook listed in the Show Notebooks pane. This enables you to combine redundant sections or move the pages from one section to another. When you complete a section merge, you have the choice to keep the section that you merge, which is emptied of all its pages; all its pages are moved to the other section. For example, I might have a notebook dedicated to a course that I am teaching, and there is a Test section that needs to be merged into another section named Grades. I use the Merge Section dialog box to move all the pages from the Test Section into the Grades section.

To merge a section, right-click the section's tab and then select Merge into Another Section. The Merge Section dialog box opens, as shown in Figure 30.11. Expand the notebooks listed to locate the section that serves as the destination for the merge.

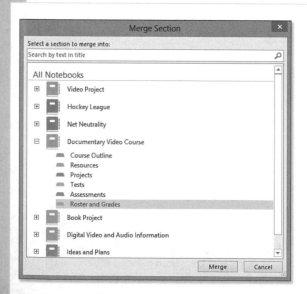

Figure 30.11
The Merge Section dialog box.

Select the destination section for the merge in the current notebook or other notebook, and then select Merge. A OneNote message box opens, asking if you are sure that you want to merge the sections. The merge cannot be undone after you perform it. Click Merge Sections to complete the merge. A second dialog box opens, allowing you to delete or keep the section that you merged. The only part that you would be keeping is the empty section because its pages have been moved into the other section you specified.

Creating a Section Group

A section group is a higher-level organizational container (than a section) and can be used to group sections in a notebook. Section groups are useful when you have many sections in a notebook and want to further organize a more complex notebook.

After you create a section group, you can move existing sections into the group or create new sections in the section group. To create a new section group, right-click any of the section tabs in the current notebook and then select New Section Group. The new section group appears to the right of the section tabs in the notebook (just below the Ribbon). The icon for a section group consists of several small section tabs. You can type a name for the section group in its name box.

After you create the section group, you can drag sections into the group. A Create New Section tab is also provided in the group, to enable you to quickly create new sections within the section group. Figure 30.12 shows a section group and the sections that it contains.

Figure 30.12
A section group and its sections.

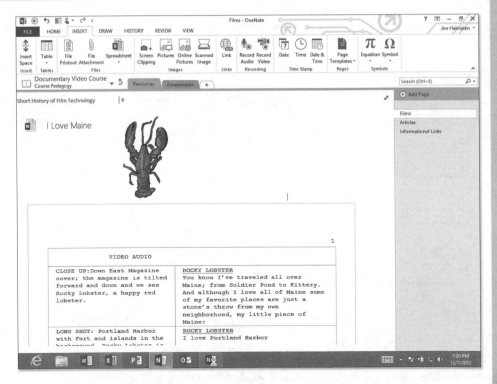

You can also rearrange sections in a group as needed. To close a group and return to the main section tabs in a notebook, select the Navigate to Parent Section Group button to the right of the section name.

Working with Pages

The pages in the various sections of your notebook hold the notebook's content, such as notes, pictures, links, and drawings. You can add pages to the current section by selecting Add Page in the Page Tabs pane. A new page appears in the section. Type a title for the page above the page time stamp. The title also appears on the tab that represents the page in the Page Tabs pane.

You can delete a page if you no longer need it: Right-click the page in the Page Tabs pane and then select Delete. You don't get to confirm the deletion; the page is immediately removed. You can use the Undo button to reverse a page deletion. You can also restore pages from the notebook Recycle Bin, if necessary, which is discussed later in this chapter.

Creating Pages Using Templates

You can create new pages based on templates. OneNote provides many different page templates, including academic page templates for lecture notes and business page templates for meeting notes. To create a new page based on a template, select the Insert tab on the Ribbon. The Page Templates command is in the Pages group. Select the Pages Templates command and then select Page Templates on the menu (the menu also includes a list of any templates you have used recently). The Templates pane appears on the far right of the OneNote workspace, as shown in Figure 30.13.

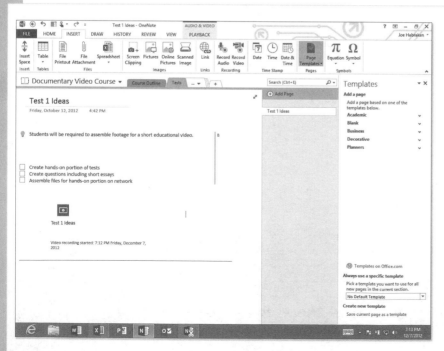

Figure 30.13
The Templates pane provides page templates.

Expand one of the template categories, such as Academic, Business, or Decorative. Select the template that you want to use to create the new page. The new page appears in the Page Tabs pane. You can edit the title of the new page to fit your needs. You can also add pages based on other templates. When you have finished working with the Templates pane, click its Close button.

The page templates can help you quickly put together a page that holds information of a particular type. For instance, the meeting note templates (such as the Detailed Meeting Notes template) set up the new page with different headings, such as Meeting Details, Attendees, and Summary. All you have to do is provide the specific information for the meeting under the appropriate note heading on the page.

Creating Subpages

You can also create subpages in a OneNote notebook. A subpage is subordinate to an existing page in a notebook section. Not unlike subordinate items in an outline, a main page can have several subpages. The point of the subpage is to add another level to the organizational structure of the notebook. For example, you might have a meeting page with subpages that provide details of each meeting listed on the meeting page. A subpage appears as its own separate page when you select it in the Page Tabs pane, but it is listed under the page to which it is subordinate.

 tip

You can promote a subpage to a "regular" page. Right-click the subpage in the Page pane and select Promote Subpage.

A subpage is subordinate to the page that is listed above it in the Page pane. You can make any existing page a subpage, or you can create a new page and then make it a subpage. Think of a subpage as a secondary level in an outline where the page above the subpage (in the page list) is at the outline's primary level. To create a new subpage for a page, create a new page directly below it in the Page list. Then right-click the new page and select Make Subpage. As with any new page, you can type the page name in the header area of the page above the time stamp.

You can also make an existing page a subpage by right-clicking that page and selecting Make Subpage from the shortcut menu. You can add as many subpages for a particular page as you need. You can also quickly promote a page from a subpage to a "regular" page by right-clicking the subpage and then selecting Promote Subpage.

When you have a subpage or subpages under a main page, you can collapse or expand the subpages for that particular page. A collapse/expand button is available to the right of the main page (the page that has the subordinate subpages). You can also arrange the subpages under a main page by dragging a particular subpage to a new position. However, if you drag a subpage under a new main page in the Page pane, the page is promoted and is no longer a subpage. Remember that subpages are no different than "regular" pages in a section. It still can hold notes, attachments, and tables. Subpages are really just another layer for organizing the information in your notebook.

Restoring Sections and Pages from the Notebook Recycle Bin

If you inadvertently delete a section or page from a notebook, you can go to the notebook's recycle bin and restore that section or page. You can also undelete a section or page that has been deleted by another user who has access to a shared notebook. The Notebook Recycle Bin command is on the Ribbon's History tab in the History group.

When you select the Notebook Recycle Bin command, it provides a menu that enables you to access the recycle bin, empty the recycle bin, or disable the history feature for the current notebook. If you disable the history feature, you are not able to restore deleted sections or pages or to view different page versions, which are accessed via the Page Versions command.

When you open the Recycle Bin for the current notebook, you find that it is arranged as a notebook. Figure 30.14 shows the Recycle Bin for a notebook.

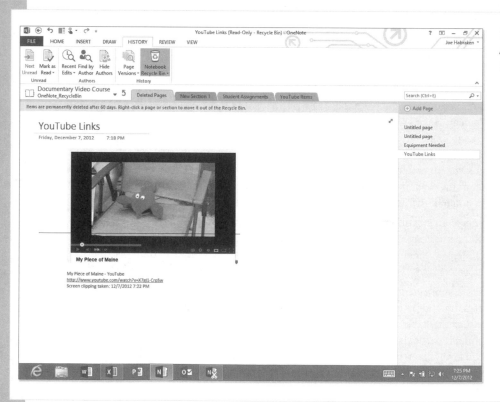

Figure 30.14
A notebook's Recycle Bin.

The easiest way to move a section from the Recycle Bin to the current notebook or any open notebook is to open the Notebook pane and then pin it to the workspace. You can now drag deleted sections from the Recycle Bin to the current notebook or another notebook.

You can also drag pages from the Recycle Bin to restore them to a notebook. Select a particular deleted section in the Recycle Bin to view the pages in that section. Pages that were deleted but were not associated with a particular section are found in the Deleted Pages section that is included in a notebook's Recycle Bin. To restore a page to the current notebook or to another notebook in the pinned Notebook pane, expand the target notebook and then drag the page from the Page pane to the section in the notebook (in the Notebook pane).

You can also move or copy a section or page found in a notebook's Recycle Bin by accessing the Move or Copy command. To access the Move or Copy dialog box for a section, right-click the section and then select Move or Copy. To access the Move or Copy dialog box for a page, right-click the page and then select Move or Copy.

When you have finished working in the notebook's Recycle Bin, click the Notebook Recycle Bin command to deactivate the Recycle Bin and return to the current notebook. You can also exit the Recycle Bin by clicking the Navigate to Parent section group on the right side of the Recycle Bin icon in the sections area at the top of the workspace.

Inserting and Formatting Notes

In OneNote, the note is the basic informational object on your notebook pages. Notes give you a container for your thoughts, ideas, lists—any text entry that you need to make. You can click anywhere on a page and quickly insert a note. As you type, the note box sizes itself to accommodate the text that you enter. To place blank lines in a note, press the Enter key.

You can move a note on a page as needed; just drag it to a new location. You can also resize notes to any dimensions that you require. If you need to delete a note, select the note and then press the Delete key.

You can format the text in your notes using the commands provided on the Home tab's Basic Text group. This group provides commands for font attributes, such as font size and color, and provides paragraph attributes, such as indents and text alignment. To format all the text in a note, select the note's frame. You can then apply formatting attributes as needed by selecting a specific command or commands.

In addition, you can select text within the note box to apply formatting attributes. This enables you to take such actions as placing a bold title at the top of the text box or assigning different font colors to text lines within the note. You can clear formatting for text in a note using the Clear Formatting command in the Basic Text group.

The Basic Text group also enables you to create notes that contain bulleted or numbered lists. Click a page to place the insertion point, and then select the Bullets or Numbering command to create the list.

The Bullets command provides a drop-down arrow that enables you to access the Bullet Library. You can specify the bullet style that you want to use by selecting a particular style in the library.

The Numbering command provides a Numbering Library that you can access via the drop-down area on the right of the Numbering command. The library provides different numbering formats that use numeric, alphanumeric, and Roman numerals. You can customize the numbers for a list by selecting the Customize Numbers command in the Numbering Library. This opens the Customize Numbering pane, shown in Figure 30.15.

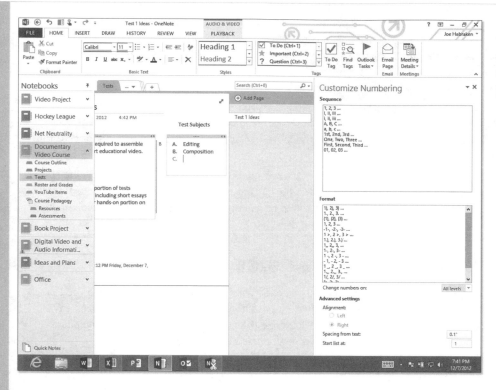

Figure 30.15
The
Customize
Numbering
pane.

You can specify a particular sequence type for the custom list, and you can apply a specific format to the sequence. You can also adjust advanced settings for the numbered list, such as the alignment and spacing of the number from the text. When you have built your list, you can close the Customize Numbering pane by clicking its Close button.

> **note**
>
> If you are using a tablet, smartphone, or touchscreen, you can write your notes directly on a page.

You can also format note text using the Styles gallery. The Styles gallery can be accessed via the Styles group on the Ribbon's Home tab. You can apply a style to all the text or to selected text in a note. To view the entire Styles gallery, click the More button on the right of the Styles gallery.

Using Tags

Another way to differentiate the notes on your notebook pages is to use tags. A tag is a way to assign a category to a note. Each tag category also assigns a distinct icon to the note. For example, there is an Important tag, a Question tag, and a Contact tag, among others. You can tag existing notes, or you can create a new note by selecting the tag first and then typing the note.

You can access the Tags gallery in the Tags group on the Ribbon's Home tab. Select the More button to view the entire gallery. Figure 30.16 shows the Tags gallery.

Figure 30.16
The Tags gallery.

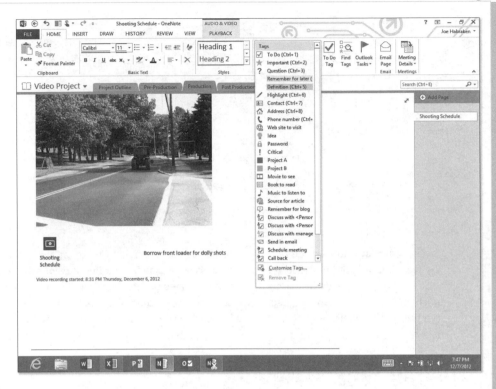

Click a tag in the gallery to start a new tagged note, or select an existing note and apply a tag to it. You can apply multiple tags to a note. If you want to remove a tag from a note, right-click the tag and select Remove Tag. The text in the note is not affected.

You can modify existing tags and create new tags in the Customize Tags dialog box. Select Customize Tags in the Tags gallery to open the Customize Tags dialog box. You can reorder the existing tags in the gallery by using the Move Tag Up and Move Tag Down buttons. To modify an existing tag, select Modify Tag. This opens the Modify Tag dialog box, which enables you to specify the name, symbol, font color, and highlight color for a tag.

Instead of spending a lot of time customizing existing tags, it might make more sense to create your own tags. This way, you can create tags that you use a lot. You can then move your custom tags to the top of the Tags gallery to make them easily accessible.

To create a new custom tag, click the New Tag button in the Customize Tags dialog box. The New Tag dialog box appears. Figure 30.17 shows both the Customize Tags and New Tag dialog box.

 note

Customizing a tag does not affect notes that have been previously tagged with that tag.

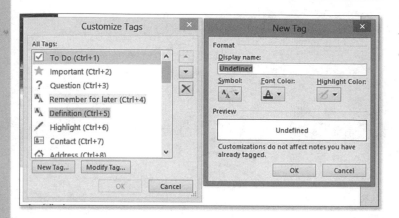

Figure 30.17
The Customize Tags and New Tag dialog boxes.

Specify a display name for the tag. You can then specify a symbol for the tag using the Symbol gallery (see Figure 30.17) and also set an optional font color and/or highlight color for the tag. The tag settings that you specify for the new tag are previewed in the New Tag dialog box. When you have finished creating the new tag, click OK. The tag is listed in the Customize Tags dialog box. Click OK to return to the OneNote workspace. You can now access your custom tag directly from the Tags gallery.

Finding Tagged Notes

You can use the Tags Summary pane to quickly list the tags that you have used in a notebook or notebooks. This enables you to view tagged notes by the tag type you assigned to a note or notes. You also can use a tagged note listed in the Tags Summary pane to immediately move to the page that contains that particular tagged note.

To open the Tags Summary pane, select the Find Tags command in the Tags group on the Ribbon's Home tab. The Tags Summary pane opens, as shown in Figure 30.18.

The tagged notes in the current notebook are listed and grouped by tag name. You can use the Group tags by drop-down list to change how the tagged notes are grouped. As already mentioned, tags are grouped by tag name by default, but you can also group the tagged notes by section, title, date, and note text. You can use the listed tagged notes in the Tags Summary task pane to navigate to a particular tagged note; simply select the note in the Tags Summary pane. The page containing the note becomes the active page, and the tagged note is selected.

The Tags Summary pane also provides a Search drop-down box at the bottom of the pane. By default, the Tags Summary pane searches for only tagged notes in the current notebook. However, you can use the Search drop-down box to search for notes in the current section or section group. You can also search the current notebook or all your notebooks, and you can search for notes by the time frame in which they were inserted. For example, you can search for notes that you added today (Today's Notes), or you can use other time-related options, such as Yesterday's Notes or This Week's Notes.

Figure 30.18
The Tags
Summary
pane.

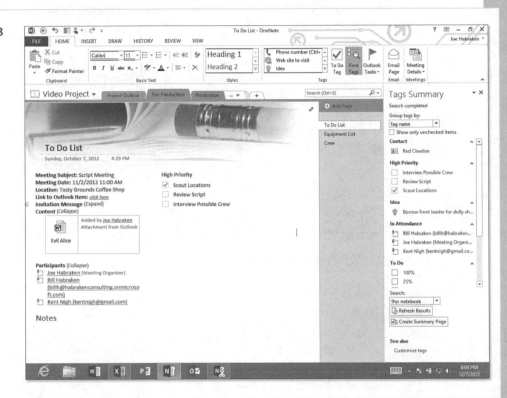

Using Tables to Store Information

Another way to organize text or other objects on a notebook page is to use a table. A table enables you to arrange text and other objects in a tabular format using rows and columns. Each intersection of a row and a column is referred to as a cell. You can type text in a cell, insert a picture into a cell, or place a link in a cell. You can even sort the data in the table.

OneNote 2013 expands the possibilities for table formatting and now includes shading options. You can also insert a blank Excel worksheet onto a page, which provides you all of Excel's capabilities as you are building a complex table on the page. Existing tables in a notebook can also be converted to an Excel worksheet.

When you insert a table into a notebook page, you are creating a note. The table resides in a note box just like any text note that you place on a page. You can move the table to a different location on the page and size the frame around the table to change its dimensions. To insert a table follow these steps:

1. Click on the page to place the insertion point where you want to insert the table.

2. Select the Insert tab on the Ribbon.

3. Click the table command, and then use the Insert Table grid to specify the number of rows and columns in the table using the mouse.

4. When you release the mouse, the table is inserted into the page.

When you enter the table, you can move forward through the table from cell to cell by pressing the Tab key. If you need to move backward from cell to cell, use Shift+Tab.

When the insertion point is in the table, or if the table is selected, the Table Tools Layout tab becomes available on the Ribbon. Figure 30.19 shows the Table Tools Layout tab on the Ribbon and a table in the OneNote workspace.

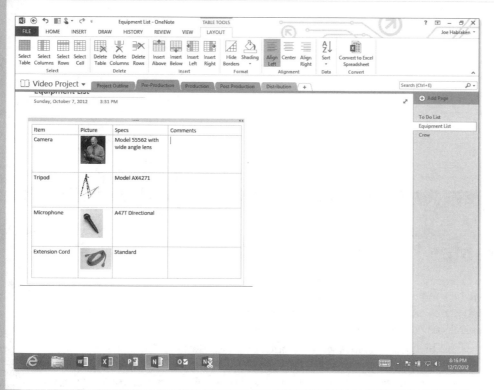

Figure 30.19
The Table Tools Layout tab.

The Table Tools Layout tab provides you with all the commands you need to modify the table. The Table Tools Layout tab's command groups are as follows:

■ **Select:** This group provides commands for selecting the table, columns, rows, or a cell. Selecting the table, columns, rows, or a cell enables you to then apply text-formatting attributes to the selected area of the table using the text-formatting commands on the Home tab. You can select a column or row by placing the mouse at the top of a column or the left of a row and then clicking when the selection arrow appears. You can also click and drag to select a group of cells.

■ **Delete:** This group provides commands for deleting the table or deleting either a column or a row. You can also select multiple columns or rows and then delete them.

■ **Insert:** This group provides commands that enable you to insert rows or columns into the table. For example, if you click in a row, you can use the Insert Above command to place a new row above the current row. If you select multiple rows, you can insert that number of rows above or below the selected rows. You can also insert single or multiple columns using the Insert Left or Insert Right commands.

■ **Format:** This group provides the Hide Borders command and the Shading command. The Hide Borders command removes the borders from the table, but not the row and column boundaries that create the cells in the table. Removing the borders enables you to align items in the table and then have them seemingly floating on the page because the table borders cannot be seen. This group also provides the new Shading command. When you select Shading, you are provided with a color palette that you can use to shade selected cells in the table.

■ **Alignment:** This group provides you with commands for changing the horizontal alignment of text or other objects within a cell or selected cells. These commands are Align Left, Center, and Align Right.

■ **Data:** This group provides the Sort command, and you can sort your table data in ascending or descending order. An option also enables you to sort selected rows in a table. You can sort the records (rows) in a table by clicking in a particular column. Make sure you set up your tables to have a header row that contains column names. You can then click in a particular column, such as last names, and sort the table by last name by selecting Sort Ascending.

■ **Convert:** This group provides the Convert to Excel Spreadsheet command. Make sure that the insertion point is in the table that you want to convert; then select Convert to Excel Spreadsheet. When you work on the converted table, you have access to Excel, so the table opens in Excel. When you close Excel, you return to OneNote.

You can apply tags to text in your tables and apply quick styles to text entries in cells. As already mentioned, you are not limited to text entries in the table's cells. You can also insert pictures, links, file attachments, and other items, such as time stamps and symbols, from the Ribbon's Insert tab.

For information on adding links or file attachments to OneNote pages, check out the information in Chapter 32, "Integrating OneNote with Other Office Applications."

WORKING WITH NOTEBOOK PAGES

OneNote notebooks provide a convenient organizational container that can be subdivided using section groups and sections. The actual information that you work with is located on the notebook pages. OneNote enables you to easily manage pages in a notebook and copy, move, or delete pages as needed. You can also view different versions of a page, which can be particularly useful when multiple users are contributing to a shared notebook.

In this chapter, we look at managing and configuring pages and discuss the different ways to search for information in a notebook. We also discuss page versions and the possibilities for viewing recent edits and changes on notebook pages. In addition, we cover adding items such as time stamps, pictures, and clip art, along with how to directly record audio and video onto a notebook page.

Managing Pages

Organizing your notebooks is all about managing the notebook pages, which, after all, contain the actual information in the notebook. Sections might provide structure to the notebook, but the page sequence in a section gives the chronological structure for the information. Most projects are executed according to a schedule or a logical sequence of steps, and the pages in each section should relate this chronology when viewed.

Keeping a notebook in proper shape might thus require rearranging pages. Pages can easily be copied, moved, or deleted. You can copy or move a page or pages within a notebook or between notebooks.

To move a page from one section to another in the notebook, select the page in the Page Tabs pane and then drag it to any of the section tabs at the top of the current notebook. You can also drag a page from the Page Tabs pane to a section in another notebook. Drag the page to a section in a notebook that is displayed in the expanded navigation pane.

You can also drag pages within a section, as needed. Drag a page to a new location in a section via the Page Tabs pane.

Using the Move Copy Dialog Box

You can also move or copy pages to another section of a notebook or to another current notebook in OneNote using the Move or Copy Pages dialog box. This enables you to easily expand notebooks to view the sections that they contain and gives you easy access to other notebooks listed in the OneNote navigation pane.

Select the page or pages (hold down the Ctrl key when selecting multiple pages) in the Pages Tabs pane, and then right-click the selected page or pages and select Move or Copy. The Move or Copy Pages dialog box opens, as shown in Figure 31.1.

tip

You can rename a page by changing the page name in the page's name area, which is directly above the date stamp on the page.

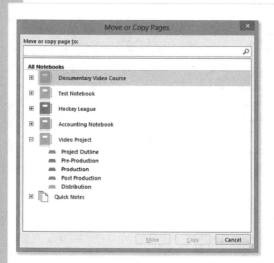

Figure 31.1
The Move or Copy Pages dialog box.

You can type a search string in the Search box to show any sections in all current notebooks that match the string. For example, you can type "pro," and any sections with "pro" in their name, such as "production" or "project," are listed in the Move or Copy Pages dialog box. The Search box gives you a quick way to filter all the sections available in your notebooks into a specific subset. You can also expand any of the notebooks listed to view the sections in the notebook if you want to locate the destination section manually.

After you specify the destination section, click Move to move the pages from their current location to the destination section, or select Copy to make a copy of the pages. The Move or Copy Pages dialog box closes, and your pages are moved or copied, depending on your selection.

Making More Space Available on a Page

If you add a lot of notes and other objects to a particular page, you might fill up the space provided on a page. You can insert additional space on a page so that you can continue to add information as needed. This can be particularly useful if you are inserting large pictures or potentially large objects, such as the file printout or scanner printout objects on a page. The file printout and the scanned objects are actually printed copies of a file that is rendered onto the notebook page as a page using the File Printout command or the Scanned Image command, respectively. (For more on the File Printout command, see Chapter 32, "Integrating OneNote with Other Office Applications.")

Imagine that you want more working space on a page. You can expand a page using the Insert Space command on the Ribbon's Insert tab. You can add the space between items on a page or at the bottom of the page.

Select the Insert Space command on the Ribbon's Insert tab. The mouse pointer becomes a sizing tool. Drag down on the bottom of the page; an expanding arrow appears showing the amount of space you have added to the page. Figure 31.2 shows space being added between a checklist and a photo on a page.

Figure 31.2 Use the Insert Space command to add space to a page.

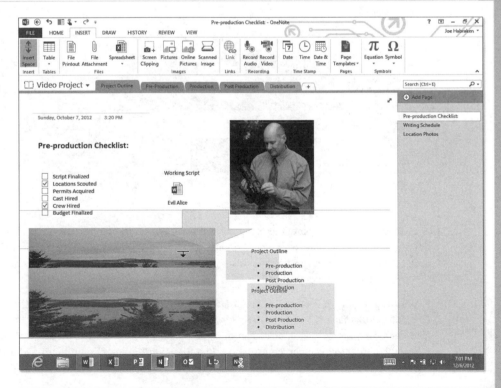

When you have added the required space, release the mouse button. You can also use the Insert Space command to decrease the amount of space available on a page, if required.

➥ *For information on using the File Printout command in OneNote, **see** "Using File Printout," p. 916.*

Modifying the Page Setup and View

You have control over many different page configuration options, such as the page background color, rule lines on the page, and the paper size and margins for a page. The Page Setup group, which contains the commands for modifying page settings, is located on the Ribbon's View menu. The commands in the Page Setup group are as follows:

- **Page Color:** This command provides a color palette that contains many different colors. Select a color to change the page background.

- **Rule Lines:** This command provides a gallery of both rule lines and grid lines, as shown in Figure 31.3. When you add rule lines or grid lines to the page, you can use the Rule Line Color command in the Rule Lines gallery to specify a color for the rule or grid lines on the page. An Always Create Pages with Rule Lines is available in the gallery so that all new pages are created with rule lines.

Figure 31.3
The Rule Lines gallery.

- **Hide Page Title:** This command claims that it enables you to hide the page title, but it actually deletes the title and date stamp on the page. Use this only if you intend to remove the header area of the page that contains the name and default time stamp. A message box appears, requiring you to confirm the deletion.

- **Paper Size:** When you select this command, the Paper Size pane opens on the right side of the OneNote workspace. By default, the page size is Auto. You can change the size to a different size, including Letter, Legal, or Postcard, by selecting the Size drop-down arrow. If you select a specific page size, you can control the orientation, width, height, and margins for the page. Figure 31.4 shows the Paper Size task pane with the selected size set to Letter.

Figure 31.4
The Paper Size pane.

The View tab also provides you with the Zoom group. This group supplies commands that enable you to zoom in and out on the current page and specify different zoom levels. OneNote does not provide a Zoom slider as the other Office applications (such as Word or Excel) do. In fact, OneNote does not have a status bar, which is where the Zoom slider is located in the other applications. The Zoom group is thus your only recourse for changing the zoom settings as you work in OneNote.

 tip

You can toggle in and out of the Dock to Desktop view using the keyboard shortcut Ctrl+Alt+D.

The View tab grants access to the Views group, which provides the Normal View, Full Page View, and Dock to Desktop options. Normal view is the default view and provides a view of the current page, the Notebook pane, and the Page pane.

When you select Full Page View or press F11, you get a view of the current page using the entire screen. This enables you to better see the various objects on the page. You can continue to work on the current page in Full Page view. When you are ready to return to Normal view, press F11 or deselect the Full Page View icon on the Quick Access Toolbar.

Dock to Desktop view pushes the OneNote window against the right side of the Windows desktop and greatly reduces the width of the application window (which you can change, if needed, by dragging the left border). This view is ideal when you want to take notes in OneNote as you work in another Office application or surf the Web. You can return to Normal view by selecting the Normal View icon at the top of the docked OneNote window (the icon is a double-headed arrow).

Viewing Page Versions

You can view the different versions of the pages in your OneNote notebooks. This feature is meant to be used when you share a notebook with other users. Page versions are listed by date and author. As the "owner" of the notebook, you can go through the different versions of a page and restore a particular version, if necessary.

The Page Versions command is in the History group on the Ruler's History tab. The Page Versions command enables you to view the versions of a page (if any exist) and to delete versions in a section, section group, or notebook. To view the versions of a page, follow these steps:

1. Navigate to the appropriate notebook section and use the Page pane to select the page you want to check for page versions.

2. Select History on the Ribbon.

3. Select the Page Versions command. The command's menu opens.

4. Select Page Versions.

The page versions for the selected page appear in the Pages pane below the page title. The page versions are ordered by date. Figure 31.5 shows the Page Tabs pane and two different versions of the same page.

Figure 31.5
Two versions of a notebook page are found using the Page Versions command.

To view a particular page version, select the version in the Page pane. Remember that OneNote saves a page version for 60 days; after that, the page version is deleted.

You have three options when viewing a page version. You can do nothing and let the page version be deleted after 60 days. You can delete the page version immediately. Or you can restore the page version, replacing the current version of the page.

To delete a page version, right-click the page version in the Page Tabs pane and then select Delete Version. The page version is deleted; no warning message precedes this—it is just gone. The page version cannot be retrieved from the Notebook Recycle Bin as can regular pages that have been deleted.

If you have determined that a particular page version should be the current version of the page, you can restore the page version. This replaces the current version of the page with the page version that you restore: Right-click the page version and select Restore Version.

Fortunately, this action is reversible. The page version that you replaced when you restored one of the page versions is added to the list of page versions for that page. It is the most recent version of the page. You can always restore it if you need to get things back the way they were before you started playing with the different page versions.

When you have finished viewing the page versions for a particular page, you can clear the page versions from the Pages pane. Click the Page Versions command in the History group so that it is no longer selected.

Viewing Recent Edits

You can view a list of pages that have been changed in a notebook based on a particular timeframe. For example, you can view recent edits to pages that were made today, since yesterday, in the last 7 days, or in the last 6 months; a number of other timeframes are also provided. You can also choose to view a list of all the pages in a notebook, which groups the pages according to when they were last edited using timeframes such as yesterday, this week, and last week.

You can view recent edits using the Recent Edits command, which is in the Authors group on the Ribbon's History tab. Viewing the recent edits in a shared notebook enables you to keep track of the individual page changes made by all the users who have access to the shared notebook. The capability to view recent edits can also be useful even when you have not shared a notebook. You can track changes that you made and quickly navigate to the pages in the notebook that changed most recently.

When you select the Recent Edits command on the History tab, you are provided with a menu of different timeframes: Today, Since Yesterday, Last 6 Months, and so on. As previously mentioned, you also have an All Pages Sorted by Date option.

Select the timeframe that you want to use for viewing recent edits on the Recent Edits menu. The Search Results task pane opens, as shown in Figure 31.6. The figure shows the pages in a notebook that have changed when Last 7 Days was selected on the Recent Edits menu.

 tip

You can view all the notes that have been tagged in a notebook via the Tags Summary pane, which shows all tagged notes grouped by tag name. Select the Find Tags command on the Home tab to open the Tags Summary pane.

Figure 31.6
View recently edited pages in a notebook.

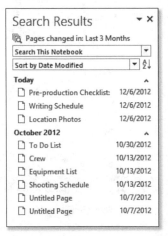

You can navigate to a specific page by clicking a page link provided in the Search Results task pane. You can also use the Search This Notebook box to search the current workbook by keyword if you want to find pages containing a specific search string.

By default, the pages are sorted by Date Modified. You can use the Sort By box to change how the pages are sorted, and you can list them in the Search Results pane by section, title, or author. The changes that you made to a particular page within the edit time range you specified are highlighted in yellow. When you have finished working with the Search Results task pane, you close it by clicking its Close button.

Viewing Changes by Author

When you work on a shared notebook, the notes and other items added to the notebook pages by other authors are tagged with the authors' initials. Keeping track of who has added what to the pages in a shared notebook is easy. Figure 31.7 shows a notebook page containing the initials of an author sharing the notebook. Note the initials BH just to the right of the Tentative Schedule check boxes.

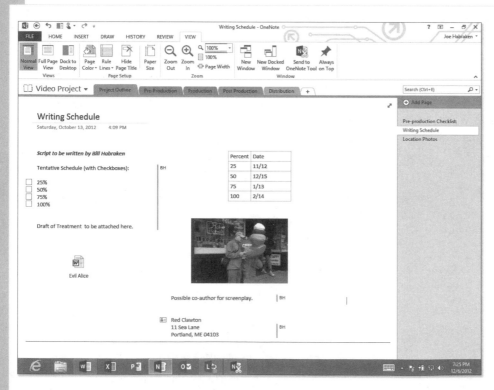

Figure 31.7
Additions and changes made by other authors are shown by default on notebook pages.

You can view the name of the author and the date the change was made. Place the mouse on the author's initials. You also can toggle off the author's initials so that they do not appear on the notebook pages. Select the Hide Authors command on the Ribbon's History tab (look in the Authors group). You can toggle the author information back on by clicking the Hide Authors command again.

You can search in a notebook for notes based on author. When you select the Find by Author command in the Authors group on the History tab, the Search Results pane opens on the right of the OneNote window, as shown in Figure 31.8, and provides the Changes by Author.

 tip

You can insert a time stamp and the author name directly into a note by right-clicking an author's initials associated with that note. Then select the author name and time stamp shown at the bottom of the shortcut menu.

Figure 31.8
View changes by each author of a shared notebook.

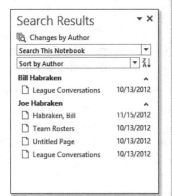

Each author for the shared notebook is listed in the Search Results pane. Click the expand button to the right of an author name to view all the pages that contain changes contributed by that author. By default, the Changes by Author list is sorted by author name. You can also change the list so that it is sorted by date modified.

Adding Objects to Notebook Pages

You can add different object types to your notebook pages. The Ribbon's Insert tab gives you options for adding tables, spreadsheets, file attachments, photos, links, meetings, files, recordings, time stamps, and symbols. The capability to add different types of objects to a notebook makes the notebook not unlike a scrapbook (or a daily planner). You can insert all sorts of information in different media right onto the pages of your notebook. The possibilities go way beyond the basic text information you can place in a note. Figure 31.9 shows the Ribbon's Insert tab.

Figure 31.9
The OneNote Ribbon's Insert tab.

For example, you can insert an Excel workbook on a page that contains information related to the budget for a project. Or you can include pictures of new appliances that you want to order as you plan a kitchen renovation. No matter what the purpose of the notebook is, you have great flexibility in gathering the information that goes into the notebook.

Each command group on the Insert tab enables you to place different types of objects onto a page. The Ribbon's Insert tab command groups are as follows:

- **Insert:** This group provides the Insert Space command, to add more space to a page.

- **Table:** Insert a table using this command. Tables are discussed in Chapter 30, "Requisite OneNote: Essential Features."

- **Files:** This group enables you to insert a new or existing Excel spreadsheet into a notebook page. The group also provides access to the File Printout and File Attachment options. File Printout enables you to print a file onto a notebook page. The text isn't editable when you use File Printout, but it does supply you with an image of the file's contents. You also have the option to attach any variety of file type, such as a Word document, PowerPoint presentation, or any other type of file.

- **Images:** This group enables you to insert pictures from your computer or insert online pictures from your SkyDrive or the Web. The Online Pictures command includes clip art and royalty-free photos from Office.com. You can also insert your own pictures directly from Flickr.com (if you have an account). In addition, the image group supplies the Scanned Image command, which you can use to insert an image from your scanner directly into a notebook page.

- **Links:** You can insert links to web pages and files that are on your computer or on your network.

- **Recording:** This group provides access to the Record Audio and Record Video commands. If your computer has a built-in microphone and camera, or if you have attached an external microphone or camera to the computer, you can record audio and video directly into your notebook pages.

- **Time Stamp:** This group provides different time stamp commands for adding the date and/or time to a page. This enables you to time-stamp items that are placed on the page, such as notes or other objects.

- **Pages:** This group provides the Page Templates command. Page templates and their use are discussed in Chapter 30, in the section "Working with Pages."

- **Symbols:** You can use the commands in this group to add equations or symbols to your notebook pages.

Many of the options provided by the Insert tab enable you to make information that already exists in pictures, files, or web pages part of a OneNote notebook. Let's look at some of the object types that can be inserted into a notebook page. Chapter 32 looks at some of the other options the Insert tab provides.

➥ *For information on integrating items from other Office applications into a notebook,* ***see*** *"Using File Printout," p. 916.*

Adding Pictures

You can insert pictures into your notebook pages. You can thus add visuals that complement other information on the page, such as notes or tables of text. The options for working with a picture in OneNote are much more limited than the possibilities provided by Word or PowerPoint—those programs enable you to adjust and correct a picture, apply styles to a picture, and remove the picture's background.

You can move and size a picture that you insert onto a OneNote page. The Ribbon's Draw tab also provides an Edit group that contains commands that enable you to rotate or flip a picture or arrange several pictures that are layered.

To add a picture to a page, click the page and then select the Picture command on the Insert tab. The Insert Picture dialog box opens. Locate the picture you want to insert and then click Open. The picture is inserted onto the page, as shown in Figure 31.10.

Figure 31.10
Insert a picture on a page.

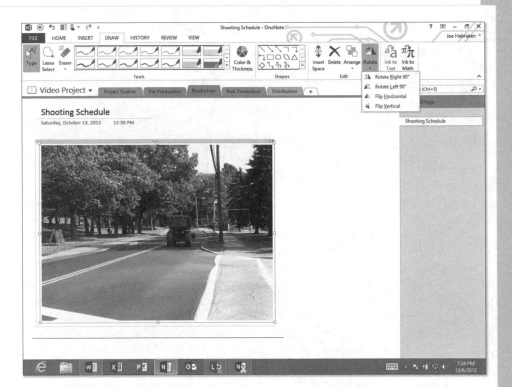

You can drag the picture to any location on the page. When the picture is selected, you can use the sizing handles to size the picture as needed.

Recording Audio

If you have either a built-in or externally attached microphone on your computer, you can add audio notes to your notebook pages. This enables you to add audio messages to other users of a shared notebook or just add ideas or other thoughts to a notebook page in the form of a recorded audio file.

If you have your Windows 8 configuration up to date, you should be able to record audio without fine-tuning your operating system settings. If you are using Windows 7, make sure that you have the latest version of DirectX and the Windows Media player installed on your computer. You can go to the Microsoft Download Center and download any updates you might need if you are unable to record audio within OneNote.

Recording audio onto a notebook page is straightforward. Click the page where you want to insert the recorded audio. Then click the Record Audio command on the Insert tab; speak into your microphone and record your audio.

The Audio & Video tab appears on the Ribbon, as shown in Figure 31.11. You can pause your recording by selecting the Pause button. You can click the Pause button again to continue recording.

Figure 31.11
The Audio & Video controls appear on the Ribbon when you record audio or video.

When you have finished recording your audio, select Stop on the Ribbon. The audio recording is represented on the page by an audio file box that uses the page's title as the name for the audio placeholder. A headphones icon is present in the audio box, and a time stamp detailing the start time and date for the recording is also inserted directly below.

When you select an audio recording on a page, the audio and video playback controls become available on the Ribbon. You can play a previously recorded audio file, and you can use the controls provided to rewind or fast-forward the audio recording, as needed. Because the audio recording is in a note, you can drag the audio note anywhere on the notebook page as you would any other note (the time stamp does not move with the audio box, however). To delete an audio note, select the note box and then press Delete on the keyboard.

If you find that the recording level was low or that you need to fine-tune the settings related to making an audio recording directly from OneNote, you might have to change settings in the Windows

Control Panel. You can set other settings related to audio and video recording in the OneNote Options window; select the Audio & Video Settings command on the Audio & Video tab. This opens the OneNote Options window with the Audio & Video settings selected. You can specify the device to be used for recording and the codec used for the audio recording, which is one of the Windows Media codecs installed on your computer. (A codec is software used to *co*mpress and *deco*mpress recorded media such as audio or video.)

Recording Video

Recording video directly into OneNote is similar to recording audio. When you are ready to record, select the Record Video command on the Insert tab. A video window opens showing the live feed that your video camera is recording—so it's "lights, camera, action" within a split-second. Figure 31.12 shows the Video window and the Audio & Video commands available on the Ribbon as you record your video.

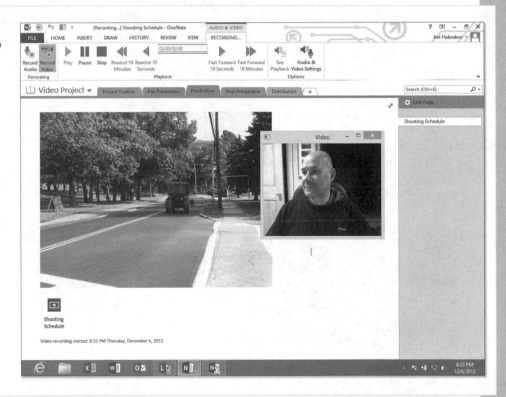

Figure 31.12
Record video onto a note-book page.

You can pause the recording as needed using the Pause button. When you have finished making the video recording, click the Stop button.

As with an audio recording, you can use the Audio & Video commands to play back any selected video note that you have inserted onto a notebook page. You can move the video recording on the page, and you can cut, copy, and paste the video note as needed.

Adding Drawings to OneNote Pages

Other possibilities for adding visuals to your notebook pages are the various drawing tools on the Ribbon's Draw tab. You can draw freehand using pens in a variety of color and sizes. You can also choose from different highlighters. The Draw tab provides a Shapes gallery as well that enables you to insert a number of shape types, including squares, circles, and lines.

 note

If you are using OneNote on a device that actually lets you draw freehand, such as a tablet or touchscreen, the drawing tools are even more useful.

You can use these tools to create diagrams or other freehand drawings on a page. You can layer different drawn objects and then use the Arrange command to specify where a particular object is in a series of layered drawn objects. Figure 31.13 shows the Ribbon's Draw tab. Most of the tools that you use to create drawings or shapes are found in the Tools command group and the Insert Shapes command group.

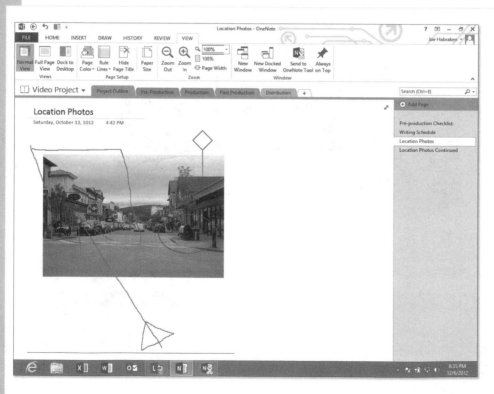

Figure 31.13
Create your own drawings on notebook pages.

To view all the pens available in the Tools gallery, click the More button on the right of the gallery. You can then select one of the built-in pens provided, which include both pens and highlighters.

After selecting a pen, you can draw on the page as needed. The pointer remains a pen until you click the Select & Type command in the Tools group. The Tools gallery provides several different pens providing you size and color choices.

The Tools gallery also provides options related to the use of the provided pens. By default, the pens can create both handwriting and drawings. You can change the pen's function by selecting Pen Mode in the Tools gallery. You can configure a pen so that it creates only drawings or is used only for handwriting. You even have an option to use the pen as a pointer.

In addition, you can insert shapes onto the page using the various shapes in the Insert Shapes gallery. You can select the color and thickness that you want to use for the inserted shape by using the Color & Thickness dialog box. Click the Color & Thickness command on the Draw tab to open this dialog box. Figure 31.14 shows the Color & Thickness dialog box.

Figure 31.14
The Color & Thickness dialog box.

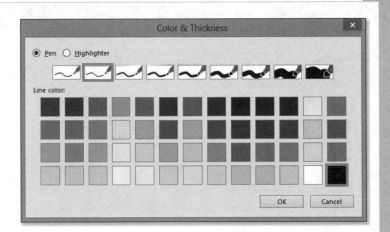

Specify a thickness and color for the pen, and then click OK. You can now select a shape from the Insert Shapes gallery and use the mouse (or your finger or tablet pen) to draw the shape on the page.

When you draw shapes, the mouse pointer returns to the I-beam as soon as you complete the shape by releasing the mouse. You do not have to click the Select & Type command to return to the typing mode as you do when you use one of the pens in the Tools gallery.

 tip
You can select any pen drawing or shape and then change its color and thickness using the Color & Thickness dialog box.

When selecting drawn objects or shapes on the page, you can use the I-beam as you would to select a note box or picture. You can also use the Lasso Select tool provided on the Draw tab to select items by drawing a lasso around the drawings or shapes that you want to select. When you create drawings and shapes, they are contained in a box much like a note.

You can drag the drawing or shape to any position on the page and also size the drawing or shape using the sizing handles provided when the object is selected.

Printing Notebook Pages

Although OneNote is designed for creating electronic notebooks, you can print pages in a notebook, if needed. You can print a specific page, a group of pages, or all the pages in a particular section.

The Print command and print preview are accessed via the OneNote Backstage. To access the Backstage, select File on the Ribbon. When you select Print in the Backstage, the Print window for OneNote contains two possibilities: Print and Print Preview.

When you select Print, the Print dialog box opens, as shown in Figure 31.15. The Print dialog box enables you to specify the printer to be used for the print job, and you can specify preferences related to the selected printer.

Figure 31.15
The Print dialog box.

In terms of the actual printout, you can specify that all pages be printed, select the current selection to be printed, or choose a particular range of pages (in the current section) to be printed. When you are ready to print the page or pages, select the Print button.

You might find it comforting to see a preview of the print job before you send it to the printer. This is where the Print Preview command, available in the Backstage Print window, comes in. When you select Print Preview, the Print Preview and Settings dialog box opens, as shown in Figure 31.16.

The Print Preview and Settings dialog box gives you more options for the print job than are provided in the Print dialog box. More important, it gives you a preview of your printout. It also enables you to move backward and forward if you select multiple pages for the print job (just select more than one page in the Page Tabs pane before opening the Print Preview and Settings dialog box) or if you are going to print a page group, which consists of a main page and subpages.

Figure 31.16
The Print
Preview and
Settings dialog
box.

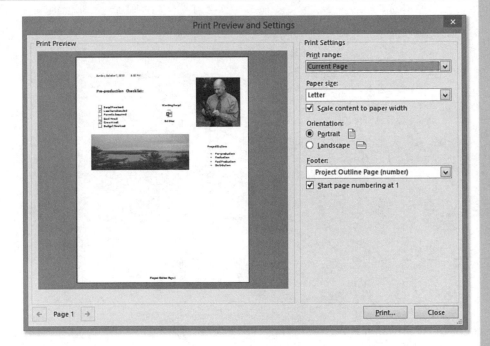

You can cycle through the pages when you have selected multiple pages or you are printing a page that contains subpages by using the Next Page and Previous Page buttons on the lower left of the dialog box.

Print settings provided by the Print Preview and Settings dialog box include the print range, the paper size, and the orientation of the printout. By default, a footer is also included on the printed page that includes the page name and the page number. You can change the footer setting so that it prints only the page number or the page title rather than both, as the default setting does. If you do not want a footer to print on the page or pages printed, select None in the Footer drop-down box.

When you are ready to print your page or pages, click the Print button. This opens the Print dialog box, discussed earlier in this section. Select the printer, printer preferences, and number of copies, and then click the Print button to send the printout to your printer.

INTEGRATING ONENOTE WITH OTHER OFFICE APPLICATIONS

OneNote notebooks make it easy for you to insert information onto your notebook pages using different objects; there are notes, pictures, and tables, and you can also insert links that point to files on your computer or to specific website addresses. OneNote also enables you to include file attachments on notebook pages and insert screen clips of other application windows.

OneNote makes it a relatively carefree process to get information that was created in one of the other Office applications onto a notebook page. This includes the capability to take notes as you work in another application, such as Word or Excel, and to insert information that has already been recorded in Microsoft Outlook onto a page.

In this chapter, we look at OneNote tools that enable you to better integrate information from the other Office applications into your OneNote notebooks. We look at how to include Office file information on a notebook page using the File Printout feature, links, and file attachments. We also look at how to integrate Outlook and OneNote information.

Taking Linked Notes

OneNote enables you to take linked notes. This is extremely useful when you are working in one of the other Office applications, such as Word or PowerPoint, and you want to take notes as you work. The Linked Notes feature takes advantage of a docked window. The OneNote window is relocated to the far right of the Windows desktop, with just enough room available to record notes as you use the remainder of the Windows desktop to work in the other application.

The OneNote Linked Notes mode can be used to take notes no matter what application you are working with as you take your notes. However, it is really helpful when you are working in Word, PowerPoint, or Internet Explorer. The notes you create are automatically linked to the application you are using.

As you take notes in the OneNote docked window and work in Word or PowerPoint, the notes that you create are tagged with an application icon. When you place the mouse on the icon, you are provided with a thumbnail of the page or slide that you were working with (in the other Office application) when you created the note. For example, if you are working on a PowerPoint slide presentation and you take a linked note related to the current slide, the note is tagged with the PowerPoint icon. When you place the mouse on the icon, a thumbnail of that slide appears. This not only enables you to immediately determine the application that the linked note was created for, but it also gives you a visual of the actual slide to which the linked note pertains.

When you open the notebook later, you can use the application icon to quickly launch PowerPoint, which loads the presentation that contains the slide referred to in the linked note.

When you are working in Word, the thumbnail is a representation of the current page in the Word document. You can use the linked icon to quickly open the Word document that contains the page associated with the linked note.

Linked notes are also created when you use Internet Explorer and take notes in the OneNote docked window. An Internet Explorer icon is used to tag the note, and a thumbnail is created that provides a preview of the web page associated with the linked note. The URL (uniform resource locater, or web address) is also provided for the web page on the thumbnail. You can quickly navigate to the page in your web browser by selecting the thumbnail provided by the linked note.

To take advantage of the OneNote docked window and linked notes, open OneNote and the other applications that you want to use, such as Word or PowerPoint. In OneNote, navigate to the Ribbon's Review tab and then click the Linked Notes command. The Select Location in OneNote dialog box opens, as shown in Figure 32.1.

The Select Location in OneNote dialog box lists sections and pages you recently accessed in the Recent Picks list. All your current notebooks are available in the All Notebooks list. Expand a notebook to select a section, and then select the page that you want to use as you take the linked notes. After you have selected the page, click OK in the dialog box.

You can now use the Windows taskbar to navigate to the application that you want to use as you take your linked notes. If you haven't opened the application, use the Windows Start menu and open the application. As you work in the application window, the OneNote Linked Notes pane remains on the right side of the Windows desktop. Figure 32.2 shows the PowerPoint application window and the OneNote Linked Notes pane on the Windows desktop.

 note

You can also create manual links to files, so any notes related to another application file that you are working with can include a link to that file. Creating links is discussed later in this chapter in the section, "Adding Links."

Figure 32.1
The Select Location in OneNote dialog box.

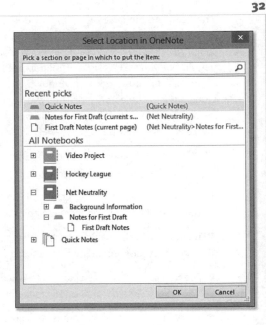

Figure 32.2
PowerPoint and the
OneNote Linked Notes
pane open on the
Windows desktop.

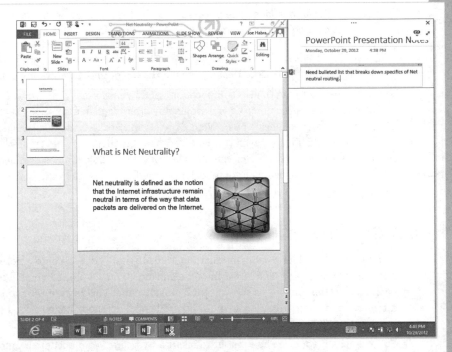

The OneNote Linked Notes pane (or docked OneNote window, if you prefer) can do more than just take notes related to what you are doing in the other application window. A Ribbon accessed at the top of the docked windows provides you with options and commands related to OneNote notebook pages. The linked OneNote Ribbon is hidden by default. All you have to do is click on the ellipsis (...) at the top of the docked windows, and the Ribbon tab appears. The Linked Notes Ribbon provides most of the commands that you have access to when working in OneNote (which makes sense because you are working in a "condensed" OneNote window). The following tabs are provided on the Linked Notes Ribbon:

- **File:** This tab opens the OneNote Backstage. It is the same Backstage that you open when you are working in the OneNote window and select File.

- **Home:** This tab provides access to the Clipboard group and the Basic Text commands for formatting text. This tab also includes commands for inserting note tags and Outlook tasks.

- **Insert:** This tab enables you to insert tables, file printouts, screen clippings, and links. You can also insert meeting details and record audio or video.

- **Draw:** This tab provides access to the different ink styles, a selection tool, and an eraser tool. The Insert Space command is also available on this tab.

- **View:** This tab enables you to switch back to Normal view (you are currently in the Dock to Desktop view) and access page colors, rule line settings, and different zoom commands.

- **Pages:** This tab provides page navigation commands and the Search command. It also gives you commands for creating a new page, deleting a page, and moving the current page.

When you have finished working with the OneNote docked window, you can close the window, or you can toggle off the Dock to Desktop icon at the top of the Linked Notes pane.

When you return to the OneNote application window in Normal view, you can access the page that contains the linked notes as you would any other page in a notebook section. You can use any of the linked notes to quickly open Word, PowerPoint, or the website associated with the linked notes. Using linked notes saves you time because you do not have to create a link to the Word or PowerPoint file; it is created for you automatically. Using linked notes also negates the need to add a lot of file attachments to your notebook pages, which slows the synchronization of a notebook stored online or on a network server.

Using File Printout

Another useful tool for placing information from other applications onto a notebook page is the File Printout command. The File Printout command creates a printed version of a file and places each page in the printout on the current notebook page. This feature is useful if you want to place a printout of a short Word document or other file on a notebook page instead of creating a link or inserting a file attachment.

For example, if you use File Printout to insert a two-page Word document onto a notebook page, the pages appear the same as they would on the printed page—including the size of the printed page. Each page in the printout can be sized or deleted as needed. You can search the text contained in

File Printout pages using the OneNote Search feature as you would text on your notebook pages. Figure 32.3 shows a Word document (a single-page flyer) that has been inserted onto a notebook page using File Printout.

tip
You can press Ctrl+Alt+D to toggle off Linked Notes mode.

When you insert a file printout, an application icon and a file link are also created for the file represented in the printout. The printout gives you a look at the contents of the document or other file, and you can double-click the file icon or click the link provided (yes, both are provided) to quickly open the original file if you need to access it.

Figure 32.3
Insert file printouts onto your notebook pages.

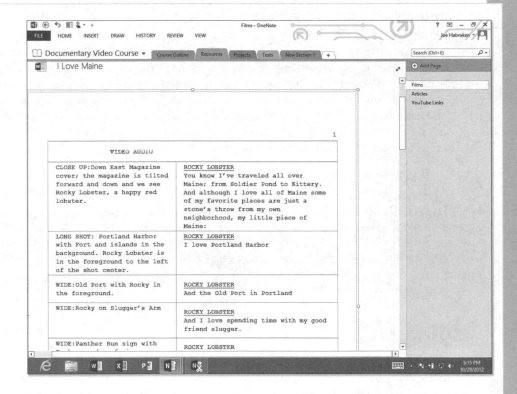

Although the printout pages look a lot like pictures, you can copy and paste information from the printout to OneNote notes. Right-click on a printout page, and you can then use the shortcut menu commands to copy the text from the current page of the printout or all the pages of the printout. You can then paste this text onto a notebook page as you require.

To insert a file printout using the File Printout command, follow these steps:

1. Navigate to the page that you want to contain the file printout.

2. Select the File Printout command on the Ribbon's Insert tab. The Choose Document to Insert dialog box opens.

3. Locate the file you want to insert and select it.

4. Click the Insert button.

Inserting the printout might take a moment, depending on the size of the document. You can use the Insert Space command on the Insert menu to lengthen the current page or remove unneeded whitespace before the printout. You can also delete an individual printout page by selecting a specific page and then pressing Delete. Each printout page is similar to a picture of a page, although, as mentioned previously, you can search and copy the text from a printout page. You can size and arrange the pages using the commands available on the shortcut menu that appears when you right-click on a printout page.

You can also quickly place a printout into a notebook using the Send to OneNote tool (which also provides access to the Screen Clipping tool). The Send to OneNote tool is useful when you are working in one of the other Office applications, such as PowerPoint or Excel, and you want to quickly send a file printout to a particular OneNote notebook. Just select the Send to OneNote icon on the Windows 8 taskbar (the Send to OneNote tool is loaded automatically when you start OneNote). Click the Send to OneNote tile in the Send to OneNote window. The Select Location in OneNote dialog box opens. Specify the location for the printout, and then click OK.

 caution

If you attempt to use File Printout on a document that contains a large number of pages, you might get a message at the top of the OneNote notebook page that not all the pages of the printout could fit on the notebook page. The File Printout tool isn't designed for inserting a large document into a OneNote notebook. If you want to include a Word document or other file with a lot of pages in it, you might be better off linking the file to a OneNote page or including the file in the notebook as a file attachment. Both these options are available on the Ribbon's Insert tab.

Adding Links

You can access files, content on websites, email addresses, or pages in a OneNote notebook (either the current notebook or another one) by taking advantage of links. Links are exactly as advertised; they are pointers to a file location, a website URL, an email address, or a page in a notebook. When you select a link, the appropriate application opens to provide you with the linked item. For example, in the case of a linked Word document, Word opens and loads the file referenced in the link. If the link is a web page URL, your web browser opens and loads the page. For an email address, your default email client (probably Outlook because you are using Office) starts and opens a new email for the contact referenced in the email link. For a page link in a OneNote notebook, the link takes you to that notebook page.

Links are extremely useful in OneNote notebooks because they point to files or other items but don't really add appreciable size to your OneNote notebook as file attachments do. It makes sense to take advantage of links when you are using a shared notebook that is stored on a file server or the Web and you don't want to extend the time it takes to synchronize the notebook by adding a lot of file attachments or file printouts to the notebook pages.

The Link command is located in the Links group of the Ribbon's Insert tab. To insert a new link, click on the current notebook page to begin a new note, and then click the Link command. The Link dialog box opens, as shown in Figure 32.4.

Figure 32.4
The Link dialog box.

Enter the text that serves as the link name for the link in the Text to Display box. This is the text that represents the link on the OneNote page (in a note). The link is formatted with a blue font color and underlining (as most text links are formatted on web pages). After entering the link's text, you need to specify the address or path of the link.

To create a link to a website, click the Browse the Web button to open the browser. Navigate to the site that you want to use for the link. Select the website's URL (address) in your web browser's address box, and then use Ctrl+C to copy the address. Return to the Link dialog box, and paste the address into the address box using Ctrl+V.

If the link is for a file on your computer or your network, use the Browse for File button in the Link dialog box to open the Link to File dialog box. Locate and select the file, and then click Open. The path to the file appears in the Address box.

You can also create a link to a location in another OneNote notebook. Use the All Notebooks list to specify a page (in a notebook) that serves as the link. An address to the page is inserted into the address box.

After you have provided the text for the link and the source for the link (web page, file, or OneNote page), click OK. The link appears on the page in the note. You can use the link to quickly open the web page, file, or OneNote page that you specified as the address for the link.

You can copy or move links on your notebook pages. If you need to delete a link, select the note containing the link and then press the Delete key.

Attaching Files

Another way to add information to a OneNote notebook is to attach files to notebook pages. This enables you to quickly access a file such as an Excel workbook, PowerPoint presentation, or Word document (just double-click on the attachment icon). Any file type can be attached to a notebook page. If you have the application used to create the file installed on your computer, you can quickly open the file in that application.

Attaching files to a shared notebook is also an easy way to share files with other users who have access to the shared notebook. The downside of file attachments is that they increase the overall size of the OneNote notebook. This can be an issue when a shared notebook is synchronized over a slow network or Internet connection. It might take a fair amount of time to totally sync a notebook with a lot of file attachments.

To attach a file to a page, click on the page to start a new note. Then select the File Attachment command on the Ribbon's Insert tab. The Choose a File or a Set of Files to Insert dialog box appears. You can select one file to attach, or you can select multiple files in the same folder location. To select multiple files, click the first file and then hold the Ctrl key as you click subsequent files. You can select a contiguous series of files by clicking the first file in the folder list and then holding the Shift key when you click the last file in the series.

When you are ready to attach the selected files, click the Insert button. The Insert File dialog box opens, with two choices: Attach File and Insert Printout. To attach the file or files, select Attach File (the Insert Printout option inserts a file printout on the page). The files are attached to the current page. The attached files are represented on the page by an application icon that denotes the application used to create them. The names of the files are inserted below the application icon.

 caution

When you attempt to open an attached file, a warning box opens, letting you know that file attachments can harm your computer. File attachments opened from a shared notebook could consist of harmful malware, although the risk is pretty minimal if you share notebooks with people you know.

After you attach a file, you can access the file whenever required. This is also true for other users who have access to the shared notebook. Double-click on an attached file icon to open that file in the source application. For example, if you double-click on an Excel icon that represents an Excel workbook, Excel opens and loads the workbook.

When you attach a file to the OneNote notebook, you are creating a copy of the file. If the original file on your computer or the network is moved or inadvertently deleted, the file attached to the notebook page is not affected (as a link would be), and you can still open the file when needed.

Inserting Screen Clips

Another way to insert information created in other applications is to use the Screen Clipping command. This command is housed in the Images command group on the Ribbon's Insert tab (you also can access the Screen Clipping command via the Send to OneNote tile on the Windows 8 taskbar). You can capture a screen clip of any application window by using the mouse. This means that you can include a screen clip of a web page or a portion of an Excel worksheet or a presentation slide in PowerPoint. Anything that you can open on your computer screen is fair game for creating a screen clip using the Screen Clipping command. Figure 32.5 shows a screen clip of a PowerPoint slide that has been inserted into a notebook page.

Figure 32.5
Insert screen clips into your notebook pages.

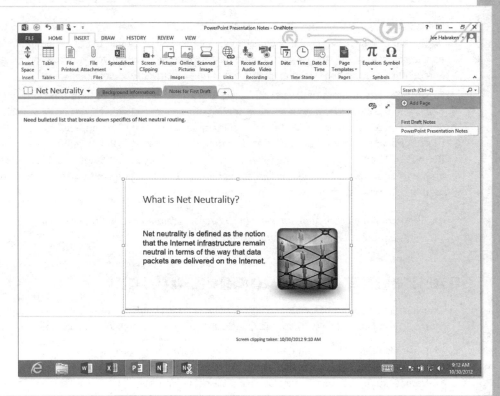

This feature is similar to the Screenshot command provided in the other Office applications, such as Word, Excel, and PowerPoint. However, the Screen Clipping command in OneNote has one huge advantage over the Screenshot command found in Word or Excel: When you insert a screen clip into OneNote, any of the text contained in the screen clip picture can be searched using the OneNote Search feature.

To insert a screen clip, follow these steps:

1. Open the application that contains the information that you want to capture as the screen clip. This can be an Office application such as Word or Excel, your web browser, or any other application.

2. On the OneNote Ribbon's Insert tab, click the Screen Clipping command. You are immediately switched to the other open application window.

3. Use the mouse pointer to select the area of the application screen that you want to capture as the screen clip.

4. When you release the mouse, the screen clip is inserted onto the notebook page in OneNote.

The screen clip is automatically time- and date-stamped. You can drag the screen clip to relocate it on the page, if necessary. Screen clips can also be copied or moved using the commands available on the shortcut menu (the Copy, Cut, and Paste commands) when you right-click on the screen clip. Screen clips cannot be resized as pictures can be on your notebook pages.

As with the file printout tool, you can access the screen-clipping tool from the Send to OneNote pane when you are working in another application window, such as Word or PowerPoint. Select the Send to OneNote tile on the Windows 8 taskbar. Select Screen Clipping, and then select the area of the screen you want to clip. The Select Location in OneNote dialog box opens, enabling you to specify the OneNote notebook and page where the clip should be sent. Select Send to Selected Location, and your clip is placed in the appropriate notebook. You can then continue working in the other application, with minimal interruption of your workflow.

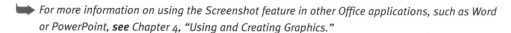 *For more information on using the Screenshot feature in other Office applications, such as Word or PowerPoint, **see** Chapter 4, "Using and Creating Graphics."*

Integrating OneNote and Outlook

OneNote gives you three commands on the OneNote Ribbon's Home tab that enable you to quickly interact with Outlook as you work in OneNote. These Outlook-associated commands are as follows:

- **Outlook Tasks:** This command (in the Tags group) enables you to insert a new task into a note on the current notebook page. The task, which can be time-stamped using a number of timeframes, such as Today, Tomorrow, Next Week, or No Date, is replicated to your Outlook Tasks list. When you open the task in Outlook, a link is provided that makes it easy to open the associated OneNote notebook directly from Outlook.

- **Email Page:** This command (in the Email group) enables you to email the current OneNote page to a recipient or recipients.

- **Meeting Details:** This command (in the Meetings group) enables you to insert meeting details from your Outlook calendar. After you insert the meeting information into OneNote, you can add notes to the OneNote page related to the meeting.

The three Outlook-related commands in OneNote are more examples of how OneNote has been tightly integrated with the other applications in the Office 2013 suite. OneNote is designed to collect and organize information, and it does so well in terms of its interactivity with the other Office applications. Let's look at how to take advantage of each of these commands.

Adding Outlook Tasks

As you work in OneNote adding notes and other items to a page, you will probably create a list of tasks or To Do items. Although you can use tags to arrange tasks in a list with check boxes or mark the note item as important, it makes sense to create tasks in OneNote that can also be tracked along with the other tasks that you are compiling in your Outlook Tasks list.

To insert an Outlook task into a note, click on the page where you want to place the new task. Then select the Outlook Tasks command in the Tags group (on the Home tab). The Outlook Tasks command provides a gallery of different time stamps that can be used for the task, such as Today and Tomorrow, as shown in Figure 32.6.

Figure 32.6
The Outlook
Tasks gallery.

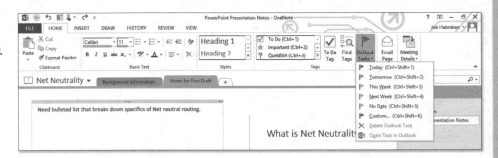

Select one of the time stamp options provided. This inserts a Task icon into the current note. Enter explanatory text for the task in the note.

If you want to create a custom task where you specify the subject, date, and other settings related to the task, select the Custom option. A new Outlook Task window appears, as shown in Figure 32.7.

tip
You can delete a task from the page and the Outlook Tasks list by pressing Ctrl+Shift+0 on the keyboard.

Provide the information for the task, such as start date, due date, and priority. When you have finished configuring the task, select Save & Close to return to the OneNote application window.

After you insert an Outlook task onto a notebook page, you can open the task from either OneNote or Outlook (because the task is saved to your Outlook Tasks list). To open the Task window from OneNote, select the OneNote note containing the task, or place the insertion point in the text you entered for the task (on the OneNote page). Select the Outlook Tasks command on the Ribbon, and then select Open Task in Outlook. The task's window opens. You can now add information to the task's body, change the start or due date, or mark the task as complete. Anything that you would do to an Outlook task created in Outlook can be done to an Outlook task that is generated from OneNote.

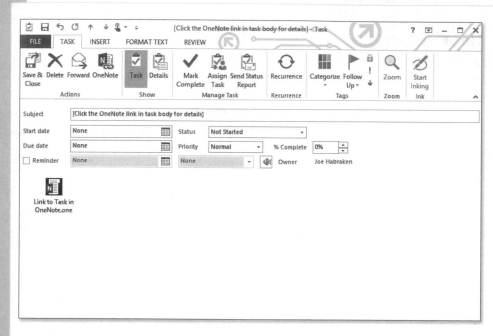

Figure 32.7
The Custom task option opens a new Outlook Task window.

As already mentioned, when you are in Outlook, your OneNote-generated tasks appear in your Tasks list (as do any tasks you create in Outlook). The OneNote tasks include a link in the body of the task that enables you to quickly open the OneNote notebook page that contains the task.

You can delete a task from a notebook page by selecting the note containing the task and then pressing Delete. This does not remove the task from Outlook, however. If you want to delete a task that you have inserted onto a notebook page and you want to delete the task from Outlook, you need to click in the task's note box and then select Delete Outlook Task from the Outlook Tasks command's gallery (or you can right-click on the task and select Delete Outlook Task from the shortcut menu).

 tip

You can open an Outlook task in Outlook from your OneNote notebook page. Right-click on the task's tag (the flag), and then select Open Task in Outlook. The Outlook Task window opens for the task. Make any changes required, and then click Save & Close in the Task window to return to your OneNote notebook.

➡ *For more information on working with Outlook tasks, **see** Chapter 24, "Using the Calendar for Appointments and Tasks."*

Emailing a Notebook Page

You can quickly email the current notebook page in your OneNote notebook to coworkers or colleagues. This can be useful when you want to share information from an OneNote notebook that you haven't shared with others (or you want to send info to someone you didn't share the notebook with).

To email the current page, select the Email Page command on the Home tab. A new Outlook email message opens, as shown in Figure 32.8.

Figure 32.8
A new Outlook mail message containing the OneNote page content.

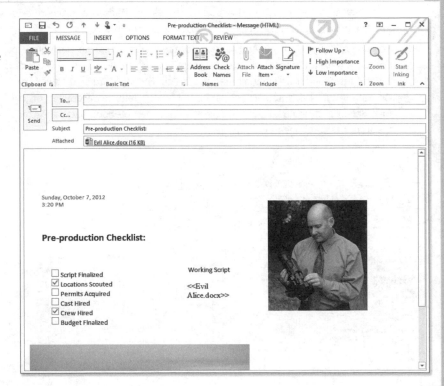

The subject of the mail message is the title of the page you are emailing. You can edit the subject line, if you choose. The content of the notebook page appears in the body of the mail message. If the notebook page contains any file attachments, the files are attached to the email message and listed in the Attached box of the message (just above the body of the message).

Address the message to the recipients, and then click Send. You are returned to the OneNote application window. When the recipient receives the message, the notebook page appears as text, but it functions more like a picture (meaning that the text isn't editable). The recipient can view all the information on the page, such as the notes or other items, but is not able to interact with most of the objects on the page. The recipient has access to any file attachments that were on the page because these are attached to the email message. The recipient also can click any links that were available on the page, such as email addresses included in meeting notes. When viewing emailed notebook pages, you get a bigger and better view of the OneNote page if you open the email in its own window.

Inserting Meeting Details

You can also insert information from an Outlook meeting into a note on a notebook page. This enables you to include the meeting information on a notebook page that also contains other information that might be related to the meeting; it also enables you to record additional notes or add links and file attachments related to the meeting's discussion.

You can quickly insert meeting details for meetings that occur during the current day. You can also specify a date and insert any meeting that you have listed in your Outlook calendar. To insert the meeting details for an Outlook meeting, select the Meeting Details command (on the Insert tab). Any meetings that you have scheduled for the current day are listed on the Meeting Details gallery. Select a meeting to insert its details onto the notebook page. Figure 32.9 shows the details of a meeting that has been inserted onto a page.

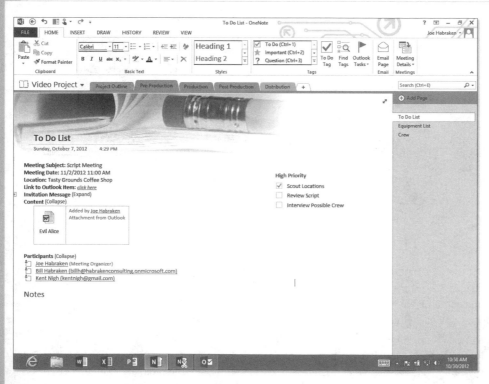

Figure 32.9 Insert Outlook meeting details into your notebook pages.

If the meeting details you want to insert into your page are for a meeting that does not occur on the current day, you can easily select a meeting from another date. Select the Choose a Meeting from Another Day option from the Meeting Details gallery. This opens the Insert Outlook Meeting Details dialog box. The dialog box shows the current date. You can use the Previous Day and Next Day buttons to move backward and forward in your calendar to find the day when the meeting was (or is) scheduled. If you want to view a calendar and specify the date when the meeting is scheduled, select the Calendar icon on the right side of the Insert Outlook Meeting Details dialog box. Figure 32.10 shows the Insert Outlook Meeting Details dialog box and the accompanying calendar.

Figure 32.10
Specify the meeting's date in the Insert Outlook Meeting Details dialog box.

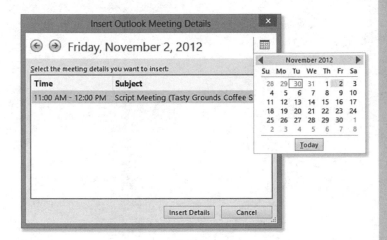

When you select a date on the calendar, the meetings scheduled for the day are listed in the dialog box. Select the meeting from the list, and then click the Insert Details button.

After you have inserted meeting details onto the page, you can add notes related to the meeting using the Notes area that is provided in the Notes box that holds the meeting details. As with other page notes, you can move the meeting details note box on the page and size the note box, if needed. If you want to delete the meeting details, select the note box and then press Delete, or right-click on the meeting details and select Delete from the shortcut menu.

 tip

After you have inserted meeting details onto a notebook page, you can quickly send that page to the meeting participants listed in the meeting details note. Select Email Page on the Home tab. An Outlook message window opens, and the email addresses of the participants listed in the note are already included in the message's To box.

OFFICE APPLICATION INTEGRATION

The Office 2013 application suite provides specific software applications for specific jobs: Word for documents, Excel for spreadsheets, PowerPoint for presentations, and Outlook for email management. However, Office isn't just a collection of unrelated software tools; it is a suite of well-integrated applications.

In this appendix, we look at how you can integrate information from an Office application into another application. For example, you might want to insert an Excel workbook into a Word document. We also look at the two different ways of sharing data between applications: linking and embedding.

Sharing Application Data

Many of us share information on corporate networks via network shares and file servers. Users on a corporate network or users taking advantage of the Enterprise Office 365 subscription can also typically access SharePoint sites that provide a place for users to share files. Office 2013 fully integrates the use of SharePoint sites into the suite applications.

Users not attached to a corporate network can take advantage of the file-sharing capabilities provided by Microsoft's SkyDrive, including use of the Office Web Apps. And we all fall back on the use of emails with file attachments as a way for sharing files with others.

> ➡ *Microsoft's SkyDrive and the Office Web Apps are discussed in Chapter 5, "Using the Office Web Apps."*

Office 2013 also provides another possibility for organizing and sharing information including file attachments: Microsoft OneNote. Notebooks created in OneNote can contain attached files and you can share these notebooks with other users. As you stay organized with OneNote, you can allow collaborators access to the materials that you are collating in the OneNote notebook.

➡ *Microsoft OneNote is discussed in Part VII, "OneNote."*

Sharing files is certainly not rocket science, considering all the connectivity possibilities that corporate networks and the Internet provide, including SharePoint sites and SkyDrive. However, all these shared files are not worth a lot if we cannot massage all that information into some kind of meaningful output.

Almost more important than file-sharing capabilities (at least, in my mind) is the capability of the Microsoft Office suite to share information from one member application to another. Being able to pull together information that resides in different applications into a report or a presentation without converting any of the data is virtually priceless. For example, you can perform a mail merge in Microsoft Word, which uses recipient information contained in your Contact folder in Outlook, to generate form letters.

➡ *Mail merges are discussed in Chapter 9, "Managing Mailings and Forms."*

Consider other examples of the cooperative abilities of Word and Outlook. Word functions as the Outlook email editor (providing you with all of Word's features when composing emails), and Smart Tags in Word documents can be used to automatically input information into Outlook. Word and Outlook are truly integrated in their capability to work together.

These collaborative capabilities found in Word and Outlook are certainly not the exception. As already mentioned, the capability to seamlessly share information between applications is a huge benefit—you can share information in Excel with Word (or vice versa) and application data with PowerPoint or Publisher. All the Office applications provide a platform for commingling data from the various suite members. The basis for much of this data sharing is called object linking and embedding.

Understanding Object Linking and Embedding

Microsoft's object linking and embedding, or OLE, has been around since the early 1990s. With OLE, you can create "compound" documents that consist of data from more than one application. Breaking down the name (object linking and embedding) into its component parts is the easiest way to define what OLE actually is. An object can be anything from worksheet data or a chart in Excel, to a slide in PowerPoint, to an image in a Word document, to pretty much any selectable entity in any of the Office applications. So OLE works with application objects.

Now let's tackle linking. When you link an object to a document or other application file, you are creating a connection between the source file and your current document, the container file. The object does not reside in the container; it is represented there by a linking code. When you update the object, the update occurs in the original source application, and the results of the update are seen in the container. For example, you can link a Microsoft Excel worksheet to a Word document. When you activate the workbook with a double-click (or by right-clicking on the worksheet and selecting

Open Source), its source application (Microsoft Excel) is started and the linked workbook is opened in it. Figure A.1 shows a linked workbook in Word that has been opened in Excel.

Figure A.1
A linked worksheet in a Word document with the Excel Source data.

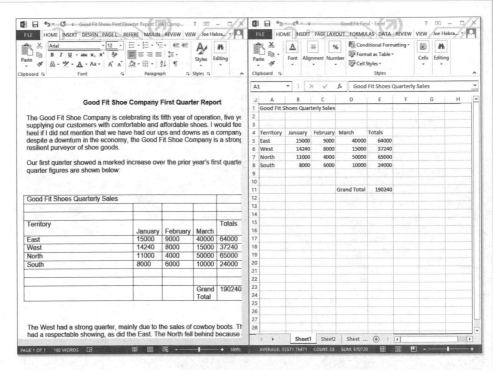

Embedding gets the data into a document or presentation, but the information is no longer linked to the original source information in the other application, such as an Excel worksheet or chart. An embedded object becomes part of the destination file and increases that file's size. It is basically a transplanted copy of the original data. Because the embedded file resides in the destination file, updating the original file in the original application does not update the embedded copy; there is no link between the two.

Embedded objects are dynamic, meaning that you can edit them. However, because they now reside in a destination application such as Word or PowerPoint, the information is edited or manipulated within that particular destination application, but in a rather unusual way. When you activate an embedded object (double-click it), the server application opens inside the current application. For example, if you activate an Excel object such as an embedded worksheet in Word, the Word Ribbon is replaced by the Excel Ribbon while the worksheet object is activated. So, in essence, you are running the server application (Excel) from inside the application (Word) that holds the embedded object.

Another example of an embedded object is an Excel workbook (such as sales figures for your company) embedded in an Outlook appointment. You double-click the embedded Excel object to activate it. Figure A.2 shows an embedded Excel worksheet that has been "activated" in an Outlook event (appointment).

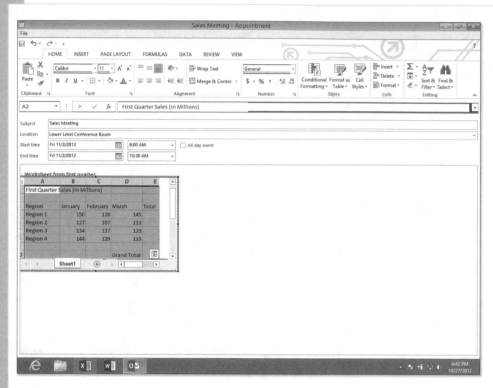

Figure A.2
An embed-
ded Excel
workbook
that has
been acti-
vated in an
Outlook
appointment.

Note in Figure A.2 that the Ribbon typically found in the Appointment window has been replaced with the Excel Ribbon. When you click outside the embedded worksheet, the various Appointment commands return to the Ribbon.

Choosing Between Linking and Embedding

You might be wondering when it's best to link and when you should embed. This depends on the type of information that you want to place in a particular file. Objects that are dynamic (the information in them updates continually), such as worksheets built in Excel or reports written in Word, are best linked to your container file. This enables you to update the object in the application you created it in and still have the current results linked to several containers. For example, the same Excel worksheet (which is being updated weekly) could be linked to a Word report (container one) and a slide in a PowerPoint presentation (container two).

Objects such as Excel worksheets that contain information from past quarters or a completed PowerPoint presentation attached to an upcoming meeting appointment in Outlook—any items that are static and not updated over time—can be embedded into your application files, making them part of the file rather than linked content.

Linking Objects

You have different possibilities for linking objects from one application to another. One option uses Copy and Paste Special, a tried-and-true method of quickly linking data (it's been around nearly as long as the Office applications).

Another possibility takes advantage of the Paste Options gallery, which is available when you select the Paste command in the Clipboard group. Interestingly, a link created by using one of the new Paste Options does create a link to external content but does not create the same kind of link that Paste Special does (we look at the differences in a moment).

The third possibility for creating a link to external data is to use the Object command on the Ribbon's Insert tab. This enables you to specify a filename (you can actually browse to locate the file) that you want to link to the current document (say, in Word) or other application file type (such as an Outlook email, an event, or a PowerPoint slide). Let's take a look at the mechanics of each of these linking possibilities.

Linking with Paste Special

When an object copied in an application is pasted into a document or other file type with the regular Paste command, the data is dropped in with no information about its origin. In contrast, when an object is pasted into a document using Paste Special options such as Paste Link, several pieces of information about the object are stored in the container file. These include the source file's name and location, the server application, and the location of the object within the source file. This extra information makes it possible for the linked object to update whenever the source file updates.

Open the application that serves as the destination (container file) for the linked information. Then to link with Paste Special, follow these steps:

1. Open the application that contains the information you want to link (such as an Excel workbook).

2. Select the information that will serve as the object.

3. Select the Copy command on the Ribbon's Home tab.

4. Return to the application (click the Application's icon on the taskbar) that will receive the linked information.

5. Select the Paste command (in the Clipboard group) and then select Paste Special. This opens the Paste Special dialog box, shown in Figure A.3.

6. In the dialog box, select the object that you want to place into the current application (Figure A.3 shows a Microsoft Excel Worksheet Object).

7. Select the Paste Link option button.

8. Click OK.

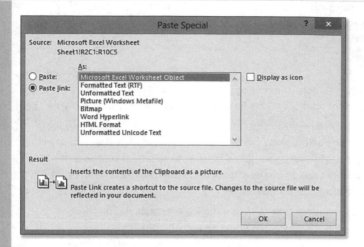

Figure A.3
The Paste Special dialog box.

The object is pasted into the application file (such as a Word document). The object that you have linked really looks no different from any information that you have pasted into a document or other file. However, the information is linked into the file; you can view the link at any time by pressing Alt+F9, which allows you to view field codes in a document or other file. Figure A.4 shows the linking field code that was inserted into a Word document using the steps discussed in this section.

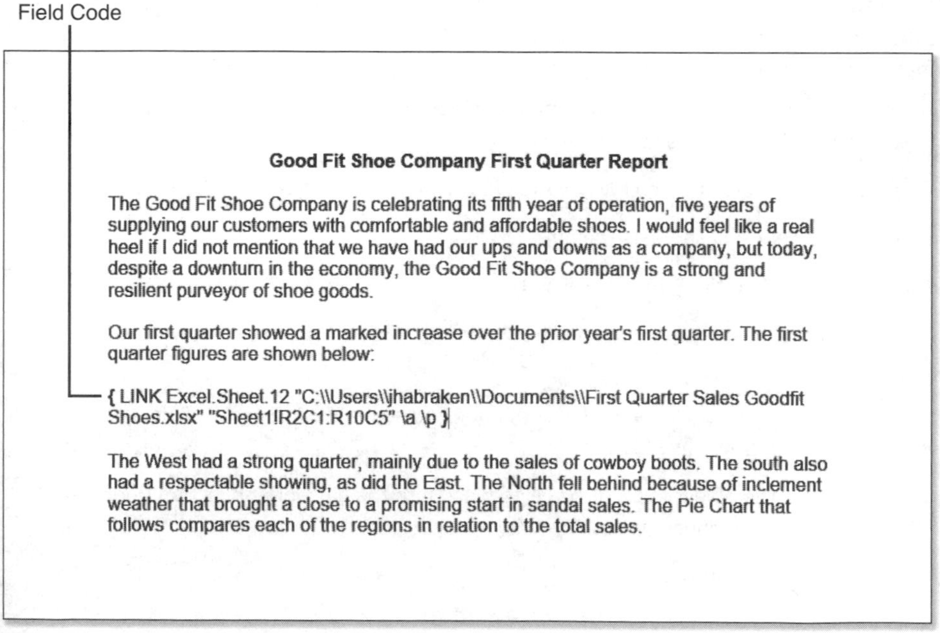

Field Code

Figure A.4
The link field code for a linked object in a Word document.

Good Fit Shoe Company First Quarter Report

The Good Fit Shoe Company is celebrating its fifth year of operation, five years of supplying our customers with comfortable and affordable shoes. I would feel like a real heel if I did not mention that we have had our ups and downs as a company, but today, despite a downturn in the economy, the Good Fit Shoe Company is a strong and resilient purveyor of shoe goods.

Our first quarter showed a marked increase over the prior year's first quarter. The first quarter figures are shown below:

{ LINK Excel.Sheet.12 "C:\\Users\\jhabraken\\Documents\\First Quarter Sales Goodfit Shoes.xlsx" "Sheet1!R2C1:R10C5" \a \p }

The West had a strong quarter, mainly due to the sales of cowboy boots. The south also had a respectable showing, as did the East. The North fell behind because of inclement weather that brought a close to a promising start in sandal sales. The Pie Chart that follows compares each of the regions in relation to the total sales.

You can toggle off the field view by pressing Alt+F9. Linked content differs from information that you've pasted, in that you can select it (when you click on it) only as a complete object. For example, clicking on linked Excel worksheet data selects all the data; you don't have the option of changing individual cells in the container application.

Linking with the Paste Options Gallery

You can also paste a link using two of the commands in the Paste Options gallery. After you select and copy the object to be inserted as a link (in the source file), return to the application and the file that serves as the linking container.

In the container application, select Paste (on the Home tab). The Paste Options gallery opens, as shown in Figure A.5. The two option commands of interest in the gallery are the third and fourth commands from the left.

Figure A.5
Create the link using the Paste Options linking commands.

The third Paste Options command is Link & Keep Source Formatting (F). If you hover over this command with the mouse, you see what the pasted link will look like in the container file. Select this option if you want to have the link created and keep the formatting for the object that was assigned to it in the source file.

If you want to create the link but take advantage of styles and formatting in the destination file (the container file), select the fourth command: Link & Use Destination Styles (L). For example, if you are pasting a link for Excel worksheet data into Word, the pasted information is formatted using the default table style for the current document.

Either of these Paste Options commands inserts the link into the document. You can view the link code by pressing Alt+F9. These links, however, are different from the link that you get when you use the Paste Special dialog box, discussed in the previous section.

When you double-click the link created using the Paste Special dialog box, the source application opens and you can update the data as needed. When you use the Paste Options commands, double-clicking on the linked information does not open the source application. However, when you update the information in the source file, the linked information is still updated. This might seem odd, but this is the way these two different linking techniques work.

You can, however, still open the source file for a link even if you have used the Paste Options command. Right-click on the linked object and then point at the object name (such as Linked Worksheet Object) on the shortcut menu. Then select Links; the Links dialog box opens. Select the link in the Links list. Then click the Open Source button to open the source file for that particular link.

Linking Using the Object Command

You have a third option for creating links: You can create a link using the Object command on the Ribbon's Insert tab. This option enables you to link an entire file to the container (destination) file. Because Word is often used as a container file, let's look at how to link into a Word document. Follow these steps:

1. Place the insertion point where you will place the linked object.

2. Select the Insert tab.

3. Select the Object command (in the Text group), and then select Object. The Object dialog box opens.

4. Select the Create from File tab in the Object dialog box, as shown in Figure A.6.

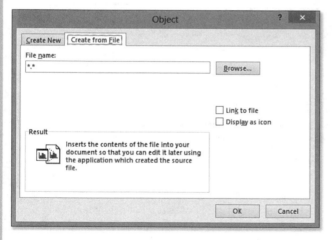

Figure A.6
Create the link using the Create from File tab.

5. Use the Browse button to locate the file that you want to link into the current document. In the Browse dialog box, select the file and then click Insert.

6. Select the Link to File check box in the Create from File dialog box.

7. Click the OK button.

The information links into the current document. When you double-click the linked object, the source application opens, showing the linked file data.

Updating and Breaking Links

When you link objects to a file, you have complete control over that link; you can configure how the link data should update, and you can break the link while retaining the currently shown information from the data source in your container file. Links (by default) update when you open the container file; any changes made in the source file should be present in the linked content when you open it. For example, if an Excel worksheet links into a Word document, any changes made to the Excel data since the last time you opened the Word document update when you open the Word document.

You have control, however, over whether the link updates when you open the document. A Microsoft Word information box opens (see Figure A.7) and asks whether you want to update the links in the document. Click Yes or No, depending on whether you want the links to update. If you don't update the link, don't worry; you can update the links manually (which we discuss in a moment) or update the links the next time you open the container file.

Figure A.7
You determine whether the links should be updated.

In some cases, you might want to configure a link so that it is updated only when you want (and need) to see the updated content. This is particularly useful when you have linked source files that might be updated by a number of users. You can wait until you are sure that the source data is in its final form before you manually update a link.

You can specify the update settings for links in a file in the file's Info window. Let's look at a Word document containing links as an example. Select File to open the Backstage; then click Info.

The Info window provides access to settings related to permissions and sharing settings for the current document. To access the Links dialog box, select the Edit Links to Files command in the Related Documents area of the window (the bottom right). Figure A.8 shows the Links dialog box.

 note

You can prevent a link from updating (automatically or manually) in a document by locking the link. This can be useful when you are not sure about the linked content and whether it originates with a trusted source. Select the link and click the Locked check box in the Links dialog box.

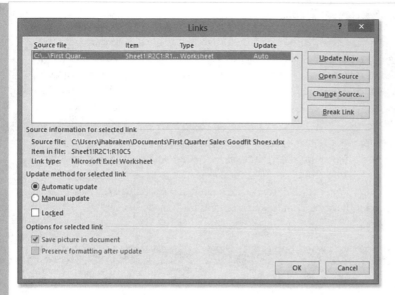

Figure A.8
The Links dialog box.

The Links dialog box gives you complete control over the links in your document or other file. Four buttons in the dialog box provide commands related to your links as follows:

- **Update Now:** You can update a selected link by clicking the Update Now button.

- **Open Source:** If you want to view the source file for a particular link, select the link and then click Open source.

- **Change Source:** This command opens the Change Source dialog box. You can browse for a file in the dialog box and then open the file to replace the source file in the currently selected link.

- **Break Link:** You can break the current link to the source file. This enables you to retain the current content in the source file in your container document, but it no longer updates when the source file is edited.

For our discussion in this section relating to automatic versus manual updates, two option buttons provided in the Links dialog box are important: Automatic Update and Manual Update. By default, the Automatic Update option button is selected for each link. If you want to change a link to manual updating, select the link and then click Manual Update. When you finish working in the Links dialog box, click OK.

In the future, you can update links manually from the Links dialog box (select a link and then click Update Now). You can open the Links dialog box from the Backstage as previously discussed. Alternatively, you can right-click an object in the container file, point at the object name on the shortcut menu (such as a linked Worksheet object), and then click Links on the shortcut menu.

You can also update a link within the container file, such as a Word document, without opening the Links dialog box: Right-click the linked object in the document and then click Update Link on the shortcut menu.

When breaking links, you might want to keep the data currently provided by the link in your container file (such as a Word document or PowerPoint slide) and not allow the object to be updated when the source file is edited (such as an Excel worksheet). This enables you to take a snapshot of the current data and include it in your document.

To break a link, open the Links dialog box and select the link that you want to break. Click Break Link. A message box opens, asking whether you are sure that you want to break the selected link (or links); click Yes to break the link. Then click OK to close the Links dialog box.

Editing Linked Objects

After you create a linked object, you might want to edit and update the information in the object. At this stage, you realize the full benefit of an OLE link because you can edit the object one time and have it update in every document to which it is linked.

You can edit a linked object in two ways. The first is to start at the source file, using the server application to make changes to the object. The second is to start at the container file and let the link information lead you to the correct source file and server application. With the second method, you do not have to remember the name of the source file or even which server application created it.

To edit a linked object starting from the source file, start the server application, and then open the source file that contains the object you want to edit. Edit and make changes to the object as needed. When you open the container file containing the linked object, the link updates (or you can update it manually) and the most current version of the data's object is provided in the container file.

Editing from the container file is quick and easy because you do not have to find and open the server application manually. To edit a linked object from the container file, double-click the linked object that you want to update. The server application starts and displays the source file. If double-clicking the object does not start the server application, right-click on the object and point at the object name on the shortcut menu. Then select Links to open the Links dialog box. Select the link you want to edit and click the Open Source button. The server application starts.

Edit the information in the server application and then save the changes that you have made. You can then close the server application. When you return to the container application, the data should have updated in the linked object.

Embedding Objects

If you want to embed data into a destination file, you can embed with the Paste Special dialog box or use the Object command on the Insert tab. Remember that embedding places the information into the destination file but does not create a link to the source, so editing embedded objects is a

 tip

You can select multiple links in the Links dialog box if you want to change multiple link settings, such as configuring the links for manual update. Select the first link, and then hold the Ctrl key as you select other links as needed.

note

Linked objects provide a great way to get multiple sources of information from different users into a particular destination application.

different process from editing linked objects. Remember, after you embed information, it becomes a part of the destination file (such as an Excel worksheet that you have embedded in a Word document).

Embedding with Paste Special

Embedding information from one application into another application using Paste Special is similar to linking an object. However, no actual link is created. Only a copy of the information in the source file is placed into your destination file. Follow these steps to embed information using Paste Special:

1. Open the application that contains the information that you want to embed.

2. Select the data, text, or other item that will serve as the object.

3. Select the Copy command in the Clipboard group, or press Ctrl+C.

4. Open (or navigate to) the application that provides the file that will serve as the destination for the embedded object. If necessary, open the specific file.

5. In the destination file, select the Paste command and then select Paste Special. The Paste Special dialog box opens.

6. Select the object type in the As box (such as Microsoft Excel Worksheet Object).

7. Select OK.

The Paste Special dialog box closes, and the object is embedded into the current document. Note that when you click on the object, particularly if the object is Excel worksheet data, you cannot place the insertion point in any of the sheet cells. You can select only the entire object.

Embedding Using the Object Command

If you want to embed an entire file as an object or create a new object, you can use the Object command. For example, let's say that you want to insert an Excel worksheet into a PowerPoint slide. You can use the Object command to do this.

You might wonder why you would want to create a new object in a destination file. If you look back at the description of embedding, it creates an object in a destination file that is then edited using the server application. So if you want to put a very complex table in a PowerPoint slide or Word document and you want to have the capabilities of Excel (in terms of Excel functions) available when you edit the object, it makes sense to embed an Excel object. The real power of embedded objects is that they are edited using all the capabilities of the server application without leaving the destination application.

To embed an existing file as an object into a destination file, open the destination file. Sticking with our Excel object on a PowerPoint slide, make sure you have the presentation that contains the destination slide for the Excel object. Make sure you are on the specific slide, and then select the Object command on the Ribbon's Insert tab. The Insert Object dialog box opens. Select the Create from File option button (in PowerPoint) and then use the Browse button to locate the file you want to embed.

After you locate the file in the Browse dialog box, select the file and then click OK. The filename appears in the File box on the Insert Object dialog box, as shown in Figure A.9.

To embed the object and close the Insert Object dialog box, click OK. The object appears in the container file (a document, slide, or other file type). You can relocate the object as needed. For example, on a PowerPoint slide, the object can be repositioned as any other object—such as an image or chart that can be dragged and sized.

note

In Word, the Object command opens the Object dialog box, as opposed to the Insert Object dialog box found in PowerPoint.

Figure A.9
The Insert Object dialog box in PowerPoint.

Embedding New Objects

You can also embed new objects in a destination application file such as a document or presentation. Use the Object command to open the Object (Word) or Insert Object (PowerPoint) dialog box. In PowerPoint, select the Create New option and select an object type in the Object Type list. Then click OK to insert the object. In Word, use the Object Type list on the Create New tab of the Object dialog box to select an object type, and then click OK.

In either case (PowerPoint or Word), a new object is placed in the file. The server application's Ribbon (an application such as Excel) replaces the destination application's Ribbon. Edit the new object as needed. To return to the destination application's Ribbon, click outside the object.

Editing Embedded Objects

Editing embedded objects is extremely straightforward. Remember that, although the object doesn't have any association with specific content in a source file, it is a copy of that source file and is still tied to the server application that was used to create it.

To edit an embedded object, double-click the object. This action evokes the server application and provides you with the Ribbon and commands found in that application. For example, when you double-click an Excel object in a PowerPoint slide, Excel basically takes over the PowerPoint application window. You are still in PowerPoint, but you now have all the capabilities of Excel to edit the object. Figure A.10 shows an activated Excel object embedded in PowerPoint.

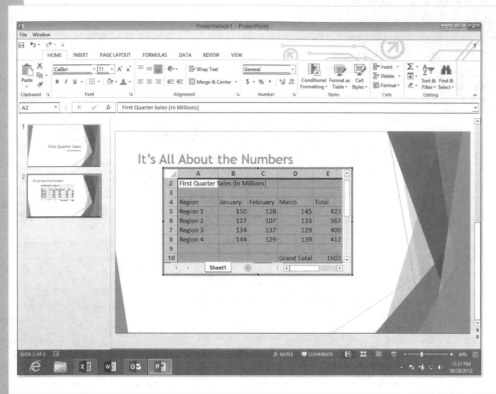

When you finish editing the object using the server application tools, you can return to the desti-nation application. Click anywhere outside the object. The Ribbon for the destination application returns, and you can continue to work in the application as needed.

Sharing Data with Outlook Using Actions

You can share data between Word and Outlook using actions. Several actions are available in Word, including the Date, Person Name, and Telephone Number actions. An action such as the Date action or Person Name action requires that you right-click on a text item (such as a Date or person's name) to complete the action; the action would actually be scheduling an event in Outlook (related to the date) or adding a person's name to your Outlook people folder. Unfortunately, there isn't a visual cue (such as underlining or highlighting) to let you know that a particular type of information can be manipulated by an action. You can tell only by right-clicking on an item (again, such as a date or a person's name) and checking whether Additional Actions is one of the choices on the short-cut menu. Placing the mouse on Additional Actions shows you the actions that are available. For example, right-clicking on a date and then pointing at Additional Actions provides actions such as

Schedule a Meeting and Show My Calendar; both of these action possibilities open Outlook, and either opens a new event to schedule a meeting or open your calendar to that particular date.

To take advantage of the actions provided in Word, you need to enable them. This is accomplished via the AutoCorrect dialog box, which you access via the Word Options window. To enable actions in Word, follow these steps:

1. In Word, select File to open the Backstage.

2. Select Options to open the Word Options window, and then select Add-Ins. The Word Add-Ins options are listed.

3. To enable the available actions, select the Manage drop-down list at the bottom of the Add-Ins window and then select Actions from the list.

4. Click Go to the Right of the Manage drop-down list. The AutoCorrect dialog box opens.

5. Select the Enable Additional Actions in the Right-Click Menu check box, as shown in Figure A.11.

Figure A.11
Enable actions in the AutoCorrect dialog box.

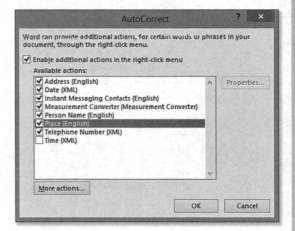

6. You can enable any of the available actions listed, such as Date, Person Name, Place, and Telephone Number, by selecting the appropriate check boxes.

7. After making your selections, select OK to return to the Word application window.

 tip

You can also access the AutoCorrect options via the Proofing page of the Word Options. Open the Word Options from the Backstage (Options) and then select Proofing. Select the AutoCorrect Options button. In the AutoCorrect dialog box, select the Actions tab.

To use an action to place information in Outlook, place the mouse on an item, such as a name or date, and then right-click. On the shortcut menu, point at Additional Actions. The Additional Actions submenu gives you choices related to placing the information into Outlook or allowing Outlook to use the information to perform a particular action. For example, in the case of right-clicking on a name (the Person Name action) you are provided with choices such as Send Mail, Schedule a Meeting, Open Contact, or Add to Contacts. All of the choices request that Outlook perform an action based on the text in the Word document.

Enabling the Word AutoCorrect actions is worthwhile. It is just another possibility for quickly taking information in a Word document and using it to interact with another Office application: Outlook.

OFFICE MACROS

The Office applications provide easy access to commands and features via the Ribbon, the standard command and control tool in Office 2013. File management and print commands (as well as access to an application's options settings) have been nested in the Backstage. Although it might seem that getting things done in your Office applications does not require anything other than the standard commands and features, you might find an occasion when you want to have more control over a process. You might want to automate a particular series of commands by recording a macro.

In this appendix, we take a basic look at the process of recording your keystrokes and mouse clicks as part of a macro script. This macro primer includes information on how to add the Developer tab to the Ribbon and enable macros in the Office Trust Center.

Macros and Office 2013

The capability to record software commands via keystrokes (and, eventually, mouse clicks) and save them in the form of a short script or mini-program has been available in the Office applications for years. This series of recorded commands that is saved as a short script or routine is called a *macro*. The great thing about macros is that they can help you automate repetitive tasks.

Another great thing about macros is that you don't have to be a programmer to create some useful macros. You don't have to write the code for the macro—you simply record it (although a special form of the Visual Basic programming language is designed for use with the Office applications).

Each of the Office applications—Word, Excel, PowerPoint, Outlook, and Publisher—provides you with the capability to create your own macros. Even simple macros can reduce the drudgery associated with certain tasks. For example, you might create a macro in an Excel worksheet that helps you insert a new row into a spreadsheet and then copies the necessary formatting and formulas into the new row from the previous row in the sheet. This macro is extremely simple to create and enables you to make a routing Excel task more efficient. Or let's say that, in Word, you create a macro that saves and prints a form based on a template that you created. This type of macro greatly simplifies the task of completing an online survey for your network users.

In terms of creating macros, you can write the code for a macro or you can record a macro (depending on the application you are working with). Word and Excel enable you to record macros; PowerPoint, Publisher, and Outlook require that you write the macro. So you might want to start exploring macros in Word and Excel because you can record the macros, which doesn't require a great deal of knowledge of the coding language (Visual Basic for Applications).

The types and complexity of macros that you ultimately create are up to you. Macros provide you with a great deal of flexibility in automating routine tasks in the Office applications; definitely consider them as a resource in reducing the number of steps for often-required tasks.

Adding the Developer Tab to the Ribbon

The various macro-related commands are on the Ribbon's Developer tab; however, by default, the Developer tab is not included as one of the Ribbon's tabs. (This is true for all the Office applications.)

If you want to record a macro in Word or Excel, you need to add the Developer tab to that application's Ribbon. For example, in Excel, follow these steps to add the Developer tab to the Ribbon:

1. On the Ribbon, select File to open the Backstage.

2. Select Options to open the Options window for the application.

3. In the application's Options window, select Customize Ribbon. Figure B.1 shows the Excel Options window with the Customize the Ribbon pane open.

4. Make sure that Main Tabs is selected in the Customize the Ribbon drop-down box (on the right of the pane).

5. In the Main Tabs list, select the Developer check box.

6. Click OK to close the application's Options window.

You are returned to the application window. The Developer tab is now included on the Ribbon.

 note

You can create macros in most of the Office Suite members, such as Excel, Word, and PowerPoint; however, Microsoft OneNote does not enable you to record macros.

Figure B.1
Use Excel's Options window to add the Developer tab to the Ribbon.

Enabling Macros in the Trust Center

Macros are a security risk; remember that macros are, in effect, programs. This means that a macro can contain all sorts of code, including code that can do bad things to your Office applications and, potentially, your computer. And antivirus software isn't always capable of catching malware (malicious software) that comes in the form of a macro.

Because macros pose a potential security risk to your computer, macros are disabled in your Office applications by default: The default setting in the Trust Center is Disable All Macros with Notification. This means that a security box notifies you if you open a file that contains macros. You are given the opportunity to keep the macros disabled or allow them to be enabled in the file. This gives you complete control over whether the macros remain disabled when you open a particular document, presentation, or workbook.

Depending on the environment you work in, the macro settings in the Trust Center might have been changed from the default to protect the computers on the network. For example, if you work on a corporate network, your network administrator might have changed the setting in the Trust Center to Disable All Macros Except Digitally Signed Macros. This requires you to digitally sign your macros before using them.

For information on digitally signing macros, **see** "Digitally Signing Macros," **p. 959**.

note

Macro viruses have long been the bane of email users around the world; macro viruses can spread like wildfire and are somewhat easy to create—think of the Melissa virus, which infected thousands of computers. Be very careful opening emails in Outlook with unknown attachments, which can contain macros. Also be careful opening Office files that contain macros that you have downloaded from the Web. Remember that macro viruses were the first cross-platform viruses and spread between computers running Windows and the Mac OS.

If you work in a home office environment and plan to use only macros that you create, you might want to change the macro setting in a particular Office application to the Enable All Macros (Not Recommended; Potentially Dangerous Code Can Run) option. This gives you the most flexibility in running your own macros, but it can potentially open your computer to attack via a macro virus if you run macros in other files, particularly those that you download from the Web.

How you approach your application security is up to you. If you are going to be working with your own macros in an application, you might want to edit the macros using the Trust Center. To access the Trust Center for an application, follow these steps:

1. On the application's Ribbon, select File to open the Backstage.

2. Select Options to open the Options window for the application.

3. In the application's Options window, select Trust Center.

4. In the Trust Center pane, select Trust Center Settings. This opens the application's Trust Center.

5. To change the macro settings for the application, select Macro Settings. Figure B.2 shows the Word Trust Center and the default macro settings.

6. Select the macro setting that you want to use for the application, and then click OK.

The Trust Center closes, and you return to the application's Options. Click OK to return to the application window.

➡ *For more about the Trust Center, **see** Chapter 2, "Navigating and Customizing the Office Interface."*

Figure B.2
The Word macro settings in the Trust Center.

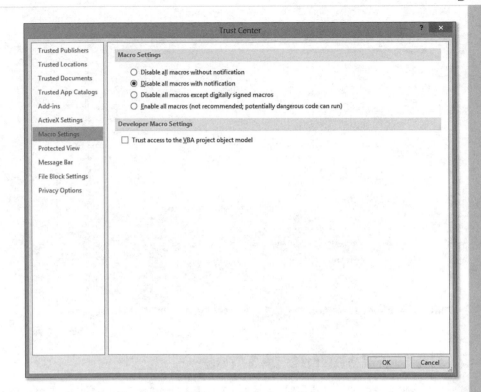

Creating Macro-Enabled Office Files

An alternative to adjusting the macro settings in the Trust Center is to save your Word document or Excel workbook in a file format that enables the macros that you have created and stored in the file. With the exception of Microsoft Outlook, all of the Office applications provide you with this capability. This approach to enabling macros in a file does not present the same level of risk as allowing an application to enable all macros via the Trust Center macro settings.

So let's say that you want to save a PowerPoint presentation as a PowerPoint macro-enabled presentation. You can create a new presentation and save it in the macro-enabled file format, or you can use the Save As command to save a macro-enabled copy of any presentation that you have previously created.

Whether you are saving a presentation for the first time (with Save) or using Save As to create a macro-enabled version of the presentation, the Save As dialog box opens. In the Save As Type drop-down list, select PowerPoint Macro-Enabled Presentation, as shown in Figure B.3.

Then all you have to do is supply a filename (if you are saving the presentation for the first time) and a location for the saved file. Then click Save. Now you can create macros as needed in this presentation, and they will be enabled.

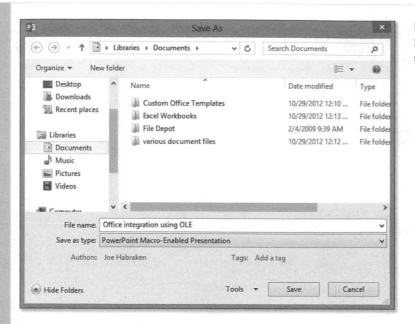

Figure B.3
Saving a macro-enabled presentation.

Understanding Macros

Macros created in the Office applications are saved in a scripting language called Microsoft Visual Basic for Applications, or VBA. Creating macros in VBA only scratches the surface of what you can accomplish using the VBA scripting language. Developers use VBA to create add-ons and other special tools for the various Office applications. VBA can enhance the user interface for an Office application by creating new Ribbon tabs and commands for those tabs.

VBA is an object-oriented programming language. This means that it is designed to manipulate different classes of objects, which is exactly what is necessary for a programming language to work in an environment such as Office, where many different object types are found in the different Office applications. In fact, VBA is designed so that developers can create new object classes, if necessary, as they design and code tools and application add-ons.

When you record VBA code for a macro, the code is contained in what is referred to as a module. Each application has its own module for the macros that you create for that application.

Each individual macro consists of a subroutine that dictates what the macro does when you run it. Figure B.4 shows the subroutine code for a simple Excel macro.

Because we are primarily exploring the recording of macros (rather than writing code), you don't have to worry too much

 note

A complete discussion of VBA as a programming tool and language is far beyond the scope of this appendix and this book. If you want to delve further into VBA programming, I recommend acquiring a book on VBA, such as Que's *VBA and Macros: Microsoft Excel 2010*, by Bill Jelen. You can also check out other VBA-related titles published by Que at www.quepublishing.com/.

about the actual code created during the process, although you can edit the code in the Microsoft VBA editor (which we touch on later in this appendix). You only need to turn on the macro recorder and then perform the steps that make up the macro's routine.

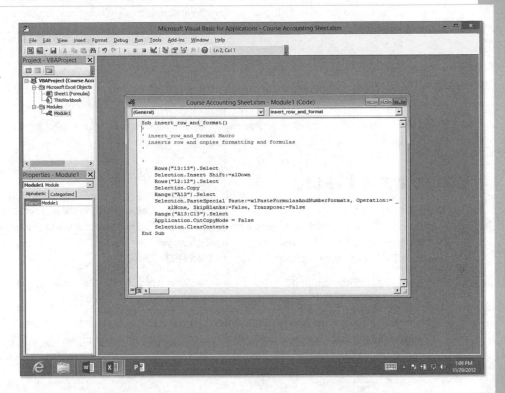

Figure B.4
Macros consist of VBA code subroutines.

Another subject area that you should understand before you begin to create your macros relates to where your macros are saved after you create them. Each Office application offers slightly different options. The following list provides the options for each member of the Office suite discussed in this book (precluding OneNote, as already mentioned):

- **Word:** Macros recorded in Word can be saved to the Normal template (Normal.dotm), which makes the macros available to all documents based on that template. You can also save macros to a specific template or to the current document.

- **Excel:** Macros recorded in Excel can be stored in the current workbook, a new workbook, or a macro catch-all workbook called the Personal Macro workbook. Macros stored in the Personal Macro workbook are available globally, meaning in all your Excel worksheets.

- **PowerPoint:** Macros in PowerPoint can be saved in the current presentation or all currently open presentations (when you use the macro recorder). You can also use the Save As Type list to save presentations, templates, and even shows (meaning that the macros can be run while you show the presentation) using the macro-enabled file types.

- **Outlook:** Outlook saves macros with the application's dataset so that you can access any macros you create in Outlook anytime you need them.

- **Publisher:** Macros in Publisher are stored in the Publisher publication that is open when you record the macro. You can also use the Save As command to save a Publisher file as a Word document containing the recorded macros using the Word Macro-Enabled Document file type.

One other important point relates to macros: They require a great deal of trial and error because they do not always work as intended. For example, sometimes the VBA code that you create when you record a macro doesn't define an object correctly (such as a range you selected in an Excel worksheet), or the macro (when played) has a problem relocating a particular object.

Simple, well-thought-out macros typically work as you intended. More complex macros might require more research into VBA if you want to create them.

Creating a Macro

The macro-related commands are in the Developers tab's Code group. Word and Excel don't provide exactly the same macro-related commands; however, some commands are common to both. For example, to record a new macro in Word or Excel, you use the Record Macro command. Other macro-related commands common to Word and Excel are as follows:

- **Visual Basic:** This command opens the Visual Basic editor. The editor has its own toolbar that you can use to create VBA modules and subroutines from scratch.

- **Macros:** This command opens the Macros dialog box. It enables you to view the list of macros. Commands are available for editing, deleting, and running macros in the list. The Macros dialog box also provides access to the Organizer, which you can use to copy macros from one file to another.

- **Record Macro:** This command starts the macro-recording process.

- **Stop Recording:** In Word and Excel, you use the Stop Recording command when you have finished recording the macro.

- **Macro Security:** This command opens the Trust Center's macro settings.

Before recording steps in the macro, you must supply a name for the macro, and you have the option of specifying a shortcut key for the macro. Keyboard shortcuts for macros can include the use of the Ctrl, Alt, and Shift keys, as well as the function keys and the alphanumeric keys on the keyboard. As already discussed in the previous section, you might also have the capability to choose where the macro is stored, depending on the specific Office application you are using (you definitely have options in Word and Excel).

In terms of naming conventions for macros, you must follow some rules. First, the macro can be up to 80 characters and must begin with a letter or an underscore. The remaining characters in the macro name can be letters, numbers, or the underscore symbol. You cannot use spaces in your macro names or special characters such as *, /, and :. Finally, your macro name cannot be a duplicate of an Excel built-in name or an object that already exists in the workbook. If you violate any of these rules, a warning box opens to let you know that the name that you entered is not valid. This is no big deal because you can close the box and re-enter a name for the macro that follows all the rules.

One other aspect of creating your macro to take into account before you turn on the macro recorder relates to planning. It makes sense to plan a macro in terms of the series of commands and actions that you will record. Definitely consider practicing or even writing down the steps in the macro before you actually record it.

If you create a macro that doesn't function correctly, it is certainly no big deal. You can easily delete a macro that doesn't operate properly. You also have the option of editing a macro, which we discuss later in this appendix—but you might find that deleting a bad macro and attempting to record it again is as easy (particularly for short macros) as trying to debug and edit your problem-child macro.

Recording a Macro

The macro-recording process is pretty much the same for the various Office applications, although you will find slight differences; it is definitely the same for Excel and Word, which are two of the most-often-used Office applications. Let's walk though how you record a macro in Excel and then look at creating a macro in Word and assigning it to the Quick Access Toolbar as a button. Follow these steps:

 note

When the macro recorder is running, you lose some functionality normally attributed to the mouse; for example, you cannot select text in a Word document. Use keyboard shortcuts as much as possible when you are recording your macros.

 note

The Record Macro dialog box in Word provides a Button command that enables you to assign the macro you are recording to a button, which can then be placed on a toolbar such as the Quick Access Toolbar. You are also provided the option of assigning a keyboard shortcut to the macro (using the Keyboard button).

1. In the Developer's tab's Code group, select Record Macro. This opens the Record Macro dialog box, shown in Figure B.5.

Figure B.5
Excel's Record Macro dialog box.

2. Enter a name for the macro in the Macro Name box.

3. Set the shortcut key for the macro.

4. Use the Store Macro In drop-down box to select where you want to store the macro.

5. Provide an optional description for the macro in the Description box and then click OK.

6. Perform the actions that will be recorded in the macro. You can access the various Ribbon tabs as needed to access commands, and you can use the keyboard or mouse to move in the worksheet.

7. When you have finished recording the macro, click Stop Recording.

The macro is stored as you specified in Step 4. You can view the list of macros available, including the new macro that you have recorded: Select Macros in the Code group.

Assigning a Macro Button to the Quick Access Toolbar

Word makes it easy to create a new macro and assign it to the Quick Access Toolbar. This is extremely useful if you create a macro that opens a weekly report form or an invoice that you use frequently. You can use the macro to open a new document based on a template that you have created (such as an invoice template).

➡️ *For more on creating forms using form controls, **see** Chapter 9, "Managing Mailings and Forms."*

 tip

If you are creating a macro in Excel to move a certain number of cells from a cell of origin (but for use with a variable starting cell), select the Use Relative References command in the Code group before recording the macro.

To create a macro in Word and assign it to a button on the Quick Access Toolbar, follow these steps:

1. In the Developer's tab's Code group, select Record Macro. This opens the Record Macro dialog box.

2. Enter a name for the macro and provide an optional description.

3. Select Button. This opens the Word Options with the Quick Access Toolbar settings selected, as shown in Figure B.6.

 caution

When the macro recorder is running in Word, you lose some of the functionality of the mouse (such as selecting text or double-clicking in the header area). Best practices related to getting around this issue are to use keyboard shortcuts, Ribbon commands, and even the arrow keys (if necessary) to record the proper sequence of actions for the macro.

 note

If you want to create a template in Word that contains its own macros, such as for an online form, save the template as a Word Macro-Enabled Template file type.

Figure B.6
The Quick Access
Toolbar settings.

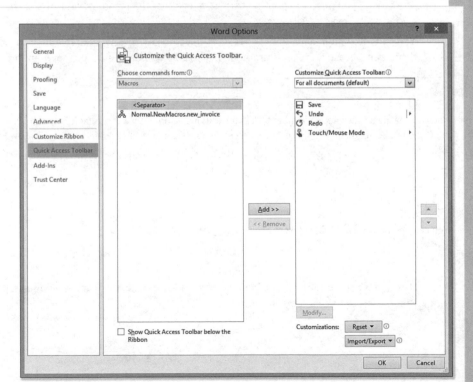

4. In the Command pane, choose the icon that represents your new macro.

5. Click Add to add the macro button to the Quick Access Toolbar pane, and then click OK.

6. Perform the actions that are included in the macro; then click Stop Recording.

The new macro is stored in the Normal template. The button for the new macro is included on the Quick Access Toolbar. You can run the macro using the button.

You can also add macros to the Quick Access Toolbar in the other Office applications, such as Excel, Outlook, and PowerPoint. Open the Backstage (select File and then Options) in the application and then select Quick Access Toolbar. In the Choose Commands From drop-down list, select Macros.

You can add any of the macros listed to the Quick Access Toolbar. Select a macro and then click the Add button.

Running Macros

Macros can be run in a variety of ways. You can run a macro using the shortcut key that you have assigned to that macro. You can also run a macro from an assigned button on the application's Quick Access Toolbar.

Before you run a macro, you need to make sure that you provide the appropriate conditions in your application required by the macro. For example, if the macro performs a particular task in an Excel worksheet, you need to be in the correct cell so that the macro navigates the sheet correctly as it performs its tasks.

You can also run macros from the Macros dialog box. To view available macros, select the Macros command (on the Developer tab). The Macros dialog box opens, as shown in Figure B.7.

 tip

You can specify a Quick Access Toolbar button for your macro other than the default in the Quick Access Toolbar settings (in Options). Select the macro in the Quick Access Toolbar list and then click Modify. Select a new button and then click OK.

 tip

You can open the Macros dialog box at any time by pressing Alt+F8.

To run a macro from the Macros dialog box, select the macro. Then all you have to do is select the Run button to have the macro run.

Figure B.7
The Macros dialog box.

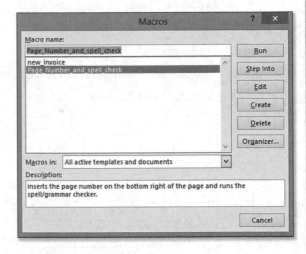

Editing Recorded Macros

As already mentioned in the previous section, macros can be accessed via the Macros dialog box. The Macros dialog box also enables you to open a macro in the VBA editor.

Although it isn't exactly editing, you can delete unwanted macros from the list. To delete a macro from the Macros dialog box, select a macro and then click Delete. A message box opens and asks whether you want to remove the selected macro; click Yes to confirm the deletion.

Exploring the VBA Editor

To view the VBA code in a macro and edit it, you need to open the VBA editor. Select a macro in the Macros dialog box and then click Edit. The VBA Editor opens, as shown in Figure B.8.

The VBA editor window shown in Figure B.8 shows the NewMacros module, which contains the subroutines for two different macros: new_invoice and page_number_and_spell_check (note that neither macro name uses special characters or spaces). The editor is basically a standalone application and provides a menu system and command toolbar structure much like the Office application interfaces were before Office 2007.

The VBA Editor window is divided into three panes:

- **Project Explorer:** This pane provides a list and is used to access the projects available in the current application session. You can use it to navigate (and select) available objects in the projects. These objects include modules such as the NewMacros module and other objects, including the current document (or worksheet) and references to other objects, such as templates.

- **Properties:** This pane provides a list of the properties for the object currently selected in the Project Explorer.

- **Code Window:** This is the largest pane of the editor's pane and contains the actual VBA code for the selected module.

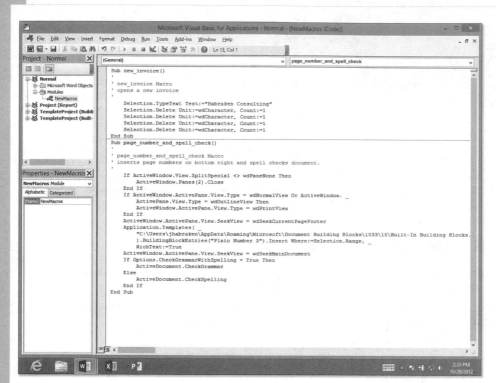

Figure B.8
The VBA Editor.

The geography of the VBA code in the macro is straightforward; each subroutine (for a macro) begins with the Sub line followed by the name of the macro. Directly under the Sub line, the name of the macro is repeated (followed by the word *Macro*). The next line consists of the description that you provided for the macro.

Below the macro's name and description (which typically appear in a green font), the actual lines of code that make up the macro (and relate to the actions that you performed) are listed. The macro subroutine ends with the code line End Sub.

In terms of editing the code lines, one of the simplest possibilities is changing references to specific files or objects specified in the macro. For example, if the macro opens a new file from a template named `cyclone.dotm` and you have modified the template and renamed it to `newcyclone.dotm`, you can change the reference within the specific code line that refers to the template. Or let's say that you have a macro that inserts a particular building block into an Excel worksheet. You can edit the name of the building block in the macro to refer to any building block in your building block galleries, as long as you only edit the name and do not delete or disturb any of the other text in the code line.

Any addition of code lines to a macro requires that you enter the VBA code in the correct syntax and in the appropriate context. For example, the `Selection` code is used to specify a command from the keyboard. If you want to specify that selected text be cut by the macro, you add a code line: `Selection.Cut`.

Obviously, you have to specify the text to be selected in a code line that comes before `Selection.Cut`. To specify the text selection, use the code line `Selection.Extend` followed by `Selection.MoveDown Unit:=wdLine, Count:=3`. This means that you turn on the Extend feature (which is F8; you can't drag with the mouse to select text when the Macro Recorder is on) and then use the down arrow key to move down three text lines to select that text. You see that you can read and understand the VBA code lines. As you add more code vocabulary to your repertoire, you will have more confidence in editing macros and potentially writing your own VBA code.

Stepping Through a Macro

A good way to troubleshoot a macro that is not working correctly is to step through the macro. This process enables you to go through the code lines one at a time. The best way to perform a step debugging is to open the VBA Editor window and then rearrange the open windows so that you can see the editor and the application window (such as Word) either side by side or top and bottom. This enables you to see what happens in the application window as you execute each line of code.

Open the Macros dialog box and then select the macro that you want to step through. Click Edit to open the VBA Editor. When you have the editor and the application arranged on your screen so that you can see them both, follow these steps to step through the macro:

1. Place the insertion point in the macro subroutine where you would to begin stepping through.

2. Press F8 to execute that line of code. The code is highlighted yellow.

3. To step to the next line of code, press F8.

4. Continue to press F8 to execute each line of code until you come to the End Sub line.

5. To end the debugging process, click the Reset button (the button with the blue square in the middle) on the editor's toolbar.

As you step through each line of code, take note of what is happening in the application window as each code line executes. This enables you to find the specific line of code that is misbehaving in a macro that does not work correctly.

Digitally Signing Macros

We have already discussed the fact the macros can be a security risk and that the security settings for the Office applications are geared toward not allowing macros to run by default. So another alternative for verifying that your macros are not malware is to digitally sign the macro project (which can contain a number of macros). This enables you to use and share the macros without enabling macros in the Security Center and lessens the possibility of executing a "bad" macro.

After you digitally sign your macro projects, you can change the macro settings in the Trust Center to use the Disable All Macros Except Digitally Signed Macros option. Collaborators and other users who might use your templates or other files that contain macros can also use this setting, which enables you to share the macros but doesn't open any of your colleagues to a macro attack.

Digitally signing a macro project requires that you obtain a digital certificate. Digital certificates can be provided by a certifying authority. For example, you can obtain digital certificates from online certifying authorities such as A-Trust (www.a-trust.at), VeriSign (http://digitalid.verisign.com), and a host of other certifying authorities (just do a search at microsoft.com for Microsoft Root Certificate program members). Some companies also have their own in-house certifying authority.

So you can purchase a digital certificate from a certifying authority for your VBA code, or you can ask your digital certificate overlord (a network administrator or CIO, perhaps) at your company for a digital certificate for your VBA projects. If neither of these options is open to you, you can still create your own digital certificate using an Office 2013 utility program named Digital Certificate for VBA Projects. To create a digital certificate using the Digital Certificate for VBA Projects utility, follow these steps:

1. On the Windows 8 Desktop (click the Desktop tile on the Windows Start page), open the File Explorer.

2. Navigate to the `Program Files\Microsoft Office\Office15` folder.

3. Locate the file `SELFCERT` (in the `Office 15` folder) and double-click the file to open the Create Digital Certificate window.

4. Navigate to the `Program Files\Microsoft Office\Office15` folder.

5. Type a name for the new digital certificate and then click OK.

6. A dialog box opens and states that your certificate was successfully created. Click OK to close the message box.

When you have a digital certificate (self-generated or provided by a certificate authority), you can use it to digitally sign your macro projects. This process takes place in the VBA editor. Follow these steps:

1. On the Developer's tab, click the Macros command to open the Macro dialog box.

2. Select a macro in the Macro Name list and then click Edit to open the VBA editor.

3. In the Project Explorer, select the name of the VBA project (it is in the project tree under the `Modules` folder) that you want to digitally sign.

4. Select the editor's Tools menu and then select Digital Signature. This opens the Digital Signature dialog box, as shown in Figure B.9.

5. Select the Choose button in the Digital Signature dialog box. A Windows Security box opens showing the certificate that you created.

6. Click OK, and you are returned to the Digital Signature dialog box. The name of your certificate is now listed as the certificate name in the dialog box.

Figure B.9
The Digital Signature dialog box.

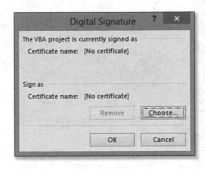

7. Click OK.

You can now close the VBA editor. The Project module (and all the macros that it contains) is now digitally signed.

You probably have digitally signed the macro project so that it is easy for others to use your macros in templates or other documents, worksheets, and so on. You plan to share it on the network or email it to another user. You have a problem, however.

Because you generated the digital signature certificate, it is not considered a certificate from a trusted source. When a user on another computer attempts to open the document or use the template, the Office application being used checks the certificate to see if it is from a certifying authority on the trusted list. Because you aren't really a certifying authority, any user opening your document or template containing the macros sees a security message in the application (just below the Ribbon) detailing that the macros have been disabled.

A quick workaround can remedy this problem. Users can add your certificate to their trusted root certificate authority's store. The macros can then be enabled. So this set of tasks should be performed on the computer of the other users.

Select the Options button in the security warning that has appeared in the application. This opens the Microsoft Office Security Options dialog box. At this point, there is no way to activate the macros. In the dialog box, click the Show Signature Details link. This opens the Digital Signature Details dialog box, which shows the details related to your digital certificate. To view the certificate, select the View Certificate button.

The Certificate dialog box doesn't really provide any more information than the digital Signature Details dialog box, but it does grant access to the Certificate Import Wizard, which is where we need to end up to add the certificate to the trusted store.

Select the Install Certificate button in the Certificate dialog box. The Certificate Import Wizard opens. By default, the certificate store is set to Current User. This means that the certificate is installed for the current user only. If you want to authorize the certificate for all users, select Local Machine in the Store Location box. Click Next to move to the next wizard window.

In the next wizard window, click the Place All Certificates in the Following Store option button, and then click the Browse button. This opens the Select Certificate Store dialog box, shown in Figure B.10.

Figure B.10
The Select Certificate Store dialog box.

In the certificate store list, select the Trusted Root Certification Authorities folder. Then click OK. Now you can click Next. The final wizard screen appears, showing the settings that you have selected, such as the certificate store. Click Finish.

A security warning dialog box opens and details that you are about to install a certificate and that Windows cannot validate that the certificate is authentic. Select Yes to install the certificate. A Certificate Import Wizard message box opens and lets you know that the import was successful. Click OK. Then click OK two more times to return to the Microsoft Office Security Options dialog box, which is where you started this entire process.

As you can see from Figure B.11, the macro-related options available have been expanded because the digital certificate was added to the store.

Figure B.11
The options for enabling your macros.

The possibilities are as follows:

- **Help Protect Me from Unknown Content (Recommended):** This option was initially the only possibility in the dialog box. It is still the default but can be changed to allow the macro to run in the application.

- **Enable Content for This Session:** This option enables the macros for this session. When you open the file in the future, the macros will be disabled and the application will provide a warning. However, you can use this same option (each time) to enable the macros.

- **Trust All Documents from This Publisher:** This option enables the user to open files with the macros enabled, and no macro-related warning appears when you open the file in an application.

After you have changed the security settings related to the macros in the document or file, you can click OK. If you have selected the second or third possibility, the security warning closes in the application. Now the macros can be run in the application as needed.

INDEX

Envelopes and Labels dialog
box, 230-231, 232

eps (Encapsulated PostScript),
182

equations, 556

error alerts for invalid data,
482-483

error bars (chart), 430-431

Error Checking dialog box,
400, 484

error checking validation rules,
484

error messages, 397-398

Event dialog box, 713-714

events
creating
in Calendar, 713-714
from notes, 775-776
deleting, 715
editing, 714-715
moving, 714-715
scheduling, 713-714
viewing, 706

Excel
capabilities, 15, 289, 367
data analysis features, 479
data validation features, 479
databases, 439-440
Document Inspector, 308-309
external data, 459-469
file extensions, 54
Flash Fill feature, 293-294,
395
macros, 951
Name Manager, 364
new features, 289-294
Quick Analysis gallery, 7-8
Quick Analysis tool, 291-292
Recommended Charts
feature, 292-293, 415
Ribbon, 294-296
Start screen, 289-290, 294
task panes, 13
Web App, 119-123

Exchange ActiveSync feature
(Outlook), 636, 638

Exchange Server (Outlook),
637-638, 696

exporting
Outlook data, 651, 653-654
presentations, 631-632
styles, 205-206

Extend feature, 146

External Data Properties
dialog box, 469

external data, working with in
Excel, 459-469

Extra Content task pane,
847-848

F

F1 key (Help), 20

Facebook, connecting Outlook
with, 751-753

field codes
copying, 249
cutting, 249
deleting, 249
formatting, 248
hiding, 249
inserting, 248-249
pasting, 249
showing, 249
viewing, 249

Field dialog box, 179-180,
248-249

Field Options dialog box, 261

fields
contacts, 741
documents, 179-180, 248-249

File Explorer, 66

file extensions
Excel, 54
PowerPoint, 54
Word, 54

file formats, 53-58

File Printout command,
916-918

FileName field, 249

files. *See also* documents
Adobe Acrobat files
editing, 13, 134
viewing, 55-56
attaching
to email, 112, 678-680,
783, 787-789
to Journal entries, 767-768
to notebooks, 920
AutoRecover feature, 65-66
browsing, 65-66
Check Accessibility tool, 72
Check Compatibility tool, 72
compatibility, 72
converting to different file
types, 57-58
creating, 60-62
digital signatures, 70-72
Documents folder, 63
editing, 70
encrypting, 70
finding
File Explorer, 66
Open dialog box, 67
Inspect Document tool, 72
inviting people to access
files on SkyDrive, 111
library, 64-65
macro-enabled Office files,
949
managing, 53, 62-63
marking as final, 70
naming conventions, 63
organizing, 62-63
password-protection, 70
passwords, 70
PDF documents, 13
posting files to social
networks, 112
protecting, 69-72
recovering, 65-66
restricting access, 70
restricting editing, 70
saving
cloud storage, 10-11,
108-110
to different file types,
56-57
Save File options, 58-60

How can we make this index more useful? Email us at indexes@quepublishing.com

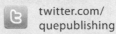
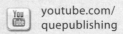
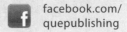

Office 2013

FREE
Online Edition

IN DEPTH

Joe Habraken

Your purchase of **Office 2013 In Depth** includes access to a free online edition for 45 days through the **Safari Books Online** subscription service. Nearly every Que book is available online through **Safari Books Online**, along with thousands of books and videos from publishers such as Addison-Wesley Professional, Cisco Press, Exam Cram, IBM Press, O'Reilly Media, Prentice Hall, Sams, and VMware Press.

Safari Books Online is a digital library providing searchable, on-demand access to thousands of technology, digital media, and professional development books and videos from leading publishers. With one monthly or yearly subscription price, you get unlimited access to learning tools and information on topics including mobile app and software development, tips and tricks on using your favorite gadgets, networking, project management, graphic design, and much more.

Activate your FREE Online Edition at
informit.com/safarifree

STEP 1:   Enter the coupon code: USFFXBI.

STEP 2:   New Safari users, complete the brief registration form.
          Safari subscribers, just log in.

If you have difficulty registering on Safari or accessing the online edition,
please e-mail customer-service@safaribooksonline.com